THE CAMBRIDGE HISTORY OF MEDIEVAL PHILOSOPHY

The Cambridge History of Medieval Philosophy comprises over fifty specially commissioned essays by experts on the philosophy of this period. Starting in the late eighth century, with the renewal of learning some centuries after the fall of the Roman Empire, a sequence of chapters takes the reader through developments in many and varied fields, including logic and language, natural philosophy, ethics, metaphysics, and theology. Close attention is paid to the context of medieval philosophy, with discussions of the rise of the universities and developments in the cultural and linguistic spheres. A striking feature is the continuous coverage of Islamic, Jewish, and Christian material. There are useful biographies of the philosophers, and a comprehensive bibliography. The volumes illuminate a rich and remarkable period in the history of philosophy and will be the authoritative source on medieval philosophy for the next generation of scholars and students alike.

ROBERT PASNAU is Professor of Philosophy, University of Colorado, Boulder. His publications include *Theories of Cognition in the Later Middle Ages* (1997), *The Cambridge Translations of Medieval Philosophical Texts*, vol. III: *Mind and Knowledge* (2002), and *Thomas Aquinas on Human Nature: A Philosophical Study of Summa Theologiae, 1a 75–89* (2002).

The Cambridge History of Medieval Philosophy

Volume II

EDITED BY
ROBERT PASNAU

ASSOCIATE EDITOR
CHRISTINA VAN DYKE

CAMBRIDGE
UNIVERSITY PRESS

CAMBRIDGE UNIVERSITY PRESS

Cambridge, New York, Melbourne, Madrid, Cape Town, Singapore, São Paulo,
Delhi, Dubai, Tokyo

Cambridge University Press
The Edinburgh Building, Cambridge CB2 8RU, UK

Published in the United States of America by Cambridge University Press, New York

www.cambridge.org
Information on this title: www.cambridge.org/9780521866729

© Cambridge University Press 2010

First published 2010

Printed in the United Kingdom at the University Press, Cambridge

A catalogue record for this publication is available from the British Library

Library of Congress Cataloguing in Publication data
The Cambridge history of medieval philosophy / Robert Pasnau, editor ; Christina Van Dyke,
associate editor.
p.   cm.
Includes bibliographical references and index.
ISBN 978-0-521-76216-8 (v. 1 : hardback) – ISBN 978-0-521-86672-9 (set : hardback)   1. Philosophy,
Medieval–History.   I. Pasnau, Robert.   II. Dyke, Christina van, 1972–   III. Title.
B721.C355   2009
189 – dc22   2009032501

Volume II ISBN 978-0-521-76218-2
Available only as set: ISBN 978-0-521-86672-9 Hardback

CONTENTS

VOLUME II

VII

POLITICAL PHILOSOPHY

39

RELIGIOUS AUTHORITY AND THE STATE

ANTONY BLACK

Religious authority and the state were conceived very differently in the Byzantine world, the Muslim world, and Latin Europe. This last was the only civilization in which the age-old and nearly universal notion of sacred monarchy was consistently and increasingly challenged.[1] In the Byzantine and Muslim worlds (except among the Shī'ites), the ruler remained a focal point of living religious authority. The Latin West was also distinguished by the variety of views expressed on this subject and the variety of forms which the relationship between church and state took. In some places the bishop was also temporal ruler, whereas in self-governing cities clergy had no overt political role. In feudal kingdoms, bishops were major landowners and often state counselors, but they owed their position partly to royal favor. Moreover, the way in which the church–state relationship was understood and theorized in the West changed as time went by. In Byzantium, by contrast, it never changed, while in the Muslim world, changes were rarely registered in what people wrote down.

BYZANTIUM

Eastern Christendom drew its notion of sacred monarchy from Roman imperial ideology, christianized by Eusebius of Caesarea (*ca.* 260–340). The one emperor was supposed to reflect the one God; he ruled "by God's favor" as "God's deputy." The common form of address to a Byzantine emperor was "O most divine emperor."[2] For more than a thousand years, the Eastern church regarded the empire as an essential part of the expression of Christ in the world. In 1391, for instance, the patriarch of Constantinople told the prince of Moscow: "it

---

[1] Francis Oakley, *Kingship: The Politics of Enchantment* (Oxford: Blackwell, 2006); Antony Black, *The West and Islam: Religion and Political Thought in World History* (Oxford: Oxford University Press, 2008).

[2] Ernest Barker, *Social and Political Thought in Byzantium: From Justinian I to the Last Palaeologus* (Oxford: Clarendon Press, 1957) p. 478. See also Averil Cameron, *Christianity and the Rhetoric of Empire: The Development of Christian Discourse* (Berkeley: University of California Press, 1991).

is not possible for Christians to have a church and not to have an empire."[3] Byzantium also transmitted its ideology to the peoples they converted, notably those in Bulgaria, Serbia, and Russia.

Within the Byzantine church itself, the emperor had considerable say in senior church appointments and played a leading, though not necessarily decisive, role in the councils that determined doctrine and discipline. In return, emperors enforced current church orthodoxy, sometimes on recalcitrant populations. This has been called "Caesaropapism."

LATIN EUROPE

Most of these Byzantine notions were rejected in the West. In a statement quoted throughout the Middle Ages (though with a variety of meanings), Pope Gelasius I (ruled 492–6) ruled out Caesaropapism, declaring that there are two powers: one of bishops, and the other of kings; "the sacred authority of bishops" carries greater weight, however, than the royal power. Christian emperors, Gelasius claimed, hold power from God only over state affairs; in what affects the salvation of the soul, emperors must "obey rather than control the religious establishment."[4] An emperor could have no role in decisions about religious doctrine or church discipline. Although this had parallels in some eastern theology, Roman bishops – unlike the patriarchs of the East – were able actually to assert their independence from the emperor. Eventually, under Pope Gregory VII (ruled 1073–85) and his successors, they produced a very different theory of church and state.

What most of all distinguished the Latin West from other medieval cultures was the development of a religious authority not only independent from, but claiming superiority over, the actual rulers. In neither Islam nor Byzantium was there any suggestion that religious leaders have legal or institutional authority over a king. What made this Latin development possible was the unique position of the papacy. It was an office with a strong claim to divine authorization (the pope was "the vicar of Christ"). At the same time, it was politically strong enough – due both to its prestige and influence and to the collapse of the empire in the West – to assert itself as an independent and, at times, dominant

[3] See Donald M. Nicol, "Byzantine Political Thought," in J. H. Burns (ed.) *The Cambridge History of Medieval Political Thought c.350–c.1450* (Cambridge: Cambridge University Press, 1988) p. 73.

[4] Francis Dvornik, *Early Christian and Byzantine Political Philosophy: Origins and Background* (Washington, DC: Dumbarton Oaks Center for Byzantine Studies, 1966) pp. 804–7; Walter Ullmann, *The Growth of Papal Government in the Middle Ages* (London: Methuen, 1955) p. 21; Joseph Canning, *A History of Medieval Political Thought 300–1450* (Cambridge: Cambridge University Press, 1994) pp. 35–6.

political force. Spiritual or ecclesiastical authority was constantly distinguished from temporal or secular authority.

The most determined attempt to bring secular rulers under the control of religious authorities was the papal revolution of the later eleventh century, when the papacy attempted, with partial success, to wrest control of the appointment of senior clergy from the emperor. This dispute generated a propaganda war unprecedented in Europe, and probably in the world. Gregory VII, the most dynamic leader of this reform movement, interpreted Augustine's idea of the heavenly and earthly cities to mean that states derive their actual legitimacy from the church.[5] A legitimate ruler has to be ratified by the church (which, in this context, usually meant the papacy), and such a ruler may be deposed by it if he fails in his duties. As Hugh of St. Victor put it, "the spiritual power has to institute the earthly power and to judge it if it turns out not to be good" (*De sacramentis* II.2.4). For, according to Gregory's *a fortiori* argument: "if the see of blessed Peter [namely, the Roman bishopric or papacy] pardons and judges heavenly and spiritual matters, how much more earthly and secular ones?"[6] In 1245, Pope Innocent IV deposed the last seriously powerful Germano-Roman emperor, Frederick II, and absolved his subjects from their oath of allegiance. In this view – referred to as "papalism" – there is nothing sacred about earthly kingship.[7] Papalism was a complete reversal of Eusebian ideology, which remained the official doctrine of the Eastern church.

In the period between the Gregorian reform and the Protestant Reformation, the church–state controversy affected the whole of Latin Europe. As well as being a prominent topic in the new and burgeoning disciplines of canon law and theology, numerous tracts by politicians, academics and propagandists on all sides were devoted exclusively to this subject. Indeed, this was probably the most written-about topic in political theory (which became recognized as a separate area of discourse following the recovery of Aristotle's *Politics* in the mid-thirteenth century).

There were innumerable attempts to balance the competing claims of king and clergy, emperor and pope. Which cases should be tried in royal courts, which in church courts? Where is the final court of appeal? Who controls the appointment of bishops, upon whom a king had to rely as part of the command structure of the realm? Could the pope, or the king, tax the clergy? Most

---

[5] Henri Xavier Arquillière, *L'augustinisme politique: essai sur la formation des théories politiques du Moyen-Age*, 2nd edn (Paris: Vrin, 1955).

[6] *Registrum*, ed. Caspar, pp. 295, 338, 550. See Gerd Tellenbach, *The Church in Western Europe from the Tenth to the Early Twelfth Century* (Cambridge: Cambridge University Press, 1993) pp. 331, 337–8.

[7] Walter Ullmann, *Medieval Papalism: The Political Theories of the Medieval Canonists* (London: Methuen, 1949).

crucially of all, what authority did the pope have over kings? What authority did kings have over the clergy in their kingdoms? At stake was the fundamental question of the boundary between the legitimate authority of two systems of law and government.

Papalists argued that the pope as vicar of Christ has fullness of power and therefore holds – *de iure* and in principle – all power, temporal as well as spiritual; normally, however, the pope only exercises his spiritual power, leaving temporal power to be exercised by others, on his behalf and at his request ("by his nod"). This meant that he could, if necessary, intervene in a king's exercise of temporal power – not by taking it over himself, but by sanctioning or even deposing a recalcitrant ruler and releasing subjects from their oath of allegiance. This could trigger a change of ruler or even of dynasty. Pro-papal writers also made a distinction between moral issues (the sphere of sin) and purely pragmatic issues: the pope would only intervene in the former.[8] In a dispute between Philip IV of France and Pope Boniface VIII over whether the king had the power to tax the clergy, the pope declared that both the "material sword" and "the spiritual sword" belonged to the church.[9]

Supporters of the independent power of secular rulers countered, for the most part, by insisting that the separation between church and state was fundamental. They interpreted Matthew 22:21 ("render unto Caesar the things that are Caesar's, and unto God the things that are God's") and Pope Gelasius's *dictum* to mean that the clergy, although spiritually superior, did not have any direct control over rulers in secular matters. John of Paris, for instance, argued that the clergy had only an indirect power in the political sphere; they could merely exert influence by their "right of preaching."[10] Such distinctions were always tricky, however, both because of the indefinable boundary between the spiritual and the purely mundane, and because few disputed the clergy's (and the papacy's) right to excommunicate serious delinquents. If a pope chose to excommunicate a king, then, this meant any person coming into contact with the king put him or herself in spiritual danger.

One result of the church–state dispute in medieval Europe was the emergence of an attempt to find arguments for the legitimate independence of secular authority that did not rest on reinterpretation of sacred texts, where the dice tended to be loaded in favor of the spiritual power. Indeed, the European theory of the state may be seen as a long-term reaction to clerical claims to

---

[8] See John A. Watt, "Spiritual and Temporal Powers," in Burns, *The Cambridge History of Medieval Political Thought*, pp. 397–402.

[9] As quoted in Antony Black, *Political Thought in Europe, 1250–1450* (Cambridge: Cambridge University Press, 1992) p. 48.

[10] As quoted in Black, *Political Thought*, p. 53.

hegemony. During the dispute between Philip and Boniface, for instance, some supporters of the secular monarchy used Aristotle and Cicero to demonstrate the "intrinsically natural and ethical origin and function of government."[11] This led to a dualist position in which the two powers were seen as altogether distinct: the pope is not superior in the temporal sphere, and neither pope nor king must interfere in the affairs of the other.

Even granted some kind of dualist position, however, there was still the question of who was to decide the boundaries between church and state. Even some royal supporters held that the pope may intervene on an occasional basis when a religious issue is clearly involved; for example, if the king commits the heresy of persistent defiance of the Roman church,[12] the pope can absolve subjects from the oath of allegiance. A few pro-secular authors, such as the radical English reformer John Wyclif,[13] went even further and argued that it was the king, not the pope, who was the vicar of Christ and who represented God on earth. These authors wanted to subordinate the clergy to the secular power. This move beyond dualism and its attendant problems was taken most decisively by Marsilius of Padua, the most original political thinker of the Middle Ages. Writing in support of the emperor-elect Ludwig of Bavaria against the papacy, Marsilius's *Defensor pacis* (1324) asserts the unequivocal superiority of the secular ruler even in the religious sphere. It does so by making a categorical distinction between coercive and persuasive forms of power, and insisting that only a secular ruler authorized by the whole people (in order that they may fulfill their natural aspirations) can legitimately possess coercive power. On such a position, the clergy would teach and administer the sacraments but hold no coercive jurisdiction. Few agreed with Marsilius, though (or, at least, would say so openly), and proponents of this view tended to be condemned as heretics.

At the same time, by about 1350, the natural or secular origin and purpose of government were becoming clearer in many people's minds. Theorists such as Thomas Aquinas and Dante Alighieri had staked out an area that was ethical but not specifically religious – namely, the promotion of virtue in a pre-Christian, Aristotelian-influenced sense. On such theories, there was now a legitimate society that was not a church. It is here, as much as in the ideology of the Italian city-states,[14] that we find the beginnings of the Western theory of the state,

---

[11] See Watt, "Spiritual and Temporal Powers," p. 406.   [12] See ibid., p. 407.

[13] See K. B. McFarlane, *John Wycliffe and the Beginnings of English Nonconformity* (London: English Universities Press, 1952); Michael Wilks, "Reformatio Regni: Wyclif and Hus as Leaders of Religious Protest Movements," *Studies in Church History* 9 (1972) 109–30.

[14] Quentin Skinner, *The Foundations of Modern Political Thought* (Cambridge: Cambridge University Press, 1978) vol. I.

including the origin of the notion of a secular authority, which is to this day problematic in the Muslim world.

These developments in political theory assumed greater importance because rulers in this period were developing and expanding the sinews of government, and were becoming increasingly capable of putting this theorizing into practice. The papacy itself had led the way with its bureaucratic system; its theory of judicial and legislative sovereignty became one model for the secular state. Secular rulers were, furthermore, developing means of obtaining the popular approval and support deemed necessary to raise taxes, wage wars, and govern effectively – usually by means of parliaments. The role of the wider public – barons, bishops, towns – was crucial to the strength of a state, both in practice and in theory.

The church–state controversy by its very nature led to a development of the role of the people (which, in this period, almost always meant the structured community as a whole) in the authorization of government and in the political process. Such ideas could be deployed against papal authority as well. For example, one riposte to papalist claims was to assert the authority within the spiritual realm of a general council of bishops – supposedly representing the church as a whole – over the pope himself.[15]

Marsilius constructed his argument by means of Aristotelian syllogisms. Starting from first principles purportedly based on observation, Marsilius concludes that the ruler's power is what it is because of a delegation by the community as a whole. This simultaneously reinforces the argument for the purely secular nature of political authority *and* locates that authority exclusively in the whole body of citizens – thus anticipating, in essence, the course taken by modern Western political theory. Marsilius goes on to apply these same principles to the church: excommunication can be imposed only by the whole community of the faithful or by someone acting on their behalf.

Marsilius's contemporary, William of Ockham (also a supporter of Ludwig), seems to have established individual conscience as the final judge in all moral and theological questions. In what was probably the most complex discussion of church and state ever undertaken to that point, his *Dialogus* explores in meticulous detail the relationship between church and state, as well as every conceivable option for the constitution of both church and secular states. It is not always clear, however, what Ockham's own view is. Although he assigns an increased role to councils and parliaments, he recognizes that these are also fallible; he therefore tends to offer a final say to the people at large, but only

---

[15] See Watt, "Spiritual and Temporal Powers," p. 408. Marsilius perceptively found precedents in the late Roman and Byzantine church (Black, *Political Thought*, p. 70).

if they are well informed and well intentioned. In other words, it is up to individuals to make up their own minds conscientiously on the basis of all available information.

The church–state controversy, and papalism in particular, encouraged the view that the people may depose their ruler. The theory and practice of the papacy itself provided a precedent: a king who broke church law, or who disobeyed the clergy on a serious matter, was no longer fit to rule his people, and the church authorities could therefore release his subjects from their oath of allegiance.[16] This was one way of legitimizing rebellion. As John of Paris puts it in the later thirteenth century, if a king is heretical, incorrigible, and refuses church censure, the pope can encourage the people to depose him, and excommunicate those who still obey him. To explain such a case, John appeals to the Aristotelian distinction between *per se* and *per accidens* (direct and indirect) causes: "the people, and the pope *per accidens*, would depose him."[17]

ISLAM

Medieval Muslim views on religious authority and the state were quite different from Christian views. In the original message of Muhammad and his followers, there was no separation between religious and political spheres or authorities. All aspects of life and conduct were supposed to be covered by the divinely ordained *Sharīʿa* (religious code); religion *meant* "law" or "right" (*sharʿ*).[18] The *Sharīʿa* embodied justice. Political activity consisted in "commanding right and prohibiting wrong" – that is, ensuring that the standards of the *Sharīʿa* were upheld in practice.[19]

Muslims believed that God had given them the task of spreading Islam and, at the same time, subduing the whole world to their rule. This holy mission thus involved conquering and ruling as well as preaching and morality. "Holy war seems to have been widely regarded as an obligation comparable to prayer."[20] This was what inspired the conquests of Iraq, Palestine, Syria, Egypt, Persia, North Africa, Spain, and Central Asia. Muslim leaders claimed (in effect) that they were establishing a new kind of political society, based on a revelation concerning – among other things – social and economic justice. Thus, they did

---

[16] See Gregory VII, *Registrum*, ed. Caspar, pp. 208, 487, 554; Tellenbach, *The Church in Western Europe*, pp. 218, 237.
[17] As quoted in Watt, "Spiritual and Temporal Powers," p. 408.
[18] Patricia Crone, *Medieval Islamic Political Thought* (Edinburgh: Edinburgh University Press, 2004) p. 8.
[19] Michael Cook, *Commanding Right and Forbidding Wrong in Islamic Thought* (Cambridge: Cambridge University Press, 2000).
[20] Crone, *Medieval Islamic Political Thought*, p. 363.

not really distinguish the political from the religious, nor the secular from the sacred or spiritual. When we use such terms we are putting a Western template on Muslim thought and language.

It was generally believed that Muslims formed a single community of believers – the *umma* – which God, through Muhammad, had ordained was to be ruled by the caliph (Muhammad's deputy), who was the leader or imam of the community. The caliph's authority was (in Western terms) religious as well as political and military. Although secular rulers from time to time issued supplementary decrees (*qanun* [sing.]), law meant the *Sharīʿa*.

In theory, the caliph held a monopoly on the legitimate means of coercion over both the *umma* and the world. He was also an essential part of the religious structure: without a caliph there is no community, and the community is the vehicle of salvation. Certain aspects of the religious law required his participation or consent, tacit or explicit; without a caliph there could be no valid contracts. Within the (religious) community there were also other posts decreed by revelation that Westerners would probably see as partly – or wholly – secular or political in character: judges, for instance, and market regulators (overseers of public morals).[21] Only the caliph or his representative could appoint judges; the market regulator was usually appointed by the judge. According to the great theologian al-Ghazālī, without a caliph "there would be no Friday prayer, no collection of taxes, no missionary jihad, no judges and no execution" of *Sharīʿa* punishments.[22]

The Abbasid dynasty (claiming descent from an uncle of the Prophet and initially supported by some Shīʿites as well) established (from 750) a single caliphate for the whole Muslim world, ruling from Baghdad. This, however, lost effective power after about a century. The entire Muslim world soon fragmented (not unlike Western Europe) into a series of dynastic territories, ranging from the Umayyads in Spain to the Ghaznavids in central Asia.

The Shīʿa and Sunnī held very different notions of religious authority. The most widely accepted Sunnī view of the caliphate was that expressed by the jurist al-Māwardī. Writing in the early eleventh century, when the Abbasid caliphs had lost political power and been reduced to figureheads, al-Māwardī reasserted the caliphate as the fulcrum of (in Western terms) the political as well as religious aspects of the Muslim community. He insisted that the by now independent sultans must recognize the formal sovereignty of the caliph, and that they held their power as legitimate Muslim rulers by formal delegation from him. Al-Māwardī also re-described the Muslim polity in such a way as to make the caliphate cover secular as well as religious governance, for he held that

---

[21] *Encyclopaedia of Islam*, ed. H. A. R. Gibb (Leiden: Brill, 1960–97) s.v. *kadi, muhtasib*.
[22] As quoted in Crone, *Medieval Islamic Political Thought*, p. 22; see also pp. 238, 242, 292.

the caliph was still the political as well as the religious leader of the *umma*. In general, orthodox jurists continued to insist that the caliph was Leader of the People in the original unitary sense.

Numerous early sects held much stricter views about what qualifies a person to be caliph than did supporters of the rather worldly Umayyads (661–740s) or of the Abbasids.[23] Above all, the Shī'ites recognized only direct descendants of 'Alī (the Prophet's son-in-law), each chosen through "designation" by his predecessor. The Imami or Twelver Shī'ites held that the twelfth of these had "gone into hiding" *ca.* 945 and would return at the end of time.[24] Hence, current existing caliphs have no religious status and no legitimacy whatsoever. For these Shī'ites, the separation between religious authority and the state was, consequently, as complete as it could be; they became quietists. The only "politics" they knew was the conduct, sometimes secretive, of their own communal affairs. They would undertake government service only if this would be of service to their fellow Shī'a.

The Twelfth or Hidden Imam was, at least in a spiritual and mystical way, the ultimate authority in all matters for these Shī'ites, and they said the sorts of things about him that Christian papalists said about the pope. Indeed, the twelve true imams were thought to be necessary to the constitution of the universe. As Heinz Halm puts it, "since the ruling caliphs are notoriously sinful and fallible and act tyrannically, there must be a Hidden Imam; without the latter's existence mankind would be forsaken by God, and man would indubitably go astray."[25]

A separation between religion and government emerged in the majority Sunnī community as well. During the first two centuries after Muhammad, certain religious scholar–teachers – the *'ulama* (literally, "the learned") – became recognized as the experts on the Quran and the Hadith (sayings of the Prophet), as well as on the burgeoning discipline of religious law. It was these religious experts rather than the caliph who became the acknowledged moral guides and social leaders of the majority of Muslims. It was they and not, as had at first seemed possible, the caliphs, who appropriated the right to decide what was or was not orthodox doctrine, and also to interpret the *Sharī'a*.[26] This meant that justice was defined independently of the actual ruler; the religious, social, and economic rules of the *Sharī'a* were interpreted primarily by the *'ulama*, especially those who were recognized authorities in jurisprudence (the *fuqaha*).

---

[23] See ibid., pp. 54–124, 197–219.
[24] The Sevener or Ismā'īlī Shī'ites, to whom the Fatimids adhered, believed this of the Seventh Imam. Since about the late eleventh century, the great majority of Shī'ites have been Twelver. 'Shī'a' means literally *party* or *sect*.
[25] Heinz Halm, *Shiism* (Edinburgh: Edinburgh University Press, 1991) pp. 55–6.
[26] Patricia Crone and Martin Hinds, *God's Caliph: Religious Authority in the First Centuries of Islam* (Cambridge: Cambridge University Press, 1986).

Thus, the ʿulama emerged as a specifically religious coterie of authoritative teachers in Islam, separate from the seats of political and military power. It was claimed that the "verse of the commanders" (*amirs*) in the Quran, which refers to "those in authority among you" (4:62), refers to ʿulama rather than to military leaders or rulers. Meanwhile, from the mid-ninth century onward, the caliphate itself was crumbling into a series of separate sultanates (power states). Having lost political power and been reduced almost to a figurehead in both the 'religious' and the 'political' spheres, all the caliph had now was his religio-legal position as the indispensable figurehead of Sunnī Muslims. Although the majority of Muslims still looked up to the hereditary Abbasid caliphs of Baghdad as legitimate deputies of the Prophet, these now depended for military power on the Saljuk Turks who ruled the Muslim heartland of Iraq and western Iran. The Saljuk vizier Nizam al-Mulk (d. 1092) also took it upon himself to promote religious learning by establishing madrasas in major cities.

What was emerging, therefore, was a *de facto* separation between religious and political authority. The original union between religion and politics began to dissolve into a division of roles between various leaders. Muslim jurists paid detailed attention to the relationship between caliph and sultan; regarding the caliph and the ʿulama, however, "the dividing-line between the two jurisdictions remained not just fuzzy, but studiously unexplored."[27] It seemed that there was after all to be a separation between religious and political power in Islam. Al-Ghazālī saw Muslims as belonging (in Patricia Crone's words) "to two different communities, one religious and the other political, one the *umma* and the other the secular kingdoms into which it was divided."[28] Increasingly, religious authority was vested in the international coterie of the ʿulama, and political power in the sultans of various territorial states. The ʿulama taught the faith and adjudicated the *Sharīʿa*; the sultan commanded the military and extracted a tax surplus. It is here that one finds some parallel to church and state in Western Europe.

The two genres of writing that explicitly discussed the relationship between religious authority and the state were religious jurisprudence (*fiqh*)[29] and Advices to Kings.[30] The Advice literature seems to allude in a somewhat haphazard and gnomic way to the relationship between sultan and the ʿulama in his domain. In these works and also, so far as one can make out, among the public at large, it also became natural to distinguish between *din* (religion) and *dawla* (state or

---

[27] Crone, *Medieval Islamic Political Thought*, p. 132.   [28] Ibid., p. 243.

[29] Joseph Schacht, *The Origins of Muhammadan Jurisprudence,* corr. edn (Oxford: Clarendon Press, 1967).

[30] *Encyclopaedia of Islam*, s.v. Nahisat al-muluk.

dynasty), but always with the proviso that "kingship and religion are twins"[31] or, as some put it, "The pen and the sword are brothers; neither can do without the other."[32]

In general, what distinguishes what went on in the Muslim world from what went on in the Christian world of Latin Europe was the lack of discussion on this whole subject. This may have been because of the embarrassing disjunction between Islamic principles and the actual situation; people preferred to gloss over it. One of the very few references to a distinction between religious authority and the state comes in a twelfth-century Advice book: "God has singled out two groups of men and given them preference over others: one prophets, and the other kings."[33] The power of prophets was a thing of the past, however, and nothing further is said about how these two categories relate to each other.

The ancient Persian saying "Religion is the foundation of kingship, and kingship the protector of religion" was explained by the tenth-century philosopher al-ʿĀmirī as follows: "the relationship of religious to royal authority is like that of the foundation to the building erected upon it, and the relationship of the ruler to religion is like that of the person who undertakes the basic obligations of a covenant to the basic obligations themselves."[34] This might seem to give the religious aspect a certain superiority; but "religion" is not equated here with the ʿulama, or with any living persons, or with any institution. This is surely not, therefore, comparable to the conception of church and state in either Eastern or Western Christianity. What we seem to find in the expressions of Muslim authors is interdependence, rather than separation, between religion and government. Whatever concerns people may have had about the one encroaching on the other were not voiced.

A separation between religion and politics may also be seen in the way in which, after the violent civil wars of early Islam, proto-Sunnīs, as well as Shīʿa, emphasized how unwise – and even impious – it is to engage in politics. Having started as a religion of political activism, Islam became in the medieval period largely a religion of quietism. Indeed, the good religious life was seen by many as incompatible with politics. Government service is dangerous, leads to immorality, and is to be avoided whenever possible. As a twelfth-century mirror

[31] Said Amir Arjomand, *The Shadow of God and the Hidden Imam: Religion, Political Order, and Societal Change in Shiʿite Iran from the Beginning to 1890* (Chicago: University of Chicago Press, 1984) pp. 93–4.

[32] Anonymous, *The Sea of Precious Virtue*, tr. Meisami, p. 294.

[33] Ann Lambton, *Theory and Practice in Medieval Persian Government* (London: Variorum Reprints, 1980) IV: 105.

[34] As quoted in Franz Rosenthal, "State and Religion according to Abū l-Ḥasan al-ʿĀmirī," *Islamic Quarterly* 3 (1956) 42–52.

for princes says, "the worst kings are those who keep themselves distant from the ʿulama, and the worst ʿulama are those who seek closeness to kings."[35]

The Abbasid caliphate was destroyed by the Mongols in 1258. Thereafter, there was no caliph; rather, sultans came to be regarded as exercising the functions of caliph within their own territories. It is interesting, however, that almost immediately after the fall of the caliphate, Ibn Taymiyya – the greatest jurist of the age – reaffirms the necessary connection between religion and politics. God, he says, has joined "knowledge and the pen, with their task of apostolate and persuasion, to power and the sword, with their task of victory and domination." He goes on: "Religion without sultan [power], holy war and wealth, is as bad as power, wealth and war without religion."[36] Ignoring the caliphate, Ibn Taymiyya calls upon the Mamluk sultan and other Muslim rulers to fulfill their religious duties by ensuring that the *Sharīʿa* was implemented, and by undertaking holy war. He also deplores the political indifference of the ʿulama and urges them to reengage with politics. In other words, he encourages sultans to assume a 'religious' role in accordance with their position after the demise of the Abbasid caliphate as *de facto* caliphs in their own lands, and he encourages the ʿulama to take a 'political' stand whenever this is required in order to teach and implement the *Sharīʿa*.

In marked contrast, Ibn Jamāʿa – a contemporary of Ibn Taymiyya but in Mamluk pay – is the jurist who goes furthest toward accepting the separation between religion and politics. He is prepared to go to extraordinary lengths to adapt religio-legal regulations in order to show that current political practice is acceptable from the viewpoint of the *Sharīʿa*. Even if someone with no religious learning seizes power by force of arms and without the consent of community leaders, Ibn Jamāʿa argues that he should be recognized as a legitimate ruler: "obedience to him is obligatory, so as to maintain the unity of the Muslims," even "if he is barbarous or vicious."[37] Given this approach, it is difficult to bring religious, moral, or legal sanctions to bear on any unjust ruler.

We have found very significant differences in the way relations between religious authority and the state were perceived in Byzantium, the Latin West, and Islam. These differences continued to play a major role in religious thought, political development and social behavior long after the Middle Ages.

[35] Anonymous, *Sea of Precious Virtue*, p. 297.

[36] As quoted in Antony Black, *The History of Islamic Political Thought: From the Prophet to the Present* (London: Routledge, 2001) p. 155.

[37] As quoted in Bernard Lewis, *The Political Languages of Islam* (Chicago: University of Chicago Press, 1988) p. 102. On Ibn Jamāʿa, see Ann Lambton, *State and Government in Medieval Islam: An Introduction to the Study of Islamic Political Thought: The Jurists* (Oxford, Oxford University Press, 1981) pp. 138–44.

INDIVIDUAL AUTONOMY

CARY J. NEDERMAN

Some readers may find it surprising to encounter a chapter on "individual autonomy" in a survey of medieval philosophy, especially in connection with political
philosophy. After all, an established tradition of historical scholarship insists that
the Middle Ages was a period in which hierarchy, interdependence, and communal holism were emphasized to the virtual exclusion of the individual. The
recovery of Aristotle's writings on ethics and politics during the course of the
mid-thirteenth century would seem only to reinforce the generally "communitarian" and anti-individualistic orientation commonly ascribed to medieval
thinkers.[1] Recently, the image of medieval Europe as hostile to the individual
has been reaffirmed by its depiction as a "persecuting society."[2] Thus, according
to the conventional view, the Renaissance and the Reformation constituted the
watershed for the appearance of the individual as a moral and political category
worthy of philosophical consideration.[3]

Yet medieval political thinkers, both before and after the dissemination of
Latin translations of Aristotle's work, were surprisingly attuned to the standing
of the individual and the role of free choice in public affairs. In their emphasis
on the centrality of private property and consent to government, as well as their
insistence on the ability of individuals to enjoy forms of personal liberty (such
as free thought, judgment, and speech), these authors resisted the supposedly
hierocratic (even authoritarian) tendencies that scholarship often ascribes to the
Middle Ages. In turn, the ability of high and late medieval writers to establish
a firm grounding for the individual in relation to religious as well as political
authority depended upon their access to a wide range of pagan and Christian sources that yielded philosophical and theological principles supporting

---

[1] Samuel Beer, "The Rule of the Wise and the Holy: Hierarchy in the Thomistic System," *Political
Theory* 14 (1984) 391–422.
[2] R. I. Moore, *The Formation of a Persecuting Society: Power and Deviance in Western Europe, 950–1250,*
2nd edn (Oxford: Blackwell, 2007).
[3] John Martin, "Inventing Sincerity, Refashioning Prudence: The Discovery of the Individual in
Renaissance Europe," *American Historical Review* 102 (1997) 1309–42.

personal autonomy.[4] For example, the political and legal traditions inherited from Rome endorsed such values as liberty, philosophical skepticism, and economic freedom.[5] Christian theologians and canon lawyers contributed ideas of free will, conscience, and human rights that were elaborated throughout the patristic and early medieval periods.[6] By the twelfth century, it is entirely plausible to speak of "the discovery of the individual" in a wide range of intellectual disciplines and endeavors.[7] A figure such as Peter Abaelard, whose major work on ethics is entitled *Know Thyself*, typifies the individualistic outlook present among many medieval thinkers.

The wealth of sources for personal autonomy and related doctrines, when applied to questions of political life, produced a number of philosophical examinations of the relation between individual and community. Although some Jewish and Islamic thinkers (such as Moses Maimonides and al-Fārābī) touched on related themes (such as mild skepticism about the ability of the human mind to attain religious knowledge with certainty[8]), these authors seem to have contributed at best secondarily to the promotion of individualism. For the most part, emphasis on the status of the individual was a Western Christian phenomenon. The present chapter will briefly survey several important examples of this effort, starting with John of Salisbury in the middle of the twelfth century and moving forward through John of Paris, Marsilius of Padua, and William of Ockham.

JOHN OF SALISBURY

John of Salisbury is one of the central figures in the emergence of a humanistic spirit associated with the so-called "Renaissance of the Twelfth Century," as well as the first author of an extended medieval treatise on public affairs and

---

[4] See Antony Black, "Society and the Individual from the Middle Ages to Rousseau: Philosophy, Jurisprudence and Constitutional Theory," *History of Political Thought* 1 (1980) 145–66.

[5] Chaim Wirszubski, *Libertas as a Political Idea at Rome during the Late Republic and Early Principate* (Cambridge: Cambridge University Press, 1950); Charles Schmitt, *Cicero Scepticus* (The Hague: Nijhoff, 1972) pp. 18–42; Odd Langholm, *The Legacy of Scholasticism in Economic Thought* (Cambridge: Cambridge University Press, 1998) pp. 30–42.

[6] See Simon Harrison, "Do We Have a Will? Augustine's Way in to the Will," and Simo Knuuttila, "The Emergence of the Logic of the Will in Medieval Thought," both in G. Matthews (ed.) *The Augustinian Tradition* (Berkeley: University of California Press, 1999) 195–221; Odon Lottin, *Psychologie et morale aux XIIe et XIIIe siècles* (Gembloux: Duculot, 1948) vol. II, pt. IV; Brian Tierney, *The Idea of Natural Rights: Studies on Natural Rights, Natural Law and Church Law, 1150–1625* (Atlanta, GA: Scholars Press, 1997).

[7] Colin Morris, *The Discovery of the Individual 1050–1200* (New York: Harper and Row, 1972). See also Ineke van't Spijker, *Fictions of the Inner Life: Religious Literature and Formation of the Self in the Eleventh and Twelfth Centuries* (Turnhout: Brepols, 2004).

[8] Al-Fārābī, *On the Perfect State*, ed. Walzer, pp. 279–85.

political community, the *Policraticus*, which was completed in 1159 (about a century before the translation of Aristotle's *Nicomachean Ethics* and *Politics*).[9] John's philosophical role model is Cicero, many of whose works he knows and whose style he imitates. In particular, John embraces the New Academy skepticism advocated by Cicero in order to develop a theory of the connection between personal virtue and forms of social and political liberty. John believes that both virtue and good political order assume extensive freedom of choice and expression, and that such freedom must be respected and indeed protected by other individuals as well as by the healthy public body. Such freedom is necessary on account of the fallibility of the human intellect: since we cannot be certain, in many matters connected with human goodness and earthly well-being, what the correct action may be, we must respect persons who have different conceptions of goodness and who seek to realize them in different ways.

John himself is aware of the connection between his Academy-influenced skepticism and the necessity for a wide band of free judgment and expression. He remarks that his own "spirit of investigation corresponds to Academic practices rather than to the plan of a stubborn combatant, so that each is to reserve to himself freedom of judgment in the examination of truth, and the authority of writers is to be considered useless whenever it is subdued by a better argument" (*Policraticus* VII prol.). The approach of the Academy requires that in all matters not settled beyond reasonable doubt, it is the force of the evidence alone that should prevail. Authorities should not be granted superior wisdom if a more cogent viewpoint opposes them. Likewise, the determination of what position seems most plausible or defensible lies with the individual. In view of his skeptical predilections, John raises the priority of individual judgment to a universal principle.

On more than one occasion in the *Policraticus*, freedom of judgment is desig-nated as a *ius*, a right that pertains to human beings. The medieval understanding of *ius* entailed acknowledgment of a fixed and defensible sphere of activity whose exercise is independent of external infringement or control. This seems to be precisely what John has in mind when insisting upon the right of free inquiry and determination: "The Academy of the ancients bestows upon the human race the leave that each person by his right (*ius*) may defend whatever presents itself to him as most probable" (ibid., II.22). Or, as he remarks in another pas-sage, "It is a very ancient rule of the Academics that each person may of his own right (*ius*) defend that which presents itself to him as most probable" (ibid.,

---

[9] See Cary Nederman, *John of Salisbury* (Tempe: Arizona Center for Medieval and Renaissance Studies, 2005).

VII.6). One's freedom to form one's own judgments derives from the fallible nature of the human mind and the uncertain character of many knowledge claims.

In turn, if we each enjoy a right to draw conclusions and construct arguments regarding those matters open to rational disagreement, then it follows that others (regardless of their status or power) likewise have a duty to respect our thoughts even if they do not endorse them. This is underscored in the *Policraticus* by John's remark that, regarding unsettled issues, "one is free to question and doubt, up to the point where, from a comparison of views, truth shines through as though from the clash of ideas (*rationum collisione*)" (ibid., VII.8).[10] Such a statement suggests that John understands very well the implications of his skeptical philosophy: the quest for truth in matters of practical as well as philosophical import demands the maintenance of openness and dissent. It is the responsibility of the wise person, not to mention the wise ruler or prelate, to uphold and defend the grounds of public debate. The realization of truth is hampered, not aided, by the suppression of divergent positions and the persecution of their adherents.

As a consequence, John maintains a central role for human liberty in his moral and political thought. In the *Policraticus*, he defends a conception of open personal expression that is vast even judged by far later standards. He counsels a doctrine of "patience" for the opinions and deeds of others.

The best and wisest man is moderate with the reins of liberty and patiently takes note of whatever is said to him. And he does not oppose himself to the works of liberty, so long as damage to virtue does not occur. For when virtue shines everywhere from its own source, the reputation of patience becomes more evident with glorious renown.

(ibid., VII.25)

The patient man respects the liberty of others to state their own honest opinions, and he attempts to improve himself by patiently regarding his fellows. "The practice of liberty," John observes, "displeases only those who live in the manner of slaves" (ibid., VII.25). Free men are reciprocally respectful of the freedom of others, even when they are the objects of criticism. John praises the Romans for "being more patient than others with censure," since they adhered to the principle that "whoever loathes and evades [criticism] when fairly expressed seems to be ignorant of restraint. For even if it conveys obvious or secret insult, patience with censure is among wise men far more glorious than its punishment" (ibid., VII.25). The *Policraticus* supports this claim in characteristic form with

---

[10] The phrase *rationum collisione* is also used at VII.6 (ed. Webb, II: 113).

numerous examples of wise people who spoke their minds straightforwardly and of wise rulers who permitted such free expression to occur.

While John upholds a realm of personal discretion in decision-making with which no one may interfere, he also insists that patient endurance of the liberty of others must be matched by a liberty of critical speech. John asserts that "it is permitted to censure that which is to be equitably corrected" (ibid.). While we may not properly force people to do good, we must equally be respected and tolerated when we point out the error of their ways. In other words, if you are free to do wrong, then I must also be free to correct or reprove you. John emphasizes this point: "Liberty ... is not afraid to censure that which is opposed to sound moral character... Man is to be free and it is always permitted to a free man to speak to persons about restraining their vices" (ibid.). John claims that this liberty to censure is not merely a privilege: "It is not necessary to obtain confirmed permission for such remarks which serve the public utility" (ibid.). Freedom to speak one's mind about both personal misconduct and the ills of society – the church as well as temporal communities – follows from the exercise of legitimate liberty (ibid., I.5).

JOHN OF PARIS

The translation of Aristotle's major works of moral and political philosophy into Latin, alongside the rise of the scholastic curriculum of the universities, did not mean an end to the humanistic flowering of "individualism" associated with earlier times. Rather, scholastics from the thirteenth century onward continued to insist upon the individual as a central category of political analysis. Thomas Aquinas, for instance, who is often taken as the quintessential Christian Aristotelian, may nonetheless be read as rejecting the hyper-communalism of Aristotle's political theory, at least in the *Summa theologiae* and in his commentary on the *Politics*. Instead, Aquinas stresses how the goodness of the human will, in conjunction with conscience and reason, might lead individuals to fulfill their natural sociability through knowing and acting upon natural law.[11] Even if Aquinas himself does not always follow through with the full implications of personal autonomy for politics (he did not, for instance, set out a theory of consent to government), many other scholastic authors took up this mantle.[12]

One of the most prominent proponents of the individual's centrality to communal life was John of Paris, a Thomist who attained the status of master of

---

[11] I follow here the interpretation of Aquinas posited by Mary Keys, *Aquinas, Aristotle and the Pursuit of the Common Good* (Cambridge: Cambridge University Press, 2006).

[12] Brian Tierney, "Hierarchy, Consent and the 'Western Tradition,'" *Political Theory* 15 (1987) 646–54.

arts at the University of Paris, flourishing around 1300. John's major work of political theory, *De potestate regia et papali* (*ca.* 1302), was composed in the midst of the notorious conflict between the French king Philip IV and the reigning pope Boniface VIII concerning their mutual rights over the material goods of the church. John's thought has been located at the root of an intellectual tradition regarding private property and political power that culminates in the seventeenth-century liberalism of John Locke's *Second Treatise of Government*. Although the building blocks of the *De potestate's* doctrine are largely conventional – in some cases directly adapted from the slightly earlier writings of Godfrey of Fontaines and from Roman law ideas of market exchange – the scenario he constructs is innovative in a manner that presages early modern natural rights theory.[13]

De potestate takes as one of its main themes the differentiation of the types of rights over property that persons of various ranks and statuses (lay versus clerical conditions, secular versus ecclesiastical rulers) may claim. John sharply distinguishes throughout the work between *dominium* (lordship) and *iurisdictio* (jurisdiction), arguing that powers conferred by the former are primary and antecedent in relation to the latter. Thus, a political official (spiritual or temporal) may be able to judge in certain circumstances whether a member of the secular community is putting his property to an unjust use, as this pertains to the realm of jurisdiction. But such judgment does not amount to a denial of the preexisting ownership of the property nor of the rightful control over property exercised by its *dominus*. Rather, John declares, "the temporalities of laymen are not communal" (ed. Bleienstein, p. 82). The earthly goods of non-clerics are rightfully apportioned by some means other than assignment by clergy or princes.

If the authority to use property does not in the first instance derive from a political/legal act or a moral/theological assessment, then whence does it arise? John gives a summary of his answer in Chapter 3 of *De potestate*: "Each is lord (*dominus*) of his own property as acquired through his own industry, therefore there is no need for a single person to dispense lay temporalities in common, since each is his own dispenser to do with his own at will (*ad libitum*)" (ibid., p. 82). This point is developed at greater length in Chapter 7:

---

[13] Janet Coleman, "*Dominium* in Thirteenth- and Fourteenth-Century Political Thought and its Seventeenth-Century Heirs: John of Paris and Locke," *Political Studies* 33 (1985) 73–100; "Poverty, Property and Political Thought in Fourteenth Century Scholastic Philosophy," in C. Wenin (ed.) *L'homme et son univers au moyen age* (Louvain-la-Neuve: Éditions de l'Institut Supérieur de Philosophie, 1986) pp. 845–55; Odd Langholm, *Economics in the Medieval Schools: Wealth, Exchange, Value, Money and Usury According to the Paris Theological Tradition, 1200–1350* (Leiden: Brill, 1992).

The external goods of the laity are not granted to the community, as is ecclesiastical property, but are acquired by individual people through their own art, labor, or industry, and individual persons, insofar as they are individuals, have right (*ius*) and power and true lordship over them. And each person is able to order, dispose, dispense, retain, and alienate his own [goods] according to his will (*pro libito*) without injury to others, since he is lord. And therefore such goods do not have order and connection amongst themselves nor towards one common head who has them to dispose and dispense, since each one may order his things according to his will (*pro libito*). And therefore neither the prince nor the pope has lordship or the power of dispensing such things.

(ibid., pp. 96–7)

Property is antecedently private and individual, and takes on a communal bearing only by virtue of the will of its owner. Individuals enter voluntarily with one another into an exchange relationship, the existence of which derives its entire legitimacy from the liberty of the participants. As John underscores at the close of Chapter 7 of *De potestate*, "Each one disposes of his own as he wills" (ibid., p. 98). The exercise of this freedom is in accordance with right and in itself harms no one.

But what about the jurisdiction enjoyed by rulers over the just and unjust uses of temporal goods? Does this not constitute a severe constraint on the liberty associated with private lordship over property? John constructs very precisely the connection between individual property and the political/legal authority of both the church and the secular ruler. Jurisdiction is rendered necessary by the entry of private proprietors into voluntary mutual relations with one another:

Because it sometimes happens that the common peace is disturbed on account of such external goods, as when someone takes that which is another's, and also at times because some people, who are excessively fond of their own, do not convey it according to what the needs and utility of the country require, therefore a ruler is instituted by the people to restrain such acts, in the manner of a judge discerning the just and the unjust, a vindicator of injuries, and a measurer of the just proportion owed to each for the common needs and utility.

(ibid., p. 97)

According to John, the temptation on the part of some to override the liberty of others, in conjunction with a failure of self-absorbed individuals to calculate and acknowledge the social costs of the profit they obtain by entering into reciprocal economic intercourse, comprise the only justifications for the jurisdiction of rulers. Hence, only those who antecedently enjoy private property rights can authorize the appointment of a judge and executor over themselves and their goods. If something falls within my exclusive dominion, then only my consent can confirm jurisdiction over my property upon someone else. John of Paris thus proposes an extensive notion of the free sphere of individual action.

MARSILIUS OF PADUA

The generation of political thinkers following John of Paris continued to reflect on the problem of the limits of clerical as well as temporal authority over the members of the political community. One of the most heralded responses dating from the early fourteenth century was the *Defensor pacis* by Marsilius of Padua, completed in 1324.[14] Although Marsilius is commonly conceived to be an arch-Aristotelian, he in fact rejects much of the communitarian orientation found in the *Nicomachean Ethics* and the *Politics*. Instead, the first discourse of the *Defensor*, which addresses the natural foundations and proper institutions of temporal community, enunciates a quite eclectic doctrine that licenses private self-interest as the source for a thoroughgoing principle of individualized consent to all facets of the exercise of political power. He has powerful reasons for adopting this stance: it permits him to eliminate any claim on the part of the pope or the priesthood to the power to interfere with the earthly lives of Christian citizens or governors, since their spiritual authority does not extend to any temporal affairs.

Marsilius's pursuit of this line of reasoning depends heavily upon his postulation of a sharp distinction between temporal and spiritual realms in the *Defensor pacis*. He acknowledges that human ends "fall into two kinds, of which one is temporal or earthly, while the other is usually called eternal or heavenly" (I.4.3). Temporal ends are for the most part indifferent to spiritual goals. The term 'spiritual,' Marsilius says, "refers to every immanent action or passion of human cognitive or appetitive power" (II.2.5), where "immanent" acts are understood as wholly internal and self-regarding. Immanent acts are spiritual in the sense that they do not transgress the boundaries of the soul, and hence are invisible to human observation and known only to God. By contrast, the temporal activities of a human being, Marsilius believes, are of concern to other people to the extent that they are "transient," that is, have an impact on someone else. Consequently, "transient" acts are the proper object of regulation by the laws and rulers of the political community (I.5.7). When transient behavior is performed in due proportion, it results in benefits to others as well as to oneself. When transient action is excessive, however, it disadvantages another person.

---

[14] See Cary J. Nederman, *Community and Consent: The Secular Political Theory of Marsiglio of Padua's Defensor Pacis* (Lanham, MD: Rowman and Littlefield, 1995).

On the basis of this distinction, Marsilius enshrines temporal advantage as a fundamental and entirely legitimate goal of human conduct. Indeed, he establishes "as the starting-point of everything to be demonstrated . . . that all human beings not deformed or otherwise impeded naturally desire a sufficient life, and avoid or flee what is harmful thereto" (I.4.2). Marsilius then quotes Cicero's proclamation in *De officiis* that the basic purpose of all living creatures is self-preservation. The advantage of human beings is achieved by gaining those conditions of existence that confer upon them a physically adequate life. Although Marsilius makes passing mention of the Aristotelian conception of living well, constituted by the exercise of the practical and theoretical virtues, the material sufficiency of human life receives the overwhelming measure of his attention.

Marsilius formulates a reconstruction of the origins of human association and of government that serves as an explanation of both the purpose of civil life and its relation to human nature. The preservation of individuals is achieved most fully and naturally under conditions of human cooperation in the context of an ordered and organized community. Marsilius holds that "human beings came together in the civil community in order to pursue advantage and a sufficient life and to avoid the opposite" (I.12.7). Human desire for mutual advantage grounds communal life in the *Defensor pacis*. The "perfected" community for Marsilius emerges along with the differentiation of the functions necessary for a materially sufficient existence, these tasks being defined by the various arts created by humankind in order to redress their physical infirmities (I.3.2–5). Marsilius thus posits that the commission of "transient" acts is absolutely necessary for human beings to attain a sufficient life. Successful self-preservation demands perpetual interaction between human beings, each of whom makes a particular contribution through the exercise of his specialized task (I.4.5). Marsilius expressly specifies these functions in terms of the occupations necessary to maintain the physical well-being of the community: farmers, merchants, craftsmen, and warriors (I.5.6–9). Since all of these jobs contribute essentially to achieving a sufficient temporal life, none are to be denigrated. These needs and the means to their fulfillment are defined by nature, but the organization of the occupations (or "offices") that perform forms of necessary labor is determined by the community. Thus, all functions requisite for communal and personal welfare have a political dimension, as a result of which Marsilius insists that politics must be inclusive. That is, citizenship in the community is conferred on a functional basis, judged according to the usefulness of various human activities for the meeting of material human needs.

Marsilius intends citizens within the community to take an active role in their own governance, locating popular consent at the center of his theoretical framework. Such consent arises directly from the functional character of the community. First, all whose interests are served or affected by a community must agree to the conditions of association (that is, law and rulership). Second, having so consented, all such citizens are absolutely bound to obey the law and the determinations made by rulers in accordance with it. In other words, people must individually as well as collectively submit to the terms of their cooperation, after which they can be held strictly accountable for excessive "transient" actions that are detrimental to the advantage of fellow citizens. As a consequence, the *Defensor pacis* holds that the legitimacy of both laws and rulers depends wholly upon their "voluntary" character, that is, the extent to which those subject to their jurisdiction have publicly and overtly consented to their authority (I.9.5, I.12.3). What Marsilius in fact regards as distinctive of citizenship is the ability to express one's will in the political venue, by judging for oneself the validity of prospective rulers and laws. This implies for Marsilius not merely formal, corporative assent, but an extensive privilege on the part of each individual citizen to examine prospective laws and rulers:

Common measures must be laid before the assembled whole body of citizens for their approval or disapproval, so that if any citizen thinks that something should be added, subtracted, changed, or completely rejected, he can say so . . . For, as has been said, the less learned citizens can sometimes perceive something that must be corrected in a proposed law even though they could not have discovered the law itself. Also, the laws thus made by the hearing and consent of the whole multitude will be better observed, nor will anyone have any protest to make against them.

(I.13.8)

Each and every member of the community reserves to himself final judgment about all matters of public regulation. This is required, Marsilius contends, because a government's very legitimacy depends upon its congruence with the voluntary acquiescence of those over whom it rules. And the only way to assure such congruence is by a prior act of explicit consent on the part of citizens. Then, should the private conduct of some citizen lapse over into an "excessive transient" deed – one that harms another person – the execution of the law by the ruler will be seen to be authorized by the community (including, indeed, the offending citizen himself) (I.12.6).

According to what criteria, what point of reference, do citizens discern the worthiness of legislative measures and candidates for rulership? Marsilius answers that every person correctly and adequately evaluates laws and rulers when he measures them against the yardstick of his own self-interest. Marsilius asserts, "Those matters, therefore, that can touch upon the advantage and disadvantage (*commodum et incommodum*) of everyone ought to be known and heard by everyone, so that they can obtain advantage and repel its opposite" (I.12.7). Marsilius cleverly recasts a conventional (and highly elastic) dictum of medieval political and legal thought: "What touches all must be approved by all" (*quod omnes tangit ab omnibus approbatur*).[15] In his hands, the vague term *tangere* becomes noticeably concrete: it refers to the material well-being designated by *commodum*. Citizens must be accorded a role in consent to law and government inasmuch as statutory dictates and the execution of those dictates impact their direct interests.

Consequently, the common good for Marsilius comes to be coextensive with the aggregate advantage of each of the individuals within the community. No power may legitimately be imposed upon the polity that is inconsistent with the interests of its citizens. Therefore, by consulting one's own direct benefit in the evaluation of public affairs, one simultaneously discovers the communal benefit:

> The common utility of a law is better noticed by the whole community, because no one knowingly harms oneself. Anyone can look to see whether a proposed law leans toward the advantage (*commodum*) of one or a few [citizens] more than of the rest or of the community and can protest loudly in opposition; this would not be so, however, if the law were to be made by one or a few.
>
> (I.12.5)

Left to their own devices, unchecked by the consent of the body of citizens, people in power will quite naturally and unavoidably create laws and make decisions that will favor themselves. But if every citizen considers a statutory proposal (or prospective governor), and none finds any detriment to his own interests, then the decision must be a good one, since it withstands the ultimate test of the common good as conceived by Marsilius: can this measure harm me in any discernible way? Or will I instead derive some tangible benefit from it? Only when laws and officials are evaluated according to purely individual determinations of personal welfare can a valid realization of the public good be ensured.

WILLIAM OF OCKHAM

Marsilius advocated the cause of the German king (and would-be emperor) Ludwig of Bavaria against the papacy (especially Pope John XXII), eventually entering into the royal court as an advisor. Also present at Ludwig's court was another important figure, the philosopher and theologian William of Ockham. Ockham previously spent several years at the papal court in Avignon under

---

[15] On the variety of usages of this slogan, see Gaines Post, *Studies in Medieval Legal Thought: Public Law and the State 1100–1322* (Princeton, NJ: Princeton University Press, 1964) pp. 163–238.

house arrest while his theological writings were investigated for containing heretical errors, during which time he became convinced that the pope himself had slid into heresy. Most philosophers know of Ockham as a leading advocate of nominalism (see Chapters 12 and 48). Fewer people realize, however, that after about 1327, Ockham gave up his philosophical and theological pursuits in order to become a full-time propagandist on behalf of Ludwig, and especially against the papacy. In the following two decades, he produced about a dozen, often lengthy, treatises opposing papal pretensions to earthly power and justifying Ludwig's claim to be emperor.

There is no persuasive evidence that Ockham consciously brought his nominalist logic directly to bear on his political doctrines. But he does embrace several ideas that demonstrate a high degree of regard for the individual, especially in connection with the religious authority of the church and its hierarchy.[16] Thus, unlike Marsilius, who had proposed that the general council formed the supreme and unerring legislative authority within the church, Ockham refuses to accept that a council was any more a necessary witness to truth than, say, the pope or the college of cardinals. Indeed, although Ockham contends that the true church could never die out on earth, he holds that the truth of the faith might reside in a single individual, regardless of social status (or even gender or age!) (*Dialogus* I.5.1–35). Moreover, he countenances individual opposition on the part of any Christian whomsoever – priest or layman, rich or poor, male or female – to notorious (that is, publicly proclaimed) heresy, even if it stretches to the upper reaches of the church's official structure (ibid., I.7.10).

Ockham thus evinces a high level of confidence in the capacity of individuals to form judgments about fundamental truths for themselves, separate and distinct from communities or institutional authorities. His grounding for this seems to be a theory of imprescriptible natural rights and natural liberty granted by God (through nature) to mankind. He insists that "the pope cannot deprive any persons of their right, particularly in that they hold it not from him, but from God or nature or another man; and for the same reason he cannot deprive any persons of their liberties, which were granted by God and nature" (*De imperatorum et pontificum potestate* [*Opera pol.* IV: 287]). Human rights and liberties include *dominium*, of course; both individual possession and the powers of earthly governance are shielded from intrusion by the pope or other religious officials (ibid., pp. 299–301). Yet these rights and liberties also include a considerable freedom of individual understanding in connection with knowledge of religious

---

[16] As emphasized by both A. S. McGrade, *The Political Thought of William of Ockham* (Cambridge: Cambridge University Press, 1974), and Janet Coleman, *A History of Political Thought from the Middle Ages to the Renaissance* (Oxford: Blackwell, 2000) pp. 169–92.

and moral truths. God has granted humanity reason and sense, in Ockham's view, so that each person may determine for himself (or herself, apparently) what is required for the sake of one's own salvation. The church may act as a guide, but it lacks any authority to coerce when confronted with persons who shun its direction. This stems from Ockham's conception of the predicament in which the faithful find themselves: on the one hand, all Christians seek the truth; on the other hand, all people are fallible such that no one can establish beyond doubt who enjoys certain access to the truth. Each individual thus possesses, in a sense, the right to be wrong, even in the face of contrary claims by ecclesiastical authorities.

Ockham thereby advocates a method of philosophical and theological analysis that requires suspension of coercive judgment in matters concerning heretical belief. In his view, the onus for demonstrating that an individual's belief stands in error pertains to the person who performs the correction. If an individual who upholds such supposed error clings to it because he does not grasp the manner of his own alleged mistake, it is unwarranted for clerical authorities to punish him via excommunication and for temporal powers to impose earthly penalties upon him (*Dialogus* I.4). In part, this is because prelates (and rulers) themselves are often ignorant and fallible in matters of faith. But, more importantly, Ockham maintains that the only reason one may legitimately employ coercion is to correct a person who explicitly admits that his position is erroneous and still refuses to surrender it – in other words, a person entirely lacking in powers of reason (which he seems to think is rare indeed). The individual who cannot or does not acknowledge that he is in error because he does not accept the reasoning presented to him must be accorded patient forbearance, not be subjected to persecution. To persecute, according to Ockham, is to misuse the corrective power granted to the church.[17] The right and liberty of individuals (including members of the laity) to maintain or refuse a belief until its error or truth is proven to their own satisfaction, even when confronted with the claim of superior political or ecclesial authority, form a centerpiece of Ockham's teaching. He thus pushes medieval thinking about individual autonomy to new and apparently quite extreme lengths.

The thinkers who have been surveyed in the present chapter are usually accounted among the most important figures in medieval Latin political thought. On the one hand, their theories were highly original and sometimes intentionally provocative, inasmuch as they adopted attitudes that were meant to be critical of both secular and ecclesiastical practices. Yet, on the other hand,

---

[17] See Takashi Shogimen, "From Disobedience to Toleration: William of Ockham and the Medieval Discourse of Fraternal Correction," *Journal of Ecclesiastical History* 52 (2001) 599–622.

all of the thinkers mentioned (even those suspected or accused of heresy, such as Marsilius and Ockham) based their teachings about the individual and his (or her) role in society upon orthodox and widely endorsed legal and theological principles, such as might be found in canon and Roman law, in Scripture, and in conventional scholastic writings. Thus, it would be misplaced to dismiss ideas of individual autonomy during the Latin Middle Ages as the work of a few cranks or outliers who were at odds with the intellectual mainstream. Rather, these authors represented the extension and application of teachings about the political implications of individual liberty that were firmly rooted in the medieval worldview.

41

LAW AND NATURE

G. R. EVANS

The sources for what we know of medieval thinking on law and nature include the Church Fathers and scholastic theologians, as well as Roman legal writings, and the somewhat confused cluster of texts that were drawn together in the twelfth and thirteenth centuries to constitute a body of recognized "canon law" for academic study. Of the first importance here is Gratian's *Decretum* from the 1140s, the ground-breaking manual of canon law on which many subsequent treatises and commentaries would rely. These sources show how the classical understanding of a right (*ius*) as the subjective right of an individual contrasts with the characteristically medieval understanding of *ius* as "a system of objectively right relationships."[1] Medieval discussions of these issues pass through a complex set of questions about law and human nature, until the point where thinkers begin to stand away from tradition and ask radical questions. This leads through early modern political thought to a conventionalism that says morality is a mere convention that depends on the interaction between individuals.[2]

DEFINITIONS AND CONCEPTS: 'LAW' AND 'NATURE'

For the clusters of concepts for which we use the modern English words 'law' and 'nature,' a series of Latin terms were used from the ancient world to the Middle Ages, often equivocally, and with a shifting range of meanings.

In one of its medieval meanings, *natura* was 'nature' – the natural world, the Latin counterpart of the Greek *physis*. Boethius, in a passage in *De Trinitate* (ch. 2), uses *naturalis* in this sense. He distinguishes the study of *speculativa*, purely abstract, theoretical matters; *mathematica*, in which things which are

---

[1] Brian Tierney, *The Idea of Natural Rights: Studies on Natural Rights, Natural Law and Church Law, 1150–1625* (Atlanta, GA: Scholars Press, 1997) p. 22.

[2] Knud Haakonssen, "The Moral Conservatism of Natural Rights," in I. Hunter and D. Saunders (eds.) *Natural Law and Civil Sovereignty: Moral Right and State Authority in Early Modern Political Thought* (Houndmills, Basingstoke: Palgrave, 2002) 13–26; see esp. pp. 13–14.

really concrete are studied as though they were abstract; and *naturalis*.[3] By this he means what might now be called natural science, which deals with those parts of the universe that can be measured and observed. Boethius's contemporary, Cassiodorus, describes *philosophia* in his *Institutiones* as the study of things human and divine, and natural philosophy as a branch of philosophy "in which any aspect of nature is discussed" (ed. Mynors, pp. 110–11).

Natura also emerged in the patristic period in the Latin West as a synonym for *substantia* or *essentia*. Augustine employs it in this way in the *De Trinitate* in his discussion of the divine "nature" (II.18.35). The driving force here was the need to identify a Latin terminology in which to carry on the heated debate about the number of "natures" and "persons" in the Incarnate Christ which had preoccupied the Greek-speaking half of the empire in the period of the Arian controversy and beyond. Boethius uses 'nature' like this, for instance, in discussing the "two natures" of Christ in *Contra Eutychen* I.

This usage, where *natura* is more or less interchangeable with *substantia* or *essentia*, permitted discussion of "human nature." For example, it is suggested that the nature of the spirit is to be invisible and that of the flesh is to be visible, as Alcuin puts it in the eighth century.[4] In the twelfth century, Aelred of Rievaulx writes within this same frame of reference about the contrast between God's nature and that of human beings. God's nature is *aeternus, intemporalis, incommutabilis*; ours is *mutabilis et temporalis*. God made a way for our nature to become more like his by becoming mutable himself.[5] This usage shades into a somewhat broader sense of 'nature' as a kind of thing or a property, as when Andrew of St. Victor suggests in the mid-twelfth century that "it is the nature of music to make someone who is happy happier and someone who is sad sadder still."[6]

The area of meaning with which we shall be primarily concerned in thinking about law and nature is the first – that of *nature* as the natural world or natural order, and the place of human beings in that natural world, for those things were governed by the *laws* of nature. When David Hume wrote that nature is "blind, impregnated by a great vivifying principle, and pouring forth from her lap, without discernment or parental case, her maimed and abortive children" (*Dialogues conc. Nat. Religion* 11), he was challenging a normative view that had been formed in the classical world of an essentially orderly overflowing of creative power. Plato, for instance, had thought that this flow was an indication

---

[3] Other Latin authors use *physica* in this sense – see, e.g., Cicero, *De divinatione* I.110, and Macrobius, *Saturnalia* VII.xv.14.

[4] *Commentaria in S. Iohannis Evangelium* (ed. Migne, *Patr. Lat.* 100: 779).

[5] *De Iesu puero duodenni* 1 (*Opera* I: 249).   [6] *Expositio Hystorica in Librum Regum* 16 (*Opera* II: 57).

of the sheer abundance of the Good, but that the goodness diminished as created things moved further from their origin, the supreme and supremely generous Good. There remained room for a vigorous patristic and medieval debate about the degree to which God planned for his creation and kept control of it, and especially whether there was a great providential plan. Under the influence of Aristotle, later mediated through discussions in Thomas Aquinas, this plan could be seen as involving rules or laws that governed the way nature worked.

Medieval Christian theologians were confident that nature had been created by God with a plan and a shape and an order which, as Genesis describes it, had been disrupted in part by the sin of Adam but never thrown wholly out of divine control. When Alan of Lille wrote the *Complaint of Nature* in the second half of the twelfth century, he personified Nature in a pseudo-classical way, as a goddess-like figure, with a list of substantive attributes that evince this; she is:

> Virtue, rule, power (*Virtus, regimen, potestas*)
> Order, law, end, way, leader, origin (*Ordo, lex, finis, via, dux, origo*).
> (VII/metr. 4)

Nature's "complaints" concern the disorderly behavior of Alan's contemporaries, behavior that was believed to go against nature, such as homosexual acts. Nature's biggest complaint is that human beings, alone in created nature, seek to behave as though they are not subject to nature's laws.

The history of the terminology of 'nature' thus had a strong theological and philosophical emphasis. The vocabulary associated with law – words such as *lex, ius, iustitia* – was also familiar in such contexts from its frequency in the Vulgate Bible, particularly the Old Testament. Marsilius of Padua, for example, recognizes in his *Defensor pacis* (*ca.* 1324) the equivocal way *lex* is used, and he has no difficulty in giving a series of biblical examples to illustrate his point (Dictio I.10). When he takes up the many meanings of *ius*, with particular reference to the contemporary poverty debate (see below, and Chapter 42), the Bible again provides him with a range of examples (Dictio II.12).

The term *iustitia* poses a particular difficulty because it can be rendered in modern English as "justice" or as "righteousness," with the Old Testament connotations of that word. The emphasis in secular classical usage is on justice as a mode of proper *citizenly* behavior, however, rather than on the Judaic notion of the *righteousness* that involves being in a right relationship with God. In a passage well known to medieval authors, Cicero – who became perhaps the most important Hellenistic source for natural law ideas – defines *iustitia* as a "habit of mind" that affords the appropriate respect to each person, while serving the common good (*De inventione* II.liii.160). The citizen is also a good neighbor, and the definition thus provided medieval authors with a basis for their own comments as Christians, commanded by God to "love thy neighbor as thyself." Alcuin, for instance, takes Cicero's definition and adds to it the observation that *iustitia* protects the worship of God and the laws of mankind and equity in living (*De rhetorica et de virtutibus* 44). These modified Ciceronian echoes persisted into the twelfth century and beyond.[7]

In the thirteenth century, Aquinas defined *ius* as "that which is just," but he knew that it was not as simple as that (*Summa theol.* 2a2ae 57.1). *Ius* in Roman law can refer not only to a concept or a general state of things (as in 'right order') but also a body of legal precepts (*ius civile, ius gentium*), or even a single precept in such a code. It can mean "right" in the sense of a person's legal rights, including personal standing in such matters as being a free man, and it can refer to legal rights over others, or *jurisdiction*. According to Ulpian, "Justice is . . . to assign to each one his *ius*"; it is about getting one's deserts, in the sense of "the just share, the just due, of someone within an established structure of social relationships, varying with each person's status and role."[8] In this sense, the word *ius* could imply disadvantage to an individual as well as the advantages usually associated with having a right,[9] and it has connotations that link it with the key passage of Cicero already cited in the discussion of *iustitia*. The range of possible classical meanings of *lex* matches those of *ius* at a number of points, although *leges* can also be specific measures or standards.[10] Conversely, *ius* often stands in for *lex*, as when authors speak of the natural law as the *ius naturale*.

In the sixth century, Isidore of Seville had provided a number of influential definitions in his short encyclopedia, the *Etymologiae*. Trying to tease out the difference between what is just, law, and custom (*ius, lex, mos*), he suggested that *ius* is the more general word, while *lex* and *mos* are the two species of *ius*. Law may be identified by being written, whereas custom need not be. Custom is what is sanctioned by long use; it is applied as though it were law when written law is lacking (*Etymol.* V.3). Merely writing law down is not enough to make it law, however. Isidore insisted that it has to be authorized, or agreed on in some way. For him, "Law is a constitution of the people by which the more highly born together with the common people sanction something" (ibid., V.10). It is also of no small importance that Isidore was hard to better even as late as the twelfth century, when the academic and practical study of law was taking on a new direction and proceeding with a new energy, in directions which

---

[7] For instance, *iustitia*, says Clarembald of Arras, is "the constant and perpetual will to distribute equality" (*Life and Works*, p. 219).

[8] *Liber regularum* 2 (in Justinian, *Digest* 1.1.10 pr. 2 [*Corpus juris civilis* vol. I]). See Brian Tierney, "Tuck on Rights: Some Medieval Problems," *History of Political Thought* 4 (1983) 429–41.

[9] Tierney, *The Idea of Natural Rights*, pp. 16–17.

[10] See, for instance, Aelred of Rievaulx, *Sermo* 43 (*Opera* II: 336).

had not been envisaged in the age of Isidore. The political and constitutional realities in which these definitions were originally framed make it important to try to understand them in context. At the same time, they purport to be of general application and were treated in that way by later authors who relied on them in their own work.[11] Gratian, for instance, relies heavily on Isidore in setting out the basics at the beginning of the *Decretum*. He holds, for instance, that promulgation is constitutive of the making of law, remarking that "laws are instituted when they are promulgated" (P. I d. iv). Aquinas, citing Gratian, agrees that promulgation is part of what defines or makes law (*Summa theol.* 1a2ae 90.4). The law has to be published in order to be law; if it has not been, no one can be blamed for not obeying it. Thus, the person who acts against a law of whose existence he has not been informed should not be treated as an offender.

Summaries and statements of this cursory and often inconsistent sort served less well once the academic study of law began seriously in the twelfth century, with the emergence of universities; nevertheless, the authority of their authors meant that they lingered on in use, out of context, bearing the appearance of philosophical axioms and blithely unaffected by the political realities of lawmaking. Ideas about the nature of law did not depend on the study of the differences between civil and canon law, or of varieties of legal codes and systems in different places.

THE 'LAW OF NATURE' IN THE HIERARCHY OF LAWS

Isidore's starting point was that all laws are either divine or human (*Etymol.* V.2). Laws of nature fall into the divine category and therefore do not change, but human laws vary from race to race, nation to nation, and people to people. Divine law is right (*ius*) in the sense of being "good" (*fas*), while human law is merely right.[12] Isidore suggested that "natural law" should be divided into civil law and the law of nations, by which he had in mind the difference between laws that are appropriate in all societies (*ius gentium*) and those that belong only to particular communities (*ius civile*) (*Etymol.* V.4). Into the first category fall the laws that govern situations involving the laws of more than one jurisdiction – roughly "international law." In practice, this seems to pertain to what happens in time of war, when nations are most likely to find themselves in action on the

---

[11] The Carolingian "Isidorian" Decretals are now known to be almost entirely forged, but their attribution to Isidore may have encouraged Gratian and others to look to the genuine Isidore for guidance about the basics.
[12] Ambrose of Milan had also put the law of nature ahead of the creation of particular laws (*De Abraham* I.2.8).

territories and physically within the territorial jurisdictions of other nations; it includes, for example, the rules for the treatment of captives and the conduct of sieges (ibid., V.6), although Isidore also identified a specific military law (*ius militare*) (ibid., V.7).

Aquinas's is perhaps the best-known medieval hierarchical breakdown of the types of law. He distinguishes between four kinds of law: eternal, divine, natural, and positive. *Divine law* is constituted by the moral and legal precepts in the Bible; this is revealed law, the subject of revelations to God's rational creatures.[13] *Eternal law*, in contrast, transcends the natural world altogether, for it existed before God made the natural world.[14] Eternal law governs everything. It embraces God's plan, God's providence, and God's idea of how things are and should be.[15] All rational law derives ultimately from these absolutely fundamental ground rules.[16] This then raises a question: how do we know what this law comprises, when it is not conveniently set out in the codifications of Scripture? Medieval thinkers were familiar with the questions of whether such knowledge could be reached by speculation (reasoning), whether it required divine revelation for us to have any idea of the nature of eternal law, or whether God had arranged for the two sources to work together. (Augustine had even postulated that Plato had some contact with the Old Testament prophets [*De civitate Dei* VIII.11–12].) Part of the point of the need to connect reason and revelation here was that "law" of this kind resembles the laws of physics and metaphysics as much as laws of conduct.

The eternal law is the law by which God does all that he does, and so it includes his will for rational creatures. Aquinas sees this, as Aristotle had, in terms of a teleology – a purpose of completing and perfecting. Hence it guides the *natural law* that governs human behavior.[17] This *lex naturalis* is within us as a "participation of the eternal law in a rational creature" (*Summa theol.* 1a2ae 91.2c). It takes the form of innate principles of rational action, all operating ultimately within the framework of eternal law. For Aquinas, natural law is in rational beings alone. Its link to rationality is important, and it is understood to be divinely implanted.[18] It has been suggested that Aquinas understands this "participation" in the divine as involving both causality (since the eternal law

---

[13] The medieval canonists also use *ius divinum* (or sometimes, confusingly, *ius naturale*) to refer to explicit divine commands found in the Bible, such as the Decalogue. See, for instance, the opening of Gratian's *Decretum*. See, too, Tierney, *The Idea of Natural Rights*, p. 22.

[14] See Aquinas, *Summa theol.* 1a2ae 91.4–5 and qq. 98–108.

[15] Norman Kretzmann, "Lex iniusta non est lex: Laws on Trial in Aquinas' Court of Conscience," in J. Finnis (ed.) *Natural Law* (Aldershot: Ashgate, 1991) II: 99–121, esp. p. 119.

[16] Aquinas *Summa theol.* 1a2ae 91.1 and qq. 93.   [17] Tierney, *The Idea of Natural Rights*, p. 25.

[18] As Tierney puts it, "Natural *ius* is called a *facultas* of discerning good from evil with approbation of the one and detestation of the other" ("Tuck on Rights," p. 438), citing other twelfth-century parallels.

is the cause of this natural law within human beings) and likeness or imitation (insofar as it resembles or is analogous with the eternal law, and it is from this resemblance that natural law gets its lawfulness).[19] In accordance with this picture, Aquinas holds that the law of nature cannot change (*Summa theol.* 1a2ae 94.5), and that all virtuous acts are done according to natural law (ibid., 94.3). Importing all this into an Aristotelian teleology, Aquinas takes this inbuilt law of nature to mean that practical reason orientates itself towards the pursuit of the good. Thus every agent acts for an end that has the nature of a good (ibid., 94.2).

Various features of human life fall within the scope of natural law and hence are subject to its reasonable rules. For instance, the sexual union of men and women leading to the birth of children was taken to follow a natural law that imposed upon the parents a duty of raising the offspring. Isidore had set out various such implications (*Etymol.* V.4), and subsequent medieval discussions routinely took up these elements of the natural law. Gratian, for instance, lists much the same *ius naturale* basics – including the union of men and women, procreation and the education of children, the liberty of all equally, and the right to keep things captured on land, sea, or air. The idea that natural law includes "the common possession of all things," found both in Isidore (ibid.) and Gratian (*Decretum* D. 1 c. 7), would have its impact in the later medieval poverty debates (see Chapter 42).

Human or positive (meaning imposed) law is the lowliest in Aquinas's hierarchy. It is devised by humans for their own governmental purposes – that is, for the better ordering of society. Still, the conditions that pertain to the essence of law must be met in framing it (*Summa theol.* 1a2ae 91). Isidore had earlier identified a series of such conditions: the law ought to be upright, just, possible, in accord with nature and local customs, appropriate to place and time, necessary, useful, evident, and written for the general utility of citizens (*Etymol.* V.21).

LAW AND HUMAN NATURE

Cicero began his *De legibus* by reflecting on what nature bestows on humanity, and on its implications for the purpose of life and the way human beings are able to form a natural society. These, he suggests, are the fundamentals that must be clear before any theory of law and justice can be developed (I.5.16). Here, he is consciously posing a challenge to those among his contemporaries who would say that the study of law should begin from actual codes of legislation and not from such philosophical principles. According to Cicero, the deep

[19] John Finnis, *Natural Law and Natural Rights* (Oxford: Clarendon Press, 1979) p. 399.

questions about the nature of law (*ius* and *lex*) cannot adequately be resolved by considering things at the level of the particular, such as a client's questions about a particular case.

The question "Is this just?," for instance, may raise the particular issue of whether something is lawful, according to positive law, or it may ask the deep question of whether the law in question is itself just.[20] Aquinas, among many others, denies that an unjust law can be law at all. When someone purports to make a law that goes beyond his legitimate powers, the result is not law. It is a form of violence, says Aquinas, and a person should submit to such "laws" only for the sake of avoiding a scandal or disruption. Another kind of non-law would be a legislative act contrary to divine law – for example, a law made by a tyrant encouraging idolatry. There may, in fact, be a duty *not* to obey these unlawful laws. We should obey God rather than human beings (Acts 5:29). This line of argument can be traced back to Augustine, who had also said that what was unjust did not seem to him to be law (*De libero arbitrio* I.5.11). Somewhere behind Augustine, although unlikely to be his direct source, stands Plato's argument in *The Laws* (715B) that enactments that are not for the common interest of the community are not true laws.

What is the relationship between law and morality? For Gratian, natural law is what is found in biblical law and in the Gospels and answers to the rule that you should do to others what you would want them to do to you, for that is "all the law and the prophets" (*Decretum* D. I c. 1, quoting Mat. 22:40). The hard question is whether every sin is or ought to be made a legal offence, or even a crime. Aquinas discusses the possibility of disagreement between morality and law. His position is that morality depends on Christian theology, and that legality depends on what the state legislates for. Here, too, an Augustinian discussion stands in the background. While Aristotle described a society of "political animals," and sees it as a part of the very definition of human beings that they should form societies with structures and laws, Augustine took the view that human society was originally intended by the Creator to work without such constraints, and that it had been made necessary for it to become political only after the Fall. Sin encouraged bad behavior and resulted in the weak needing protection from the strong. Had it not been for the Fall, ordinary human conduct would have continued to be naturally virtuous, and there would have been no need for laws to protect the weak and to keep the strong in order.

---

[20] Kretzmann, "Lex iniusta non est lex," p. 99, citing H. L. A. Hart, *The Concept of Law* (Oxford: Clarendon Press, 1961) p. 7.

RIGHT REASON, LAW, AND NATURE

Cicero had argued that the nature of law (*natura iuris*) can be understood only in terms of a study of human nature (*De legibus* I.5.17). Accordingly, echoing Aristotle's claim that rationality is central to being human, Cicero takes *lex* to be *ratio* – the reason inherent in human nature and according to which a person ought to direct his actions. On this analysis, law is really *prudentia*, or wisdom *(De legibus* I.6.19). This accords well enough with Aquinas's Christian version of the same basic cluster of ideas. The belief that natural law is innate in human nature and is known by reason rather than biblical revelation also provides a basis for rational assessment of positive law. Positive law ought to be in accord both with what is implied in the eternal and divine law (for example, not committing murder) and also with a generally rational way of behaving (for example, obeying laws that are designed to make life proceed smoothly and for the general good, of which modern examples might be stopping a car at red traffic lights or obeying the speed limit).[21]

Elsewhere, Cicero defined law as "right reason in harmony with nature" (*De republica* III.33). On Cicero's theory, to live in accord with nature one must reason by taking account of the whole plan of nature and continuing to ask whether one's own nature is in harmony with universal nature. That is the way to a happy life (*De finibus* III.7.26). In this way, one can locate in the framework of the natural universe the laws that are its ground rules, such as "adjust what you do to the needs of the occasion, follow God, know yourself, nothing to excess" (ibid., III.22.73). Cicero's idea thus seems to have been that what is reasonable behavior is to be determined by reference to the laws of nature. *Ius* is not a matter of opinion but "constituted by nature" (*De legibus* I.10.30). The just is, however, commonly understood as such, so that all humans as rational beings share the same assumptions (*De legibus* I.12.33). The principles on which a society or state ought to be run likewise owe something to these laws of nature and reasonableness, and Cicero set these principles out in his now fragmentary *De republica*.

The addition of the dimension of sin in Christian discussions made for an important change of emphasis. Augustine, for instance, was influential in getting later generations to accept that sinfulness is irrational behavior.[22] A law is to be obeyed simply because it is just and right and reasonable, and it is appropriate for a rational being to have regard for it; it is not the fact that someone has the naked power to enforce it that makes it lawful. Is there a deep instinctual

---

[21] Aquinas, *Summa theol.* 1a2ae 91.3 and qq. 95–7.
[22] See G. R. Evans, *Augustine on Evil* (Cambridge: Cambridge University Press, 1982).

mode of behavior, then, that derives from the very nature of humanity, in its unfallen state, and that these now necessary laws are seeking to restore? Aquinas appears to think so. He puts the thought in Aristotelian terms when he suggests that every agent acts with reference to an end or purpose that is given its "direction" by the good (*Summa theol.* 1a2ae 94.2). Laws should, then, align themselves in a direction that will make those subject to them behave better. Aquinas attempts to deal with the conflict that arises between Aristotle and Augustine from the absence in Aristotle of the Christian idea of sin. Separating the sphere of legal obligation from that of moral obligation,[23] he speaks of the "court of conscience" (ibid., 96.4c) in which the individual can consider for himself whether a particular law is in accord with eternal law, what its authority is, and whether the benefits of a law in terms of its promoting the common good are proportionate to the benefits to the individual.

NATURAL RIGHTS: DOMINION AND JURISDICTION AND THE QUESTION OF PROPERTY RIGHTS

Natural rights fall under the topic of law and nature, partly because of a confusion of usage that bedevils the technical terminology both here and elsewhere. Classical Latin seems to allow *dominium* (lordship) and *ius* (here meaning *right*) to inhere in the same subject: to have lordship over something or someone is also to have rights in or over him or it.[24] The Romans had a concept of power over persons or things, which they called *dominium*,[25] but Roman jurists recognized that the power to enjoy or use one's property is a practical matter (*de facto*), not solely a right. In the case of consumables, for instance, it is far from easy to separate use from the rights attaching to possession.[26] If I have use and enjoyment of your apple by eating it, then there is nothing but the core left for you to possess, and your lordship or control of the apple becomes an empty authority.

The Franciscans' internal disputes after the death of Francis of Assisi prompted a radical rethinking of the ground rules of property rights. In the debates of the high Middle Ages about poverty, some went to great lengths to argue that a member of a religious order who had made a vow of poverty was not necessarily breaking that vow if he had the "use" or "enjoyment" of things without actually owning them. In 1279, the Bull *Exiit qui seminat* of Nicholas III provided a list of

---

[23] Kretzmann, 'Lex iniusta non est lex," p. 129.   [24] Tierney, *The Idea of Natural Rights*, pp. 16–17.
[25] A *dominus* did not have a power of usufruct (use and enjoyment) over other persons, however, even if they were his property.
[26] Tierney, *The Idea of Natural Rights*, p. 151.

aspects to be considered with reference to temporal things: property, possession, enjoyment, right of use, and actual use.[27] The pope said the Franciscans had given up everything but actual use and that this was the way of Christ and the Apostles. Others argued that it was a Christ-appointed law, as some of the Franciscans taught, that the observation of perfect poverty as exemplified by Christ involved renunciation not only of property but also of the "right of use in exterior things" – and even, perhaps, the actual use. Pope John XXII stated in 1323 that this was to be deemed heresy. The right of use was generally acceptable as a solution to all but the most extreme of the poverty questions, although Ockham began to challenge this on the assumption that the right in question is a power; Ockham, like John Wyclif and others in succeeding generations, was wary of anything that seemed to shift all these questions towards an exercise of power that amounted to dominion.[28] (See Chapter 42 for further discussion.)

Behind these refinements loomed still more fundamental questions. How, for example, could one justify the first appropriation for personal use of property taken from a stock of creation God gave to everyone, so that some came to possess what others did not, while those others were deprived even of the freedom to use it? This question was attributed to Augustine in a text quoted in Gratian's *Decretum* (Dist.8.c.1): Do we possess things by divine or human law? By human law, Augustine says. God made one earth, on which live both rich and poor. It is human law that makes the rich rich and the poor poor, and that law is needed only because of sin, which is the origin of personal greed.[29]

The commonly voiced claim that "In times of necessity all things are common" asserts that the poor may rightly take what they need in time of want without committing theft.[30] In a similar vein, Henry of Ghent posed the question of whether someone condemned to death can legitimately flee (*Quodlibet* IX.26). His interest was in the effect of extreme necessity on decisions about moral acts. He distinguishes between different kinds of power that could be exercised by different persons or authorities over the same thing or person. When someone is desperately hungry, he suggests, necessity excuses theft. Does someone have an excuse for running away, then, when condemned to death, or does that person's body belong to the judge? Henry claims the criminal can take away what is necessary to sustain life – which, in this case, is his body.[31]

---

[27] *Bullarium Franciscanum*, ed. G. G. Sbaraglia (Rome, 1759–68) III: 404–16.
[28] Tierney, *The Idea of Natural Rights*, p. 29.
[29] The *Decretum* also contains a pseudo-Isidorian item, which says that the differentiation of possessions came about through iniquity (C.12 q.1 c.2). So, for instance, only avarice makes it necessary to protect property from thieves.
[30] See, e.g., Aquinas, *Summa theol.* 2a2ae 66.7. See also Tierney, "Tuck on Rights," p. 436.
[31] Tierney, *The Idea of Natural Rights*, pp. 83–9.

Another question of the same type concerns the right of self-preservation, and whether it is in fact a duty. Franciscans who said they had renounced all rights were attacked for implicitly condoning suicide. More generally, are there rights that cannot be renounced?[32] The answer to that question depends, perhaps, on whether rights derive from the will of an omnipotent God or whether they have simply an internal coherence, and so can change along with societal conventions. The founder of modern natural law theory, Hugo Grotius, would insist on the first, asserting that the laws of nature would hold "even though we should even grant what without the greatest wickedness cannot be granted, that there is no God, or that he takes no care of human affairs."[33]

One of the leading medieval authors who helped focus attention on the conception of *dominium* as lordship over material property was John of Paris. His *De potestate regia et papali* (1302/3) concentrates in this respect on secular sovereignty over temporal things. According to John's contemporary Giles of Rome, there were judges before there were kings, and these judges ruled the people with an authority entrusted to them by priestly powers. Those who became lords (*domini*) either usurped their power or acquired it by this proper route. The only proper way for individuals to possess particular things, however, was by agreement with other people. The "natural" state of affairs is the holding of property in common.[34] Marsilius of Padua also wrestles with the range of meanings of *ius* and *dominium* in his *Defensor pacis*, as he tries to articulate the modes of possible power over things (*Dictio* II.12). Wyclif, in turn, writing the *De dominio divino* as the starting point of an approach to systematic theology, accepts that dominion is in a reciprocal relationship with service, for lords have servants and servants have lords, and this is possible only in the case of rational beings (Bk. I, ed. Poole, p. 6). From these two authors was to flow an important debate running beyond the Middle Ages about the place of dominion in temporal and spiritual affairs and the circumstances in which, by abuse of power, an individual might be deemed to have lost the right of dominion.

---

[32] Ibid., p. 79.   [33] Haakonssen, "The Moral Conservatism of Natural Rights," p. 28.
[34] Janet Coleman, "Medieval Discussions of Property: Ratio and Dominium according to John of Paris and Marsilius of Padua," *History of Political Thought* 4 (1983) 209–28.

POVERTY

MICHAEL F. CUSATO

THE EFFECTS OF THE AGRARIAN AND COMMERCIAL REVOLUTIONS, 950–1300

The seismic economic changes that occurred in Western and Central Europe roughly between 950 and 1300 and known to historians as the Agrarian and Commercial revolutions had profound, long-term ramifications on the life and societal structures of the continent. Indeed, so dramatic were these socio-economic developments that modern Anglo-Saxon historians in particular feel justified in distinguishing the former period from the one that followed: an early from a high Middle Ages. The classic accounts of this transformation of the European mainland relate how, with the cessation of the last of the external threats to the region known as the Great Invasions – the defeat in 951 of the Magyar forces in central Germany by Otto the Great at the Lech River – a period of relative internal calm descended upon Europe.[1] The elimination of open warfare and defensive entrenchment paved the way for a resurgence of agricultural productivity, the renewed movement of trade surpluses across regions, the redevelopment of the old Roman road system, the rebirth of town life (especially in northern Italy and Flanders), the revival of commerce within these urban spaces and, most characteristically, the reemergence of the use of money (coin) as a neutral means of exchange between diverse peoples, with the subsequent development of the concomitant institutions of lending and banking.

The appearance of these interrelated trends profoundly altered the structure of the European economy in a number of ways. First, the sudden upsurge in agricultural and commercial productivity led to a definite but widely uneven increase in the level of economic prosperity for peoples across the region: the

---

[1] Robert S. Lopez, *The Commercial Revolution of the Middle Ages, 950–1350* (Cambridge: Cambridge University Press, 1976); Carlo Cipolla, *Before the Industrial Revolution: European Society and Economy, 1000–1700*, 2nd edn (New York: Norton, 1980); Norman Pounds, *An Economic History of Medieval Europe*, 2nd edn (London: Longman, 1994).

famous economic boom noted by economic historians of this period. Second, these same events also spurred the evolution of the economy from a manorial-based system decidedly rooted in the countryside to one in which the rural economy began to work more in tandem with and to serve the needs of the new urban centers. Third, this migration from the manor then prompted the transformation of the traditional feudal definitions of the ownership of property. Indeed, by the mid-eleventh century, allodial holdings – that is, independent of strict vassalage – began to constitute the principal form of property.[2] Fourth, these dramatic economic changes, in turn, also had profound repercussions upon the very structure of social relationships whereby the ties between feudal lord, vassal, and serf were no longer as clearly defined as they had once been in the early Middle Ages. For although the vast majority of the population by 1300 still lived out in the country and worked in agriculture, a sufficiently large number of people had migrated from the manor to live closer to or even within the towns themselves (often far from their native regions) so as to significantly alter the ways of identifying and defining one's place in the social fabric. This was particularly true with respect to the peasantry – that largest and most diffuse social class whom we can call "the poor."[3] Indeed, their migration towards the cities was accompanied by a simultaneous development that had been virtually unknown in the early Middle Ages: the problem of economic poverty.

WHO ARE THE POOR?

Using the vocabulary employed by canonists and moral theologians in the thirteenth century, the predominant category used to describe the traditional social relationship of the poor to others is that of *dominus/servus*. The *servus* was one who submitted to a certain number of obligations and possessed rights limited by those who acted as master or *dominus*. The *dominus* was the proprietor: the owner of land and the owner of the *servi* attached to that land. Indeed, he drew revenues from the exploitation of both. The *dominus* was said to possess *dominium* (ownership) over such things. But the *dominus* also possessed jurisdiction: the authority to govern, to mete out justice, to wage war and to levy taxes in return for protecting his *servi/subditi*.[4]

---

[2] Janet Coleman, "Property and Poverty," in J. Burns (ed.) *The Cambridge History of Medieval Political Thought* (Cambridge: Cambridge University Press, 1988) 607–48; specific reference here to p. 607. Parts of this chapter are very much indebted to this magisterial article.

[3] On the poor in the Middle Ages, see the work of Michel Mollat, particularly *Les pauvres au Moyen Age: étude sociale* (Paris: Hachette, 1978).

[4] Coleman, "Property," p. 626.

In the Carolingian period, to use the expression made famous by Karl Bosl,[5] the *dominus* was thus a *potens* in contrast to the *pauper*: the one with authority in relation to the dependent and powerless *servus*. The poor man had no rights or weapons; he was usually not a free man and he worked for his survival and that of his family. Thus, in the early Middle Ages, his status as *pauper/impotens* was only in part ascribed to his economic circumstances. Indeed, he (and his family) had a level of subsistence that was provided by – assured by – the manorial system. His status as *pauper* was, in other words, more social than economic: he was poor to the extent that he was dependent on the system controlled by his lord and was powerless to change his social condition. His economic needs were modestly provided for; he and his family lived in neither penury nor destitution.

This definition would change, however, with the economic upsurge of the Agrarian and Commercial revolutions and the options opened to those enterprising and daring individuals who attempted to break free of the feudal ties to the land of the *dominus*. Only then did poverty become a synonym for social dislocation and economic penury. One's social poverty (dependence/powerlessness) now became linked to the real possibility of economic poverty as well (deprivation/indigence). Those who took the risk of forsaking the assurances provided by the manor in favor of a new life in the cities often encountered a lack of employment, ramshackle housing, severe hunger and privation, and the constant threat of theft or physical assault by others of like condition – in short, poverty as we moderns know it.

In a time when agriculture was still the dominant means of subsistence, the poor may be defined – according to the metric proposed by Janet Coleman – as those who do not possess a minimum of arable land sufficient to support a family. In the thirteenth century, for example, a family of four would have required four hectares to survive.[6] Hence, poverty is measured against subsistence: the ability of one to subsist as a human being and to care for one's family. And in spite of the economic boom experienced by some in Western Europe due to the Agrarian and Commercial revolutions, the rise of the commercial economy actually affected in a positive manner only a small minority of peasants, accelerating the social (and now economic) differentiations between rich and poor.

Indeed, beginning with Gratian's twelfth-century *Decretum* – the foundational medieval treatise on canon law – the term *miserabiles personae* came to be used to describe that category of persons in dire need of (and thus worthy of)

---

[5] Karl Bosl, "*Potens und Pauper*," in A. Bergengruen and L. Deike (eds.) *Alteuropa und die Moderne Gesellschaft: Festschrift für Otto Brunner* (Göttingen: Vandenhoeck und Ruprecht, 1963) 60–87.

[6] Coleman, "Property," p. 625.

legally sanctioned benevolence. Included here were widows, orphans, and the economically destitute: those who would not have the means to pay to defend or obtain their rights in court. *Miserabiles personae* were those deprived of the protection of the manorial family and whose sudden dislocation to the cities, abandonment of customary sources of security, and resultant material poverty left them solitary and on the edge of survival. According to canon law, *pauperes* were those who had but one right: the right to receive alms precisely because of their situation of penury. Moreover, in a society that recognized authority in degrees (according to rank), the poor were placed at the very bottom of the social scale as those having no authority or power.

Contrasted with this social category were the rich, the *divites*, who were obliged to give alms to these poor. By the twelfth century, oppositional categories such as *nobiles/ignobiles, divites/pauperes*, and *civis/pauper* expressed a social status and value that came to be measured increasingly in economic terms of material possession (the ownership of property) and money – or the lack thereof. The social meaning associated with this economic status included rights-bearing, civic capacity or its opposite – social insignificance and worthlessness. This social disparity between rich and poor was an acknowledged fact by the mid-to-late twelfth century, a fact that was mirrored by two new developments: the creation of charitable institutions in the cities to address the needs of the destitute, and the rise of literature stressing justice for and the rights of the poor.

RELIGIOUS RESPONSES TO THE NEW ECONOMY

The new money economy, with its divergent effects upon rich and poor, also gave rise to a series of religious responses that spurred the creation of new forms of religious life hitherto unseen in Western Europe.[7] On the one hand, when the prosperity enjoyed by the great landowning monasteries during the agrarian revolution led to unprecedented levels of comfort and concomitant religious laxity, some took it upon themselves to seek out lives of greater austerity and spiritual intensity – through a deeper withdrawal into the solitude of the forests, or the creation of small eremitical communities like the Camaldolese or the Carthusians, or the establishment of more rigorous forms of cenobitical living like that of the Cistercians. On the other hand, and at a slightly later moment (in the later eleventh and twelfth centuries), the growing and increasingly visible gap between rich and poor in the cities prompted others (both clerics and lay people

---

[7] Lester K. Little, *Religious Poverty and the Profit Economy in the High Middle Ages* (Ithaca, NY: Cornell University Press, 1978).

alike) to call on the whole church to return to the life of the apostolic community as depicted in Acts 4:32–6, in which all goods were shared in common and where no one lived in crushing need. Such groups and individuals, increasingly of lay inspiration by the end of the twelfth century (such as the Waldensians of southern France or the Humiliati of northern Italy), challenged the church – either directly by their preaching or indirectly by the example of their own lives of voluntary poverty – to abandon its wealth and to be attentive to the poor who were now seen as the contemporary face of Christ and his Apostles. Indeed, for such men and women, it was imperative that the church and its leaders come to terms with the new wealth and poverty coexisting visibly and uneasily within the towns of Western Europe. It is not by accident that, by the end of the twelfth and the start of the thirteenth century, this growing disparity between rich and poor was paralleled by the appearance of two other related trends. First, there was the creation and proliferation of the means of charitable assistance available to the disadvantaged and indigent, in the form of hospices, alms-houses, care for lepers, and so on.[8] Second, there was an evolution in the notion of Christian responsibility, from an emphasis on the obligations of charity to the demands of justice, in order to rectify the social conditions that gave rise to such misery in the first place. It is in this environment that canonists and theologians began to address themselves to the moral implications of the problem of poverty and the poor.

THEORISTS OF THE RIGHTS OF THE POOR

While the socioeconomic context of these innovative responses to the new realities of poverty and penury is the expansion of the economy and its attendant (if uneven) increase in prosperity, the theoretical context pivots on the issue of property and the purpose and use of the goods of the earth given by a provident God. This reflection on property was first directed at the church itself: namely, the ownership of property by its bishops and clergy. By the mid-twelfth century, with the revival of the science of canon law from Gratian onwards, canonists had developed a doctrine of property ownership that was consistent with ecclesiastical legislation and the writings of the Fathers of the church in late antiquity, and that also began to take account of the more recent and pointed criticisms of those who were demanding that the church be a more faithful reflection of the early Christian community, with its collective

---

[8] See Michel Mollat, "Hospitalité et assistance au début du XIIIe siècle," in D. Flood (ed.) *Poverty in the Middle Ages* (Werl: Coelde, 1975) 37–51.

ownership of goods. They were calling, in other words, for a church that was poorer – in lands, in properties, in wealth – than it presently was.

In the *Decretum*, for instance, just as Peter Abaelard had done in his famous *Sic et non*, Gratian simply gathers together sayings from the Fathers that defended the use and possession of wealth by the church and places them alongside those texts that appeared to condemn private property based on this same apostolic model. The result is a concordance of discordances that, without proposing any definitive resolution, at least lays out the problematic. For Gratian, the human race is ruled by two norms: natural law and what he calls "custom." It is, he says, by natural law that all things are common to all. But the law of custom (that is, what is established by the legal enactments of emperors and kings) does allow human beings to claim some things as their own: mine, rather than yours or ours. The closest Gratian comes to resolving this tension and potential conflict is to state that where the natural law is contrary to customary law, it is the latter that is null and void (see also Chapter 41).

Shortly after, the *Summa Parisiensis* (1159) – a commentary on Gratian's *Decretum* – claims that, in accord with the dictates of natural law, the initial human institution was common property. Rufinus, however, writing around the same time, argues that while some parts of natural law are indeed immutable, others are not necessarily to be construed as morally binding on all people at all times. For him, the common ownership of property is one such example. Hence, the depiction of Christian life in the Acts was a time-bound description; it was not meant to depict a divine mandate for all time (*Summa decretorum* dist. 1 [ed. Singer, p. 7]). The lines for the debate which was to unfold during the next century were thus clearly drawn.

Huguccio, the most important canonist of his day, states in his seminal commentary on Gratian's *Decretum* (probably in the early 1190s) that natural law (and thus natural reason) tells us that all things are common and, therefore, to be shared in times of necessity with all those in need.[9] Huguccio thus (re)introduces two new terms into the medieval discussion of property and the human person: the notions of *ius* (in the sense of natural law but also in the sense of a legal right) and *necessitas*.[10] Natural reason tells us that we should keep for ourselves only what is necessary and then to distribute what is left to our neighbors who

---

[9] Huguccio, as cited in Odon Lottin, *Le droit naturel chez Thomas d'Aquin et ses prédécesseurs*, 2nd edn (Bruges: Beyaert, 1931) p. 110. See also Brian Tierney, *Medieval Poor Law* (Berkeley: University of California Press, 1959).

[10] On the principle of extreme necessity, see *Decretum* D. 86 c. 21 and D. 42 c. 1. Cf. Scott G. Swanson, "The Medieval Foundations of John Locke's Theory of Natural Rights: Rights of Subsistence and the Principle of Extreme Necessity," *History of Political Thought* 18 (1997) 403–12 (for the medieval background). For a more recent overview, see Diana Wood, *Medieval Economic Thought* (Cambridge: Cambridge University Press, 2002) esp. pp. 42–68 ("Wealth, Beggary, and Sufficiency").

might still be in need. This is a rather astonishing position, for it heralds a radical shift from the simple notion of charity to the needy – an obligation imposed on all Christians by virtue of their baptism – to the demands of doing justice to the poor. The Pisan canonist, in other words, is calling his fellow Christians to move beyond individualistic acts of succor for the disadvantaged (done perhaps with an averted glance or disdainful look) towards a more sweeping social ethic of distributive (or redistributive) justice.[11]

Huguccio's ideas passed into the *Glossa ordinaria* of Johannes Teutonicus (*ca.* 1215), who likewise affirms that all things are common to all since, in time of need, we know instinctively (that is, by reason) that such things are to be shared out to the less fortunate. Both men, in fact, were building on ideas already present (if hitherto forgotten) in the writings of the early Church Fathers.[12] Authors like Ambrose, for example, stated quite clearly that, in times of necessity, any surplus wealth is to be regarded as common property that is to be shared with those who are in need. Nonetheless, such thinking on the ownership of superfluities never develops into any full-scale theory denouncing the ownership of property *per se*; rather, harking back to Roman law, these medieval commentators simply urge that human beings not use their property "badly," that is, for the satisfaction of themselves alone to the neglect of those in real need.[13]

Authors like Johannes Teutonicus, therefore, are not espousing a theory of the total lack of ownership for clergy and Christians alike.[14] Under pressure from the radical reformers of the age, however, theorists begin to couch the question of ownership (and especially the ownership of goods by the church) either in terms of corporate ownership (by groups of clerics or canons) or, more commonly, in

---

[11] Cf. Gilles Couvreur, *Les pauvres ont-ils des droits? Recherches sur le vol en cas d'extrême nécessité depuis la Concordia de Gratien (1140) jusqu'à Guillaume d'Auxerre († 1231)* (Rome: Libreria Editrice dell'Università Gregoriana, 1961) and *La pauvreté: des sociétés de pénurie à la société d'abondance* (Paris: Fayard, 1964) pp. 13–37.

[12] As cited by Coleman, "Property," p. 618 n. 37.

[13] For a succinct overview of how property was used in Roman law, see Coleman, "Property," pp. 609–12. Regarding Ambrose, the *Decretum* of Gratian (Dist. 48, pars I, c. 8) cites a famous text on ownership that is attributed to Ambrose (Sermo 81) (cf. Migne, *Patr. Lat.* 187: 247–8). In reality, however, the text is actually a partial Latin translation made by Rufinus of Aquileia (*ca.* 397) of a sermon of Basil the Great (cf. Migne, *Patr. Graeca* 31: 1752A). The important lines are cited, in the truncated Latin version but with a French translation of the original Greek sermon, in Stanislas Giet, "La doctrine de l'appropriation des biens chez quelques-uns des pères," *Recherches de science religieuse* 35 (1948) pp. 67–9. The Latin abridgement in the *Decretum* also appears in an English translation in Tierney, *Medieval Poor Law*, p. 34.

[14] The radical positions in this direction of men like Arnold of Brescia, the fiery canon of the twelfth century, were certainly exceptions to the more measured approaches that were developing among literate clergy and canonists who based themselves less on a prophetic challenge grounded in the gospels than on a careful reading of ecclesiastical law and history (see Coleman, "Property," p. 620 n. 46).

terms of the view that all ownership of ecclesiastical goods ultimately inheres in God or in the poor themselves. Innocent IV (the expert canonist Sinnibaldo dei Fieschi) goes a bit further, stating that since the church is the mystical body of Christ, the property of the church belongs to the whole Christian community (*Apparatus* X.2.14.4). Hostiensis, a canonist contemporary to Innocent, goes further still: ownership (*dominium*) of ecclesiastical property belongs to the body, the *congregatio fidelium*. Hence, the poor and needy are to be supported from the goods of the church because they have a right (*ius*) to this support from the common property of the church. Increasingly, therefore, the arguments in favor of providing succor for the poor pivot on the notions of necessity and rights: a necessity created by the difficult socioeconomic conditions of the day and the God-given right (*ius naturale*) to sustenance grounded in the natural law whereby, in conformity with the will of God, all things are viewed as being ultimately in common. In this light, the use of church property is no longer to be construed as simple charity but as a legal, lawful use of public property whose purpose is the maintenance of the common welfare but most especially the sustenance of the needy poor.

Thomas Aquinas, a Dominican friar, likewise added his voice during the middle of the same century to the discussions on the issues of property, ownership, and the plight of the poor. A member of an order that espoused voluntary poverty (although understood, as we will see, in a way somewhat different from their contemporaries, the Franciscans), Aquinas had chosen this way of life on the basis of certain ideas about the material world. Not surprisingly, he develops a systematic approach to the matter (*Summa theol.* 2a2ae 66). Human beings, he says, have two primary goals: happiness in this life and beatitude in the life to come. The material goods of the earth – be they wealth, property, food, or possessions – are but a means to the achievement of that higher end. They are, in other words, to be subordinated to that goal rather than enjoyed in their own right. Human beings can legitimately and with good conscience own things. But although private property is not wrong, it is a mode of possession that must always be directed towards the higher goal. Indeed, ownership prevents chaos in society: a situation that would ensue if all things were claimed by all people. The goods of the earth, while originally intended for the use of all human beings (*dominium naturale*), eventually came to be construed as possessions. Natural law does not specify how private property should be determined and arranged; historical situations determine distribution. But when the common welfare is at stake, civil law must always regulate property in the interest of society as a whole.

Thus far, Aquinas's view is quite unexceptional. His commitment to a life of poverty – a conception of poverty quite different from what is normal today – emerges when he considers situations of superfluity. For when there is a superfluity of goods, there can be no justification for their being maintained as private. Natural law teaches that this surplus is owed to the poor. Human needs have to be met with material goods sufficient to sustain life. In short, a surplus can thus be justified only in terms of its social use. Thus, similar to Huguccio, Thomas notes that whenever dire necessity exists, it is permitted to expropriate a surplus held privately by another without being considered a thief. In extreme necessity, a starving person may take what is necessary to free him or herself from imminent conditions of death (ibid., 66.7).

It is in this context – the sustenance necessary for human life – that the matter of alms came to play such a prominent role in the discussions of the twelfth and thirteenth centuries.

ALMS

In his *Verbum abbreviatum* (before 1187), an instruction for preachers and teachers, Peter the Chanter, master at the cathedral school of Notre Dame in Paris, follows up his remarks on the necessity of mercy in society with five chapters on alms. While extolling the heavenly reward that almsgivers will receive in return for the giving of alms, he urges his listeners to give to everyone who is in need, but most especially to the just (ed. Migne, 205: 286–92). That is to say: Peter distinguishes the deserving from the undeserving poor. No such distinction, however, is found in the writings of his contemporary, the Parisian theologian Radulphus Ardens. In the same vein as Huguccio, he states that the poor have a right to the superfluities of the rich. "When we give alms to the poor, we do not give them what belongs to us. Rather, we return what [in fact] belongs to them" (*Homilia* 34, in Migne, *Patr. Lat.* 155: 1787B). Indeed, we use the goods of the earth properly by serving God and neighbor with them. For if we do not distribute to the needy what God has first given us, we create the conditions for their death. In short, by such niggardly acts, we "murder the poor" (*Homilia* 70, ibid., 1932B). All things come from God and all things ought to be given back to him in service to his creatures. As he notes: "let us serve God with his gifts. And let us refer all things back to him who alone is alpha and omega, the beginning and end of all good things."[15] Human beings praise their Creator by the manner in which they take care of the least among us.

---

[15] Migne, *Patr. Lat.* 155, 1787B. The same Latin phraseology will be used by a man of vastly different education and temperament – Francis of Assisi – in his Early Rule (*Regula non bullata*), referring, according to the historian David Flood, not merely to "all things" (that is, generically, to everything) but to "all the goods of the earth." See Flood's "Assisi's Rules and People's Needs," *Franzikanische Studien* 66 (1984) 91–104.

Another twelfth-century preacher, Peter of Poitiers (the Victorine canon, d. *ca.* 1216), vividly described to a group of gathered clergy a scene of the starving needy looking at the waste of the ecclesiastical rich. In exasperation, he has them crying out to the churchmen: "What you waste belongs to us!"[16] One cannot imagine that the needy would ever say such things for fear of being deprived of the alms they needed for their own survival; nevertheless, similar expressions of repugnance against the rich would be made at the turn of the next century by the fiery Franciscan preacher, Ubertino da Casale, in his *Arbor vitae crucifixae Iesu* (1305), where the excesses of the clergy (and by this time his fellow Franciscans) would be denounced for stripping the poor Crucified One in the person of his poor, who had a right to be sustained in dignity by creation (I.1).

FRANCIS OF ASSISI AND THE EARLY MINORITE MOVEMENT

Sentiments such as these – whether expressed in the genre of sermons or commentaries on canon law – were quite commonplace in the religious world of the early thirteenth century. To what extent they might have fueled some of the evangelical fervor of the men and women who took on lives of voluntary dispossession and gospel poverty in this period is quite unclear; documentation on such groups as the Waldensians, the Poor Catholics, and the Poor Lombards is all too sparse. Fortunately, we do have a goodly amount of material about the early followers of Francis of Assisi (commonly known as the Poverello, or "little poor one"), the person most closely associated with the life of voluntary poverty. This material is found most notably in the Early Rule of the Franciscan order, the so-called *Regula non bullata*,[17] which shows us that these same ideas were not only prevalent in academic disputations and homiletic instructions but also had penetrated into the lived ideals of those men and women who saw themselves as the new *pauperes Christi* in the thirteenth century.

The Franciscan movement takes its origin and inspiration from the conversion experience of its founder. Francis's famous encounter with lepers outside the city of Assisi in 1205 brought him face to face, perhaps for the first time in his life, with a world of suffering human beings who hitherto had virtually been invisible to him and whom he had been socialized by his upbringing to

---

[16] Cited in Jean Longère, "Pauvreté et richesse chez quelques prédicateurs durant la seconde moitié du XIIe siècle," in M. Mollat (ed.) *Études sur l'histoire de la pauvreté* (Paris: Publications de la Sorbonne, 1974) I: 259–60.

[17] *Regula non bullata*, in Francis of Assisi, *Opuscula*, pp. 377–402. A slightly updated critical edition of this text has just been published by Carlo Paolozzi in *Archivum Franciscanum Historicum* 100 (2007) 5–148.

ignore and account for nothing. Through his encounter with these *miserabiles personae*, Francis came to a conception of the universal fraternity of all creatures, in which every human being without exception was seen to be graced with the same inestimable worth and dignity given by God, *fratres et sorores*, one to another. It was in this moment, according to his Testament, that he began to "do penance" – a decision to distance himself from all actions and attitudes that threatened to violate the sacred character of this human fraternity, dividing human beings from each other, placing one over and against the other.[18] He included in such deleterious actions all violence and warfare, the exploitative nature of money,[19] and the hoarding and ownership of property, which serves to increase the hunger and misery of the powerless and voiceless poor.[20] Thus, in a gesture of profound human solidarity, he and his followers decided to live poor among the poor and for the sake of the poor: working as they worked, assisting them in their pain, and calling the powerful of the world to build a society where all human creatures would receive the mercy and justice that creatures of God were due simply by virtue of their creation.[21]

The freely chosen poverty of the early friars – before it came to be narrowed to a legal concept that defined it as the renunciation of ownership – was premised on a positive ethic of creation: namely, that the earth and all within it ultimately belonged to God. No one could rightly claim ownership of it; human beings were its stewards. But they were stewards with a responsibility: to ensure – just as canonists and theologians were insisting – that the resources of the earth were properly used for the good of all, especially those most in need. Indeed, the friars believed that God had so blessed the earth that all men and women could be – and had a right to be – sustained by the resources of creation.

By contrast, the poverty of the early Dominicans had a very different motivation. Cognizant of the failure of the Cistercians, with their retinues of horses and supplies, to win back followers of the dualist Cathar heresy (see Chapter 52) to orthodox Catholicism in the Languedoc, Dominic had become convinced that he and his friars, in order to be persuasive, needed to adopt the same simplicity of dress that characterized the Cathar preachers. For Dominic, in other words, evangelical poverty was more of a strategy for effective preaching than

---

[18] See Michael F. Cusato, "The Renunciation of Power as a Foundational Theme in Early Franciscan History," in M. Gosman *et al.* (eds.) *The Propagation of Power in the Medieval West* (Groningen: Forsten, 1997) 265–86, esp. pp. 274–7.

[19] Peter Spufford, *Money and Its Use in Medieval Europe* (Cambridge: Cambridge University Press, 1988); and Wood, *Medieval Economic Thought*, pp. 69–88.

[20] Tierney, *Medieval Poor Law*, pp. 22–44 (although the focus is on the English context).

[21] *Regula non bullata* chs. 1, 7–9 and 14; David Flood, *Francis of Assisi and the Franciscan Movement* (Quezon City, Philippines: FIA Contact Publications, 1989); Michael F. Cusato, "To Do Penance/ *Facere penitentiam*," *The Cord* 57 (2007) 3–24.

an ethic about the proper use of creation. Indeed, this explains why, in the
1250s, the Dominicans could revert back quite easily to the practice of individual poverty and collective ownership: a posture that was more characteristic of
canons regular which, in fact, they originally were.[22]

The Franciscans, however, approached the issue of poverty as essential to the
very core of their identity: they were poor, using creation on the basis of honest
human need, because this was the use of creation intended by God and shown by
Jesus of Nazareth. Moreover, this same ethic of creation also sheds light on their
understanding of the role of begging in their lives. For although they shared the
same ecclesial designation with the Dominicans as mendicant orders, the early
Franciscans' understanding of their mendicancy likewise flowed from the same
ethic. The early Franciscans went out and begged only when remuneration for
their work was not sufficient to cover their needs. Begging, in other words,
was not a way of life but an extreme remedy when work did not adequately
sustain them. Indeed, the statement in chapter 9 of their Early Rule is one of
the most eloquent expressions in the Middle Ages of the right of all human
beings, especially the poor, to a basic level of sustenance:

And when it is necessary, let them go for alms. And let them not be ashamed and
remember, moreover, that our Lord Jesus Christ . . . set his face like flint and was not
ashamed . . . And when people revile them and refuse to give them alms, let them thank
God for this because they will receive great honor before the tribunal of our Lord Jesus
Christ for such insults. Let them realize that a reproach is imputed not to those who
suffer it but to those who cause it. Alms are a hereditary right and a justice due to the
poor that our Lord Jesus Christ has acquired for us.

(*Regula non bullata* ch. 9)

Unschooled though most of them were, their Early Rule captured the very
essence of the reflections on the same subject by the greatest theologians and
canonists of their age. The difference is that they not only theorized about the
intention of creation, but they lived it every day among the poor as a matter
of conscience and conviction. Accordingly, when the proper understanding
of mendicant poverty became controversial in the later thirteenth century, it
was primarily a dispute between Franciscans. Consequently, the many treatises

---

[22] Priests in the order of canons regular take a vow of poverty but own things in common (cf. Acts
4:32–5). The transition to a more thoroughgoing form of poverty occurred, according to early
Dominican and Franciscan hagiography, when Dominic, upon meeting Francis *ca.* 1220, decided
to embrace the latter's following of absolute poverty. This shift from the early Dominican approach,
however, was never fully embraced by the order. The abandonment of this approach, and the return
to the practice of common ownership is associated with the generalate of Humbert of Romans
(1254–63).

written on this topic (with its wider ramifications for issues such as ownership, use, and property) were also largely written by Franciscans.

THE DISPUTE OVER FRANCISCAN POVERTY

With the entrance into the Franciscan order of an increasing number of clerics from outside the Spoleto Valley, especially after the death of Francis in 1226, the friars began to redefine and refine – to the great dismay of the early companions of the saint – the meaning of their poverty.[23] Trained in the schools and steeped in the categories and distinctions of law, these friars came to see their uniqueness within the church as consisting in their vow of *gospel* poverty, which they defined as absolute poverty in the sense of the total renunciation of the legal ownership of all things. The papacy of Gregory IX was particularly obliging in this regard – in the bull *Quo elongati* (1230) – by articulating this understanding in legal terms through the famous distinction between *dominium* (which the friars renounced) and *usus* (which they retained).[24] Yet if the friars renounced *dominium*, who then held it over the goods they used? In *Ordinem vestrum* (1245),[25] Innocent IV declared that the ownership of the friars' goods would henceforth be retained by the papacy itself.

William of St. Amour and Gerard of Abbeville, mid-thirteenth-century secular masters at the University of Paris (that is, masters unaffiliated with any religious order), contested these distinctions on legal grounds, claiming that *usus* and *dominium* were not in fact separable with respect to consumables. As such, not only were the friars hypocrites (professing to have given up all things while using all things) but – more to the point – their justifications for their life were insupportable in the law.[26] In defense of the Franciscan claim, Bonaventure, in his *Apologia pauperum* (1269), claimed that the friars had indeed renounced all *dominium* (*proprietas, possessio, ususfructus*, and *usus iuris*) and retained only the right of *usus simplex*: the use of a thing necessary for life, or the use of the

---

[23] The recasting of the meaning of poverty, in conjunction with the acceptance of new and important ecclesial roles by the clerical friars in response to the desires of the papacy, progressively resulted in the abandonment of the original social location of the friars among the lesser members of society (the *minores*) and prompted a severe reaction to these changes among the companions of Francis, who steadfastly remained well outside the cities in their poor and remote settlements (*eremi*). This is the root of the struggles within the Franciscan order throughout the rest of the Middle Ages.

[24] *Quo elongati*, in G. G. Sbaraglia (ed.) *Bullarium Franciscanum* (Rome, 1759–68) I: 168–70.

[25] Ibid. I: 400–2.

[26] William's specific contributions to the debate have been edited by Andrew Traver, "William of Saint-Amour's Two Disputed Questions '*De quantitate eleemosynae*' and '*De valido mendicante*'," *Archives d'histoire doctrinale et littéraire du moyen âge* 62 (1995) 295–342; see also the *magnum opus* of Gerard of Abbeville, *Contra adversarium perfectionis christianae*, which became the touchstone for Bonaventure's response in the *Apologia pauperum*.

necessities of life (11.5; *Opera* VIII: 312a). Simple use concerned consumables such as clothing, shoes, food, dwellings, and books. Such use of goods, however, did not allow the friars to buy, exchange, or lend anything since, in their total renunciation, they had also given up all legal right over everything. Indeed, Bonaventure likens the friars to children who use a father's goods through the right of *peculium*, the use of a thing without having legal possession or owner-ship (ibid., 11.9). For the friars, that ownership was invested in the church (in general) or the pope (in particular).

Nicholas III, in his famous bull *Exiit qui seminat* (1279), extends Bonaventure's line of thinking, defending the friars' right to use the necessities of life without ownership (*usus simplex*) but by employing a term – *usus facti* – that was legally neutral, implying that the friars had been (implicitly) granted permission (by the owner) to use such things without claiming any right over them.[27] The Francis-can argument, in other words, addressed the legal questions of their opponents by avoiding them. This would become the standard Franciscan response until William of Ockham took up the question once again in the 1330s.[28]

Doubts about the legitimacy of the Franciscan position nonetheless persisted; indeed, it would take another pope with expert legal training – John XXII – to expose the latent contradictions in the Franciscan position. John was no friend of the Franciscans. Indeed, his theological formation led him to have a more natural affinity to the Dominicans and their theologians.[29] As archbishop of Avignon during the debates in 1309–11 over the observance (or non-observance) of poverty between the Spiritual Franciscans and the leadership of the Order,[30] John had become increasingly disenchanted with the internal squabbling between the two factions, as well as by the legal imprecision of their position on using goods without any right to do so. Like William of St. Amour before him, he regarded the distinction between *dominium* and *usus facti* to be legally impossible, especially in relation to consumables. Thus, when the issue of Christ's poverty was brought to him as pope for adjudication in 1321 (in the context of a theological debate between a Dominican inquisitor

---

[27] Sbaraglia, *Bullarium Franciscanum* III: 404–16. See Virpi Mäkinen, "The Franciscan Background of Early Modern Rights Discussion: Rights of Property and Subsistence," in J. Kraye and R. Saarinen (eds.) *Moral Philosophy on the Threshold of Modernity* (Dordrecht: Kluwer, 2005) 165–80.

[28] For Ockham, a right (*ius*) was a licit power of using; it was distinct from *usus facti*, which was simply an *actus utendi* (an act of using), such as the action of eating, drinking, riding a horse, wearing clothes, or dwelling in a place. Such use was not to be construed as a right; it was the use of an object in which the user claims no right or dominion in the act of using. See his *Opus nonaginta dierum* chs. 2 and 4 (*Opera politica* I: 302, 335–6).

[29] It was during the pontificate of John XXII, in 1323, that Thomas Aquinas was canonized.

[30] David Burr, *The Spiritual Franciscans: From Protest to Persecution in the Century after Saint Francis* (University Park: Pennsylvania State University Press, 2001).

and Franciscan lector), the stage was set for John's famous series of bulls against the Franciscan notion of absolute poverty.[31] By claiming use without the right of use, the friars' way of life, he claimed, was neither just nor based on right; it was, therefore, illicit. By contrast, the Dominican approach to evangelical poverty, which had distanced itself from the renunciation of the ownership of all things and contented itself with limited communal possession, avoided such pitfalls of legal nonsense.

What John was ruling against, however, was not in fact the early Franciscan notion of poverty but rather the narrowing of that original concept to a legal – and ultimately untenable – construct. This lies quite far away from the original understanding of poverty, which had been grounded in an ethic about the use of the goods of the earth and its relationship to the life of the real poor of the world.

THE RIGHT TO SUBSISTENCE

These arguments over *dominium* and *usus* in the Franciscan poverty controversy rest on a fundamental question concerning involuntary poverty and hunger: namely, can a human being, friar or not, ever renounce the right to subsistence? Can a friar claim – as some Franciscan theorists were claiming – that having given up not only all *dominium* but also all right (*ius*) to *dominium*, they have also given up all rights, even those to subsistence? This logical extension of the Franciscan position as it had been articulated by Bonaventure seemed to many thinkers outside the Franciscan order to be extreme, and to some nonsensical.

Nicholas III had seen the problem and, while supporting the right of the friars to renounce all *dominium*, tried to address the issue more reasonably in *Exiit qui seminat*:

And . . . the brothers, like anyone else, in the pinch of extreme need, would still have available to them the so-called right of existence – that is, to provide for their natural sustenance – a path conceded to every person in the grip of dire necessity, since such a condition is exempt from any law.

(*Bull. Franc.* III: 408)

Both Henry of Ghent and Godfrey of Fontaines, secular theologians who contested the more radical claims of Franciscan renunciation, echoed this more reasonable approach while insisting that, in the matter of consumables (sustenance), one cannot possibly surrender the right (*ius/dominium*) to use such things. Godfrey articulates this objection in *Quodlibet* XII.9:

---

[31] *Quia nonnunquam* (Sbaraglia, *Bullarium Franciscanum* V: 224–5); *Ad conditorem* (ibid. V: 233–46); and *Cum inter nonnullos* (ibid. V: 256–9).

From this it follows, however, that no one can in this way renounce temporal goods, since in extreme necessity anyone has a right to use (*ius utendi*) temporal goods to the extent that is sufficient for one's sustenance. No kind of perfection whatsoever will demand or permit someone to renounce this right (*ius*) and *dominium*. Thus, a person who cannot renounce the use of some thing should not [do so]. Similarly, in such a case, one cannot or should not renounce the *dominium* or faculty or right of using (*ius utendi*) those things.

(*Phil. Belges* V: 143)[32]

Everyone has a right to subsistence – a right that he or she can never renounce. This applies to the mendicant orders because it applies to all members of society.

The profound socioeconomic changes in Europe that were a result of the Agrarian and Commercial revolutions not only prompted a slow migration of the peasant classes into revitalized towns and villages but also spawned a new socioeconomic reality: poverty in its modern cast of privation, hunger, and misery. By the mid-twelfth century, theologians attempted to address this new social reality, eventually confronting the vexed problem of a creation that was intended by God for the sustenance of all, but that historically has never fulfilled its original promise. Still, some writers – and such figures as Francis of Assisi – insisted that humanity must do better; that creation ought to be able to sustain its creatures; and that those with power ought to strive for this higher end. By the end of the Middle Ages, the right to subsistence had been recognized as an absolute right of all human beings.

[32] See Virpi Mäkinen, "Godfrey of Fontaine's Criticism concerning Franciscan Poverty and the Birth of Individual Natural Rights," *Picenum seraphicum* 19 (2000) 69–85; and "The Rights of the Poor: An Argument against the Franciscans," in M. Korpiola (ed.) *Nordic Perspectives on Medieval Canon Law* (Helsinki: Matthias Calonius Society, 1999) 41–9.

43

JUST WAR

FREDERICK H. RUSSELL

Just war theories of any age have the difficult dual purposes of restraining and justifying violence. Augustine's thought, crucial for medieval Christian theory, reflected both purposes, but was casual and unsystematic. Medieval (and later) thinkers in the Latin West tried to give his scattered comments a specious doctrinal precision, packaging and repackaging the few familiar Augustinian phrases in ways that make it difficult to determine when a real shift in thought has occurred. For instance, the basic Augustinian criteria for just war were just cause, proper authority, and right intention, but agreement on these superficial generalities often masked real differences of medieval opinion.

Medieval theorizing was made more complex by the fact that warfare was not clearly distinguished from other forms of legitimate violence. Moreover, the sovereign state was supplanted by the decentralized lordships of feudalism, whereby every feudal lord had the right to use violence in his own defense. It was only when sovereign states with their monopoly of legitimate violence reappeared in the thirteenth century that something like Augustine's idea of the just war could reemerge. The internal tensions in this theory between a suspicion of all physical violence and its ardent support are best seen in the halting justification of the Crusades. Churchmen were leery of involving the church too directly in bloodshed, and yet they championed the Crusades. That they had no term to approximate 'Crusade' indicates their reticence, however, and so they had trouble including the Crusades within their rubric of just war. This is just one indication that the best minds of the Middle Ages did not devote sustained and systematic reflection to the problems of warfare. Even so, their views have had a lasting impact on modern thinking about the topic.

THE AUGUSTINIAN BACKGROUND

Medieval just war theory is encapsulated in Augustine's four-word phrase: *iusta bella ulciscuntur iniurias*, "just wars avenge injuries."[1] Augustine's actual wording, from a minor biblical commentary, is "just wars are accustomed to be defined as those that avenge injuries." This phrasing indicates how tentative he himself considered his definition; it was others who later rendered it definitive. Augustine had an ambivalent set of precedents to work with. Aristotle applied the term "just war" to wars of Hellenes against non-Hellenes, while Cicero added a legal dimension by saying that just wars were to recover lost goods (*pro rebus repetitis*), and to repel or punish an enemy (*De officiis* 1.11.36; *De republica* 2.23.35). The Old Testament describes the wars of the Israelites as justified by God, and in the New Testament Christ had used violence and yet had counseled non-violence. The early church witness was primarily pacifistic, but after Constantine the Church Fathers justified participation in warfare. The Manicheans advocated a rigid pacifism. Out of these countervailing vectors, Augustine cast

---

[1] *Quaestiones in Heptateuchum* 6.10. Much of this chapter is based on my *The Just War in the Middle Ages* (Cambridge: Cambridge University Press, 1975); the discussion of Augustine is found on pp. 16–26. Literature on the just war, both historical and systematic, is voluminous and of varying quality. Sometimes a philosophically rigorous theory makes for bad history, and vice versa. More historical treatments include David Bachrach, *Religion and the Conduct of War c. 300–1215* (Woodbridge, Suffolk: Boydell Press, 2003); Jonathan Barnes, "The Just War," in N. Kretzmann et al. (eds.) *Cambridge History of Later Medieval Philosophy* (Cambridge: Cambridge University Press, 1982) 771–84; James Johnson, *Ideology, Reason, and the Limitation of War. Religious and Secular Concepts, 1200–1740* (Princeton, NJ: Princeton University Press, 1975), and *Just War Tradition and the Restraint of War. A Moral and Historical Inquiry* (Princeton, NJ: Princeton University Press, 1981); James Muldoon, *Popes, Lawyers, and Infidels: The Church and the Non-Christian World, 1250–1550* (Philadelphia: University of Pennsylvania Press, 1979); Yasuaki Onuma, *A Normative Approach to War. Peace, War and Justice in Hugo Grotius* (Oxford: Oxford University Press, 1993). More systematic treatments include Jean Bethke Elshtain (ed.) *Just War Theory* (New York: New York University Press, 1992); National Conference of Catholic Bishops, *The Challenge of Peace: God's Promise and our Response* (Washington, DC: United States Catholic Conference, 1983), my assessment of which is "The Historical Perspective of the Bishops' Pastoral Letter: The View of One Medievalist," in C. J. Reid, Jr. (ed.) *Peace in a Nuclear Age: The Bishops' Pastoral Letter in Perspective* (Washington, DC: Catholic University of America Press, 1986) 86–97; Oliver O'Donovan, *The Just War Revisited* (Cambridge: Cambridge University Press, 2003); Paul Ramsey, *The Just War: Force and Political Responsibility* (New York: Scribner, 1968); William Stevenson, Jr., *Christian Love and Just War: Moral Paradox and Political Life in St. Augustine and his Modern Interpreters* (Macon, GA: Mercer University Press, 1987); Michael Walzer, *Just and Unjust Wars: A Moral Argument with Historical Illustrations* 4th edn (New York: Basic Books, 2006). The state of the question is in Richard Sorabji and David Rodin (eds.) *The Ethics of War: Shared Problems in Different Traditions* (Aldershot: Ashgate, 2006) esp. ch. 1. For a recent anthology, see Gregory Reichberg et al., *The Ethics of War: Classic and Contemporary Readings* (Indianapolis, IN: Wiley-Blackwell, 2006). For Augustine, see R. A. Markus, "Saint Augustine's Views on the 'Just War'," in W. J. Sheils (ed.) *The Church and War* (Oxford: Oxford University Press, 1983) 1–13; Herbert Deane, *The Political and Social Ideas of St. Augustine* (New York: Columbia University Press, 1963) ch. 5; and Alan Watt, "Which Approach? Late 20th Century Interpretations of Augustine on War," *Journal of Church and State* 46 (2004) 99–113.

the die for what later becomes the prevailing medieval view: that war might be just.[2]

Augustine's first task was to harmonize the evangelical precepts of patience with Roman legal notions, and to situate wars within God's providence. On his view, war was both a consequence of sin and a remedy for it. The real evil in war was not killing in and of itself, but rather the violence, cruelty, greed, and desire for domination that went with it.[3] (Later this would fall under the broad category of "intention.") Wars punished peoples for sins and crimes – even those unrelated to the wars themselves. Even wicked people could serve providence by punishing the sins of other peoples. War was also understood as an instrument of peace;[4] the just warrior restrained sinners from evil, thus acting against their will but in their own best interest.[5] Punishment of evil-doers that prevented them from doing further wrong was an act of love. The precept "resist not evil" (Matt. 5:39) did not prohibit wars, for the real danger was not military service itself but the malice that often accompanied it; Christ's command to "turn the other cheek" (Luke 6:29) referred to the inner disposition of the heart (*praeparatio cordis*), not to the outward deed. Love for one's enemies did not preclude a "benevolent severity."[6] By this distinction between inward attitude and outward behavior, Augustine sought to reconcile war with the teachings of the New Testament. This problematical reconciliation was generally accepted in the Middle Ages.[7]

Augustine required a just war be waged on legitimate authority. Either God or the ruler had the responsibility to decide whether a war was just, and soldiers alone were the proper officials for waging war.[8] Since obedience to kings was a general human convention, Augustine advised a soldier to obey even a sacrilegious king, and to fight even an unjust war unless the ruler ordered deeds that clearly violated divine precepts.[9] When an official killed on orders, he was not guilty of murder, and if he disobeyed an order to kill, he was guilty of treason (*City of God* I.21). Augustine thus absolved the individual soldier of moral responsibility for his official actions.

---

[2] See Russell, *Just War*, pp. 8–18, and Louis J. Swift, "Augustine on War and Killing: Another View," *Harvard Theological Review* 66 (1973) 369–83.

[3] *Contra Faustum Manicheum* 22.74: "Desire to harm, cruelty of punishment, implacable intent, severity or rebellion, the desire for domination, these are what are culpable in war."

[4] *De civitate Dei* XIX.12–13, 15; *Enarrationes in Psalmos* 73.7–8; *Contra Faustum* 22.75; *Epist.* 139.6.

[5] *Contra Faustum* 22.74, 78; *Epist.* 138.2.14.

[6] *Sermo* 302.15; *De sermone Domini in monte,* 1.19.59; 1.20.63; *Contra Faustum* 22.75; *Epist.* 47.5; *Epist.* 138.2; *Epist.* 189.4.

[7] I attempted to deal with this in my "Love and Hate in Warfare: The Contribution of Saint Augustine," *Nottingham Medieval Studies* 31 (1987) 108–24.

[8] *Contra Faustum* 22.74–5; *Quaestiones in Heptateuchum* 6.10.

[9] *Confessiones* 3.8.15; *Enarrationes in Psalmos* 124.7.

Whenever Augustine discussed authority he naturally turned to God himself. The *City of God* enumerated instances in which divine authority made exceptions to its own prohibition on killing. Some men waged war in obedience to a direct divine command while others, acting in conformity with God's ordinance, put wicked men to death (ibid.). Divine sanction of the right to punish wickedness was Augustine's strongest justification of the right to wage war. Nowhere is Augustine's critique of early Christian pacifism clearer than in his treatment of wars endowed with a divine purpose.

Augustine's just war did not distinguish between offensive and defensive warfare. Although a simple war of conquest was unjust, the concept of avenging injuries rather than defense was the starting point for every justification of war. In medieval retrospect, this expansion of the just war would also draw on Augustine's acceptance of religious persecution. Since wickedness includes improper belief, Augustine saw a divine purpose in punishing deviation from orthodoxy. Although, unlike his later interpreters, he never discussed warfare in this context, his justification of persecution shared common elements with it. He concluded that church authorities had both the right and the duty to seek imperial coercion against the Donatist heretics,[10] and he saw punishment of heretics as a form of charity:[11] in applying coercion to heresy, the church imitated God himself (*Epistle* 185.6.23). The clergy is able to compel people to the good,[12] but in so doing they must seek the aid of the emperors, who serve God by chastising heretics.[13] Thus, Augustine established the rationale by which medieval prelates appealed to secular authorities for aid against enemies of the church.

While "just wars avenge injuries" appears merely to echo Cicero's "recovery of lost goods" account, medieval interpretations of the phrase wandered between that narrow, Ciceronian view and a broader, more theocratic view. The narrow view required a clear violation of preexisting rights of the injured party, and was limited to redress of grievances and compensation for losses, a return to the *status quo ante bellum* akin to compensatory damages. Theoretically, at least, the broader interpretation saw the just war as a punishment comparable to punitive damages and unlimited in its use of violence, for it avenged the moral order. Sins against God as well as crimes could be punished. Any violation of God's laws, and any violation of Christian doctrine could be seen as an

---

[10] See Deane, *The Political and Social Ideas of St. Augustine*, ch. 6, and my "Persuading the Donatists: Augustine's Coercion by Words," in W. Klingshirn and M. Vessey (eds.) *The Limits of Ancient Christianity. Essays on Late Antique Thought and Culture in Honor of R. A. Markus* (Ann Arbor: University of Michigan Press, 1999) 115–30.

[11] *Epist.* 93.2, 6, 8.; *Contra Epist. Parmeniani* 3.1.3; 3.5.26.; *Epist.* 173.2.

[12] *Contra Gaudentium* 1.25.28; *Sermo* 112.8.

[13] *Epist.* 87.8; *Epist.* 185.7.28; *Epist.* 93.3.9–10; *De catechizandis rudibus* 1.27.53

injustice. Furthermore, punishment of the enemy population could be inflicted without regard for the distinction between soldiers and civilians, guilty and innocent.

Coupled with the concept *to avenge injuries*, the appeal to divine authority enabled the later development of holy wars and Crusades within the just war. Underwritten by divine activity, Augustine's just war became a more multipurpose institution than the Roman just war. Moreover, a divinely inspired just war could be linked to the Pauline derivation of ruling authority from God, so that wars to defend righteousness could be waged by rulers even without an express divine command.

In reality, Augustine's thoughts on the just war were only a minor theme in his thought and never systematized, constituting not so much a coherent position as a cluster of ideas, grouped around the *avenging injuries* concept. Not surprisingly, there were unresolved tensions. On the one hand, he lamented at greater length than indicated here the moral evils of warfare in general, and the faulty justice that it can at best accomplish. On the other hand, he gave grudging acceptance to just warfare under certain restrictions. Until the power of love overcame the love of power, just wars would remain a sad necessity, often justifiable, but never fully just. It is ironic that the founder of Christian just war thinking so hated warfare. Augustine's medieval successors in just war thinking often transformed his reticence into enthusiasm for the just war.

ROMAN LAW

There was little just war theory in the early Latin Middle Ages. But with the revival of learning and the rise of universities in the twelfth century, three disciplines emerged that considered these issues in detail: Roman law, canon law, and theology.

The Roman lawyers or Romanists "glossed" or commented upon Justinian's *Corpus juris civilis*, beginning in the late eleventh century. The University of Bologna was especially prominent in this movement. One of its main leaders from the late twelfth century was Azo, followed by Accursius (who produced a massive *Glossa ordinaria* [*ca.* 1230]), and then by the post-glossators or commentators. The ancient Roman hostility to barbarians, pagans, and heretics endured during this period, with Azo treating all those who deviated from orthodoxy – such as heretics, Jews, pagans, and infidels – as liable to violent punishment for their beliefs alone; Accursius also compared heresy to treason.[14] Both of these opinions enriched the canonists' later justification for the Crusades.

---

[14] Azo, *Summa Codicis*, to Cod. 1.11; Azo, *Lectura in Codicem*, to Cod. 8.4.7 v. *vel apud homines quoslibet*; Accursius, *Glossa ordinaria*, to Cod. 1.5.4, v. *subire*.

The primary concern of the Romanists was to define the legal conditions of belligerency, and so they propounded more a doctrine of licit war (*licitum bellum*) than of just war. Wars were justified according to the *ius gentium*, that complex of rights observed by all peoples.[15] The Romanists insisted that no hostile encounter could be licit without public authority. When public authority was shared among many feudal lords, most Romanists concluded that only the emperor could legally wage war; the *Libri feudorum* (*ca.* 1170), however, obliged a ruler to proceed judicially to end any *guerra* or war between his subordinates (II.27.8). Feudal custom required a vassal to aid his lord in a *guerra*, but what if that *guerra* was unjust? The Romanist debates were inconclusive. They distinguished between three distinct levels of licit warfare: the Roman just war, the *guerrae* of kings, lords, and vassals independent of the Holy Roman Emperor, and, more hesitantly, just wars in defense of the *patria* by kings who commanded the primary allegiance of all their feudal and non-feudal subjects.[16] Medieval Roman lawyers also had to deal with the complex of legal rights to inflict private violence that had developed with feudalism and were not directly dependent on the Holy Roman Emperor. Private persons had a limited right of self-defense in Roman law, for "all laws and rights permit to defend against force with force."[17] This, however, was not a war, and so such defense must be done immediately (*incontinenti*), before turning to other pursuits,[18] and be done with moderation to prevent vengeance.[19]

CANON LAW[20]

The basic text of canon law was Gratian's *Decretum* (*ca.* 1140), a systematic collection of legislation and opinions. The just war was central to Gratian, as it was not to Augustine. Gratian embeds war within other forms of coercion. Augustine's "inner disposition of the heart" becomes the hinge upon which all his discussions turn, as when he describes the moral dangers of greed and love of violence faced by knights (C. 23 q. 1 *passim*). His account of the just war has two fundamental components: authority and an injury to be avenged. Quoting first Isidore of Seville's definition of the just war as one waged on formal declaration to recover lost goods or to repel and punish enemies (*Etymologiae* 18.1.2–4), and then the Augustinian definition cited at the start of this chapter,

---

[15] Taken over via Isidore by Gratian, *Decretum* D. 1 c. 9.
[16] See Gaines Post, *Studies in Medieval Legal Thought* (Princeton, NJ: Princeton University Press, 1964) pp. 341–3, 445–8, 473–81.
[17] *Corpus iuris civilis*, Digest 9.2.45.4; taken over via Isidore of Seville by Gratian, *Decretum* D. 1. c. 7.
[18] *Corpus iuris civilis*, Digest 43.16.3.9.   [19] Ibid., Codex 8.4.1.
[20] For the structure of canonists' debates, see James Brundage, *Medieval Canon Law* (London: Longman, 1995).

Gratian proposes a definition that combined elements of both: "a just war is waged by an authoritative edict to avenge injuries." To prevent this definition from justifying vengeance, Gratian appeals to authority – wars should be waged only on the command of God or some legitimate authority (C. 23 q. 2 d. p. c. 2). Following Augustine after his fashion, Gratian enlarges the just war when he invokes God, thus linking just wars with divine authority for church wars. He justifies religious persecution of the church's enemies – infidels, pagans, and heretics – but he only implicitly conflates just wars and religious persecution, and is unclear about whether the church has the right to authorize wars, and how directly it could be involved. He never explicitly discusses the Crusades.

Gratian's account raised more questions than it answered, and so the so-called Decretists "glossed" the *Decretum* to about 1190. They first had to explicate the just war formula. Most terse was the account of Huguccio, for whom the just war was waged by the just edict of a prince (*Summa* to C. 23 q. 2 pr). To prevent vengeance, the Decretists restricted the rights of self-defense by requiring recourse to judicial authority, for, as Huguccio said, no one could act as judge in his own cause.[21] Decretists agreed that the necessity of defense sometimes justified armed violence, but it was Huguccio who narrowed what could count as a just cause for war when he prohibited a purely aggressive war of attack (ibid.). What the Decretists lacked was an effective distinction between war and the exercise of jurisdiction over one's subjects; they were concerned to limit the petty violence of the feudal nobility, but they placed no similar restrictions on the violence of wars between full-fledged authorities.

For Huguccio, wars against heretics were justified by both divine and human law (*Summa* to D. 1. c. 9), but many Decretists were unclear as to whether the just cause in this case was heresy itself, or the heretics' resort to violence. Defense of the church, the Holy Land, and the faith often overrode their cautions, though, and enabled them to envision wars based on the church's authority. Since heretics transgressed divine law and persecuted the church, they were denied the protection of human law and could even have their property confiscated.[22] Popes and prelates could summon princes and urge Christians to attack all those who disturbed the *patria*, meaning here the church.[23]

The Decretists took a major step when they transformed the Crusades from a nebulous holy war into a just war of the church. Overall, they confirmed the principle that any use of violence other than immediate self-defense was the

---

[21] *Summa* to D. 46 c. 8; for other texts, see Russell, *Just War*, p. 97 n. 14.
[22] Russell, *Just War*, p. 114 n. 98.   [23] Ibid., p. 116 n. 107.

monopoly of legitimate authority. The just war became the province of princes, popes, and prelates justified by defense of the *patria* and the church. The clearest justification for the Crusade was Muslim occupation of the Holy Land. Lacking in their debates, however, was an awareness of the subtle differences between authorizing, promulgating, declaring, and directing hostile operations from afar.

Around 1190, canon lawyers began glossing papal decretal letters; the disagreements between these canonists, known as Decretalists, provide a richness of debate. Their first task was to refine the formulation of the just war. Five distinct components of a just war – *persona, res, causa, animus,* and *auctoritas* – entered into general use in the *Summa de paenitentia* of Raymond of Pennafort (*ca.* 1221). According to Raymond, all five criteria must be met for a war to be just (2.5.12.17). First, the person waging war must be a layman. Second, the *res*, or object, of the war must be recovery of property or defense of the *patria*. Third, the *causa*, or immediate circumstances necessitating the war, must be that hostilities had already begun. Fourth, the *animus*, or attitudes, included piety, justice, and obedience, and excluded hatred, cruelty, and cupidity. Fifth, the war must be waged on princely authority.

Of course, such broad formulations only opened debate. A key part of this debate concerned how to clarify Augustine's phrase "avenge injuries." By common consensus, "avenge" came to mean the simple repulsion of injuries, in line with Roman law, and "injuries" usually meant violence to be repelled immediately if the defense was moderate. Gradually, however, the concept of avenging disappeared, a shift that enabled the Decretalists to explore the underdeveloped notion of defense. Another question, which particularly vexed the Decretalists, concerned the proper authority for a just war. Some felt that princes in general, and even Italian cities, had the right to declare war. In contrast, Hostiensis claimed that the just war could be waged only on the authority of emperor, pope, or a judge possessing sovereign powers (the *merum imperium*). He condemned all wars between Christians as treason.[24] Around 1250, the most prominent among the Decretalists, Innocent IV (Sinibaldo dei Fieschi), probably the most accomplished lawyer to sit as pope, adopted a middle position. Taking into account contemporary practice, Christian legal norms, and differences in levels of jurisdiction, he distinguished between a just war against external invaders and exercise of internal jurisdiction. These licit military actions of inferior princes were not just wars, he claimed.[25] The legal conditions under which violence

---

[24] Copious references ibid., p. 141f.
[25] *Commentaria* to X.2.13.12, par. 7–8 (ed. 1570, ff. 231va–232ra).

was inflicted, rather than the nature of the violence itself, determined its legal status.

Concomitant with the issue of authority was the question of obedience. Common opinion held that a vassal was not bound to aid his overlord when the latter unjustly attacked, or when obedience would lead to sinful activities,[26] but such disobedience in an unjust war clearly opposed feudal custom. Taking this into account, Innocent IV applied Roman private law to the feudal relationship, stating that a vassal could sue his lord for damages incurred in a just war, but not in an unjust war.[27] Lords and vassals thus had to confront both moral and material risks when they engaged in violence.

Rules of conduct, whether customary or canonical, were based more on military expediency and moral justification than on the inherent rights of bystanders. Common opinion applied the Truce of God – a temporary cessation of hostilities based on the liturgical year – only to wars of attack, while a just defensive war could be waged at any time. Especially deadly weapons could be used in a just war even against Christians, but not in unjust wars. According to William of Rennes, just warriors should limit their violence according to current practices, or, as he put it, by the "industry and custom of those fighting with good faith." Restitution for damages in an unjust war was obligatory, but not in a just war unless moderation had not been observed.[28] Innocent IV and Hostiensis – who were in general concerned less with the justice of war and more with its legal consequences – linked property rights to three levels of licit violence. The highest, a just war between independent adversaries, carried the full legal consequences of confiscation of the Roman just war, including capture of enemies and confiscation of their property. The second, waged by a prince with some jurisdiction over his enemy, limited a prince to, in effect, a just battle rather than a just war, in which he could exercise jurisdiction over enemy property but could not confiscate it. The third, most restrictive type was simple defense against invasion, where the only right was simple repulsion, without increased property rights.[29]

Debates about the church's involvement in hostilities focused on ecclesiastical regulation of lay wars and on the authority of the prelates to declare war. Johannes Teutonicus spoke for most when he claimed church competence to

---

[26] Johannes Teutonicus, *Glossa ordinaria*, to C. 22 q.5 c. 18 v. *honestum*; to C. 22. q. 5 c. 1 v. *et miles*.
[27] The fuller argumentation is in Russell, *Just War*, pp. 149–55.
[28] See William's *Glossa* on Raymond of Pennafort's *Summa de paenitentia* II.5.12.19, v. *sibi dato* (ed. 1603, p. 188a).
[29] Russell, *Just War*, pp. 175–9; cf. Maurice H. Keen, *The Laws of War in the Late Middle Ages* (London: Routledge, 1965) pp. 67–72.

judge the moral status of a particular war.[30] Innocent IV insisted, however, that Christians could not make war on infidels merely because of their infidelity, but only when infidels attacked Christians.[31] On the other hand, when the Holy Roman Emperor made war on the church, Hostiensis obliged all Catholics including imperial vassals to come to its defense. The *Glossa ordinaria* to the Gregorian decretals of 1234 gave the church alone authority to declare war on enemies of the faith, since it alone could promote such wars by granting indulgences. For Hostiensis, without the papal preaching of the cross, no church war enjoyed the status of a Crusade, and he distinguished between Crusades to the Holy Land and Crusades within Europe, finding these latter more reasonable and just.[32] Now domesticated by papal authority, the Crusade became *the* papal just war. In effect, the Decretalists distinguished three levels of the church's wars against its enemies: it could first invoke the secular arm, then prelates could take the initiative, and finally the pope could preach and direct the Crusade. Theory had finally caught up with practice.

THEOLOGIANS

Since the basic theology text in the schools, the *Sentences* of Peter Lombard (*ca.* 1150), did not explicitly discuss warfare, theologians used Gratian extensively in their discussions. Even so, theology and canon law diverge quite significantly, especially after 1250, when Aristotle joined the Bible and Augustine as a major authority in medieval discussions. In general, theologians placed more emphasis on the moral dimensions of warfare than canonists did, betrayed more suspicion of military service, and also placed greater emphasis on the individual soldier's responsibility. In addition, they continued to emphasize avenging injuries long after the canonists had discarded it. John of La Rochelle, for instance, repeated the canonist Raymond of Pennafort's five criteria mentioned above and added that, if all five criteria were not met, the war was not only unjust but rapacious.[33] Proper authorities included kings and the emperor, and just causes included protection of the *patria*, the faith, and peace. Following Augustine's durable definition but subdividing it differently, the Franciscan Alexander of Hales distinguished six requirements for the just war: authority, attitude, intention, condition, merit, and cause. Authority and attitude concerned the person declaring the war, intention and condition referred to those fighting the

---

[30] *Apparatus glossarum in Compilationem quartam* to 2.9.2 (X.2.24.29) v. *iniuste*.

[31] *Commentaria* to X.3.42.4, para. 5 (ed. 1570, f. 456rb). See Muldoon, *Popes, Lawyers and Infidels*.

[32] Russell, *Just War*, pp. 199–205.

[33] *Summa de vitiis*, v. *de his rapiuntur in bello* (ms. Paris, Bibl. Nat. Lat. 16417, f. 151ra).

war, and merit referred to the enemy, which came under Augustine's rubric of avenging injuries. The just cause, Alexander's sixth criterion, became the overriding moral purposes of Augustine's just war: the relief of good people, the coercion of the wicked, and peace for all.[34] By placing this last, Alexander emphasized the teleological view of the just war that Thomas Aquinas would develop more fully.

Opinion was divided over whether knights could serve in an unjust war, or withhold their obedience, but discussion was casuistic and inconclusive. More systematic was Alexander of Hales's later distinction between two elements of his just war formula: a king's war could be unjust but still the knights had the duty to obey him (*Summa theol.* III n. 467 ad 1–2). This returned the requirement to Augustine's position. Theologians privileged defense against attack in their analysis of cause, and since defense cost money, they justified as incentives the payment of salaries to mercenaries and rewards from spoils.[35] Like the lawyers, theologians felt that plunder seized in a just war became one's own, but observed that just title was often difficult to determine. Their advice was to seek the judgment of a church court, and, in the confessional, to render restitution in dubious cases.[36] On Crusades against infidels and heretics, theologians before Aquinas basically reflected received opinion.

With the infusion of Aristotle's thought from around 1250, theology became more speculative and systematic, incorporating Aristotle's naturalness of political authority, the teleology of communal life, and the superiority of the common good into the earlier Augustinian framework; in the process, it both emancipated the theology of war from the canonists and neglected the messy complexities of feudalism. Aquinas's most extensive treatment of war, in his *Summa theologiae*, places warfare within an overall moral scheme of Christian salvation. To the objection that the evangelical precepts made war illicit, Aquinas first cites Augustine's reference to the inward disposition of the heart, and then cites the Aristotelian defense of the common good, which was in effect the divine good.[37] Fighting enemies is both for their own good and for that of others. One can do harm to enemies to avoid greater evils or to support greater goods such as justice (*Sent* III.30.2), but wars waged not for the common good but for greed and vainglory are dangerous to both the soul and the community (*De regimine principum* I.8). Aquinas justifies princely authority to wage war, since princes are instituted by God to further the common good (*Epistola ad ducissam*

---

[34] *Summa theologica* III n. 466 resp. and ad 3 (ed. Quaracchi, IV: 684–5). Cf. Russell, *Just War*, pp. 219–20.

[35] Russell, *Just War*, pp. 241–3.   [36] Ibid., pp. 250–1.

[37] *Summa theol.* 2a2ae 40.1 obj. 1, ad 1; *In Ethic.* X.11 (to 1177b).

Brabantiae 6). Dispelling any lingering doubts over whether killing could be justified, he divinizes the teleology of the just war, going far beyond Augustine's more somber estimate of what just warfare could accomplish.

Aquinas proposes three requirements for a just war: authority, just cause, and just intention (*Summa theol.* 2a2ae 40.1c). Meriting first place is the authority of a prince committed to the common good. The second requirement is the guilt of an enemy, rendering him worthy of attack. Third, the warriors themselves must be motivated by righteous intentions to promote good and to avoid evil. Aquinas further requires the fulfillment of all three criteria, such that even if the first two are met, the war can still be rendered illicit by wicked intentions. Aquinas also insists that a war be not only justified but also justly waged. The Thomistic formula for the just war thus recast the simple if problematic Augustinian definition in a new and concise form.

Aquinas at least obliquely raises the issue of non-combatant immunity when he argues that just men should not kill innocent men (ibid., 188.3 ad 1). He feels that someone who kills a just man sins grievously, yet he retreats from this because a just man unjustly killed would be led to glory by God (ibid., 64.6 ad 2). These passages could support non-combatant immunity, but Thomas does not mention warfare in this context, remaining safely within the confines of Augustine's theory of war guilt.[38] Aquinas supports the right of just warriors to retain their plunder, provided their pillaging was motivated by justice rather than cupidity (ibid., 66.8 ad 1, 3).

Aquinas has little new to say about wars of the church. He holds that the crusading (military) orders could justly wage war at the behest of a prince or the church (*Summa theol.* 2a2ae 188.3 ad 4). Like Innocent IV, he makes concessions to existing infidel societies: mere infidelity does not justify warfare against non-Christian lands, but attacks on Christians and their rightful territory do. Following Aristotle, Aquinas is convinced that any human community has a natural right to an independent existence regardless of its religious beliefs. Nevertheless, he denies such toleration to heretics.[39] In general, Aquinas synthesizes the older Augustinian notion of war as punishment with the newer Aristotelian *raison d'état*; his bold application of Aristotle's politics to warfare prevents him from transforming the church's spiritual superiority into the legal supremacy advocated by Hostiensis. In effect, Aquinas proposes two separate but complementary formulas: one is the standard formula of avenging injuries,

---

[38] Vincent of Beauvais hinted at non-combatant immunity when he obliged a knight who waged a just war to refrain from punishing the subjects of his enemy who had refused aid and counsel to their ruler (*Speculum doctrinale* 7.28, ed. 1624, p. 576).

[39] *Summa theol.* 2a2ae 11.3c. Also, heretics could be compelled to fulfill their promises by coercion (*Summa theol.* 2a2ae 10.8c, ad 3).

while the other treats the just war as a defense of the community and the common good. This approach points toward the modern distinction between offensive and defensive wars and to the age of the standing army.

CONCLUSIONS

Just war theories were the best compromise between human aggression and Christian pacifism that the church could devise. Even so, the problem defied consistent and sustained philosophical attempts at solution. Part of the difficulty was that medieval thought on war developed largely through commentaries on key texts. If unmentioned in the text, an issue often did not receive attention, while mention in turn often provoked pointless repetition. In addition, debates often applied texts to contemporary feudal and papal realities; when these time-bound realities changed, such debates became less relevant. The response of late medieval legists to these changed conditions was a sort of quotation-mongering deficient in practical viability and new thought. Canonistic treatments became more detailed and specific, while theologians became increasingly abstract. Finally, in the seventeenth century, Hugo Grotius ushered in modern just war theory when he secularized the just war by removing medieval religious considerations from it.[40]

When Innocent IV limited a just war to authorities with no superior, he buttressed the right of secular monarchs and independent city-states to develop their monopoly of legitimate violence (see Chapter 39). As a result, the just war could not only support clerical purposes, but could be turned against them, as it was in the conflicts between kings and popes after 1300. Royal laws punishing disobedience as treason eroded the capacity of vassals to wage private warfare, and increasing use of standing armies weakened the power of vassals to disobey. What had begun with Augustine as an issue of morality and scriptural exegesis ended up as a tool of statecraft, as a *bellum legale*, waged in defense of legality rather than morality, and also made possible ever-larger wars. Similarly, the crusading ideology helped justify later European states in their imperialism outside Europe. The real victors of the medieval concept of the just war were the monarchs of early modern Europe.

The assessment of just war theories of any age is bound to be ambivalent, for they are an unstable compound always in danger of splitting into their

---

[40] See Karma Nabulsi, "Conceptions of Justice in War: From Grotius to Modern Times," in Sorabji and Rodin, *The Ethics of War*, 44–60; Richard Tuck, "Grotius' *Of the Law of War and Peace*," in J. H. Burns (ed.) *The Cambridge History of Political Thought, 1450–1700* (Cambridge: Cambridge University Press, 1991) 514–22.

component parts. The greatest weakness of all medieval theories is their dependence on an assessment of prior guilt. Without a competent tribunal to judge the justice of a war, the authority declaring the war is both morally and legally compromised, and both sides can claim justice. The just war is really an ethical and religious doctrine covered with a thick veneer of legality. At the very least, however, the medieval just war placed the burden of proof on just warriors to rationalize the grounds for their actions according to accepted principles.

VIII

METAPHYSICS

44

THE SUBJECT OF THE ARISTOTELIAN
SCIENCE OF METAPHYSICS

REGA WOOD

Aristotelian science conveys understanding by showing the necessary relationship between immediately evident first principles and conclusions about the natural world. To take a trivial example: induction from repeated experience teaches us that all broad-leaved plants are deciduous. We discover that grapevines have broad leaves. We infer that grapevines are deciduous, and thereby we also learn that they lose their leaves in winter because they are broad-leaved (see Aristotle, *Post. An.* II.16–17).

Aristotelian science explains a subject's possession of an attribute (the *explanandum*) by identifying the possession of that attribute with membership in a species, and then citing as *explanans* the inclusion of that species within a prior genus. In the present example, the property is "losing its leaves in winter," the species is "grapevines," and the genus is "broad-leaved plants." The explanation is then presented in the form of a syllogism. In the first premise an attribute (being deciduous) is predicated of a subject (broad-leaved plant). The second premise introduces a new subject that belongs to the class described by the subject of the first premise, allowing us to conclude that the second subject shares an attribute of the first.

Aristotle describes this demonstration as *propter quid* science because it explains why grape leaves fall. If the deduction were valid, but its premises were not explanatory, it would count as *quia* science: knowing a fact without understanding why it obtains (ibid., I.13, 78a22–b3) (see also Chapter 26).

A great strength of Aristotelian science is its claim systematically to explain the world as a whole. It explains not only the movement of celestial bodies and the tendency of heavy bodies to fall but also the generation and growth of plants and animals, their absorption of nutrients, and their eventual decay. Another strength of the approach is that it offers reliable knowledge of a changing world using a method that takes advantage of the strengths of induction, observation, and deduction.

A SCIENCE OF METAPHYSICS?

A weakness of Aristotelian science is that the method threatens to collapse precisely at the point where it should be strongest – namely, when it deals with the most general science, metaphysics. Metaphysics is central to the structure of Aristotelian science because it validates the principles and concepts assumed in the particular sciences.[1] One sign of the problem is an inconsistency between the work that explains scientific method and the work that describes the most general science: the *Posterior Analytics* and the *Metaphysics*, respectively.

In his *Posterior Analytics*, Aristotle establishes that a science proceeds from indemonstrable first principles to demonstrate and thereby explain the attributes of a unified subject (I.2, 71b9–19; I.10, 76b11–22). He holds that a science is unified if its indemonstrables, its subject, and its attributes belong to one single genus (I.28).

In his *Metaphysics*, however, Aristotle says that the subject of metaphysics is *ens qua ens* (*to on hē on*).[2] Usually this phrase is translated as "being *qua* being," but though 'entity' (*ens*) signifies a subject, 'being' signifies an attribute rather than a subject of which attributes are predicated. Attributes as such, however, cannot be the subject of an Aristotelian science. So here we will refer to "entity *qua* entity."[3] But the basic problem is not with how to translate the word *ens*; it is with its ontological status. For since *ens* is not a genus,[4] it seems it could not be the subject of an Aristotelian science. There cannot be a science of entity, as science is defined in the *Posterior Analytics*, since there is no common nature or most general genus that includes both substance and accidents.

Moreover, were we to overlook that obstacle and suppose that entity is a genus, we would find then ourselves predicating a genus (entity) of species and *differentia*, which is improper.[5] Thus while it is proper to say 'an animal is a substance,' we cannot say that 'substance is animal,' since it is wrong to predicate the less general of the more general category. But while we cannot say 'substance is animal' or 'animal is man,' we do rightly say 'substance is an entity' and 'substance is unified,' and that would not be possible if entity were a genus. Therefore, entity cannot be a most general category or genus (see *Metaphys.* II.3, 998b14–28).

---

[1] See Aristotle, *Metaphys.* IV.3, 1005a19–b34; VI.1, 1025b4–18. For a challenge to this view see Alfonso Gómez-Lobo, "Arisotle's First Philosophy and the Principles of Particular Disciplines," *Zeitschrift für philosophische Forschung* 32 (1978) 183–94.

[2] *Metaphys.* IV.1, 1003a21–22, but see I.2, 982b7–10; VI.1, 1025b3–4; 1026a16–18.

[3] Another problem with the usual English 'being as being' is that that phrase would normally translate the Latin '*esse qua esse*,' not '*ens qua ens*.' Still, '*ens*' is a participle and 'entity' is an abstract noun, so no solution is really satisfactory.

[4] *Post. An.* II.7, 92b14; *Metaphys.* III.3, 998b22.   [5] See Aristotle, *Topics* VI.6, 144a31–b3.

AVICENNA AND AVERROES

As these last puzzles show, the problem is not just that Aristotle is not entirely consistent, but that the puzzles he himself states early in the *Metaphysics* seem to show that there could not be a most general science. Faced with this problem, medievals turned to Avicenna and Averroes. Avicenna agrees with Aristotle that the subject of metaphysics is entity as entity and its causes. In its search for understanding of entity as entity – that is, entity insofar as it is entity – metaphysics demonstrates the existence of God. It has four parts: (1) It investigates divine being, entirely removed from matter, as it seeks to discover the final causes of caused beings as beings. (2) It seeks to understand caused beings connected with but not constituted by matter, by considering them insofar as they are caused by the first cause. Also, (3) it enquires about the attributes and dispositions that characterize indifferently both being that is connected with and being that is unconnected with matter – specifically mentioned are the attributes of unity and causality. Finally, (4) metaphysics establishes the first principles of the particular sciences that deal with beings connected with matter.[6]

Averroes agrees with Avicenna that metaphysics establishes the principles of the particular sciences, and like Avicenna he lists this as the last part of the study of metaphysics.[7] But it is the last of three, not four parts, since Averroes eliminates the distinction between the second and third parts of metaphysics Avicenna described. Accidents need not be studied separately, since the nine accidental categories are all attributes of the first category of substance (*In Metaphys.* IV.2–3). Obeying the logic of the *Posterior Analytics*, Averroes holds that metaphysics considers only a single genus, substance.[8] Entity as such cannot be the subject of a science, since it does not constitute a genus. Moreover, the principal subject of metaphysics, according to Averroes, is unqualified entity, by which he means substantial forms removed from matter. Such forms removed from matter are those of the most noble causes, and hence God and separated substances are the subject of metaphysics, but proving their existence is not the task of metaphysics. The existence of separated substances is established in the science of physics (*In Phys.* I.83; *In Metaphys.* IV.1).

---

[6] Avicenna, *Liber de philosophia prima* I.1–2 (ed. Van Riet, I: 8–17). For the suggestion that metaphysics has only three parts, since the first two parts of this science should not be distinguished see Gerard Verbeke, ibid., pp. 21*–23*. By contrast, Olivier Boulnois refers to four parts in "Le besoin de métaphysique. Théologie et structure des métaphysiques médiévales," in J.-L. Solère and Z. Kaluza (eds.) *La servante et la consolatrice* (Paris: Vrin, 2002) pp. 70–2.

[7] Averroes, *Epitome in librum Metaphysicae Aristotelis*, tr. 1 (ed. 1562, VIII: 357r).

[8] Cf. Aristotle *Metaphys.* IX.1, 1045b28–33.

SCHOLASTIC APPROACHES

Albert Zimmermann distinguishes three principal scholastic approaches to the problem. The first does not aim for a unified subject, but makes God one of many subjects of metaphysics. The second includes God, but as the cause of metaphysics' subject rather than as its subject. The third includes God as a part of a unified subject of metaphysics. The three most famous medieval philosophers, Thomas Aquinas, John Duns Scotus, and William of Ockham each espouse one of these three approaches: Aquinas, the second; Scotus, the third; and Ockham, the first.[9] To this list a fourth approach should be added, according to which substance is the subject of metaphysics. Though the fourth approach was rarely advocated by scholastics, related views are widely held today.[10] So we will consider advocates of all four approaches in chronological order, beginning with an advocate of the fourth view.

Richard Rufus of Cornwall

Denying Averroes's claim that God and separated substances are the subject of metaphysics and accepting his claim that entity cannot strictly speaking be its subject, Richard Rufus proposes that the subject of metaphysics is substance. Rufus does not see himself as thereby rejecting Aristotle's claim that entity as entity is the subject of metaphysics. Rather, following Averroes (*In Metaphys.* IV.2), Rufus holds that substance is the primary meaning of 'entity,' which is an analogous term referring *per posterius* to entities other than substance – that is, to quality and quantity and the other accidental categories.[11] Modern proponents of this approach refer not to analogy but to *pros hen* equivocation or to focal meaning.[12] They basically agree with Rufus and Averroes, however, that 'entity' primarily signifies substance. Thus proponents of the fourth approach hold that when Aristotle speaks of the science that studies entity as entity, he is referring to the science of substance, which is a science that also considers substance's

---

[9] See Albert Zimmermann, *Ontologie oder Metaphysik* (Leuven: Peeters, 1998) pp. 200–22, 294–329, 389–98.

[10] See Alan Code, "Aristotle's Metaphysics as a Science of Principles," *Revue internationale de philosophie* 51 (1997) 357–78; Kyle A. Fraser, "Demonstrative Science and the Science of Being *qua* Being," *Oxford Studies in Ancient Philosophy* 22 (2002) 43–82.

[11] *Dissertatio in Metaphys.* 4.1.E2 (Salamanca, Bibl. Gen. Hist. cod. 2322, f. 75rb). See also Albert Zimmermann, "Some Aspects of the Reception of Aristotle's Physics and Metaphysics in the Thirteenth Century," in M. Jordan and K. Emery (eds.) *Ad litteram: Authoritative Texts and their Medieval Readers* (Notre Dame, IN: University of Notre Dame Press, 1992) pp. 220–2.

[12] Modern discussion of focal meaning was pioneered by G. E. L. Owen, "Logic and Metaphysics in Some Early Works of Aristotle," in G. Owen and D. Ingemar (eds.) *Aristotle and Plato in the Mid-Fourth Century: Papers of the Symposium Aristotelicum* (Gothenburg: Elanders, 1960) 163–90.

attributes and its principles, and thus by extension all entities. The accidents of substance are also considered by other sciences – number, for example, by a mathematician. But it pertains to the metaphysician alone to consider them unqualifiedly as entities.

Unlike modern advocates of this approach, Rufus does not include the first cause in the science of metaphysics, but limits the subject of metaphysics to caused entities. Here Rufus's belief that the subject of metaphysics includes only caused substances and its passions may reflect the influence of Avicenna. Though Rufus rejects Avicenna's claim that the subject of metaphysics includes the divine final cause of being as being, Rufus seems to agree with Avicenna that metaphysics deals with the causes of caused entities insofar as they are caused.[13]

Since substance is a genus, and its attributes can be understood as a consequence of its first principles, it meets the requirements stated in the *Posterior Analytics*. But Rufus adds that the subject of a science must have not only generic unity but also share a single nature that can be measured by a common minimum in much the same way that all numbers are measured by a single unit. Partly for this reason, God cannot be the subject of the science of metaphysics, or a part of its subject. God enters into the science of metaphysics only as a cause, and not as an intrinsic but as an extrinsic cause.[14] Hence, the subject of metaphysics is limited to created substance, and its utility is to supply such knowledge of created entities as is possible in this life. Despite having denied that God is the subject of metaphysics, Rufus holds that the final end of metaphysics is to speak of God as the final cause, which is a thought that would resonate with his successors.[15]

In some respects Rufus's is an incomplete and unsatisfactory account of the subject of metaphysics. It is sketchy, and he does not tackle the problem of the relationship of metaphysics and theology. Perhaps for this reason, he does not appear to qualify the requirements for an Aristotelian science in defining the subject of metaphysics, except perhaps by unduly restricting the subject. By contrast, most scholastics compromise the requirements stated in the *Posterior Analytics* for a unified science and come closer to the views stated by Avicenna. Moreover, they also seek to preserve some aspect of Averroes's claim that God is its primary subject.

---

[13] Avicenna, *Liber de philosophia prima* I.2, ed. Van Riet, I: 14–15. Averroes by contrast speaks not of caused things but of transmutable or sensible things. See Averroes, *In Metaphys.*, IV.1; *Epitome in Metaphys.*, tr. 1 (ed. 1562, VIII: 357r).

[14] Rufus, *Dissertatio in Metaphys.* prol. (ed. in Zimmermann, *Ontologie oder Metaphysik*, pp. 113–15).

[15] Rufus, *Dissertatio in Metaphys.* prol. (UB Erfurt, Dep. Erf. CA Quarto 290, f. 2va). Cf. Thomas Aquinas, *Summa contra gentiles* III.25.

Thomas Aquinas

Aquinas's solution to the problem is closer to Avicenna's than to Averroes's.[16]
For though, like Averroes, Aquinas holds that metaphysics is principally about
substance,[17] Aquinas agrees with Avicenna that the subject of metaphysics is
entity *qua* entity and not God and separated substances. Most of the elements
of Aquinas's solution are drawn from either Aristotle or Avicenna, and yet he
goes beyond these authors, often in a manner dictated by Christian doctrine.[18]
Specifically, Aquinas carefully distinguishes a divine science based on revelation
from the divine science of metaphysics, and he provides an alternative account
of the unity of metaphysics, a negative unity that we will discuss below.

According to Aquinas, God is related to metaphysics as the cause of its subject.
From this it would seem to follow that metaphysics investigates God, since every
science has to consider its principles.[19] So in making the case for theology as
a separate science, Aquinas explains why we need to postulate a science other
than metaphysics that considers God. The positive case is based on the claim
that God and separated substances are special kinds of causes; the negative case
is based on our limited epistemological capacity.

Theology can be a separate science because, though every science investigates
the principles of its subject,[20] it is not always the sole science that does so,
according to Aquinas. What determines whether causes are treated in more than
one science is whether they exist independently. Non-self-subsisting principles
are studied only by the science whose subjects they cause. However, complete,
self-subsistent causes must also be studied in a separate science without reference
to the things they cause. Just as the elements of fire, air, water, and earth
are studied apart from the compounds based on them, so God and separated
substances are studied in theology.

The negative case is based on the claim that God is a non-natural cause
and presupposes the psychological definition of an Aristotelian science. An
Aristotelian science is an intellectual habit or disposition concerning a demonstrated truth about a unified subject matter.[21] The science of metaphysics, like
other natural sciences, is a habit of the possible intellect, a faculty whose objects
are sensed before they are abstracted, and hence a faculty whose sole access
to knowledge of God is *a posteriori*, since natural reason can know only God's
effects in the world. Though God is maximally intelligible, our intellects are

---

[16] See John F. Wippel, *The Metaphysical Thought of Thomas Aquinas* (Washington, DC: Catholic
University of America Press, 2000) p. 18.
[17] Aquinas, *In Metaphys.* V.7 (ed. Cathala and Spiazzi, n. 842); VIII.1 n. 1682; XI.1 n. 2155.
[18] See Zimmermann, *Ontologie oder Metaphysik*, p. 214.   [19] See Aristotle, *Phys.* I.1, 184a12–14.
[20] See Aquinas, *In Metaphys.* VI.1 n. 1145 (re. 1025b5–7).
[21] See Aristotle, *Nic. Ethics* VI.3, 1139b26–35; *Post. An.* I.28, 87a38–87b4.

blind to him; he cannot be a direct object of natural understanding.[22] Since the relation of a science to its subject is the same as the relation of an intellectual habit to its object (*Summa theol.* 1a 1.7), theological understanding – which has a different subject, namely, God as described by Scripture – must be a scientific habit different from metaphysics (*In De Trinitate* 5.4).

So far Aquinas has shown only that God cannot be the subject of a natural science of metaphysics, but must instead be the subject of a distinct science, not naturally acquired. The more daunting task, however, is to show the unity of the subject. Since the unity of a science requires the unity of its principles as well as the unity of its subject, Thomas discharges this obligation in part by his account of God as a principle of entity.[23] Here Aquinas is drawing on a distinction stated by Avicenna between two ways in which a principle can be common: a principle can be common as a universal is common, and in that case it can be predicated of all particular things that share it. By contrast, an efficient cause can be common as the shared primary origin of things.[24] Aquinas revises this distinction, contrasting common predicables with principles having general causal power. For both Avicenna and Aquinas the common causes of entity as such are beyond the natural realm – non-natural for Avicenna, and maximally actual, complete, incorruptible, and immaterial for Aquinas (*In De Trinitate* 5.4). Thus the subject of metaphysics is united in part because all being or entity shares a common cause.

The more obvious problem is the unity of entity itself as a subject of inquiry. Sometimes in this context Thomas describes entity as a genus, though, of course, strictly speaking it is not (*In Metaphys.* proem.).[25] Moreover, Thomas faces another problem since he has denied that God is the subject of metaphysics: for if entity as such is the subject of metaphysics, then God cannot be an entity. At some points, Thomas seems to accept this consequence. He excludes God from the subject of metaphysics by defining entity as what finitely participates in being or what God causes (*In De causis* 6).[26] But at other points Aquinas includes God as an entity.[27]

[22] Aquinas, *In De Trinitate* 5.4 (re. Aristotle, *Metaphys.* II.1, 993b10, and Romans 1.20). Cf. *Summa theol.* 1a 84.7 ad 3.
[23] *In Post. an.* I.41, lines 242–300 (re. Averroes, *In Post. an.* I.179; Aristotle, *Post. an.* I.27, 87a38–b4).
[24] Also common is the shared primary end for which natural things were intended (Avicenna, *Liber primus naturalium* 1.2, ed Van Riet, pp. 22–3). Cf. Wippel, *Metaphysical Thought*, pp. 15–16.
[25] See Wippel, *Metaphysical Thought*, p. 20.
[26] Less radically, elsewhere Thomas denies only that God is included with everything that is a *common* entity. See *In De divinis nominibus* 5.2.660, and *Summa theol.* 1a2ae 66.5 ad 4.
[27] Zimmermann, *Ontologie oder Metaphysik*, pp. 219–21, lists the passages and suggests that Aquinas may simply be inconsistent on this point.

Restricting the significance of 'entity' bears some resemblance to Rufus's claim that metaphysics concerns only caused being. This is an approach that Thomists consider uncongenial to Aquinas,[28] so fortunately there is another, more consistent strategy, which rests on a variation of Aristotle's distinction between physical, mathematical, and metaphysical abstraction. As traditionally interpreted by Averroes, physics abstracts only the general from the particular and deals with objects abstract from matter neither in being nor in definition, whereas mathematics deals with objects abstract in definition but not in being, and metaphysics deals with abstract objects, independent of matter in their being (*In Metaphys.* VI.2 [re. 1026a19]).

For Thomas, the metaphysician separates rather than abstracts (*In De Trinitate* 5.3) – that is, the metaphysician judges not just that being can be considered separately from matter, but that its nature is unconnected with matter.[29] Things are separated from matter in two ways according to Thomas: on the one hand, there are things that cannot be combined with matter, such as God and angels; on the other hand, there are things that can exist with or without matter and do not depend on it, such as entity and substance, act and potency (ibid., 5.4; *In Metaphys.* proem.). The human science of metaphysics, which Thomas describes as philosophical theology, deals with the former as the cause of its subject. Its proper subject, however, is entity judged to be independent of matter in the latter sense (*In De Trinitate* 5.4). That subject is unified negatively, not by being positively distinct from matter, but by being as capable of existing apart from matter as conjoined with it.[30]

Sharing with Avicenna the view that the subject of metaphysics is entity as entity, Thomas goes beyond Avicenna in justifying the unity of metaphysics by reference to the requirements stated for an Aristotelian science in the *Posterior Analytics*. Aquinas also has provided a carefully reasoned response to Averroes's claim that God and separated substances are the subject of metaphysics. Thomas makes them instead the causes of its proper subject and the subject of a different science.[31] But though God is not the subject of metaphysics, it aims at knowledge of God as its final end, for Aquinas (*Summa contra gentiles* III.25) as for Rufus.

---

[28] Ibid., p. 222.
[29] See John F. Wippel, "Metaphysics and *Separatio* According to Thomas Aquinas," *Review of Metaphysics* 31 (1978) 431–70.
[30] See Wippel, *Metaphysical Thought*, p. 17; Zimmermann, *Ontologie oder Metaphysik*, p. 211.
[31] As Zimmermann points out, God and separated substances are not the subject of science in anything like the same sense for Thomas (*Ontologie oder Metaphysik*, pp. 217–18).

John Duns Scotus

Like Aquinas, John Duns Scotus carefully distinguishes theology from metaphysics, a discussion we cannot consider here. And, like Aquinas, Scotus emphasizes that knowledge of God in metaphysics must be *a posteriori* (*Quaest. in Metaphys.* I.1 nn. 30, 136) and seeks a compromise that can acceptably include the study of God in metaphysics. Unfortunately, his most influential discussion of the subject of metaphysics, the first of his *Questions on the Metaphysics*,[32] is also terribly difficult. Not only is it apparently incompatible with his other discussions of the topic, but even great Scotists find it aporetic and so deeply perplexing as to be beyond human capacity.[33] We consider it here because it strongly influenced Ockham and later authors and also usefully situates Scotus's position relative to Islamic approaches.

In *Metaphysics* I.1 Scotus sets out to show that neither Avicenna nor Averroes satisfactorily solved the problem. In so doing, he undermines his own commitment elsewhere to the claim that entity is the subject of metaphysics.[34] He even states non-committally his famous claim that there is a common concept of entity, univocally predicated of God and creatures.[35] More straightforwardly, Scotus shows that nothing can be predicated of entity in all its generality, since attributes predicated of a subject in scientific propositions must be distinct from their subject.[36] And because not even unity and actuality can be predicated of entity in all its generality, no science can consist of propositions about entity (*Quaest. in Metaphys.* I.1 nn. 86–91).

Avicenna cannot be right about the subject of science, since he agrees that the aim of metaphysics is to learn about God. However, if we could learn about God by studying entity, then information about God would have to be virtually contained in the concept of entity, which is impossible since cognition of the more perfect cannot be contained in cognition of the less perfect. Also, our highest happiness would have to consist in knowing entity as entity, which is false, since it is the most imperfect being (ibid., n. 123).

---

[32] Ibid., p. 295.

[33] See Hugo Cavellus, scholium 9 to *Quaest. Metaphys.* I.1 (ed. Wadding IV: 521). See also Ludger Honnefelder, *Ens inquantum ens: der Begriff des Seienden als solchen als Gegenstand der Metaphysik nach der Lehre des Johannes Duns Scotus* (Münster: Aschendorff, 1979) p. 10.

[34] Cf. Peter King, "Scotus on Metaphysics," in T. Williams (ed.) *The Cambridge Companion to Duns Scotus* (Cambridge: Cambridge University Press, 2003) pp. 17–18. Compare Scotus, *Quaest. in Metaph.* 1.91 (*Opera philosophica* III: 46).

[35] Scotus, *Quaest. in Metaphys.* I.1 nn. 85, 153.

[36] See Aristotle, *Metaphys.* VII.6, 1031b21–7. Or, as Scotus would put it, they must not be contained in the subject's essence.

Scotus's initial positive account is a defense of the claim that substance is the subject of metaphysics. Scotus argues against entity as its subject,[37] since there is no unity more general than the ten categories, no concept common to the categories, and no property common to them. Thus the only subject that meets the conditions for a science – namely, to have proper passions demonstrable of it *a priori* – is substance. And although substance is its principal subject, metaphysics also considers everything else in so far as such things are attributes of substance. Like Rufus,[38] Scotus here holds that substance is the primary subject of a *propter quid* science and glosses the claim that *ens qua ens* is the subject by holding that the other categories are included as attributes of substance (ibid., nn. 91–6).

After reaching this conclusion, however, in a subsequent addition that may have been written many years later,[39] Scotus states yet another position. Objecting to the claim that substance is the subject of metaphysics, Scotus asks what metaphysical attribute is predicated of substance, and he considers only one option: prime entity. After suggesting that this attribute cannot be accounted for either as a quantity or a relation predicated of substance, Scotus offers another alternative. That alternative gives up the search for a unified science of metaphysics. Perhaps the science of metaphysics is simply an aggregate of propositions, premises, and conclusions all related to a single primary subject. Given this weaker requirement for unity, God can be the subject of the science of metaphysics.

According to this later addition – which may be Scotus's last statement on the topic – the metaphysician considers all entities insofar as they are attributed not to substance but to the first entity, namely God (ibid., n. 134). Prime entity is the first, but not the only subject of metaphysics. The subjects of metaphysics include first entity and other entities as such and insofar as they are attributed to first entity in our search for knowledge of God (ibid., nn. 136–7).

Scotus also radically separates himself from earlier members of the tradition in other respects. He gives up the claim that metaphysics is an explanatory *propter quid* science, calling it instead a *quia* science. Finally, Scotus allows that a science can demonstrate its subject,[40] since it need presuppose only the concept of its

---

[37] Cf. *Ordinatio* I.3.1.3 n. 128 and King, "Scotus on Metaphysics," p. 17. See also Scotus, *Quodlibet* III.1 (ed. Alluntis n. 9), where Scotus describes *ens* in its most general sense, as whatever does not involve contradiction, as the first object of the intellect.

[38] Not only does Scotus agree with Rufus about the subject of metaphysics, but he seems sympathetic to the claim that perhaps only created entity is meant by the famous phrase '*ens qua ens*'; see *Quaest. in Metaphys.* I.1, nn. 84, 134.

[39] For a discussion of the different dating of parts of the same question in this work, see Giorgio Pini, "Univocity in Scotus' *Quaestiones super Metaphysicam*: The Solution to a Riddle," *Medioevo* 30 (2005) 69–110.

[40] Cf. Aristotle, *Post. An.* I.10, 76a31–36.

subject, and it can demonstrate its subject's existence from its effects. Indeed, more than one science can demonstrate *a posteriori* the existence of the same thing, albeit from different effects. Specifically, both physics and metaphysics show the existence of God from his effects in the world, but they only accidentally consider the same object since their proofs rest on different descriptions of God. Physics considers God as a mover, whereas metaphysics considers God as entity, a description that more immediately pertains to his quiddity (ibid., nn. 111–14, 135, 163).

Scotus does not fully commit himself either to substance or to God as the subject of metaphysics (ibid., n. 104). Of Scotus's two answers to the questions of what the subject of metaphysics is and how it is unified, the first denies that there is a unified *propter quid* science of entity as such. By contrast, the second posits such a science as a part of a larger *quia* science of metaphysics, whose subject is first entity (ibid., nn. 140, 150). So the question arises: why not consider the study of first entity as a part of the more general science of entity as such (ibid., n. 137)? Also, if we admit that the metaphysician is chiefly concerned with the first entity, why not consider this the end but not the subject matter of metaphysics, as Thomas had done (ibid., n. 147)? Finally, if entity can be posited univocally of God and other entities, why not make entity the subject, since it includes God as well as other entities (ibid., n. 152)?

Scotus's replies to these questions revolve around an idea that played a minor role in the thought of Rufus and Aquinas: God as the purpose of metaphysics.[41] This thought prompts Scotus not only to claim that God is the subject of metaphysics, but also to use the phrase "subject of a science" in a very different sense than Scotus himself and other authors commonly use. According to Scotus in his other works, the subject of a science virtually contains the truths it demonstrates and serves as a starting point. By contrast, in the *Metaphysics*, Scotus says that God as subject serves not as the starting point but as the end pursued by metaphysics.[42] Knowledge of God is what metaphysicians principally intend to acquire; it is prior in our intention, not as a source of knowledge (ibid., n. 140). We study metaphysics for the sake of knowledge of God, not knowledge of entity (ibid., nn. 148, 153). Metaphysics aims at perfect knowledge of entity, which is knowledge of the first entity (ibid., nn. 117, 161).

Scotus's *Metaphysics* offers a choice between a strongly unified science of substance and a weakly unified science of God. The weakly unified aggregate

---

[41] Albert Zimmermann has called attention to most of the relevant texts in which Scotus argues that God is the subject of metaphysics, and at the same time Zimmermann reminds us that God is the subject in a very different sense than Scotus himself and other authors commonly use (*Ontologie oder Metaphysik*, pp. 310–11). See also Avicenna, *Liber de philosophia prima* I.3, ed. Van Riet, I: 26.

[42] Zimmermann, *Ontologie oder Metaphysik*, pp. 310–11.

science of metaphysics, however, includes a *propter quid* science of entity that is quite close to Scotus's better-known description of metaphysics as a science of entity *qua* entity. Hence we might expect later authors to prefer the latter.

William of Ockham

Far from seeking to preserve a science of entity as such, however, Ockham chooses to give up the notion of a unified Aristotelian science altogether. Not just the problematic general science of metaphysics, but even the special sciences, such as mathematics and physics, have only collective, aggregate unity. Moreover, Ockham denies that the subject of a science implicitly contains the truths demonstrated in that science.[43]

Ockham, like Aquinas, starts from the psychological definition of science as an intellectual disposition concerning a demonstrated truth. But for Ockham these are truths stated in individual propositions, a different science for the subject of every demonstrated conclusion. Restricting science strictly speaking to such habits, Ockham does not allow that there can be a habit that pertains to a variety of related conclusions. There can, however, be an ordered collection of habits, and it is in that sense that metaphysics is a unified science.[44] Unlike Scotus,[45] however, Ockham does not allow that particular habits can virtually incline us to a more general science. Sciences are not unified in the strong sense and, contrary to Aristotle (*Post. An.* I.7), it is not important to maintain a generic distinction between sciences. Indeed, the same proofs can equally well pertain to different sciences.[46]

It does not make sense to seek a single unified subject for a science, just as it does not make sense to try to find out who is the single world sovereign, since there is none. Sciences are no more unified in their subject than cities or armies.[47] Thus, for Ockham, the traditional Aristotelian sciences have many distinct parts, each of which has a different subject. However, he allows that these subjects constitute an ordered group, and he makes some of the traditional claims. In a manner reminiscent of Scotus, Ockham holds that God is the primary subject of metaphysics, if we are inquiring about the primacy of perfection, while in the order of predication and attribution, entity is the primary

---

[43] *In Phys.* prologue (*Opera phil.* IV: 9); *Sent.* prol. q. 9 (*Opera theol.* I: 262–3).

[44] *In Phys.* prologue (*Opera phil.* IV: 6–7); *Sent.* prol. q. 1 (*Opera theol.* I: 8–9), q. 9 (I: 255–7).

[45] Scotus, *Quaest. in Metaphys.* VI.1 nn. 39–40. See also Aquinas, *Summa theol.* 1a2ae 54.2 ad 2, 54.4 ad 3.

[46] Ockham, *In Phys.* prologue (*Opera phil.* IV: 9–10); *Sent.* prol. q. 1 (*Opera theol.* I: 13–15). Indeed, theology can be subalternated to metaphysics, just as metaphysics can be subalternated to theology.

[47] Ockham, *In Phys.* prologue (*Opera phil.* IV: 7, 10); *Sent.* prol. q. 1 (*Opera theol.* I: 13), q. 9 (I: 259).

subject of metaphysics. Thus Avicenna and Averroes may have disagreed about the subject of metaphysics, but they need not have done, since there is no single subject of the science as a whole; instead there are many subjects: one of which is God; another, entity.[48]

The medieval debate over the subject of metaphysics illustrates the pervasive influence of Arabic thought on the Latin West, and at the same time the innovativeness that Latin authors brought to these discussions. Even Ockham's approach to the unity of a science addresses the concerns of Avicenna and Averroes, though for him the problems posed by their disagreement were hardly pressing.

Ockham's approach may seem refreshingly modern, but his lack of concern for the generic unity of sciences seems unjustified. For he continues to operate with the paradigm of Aristotelian science, and this derives explanations for why things are as they are (and could not be otherwise) from truths about generic natures as determined by specific *differentiae*.

In this respect even the high prices Ockham's predecessors paid as they wrestled with the problem seem preferable. For Rufus the price for a unified science of metaphysics was to exclude the first cause from its subject matter, an approach Aristotle would surely not endorse. Aquinas's theory provides a neat solution to the problem of how to incorporate consideration of God into metaphysics. But if Rufus were to object that God is only an external cause of the substances metaphysics studies and hence not an intrinsic part of metaphysics, it is not clear how Thomas would reply, and neither is it clear how Thomas's description of metaphysical abstraction addresses the question whether entity can be considered a genus. Scotus's description of entity as a thing whose being does not include contradiction is an elegant solution to that problem. It comes at the cost, however, of providing a negative description of entity, lacking any nature. Equally elegant is Scotus's solution to the problem of integrating God into the science of metaphysics – namely, to admit that metaphysics as a whole is not science in the strict sense required for explanatory, *propter quid* science. But though all would agree that *a propter quid* science of a freely acting God is impossible, that is a heavy cost, a measure perhaps of the toughness of the problem Avicenna and Averroes set for their Western successors.[49]

---

[48] Ockham, *Sent.* prol. q. 9 (*Opera theol.* I: 256–8); *In Phys.* prologue (*Opera phil.* IV: 10).

[49] See Gerhard Endress, *Der arabische Aristoteles und sein Leser* (Münster: Aschendorff, 2004) pp. 13–14, 20–1.

45

ESSENCE AND EXISTENCE

JOHN F. WIPPEL

SOURCES FOR THE SCHOLASTIC DEBATE

At least two issues contributed to the extensive discussion of essence and existence by Latin thinkers in the thirteenth and early fourteenth centuries. First, there was a need to explain the metaphysical structure of immaterial entities other than God (angels, within the Christian tradition) in a way that would distinguish them from the absolute simplicity of God, especially for those who rejected the possibility of matter–form composition both for such entities and for human souls (see Chapters 21 and 46). Second, there was a need to account metaphysically for the distinction between God, the uncaused cause who necessarily exists, and all other beings, which depend on something else for their existence.

This famous scholastic dispute over the relationship between essence and existence has its roots in earlier Latin and Arabic discussions. Among Latin sources, Boethius was especially influential. He begins his *De hebdomadibus* by listing a series of axioms, some of which compare and contrast that-which-is (*id quod est*) and being (*esse*). Consider, for instance, Axiom II: "Being and that-which-is are diverse"; Axiom VII: "Every simple entity has its being and that-which-is as one"; and Axiom VIII: "In every composite entity its being and that-which-is are diverse." With some exceptions, modern interpreters of Boethius do not see in this contrast a real distinction between essence and existence (*esse*) as two distinct intrinsic principles of being. Rather, according to many of these interpreters, Boethius compares and distinguishes between a concrete entity (that-which-is) and a form in which it shares (*esse*). In simple beings they are identical, whereas in composite beings they are diverse.[1]

---

[1] For a variety of interpretations of Boethius's understanding of these axioms and of *esse* see Hermann Brosch, *Der Seinsbegriff bei Boethius mit besonderer Berücksichtigung der Beziehung von Sosein und Dasein* (Innsbruck: Felizian Rauch, 1931); M.-D. Roland-Gosselin, *Le "De ente et essentia" de s. Thomas d'Aquin* (Paris: Vrin, 1926) pp. 142–5; Cornelio Fabro, *La nozione metafisica di partecipazione secondo*

Equally influential on medieval discussions of this issue was Avicenna's *First Philosophy* or *Metaphysics*. He begins Book I, chapter 5 by observing: "We will say therefore that *thing* (*res*) and *being* (*ens*) and *the necessary* (*necesse*) are such that they are immediately impressed on the soul by a first impression, which is not derived from other things better known than themselves."[2] He notes the similarity between such primary notions at the level of concepts and first principles at the level of judgment. If every concept were to require another and prior concept, this would lead either to an infinite regress or to circularity.[3] Best suited to be conceived in themselves are those concepts that are common to all things, and he again mentions *thing* (*res*) and *being* (*ens*), but adds *one* (*unum*). He also writes: "I say therefore that the meaning of 'being' (*ens*) and the meaning of 'thing' (*res*) are conceived in the soul as two meanings (*intentiones*). 'Being,' however, and 'something' are different words with the same meaning."[4] Avicenna also notes that each thing has a nature (*certitudo*) by which it is what it is. He comments that we might, perhaps, refer to this as its "proper being" (*esse proprium*), but explains that this is different from the meaning that 'existence' (*esse*) has insofar as it is asserted of something or, according to the Latin translation, insofar as that term is synonymous with the term 'something' (*aliquid*).[5]

From these texts, it is clear that Avicenna defends a distinction between quiddity or essence, on the one hand, and existence taken as that which is

---

S. Tommaso d'Aquino, 3rd edn (Turin: Società Editrice Internazionale, 1963) pp. 102–3, 33–7; Pierre Hadot, "La distinction de l'être et de l'étant dans le 'De Hebdomadibus' de Boèce," in *Die Metaphysik im Mittelalter* (Berlin: De Gruyter, 1963) pp. 147–53; "Forma essendi: interprétation philologique et interprétation philosophique d'une formule de Boèce," *Les Études Classiques* 38 (1970) 143–56; Ralph McInerny, *Boethius and Aquinas* (Washington, DC: Catholic University of America Press, 1990) pp. 161–98 (survey of other opinions); John Marenbon, *Boethius* (Oxford: Oxford University Press, 2003) pp. 88–90; Alain Galonnier's commentary in *Boèce. Opuscula Sacra* (Louvain: Peeters, 2007) I: 336–45. McInerny, *Boethius and Aquinas*, maintains that Aquinas's understanding of *esse* and its distinction from "that which is" is present in Boethius, whereas Schulz and Synan's introduction to Aquinas's *On the Hebdomads* has recently argued in support of the majority view that it is not (pp. xxxvii–liv). For Aquinas see *De ente et essentia* 4 (ed. Leonine, XLIII: 377 [lines 165–6]); *In De hebdomadibus* 2 (ed. Leonine, L: 272–3 [lines 201–49]).

[2] Ed. Van Riet, I: 31–2. For a translation from the Arabic see *Metaphysics* I.5, tr. Marmura, p. 22: "We say: The ideas of 'the existent,' 'the thing,' and the 'necessary' are impressed in the soul in a primary way. This impression does not require better known things to bring it about."

[3] Ed. Van Riet, I: 32–3; tr. Marmura, pp. 22–3.

[4] Ed. Van Riet, I: 33; 34; tr. Marmura, p. 23: "As for example, 'the existent,' 'the one thing,' and others"; p. 24: "The meaning of 'existence' and the meaning of 'thing' are conceived in the soul and are two meanings, whereas 'the existent,' 'the established,' and 'the realized' are synonyms." For a different translation of the first passage (following the Latin) see Thérèse-Anne Druart, " 'Shay' or 'Res' as Concomitant of 'Being' in Avicenna," *Documenti e studi sulla tradizione filosofica medievale* 12 (2001) pp. 125–6.

[5] Ed. Van Riet, I: 34; tr. Marmura, p. 24.

affirmed of something, on the other.[6] His ensuing discussion builds on this, distinguishing between the one being that is a necessary existent in itself (God), and all others which, while being possible existents in themselves, may be rendered necessary by something else. The necessary existent in itself has no cause (I.6) and can only be one (I.7). Avicenna reaffirms in VIII.4 that it is one (unique), and he states that its quiddity is identical with its individual existence.[7]

Avicenna distinguishes between a quiddity "in which the one and the existent occur accidentally and the one and the existent inasmuch as it is one and existent."[8] By restricting the latter to the necessary existent alone, Avicenna defends its absolute simplicity. There is no quiddity for it other than "its being the Necessary Existent," and Avicenna identifies this with its "thatness," or its individual existence. Indeed, he goes on to write that the First has no quiddity.[9]

Among later Latin authors, the essence–existence distinction begins to assume a prominent place in the early thirteenth century with William of Auvergne. In his *De Trinitate* 1 (ed. Switalski, pp. 16–17), he writes that 'being' (*ens*) and 'existence' (*esse*) have various meanings (*intentiones*). Thus, we speak in one sense of (a) being (*ens*) whose essence is its existence (*esse*), and whose essence we predicate when we say it "is," so that it and its existence are one thing (*res*) in every respect. In another sense, we speak of being (*ens*) by participation insofar as it has something – its *esse* – that in no way forms one thing with its essence nor is a part of that being's essence. Its *esse* is completely outside the intelligible content (*ratio*) of the substance or essence of that being. In support he cites Axiom VII from Boethius's *De hebdomadibus*, quoted above.

In chapter 2, William notes that the word *esse* has two meanings: (1) the substance, or quiddity, or essence of a thing, and (2) what is expressed by the verb 'is' when this is affirmed of something. When *esse* is taken in this second way, it is not included in the intelligible content (*ratio*) of any thing we may apprehend, such as a human being or a donkey, with one sole

---

[6] See Druart, " 'Shay'," p. 135; Robert Wisnovsky, "Avicenna and the Avicennian Tradition," in P. Adamson and R. Taylor (eds.) *The Cambridge Companion to Arabic Philosophy* (Cambridge: Cambridge University Press, 2005) pp. 108–9. Robert Wisnovsky, *Avicenna's Metaphysics in Context* (Ithaca, NY: Cornell University Press, 2003) chs. 7–9, shows that Avicenna's distinction between essence and existence owes much to earlier discussions within Islamic *kalām* on the relationship between 'thing' and 'existent,' although for Avicenna these two relationships are not identical. Also see Druart, " 'Shay'," pp. 127–8 on the *kalām* background for 'thing.'

[7] Following the translation of Marmura, p. 274: "The First has no quiddity other than His individual existence" (ed. Van Riet, II: 398–9). Also see ibid., tr. Marmura, p. 276; ed. Van Riet, II: 401.

[8] *Metaphysics* VIII.4, tr. Marmura, p. 274; ed. Van Riet, p. 399.

[9] Ibid., tr. Marmura, p. 276; ed. Van Riet, pp. 401–2. On this see Wisnovsky, "Avicenna and the Avicennian Tradition," pp. 126–7.

exception – namely, that one being of which it is said essentially because it and its *esse* are entirely the same. The implication is that in all other entities, essence or quiddity is not one and the same as *esse*. Whether he means by this that they are really distinct or only conceptually distinct, however, is disputed by modern scholars.[10] Certain texts, such as *De Trinitate* 7, strongly suggest that William has in mind a real distinction (ed. Switalski, pp. 43–4).[11] In *De universo* Ia I ch. 3, however, William refers to the existence of every caused being as separable from such a being "at least by the intellect" – thereby suggesting hesitation about whether they are also really distinct.[12]

Beginning especially with Thomas Aquinas and continuing onward into the early fourteenth century, various thinkers attempted to specify more precisely the nature of the relationship between essence and existence in created beings. Three major lines of interpretation may be discerned if one allows for variation between individual representatives of each: essence and existence are (1) really distinct, (2) really identical but conceptually distinct, or (3) distinct in some intermediate way.

REAL DISTINCTION BETWEEN ESSENCE AND EXISTENCE

It is generally agreed today that in his youthful *De ente et essentia* (1252–6) and continuing throughout his career, Thomas Aquinas defended a real distinction and composition of essence and existence (*esse*) in all finite beings – that is, a distinction that obtains in reality apart from the mind's consideration.[13] In *De ente* ch. 4 he introduces this theory after rejecting matter–form composition in created separate substances (angels). To show that they are, nevertheless, composed of actuality and potentiality, he offers a three-stage argument.

The first stage reasons from the fact that we can think of something such as a human being or a phoenix without knowing whether or not it exists, and it quickly concludes that there is a distinction between essence and existence

---

[10] See Roland-Gosselin, *Le "De ente"*, p. 163; Kevin Caster, "William of Auvergne and St. Thomas Aquinas on the Real Distinction between Being and Essence," in J. Hackett *et al.* (eds.) *Being and Thought in Aquinas* (Binghamton, NY: Global Academic Publications, 2004) 75–108 (William defends a real distinction). Étienne Gilson denies this in "La notion d'existence chez Guillaume d'Auvergne," *Archives d'histoire doctrinale et littéraire du moyen âge* 15 (1946) 55–91, esp. pp. 80–4.

[11] Ed. Switalski, pp. 43–4. Caster, "William of Auvergne" p. 106 nn. 75, 76, cites some other texts in this vein from William's *De universo* IIa IIae ch. 8 (ed. 1674, I: 852aG–H).

[12] Ed. 1674, I: 594b. See Maurer's introduction to Thomas Aquinas, *On Being and Essence* (Toronto: Pontifical Institute of Mediaeval Studies, 1968) pp. 23–4; Roland-Gosselin, *Le 'De ente'*, p. 163 n. 3.

[13] For a few scholars who have denied this, see the references in John F. Wippel, *The Metaphysical Thought of Thomas Aquinas: From Finite Being to Uncreated Being* (Washington, DC: Catholic University of America Press, 2000) p. 136 n. 11.

(*esse* = act of existing) within any such being. Possibly anticipating the objection that this establishes only a conceptual distinction between the two, in a second stage Aquinas uses a process of elimination to show that if, perhaps, there is a being in which essence and act of existing are identical, this being must be unique. In every other entity, therefore, essence and act of existing cannot be identical but must be distinct. Moving from this to the third stage, Aquinas reasons that every being in which essence and act of existing are distinct must receive its existence from something else. From this, he reasons to the actual existence of an uncaused cause of existence in which essence and act of existing are identical – namely, God. Since the act of existing (*esse*) of every other being is received by its essence, in all such beings this *esse* is related to essence as act to potency, resulting in an act–potency composition even within created spiritual beings.[14] This sets the stage for his subsequent insistence in other writings that the act of existing not only accounts for the fact that created beings exist, but is also an intrinsic principle of perfection within every such being; it is the "actuality of all acts and the perfection of all perfections," not a "thing" or entity.[15]

In later writings Thomas offers several kinds of argumentation to support the real distinction and composition of essence and existence in creatures. He favors in particular those that, like stage two in the *De ente*, show that there can be at most one being in which essence and existence are identical, and that, by contrast, they must be distinct in all others.[16] He connects his views on essence and existence with the metaphysics of participation he gradually develops, and holds that every finite being may be viewed as participating in (1) the act of existing (*esse*) taken universally (*esse commune*), (2) self-subsisting *esse* (God), as in its efficient cause, and (3) its own act of existing.[17]

During Aquinas's second teaching period at Paris (1268–72), Giles of Rome, a young bachelor in theology there, was developing his own views on the essence–existence relationship. Foreshadowings of Giles's final position appear already in his Commentary on I *Sentences* (*ca.* 1271–3) and in his slightly later *Theoremata de corpore Christi* (*ca.* 1274); he works out his view in detail and defends it with many arguments in subsequent writings such as his *Theoremata*

---

[14] Ed. Leonine, XLIII: 376–7. See Wippel, *Metaphysical Thought of Thomas Aquinas*, p. 136 n. 11 for references to other readings of this text; see ibid., p. 137 n. 14 for his dispute with Owens. Also see R. E. Houser, "The Real Distinction and the Principles of Metaphysics: Avicenna and Aquinas," in R. E. Houser (ed.) *Laudemus viros gloriosos. Essays in Honor of Armand Maurer, CSB* (Notre Dame, IN: University of Notre Dame Press, 2007) 74–108.

[15] See *Quaest. de potentia* 7.2 ad 9; *Summa theol.* 1a 3.4; Wippel, *Metaphysical Thought of Thomas Aquinas*, pp. 32–4, 173–5; Cornelio Fabro, *Participation et causalité selon S. Thomas d'Aquin* (Louvain: Publications universitaires,1961) p. 195.

[16] For these see Wippel, *Metaphysical Thought of Thomas Aquinas*, pp. 150–7.

[17] See ibid., pp. 110–24.

de esse et essentia (1278–85) and *Quaestiones disputatae de esse et essentia* (1285–7).[18] According to Giles, just as generation makes us understand that matter is different from form, so creation makes us realize that essence is different from existence. Hence, just as form is a certain actuality and perfection of matter and really differs from it, so *esse* is a certain actuality and perfection of essence and really differs from it.[19] Moreover, it is because essence receives and limits a really distinct existence that existence in created beings is participated and limited. Finally, such a distinction is needed to account for the fact that one can be aware of the essence of a creature even when one knows that it does not exist.[20]

At times, however, Giles refers to essence and existence as "things" (*res*) and to the distinction between them as between "thing" and "thing."[21] This language has been denounced by many as an inaccurate presentation of Aquinas's theory, and so it would be if Giles had intended his theory simply to be a repetition of Aquinas's position. Even when viewed as a theory Giles was developing in his own right, however, this particular terminology is easily subject to misinterpretation and criticism. Thus, as Henry of Ghent and Godfrey of Fontaines would point out, if one appeals to an essence "thing" and an existence "thing" to account for the metaphysical structure and created character of a finite being, the same logic should lead one to posit "sub-things," inasmuch as

---

[18] On the dates for *Sent.* Bk. I and *Theoremata de corpore Christi* see the discussion by Robert Wielockx in *Giles of Rome, Apologia* (Florence: Olschki, 1985) pp. 236–40; Silvia Donati, "Studi per una cronologia delle opera di Egidio Romano. I: Le opera prima del 1285 – I commenti aristotelici," *Documenti e studi sulla tradizione filosofica medievale* 1 (1990) pp. 21–5, 71. Pasquale Porro, however, in "An Historiographical Image of Henry of Ghent," in W. Vanhamel (ed.) *Henry of Ghent. Proceedings of the International Colloquium on the Occasion of the 700th Anniversary of his Death (1293)* (Leuven: Leuven University Press, 1996) p. 391, places this *Theoremata* in 1271. In *Sent.* I.8.2.1.2 (ed. 1521, f. 52v), Giles denies that the divine existence (*esse*) differs from the divine quiddity or enters into composition with it, implying that the opposite is true of a creature's existence. See also *Sent.* I.8.2.2.1 (f. 54ra), where in the *In contrarium* he introduces the argument based on the fact that every created existence (*esse*) is limited, and in his Response argues that every creature is composed of *quod est* and *esse*. See as well *Theoremata de corpore Christi* (ed. 1481, f. 19rb–vb), where he implies that separability of actual existence from essence indicates a real distinction, and notes that only the divine essence is its *esse* and that in other beings *esse* is something added to the nature of the creature and received in it. On this see Adriaan Pattin, "Gilles de Rome, O.E.S.A. (*ca.* 1243–1316) et la distinction réelle de l'essence et de l'existence," *Revue de l'Université d'Ottawa* 23 (1953) pp. 85*–8*; Wippel, "The Relationship Between Essence and Existence in Late Thirteenth-Century Thought: Giles of Rome, Henry of Ghent, Godfrey of Fontaines, and James of Viterbo," in P. Morewedge (ed.) *Philosophies of Existence Ancient and Medieval* (New York: Fordham University Press, 1982) pp. 134–6.

[19] See *Theoremata de esse* 5 (ed. Hocedez, pp. 19–20); *Quaest. de esse* 9 (ed. 1503, ff. 20vb–21ra).

[20] *Quaest. de esse* 11 (ed. 1503, ff. 24vb–25ra).

[21] See *Theoremata de esse* 16 (ed. Hocedez, p. 101), 19 (pp. 127, 134): "Just as matter and quantity are two things (*duae res*), so essence and *esse* are two really different things"; *Quaest. de esse* 9 (ed. 1503, f. 20vb); 11 (f. 24vb); 12 (f. 28ra): "*esse* itself is a certain absolute thing (*res*) superadded to essence."

existence, conceived of as a "thing," would require its own "sub-essence-thing"
and "sub-existence-thing," and so on *ad infinitum*. To avoid this, one should
admit that the original essence exists without the addition of a distinct "thing"
known as *esse*.[22] It should be noted, however, that earlier in his *Theoremata de
corpore Christi* Giles, while still developing his position, had explicitly denied that
the existence of a given entity is itself an essence, making it unlikely that he then
viewed it as a thing (ff. 19vb–20ra). Unfortunately, his later talk of a distinction
between "things" soon came to be accepted by critics as a standard way of
referring to all theories of real distinction between essence and existence.[23]

IDENTITY BETWEEN ESSENCE AND EXISTENCE

At the opposite end of the spectrum lie positions that completely reject any
kind of real distinction and composition of essence and existence in finite
beings, including created separate substances. In the early to mid-1270s the
Paris master of arts, Siger of Brabant, defends such a view in his *Quaestiones
in Metaphysicam*, Introduction, q. 7. There he seeks to ascertain whether the
being (*ens*) or existence (*esse*) of caused beings belongs to their essence or is
something added to it.[24] He introduces his own solution by listing different
positions. Some (Avicenna and Albert the Great) hold that because the terms
'thing' (*res*) and 'being' (*ens*) do not have the same meaning (*intentio*), *esse* must
be something added to essence. In rejecting this position, Siger considers the
argument in its favor that if existence (*esse*) pertains to the essence of something,
then that thing exists of itself and is uncaused. He counters that the term 'of'
(*ex*) is equivocal when applied to causation. To say that a thing exists *of itself* can
denote the order of formal causality (which is compatible with a thing's being
caused efficiently) or of efficient causality (which is not).[25]

---

[22] See Henry of Ghent, *Quodlibet* I.9 (*Opera* V: 51) and Godfrey of Fontaines, *Quodlibet* III.1, arg.
3 (*Philosophes Belges* II: 164 [long vers.], II: 303 [short vers]). Godfrey refers to Averroes's critique
of Avicenna for having regarded *ens* and *unum* as dispositions added to the essence of a thing (for
Averroes see *In Metaph* IV.3 [ed. 1562, VIII: 67ra]).

[23] For emphasis on the difference between Giles's theory and that of Thomas see Edgar Hocedez's
introduction to Giles of Rome, *Theoremata de esse*, pp. 62–7, 116–17; Jean Paulus, *Henri de Gand.
Essai sur les tendances de sa métaphysique* (Paris: Vrin, 1938) pp. 283–4; Peter Nash, "Giles of Rome
on Boethius' 'Diversum est esse et id quod est'," *Mediaeval Studies* 20 (1950) pp. 57–8, 90–1;
"Accidentality of *Esse* According to Giles of Rome," *Gregorianum* 38 (1957) 103–15. For more
positive evaluations of Giles's theory see Gregorio Suárez, "El pensamiento de Egidio Romano
en torno a la distinción de esencia y existencia," *La Ciencia Tomista* 75 (1948) 66–99, 230–72, esp.
pp. 251–4, 262–3, 266–8, 270–1; Pattin, "Gilles," pp. 80*–116*.

[24] Munich ms. (ed. Dunphy, p. 41); Cambridge ms. (ed. Maurer, p. 30).

[25] The Munich ms. (pp. 43–4) assigns this to Avicenna, whereas according to the Cambridge ms.
(p. 32) both Avicenna and Albert were deceived by it.

Siger next assigns an intermediate position to some (Thomas Aquinas) who hold that existence (*esse*) is something added to the essence of a thing – something that does not pertain to that thing's essence, is not an accident, and is, as it were, constituted by (*per*) the essence or the principles of the essence. While Siger comments that this position is true, he acknowledges that he does not understand the way it is presented. He counters that to hold that the *esse* of a thing is not identical with (1) the thing itself, nor (2) a part of its essence, such as matter or form, nor (3) an accident, is to posit some fourth nature among beings. Moreover, to say that the *esse* of a thing is constituted by the principles of its essence is really just to say that it is the thing itself.[26]

Siger himself holds that the *esse* of a caused thing does belong to its essence. It is not something added to the essence in such a way that 'thing' and 'being' would signify different "intentions"; rather, they signify one intention.[27] In support, he notes that some names signify the same essence, but according to different modes of signifying – one through the mode of act and the other through the mode of habitual condition (*habitus*). It is in this way that 'being' (*ens*) and 'thing' (*res*) signify the same essence: 'being' signifies *per modum actus*, and 'thing' signifies *per modum habitus* or *per modum potentiae*. Accordingly, this is how *esse* (existence) stands in relation to thing or essence.[28] Siger follows Averroes in criticizing Avicenna for failing to distinguish between names that signify different intentions or essences and names that signify the same essence in different modes.[29]

Siger rejects an opening argument (which he attributes to Thomas) that bases itself on the claim that everything other than the First Being must recede from its simplicity by being composed and that separate intelligences, not being composed of matter and form, must be composed of essence and existence. In a first rebuttal (which Siger claims is not definitive), he counters that such entities recede from the First Being (pure act) simply because they approach the nature of potentiality to a greater or lesser degree. His second rebuttal is based on the distinction in such entities between their substance and the intelligible

---

[26] Munich ms. (pp. 44–5); Cambridge ms. (pp. 32–3). Siger is paraphrasing and reacting to Aquinas, *In Metaph.* IV.2 (ed. Cathala and Spiazzi, n. 558). See Wippel, "Thomas Aquinas and Siger of Brabant on Being and the Science of Being as Being," *Modern Schoolman* 82 (2005) pp. 155–6; Ruedi Imbach, "Averroistische Stellungnahmen zur Diskussion über das Verhältnis von *Esse* und *Essentia*: von Siger von Brabant zu Thaddeus von Parma," in A. Maierù and A. Paravicini Bagliani (eds.) *Studi sul xiv secolo in memoria di Anneliese Maier* (Rome: Edizione di Storia e Letteratura, 1981) pp. 309–16.

[27] Munich ms., p. 45; Cambridge ms., p. 33.   [28] Munich ms., p. 45; Cambridge ms., pp. 33–4.

[29] Munich ms. (which speaks of different "intentions"), pp. 45–6; Cambridge ms. (different "essences"), p. 34.

species by means of which they understand.[30] Surprisingly, however, in his final *Quaestiones in Librum de causis*, he uses language in certain passages concerning intelligences that reflects Aquinas's texts and that seems to imply that Siger ended by adopting a view similar to Thomas's theory of the real distinction and composition of essence and *esse*.[31]

Godfrey of Fontaines, a student in arts at Paris during Siger's period as a master in that faculty and subsequently himself master in theology, was familiar with many of Siger's views. This is evident from writings contained in various manuscripts in Godfrey's personal library, including an abbreviated copy of Siger's *Quaestiones in Metaphysicam*.[32] In his *Quodlibet* II, q. 2 (Easter 1286), Godfrey comments that one might hold that existence is the act of essence and therefore a thing (*res*) that is really distinct from it (as Giles of Rome believed), or that *esse* is really identical with essence and differs from it only logically (which will prove to be Godfrey's view) or intentionally (Henry of Ghent's position; see below). Here he comments only that it is more probable that existence (*esse existentiae*) is not a distinct thing from essence (*Phil. Belges* II: 60), thereby setting the stage for his subsequent definitive rejection both of a real distinction and of an intentional distinction between them.

In *Quodlibet* III, q. 1 (Christmas 1286), Godfrey presents at length and criticizes extensively Giles's theory of a real distinction between existence and essence as well as, in lesser detail, Henry's view that they are intentionally distinct.[33] Among his arguments against a real distinction is one that Godfrey connects with Aristotle's *Metaphysics* IV.2 (1003b26–35) and with Averroes's commentary on the same, to the effect that being involves less addition than

---

[30] Munich ms., pp. 42 (arg. 7), 47–8 (ad 7); Cambridge ms., pp. 31 (arg. 7), 35–6 (ad 7).

[31] *Quaest. in Librum de causis* 22 (ed. Marlasca, p. 93 [lines 60–8]; 53 (p. 184 [33–9]). On this see Marlasca's introduction, p. 21 n. 20; Fernand Van Steenberghen, *Maître Siger de Brabant* (Louvain: Publications universitaires, 1977) pp. 291–2; François-Xavier Putallaz and Ruedi Imbach, *Profession, philosophe: Siger de Brabant* (Paris: Cerf, 1997) pp. 153, 163; Wippel, "Thomas Aquinas and Siger," pp. 162–3; Catherine König-Pralong, *Avènement de l'aristotélisme en terre chrétienne* (Paris: Vrin, 2005) pp. 49–52; also pp. 37–48 (background).

[32] See Godfrey's student notebook (Paris, Bibliothèque Nationale lat. 16297). On this and other works collected and/or copied by Godfrey see J. J. Duin, "La bibliothèque philosophique de Godefroid de Fontaines," *Estudios Lulianos* 3 (1959) 21–36, 137–60; John F. Wippel, "Godfrey of Fontaines at the University of Paris in the Last Quarter of the Thirteenth Century," in J. A. Aertsen *et al.* (eds.) *Nach der Verurteilung von 1277. Philosophie und Theologie an der Universität von Paris im letzten Viertel des 13. Jahrhunderts* (Berlin: De Gruyter, 2001) 359–89. For further information on Godfrey's student notebook, see Andrea Aiello and Robert Wielockx, *Goffredo di Fontaines, aspirante baccelliere Sententiario: le autografe "Notule de scientia theologie" e la cronologia del ms. Paris BNF Lat. 16297* (Turnhout: Brepols, 2008).

[33] His presentation of certain arguments in support of a real distinction confirms his knowledge of Giles's position; see John F. Wippel, *The Metaphysical Thought of Godfrey of Fontaines: A Study in Late Thirteenth-Century Philosophy* (Washington, DC: Catholic University of America Press, 1981) pp. 47–53.

does unity to that of which it is affirmed. But since unity adds nothing real to essence, neither does being (*ens*) and, therefore, neither does *esse*. Moreover, unless one grants that each thing is a being (*ens*) by reason of itself and not by some superadded *esse*, one would have to account for the being of this super-added factor in the same way to infinity.[34] In defending the real identity of essence and existence, Godfrey argues that a concrete noun, an abstract noun, and a verb do not signify really distinct things, but differ merely in their mode of signifying. If this is true of *currens* (a runner), *cursus* (race), and *currere* (to run), so is it true of *ens* (being), *essentia* (essence), and *esse* (to exist).[35]

Godfrey rejects the argument that without a real distinction of essence and existence, the existence (*esse*) of created entities would not be participated and they would be as simple as God. In *Quodlibet* III, q. 1 he counters that the essence of a created being is participated and more composite than the divine essence not by including diverse things (*res*), but by reason of one and the same thing that is both potential in relation to more perfect things and actual in itself.[36] In *Quodlibet* VII, q. 7, he explains that even if angels do not fall into a natural genus, they do fall into a logical genus because any such being may be regarded as potential insofar as it is less perfect than higher beings and as actual insofar as it is more perfect than lower beings (III: 355, 357–9). In support he cites Proposition 2 from Proclus's *Elements of Theology*: "That which participates in the One is both one and not one." Godfrey maintains that this kind of act–potency composition is not purely imaginary or fictitious, even though it does not involve really distinct things. In developing this solution he was likely influenced by the one anticipated by Siger of Brabant (at note 30 above), and certainly by an anonymous set of questions contained in a manuscript in his personal library.[37]

INTERMEDIATE DISTINCTION BETWEEN ESSENCE AND EXISTENCE

In his *Quodlibet* I, q. 9 of 1276, Henry of Ghent addresses the question of whether the essence of a creature is its own existence (*esse*). He presents a

[34] *Phil. Belges* II: 164–5, 303–4 (short vers.). For Averroes see *In Metaph.* IV.3, ff. 67ra–va.

[35] *Phil. Belges* II: 164–5, 303–4 (short vers.). For similar reasoning see his late *Quodlibet* XIII. 3 (*Phil. Belges* V: 207–8), dating *ca.* 1297–8.

[36] *Phil. Belges* II. 306 (short vers.). Also see *Quodlibet* III.3 (*Phil. Belges* II: 186 [long vers.], II: 309 [short vers.]).

[37] Paris, Bibliothèque Nationale lat. 16096. On this see John F. Wippel, "Possible Sources for Godfrey of Fontaines' Views on the Act-Potency Composition of Simple Creatures," *Mediaeval Studies* 44 (1984) 222–44; Robert Wielockx, "Le ms. Paris Nat. lat. 16096 et la condemnation du 7 mars 1277," *Recherches de théologie ancienne et médiévale* 48 (1981) 227–37.

series of opening arguments in support of a real distinction between them, based apparently on his knowledge of the position already developed by Giles of Rome in the earlier 1270s, and he submits this position to severe criticism, drawing on certain arguments already advanced by Siger of Brabant.[38] Henry himself refuses to say that any creature is pure and subsisting *esse;* at the same time, he does not want to deny completely that a creature is its *esse,* since the creature is not really distinct from it.

Drawing upon Avicenna's *Metaphysics* V, Henry distinguishes between a certain *esse* that a thing has essentially of itself ("essential being" [*esse essentiae*]), and an existential *esse* that it receives from something else (its "being of actual existence" [*esse actualis existentiae*]). A creature has the first kind of *esse* essentially, but nonetheless by participation insofar as it has a formal exemplar idea in God's intellect. By reason of this *esse* it falls under one of the ten Aristotelian categories of being and can be conceptualized before it actually exists. As for the second kind of *esse* (actual existence), a creature possesses this not through its essence but only from God as an effect of the divine will, which produces it in accord with its exemplar in the divine mind. This kind of *esse* has the mode of an accident insofar as it is added to essence, but it is not an accidental thing (*res accidentalis*). Rather it is through it that a thing exists (*Opera* V: 53–4).

The first kind of *esse* (*esse essentiae*) differs from the essence of a creature only conceptually, and so the essence can be said to be its *esse* taken in this sense.[39] The second, existential *esse* (*esse actualis existentiae*), although not really distinct from the essence of a creature, differs from it not merely conceptually but also according to intention (a new and intermediate kind of distinction that Henry has introduced). Accordingly, a creaturely essence cannot be said to be identical with its *esse* taken in this sense – that is, with its existential *esse*. Only God is identical with his *esse* understood this way (*Opera* V: 54–5).

In *Quodlibet* X, q. 7 (Christmas 1286), Henry replies to a lengthy discussion and critique of his position in Giles of Rome's *Quaestiones disputatae,* qq. 9, 11

---

[38] On Henry's knowledge of Siger's argumentation see Imbach, "Averroistische Stelllungnahmen," pp. 316–19; König-Pralong, *Avènement,* pp. 64, 67. Henry's references to Giles's position are so pointed that some suggest Giles may have participated actively in Henry's *Quodlibet* I. See Hocedez's introduction to Giles of Rome, *Theoremata de esse,* p. 39; Porro, "Historiographical Image," p. 391.

[39] Some years later, however, Henry would change his position concerning this and propose an intentional distinction even between essence and its *esse essentiae.* See his *Summa quaest. ord.* 21.4, in the reworked version in José Gómez Caffarena, *Ser participado y ser subsistente en la metafísica de Enrique de Gante* (Rome: Pontificia Universitas Gregoriana, 1958) pp. 263–6 (text) and 103–4 (discussion). Also see Paulus, *Henri de Gand,* pp. 311–14; Walter Hoeres, "Wesen und Dasein bei Heinrich von Gent und Duns Scot," *Franziskanische Studien* 47 (1965) pp. 146 n. 77, 156 n. 14; Pasquale Porro, "Possibilità e *Esse essentiae* in Enrico di Gand," in Vanhamel, *Henry of Ghent: Proceedings of the International Colloquium on the Occasion of the 700th Anniversary of his Death,* pp. 235–6; Wielockx, "Henry of Ghent," 298–9.

(1285–6).[40] Here, Henry reaffirms the position he had defended in his *Quodlibet* I. Against Giles, he denies that actual existence adds anything absolute to essence that would be added to it as form is added to matter; it simply adds a relationship to God as its (efficient) creating and conserving principle, and therefore should be viewed not as a distinct thing added to essence, but as another "intention" (*Opera* XIV: 152–61). Therefore actual existence (*esse existentiae*) does not differ really from essence, nor merely according to reason, but in an intermediary fashion, intentionally, as do rational and animal, which, he explains at some length, differ more than merely conceptually, but less than really (*Opera* XIV: 164–6). In his *Quodlibet* XI, q. 3, Henry explains that from his denial that actual existence (*esse existentiae*) adds anything real to essence it does not follow that a creature's essence is identical with its actual *esse*; for actual existence adds a relation involving another "intention," which is added to a creature's essence as something accidental. It is added not as a real accident, however, but as an intentional accident.[41]

Succeeding Giles of Rome in the Augustinian chair of theology at Paris in 1292 or 1293,[42] James of Viterbo nicely summarizes, in his *Quodlibet* I q. 4, the three major positions on the essence–*esse* relationship as represented above by Giles, Henry, and Godfrey. While not in full agreement with any of them, James diplomatically tries to find some good in each as he presents his own position as probable (ed. Ypma, pp. 46–7, 54–6). Just as to give light (*lucere*) is to light (*lux*), he claims, so is *esse* (taken as *to exist*) to essence – that is, as the concrete is to the abstract. While the concrete term '*esse*' signifies the same thing as the abstract term '*essence*' in its primary meaning, in creatures '*esse*' includes in its secondary meaning something more than essence: namely, other features (accidents) that must be joined with essence when it exists actually. Therefore, in its secondary meaning '*esse*' signifies something in addition to essence that really differs from it. And since being (*ens*) is expressed as a concrete subject (*suppositum*), James equates the distinction between *esse* and essence with that between a *suppositum* and essence.[43] Therefore, when one takes *esse* in its primary meaning, it cannot

---

[40] On the controversy between Henry and Giles see Paulus, "Les disputes"; Köning-Pralong, *Avènement*, pp. 67–99.

[41] Ed. 1518, II: 441rv, ad 5. Here Henry is responding to six truths that Giles had maintained (*Quaest. de esse* 11) cannot be defended without acceptance of the real distinction.

[42] Eelcko Ypma, "Recherches sur la carrière scolaire et la bibliothèque de Jacques de Viterbe +1308," *Augustiniana* 24 (1974) 247–82; "Recherches sur la productivité littéraire de Jacques de Viterbe jusqu'à 1300," *Augustiniana* 25 (1975) 223–82. On James's date of promotion, see John F. Wippel, "The Dating of James of Viterbo's Quodlibet I and Godfrey of Fontaines' Quodlibet VIII," *Augustiniana* 24 (1974) 348–86.

[43] *Quodlibet* I.4, ed. Ypma, pp. 47–9, 56. See Mark Gossiaux, "James of Viterbo on the Relationship between Essence and Existence," *Augustiniana* 49 (1999) 73–107. On the similarity between James's solution to this issue and Godfrey's solution to the nature–supposit relationship see John F. Wippel,

be said to be really distinct from essence, as defended either by Thomas or by Giles.

A real distinction between *esse* and essence would also be rejected by most subsequent thinkers outside the Thomistic tradition: for instance, by John Duns Scotus, John of Jandun, the early fourteenth-century Italian Latin Averroist Thaddeus of Parma, William of Ockham, and also, more surprisingly, by the early fourteenth-century Dominican promoter of Aquinas and his cause, Hervaeus Natalis.[44]

"James of Viterbo on the Essence-Existence Relationship (Quodlibet 1, q. 4), and Godfrey of Fontaines on the Relationship between Nature and Supposit (Quodlibet 7, q. 5)," in *Sprache und Erkenntnis im Mittelalter* (Miscellanea Mediaevalia 13/2) (Berlin: De Gruyter, 1981) 777–87.

[44] For Scotus see *Ordinatio* IV.11.3 n. 46 (ed. Vivès) and *Ordinatio* I.8.1.2, nn. 32–4 (ed. Balić), on the qualified "composition" he assigns to created intelligences. On whether Scotus assigns a formal distinction or a modal distinction to essence and existence, see A. J. O'Brien, "Duns Scotus' Teaching on the Distinction between Essence and Existence," *New Scholasticism* 38 (1964) 61–77; Allan B. Wolter, "The Formal Distinction," in J. K. Ryan and B. M. Bonansea (eds.) *John Duns Scotus, 1265–1965* (Washington, DC: Catholic University of America, 1965) 45–60, esp. pp. 54–6. For Ockham see *Summa logicae* III-2 ch. 27 and *Quodlibet* II.7. On this see Armand Maurer, *The Philosophy of William of Ockham in the Light of its Principles* (Toronto: Pontifical Institute of Mediaeval Studies, 1999) pp. 60–2. On Buridan and on Thaddeus of Parma see Imbach, "Averroistische Stellungnahmen," pp. 326–39; on Hervaus, see ibid., pp. 324–5.

46

FORM AND MATTER

ROBERT PASNAU

The first unquestionably big idea in the history of philosophy was the idea of form. The idea of course belonged to Plato, and was then domesticated at the hands of Aristotle, who paired form with matter as the two chief principles of his metaphysics and natural philosophy. In the medieval period, it was Aristotle's conception of form and matter that generally dominated. This was true for both the Islamic and the Christian tradition, once the entire Aristotelian corpus became available. For this reason, although there is much to say about the fate of Platonic Forms in medieval thought, the present chapter will focus on the Aristotelian tradition.[1]

Aristotelian commentators have been puzzled by form and matter for as long as there have been Aristotelian commentators. Indeed, it would not be too much to say that these are topics about which Aristotelians have never formed a very clear conception, and that their failure to do so was the principal reason why Aristotelianism ceased to be a flourishing research program from the seventeenth century onward. For those who aspire to a modern revival of Aristotelianism, the concepts of *form* and *matter* can easily take on the aspect of a kind of Holy Grail, such that if only we could get these ideas clearly in focus, we could see our way forward on any number of philosophical fronts, such as the union of mind and body, the coherence and endurance of substances, the nature of causality, and so on. The historical record, however, suggests that this hope is a snare and a delusion, insofar as there has never been any such thing as

---

[1] Since medieval Latin before 1200 proceeded in ignorance of Aristotle's metaphysics and natural philosophy (see Chapter 4), one might suppose that it would have little to say about form and matter in anything like an Aristotelian sense. In fact, this is not always the case. Peter Abaelard works with a sophisticated conception of form and matter, although he treats these concepts in a highly reductive fashion. See Peter King, "Peter Abelard," in E. Zalta (ed.) *The Stanford Encyclopedia of Philosophy*: http://plato.stanford.edu. Gilbert of Poitiers likewise gives form an important role in his thought (see John Marenbon's entry on Gilbert of Poitiers in J. Gracia and T. Noone, *A Companion to Philosophy in the Middle Ages* [Oxford: Blackwell, 2003] p. 264). See also Chapter 49.

the theory of form and matter. Although medieval philosophers of all kinds used this terminology incessantly, it had no more of a fixed meaning than does the ubiquitous contemporary philosophical talk of "properties." Hence, the most a general survey of the topic can do is consider some of the more important areas of agreement and disagreement.

UNIVERSAL HYLOMORPHISM

Our default theory of bodies today is taken from the seventeenth century, though it springs largely out of ancient atomism: we take material substances to be constituted by their integral parts, and to be nothing more than the sum of those parts. On this picture, the bodies we are ordinarily acquainted with are just a collection of smaller bodies, perhaps with the further proviso that the whole be assembled in a certain way. The rightness of this picture can seem so self-evident as to require no defense. To medieval philosophers working in the Aristotelian tradition, however, this analysis would seem so incomplete as to be laughable. On their model, although bodies are composed of other bodies, this sort of analysis never gets to the fundamental constituents of the material world, however far down it goes, because it frames the analysis in the wrong way. For an Aristotelian, the fundamental constituents of physical bodies are not integral parts, but the metaphysical parts of form and matter.

On one understanding of matter, it is the counterpart of form – the stuff that gets informed – so that whenever there is a form there must also be some matter that serves as its subject. On this conception, there will often be hierarchies of matter, with the most basic stuff, *prime matter*, at the bottom, and various form–matter composites at higher levels, which may themselves be conceived as the matter for some further form. Wood, for example, is a form–matter composite that can itself serve as the matter of a bed (see Aristotle, *Phys.* II.1).

This conception of matter lends itself naturally to universal hylomorphism: the doctrine that every (created) substance is a composite of form and matter. Perhaps the most influential proponent of this view was Solomon ibn Gabirol, the eleventh-century Jewish philosopher and poet. According to Gabirol, everything that exists has a form, because "every existence of a thing comes from form," and moreover "every difference [between things] occurs only through form" (*Fons vitae* III.39). These claims are relatively uncontroversial, inasmuch as all beings, material and spiritual, were standardly viewed as containing some form, and such forms are what give character to otherwise homogeneous matter. Gabirol's further, highly controversial claim is that all created substances also contain matter:

[A]ll things are composed of matter and form. That is to say, a body at the lower extreme [of the hierarchy of being] – namely, a substance having three dimensions – is composed of matter and form. And if the whole of what exists is a continuum extended from the highest extreme to the lowest extreme, and the lowest extreme is composed of matter and form, then it is clear from this that the whole of what goes from the uppermost extreme high to the lowest extreme is also composed of matter and form.

(*Fons vitae* IV.6)

Many early scholastic authors, especially Franciscans, embraced this sort of view. From the time of Albert the Great and Thomas Aquinas, however, the view fell entirely out of favor, replaced by the idea that matter occurs only in the corporeal realm. Hence there arose the linkage we take for granted today, between corporeality and materiality, so that to be a body (*corpus*) is just to have matter.[2]

One way to confine matter to a narrower range of entities would be to restrict form as well to the corporeal realm. This strategy does not go very deep, however, inasmuch as it leaves untouched the principal rationale for universal hylomorphism – namely, to account for the mix of actuality and potentiality found everywhere among creatures, material and spiritual. That forms are what give actuality to their subjects, whereas matter is the corresponding potentiality for that subject to enter into a certain state, by acquiring a form – these are perhaps the only truly uncontroversial things that can be said about form and matter. This suggests that wherever there is the capacity for change, there will be both form and matter.

In response, one might try denying that spiritual entities – celestial intelligences, human souls – have any sort of potentiality for being affected in any way. This, however, would introduce a radical discontinuity among creatures that medieval authors were generally unprepared to accept. Aquinas, for

---

[2] On hylomorphism among the early scholastics, see Erich Kleineidam, *Das Problem der hylomorphen Zusammensetzung der geistigen Substanzen im 13. Jahrhundert, behandelt bis Thomas von Aquin* (Breslau: Tesch, 1930); Odon Lottin, *Psychologie et morale aux XIIe et XIIIe siècles* (Gembloux: Duculot, 1948–60) I: 427–60; Richard Dales, *The Problem of the Rational Soul in the Thirteenth Century* (Leiden: Brill, 1995); R. James Long, "Of Angels and Pinheads: The Contributions of the Early Oxford Masters to the Doctrine of Spiritual Matter," *Franciscan Studies* 56 (1998) 237–52. Among Franciscan authors, see Bonaventure (*Sent.* II.3.1.1.1c, II.17.1.2c) and John Pecham (*Quaest. de anima* 4), and the detailed discussion in Theodore Crowley, *Roger Bacon: The Problem of the Soul in his Philosophical Commentaries* (Leuven: Institut Supérieur de Philosophie, 1950) ch. 2. For Albert the Great, see *Sent.* II.3.4c, *In De an.* III.2.9, and James Weisheipl, "Albertus Magnus and Universal Hylomorphism: Avicebron," in F. Kovach and R. Shahan (eds.) *Albert the Great Commemorative Essays* (Norman: University of Oklahoma Press, 1980) 239–60. On Gabirol, and especially the Neoplatonic background to his thought, see Lenn Goodman (ed.) *Neoplatonism and Jewish Thought* (Albany, NY: State University of New York Press, 1992).

instance, accepts Gabirol's basic assumption in the passage quoted above, that what is found at the lower levels of creation will be found at the higher levels. *All* created substances exhibit complexity and changeability, which is to say that they exhibit potentiality and actuality. But Aquinas insists that not all potentiality is material potentiality:

> To receive, to be subjected, and other such things do not apply to the soul and to prime matter in the same way (*rationem*), because prime matter receives a thing through transformation and motion. And because all transformation and motion goes back to local motion as to what is first and most common (as is proved in *Physics* VIII), we get the result that matter is found only in those cases where there is the potentiality for location. But only corporeal things, which are circumscribed to some place, are of this sort. Hence matter is found only in corporeal things, with respect to how the philosophers have talked about matter, unless one wants to use 'matter' equivocally.
>
> (*Quaest. de anima* 6c)

The argument aims to establish a general characterization of material change, so that it can be distinguished from spiritual change. Only things whose changes occur in virtue of local motion – and so only things that occupy place – can undergo material change. This limits material change to bodies, and so limits matter to bodies.[3] Aquinas's closing reference to a possible "equivocal" use of matter recognizes that someone might want to treat any sort of potentiality as matter, thereby retaining universal hylomorphism. Since Aquinas accepts that all creatures contain potentiality, inasmuch as they are a composite of being and essence (see Chapter 45), he can object to this locution only on the grounds that it would equivocate between very different senses of what matter is. It is much better, he claims, to restrict matter to the corporeal realm.

PRIME MATTER

When matter is restricted to the corporeal realm, the notion of *prime matter* takes on a more precise meaning – not just as the basement level of any hylomorphic hierarchy, but more specifically as the stuff in virtue of which substances count as *corporeal* substances. This, at any rate, is what the rationale that leads to restricting matter to the corporeal realm naturally suggests. At the same time, however, the

---

[3] Aquinas's argument is liable to misinterpretation in several respects. First, although the text literally says that all change "reduces" to local motion, Aquinas does not mean – and does not understand *Physics* VIII (at 260a27–261a27) to assert – that a reductive account of qualitative change in terms of local motion is possible. He means only that, since bodies act on other bodies in virtue of spatial proximity, local motion is always a basic and necessary condition for the onset of any material change. Second, Aquinas believes that spiritual substances can literally have location. God, for instance, is literally everywhere (*Summa theol.* 1a 8.3). But the actions of spiritual agents *need not* involve any sort of local change.

logic of the form–matter distinction tends to drain the concept of *prime matter* of all content, making it very hard to see what exactly prime matter might be, or might do. This tendency appears in its most extreme form in Aquinas, who treats prime matter as pure potentiality to such a degree that it cannot possibly exist on its own, or even be understood on its own, not even by God.[4] Yet although it would become a scholastic platitude to describe prime matter as pure potentiality, few later scholastics were willing to go as far as Aquinas in depriving prime matter of all actuality. Even Domingo de Soto, an influential sixteenth-century Thomist, would feel obliged to postulate within prime matter an "essential metaphysical actuality" that gives matter its distinctive character – a conclusion that, he remarks, "seems so certain to me that there can be no question about it, except in name" (*In Phys.* I.5).

The worry that prime matter, conceived of as nothing but potentiality, would lack character entirely, was stated forcefully by John Duns Scotus and then William of Ockham. Contrary to Aquinas's claim that prime matter by itself would lack even existence, Ockham claims that "matter is a kind of thing that actually exists in the natural realm" (*Summula philosophiae naturalis* I.9). It must be so, he argues, because matter is a real principle of corporeal substances, but "that which is not an actual entity can be a part or principle of no being" (ibid., I.10). Scotus had said much the same thing, but in somewhat more cautious terms, remarking that "if you ask whether or not matter ought to be called an actuality, I have no wish to dispute over names." What is important, according to Scotus, is that "matter is a true reality" and "a positive being" (*Lectura* II.12 [ed. Vatican XIX nn. 38, 37]). On the usual reading of Aquinas, these are claims to which he, too, would assent; this raises the possibility that the dispute over whether matter has some actuality just is, in large part, a terminological dispute. Scotus, however, treats the strict "pure potentiality" line as tantamount to denying that matter is a thing in its own right, distinct from form, and there is indeed room to wonder whether this is correct, or even whether it might be Aquinas's intended view.[5]

The chief argument for prime matter having actuality was that it could not otherwise serve as the stuff that endures beneath every change, both substantial

---

[4] For Aquinas on prime matter's dependence on form, see *Quodlibet* III.1.1; on its intelligibility, see *Quaest. de veritate* 3.5c and *Summa theologiae* 1a 15.3 ad 3 (see also John Wippel, *The Metaphysical Thought of Thomas Aquinas: From Finite Being to Uncreated Being* [Washington, DC: Catholic University of America Press, 2000] ch. IX). The tendency appears in many other authors. Gabirol, for instance, insists that matter without form must lack being (*Fons vitae* IV.5), as does Avicenna (*Metaphysics* II.3).

[5] For Scotus on prime matter, see also *Quaest. in Meta.* VII.5. For a reading of Aquinas as denying that prime matter has any real ontological standing, see Robert Pasnau, *Thomas Aquinas on Human Nature* (Cambridge: Cambridge University Press, 2002) ch. 1.

and accidental. On this conception of prime matter's role, it may not need any special sort of character. But if matter is also to play a role in explaining the corporeality of physical substances, then it must presumably be more than just a bare, purely potential, substratum. Specifically, since the defining character of *body* is three-dimensionality, prime matter might naturally be supposed to account for extension. This idea, however, was extremely controversial. The usual medieval stance was to distinguish prime matter from extension, but there was a wide range of possible views. Both Avicenna and Averroes, for instance, had conceived of extension as a form that inheres directly in prime matter, prior to the substantial form that makes the matter be a stone or a horse. They disagreed, however, on how to characterize that form. For Avicenna, extension results from a substantial form – what would be known as the *forma corporeitatis* – that endures through all change and accounts for the corporeal character of matter. Averroes, in contrast, conceived of extension as an accidental form that inheres in prime matter perpetually but in such a way that prime matter apart from subsequent forms has merely "indeterminate" dimensions. Both of these views were influential on the later Latin tradition, but competed against the view – associated with Aquinas – that extension (or quantity) is posterior to the substantial form, just as other accidents are. On this view, when prime matter is conceived of apart from form, it lacks extension altogether.[6]

The notion of extensionless prime matter is, of course, puzzling – in part because it is unclear how we are to conceive of prime matter, if not as extended. Averroes took the rather surprising position that prime matter is numerically one everywhere it exists, even within corporeal substances:

> We have already said elsewhere that prime matter is numerically one. Let us then demonstrate how numerically one thing can be found in many places. This is not found in what is actual. But in what is potential it can be said that a thing is numerically one and common to many, and that it does not have the differentiating features by which [the many] differ from each other in singular individuals. And because they have no indivisible differences and they lack forms, through which is found numerical plurality, these things are said to be one.
>
> (*In Meta.* XII.14)

Averroes's view seems to be that prime matter is located throughout space, but that since it is the same everywhere, this does not count as being extended. This sort of extensionless spreading out, so as to exist wholly in multiple

---

[6] For Avicenna, see *Metaphysics* II.2–3, and the discussion in Abraham Stone, "Simplicius and Avicenna on the Essential Corporeity of Material Substance," in R. Wisnovsky (ed.) *Aspects of Avicenna* (Princeton, NJ: Markus Wiener, 2001) 73–130. For Averroes, see *De substantia orbis* ch. 1, and Arthur Hyman, "Aristotle's 'First Matter' and Avicenna's and Averroes' 'Corporeal Form'," in S. Lieberman *et al.* (eds.) *Harry Austryn Wolfson Jubilee Volume* (Jerusalem: American Academy for Jewish Research, 1965) pp. 400–6.

places at the same time, is more often associated with immaterial entities like the soul, or else with universal properties. Averroes, however, denies that a form, or anything actual, could be present in many places. This mode of existence is possible for prime matter, however, given its lack of actuality, inasmuch as there is nothing to distinguish one bit of matter from another. This is a view that would be defended in the early fourteenth century by the leading Latin proponent of Averroism, John of Jandun (*In Phys.* I.24).

If prime matter is strictly and purely potential, then it must lack any intrinsic distinctness. Thus, according to the fifteenth-century Thomist John Capreolus, prime matter is "actually indivisible and one, but potentially divisible, multiple, and plural." Or, to avoid the impression that prime matter is *actually* anything, he goes on to gloss "actually indivisible" as "not actually divisible" (*Defensiones* II.13.1.3). To others, however, it seemed that prime matter had to have some feature that at least lent itself to extension. According to Scotus, prime matter is not intrinsically extended, but nevertheless it has "substantial parts" – parts not necessarily spread out in space, but there nevertheless, and apt to be spread out, when informed by quantity.[7] Scotus's idea that prime matter could have parts and yet lack extension struck Ockham as needlessly obscure, as did the Averroistic view that prime matter could be spread out without having parts at all, being numerically one at each location. Ockham's own conclusion, instead, is that prime matter is intrinsically extended:

> It is impossible for matter to exist without extension, because it is not possible for matter to exist unless it has part distant from part. Hence although the parts of matter can be united in the way in which the parts of water and air can be united, still the parts of matter can never exist in the same place.
>
> (*Summula* I.13)[8]

On this view, prime matter is necessarily spread out in space, part-wise, in virtue of its own nature. Since this is a theory of prime matter, not of body, we are still a long way from Descartes's later identification of body with extension. Still, building extension into the notion of prime matter gives Ockham the resources to reduce much of the standard scholastic ontology – especially the accidental category of Quantity – to nothing more than matter variously situated. This move thus serves as a critical foundation for his parsimonious, nominalistic ontology (see Chapter 48).

---

[7] Scotus, *Reportatio* II.12.2 n. 7 (ed. Wadding XI: 322b; cf. VI.2: 683). See also Paul of Venice, *Summa philosophiae naturalis* VI.13. For another statement of the Thomistic view, see Robert Orford (?), *De natura materiae* ch. 5 n. 390.

[8] See also Marilyn McCord Adams, *William Ockham* (Notre Dame, IN: University of Notre Dame Press, 1987) pp. 671–95.

SUBSTANTIAL FORM

Although the obscurity of prime matter is naturally captivating, of far greater significance to medieval philosophy is the conception of form, which serves as the chief analytic tool in nearly every area of Aristotelian thought. There are two basic kinds of form, substantial and accidental. Although the status of accidental forms was one of the most controversial issues in later medieval philosophy, the focus here will be on substantial form, leaving the dispute over accidents for elsewhere (Chapters 47–9). To concentrate on substantial form and prime matter, leaving aside accidental forms, is in fact to concentrate on the substance itself, since on the standard medieval Aristotelian understanding, a human being or a horse is just a composite of prime matter and substantial form.[9] Thus, the substance's color, size, and shape *inhere* in it, but are not strictly speaking a *part* of it. (When Locke and other critics of scholasticism call into question our grasp of substance, they have in mind this notion of the substance as the thing itself, apart from its accidents.) In terms of Aristotle's often-cited example, a white man is not a genuine substantial unity, because it is a composite of a substance (the man) and an accidental form (whiteness). In contrast, what became known as the "essential parts" of a human being (prime matter and substantial form) make a thing that is one *per se* – that is, yield the sort of unity characteristic of substances.[10]

It is not at all easy to account for the unity of a form–matter composite, however, when form and matter are understood as distinct things. Scotus, for one, thinks there simply is no such explanation, but that instead their unity is a brute fact:

> If you ask why there is one thing *per se* in one case more than in another, I reply that just as, according to *Metaphysics* VIII, there is no question of why one thing is made from actuality and potentiality, except that this is actuality *per se* and that potentiality *per se*, so too there is no cause for why one thing *per se* is made from this actuality and that potentiality, either in things or in concepts, except that this is potentiality with respect to that, and that is actuality.
>
> (*Ord.* IV.11.3 n. 53 [ed. Wadding VIII: 652]).

What Aristotle had said is that "if one is matter, the other form, one in potentiality, the other in actuality, then the question [of their unity] will no longer

---

[9] Admittedly, this oversimplifies the views of some authors, who would add certain further ingredients to a substantial composite, such as Averroes's indeterminate quantity, Scotus's haecceity, or even multiple substantial forms (see below).

[10] For the case of the white man, see *Metaphysics* VII. On the *per se* unity of substances, see, e.g., Aquinas, *De ente* 6 (ed. Leonine XLIII: 380.23–49); Scotus, *Lectura* II.12.1 nn. 45–51. I discuss Locke's view in a forthcoming book on the origins of seventeenth-century philosophy.

appear to be puzzling" (1045a23–5). Rather than try to explain *why* there is no longer a puzzle at this point, Scotus contends that the appeal to potentiality and actuality is the end of the story, leaving nothing more to be said. This is an unorthodox conclusion, but it captures the unsettled state of the discussion over how a hylomorphic account might explain the unity of soul and body, or of any other hylomorphic compound.

A substantial form is more than just a cluster of necessary properties, and more even than just those properties that give a thing its essential nature as a thing of some kind (*horse, gold*, etc.). To be sure, the substantial form is closely associated and sometimes identified with the essence of a thing.[11] But an essence is more than just a certain sort of defining property – an essence defines a thing because it plays a critical functional role within a substance, explaining the various characteristic properties of a thing, both necessary and accidental. This is not to say that the essence explains *every* property of a thing, however; some properties, like having a scar, have extrinsic causes. Thus, according to Avicenna, "among accidents, there are some that occur from without and some that occur from the substance of the thing" (*Sufficientia* I.6). Drawing on Avicenna's discussion, Aquinas remarks that "everything that holds true of something is either caused by the principles of its nature, as is a human being's capacity for laughter, or comes to it from an external principle, as light in the air comes from the sun's influence" (*De ente* 4 [ed. Leonine XLIII: 377.127–30]). This idea runs through all of medieval Aristotelianism. Water, to take a common example, was thought to have all its various characteristic features – the tendency to be cold, to freeze at a certain point, to be transparent, etc. – in virtue of its essence. And just as the features of a substance that distinguish it as a natural kind stem from the kind of substantial form it has, so a substance's intrinsic individual properties are often said to stem from the distinctive features of an individual's substantial form. (Thus, it is *my* soul that accounts for the intrinsic accidental features that are distinctive of me in contrast with other human beings.) For medieval Aristotelians, the need to postulate some such intrinsic explanatory principle was the undisputed rationale for postulating substantial forms.[12]

Once substantial forms are justified in terms of this specific causal framework, the theory becomes at once more concrete and more vulnerable. There is no temptation to embrace any sort of conventionalism about essences, inasmuch

---

[11] There was a running medieval dispute over whether the essence of a thing should simply be identified with its substantial form, as Averroes had argued (*In Meta.* VII.34), or whether, as Aquinas had argued (*Summa theol.* 1a 75.4c), a thing's essence is its substantial form together with its common matter (those general features of its matter that it shares with all members of the species).

[12] For further discussion, see Robert Pasnau, "Form, Substance, and Mechanism," *Philosophical Review* 113 (2004) 31–88.

as it is clearly more than convention that explains why water has its distinctive characteristics. But in taking on the aspect of a kind of proto-scientific hypothesis, the theory loses touch with its more metaphysical roots as an abstract principle of analysis. In Aristotle, these two aspects of form – proto-scientific and metaphysical – exist side by side, so that sometimes forms are conceived of on the model of souls, where souls are thought to have certain causal powers, whereas at other times forms are conceived of as abstract, functional principles, offering explanations at a level that is quite independent of whatever causal, physical story might be told about the natural world. Both of these aspects of form are present in medieval discussions as well, but the more pronounced tendency as time went on was to think of forms as causal agents. Hence, Francis Bacon would complain that in the natural philosophy of his day "forms are given all the leading parts" (*De principiis*, p. 206).

THE PLURALITY OF FORMS

The doctrine of substantial form was never seriously challenged during the Middle Ages. There was, however, a very contentious dispute over how many substantial forms to postulate within a single substance. Avicenna's corporeal form, described above, marks him as a pluralist, and Gabirol postulates an even larger hierarchy of forms within living things (*Fons vitae* IV.3, V.34). Averroes, in contrast, seems to take the unitarian position, arguing that a substantial form can inhere only in prime matter, not in an actualized matter–form composite, and that therefore "it is impossible for a single subject to have more than one form."[13] Among Latin authors, the initial tendency was pluralistic, at least until Aquinas forcefully defended the unitarian position. Although unitarianism was condemned at Oxford in 1277 and again in 1284, Aquinas's influence endured, and the result was a persistent division on the topic.[14]

---

[13] *De substantia orbis* ch. 1, quoting from the medieval Latin translation (ed. 1562, IX: 3vK). Most Hebrew manuscripts have the inverted claim that "it is impossible for one form to have more than one subject." But the context of the passage, and the commentary tradition on the passage, suggest that the intended sense is as quoted (see *De substantia orbis*, ed. Hyman, p. 50n).

[14] On the thirteenth-century debate, see Roberto Zavalloni, *Richard de Mediavilla et la controverse sur la pluralité des formes* (Louvain: Éditions de l'Institut Supérieur de Philosophie, 1951), and Dales, *Problem of the Rational Soul*. For Aquinas, see, e.g., *Summa theol.* 1a 76.3–4, *Quaest. de anima* 9, 11. On the controversy in Oxford, see Francis Kelley's introduction to Richard Knapwell, *Quaest. de unitate formae*. For the Thomistic defense, see Frederick Roensch, *Early Thomistic School* (Dubuque, IA: Priory Press, 1964). Prominent pluralists include Henry of Ghent (*Quod.* IV.13), Scotus (*Quod.* IV.11), Ockham (*Quod.* II.10–11), and Paul of Venice (*Summa philosophiae naturalis* V.5). Unitarians include Thomists such as Giles of Lessines (*De unitate formae*) and Capreolus (*Defensiones* II.15), and also Gregory of Rimini (*Sent.* II.16–17.2), John Buridan (*Quaest. Metaphys.* VII.14), Albert of Saxony (*Quaest. de gen. et cor.* I.5), and Marsilius of Inghen (*Quaest. de gen. et cor.* I.6). Francisco Suárez offers an extended defense of unitarianism in *Disputationes metaphysicae* XV.

In a sense, however, this ongoing dispute obscures the real story: although Aquinas's unitarian account was attacked for centuries, the consensus throughout was that such an account was preferable when available. When Henry of Ghent argued against the unitarian conception, for instance, he did so only for the special case of human beings, and even there he postulated only two substantial forms. Scotus likewise argued only for two forms, and only in the case of living things. Ockham was relatively extravagant in positing three substantial forms within a human being: a rational soul, a sensory/nutritive soul, and a form of the body. (Ockham was also unusual in his willingness to describe a human being as having two souls.) All three, however, agreed with Aquinas in the case of non-living things, and they also agreed that the default view should be the unitarian one, unless special considerations make it untenable. Aquinas thus succeeded in changing the terms of the debate. The kind of pluralism he attacked had posited a substantial form corresponding to each of a thing's necessary properties; the force of his arguments was such that this kind of promiscuous pluralism ceased to be a live view.

Although it is not immediately obvious that very much rests on the question of whether a human being has one substantial form or more, the debate in fact raises some fundamental metaphysical questions. The principal benefit of unitarianism is the work it does in accounting for substantial unity. Because of the substantial form's role in explaining the properties of a thing, one can say that a substance has its enduring character over time in virtue of having a single substantial form that gives rise to those characteristics. Pluralists, with their multiple substantial forms, need to have some further story about what unifies a living organism. By treating the rational soul as distinct from the form of the body, they in effect abandon the promise of hylomorphism to explain the unity of mind and body. Balanced against that cost, however, are the resources available to pluralism to explain various puzzling features of substantial change. Intuitively, it seems that in many cases where a thing goes out of existence, part of that thing remains. An animal dies, but its body remains. A statue is smashed, but the clay remains. Philosophers have sometimes been tempted to deal with these sorts of cases by holding either that there is no real substantial change (that is, nothing goes out of existence) or that in fact there were two substances overlapping for a time (the statue *and* the clay), only one of which remains. Pluralists are able to say something less strange: there is only one substance, but its identity is centered on two axes, as it were, around one or the other of which its various properties revolve. The animal is a single substance, then, and *it* goes out of existence when it dies, but nevertheless part of it endures, in virtue of its corporeal form. A unitarian must instead say that when a substance goes out of existence, it *wholly* goes out of existence. Thus when an animal dies, not only is the corpse not that same body, but nothing about that corpse is the same. The corpse may have qualitatively the same properties, but those properties are numerically distinct. It was this implausible consequence – and the difficulty of explaining *why* a numerically distinct corpse should happen to have the same properties as the living body – that fueled the philosophical opposition to unitarianism.[15]

---

[15] For Aquinas, see, e.g., *Summa contra gentiles* II.72, *Summa theol.* 1a 76.8 (see also Wippel, *Metaphysical Thought of Thomas Aquinas*, pp. 327–51). Aristotle suggests this sort of view at *Meteor.* IV 12, 389b31–390a19, *De an.* II 1, 412b20–2. Pluralists had other, theological objections to unitarianism. For objections of both kinds, see Adams, *William Ockham*, pp. 647–69; Richard Cross, *The Physics of Duns Scotus* (Oxford: Clarendon Press, 1998) pp. 47–93. Because statues are artifacts, they would not generally have been regarded as substances, and so the analysis in such a case would run rather differently than in the case of a true substance like an animal.

47

REALISM

ALESSANDRO D. CONTI

Realism and nominalism were the two major theoretical alternatives in the later Middle Ages concerning the reality of general objects: realists believed in the extramental existence of common natures or essences; nominalists did not. This so-called "problem of universals" was only one of the main questions at issue between realists and nominalists, however, whose disputes ranged widely over the status and mutual relationships of the basic items of the world (individual and universal substances, individual and universal accidents) as well as their connection to language. For scholastic authors, these questions arose first and foremost in the context of Aristotle's *Categories*. As a consequence, the medieval realist–nominalist dispute included also the problem of the status and number of real categories. Realists held that the division into categories is first of all a partition of things made on the basis of ontological criteria and only secondarily a classification of terms (which could be mental, written, or spoken), and therefore that the world is divided into ten fundamental kinds of things (in a broad sense of 'thing'), no one of which can be reduced to any other. In contrast, nominalists maintained that Aristotle's division into ten categories is a partition of terms on the basis of semantic criteria, and that there are only two or three real categories (Substance and Quality, and perhaps Quantity too). Even though from a purely logical point of view these opinions on categories and universals are independent of each other, historically, in the later Middle Ages, realism concerning categories was always matched by a realistic conception of universals, whereas nominalism on the question of categories was always paralleled by a nominalistic position on universals.

This chapter outlines the main medieval forms of realism, trying to indicate how the debate over universals and categories evolved. First, it sketches the chief features of the standard realist doctrine on universals and categories as it was worked out between the thirteenth and fourteenth centuries. Second, it summarizes William of Ockham's attack on this traditional view and Walter Burley's reply on behalf of realism. Finally, it considers the most important realist theories of the later Middle Ages, which were proposed in order to avoid both Ockham's criticisms and the "exaggeration" of Burley's version of realism.

TRADITIONAL "MODERATE" REALISM

What has come to be known as "moderate realism" is a view endorsed by a long list of authors from the thirteenth and early fourteenth centuries, including Albert the Great, Thomas Aquinas, Henry of Ghent, Simon of Faversham, John Duns Scotus, Thomas of Sutton, Giles of Rome, and Walter Burley (pre-1324). We can approach this view by considering its semantic origins, which are evident as early as Robert Kilwardby's formulation of the problem of universals in his commentaries on the *Ars vetus* (1235–40). According to the semantics of the traditional moderate realist, universals are the real *significata* of general nouns (such as 'man' and 'whiteness'), and are thus extramental entities that are common to many individual items. Moderate realists investigated the metaphysical composition of such universals from a point of view that we can call "intensional." Only by associating common nouns with such entities as their proper *significata* did they think the fact could be explained that a general noun can be used predicatively to ascribe a given property (say, being a human being or being white) to many individuals at the same time. According to them, a general noun stands (supposits) for a certain set of individual items only by way of the common nature (the universal) that it directly signifies – a common nature that is present in that set of individuals as their intelligible essence. (On supposition and signification, see Chapter 11.)

This emerges quite plainly in the common reading of *Categories* 5, where Aristotle maintains that primary-substance terms signify a single item (*hoc aliquid* in Latin), whereas secondary-substance terms signify a "qualifying" (and therefore common or universal) item (*quale quid* in Latin) – even if they seem to signify a single item.[1] Medieval realists identified the secondary substance with the *quale quid* and the primary substance with the *hoc aliquid*, and therefore identified secondary substances (namely, the universals of the category of substance) with the *significata* of general nouns of that category (such as 'man') and primary substances (namely, the individuals of the category of substance)

---

[1] See *Cat.* 5, 3b10–15: "All substances appear to signify something individual. In the case of primary substances it is indisputably true that they signify something individual, since what is shown [by them] is something indivisible and unitary. In the case of secondary substances, the form of naming gives the impression that we are also signifying something individual when we speak, for instance, of man or animal, but this impression is not true. On the contrary, we are signifying [a type, i.e.] something with a certain qualification."

with the *significata* of individual expressions of that category (such as 'this man'). Furthermore, they assumed that secondary substances specify which kind of substance a certain individual substance is. As a consequence, they thought of universals and individuals as linked together by a sort of relation of instantiation. Moreover, they agreed with Aristotle (*Cat.* 5, 2a35–2b6) that if primary substances did not exist, it would be impossible for anything else to exist, since everything else depends on them for its own being. Accordingly, the question of the status of universals became the question of their relation to individual substances. For these authors, universals are not self-subsistent entities, but exist only in and in virtue of individual entities, inasmuch as universals have no being outside the being of their instantiations.[2]

Medieval realists distinguished between three kinds of universals:

- *ante rem* – the ideas in God;
- *in re* – formal universals, the common natures (or essences) present in individual things;
- *post rem* – the mental signs (or concepts) by which we refer to the universals *in re*.

Formal universals were conceived of in two different ways, as first intentions and as second intentions. Conceived of as first intentions, universals are natures of a certain kind, identical with their own individuals. (For example, *man* would be the same thing as Socrates.) Conceived of as second intentions, formal universals were regarded as properly universal and distinct from their own individuals, considered *qua* individuals. So conceived, universals and individuals had to be distinct, because of their opposing constitutive principles: on the one hand, the generality, or natural tendency to be common (*communicabilitas*) that characterizes universals; on the other hand, the thisness, or impossibility of being common (*incommunicabilitas*) that characterizes individuals.[3]

These dual conceptions necessarily required a flexible approach to defining and classifying the types of identity and difference, given that universals were considered at the same time not totally identical with and not totally different from their own individuals. Indeed, initial scholastic accounts of identity and

[2] For statements of the general semantic account described here, see Kilwardby, *In Porphyrium* 2 (Peterhouse ms. 206, f. 34vb); *In Praedicament.* 7 (Peterhouse ms. 206, f. 47ra–b); Albert the Great, *De praedicament.* 2.4, 2.8; Simon of Faversham, *Quaest. super Praedicamenta* 7; Sutton, *In Praedicament.* [*De substantia*], ed. Conti, in "Thomas Sutton's Commentary," pp. 203–4; Scotus, *Quaest. super Praedicamenta* 13 (*Opera phil.* I: 369–72, 377); Burley, *De suppositionibus*, ed. Brown, pp. 35–6; *Tractatus super Praedicamenta* [*De substantia*] (Peterhouse ms. 184, ff. 177va, 178ra–b); *Commentarius in Periherm.*, ed. Brown, p. 85.

[3] Albert the Great, *De quinque universalibus* 1.3, 1.5; Simon of Faversham, *Quaest. super Porphyrium* 4; Scotus, *Quaest. in Porphyrium* 3 (*Opera phil.* I: 19–20).

difference appealed to two kinds of distinctions: a real distinction and a distinction of reason. At the end of the thirteenth century, attempts were made to introduce a third, intermediary distinction. Henry of Ghent, for instance, spoke of an intentional distinction (*Quodlibet* X.7), whereas Scotus spoke of a formal distinction.[4] In the *Lectura* (I.2.2.1–4) and in the *Ordinatio* (I.2.2.1–4; II.3.1.6), Scotus describes this as a symmetrical relation between two entities that cannot exist separately; in the *Reportatio Parisiensis* (I.33.2–3; I.34.1), he defines it as an asymmetrical relation between a whole reality and one of its constitutive elements. Although none of these intermediary distinctions was specifically intended to offer an answer to the problem of universals, they nevertheless served as a potentially useful tool, for by means of them, moderate realists were trying to explain how it is possible to distinguish between many different real aspects internal to the same individual thing, without breaking its unity.

As far as the problem of the status and number of real categories was concerned, some moderate realist thinkers – such as Kilwardby, Henry of Ghent, Simon of Faversham, and "the first" Burley (in contrast with his later views, described below) – held a sort of reductionist position regarding the number of real categories: they judged only the items falling into the three "absolute" categories (Substance, Quantity, and Quality) to be things (*res*) in the strict sense of the term, considering the remaining ones to be merely "real aspects" (*respectus reales*) of the former, albeit still somehow distinct from them.[5] Others, such as Albert the Great, Thomas of Sutton, and Scotus, defended a real distinction between all ten categories, as things in the world, irreducible to one another.[6] With the sole and remarkable exception of Scotus, who maintained that the distinction among the ten categories is based on their different natures, all of these authors regarded categorial items as made up of two main components: an inner nature or essence, and a distinctive mode of being or of being predicated (*modus essendi, modus praedicandi*). The categories were understood to divide items according to these modes, rather than according to their essences.

---

[4] On Henry's doctrine of intentional distinction see John F. Wippel, "The Dating of James of Viterbo's Quodlibet I and Godfrey of Fontaines' Quodlibet VIII," *Augustiniana* 24 (1974) 348–86; on Scotus's formal distinction see Peter King, "Duns Scotus on the Common Nature and Individual Difference," *Philosophical Topics* 20 (1992) 51–76, and Stephen Dumont, "Duns Scotus's Parisian Question on the Formal Distinction," *Vivarium* 43 (2005) 7–62.

[5] Kilwardby, *In Praedicament.* prooem. (Peterhouse ms. 206, f. 41ra) and ch. 5 (ff. 44vb–45ra); Henry of Ghent, *Summa quaest. ord.* 32.5 (*Opera* XXVII: 79–80); Simon of Faversham, *Quaest. super Praedicamenta* 12; Burley, *Tractatus super Praedicamenta* [*De numero praedicament.*] (Peterhouse ms. 184, ff. 175rb–76rb).

[6] Albert the Great, *De praedicamentis* 1.7; Sutton, *In Preadicament.* [*De numero praedicament.*], ed. Conti, p. 196; Scotus, *Quaest. super Praedicamenta* 1 (*Opera phil.* I: 250–1).

OCKHAM'S CRITIQUE AND BURLEY'S EXTREME REALISM

In the second and third decades of the fourteenth century, Ockham argued that the common realist account of the relationship between universals and individuals was inconsistent with their being really identical. His central argument was that if universals are something existing *in re*, really identical with their individuals, then whatever is predicated of individuals must be predicated of their universals too. Hence a unique universal entity (say, human nature) would possess contrary attributes simultaneously (short and tall, young and old), just as different individuals do. This is clearly unacceptable (*In Praedicament.* 8.1; *Summa logicae* I.15).

Such an inconsistency had been foreseen by moderate realists, who had tried to avoid it by introducing the sorts of intermediary distinctions described earlier between individuals and universals considered as second intentions. On the one hand, according to traditional realists, the real identity of universals and individuals had to be maintained in order to safeguard the division of predication into essential and accidental, as well as to maintain the difference between substantial and accidental forms. Like accidental forms, universal substantial forms are somehow present in individual substances and cannot exist without them; so if they, unlike accidental forms, had not been identical with individual substances, as constitutive parts of their being, then they would have been indistinguishable from accidents. Consequently, moderate realists had been forced to speak of identity between universals and individuals. On the other hand, it was evident that not all that was predicated of individuals could be predicated of universals, and vice versa. For instance, it was a common topic in commentaries on *Categories* 3, 1b10–15 that one cannot infer from 'Socrates is a man' and 'man is a species' that 'Socrates is a species,' notwithstanding the identity between *homo* and Socrates.[7] For this reason, it was necessary to limit in some way the transitivity of predication between universals and individuals. The intermediary distinctions considered earlier were the vehicle for satisfying both of these demands.

According to Ockham, there is no room for any further distinction beyond the real one, since any other possible kind of distinction necessarily implies identity (or else it would count as a real distinction), and identity is a transitive, symmetrical, and reflexive relation (*Ordinatio* I.2.6; I.33.1). Hence, the transitivity of predication cannot be limited by this strategy. Moreover, Ockham

---

7 Kilwardby, *In Praedicament.* 4 (Peterhouse ms. 206, f. 44va); Albert the Great, *De praedicamentis* 1.6; Sutton, *In Praedicament.* prolog., ed. Conti, p. 187; Simon of Faversham, *Quaest. super Praedicamenta* 3; Scotus, *Quaest. super Praedicamenta* 9; Burley, *Tractatus super Praedicamenta* [*De regulis praedicationis*] (Peterhouse ms. 184, f. 174va).

accepts the indiscernibility of identicals. As a consequence, he concludes that it is impossible for contradictory properties to be truly asserted of the same thing. Instead, the bearers of those contradictory properties have to be really distinct and independent things (*Ordinatio* I.2.1; I.2.6; I.2.11; *Summa logicae* I.16).[8] Later medieval realists acknowledged that Ockham's critique showed that the traditional realist description of the relation between universals and individuals is untenable, but they were convinced that realism as a whole is still defensible. Two fundamental strategies emerged for formulating a revised form of realism: either to affirm a real distinction between universals and individuals, or to elaborate new notions of identity and difference. The first strategy was that of Burley. At the beginning of his academic career, he was a supporter of moderate realism, but beginning in 1324, in response to Ockham, he developed an original form of Platonic realism. On this view, universals, conceived of as general forms, fully exist outside the mind and are *really distinct* from the individuals in which they are present. In many of his last works he expounds on his new ontology, which is based on a threefold *real* distinction: between universals and individuals; between categorial items (*incomplexa*) and real propositions or states of affairs (*propositiones in re*); and between each of the ten categories.[9]

Like Ockham, Burley rejects any kind of distinction in addition to the real one. He considers identity a transitive, symmetrical, and reflexive relation, and identity and difference two mutually incompatible relations.[10] On the other hand, he claims that universals *in re* fully exist outside the mind and are really distinct from the individuals they are in and are predicated of. Two startling conclusions follow from this. First, a universal has its own being, distinct from the being of the individual that instantiates it. Second, a universal is not a part of that individual. Instead, individual substances are composed of nothing but singular form and matter. The base-level species (*human being*, for instance, or *horse*) is not a constitutive part of the individuals it is in and is predicated of, but is only a form coming together with those individual essences and making their metaphysical structure known: it is the species (namely, the type) that individuals belong to (or instantiate). Once universals are no longer constitutive

---

[8] On real sameness and distinction in Ockham, see Marilyn McCord Adams, "Ockham on Identity and Distinction," *Franciscan Studies* 36 (1976) 5–74.

[9] On Burley's new ontology see Alessandro Conti, "Ontology in Walter Burley's Last Commentary on the *Ars Vetus*," *Franciscan Studies* 50 (1990) 121–76; on the development of his semantic theory see Alessandro Conti, "Significato e verità in Walter Burley," *Documenti e studi sulla tradizione filosofica medievale* 11 (2000) 317–50, and Laurent Cesalli, "Le réalisme propositionnel de Walter Burley," *Archives d'histoire doctrinale et littéraire du moyen âge* 68 (2001) 155–221.

[10] Burley, *Expositio super Praedicamenta* [*De oppositione*], ed. 1509, f. 44rb; *Tractatus de universalibus*, ed. Wöhler, p. 22.

parts of their own individuals, the inconsistencies stressed by Ockham vanish.[11]

The other two main theses of Burley's ontology also depend on what he takes to be necessary in order to defend a realist view of universals. Because he gives up intentional and formal distinctions, and so can no longer reduce the being of universal substantial forms and that of accidental forms to the being of individual substances, Burley is compelled to make the ontological status of *propositiones in re* stronger than it was before. Whereas in his youth he had clearly stated that mental propositions exist in our minds as in their own subjects of inherence, and that real propositions exist in our minds as their intentional objects, in his last commentary on the *Ars vetus* (1337) he affirms that a real proposition (which is the *significatum* of a mental proposition) is a "molecular being" (*ens copulatum*) formed by the entities for which the subject and the predicate of the corresponding mental proposition stand, together with an identity-relation (if the proposition is affirmative) or a non-identity-relation (if the proposition is negative).[12] Moreover, with respect to the problem of the ontological value of the Aristotelian categories, he claims that the division into categories is first and foremost a division of things (*res*) existing outside the mind – using *res* in its strictest sense for an irreducible, fully existing entity. Accordingly, the things in one category are really distinct from those in others. Burley rejects any sort of reductionism, arguing that this compromises the actual goal of a correct categorial theory – namely, the classifying and putting in hierarchical order of all the world items according to their nature, metaphysical structure, and distinctive modes of being.[13]

Despite these new views (namely, that there is a real distinction between universals and individuals, and that the ten categories are all irreducibly real), Burley keeps on supporting without qualification the Aristotelian principle that primary substances are the necessary condition of existence for all other categorial items, including universals (*Cat.* 2b5–6).[14] This is still possible because he holds that universals are forms, and therefore existentially incomplete and

---

[11] Burley, *Expositio in Phys.* prooem., ed. 1501, ff. 8rb–9vb; *Expositio super Praedicamenta* [*De subiecto et praedicato*], ed. 1509, f. 20rb and [*De substantia*], ff. 23rb–vb, 24va; *Expositio super Periherm.* [*De oppositione enuntiationum*], ed. 1509, f. 74rb–va; *Tractatus de universalibus*, ed. Wöhler, pp. 14–40.

[12] Burley, *Expositio super Praedicamenta*, prooem., ed. 1509, ff. 17vb–18va; [*De subiecto et praedicato*], ed. 1509, f. 20rb; [*De priori*], ed. 1509, f. 47va; *Expositio super Periherm.*, prooem., ed. 1509, f. 66ra-b. For his earlier view of propositions, see *Quaest. in Periherm.* 3 and *Commentarius in Periherm.*, ed. Brown, pp. 61–2.

[13] Burley, *Expositio super Praedicamenta* [*De numero praedicament.*], ed. 1509, ff. 21ra–b, 21va–b, 22ra. For Burley's earlier views, see the reference in note 5.

[14] Burley, *Expositio super Praedicamenta* [*De substantia*], ed. 1509, f. 24va.

dependent entities whose existence requires the existence of at least one individual substance. Since he is faithful to Aristotle rather than to Plato on this point, Burley has to build up a sort of mixed theory, where principles of Aristotelian ontology go alongside principles of Platonic ontology. Two difficulties arise from his new system, however. First, it becomes difficult to distinguish essential from accidental predication, since universal substances necessarily presuppose individual substances for their existence, in the same way that accidental forms do. Second, the conclusion that universals have their own being distinct from the being of individuals seems dangerously close to Plato's theory of Forms. As a consequence, many late medieval realists would try other ways of replying to Ockham's charges.

LATE MEDIEVAL REALISM

Because Burley was persuaded that Ockham's arguments were valid, he sought to escape from the resulting inconsistencies by moving toward Platonism. In particular, he renounced his support for the thesis that universal forms have no being apart from the being of individuals. Most later medieval realists, in contrast, retained that anti-Platonic thesis. To escape the contradictions Ockham had described, they instead revised the notions of identity and difference to make room for the distinctive relation of partial identity and difference that they claimed holds between universals and individuals. There were two main lines of strategy. The first was that of some Italian Dominican masters, such as Francis of Prato and Stephen of Rieti in the 1340s, who worked out new definitions for identity and distinction that were inspired by Hervaeus Natalis's notion of conformity. The second approach was that of the most important school of later medieval realists: the so-called "Oxford Realists," started by John Wyclif. Besides Wyclif himself, this school includes the Englishmen Robert Alyngton, William Milverley, William Penbygull, Roger Whelpdale, and John Tarteys, as well as the German John Sharpe and the Italian Paul of Venice. According to the Oxford Realists, universals and individuals are *really* identical but *formally* distinct. In addition, they claimed that the two notions of formal difference and real identity are logically compatible, that predication is a *real* relation between things, and that the ten Aristotelian categories are ten really distinct kinds of things (*res* in the strict sense).[15]

---

[15] On this last point see Wyclif, *De ente praedicamentali* 4; Alyngton, *Super Praedicamenta* [*De numero praedic.*], ed. Conti, pp. 252–3; Paul of Venice, *Super Praedicamenta* [*De numero praedic.*], ed. 1494, ff. 50rb–51ra.

Francis of Prato and Stephen of Rieti both attempt to defend realism by rethinking the relation between universals and individuals.[16] Their goal is to avoid the inconsistencies pointed out by Ockham without going as far as Burley's real distinction between individuals and universals. Toward this end, they develop some of Aquinas's and Hervaeus Natalis's chief intuitions.[17] Like them, Francis and Stephen reject any kind of distinction midway between a real distinction and one of reason. Their basic ideas are that universal forms have no being outside the being of their individuals[18] and that real identity may be more or less close. This is to say that the limit of real identity is entirely real identity, but that two things can be not entirely really identical without being really non-identical and, hence, without being really different.[19] Although the idea that identity comes in degrees is a distinctive one, Francis and Stephen clearly fall into the moderate realist tradition with respect to the problem of universals.[20] The same is true for their defense of the reality and real distinctness of each category. In his *Logica* (I.5.1), Francis observes that all ten Aristotelian categories contain things, but in two different senses of the term, for *res* can signify either a real essence or the mode of being of a real essence. The three absolute categories are things in the former sense of the term, whereas the other seven categories are said to be things in the latter sense.

The most influential of the later scholastic realists was Wyclif.[21] Like the moderate realists, he recognizes three main kinds of universals – ideal universals, formal universals, and intentional universal – and he holds that formal universals

---

[16] On Francis's and Stephen's lives, works, and theories see Fabrizio Amerini, *I trattati De universalibus di Francesco da Prato e Stefano da Rieti (secolo XIV)* (Spoleto: Centro italiano di studi sull'alto medioevo, 2003) 1–56, Christian Rode, *Franciscus de Prato* (Stuttgart: Steiner, 2004), and Fabrizio Amerini, *La logica di Francesco da Prato: con l'edizione critica della* Loyca *e del* Tractatus de voce univoca (Florence: SISMEL, 2005) 1–248, and "What is Real? A Reply to Ockham's Ontological Program," *Vivarium* 43 (2005) 187–212.

[17] Thomas Aquinas, *In Metaphys.* VII.11, VII.13; Hervaeus Natalis, *Quodlibet* I.2 (ed. 1513, f. 7rb–va), I.9 (ff. 19ra–vb, 20rb), II.7 (f. 47rb).

[18] Francis of Prato, *De universalibus* 5, ed. Amerini, p. 110; Stephen of Rieti, *De universalibus*, ed. Amerini, pp. 142–3.

[19] Francis of Prato, *De universalibus* 4, ed. Amerini, pp. 99–100.

[20] Stephen of Rieti, *Super Porphyrium* 1, ed. Amerini, pp. 159–61.

[21] On Wyclif's form of realism see Anthony Kenny, *Wyclif* (Oxford: Clarendon Press, 1985) 1–30; Paul Vincent Spade, "Introduction," in John Wyclif, *On Universals*, tr. A. Kenny (Oxford: Clarendon Press, 1985) vii–xlvii; A. Kenny, "The Realism of *De Universalibus*," in A. Kenny (ed.) *Wyclif in his Times* (Oxford: Clarendon Press, 1986) 17–29; Alessandro Conti, "Analogy and Formal Distinction: On the Logical Basis of Wyclif's Metaphysics," *Medieval Philosophy and Theology* 6 (1997) 133–65; Laurent Cesalli, "Le 'pan-propositionnalisme' de Jean Wyclif," *Vivarium* 43 (2005) 124–55; Paul Vincent Spade, "Insolubles," in E. Zalta (ed.) *The Stanford Encyclopedia of Philosophy*: http://plato.stanford.edu; and Conti, "Wyclif's Logic and Metaphysics," in I. C. Levy (ed.) *A Companion to John Wyclif* (Leiden: Brill, 2006) 67–125.

are really identical with their individuals. In his view, universals and individuals share the same reality – that of the individuals – but have opposite constituent principles. On his terminology, they are really (*realiter*) the same but formally (*formaliter*) distinct. In this way, Wyclif both accepts the very core of the traditional realist account of the relationship between universals and individuals and tries to improve on it by defining its predicative structure more accurately. Because of the formal distinction, not everything predicable of individuals can be directly attributed to universals and vice versa, although an indirect predication is always possible. As a consequence, Wyclif distinguishes three non-mutually exclusive types of predication, each more general than the preceding one. In the *Tractatus de universalibus* (1, ed. Mueller, pp. 28–30, 34–6) they are described as formal predication, predication by essence (*secundum essentiam*), and habitudinal predication (*secundum habitudinem*). Habitudinal predication does not require any kind of identity between the item(s) signified by the subject term and the item(s) signified by the predicate term, but formal predication and essential predication do. Thus, the ontological presuppositions of the most general type of predication are different from those of the other two. Wyclif aims to unify the various kinds of predication by means of a unique basic relation of partial identity, the formal distinction, which he characterizes as that by which things differ from each other even though they are constitutive elements of the same single essence or supposit (ibid. 4, pp. 90–1). The formal distinction is the main kind of transcendental relation holding among the items in Wyclif's world (a transcendental relation being one that does not fall into the category of Relation and that can connect items belonging to different categories or not belonging to any category). It is intended to explain both why one and the same individual substance (say, Socrates) is *one thing*, even if it contains in itself a lot of simpler entities, and how many different entities can constitute just one thing. Moreover, the formal distinction accounts for the relations between a concrete accident and its substance – for instance, between being white (*album*) and the substance in which the corresponding abstract form, whiteness, inheres. Consequently, the formal distinction also plays a central role in discussions of the categories.

Wyclif is a realist with respect to the categories: he holds that the extramental world is divided into ten genera of beings, none of which can be reduced to another. Thus, like Burley, he insists that the items falling into the accidental categories, considered by themselves, in an absolute manner, are forms inherent in composite substances. In this way, Wyclif attempts to safeguard the reality of accidents as well as their distinctness both from substance and from one another. At the same time, he affirms that accidents depend on substances for their existence, since he subscribes to the Aristotelian thesis that primary substances are a necessary condition for the existence of all other categorial items.[22] Indeed, Wyclif can insist on this doctrine in a very strong form, since accidents considered from the point of view of their existence as concrete beings are only *formally*, but not *really* distinct from the substance in which they are present and that they affect. Opposed to the separability of accidents from their substance (a view that became notorious because it clashed with the doctrine of transubstantiation), Wyclif describes accidents as mere modes of that substance.[23]

Wyclif's philosophy exercised an enormous influence on the forms of later medieval realism. In particular, his intuitions concerning universals, predication, and categories played a large role in the logic and metaphysics of many authors, especially of the Oxford Realists.[24] According to these authors, formal universals are common natures in virtue of which the individuals that share them are what they are. Humanity, for instance, is the form by which every human being is formally a human being. Like Wyclif, the Oxford Realists agree that common natures exist *in actu* in the external world and that they are really identical to, but formally distinct from, their own individuals.[25] Different authors, however, analyze predication and identity in different ways. Alyngton – and, some years later, Sharpe, Milverley, and Tarteys – divide predication into formal predication and predication by essence, which Alyngton also calls "remote inherence" (*inhaerentia remota*). Predication by essence requires only a partial identity between the real subject and predicate. These need to share some, but not all, metaphysical component parts. Formal predication, in contrast, requires the direct presence in the entity denoted by the subject term of the

---

[22] Wyclif, *De ente praedicamentali*, 4 (ed. Beer, pp. 30–2), 5 (pp. 42–3), 6 (pp. 48–50), 7 (pp. 61–2).

[23] Wyclif, *De actibus animae* 2.4 (ed. Dziewicki, *Miscellanea philosophica* pp. 122–3, 127). For Wyclif's treatment of accidents as it pertains to the Eucharist, see Kenny, *Wyclif*, 68–90; see also Paul Bakker, "Réalisme et rémanence: la doctrine eucharistique de Jean Wyclif," in M.-T. Fumagalli Beonio Brocchieri and S. Simonetta (eds.) *Wyclif: logica, teologia, politica* (Florence: SISMEL, 2003) 87–112.

[24] For analyses of their main works and doctrines and information on Wyclif's influence see Alessandro Conti, "Teoria degli universali e teoria della predicazione nel trattato *De universalibus* di William Penbygull: discussione e difesa della posizione di Wyclif," *Medioevo* 8 (1982) 137–66; Alessandro Conti, "Studio storico-critico," in John Sharpe, *Quaestio super universalia* (Florence: Olschki, 1990) pp. 211–38, 295–336; Alain de Libera, "Questions de réalisme: sur deux arguments antiockhamistes de John Sharpe," *Revue de métaphysique et de morale* 97 (1992) 83–110; Alessandro Conti, "Linguaggio e realtà nel commento alle *Categorie* di Robert Alyngton," *Documenti e studi sulla tradizione filosofica medievale* 4 (1993) 179–242; Alain de Libera, *La querelle des universaux de Platon à la fin du Moyen Age* (Paris: Seuil, 1996) pp. 402–28; Alessandro Conti, "Johannes Sharpe's Ontology and Semantics: Oxford Realism Revisited," *Vivarium* 43 (2005) 156–86; Conti, "Wyclif's Logic and Metaphysics," 118–25.

[25] Alyngton, *Super Praedicamenta* [*De substantia*], ed. Conti, p. 268; Penbygull, *De universalibus*, ed. Conti, pp. 181, 189; Milverley, *Compendium de quinque universalibus*, ed. Conti, p. 163; Tarteys, *Problema correspondens libello Porphyrii*, ed. Conti, pp. 178–9; Whelpdale, *Tractatus de universalibus*, ed. Conti, pp. 193–4; Sharpe, *Quaestio super universalia*, ed. Conti, pp. 91–2; Paul of Venice, *Quaestio de universalibus*, ed. Conti, p. 199; *Super Porphyrium* [*De genere*], ed. 1494, f. 14vb.

form connoted by the predicate term. Instances of predication by essence (or remote inherence) are '(What is) singular is (what is) common' (*Singulare est commune*) and 'Humanity is (something) running' (*humanitas est currens*).[26] 'Man is an animal' and 'Socrates is white' are instances of formal predication.

Unlike the others, Penbygull and Whelpdale add a third, causal kind of predication. According to them, there is causal predication when the item signified by the predicate term is not present in any way in the item signified by the subject term, but the subject has been caused by the predicate (for example: *A day is the effect of the sun around the earth*).[27] These authors differ in other ways as well. Penbygull and Milverley, for instance, distinguish between non-identity and difference, deny that difference implies non-identity, and affirm that the two notions of difference and real identity are logically compatible, thus admitting that there are degrees of distinctness.[28] Sharpe, in his turn, treats identity and difference as the two possible inverse measures of the coincidence of the metaphysical components of two given entities. On his view, although formal identity is stronger than real identity (since the former entails the latter), a real distinction is stronger than a formal distinction (since the latter is entailed by the former). Sharpe also recognized degrees within the formal distinction (*Quaest. super universalia*, ed. Conti, pp. 91–2).

Among the Oxford Realists, the most original was Paul of Venice, who studied in Oxford in 1390–3 before returning to Padua, where he spread Oxford Realism to a wider audience.[29] He fully developed the new form of realism started up by Wyclif, but was open also to influences from other directions, giving serious attention to moderate realism and critically discussing the doctrines of the main fourteenth-century nominalists. Paul's world consists of finite beings (such as human beings and horses), which are aggregates of an individual substance and a host of formal items (substantial and accidental forms, both universal and singular) existing in and through that individual substance. The components of finite beings are nothing but the categorial items themselves, together with their own modes of being. All these items are real, in the sense that they are mind-independent beings, none of which can be reduced to another; still, only individual substances *exist*, inasmuch as only they are actual beings

---

[26] Alyngton, *Super Praedicamenta* [*De substantia*], ed. Conti, p. 289; Milverley, *Compendium*, p. 160; Tarteys, *Problema*, Lambeth Palace ms. 393, ff. 204(235)r–v, 209(240)r–v; Sharpe, *Quaestio super universalia*, ed. Conti, pp. 89–91.

[27] Penbygull, *De universalibus*, ed. Conti, pp. 186–8; Whelpdale, *Tractatus de universalibus*, ed. Conti, pp. 190–2.

[28] Penbygull, *De universalibus*, ed. Conti, pp. 190–1; Milverley, *Compendium*, ed. Conti, p. 163.

[29] On Paul of Venice's form of realism see Alessandro Conti, *Esistenza e verità: forme e strutture del reale in Paolo Veneto e nel pensiero filosofico del tardo medioevo* (Rome: Edizioni dell'Istituto Storico Italiano per il Medio Evo, 1996).

(*entia in actu*). Individuation thus involves the passage not just from universal to individual, but also from being (*esse*), which is the universal condition of reality for every kind of entity,[30] to existence (*existentia*), which is the mode of being peculiar to individual substances only. Common natures, which correspond to the ideas in the mind of God, are the main type of beings within Paul's world; individuals exist only as material substrates (*partes subiectivae*) of the natures themselves, since the principle of individuation (the *haecceitas*, *ratio individualis*, or *suppositalis*) within the individual compound plays the role of the matter that is to be determined, while the common nature plays the role of the determining form.[31]

Like the other Oxford Realists, Paul claims that universals and individuals are really the same and only formally distinct. Yet, since common natures have a kind of being of their own, if all the individuals belonging to some natural species were annihilated, their corresponding nature would continue to have being, even though only potentially, as a mere metaphysical possibility (*Super Porphyrium* prooem. [ed. 1494, f. 8va]). In commenting on Aristotle's seemingly contrary claim at *Categories* 2b5–6, Paul restates that same thesis, adding that a certain common nature would be annihilated if and only if all the individuals belonging to the corresponding natural species were destroyed not only in relation to their actual existence, but also in relation to their potential being.[32] Since the potential being of individuals is nothing but the essential being proper to universals,[33] the destruction of the individuals in relation to their potential being just *is* the destruction of universals themselves.

CONCLUSION

If we consider the moderate realist view of universals, it is easy to see that it is determined by a general evaluation of the *Categories*, together with the main principles and theses stated by Aristotle in that book. When moderate realists interpret the relation between universals and individuals in terms of identity, they are trying to save the ontological primacy of individual substances, while at the same time reading in a realist way the nature and division of predication, and the twofold partition (into substantial and accidental, individual and universal items) described in the second chapter of the treatise. On the one hand, they assume

---

[30] Paul of Venice, *In Metaph.* IV.1.1 (Pavia ms. 324, f. 125vb); *Super Porphyrium* [*De specie*], ed. 1494, f. 22rb.
[31] On Paul's theory of individuation see Alessandro Conti, "Paul of Venice on Individuation," *Recherches de théologie et philosophie médiévales* 65 (1998) 107–32.
[32] *Super Praedicamenta* [*De substantia*], ed. 1494, f. 57va–b.
[33] *Summa philosophiae naturalis* VI.1 (ed. 1503, ff. 92vb–93ra), VI.5 (ff. 95vb–96ra).

that being a universal is equivalent to being said of something as a subject; on the other hand, they consider the being-said-of relation as a real relation between two different kinds of beings. As a result, they are compelled to postulate a form of identity between universals and individuals: universals are (metaphysical) parts of their individuals. Otherwise, it would be impossible to distinguish the being-said-of relation (essential predication) from the relation of being in something as a subject (accidental predication, or inherence). Both universal substances and accidents are somehow present in individual substances and neither can exist apart from individual substances, but universals are parts of individuals and accidents are not (*Cat.* 2, 1a24–5). Still, universals and individuals cannot be entirely identical, since there is not a complete transitivity in predication between them.

Realists of the fourteenth century elaborate new notions of identity and distinction, judging that the logical machinery they have at their disposal is insufficient for their purposes. Because of Ockham's critique of moderate realism and the formal distinction, almost all the realists of the later Middle Ages become dissatisfied with Henry's and Scotus's formulations of distinctions midway between the real distinction and the distinction of reason. They therefore try to improve the realist theory of universals by modifying both the standard Aristotelian analysis of predication and the notion of formal distinction. Indeed, the only other possible way of overcoming Ockham's arguments against realism is to assume, as Burley does, that universals and individuals are really distinct – a choice that entails a change from an Aristotelian to a Platonic metaphysics and that leads to a paradoxical result: the partial dissolution of the Aristotelian doctrine of categories. Within the new metaphysical system of the Oxford Realists, universals and individuals, as well as essential and accidental predication, are far removed from their Aristotelian patterns. According to the moderate realists of the second half of the thirteenth century, the actual existence of at least one individual is necessary in order to guarantee the existence *in potentia* of the corresponding universal. In Paul of Venice's view, in contrast – which is the final culmination of the realist tradition initiated by Wyclif – the being of a universal essence is a necessary condition for the existence of individuals, but not vice versa. Thus the metaphysics proper to the Oxford Realists is substantially a Platonic metaphysics, where universal essences, and not individual substances, are the main kind of being.[34]

---

[34] A comprehensive survey of the connected problems of universals and of categories in the late Middle Ages is provided in Alessandro Conti, "Categories and Universals in the Later Middle Ages," in L. Newton (ed.) *Medieval Commentaries on Aristotle's* Categories (Leiden: Brill, 2008) 369–409.

48

NOMINALISM IN THE LATER MIDDLE AGES*

JOËL BIARD

There is no dispute that nominalism is a major movement in logic and philosophy during the later Middle Ages. Not only are some major thinkers connected with it, such as William of Ockham and John Buridan, but it is the place where some decisive innovations fully unfold, such as the theory of mental language and of the universal as sign. Even so, the term 'nominalism' seems uncertain and equivocal, for several reasons.

First, it is commonly admitted that there are two great periods of medieval nominalism: the twelfth century and the fourteenth century. The historical and theoretical links between the two are, however, far from clear. The questions that constitute the conceptual core of the confrontations between schools in the dialectic of the twelfth century – such as the question of the unity of names, the nature of inference, and the reality of relations within the Trinity – are not found in the same terms two centuries later; as for universals, although Abaelard criticizes the theory of real universals, he posits a *status* which, without being a thing, must account for the imposition of universal names, and for which no equivalent is found in the fourteenth century. The rapprochement of the two periods, the exaggerated place accorded to the problem of universals, and the major role attributed to Abaelard are due to a historiography that began in France in the nineteenth century with Victor Cousin, but that current knowledge renders more and more problematic.

Second, the nominalism of the later Middle Ages embraces authors whose doctrines present important differences. Although Ockham and Buridan offer similar analyses of language, the status they attribute to concepts is different. Their theories of the reference of terms also diverge in various ways. This does not preclude a rapprochement, but it leads one to wonder whether the label 'nominalism' is not sometimes too imprecise to characterize these doctrines. This is even more the case if one considers the diverse views of

---

* Translated from the French by Amandine Catala.

fourteenth-century authors like Gregory of Rimini and Peter of Ailly, or the fifteenth-century Jerome Pardo.

Finally, it must be recalled that no author of the fourteenth century claims to be a nominalist, even though in the twelfth century there was indeed a sect of Nominales. The designation is therefore retrospective. Although from the beginning of the fifteenth century there begins to be talk of "terminists" to designate those logicians who study the properties of terms, this does not exclusively designate nominalists, and the term 'nominalist' itself comes even later. It seems that clans confronting each other in Paris in the fifteenth century begin to identify themselves as belonging to "schools," even if their conflicts arose out of institutional as much as doctrinal reasons. The famous letter sent by the nominalists to Louis XI serves as a landmark. It is this text that defines how 'nominalist' was understood at the time, and that accounts for the picture we still have today of later medieval nominalism.[1] Let us consider the core of this letter.

In 1474, Louis XI issued a decree against the Nominales. The latter responded with a manifesto that makes clear how they saw the cleavage:

We call *nominales* those doctors who do not multiply things that are chiefly signified by terms according to the multiplication of terms. We call *reales*, by contrast, those who hold that things are multiplied with the multiplicity of terms... Further, we call *nominales* those who pay attention and study to know all the properties of terms, upon which depend the truth and falsity of propositions and without which one cannot make any definitive judgment about the truth and falsity of propositions.

What can we conclude from this? First, the importance granted to the analysis of language. Second, the use of a tool for that analysis, namely the theory of the properties of terms, which in itself is not nominalist (since it was framed in the thirteenth century by realist masters), but which afterward was the object of notable improvements by Ockham and Buridan (see Chapters 11 and 12). That which, by contrast, is not evoked at all is the ontology of the singular. This can, no doubt, be read into the first remarks – namely, the demand not to multiply things according to the categories of terms, although this also has a narrower sense in the context of disputes over the reality of Aristotle's ten

---

[1] On the doctrinal and institutional history of these cleavages, see Zénon Kaluza, "Les sciences et leurs langages. Note sur le statut du 29 décembre 1340 et le prétendu statut perdu contre Ockham," in L. Bianchi (ed) *Filosfia e teologia nel trecento: studi in ricordo di Eugenio Randi* (Louvain-la-Neuve: Fédération internationale des instituts d'études médiévales, 1994) 197–258. For Victor Cousin, see *Ouvrages inédits d'Abélard pouvant servir à l'histoire de la philosophie scolastique en France* (Paris: Imprimerie Royale, 1836). The text of the exchange between Louis XI and the nominalists is edited in Franz Ehrle, *Die Sentenzenkommentar Peters von Candia, des Pisaner Papstes Alexanders V* (Münster: Aschendorff, 1925) pp. 322–6.

categories, as we will see below. Also missing are several theses at the crossroads between theology and logic, such as the radical contingency of the created world and the methodological use of God's "absolute power" to emphasize the ontological structure of the created world. As for the forefathers they give themselves, nominalists of the time cite Ockham, followed by a more or less heterogeneous list of authors, such as John of Mirecourt, Gregory of Rimini, Buridan, Peter of Ailly, Marsilius of Inghen, and Albert of Saxony. But in fact their true inspiration, as we will see, is John Buridan, and this will remain true up to the time of John Major, who teaches in Paris in the first decades of the sixteenth century.

NOMINALISM AND LANGUAGE

Although all of the Middle Ages paid special attention to language, the nominalist attitude goes further. The critique of language is treated as the necessary precondition for any philosophical or scientific analysis (including theology, considered as a science). It is this critique of language and its illusions that allows for a solution to the problem of universals and the status of abstract terms by rejecting various linguistic illusions. This critique also allows for the development of a metaphysics whose ontology remains parsimonious, and for the analysis of the language of physics and theology. The paramount question for understanding the nature of later medieval nominalism is, thus, the status of language and the signs that compose it.[2]

SIGNS AND THEIR PROPERTIES

Ockham begins his *Summa logicae* with a discussion of the nature of a sign and its divisions. A term, which is the elementary component of language, is a sign. William takes, with modifications, the Augustinian definition of a sign;[3] for him, it is "anything that, when apprehended, makes something else be known" (*Summa logicae* I.1). Signs can be of three kinds: written, spoken, or mental. A sign corresponds to something other than itself (except in cases where it reflects itself as sign), but the logical sign, unlike other signs (a fire, a storefront sign), is part of a set that is composed according to certain rules, and it has properties that are connected to this regulated use. Finally, any sign corresponds directly to the thing it signifies (its significate), and for which it substitutes. This means that the signification of a spoken sign is defined in relation to

---

[2] See Joël Biard, *Logique et théorie du signe au XIVe siècle* (Paris: Vrin, 1989).
[3] Augustine, *De doctrina christiana* II.1.1.

the signified thing itself rather than to the associated concept to which it is subordinated, even though this concept is itself also a sign. Thus, among signs, some are conventional (namely, written and spoken signs), whereas others are natural (namely, concepts). The naturalness of conceptual signification can be understood either through a natural relation of resemblance or through a relation of causality between the signified thing and the concept that arises – it is this second relation that Ockham privileges in his definition of the conceptual sign (*Summa logicae* I.12).

Inasmuch as they are destined to be part of propositions, linguistic signs have, in addition to their signification (that is, their relation of possible substitution with regard to real things), other semantical properties they exert in virtue of their propositional use. These are the "properties of terms," such as supposition (the reference of a term in a certain propositional context) and its variations (ampliation, restriction), as well as appellation or connotation (namely, the signifier's correspondence to something other than that for which the term supposits, as the term 'white' refers to an individual and connotes a quality: such or such whiteness) (see Chapter 11).[4]

Language is not, however, composed only of such categorematic terms. It also includes terms that do not have a proper signification determined by themselves, the so-called syncategorematic terms (see Chapter 11). Logic devotes considerable space to the study of these terms, both with respect to their mode of signification (beginning with Peter of Ailly, it is said that they signify not some thing or things [*aliquid, aliqua*], but somehow [*aliqualiter*]), and with respect to the effects they produce in the proposition.

John Buridan subsequently articulates a somewhat different connection between spoken terms and mental terms.[5] For him, the spoken term has both an immediate signification, which is the concept, and an ultimate signification, which is the thing. The concept is the reason according to which a spoken term signifies, which leads to an original theory of the "appellation of reason" – that is, of the term's evoking, in certain contexts (for example, in the context of aspectual verbs such as 'to know' or 'to promise'), the concept according to which it corresponds to such or such thing.[6]

---

[4] See Marilyn Mc Cord Adams, *William Ockham* (Notre Dame, IN: University of Notre Dame Press, 1987); Cyrille Michon, *Nominalisme: la théorie de la signification de Guillaume d'Ockham* (Paris: Vrin, 1994).

[5] *Summulae* IV (*De suppositionibus*) 1.2, and esp. *Summulae* IX (*De practica sophismatum*) 1. See also Biard, *Logique,* pp. 162–202; Jack Zupko, *John Buridan: Portrait of a Fourteenth-Century Arts Master* (Notre Dame: University of Notre Dame Press, 2003) pp. 150–63.

[6] *De suppositionibus* 5.3.

On these semiological and semantic questions, the Ockhamist position is taken again by Albert of Saxony, then by Peter of Ailly. We still find its echoes in Blasius of Parma in his *Quaestiones* on Peter of Spain at the end of the fourteenth century and the beginning of the fifteenth. Marsilius of Inghen's treatises on the properties of terms, however, follows Buridan, even while modifying certain details.

MENTAL LANGUAGE

It is on the basis of this semantic theory that Ockham can develop in an unprecedented way the theory of mental language.[7] He refers both to Boethius's three kinds of propositions and to Augustine's doctrine of the inner word, but in fact his theory has no antecedent. The mental domain can be considered as a collection of conceptual elements that themselves carry semantic properties, combined according to certain syntactic rules. So, while Ockham takes and improves on the already well-established theory of the referential properties of terms, he treats concepts as what first carry these properties.

Mental language includes diverse elements that assume different functions, and that have properties mirroring those of spoken language. It includes names (nouns and adjectives), verbs, pronouns, adverbs, conjunctions, and prepositions, with accidents for names such as case, number, and comparison.

Many debates have arisen, as much among scholars today as among medieval authors, about the structure of mental language, including whether there are connotative terms or synonyms among mental terms, and whether the act corresponding to a "mental proposition" is simple or composite. With respect to this last issue, Gregory of Rimini holds that since the mind is not extended, a proposition in mental language cannot strictly have any parts. This is so, at least, in what is properly referred to as mental language, which is prior to spoken language and which must be distinguished from mental language loosely speaking, which is a mere mental image of vocal language. This question would be debated into the sixteenth century.[8] The Buridanian tradition also emphasizes the linguistic structure of the mental proposition. As for Peter of Ailly, his treatise on *Concepts* radicalizes the subordination of spoken language to mental language, claiming that the structure of mental language is the first and proper syntactic

---

[7] Claude Panaccio, *Le discours intérieur de Platon à Guillaume d'Ockham* (Paris: Seuil, 1999).

[8] E. J. Ashworth, *Language and Logic* (Boston: Reidel, 1974); "Theories of Propositions: Some Early Sixteenth Century Discussions," *Franciscan Studies* 38 (1978) 81–121; "Mental Language and the Unity of Propositions: A Semantic Problem Discussed by Early Sixteenth Century Logicians," *Franciscan Studies* 41 (1981) 61–96.

combination from which the elements of spoken language draw their rules of construction.

UNIVERSALS AS SIGNS

However it is defined, nominalism entails the ontological thesis of the singularity of being; thus, there are only individuals. Assuredly, no one imagines that common natures exist in the way singular things do, but many have found it indispensable to grant them *some* form of being or subsistence. The nominalist denies that beings can take on any such forms or degrees of being: for the nominalist, in contrast to what the Neoplatonist tradition suggested, anything that is, is singular – and, consequently it is so by itself, without the need to be individualized out of natures or essences. Ockham constantly asserts this irreducible singularity: "Anything one can imagine is, by itself, without anything being added to it, numerically one, singular thing" (*In Porphyr.* proem. sec. 2, ed. *Opera phil.* II: 10). Similarly, for Buridan, "all beings exist in a singular way" (*Quaest. de anima* I.5; *De differentia universalis ad individuum*, p. 153).

This is why, according to the nominalists, the question of universals[9] should not be addressed by focusing chiefly on the being of the universal. Rather, one must admit from the start that the universal is a sign. If one accepts the previously established principles of semiology, the question might thus seem to be settled as soon as it is asked. This is not the case, however, because language inherently carries realist illusions, if only by using common names. Moreover, it is not clear what an individual is: there are changing realities (such as a human being who remains numerically the same through the different stages of life), collective entities (France, for example, or the Franciscan Order), mass nouns (such as 'water'), and so on. Ontological nominalism will thus have to be justified not by a direct proof (it functions here as a first principle), but by the critique of any form of realism.

Accordingly, Ockham strives to show the contradictions in John Duns Scotus's doctrine of common natures (see Chapter 47). After having posited in *Summa logicae* I.14 that the universal is a sign, principally a mental sign, he immediately goes on in the next chapter to criticize the idea of the universal as a substance, whether it be something numerically the same or else multiple. Still, one might maintain that the universal is somehow in individuals without positing it as subsisting by itself. It is therefore necessary to mount a direct attack on Scotus's position (in I.16). The basis of this critique is a strict account of

---

[9] On this question, see the detailed study by Alain de Libera, *La querelle des universaux de Platon à la fin du Moyen Âge* (Paris: Seuil, 1996).

distinctions that – setting aside mere differences in manner of signification – admits only of real distinctions. If there are two really distinct things, then God could make one exist without the other, even if they are naturally inseparable. Thus armed, Ockham resists both the idea of a common nature that would be really identical to the individual, yet formally distinct, as well as the idea of an individualizing difference such as 'Socrateity.' He concludes that the universal is a sign that is predicable of more than one individual, where the Aristotelian idea of a predicable (which had been ontologized by Porphyry) is understood in a decidedly semiological sense: "Any universal . . . is universal only by signification, because it is the sign of several things" (*Summa logicae* I.14). The universal is thus nothing like a *flatus vocis*, as the twelfth-century nominalist Roscelin famously held; it is not an empty sound, but on the contrary a signifying term.

Yet what does the universal signify? It cannot signify a common *nature*, since only individuals exist. According to Ockham, its signification is explained by *multiple reference*: it signifies a plurality of things. From the cognitive point of view, this thesis relies on a theory of the concept, explained in his *Commentary on the Sentences*, according to which concepts arise out of some sort of initial contact with things.[10] The concept is the act of conceiving one or more things, either intuitively or abstractively. From the logical–linguistic point of view, the concept signifies this plurality in a confused way; depending on how it is placed within a proposition, it can refer either to the whole of this plurality ('dogs are mammals') or to a part ('Labradors are dogs').

One may, nonetheless, wonder how to explain this multiple reference.[11] For Ockham, it is founded on a certain resemblance: individuals can be similar, and even "maximally similar" in the case of individuals of the same species. This resemblance is not a real relation in the sense of being some further entity beyond the items that resemble one another; it is not a "little thing among things." It is instead the fact that identical qualities or properties can be signified by the same mental sign, if I apply that sign to these individuals not discretely (to one or the other) but jointly (to all of them at once).

John Buridan discusses universals in various places, especially in his *Questions on Porphyry*. There he distinguishes between four senses of the universal. First, in logic, a quantifier such as 'all' or 'no' is said to be universal. Second, universal

---

[10] See, e.g., *Ordinatio* prol., q . 9 and *Quaest. Phys.* 7. See also Joël Biard, *Guillaume d'Ockham: Logique et philosophie* (Paris: Presses Universitaires de France, 1997) pp. 67–75.

[11] Claude Panaccio, *Les mots, les concepts et les choses. Le sémantique de Guillaume d'Occam et le nominalisme d'aujourd'hui* (Montréal: Bellarmin, 1991) pp. 253–67.

propositions are distinguished from particular and singular propositions. Third, one speaks of a universal cause or a universal by causality. This designates entities that are causes of many effects, as God or the celestial intelligences are. This idea also evokes realist theories of the universal such as that of Robert Grosseteste in the thirteenth century, for whom universals are both principles of being and principles of knowledge, in a hierarchical conception of causes (*In Post. anal.* I.7). In Buridan, the sense is weakened, but the idea of a "cause of many" remains. It is only in this sense that the universal can be a substance. For Buridan, however, this sense is irrelevant to the question raised by Porphyry, that of the being and subsistence, separated or not, of genera and species. Only the fourth, final sense is relevant: the universal by predication, signification, and supposition. This universal is such because it signifies many things, and when it assumes a certain role (subject or predicate) in a proposition, it is able to refer to them.[12]

After Ockham and Buridan, the nominalist account of universals remains unchanged at its core: the universal is a sign, either conceptual or vocal. Later authors, beginning with Albert of Saxony,[13] adopt those expressions by Buridan that underline the exclusively logico–linguistic interpretation of predication.[14] And, when faced with various resurgences of realism in Oxford and Paris, nominalists generally respond with these Buridanian theses.

At the beginning of the sixteenth century, John of Celaya, a student of John Major, lectures on Aristotle "*secundum triplicem viam beate Thome, realium et nominalium.*" Thus discussions of schools or movements – the Thomistic way, the way of the *reales* (in this case, the Scotists), and the way of the Nominales – have become an integral part of reflection and exposition in logic and in philosophy. John of Celaya himself leans toward the last of these ways; he sets forth five main positions regarding universals, the last of which is then considered under several interpretations (*Expositio in librum Porphyrii* [ed. 1516, f. 5rb]).

The first, attributed to the Epicureans, is that the soul is material and the universal is nothing. It is quickly pushed aside because it would make science

---

[12] See *Quaestiones libri Porphyrii* 4 (ed. Tatarzynski, p. 139): "In the fourth way, which is more relevant here, something is called 'universal' by predication – that is, because it is naturally apt to be predicated of many things. And in this way a universal is a significant term that can be the subject or the predicate in a categorical proposition." See also *Summulae* II (*De praedicabilibus*) 2.1.2 and *Quaest. de anima* I.5.

[13] *Quaest. in artem veterem* prooem. secs. 60–1; *Quaest. circa logicam* 10; *Perutilis logica* I.10–11. See also Christoph Kann, *Die Eigenschaften der Termini: eine Untersuchung zur "Perutilis logica" Alberts von Sachsen* (Leiden: Brill, 1994).

[14] "Such a universal by predication is called a universal by signification, because it signifies indifferently many things, and is called a universal by supposition because it supposits indifferently for many things" (Buridan, *Quaest. Porph.* 4, p. 139).

impossible. The second opinion is that of Plato and the Stoics. For them, universals, called ideas, exist by themselves and are exemplary causes of things. This position is rejected because of the separation that would make impossible any connection between the universal and that of which it is a universal. The third posits the universal as innate in us rather than the result of abstraction. No names are mentioned, but this view suggests Augustinianism. The fourth claims that the universal arises from an agent intellect that is God or an intelligence, and seems to evoke (here again without any names being mentioned) Greco-Arab Aristotelianism and its revivals in thirteenth-century scholastics like Albert the Great. The fifth and last opinion is that of Aristotle and his followers, who hold that the universal is *in* the many, but that it is still one thing, beyond the many things. Only this view is retained; it becomes the object of the three interpretations that John develops: one according to the doctrine of Thomas Aquinas, another according to the realism of the Subtle Doctor (Scotus), and a third according to the nominalists, whose doctrine is from the start characterized as "the most likely of all."

John of Celaya's attacks on realism rely on positions defended by George of Brussels at the end of the fifteenth century. The universal is defined as "a simple, univocal, formally common categorematic term." The expression "formally common" is explained in the following way: "By the term 'formally common,' it is meant that this term has a common connotation if it is a connotative term, and that if it is an absolute term, then it is a common one" (ibid., f. 7va). There are three kinds of universal (written, mental, and spoken), and the mental universal signifies naturally. In sum, John of Celaya embraces the conception of the universal as a term, with the result that the sciences are sciences of propositions, in which terms represent things.

Yet although universals are a central issue for the nominalists, no less important is the question of the ten Aristotelian categories.

THE CATEGORIES AS MODES OF SIGNIFICATION

From late antiquity, there is a question of whether the categories are names, thoughts, or things. Late medieval nominalism, addressing this issue, criticizes realist accounts of the categories but transforms the problem. The categories are not "genera of being" but types of terms, and so types of signs, either vocal or conceptual, classified according to the type of question to which they provide an answer: *quid? quale? quantum?* and so on. A term from the category of Substance is that which provides a correct answer to the question "what is?" (*Quid est?*)

This semiological conception of the categories is just as strong in John Buridan:

certain predicable terms signify the substance, without any extra connotation, and they fall under the category of Substance. Others signify or connote something about the substance (*circa substantiam*), so that, when said of primary substances, they signify not only what it is but how it is (*qualis est*), and they fall under the category of Quality, and similarly of Quantity and of others.

(*Summulae* III [De praedicamenta] 1.8)

Earlier in the fourteenth century, Walter Burley, in defending a competing form of realism, draws two interpretative lines: one, which he dates back to Boethius and Simplicius, according to which Aristotle's *Categories* deals chiefly with significative vocal sounds (*de vocibus significativis*); another, found in Avicenna and Averroes, according to which category theory deals "chiefly with things, and with vocal sounds in a secondary manner and by way of consequence" (*Expositio super artem veterem, Comm. Cat.*, Prol.). Two centuries later, John of Celaya also mentions a *magna controversia inter doctores*, and literally copies Burley's terms, simply adding a few more recent authors in one or the other of these interpretative lines, including Burley himself and Paul of Venice on the "realist" side (see Chapter 47). But, as a good student of John Major, Celaya holds as more true the opinion according to which categories are only signs.

The controversy about the categories is not exhausted by these general considerations about their status. Behind this first question another immediately follows – namely, which categories of terms properly and directly correspond to things. As such, this question concerns the furnishing of the world. For Ockham, there are only two kinds of terms that properly and directly correspond to real things: substantial terms and qualitative terms. Beyond individual substances, Ockham admits only particular qualities (this white, that black); he rejects at length anything that would turn quantity into something distinct from substance. Thus, quantitative terms signify only certain dispositions of substances or qualities. The thesis is a delicate one because it has consequences for the doctrine of transubstantiation: Aquinas had assigned quantity as the real subject of qualities during the substantial change occurring in the sacrament of the altar. In his theological texts, Ockham strives to show that God can, in virtue of his omnipotence, separate the quality from the substance that is normally its subject (see, in particular, his *Tractatus de corpore Christi*). Buridan, in contrast, has a more nuanced position on this point: in *Summulae* III he sticks with an analysis of the modes of predication dealing with quantitative terms (*De praedicamenta* 3.3), but in his *Physics* he wonders whether the substance and the quantity are really identical. Relying on physical arguments, he leans there toward a real distinction between substance and what he calls "magnitude" (*Quaest. Phys.* I.8).

The other most controversial category undergoing "reduction" is Relation. Ockham wants to show that it is by no means a "little thing among things," something real through which substances would be linked with one another.[15] It is, rather, only a way of signifying several things that happen to have certain qualities, with respect to which it might be said, for example, that they resemble each other, or that one is the father of the other. Later nominalists add only nuances to this schema, without fundamentally calling it into question. Albert of Saxony, for example, emphasizes the conceptual aspect of the relation by making it "an act of the mind that links one thing to another."[16]

A COMMON APPROACH, AND A HISTORY

In addition to a few shared theses, one could mention numerous divergences among the nominalists. Thus, with respect to the signification of a proposition, one encounters a whole range of positions, going from Buridan's rejection of any proper and adequate significate of the proposition (beyond what the terms signify) all the way to Gregory of Rimini's defense of such a proper significate (which he calls the *complexe significabile*), and in between the different ways of treating propositions as *modi rerum*. (Although modes are usually understood as features of substances, they are sometimes assimilated to propositions or states of affairs – in the work of Nicole Oresme, for instance, and also sometimes in Albert of Saxony, and later in Jerome Pardo.)[17] Such cleavages do not neatly overlap with nominalism or realism. In fact, the nominalism of the later Middle Ages is not exhausted by a set of theses, let alone by a list of authors; it is characterized rather by a common approach, a way of doing philosophy.

The leading characteristic of this approach is the conviction that the logical analysis of language is an indispensable prerequisite for developments in other disciplines – it being only through words that we can get to things. Moreover, as is evident in their analyses of the categories, nominalists reject any logico–linguistic parallelism. Indeed, they are convinced that many difficulties come from the fact that we project certain traits of language onto the structure of the world. This does not prevent them from developing philosophical or theological theories; on the contrary, they are convinced that many errors in

---

[15] See *Summa logicae* I.49–51; *Expositio in librum Praedicamentorum* 12; *Ordinatio* 30.3; *Quodlibet* VI.16 (where he speaks scornfully of a "little thing" [*parvam rem*]).

[16] *Quaest. in artem veterem, In Praed.* q. 4a sec. 569.

[17] See Joël Biard, "Les controverses sur l'objet du savoir et les 'complexe significabilia' à Paris au XIVe siècle," in S. Caroti (ed.) *Quia inter doctores est magna dissensio. Les débats de philosophie naturelle à Paris au XIVe siècle* (Florence: Olschki, 2004) 1–31; Alain de Libera, *La référence vide: théories de la proposition* (Paris: Seuil, 2002).

natural philosophy, in metaphysics, in theology, and perhaps in ethics arise from a misunderstanding of our language. It is thus understandable that, at the end of the Middle Ages, Ockham's theories are not invoked only in logic, but also in theology, regarding, for example, the status of created charity as separated or not in the soul, the nature of the divine act that justifies or condemns, and the contingency of the divine commands that ground the moral law.[18] The theology with which Martin Luther had to reckon in the early sixteenth century is that of Gabriel Biel, who is strongly influenced by Ockham.

Second, the principle of parsimony known as "Ockham's Razor" becomes meaningful in this context. To be sure, equivalent formulas are present in Scotus. But, given that no one wants to multiply entities beyond necessity, it still remains to be determined which ones are in fact necessary. It is true that nominalists generally have a more parsimonious ontology than their adversaries. But this becomes understandable only against the background of their theory of language, which reduces the real scope of the categories or posits that certain abstract nouns are simply synonyms of concrete nouns (for example, 'humanity' is synonymous with 'human being') (see Chapter 12).

That is why, third, the nominalists craft a conception of signification that incorporates a direct relation to individuals. This yields an extensional conception of signification. Very quickly, however, an author such as Buridan underlines the need to take into account phenomena that are not reducible to this sort of direct reference to collections of individuals. Even so, it is from this relation, and from the redefinition of the semiotic relations it entails, that he designs a theory to account for phenomena such as those that are linked to verbs of propositional attitude.

The nominalism of the later Middle Ages is thus also a history – a history of internal debates just as much as of confrontations with competing positions. There is no Ockhamist school, because of the ecclesiastical trouble that stopped the career of the *Venerabilis inceptor*. There is not really a Buridanian school either, because the positions of the closest of the contemporaries and successors of the Picardian master (Albert of Saxony, Marsilius of Inghen, Nicole Oresme) diverge as much in semantics as in physics. Even so, Buridan's theories exert a lasting influence. One only has to read John Major's logic to see that Buridan is his guide: he takes from him characteristic notions such as the appellation of reason and a reductive analysis of the significate of the proposition. Extending the teaching of Thomas Bricot and George of Brussels, Major gathers around

---

[18] See Paul Vignaux, *Justification et prédestination au XIVᵉ siècle. Duns Scot, Pierre d'Auriole, Guillaume d'Ockham, Grégoire de Rimini* (Paris: Leroux, 1934; repr. Paris: Vrin, 1981); Joël Biard, *Guillaume d'Ockham et la théologie* (Paris: Cerf, 1999) pp. 101–13.

him a whole group of students who will perpetuate this teaching. It is during this era, at the start of the sixteenth century, that nominalism becomes a "way." The confrontations that, two centuries earlier, arose from the particularities of various questions and answers are from now on labeled and catalogued into preestablished doctrines.

In these confrontations, nominalism was not always the predominant position. It is so in Paris at the beginning of the sixteenth century, presenting itself in opposition to Thomism and Scotism (assimilated to realism). It had been overturned, however, during the fifteenth century in Louvain, Cologne, and Central Europe, replaced by a doctrine of the universal that relied strongly on Albert the Great and that opposed not just Buridanism but also Scotism. At the same time it is attacked in Italy by Lorenzo Valla, who knows well the views of both Ockham and Paul of Venice, but who seeks to revalorize both rhetoric (the study of spoken language in discursive situations) and dialectic (reasoning concerning what is merely probable). Still, the memory of nominalism does not disappear. It rises again in the seventeenth century, in authors such as Thomas Hobbes, who develops a theory of universals as names, and in Leibniz, who mentions Ockham in his 1670 preface to Marius Nizolius's *De veris principiis* (*Philos. Schriften* IV: 157), and praises "the nominalist sect, the most profound of all the scholastics, and the most consistent with the spirit of our modern philosophy."

49

ACCIDENTS AND MODES

CALVIN G. NORMORE

The Middle Ages inherited from antiquity an approach to metaphysics which supposed both that, to provide an account of being, one provides a theory of categories, and that a division into substance and accident is fundamental to such an account. During the thousand years between Boethius and Descartes, this fundamental division was subjected to careful scrutiny and modified dramatically. Eventually even the term 'accident' was partially eclipsed by a competing term, 'mode,' which bespoke a competing metaphysical picture; by the mid-seventeenth century Descartes was able to contrast his ontology of substances and modes with an ontology of substances and "real" accidents.

The doctrine of real accidents that Descartes rejects has two medieval roots. One lies in the related theological mysteries of the Eucharist and the Incarnation, and the other lies in the perceived need for real accidents to account for at least some physical phenomena. This chapter explores how these roots formed and developed, how accidents came to be "real," and how real accidents came to be perceived as a philosophical mistake.

THE *CATEGORIES* FRAMEWORK

In his *Categories* chapter 4, Aristotle lists ten heads under which nouns and adjectives fall: Substance, Quality, Quantity, Relative, Place, Time, Situation, Habit, Action and Passion. Although there is little reason to think Aristotle was wedded to this list, it had special salience in the early medieval period, both because the *Categories* was translated and commented on by Boethius and because the list was also found in "On the Ten Categories" (*De decem categoriae*), a work attributed to Augustine (but likely from a hand influenced by Themistius). The list yields a motley crew, and the author of the *De decem categoriae* divides it into items that are intrinsic – Quality, Quantity, and Situation – and the rest, which are extrinsic. The intrinsic ones help in some way to constitute the substance, the extrinsic ones to situate it among others. The author makes very clear that it is not possible for there to be substances without accidents, and – while not going as far as Boethius to suggest that substances are individuated by their accidents – certainly leaves open that possibility.

The *Categories* also distinguishes items along two further dimensions: whether they are "said of" other items and whether they are "in" other items. Primary substances (individual animals or terms referring to them are Aristotle's paradigms) are neither in a subject nor said of a subject, secondary substances (kinds of primary substances or terms referring to them) are "said of" a subject, and other items are "in" a subject but not said of the subject they are in. Since the items that are in a subject but not said of that subject correspond to the items that fall under the heads other than Substance in the list from *Categories* chapter 4, it would be natural enough to group these together and to have a common name for them – although Aristotle does not himself do this. 'Accidents' is that name. Aristotle does not tell us much in the *Categories* about what it is to be "in" a subject other than to deny that it is to be "a part of" the subject. He does suggest that the accidents that are in a primary substance are individual, like the primary substance itself, and that they cannot exist apart from and perhaps are individuated by the primary substance in which they are, but he does not tell us whether accidents of different categories are in their subject in a univocal sense of "in," whether accidents could themselves be subjects of other accidents, or whether substances and accidents have different existence conditions.

Answers to some of these questions can be gleaned from (or read into) Aristotle's *Physics* and *Metaphysics*; yet, while the *Categories* with Boethius's commentaries and the *De decem categoriae* were available throughout the early Middle Ages, the *Physics* and *Metaphysics* were translated only in the twelfth century. Not having Aristotle's more articulated discussions of the structure of substance, the equivocity of being, and the differences between what it is to be a substance and what it is to be an accident, early medieval Latin writers were free to speculate about these issues.

Although interest in the *Categories* never died in the Latin West and there were between the sixth and the late eleventh century a number of authors who developed accounts of real interest (John Scottus Eriugena and Anselm of Canterbury, for example), it is not until the very end of the eleventh century that we find a picture that would deeply influence later developments. We find this picture in a *Dialectica* attributed to one Garlandus and possibly dated as early as 1075; there is, in fact, reason to think that this *Dialectica* was one product of a movement which may have begun even earlier and which came to include

Roscelin of Compiegne, one of Peter Abaelard's teachers.[1] Garlandus posits an ontology of what he calls *res*, and he then treats the categories as categories of words that can apply to these *res*. As Garlandus uses it (and as Abaelard was to use it later) the term *res* signifies any item there is (*Dialectica* pp. 23–3). Any *res* can be classified using terms from the *Categories*. Indeed, Garlandus seems to think that any *res* can be classified using terms from each one of the Aristotelian categories – a given *res* might be Socrates, human, pale, and in the marketplace, and these predicates would apply to it with equal propriety. Thus, to think of Garlandian *res* as substances would be as improper as to think of them as accidents.

Abaelard studied with Roscelin and was much influenced by this picture. We have from his pen a much larger and more elaborated oeuvre than we have from Garlandus and so we can fill in more detail, but much of Abaelard's ontology is still badly understood. What is clear is that there are individual *essentiae* (a term that in Abaelard and his contemporaries does not mean essence as this is understood in, for example, Aquinas) and that these are all things (*res*). Individual *essentiae* informed by forms have "statuses" (*status*) that are picked out by such phrases as 'being human,' 'being pale,' and so on. There are far more statuses than forms and it is the statuses that are classified by the categories. Thus, for Abaelard a substance is an *essentia* with a substantial status – a status it presumably has by virtue of a substantial form. Abaelard holds that if a form F informs an *essentia* E it is correct to say that E is F. He also expressly maintains that a brightness may inform a whiteness (so that we may say the whiteness is bright), and that while a body may sustain that brightness (in virtue of sustaining the whiteness which it informs), the brightness does not inform the body (which is why we may not properly say that the body is bright). Thus Abaelard distinguishes a subject of predication, which is the subject of inherence, from what we might think of as a subject of constitution. One significant dimension along which substances and accidents differ is that it was widely believed by Christians (though not by Aristotle) that only God could produce a substance while humans and other natural agents could produce accidents. Abaelard held this view – and with it the view that material substances are distinguished from artifacts by the degree of unity among their parts.

---

[1] The identity of the author of the *Dialectica*, its date and its relation to the work of Roscelin and that of a Master Johannes mentioned by the author of the *Historia Francia* are all disputed. For a path into the controversies see John Marenbon, "Medieval Latin Commentaries and Glosses on Aristotelian Logical Texts, Before c. 1150 AD," in C. Burnett (ed.) *Glosses and Commentaries on Aristotelian Logical Texts* (London: Warburg Institute, 1993) 77–127.

LATER MEDIEVAL DEVELOPMENTS

The translation of Aristotle's corpus into Latin together with both a number of Arabic commentaries and a number of independent Arabic treatises introduced a new complexity into an already complex story about accident. The standard Arabic term translated as *accidentia* in Latin is ʿaraḍ, and that term had been used by theologians (the *mutakallimūn*) to refer to anything that is not *jawhar*, a term that is typically translated as *substantia*. Since the *mutakallimūn* talked freely about all manner of items not in the Aristotelian categories, this raised a complex set of issues about whether these should be regarded as accidents. There was also the question that we saw above in the early Latin tradition of whether the very same item could be described as both a substance and an accident. For example, Solomon ibn Gabirol maintained that it could, Abraham ibn Daud that it could not. When Ibn Gabirol's major philosophical work, the *Fons vitae*, was translated into Latin in the second half of the twelfth century, this reinforced the already prevalent view that the division between substances and accidents is not absolute.[2]

All of this changed in the middle of the thirteenth century, when Albert the Great and Thomas Aquinas undertook to put a new and more authentically Aristotelian foundation under the *Categories*. From the very beginning of his career, as evidenced, for example, in his *De ente et essentia*, Aquinas presents a clear and largely novel account of the relations between substance and accident. Taking on board a wider variety of Aristotle's work than had been hitherto available, Aquinas proposes that, for accidents as Aristotle understands them, *esse est inesse* − "to be is to be in" (*In Post. an.* I.2). Thus it is, for Aristotle, simply conceptually impossible for an accident to exist without the subject in which it inheres. In his theological work, however, Aquinas himself maintains that this is not conceptually impossible, because what it is to be a particular quantity of two kilograms (say) is to have a natural tendency to be the quantity of some subject. It is not part of what it is to be a quantity that that tendency is actualized. Thus on Aquinas's view it is not essential to every accident to be an accident of anything (*Sent.* IV.12.1.1.1).

It is not clear, however, whether Aquinas means to apply this picture to every type of accident or only to quantity. On the picture that seems to be Aquinas's 'natural' reading of Aristotle, accidents are not only in their subjects in such a way that they exist only because their subjects do, but they are also individuated

---

[2] See Resianne Fontaine, *In Defence of Judaism, Abraham ibn Daud: Sources and Structure of ha-Emunah ha-ramah* (Assen: Van Gorcum, 1990) p. 15 and the references therein.

by their subjects so that they are the very individual accidents they are in virtue of their being the accidents of the very subjects in which they are. From this it would seem to follow that a difference in the subject would make for a difference in the accident, and this is the line Aquinas takes with the death of a human being. When a human dies all of the accidents that were previously present are destroyed and many very similar accidents come into existence. However, Aquinas holds that in the case of the Eucharist, where the substance of the bread and wine are destroyed, numerically the same qualitative accidents remain.

As Aquinas understands it, what happens in the Eucharist is that the bread of the host and the wine in the cup are destroyed, and the body of Christ comes to be where they were. Nonetheless the qualitative accidents of the bread and wine remain and they do not remain as accidents of the body of Christ (*Summa theol.* 3a 77). How then do they remain? These accidents are accidents, and so they are individuated by a relation they bear to something else. What exactly is that something else?

Accidents for Aquinas are accidental forms, and forms for Aquinas are neither universal nor individual in themselves. Since they are not individual of themselves, Aquinas thinks they have to be made individual. Accidental forms are individuated by the subject in which they inhere, but since he also holds that almost all of these subjects are composites of matter and substantial form, one might well inquire whether it is the matter, the substantial form, or the composite as a whole that is properly the subject of the accidents. Aquinas suggests that the substantial forms of material substances are individuated by the matter that they inform. But on Aquinas's view the only matter in a substance is prime matter (see Chapter 46). Prime matter is not of itself individual any more than substantial forms are. How could two principles that are not individual combine to make something that is? Aquinas seems to handle this problem by suggesting that matter is individuated prior, logically, to its being informed by a substantial form. Matter is individuated by being under dimensions. Since matter never exists except as the matter of something, it always appears under determinate dimensions, but what makes matter as such individual is indeterminate quantity. This makes quantity – which is, after all, an accident for Aristotle – a very strange accident indeed.

Aquinas holds that accidents in the eight accidental categories other than Quantity can remain after transubstantiation because those accidents are individuated by another accident – namely, the dimensive quantity of the bread and wine – and this accident is in turn individuated of itself, depending on the bread and wine that sustain it only with respect to its existence, not with respect to being the very quantity that it is. Since God can supply any causal power a created substance can, God can sustain the dimensive quantity and the other accidents in existence. And since the dimensive quantity needs nothing further to individuate it, and the other accidents are individuated through it, Aquinas concludes that numerically the same accidents present before the transubstantiation can be present afterwards.

Aquinas's thought seems to be that in the ordinary case both material substances and material accidents are individuated by being in individual parcels of matter that are themselves primary subjects of quantities with dimensions through which the accidents are immediately individuated. In the special case of the Eucharist, the matter is transformed into the matter of the body of Christ, but the dimensive quantity remains as a subsistent item that still serves as the basis for (and can be regarded as the subject of) other accidents.

If this is right, then we see in Aquinas's account of the Eucharist that quantity can serve as the subject of qualitative accidents. Moreover, we see that while for Aquinas quantity cannot naturally exist apart from substance, it supernaturally can: there is nothing in what the quantity is that involves its being in a substance as a subject, even though it is part of what quantity is to require something to sustain it in existence. And although it is part of what other accidents are to require a subject, that subject need not be substance: it could be and in the Eucharist is dimensive quantity.

One fairly minimal way of understanding the tag that for an accident to be is for it to be in a subject is as holding that to say that an accident exists is at least necessarily equivalent to saying that some substance is so modified. Different morals can be drawn from this. One would be that every predication such as 'Socrates is white' involves *two entities* – namely, Socrates and a whiteness – but that to speak of Socrates as an entity and to speak of the whiteness as an entity is to speak analogically. The other would be that to say a whiteness exists is just to say that some singular sentence such as 'Socrates is white' is true and that in *that* sentence no reference is made to an entity other than Socrates. On this reading, simply predicating existence in the accidental categories does not carry any ontological commitment over and above a commitment to the subjects of the accidents in question. From this perspective there may or may not be additional ontological commitments involved in particular accidental predications, but they are not signaled merely by the predication relation itself.

The first reading was Aquinas's. Aquinas maintains that each distinct category introduces new being, though equivocally, and this became the majority tradition within the Thomist school – numbering John Capreolus, Cajetan, Sylvester of Ferrara, and John Poinsot (John of St. Thomas) among its adherents. Perhaps surprisingly, the view that each category introduces new being was also adopted by John Duns Scotus, who thereby set the stage for what is perhaps the most fundamental debate about 'realism' in the later Middle Ages.[3] While Scotus defended the position that accidents simply in virtue of being accidents are additional beings over and above the beings that are their subjects, a position defended by most of those prepared to call themselves Scotists, this position was vehemently rejected by Ockham and the entire tradition identified as nominalist (see Chapters 47–8).

The second reading was, however, more common, at least from the mid-thirteenth century on, and writers as diverse as Henry of Ghent, Peter of John Olivi, William of Ockham, and John Buridan subscribed to it. Some who understood predication in the accidental categories in this second way (Ockham and Buridan, for example) understood Aristotle's view to be that there was no need to suppose that any accidental category introduced beings not already introduced by the category of Substance. This position (reminiscent of that in the *Dialectica* of Garlandus) was generally not thought to be orthodox, however, because it seemed to leave no explanation of how, in the Eucharist, when the bread was transubstantiated into the body of Christ, the appearances of the bread could remain without the bread itself and without becoming accidents of the body of Christ. There was also thought to be physical evidence against it. Buridan, for example, holds that we cannot explain the facts of the *limits* on the rarefaction and condensation of bodies (that is, their expansion and contraction) without supposing that there is a real quantity or magnitude that a given body possesses. In his *Questions on the Physics* I.8, he canvasses the available explanations for the behavior of gas when heated or cooled and concludes that only by supposing a magnitude distinct from the thing can we save the phenomena. He then proposes that: "[J]ust as a thing already white is not able to become whiter except by the generation in it of whiteness together with the existing whiteness . . . so a thing already extended is not able to become greater without some generation of magnitude together with the existing magnitude" (ed. 1509, f. 11rb).

Although the view that there were *no* items picked out by terms in the nine categories of accident that were not picked out by terms in the category of Substance was rare in the later Middle Ages, there was a regular industry of trying to reduce the kinds of additional entities. Henry of Ghent, for example, posited that besides items in the category of Substance there were items picked

---

[3] Whether Scotus would agree with Aquinas that beings picked out by terms in the accidental categories exist in the same sense that substances exist is a complex issue. See Giorgio Pini, *Categories and Logic in Duns Scotus: An Interpretation of Aristotle's Categories in the Late Thirteenth Century* (Leiden: Brill, 2002) for an extensive recent discussion.

out by terms in the categories of Quality and Quantity. Each of these is a *res* in its own right, and although each of them ordinarily exists in a substance, this is not part of what it is to be the *res* in question. Thus, for Henry there is no contradiction in a quality or a quantity existing without being in a subject. Buridan seems to have taken a similar position.

We have seen that Aquinas held that although the whiteness, shape, and so on of the bread and wine no longer inhere in any substance after the consecration, they do inhere in something – namely, the *quantity* of the bread and wine – that is, in the Eucharist miraculously conserved. This privileging of the role of quantity is reflected also (though differently) in Henry of Ghent and in Buridan. However, Peter of John Olivi took a different line, and in this he was followed by both Scotus and Ockham. Olivi claimed that, after the consecration, the qualities of the bread and wine remain without inhering in *any* subject. He was thus led to posit *real qualities*, which could exist by the power of God in the absence of any created substance. Within this picture these qualities exist in the same way substances do, and so 'being' is univocally applied to substances and qualities. Olivi, and Ockham after him, combined this view with an attack of the distinction between a substance and its quantity and so were led to the position that substances and qualities of certain kinds exhaust the range of real beings.

Ockham distinguishes sharply between claims like 'Socrates is human' and 'Socrates is pale.' Roughly speaking, 'human' is what he calls an absolute term, and its semantic function is just to signify human beings. Since the sentence is true just in case Socrates is one of these, the truth conditions for the sentence do not require anything more than humans (indeed than Socrates himself). On the other hand, something, say Socrates, is pale on Ockham's account in virtue of its "having" a paleness and, since we say correctly that Socrates is pale but not that he is a paleness, the paleness is not signified but consignified by 'pale.' Numerically the same thing can be pale at one time and not at another just because at one time it has a paleness and at the other it does not, whereas if a thing is human it cannot cease to be human without ceasing to be altogether.

Ockham is happy to say that we need nothing more for the truth of 'Socrates is human' than Socrates himself. It is just because both 'Socrates' and 'human' signify him that the sentence is true. Suppose now that for Socrates's paleness to exist is nothing more than for Socrates to be pale (as the Thomist reading of Aristotle suggests) and that, just as in the case of 'Socrates is human,' only Socrates is required for the truth of this. Then we do not have a truth-maker for Socrates being pale over and above Socrates. But, while Socrates's existence is enough to account for his being human, it surely is not enough to account for his being pale – else he would be essentially pale (in the sense that while existing he could not but be pale). Hence it seems that 'Socrates is pale' requires the being of both Socrates and his particular paleness.

Accidental properties are precisely those such that it is in some sense contingent whether the thing that has them does indeed have them. ("In some sense" because there may be inseparable accidents, the so-called *propria*, but even these are not *metaphysically* inseparable.) But if we suppose that for those accidents to exist is nothing more than for their subject to be so qualified, we would have nothing with which to account for this contingency. Ockham is thus led to the conclusion that where there are genuine basic contingent facts about something (over and above its existence), there must either be accidents that exist in the sense of being separable from their subjects, or the subjects must have parts on whose arrangements the contingent facts supervene. On the other hand, what one might ordinarily call essential properties do not require such additional existences – though they may require that the subject be complex in some way. For example, for Socrates to be rational does not require any special being which is rationality – it is enough for Socrates to be rational that he exist – but for Socrates to exist Socrates must have a mind and Socrates is rational only if Socrates exists and his mind exists. Socrates's mind is, of course, just an essential part of Socrates himself.

Thus the doctrine of real accidents provided a solution to a number of problems in theology, physics and semantics. It did, however, have problems of its own. If substances and qualities exist in a univocal sense of 'exist' and if it is possible by God's power for qualities to exist without inhering in a subject, what then is the difference between a substance and a quality? This problem was exacerbated by another theological problem, that of the Incarnation. On the orthodox view of the Incarnation, the second person of the Trinity assumed a human nature – that is, acquired a human body and soul. You and I are, on the classical Christian Aristotelian hylomorphic picture, composites of body and soul; destroy my body and soul, and you would destroy me completely. But if Christ's body and soul were destroyed, the second person of the Trinity would not be destroyed. Each of us then simply is our body and soul. Christ, however, has a body and soul but is not simply a body and soul. What then is the relation between Christ and Christ's human nature? One suggestion, the one followed up by Scotus and the theologians most influenced by him, was that the relation between the two was analogous to that between a substance and a quality (*Ordinatio* III.1.1 n.3). As presented by Ockham (*Quodlibet* IV.7) the suggestion was that the composite of Christ's body and soul – were it to exist without being assumed – would be a human being like the rest of us. Having been assumed, it is related to the *suppositum* that is the second person of the Trinity in the way my skin color is related to my skin. A consequence of this view is that what is ordinarily a substance can, with divine intervention, behave like an accident.

REAL ACCIDENTS VERSUS MODES

The upshot of these considerations is that the categorial distinction between substance and real accident became metaphysically problematic. If accidents can behave as substances ordinarily do, and substances can behave as accidents ordinarily do, what is the difference? The short answer given by this tradition is the one we found in Aquinas – that the difference lies in what they are naturally apt to do. Accidents are naturally fitted to inhere in substances; substances are not naturally fitted to inhere in anything. God can override this natural fit but not obliterate it. However, this answer requires a robust sense of nature distinct from God's power. It is thus not available for someone who wants to derive the characteristics of nature from the features of God's power.

The natural result of all this is that someone who rejects the distinction between the power by which God operates naturally and the power by which God operates supernaturally, as Descartes does, could also be expected to reject the view that there are real accidents distinct from substances. That is, of course, what Descartes also does, and for the very reasons we might expect. For example, to Hyperaspistes he remarks that "when people believe that accidents are real, they are representing them to themselves as substances" (ed. Adam and Tannery, III: 430), and to Regius in January 1642 (ibid., III: 503) he writes: "Now we do not deny active qualities, but we say that they should not be regarded as having any degree of reality greater than that of modes; for to regard them so is to conceive of them as substances." In these passages we have the well-known Cartesian contrast between *real accidents* and *modes*. 'Mode,' like 'real accident,' is a scholastic term. In the sense Descartes has in mind it seems to go back to medieval theories of the intension and remission of forms. According to some such theories, some features, heat or color for instance, can be found in various degrees (*gradus*) of intensity. Each such distinct degree is a mode (*modus*) of the feature.

This account is taken over by Duns Scotus and widened so that being can be said to come in modes – finite or infinite, for example – and is widened still further by his followers. Scotus goes on to speak of a *modal distinction* between an item and its mode, which allows one to speak of them as distinct items but does not allow that the mode can exist without that of which it is a mode (*Ordinatio* I.8.1.3 nn. 138–40). There is also another tradition of talking about modes which interacts with the one just mentioned. We saw it at work already in the *Dialectica* of Garlandus where the categories are spoken of as signifying things in *diversis modis*. There was a long and controversial tradition of attempting to equate each category with a different mode of predicating, a tradition which sometimes tried to remain neutral on the issue of whether the modes of predicating corresponded to ways of being in the world but which in the hands of the so-called *modistae* postulated a full-fledged parallelism between modes of signifying and modes of being. These two conceptions of mode would be easy to conflate.

In the context of late medieval metaphysics, talk about modes of a thing is usually alternative to talk about real accidents. What it is an alternative to is the use of real accidents in accounting for change. Sometimes it is true to say of a given poker that it is hot; at other times it is true to say that the poker is not hot. Why? Because the temperature of the poker has changed. In what does this change of temperature of the poker consist? Two stories seem plausible: that the change consists in the subtraction of units of heat (or the addition of cold, if you prefer), or that the change consists in a difference in the *way* (*modus*) the poker is but not in the addition or subtraction of any*thing*. If we adopt the first alternative, we have the doctrine of real accidents. The second alternative is the doctrine of the modes of substance.

We can see the Cartesian theory of modes as a reasonable response to the problems raised by the late scholastic theory of real accidents and, in particular, to the suggestion that accidents might differ from substances in having a natural tendency to inhere that substances lack. On this suggestion accidents could fail to inhere and substances could inhere or do something very like inhere, but these would be unnatural states. This reliance on the distinction between the natural and the supernatural requires that we be able to make sense of a distinction between what would be natural for a thing and what would be possible for it with supernatural intervention. Moreover, it requires either that this distinction itself be metaphysically necessary or that we accept that categorial distinctions themselves be contingent. Neither of these is a happy option. That it be a contingent matter whether something is a substance or an accident is, on the face of it, very strange. That the distinction between the natural and the supernatural be itself necessary may seem less strange, but it does require that the natures of things be independent of God's choices – and it is far from clear that Descartes, at least, would accept this.

Ockham has to suppose real qualities because he does not believe that all change can be reduced to the generation and corruption of substances and the rearrangements of their parts. Early modern mechanical philosophy can be seen as the result of taking that further step; by the time we come to Descartes, all the change in extended substances is explained in terms of the rearrangements of their parts. Accordingly, there is no longer any need for real accidents (which Descartes correctly sees as little different from substances), and one can equate the existence of a mode with a substance being disposed thus and so. At bottom, that disposition is a matter of spatial arrangement either at a time or (as in the case of motion) over time.

The doctrine of modes – taken together with the view that all change is creation, annihilation, or local motion – is promising as an account of the extended universe. But Descartes has not only extended substances with their innumerable parts, but also *res cogitantes*, which are simple, and yet which he claims to be multiply modified (at least over time). From the Ockhamist point of view this is a great mystery. What is the difference between my thinking of Manhattan and my thinking of Vienna? It cannot be in parts of my mind being differently arranged, because my mind has no parts. It cannot be in there being *thoughts* that are related to my mind – that is just the despised doctrine of real accidents. So, Descartes claims, it is just for my mind to have one mode rather than another. And what is that? Modes, says he, have no being of their own – they borrow all their being from their subjects. But if the being of my thinking of Vienna is just my being, and so is the being of my thinking of Manhattan, then what can be the difference between them? One possibility is a different relation to something else: my thinking of Manhattan involves my mind and something else (Manhattan, say), and my thinking of Vienna involves my mind and another thing (say, Vienna). Let us call this externalism. Another possibility is to abandon the simplicity of the mind and to insist on its having real parts. Both are live and lively contemporary options. They arise, quite possibly, from the dialectic of the argument itself. The debate between the doctrine of real accidents and the doctrine of modes is still with us.

IX

THEOLOGY

50

PHILOSOPHY AND THEOLOGY

M. W. F. STONE AND ROBERT WISNOVSKY

THE LATIN WEST (STONE)

In the resplendent summer of 1997 an incongruous collection of scholars from the four corners of the earth assembled in Erfurt, Germany, to discuss the seemingly anodyne yet strangely engaging question: "What is Philosophy in the Middle Ages?" Sponsored by the Société Internationale pour l'Étude de la Philosophie Médiévale (SIEPM), and organized by genial hosts from the Thomas-Institut of the University of Cologne, the conference debated over long days and balmy nights the nature, scope, and point of philosophical discourse in the Middle Ages.[1] Even though the distinguished speakers and other delegates who held forth during the interminable sessions brought to bear insight and erudition in their respective analyses of the chosen theme, the conference concluded its business without reaching any firm agreement. With the conversation and *convivio* at an end, the delegates returned to their respective countries harboring quite incommensurate ideas about just what was "philosophy" in the Middle Ages, many remaining unsure whether it could or ought to be distinguished from "theology."

That unanimity on the question of the exact relationship of "philosophy" and "theology" should prove so utterly elusive, even in the context of one of the more significant gatherings of medieval scholars in recent years, is not in the least surprising when one considers that the independence, or otherwise, of philosophy from theology has been continuously contested and vicariously debated, ever since the establishment of "medieval philosophy" as a recognizable branch of the history of philosophy in the nineteenth century.[2] As such, the problem of identifying and then individuating philosophy in the Middle Ages

---

[1] The proceedings of the conference were subsequently published by Jan Aertsen and Andreas Speer (eds.) *Was ist Philosophie im Mittelalter? Qu'est-ce que la philosophie au moyen âge? What is Philosophy in the Middle Ages?* (Berlin: De Gruyter, 1998).

[2] For a history of the early years of the discipline see John Inglis, *Spheres of Philosophical Inquiry and the Historiography of Medieval Philosophy* (Leiden: Brill, 1998).

is generated by a blatant historical disparity that exists between "philosophy" (*philosophia*) as it was understood and practiced by medieval Christians, and the seemingly related discipline that graces the modern age. Nowhere is this more apparent than in the fact that those thinkers who have been acknowledged by posterity to have made a significant contribution to Western philosophy, such as Thomas Aquinas, John Duns Scotus, and William of Ockham, did not represent themselves as "philosophers" at all, but rather viewed their own efforts through the lens of "sacred doctrine" (*sacra doctrina*). As theologians (*theologi*), they sought to understand the content and meaning of their theistic beliefs, and while this endeavor could include the appropriation of "philosophical" ideas and arguments, the point of the exercise was to acquire knowledge of God and provide a rational foundation for the Christian faith.

The institutional settings

A significant aspect of the complicated relationship of philosophy and theology can be initially clarified by examining their very different institutional settings.[3] As an academic discipline, philosophy, insofar as it was practiced in medieval universities, was not studied by means of a designated core of subjects, even though disciplines such as logic and antecedent forms of more modern fields of philosophical inquiry can be discerned in medieval debates. Furthermore, the subject was not studied historically since no recognized canon of authorities existed. Even when individual thinkers such as Aristotle were lauded and valorized as "the philosopher,"[4] their writings were thoroughly policed by the perceived truths of theology, and were considered inferior to the authorities (*auctoritates*) of the Christian tradition.[5] Situated in the arts faculty, what we would recognize as elements of philosophy were taught in the context of the trivium (grammar, rhetoric, and dialectic) and the later quadrivium (geometry, astronomy, arithmetic, and music), and were a part of a more general education in the liberal arts (*artes liberales*).[6]

---

[3] See Jacques Verger, *Les universités au moyen âge* (Paris: Publications universitaires de France, 1973), and Olaf Pedersen, *The First Universities: Studium Generale and the Origins of University Education in Europe* (Cambridge: Cambridge University Press, 1997).

[4] For an important set of explanations of how this and other corresponding terms were used, see Mariken Teeuwen, *The Vocabulary of Intellectual Life in the Middle Ages* (Turnhout: Brepols, 2003) pp. 376–83.

[5] On the use of the Fathers in early and late medieval theology, see Irene Backus (ed.) *The Reception of the Church Fathers in the West: From the Carolingians to the Maurists* (Leiden: Brill, 1997).

[6] On the arts faculties see J. M. Fletcher, "The Faculty of Arts," in J. I. Catto *et al.* (eds.) *The History of the University of Oxford* (Oxford: Clarendon Press, 1984) 369–99, and James A. Weisheipl, "The Parisian Faculty of Arts in Mid-Thirteenth Century: 1240–1270," *American Benedictine Review* 25 (1974) 200–17.

From the mid-thirteenth century onwards, the pedagogical program of the liberal arts was embellished and revised in order to take account of the writings of Aristotle, as can be seen in statutes such as that of Paris in 1255. From that time, most of the *corpus Aristotelicum* became required reading in the arts faculties, and thereby formed the basis of a detailed philosophical and scientific education (see Chapter 4). It remains controversial whether we can find an autonomous or even textually identifiable "Aristotelian philosophy" among the writings of the arts masters. What is certain, however, is that the *magistri* of the medieval university accompanied Aristotle through the host of topics he broached in his encyclopedic corpus, from logic to poetics, from the physics of moving bodies through the species of plants and animals, to the movement of the heavens. With the wholesale assimilation of Aristotelian thought into the curriculum of the arts faculty, "philosophical" and "scientific" learning become intertwined, providing a comprehensive training in speculative inquiry and rational demonstration.

Such knowledge was deemed to facilitate further and more rarefied study in the faculty of theology. There, the Bible was the main resource of authoritative instruction, with the dogmatic teaching of the Church Fathers, especially Augustine, functioning in a supporting role. By the end of the twelfth century, theologians such as Peter of Poitiers, and then Peter Lombard, began to assemble the *dicta* of the Fathers as well as relevant biblical passages into collections of opinions or *sententiae*.[7] Lombard's *Sentences* became the most popular textbook in theology, and helped to shape theological reflection until the end of the seventeenth century.[8] Students in theology were expected to attend lectures on the Bible and the *Sentences* for several years. Once they had assumed the title of bachelor, they had to deliver their own lectures on these very same texts. After three to four years of offering such courses they participated in faculty disputations for at least one year prior to being admitted into the company of the masters (*magistri*) with whom they had studied. As *magistri* they were required to lecture on the Bible, hold regular disputed questions, and advance their own theological ideas through preaching. In their rehearsal and prosecution of every conceivable form of theological argument, medieval thinkers did make extensive use of logic, metaphysics, and philosophical psychology, especially in their clarification of issues such as the Trinity,[9] but their investment in these

---

[7] On this see Marcia Colish, *Peter Lombard* (Leiden: Brill, 1994), and Philipp W. Rosemann, *The Story of a Great Medieval Book: Peter Lombard's Sentences* (Peterborough, ON: Broadview, 2007).

[8] See G. R. Evans (ed.) *Medieval Commentaries on the Sentences of Peter Lombard*, vol. I: *Current Research* (Leiden: Brill, 2002).

[9] On this see the important study by Russell L. Friedman, *Intellectual Traditions in the Medieval University: The Use of Philosophical Psychology in Trinitarian Theology among the Franciscans and Dominicans, 1250–1350* (Leiden: Brill, 2008).

subjects was never gratuitous nor was it ever motivated by purely philosophical concerns.

Modern scholarly strategies

It is somewhat ironic that while medieval theologians were quite relaxed in their attitudes towards Aristotelian philosophy, and thought nothing of appropriating its dialectical methods for what they deemed to be higher ends, modern scholars of "medieval philosophy" have always been conscious of the need to assert, and to reassert, the purely *philosophical* credentials of their discipline. This is a marked feature of the subject from the days of the writings of Barthélemy Hauréau, Joseph Kleutgen, and Albert Stöckl, to the synoptic histories of Martin Grabmann, Maurice de Wulf, and Étienne Gilson, and on to the commodious introductions, learned monographs, readers, and multiple anthologies of the present era. With the exception of Gilson's highly contentious thesis that philosophy throughout the medieval period was "Christian philosophy," or the conceptual clarification and defense of the truths of revelation, many leading specialists have tried to distill the "essence" of medieval philosophy by adopting one or other of the following strategies.

In the first instance, some scholars have attempted to explain the contribution of the medieval cognoscenti to the perennial philosophical problems of the West. On this model, thinkers in the Middle Ages, like those of antiquity and early modernity, are deemed to have made a specific bequest to Western philosophical learning that can be studied both for its own sake, and for the sake of acquiring a balanced philosophical education. Second, other specialists have argued that while the practice of philosophy in the Middle Ages is altogether odd when viewed from the perspectives of the present, the subject is still of profound importance because it can be shown to be historically continuous with the efforts of modern philosophers.[10] Examples of both these tendencies have enlivened the discipline from its very early years, as when Kleutgen and Stöckl took issue with Hauréau's overtly theological understanding of the relationship between reason and revelation,[11] and De Wulf formulated the idea that a common "scholastic" patrimony existed among medieval thinkers, a patrimony

---

[10] The merits or otherwise of these different approaches are discussed in recent volumes such as David Luscombe, *Medieval Thought* (Oxford: Oxford University Press, 1997); Jorge J. E. Gracia and Timothy B. Noone (eds.) *A Companion to Philosophy in the Middle Ages* (Oxford: Blackwell, 2003); and A. S. McGrade (ed.) *The Cambridge Companion to Medieval Philosophy* (Cambridge: Cambridge University Press, 2003).

[11] On this see Inglis, *Spheres of Philosophical Inquiry*, pp. 41–61.

which he thought proved resistant to any characterization in terms of sacred doctrine.[12]

More recently, we have been invited to consider other ways in which the content of medieval philosophy can be viewed apart from theology. In the English-speaking world one influential approach has been the promotion of the opinion that a large part of the known corpus of medieval philosophy is consistent with the methods of analytic philosophy, whose own arguments and techniques, especially in logic and the philosophy of language, are thought to resemble the efforts of medieval schoolmen.[13] A similar move, albeit driven by different motives, can be seen in the approach of those who argue that medieval philosophy is the study of the transcendentals, concepts such as *Being*, *One*, *True*, *Good*, and *Beautiful*.[14] Less beholden to the methodological outlook of analytic philosophy, this theory is just as eager to emphasize the independence of medieval philosophy from theology, even though it is also moved to explain how and why authors like Thomas Aquinas used transcendental concepts in their *philosophical* account of human knowledge of God.

Against these prominent and suggestive attempts to capture the distinctiveness and independence of medieval philosophy, Alain de Libera has argued that the essence of the subject resides elsewhere. With the target of Gilson's thesis of Christian philosophy firmly in his sights, de Libera has claimed that increasing cognizance of ancient and Arabic philosophy among members of the arts faculty at Paris in the late thirteenth century not only served to challenge theological orthodoxy but also bequeathed philosophy as an autonomous intellectual pursuit, a discipline largely independent of the external control of theology. For de Libera, the *magistri* of late thirteenth-century Paris are a new intellectual class, *les philosophes*, whose theories concerning human happiness, the immortality of the soul, the eternity of the world, and the capacity of the intellect to know higher things seemed to eliminate the need for many of the Christian verities.

---

[12] See ibid., pp. 168–92. De Wulf's writings should be in seen in the light of Stöckl's influence upon him, but also viewed in synergy with the efforts of Grabmann to provide an equally comprehensive history of a generic "scholastic tradition."

[13] This view can be associated with philosophers such as Peter Geach, Anthony Kenny, and Norman Kretzmann, and is still widely followed today, as can be evinced in the current volume. The apotheosis of this approach was the completion by Kretzmann, Jan Pinborg, and Kenny of *The Cambridge History of Later Medieval Philosophy* (Cambridge: Cambridge University Press, 1982), in which the subject was largely presented by means of the history of logic and the philosophy of language.

[14] Originally advanced in a series of papers by Jan Aertsen, and set out in his *Medieval Philosophy and the Transcendentals: The Case of Thomas Aquinas* (Leiden: Brill, 1996), this approach enjoys something of a modest scholarly profile, not least in virtue of its confident reassertion in numerous doctoral dissertations published by Aertsen's former students.

Furthermore, the institutional intrigues and political machinations of this new intellectual constituency finally brought philosophy and theology into irrevocable conflict, with the infamous condemnation of 1277 apparently bearing witness to the fact that the theologians were minded to bring the philosophers back within their control (see Chapter 8).[15]

And yet why should contemporary scholars expend such great effort in their quest to reveal the purely philosophical basis of their chosen discipline? This question does not invite a facile answer, but one of the reasons why the discussion of the relationship between philosophy and theology in the Middle Ages continues to occasion such spirited debate and commentary derives from the fact that current practitioners of medieval philosophy are children of a modern intellectual culture that is smitten by the view that one cannot be truly "philosophical" if one is beholden to a network of antecedent beliefs and assumptions that draw upon the resources of religious faith and divine revelation.[16] In and of itself, an uncritical acceptance of this view can lead to a serious distortion of important features of medieval intellectual life, since it will commit a scholar to seek a conception of philosophy that neatly equates with current tastes and predilections, rather than allowing the medieval ideas and opinions to stand on their terms. Whether one likes it or not, the practice of specific aspects of "philosophy" among members of the arts faculties was bound up with various forms of "scientific" learning as well as with the pursuit of the liberal arts: the discipline as we recognize it did not exist. In the faculty of theology, theories and arguments gleaned from the texts of Aristotle and some others were utilized and then placed in the service of *sacra doctrina*. These sober facts surely enjoin us to resist any temptation to recast philosophy in the Middle Ages in our own self-image; anachronism is no friend to medieval scholarship.

Philosophy in the context of theology

In the matter of specifying the precise relationship of philosophy to theology, we have much to learn from medieval thinkers themselves, who, unburdened by our concerns and limitations, developed original philosophical arguments in the

---

[15] De Libera's understanding of the events of 1277 and every other conceivable aspect of Bishop Tempier's condemnation are explored and debated in the volume by Jan A. Aertsen, Kent Emery, and Andreas Speer (eds.) *Nach der Verurteilung von 1277: Philosophie und Theologie an der Universität von Paris im letzten Viertel des 13. Jahrhunderts: Studien und Texte* (Berlin: De Gruyter, 2001).

[16] Here one thinks of Bertrand Russell's often quoted yet egregiously silly remark that Thomas Aquinas lacked "the true philosophic spirit" because he already knew the truth to be declared in the Catholic faith. See *A History of Western Philosophy* (London: Allen and Unwin, 1946) p 484.

context of theology. By extending the purview of speculative investigation into every area of the natural and supernatural worlds,[17] medieval *theologi* addressed problems and perplexities that derived from their earnest reflection on religious faith and the search for its rational basis. In many works the conversion or ascent of philosophy to faith is the central theme, as can be witnessed in Boethius's *Consolation of Philosophy*, where the figure of philosophy reminds the author of those verities without which his faith cannot be restored. One of the more enduring models of reflection on divine matters was presented by Anselm of Canterbury in his *Proslogion*. Building on the intellectual heritage of Augustine and his monastic interpreters, he used the phrase *fides quaerens intellectum*: "faith seeking understanding." We can clearly see this strategy at work in what was known to medieval writers as the *ratio Anselmi* (later baptized by Immanuel Kant as the "ontological argument") in *Proslogion* chs. 2–3 (see Chapter 53).[18] It can be argued that one does much better justice to Anselm's intentions if one views "the argument" (such as it may be) not as a demonstration of the existence of God, but as a systematic investigation into God's mode of existence. As a person seeking understanding (*fidelis quaerens intellectum*), Anselm begins from a faith that provides the conceptual parameters of his philosophical reflection, and then attempts to win his way through to a better understanding of the divine nature.[19]

In terms loosely contiguous with Anselm's project, other medieval authors clarified the relation between philosophy and theology by insisting that philosophy must be studied thoroughly before proceeding to theology. The absorption of elements of Aristotelian philosophy into theological discourse in the second half of the thirteenth century only served to make the discussion of issues concerning the immortality of the soul, angels, and the Trinity more sophisticated and susceptible to further clarification and reasoned analysis.[20] Examples of this preference can be found in thinkers as diverse as William of Auvergne, Robert Grosseteste, and Bonaventure, or in the work of Albert the Great and Roger Bacon, whose own commitment to active research in natural philosophy enabled them to provide a detailed account of the hierarchy of human

---

[17] On this see the eloquent description of Richard W. Southern, *Scholastic Humanism and the Unification of Europe*, vol. I: *Foundations* (Oxford: Blackwell, 1995) pp. 17–18. See also Alexander Murray, *Reason and Society in the Middle Ages* (Oxford: Clarendon Press, 1978).

[18] For a history of this form of reasoning throughout the high medieval period see the dated, if still useful, Augustinus Daniels, *Quellenbeiträge und Untersuchungen zur Geschichte der Gottesbeweise im XIII. Jahrhundert* (Münster: Aschendorff, 1909).

[19] See Georgi Kapriev, *Ipsa vita et veritas: der ontologische Gottesbeweis und die Ideenwelt Anselms von Canterbury* (Leiden: Brill, 1998).

[20] The best general guide to these diverse debates is still A. M. Landgraf, *Dogmengeschichte der Früh Scholastik* (Regensburg: Pustet, 1952–6).

knowledge, beginning with what we know in the physical sciences and the liberal arts, and concluding with the heady heights of theology.[21]

When we peruse the intellectual achievements of the last quarter of the thirteenth and the first half of the fourteenth century, and acquaint ourselves with the works of Aquinas, Henry of Ghent, Giles of Rome, Duns Scotus, Durand of St. Pourçain, Peter Auriol, Robert Holcot, and Ockham, we find there a profound illustration of the range and diversity of the engagement of medieval theologians with the Aristotelian inheritance, especially the Organon, and also a deep commitment to utilize rational thought for the analysis, clarification, and vindication of dogmatic truth.[22]

Aquinas, for instance, holds that theology (*theologia*) employs, improves, and then perfects the best of ancient philosophy. He extends great deference to pagan philosophers, especially Aristotle, but whenever he speaks in his own voice he systematically transforms most of the Aristotelian doctrines he discusses, often in directions quite opposed to the Stagirite's original intentions.[23] Henry of Ghent utilizes the multifarious resources of philosophy, including selected insights gleaned from Averroes, Avicenna, Aristotle, and the Neoplatonic tradition in his account of creatures and creator, and in his distinctive metaphysical proofs of the existence of God.[24] Scotus, on the other hand, begins by candidly refusing to accommodate everything of Aristotle into theology; nevertheless his approach to divinity is nothing but a complex *mélange* of his utilization of the theological legacy of Augustine, the philosophical deposit of Neoplatonism, a considered reaction to the work of his contemporaries (especially Thomas and Henry), and a reading of Aristotle refracted through the glass of Latin Averroism.[25]

In the writings of the dominant theologians of Paris and Oxford in the first half of the fourteenth century, the place of philosophical reasoning in

---

[21] For contrasting readings of these developments see Edward Grant, *God and Reason in the Middle Ages* (Cambridge: Cambridge University Press, 2001); and Steven P. Marrone, *The Light of Thy Countenance. Science and Knowledge of God in the Thirteenth Century* (Leiden: Brill, 2001).

[22] Dominik Perler and Ulrich Rudolph, *Logik und Theologie: das Organon im arabischen und im lateinischen Mittelalter* (Leiden: Brill, 2005).

[23] Aquinas's appropriation of Aristotelian philosophy for theological purposes has long and famously been disputed by scholars. For contrasting approaches see Étienne Gilson, *Le thomisme: introduction au système de Saint Thomas d'Aquin* (Strasbourg: Vix, 1919; 6th edn Paris: Vrin, 1983); Fernand van Steenberghen, *Le problème de l'existence de Dieu dans les écrits de S. Thomas d'Aquin* (Louvain-la-Neuve: Institut Supérieur de Philosophie, 1980); and Eleonore Stump, *Aquinas* (London: Routledge, 2003).

[24] On Henry's theology see Guy Guldentops and Carlos Steel (eds.) *Henry of Ghent and the Transformation of Scholastic Thought: Studies in Memory of Jos Decorte* (Leuven: Leuven University Press, 2003) esp. pp. 259–408.

[25] Different perspectives on Scotus's philosophical theology can be found in Oliver Boulnois, *Être et représentation: une généalogie de la métaphysique moderne à l'époque de Duns Scotus (XIIIe–XIVe siècle)* (Paris: Publications universitaires de France, 1999); and Richard Cross, *Duns Scotus on God* (Aldershot: Ashgate, 2004).

theological discourse is evident for all to see. This age not only witnessed the full appropriation of logic into Trinitarian theology,[26] but is further noteworthy for its expansive discussion of a whole host of philosophical issues in metaphysics, especially the topic of relations, as they impinged upon several subjects germane to theological reflection. Durand of St. Pourçain, for instance, made a distinguished contribution to this topic and to philosophical psychology,[27] as did the Franciscan theologian Peter Auriol, whose own work challenged several of the basic assumptions of late thirteenth-century thought, and ushered in new horizons of thought in ontology and the theory of knowledge.[28] That said, the profusion of sophisticated philosophical arguments in the early fourteenth century can often disguise a more general awareness on the part of *theologi* of the limits of rational enquiry and of their increasing realization that some of the more recondite pronouncements of Christian dogma, such as the Trinity, must be accepted by faith alone.[29]

At Oxford, thinkers such as the Dominican Robert Holcot debated, among other things, whether Aristotelian logic was sufficient for dealing with theological antinomies, and Thomas Bradwardine, like countless others before and after him, wrestled with the problem of divine foreknowledge. One of the greatest English theologians of the century, Ockham, saw fit to repudiate some of the central features of the metaphysics espoused by his forebears, but he repeatedly sought to use Aristotle's work to support his own innovative philosophical views while he aspired to be perceived as a faithful theologian.[30] In succeeding years, "nominalist" and "Augustinian" thinkers as gifted and as radically different as Gregory of Rimini,[31] Marsilius of Inghen,[32] and Gabriel Biel[33] continued to appropriate philosophical arguments and theories for theological ends. Far from reducing late medieval theology to a state of "decadence," as

---

[26] See Hester Goodenough Gelber, *It Could Have Been Otherwise: Contingency and Necessity in Dominican Theology at Oxford, 1300–1350* (Leiden: Brill, 2004).

[27] See Isabel Iribarren, *Durandus of St. Pourcain: A Dominican Theologian in the Shadow of Aquinas* (New York: Oxford University Press, 2005).

[28] Chris Schabel, *Theology at Paris 1316–1345: Peter Auriol and the Problem of Divine Foreknowledge and Future Contingents* (Aldershot: Ashgate, 2000).

[29] See Friedman, *Intellectual Traditions in the Medieval University*.

[30] On Ockham's theology compare the contrasting approaches of Marilyn McCord Adams, *William Ockham* (Notre Dame, IN: University of Notre Dame Press, 1987); and Armand Maurer, *The Philosophy of William of Ockham in the Light of its Principles* (Toronto: Pontifical Institute of Mediaeval Studies, 1999).

[31] For an illuminating discussion of late medieval Augustinian theology see Eric Saak, *High Way to Heaven: The Augustinian Platform between Reform and Reformation, 1292–1524* (Leiden: Brill, 2002).

[32] See Maarten J. M. Hoenen and Paul J. J. M. Bakker (eds.) *Philosophie und Theologie des ausgehenden Mittelalters: Marsilius von Inghen und das Denken seiner Zeit* (Leiden: Brill, 2000).

[33] See Heiko Oberman, *The Harvest of Medieval Theology: Gabriel Biel and Late Medieval Nominalism* (Cambridge, MA: Harvard University Press, 1963).

Gilson and other Thomistically inclined scholars of medieval philosophy once argued, these thinkers refreshed and ameliorated the speculative quality of theological discourse in the years leading to the Reformation, helping to create a pluralistic discipline open to a diversity of influences.[34] Even with the rise of less "scholastic," more apophatic, and even humanistic forms of theology that can be found in the writings of John Gerson, Nicholas of Cusa, Heymeric de Campo, and Denys the Carthusian, recognizably philosophical ideas and methods are never far from view (see Chapter 52).

What all this demonstrates is that for thinkers of the high and late Middle Ages, philosophical concepts and methods were simply indispensable to the more rarefied aspects of theological debate; human reason, even in its fallen state, could make a substantial contribution to acquiring genuine knowledge of the natural and supernatural orders. While the *theologi* accepted that Christian verity extended far beyond the purview of the ideas of the ancient philosophers, they were always mindful of the uses to which speculative reflection could be put, and were prepared to experiment with a wide range of philosophical notions in their theological labors.

ISLAM (WISNOVSKY)

One of the main axes of Islamic intellectual culture in the Middle Ages was the relationship between *kalām* (the Arabic term for *speech* or *discourse*, but usually taken to mean simply *theology*) and *falsafa* (the Arabic transliteration of the Greek *philosophia*). The present chapter will argue that, far from being wholly distinct categories, *kalām* and *falsafa* were less oppositional than is generally assumed. It appears in fact that both *kalām* and *falsafa* fall on one side of a larger distinction in Islamic thought, the distinction between knowledge that arises from *intellect* and knowledge that arises from *transmission*; and even this distinction is not hard and fast.

The tendency toward taxonomy

Writing in the late fourteenth century, the North African historian Ibn Khaldūn grumbled that unlike the good old days, when *kalām* and *falsafa* were discrete enterprises, "among these moderns the two methods have become so intermingled and the problems of *kalām* have become so conflated with the problems

---

[34] This aspect is especially well brought out in the important study by Paul J. J. M. Bakker, *La raison et le miracle: les doctrines eucharistiques (c. 1250–c.1400). Contribution à l'étude des rapports entre philosophie et théologie* (Nijmegen: Katholieke Universiteit Nijmegen, 1999).

of *falsafa* that the one discipline is indistinguishable from the other."[35] Ibn Khaldūn's statement is worth citing not just for what it says about the changing relationship between *kalām* and *falsafa*. Their increasing synthesis is a plain fact about medieval Islamic civilization, a development that is clear to anyone who reads the works of post-classical (that is, post-1050) Muslim thinkers.[36] What is more striking is Ibn Khaldūn's acknowledgment that their relationship had changed, and with that an implicit recognition that intellectual activity, like any other human activity, is not static but evolutionary. As obvious as such a notion may seem, it flies in the face of how Islamic thought has generally been conceived. The tendency to treat *kalām* and *falsafa* as unchanging categories is detectable in the works of medieval Muslim doxographers, writers who concerned themselves with cataloguing the many different Muslim schools and sects. And since their works have served for the past two centuries as the primary textual sources for Western scholars of Islamic intellectual history, these supposedly rigid categories have permeated modern scholarship as well. In other words, the Muslim doxographers, and the Western scholars who swallowed their taxonomies of thought, viewed *kalām* and *falsafa* much as a Neoplatonizing Aristotelian philosopher viewed the species we find in the world: as stable and natural, with each possessing a specific *differentia* that could always be relied on to distinguish one species from another of the same genus. Thus a doxographer could distinguish the Muʿtazilī species of *kalām* from the Sunnī species of *kalām* by appealing to the fact that the Muʿtazilīs had always held (and presumably always will hold) that the Quran was created; the Sunnīs, by contrast, held that the Quran was uncreated.[37] (Their position on human free will was also used as a distinguishing feature, with the Muʿtazilīs tending towards greater human autonomy and the Sunnīs tending towards less.) The Shīʿīs could then be differentiated from the Sunnīs by appealing to the fact that the Shīʿīs held

---

[35] Ibn Khaldūn, *Kitāb al-ʿibar*, ed. 1961, I: 837.2–4; cf. I: 836.6–8 and, more generally, I: 921.8–923.12.

[36] Recent work on this synthesis and on the relationship between *kalām* and *falsafa* include Jean Michot, "La pandémie avicennienne," *Arabica* 40 (1993) 287–344; Frank Griffel, "Al-Ghazālī's Concept of Prophecy: The Introduction of Avicennan Psychology into Ashʿarite Theology," *Arabic Sciences and Philosophy* 14 (2004) 101–44; Robert Wisnovsky, "One Aspect of the Avicennian Turn in Sunnī Theology," *Arabic Sciences and Philosophy* 14 (2004) 65–100, and "Avicenna and the Avicennian Tradition," in P. Adamson and R. Taylor (eds.) *The Cambridge Companion to Arabic Philosophy* (Cambridge: Cambridge University Press, 2005) 92–136.

[37] The best concise discussion of this debate remains Wilferd Madelung, "The Origins of the Controversy Concerning the Creation of the Koran," in J. M. Barral (ed.) *Orientalia Hispanica sive studia F.M. Pareja octogenario dicata* (Leiden: Brill, 1974) 504–25. For a more detailed philosophical survey see Harry A. Wolfson, *The Philosophy of the Kalam* (Cambridge, MA: Harvard University Press, 1976) pp. 235–303. The most up-to-date and comprehensive discussion is now Josef van Ess, *Theologie und Gesellschaft im 2. und 3. Jahrhundert Hidschra: eine Geschichte des religiosen Denkens im fruhen Islam* (Berlin: De Gruyter, 1991–97) IV: 179–227 and 625–30 (analysis), and VI: 402–27 (translations).

that the imamate, or religio-political leadership of the Muslim community, had passed directly from Muhammad to his cousin and son-in-law ʿAlī following the Prophet's death in 632. The Sunnīs, by contrast, believed that ʿAlī's claim to leadership reflected the historical order in which the Rightly Guided Caliphs actually succeeded the Prophet. (The Muʿtazilites held varying positions on the imamate, with some leaning toward the Sunnī position and others toward the Shīʿīs.)

As is the case in the Neoplatonists' natural world, each of these three great species of *kalām* – the Muʿtazilīs, the Sunnīs, and the Shīʿīs – can in its turn be construed as a genus containing species. The genus of Muʿtazilism comprised two main species, the Baghdādīs and the Baṣrans, differentiated by the doxographers on the basis of the answers each sect gave to the question, "Is God under an obligation to do what is best (*al-aṣlaḥ*) for his creatures?" The Baghdādīs answered yes and the Baṣrans no. The Sunnī genus itself comprised the species Ashʿarism, Māturīdism and Ḥanbalism. The Ashʿarīs and the Māturīdīs were differentiated from each other by their position on the divine attributes. Attributes such as "creating" and "providing sustenance," which necessarily implied the existence of creatures, were labeled by the *mutakallimūn* (the practitioners of *kalām*) "attributes of action" (*ṣifāt al-fiʿl*); these attributes were distinct from God's "attributes of self" (*ṣifāt al-dhāt* or *ṣifāt al-nafs*), such as "knowing" and "being powerful", which did not necessarily imply the existence of creatures. The Ashʿarīs held that while God's attributes of self were eternal, God's attributes of action came into existence at the moment of creation; to maintain otherwise could imply that creatures – the objects of those attributes of action – were similarly eternal, which is untenable. The Māturīdīs, by contrast, held that God's attributes of action were eternal just as God's attributes of self were; to maintain otherwise could imply that God underwent change at the moment of creation, which is untenable. Standing aloof from their Sunnī colleagues, the Ḥanbalīs would in fact have regarded themselves as *muḥaddithūn* – scholars of Hadith, the transmitted accounts of the Prophet Muhammad's words and deeds – and not as *mutakallimūn*. Nevertheless, many Ḥanbalīs were actively engaged in debates over central issues in *kalām*. In particular, the Ḥanbalīs held that they alone were the true "upholders of the divine attributes." This is because the Ḥanbalīs insisted on a literal understanding of Quranic references to divine actions such as God's rising up on his throne, actions that the more rationalist Ashʿarīs and Māturīdīs held were understandable only through allegorical interpretation. Similarly, the Shīʿīs can be seen as a genus of *kalām* comprising the species Zaydīs (or "Fivers"), Ismāʿīlīs (or "Seveners") and Ithnā-ʿAsharīs ("Twelvers"), each distinguished from the other by the essential differentiating characteristic of which particular imam or descendant of ʿAlī – the fifth, the seventh, or the twelfth – they believed went into a state of occultation until the end times, when that imam will reappear on earth as the Mahdī.

This taxonomic approach rests on the assumption that any given species of thought is stable over time and can reliably be differentiated from another species of thought by appealing to its essential doctrinal characteristic. The problem here is that these different schools of *kalām* underwent major evolutions during the twelve centuries of classical and post-classical Islamic intellectual history. Although the Muʿtazilīs in most respects ceased to exist as a school after the thirteenth century, some key Muʿtazilī doctrines were taken over by the Ithnā-ʿAsharī Shīʿīs and others were taken over by the Zaydī Shīʿīs. The Ashʿarīs and the Māturīdīs, two Sunnī schools of *kalām*, themselves underwent a period of synthesis in the fourteenth century, with the result that prominent Ashʿarī *mutakallimūn* such as al-Taftāzānī took over the Māturīdī doctrine of the eternality of the divine attributes of action.[38]

What about the larger distinction between the genus *kalām* and the genus *falsafa*? As was the case with the different *kalām* schools, whose members some-times advanced the taxonomies of the doxographers for the rhetorical purpose of hardening their own school's sense of identity, so too did the *mutakallimūn* and the *falāsifa* often promote the idea that *kalām* and *falsafa* were irreducibly distinct. There were certainly doctrinal differences between the *mutakallimūn* and the *falāsifa*, the most comprehensive of which was the *mutakallimūn*'s adherence to the atomistic doctrine that the universe was composed of tiny, discontinuous parts, in contrast to the *falāsifa*'s Aristotelian belief in the continuity of matter and their rejection of the void – that is, the empty "space" between the *mutakallimūn*'s atoms. Not even this distinction was watertight, however, since the ninth-century Muʿtazilī *mutakallim* al-Naẓẓām did not hold an atomistic worldview, while the slightly later *faylasūf* and doctor Abū Bakr al-Rāzī did. Even if it were watertight, this doctrinal difference is in itself not sufficient to justify calling *kalām* "theology" and *falsafa* "philosophy."[39] If that were the case, a number of important ancient thinkers – Leucippus, Democritus, Epicurus and their followers – would similarly have to be labeled theologians rather than philosophers. What about the three crucial doctrines of the *falāsifa* that, according to the Ashʿarī *mutakallim* al-Ghazālī in his *Incoherence of the Philosophers* (*Tahāfut al-falāsifa*), warranted an accusation of unbelief (*takfīr*): their belief in the world's co-eternity with God, their denial of God's knowledge of particular

---

[38] Al-Taftāzānī, *Sharḥ al-ʿaqāʾid al-nasafiyya* (*Commentary on Nasafī's Creed*), ed. 1916, pp. 308.3–324.10 (top-inside box); tr. Elder, pp. 67–73.

[39] On this now see A. I. Sabra, "*Kalām* Atomism as an Alternative Philosophy to Hellenizing *falsafa*," in J. Montgomery (ed.) *Arabic Theology, Arabic Philosophy: From the Many to the One: Essays in Celebration of Richard M. Frank* (Leuven: Peeters, 2006) 199–272.

things and their denial of bodily resurrection?[40] Surely these doctrines of the *falāsifa* were stable enough to provide the kind of perpetual differentiating characteristic the doxographers were searching for. Yet two centuries earlier we find al-Kindī, the first great Muslim *faylasūf*, promoting the world's createdness-in-time, and in the fourteenth century we find the Ḥanbalī thinker Ibn Taymiyya advocating a version of the co-eternity position.[41] And in the fifteenth century, we find the Ashʿarī *mutakallim* al-Dawwānī advocating a nuanced and sympathetic reading of Avicenna's denial of bodily resurrection and the doctrine that God knows particulars in a general way.[42] Although it is true that some doxographers allowed for a distinction between earlier generations (*ṭabaqāt*) of a school and later generations, the doctrinal *differentiae* they relied on made their taxonomies hopelessly brittle.

By contrast, the *falāsifa* themselves suggested an epistemological rather than a doctrinal basis on which to draw the distinction between themselves and the *mutakallimūn*: while the *falāsifa* employed demonstrative syllogisms – that is, syllogisms that produce a scientific understanding of a thing – in their discussions, the *mutakallimūn* employed only dialectic, and in particular dialectic that employed theorems specific to the Islamic religion and which thus produced conclusions without universal applicability[43] (see Chapter 26). But this too is a mischaracterization of the difference between *falsafa* and *kalām*. For whatever the *falāsifa* may have said about the role of demonstration in their epistemology, the fact remains that in much if not most of their work it is dialectical methods rather than demonstrative syllogistic that they use. In this respect the *falāsifa* were in fact following Aristotle, who himself employed dialectic widely, often starting his investigations by listing puzzles (*aporiai*), for example, rather than starting from the necessarily true first principles required in demonstrative syllogisms. Indeed the role of dialectic in arriving at those same first principles appears to have been a crucial element of Aristotelian epistemology. For better or worse dialectic was the primary mode of argumentation in Islamic thought just as it was

---

[40] Al-Ghazālī, *Tahāfut al-falāsifa*, *passim*.

[41] On Ibn Taymiyya's criticism of the Ashʿarīs, which verges on an advocacy of the eternity of the world construed as an infinite series of temporally originated events, and on his appropriation of Avicennian cosmological positions, see Jon Hoover, "Perpetual Creativity in the Perfection of God: Ibn Taymiyya's Hadith Commentary on God's Creation of the World," *Journal of Islamic Studies* 15 (2004) 287–329, and "Ibn Taymiyya as an Avicennan Theologian: A Muslim Approach to God's Self-Sufficiency," *Theological Review* 27 (2006) 34–46.

[42] Specifically, in his *Sharḥ al-ʿaqīdat al-ʿAḍudiyya (Commentary on al-Ījī's Creed)*, ed. in S. Dunyā, *Al-Shaykh Muḥammad ʿAbduh bayna al-falāsifa wa-al-kalāmiyyīn* (Cairo: ʿĪsa al-Bābī al-Ḥalabī, 1958) pp. 339ff. and 606ff.

[43] This position is set out in Dimitri Gutas, "The Logic of Theology (*kalām*) in Avicenna," in D. Perler and U. Rudolph (eds.) *Logik und Theologie: das Organon im arabischen und im lateinischen Mittelalter* (Leiden: Brill, 2005) 59–72.

in Aristotelian thought, as Aristotle scholars have begun recognizing since the 1960s.[44] Similarly, the entire post-classical Islamic discipline of "ground-rules of research" (*ādāb al-baḥth*) presupposes the universal applicability of dialectic. A major work of this discipline, by al-Samarqandī, contains case-studies of dialectic's applicability not just to classic problems of *kalām* and Islamic law (*fiqh*), but also to those of *falsafa* – although *falsafa* is now referred to by the less foreign-sounding *ḥikma*, the Arabic translation of the Greek *sophia*.[45] The most that could be said in this regard is perhaps that the *mutakallimūn* and the *falāsifa* appropriated different goals from the ideals of the exact sciences. With the *falāsifa*, what was taken from the exact sciences was the ideal of mathematical proof, the kind of proof that exhibited necessity both in the premises of an argument and in the way the conclusion inexorably emerged from those necessary premises. With the *mutakallimūn*, it was the idea of precision: just as the mathematical astronomers aimed at greater and greater precision in their models, so too the *mutakallimūn* aimed at greater and greater precision in the dogmatic formulas they painstakingly constructed. Nevertheless, both *mutakallimūn* and *falāsifa* shared the goal of achieving a state of impregnability in their arguments.

So much for doctrines and epistemology; could the subject matter of *falsafa* and *kalām* serve to distinguish the two? There was doubtless a set of problems specific to the Islamic religion, problems that works of *kalām* normally included but which did not find a home in *falsafa* books, such as the question of whether or not a dead sinner feels pain in the grave (in anticipation of the punishments that will follow the Day of Judgment). And yet the *falāsifa* and the *mutakallimūn* shared so many core interests, including logic and philosophy of language, general metaphysics (i.e. ontology) and special metaphysics (i.e. theology), natural philosophy and cosmology, philosophy of mind, and epistemology, that the non-overlapping topics such as punishment in the grave appear quite marginal.

Even the periodization that Ibn Khaldūn mentioned above – the modern (*al-mutaʾakhkhirūn*, lit. "those who come later") Muslim thinkers as opposed to the classical (*al-mutaqaddimūn*, lit. "those who come before") Muslim

[44] The classic articulation of this corrective to the medieval view that demonstration lay at the heart of Aristotelian epistemology is G. E. L. Owen, "*Tithenai ta phainomena*," in J. Barnes *et al.* (eds.) *Articles on Aristotle*, vol. I: *Science* (London: Duckworth, 1975) 113–26.

[45] See L. B. Miller, "Islamic Disputation Theory: A Study of the Development of Dialectic in Islam from the Tenth through Fourteenth Centuries" (Ph.D. dissertation: Princeton University, 1984) pp. 234–5; for a list of commentaries on al-Samarqandī's work, see Robert Wisnovsky, "The Nature and Scope of Arabic Philosophical Commentary in Post-Classical (*ca.* 1100–1900 AD) Islamic Intellectual History: Some Preliminary Observations," in P. Adamson *et al.* (eds.) *Philosophy, Science and Exegesis in Greek, Arabic and Latin Commentaries* (London: Institute of Classical Studies, University of London, 2004) II: 169–70.

thinkers – was itself an unstable distinction that various writers applied differently across disciplines. Avicenna, for instance, whom we regard as a classical Muslim thinker, often used the term 'moderns' to refer to himself and his philosophical contemporaries and thereby distinguish them from their ancient and late antique Greek forebears such as Plato, Aristotle, Alexander of Aphrodisias, and John Philoponus, who were called the "ancients."[46] The Muʿtazilīs themselves distinguished between the founding generations of their school (al-qudamāʾ or al-salaf min aṣḥābinā) in the eighth and ninth centuries and subsequent generations. The distinction between ancients and moderns was also standard in medieval Arabic literature, with the sinewy power of classical pre-Islamic and early Islamic Arab poetry (late sixth to the mid-eighth century) contrasted with the effete and ornate new poetry of the Abbasid period (late eighth to tenth century).[47]

Actors' categories and historians' categories

Given all these counterexamples, which make hard distinctions between species of Islamic thought impossible to maintain, what can we say in general about how the intellectual trends that correspond to the Western labels 'philosophy' and 'theology' played out in the Islamic context? Contemporary historians of early modern European science are committed to narratives that foreground "actors' categories": that is, the conceptual scheme in use among the historical protagonists themselves. But are the actors' categories employed by the Muslim doxographers so hopelessly embedded in rigid Neoplatonic and Aristotelian notions of what it means to be a species that they are useless to us when we try to describe a dynamic intellectual scene? It may well be true that the categories *philosophy* and *theology*, which arose and were deployed in a specific medieval European institutional context, cannot be imported and applied directly to *falsafa* (or its later version, *ḥikma*) and *kalām*.[48] It may also be true that the firm boundaries drawn by the doxographers and by the thinkers themselves – boundaries drawn on the basis of doctrine, epistemology, subject matter, and periodization – turn out to be so tenuous that the various strands of Islamic

---

[46] See, e.g., *Kitāb al-shifāʾ/Ilāhiyyāt (2)*, ed. Mūsā et al., p. 399.10 (= *Liber de philosophia prima sive scientia divina V-X*, ed. Van Riet, pp. 472.57–473.58).

[47] See Daniel Gimaret, "Muʿtazila," in P. Bearman et al. (eds.) *Encyclopaedia of Islam*, new edn (Leiden: Brill, 1993) VII: 783–93, and G. J. H. van Gelder, "Ancients and Moderns," in G. Krämer et al. (eds.) *Encyclopaedia of Islam*, 3rd edn (Leiden: Brill Online, 2008).

[48] For an interesting recent discussion of how an analogous Western distinction came to be imported into and naturalized in the Japanese context, see G. C. Godart, "'Philosophy' or 'Religion'? The Confrontation with Foreign Categories in Late Nineteenth-Century Japan," *Journal of the History of Ideas* 69 (2008) 71–91.

thought can be said to be intertwined in an irreducibly complex way. But this in itself does not mean that historians should resist foregrounding all such actors' categories when analyzing Islamic intellectual history.

Instead, we can apply the overarching distinction that was favored by the majority of Muslim thinkers themselves: that between knowledge that arises from the "intellect" (*ʿaql*) and knowledge that arises from "transmission" (*naql*, sometimes referred to as *samʿ*, meaning *audition* or *hearing* – that is, hearing a report from someone else). This distinction referred at its most basic level to the two different ways that Muslim scholars and thinkers understood how one arrives at the truth with certainty. For those tending towards an intellectualist, *ʿaqlī*, position, truth was construed rationalistically, as a function of logical validity, as the product of sound argumentation – argumentation that started with axioms or from generally accepted opinions and proceeded according to the rules of syllogistic or dialectic towards a necessary conclusion. By contrast, those tending towards a transmission-based, *naqlī*, position, saw truth historiographically, as a function of the truthfulness of individuals, as the product of sound chains of trustworthy transmitters who could be verified, through historical research, as having been at the right age in the right place at the right time, and having been in possession of a sufficiently upright character to pass along accurately the utterance each had received from his predecessor in the chain – a chain that passed through the Prophet's Companions (*al-ṣaḥāba*), whose righteousness was very great, and stretched ultimately to the Prophet Muhammad himself, whose truthfulness is unimpeachable. These two actors' categories, *ʿaql* and *naql*, are elastic enough to contain both *falsafa* and *kalām* in the category of "rational sciences" (*al-ʿulūm al-ʿaqliyya*), and thus be useful to the historian of Islamic thought. In other words, the hard distinction between *falsafa* and *kalām* should be set aside as a rhetorical artifact of the multiple processes of school formation that occurred in Islamic intellectual history, and replaced by the larger distinction between *ʿaql* and *naql*. With *falsafa* and *kalām* both included in the broad category of rational as opposed to transmitted sciences, the historian of Islamic thought can give proper attention to the common set of conceptual tools employed by both the *falāsifa* and the *mutakallimūn*, and avoid falling into the trap of assuming that the differences between a *faylasūf* and a *mutakallim* will necessarily override their similarities.

Having said all this, many Muslim thinkers regarded even these two distinct ways of viewing the truth – *ʿaql* and *naql* – as complementary rather than in competition, and they would employ *ʿaqlī* and *naqlī* methods alternately, sometimes arguing and other times citing authority, depending on their audience and opponent. Even the Ḥanbalī theologian and jurisprudent Ibn Taymiyya, whom the Wahhābīs of the modern era regard as their intellectual grandfather, was extremely well read in *falsafa* and *kalām*, and composed a long work entitled *Rejecting the "Contradiction" between Intellect and Transmission (Darʾ taʿāruḍ al-ʿaql wa-al-naql)*.

Coming back to Ibn Khaldūn's statement, what then can be said about the relationship between philosophy and theology in the Islamic context? To start with, it is obvious that *falsafa* cannot be reduced to "philosophy" and *kalām* to "theology." There were many texts and sections of texts written by the *falāsifa* (as was the case with Aristotle himself) that they themselves labeled as theology (*ilāhiyyāt*, lit. "divine matters"), and which treated not only traditional topics in metaphysics such as ontology and causality, but also the nature of God and the relation between the divine self and the divine attributes, the question of determinism, and so on. Similarly, the *mutakallimūn* squarely addressed issues that are usually labeled philosophical: the primary components of matter, the different types of existence, and so on. Furthermore, in discussing these topics the *falāsifa* and the *mutakallimūn* shared and traded technical vocabulary, concepts, examples, distinctions, and arguments. So although *falsafa* and *kalām* were not co-extensive – although there were topics and terms and distinctions and arguments that were unique to one or the other group – they largely overlapped and were both contained within the larger *ʿaqlī* tradition in Islamic thought. Apart from their admittedly real differences, part of what has made *falsafa* and *kalām* appear to be distinct enterprises has been our own scholarly tendency to reproduce the doxographers' taxonomies. Another significant factor has been our tendency to focus on the earliest period of Islamic intellectual history – the "classical" period between 700 and 1050 – during which time *falsafa* and *kalām* overlapped the least, and then to assume that this classical distinctiveness expresses something natural in Islamic intellectual history. In other words, the classical period is viewed as the model Islamic disciplinary arrangement, with subsequent developments seen as pale reflections or decadent versions of the pristine, "true" relationship between *falsafa* and *kalām*. More historically justifiable would be to determine the nature of the relationship between *falsafa* and *kalām* on the basis of evidence contained in texts produced during the longest segment of Islamic intellectual history. In the broader context of Islamic thought, where the 850-year span between 1050 and 1900 is taken as the defining period, rather than the classical era that preceded it or the era of European-style modernity that followed it, *falsafa* and *kalām* come across as a single hybrid enterprise.

51

FAITH AND REASON

WILLIAM E. MANN

The epistemology of religious belief, a central topic among medieval philosophers, shows no signs of disappearing from the public's consciousness or the philosophers' agenda. The reason why is not hard to find. Large-scale advances in science, rightly heralded as triumphs of reason, have been alleged to have implications for the rationality of religious faith: one need only think of the development of evolutionary biology in the past 150 years and of physical cosmology in the past fifty. Of course, the medieval philosophers knew nothing of evolutionary biology. And although they speculated about one big issue in physical cosmology – whether the world was created or has existed forever – their speculations were shaped not by experimental evidence but by Scripture and Aristotelian science. Nevertheless, it does not follow that medieval debates about faith and reason have been superseded. It may well be that contemporary debates on the relation between faith and reason would benefit from a fresh examination of medieval discussions.

PRELIMINARIES

A few preliminary, terminological remarks are in order, first about reason, then about faith. First, in theological contexts, reason is sometimes contrasted with divine revelation, especially when revelation is restricted in its application to doctrines alleged to be beyond the powers of human reason. There is a more expansive conception of reason according to which reason can discover on its own some items of revelation, but this chapter will exclude discussion of that possibility. Second, reason is sometimes distinguished from understanding. Reason, it is said, is discursive while understanding is intuitive. Reason is a capacity to construct, follow, and analyze arguments and hypotheses, whereas a person who has *understanding* of a particular topic grasps the topic immediately with no need (or, at least, no need any longer) to employ reason. Understanding occupies a Janus-like position with respect to reason: it can be either the *foundation* for reasoning or the *consequence* of reasoning. Viewed as foundational, understanding is claimed to apprehend truths so pellucid that simply to entertain them is to see that they are true. Reason is then supposed to perform legitimate operations on these basic truths in order to generate further, non-basic truths. Viewed as consequential, understanding is the result of an exercise of reason – perhaps based on items previously understood. Third, although it is tempting to regard scientific inquiry as the paradigm of reason at work,[1] it is also the function of reason to construct, criticize, and defend arguments in theology and philosophy.

Two final remarks apply to faith. First, 'faith' sometimes refers to an act (or state) and sometimes to the contents or objects of that act. One might ask what sort of state faith is; for example, is it a kind of belief? One might also inquire about what the proper articles of faith are. Second, intentional attitudes such as understanding and faith (especially if faith is construed as a kind of belief) tolerate both objectual and propositional complements. One can believe Jones or believe that Jones is laconic; one can understand horses or understand that this horse is spavined. It is a fine question whether objectual constructions can always be analyzed in terms of propositional ones. Thomas Aquinas certainly thought so. Responding to the observation that the Apostles' Creed begins with the objectual "I believe in God Almighty," Aquinas holds that although the object of faith, God, is a being, apprehension of this being by the human intellect is necessarily by means of propositional complexes. Analogous remarks hold for scientific understanding, as Aquinas understands it; its objects are things in the world about which our knowledge is propositional (*Summa theol.* 2a2ae 1.2 ad 2).

This chapter supposes that both faith and reason are propositional, if only because to suppose otherwise makes it hard to see what tensions there are between them. And tensions there have been. It will help in identifying some of them if we focus on the following collection of propositions. First, here are four accepted by adherents to various religious traditions:

God's existence. God exists.
God's attributes. All of God's essential attributes – omniscience, omnipotence, goodness, and the like – are perfections.
Creator. God created the world.
Love. We are morally obligated to love God and to love our neighbors as we love ourselves.

---

[1] For a robust example, see Edward Grant, *God and Reason in the Middle Ages* (Cambridge: Cambridge University Press, 2001).

Next, here are three that have special significance for Christians:

Trinity. God is three persons in one substance.
Incarnation. At one time, Christ – the second person of the Trinity – became a man while remaining divine.
Embodiment. God cannot become a donkey, or a stone, or wood.

Finally, here are three more that had considerable philosophical authority, but that came to seem problematic in various contexts:

Past. It is impossible to change the past.
Accidents. No (instance of an) accidental property can exist without inhering in a substance.
Eternal world. The world had no beginning.

With the content of these propositions in mind, we can now turn to various views about the nature of faith and reason.

DAMIAN AND ANSELM

The eleventh century provides us with two distinctive Christian contributors to the debate about faith and reason: Peter Damian and Anselm of Canterbury. Because they flourished before the transmission into northern Europe of Aristotle's major works, they present two views that do not yet reflect the tensions that surface in the thirteenth century over the relation between Aristotelian science and revelation.

At first blush, Damian appears to be a champion of anti-intellectualism regarding matters of faith. Throughout much of his Letter 119 ("On Divine Omnipotence") he rails against dialecticians and rhetoricians who apply the tools of their trade thoughtlessly to theological matters: in the case at hand, questions dealing with God's omnipotence. He does allow for a proper use of these tools in the study of Scripture, however, so long as both the tools and the practitioners who wield them remain subservient to the text (tr. Blum, p. 356). Abuse can occur in at least two different ways. First, a person can interpret a text uncharitably. Someone might thus take the angel's exhortation to Lot, "Hurry, escape there, for I can do nothing until you arrive there" (Gen. 19:22), as evidence of a limitation on God's power (ibid., p. 346). Second, the tools themselves are sometimes inadequate. If the canons of grammar and rhetoric conflict with an item of faith, then so much the worse for the canons. Damian supplies an example of how such a conflict must be resolved. It might seem as though **Past** conflicts with the claim that God is omnipotent, if what is past is beyond

God's control. Contrary to how he is sometimes understood, Damian resolves the apparent conflict not by maintaining that God's omnipotence transcends the laws of logic, but by claiming that events that are past to us are not past to God's eternal mode of existence, in which all events, past, present, and future (relative to us), are equally present to God (ibid., pp. 381–2). Damian's point can be illustrated by contrasting two sentences:

(1) Romulus can still cause Rome, which was founded, never to have been founded.
(2) God can still cause Rome, which was founded, never to have been founded.

(1) is absurd, perhaps contradictory. But Damian regards (2) as true without supposing that God can flout the principle of non-contradiction. Understood properly, (2) is equivalent to

(2′) God can still (in his eternal present) cause Rome, which was founded (relative to the passage of human time), never to have been founded (in human time).

While Damian is willing to find a place for reason in the servants' quarters, Anselm welcomes reason into the salon. Anselm's writings display a seemingly boundless optimism about the powers of reason to achieve understanding about the content of faith. He thus provides arguments for the rational necessity of **God's existence** (most famously in *Proslogion* 2–3), **God's attributes** (see especially the strategy developed in *Monologion* 15), **Creator** (*Monol.* 7–9), **Incarnation** (*Cur Deus Homo*), and **Trinity** (*Monol.* 29–65).[2] At the same time, Anselm insists that faith precedes understanding – that is, that he would not understand these propositions unless he believed them (*Prosl.* 1). There are two questions to be asked of Anselm's position. First, does it imply that faith has only instrumental value, motivating the believer to strive for understanding, but superseded by that understanding once it has been achieved? Second, does Anselm think that all five propositions are equally amenable to reason?

In his consignment of *Cur Deus Homo* to Pope Urban II, Anselm says that the understanding that we grasp in this life stands between faith and (revelatory) vision, and that the more progress we make in understanding, the closer we get to that supremely desired vision. This passage does not entail that faith has only instrumental value, but it is tempting to conclude that it assigns greater value to understanding. Before succumbing to that temptation, however, we should examine chapter 1 of *On the Incarnation of the Word*. Here Anselm inveighs against people who try to employ their faculty of understanding in the investigation of religious matters without first having an adequate grounding in faith. They run the risk of declaring as impossible – because unintelligible to them – something that is indeed possible, something whose possibility they would have been

---

[2] For **Trinity**, see also *On the Incarnation of the Word* and *On the Procession of the Holy Spirit.*

motivated to discover had they antecedently had sufficient faith. In an arresting simile, Anselm compares them to bats and owls, who only see the heavens at night, disputing with eagles about the midday sun.[3] Such people are susceptible to two other infirmities. First, without faith they will be unable to interpret experience in the way that the person of faith is able; they will thus fail to understand the higher religious truths conveyed by that interpretation. Second, because they lack sufficient faith, the deliverances of their understanding are apt to be unstable, resulting in the subversion of what faith they might have had.

The following can be said on Anselm's behalf. Someone who holds true beliefs about religious matters and who has subsequently come to understand cogent arguments for those beliefs is in a state that is cognitively more responsible than and superior to the state of someone whose religious beliefs, even though true, are held without the appropriate understanding. The contrast here is between foundational and consequential understanding, where foundational understanding may approximate the sort of noetic certainty that Anselm ascribes to vision. At the same time, Anselm emphasizes that the faculty of understanding – that is, the human intellectual capacity – can go astray in the ways that Anselm has delineated, if it is not "cleansed" by faith (*Incarnation* 1).

Anselm clearly regards **God's existence** and **God's attributes** as demonstrable necessary truths. He takes the key to demonstrating **God's existence** to be the notion of "that than which nothing greater can be conceived." This notion also helps to establish **God's attributes**, aided by the principle that for any property P such that P is better without qualification than not-P, God possesses P (see Chapter 54). **Trinity** is also a necessary truth, by Anselm's lights, but he regards our epistemological situation with respect to it as somewhat different. Given that **Creator** is true, Anselm argues that we should expect to find (necessarily imperfect) images of his triune nature in his creation. At the same time, he takes pains to insist that though the images that he has adduced are true to the thing imaged, it cannot be explained how this is so; the nature of the Trinity is ineffable (*Monol.* 64–6).

When Anselm discusses God's activity as creator, he devotes his energies to trying to make sense of creation *ex nihilo*. If, like pseudo-Dionysius, he thought that God's creating something was a necessary consequence of God's nature, he is remarkably silent about it. One may suppose, then, that for Anselm, **Creator** is only contingently true. He must in any event regard **Incarnation** as contingently true: that God became a man is a response, ultimately, to the freely chosen, contingent fall of Adam and Eve. But if **Creator** and **Incarnation** are contingently true, they cannot be demonstrated with the same sort of rigor

---

[3] Recall the similar strategy deployed by Damian regarding **Past**.

exemplified in the proofs of **God's existence** and **God's attributes**. Anselm
seems to be fully aware of this point. In *Cur Deus Homo* I.10 he invokes two
principles – one methodological, one modal – that prove particularly applicable
to **Incarnation**:

(3) (a) One should accept no proposition concerning God if it entails any inappro-
    priateness, no matter how slight, on God's part, and (b) one should not reject
    any proposition concerning God unless it conflicts with some more reasonable
    proposition.
(4) (a) Any proposition entailing anything inappropriate concerning God entails an
    impossibility, and (b) any proposition concerning God is necessary unless it is
    contradicted by a more reasonable proposition.

Setting aside concerns about how to interpret "inappropriateness," we might
allow Anselm (3a) and (4a). (3b) and (4b) call out for explanation. Notice,
however, that (3b) does not necessarily advocate *acceptance* of just any proposition
concerning God that is not contradicted by a more reasonable proposition.
Suppose, for example, that neither 'God created an odd number of stars' nor
'God created an even number of stars' is contradicted by any proposition we have
more reason to believe. In cases like this, Anselm may have thought that what
(3b) counsels is suspension of judgment about the number of stars. Interpreted
generously, (4b) is an inchoate imputation to God of a Principle of Sufficient
Reason, supplemented by the assumption that it is never reasonable to do what
is suboptimal when one can do what is optimal. That is, God, *qua* supremely
rational being, does only what is rationally the best, what cannot be defeated by
a more rational alternative course of action. (4b) understood in this way coheres
with and helps to further the project of *Cur Deus Homo*, namely, to show that
Incarnation represents the best divine solution to a calamity brought about
by humankind. Readers expecting to find a precocious Leibniz in Anselm,
however, will be disappointed to find that he does nothing more to articulate
or apply (4b).

Anselm appears to invoke (3a) and (3b) in defense of the *pro tanto* reasonableness of his account, in *Cur Deus Homo*, of why God became a man. So far
as he knows, the account imputes no inappropriateness to God, and so does
not violate (3a). In addition, to the best of his knowledge, his account does
not conflict with any propositions more reasonable than the propositions that
constitute his account, and so it satisfies (3b).

Nevertheless, Anselm acknowledges that his account could be mistaken.
Because it involves a contingent truth, he regards his explanation of why **Incarnation** is true as epistemically vulnerable in a way in which, for instance, his
proof of **God's existence** is not.

AQUINAS

By the second half of the thirteenth century, the major works of Aristotle were exerting enormous influence, not all of it welcome, on arts and theology masters teaching in the European universities. Thomas Aquinas retrofitted much of Aristotle's conceptual framework to serve Christian philosophical theology, while recognizing that some of the content of Aristotelian thought is in tension with that theology. After sketching Aquinas's views on the nature of faith and reason, I will examine two cases in which Aquinas appeals to the content of faith to modify – some might even say reject – Aristotelian doctrines.

One way to approach Aquinas's views on faith and reason is to examine some of the salient texts he cites as authoritative. Three are especially worthy of note: one from Aristotle, one from Augustine, one from Scripture.[4] Aristotle had characterized a virtue as a "state of character that makes a person good and enables him to perform his own work well" (*Nic. Ethics* II.6, 1106a22–5). Aquinas classifies faith along with hope and charity as virtues in this generic Aristotelian sense. But faith cannot be fitted into Aristotle's dichotomy of intellectual and moral virtues. These help human beings attain the sort of happiness that can be found in the natural world; they are acquired by natural means. Aristotle had said that intellectual virtues, such as understanding, are developed by education; moral virtues like courage are acquired by habituation. Faith and the other "theological virtues," in contrast, which are necessary for humans to achieve their supernatural happiness – a kind of participation in the Godhead – cannot be acquired naturally. These virtues are "infused" into a person by an act of divine grace (see Chapters 32 and 36).

In order to pin down Aquinas's notion of faith we need to have a characterization of *belief*. Aquinas endorses the Augustinian claim that "to believe is to think with assent."[5] Belief in a proposition, *p*, fits into a family of cognitive states that can be differentiated one from another depending on the strength of conviction the agent has regarding *p*. To doubt that *p*, for example, is to waver between *p* and not-*p*; to suspect that *p* is to think that there may be more reason to assent to *p* than to not-*p*; to venture the opinion that *p* is to risk something on *p* while fearing that not-*p* might nonetheless be true. Unlike belief that *p*, doubt, suspicion, and opinion about *p* do not involve intellectual assent, since the agent is not prepared, or is not prepared fully, to regard *p* as true. One way to interpret Aquinas's view is that belief, doubt, and other such states are, like reasoning, species of discursive mental activity. Mindful

---

[4] In what follows I shall be drawing for the most part on Aquinas's *Quaest. de veritate* 14 and *Summa theol.* 1a2ae 62.1–2 and 2a2ae qq. 1–4. The three passages are cited in both works.

[5] Augustine, *De praedestinatione sanctorum* 2.

of Augustine's definition, we can call the genus of which they are species "thinking."[6]

The third text is from the Vulgate version of Hebrews 11:1: "faith is the substance of things hoped for, the evidence of things that are not seen." Aquinas's interpretation of this verse depends on a sharp distinction between seeing and believing. Aquinas extends 'seeing' to include both visual perception and intellectual apprehension: when a thing is seen, it causes either the senses or the intellect to have knowledge of it.[7] Contrary to contemporary analyses of knowledge, though, to know a thing – at least by way of seeing it – does not entail believing it. Put more strongly, knowledge by seeing renders belief otiose because knowledge by seeing involves *understanding*, and understanding precludes believing. It is true that, like belief, understanding entails assent. *Immediate* (or foundational) understanding is the assent the intellect gives to self-evident principles. The successful tracing out of entailments from self-evident principles, or *mediate* (consequential) understanding, yields *scientia,* knowledge in the strictest sense (see Chapter 26). Unlike belief, however, understanding precludes discursiveness, and thus understanding precludes believing. Immediate understanding would not be immediate if it involved thinking, and thinking ceases once *scientia* is achieved. Thus because to believe is to *think* with assent, belief cannot coexist with understanding.[8]

Thus, for Aquinas, faith cannot coexist with understanding. Recall that, for Anselm, it is possible for a person to believe a theological proposition on the basis of both faith and understanding, and that believing something on these two bases is preferable to believing it on the basis of faith alone. In contrast, Aquinas denies that any one proposition can be held by the same person at the same time on the bases of both faith and understanding. He thus allows that some people can have *scientia* regarding some theological propositions about which others, who are not trained in the rigors of theology, can have only belief. He regards the proposition that God exists, for example, as demonstrable even though the demonstrations may be beyond the intellects of many. For that reason Aquinas does not count this proposition as an article of faith, but rather as a "preamble" to the articles of faith, something that the articles presuppose. The articles of faith themselves are contained in the Nicene Creed; by Aquinas's

---

[6] This interpretation makes room for dispositional beliefs and doubts, but maintains that every dispositional belief and doubt has an ancestry in occurrent, discursive mental activity.

[7] One should interpret "thing" here to include propositions.

[8] Aquinas's cordoning off understanding from believing will strike many present-day readers as odd, inasmuch as they are inclined to think that understanding entails knowing and knowing entails believing. Things were not always so, as we can also see from Book V of Plato's *Republic,* where Plato argues for the categorical separation of knowledge from belief.

count, there are fourteen of them. Consider, for example, the proposition affirming the resurrection of the dead and life everlasting. Not even the keenest human intellect finds it to be self-evident or to be deducible from self-evident principles. The intellect is stymied here.

Aquinas's psychological theory relies on a fundamental distinction between the human intellect and the human will. The intellect is aimed at ascertaining the truth, the will at seeking goodness. They are mutually accessible; each can influence the other in various ways. When presented with a proposition about a supernatural good, namely, eternal life in communion with the font of all goodness, the will can induce the intellect to assent or decline. But the presentation itself is cloudy; humans see now "through a glass, darkly." The infused virtue of faith is what enables assent to and perseverance in the proposition. Perseverance includes, among other things, the intellect's continuing to think discursively about what it does not fully understand. Aquinas thus defines faith as "a habit of mind by which eternal life begins in us, making the understanding assent to things that are not seen" (*Summa theol.* 2a2ae 4.1c; *Quaest. de veritate* 14.2c).

One place where faith and reason might seem to clash is where **Creator** meets **Eternal world.** The Nicene Creed begins with the proposition that God is "maker of heaven and earth, of all that is, seen and unseen." Aristotelian physics, in contrast, holds that the physical world never had a beginning (see esp. *De caelo* II.1, 283b26–30). In the second half of the thirteenth century, serious disagreement arose concerning this apparent conflict between religion and science.[9] Bonaventure, for one, sought to demonstrate that the world had a beginning by showing that a beginningless, infinitely old world would entail, among other things, the "absurdity" that if the sun has already revolved around the earth infinitely many times, then an infinitely long series has been completed. Thus tomorrow's revolution cannot be added to the series, since "it is impossible to add to the infinite" (tr. Vollert *et al.*, p. 107). The reasoning here is specious,[10] however, and may have contributed to Aquinas's contrary resolution of this and related issues.

That God created the world was not at dispute. There is, however, according to Aquinas, no demonstration or scientific proof of the claim; if there were, the

---

[9] The texts of Thomas Aquinas, Siger of Brabant, and Bonaventure are translated in *On the Eternity of the World*, tr. C. Vollert *et al.* (Milwaukee, WI: Marquette University Press, 1964). See also the texts in Richard C. Dales and Omar Argerami, *Medieval Latin Texts on the Eternity of the World* (Leiden: Brill, 1991).

[10] See Grant, *God and Reason in the Middle Ages*, pp. 237–52, for an analysis of medieval discussions of the so-called paradoxes of the infinite. See, too, Richard Dales, *Medieval Discussions of the Eternity of the World* (Leiden: Brill, 1990).

claim would be out of place as an article of revelation in the Nicene Creed. What Aquinas did dispute was the epistemological status of these propositions:

(5) The world has existed forever.
(6) The world had a beginning.

Neither (5) nor (6) is demonstrable, according to Aquinas. The Aristotelian arguments for (5) fail to recognize that whether anything is everlasting depends on God's will, which is the cause of all things and which is beyond human investigation. Bonaventure's arguments to the contrary notwithstanding, however, there is no contradiction in maintaining that (6) is false, for an eternal God could have created an everlasting world. Scripture, however, favors (6), and so Aquinas accepts it on the basis of faith, not demonstration. In a rare display of agitation, he concludes his argument for the indemonstrability of (6) by pointing out that to offer unsound arguments in favor of (6) is to hand unbelievers material for ridiculing believers (*Summa theol.* 1a 46.2, tr. Vollert *et al.*, p. 66). (See Chapter 17 for further discussion of the eternity of the world.)

Another place where faith and reason meet, for Christians, is in the sacrament of the Eucharist. Aquinas articulates and defends the doctrine of transubstantiation, which maintains that in the consecration, the whole substance of the bread and wine is converted into the body and blood of Christ, leaving behind only the "accidents" or sensory qualities of the bread and wine. The account that Aquinas gives thus denies **Accidents**. In Aristotelian metaphysics an accident is "in a subject," that is, it inheres in something, but not as a part of that thing, and it cannot exist separately from that in which it inheres (*Categories* 2, 1a24–5). Despite what Aristotle says, Aquinas argues that God's infinite power can keep the accidents of the bread and wine in existence, inhering in no subject, after their natural and original host substances have ceased to exist. **Accidents** holds at best for what Aquinas calls the order of nature. Faith requires what reasoning based on sensory experience cannot disclose: that the order of nature can be overridden by a special privilege of grace (*Summa theol.* 3a 77.1).

1277 AND BEYOND

In 1277, Stephen Tempier, the bishop of Paris, issued a list of 219 condemned propositions in philosophy and theology, threatening excommunication to anyone who defended or even listened to them (see Chapter 8). Among other things, the condemnation is symptomatic of a worry that the claims of reason, exemplified by Aristotelian philosophy, were misleading believers about the claims of faith. To examine one particular strand, Aristotelian science and metaphysics made claims about what was necessary and what was impossible that contradicted a robust notion of God's omnipotence. Aquinas's position on the indemonstrability of either **Eternal world** or its negation depends on the claim that there is no contradiction in omnipotent God creating a world that has no beginning. Proposition 147 condemns the belief "that what is simply impossible cannot be brought about by God or any other agent. This is an error if it be understood as 'impossible according to nature.'"[11] It is the nature of fire to burn; it is impossible according to nature that fire not burn. Yet, an omnipotent God could suspend this natural necessity – a necessity that he, after all, had established – in order to save believers cast into Nebuchadnezzar's furnace (Dan. 3). Proposition 147 distinguishes between what is *simply* impossible (the hallmark of which is, presumably, contravention of the principle of non-contradiction), and what is *naturally* impossible. Believers are thereby entitled to accept as revelation the narrative in Daniel by supposing that natural impossibilities are not impossibilities for God.

By Edward Grant's count, at least twenty-seven propositions in the condemnation of 1277 were directed against arguments for an eternal world, and were thus also generally consistent with Aquinas's opinion.[12] Aquinas's articulation of the metaphysics of the Eucharist also did not run afoul of the condemnation, which aimed no fewer than four of its propositions at those who claimed that an accident cannot exist without a subject.[13] It is tempting from a modern perspective to regard these two cases as invoking two different conceptions of possibility. We might say on Aquinas's behalf that it is *physically* possible that the world had no beginning, inasmuch as **Eternal world** is consistent with the laws of physics. In contrast, we might suppose that Aquinas's denial of **Accidents** relies on a notion of *metaphysical* possibility: that while it is physically impossible to separate an accident from its subject, it nonetheless remains metaphysically possible. Proposition 147's distinction between simple and natural impossibility appears to parallel the distinction between metaphysical and physical impossibility.

Grant claims that a (perhaps unintended) consequence of the condemnation is that it encouraged scientific speculation along lines that depart from Aristotelian science, since the only thing that was deemed impossible is something that would violate the principle of non-contradiction.[14] The test for the possibility of a state of affairs was whether it fell within the scope of what omnipotent God can bring about. Aristotle's physics assumed the (natural) impossibility of a vacuum – that

---

[11] Henri Denifle and Émile Chatelain (eds.) *Chartularium Universitatis Parisiensis* (Paris: Delalain, 1889–97) I: 552.

[12] Grant, *God and Reason in the Middle Ages*, p. 238.

[13] Denifle and Chatelain, *Chartularium* I: 551 (propositions 138–41).

[14] Grant, *God and Reason in the Middle Ages*, pp. 213–17.

is, a region of physical space containing nothing. For all Bishop Tempier knew, the physical world actually is a vacuumless plenum. But the condemnation of 1277 insisted that it need not have been, condemning the proposition "that God cannot move the heavens in a rectilinear motion, the reason being that he would leave a vacuum."[15] To encourage this latitudinarian speculative tack has implications not only for science, however, but also for faith, inasmuch as it opens the door to a wider range of theological possibilities than Christian theologians had hitherto been willing to contemplate. This is a consequence that William of Ockham and his followers make manifest. Let us look briefly at two examples.

First, suppose that God knows that love tempers the soul, making it more receptive to humankind's ultimate happiness, union with God, a happiness that God desires for us. Then it might seem that a perfectly good God could hardly have failed to prescribe **Love**. Ockham demurs from this conclusion. God could have commanded us to hate him; had he done so, hatred of him would have been obligatory and possibly good. Obligatory, because God's commands are the foundation of obligation. Possibly good because, according to Ockham, the deformity and wickedness of an act of hating God are logically separate from the act itself, and thus can be detached from the act by God (*Reportatio* II.15, ed. *Opera theol.* V: 342). It appears, then, that on Ockham's view, when Scripture commands **Love** (Matt. 22:37–40), it is transmitting a moral mandate that we could not otherwise reliably infer by natural means even if we were in a position to demonstrate by reason that God exists and is perfectly good.

The second example comes from an anonymous work, *Centiloquium*, collected with Ockham's *Dubia et spuria*. Appealing to God's power to do anything the doing of which does not entail a contradiction, the author argues that God could assume the nature of a donkey, or a stone, or wood (*Opera phil.* VII: 384–95). One wonders how Anselm would have reacted to the author's position, which directly contradicts **Embodiment**. A major theme of Anselm's *Cur Deus Homo* is that it was eminently appropriate for Christ to become a man, because the redemption of humanity should be accomplished by a human being. For Christ to have instead assumed the nature of a donkey would have been inappropriate. It might then seem that by Anselm's principle (4a), it would be impossible for God to assume the nature of a donkey. But (4a) does not have that consequence. All that (4a) entitles Anselm to say is that Christ becoming a human being was necessary *for the purpose of human redemption*. That does not preclude the possibility that Christ became both a man and a donkey. Is there disagreement between Anselm and the *Centiloquium* author that centers

---

[15] Denifle and Chatelain, *Chartularium* I: 546 (proposition 49).

on Anselm's (4b)? According to (4b), it was necessary, given the self-induced sinful state of humankind, that God assume the nature of a human "unless it is contradicted by a more reasonable proposition." Anselm's claim depends on divine reasonableness: not to become human, under the circumstances, would be inconsistent with God's nature as supremely rational agent. Suppose that the *Centiloquium* author asserts, in the teeth of Anselm's claim, that it is not necessary for God to assume the nature of a human, not even for the purpose of redeeming humankind. The author will base his claim on God's omnipotence, insisting that, inasmuch as there is no violation of the principle of non-contradiction, God could have redeemed humankind in practically any way – for example, by assuming the nature of a donkey. There is at least the appearance of an impasse. Anselm's (4b) supports

(7) God could not have redeemed humankind by assuming the nature of a donkey.

The *Centiloquium* author's appeal to divine omnipotence endorses

(8) God could have redeemed humankind by assuming the nature of a donkey.

If (7) and (8) are jointly contradictory, then it follows that God cannot be both supremely rational and absolutely omnipotent. But perhaps (7) and (8) are not really contradictory. It might be, for example, that different modalities are at play in (7) and (8). We have already seen a distinction between physical and metaphysical impossibility in the condemnation of 1277. The *Centiloquium* author is surely invoking a notion of metaphysical possibility in (8). Anselm could agree with (8) while claiming that the notion of impossibility invoked in (7) alludes to a third kind of modality, something like rational unacceptability. (7) might then be rephrased as

(7′) It would have been inconsistent with God's standards of rational acceptability for him to have redeemed humankind by assuming the nature of a donkey.

(7′) and (8) are not contradictory. But the solution suggested here is conjectural. We must recall that the two protagonists of this philosophical drama are separated by two centuries.

52

MYSTICISM

CHRISTINA VAN DYKE

Current scholars generally behave as though the medieval traditions of mysticism and philosophy in the Latin West have nothing to do with each other; in large part, this appears to be the result of the common perception that mysticism has as its ultimate goal an ecstatic, selfless union with the divine that intellectual pursuits such as philosophy inhibit rather than support. There are, however, at least two central problems with this assumption.

First, mysticism in the Middle Ages – even just within the Christian tradition[1] – was not a uniform movement with a single goal: it took different forms in different parts of Europe, and those forms changed substantially from the eleventh to the fifteenth century, particularly with the increased emphasis on personal piety and the feminization of religious imagery that emerges in the later centuries.[2] The belief that mysticism entails the rejection or abandonment of reason in order to merge with the divine, for instance, represents only one strain of the medieval tradition. Although this view is explicitly advocated in the Christian West by such influential figures as Meister Eckhart and Marguerite Porete, the prevalent identification of the allegorical figure of Wisdom with Christ provides the grounds for equally prominent figures such as Hildegard of

---

[1] In several respects, mysticism played a more integral role in Arabic and Jewish philosophy than in Christian philosophy from late antiquity through the Middle Ages. For reasons of space, and because the importance mysticism assumes in those philosophical traditions has been more widely acknowledged, this chapter focuses exclusively on Christian mysticism. See, however, Aaron Hughes, *The Texture of the Divine: Imagination in Medieval Islamic and Jewish Thought* (Bloomington, IN: Indiana University Press, 2004); David Blumenthal, "On the Intellect and the Rational Soul," *Journal of the History of Philosophy* 15 (1977) 207–11; M. Idel and B. McGinn (eds.) *Mystical Union in Judaism, Christianity, and Islam: An Ecumenical Dialogue* (New York: Continuum, 1999).

[2] For an influential early piece on this trend, see Herbert Grundmann, "Die Frauen und die Literatur im Mittelalter: Ein Beitrag zur Frage nach der Entstehung des Schrifttums in der Volkssprache," *Archiv für Kulturgeschichte* 26 (1936) 129–61. See also Caroline Walker Bynum, "Jesus as Mother and Abbot as Mother: Some Themes in Twelfth-Century Cistercian Writing," in her *Jesus as Mother: Studies in the Spirituality of the High Middle Ages* (Berkeley: University of California Press, 1982) esp. pp. 129–46.

Bingen, Richard of St. Victor, and Henry Suso to claim that mystical union with God is actually aided by reason.[3]

Second, even when not self-consciously engaged in formal intellectual speculation, mystics often engage issues central to medieval philosophical theology, such as the nature of the Trinity, God's attributes, and the possibility of universal salvation.[4] Rather than dismissing mysticism as irrelevant to the study of medieval philosophy, then, this chapter identifies the two forms of mysticism most prevalent in the Middle Ages from the twelfth to the early fifteenth century – the apophatic and affective traditions – and examines the intersections of those traditions with three topics of medieval philosophical interest: the relative importance of intellect and will, the implications of the Incarnation for attitudes toward the human body and the material world, and the proper relation between contemplation and activity in the good life.[5]

THE NATURE AND PRACTICE OF MEDIEVAL MYSTICISM

Directly contributing to the perception of medieval mysticism as experiential, emotional, individualistic, and anti-intellective – and, hence, as inherently at odds with the highly rationalistic scholastic philosophical tradition – is general confusion over what mysticism is. Indeed, although mystic traditions appear in every major religion throughout the world, there exists surprisingly little consensus about what constitutes either a mystical experience or mysticism in general; the further question of how best to define it has proved to be a highly contentious issue which now has a loaded history.[6] This general problem is further complicated for the particular study of medieval mysticism by the fact that the term 'mysticism' itself is used for the first time only in 1736, whereas the English term 'mystick theology' is first attested in 1639, and the Latin phrase *theologica mystica* is not used to refer to what is now understood as mystic theology

---

[3] So, e.g., although Richard of St. Victor held that philosophy separated from theology is "insipid wisdom and unlearned learning," he saw mystic experiences generally as leading to an understanding of the divine that fulfills rather than empties the intellect. See, for instance, his *De Trinitate*.

[4] Julian of Norwich's *Revelations of Love* (*Book of Showings*), for instance, addresses all three of these topics.

[5] There are, of course, also numerous topics of philosophical interest that are also addressed within the mystical tradition but which (in the interests of space) cannot be addressed here, including issues in human identity and moral psychology, the proper analysis of visual perception, and the nature of being.

[6] See the first chapter of Sarah Beckwith's *Christ's Body: Identity, Culture, and Society in Late Medieval Writings* (London: Routledge, 1993) for a history of the charged politics involved in modern attempts to define mysticism.

until the sixteenth century.[7] (The difficulties involved in retroactively applying these labels parallel in many ways those that arise in discussions of whether medieval figures such as Anselm and Thomas Aquinas should be considered philosophers as well as theologians [see Chapter 50].)

In this context, attempting to provide a precise and comprehensive characterization of either mysticism or mystical experiences would be more likely to obscure than to illuminate important points of intersection between medieval mysticism and philosophical theology. Rather than seeking to distinguish exhaustively the true substance of mysticism from its accidents,[8] then, this chapter will adopt a working definition of mysticism in the twelfth through fifteenth century as having as its goal direct and immediate union of the human soul with the divine. As we will see, this attempt to "forge an unmediated relationship with God"[9] can be understood and worked toward in a variety of different ways; still, common to all these attempts seems to be the assumption of a living God and the belief that the ultimate fulfillment of human nature involves a direct relationship with that God that goes beyond the realm of normal earthly experience and yet is possible to achieve in this life.[10]

Given this general description of medieval mysticism, it is both possible and useful to distinguish between two subcategories within it – namely, the apophatic tradition (which holds that the ultimate stage of human existence is a selfless and unknowing merging with the infinite) and the affective tradition (which focuses on the way in which mystical union can be experienced and expressed in emotional, physical, and sensory terms). The apophatic mystic tradition stresses that the pinnacle of intellection is the paradoxical recognition that reason and knowledge must be abandoned in order to achieve unity with the divine.[11] Apophatic mysticism thus characterizes the ultimate goal of humanity

---

[7] For discussion of this usage, see the *Oxford English Dictionary*; also Nicholas Watson, "Middle English Mystics," in D. Wallace (ed.) *The Cambridge History of Medieval English Literature* (Cambridge: Cambridge University Press, 1999) 539–65; Michel de Certeau, *La fable mystique: XVI–XVII siècle* (Paris: Gallimard, 1982) and *Heterologies* (Manchester: Manchester University Press, 1986).

[8] Evelyn Underhill poses the question in these terms on the first page of *The Essentials of Mysticism and Other Essays* (New York: Dutton, 1920).

[9] Beckwith, *Christ's Body*, p. 19.

[10] In adopting this working definition I follow a wide range of contemporary scholars, including Sarah Beckwith, Caroline Walker Bynum, Michel de Certeau, and Barbara Newman. In "Middle English Mystics," however, Nicholas Watson argues that Richard Rolle – one of the canonical Middle English mystics – "is working with an inherited doctrine of blessedness too conservative to contain a theory of union at all" (p. 549).

[11] Although the apophatic tradition was a minority view in its own time, it is today generally perceived as representative of medieval Christian mysticism as whole. The explanation for this appears to be related to the early twentieth-century battles over the definition of mysticism: in fighting to distinguish "genuine" mystical experiences from their counterfeit rivals, figures such as Evelyn Underhill, William James, and Rufus Jones advocated a true understanding of mysticism

as anti-experiential: the annihilation of self entails the annihilation of sensory experience, and so this tradition discounts the visions of light, smells of incense, tastes of honey, and so on, that were central experiences in the lives of many medieval mystics.[12] To the extent that these experiences regularly occur on the path to true union with God, they function in the apophatic tradition not as divine signs but as potential distractions from the achievement of self-abnegation, which involves the total absence of both sensory and intellective experiences. Indeed, in his late fourteenth-century *The Scale of Perfection*, Walter Hilton explicitly warns against accepting altered physical sensations as signs of true mystic union, whether "in sounding of the ear, or savoring in the mouth, or smelling at the nose, or else [the sensation of] any perceptible heat as if it were fire, glowing and warming the breast" (1.10).

In contrast, the affective mystic tradition often expresses the experience of union with God in terms of a wide variety of emotional and sensory states, and it recognizes those states as valuable unitive experiences.[13] In this tradition, the ultimate goal of mystic union with the divine is best understood not as a selfless merging into the unknowable divine, but rather as the complete realization of the individual creature in full relation to the Creator – which is seen as including the fulfillment of the bodily senses and the emotions as well as the fulfillment of the rational soul. The general flavor of affective mysticism is perhaps best illustrated by the vision of the thirteenth-century French nun, Marguerite of Oingt, in which she began as a withered tree that revivified and flowered when watered by the river of Christ – at which point she saw the names of the five senses written on her now-flourishing branches (*Œuvres*, p. 147). True union with Christ, on this view, does not remove us from our senses or transcend physical reality in a way that renders it irrelevant; rather, it brings those senses and that physical reality into their fullest form. The goal of mystic union in the affective tradition, in other words, embraces rather than eschews embodiment.

Before turning to a closer examination of how central issues within the apophatic and affective mystic traditions intersect with medieval philosophical theology, it is important to note that the majority of extant mystical literature comes not from medieval university culture, but from convents (a term that

as transcending sensory experience entirely in a movement toward the universal and absolute. As later scholars of mysticism such as W. T. Stace and R. C. Zaehner adopted and disseminated this understanding, affective/sensory mysticism disappeared from view – and from the study of medieval mysticism.

[12] See, e.g., Denys Turner's *The Darkness of God: Negativity in Christian Mysticism* (Cambridge: Cambridge University Press, 1995).

[13] In *Margery Kempe and Translations of the Flesh*, Karma Lochrie identifies the two main features of affective spirituality as "its corporeality and the imitation of Christ's suffering humanity" (Philadelphia: University of Pennsylvania Press, 1991) p. 14.

properly applies to both monasteries and nunneries) and – in the later Middle Ages – from the religious "Third Order" of the beguines and tertiaries.[14] Moreover, because the majority of medieval Christian mystics were relatively uneducated members of religious orders and lay communities (particularly in the thirteenth through fifteenth century), both mystical experiences themselves and their interpretations were often expressed and recorded in the vernacular of the region, rather than in scholarly Latin. The words of mystics who were not themselves literate survive only through the written records of more educated people – often their hagiographers, who were frequently concerned more with presenting a certain image of their subject than reporting the mystic's own words.[15] This poses an obvious difficulty for the study of mysticism, insofar as it is challenging in these cases to reconstruct fully the actual nature of the mystic's experiences.[16] Even a focus trained exclusively on mystics who wrote down their own experiences does not guarantee a direct glimpse into their inner life, for the ways in which those mystics express their visions – and, perhaps, even the very ways in which they experienced them – were importantly shaped by then current conceptions of sanctity.[17] Although these facts help account for the relative neglect of medieval mysticism by contemporary scholars of medieval philosophy, however, and although they should be kept firmly in mind when approaching the relevant texts, certain themes emerge clearly enough throughout the Christian mystic literature of the twelfth through fifteenth century to make them well worth philosophical attention.

---

[14] The dramatic rise of the beguine/tertiary movement in the later Middle Ages has long perplexed scholars. In short, in the thirteenth century, an increasing number of women began to function as lay members of religious orders, removing themselves from normal social life and devoting themselves to prayer and religious service, but without taking vows. Often identified as a "women's religious movement," the beguines were extremely influential on forms of religious expression and piety through the later Middle Ages. See, for instance, Herbert Grundmann's classic discussion in *Religious Movements in the Middle Ages: The Historical Links between Heresy, the Mendicant Orders, and the Women's Religious Movement in the Twelfth and Thirteenth Century, with the Historical Foundations of German Mysticism* (Notre Dame, IN: University of Notre Dame Press, 1995 [orig. publ. in German, 1935]); for a treatment of the relation between the beguine movement and the apophatic mystic tradition, see Bernard McGinn's *Meister Eckhart and the Beguine Mystics: Hadwijch of Brabant, Mechtild of Magdeburg, and Marguerite of Porete* (New York: Continuum, 1994).

[15] The case of Beatrice of Nazareth's vernacular treatise and the markedly different *Vita* composed by her hagiographer offers an interesting illustration of this point. See Amy Hollywood, "Inside Out: Beatrice of Nazareth and Her Hagiographer," in C. Mooney (ed.) *Gendered Voices: Medieval Saints and their Interpreters* (Philadelphia: University of Pennsylvania Press, 1999) 78–98.

[16] See Chiara Frugoni's "Female Mystics, Visions, and Iconography," in D. Bornstein and R. Rusconi (eds.) *Women and Religion in Medieval and Renaissance Italy* (Chicago: University of Chicago Press, 1996) 130–64.

[17] See, e.g., Benedicta Ward's *Miracles and the Medieval Mind*, rev. edn (Philadelphia: University of Pennsylvania Press, 1987). The pressing concern to avoid being condemned as a heretic further affects how mystics were likely to report their experiences.

INTELLECT AND WILL IN THE APOPHATIC TRADITION

The apophatic mystic tradition reaches into the Middle Ages from Plotinus through pseudo-Dionysius the Areopagite and John Scottus Eriugena; it is often seen as culminating in the late thirteenth century with the work of the Dominican Meister Eckhart and continuing into the early Renaissance with Nicholas of Cusa's *De docta ignorantia*. The final goal of apophatic mysticism – the final goal of humanity – is complete union with the divine, where that union entails the absolute absence of self-consciousness and knowledge. As we will see, a prominent theme running throughout this tradition involves the respective roles of intellect and will in attaining this end.

"What is the last end?" asks Eckhart. "It is the hidden darkness of the eternal divinity, and it is unknown, and it was never known, and it will never be known. God remains there within himself, unknown."[18] Eckhart (echoed later by John Tauler and Nicholas of Cusa) contends that the belief that one has achieved any sort of divine knowledge or understanding is itself an indication that one has further to go on the path to genuine union with God. Although the apophatic tradition holds that the final stage of the mystic life involves the abandonment of reason, though, it does not uniformly distance itself from either the intellect or the life of the mind. Earlier figures in this tradition in particular present intellectual learning as a necessary stage along the way toward selfless union, and Eckhart also gives the intellect a central role in his account. According to pseudo-Dionysius, for instance, who is strongly influenced by Plotinus, intellectual study is required to lead us from the sensible world to the knowledge of abstract theological truths; indeed, intellective activity can lead us all the way up to the final stage of mystic truth, at which point we must relinquish reason in order to lose ourselves in God's unknowable Being.[19] This method of reaching the ultimate goal of apophatic union is retained in Eckhart, who in fact characterizes God – the absolute principle or absolute cause – not as pure being, but as pure intellect. On this view, intellect is itself unknowable and without being, whereas being (*esse*) presupposes intellect as the cause of its being.[20] Properly speaking, the soul's union with God is not a merging of self with eternal Being – it is actually the loss of being itself and the absorption of individual consciousness into the "hidden darkness" of God's intellect.

---

[18] As quoted in Bernard McGinn, *Harvest of Mysticism in Medieval Germany*, p. 142 (vol. IV of *The Presence of God: A History of Western Christian Mysticism* [New York: Crossroad, 2005]).

[19] See, e.g., pseudo-Dionysius's *On the Divine Names*. Underhill provides a classic summary of this process in *The Essentials of Mysticism*, pp. 11–24. See also Seely J. Beggiani's "Theology at the Service of Mysticism: Method in Pseudo-Dionysius," *Theological Studies* 57 (1996) 201–23.

[20] See Eckhart's *Utrum in deo sit idem esse et intelligere*.

Although central for the Neoplatonist mystics and Eckhart, the role of intellect is sharply downplayed in other figures in the apophatic mystic tradition, particularly in the fourteenth and fifteenth centuries; instead, the will comes to assume an increasingly important role in the ultimate act of union. (This is analogous to debates over intellectualism and voluntarism occurring at this period in the universities [see Chapter 30].) Marguerite Porete, for instance, who was burnt at the stake as a heretic in 1310 for refusing to recant her views, argues in *The Mirror of Simple Souls* that human beings should desire only God, to the point of abnegating personal desire altogether and surrendering their individual wills to God's uniform, unchanging will. Indeed, Porete is closely associated with the Free Spirit antinomianist movement, which held that those who attained mystic union transcended the authority of the church and had no further need for its sacraments or rules.[21] Again, a crucial component of what is renounced is knowledge or understanding; ultimately, Porete indicates, a simple act of will (namely, love) is all that remains. The final goal of humanity is the annihilation of the conscious, knowing self: "The whole is one to her without an explanation (*propter quid*), and she is nothing in such a one. Then nothing more remains for her to do concerning God than remains for God to do concerning her. Why? Because he is and she is not" (ch. 135). By letting go of reason (and the need for understanding or explanation), one is in a position to surrender the human will completely to God's will; in this way, the human being can become fully one with God.

Similar sentiments are also echoed in later fourteenth-century English works, such as the anonymous *Cloud of Unknowing*, which states simply: "Love, but not knowing, may reach to God in this life" (ch. 8). Although this treatise follows the general pattern in the apophatic tradition of providing a systematized approach to achieving true union with the divine, there is no longer any sense that formal intellectual training is a necessary part of this process; central emphasis is placed, instead, on the proper orientation of the will – which is not seen as requiring the intellectual ability to abstract to theological truths from sensible reality. Indeed, the Latin text of the *Cloud of Unknowing* draws a sharp distinction between *scientia* and *sapientia*, contrasting worldly or scientific knowledge with genuine Christian wisdom – a contrast that is also found in other late medieval apophatic works, such as Nicholas of Cusa's fifteenth-century *Idiota de sapientia* (which is heavily indebted to Henry Suso's *Horologium sapientiae*). To achieve wisdom, the

---

[21] For a discussion of Porete in relation to the Free Spirit movement – and an argument that there was no such movement in a formal sense – see Robert Lerner, *The Heresy of the Free Spirit in the Later Middle Ages* (Berkeley: University of California Press, 1972).

layperson does not require access to either formal university education or its methodology; indeed, insofar as the practice of *scientia* self-consciously involves the intellect's attempt to apprehend the truth, it is seen as potentially interfering with the soul's ability to know God in the only relevant sense – namely, through love, a pure act of the will. In addition, as is typical in the apophatic tradition, language is seen in the *Cloud* not as revealing God's nature to us but rather as obscuring the unspeakable truth of God's ultimate being (see Chapter 54). In short, "God may well be loved but not thought."

The increasing emphasis on the role of will over that of the intellect in later apophatic mysticism is further highlighted in the story of the Augustinian nun Clare of Montefalco, who, toward the end of the thirteenth century, found that she "lacked her usual light of revelations and peace of soul"[22] during the eleven years that she spent in intellectual study and in religious and political conversation with cardinals and bishops. According to Clare's *Vita*, when she eventually renounced her desire for knowledge and focused her will entirely on God, surrendering herself to his will for her, she began to experience visions again and became content. In general, although mystics in the apophatic tradition tend to describe the merging of one's soul with God as the end goal of a progression through a number of carefully delineated stages, there is a gradual shift away from characterizing this progress as requiring any sort of formal intellectual training. Rather, the path to the total loss of self in God is left open to anyone willing to pursue it.

Significantly, the increased centrality of the will in apophatic mysticism and the growing sentiment that one need not be learned (or even formally literate) to achieve union with the unknowable divine parallels the well-documented shift from the early twelfth century to the late fourteenth century in general attitudes towards the relation of knowledge and piety.[23] Due in part, no doubt, to the development of the university system and the corresponding transfer of formal intellectual training from convents to the universities (see Chapters 4–5), together with the marked distinction of power and religious authority between clergy and laity after the Gregorian reform of the late eleventh century (see Chapter 39), the later Middle Ages witnessed a sharply increased focus on personal piety – a piety that was not only accessible to those both within

---

[22] Pietro Tommaso de Töth, *Storia di S. Chiara da Montefalco secondo un antico documento dell'anno 1308* (Siena: tip. pont. S. Bernardino, 1908) pp. 26–7.

[23] For detailed discussions of this shift, see, e.g., McGinn's *The Flowering of Mysticism*; Grundmann's *Religious Movements in the Middle Ages*; and the essays in Caroline Walker Bynum's *Fragmentation and Redemption: Essays on Gender and the Human Body in Medieval Religion* (New York: Zone Books, 1992), particularly "The Female Body and Religious Practice."

and without academic centers and positions of ecclesiastical authority, but that often placed positive value on emotional and sensory responses to God. As we will see, this general shift has important consequences for affective as well as apophatic mysticism.

THE INCARNATION AND THE HUMAN BODY IN AFFECTIVE MYSTICISM

Although the apophatic tradition of mysticism has remained, however faintly, on the philosophical radar since the Middle Ages, the medieval affective tradition has been almost entirely ignored. One reason for this neglect is that emotional or sensory mystic experiences have often been flatly dismissed by modern scholars as overly concerned with material reality and irrelevant to the spiritual transcendence of "genuine" mysticism.[24] The increased concern in the later medieval period with such experiences, together with the rise of affective piety and the feminization of religious imagery has, in turn, been attributed (in many cases, negatively) to the increased influence of women on late medieval ideas of spirituality.[25] Indeed, the prevailing medieval conception of women as less rational, more emotional, and more closely associated with matter and physicality than men makes it unsurprising that women dominate the affective mystic tradition and that the male mystics associated with it – including Bernard of Clairvaux, Francis of Assisi, Richard Rolle, and Henry Suso – are often described as feminine in their theological sensibilities.

Although its association with the "lower," "feminine" realm of matter has contributed to the neglect of the affective mystic tradition, from a philosophical standpoint much of its interest stems precisely from the light this association sheds on the complex ways in which conceptions of matter and the body functioned in the Middle Ages (see Chapters 46 and 21). Affective mysticism's emphasis on the importance of physical and emotional as well as intellectual and volitional union with God, for instance, actively undermines a strongly dualist conception of human nature that identifies the self with the rational soul; in fact, by focusing on the incarnate Christ – whose bleeding, broken body plays

---

[24] So, for example, Evelyn Underhill describes episodes of ecstatic union and physical sensations as "frequently pathological, and . . . often found along with other abnormal conditions in emotional visionaries whose revelations have no ultimate characteristics" (*Essentials of Mysticism*, p. 23).

[25] In *The Religious Orders in England*, for instance, David Knowles describes the "pure spirituality" of the early Middle Ages as "contaminated" by "a more emotional and idiosyncratic form of devotion . . . deriving partly from the influence of some of the women saints of the fourteenth century" (Cambridge: Cambridge University Press, 1948–9) II: 222–3. See also Simone de Beauvoir's extremely dismissive discussion of the female mystic in *The Second Sex*.

an extremely important role in later medieval mysticism – the affective mystic tradition links matter and the physical body directly to the divine.[26]

The increase in importance of affective spirituality from the early thirteenth century onward can be understood, in part, as a reaction to Cathar dualism. In the twelfth century, the Cathars (also known as Albigensians) preached an influential (and heretical) version of absolute dualism in the tradition of Gnosticism and Manicheanism that saw the material world as a prison, created by an evil spirit eternally opposed to an equally powerful good spirit. A human being's primary spiritual duty on this view was to liberate the soul from this physical prison through a process of purification that included the total rejection of material goods and power. According to the Cathars, Jesus was a pure spirit, not a physical human being, who came to the material world in order to teach the path to spiritual transcendence; individual human beings exemplified the cosmic struggle between good and evil in their own ongoing battle between spirit and flesh.

The affective tradition countered the perception that materiality was inherently negative by placing a heavy emphasis (often seen as beginning with Anselm's *Cur Deus Homo*) on the Incarnation: if the supremely good God could take on flesh, then flesh itself could not be evil. In *De sacramentis christianae fidei*, for instance, the twelfth-century Augustinian mystic Hugh of St. Victor first affirms Christ's humanity and then gives an analogy where the union of Christ's divine and human natures in one person is compared to the union of human soul with body in one person. He concludes his description of human nature on a decidedly holistic note: "I say truly (*bene*) that the soul and the flesh is a human being . . . and again I say truly that the soul and the flesh is one person" (ed. Migne, 176: 405A). Such stress on Christ's physical humanity – a stress that continues to gain popularity and importance in the affective mystical tradition throughout the later Middle Ages – and the moral explicitly drawn from it for the case of human beings undermine a Platonic and Neoplatonic identification of self with soul and parallel more closely an Aristotelian hylomorphic conception of the human being as a unified composite of body and soul (see Chapters 21 and 34).

Within affective mysticism, the Incarnation is also seen as divinizing the material realm; the fact that Christ became human was seen as a "guarantee that

---

[26] Caroline Walker Bynum has done more to illuminate these issues than any other single scholar, particularly with respect to the relation of affective spirituality to physicality and women. See, e.g., her *Jesus as Mother, Fragmentation and Redemption*, and *Holy Feast and Holy Fast: The Religious Significance of Food to Medieval Women* (Berkeley: University of California Press, 1987), as well as her most recent *Wonderful Blood: Theology and Practice in Late Medieval Northern Germany and Beyond* (Philadelphia: University of Pennsylvania Press, 2007).

what we are is inextricably joined with divinity."[27] The remarkable increase in Eucharistic piety from the thirteenth century onwards and the central importance of the Eucharist in the mystic experiences of many figures within this tradition, for instance, underscore the popularity of the belief that human beings are most closely joined with Christ's divinity through his corporeity. It was not an uncommon event for figures in the affective mystic tradition such as Mary of Oignies, Margaret of Ypres, Christina Mirabilis of St. Trond, or Ida of Louvain to see flesh or taste honey in the Eucharistic wafer, for instance, or to see the priest hold up an infant in place of the host at the moment of transubstantiation.[28]

In general, affective mystic experiences encompass a wide variety of physical and emotional states, including visions and auditory, olfactory, gustatory, and tactile sensations. In the *Form of Perfect Living*, for instance, Richard Rolle describes the third and final "degree" of the spiritual life in terms of intensely pleasant heat: "He or she that is in this degree may as well feel the fire of love burning in their soul, as you may feel your finger burn if you put it in the fire. But that fire, if it be hot, is so delightful and wonderful that I cannot tell it" (ch. 8). Although in many cases it is difficult to determine from surviving texts whether mystics are speaking of their experiences in literal or metaphorical terms, and although treating the experiences of mystics in different regions and different centuries together obscures important and interesting differences between them, the persistently physical expression of affective mystic spirituality is striking. Thus, Beatrice of Nazareth laughed uncontrollably when experiencing the joy of Christ, Catherine of Siena endured a "mystic death," and a number of mystics – including Francis of Assisi and Catherine of Siena – received the stigmata. Standardly negative medieval attitudes towards matter and the body persist in this tradition as well, but Christ's incarnation and passion consistently provide these mystics with a means for a positive conceptualization (and experience) of the human body and the material world.

The senses and sensory perception are portrayed in the affective tradition as not merely a distraction from contemplation but also as an important means of achieving union with God. Hugh of St. Victor, for instance, describes the senses as a bridge or pathway between the material and the divine: "The body ascends by means of sense, the spirit descends by sensuality" (*De unione corporis et spiritus*, ed. Migne, *Patr. Lat.* 177: 285A). In direct contrast to the apophatic

---

[27] Bynum, *Jesus as Mother*, p. 130.

[28] See Bynum's discussion of mystic experiences involving the body of Christ in "Women Mystics and Eucharistic Devotion in the Thirteenth Century" and "The Female Body and Religious Practice in the Later Middle Ages," in *Fragmentation and Redemption*, as well as the extended discussion in *Holy Feast and Holy Fast*.

understanding of mystic union, then, which involves a radical loss of self, the affective mystic understanding of union with God can be seen as a radical fulfillment of the embodied self.

Even accepted negative associations with matter and physicality are sometimes used by medieval mystics towards a positive end: female mystics in particular often highlight their closer association with matter and their status as the "weaker vessel" to validate their religious authority. We can see an early use of this "power made perfect in weakness" approach in Hildegard of Bingen, a twelfth-century Benedictine abbess of remarkable influence and longevity.[29] Active on a wide variety of fronts, including theology, philosophy, poetry, music, and medicine, Hildegard never expresses the anxiety of Clare of Montefalco concerning the compatibility of intellective activity with her mystical visions. Still, Hildegard emphasizes both her lack of formal education and her status as a "poor little female figure" (*paupercula feminea forma*);[30] she appeals directly to her supernatural experiences to account for both her intellectual insights and her authority to share those insights, as when she explains that the knowledge of Scripture she receives in a vision is what serves as the inspiration – and the authorization – for her *Liber divinorum operum*.[31]

This sort of appeal to divine authority via personal weakness increases in the later Middle Ages, as religious authority continues to be transferred away from the laity to the clergy; it appears in the writings of many prominent female mystics of the thirteenth through fifteenth century, including Angela of Foligno, Mechtild of Magdeburg, and Julian of Norwich. In the short text of the *Revelations of Love* (*Book of Showings*), for instance, Julian first underscores the fact that she is "a woman, lewd, feeble, and frail" – and then immediately goes on to state that everything she knows and reports comes directly from "him that is sovereign teacher" (ch. 6 of the shorter *Revelations*). God's charity is what both authorizes and impels her to share her "shewings."[32]

Although mystic experiences were often used to validate the teachings of individuals outside the clergy, however, they were only rarely used to undermine orthodox ecclesiastical authority. Mystic experiences were by nature private, but

---

[29] For a more detailed discussion of this topic, see Barbara Newman's "Hildegard of Bingen: Visions and Validation," *Church History* 54 (1985) 163–75.

[30] *Epistola* 2 (ed. Pitra, *Analecta*, p. 332). The *Vita* of Jutta of Sponheim, her teacher, suggests that Hildegard may, in fact, be exaggerating her lack of intellectual training. See Anna Silvas, *Jutta and Hildegard: The Biographical Sources* (Turnhout: Brepols, 1998).

[31] See Godefridus et al., *Vita Sanctae Hildegardis*, ed. M. Klaes (Turnhout: Brepols, 1993) II.16.

[32] For a discussion of how issues of authority function in the longer text of the *Revelations*, see Lynn Staley, "Julian of Norwich and the Late Fourteenth-Century Crisis of Authority," in D. Aers and L. Staley (eds.) *The Powers of the Holy: Religion, Politics, and Gender in Late Medieval English Culture* (University Park: Pennsylvania State University Press, 1996) 107–78.

within medieval Christianity the condition of their possibility was communal. Just as Aristotle used the human body as a metaphor for human society, so in the Middle Ages Christ's body was used as a metaphor for ecclesiastical society: individual believers were understood to work together to form a single, holy unity. As we will see, the importance of this corporate identity within medieval spirituality has further implications for medieval mystic conceptions of the role of active service in the good life.

CONTEMPLATION, ACTIVITY, AND THE GOOD LIFE

Given the final goal of mystic union, particularly as that union was understood within the apophatic tradition as transcending both physicality and knowledge, we might expect medieval mystics to come down on the side of contemplation in the age-old debate about the roles of contemplation and activity in the good life (see Chapter 33). Yet, although some figures (such as Richard Rolle[33] and Walter Hilton[34]) lean in that direction, withdrawal from active life was in fact the rare exception rather than the general rule in both the affective and apophatic traditions. From Hildegard of Bingen in the twelfth century to Meister Eckhart, Catherine of Siena, and even the secluded anchoress Julian of Norwich in the later fourteenth century, active involvement with religious, social, and political communities forms an integral part of most mystics' lives.

One particularly striking example of the attitude that the individual mystic life includes active involvement with community can be seen in the life of the nuns at Helfta, Saxony in the thirteenth century,[35] particularly Gertrude the Great (author of *The Herald of Divine Love* or the *Revelations*), Mechtild of Hackeborn (author of *The Book of Special Grace*), and Mechtild of Magdeburg (author of *The Flowing Light of the Godhead*). Many of the numerous visions reported by these women were understood to have direct practical significance both for the community at Helfta and for their broader ecclesiastical and social communities. Gertrude, for instance, reports receiving a vision in which God gave her a choice between joining in unspeakable mystic union with Christ or conversing with God in such a way that she would later be able to share these

---

[33] For an argument that Rolle only grudgingly acknowledged the need for active service in the mystic's life, see Richard Kieckhefer's "Mysticism and Social Consciousness in the Fourteenth Century," *Revue de l'Université d'Ottawa* 48 (1978) 179–86.

[34] Although praising contemplation as the highest end, Hilton does concede in his *Epistle on the Mixed Life* that: "Thou shalt meddle [mix] the works of active life with spiritual works of contemplative life, and then does thou well" (ed. Ogilvie-Thomson, pp. 89–103).

[35] The classic treatment of this community is Bynum's "Women Mystics in the Thirteenth Century: The Case of the Nuns of Helfta," in *Jesus as Mother*, pp. 170–262; see also Mary Finnegan, *The Women of Helfta: Scholars and Mystics* (Athens: University of Georgia Press, 1991).

conversations with others for their instruction. Gertrude chooses the second option (*Legatus* 4.2). In another vision, Gertrude hears Christ say:

> [I]t is equally the same to me whether you rest in spiritual things or sweat in external labors, so long as you refer your will in free intention to me. For if I took pleasure only in spiritual exercises I should have so reformed human nature after the fall that it would no longer have needed food or clothing or the other things for which human industry exerts itself.
>
> (*Œuvres* Bk. 3, ch. 68)

Gertrude's assurance of divine approval for a life involving active service is common to the Helfta community at large.

The brief and remarkable life of Catherine of Siena, a fourteenth-century Dominican tertiary, further illustrates this general attitude. Although at first strongly inclined toward complete withdrawal from public life for contemplative purposes, Catherine reports receiving a vision one day of Christ standing outside the door of her cell and calling her to join her community and to care for her neighbors.[36] She spent the remaining thirteen years before her death deeply immersed in social, political, and ecclesiastical affairs – in addition to caring for the sick and working to bring peace to her native Siena, she devoted considerable energy attempting to avert and then to heal the schism that split the church in 1378, dictating countless letters (over three hundred of which survive) and traveling to Florence, Avignon, and Rome to meet with ecclesiastical authorities. At the same time, Catherine retained a deep and abiding sense of mystical union with Christ, which at times manifested itself in dramatic physical ways, including the "mystical death" in 1370 mentioned earlier, when she lay for four hours without breathing or her heart beating, and her receiving of the stigmata in 1375.

This emphasis on the importance of the active as well as the contemplative life can even be seen in the case of the late fourteenth-century anchoress, Julian of Norwich. Although physically removed from communal life and voluntarily walled up in a small cell attached to St. Julian's Church in Norwich, Julian had nevertheless gained a reputation as a spiritual counselor and advisor by the time Margery of Kempe came to consult her in 1413. This was in keeping with the general pattern for anchorites, who were encouraged to remain involved in the spiritual (and, often, educational) life of their communities even after removing

---

[36] *Legenda major* 216 (ed. in J. Bolland *et al.* (eds.) *Acta sanctorum quotquot toto orbe coluntur* [Paris: Palme, 1863–1940] p. 915). For a more detailed discussion of Catherine's attitude toward the life of active service, see Karen Scott, "'This is why I have put you among your neighbors': St. Bernard's and St. Catherine's Understanding of the Love of God and Neighbor," in D. Maffei and P. Nardi (eds.) *Atti del Simposio Internazionale Cateriniano-Bernardiniano* (Siena: Accademia senese degli intronati, 1982) 279–94.

themselves from general society in order to devote themselves more fully to spiritual devotion; so, for instance, the *Ancrene Wisse* – an extremely influential thirteenth-century English handbook for anchorites – includes explicit recommendations for balancing contemplation with obligations to one's community.[37] This recognition of the importance of and need for active service would be surprising in a book written for recluses, if not for the way in which it fits into a broader understanding of the mystic life as inherently communal.

Christian mysticism, both apophatic and affective, flourished in the later Middle Ages. Widespread reports of mystic experiences, however, led to increasing suspicion that such experiences (particularly affective ones) were not divinely inspired; as the "Age of Reason" took hold in the early modern era, mysticism diminished in both importance and popularity.

[37] For a comprehensive introduction to *Ancrene Wisse*, see Y. Wada (ed.) *A Companion to* Ancrene Wisse (Cambridge: Brewer, 2003).

53

ARGUMENTS FOR GOD'S EXISTENCE

BRIAN LEFTOW

Kant named the three main sorts of argument for God's existence "ontological," "cosmological," and "teleological." All three sorts were deployed in the Middle Ages. "Ontological" arguments are deductive and have no empirical premises. These originated with Anselm of Canterbury and flourished in the thirteenth century, but fell into disuse afterward, reemerging only with Descartes. Medieval "cosmological" arguments are also deductive, but have at least one empirical premise. Most medieval cosmological arguments depend heavily on material from Aristotle or John Philoponus; the most original medieval contributions were by al-Fārābī and Avicenna. Cosmological arguments typically first infer the existence of something, and then argue that it is God. Although medieval philosophers had much to say on the second score, for reasons of space this chapter focuses only on their existence arguments. Teleological arguments – arguments from design – were not prominent in medieval philosophical theology and mostly remained at an intuitive level.[1] The Middle Ages' real contribution to natural theology thus lies with the first two sorts, and so this chapter discusses only these.

ONTOLOGICAL ARGUMENTS

Anselm gave the first "ontological" argument in *Proslogion* 2. The key passage is this:

We believe [God] to be something than which nothing greater can be thought... The Fool... when he hears... "something than which nothing greater can be thought," understands what he hears, and what he understands is in his intellect. [But] it cannot exist in the intellect alone. For if it exists only in the intellect, it can be thought to exist also in reality, which is greater. If therefore it... exists only in the intellect, this same

---

[1] The most elaborate scientifically was Levi ben Gershom's (Gersonides). Unfortunately the "science" he drew on was astrology. The most elaborate I know of in terms of philosophical machinery was Aquinas's Fifth Way.

thing than which a greater cannot be thought is a thing than which a greater can be thought... So something than which no greater can be thought... exists... both in the intellect and in reality.[2]

Let "a G" abbreviate "something than which no greater can be thought." Then, on one reading, Anselm's crucial premises are

1. Something existing in the intellect is a G, and
2. If any G in the intellect does not exist outside the intellect, it could have been greater than it actually is.

His *reductio* runs this way. By definition, if an item *x* is a G, then no possible object in any possible state is greater than *x* actually is. It is in a state than which there is no greater. Let *g* be our G existing in the intellect. As a G, *g* is in a state than which there is no greater. According to (2), however, if *g* does not exist outside the intellect, *g* could have been greater than *g* actually is. So, according to (2), if *g* does not exist outside the intellect, *g* is not in a state than which there is no greater. So, if *g* does not exist outside the intellect, *g* both is and is not in such a state. Since that is impossible, it follows that *g* exists outside the intellect.

This argument is valid, so the only question is whether its premises are true. Soon after Anselm published it, Gaunilo of Marmoutiers replied with a parody that raises this issue:

You cannot doubt that [an] island more excellent than all other islands truly exists somewhere in reality, any more than you can doubt it to be in your mind. For it is more excellent to exist not only in the mind but also in reality. So it must... exist. For if it did not, any other island existing in reality would be more excellent.

(*Pro insipiente* 6)

Gaunilo likely misunderstood Anselm: "most excellent" does not mean what "such that no greater can be thought" does. The most excellent actual dog is such that a greater can be thought – for instance, Lassie. The right parody would be to say that if we let "a G" stand for "an island than which no greater can be thought," the resulting argument will work as well as Anselm's. As there is no such island, Gaunilo should have concluded that we know the argument is not sound, even if we do not know which premise is flawed.

Anselm did not reply well to Gaunilo's parody. But in responding, he did come up with a better argument: "Whatever can be thought and does not exist, if it existed, would be able... not to exist. [But] something than which no greater can be thought... if it existed, would not be able... not to exist – for

---

[2] Anselm, *Proslogion* 2. Ellipses here and elsewhere are used to facilitate focusing only on what is formally relevant to an argument.

which reason, if it can be thought, it cannot not exist" (*Reply to Gaunilo* 1). Anselm's reasoning is this:

3. If it can be thought that a G exists while in fact no G exists, then any G would exist contingently if it did exist.
4. It is not possible that a G exist contingently. So
5. It is not the case that it can be thought that a G exists while in fact no G exists.
6. It can be thought that a G exists. So
7. It is not the case that no G exists. So
8. Some G exists.

It would help Anselm to recast (3) as

9. If it is possible that a G exists while in fact no G exists, then any G would exist contingently if it did exist

and alter the rest of the argument accordingly. For (9) is true in the Brouwer system of modal logic, and many – perhaps most – philosophers grant that the correct logic for real metaphysical modality includes Brouwer.[3] Given this alteration, the main problem Anselm's argument faces is giving reason to believe that possibly there is a G.

Two thirteenth-century ontological arguments are also worth noting. In the 1240s, Richard Fishacre took as a premise that God is maximally simple, and reasoned that: "Something most simple . . . would be identical with its being. [Thus] anything most simple . . . would exist."[4] If "being" means *existence*, the argument is a slip, presupposing what it seeks to prove; if it means *essence*, however, we could recast it this way:

10. Possibly God exists.
11. If possibly God exists, a divine essence exists.
12. Any divine essence = God (simplicity premise). So
13. God exists.

(11) is attractive. Before ever there were hamsters, it was possible that there be hamsters. It is a reasonable thought that what made this possible was that there was a property, *hamsterhood*, that existed and could be exemplified. In the mid-1250s, Bonaventure made a similar argument from simplicity: because God

---

[3] The logic I refer to is S5. Perhaps the most prominent defender of S5 is Alvin Plantinga. See, e.g., *The Nature of Necessity* (Oxford: Oxford University Press, 1974). For arguments against S5 see Hugh Chandler, "Plantinga and the Contingently Possible," *Analysis* 36 (1976) 106–9; Nathan Salmon, *Reference and Essence* (Princeton, NJ: Princeton University Press, 1981) 229–52.

[4] Richard Fishacre, *Sent.* I.3 (tr. R. James Long, "Richard Fishacre's Way to God," in R. Link-Salinger *et al.* [eds.] *A Straight Path* [Washington, DC: Catholic University of America Press, 1987] pp. 176–7).

is simple, in 'God exists,' the existence predicated of God is identical with God. This is effectively an identity statement, and so (Bonaventure concludes) it is indubitable.[5] Though rather different from Anselm's, both arguments count as ontological in virtue of being deductive and non-empirical.

Thomas Aquinas took exception to all this. Around 1260, he wrote that God can be thought not to be due only to our cognitive limitations: that is, because we do not have cognitive access to that which is identical with God's existence. Furthermore, he claims:

> No difficulty accrues to those who posit that God does not exist. For it is no difficulty that for anything given in reality or in the intellect something greater can be thought, save to one who concedes there to be in reality something than which a greater cannot be thought.
>
> (*Summa contra gentiles* I.11)

Aquinas's reasoning is this. If there is no actually existing G, then something greater can be thought than anything given in reality. For we can think of a G. If there is none, this is a thought of something greater than anything given in reality. Now if I say that a G exists in reality and that something is greater than it is, I say that there is something that both is and is not a G – an impossible individual. So someone who believes in a G cannot also say that something greater can be thought than anything given in reality or the intellect. But if no G exists in reality, then, at most, one exists in my mind. If I say that a G exists in my mind *and* something is greater than that G is, what follows is simply that I have "in mind" an impossible individual. For if a G exists in my mind, it is really a G, though it exists only in my mind; but if something is greater than it, it is also not a G. We can have impossible individuals in mind; we do, for instance, when we conceive of a particular round square. So one can consistently deny the existence of a G – if one also holds that the concept of a G is a concept of an impossible individual. Although Aquinas does not put the issue in quite these terms, he may have been the first to point out that the claim that a G is possible needs support.

Forty years after Aquinas, John Duns Scotus tried to provide something close – namely, an argument that possibly there is a most perfect possible being. Defining a *simpliciter* perfection (s-perfection) as an attribute better to have than any positive attribute that cannot be co-exemplified with it, he reasons this way: having an s-perfection is better than having any positive attribute inconsistent with it. Consider a candidate s-perfection, F. Given the definition, if there is some positive F* such that being F* is better than being F, either F is not

---

[5] *Quaest. de mysterio Trinitatis* I.1 arg. 28 in agreement.

an s-perfection or F and F* can be co-exemplified. If being F* is equal to or incommensurable with being F, then either neither is an s-perfection or they can be co-exemplified.[6] So there are as many as two s-perfections, F and F*, only if they can be co-exemplified; in general, however many s-perfections there are, they are co-exemplifiable – that is, some single possible being in some possible state has all of them. In this possible state, Scotus thought, that being is a most perfect possible being, for nothing else has a conjunction C of positive attributes that it is better to have. For if C is possible, positive, and better to have than the conjunction of what we have previously thought were s-perfections, and C cannot be co-exemplified with that conjunction, then C is itself an s-perfection, and the previous conjunction contains no s-perfections unless it has members in common with C.[7]

If all s-perfections can be conjoined, though, does it then follow that a G is possible? Let F be the conjunction of all s-perfections. Suppose there is a further family of properties, the Hs, each of which is positive, none of which can be co-exemplified, and which stand in an ordering relation: it is better to have H^2 than H^1, better to have H^3 than H^2, etc. Suppose that infinitely many Hs stand in this relation: there is a least H-property, but no greatest H-property. Then no H is an s-perfection, since no H is better to have than every positive property incompatible with it. Suppose finally that all H-properties are compatible with being F. On these assumptions, no G is possible. For every possible F-being with an H-property, there is a greater possible being. One could easily argue that this is how things actually are: let F be the conjunction of the standard divine essential attributes, and let the Hs be contingent moral record properties (having done one good deed, having done two good deeds, three . . .). Given this, even if there are s-perfections and Scotus's argument shows that they all are compatible, more work needs to be done before we can conclude that a G is possible.

Another of Scotus's arguments for the possibility of a perfect being takes off from the following premise: "Because being able to cause does not necessarily bring with it any imperfection . . . it can exist in some nature without imperfection" (*De primo principio* 3.13). Scotus's premise amounts to this:

14. It is not the case that, necessarily for all x, if x can cause, x is in some respect imperfect.

His premise is not, in other words, that something can be perfectly able to cause, without any imperfection in its causing ability; it is, rather, that being able to

[6] Scotus does not consider the alternatives of equal or incommensurably valuable candidate s-perfections, but completeness requires their mention.
[7] *De primo principio* 4.10–11, with considerable explication.

cause is not necessarily linked with any property the having of which entails being in some respect imperfect. And (14) is plausible. For it does not seem that being able to cause strictly implies being in some respect imperfect due to any conceptual tie. So it does not seem that the first strictly implies the second at all – which is reason to assert (14). Now (14) is equivalent to:

A. It is not the case that, necessarily for all x, either x cannot cause or x is not in some respect imperfect.

(A) is, in turn, equivalent to:

B. It is possible that, for some x, it is not the case that (either x cannot cause or x is not in some respect imperfect),

and (B) is equivalent to:

15. It is possible that some x be able to cause and be in no respect imperfect.

But necessarily, what is in no respect imperfect is in all respects perfect. So, Scotus infers,

16. It is possible that some x be able to cause and be in all respects perfect.

Anything in all respects perfect would be a G, and so (16) implies that possibly there is a G. (Note that what one thinks of this argument will depend on how one views the move from "P does not imply Q due to any conceptual tie" to "P does not imply Q.")

Scotus's own argument for God's existence runs this way (*De primo principio* 3.19):

17. An uncaused cause (UCC) cannot be caused by anything. (df.) So
18. If a UCC can exist, it can exist uncaused.
19. A UCC can exist. ((14), ultimately)
20. A UCC can exist uncaused. (18, 19, modus ponens)
21. If a UCC does not exist uncaused, it cannot exist uncaused. (premise)
22. If a UCC can exist uncaused, it does exist uncaused. (21, contrapos.)
23. A UCC does exist uncaused. (20, 22, modus ponens)

This argument is "ontological": it is deductive and has no empirical premises. Unfortunately (21) is false: if there happens to be no UCC, it might still be possible that one exist uncaused, for perhaps one exists causelessly in another possible world.[8]

---

[8] James F. Ross revived Scotus's argument in the 1960s; see his *Philosophical Theology* (Indianapolis: Bobbs-Merrill, 1969).

COSMOLOGICAL ARGUMENTS

Cosmological arguments are deductive and have at least one empirical premise. Medieval philosophers developed the temporal regress and "contingency" cosmological arguments and also retailed Aristotle's argument from motion.

Temporal regress arguments

These have two main premises:

24. The universe had only a finite past[9]

(which entails that

25. The universe began to exist)

and

26. Whatever began to exist was caused to do so.

Philoponus, the sixth-century Aristotelian, based arguments for (24) on the axioms that

NT. An infinite cannot be traversed, and
NG. Nothing can be greater than an infinite number.

These axioms yielded three arguments:

PRES. Due to NT, had there been an infinity of celestial rotations, the present rotation could never have been reached.
ADD. Had there been an infinity of celestial rotations, each new rotation would add to the number of rotations. This would yield a number greater than the prior infinite. This would contradict NG.
MULT. The heavenly spheres' revolutions are multiples of one another. But "if it is not even possible to traverse the infinite once, is it not [absurd] to assume ten thousand times the infinite?"[10] For there to have been infinite rotations of the solar and lunar spheres, then, would contradict both NT and NG.[11]

---

[9] In our modern view, this is an empirical premise: there are empirical grounds to favor a Big Bang cosmology. The medievals would have disagreed. They were not in a position to argue a Big Bang cosmology, and backed (24) on conceptual grounds: as they saw it, (24) was true because it *had* to be.

[10] As reported by Simplicius, *In Phys.* (X: 1179.23–24; tr. Wildberg, *Philoponus Against Aristotle on the Eternity of the World* [Ithaca, NY: Cornell University Press, 1987] p. 146). I have cleaned up and strengthened Philoponus's presentation: where he speaks of "motions" – e.g. the generation of air from fire – I speak of past events of at least some minimum unit of duration.

[11] MULT does not really add any new consideration to ADD, since multiplication is just multiple addition. I record it only because medievals responded to it separately.

In Islamic philosophy, the Muʿtazilites and Ashʿarites picked up and developed these arguments (see also Chapter 17). Their most interesting addition was the thought that items of finite span, added together, can never compose an item of infinite span.[12] In the eleventh century, al-Ghazālī adds to MULT that if one infinite number is one twelfth as large as another, what is divisible into twelfths must be an even number (*Incoherence of the Philosophers*, tr. Marmura, p. 19).[13] But an infinite number cannot be even or odd, for either way the infinite is "in need of one" (ibid., p. 18) – if it is even, for instance, it is one less than an odd number. Yet any number must be even or odd (ibid., p. 19). If this is correct, there can be no infinite number; hence no infinite number of days; hence there cannot have been an infinite past; and hence, al-Ghazālī infers, (24) is true. Another of al-Ghazālī's arguments makes use of the Aristotelian commonplace that there could be no actually infinite collection. Were the past infinite, he notes, there would now be an infinite collection of immortal human souls (ibid., p. 19).

Some Islamic philosophers backed (26) with a "principle of determination": since prior to the universe's beginning it was equally possible for it to be or not be, there had to be a cause for its being rather than not being.[14] A principle of sufficient reason drives this inference: it is assumed that as the universe appeared contingently, there "must" have been an explanation of its appearing. That principle was not pushed as far as it might have been, however. Confident that what would later be called the problem of Buridan's Ass would not be a problem for God, al-Ghazālī is content to say that God, by sheer will, could pick a time for the world to begin without any sufficient reason to pick one time over another (ibid., pp. 21–2).

Aquinas points out against PRES that it is compatible with the past having been infinite that every interval of time (say, a day) be only finitely distant from every other particular day. Were this so, every distance between two days would be traversable: the present could be reached no matter what day one started from (*Summa theol.* 1a 46.2 ad 6). This implies part of a response to ADD – if an infinite distance is exhaustively composed of finite distances, it is composed of distances that can be added to. Aquinas makes a similar point: had the past been infinite, still the present could be added to: the part of time which came after the present would always be finite (*Summa contra gentiles* II.38).

---

[12] For a general overview of Islamic discussions, see Husām Muhī al-Dīn al-Alousi, *The Problem of Creation in Islamic Thought* (Baghdad: National Printing and Publishing, 1968) pp. 298–320.

[13] Ghazālī does not actually say that it must be even, but he takes it as obvious that something divisible into sixths must be even or odd, and it cannot be odd.

[14] Majid Fakhry, "The Classical Islamic Arguments for the Existence of God," *Muslim World* 47 (1957) p. 139.

But (the friend of ADD might reply) would not the sum of infinite past plus finite addition to the present yield something greater than the infinite past alone? Ḥasdai Crescas would deny this in the fourteenth century: the infinite is not measurable, and so one infinite cannot be greater than another, even if it includes something the other does not (*Or Adonai*, tr. Wolfson, *Crescas' Critique*, pp. 189–91).

NG implies that infinite quantities cannot be proper parts if

PP. Wholes are always greater than their proper parts,

and it implies that all infinite quantities are of equal size if

R. The relations *equal to* and *greater than* hold between infinite quantities.

So, given PP and R, NG yields MULT. Averroes denies PP and R: *equal to* and *greater than* hold only if quantities have end points, but periods without beginning or end have none (*Incoherence of the Incoherence*, tr. van den Bergh, p. 10). His thought may be that such periods have no determinate size, since size is measured between end points. Averroes replies to Ghazālī that being even or odd are properties only of finite numbers (ibid., pp. 12, 13); he might have drawn this from the denial of R, reasoning that an even number must be equal to twice some other number and greater than some odd number. Gregory of Rimini would later suggest that such terms as 'part,' 'whole,' and 'greater than' have more than one sense, and that the senses differ in such ways as to block ADD and MULT.[15] Acceptance of actually infinite collections became common in the fourteenth century. Finally, leaving the principle of sufficient reason aside, the "determination" argument is faulty. It is not obvious that the past's being finite entails that the world need not have existed: it could be necessary that the world exist at every time it does exist, without its being necessary that every time have had a predecessor.

"Contingency" arguments

In the early tenth century, al-Fārābī gave the first contingency argument, which was in essence this:

All contingent beings are caused to exist.
The cause of any contingent being either is or is not contingent.
A series of contingent causes cannot continue infinitely or be circular.

---

[15] Gregory of Rimini, *Sent.* dd. 42–44, q. 4, as quoted in John Murdoch, "Infinity and Continuity," in N. Kretzmann *et al.* (eds.) *The Cambridge History of Later Medieval Philosophy* (Cambridge: Cambridge University Press, 1982) p. 572 n. 23.

So, the series must terminate in an uncaused cause, which as uncaused is not contingent.[16]

Historically, however, Avicenna's subsequent version was the most important, being adopted by, among others, Averroes, Scotus and Francisco Suárez. Avicenna asks us to suppose that some contingent being's existence has causes all of which coexist and exist contingently. In this case, he argues:

> Their total . . . whether . . . finite or infinite, is either necessary of existence . . . or contingent. If it is necessary . . . but each of its units is contingent, then the necessary . . . would be composed of contingents, which is absurd. And if it is contingent, the total needs . . . something to bestow existence. This will be either external . . . or internal to it. If it is internal . . . a cause of the total is primarily a cause for the existence of its parts . . . and thus it will . . . cause [its own] existence . . . [Thus] it is external to the total and [so] not contingent.[17]

Let T be the "total" these causes compose. Then Avicenna's reasoning is this:

27. T is either necessary or contingent.
28. No necessary whole is composed entirely of contingent parts.
29. All of T's parts are contingent. So
30. T is contingent.
31. Every contingent being's existence is caused. So
32. T has a cause.
33. T's cause either is or is not part of T.
34. If it is part, it causes itself to exist.
35. Nothing can cause itself to exist. So
36. It is not part of T.
37. T includes all contingent causes of the posited contingent being.
38. Whatever causes T causes the posited contingent being. So
39. The cause of T is a necessary being.

The restriction to coexistent causes is doubtless to ensure that there *is* such a whole, but the argument could also be recast in terms of transtemporal series. (28) is fairly plausible: any contingent part can fail to exist, and presumably many sums of them can also fail to exist, and it is at least plausible that some parts or sums are such that the whole would not survive their absence. (34) supposes that a full cause of T's existence must be a full cause of all T's parts' existence (else an uncaused part could account for T's existence by causing all the other parts). But this seems true. If there is no cause for A, then though it is

---

[16] See the text translated in Robert Hammond, *The Philosophy of Alfarabi and its Influence on Medieval Thought* (New York: Hobson Book Press, 1947) p. 21.

[17] Avicenna, *Al-Najāt*, as translated in George Hourani, "Ibn Sina on Necessary and Possible Existence," *Philosophical Forum* 4 (1972) pp. 81–2. 'Contingent' has been substituted for Hourani's 'possible,' which although more literal nevertheless gets the sense wrong in this context.

true that if A causes all the rest of T, we can say why T exists given that A does, still we cannot say why T exists: if there is no explanation for A's existence, there is none for T's.

Al-Ghazālī replies that Avicenna had overlooked an alternative: if "contingent" just means "has a cause" and "necessary" just means "lacks a cause," then it can be the case that each contingent thing in T has a cause (another contingent thing in T), but that the whole has no cause and so is a necessary being (*Incoherence*, tr. Marmura, p. 82). But this was not Avicenna's understanding of the modal terms (nor an independently plausible one). Avicenna was clear that a necessary being is one whose non-existence would entail an impossibility and that a contingent being is one whose non-existence is neither necessary nor impossible.[18] Ghazālī's point is thus not germane.

William of Ockham would later agree that T has no one cause, but he adds that T depends on itself, by way of each part of it depending on another part of it (*Quaest. in Phys.* 135). This suggests that (38) does not in fact yield (39): perhaps T's cause is not part of T but is still contingent, because that cause is all parts of T, by each causing some other parts of T. The thought here is this: suppose that T is an infinite series of causes, mapped 1:1 to the number series . . . , −3, −2, −1, 0, 1, ... Then every cause in the series has a cause elsewhere in the series, and so the whole is in a way self-causing – not by itself, as a whole, causing itself as a whole to exist, but by way of each part causing the next, and so collectively causing all the parts, as well as their composition into a whole.

Another thought that might lie behind (28) is that if all the parts are contingent, they might all fail to exist at once – in which case the whole could not be necessary. This thought is the root of an argument by Moses Maimonides: suppose that there has been infinite time, and that all things are such that they might cease to exist. It is possible that at some time nothing is left in existence. Given infinite time, this would already have occurred: in infinite time, every possibility is eventually realized. So nothing would exist now. Thus, if there has been infinite time, it is not the case that all things are such that they might cease to exist (*Guide of the Perplexed* pt. II ch. 1). Aquinas would later adopt this as part of the third of his famous Five Ways to prove God's existence (*Summa theol.* 1a 2.3c). In so doing, Aquinas is sometimes accused of a quantifier-shift fallacy – that is, of inferring from the claim that each thing is such that at some time it ceases to exist to the claim that at some time, each thing is such that it ceases to exist (at that time). We could, however, construe the offending "then" as "then plausibly" – though the resulting argument would no longer be what

---

[18] Ibid., p. 79; cf. pp. 77, 76.

Aquinas would call a demonstration – and treat the whole argument this way: if all things might cease to exist, then plausibly they all might cease at once. If there has been infinite time, there has been enough time for this to occur if it is possible. So it is plausible that there would be nothing now, if nothing is not such that it might cease to exist. So if there has been infinite time, it is plausible that something is not such that it might cease to exist.

The argument from motion

Aristotle's argument for a first, unmoved mover that is the ultimate source of motion was championed by al-Fārābī, Maimonides, Aquinas, and hosts of lesser lights. The first of Aquinas's Five Ways (which may also stem from an argument in Maimonides)[19] gives the core of this argument (*Summa theol.* 1a 2.3c):

40. Some things are in motion.[20]
41. Whatever is in motion is being moved by another thing.
42. The regress of moved movers must terminate in a first mover. So
43. There is a first, unmoved mover.

Standard Aristotelianism used 'motion' to label changes of quality and quantity as well as place. (41) thus proved controversial.

Many Franciscans – including Bonaventure, Scotus, and Ockham – insisted that wills "move" themselves or at least that things with wills do so.[21] If there is not some sense in which this is true, then we are not genuinely free. This would not automatically imply that any material thing moves itself locally. A Cartesian, for instance, might hold that souls are the primary bearers of wills, that a will moves its associated body as something like an efficient cause, and that the soul directly "moves itself" only in a sense not involving literal locomotion.[22] Nevertheless, if it is *we* who primarily have the will and move ourselves locally by willing to do so, then if wills move themselves, something moves itself locally without being moved by another. The best response on Aquinas's behalf might be to insist that our souls are in some sense parts of us, and so this is a case not of a whole moving itself but of one part of a whole moving a different part and, thereby, derivatively moving both itself and the whole.

---

[19] *Guide* pt. II ch. 1. Aquinas's Second Way is similarly just a riff on an argument of Aristotle's in *Metaphysics* II.2. If any of the Five Ways originate with Thomas, they are the fourth and fifth.

[20] Or: "some things are being moved." There is still debate about just how to translate the Latin *moveri*.

[21] Bonaventure, *Sent.* I.37.2.2, n. 4; Scotus, *Quaest. in Meta.* IX.15; Ockham, *Quodlibet* I.16.

[22] If a writer recognizes some sense in which a soul is where its body is, then if a soul wills that its body move to a new place and its body then moves, the writer will have to grant that the soul moves itself locally, but indirectly, by way of moving the body.

Another problem concerns heavy objects, which might seem to move themselves downward. Aristotelians would gloss this by saying that their natures give them a natural impulse down which acts unless impeded. A stock medieval Aristotelian response was that in such cases the stone is really moved by what removes the impediment and what gave the stone its nature. Making this a basis for (41), however, was not healthy for the cosmological argument. Since what gave the stone its nature need no longer exist, it is then compatible with (41) that there only *was* and no longer *is* a first, unmoved mover – unless one has some argument that this sort of mover cannot cease to exist.

Scotus argues that stones do move themselves downward, contending among other things that this theory faced fewer objections than orthodox Aristotelian alternatives (*Quaest. in Meta.* IX.14, esp. nn. 45–52). Suárez, in turn, would point to hot water spontaneously cooling – a point relevant because in his day 'motion' was held to include change of temperature (*Disp. metaphys.* 29.1.7). Thrown projectiles also pose a problem for (41), since the thrower is no longer in contact with them to move them along. The problem led eventually to impetus theories of motion (see Chapter 18); such later Thomists as John Capreolus, Suárez, and John of St. Thomas reconcile this case with their defense of (41) by taking the impetus as the mover's instrument in moving the projectile. Eventually, the entire problematic would be transformed by the concept of inertial motion. As Newton would see it, an object in everlasting motion would need no mover to keep it going were its motion not resisted: objects in uniform motion tend naturally to maintain their motion. This is less a shocking physical discovery than a shift in explanatory paradigm: Newtonian physics makes the claim that continued inertial motion is not the sort of thing to require a physical explanation. Thereafter, defenders of the argument from motion had to take their chances on the field of metaphysics.

Naturally, (42) was also controversial. The First Way does not reason that causal series must be finite and, therefore, there must be a first cause. It reasons instead that there must be a first cause and that therefore, as it were incidentally, the series must be finite. In fact, whether a series is infinite and whether it terminates in a first cause are independent matters; as Crescas notes, it is possible that a causal series be infinite and yet terminate (*Or Adonai*, tr. Wolfson, *Crescas' Critique*, p. 225). (A descending series of positive integers is infinite, and yet it terminates at the number one.) Suárez would go further, suggesting that it is possible that a causal series be infinite despite terminating on both ends – that is, that the first cause and the final effect be separated by infinitely many intermediate causes: for (he would reason) God is infinitely perfect, any species of angel is finitely perfect, and so between God and any species of angel there is "room" for an infinite gradation of further degrees of perfection, to each of which could correspond an angel involved in a causal series (*Disp. metaphys.* 29.1.30). Aquinas himself, although he thought a first cause could be proved, did not think the world could be proved to be finite in either the past or future. The reason he nevertheless felt sure of (42) was that he thought that the causal series in question was ordered *per se*.

In a *per se* series, every cause other than a first is caused to act by another member of the series: when a hand moves a stick which moves (say) a stone, the hand causes the stick to move the stone, and does not move the stone apart from doing so by moving the stick. Thus, in a *per se* series, all causes act together to produce the final effect: the stick moves the stone and the hand also moves the stone. In such a series, the hand moves the stone by means of the stick. Since each cause earlier in the series produces the final effect by means of causes later in the series, what goes on can always be described by plugging names of causes into a sentence-frame such as '___ . . . causes effect F by means of C by means of D by means of E . . . ,' where the blank is a place holder for the first cause. Thus, if there is no first mover in a *per se* series of movers, to record what is going on we need a sentence frame of the form '___ . . . moves F by means of C by means of D by means of E . . . ' but without any subject term to plug into the blank. With nothing plugged into the blank, the purported description of what is going on is not the kind of thing that can be true. So it seems that there cannot be a true sentence asserting the existence of a *per se* series of movers with no first mover.[23] Further, if in such a case there is nothing to plug into the blank before 'moves,' then nothing does the series's moving. If nothing does the moving, there are no movers. But, of course, a series of movers with no movers in it is a contradiction in terms. Thus it seemed clear to the medievals that in a *per se* causal series, there *had* to be a first mover. Of course, it is another question whether any such series had to be traced to an absolutely unmoved mover. If the human will can move itself, then human beings are first movers in any number of *per se* causal series – unmoved insofar as involved in those series, but moved in other respects. So even if (40)–(42) are all true, someone arguing from motion has more work to do before concluding the existence of something legitimately identifiable as God.

---

[23] This paragraph is heavily indebted to Barry Miller, "Necessarily Terminating Causal Series," *Mind* 91 (1982) 201–15.

54

DESCRIBING GOD

THOMAS WILLIAMS

The philosophical problem of describing God arises at the intersection of two different areas of inquiry. The word 'describing' makes it clear that the issue is in part a logical one – in the broad medieval sense of 'logic,' which includes semantics, the philosophy of language, and even some aspects of the theory of cognition. It is the problem, first, of forming an understanding of some extramental object and, second, of conveying that understanding by means of verbal signs. But the word 'God' also indicates that the logical problems involved in description are exacerbated, or perhaps that new problems arise, because of the nature of the extramental object that we are seeking to describe.

Given the enormous ingenuity with which logical problems were debated in the Middle Ages, it is not surprising that the problem of describing God would be worked out in detail – and that many thinkers would lose sight of the specifically theological context in which the problem was ostensibly set. We see here a familiar phenomenon. Once philosophers (even scholastic philosophers) have fully domesticated a problem, discussions of the problem seldom lay bare the practical urgency that alone made the question worth pursuing in the first place; it becomes a technical question, answerable by technical means. Yet, though it is not always in evidence, the practical upshot of the issue is never entirely forgotten, as John Duns Scotus reminds us in his curt dismissal of the view that we can at best say of God what he is not: "We do not have supreme love for negations" (*Ordinatio* I.3.1.1–2 n. 10).

Attempts to resolve the problem of describing God are ultimately efforts to "save the appearances": to accommodate within a philosophically defensible framework both the data of what are taken to be divinely revealed texts and the linguistic practices of believers. The appearances to be saved of course differ somewhat from one religious tradition to another. The Christian tradition, for example, faces distinctive problems that arise in understanding and describing the triune nature of God.[1] Yet, despite these differences, the broad contours of the problem of describing God are recognizably similar in Judaism, Christianity, and Islam.

The chief reason for this similarity is that mainstream philosophical opinion in all three traditions was united in its view of those features of God that resist understanding and, consequently, expression. Philosophers taught that God is simple, which means that he lacks not only physical structure but also the *metaphysical* structure that our ordinary subject–predicate language implies. He is also far removed from the ordinary objects of the senses, which are the most accessible objects of knowledge and (for Aristotelians, at least) the ultimate source of the concepts that give meaning to our language. Finally, God has nothing in common with the objects of our ordinary experience; he shares no feature with them and belongs to no genus that includes them. Consequently, it is hard at first glance to see how any concepts or words that apply to the objects of our ordinary experience could also apply to God.

ANSELM

Anselm's approach to the problem of describing God makes a useful introduction to the topic, because Anselm sees the issues involved clearly and offers a resolution that does not depend on the more elaborate semantic theories to which later writers would appeal.[2] The issue initially arises for Anselm in the context of his natural theology in the *Monologion*. Noticing that his arguments all involve relating or comparing God to creatures – God is best, highest, and greatest; he is the creator and sustainer of all other things – Anselm asks whether he has yet managed to say anything about the *substance* of God: that is, about what God is in himself, rather than how God is related to other things (ch. 15). So he excludes relative terms from consideration and divides all other predicates into two mutually exclusive and jointly exhaustive classes. For any feature F, either (a) what has F is, as such, better than what lacks F, or (b) it is not the case that what has F is, as such, better than what lacks F. Following later medieval usage, let us call the features that fall in class (a) "unqualified perfections" (*perfectiones simpliciter*). The predicates that name the unqualified perfections – such predicates as 'living,' 'wise,' 'powerful,' and 'just' – can all be applied to God. Moreover, they do not express merely what God is *like* (*quale est*), but what

---

[1] The scholarly literature has paid scant attention to how frequently medieval Christian writers situate their discussions of religious language in an explicitly Trinitarian context.

[2] The reading of Anselm's theological semantics presented here is defended at much greater length in Thomas Williams and Sandra Visser, *Anselm* (Oxford: Oxford University Press, 2008).

God *is* (*quid est*): in other words, these perfections are not merely predicated of God but are actually identical with God's nature. This follows from a general principle for which Anselm had already argued (in chs. 1–4): that for any F, if God is F, God is F through himself. Hence if God is just, for example, and whatever is just is just through justice, it follows that God is himself justice.

Anselm emphasizes, however, that our ability to use ordinary language to express the simple divine nature should not be taken to imply that there is any ontological overlap between God and creatures. God's being is utterly unique, because he alone has all his being from himself, whereas all other things have their being from him. And since every non-relative term that signifies God at all signifies God's being, every predicate we apply to God will have a very different significate in its theological and non-theological uses.[3]

To say that these predicates have a very different *significate* is not, however, to say that they have a very different *meaning*. Anselm does suggest, provisionally, that "if anything is ever said of [the supreme essence] in words that are common to other natures, their meaning is in no way common" (*Monologion* 65). But he cannot fully endorse this suggestion, since such discontinuity of meaning would (as he clearly sees) make all the arguments of his natural theology founder on the fallacy of equivocation. So he locates the discontinuity not in the meaning of our words, but rather in the nature of the connection between mind and world that signification establishes. He distinguishes between two ways in which a word might signify or bring something to mind: *per se* and *per aliud*. When a word signifies something *per se*, it brings that thing to mind directly or straightforwardly; when it signifies something *per aliud*, it brings that thing to mind only in virtue of some additional knowledge or some other feature of the context of utterance. The names that express unqualified perfections signify *per se* the perfections that we experience in creatures; they signify God *per aliud* by "hinting at" the divine nature "through a certain likeness" (ibid.). Our knowledge of God derived from Scripture or natural theology is the only reason that such names bring God to mind at all; even then, they do so only obliquely.

AL-FĀRĀBĪ AND AVICENNA

Classical Arabic philosophy puts particular emphasis on the claim that God is *intellect*. Both al-Fārābī and Avicenna connect God's intellectual nature with his immateriality. As al-Fārābī puts it,

---

[3] It is this point about God's metaphysical uniqueness, rather than any skepticism about the success of theological language, that Anselm means to convey when he says that "if God ever shares any name with other things, undoubtedly a very different signification must be understood" (*Monologion* 26).

Because the First is not in matter and has itself no matter in any way whatsoever, it is in its substance actual intellect; for what prevents the form from being intellect and from actually thinking is the matter in which a thing exists. And when a thing exists without being in need of matter, that very thing will in its substance be actual intellect; and that is the status of the First.

(Perfect State I.1.6, tr. Walzer, p. 71)

He adds that, since matter is also what stands in the way of intelligibility, God is also intelligible. Since God is by nature actual intellect, and he cannot depend on anything outside himself to be what he is, it follows that God thinks himself. Avicenna offers a similar account of God as self-understanding intellect, but he argues explicitly for a claim that was merely implicit in al-Fārābī: namely, that God's self-understanding does not entail any duality in God. As Avicenna puts it, "a thing's being an intelligible does not necessitate that it is intellectually apprehended by some thing, that thing being another" (*Metaphysics* VIII.6.10, tr. Marmura, p. 286).

For al-Fārābī, much of what we can say about God is reducible to claims about God's intellectual nature. "God is knowing," "God is wise," and even "God is living" all mean the same thing: that God "understands the most excellent intelligible through the most excellent intellect" (*Perfect State* I.1.10; tr. Walzer, pp. 75, 77). Avicenna offers a more complex theory, according to which we can describe God in three ways. First, we can speak of God on the basis of his unique, individual, and necessary existence. Second, we can negate any likeness between God and creatures. Third, we can attribute to God relations to creatures as their first cause. Avicenna explains these three kinds of predication as follows:

[It is evident] that, if you ascertain the truth about him, [you will find] that, after [the fact] of his individual existence, he is only described by means of negating all similarities of him and affirming to him all relations. For all things are from him, and he shares nothing in common with what [proceeds] from him. He is the principle of all things, and he is not any of the things that are posterior to him.

(*Metaphysics* VIII.5.14, tr. Marmura, p. 283)

On the basis of God's individual existence we can say that God is perfect, since he is not deficient in any way, and that he is intellect, since he is immaterial. We can also say that God is good, because the good is what everything desires, everything desires existence, and God is perfect existence. Negative and relative predications include the concept or notion of God's unique necessary existence and add to it some negation or relation. For example, if "one, without due respect, says of the First that he is a substance, he would not mean [anything] but this existence with the negation of his being in a subject." And "if he says of him 'powerful,' he would mean by it only that he is the Necessary Existent, to which is added that the existence of [what is] other than him truly comes about only from him in the manner that has been mentioned" (*Metaphysics* VIII.7.13, tr. Marmura, p. 296).

In the course of his discussion of describing God, Avicenna (unlike al-Fārābī) seems at times to understand the claim that God is intellect as meaning no more than that God is immaterial. He writes that if someone says God is "intellect, intellectual apprehender, and intelligible, he would mean in reality only that this pure being [is such that] the possibility of mixing with matter and its attachments is negated of him," and he identifies God's intellectuality with "the negation of matter from him" (ibid.). But since Avicenna holds that God knows genera and species (though not particulars), and that God's knowledge is creative, it is clear that there is more to God's being an intellect than simply lacking matter. The emphasis on immateriality in Avicenna's discussion of divine intellect simply reflects the basic Aristotelian requirements for intellectual cognition and his conviction that those requirements are perfectly fulfilled only in God.[4]

MAIMONIDES

For Moses Maimonides, it is the oneness of God – his uniqueness and simplicity – that systematically frustrates our ability to represent God in thought and to speak meaningfully about God. Maimonides discusses five kinds of affirmative predication. (1) We cannot predicate any *definition* of God, since "there are no previous causes to his existence, by which he could be defined" (*Guide of the Perplexed* I.52). (2) We cannot predicate a *part* of a definition, since God has no parts. (3) We cannot predicate any *qualities* of God, since God is not a substratum for accidents distinct from himself. (4) We cannot predicate any *relations* of God, for two reasons. First, such predications contradict the simplicity of God. (Maimonides thinks of relations as real accidents inhering in their subjects [*Guide* I.52].) Second, such predications contradict the uniqueness of God by implying that God is a member of a larger class of objects; to say

---

[4] The focus on divine intellect that we find in the Arabic Aristotelians from al-Fārābī onward is perhaps surprising, given the insistence of Islamic theology on the oneness of God. The best philosophical text on the oneness of God is al-Kindī's *On First Philosophy* chs. 3–4, which offers arguments reminiscent of Plato's in the *Parmenides* for the claim that God is the true One. For these arguments and their Platonic–Plotinian background, see Michael E. Marmura and John M. Rist, "Al-Kindī's Discussion of Divine Existence and Oneness," *Mediaeval Studies* 25 (1963) 338–52, and Peter Adamson, *Al-Kindī* (Oxford: Oxford University Press, 2006) ch. 3. (I am grateful to Deborah L. Black for impressing upon me the contested place of divine intellect in this tradition, and more generally for her help with this whole section.)

that God is more powerful than human beings is to place both God and human beings together in a single class of powerful beings (*Guide* I.56). Consequently, there is no similarity between God and creatures, and there is no truth at all in the affirmative predications that imply such similarity: "The man who affirms an attribute of God knows nothing but the name; for the object to which, in his imagination, he applies that name does not exist; it is a mere fiction and invention, as if he applied that name to a non-existing being, for there is, in reality, no such object" (*Guide* I.60).

There is only one permissible kind of affirmative predication concerning God: (5) we can predicate *actions* of God. Such predications do not purport to describe God as he is in himself; they merely attribute certain effects to the divine activity. Hence, the fact that many such predications are possible – owing to the multiplicity of God's effects – does not derogate from divine simplicity. Other affirmative predications are legitimate only insofar as they are taken as disguised negations. Negative predications do not imply plurality in God, and they "are necessary to direct the mind to the truths that we must believe concerning God" (*Guide* I.58). We can say, for example, that God exists, meaning that his non-existence is impossible, or that God is living, meaning that he is not inanimate like the four elements. Since human knowledge of God is limited to negations, which "do not convey a true idea of the being to which they refer" (*Guide* I.59), the best and most becoming response to the divine nature is silence.[5]

THOMAS AQUINAS

"We cannot know what God is," Aquinas says, "but only what he is not" (*Summa theol.* 1a 3 prooem.). In saying this Aquinas appears to embrace a position very close to that of Maimonides, and many contemporary interpreters, especially (though not exclusively) those influenced by Martin Heidegger, read Aquinas as a largely apophatic thinker. But in fact Aquinas accommodates both affirmative and negative predication about God, although the transcendence and simplicity of God entail that our affirmative predications are inevitably problematic.

Aquinas was definitely influenced by Maimonides, however, and it is instructive to consider first the grounds on which Aquinas rejects Maimonides's view.

---

[5] See further Hilary Putnam, "On Negative Theology," *Faith and Philosophy* 14 (1997) 407–22; Kenneth Seeskin, "Sanctity and Silence: The Religious Significance of Maimonides' Negative Theology," *American Catholic Philosophical Quarterly* 76 (2002) 7–24; and Diana Lobel, " 'Silence is Praise to You': Maimonides on Negative Theology, Looseness of Expression, and Religious Experience," *American Catholic Philosophical Quarterly* 76 (2002) 25–49.

He offers three reasons.[6] First, if all our affirmative predications are disguised negations, we will have no reason to affirm some things of God in preference to others. If we can say "God is alive" to express the claim that God is not an inanimate object, why can we not equally well say "God is a body" to express the claim that God is not pure potentiality, like matter? Second, it would follow that all affirmative names predicated of God would be said of him only in a derivative or secondary sense. Third, this is simply not what people mean when they speak affirmatively of God: "for in saying that God is alive, they intend to convey more than just that . . . he differs from inanimate bodies" (*Summa theol.* 1a 13.2c).

To this last point Maimonides could well respond that people who say "God is alive" do indeed intend to convey more than a mere negation, but that is only because they are confused. Aquinas, however, believes he can save more of the phenomena than Maimonides could, accommodating not only what believers do when they talk about God but also what they take themselves to be conveying by such talk. The positive content that believers intend to convey in their ordinary practice of affirmative predication is grounded in a genuine relation of similarity between God and creatures.[7] Any perfection in an effect must be found in its cause: either according to the same intelligible character (*ratio*), if the cause is a univocal cause, or in a more eminent way, if it is an equivocal cause. God is the first efficient cause of all creatures, and he is an equivocal cause. So all the perfections of creatures "preexist in God in a more eminent way" (ibid., 4.2c). Consequently, "every creature represents God and is like him insofar as it possesses some perfection" (ibid., 13.2c).

Our power to describe things rests on our power to know them. Since creatures represent God and are like him, we can come to know God, and hence describe him, on the basis of creatures. But creatures represent God incompletely, in a fragmentary and deficient way, so both our knowledge of God and our names for God will be fragmentary and deficient as well. The deficiency of our names for God entails that no name can be predicated univocally (with exactly the same meaning) of both God and creatures. When we predicate 'wise' of a human being, "we signify a perfection that is distinct from the human being's

---

[6] Aquinas uses these same three arguments (though with different examples) to oppose the view that affirmative predications about God are disguised relative predications: that to say "God is good," for example, is really to say that God is the source of the goodness of creatures. Aquinas found this view in Alan of Lille's *Regulae celestis iuris*.

[7] It is, to be sure, a one-sided relation: creatures bear a relation of similarity to God, but God does not in turn bear any relation to creatures. The denial of real relations *ad extra* in God is standard in medieval Christian thought. By contrast, Maimonides assumes that any genuine relation is *reciprocal*.

essence, and from his power and being and so forth" (ibid., 13.5c). In that way, the predicate 'wise' delimits an isolable aspect of the thing signified and brings that aspect fully under the sway of our understanding. Things are otherwise when we predicate 'wise' of God. In that case we do not intend to signify any perfection distinct from the divine essence, since there is no such thing in God. So even when we represent and name God as wise, God remains beyond our comprehension. Accordingly, we do not predicate 'wise' of God in the same sense (*secundum eandem rationem*) in which we predicate it of a human being.

In the technical language of thirteenth-century logic, our perfection terms have a "mode of signification" (*modus significandi*) that does not apply to God (*Sent.* I.22.1.2; *Summa theol.* 1a 13.3; *Summa contra gentiles* I.30). All of our concepts derive from composite creatures, in which the thing that has a form is distinct from the form itself. So our perfection terms either signify the form as simple but non-subsistent, as 'justice' does, or else signify the thing having the form as subsistent but not simple, as 'just' does, for instance, when it signifies a person who is just. Consequently, Aquinas says, "as far as their mode of signification is concerned, [our perfection terms] are not said properly of God; for they have a mode of signification that is appropriate for creatures" (*Summa theol.* 1a 13.3c). But this fact is not sufficient to render *all* our language equivocal when applied to God. The similarity between God and creatures that is grounded in God's causal activity means that the external nature signified (*res significata*) by our names for God does exist in God, although in a more eminent way than in creatures.

Thus, our names for God are neither purely univocal nor purely equivocal; they are analogical.[8] Analogical predication is intermediate between univocity and pure equivocity.[9] It happens when a single word is said of two things in a prior and a posterior sense. In the case of religious language, God is prior in reality, since creaturely perfections reflect the divine perfection. Accordingly, the names of perfections are predicated in a prior way of God, and indeed are said more properly of God than of creatures (*Summa theol.* 1a 13.6) – even though

---

[8] The proper characterization of Aquinas's doctrine of analogy is endlessly disputed. The interpretation given here is strongly influenced by E. J. Ashworth, "Signification and Modes of Signifying in Thirteenth-Century Logic: A Preface to Aquinas on Analogy," *Medieval Philosophy and Theology* 1 (1991) 39–67, and "Analogy and Equivocation in Thirteenth-Century Logic: Aquinas in Context," *Mediaeval Studies* 54 (1992) 94–135, as well as by Ralph McInerny, *Aquinas and Analogy* (Washington, DC: Catholic University of America Press, 1998).

[9] So Aquinas expressly says at *Summa theol.* 1a 13.5, notwithstanding the incredulity of Kevin L. Hughes, "The *Ratio Dei* and the Ambiguities of History," *Modern Theology* 21 (2005) p. 659 n. 7. The qualification "pure" is necessary because thirteenth-century writers classed analogical predication as a species of equivocation, corresponding to Aristotle's *pros hen* homonymy.

God is posterior in our knowledge and those names are originally imposed on the basis of our experience with creatures.

Aquinas's account of theological language suggests a close connection between semantics and cognition: our ability to use language concerning God rests on our ability to understand God, and since our understanding of God is inevitably fragmentary and deficient, so too is our language about God. His account also suggests a close connection between semantics and ontology: the possibility of non-equivocal speech about God rests upon the real similarity of creatures to God, and the impossibility of univocal speech about God rests upon the irreducible ontological diversity of God and creatures. Later medieval thinkers will suggest loosening one or both of these connections. The remainder of this chapter looks first at the connection between semantics and cognition, and second at the connection between semantics and ontology.

NAMING AND KNOWING[10]

Henry of Ghent follows Aquinas in arguing that our knowledge of God is fragmentary and incomplete in ways that make our language about God problematic, but Henry does not tie naming God to knowing God quite so closely as Aquinas had. It is possible for us to have a more adequate understanding of something than we convey in speech. Imagine two people reciting, with full conviction, the so-called Athanasian Creed. One of them is a regular person in the pew; the other is a brilliant systematic theologian. The two of them speak with equal precision, but the theologian has a far richer understanding of what is being said. Moreover, individual knowers may be incapable of expressing something to the extent to which they understand it. For example, we can grasp the immensity of God more adequately than we can express it in language (*Summa* 73.10).

Where Henry is concerned with the ways in which our knowing is keener than our naming, Scotus emphasizes the possibility of naming God more adequately than we know him. He writes: "This proposition, which is common to many opinions – I mean that 'As God is understood, so too is he named' – is false if taken strictly, because it is possible for something to be signified more distinctly than it is understood" (*Ordinatio* I.22, q. un., n. 4). This has to be the case, since otherwise we would be unable to signify anything in the category

---

[10] For additional thirteenth-century discussions of the connection between naming God and knowing God, see Alexander of Hales, *Summa theol.* I.2.1, tr. un. q. 1.1c; Bonaventure *Sent.* I.22, a. un. q. 1c; Giles of Rome *Sent.* I.22 princ. un. q. 1 ad 2; and Richard of Middleton, *Sent.* I.22.1c. See also E. J. Ashworth, "'Can I Speak More Clearly Than I Understand?' A Problem of Religious Language in Henry of Ghent, Duns Scotus, and Ockham," *Historiographia Linguistica* 7 (1980) 29–38.

of substance; we could signify only the feature of the substance on the basis of which the name was originally imposed. Thus, for example, the name 'rock' (*lapis*) would not signify anything in the genus of substance, but only something in the genus of action – namely, the "foot-hurting" (*laesio pedis*) on the basis of which the name was imposed. And we can signify distinctly a particular substance that underlies accidents as 'this being,' even if our only quidditative concept of the substance is the concept of *being*, which is the most general or common concept available. In the case of religious language, a name proper to God, distinctly signifying the divine essence as "this essence," might be imposed by God himself, or by an angel that knows God, or even by someone in this life (*Ordinatio* I.22, q. un., n. 10), even though we do not *know* God as "this essence," but only as (say) "this infinite being that does not depend on anything" (*Lectura* I.22, q. un., n. 4).

In contrast, William of Ockham's treatment of the question is much more explicitly tied to his semantic theory. For Ockham, there are some words that signify extramental things directly – that is, not through any mediating mental conception. This is not to say that such words do not have to be associated with a concept to be meaningful, only that they directly signify (that is, supposit for) things, rather than for the associated concepts (see Chapter 11). Since this is the case, "anyone who can genuinely understand that one thing is distinct from another can impose a name for the purpose of distinctly signifying that thing" (*Ordinatio* I.22, q. un. [*Opera theol.* IV: 55]); the adequacy or inadequacy of the person's conception of that thing is entirely beside the point. For instance, with the word 'man' I can distinctly signify someone who does not even exist yet. Or, I can impose the name '*a*' to signify whatever animal I am going to run across tomorrow. For me, and for anyone else who is willing to adopt this imposition, '*a*' will signify that animal, even though I do not distinctly understand the animal when I impose the name (and may well not distinctly understand it even when I run across it tomorrow). Accordingly, since human beings in this life "can genuinely understand and know that God is distinct from everything else" (ibid.), we can impose a name that signifies God distinctly. We can distinctly signify what we do not distinctly understand.

ANALOGY AND UNIVOCITY

The essential feature of Aquinas's theory of analogy is that a single term is predicated *per prius et posterius*: of God in a prior way and of creatures in a posterior way. Henry of Ghent gives a more detailed account of religious language, but his basic approach is very much like Aquinas's. Henry argues that perfection words are used in a prior way of God, reflecting the fact that such perfections are in creatures only as effects of divine perfection. It is this metaphysical relation of participation or resemblance that both saves theological language from pure equivocity and also bars univocity. Henry goes a step further than Aquinas, however, by settling a question that Aquinas had left unresolved: is an analogical term subordinated to a single concept, or to more than one? Henry holds that in an analogical predication there are two distinct, though closely related, concepts.[11]

Scotus is hostile both to predication *per prius et posterius* and to Henry's claim that a distinct concept is involved in predicating perfection terms of God. In his early logical works, Scotus argues against predication *per prius et posterius* in ways that do not depend on any specifically religious claims (*Quaest. super Praedicamenta* 4; *Quaest. super librum Elenchorum* 15).[12] But these arguments are nonetheless relevant to our topic, since they rule out analogy as a mean between univocity and equivocity. They thus provide the background to Scotus's later development of the doctrine for which he is best known: the claim that all unqualified perfections are predicated univocally of God and creatures.

Scotus has a number of arguments for univocal predication and against the doctrine of analogy (*Ordinatio* I.3.1.1–2, nn. 26–55). The most widely discussed is his argument that one can be certain that something is a being and yet uncertain whether that thing is a finite or an infinite being. Such a state is possible only if the concept of *being* is univocal between finite and infinite. (Compare: I can be certain that someone is a mother while being in doubt whether she is a good mother or a bad mother. This combination of certainty and doubt is intelligible only on the supposition that 'mother' is predicated univocally of good mothers and bad mothers.)

Moreover, according to Scotus, any recognizably Aristotelian view of concept formation entails univocity. Aquinas and Henry of Ghent agree that all our concepts are derived ultimately from our experience of sensible creatures. But, Scotus argues, if this is the case, then the concepts that give meaning to our language about God will also derive from creatures. They will not merely be *like* the concepts that come from creatures, as in analogous predication; they will have to be the very same concepts that come from creatures, which entails univocal predication. Either we have the same concepts for God and creatures, or we have no concepts of God at all, in which case it would be impossible to speak about God.

---

[11] For discussion and references, see Ashworth, "Analogy and Equivocation," p. 124.

[12] See Robert Prentice, "Univocity and Analogy According to Scotus's *Super libros Elenchorum Aristotelis*," *Archives d'histoire doctrinale et littéraire du moyen âge* 35 (1968) 39–64, for a discussion of Scotus's early views.

In a similar vein, Scotus argues that univocity is necessary to preserve the character of theology as a science: that is, as an argumentative discipline. Just as our power to describe God rests on our having concepts under whose extension both God and creatures fall, so too our ability to draw inferences about God depends on the univocity of the terms in which we carry on argument and the unity of the concepts that underwrite the intelligibility of such language. Without univocity, any attempt to draw inferences about God will founder on the fallacy of equivocation.

Scotus's doctrine of univocity breaks the close association between semantics and ontology – between naming and knowing – that we have seen not only in Thomas Aquinas and Henry of Ghent but in their Muslim and Jewish predecessors as well. These other thinkers all insisted, in their various ways, that some change of meaning or conceptual slippage or linguistic indirectness had to result from our attempts to apply to God the words and concepts by which we name and understand creatures – precisely because creatures are irreducibly distinct from God. These divergences from ordinary usage were, so to speak, the semantic epicycles apart from which the appearances could not be saved. For Scotus, by contrast, our describing God requires no such epicycles. Ordinary words, with their ordinary meanings, apply straightforwardly to a metaphysically extraordinary God.

55

PROVIDENCE

HESTER GOODENOUGH GELBER

Two texts framed medieval Christian discussions of the idea that God exercises providential care and governance over the created order: the biblical Book of Wisdom and Boethius's *Consolation of Philosophy*. In the Book of Wisdom, the term 'providence' occurs at 6:17, where Wisdom "presents herself in all providence," and again at 14:3, which says: "Father, your providence rules because you have provided a way even on the sea and a most solid path among the waves." These passages provided both warrant and mandate for theologians to investigate how God's omniscience and omnipotence were manifest in the providential governance of the created order; it was Boethius, however, who set the philosophical parameters for that investigation.

Boethius defines God's providence as the "unfolding of temporal events as this is present to the vision of the divine mind" (*Consolation* IV prose 6). He goes on to claim that:

Fate moves the heavens and the stars, governs the elements in their mixture, and transforms them by mutual change; it renews all things that are born and die by the reproduction of similar off-spring and seeds. This same power binds the actions and fortunes of men in an unbreakable chain of causes and, since these causes have their origins in an unchangeable providence, they too must necessarily be unchangeable. In this way things are governed perfectly when the simplicity residing in the divine mind produces an unchangeable order of causes. This order, by its own unchanging nature, controls mutable things which otherwise would be disordered and confused.

(ibid.)

Boethius grapples with the question of how such an unbreakable chain of causes grounded in the divine mind could be compatible with free will and human accountability for moral evil (ibid., V prose 3). He has his interlocutor, Lady Philosophy, claim that there is free will, "and that no rational nature can exist which does not have it. For any Being which by its nature has the use of reason, must also have the power of judgment by which it can make decisions and, by its own resources, distinguish between things that should be desired and things that should be avoided" (ibid., V prose 2). Boethius famously concludes that because God's knowledge is outside time and God knows everything as "present" in itself, the only necessity that attaches to acts of free will is a "conditional necessity" of the sort that arises from the necessity of the principle of non-contradiction: if a woman chooses to be sitting, she must necessarily be sitting, not standing, because to stand and sit at the same time would violate the principle. If that woman chooses to sit, no necessity compels her choice and she could just as easily have chosen to stand. The "absolute freedom" of her own nature is not compromised in any way as a result of God's necessary knowledge of everything that happens (ibid., V prose 6).

Yet to square human freedom with divine knowledge is not yet to square it with divine providence. Boethius's contention that God's providence orders everything through unbreakable chains of causes without compromising the absolute freedom of judgment that rational creatures exercise through freedom of the will created a philosophical conundrum for medieval schoolmen. What is the nature of causality, and what is the nature of the will in relation to causality that would make this position tenable? Throughout the Middle Ages, discussions of divine providence revolved around these issues.

Although Arabic philosophy had significant impact on Latin scholastic philosophy and theology, both positively and as a goad for deeper reflection where those in the Christian tradition disagreed with their Muslim counterparts, there is not much direct dialogue regarding providence. Matthew of Aquasparta expressed concern that Averroes had restricted providence to species rather than extending it to individuals, and Thomas Bradwardine cited Arabic thinkers along with everyone else in massive lists of authorities to justify his determinist views. Nevertheless, it was the scriptural warrant for taking up the term and the Boethian legacy that provided the imperative and the frame for the ensuing discussion. Although Islamic and Jewish authors discuss the problem of divine foreknowledge (see Chapter 29), the question of how to reconcile human free will with God's providential oversight over every particular aspect of creation was a more pressing question among Latin authors than among the best-known Arabic ones. What follows provides a short history of the term 'providence' as Christian theologians understood it during the high Middle Ages – the thirteenth and fourteenth centuries – in light of the problem Boethius bequeathed.

THE THIRTEENTH CENTURY

The recovery of Aristotle's natural philosophy in the Latin West (and, in particular, his discussion of causality in *Physics* II.3) provided a new vocabulary for analyzing providence. Over the course of the thirteenth century, Alexander of Hales, Thomas Aquinas, and Matthew of Aquasparta adapted the Aristotelian distinction between efficient, formal, material, and final causality to probe the relation between divine governance and human freedom.

Alexander of Hales

The first book of Alexander's *Summa theologica* defends at length the idea of a providential order. He argues that power, wisdom, and goodness are all attributed to God through the nature of his causality. Thus, "power is attributed to him as he is the efficient cause, wisdom as he is the formal, exemplary cause of things, and will or goodness as he is the final end" (I.1.5.2.3.1, ed. Quarrachi, I: 285a). Importantly, Alexander claims that God's formal and final causality – but not his efficient causality – are operative in the exercise of divine providence. He calls attention to the root and prefix of the term *providentia*: the root *videntia* connects with divine wisdom, and thus with formal causality; the prefix *pro* denotes the causality of governance or ordination of God's good pleasure or will, and thus God's final causality (ibid., I: 286b–87a). With respect to texts that seem to equate providence with God's power and thus with efficient causality, Alexander argues that God's power in these instances should be understood not as separate from God's wisdom and goodness or will, but as integral to them. Hence it is not God's power as an efficient cause or agent of change that is the causality directly operative in providence (ibid., I: 287b). Alexander's analysis, unlike that of either Boethius before him or Aquinas after him, emphasizes that understanding providential causality requires defining the roles of both the divine intellect and the divine will.

Restricting providence to formal and final causality opens space for freedom of the will: God's governing in this way enables the unfolding of the divine plan for creation without God's coercing particular acts of human willing as their immediate efficient cause. Alexander borrows a distinction from John of Damascus between providence understood as "acceptation" and providence understood as "concession" to work out the exact relationship. The providence of acceptation occurs when providence encounters no resistance, as in the case of natural things (like the sun's rising and setting) that operate in an orderly way and cannot be otherwise. The providence of concession comes into play where there can be resistance, as in the case of creatures with free will. God concedes to those with free will the power freely to consent to or reject good and evil and God does not coerce such choices (ibid., I: 294b); nevertheless, these acts of free will do not escape from providential governance or necessity because of their freedom. To explain this, Alexander invokes a distinction between two forms of relative necessity: "necessity *ab hoc*," which is the necessity that arises from force, violence, or the intrinsic nature of things, and "necessity *ad hoc*," which is the necessity that arises after the fact, imposing order on what has previously come about (ibid., I: 302a–b). In the case of acts of free will, whether the will chooses well or ill, those acts are always providentially ordered to some good after the fact, whether that be the good of just punishment or of just reward (ibid., I: 302b, I: 285a–b).

Thomas Aquinas

Like Alexander, Aquinas seeks to reconcile God's providential governance with Aristotelian causality; like Boethius and unlike Alexander, however, he locates providence in God's intellect and not in both his intellect and his will. Aquinas argues that God conceives of the overall good of creation as the order all created things have toward their end, and especially toward their ultimate end, the divine goodness itself. The good each individual thing has through its substantial form is complemented by its innate ordering to an end, which, in turn, is ordered to the greater overarching divine good, and the whole system is enacted according to God's governance. Hence, prior to creation, God understood the order of everything to its ultimate end. Aquinas concludes that "the understanding of the things to be ordered to an end is in a strict sense providence" (*Summa theol.* 1a 22.1c).

This exposition of providence follows the Aristotelian formulation of final causality as the end or sake for which something is done – a principle of change located in reason, not action (and by implication not the will) (*Phys.* II.3, 194b33–95a3; II.9, 200a5–24). God acts providentially inasmuch as he is the final cause of creation. Thus, divine providence completes Aquinas's analysis of God's creative act in terms of the Aristotelian picture of causality: God is not only the first efficient and the first formal cause of everything as enacted through his will, but also, through his reason, the ultimate final cause (*Summa theol.* 1a 19.4c).

Aquinas rejects the Aristotelian legacy that restricted divine final causality to species, exclusive of individuals. He asserts that divine providence rules all things – not just universal natures, but even singulars:

That this is so is evident: for since every agent acts on account of an end, the ordination of effects to an end extends itself as far as the causality of the first agent... But the causality of God, who is the first agent, extends to every being, not only as to the ground of their species but also to their ground as individuals, not only to incorruptible things but also corruptible things. Whence it is necessary that everything that has being in some way is ordained by God to an end.

(ibid., 22.2c)

As Boethius had shown, however, such complete divine control over events threatens to preclude human free will as a part of the providential order. In response, Aquinas argues that God does not determinately fix in advance the operative power of human willing to one outcome. Human beings are rational creatures who deliberate and choose through free will. But, because the act of free will is itself reduced to God as its ultimate cause, it is necessary that those things done from free will fall under divine providence. The "providence" of human beings is contained under the "providence" of God, as a particular under a universal cause (22.2 ad 4).

A form of "gentle" compatibilism emerges when Aquinas makes clear just how God's exertion of providential power extending even to each individual is conjoined with the human exercise of free will. Discussing the text of Romans 8:20 ("all things work together for the good for those who love God"), he asserts that "God has providence over just human beings in a more excellent way than he does over the impious, in that he allows nothing to happen to them that would ultimately obstruct their salvation" (ibid.). Those whom God has elected can exercise their free will, but the circumstances under which they exercise it are such that God preserves their eventual salvation. This form of compatibilism is "gentle" because, although God determines the circumstances under which each human being wills and he knows how each will choose under those circumstances, he does not in any way interfere with the act of willing itself. Hence, whereas Alexander had looked to God's ultimate retributive justice to bring all free acts of will under the aegis of providence, Aquinas perceives God as playing a more directive role to safeguard the predestined salvation of the just.

In general, Aquinas's systematic exposition of providence provides for an overarching order immediately present in God's understanding and understood in terms of final causality; it is also worked out in terms of secondary causes and in terms of both necessary and contingent proximate causes that include room for both necessary and contingent effects (ibid., 22.4c). God's governance is achieved through such secondary causes, whose effects are perfectly foreseen (ibid., 22.3c). In addition, God's goodness guarantees space for human free will and its contingent willing as integral to the perfection of the divine order. God contains the outcome of such acts of free will by managing the causal contexts within which people exercise their acts of free choice, preventing any circumstances that would keep those chosen for salvation from exercising their free wills in a way sufficient for that end.

Matthew of Aquasparta

Toward the end of the thirteenth century, Aquasparta compiled a set of disputed questions on providence. In these questions, he argues against the "many errors of the ancients" with considerable vehemence: "Having repulsed, rejected and repudiated these errors, one should say that the whole world is undoubtedly governed by divine providence, as are all those things that are in the world: superior and inferior, heavenly and terrestrial, incorruptible and corruptible, spiritual and corporeal, universal and particular, natural and voluntary" (q. 1, ed. Gál, pp. 240–1).

The ancients were Aristotle, Averroes, Cicero, and others who espoused limits on the reach of providence into the particular workings of the world (ibid., pp. 237–40). It is not clear whether he has more recent Aristotelians in his sights. But his assertion of God's causal power remains Aristotelian in form, even while combating Aristotelian restrictions on the extent of that power. God is the cause of things according to a threefold kind of causality: efficient, formally exemplary, and final: "For God makes everything by himself and through himself and for himself, just as the Apostle says in Romans 11:36, 'Since all things are from him and through him and in him; glory to him'" (ibid., p. 241). Divine providence is evident with respect to the world because of its perfection, its beauty and propriety, the apparent rules governing change, and the mutual connections among things. All of the completeness, proportion, regularity, and ordered relationships within the world evince God's providential intention (ibid., pp. 242–6). God does not impose undue necessity on the world through his providential guidance, however, because God's will is open to more than one effect, and God acts through a chain of mixed causes, some necessary and some contingent. The effect of any such mixed chain is assigned the mode of contingency, not necessity. Thus, even though divine providence is a first cause that acts on everything else through itself, its effects do not happen of necessity because providence also operates to cause its effects in conjunction with secondary, inferior, and particular causes (ibid., ad 7).

Aquasparta thus makes space for according special status to rational creatures with free will. Where irrational creatures are concerned, providence preserves them because preservation of their species is necessary for the perfection of the world. Since irrational creatures lack free will, they are not subject to praise or blame and are not suitable subjects for beatitude. Furthermore, they are preserved not indefinitely, but only as long as the world lasts. Rational creatures, however, do have free will and are fit for beatitude and immortality. With free will, they have dominion over their acts, and their acts are thus laudable or blameworthy, meritorious or sinful. Only merits qualify someone for beatitude, moreover, and merits consist in observance of some law; therefore, law is given to rational creatures, and observance of legal precepts results in beatitude. Still, even those who sinfully transgress those precepts may be set free through prayers. Citing John of Damascus's distinction that we saw Alexander employ earlier, Aquasparta claims that God provides for rational creatures "according to acceptance and permission," either rewarding or punishing them according to the laws of justice, so that if they depart from the assigned order, they will necessarily fall back into another order (ibid., pp. 247–8).

As we have seen, an Aristotelian analysis of divine providential causality appears to be the norm at the end of the thirteenth century. Aquasparta, like Aquinas, provides space for contingency through secondary causes. Some differences are also apparent, however. For one, where Aquinas had specifically identified providence with God's exercise of final causality, Aquasparta identifies it with the exercise of God's causal power more generally. Also, where Aquinas, citing Romans, had emphasized God's management of the circumstances surrounding those whom he has chosen for election so that nothing will impede their eventual salvation, Aquasparta turns away from compatibilism and lays the emphasis on God's provision of laws and on the free ability people have to conform to them.

THE FOURTEENTH CENTURY

With the onset of the following century, John Duns Scotus, William of Ockham, and their successors at Oxford adopted a number of ideas that greatly strained thirteenth-century views about providence. First, Scotus rejects the idea that contingency might arise at the level of secondary causes, insisting that for contingency to exist in the world it must originate in God's own contingent will (*De primo principio* IV.15).[1] Second, and even more fundamentally, Ockham criticizes Aristotle's analysis of causality as a model for understanding God's causal relationship with the world. Finally, an entirely different model for understanding providence emerges with the spread of what Heiko Oberman has called "covenantal theology."[2]

John Duns Scotus

In the *Ordinatio* version of his lectures on the *Sentences*, Scotus directs a powerful attack against the idea that there could be any "simply necessary natural connection of cause and effect in creatures." He argues that, since every effect in the natural order depends upon the first cause, and the first cause only causes contingently, every subsequent cause must also cause its effects contingently. The necessity that seems to obtain within the natural order in some chains of

---

[1] See Hester Goodenough Gelber, *It Could Have Been Otherwise* (Leiden: Brill, 2004) pp. 123–38.
[2] Heiko Oberman, *The Harvest of Medieval Theology* (Cambridge, MA: Harvard University Press, 1963).

causality is only a relative (*secundum quid*) form of necessity, ultimately sub-ordinate to the overarching contingency that anything God causes could be otherwise than it is (*Ordinatio* I.8.2 q. un [ed. Vatican, IV: 328]). Scotus's cri-tique entails that contingency arises at the level of God's causality, not at the level of secondary causes, as Aquinas had proposed. Providence – not an idea that Scotus seems to have addressed using that very term, but which he in effect discusses under the heading of divine willing – functions in the immediate present with the cooperation of the contingent and free human will as one part of the single moment of eternal creation to effect what is.[3] Scotus's critique nullifies the idea of divine "foreseeing," so that whatever 'providence' might mean, it cannot mean something prior to the immediacy of God's single act of contingent creation. His apparent disinterest in the term 'providence' makes sense if God wills everything all at once in a single moment of eternity and if the divine and human wills are cooperative co-causes of human action within that eternal moment. It would take some explaining to make a space for the term 'providence,' and Scotus instead simply chooses not to use it.

William of Ockham

In his *Quodlibetal Questions*, Ockham disputes the traditional assumption that Aristotelian causality is demonstrably applicable to God. At best, he claims, human reason can be plausibly persuaded only that God is the first efficient cause (*Quodlibet* II.1, IV.2). When it comes to final causality, there is even less to be said. Ockham defines final causality in *Quodlibet* IV.1:

> I say that the causality of the end is nothing but to be loved and desired by an agent efficiently, on account of which that which is loved is put into effect. Whence just as the causality of matter is nothing but to be informed with a form, and the causality of form is nothing but to inform matter, so the causality of the end is to be efficiently loved and desired, without which love and desire there would be no effect.
>
> (*Quodlibet* IV.1 concl. 1)[4]

He specifically sets his view apart from the more traditional definition, familiar from Aquinas, of final causality as the "end intended by the agent, which although it is first in intention, is yet last in execution; and such an end is always the produced terminus or produced operation" (IV.2 art. 1).[5] Ockham argues

---

[3] See William Frank, "Duns Scotus on Autonomous Freedom and Divine Co-Causality," *Medieval Philosophy and Theology* 2 (1992) 142–64.

[4] On Ockham's views regarding final causality in general, see Marilyn McCord Adams, "Ockham on Final Causality: Muddying the Waters," *Franciscan Studies* 56 (1998) 1–46.

[5] See also Ockham, *Expositio Phys.* II.5 sec. 6.

that God is clearly not such an end because then God would be posterior to that which is the end, as the produced effect is posterior to the producing agent (ibid.).

Ockham does allow that we can know with certainty that God is a final cause of effects produced by free agents here on earth, but he explains that this is because human beings have the evident experience of acting in order to honor God (ibid., concl. 3).[6] If the human will determines its acts out of love for God, then God as the object of the will's love will serve as the final cause of such a will. But this is a far cry from the traditional view of final causality as operative on the created order, drawing each thing of necessity to its preordained end.

Covenantal theology

While Aristotelian causality was undergoing scrutiny in the fourteenth century in ways that made the thirteenth-century approaches to providence less feasible, another way of conceiving the relationship between God and human beings was taking shape that could substitute for the thirteenth-century view – namely, covenantal theology.[7] Covenantal theology binds together the moral order through a pact or covenant God makes with the faithful. Although the requirements that God places on believers are not intrinsically worthy of merit, God has bound himself to accept them as meritorious under his various covenants. Under this pact, God promises that he will not deny grace to those who do their best to conform their wills to what they believe he wants them to do as revealed through Scripture and through the determinations of the church.[8]

A leading adherent of covenantal theology is the Dominican Robert Holcot.[9] As noted at the start of the chapter, the Book of Wisdom provided the scriptural touchstone for discussions of providence, and Holcot wrote a lengthy and much circulated commentary on it. Although Holcot, like many of his British contemporaries, omitted treatment of the term 'providence' in his other works, this scriptural text made addressing it mandatory in his commentary. Holcot

---

[6] Ockham, *Quaest. variae* 4, provides arguments for a position something like his own, which the editors suggest is that of the Scotist John of Reading, meaning that Ockham may not have been the first to propose such a view (see *Opera. theol.* VIII: 101 n. 12). For discussion, see Marilyn McCord Adams, *William Ockham* (Notre Dame, IN: University of Notre Dame Press, 1987) I: 143–313.

[7] Oberman's *Harvest of Medieval Theology* documents the emergence of covenantal theology in the fourteenth century, portraying Scotus, Ockham, Robert Holcot, and a number of others as proponents.

[8] See William Courtenay, "Covenant and Causality in Pierre d'Ailly," *Speculum* 46 (1971) pp. 116–19, and Gelber, *It Could Have Been Otherwise*, pp. 191–200.

[9] Oberman, *Harvest of Medieval Theology*, pp. 235–43.

explicates Wisdom 6:17 ("In every providence [Wisdom] proffers herself") as
follows:

> In every kind of providence, God proffers himself to the faithful, informing them about
> what is expedient for them to ponder, what to practice, what to expect. The Holy
> Spirit, therefore, wishes to say that God himself proffers himself to the faithful in every
> providence – that is, he bestows grace, not only by ordaining the present well, but also
> by providing for the future.
>
>   (*Super libros Sapientiae* VI.82, ed. Hagenau, f. o8vb)

This explication could easily continue with a fairly traditional account of providence; yet, when Holcot sets out the various ways providence functions, his
explication is anything but traditional. He distinguishes four kinds of providence necessary for the perfect governance of human life: the providence of
legal statutes, of temporal treasure, of personal merits, and of rule-governed
responses, each of which requires human beings to live up to certain God-given
responsibilities (ibid.). Rather than seeing providence as God's final causality or as a constantly guiding hand, Holcot interprets it as God's proffering
human beings instructions, obligations, and responsibilities – in other words, a
covenantal relationship that they will be answerable for at judgment. Each type
of providence has a particular provenance. So, for example:

> the first providence is instituted to make kings, princes, prelates, counselors, and royal
> ministers institute laws fairly such that they apply consistently and in common to both
> rich and poor. And this providence ought to proceed from the treasury of sacred scripture.
> For a law in opposition to sacred scripture, to the decrees of the church, and to good
> customs ought to be of no account.
>
>   (ibid.)

The second providence, in turn, enjoins all those with wealth at their disposal,
and clerics in particular, to care for the poor. The third providence lays responsibility on everyone to live virtuously, returning good for evil, providing alms and
fasting. The fourth providence, finally, asks all to live their lives giving thought
to the state of their souls at death so that they will not sin, and so that God may
judge them worthy of salvation (ibid., ff. o8vb–p1rb).

   Although Holcot cites Cicero, Augustine, and Boethius, he hangs his discussion on a latticework of scriptural citations commensurate with his view
that providence lies in God's revealed instructions to us. Where Aquasparta
had connected providence with the order evident in the natural world, and
he, Alexander, and Aquinas had tied it to Aristotelian causality, Holcot turns
the discussion back to revelation as the source for God's instructions to human
beings about what he expects of them.

Thomas Bradwardine took deep offense at the covenantal theology of his time, arguing strenuously against those who, in his view, attributed too much power to human beings at the expense of God's imminent action in the world. As part of his critique, he brought back the idea of providence and put it at the center of his theology. In his *De causa Dei* (*On Behalf of God* [1344]), Bradwardine throws down the gauntlet to those he calls the "Pelagians" of his age, among whom he includes Ockham, Holcot, and other covenantal theologians.[10] Bradwardine aims to defend God's effective causal engagement with every facet of the created world order, and the idea of divine providence figures prominently in his argument. When he reaches chapter 27 of Book I, asserting that "everything happens from divine providence," he has already built an argument about the nature of God's knowledge and his unimpedible will that makes his conclusion about God's providence seem undeniable. He begins the chapter with a definition: "For what is providence except the intellect seeing or foreseeing at a distance, along with the willing or prewilling of the will at a distance?" (ed. 1618, p. 261). He then lists five previously demonstrated propositions in support:

(1) God has distinct true knowledge of everything (I.6).
(2) The divine knowledge, which is his simple understanding, is also truly the cause of everything that is made and not just the cause *sine qua non* (I.17, coroll. 220).
(3) God has effective positive or negative volition in regard to everything (I.22).
(4) Both the knowledge and the will of God are immutable in every way (I.23).
(5) The divine will is universally efficacious, insuperable, and necessary in its causing, and can in no way be impeded or thwarted (I.10).

Bradwardine concludes: "It is therefore evident that everything that happens, happens from divine providence" (I.27, ed. 1618, p. 261). The unimpedible and immutable divine will, as the efficient cause and mover of all motion, directly and efficaciously causes everything that happens, whether God acts as the most loving progenitor, nurse, or vivifying conserver of everything in creation (I.9, I.22).

Bradwardine compares God's providential care to the responsibilities of a paterfamilias, who provides for everyone and everything in his household so that there is nothing out of order. In support of such proper governance, he cites Aristotle's discussion of the well-ordered household in *Economics* I.6, where Aristotle writes that "masters ought to rise earlier than their slaves and retire

---

[10] Obermann, *Harvest of Medieval Theology*, identifies Ockham and his followers as those most closely identified with covenantal theology. A touchstone for identifying a member of this group would be use of the phrase *facere quod in se est*, or doing the best that is in one, as what is needed for salvation within God's covenanted agreement.

to rest later, and a house should never be left unguarded any more than a city, and when anything needs doing it ought not be left undone, whether it be day or night" (1345a13–16). So Bradwardine says: "How much more that great *Paterfamilias*, of whose abundance there is no end, and of whose wisdom there is no measure, whose goodness is immense, will govern his whole great house with all it contains, providentially for all time?" (*De causa Dei* I.27, ed. 1618, p. 262). Bradwardine ends his discussion with a reference to Matthew 10:29 and a rejection of Epicurean chance: "Since the Savior says a sparrow does not fall to earth without the will of God . . . even the most common and humble particles are ruled by divine providence, and not disturbed by fortuitous motions, whose causes we cannot comprehend" (ibid., p. 264).

There are several striking aspects of Bradwardine's view. God's providential care for the world is a necessary adjunct of his omniscient intellect and omnipotent will, and at the same time it is a personal loving concern for even the least of creatures. Divine providence is self-evident, all-pervasive, and intimate. But while Bradwardine cites quantities of authorities for his position, including Scripture, the Church Fathers, and Greek and Arabic philosophers, his take on providence is atypical and constitutes part of his strong reaction against the scholastic currents of his day. God's efficient causality extends to everything, even to the human will. Nothing escapes the necessity his care imposes (III.1). Of course, this leads directly to questions about human freedom. Free will is not the freedom to enact different outcomes, but rather the "spontaneous rational capacity to choose the good" (II.2, ed. 1618, p. 448), a freedom completely in harmony with God's effective and efficient necessitation of the will's choice. Bradwardine rejects the idea that the human will could in any way resist the divine will. This view, a minority one in Bradwardine's own time, foreshadows the stress the Protestant reformers would put on God's providential presence in every aspect of human life.[11]

---

[11] See Alexandra Walsham, *Providence in Early Modern England* (Oxford: Oxford University Press, 1999); Michael Winship, *Seers of God: Puritan Providentialism in the Restoration and Early Enlightenment* (Baltimore, MD: Johns Hopkins University Press, 1996).

56

THE PROBLEM OF EVIL

ELEONORE STUMP

THE AUGUSTINIAN BACKGROUND

The problem of evil is raised by the combination of certain traditional theistic beliefs and the acknowledgment that there is evil in the world. If, as the major monotheisms claim, there is a perfectly good, omnipotent, omniscient God who creates and governs the world, how can the world such a God created and governs have evil in it? In medieval philosophy in the Latin-speaking West, philosophical discussion of evil is informed by Augustine's thought. But even those medieval philosophers not in the Latin-speaking world and not schooled in the thought of Augustine in effect share many of his views. For these reasons, it is helpful to begin an overview of medieval responses to the problem of evil with a brief description of Augustine's position.[1]

Augustine struggled with the question of the metaphysical status of evil; his ultimate conclusion, that evil is a privation of being, was shared by most later medieval philosophers. But 'privation' here is a technical term of medieval logic and indicates one particular kind of opposition; its correlative is 'possession.' A privation is the absence of some characteristic in a thing that naturally possesses that characteristic. So, on Augustine's view, evil is *not* nothing, as he is sometimes believed to have maintained. Rather, it is a lack or deficiency in being in something in which that being is natural. Nothing about this metaphysical position constitutes a solution to the problem of evil; nor did Augustine or any later medieval philosophers suppose it did.[2]

---

[1] The literature on Augustine's reflections on goodness is vast; but see, for example, Christopher Kirwan, *Augustine* (London: Routledge, 1989), and G. R. Evans, *Augustine on Evil* (Cambridge: Cambridge University Press, 1982) for helpful introductions. For more recent discussion, see N. Kretzmann and E. Stump (eds.) *The Cambridge Companion to Augustine* (Cambridge: Cambridge University Press, 2001). For a good overview of the problem in the context of medieval philosophical theology, see Ingolf Dalferth, *Malum: Theologische Hermeneutik des Bösen* (Tübingen: Mohr Siebeck, 2008).

[2] For a general discussion of this Augustinian position in later medieval philosophy, see, e.g., Scott MacDonald (ed.) *Being and Goodness. The Concept of the Good in Metaphysics and Philosophical Theology* (Ithaca, NY: Cornell University Press, 1991).

Augustine did puzzle over the introduction of evil into a world created by a good God, and his solution has roots in his understanding of the metaphysics of evil. As he sees it, evil is introduced into creation by the misuse of free will. So-called natural evil, suffering not generated by human free will but arising from events in nature, is explained as the natural concomitant to fallen humanity. The primary cause of all suffering in the world is therefore the evil willed by God's creatures. For Augustine, however, there is *no* cause of a morally wrong act of will, and to that extent there is also no explanation for it. If we want to know the explanation why a good creature of a good creator forms a morally wrong act of will, there is nothing there to know, if the explanation we are seeking is the cause of the evil in that will. A morally wrong, free act of the will is deficient in being, as it is deficient in reason, and there is no efficient cause of this deficiency.

A theodicy is an attempt to show the compatibility of God and evil in the world. Typically, a theodicy tries to provide a morally sufficient reason for an omniscient, omnipotent, perfectly good God to allow evil. Augustine gave varying suggestions for such a reason. One suggested reason is that the suffering permitted by God contributes to the beauty and goodness of the whole universe, just as a dark patch may contribute to the lightness and beauty of a painting.

Another suggested reason ties suffering to the human propensity for wrong-doing and the remedy for that propensity, divine grace. On Augustine's view, the proclivity to moral wrongdoing is universal among human beings, and the remedy for it requires God's aid. At the end of his life, Augustine was intensely occupied by the Pelagian controversy. On Augustine's fiercely anti-Pelagian position, without the aid of divine grace it is not possible for there to be any good in a human will. Augustine himself felt that he had failed to find the solution to the philosophical and theological difficulties engendered by this anti-Pelagian position, but he was not on that account inclined to abandon it. For Augustine, there is a bentness in the human will that human beings themselves are unable to cure. Grace is necessary for redemption from it; but, in a way not easy to explain, suffering also somehow works together with grace to effect an antidote to it.[3]

GREGORY THE GREAT

For a large part of the subsequent history of medieval philosophy, consideration of the problem of evil either is influenced by Augustine's views or is reacting

---

[3] For Augustine's views on these issues, see, for example, my "Augustine on Free Will," in N. Kretzmann and E. Stump (eds.) *The Cambridge Companion to Augustine* (Cambridge: Cambridge University Press, 2001) 124–47.

to metaphysical and theological views analogous to his. Augustine's suggestion that evil is like a dark patch that contributes to the overall beauty of a picture did not altogether disappear from later medieval discussion, but it is his connection between suffering and redemption from the universal human tendency to wrongdoing that is central to later discussions of the problem of evil.

The typical medieval development of this attitude can be found already in the work of Gregory the Great, in his sixth-century commentary on the biblical book of Job. Like many other commentators on that book, Gregory puzzled over the way in which suffering and prosperity are distributed in the world, and he confessed himself mystified about how to square that distribution with the existence of a perfectly good, omnipotent, omniscient God. But Gregory's puzzle is at the antipodes from that customary in the modern period. The ways of providence are often hard to understand, Gregory said, but they are

still more mysterious when things go well with good people here, and ill with bad people . . . When things go well with good people here, and ill with bad people, a great uncertainty arises whether good people receive good so that they might be stimulated to grow into something [even] better or whether by a just and secret judgment they see the rewards of their deeds here so that they may be void of the rewards of the life to come . . . Therefore since the human mind is hemmed in by the thick fog of its uncertainty among the divine judgments, when holy people see the prosperity of this world coming to them, they are troubled with a frightening suspicion. For they are afraid that they might receive the fruits of their labors here; they are afraid that divine justice detects a secret wound in them and, heaping external rewards on them, drives them away from internal ones . . . Consequently, holy people are more fearful of prosperity in this world than of adversity.

(Bk. V, intro.)[4]

In other words, since in Gregory's view it is so difficult to understand how a just and benevolent providence could allow *good* things to happen to *good* people, when good people see there is no adversity in their lives, they cannot help but wonder whether they are not after all to be counted among the wicked. For that reason, prosperity is more frightening to them than adversity.

THE MEDIEVAL STANDARD OF VALUE

The medieval period certainly does not speak with one voice about the problem of suffering. Nonetheless, the worldview underlying Gregory's lines is common throughout the Middle Ages. To understand the medieval appropriation and development of the Augustinian position as formulated in this quotation from

---

[4] Although I have preferred to use my own translation, there is a nineteenth-century translation of the whole work by James Bliss; for this passage see pp. 241–2. (A partial contemporary translation by James O'Donnell is also available online.)

Gregory, it is necessary to recognize that the problem of evil will appear differently to different thinkers grappling with it depending on the worldview they bring to it.

One important part of any worldview is the standard of value adopted. The problem of suffering challenges religious belief to produce a morally sufficient reason for a perfectly good, omniscient, omnipotent God to allow human beings to suffer. But to ask for such a reason is to ask whether there is any benefit that can defeat suffering.[5] Even to consider this question, then, requires reflecting on standards of value. What is a benefit for human beings, and on what scale could it outweigh suffering? How shall we measure the good for human beings?

On views common to many medieval authors, the genus within which the greatest goods for human beings fall is *personal relationship*. That is because, on these medieval views, it is possible for a human person to be united with God. The greatest good for a human being is to be in personal relationships of love, and the greatest personal relationship of love is union with God. Furthermore, the hallmark of a great good is that it is shareable, that it is not diminished by being distributed. Union with God, which is the greatest of goods for a human being and the best of personal relationships, is therefore also the most shareable. The love of one human being for another is also a shareable good, and human loves can themselves be woven into the shareable love between God and human persons. Heaven, then, is this best thing for human beings made permanent and unending.

If a shared loving personal relationship of this sort with God is the best thing for human beings, the worst thing is its absence. Because a human will is free, it is possible for a human being never to want or to achieve real closeness or love with God or with any human persons. Furthermore, because human beings are permanent and not transitory things, a human being is capable of being in such a condition forever; and this is hell.[6]

This view of the best thing and the worst thing for human beings thus marks out a scale of value on which human suffering and the benefits which might be thought to redeem it can be measured. The scale comes in degrees, because it is possible to have more or less of a loving relationship with any person, or to be more or less distant from a person. But the scale also has limits. The complete

---

[5] 'Defeat' is a technical term in this connection. There are different formulations of the notion of defeat, but basically the idea is this. A benefit defeats suffering only if the benefit outweighs the suffering and could not be gotten without the suffering (in some suitable sense of the modality in question).

[6] This view of the best thing and the worst thing for human beings is made graphic and vivid in the *Divine Comedy* of Dante, who was himself an impressive student of medieval philosophy and theology.

and permanent absence of loving personal relationships is an extrinsic limit on one end.[7] The shared and unending loving union with God is the intrinsic limit on the other end.

THE ROLE OF SUFFERING

In varying ways, on typical medieval views, suffering is understood as one important means by which the worst thing for human beings is warded off and the best thing for human beings is achieved. Human proclivities to moral wrongdoing are an obstacle to union with God and can result in permanent separation from God. God's grace is sufficient to bring everyone to union with him, provided only that a person does not reject that grace. Suffering is a means by which a person can be brought to surrender to the help of grace. And so, on these medieval views, suffering is seen as medicinal. Because it can melt resistance to God's grace, it can be therapeutic for spiritual health.[8]

Thomas Aquinas

In his commentary on the biblical book of Job, Aquinas says,

> Someone's suffering adversity would not be pleasing to God except for the sake of some good coming from the adversity. And so although adversity is in itself bitter and gives rise to sadness, it should nonetheless be . . . [acceptable to us] when we consider its usefulness, on account of which it is pleasing to God . . . For in his reason a person rejoices over the taking of bitter medicine because of the hope of health, even though in his senses he is troubled.
>
> (ch. 1, secs. 20–1)

In fact, on Aquinas's view, the better the person, the more likely it is that he will experience suffering. The moral strength and spiritual greatness of a person render him more, rather than less, likely to suffer. That is because strenuous medical regimens are saved for the strongest patients. In the case of a person who is comparatively psychically healthy, the point of the suffering is not so

---

[7] By speaking of this point as an extrinsic limit on loving relationship, I do not mean to imply that absence of personal relationship with God does not come in degrees. Zero is the extrinsic limit on the continuum of the positive integers, but there is a continuum of integers below zero. On typical medieval views of the sort exemplified by Dante in the *Inferno*, for example, although there is no mutual loving relationship between God and any persons in hell, some people in hell are more distant from that love than others.

[8] For a detailed exposition of this medieval theodicy and an examination of the underlying worldview in which it is set, see my *Wandering in Darkness: Narrative and the Problem of Suffering* (Oxford: Oxford University Press, forthcoming). See also the chapter on providence in my *Aquinas* (London: Routledge, 2003).

much warding off the worst thing as it is enabling as much as possible of the best thing, the shared union with God, which is the glory of a human being.

Because Aquinas is Christian, on his view there is a theologically important connection between suffering in its redemptive role and the suffering of Christ. Christ's passion and death are the primary means by which divine grace is brought to human beings, and it also provides consolation for human beings who are suffering. But, however important it is in Aquinas's philosophical theology, the connection between Christ's suffering and redemptive human suffering is too complicated to be explored adequately in passing here.[9]

Saadiah Gaon

In all but its specifically Christian respects, Aquinas's account is representative not only of views in the Latin-speaking medieval world but also of attitudes in Jewish thought. Consider, for example, the theodicy given by the tenth-century Jewish thinker Saadiah Gaon.[10] Aquinas and Saadiah share certain basic theological and ethical views. Unlike the fourteenth-century Jewish philosopher Levi ben Gershom (Gersonides), for example, who seems to think that God's providence does not extend to all individual human beings,[11] Saadiah, like Aquinas, assumes that God knows and cares about every individual human being. Furthermore, like Aquinas, Saadiah also supposes that God is justified in allowing some unwilling innocent to suffer only in case the benefit that justifies the suffering goes primarily to the sufferer. In his commentary on Job, Saadiah says that:

God's creating suffering, sickness, and injury in the world is also an act of beneficence and in the interest of humanity ... What is true of sufferings felt without affecting the

---

[9] For some discussion of it, see the chapters on atonement and on faith in my *Aquinas*.

[10] For detailed consideration of Saadiah's account of the problem of evil in comparison with that of Aquinas and that of Maimonides, see my "Saadya Gaon and the Problem of Evil," *Faith and Philosophy* 14 (1997) 523–49.

[11] See, for example, Levi ben Gershom, *The Wars of the Lord*, Bk. IV ch. 4 (tr. Feldman, p. 174): "It is evident that individual providence must operate in some people but not in others ... It is evident that what is more noble and closer to the perfection of the Agent Intellect receives the divine providence to a greater degree and is given by God the proper means for its preservation ... Since man exhibits different levels of proximity to and remoteness from the Agent Intellect by virtue of his individual character, those that are more strongly attached to it receive divine providence individually. And since some men never go beyond the disposition with which they are endowed as members of the human species ... such people are obviously not within the scope of divine providence except in a general way as members of the human species, for they have no individual [perfections] that warrant [individual] providence. Accordingly, divine providence operates individually in some men ... and in others it does not appear at all." For helpful discussion of Levi ben Gershom's work, see T. M. Rudavsky, "Gersonides," in E. Zalta (ed.) *Stanford Encyclopedia of Philosophy*: http://plato.stanford.edu.

body is true also of those that do affect it: the Creator does not so afflict His servant except in his [the servant's] own interest and for his own good.

(tr. Goodman, pp. 124–5)

Saadiah's scale of values by which the good for human beings is measured resembles Aquinas's as well. To begin with, Saadiah believes that a human life does not end with death but that it continues forever, after death, in a state dependent on its condition at death. In fact, not only does Saadiah hold this belief, but in his view so does every Jew. In his *Book of Beliefs and Convictions* he says:

as far as the resurrection of the dead is concerned . . . it is a matter upon which our nation is in complete agreement . . . The reason why [man] has been distinguished above all other creatures is that he might serve God, and the reward for this service is life in the world of recompense . . . We . . . do not know of any Jew who would disagree with this belief.

(tr. Rosenblatt, p. 264)

For Saadiah, the standard of value for human beings also is a function of relationship with God. So, for example, in describing the highest good to be expected in the afterlife, Saadiah describes it in terms of being gathered gloriously to God:

God has made us great and liberal promises of the well-being and bliss and greatness and might and glory that He will grant us twofold . . . for the humiliation and misery that have been our lot . . . [W]hat has befallen us has been likened by Scripture to a brief twinkling of the eye, whereas the compensation God will give us in return therefore has been referred to as His great mercy. For it says: *For a small moment have I forsaken thee; but with great compassion will I gather thee.*

(ibid., p. 292)

The worst thing for human beings, as well as the best thing, is what is to come in life after death:

the reward and the punishment . . . will be everlasting, [and] their extent will vary according to the act. Thus, for example, the nature of a person's reward will be dependent upon whether he presents one or ten or one hundred or one thousand good deeds, except that it will be eternal in duration . . . Likewise will the extent of a person's punishment vary according to whether he presents one or ten or a hundred or a thousand evil deeds, except that, whatever the intensity of the punishment may be, it will be everlasting.

(ibid., pp. 347–8)

For Saadiah, as for Aquinas, suffering has a role to play in warding off the worst thing and providing the best thing for human beings.

On Saadiah's account, which is more explicit and developed in this respect than Aquinas's is, suffering serves this function in three differing ways. First, there is the sort of suffering which constitutes training and character-building. Saadiah says, "Although these may be painful for human beings, hard, wearying, and troubling of mind, all this is for our own good. Of this the prophet says, *the chastening of the Lord, my son, despise not*" (*On Job*, p. 125). Second, there is "purgation and punishment." If the first case can be thought of as making a basically good person better, this second case can be thought of as keeping a person who has done something bad from getting worse and/or rectifying his accounts so that he is not in moral debt any more. Third, there is suffering such as Job's. To explain this sort of suffering, we need yet a third category, on Saadiah's view. This is the category of trial:

> The third case is that of trial and testing. An upright servant, whose Lord knows that he will bear sufferings loosed upon him and hold steadfast in his uprightness, is subjected to certain sufferings, so that when he steadfastly bears them, his Lord may reward and bless him. This too is a kind of bounty and beneficence, for it brings the servant to everlasting blessedness.
>
> (ibid., pp. 125–6)

That is why, Saadiah maintains, one kind of goodness that God shows his creatures is "recompense for tribulations . . . [God] records all to our account in His books. If we were to read these ledgers, we would find all we have suffered made good, and we would be confirmed in our acceptance of His decree" (ibid., p. 127). (See Chapter 33 for further discussion of Saadiah's views in this area.)

COMPLICATIONS AND VARIATIONS

In the period after Aquinas, an increasing tendency to tie morality to God's will complicates the attitude toward the problem of evil represented by Saadiah's and Aquinas's theodicies. So, for example, William of Ockham holds that God has no moral obligations but that whatever God does is done justly in virtue of the fact that God does it. In a famous passage, much cited out of context, Ockham claims that if God commanded a person to hate God, then it would be just for that person to hate God, in heaven as well as on earth (see Chapter 51).[12] Although the lineaments remain roughly the same, theodicy and the problem of evil itself will obviously look different on this way of conceiving the standard

---

[12] See, e.g., Ockham, *Sent.* II.3–4 (*Opera theol.* V: 59) and *Sent.* II.15 (*Opera theol.* V: 343). For a discussion of these issues in Ockham's work, see, for example, Lucan Freppert, *The Basis of Morality According to William Ockham* (Chicago: Franciscan Herald Press, 1988).

of value for human beings. There is no need to search for a morally sufficient reason for God to allow evil if whatever God does is done justly in virtue of the fact that God does it. The apparent incompatibility of God and evil in the world is also harder to show if by God's justice we mean God's doing whatever he wills.

In addition, changing attitudes toward God's relationship to time and God's foreknowledge of things in time also make a difference to the role assigned to suffering in the process of redemption and thus also to its place in theodicy. John Duns Scotus's doctrine of predestination shows the point at issue here. According to Scotus, although God predestines human beings to salvation prior to foreknowing their actions, he does not destine human beings to damnation prior to foreknowing their actions. Rather, on the basis of foreknowledge of the bad actions of those not saved, God relegates them to damnation. In defense of this view and to explain why God's failing to destine some human beings to salvation does not constitute God's destining them to damnation, Scotus looks for a position which is Augustinian in its anti-Pelagian character but which nonetheless relegates some control over good actions to human beings. As Scotus explains this position, although on anti-Pelagian views a human being cannot merit divine grace, it is still open to a human being to merit the restoration of grace after a fall into sin. That is because the restoration of grace can be merited by suffering, in the doing of penance. Suffering that is penance can thus contribute to redemption. God is therefore justified in allowing suffering that is penitential and redemptive.

On this account, then, suffering still has a role to play in salvation, although in its details this is significantly different from Saadiah's or Aquinas's account.[13]

AN ALTERNATIVE ACCOUNT: MAIMONIDES

The general attitude toward suffering represented by the medieval accounts sketched so far would need considerably more discussion in order for them to seem anything other than alien to contemporary sensibilities. Even so, this brief presentation is enough to clarify the development of the Augustinian view expressed by Gregory the Great in the quotation above, which is central to the theodicies of Saadiah and Aquinas. Gregory finds it perplexing when good things happen to good people, because Gregory thinks that if these people were in fact morally healthy (relatively speaking), then God would bless them with

---

[13] For a discussion of these issues in the work of Duns Scotus, see, for example, Richard Cross, *Duns Scotus* (Oxford: Oxford University Press, 1999). Cross (p. 106) cites in this connection *Ordinatio* I.2.2.1–4, nn. 233, 235.

the medicine of suffering to move them forward to even further spiritual health. The absence of suffering in the lives of such people is therefore mysterious to Gregory. Medicinal regimes are withheld from people only in case they are so ill that the therapy cannot do them any good. And so when *good* things happen to good people, Gregory finds the ways of providence hard to understand.

The theodicies offered by Saadiah and Aquinas are at home in this sort of attitude. There are also, however, medieval accounts of suffering that are not. In addition to the account of Levi ben Gershom alluded to above, the position of Moses Maimonides is a good example here. Maimonides knows Saadiah's theodicy, and he particularly dislikes Saadiah's view of sufferings as trials. Maimonides thinks that this view is common, vulgar, stupid, and impious. He says:

> What is generally accepted among people regarding the subject of *trial* is this: God sends down calamities upon an individual without their having been preceded by a sin, in order that his reward be increased. However, this principle is not at all mentioned in the *Torah* in an explicit text ... The principle of the Law that runs counter to this opinion, is that contained in His dictum, may He be exalted: *A God of faithfulness and without iniquity.* Nor do all the *Sages* profess this opinion of the multitude, for they say sometimes: *There is no death without sin and no sufferings without transgression.* And this [the quoted view of the Sages] is the opinion that ought to be believed by every adherent of the Law who is endowed with intellect, for he should not ascribe injustice to God, may He be exalted above this, so that he believes that Zayd is innocent of sin and is perfect and that he does not deserve what befell him.
>
> (*Guide of the Perplexed*, tr. Pines, pp. 497–8)

If it is represented accurately in this passage, it is hard to see Maimonides's own account of suffering as more palatable than the view of Saadiah which Maimonides is attacking, since Maimonides's account apparently claims that there is no suffering without preceding transgression. It is not always easy to know what Maimonides's own opinions are, however, given the commitment to caution and secrecy evinced in the *Guide*; perhaps Maimonides here means to be presenting only religious views suitable for the unlearned. But there are certainly passages in which Maimonides appears to be arguing explicitly for the view that every sufferer deserves exactly what he suffers. So, for example, he says:

> It is likewise one of the fundamental principles of the Law of *Moses our Master* that [1] it is in no way possible that he, may he be exalted, should be unjust, and that [2] all the calamities that befall men and the good things that come to men, be it a single individual or a group, are all of them determined according to the deserts of the men concerned through equitable judgment in which there is no injustice whatever. Thus if some individual were wounded in the hand by a thorn, which he would take

out immediately, this would be a punishment for him, and if he received the slightest pleasure, this would be a reward for him – all this being according to his deserts. Thus he, may he be exalted, says: *For all his ways are judgment.*

(ibid., p. 469)

As a palliative for what seems to be the manifest mistakenness of his position, Maimonides adds that human judgment of the moral state of others is often wrong, for "we are ignorant of the various modes of deserts" (ibid.).[14] On this position, there is nothing perplexing about God allowing good things to happen to good people.

THE END OF THE MEDIEVAL PERIOD

Even Maimonides's position has this much in common with that of Saadiah and Aquinas: Maimonides takes himself to have a satisfactory theodicy, and he supposes that suffering can be understood in terms of its connection to or effects on the person who suffers. Even as punishment, suffering is somehow – directly or indirectly – good for the person who suffers, and it is allowed by God for just that reason. In marked contrast to this attitude, however, is the one expressed by an adherent to the *devotio moderna*, a religious movement important in the Netherlands in the fifteenth century. Commenting on the death of a recently appointed principal of a school for religious instruction, an anonymous adherent of the *devotio moderna* raises the problem of evil in a way that is quite devout but that has an almost contemporary sound to it:

Permit me to take a moment here to allude to the wondrous and secret judgments of our Lord God, not as if scrutinizing them in a reproachful way but rather as humbly venerating the inscrutable. It is quite amazing that our fathers and brothers had set out with a single will and labored at their own expense, to the honor of God and for the salvation of souls, to erect a school here in Emmerich to do exercises with boys and clerics . . . And now after much care and trouble, everything had been brought to a good state: we had a learned and suitable man for rector, the venerable Master Arnold of Hildesheim . . . Then, behold . . . our Lord God, as if totally unconcerned with all that we had in hand, which had just begun to flower, suddenly and unexpectedly threw it all into confusion and decline, nearly reducing it to nothing. For just as the sheep are dispersed when the shepherd is struck down, so when our beloved brother [Master Arnold] died the whole school was thrown into confusion. The youths left in swarms . . . not, it is to be feared, without some danger to their souls . . . Nonetheless, to

---

[14] David Shatz has pointed out to me the need for caution with regard to Maimonides's position on deserts. It is complicated by Maimonides's unusual account of providence, which makes an individual's intellectual development a primary value for divine providence.

[him] be the honor and the glory now and through the ages, to him whose judgments, though hidden, are yet never unjust.[15]

Here we find an attitude towards the problem of evil that is not difficult for us, even with our current sensibilities, to understand. This pious author, dealing just with the establishment of a school for children, finds adversity fundamentally inexplicable, not only as regards the application of the theory of a theodicy to this particular instance of evil but even within the theological theory of theodicy. It certainly does not occur to him to tie the suffering of the loss of the school to the spiritual condition of those who suffer. However religiously committed this fifteenth-century author may be, the worldview with which he approaches the problem of evil is no longer medieval. He is focused on goods of this world, and he is not inclined to see suffering as instrumental to otherworldly goods, such as spiritual well-being; consequently, he finds an acceptable theodicy hard to imagine. His response to suffering in the world thus has more in common with modern views than with those in the medieval period.

[15] John van Engen (tr.) *Devotio Moderna: Basic Writings* (New York: Paulist Press, 1988) p. 151. I am grateful to Van Engen for calling my attention to the intriguing material in this book.

APPENDICES

Appendix A

DOCTRINAL CREEDS

1. THE NICENE CREED
THOMAS WILLIAMS

The Nicene Creed was adopted by the First Council of Nicaea (325) and revised by the First Council of Constantinople (381). Its original Greek text was in the first-person plural – "We believe" – reflecting the Creed's role as a statement of the essential faith of the Church. The most familiar Latin text, however, is in the first-person singular, recited by the priest alone at a time when the people no longer participated vocally in the Eucharistic liturgy. A strictly literal translation of the Latin text is given below.

For medieval Christians, the Nicene Creed held a unique status as a touchstone of orthodoxy. As the statement of ecumenical councils held by the undivided Church, it was (and remains) preeminently authoritative. There was nothing comparable in medieval Judaism and Islam, which had no authoritative mechanism or centralized hierarchy for determining the boundaries of correct belief.

> I believe in one God, the Father omnipotent, Maker of heaven and earth, and of all things visible and invisible.
>
> And [I believe] in one Lord, Jesus Christ, the only-begotten Son of God, and born from the Father before all ages: God from God, Light from Light, true God from true God; begotten, not made; consubstantial with the Father. Through him all things were made. For the sake of (*propter*) us human beings, and for the sake of our salvation, he descended from heaven. And he was incarnate by the Holy Spirit from the Virgin Mary, and became human (*homo factus est*). He was also crucified for us under Pontius Pilate, suffered, and was buried. And on the third day he rose again in accordance with the Scriptures. And he ascended into heaven [and] sits at the right hand of the Father. And he will come again with glory to judge the living and the dead. His kingdom will have no end.
>
> And [I believe] in the Holy Spirit, the Lord and Life-giver, who proceeds from the Father and the Son.[1] He is worshiped and glorified together with the Father and the Son. He has spoken through the prophets. And [I believe]

---

[1] The phrase "and the Son" (*filioque*) was added by the Synod of Toledo in 447 and gradually came to be accepted in the West. The *filioque* has never been accepted by the Eastern churches.

one holy, catholic, and apostolic Church. I acknowledge one baptism unto remission of sins. And I look for the resurrection of the dead and the life of the age to come. Amen.

2. CREEDS IN ISLAM

DIMITRI GUTAS

Due to the particular historical circumstances of its growth and spread, the religion of Islam did not develop a centralized institutional authority that would define doctrine and impose it as orthodox. By the same token, because the Arabic text of the Quran is considered to be the very words of God – a fundamental doctrine of Islam unparalleled in both Judaism and Christianity – the holy Book itself constitutes the "creed" that is incumbent upon all Muslims to believe in and follow. For both reasons Islam does not have a creed in the sense of the Christian Nicene Creed. Muslim religious scholars throughout history have composed numerous documents summarizing the principles of their faith as they saw it, but all of these documents, because they were generated in concrete historical circumstances that called for the defense of the views of their adherents, are not so much creeds as distilled statements of a theological position. Their main purpose is to define and establish the doctrinal core of their author and refute as heterodox the positions of his opponents. Every major legal and theological school in Islam has documents of this sort, but they have never had doctrinal force or liturgical function for Muslims at large.[2]

The basic creed of Muslims can be summarized in the Profession of Faith, the *Shahāda* (literally, bearing witness to the fact that)

There is no god but God, Muhammad is the Messenger of God.
   (*lā ilāha illā llāh, Muḥammadun rasūlu llāh.*)

This formula in its composite form is not found as such in the Quran, though its two parts are (Q37:35 and Q48:29). The public profession of this statement constitutes legally valid conversion to Islam. Beyond this kern of Islamic faith, what comes closest to a creed in the Quran, and something that the Muslims themselves have considered as such, are the following verses (Q4:135):[3]

> O believers, believe in God and His Messenger
> and the Book He has sent down on His Messenger
> and the Book which He sent down before.
> Whoso disbelieves in God and His angels
> and His Books, and His Messengers,
> and the Last Day, has surely gone astray
> into far error.

---

[2] A selection of them is available in English translation in W. M. Watt, *Islamic Creeds* (Edinburgh: Edinburgh University Press, 1994). A succinct and up-to-date presentation of the subject is offered in the article "Creeds" by Sabine Schmidtke in J. D. McAuliffe (ed.) *Encyclopaedia of the Qur'ān* (Leiden: Brill, 2001–6).

[3] Cited in the translation by A. J. Arberry, *The Koran Interpreted* (London: Macmillan, 1955).

Beyond this, there are certain elements of doctrine, all of them ultimately deriving from the Quran, that constitute the basis of Islamic faith and are included in the credal documents written by the religious scholars mentioned above. W. M. Watt has presented a summary of them, and it is useful to extract its highlights here.[4] Watt's summary may be tilted toward the main Sunnī theological position of the Ashʿarites, but for the most part it is quite representative. Each of these twenty articles has some basis in the Quran, and some are direct translations from various verses. They were all the object of intense theological debates in the history of Islam, and an elucidation of them, even a bare annotation, would essentially constitute a history of Islamic theology. It will be noticed, moreover, that some formulations bear distinct traces in terminology of the philosophical background and context of the debates.

1. God is one, there is no god except Him; He has no partner nor wife; He neither begets nor is begotten.
2. God exists; His existence is rationally proved from the originated character of the world.
3. God is eternal; His existence has neither beginning nor end.
4. God is different from created things. He is not a body nor a substance nor the accident of a substance. He sits on the throne, but only in the sense in which He Himself intended.
5. God will be seen by the faithful in the world to come.
6. God is eternally omnipotent, omniscient, living, willing, hearing, seeing, speaking. These attributes are eternal; they are not God, yet no other than God.
7. The Quran is the eternal and uncreated speech of God.
8. God's will is supreme and always effective; what He wills exists, and what He does not will does not exist. Actions are good and bad because He commands or forbids them, and not in themselves.
9. Man's acts are created by God, but are nevertheless properly attributed to man.
10. The punishment of the tomb – between death and the resurrection – is a reality, as are the signs portending the Last Day.
11. God will judge all men on the Last Day.
12. Certain persons, and notably the Prophet, will be permitted by God to intercede for others.
13. Paradise and Hell already exist, and will continue to exist eternally. Grave Muslim sinners will be punished in Hell, but not eternally. No monotheist will remain eternally in Hell.
14. Prayers for the dead and alms offered on behalf of them are advantageous to them.
15. God has sent to mankind prophets, who are above saints and angels. Muhammad is the seal of the prophets: the final and most excellent of them.
16. Prophets are preserved from all sin by God.
17. The best of men after the prophets, according to the Sunnīs, are Abū Bakr, then ʿUmar, then ʿUthmān, then ʿAlī. According to the Shīʿites, in contrast, ʿAlī and his descendants, the imams, are best.

---

[4] W. M. Watt, "Aḳīda," in H. A. R. Gibb *et al.* (eds.) *Encyclopaedia of Islam*, 2nd edn (Leiden: Brill, 1960–2004).

18. Unbelief does not necessarily follow the commission of sin by a believer.
19. Faith is knowing in the heart, confessing with the tongue, and performing works. It increases and decreases.
20. Faith and unbelief are due to God's guidance and abandonment respectively.

3. MAIMONIDES'S THIRTEEN PRINCIPLES OF FAITH

SARAH PESSIN

The question of whether Judaism has fundamental principles of belief at all is subject to much debate.[5] One can find a broad array of arguments against Judaism's having foundational beliefs: from Heinrich Graetz's insistence that Judaism is about ethical action rather than beliefs,[6] to Jewish theological reformers who see Judaism as infinitely fluid (and, hence, absent any list of basic beliefs), to even more traditional Jewish Rabbinic thinkers who, like Rabbi Isaac Abarbanel in the fifteenth century, maintain that every claim in the Torah holds equal weight, and that therefore any attempt to highlight the "most central claims" is untenable and ultimately foreign to Judaism.[7] On the other hand, there is the centuries-old theological pervasiveness of Maimonides's Thirteen Principles of Faith, heralded within many Jewish circles as the defining statement of Jewish creed. While not the first to list principles of Judaism, Maimonides is nonetheless frequently seen within Jewish theological history as the thinker responsible for most fully and definitively penning a list of such foundational beliefs.

The Thirteen Principles are taken from Maimonides's commentary on the tenth chapter of the Mishnaic tractate *Sanhedrin*, itself part of a multi-volume commentary on the Mishnah. Maimonides immediately follows up these Principles with the dual claims that anyone who understands and believes them enters the community of Israel, and that anyone who doubts any of these foundations is not simply a sinner, but is no longer a member of the community of Israel. However, despite these remarks, and despite the prevalence of the Thirteen Principles in modern Jewish theological rhetoric − appearing everywhere from prayer books to greeting cards − it is not clear that Maimonides took himself to be crafting a definitive statement of Jewish creed, or that these principles were ever actually treated as such by Jewish rabbis and theologians through the ages.[8] Maimonides does not issue these principles as part of an authoritative public proclamation on orthodoxy; instead, they are found in the closing pages of a much longer commentary.

---

[5] For a bibliography of sources on dogma in Judaism, see Menachem Kellner, "Dogma in Medieval Jewish Thought: A Bibliographical Survey," *Studies in Bibliography and Booklore* 15 (1984) 5–21; see, too, Louis Jacobs, *Principles of the Jewish Faith: An Analytical Study* (New York: Basic Books, 1964) pp. 7–8, 30–2; and Marc Shapiro, *The Limits of Orthodox Theology: Maimonides' Thirteen Principles Reappraised* (Oxford: Littman Library of Jewish Civilization, 2004) pp. 1–37.

[6] See Heinrich Graetz, "The Significance of Judaism for the Present and the Future," *Jewish Quarterly Review* 1 (1888) 4–13.

[7] Isaac Abarbanel (sometimes transliterated as Abravanel) explores this in his *Rosh Amanah*. For discussion, see Menachem Kellner, *Dogma in Medieval Jewish Thought: From Maimonides to Abravanel* (Oxford: Oxford University Press, 1986) pp. 179–95.

[8] For an argument to this effect, see Shapiro, *The Limits of Orthodox Theology*.

One approach to these Thirteen Principles (championed by Abarbanel and others)[9] is that Maimonides intended this as a creedal list only for the "religious masses" not able to use their intellects to attain the true principles of being. A hint of this idea can be seen in the pages leading up to his statement of the Principles. Commenting on the salvific rabbinic concept of "having a share in the world to come," Maimonides launches into an analysis of allegory and the art of writing, charting the contrast between esoteric "inner" meanings and exoteric "outer" texts, a theme on which he elaborates at greater length in his *Guide of the Perplexed*. Even in this earlier commentary on the Mishnah, Maimonides highlights the theme of writing-for-your-reader, stressing that "it is clear . . . that the words of the Sages contain both an obvious and a hidden meaning."[10] The masses cannot be expected to grasp hidden meanings, a point underscored by Maimonides's contention that "concerning this strange world to come, you will rarely find anyone to whom it occurs to think about it seriously . . . or to inquire what it really means." Hence Maimonides argues that it is sometimes crucial for these Sages to speak in simplistic terms, if they are to be understandable to the average person. He offers the analogy of a child who must be coaxed towards the truth with figs and honey – instrumental tools that lead to the truth, but that are not themselves the truth.[11]

Here is an abridged version of Maimonides's text, supplying just the opening claims and not the subsequent analysis for each principle:[12]

> The first foundation (*al-qā'ida*) is the existence (*al-wujūd*) of the Creator (*al-bāri'*), may He be praised. And this in the sense that there is an existent in the most perfect kind of existence, and it is the cause of the existence of all the existents.
>
> The second foundation is His oneness (*al-waḥda*), may He be exalted. And this in the sense that He, cause of all things, is one.
>
> The third foundation is the denial of corporeality to Him. And this in the sense that this One is not a body and is not a power in a body.
>
> The fourth foundation is [His] eternal preexistence (*al-qidam*). And this in the sense that this One is described as He who is absolutely eternally preexistent.
>
> The fifth foundation is that He, may He be exalted, is He Whom it is proper to worship and to praise, and to publicize His greatness and obedience to Him.
>
> The sixth foundation is prophecy.
>
> The seventh foundation is the prophecy of Moses, our Teacher.
>
> The eighth foundation is that the Torah is from heaven.

---

[9] See *Rosh Amanah*, ch. 23. For a reaction against this sort of reading, see Kellner, *Dogma*, pp. 36 and 47.

[10] As translated by Arnold Jacob Wolf in *A Maimonides Reader* (ed. I. Twersky 1972) p. 409.

[11] Ibid., pp. 403–5.

[12] The translation is from the Arabic original of the *Mishnah im Perush* (ed. and [Hebrew] tr. Kafih, pp. 210–17), and partially follows David R. Blumenthal (as printed in Kellner, *Dogma*, pp. 11–16) as well as Kafih's Hebrew notes and translation.

The ninth foundation [regards] abrogation (*al-naskh*). And this in the sense that the Law of Moses shall not be abrogated [or changed] and that there shall not arise from God any Law other than this one.

The tenth foundation is that He, may He be exalted, knows the acts of men and does not overlook them.

The eleventh foundation is that He, may He be exalted, rewards him who obeys the commands of the Torah and punishes him who violates its prohibitions.

The twelfth foundation is the days of the Messiah, namely, the belief in (*al-ʾīmān*) and assent to [the truth of] (*al-taṣdīq*) his arrival.

The thirteenth foundation is the resurrection.

Appendix B

MEDIEVAL TRANSLATIONS

1. GREEK ARISTOTELIAN WORKS TRANSLATED INTO LATIN

The information in this table is adapted, with a few revisions, from Bernard G. Dod's table in the *Cambridge History of Later Medieval Philosophy*.[1] The most popular translations (judging from the number of extant manuscripts) are marked with a star (★). Translations made via the intermediary of an Arabic text are marked with an obelisk (†). Volumes published (or available electronically) through the series *Aristoteles Latinus* are indicated by AL (or ALD for volumes as yet available only electronically). Working texts of translations not yet edited as part of that series can often be found in editions of the commentaries of Thomas Aquinas and others. These other abbreviations are also used: CLCAG = *Corpus Latinum Commentariorum in Aristotelem Graecorum*; ASL = *Aristoteles Semitico-Latinus*.

Title Commentator	Translator	Date
Categories	a. Boethius★ (AL I.1)	*ca.* 510–22
	b. William of Moerbeke (AL I.3)	1266
Simplicius	William of Moerbeke (AL I.4; CLCAG V)	1266
De interpretatione	a. Boethius★ (AL II.1)	*ca.* 510–22
	b. William of Moerbeke (AL I.2)	1268
Ammonius	William of Moerbeke (CLCAG II)	1268
Prior Analytics	a. Boethius★ (AL III.1–2)	*ca.* 510–22
	b. Anonymous (AL III.3)	twelfth century
Posterior Analytics	a. James of Venice★ (AL IV.1)	1125–50 (?)
	b. Ioannes (AL IV.2)	before 1159
	c. † Gerard of Cremona (AL IV.3)	before 1187
	d. William of Moerbeke (AL IV.4) (revision of [a])	*ca.* 1269 or earlier
Themistius	† Gerard of Cremona	before 1187

(*cont.*)

---

[1] For up-to-date details, see Jozef Brams, *La riscoperta di Aristotele in Occidente* (Milan: Jaca, 2003), as well as the Aristoteles Latinus web page: www.hiw.kuleuven.ac.be/dwmc/al.

Title Commentator	Translator	Date
Topics	a. Boethius★ (AL V.1–2)	*ca.* 510–22
	b. Anonymous (AL V.3)	twelfth century
Sophistici elenchi	a. Boethius★ (AL VI.1)	*ca.* 510–22
	b. James of Venice (AL VI.2)	1125–50 (?)
	c. William of Moerbeke (AL VI.3)	*ca.* 1269 or earlier

Pseudo-Alexander
    (Michael of
    Ephesus)
	James of Venice (CLCAG VII)	1125–50 (?)

Physics	a. James of Venice★ (AL VII.1)	1125–50 (?)
	b. Anonymous ('Physica vaticana') (AL VII.2) (same translator as the *media* of the *Metaphysics*)	mid-twelfth century (?)
	c. † Gerard of Cremona	before 1187
	d. † Michael Scot (?)★	*ca.* 1220–35
	e. William of Moerbeke★	*ca.* 1260–70 (?)
De caelo	a. † Gerard of Cremona★ (ed. Opelt, in Albert the Great, *Opera* V.1)	before 1187
	b. † Michael Scot	*ca.* 1220–35
	c. Robert Grosseteste (ALD VIII.1)	after 1247 (?)
	d. William of Moerbeke★ (ALD VIII.2)	*ca.* 1260–70 (?)
Simplicius	a. Robert Grosseteste	after 1247 (?)
	b. William of Moerbeke★ (CLCAG VIII)	1271 (Viterbo)
De generatione et *corruptione*	a. Burgundio of Pisa★ (AL IX.1)	mid-twelfth century
	b. † Gerard of Cremona	before 1187
	c. William of Moerbeke★ (ALD IX.2)	before 1274
Meteorologica	a. Henry Aristippus (Bk. IV)★	before 1162
	b. † Gerard of Cremona (Books I–III)★ (ASL XII)	before 1187
	c. William of Moerbeke★ (ALD X.2)	*ca.* 1260 (?)
Alexander	William of Moerbeke	1260 (Nicea)
De anima	a. James of Venice★ (ALD XII.1)	1125–50 (?)
	b. † Michael Scot (?)★	*ca.* 1220–35
	c. William of Moerbeke★ (ALD XII.2)	before 1268 (?)
Philoponus (Bk. III)	William of Moerbeke (CLCAG III)	1268 (Viterbo)
Themistius	William of Moerbeke (CLCAG I)	1267 (Viterbo)

Title Commentator	Translator	Date
De sensu	a. Nicholas of Reggio (?)★ (ALD XIII.1)	later twelfth century
	b. William of Moerbeke★ (ALD XIII.2)	1260–70 (?)
Alexander	William of Moerbeke	1260–70 (?)
De memoria	a. James of Venice★ (ALD XIV.1)	1125–50 (?)
	b. William of Moerbeke★ (ALD XIV.2)	1260–70 (?)
De somno	a. Anonymous★ (ALD XV.1)	twelfth century
	b. William of Moerbeke★ (ALD XV.2)	1260–70 (?)
De longitudine	a. James of Venice★ (ALD XVI.1)	1125–50 (?)
	b. William of Moerbeke★ (ALD XVI.2)	1260–70 (?)
De iuventute	a. James of Venice (ALD XVI.1)	1125–50 (?)
	b. William of Moerbeke★	*ca.* 1260–70
De respiratione	a. James of Venice (ALD XVI.1)	1125–50 (?)
	b. William of Moerbeke★	1260–70 (?)
De morte	a. James of Venice (ALD XVI.1)	1125–50 (?)
	b. William of Moerbeke★	1260–70 (?)
De animalibus (comprising *Historia, De progressu, De motu, De partibus, De generatione*)	a. † Michael Scot (*Hist., De part., De gener.*)★ (ASL V)	before 1220
	b. Anonymous (*De motu*) (ALD XVII.1)	early thirteenth century (?)
	c. Anonymous (*De part. an.*)	thirteenth century (?)
	d. William of Moerbeke★ (AL XVII.2)	1260 (Thebes)
Metaphysics	a. James of Venice (AL XXV.1) (Bks. I–IV.4; '*vetustissima*')	1125–30 (?)
	b. Anonymous (AL XXV.1a) ('*vetus*'; revision of [a])	1220–30
	c. Anonymous (AL XXV.2) ('*media*'; lacks Bk. XI) (same translator as the *Vaticana* of the *Physics*)	twelfth century
	d. † Michael Scot★ (?) ('*nova*') (lacks Bk. XI)	*ca.* 1220–35
	e. William of Moerbeke★ (AL XXV.3) ('*novae translationis*'; revision and completion of [c])	before 1272

(cont.)

Title Commentator	Translator	Date
Nicomachean Ethics	a. Burgundio of Pisa★ (AL XXVI.1) (Bks. II–III; '*vetus*')	mid-twelfth century
	b. Burgundio of Pisa★ (AL XXVI.2) (Bk. I and fragments of II–X; '*nova*')	mid-twelfth century
	c. Robert Grosseteste★ (AL XXVI.3)	1246–7 (?)
	d. William of Moerbeke★ (AL XXVI.3) (revision of [c])	1250–60
Eustratius (I), Aspasius (VIII), Michael of Ephesus (IX–X)	Robert Grosseteste (CLCAG VI.1, VI.3)	1246–7 (?)
Eudemian Ethics (De bona fortuna)[2]	a. Anonymous★	thirteenth century (?)
	b. Anonymous (fragments)	thirteenth century (?)
Politics	a. William of Moerbeke (AL XXIX.1) (Books I–II; early draft)	1260–4
	b. William of Moerbeke (complete)★ (ALD XXIX.2)	1260 (?)
Oeconomica	a. Anonymous	mid-thirteenth century (?)
	b. William of Moerbeke (rev. of [a])	
	c. Durandus de Alvernia★	1295
Rhetoric	a. Anonymous (AL XXXI.1)	mid-thirteenth century (?)
	b. † Hermann the German	1240/50
	c. William of Moerbeke★ (AL XXXI.2)	before 1270
Rhetorica ad Alexandrum	Anonymous	fourteenth century (?)
	Anonymous	fourteenth century (?)
Poetics	William of Moerbeke (AL XXXIII)	1278
PSEUDO-ARISTOTELIAN AND RELATED WORKS		
Categoriae decem[3]	Anonymous (AL I.5)	350–80
Problemata	Bartholomew of Messina★ (ALD XXII)	1258–66

[2] The work circulating under this title consists of a single chapter of the *Eudemian Ethics* (VII.14) combined with a chapter from the pseudo-Aristotelian *Magna moralia* (II.8) (see below).

[3] A pseudo-Aristotelian work that is, at least in part, a translation of an unknown Greek text.

Title Commentator	Translator	Date
Physiognomia	Bartholomew of Messina★	1258–66
De mirabilibus auscultationibus	Bartholomew of Messina (ALD XXI)	1258–66
De principiis (Theophrastus, *Metaphysics*)	Bartholomew of Messina	1258–66
De signis aquarum	a. Bartholomew of Messina b. Anonymous	1258–66 thirteenth/fourteenth century (?)
De lineis insecabilibus	Robert Grossesteste★	*ca.* 1240–50 (?)
De mundo	a. Bartholomew of Messina (AL XI.1) b. Nicholas of Sicily★ (AL XI.2)	1258–66 before 1240 (?)
Magna moralia (*De bona fortuna*)⁴	a. Bartholomew of Messina★ (ALD XXVII) b. Anonymous★	1258–66 thirteenth century (?)
De coloribus	a. Bartholomew of Messina★ b. William of Moerbeke	1258–66 1260–70 (?)
De inundatione Nili	Anonymous★	thirteenth century (?)
De intelligentia (anonymous introduction to the *Physics*)	James of Venice★	1125–50 (?)
De causis (Proclus)	† Gerard of Cremona★ (ed. Pattin 1966)	before 1187
Enigmata Aristotelis	Anonymous	twelfth century
Vita Aristotelis	Anonymous★	twelfth to thirteenth century
Isagoge (Porphyry)	Boethius★ (AL I.6)	*ca.* 510–22
De laudabilibus bonis	Robert Grosseteste	1240–53 (?)
Epistola ad Alexandrum (an anonymous introduction to the *Rhetorica ad Alexandrum*)	Anonymous★	thirteenth century

---

⁴ See note 2.

2. GREEK PHILOSOPHICAL WORKS TRANSLATED INTO LATIN

MICHELE TRIZIO

The following table lists non-Aristotelian philosophical works written in Greek and translated into Latin. Authors are listed chronologically. The table is limited to philosophical material and to those theological and scientific works of philosophical interest.[5] Translations from Arabic are marked with an obelisk (†). An asterisk (*) marks those works that, although translated, had little or no influence in the Middle Ages.

Author and Work	Translator	Date
PLATO		
Timaeus	*a. Cicero (27d–37c; 38c–43b, 46c–47b) (ed. Plasberg and Ax 1938)	first century BCE
	b. Calcidius (to 53c) (ed. Waszink 1975)	first century BCE
	*c. Apuleius (?) (lost)[6]	second century
Protagoras	*Cicero (only fragments extant)	first century BCE
Phaedo	*a. Apuleius (lost)[7]	second century
	*b. Henry Aristippus (ed. Minio-Paluello 1950)	1156
Meno	*Henry Aristippus (ed. Kordeuter and Labowsky 1940)	1154/60
Parmenides	William of Moerbeke (126a–142a) (ed. Steel, in Proclus 1982–5)	1280/6
EUCLID		
Elements	† a. Adelard of Bath (ed. Busard 1983)	*ca.* 1120s
	† b. Hermann of Carinthia (ed. Busard 1967–77)	*ca.* 1140s
	† c. Gerard of Cremona (ed. Busard 1984)	before 1187
	*d. Anonymous (ed. Busard 1987)	mid-twelfth century

---

[5] For a useful although now out-of-date list that includes more theological works, see J. T. Muckle, "Greek Works Translated into Latin before 1350," *Mediaeval Studies* 4 (1942) 33–42, 5 (1943) 102–14. Another important source is the encyclopedic *Catalogus translationum et commentariorum: Mediaeval and Renaissance Latin Translations and Commentaries*, ed. P. O. Kristeller *et al.* (Washington, DC: Catholic University of America Press, 1960–).

[6] See. W. S. Teuffel, *Geschichte der Römische Literatur*, 6th edn (Teubner: Leipzig, 1910–16) 366.8 (III: 104).

[7] See ibid.

Author and Work	Translator	Date
PHILO OF ALEXANDRIA		
Quaestiones ad Genesim	Anonymous (ed. Petit 1973)	*ca.* fourth century
De vita contemplativa	Anonymous (ed. Conybeare 1895)	*ca.* fourth century
PTOLEMY		
Almagest	† a. Abdelmessie Wittoniensis	*ca.* 1130
	b. Anonymous (Sicily)	1160
	† c. Gerard of Cremona	before 1187
GALEN		
De alimentis	William of Moerbeke (ed. Camps 1987)	1277
De causis contentivis	Nicholas of Reggio (ed. Lyons *et al.* 1969)	early fourteenth century
De causis procatarcticis	Nicholas of Reggio (ed. Bardong 1937)	early fourteenth century
De complexionibus	Burgundio of Pisa (ed. Durling 1976)	twelfth century
De crisibus	Burgundio of Pisa (ed. Durling, in "Corrigenda" 1981)	twelfth century
De differentiis febrium	Burgundio of Pisa	twelfth century
De interioribus	Burgundio of Pisa (ed. Durling 1992)	twelfth century
De partibus artis medicativae	Nicholas of Reggio (ed. Lyons *et al.* 1969)	early fourteenth century
IRENAEUS		
Adversus Haereses	Anonymous (PG VII)	prob. third century
SEXTUS EMPIRICUS		
Outlines of Pyrrhonism	*Anonymous (ed. Wittwer, in *Sextus* forthcoming)	twelfth century
HERMES TRISMEGISTUS		
Asclepius	Anonymous (ed. Nock 1946)	third/fourth century
ORIGEN		
De principiis	Rufinus (ed. Crouzel and Simonetti 1978–84)	398–9
Homilies on Genesis	Rufinus (*Werke* vol. VI)	408–10 (?)
Homilies on Exodus	Rufinus (*Werke* vol. VI)	408–10 (?)
Homilies on Leviticus	Rufinus (*Werke* vol. VI)	408–10 (?)
Homilies on Numbers	Rufinus (*Werke* vol. VII)	408–10 (?)
Homilies on Joshua	Rufinus (*Werke* vol. VII)	408–10 (?)
Homilies on Judges	Rufinus (*Werke* vol. VII)	408–10 (?)
Homily on Kings	Rufinus (?)	408–10 (?)
Homilies on Job	Hilary of Poitiers (lost)	fourth century

(*cont.*)

Author and Work	Translator	Date
Homilies on Psalms 36–38	Rufinus (PG XII)	408–10 (?)
Homilies on the Song of Songs	Jerome (*Werke* vol. VIII)	384
Commentary on the Song of Songs	Rufinus (ed. Brésard and Crouzel 1991–2)	408–10 (?)
Homilies on Isaiah	Jerome (*Werke* vol. VIII)	after 390 (?)
Homilies on Jeremiah	Jerome (PG XIII)	381 (?)
Homilies on Ezekiel	Jerome (*Werke* vol. VIII)	381 (?)
Commentary on St. Matthew	Anonymous (*Werke* vols. X–XI)	
Homilies on Luke	Jerome (*Werke* vol. IX)	after 390 (?)
Commentary on Romans	Rufinus (ed. Hammond Bammel 1990–)	408–10 (?)
PORPHYRY		
Isagoge	a. Marius Victorinus (fragments) (ed. Minio-Paluello, in Porphyry 1966)	*ca.* fourth century
	b. Boethius (ed. Minio-Paluello 1966)	*ca.* 500
BASIL OF CAESAREA		
Homilies on the Hexaemeron	*Eustathius (PL 53)	440
GREGORY OF NAZIANZUS		
Nine Homilies	Rufinus (ed. Wrobel and Engelbrecht 1910)	fourth century
GREGORY OF NYSSA		
De hominis opificio (*De creatione hominis, De imagine*)	a. Dionysius Exiguus (PL 67)	sixth century
	b. John Scottus Eriugena (ed. Cappuyns 1965)	after 862
NEMESIUS OF EMESA		
De natura hominis	a. Alphanus (*Premnon physicon*) (ed. Burkhard 1917)	mid-eleventh century
	b. Burgundio of Pisa (ed. Verbeke and Moncho 1975)	*ca.* 1165
On the Elements (*De natura hominis*, ch. 6)	† Anonymous (Constantine the African?) (ed. Burnett, in "Physics" 2002)	twelfth century
PROCLUS		
Elementatio theologica	William of Moerbeke (ed. Boese 1987)	1268
Parmenides Commentary	William of Moerbeke (ed. Steel 1982–5)	1280/6

Author and Work	Translator	Date
Timaeus Commentary	William of Moerbeke (fragment) (ibid.)	*ca.* 1280 (?)
Tria Opuscula (*De decem dubitationibus, De providentia, De malorum subsistentia*)	William of Moerbeke (ed. Boese 1960)	1280

PSEUDO-DIONYSIUS

Corpus Dionysianum (*De divinis nominibus, De coelesti hierarchia, De ecclesiastica hierarchia, De mystica theologia, Epistulae*)	a. Hilduin (ed. Théry, in *Études* 1937)	after 827
	b. John Scottus Eriugena (PL 122)	*ca.* 860–2
	c. John the Saracene (ed. in Denys the Carthusian, *Opera* vols. XV–XVI)	*ca.* 1167
	d. Robert Grosseteste	after 1235
	e. Thomas Gallus (paraphrases) (ed. in Denys the Carthusian, *Opera* vols. XV–XVI; *De mystica theologia* ed. and tr. McEvoy 2003)	1233–43
	All of the above are edited by Chevallier 1937–50	

MAXIMUS THE CONFESSOR

Ambigua ad Iohannem	John Scottus Eriugena (ed. Jeauneau 1988)	after 860
Centurae de caritate	Cerbanus (ed. Boronkai 1975)	twelfth century
Life of St. Maximus the Confessor	Anastasius Bibliothecarius (ed. Allen and Neil 1999)	ninth century
Mystagogia (extracts)	Anastasius Bibliothecarius (ed. 1905)	ninth century
Quaestiones ad Thalassium	John Scottus Eriugena (ed. Laga and Steel 1980–90)	after 860

JOHN OF DAMASCUS

De centum haeresibus	Robert Grosseteste (ed. Holland 1980)	1235–42
De fide orthodoxa	a. Burgundio of Pisa (ed. Buytaert 1955)	1154/5
	b. Cerbanus (ibid.)	twelfth century
	c. Robert Grosseteste (rev. of [a])	1235–42
De hymno trisagio	Robert Grosseteste (ed. Holland 1980)	1235–40
Dialectica	Robert Grosseteste (ed. Colligan 1953)	1235–42
Elementarius dogmatum	Robert Grosseteste (ed. Holland 1980)	1235–42

3. GREEK PHILOSOPHICAL WORKS TRANSLATED INTO ARABIC

DIMITRI GUTAS

The Graeco-Arabic translation movement, during which the vast majority of the works listed here were translated, lasted over two hundred years, from shortly after the foundation of Baghdad in 762 until almost the end of the tenth century. It was a complex cultural process that traversed a number of stages and reflected a constant interaction between the needs and demands of scholarship and administration on the one hand and, on the other, the ability and availability of those who could supply the information needed in terms of translated texts. Its history in detail remains largely to be written, and although scholarship has made great strides in the past few decades, we are still not in a position to draw accurate lists of translations complete with dates and names of translators. For this reason this information has not been provided in the list that follows – and, in any case, the precise date of a translation and its author are of immediate interest only to the specialist of Arabic philosophy during the period of the translation movement, and these scholars can appreciate and analyze the problems involved on their own.[8]

In the table below, the Greek authors and their works are listed, in order to avoid ambiguities, according to the *Thesaurus Linguae Graecae, Canon of Greek Authors and Works* (*TLG*) by Luci Berkowitz and Karl A. Squitier (Oxford: Oxford University Press, 1990), and provided with the following information:

(a) If the Arabic translation of the work in question is extant and published, reference is given when possible by its number in Hans Daiber's *Bibliography of Islamic Philosophy* (Leiden: Brill, 1999–2007). (In general, editions are included in this volume's bibliography only if they are not found in Daiber.) If there is more than one edition,

---

[8] For a discussion of some of these problems see Dimitri Gutas, *Greek Thought, Arabic Culture* (London: Routledge, 1998) pp. 136–50, as well as Gerhard Endress and Dimitri Gutas, *Greek and Arabic Lexicon* (Leiden: Brill, 1992–) I: 1*–9*. A number of articles and book chapters offer narrative surveys of the information presented here in tabular form. For the earliest Greek philosophical texts available in Arabic see Gerhard Endress, "Building the Library of Arabic Philosophy. Platonism and Aristotelianism in the Sources of al-Kindī," in C. D'Ancona (ed.) *The Libraries of the Neoplatonists* (Leiden: Brill, 2007) 319–50. Conveniently located in the same volume, for the purposes of comparison with the information provided by Endress, is the survey of Syriac translations by Henri Hugonnard-Roche, "Le corpus philosophique syriaque aux VIᵉ–VIIᵉ siècles," 279–91. A bibliographically thorough survey of "Le opere tradotte" is offered by Cristina D'Ancona in the book edited by her, *Storia della filosofia nell' Islam medievale* (Turin: Einaudi, 2005), pp. 201–41, the most reliable and comprehensive general history of the classical period of philosophy in medieval Islam. A fundamental survey of medieval Arabic philosophical and scientific literature with full bibliography, to the time of its appearance, is offered in the book-length articles by Endress, "Die wissenschaftliche Literatur," in *Grundriss der Arabischen Philologie*, ed. H. Gätje and W. Fischer (Wiesbaden: Reichert, 1987–92) vols. II and III. A brief bibliographical guide on Greek works translated into Arabic, including philosophy, can be found in Gutas, *Greek Thought, Arabic Culture*, pp. 193–6. Indispensable, finally, for a complete account of the Arabic versions of works by individual philosophers, are the entries under their name in the *Dictionnaire des philosophes antiques*, ed. R. Goulet (Paris: CNRS, 1999–).

reference is generally given only to the latest (in whose introduction earlier editions are normally mentioned), or to the critically most sound. If none is satisfactory, then I list them all chronologically.

(b) If the Arabic translation is extant but not published, reference is given to the bibliographical source which lists the manuscripts and other sources in which it is extant.

(c) If the Arabic translation, to the best of our current knowledge, is not extant but there is a reference to it, in the Arabic bibliographical sources (mainly in Ibn al-Nadīm's *Fihrist*), as having existed, its title is put in square brackets. The information provided by such sources is still unprocessed by modern scholarship, so that its nature cannot be ascertained. Specifically, we cannot tell whether such a translation existed in Syriac or in Arabic, whether Ibn al-Nadīm and other bibliographers saw the actual translation or merely heard about it from their own sources, and finally whether the attribution of the work to the philosopher concerned is authentic or not.

Titles listed in *TLG* are given in Latin as they appear there; all others are given in English translation of the Arabic title in the sources.

Further, to help the user in assessing the significance and nature of the Arabic translations, the following signs precede the authors' names and titles of works:

* before an author's name: some works by this author that are not extant in Greek are preserved in Arabic;

\+ before the title of a work: work extant in Arabic only;

\> before the title of a work: the Arabic translation contains more text than the extant Greek original;

[ ] titles in brackets: the work is listed or mentioned in Arabic sources but no manuscript of it has so far been recovered; extant fragments are normally listed.

These abbreviations have also been used:

D	Daiber, *Bibliography of Islamic Philosophy* (1999). The references are to Daiber's serial numbers, followed by the letter *S* for those in the *Supplement* (2007).
DPhA, DPhAS	*Dictionnaire des Philosophes Antiques* (1999); *Supplément* (2003) (ed. Goulet)
F	Ibn al-Nadīm, *Kitāb al-Fihrist* (ed. Flügel)
GALex	*A Greek and Arabic Lexicon*, vol. I (ed. Endress and Gutas)
GAP	Endress, "Die wissenschaftliche Literatur," in *Grundriss der Arabischen Philologie*
GAS	*Geschichte des arabischen Schrifttums* (Sezgin)
GCAL	*Geschichte der christlichen arabischen Literatur* (Graf)
Ullmann *Med.*	Ullmann, *Die Medizin im Islam*
Ullmann *Natur*	Ullmann, *Die Natur- und Geheimwissenschaften im Islam*

AETIUS Doxogr. [Ps.-Plutarchus Chaeronensis]
  >*De placitis reliquiae*; ed. and tr. Daiber (D2130)

*Alexander Phil. Aphrodisiensis

(As listed in the entries in *DPhA* (Goulet and Aouad) and *DPhAS* (Fazzo), which should be consulted in all instances; the numbers before the titles refer to their numbers.)

(1) [*In Aristotelis analyticorum priorum librum i commentarium*]; F249,7–8

(2) [*In Aristotelis topicorum libros octo commentaria*]; F249,18–24

(3) [*In Aristotelis meteorologicorum libros commentaria*]; F251,9

(4) *In Aristotelis metaphysica commentaria*; F251,27–8; frg. ed. Freudenthal (D3179); *GAP* III,32n49

(5) +*Commentary on Categories*; F248,25; frg. ed. Zonta (D9497/1)

(6) [*Commentary on De Interpretatione*]; F249,2

(9) [*In analytica posteriora commentaria*]; F249,13; F252,27–8

(10) [*In Aristotelis sophisticos elenchos commentarius*]; F249,29

(11) +*Commentary on Physics*; F250,7; F252,27; frg. ed. Badawī (D795); frg. ed. and tr. Giannakis (D3540)

(12) [*Commentary on De Caelo*]; F250,29

(13) +*Commentary on De Generatione et Corruptione*; F251,4; ed. and tr. Gannagé (D3301/3S), tr. E. Gannagé (2005).

(16) *On the Soul*; cf. Gätje (D3400), pp. 69–70; frg. ed. Günsz (D3798)

(19a–p) >Ἀπορίαι καὶ λύσεις; various *Quaestiones* extant in Arabic (some are by Philoponus); see the lists in *DPhA* and *DPhAS*

(21) >*De anima libri mantissa*; various treatises extant in Arabic; see the list in *DPhA* and *DPhAS*

(22) +*On Providence*; F253,8; ed. and tr. Thillet, 2003

(23) +*On Time* (= *Refutation of Galen on Time and Place*, F253,5–6 ?); ed. Badawī (D385)

(24) +*On the Principles of the Universe*; F253,7; ed. and tr. Genequand (D3431/1S); ed. Endress (D2641/1S)

(25) +*Refutation of Galen's Critique of Aristotle on the Theory of Motion*; ed. and tr. Rescher and Marmura (D395)

(26) +*Refutation of Xenocrates on Form and Genus*; ed. Badawī (D382); tr. Pines (D7058)

(27) +*Refutation of Galen on the Possible* (?); frg. ed. and tr. Rescher and Marmura (D7503)

(28) +*On the Conversion of Premises*; F253,6–7; ed. Badawī (D377)

(29) +*On the Specific Difference*; F253,11; ed. and tr. Dietrich (D2344)

(30) +*On the Governance of the Spheres* (= a parallel version of *On Providence*, no. 22 above); ed. and tr. Ruland (D7695)

(31) +*On Sound*; ed. Badawī (D383)

(32) *On Form*; ed. Badawī (D384), tr. Badawī (D1119)

(33) (Ps.-Alexander = Philoponus) *That the Act is More General than Motion*; ed. and tr. Hasnawi (D4019)

(34) +*On the Division of Genera*; ed. Badawī (D379), tr. Badawī (D1119)

(35) (Ps.-Alexander = Philoponus) *On Creation ex nihilo*; F254,9; ed. and tr. Hasnawi (D4019)

(36) (Ps.-Alexander = Philoponus) *That Every Separate Cause is in All Things and in None*; ed. and tr. Zimmermann (D9484)

(37) *On the Celestial Sphere*; MS Istanbul, Carullah 1279, ff. 53b–54a; part of (24) above

(38) Ps.-Alexander (?), *Poetic Gleanings*, actually on topics; see Zimmermann (D9486)

(39) +*On the Cause*; ed. Endress (D2641/1S); ed. and tr. Genequand (D3431/1S)

(43) [*On Melancholy*]; F253,11

(57) [*That Being Is Not of the Same Genus as the Categories*]; F253,7–8

(59) >*Problemata*; *GAP* III,139n3; cf. Filius (D3084S) p. xvi

*Alexandri Magni Epistulae, *see* Aristoteles, *Epistulae*

*Alexandrini Philosophi, *see* Summaria Alexandrinorum

*ALLĪNŪS (?)
[*Commentary on the Categories*]; F248,21
+Frg. tr. F. Rosenthal (D7618)

AMMONIUS Phil. Alexandrinus
[*On the Purposes of Aristotle's Books*]; F253,22
[*In Aristotelis Categorias commentarius*]; F248,21
[*Commentary on the Topics*]; F249,19–24
[*Commentary on Aristotle on the Creator*]; F253,22
[*Aristotle's Proof of the Oneness (of God)*]; F253,22–3

ANACHARSIS Scythicus
+Sayings; in Arabic gnomologia, cf. Gutas (D3818)

ANONYMI *De Anima Paraphrasis*
+ ed. and tr. Arnzen (D879)

ARISTOTELES Phil. et CORPUS ARISTOTELICUM
Analytica priora ed. Badawī (D757), ed. Jabr (1999) I: 169–416
Analytica posteriora; ed. Badawī (D758); ed. Jabr (1999) I: 417–620
De anima; survey of the transmission in Arabic by Gätje (D3400); ed. Badawī (D762, 1088); medieval Hebrew tr. from the Arabic ed. Bos (D763); medieval Latin tr. from the Arabic ed. Crawford (D4522), tr. of the Latin by Taylor (2009); cf. *GAP* III,29n27, 33n57. See also Anonymi, *De Anima Paraphrasis*
De caelo; survey of the transmission in Arabic by Endress (D2643); ed. Badawī (D1089), ed. Endress (forthcoming); cf. *GALex* I: 17*
Categoriae; ed. Bouyges (D4550); ed. Badawī (D761); ed. Jabr (1999) I: 1–96
[*De coloribus*]; apparently not translated; cf. Gätje (D3404) p. 285
De divinatione per somnum, see *Parva naturalia*
Divisiones aristoteleae; ed. Kellermann (D5005); *GALex* I: 33*
+*Epistulae*; survey of the transmission in Arabic by Gutas, "Epistolary 'Novels'" (forthcoming); cf. Gutas *Greek Thought* (1998) pp. 194–5; ed. Maróth, in *Correspondence* (2006)
Ethica Nicomachea; unpublished ed. and tr. Dunlop; ed. Akasoy and Fidora (D778, 778S)
De generatione animalium; ed. Brugman and Drossaart Lulofs (D765)

De generatione et corruptione; survey of the transmission in Arabic by Eichner (D4537/1S, pp. 291–332); medieval Hebrew translation from the Arabic translation ed. Tessier (D768)

Historia animalium; ed. Badawī (D779)

De insomniis, see *Parva naturalia*

De interpretatione; ed. Badawī (D770); ed. Jabr (1999) I: 97–166

De longitudine et brevitate vitae, see *Parva naturalia*

Magna moralia; ed. Kellermann (D5005); *GALex* I: 20*

Mechanica; extant paraphrastic summary ed. and tr. Abattouy (2001)

De memoria et reminiscentia, see *Parva naturalia*

Metaphysica; survey of the transmission in Arabic by Bertolacci (D1432/1S); ed. Bouyges (D1591), ed. Badawī (D786), ed. Mishkāt (D787)

Meteorologica; the Arabic and medieval Latin tr. from the Arabic ed. Schoonheim (D7978S); cf. *GAP* III,28n22

[*Mirabilium auscultationes*]; no trace has so far been found in Arabic; the entry on it in Peters *Aristoteles Arabus* (1968) p. 61 is based on a mistaken reference by Walzer, corrected by Walzer later in his *Greek into Arabic* (1962) 140n5–6

De mundo; ed. Brafman (D1603); cf. *GAP* III,30n41

Oeconomica; ed. Maʾlūf (D793), tr. Shunnar (D9049); cf. Peters *Aristoteles Arabus* (1968) pp. 62–3

De partibus animalium; ed. Kruk (D773)

Parva naturalia; survey of the transmission in Arabic by Gätje (D3400) pp. 81–92; ed. Hansberger, in *Transmission* (2006)

Physica; ed. Badawī (D795)

Physiognomica; ed. and tr. Ghersetti, in *Il Kitāb Arisṭāṭalīs* (1999)

Poetica; ed. and modern Latin tr. Margoliouth (D5935), ed. and modern Latin tr. Tkatsch (D8661), ed. Badawī (D797), ed. ʿAyyād (D798)

Politica; tr. of parts only; cf. Pines (D7037), Brague (D1607)

>*Problemata*; ed. Filius (D3084S); cf. *GAP* III,139n3

[*Protrepticus*]; cf. Fakhry (D2789)

Rhetorica; ed. Lyons (D801)

Sophistici elenchi; ed. Badawī (D803); ed. Jabr (1999) II: 897–1203

De sensu et sensibilibus, see *Parva naturalia*

De somno et vigilia, see *Parva naturalia*

Testamentum; ed. and modern Latin tr., references in *GALex* I: 23*

Topica; ed. Badawī (D809); ed. Jabr (1999) II: 627–896

De virtutibus et vitiis; ed. Kellermann (D5005); *GALex* I: 34*

>Sayings, ed. Gutas (D3809); cf. Gutas (D3818)

+Ps.-Aristoteles

+*De lapidibus*, ed. Ruska; see Peters, *Aristoteles Arabus* (1968) p. 60

+*De pomo*, ed. Khayrallāh (D775); see Aouad in *DPhA* I: 537–41; cf. Kotzia, Περί του Μήλου (2007)

+Pseudepigrapha; see Peters, *Aristoteles Arabus* (1968) 55–75, *GAP* III,31n42

+*Secretum secretorum*, ed. Badawī (D780), ed. al-Aʿwar (D802); cf. Forster, *Das Geheimnis der Geheimnisse* (2006).

*Bryson Phil.
+Οἰκονομικός; ed. Plessner (D7146)

Cebes Phil.
Cebetis tabula; see Gutas in *DPhA*; cf. F. Rosenthal (D7647)

*Corpus Hermeticum
Numerous works ascribed to Hermes are preserved in Arabic. The degree to which these are actually translations from the Greek or correspond to surviving works and fragments in Greek has been little investigated. See Goulet in *DPhA* III: 649–50; *GAS* IV,38–44; Ullmann *Natur* 165–70; *GAP* III,144–5; van Bladel, *Hermes Arabicus* (2004).

*Diogenes Phil. et Trag.
>Sayings; tr. Gutas (D3820)

*Eudemus Phil. Rhodius
+Sayings; ed. and tr. Gutas (D3807/1S)

*Galenus Med. Pergamenus
(Only philosophically relevant works are given, as listed in the entry by V. Boudon in *DPhA*, which should be consulted in all instances; the numbers before the titles refer to her numbers.)

(1) *Adhortatio ad artes addiscendas (Protrepticus)*; *GAS* III,138 (#151); Ullmann *Med.* 53 (#73); extant Arabic epitome ed. Badawī (D3283)

(3) *Quod optimus medicus sit quoque philosophus*; ed. and tr. Bachmann (D1065)

(4) *De sectis ad eos qui introducuntur*; ed. Sālim (1977)

(6) [*De placitis Hippocratis et Platonis*]; *GAS* III,105 (#37); Ullmann *Med.* 40 (#12)

(7) *Quod animi mores corporis temperamenta sequantur*; ed. and tr. Biesterfeldt (D1457, D1456)

(8) (8a) [*De propriorum animi cuiuslibet affectuum dignotione et curatione*]; Ullmann *Med.* 51 (#65)

(9) *De consuetudinibus*; ed. and tr. Klein-Franke (D5210)

(10) [*Institutio logica*]; Ullmann *Med.* 51 (#63)

(12) *De elementis secundum Hippocratem libri ii*; cf. *GAP* III,120n25; ed. Sālim (1987)

(14) [*On the Authentic and Inauthentic Book by Hippocrates*]; Ullmann *Med.* 53 (#72); *GAS* III,137 (#146)

(15) +*On Cohesive Causes*; ed. and tr. Lyons (1969).

(16) [*On Antecedent Causes*]; Ullmann *Med.* 57 (#91); *GAS* III,135 (#138)

(17) [*An Outline of Empiricism in Medicine*]; Ullmann *Med.* 52 (#67); *GAS* III,131 (#118)

(18) +*On Affections and their Cure, III*; see Steinschneider, *Die hebräischen Übersetzungen* §415,13

(19) +*De experientia medica*; ed. and tr. Walzer (D3284)

(20) =(8)

(21) +*That Good Men Benefit from Their Enemies*; Ullmann *Med.* 65 (#117)

(22) >*De demonstratione*; Ullmann *Med.* 62 (#12); *GAP* III,31 and 53n180; for ed. frg. see *DPhA*

(23) *De propriis placitis*; Ullmann *Med.* 51 (#64); for the surviving parts see *DPhA*

(24) +*De nominibus medicinalibus*; ed. and tr. Meyerhof and Schacht (1931)

(25) +*De moribus*; ed. Kraus (D3286), tr. Mattock (D6129)

(26) >*In Platonis Timaeum commentarius* (Περὶ τῶν ἐν τῷ Πλάτωνος Τιμαίῳ ἰατρικῶς εἰρημένων); *GAS* III,126 (#90); Ullmann *Med.* 64 (#115); frg. ed. P. Kahle (1934).

(27) +*Compendium Timaei*; ed. and tr. Kraus and Walzer (D3279), ed. Badawī (D3280); see Gutas, "Plato Arabus," in *DPhA*

(28) +*Compendium Rei publicae*; Ullmann *Med.* 64 (#114b); used by Averroes for his *Middle Commentary*, ed. and tr. E. I. J. Rosenthal (D4558; cf. D4559–62); see Gutas, "Plato Arabus," in *DPhA*

(29) +*Compendium Legum*; Ullmann *Med.* 64 (#114c); epitomes by al-Fārābī and Ibn al-Ṭayyib (see Gutas D3808), ed. and tr. Gabrieli (D2965), ed. Druart (D2510/1); see Gutas, "Plato Arabus," in *DPhA*

(30) +[*Compendium Phaedonis*]; Ullmann *Med.* 64 (#114d); cf. Rowson (D7660) pp. 29–41; see Gutas, "Plato Arabus," in *DPhA*

    (30.1) +[*Compendium of Cratylus*]; see Gutas, "Plato Arabus," in *DPhA*

    (30.2) +[*Compendium of Sophist*]; see Gutas, "Plato Arabus," in *DPhA*

    (30.3) +[*Compendium of Politicus*]; see Gutas, "Plato Arabus," in *DPhA*

    (30.4) +[*Compendium of Parmenides*]; see Gutas, "Plato Arabus," in *DPhA*

    (30.5) +[*Compendium of Euthydemus*]; see Gutas, "Plato Arabus," in *DPhA*

(32) [*De dolore evitando*]; Ullmann *Med.* 65 (#118); for frg. see *DPhA*

(33) +*In primum movens immotum*; Ullmann *Med.* 65 (#116); see *DPhA*

(34) [*On the Providence of the Creator*]; see *DPhA*

(36) [Περὶ οὐσίας τῆς ψυχῆς κατ' Ἀσκληπιάδην]; Syriac tr. Degen, in "Galen im Syrischen" n. 124

(41) [Περὶ τοῦ τῶν συλλογισμῶν ἀριθμοῦ]; Syriac tr. Degen, ibid., n. 115

(48) [*On the Possible*]; see *DPhA*

(95) +*Platonicorum dialogorum compendia octo*; see *GAP* III,31n43, 43n121; Ullmann *Med.* 63 (#114); Gutas, "Plato Arabus," in *DPhA*

(98) [*Commentary on De Interpretatione*]; F249,2–3

Ars medica (*parva*); *GAS* III,80 (#4); Ullmann *Med.* 45 (#38); *GAP* III,120n25

De usu partium; *GAS* III,106 (#40); Ullmann *Med.* 41 (#15)

In Hippocratis aphorismos commentarii; *GAS* III,123 (#71); Ullmann *Med.* 50 (#58)

[*De libris propriis*]; *GAS* III,78 (#1); Ullmann *Med.* 35 (#1)

[*De ordine librorum suorum ad Eugenianum*]; *GAS* III,79 (#2); Ullmann *Med.* 35 (#2)

+*In Hippocratis de aere aquis locis commentaria*; *GAP* III,119n24; *GAS* III,123 (#81); Ullmann *Med.* 61 (#107); ed. Strohmaier in preparation

+*De examinando medico*, ed. Iskandar (*GAP* III,120n25, 127n73); Ullmann *Med.* 52 (#70)

+*De partibus artis medicativae*, ed. Lyons; *GAS* III,112 (#49); Ullmann *Med.* 52 (#69)

+*De somno et vigilia*; *GAS* III,126 (#92); Ullmann *Med.* 55 (#84)

+[*De voce*]; *GAS* III,103 (#30); Ullmann *Med.* 54 (#79)

*Pseudo-Galenus Med.

[*Definitiones medicae*]; *GAS* III,138 (#153); Ullmann *Med.* 38 (#3)

+*De Plantis*; *GAS* IV,314

+*Book of Poisons*; *GAS* III,121 (#67); Ullmann *Med.* 61 (#106)

+*On the Soul*; ed. Jellinek (1852)

+*In Hippocratis legem commentarius*; ed. F. Rosenthal: *GAS* III,123 (#70); Ullmann *Med.* 62 (#111)

+*Oeconomica*; see Plessner (D7146), pp. 205–13

Georgius Gemistus Plethon

Works preserved in Arabic translation in MS Istanbul, Ahmet III, 1896; cf. Tardieu, "La recension arabe" (1995) pp. 157–8.

*Hippocrates Med. et Corpus Hippocraticum

(Only the philosophically relevant works are listed, as discussed by J. Jouanna and C. Magdelaine in *DPhA* III, 786–90)

[*De prisca medicina*]; *GAS* III,43 (#24); Ullmann *Med.* 31 (#13)

De aere aquis et locis; ed. Mattock and Lyons (*GALex* I: 27*–28*); *GAS* III,36 (#8); Ullmann *Med.* 27 (#3)

Aphorismi; ed. Tytler (*GALex* I: 28*); *GAS* III,28 (#2); Ullmann *Med.* 28 (#4)

Jusjurandum; ed. and tr. see Ullmann *Med.* 32 (#25); *GAS* III,28 (#1); *GAP* III,119n23

Lex; ed. and tr. see Ullmann *Med.* 33 (#27); *GAS* III,38 (#11)

De humoribus; ed. Mattock (*GALex* I: 29*); *GAS* III,35 (#6); Ullmann *Med.* 30 (#9)

De natura hominis, ed. Mattock and Lyons (*GALex* I: 29*–30*); *GAS* III,37 (#9); Ullmann *Med.* 27 (#2)

De ventis; Ullmann *Med.* 32 (#22); *GAS* III,46 (#8)

[*De carnibus*]; *GAS* III,46 (#11)

De alimento; ed. and tr. Mattock (*GALex* I: 28*); Ullmann *Med.* 30 (#10); *GAS* III,41 (#16)

[*De medico*] (?); Ullmann *Med.* 33 (#28)

>*De septimanis*; Ullmann *Med.* 32 (#20); *GAS* III,40 (#14)

*Pseudo-Hippocrates Med.

>*Epistulae*; *GAS* III,43 (#21); Ullmann *Med.* 34 (#30)

Testamentum; tr. F. Rosenthal (Ullmann *Med.* 33, #26; *GAS* III,39, #12)

+*Secreta Hippocratis / Capsula eburnea*; *GAS* III,39 (#12b); Ullmann *Med.* 33 (#29)

Hippolytus Scr. Eccl. Romanus

Refutatio omnium haeresium; partially preserved in "Ps.-Ammonius," ed. Rudolph (D7681); see *GAP* III,30n37, 146n52

Historia et Sententiae De Ahiqar

Historia et sententiae de Ahiqar; ed. in Conybeare *et al.*, *The Story of Ahikar* (1898)

*Iamblichus Phil.

[*Commentary on the Categories*]; F248,23

[*Commentary on De Interpretatione*]; F249,2

+*Commentaria in Carmen aureum Pythagorae*; ed. Daiber (D2158)

Isocrates Orat.
+Sayings; ed. Alon (D436)

*Joannes Philoponus Phil. Alexandrinus
  [*In Aristotelis meteorologicorum libros commentaria*]; *GCAL* I,418 #4
  [*In Aristotelis libros de generatione et corruptione commentaria*]; *GCAL* I,418 #4
  >*In Aristotelis physicorum libros commentaria*; F250,18, 255,2; ed. Badawī (D795); tr.
    Giannakis (D3541); tr. Lettinck (D7012); ed. and tr. of the corollaries on place and
    void Giannakis (D3542/1)
  De aeternitate mundi contra Proclum; F254,25; frg. (from Bīrūnī) ed. and tr. Giannakis
    (D3541/1S); see above, Alexander Aphrodisiensis, nos (33) and (35), and Hasnawi
    (D4019)
  +*Contra Aristotelem*; F254,27; frg. ed. and tr. Mahdi (D5784, D5773); frg. ed. and tr.
    Kraemer (D5265); frg. tr. Wildberg (D9267)
  +*De contingentia mundi*; *GCAL* I,418 #1; ed. and tr. Troupeau (D8713); tr. Pines
    (D7036)
  +*In Galeni libros commentaria*; F255,1; *GCAL* I,418 #4
  [*Every finite body has a finite power*]; F254,25–6
  [*Commentary on Aristotle's Problemata*]; F254,26–7

Nemesius Theol.
  De natura hominis; F255,10; ed. Weisser, in *Buch über das Geheimnis* (1980); cf. Samir
    (D7873)

*Nicolaus Hist. Damascenus
  +*De plantis*; *GAS* IV,312–3; *GAP* III,30n40; ed. and tr. Drossaart Lulofs (D2491)
  +*Epitome of Aristotle's philosophy*; F254,4; frg. ed. and tr. Drossaart Lulofs (D2489); frg.
    ed. and tr. Takahashi (D8501/6S)
  [*Summary of Aristotle's De anima*, one book]; F254,3
  [*Summary of Aristotelian zoology*]; F251,23; Ullmann *Natur* 9
  [*Refutation of those who make the act and what is acted upon identical*]; F254,4

Nicomachus Math. Gerasenus
  Introductio arithmetica; ed. Kutsch (*GAP* III,65n20)

Olympiodorus Alchim.
  Εἰς τὸ κατ' ἐνέργειαν Ζοσίμου; see Endress, "Building the Library" (2007)
    327n18

*Olympiodorus Phil.
  [*Commentary on Plato's Sophistes*]; F246.12
  [*Commentary on De Generatione et Corruptione*]; F251,5
  +*In Aristotelis Meteora paraphrasis*; F251,8; ed. Badawī (D6911)
  [*Commentary on De anima*]; F251,13–14

Oracula Chaldaica
  Oracula; frg. ed. and tr. Tardieu, in "La recension arabe" (1995)

PLATO Phil. (See Gutas, "Plato Arabus," in *DPhA*)

No dialogue of Plato is known to have been fully translated into Arabic, and none survives. Some portions of the more famous dialogues were literally translated, but for the most part the works of Plato were known in Arabic through the epitomes of Galen (for which see under Galen), citations in the works of other authors who quoted him (notably Galen and Aristotle in *Metaphysics* A and M–N), and doxographies and gnomologia, the most significant among which is al-ʿĀmirī's (?) *Al-Saʿāda wa-al-isʿād* (for which see Arberry, D736). Of the dialogues that were known the best, three were known by name, *Laws* (Gutas, D3808), *Republic* (Reisman, D7457/4), and *Timaeus* (evidence of an abbreviated translation by Ibn al-Biṭrīq in al-Kindī's work: Rescher, D7483), and one anonymously, *Phaedo* (Rowson, D7660). For the *Symposium*, see Gutas (D3817); for the *Meno*, see Endress (D2642). For his sayings see Gutas (D3809).

PLOTINUS Phil.

Enneades IV–VI; ed. and tr. Dieterici (D804, D2340); ed. Badawī (D806); tr. Lewis (D7155); see *GAP* III,30n35, and Adamson (D218/4S)

PLUTARCHUS Biogr. et Phil. Chaeronensis (see Gutas [D3818] 4944n5)

[*De cohibenda ira*]; F254,8

[*On the Soul = De animae procreatione in Timaeo?*]; F254,8

[*De capienda ex inimicis utilitate*]; F254,7–8

Pseudo-PLUTARCHUS

Placita Philosophorum, see Aetius

[*On Training =* Περὶ ἀσκήσεως]; F254,8; cf. Gutas (D3818) 4944n5

Pseudo-POLEMON

Physiognomica; ed. and tr. Hoyland (2007)

PORPHYRIUS Phil. vel Malchus (see Walzer [D9152])

Vita Pythagorae; see F. Rosenthal (D7644)

Isagoge sive quinque voces; ed. Badawī (D7184); ed. Ahwānī (D7185); *GALex* I: 32*–33*

[*In Aristotelis Categorias*]; F248,20

[*Commentary on De Interpretatione*]; F249,2

[*Introduction to Categorical Syllogisms*]; F253,15–16

[*Commentary on Physics*]; F250,21–2

[*On the Elements*]; F253,17

+*On the Soul*; ed. and tr. Kutsch (D5362)

[*On the Intellect and the Intelligible =* Ἀφορμαὶ πρὸς τὰ νοητά?]; F253,16

[*Refutation of ? on the Intellect and the Intelligible*]; F253,16–17

[*Commentary on Nicomachean Ethics*]; F252,2

[*Epistula ad Anebonem*]; F253,16; frg. tr. F. Gabrieli (D3261)

Fragmenta; ed. Wasserstein (D7183)

[*Historia philosophiae*]; F253,18; frg. ed. F. Rosenthal (D7614)

*PROCLUS Phil. Atheniensis (see G. Endress, *Proclus Arabus* [1973] = D2656)

[*In Platonis rem publicam commentarii*]; Endress, *Proclus Arabus* 29

Institutio theologica; *GAP* III,30n36; ed. Endress (D2656); frg. ed. Badawī (D7123); see
   also Alexander Aphrodisiensis, no. 36 – *De causis*; Endress, *Proclus Arabus* 18–24; ed.
   Badawī (D782); ed. and tr. Taylor (D8565); ed. Badawī (D7207)
[*Institutio physica*]; Endress, *Proclus Arabus* 27
In Platonis Timaeum commentaria; Endress, *Proclus Arabus* 24; frg. tr. Pfaff (D7205)
[*De decem dubitationibus*]; Endress, *Proclus Arabus* 27–8
+*De aeternitate mundi*; Endress, *Proclus Arabus* 15–18; frg. ed. Badawī (D7206); tr.
   Badawī (D1119); tr. Anawati (D645); ed. and tr. Maróth (D5998)
+*Problemata physica*; Endress, *Proclus Arabus* 26; ed. Badawī (D7208)
+(Ps.-Proclus?)[9] *Comm. in Carmen aureum Pythagorae*; Endress, *Proclus Arabus* 26–7;
   ed. Linley (D5575)
[*In Platonis Gorgiam commentaria*]; Endress, *Proclus Arabus* 28
[*In Platonis Phaedonem commentaria*]; Endress, *Proclus Arabus* 28–9
[*In Aristotelis De Interpretatione commentaria*]; Endress, *Proclus Arabus* 29–30
[*On the Supernal Substances*]; Endress, *Proclus Arabus* 30
[*On the Atom*]; Endress, *Proclus Arabus* 30

Claudius PTOLEMAEUS Math.
   Syntaxis mathematica; *GAS* VI,88–9; *GAP* III,89n23
   Tetrabiblos; *GAS* VII,43 (#1); *GAP* III,105n7

*Pseudo–PTOLEMAEUS
   Fructus; *GAS* VII,44–5 (#2); *GAP* III,105n8

*PTOLEMAEUS Pinacographus, 4 A.D.?
   +*Vita Aristotelis et pinax*; F255,11–12; tr. Plezia (D7150); cf. Düring (D2554), Gutas
      (D3822)

<PYTHAGORAS> Phil.
   Carmen aureum; *GAP* III,39n91; cf. Endress, "Building the Library" 331n30; ed.
      Cheikho (D7239); ed. Ullmann (D8820)
   >Sayings; ed. and tr. Gutas (D3809); cf. Gutas (D3818)

Secundus, *see* Vita et Sententiae Secundi

<SEPTEM SAPIENTES> Phil.
   >Sayings in Arabic gnomologia; cf. Gutas (D3818)

SIMPLICIUS Phil. (see Gätje [D3399])
   [*In Aristotelis Categorias commentarium*]; F248,21; cf. Türker (D8735)
   [*In Aristotelis libros De anima commentaria*]; F251,15
   [*Commentary on the Introduction of Euclid's Elements*]; F268,15

SOCRATES Phil. Atheniensis
   >Sayings; ed. and tr. Gutas (D3809); ed. and tr. Alon (D438, D439)

---

[9] See L. G. Westerink, "Proclus commentateur des *Vers d'Or*," in G. Bos and G. Seel (eds.), *Proclus et son influence* (Zurich: Éditions du Grand Midi, 1987), 62–78.

Stephanus Phil. Alexandrinus, Constantinopolitanus
[*Commentary on Categories*]; F248,20–1

Summaria Alexandrinorum
[*On De anima*]; F251,15–16

Syrianus Phil. Atheniensis
[*In Aristotelis Metaphysica B commentaria*]; F251,31

*Thales Phil.
>Sayings; in Arabic gnomologia, cf. Gutas (D3818)

*Themistius Phil. et Rhet.
Περὶ φιλίας; Syriac tr. ed. Sachau (D7759)
Περὶ ἀρετῆς; Syriac tr. ed. Mach (D8613)
[*Commentary on Categories*]; F248,21
[*In Aristotelis Analyticorum priorum paraphrasis*]; F249,8
Against Maximus, on the Reduction of the Second and Third Figure to the First; ed. Badawī (D8612)
[*In Aristotelis Analyticorum posteriorum paraphrasis*]; F249,12–13
[*Commentary on Topics*]; F249,23
[*Commentary on Poetics*]; F250,5
[*In Aristotelis physica paraphrasis*]; F250,22
Commentary on De caelo; F250,30; ed. Landauer (D8604)
[*Commentary on De generatione et corruptione*]; F251,6
In Aristotelis libros de anima paraphrasis; F251,12–18; ed. Lyons (D8603); partial tr. Gätje (D3385)
+*Epitome of Aristotelian zoology*; Ullmann *Natur* 9–10; ed. Badawī (D8608)
+*Commentary on Book Lambda of the Metaphysics*; F251,30; ed. Landauer (D8606); ed. Badawī (D8605, D 8607)
[*Commentary on Nicomachean Ethics*]; F252,3
[*On the Soul = De anima paraphrasis?*]; F253,27
+*Letter to Julian, on politics*; F253,26–7 mentions two letters without indication of their identity; ed. Cheikho (D8609); ed. Sālim (D8610); ed. Shahid (D8611)

*Theon Smyrnaeus
+*Life and Works of Plato*; F246,4; 255,12–13; ed. in Ibn al-Qiftī, ed. Lippert (D7291) 17–25; cf. Lippert (D5577)

Theon (?)
[*Commentary on Categories*]; F248,22

Theophrastus Phil.
[*De causis plantarum*]; F252,9–10; *GAS* IV,313
[*De sensu et sensibilibus*]; F252,8
Metaphysica; ed. Gutas (forthcoming)
[*Commentary on Categories*]; F248,21; F252,10–11
[*Commentary on De Interpretatione*]; F249,3

+*Meteorologica*; ed. and tr. Daiber (D2154); frg. ed. and tr. Takahashi (D8501/6S)
[*On the Soul*]; F252,7
[*On Education*]; F252,8
+Sayings; ed. Gutas (D3811)
+Fragments; ed. and tr. Gutas (D8617), ed. and tr. Daiber (D2171)

VITA ET SENTENTIAE SECUNDI
  Vita Secundi; ed. Perry (D6991)
  >Sayings; in Arabic gnomologia, cf. Gutas (D3818)

4. ARABIC PHILOSOPHICAL WORKS TRANSLATED INTO LATIN
CHARLES BURNETT

The following table lists translations according to the chronological order of the author
in the Arabic original. Works that have not survived in Arabic, or in the Latin translation,
or that have not been identified, are marked with an asterisk (*). Translations made via
the intermediary of a Hebrew text are marked with an obelisk (†). Certain works that
primarily belong to other genres, such as mathematics and medicine, have been added
because they include substantial discussions of topics germane to *falsafa*. The following
abbreviations have been used: AL = *Aristoteles Latinus*; ASL = *Aristoteles Semitico-Latinus*;
AvL = *Avicenna Latinus*. A previous version of this table published in the *Cambridge
Companion to Arabic Philosophy* contains fuller bibliographical details, and extends into
the Renaissance.

Author and Work	Translator	Date
ARISTOTLE		
Posterior Analytics	Gerard of Cremona (AL IV.3)	before 1187
Rhetoric	Hermann the German	1240/50
Physics	Gerard of Cremona	before 1187
De caelo	Gerard of Cremona	before 1187
De generatione et corruptione	Gerard of Cremona	before 1187
Meteora I–III, paraphrase of Yaḥyā ibn al-Biṭrīq	Gerard of Cremona (ASL XII)	before 1187
De animalibus	Michael Scot (ASL V)[10] (=*Historia an., De part. an., De gen. an.*)	before 1220
PSEUDO-ARISTOTELIAN AND RELATED WORKS		
On the Pure Good (= Proclus, *Elements of Theology*)	Gerard of Cremona (*Liber de causis*) (ed. Pattin 1966)	before 1187

[10] Michael Scot also translated the *De caelo*, and perhaps the *Physics*, *De anima*, and *Metaphysics*, as part
of Averroes's Long Commentaries on these works (see Appendix B1, and below under 'Averroes').

Author and Work	Translator	Date
*On the Causes of the Properties of the Four Elements	Gerard of Cremona (Bk. I only) (ed. Vodraska 1969)	before 1187
On Plants (Nicholas of Damascus)	Alfred of Shareshill (ASL IV)	*ca.* 1200
Secret of Secrets	a. John of Seville (partial) (ed. Suchier 1883)	*ca.* 1120
	Philip of Tripoli (complete) (ed. in Roger Bacon's commentary [ed. Steele *et al.* V: 2–172])	*ca.* 1220
On the Apple (The Death of Aristotle)	† Manfred (*De pomo*) (ed. Plezia 1960)	*ca.* 1260
Summa Alexandrinorum (a compendium from the *Nicomachean Ethics*)	Hermann the German	1243–4
EUCLID		
Elements	a. Adelard of Bath (ed. Busard 1983)	*ca.* 1120s
	b. Hermann of Carinthia (ed. Busard 1967–77)	*ca.* 1140s
	c. Gerard of Cremona (ed. Busard 1984)	before 1187
PTOLEMY		
Almagest	a. Abdelmessie Wittoniensis	*ca.* 1130
	b. Gerard of Cremona	before 1175
ALEXANDER OF APHRODISIAS		
On the Intellect	Dominicus Gundisalvi ("*est cum Gond.*") (ed. Théry, in "Autour de décret" 1926)	*ca.* 1160/90
On Time, On the Senses, and *That Augment and Increase Occur in Form, not in Matter*	Gerard of Cremona (ed. in Théry, ibid.)	before 1187
THEMISTIUS		
Posterior Analytics Comm.	Gerard of Cremona (ed. O'Donnell 1958)	before 1187
NEMESIUS		
On the Elements (= *On the Nature of Man*, ch. 6)	Anonymous (Constantine the African?) (ed. Burnett, in "Physics" 2002)	twelfth century

(*cont.*)

Author and Work	Translator	Date
Pseudo-Apollonius		
On the Secrets of Nature	Hugo of Santalla (ed. Hudry 1997–9)	*ca.* 1150
Māshāʾallāh		
On the Elements and Orbs (On the Knowledge of the Movement of the Orb)	a. Anonymous b. Gerard of Cremona	before 1149 before 1187
Anonymous		
Turba philosophorum	Anonymous (ed. Ruska 1931)	
Quṣṭā ibn Lūqā		
On the Difference between Spirit and the Soul	John of Seville (ed. Wilcox 1985)	1125/52
On Physical Ligatures	Constantine the African (ed. Wilcox and Riddle 1995)	before 1198
Abū Maʿshar		
Great Introduction to Astrology	a. John of Seville and Limia (ed. Lemay 1995–6)	1133
	b. Hermann of Carinthia (ed. Lemay 1995–6)	1140
al-Kindī		
On the Five Essences	Gerard of Cremona (ed. Nagy, in *Philosophischen Abhandlungen* 1897)	before 1187
On Sleep and Vision	Gerard of Cremona (ed. Nagy, ibid.)	before 1187
On the Intellect	a. Dominicus Gundisalvi (?), *De intellectu* (ed. Nagy, ibid.)	*ca.* 1160/90
	b. Gerard of Cremona, *De ratione* (ed. Nagy, ibid.)	before 1187
Two Letters on Weather Forecasting	Anonymous, *De mutatione temporum* (ed. Bos and Burnett, in *Scientific Weather Forecasting* 2000)	
On Rays (The Theory of the Magic Arts)	Anonymous, *De radiis stellarum* (ed. d'Alverny and Hudry 1974)	
Commentary on Almagest, Bk. 1	*Hugo of Santalla	
al-Fārābī		
On the Classification of the Sciences	a. Dominicus Gundisalvi (ed. Schneider 2006)	*ca.* 1160/90
	b. Gerard of Cremona (ed. Schupp 2005)	before 1187

Author and Work	Translator	Date
On the Intellect	Dominicus Gundisalvi (? "*est cum Gond*.") (ed. Gilson, in "Les sources" 1929–30)	*ca.* 1160/90 (?)
Directing Attention to the Way to Happiness (*Kitāb al-tanbīh ʿalā sabīl al-saʿāda*)	Dominicus Gundisalvi (?), *Liber exercitationis ad viam felicitatis* (ed. Salman 1940)	*ca.* 1160/90 (?)
The Sources of the Questions[11] (ʿ*Uyūn al-masāʾil*)	Anonymous (fragment) (*Fontes questionum/Flos Alpharabii secundum sententiam Aristotelis*)	
On De Interpretatione	Anonymous (abbrev. excerpts) (ed. Grignaschi, in "Les traductions" 1972)	
*On the Syllogism	**Gerard of Cremona (not found)	before 1187
*On Posterior Analytics	Cited by Albert the Great (not found)	
Introduction to the Book of Rhetoric (*Ṣadr kitāb al-khiṭāba*)	Hermann the German (*Didascalia in Rhetoricam Aristotelis ex glosa Alpharabii*) (ed. Grignaschi and Langhade, in *Deux ouvrages* 1971)	
*On Physics	**Gerard of Cremona (*Distinctio super librum Aristotilis de naturali auditu*)[12]	before 1187
Explanation of the Problems in the Postulates of the Fifth Book of Euclid	Dominicus Gundisalvi (?) (ed. Burnett, in "Euclid and al-Fārābī" 2004)	*ca.* 1160/90 (?)
*Pseudo-Fārābī, On the Rise of the Sciences	Anonymous (Dominicus Gundisalvi?)	twelfth century
Ikhwān al-Ṣafāʾ		
Letter on Proof	Anonymous (*Liber introductorius in artem logicae demonstrationis*) (ed. Nagy, in *Phil. Abhandlungen* 1897)	
Letter on Geography	Anonymous (*Epistola fratrum sincerorum in cosmographia*) (ed. Gauthier-Dalché 1988)	

(cont.)

---

[11] A collection of comments on Aristotle's logic. See Jeanne Bignami-Odier, "Le manuscrit Vatican latin 2186," *Archives d'histoire doctrinale et littéraire du moyen âge* 11 (1938) 133–66.

[12] See a text ascribed to al-Fārābī in Lynn Thorndike and Pearl Kibre, *A Catalogue of Incipits of Mediaeval Scientific Writings in Latin* (London: Mediaeval Academy of America, 1963) col. 1253: "Liber de natura loci ex latitudine et longitudine: Quod naturam loci scire oportet in scientia naturali."

Author and Work	Translator	Date
Final Letter	Anonymous (*Liber de quatuor confectionibus*) (ed. Sannino 2000)	
Isaac Israeli		
*On the Elements	Gerard of Cremona (ed. 1515)	before 1187
*On the Description and Definition of Things	a. Dominicus Gundisalvi (?) (ed. Muckle 1937–8)	*ca.* 1160/90
	b. Gerard of Cremona (ibid.)	before 1187
Avicenna		
al-Shifā[13]		
prologue of Juzjānī	Avendauth (with the aid of an unknown Latinist) (ed. Birkenmajer, in "Avicennas Vorrede" 1970)	*ca.* 1160/80
I. Logic		
1. *Isagoge*		
Bk. 1, chs. 1 and 12	Avendauth (with the aid of an unknown Latinist)	*ca.* 1160/80
Bk. 1, chs. 2–11, 13–14, Bk. 2, chs. 1–4	Anonymous (Toledo?) (not Dominicus Gundisalvi)	twelfth century
5. *Posterior Analytics*, Bk. 2, ch. 7	Dominicus Gundisalvi, *De convenientia et differentia scientiarum* (within his *De divisione philosophiae* [ed. Baur 1903])	*ca.* 1160/90
8. *Rhetoric* (excerpts)	Within Hermann the German's translation of Aristotle's *Rhetoric*	1240/50
II. Natural Science		
1. *Physics*	(*Sufficientia*)	
Bks. 1–3 (beginning only)	Anonymous (Toledo?) (AvL)	twelfth century
Bk. 3, chs. 1–10 (continuation of previous translation)	Juan Gonzalves de Burgos and Salomon (AvL)	1275–80
2. *On the Heavens*	Juan Gonzalves de Burgos and Salomon (ed. Renaud 1973)	

---

[13] For further information, see Marie-Thérèse d'Alverny, "Notes sur les traductions médiévales des œuvres philosophiques d'Avicenne," *Archives d'histoire doctrinale et littéraire du moyen âge* 19 (1952) 337–58. Most recently, see Amos Bertolacci, "A Community of Translators: The Latin Medieval Versions of Avicenna's *Kitāb al-Shifā*ʾ *(Book of the Cure)*," in C. Mews and J. Crossley (eds.) *Communities of Learning, Religious Diversity, and the Written Record 1085–1453* (forthcoming).

Author and Work	Translator	Date
3. *On Generation and Corruption*	Juan Gonzalves de Burgos and Salomon (AvL)	
4. *On Actions and Passions*	Juan Gonzalves de Burgos and Salomon (AvL)	
5. Bks. 1–2 (*Meteora*)	Juan Gonzalves de Burgos and Salomon	1275/80
Bk. 1, ch. 1 and 5 *On Stones and Metals*	Alfred of Shareshill (*De congelatione et conglutinatione lapidum*) (ed. Holmyard and Mandeville 1927)	*ca.* 1200
Bk. 2, ch. 6 (*On Floods*)	Alfred of Shareshill (?)	*ca.* 1200
6. *On the Soul*	Avendauth and Dominicus Gundisalvi (AvL)	*ca.* 1160/90
7. *On Plants*	*Liber eiusdem (Avicenne) de vegetabilibus*[14]	
8. *On Animals*	Michael Scot	
IV. *Metaphysics*	Dominicus Gundisalvi and an unknown collaborator (AvL)	*ca.* 1160/90
Letter on Medicines for the Heart	a. Avendauth and Dominicus Gundisalvi (chs. 2–7) (in Avicenna's *De anima* [AvL])	*ca.* 1160/90
	b. Arnold of Villanova	*ca.* 1300
PSEUDO-AVICENNA		
Book on the Heavens and the World	Dominicus Gundisalvi *Liber caeli et mundi* (ASL XIV)	*ca.* 1160/90
ABŪ WAFĀ' AL-MUBASHSHIR IBN FĀTIK		
Choicest Maxims and Best Sayings (1048–49)	a. Gerard of Cremona (the sayings of Ptolemy, in the preface to the *Almagest*) (ed. Burnett, "Ptolemaeus" 2009)	before 1187
	b. John of Procida (?) (*Liber philosophorum moralium antiquorum*) (ed. Franceschini 1931–2)	
al-GHAZĀLĪ		
Prologue to the Aims and the Destruction of the Philosophers	Anonymous (ed. Salmon, in "Algazel" 1936)	

(*cont.*)

[14] Only as an item in the 1338 catalogue of the library of the Sorbonne.

Author and Work	Translator	Date
The Aims of the Philosophers	Magister Johannes and Dominicus Gundisalvi (*Summa theorice philosophie*) (on logic ed. Lohr 1965; on metaphysics and physics ed. Muckle 1933)	*ca.* 1160/90
The Destruction of the Philosophers	Included within Averroes, *The Destruction of the Destruction*, q.v.	1328
RAYMOND LULL		
*Arabic logical compendium, dependent on the logic of *The Aims*	Raymond Lull (*Compendium logicae Algazelis*) (ed. Lohr 1967)	1275–6 or 1288
IBN AL-HAYTHAM		
On the Configuration of the World	a. Anonymous (Oxford, Canon. misc. 45) (ed. Mancha 1990)	late thirteenth century
	b. Anonymous (Madrid, BN, 10059) (ed. Millás Vallicrosa, in *Traducciones orientales* 1942)	before early fourteenth century
Optics	Two unknown translators (ed. Smith 2001–8)	before late thirteenth century
SOLOMON IBN GABIROL		
Fount of Life	Johannes Hispanus and Dominicus Gundisalvi, *Fons vitae* (ed. Baeumker 1892–5)	*ca.* 1160/90
AL-BITRŪJĪ		
On the Movements of the Heavens	Michael Scot and Abuteus Levita	1217
AVERROES		
*Middle Comm. on *Isagoge*	William of Luna	1258/66
Middle Comm. on *Categories*	William of Luna (ed. Hissette forthcoming)	1258/66
Middle Comm. on *De interpretatione*	William of Luna (?) (ed. Hissette 1996)	1258/66
Middle Comm. on *Prior Analytics*	William of Luna (?) (ed. 1562, etc.)	1258/66
Middle Comm. on *Posterior Analytics*	William of Luna (?) (ed. 1562, etc.)	1258/66
Middle Comm. on *Rhetoric*	Excerpt in Hermann the German's translation of Aristotle's *Rhetoric*	1240/50

Author and Work	Translator	Date
Middle Comm. on *Poetics*	Hermann the German (AL XXXIII)	1256
*Long Comm. on *Physics*	a. Michael Scot (?) (ed. 1562, etc.) b. Hermann the German (?) (only Bk. 7 [ed. Schmieja 2007] and Bk. 8, comm. 80–6) c. Theodore of Antioch (Proemium) (ed. 1562, etc.)	*ca.* 1220/35
Long Comm. on *De caelo*	Michael Scot (ed. Carmody and Arnzen 2003)	*ca.* 1220/35
Middle Comm. on *De gen. et corr*	Michael Scot (?) (ed. 1562, etc.)	
Middle Comm. on *Meteora*	Anonymous (Bk. 4 only) (ed. 1562, etc.)	
Middle Comm. on nine books of *De animalibus*	Michael Scot (?)	
*Long Comm. on *De anima*	Michael Scot (?) (ed. Crawford 1953)	*ca.* 1220/35
Epitomes of *Parva naturalia*	Michael Scot (?) (ed. Shields 1949)	
Long Comm. on *Metaphysics*	Michael Scot (?) (ed. 1562, etc.)	*ca.* 1220/35
*Middle Comm. on *Nicomachean Ethics*	Hermann the German (?) (ed. 1562, etc.)	1240
On the Substance of the Orb	Michael Scot (?) (ed. 1562, etc.)	
On the Separation of the First Principle	Afonso Dinis of Lisbon and Magister Alfonsus Conversus (Abner of Burgos) (ed. Steel and Guldentops 1997)	mid-fourteenth century
On the Possibility of Conjunction with the Active Intellect, treatises 1 and 2	*De animae beatitudine* (possibly by same as previous) (ed. Geoffroy and Steel 2001)	
Al-Damīma	Ramón Martí (*Epistola ad amicum*) (ed. Alonso, in *Teología* 1947)	
Destruction of the Destruction	Calonymos ben Calonymos (incomplete)	1328

(cont.)

Author and Work	Translator	Date
Abū Muḥammad ʿAbdallāh Ibn Rushd (the son of Averroes)		
On the Possibility of Conjunction	Anonymous (*De intellectu*) (ed. Burnett and Zonta 2000)	early thirteenth century
Maimonides[15]		
Guide to the Perplexed	† John of Palermo (?) (*Dux neutrorum*)	*ca.* 1230 (?)
Liber de uno deo benedicto (= *Guide* Bk. 2, chs. 1–2)	Anonymous	thirteenth century
Liber de parabola (= *Guide* Bk. 3, chs. 29–30, 32–49)	Anonymous	early thirteenth century

5. LATIN PHILOSOPHICAL WORKS TRANSLATED INTO GREEK

JOHN A. DEMETRACOPOULOS

From the quantitative point of view, medieval Latin philosophical literature is some dozen times bulkier than the Byzantine tradition. This sheer quantity of work, along with the language barrier, made it difficult for Byzantine thinkers to catch up with the Latins. Thus the vast majority of ancient and medieval Latin philosophical writings remained always inaccessible to the Byzantines. Still, some exceptions do exist, including some major works, including many ones by Thomas Aquinas. These Latin pieces were made known little by little in Byzantium after the capture of its capital, Constantinople, in the course of the Fourth Crusade (1204), especially on the occasion of the numerous diplomatic contacts between the churches of Constantinople and Rome, as well as between the Byzantine emperors and the Holy See, in the later thirteenth and fourteenth centuries. In the fifteenth century, George Scholarios – Gennadios II stands as an exceptional case: he explicitly advocates the superiority of scholastic thought in general as well as of the scholastic interpretation of Aristotle over the interpretation by Neoplatonic and Byzantine commentators en bloc. Scholarios was particularly impressed by Aquinas, whose works he consulted in regard to almost every topic.

The present list, in addition to those works that can be properly classified as philosophical, contains some principally theological writings too, in cases where they touch upon some philosophical matters. This list should not be taken as definitive. Several of

---

[15] For the medieval Latin translations of Maimonides, see Wolfgang Kluxen, "Literargeschichtliches zum lateinischen Moses Maimonides," *Recherches de théologie ancienne et médiévale* 21 (1954) 23–50.

the translations remain unedited;[16] and, since their manuscript tradition has not been as yet adequately explored, surprises will no doubt meet us in the future. Further, even in the cases where an edition is available, little research into the Latin provenance of these translations has yet been carried out. Finally, there are some texts (both edited and unedited) that, although passing for original Byzantine treatises, are in fact just translations (full, abridged, or enriched) from Latin.

Author and Work	Translator	Date
ALFRED OF SHARESHILL Translation of the pseudo-Aristotelian *De plantis* (Nicholas of Damascus)	Manuel Holobolos (ed. Drossaart Lulofs and Poortman 1989)	before 1314
ANONYMOUS		
De sex principiis[17]	George Scholarios – Gennadios II (*Œuvres* VII: 283–337)	1435/6
Paraphrase of *Physics* Bks. I–V	George Scholarios – Gennadios II (*Œuvres* VIII: 1–133)	*ca.* 1431
Prolegomena to the *Physics*	George Scholarios – Gennadios II (*Œuvres* VIII: 134–57)	*ca.* 1431
ANSELM OF CANTERBURY		
Cur Deus homo	Manuel Kalekas	before 1397/8
De processione Spiritus sancti	Demetrios Kydones	after 1358 (?)
AUGUSTINE		
De beata vita I.4–II.9	Prochoros Kydones	before 1370/1
De libero arbitrio I (to 13.27.90)	Prochoros Kydones (ed. Hunger 1990)	before 1370/1
De Trinitate	Maximos Planudes (ed. Papathomopoulos *et al.* 1995)	before 1281
De vera religione I.1–VIII.15	Prochoros Kydones	before 1370/1
BERNARD GUI		
Vita S. Thomae de Aquino ch. 53 ("De numero et nominibus librorum et tractatuum") and ch. 54 ("De opusculis")	Demetrios Kydones (ed. Demetracopoulos, in "Demetrius Cydones" 2010)	1364/5

(*cont.*)

[16] A recently inaugurated research project, "Thomas de Aquino Byzantinus" (National Hellenic Research Foundation, Athens; editor: John A. Demetracopoulos) is intended to offer an edition of the Byzantine translations of Aquinas's texts listed here.
[17] The translator remarks that this work "is not by Aristotle, as somebody says, but possibly by Boethius and more probably by Gilbert of Poitiers" (*Œuvres* VII: 214).

Author and Work	Translator	Date
BOETHIUS		
Consolatio philosophiae	Maximos Planudes (ed. Papathomopoulos 1999)	*ca.* 1295
De hypotheticis syllogismis	Maximos Planudes (ed. Nikitas 1982)	before 1268
De topicis differentiis	a. Manuel Holobolos (ed. Nikitas 1990)	*ca.* 1267
	b. Prochoros Kydones (ed. Nikitas 1990)	1360/7
De Trinitate	Manuel Kalekas (ed. Demetracopoulos 2005)	1396/9
PSEUDO-BOETHIUS		
A Division of the Dialectical Topoi[18]	George Pachymeres (?) (ed. Nikitas 1990)	before 1283
CICERO		
De senectute	Theodore Gazes (ed. Salanitro 1987)	1451/55
Somnium Scipionis (= *De re publica VI*)	Maximos Planudes (ed. Pavano 1992)	
Macrobius's commentary on *Somnium Scipionis*	Maximos Planudes (ed. Megas 1995)	before 1305
De amicitia (?)[19]	Theodore Gazes	before 1475
De officiis (?)	Theodore Gazes	before 1475
PSEUDO-CICERO		
Rhetorica ad Herennium, Bk. III, 16.28–24.40	Maximos Planudes or Bessarion (ed. Bernardinello 1973)[20]	late thirteenth century/ mid-fifteenth century
HERVAEUS NATALIS		
Sentences Bk. I, dist. I qq. 1–4 and 7	Prochoros Kydones	before 1370/1

[18] On the Latin provenance of this text see Sten Ebbesen, "George Pachymeres and the *Topics*," *Cahiers de l'Institut du Moyen Age Grec et Latin* 66 (1996) 169–85. For the attribution of the translation to George Pachymeres, see Börje Bydén, "'Strangle Them with these Meshes of Syllogisms!': Latin Philosophy in Greek Translations of the Thirteenth Century," in J. O. Rosenqvist (ed.) *Interaction and Isolation in Late Byzantine Culture* (Stockholm: Swedish Research Institute in Istanbul, 2004) 153–6.

[19] There is some meager evidence that Gazes translated this and the following work.

[20] According to Bernardinello, it is slightly more probable that this text was translated by Bessarion than by Theodore Gazes and much more probable that it was translated by either of these scholars than by Maximos Planudes. More recent scholars, however, have unanimously rejected the ascription to Bessarion.

Author and Work	Translator	Date
PETER OF SPAIN		
Summulae logicales, tract. I–VI	George Scholarios – Gennadios II (*Œuvres* VIII: 338–50)	1435/6
PLINY THE ELDER		
Naturalis historia II.4.12–13	Theodore Gazes	1440s
RADULPHUS BRITO		
Quaestiones super artem veterem Prooemium *Isagoge* (Intro., qq. 1–5, 10–16, 19–32) *Categories* (qq. 8–9; 12–17; 19; 21–30) *De Interpretatione* (qq. 16, 24) *Sophistici elenchi* (prooemium)	George Scholarios – Gennadios II[21] (*Œuvres* VIII: 11–18) (*Œuvres* VII: 20–9; 32–6; 48–104) (*Œuvres* VII: 132–9, 157–9; 163–71; 180–2; 188–90, 191–4; 205–7) (*Œuvres* VII: 297–300; 347–8) (*Œuvres* VII: 8–11)	*ca.* 1433/5
THOMAS AQUINAS		
De ente et essentia	George Scholarios – Gennadios II (*Œuvres* VI: 154–77)	1445/50
Armandus de Bellovisu, comm. on *De ente et essentia*	George Scholarios – Gennadios II (*Œuvres* VI: 177–326)	1445/50
Summa contra gentiles	Demetrios Kydones	1354
Compendium of the *Summa contra gentiles*	by George Scholarios – Gennadios II	1464
Summa theologiae		
1a, 1a2ae, 2a2ae	Demetrios Kydones (2a2ae: ed. Leontsinis *et al.* 1976–2002)	*ca.* 1355–8?
3a qq. 45, 49, 54–5	Prochoros Kydones	1358/70 (?)
Supplementum (76 qq.)	Prochoros Kydones	1358/70 (?)
Compendium of 1a	by George Scholarios – Gennadios II (*Œuvres* V: 338–510)	1464
Compendium of 1a2ae	by George Scholarios – Gennadios II (*Œuvres* VI: 1–153)	after 1464
Compendium of 1a2ae (qq. 1–7)	by Bessarion	mid-fifteenth century
Florilegium Thomisticum I (*Summa contra gent.* and 1a)	by George Scholarios – Gennadios II (ed. Demetracopoulos 2002)	1444/53
Florilegium Thomisticum II (*Summa contra gent.* III)	by George Scholarios – Gennadios II (ed. Demetracopoulos 2007)	1444/53

(*cont.*)

[21] See Sten Ebbesen and Jan Pinborg. "Gennadios and Western Scholasticism: Radulphus Brito's *Ars Vetus* in Greek Translation," *Classica et Mediaevalia* 33 (1981–2) 263–319.

Author and Work	Translator	Date
Extracta Thomistica (*Summa contra gent.* II–III, 1a, 2a2ae)	by George Gemistos Plethon (ed. Demetracopoulos, in *Apo tēn historia* (2004)	1414/33 (?)
De aeternitate mundi	Prochoros Kydones	before 1370/1
De potentia	Prochoros Kydones (?)	before 1370/1
De spiritualibus creaturis	Prochoros Kydones (?)	before 1370/1
De interpretatione commentary (nearly complete)	George Scholarios – Gennadios II (*Œuvres* VIII: 242–308)	1433/5
Post. Analytics commentary (I.1 nn. 1–6)[22]	George Scholarios – Gennadios II (*Œuvres* VII: 18–20)	1433/5
De anima commentary	George Scholarios – Gennadios II (*Œuvres* VI: 327–581)	*ca.* 1435
Physics commentary (I.1 nn. 3–15; II.1–12)	George Scholarios – Gennadios II (*Œuvres* VIII: 163–254)	before 1438
Metaphysics comm. (prologue)	Prochoros Kydones	before 1370/1
Quodlibet I.1	George Scholarios – Gennadios II (?) (ed. Cacouros, in "Georges Scholarios" 2000)	first half of fifteenth century (?)
Pseudo-Thomas Aquinas		
De fallaciis	George Scholarios – Gennadios II (*Œuvres* VIII: 255–82)	*ca.* 1435/6

6. ANCIENT PHILOSOPHICAL WORKS AND COMMENTARIES TRANSLATED INTO HEBREW

MAURO ZONTA

The following table lists philosophical texts originally written either in Greek or in Latin in antiquity (up to the mid-sixth century) that were translated into Hebrew during the Middle Ages, mostly in the period 1200–1500. None of them was directly translated from Greek, but instead either from a medieval Arabic version (see Appendix B3) or from a Latin version directly based upon the Greek original or upon an Arabic version of the Greek (see Appendices B1 and B2). Many of these texts are not translations of the original, but of medieval commentaries that contain literal passages or paraphrases or summaries, or questions on some points, where the contents of the original works were sometimes altered. Often, however, these commentaries are the only way by which medieval Hebrew scholars read and knew these texts. Each reference mentions either the critical edition of the text or the first edition, if any. (Editions not yet published, including those edited as part of a Ph.D. thesis, are not mentioned.)

A = translation from an Arabic version
AL = translation from an Arabic-into-Latin version

[22] See Ebbesen and Pinborg, "Gennadios and Western Scholasticism," p. 267. Scholarios himself attests to having made a translation of the entire commentary (*Œuvres* VII: 4–5), but it is lost.

L = translation from a Latin version
LC = translation from a Latin-into-Catalan version

Author and Work (with commentators)	Translator	Date
ALEXANDER OF APHRODISIAS		
De anima (Bk. I)	Samuel of Marseilles (A)	1323–40
De intellectu		
Averroes	Anonymous (A) (ed. Davidson 1988)	before 1340
ARISTOTLE		
Categories		
al-Fārābī (summary)	Three anonymous translators (A)	thirteenth century
al-Fārābī (long commentary)	Anonymous (Samuel of Marseilles?) (A) (ed. Zonta 2006)	fourteenth century (?)
Averroes (summary)	Jacob ben Makhir (A) (ed. Marcaria 1559)	1289
	revised by Samuel of Marseilles (A)	1329
Averroes (middle commentary)	Jacob Anatoli (A) (ed. Davidson 1969)	1232
	revised by Samuel of Marseilles (A)	1330 (?)
pseudo-Marsilius of Inghen (questions)	Abraham Shalom (L)	before 1492
De interpretatione		
al-Fārābī (summary)	Two anonymous translators (A)	thirteenth century
al-Fārābī (long commentary)	Anonymous (A)	before 1320 (?)
Averroes (summary)	Jacob ben Makhir (A) (ed. Marcaria 1559)	1289
	revised by Samuel of Marseilles (A)	1329
Averroes (middle commentary)	Jacob Anatoli (A)	1232
pseudo-Marsilius of Inghen (questions)	Abraham Shalom (L)	before 1492
Prior Analytics		
al-Fārābī (summary)	Two anonymous translators (A)	thirteenth century
al-Fārābī (*Short Book of Syllogism*)	Moses ibn Tibbon (A)	1255
Averroes (summary)	Jacob ben Makhir (A) (ed. Marcaria 1559)	1289
	revised by Samuel of Marseilles (A)	1329
Averroes (middle commentary)	Jacob Anatoli (A)	1232

(cont.)

Author and Work (with commentators)	Translator	Date
Posterior Analytics		
al-Fārābī (summary)	Judah ibn Tibbon (?) (A)	second half of twelfth century
Averroes (summary)	Jacob ben Makhir (A) (ed. Marcaria 1559)	1289
	revised by Samuel of Marseilles (A)	1329
Averroes (middle commentary)	Jacob Anatoli (A)	1232
Averroes (long commentary)	Calonymos ben Calonymos (A)	1314
Topics		
al-Fārābī (summary)	Moses ibn Lajis (?) (A)	thirteenth century (?)
Averroes (summary)	Jacob ben Makhir (A) (ed. Marcaria 1559)	1289
	revised by Samuel of Marseilles (A)	1329
Averroes (middle commentary)	Calonymos ben Calonymos (A)	1313
Sophistical Refutations		
al-Fārābī (summary)	Anonymous (A)	second half of twelfth century (?)
Averroes (summary)	Jacob ben Makhir (A) (ed. Marcaria 1559)	1289
	revised by Samuel of Marseilles (A)	1329
Averroes (middle commentary)	Calonymos ben Calonymos (A)	1313
Rhetoric		
al-Fārābī (summary)	Todros ben Todrosi (A)	1330–40
Averroes (summary)	Jacob ben Makhir (A) (ed. Marcaria 1559)	1289
	revised by Samuel of Marseilles (A)	1329
Averroes (middle commentary)	Todros ben Todrosi (A) (ed. Goldenthal 1842)	1337
Poetics		
al-Fārābī (summary)	Todros ben Todrosi (A)	1330–40
Averroes (summary)	Jacob ben Makhir (A) (ed. Marcaria 1559)	1289
	revised by Samuel of Marseilles (A)	1329

Author and Work (with commentators)	Translator	Date
Averroes (middle commentary)	Todros ben Todrosi (A) (ed. Lasinio 1872)	1337
Physics	Judah Messer Leon (Bks. I–IV) (L)	1473–5
Averroes (summary)	Moses ibn Tibbon (A) (ed. Marcaria 1559)	*ca.* 1250
Averroes (middle commentary)	a. Zerahyah ben Isaac Hen (A)	1284
	b. Calonymos ben Calonymos (A)	1316
Averroes (long commentary)	Calonymos ben Calonymos (A)	1315 (?)
pseudo-Robert Grosseteste (summary)	Anonymous (L)	*ca.* 1450 (?)
Albert of Orlamünde (summary)	a. Anonymous (L)	before 1400
	b. Abraham Shalom (L)	before 1492
John Letourneur (questions)	Eli Habillo (L)	1472
Thomas Bricot (summary)	David ibn Shoshan (L)	end of fifteenth century
De caelo et mundo		
Themistius (paraphrase)	Zerahyah ben Isaac Hen (A) (ed. Landauer 1902)	1284
Pseudo-Avicenna (questions) (Hunayn ibn Ishaq?)	Solomon of Melguiri (AL)	1290–1300 (?)
Averroes (summary)	Moses ibn Tibbon (A)	*ca.* 1250
Averroes (middle commentary)	Solomon ibn Ayyub (A)	1259
Pseudo-Robert Grosseteste (summary)	Anonymous (L)	*ca.* 1450 (?)
Albert of Orlamünde (summary)	a. Anonymous (L)	before 1400
	b. Abraham Shalom (L)	before 1492
John Letourneur (questions)	Eli Habillo (L)	1473
Thomas Bricot (summary)	David ibn Shoshan (L)	end of fifteenth century
De generatione et corruptione	Zerahyah ben Isaac Hen (A) (ed. Tessier 1984)	1284
Averroes (summary)	Moses ibn Tibbon (A) (ed. Kurland 1958)	1250

(cont.)

Author and Work (with commentators)	Translator	Date
Averroes (middle commentary)	Calonymos ben Calonymos (A) (ed. Kurland 1958)	1316
Albert of Orlamünde (summary)	a. Anonymous (L) b. Abraham Shalom (L)	before 1400 before 1492
John Letourneur (questions)	Eli Habillo (L)	1472
Thomas Bricot (summary)	David ibn Shoshan (L)	end of fifteenth century
Meteorology	Samuel ibn Tibbon (A) (ed. Fontaine 1995)	1210
Averroes (summary)	Moses ibn Tibbon (A)	*ca.* 1250
Averroes (middle commentary)	Calonymos ben Calonymos (A)	1316
Albert of Orlamünde (summary)	Abraham Shalom (L)	before 1492
Thomas Bricot (summary)	David ibn Shoshan (L)	end of fifteenth century
Historia animalium	Anonymous (Samuel ha-Levi?) (AL)	before 1300
De partibus animalium	Anonymous (Samuel ha-Levi?) (AL)	before 1300
Averroes (middle commentary)	Jacob ben Makhir (A)	1302
De generatione animalium	Anonymous (Samuel ha-Levi?) (AL)	before 1300
Averroes (middle commentary)	Jacob ben Makhir (A)	1302
De anima	Zerahyah ben Isaac Hen (A) (ed. Bos 1994)	1284
Averroes (summary)	Moses ibn Tibbon (A)	1244
Averroes (middle commentary)	a. Shem Tov ben Isaac (A) b. Moses ibn Tibbon (A) (ed. Ivry 2003)	*ca.* 1260 (?) 1261
Averroes (long commentary)	Baruch ibn Ya'ish (?) (AL)	before 1470
pseudo-Robert Grosseteste (summary)	Anonymous (L)	*ca.* 1450 (?)
Albert of Orlamünde (summary)	Abraham Shalom (L)	before 1492
Thomas Aquinas	Anonymous (L)	before 1448

Author and Work (with commentators)	Translator	Date
Giles of Rome	Judah Romano (L)	*ca.* 1320–30
John of Jandun (questions)	Baruch ibn Ya'ish (?) (L)	before 1475
John Letourneur (questions)	Eli Habillo (L)	1472
Thomas Bricot (summary)	David ibn Shoshan (L)	end of fifteenth century
Parva naturalia		
Averroes (summary)	Moses ibn Tibbon (A) (ed. Blumberg 1954)	1254
John Letourneur (questions)	Eli Habillo (L)	1473
Thomas Bricot (summary)	David ibn Shoshan (L)	end of fifteenth century
Metaphysics	Baruch ibn Ya'ish (L)	*ca.* 1485
Themistius (Bk. XII) (paraphrase)	Moses ibn Tibbon (A) (ed. Landauer 1903)	1255
al-Fārābī (summary)	Anonymous (A)	fourteenth century (?)
Averroes (summary)	Moses ibn Tibbon (A)	1258
Averroes (middle commentary)	a. Zerahyah ben Isaac Hen (A)	1284
	b. Calonymos ben Calonymos (A)	1317
Averroes (long commentary)	a. Calonymos ben Calonymos (?) (A)	1315 (?)
	b. Moses ben Solomon of Beaucaire (A)	1320–5 (?)
Thomas Aquinas	Abraham ibn Nahmias (L)	1490
Antonius Andreas (questions)	Eli Habillo (L)	after 1473 (?)
Nicomachean Ethics	a. Meir Alguadez (L) (ed. Satanow 1790)	*ca.* 1400
	b. Baruch ibn Ya'ish (L)	*ca.* 1480
Averroes (middle commentary)	Samuel of Marseilles (A) (ed. Berman 1999)	1321
John Letourneur (questions)	Eli Habillo (L)	after 1473 (?)
PSEUDO-ARISTOTLE		
De causis (Proclus)	a. Hillel of Verona (AL) (ed. Halberstam 1874)	*ca.* 1260 (?)
	b. Zerahyah ben Isaac Hen (A) (ed. Schreiber 1916)	1284
	c. Judah Romano (AL)	*ca.* 1313
	d. Eli Habillo (AL)	1471 or 1477

(cont.)

Author and Work (with commentators)	Translator	Date
De mineralibus	a. Anonymous (A)	before *ca.* 1300
	b. Anonymous (L)	fifteenth century (?)
De pomo	Abraham ibn Hasdai (A) (ed. Marcaria 1562, etc.)	*ca.* 1210–30
Economics (Bks. I and III)	a. Anonymous (L)	*ca.* 1440 (?)
	b. Baruch ibn Ya'ish (?) (L)	*ca.* 1480 (?)
Moral Epistle	Judah al-Harizi (A) (ed. Marcaria 1559, etc.)	*ca.* 1200
Problemata physica (pt. I)	Moses ibn Tibbon (A) (ed. Filius 1999)	1264
Secretum secretorum (short version)	Anonymous (A) (ed. Gaster 1907–8)	*ca.* 1300
Boethius		
De consolatione	a. Samuel Benveniste (LC)	1412
philosophiae	b. Bonafous Bonfil Astruc (L) (ed. Sierra 1967)	1423
Bryson		
Economics	David ibn Ya'ish (A) (ed. Plessner 1928)	*ca.* 1375
Nicholas of Damascus		
De plantis	Calonymos ben Calonymos (A) (ed. Drossaart Lulofs and Poortman 1989)	1314
Plato		
Republic		
Averroes (summary)	Samuel of Marseilles (A) (ed. Rosenthal 1966)	1320–1
Porphyry		
Isagoge		
al-Fārābī (summary)	Four anonymous translations	thirteenth–fourteenth centuries
Averroes (summary)	Jacob ben Makhir (A) (ed. Marcaria 1559)	1289
	revised by Samuel of Marseilles (A)	1329
Averroes (middle commentary)	Jacob Anatoli (A) (ed. Davidson 1969)	1232
Pseudo-Marsilius of Inghen (questions)	Abraham Shalom (L)	before 1492

Appendix C

BIOGRAPHIES OF MEDIEVAL AUTHORS

An effort has been made to provide an entry for every medieval author who has been the subject of significant philosophical research in modern times, from the eighth to the early fifteenth century. Inevitably, such an effort will be imperfect: some notable authors have doubtless been omitted, and moreover there is considerable vagueness in the boundaries of such a census. Many figures included here are not philosophers even in a very broad sense of the term. Although the entire appendix is the responsibility of one hand, a great deal of advice has been received from many contributors to the volume and also, especially, from Russell Friedman, Martin Pickavé, and Chris Schabel.

Authors are organized by first name, unless, as with most Arabic authors, that name is not commonly used. In the lists of secondary sources, items of special bio-bibliographical importance are placed first. The following works are abbreviated:[1]

BBK	*Biographisch-Bibliographisches Kirchenlexikon* (Bautz)
BCPMA	[*Blackwell*] *Companion to Philosophy in the Middle Ages* (Gracia and Noone)
BEIP	*Biographical Encyclopaedia of Islamic Philosophy* (Leaman)
CALMA	*Compendium Auctorum Latinorum Medii Aevi* (Lapidge, Leonardi, and Garfagnini)
CHLMP	*Cambridge History of Later Medieval Philosophy* (Kretzmann, Kenny, and Pinborg)
CTMPT	*Cambridge Translations of Medieval Philosophical Texts* (vol. I, Kretzmann and Stump; vol. II, McGrade, Kilcullen, and Kempshall; vol. III, Pasnau)
DBI	*Dizionario biografico degli Italiani* (Ghisalberti)
DMA	*Dictionnaire du Moyen Âge* (Gauvard, de Libera, and Zink)
Dronke	*A History of Twelfth-Century Western Philosophy*
DS	*Dictionnaire de spiritualité* (Viller)
DSB	*Dictionary of Scientific Biography* (Gillispie)
DTC	*Dictionnaire de théologie catholique* (Loth and Michel)
EI	*Encyclopaedia of Islam*, 2nd edn (Gibb)

---

[1] Three further resources worthy of special notice are Hans Daiber, *Bibliography of Islamic Philosophy* (Leiden: Brill, 1999; suppl. 2007); Rolf Schönberger and Brigitte Kible, *Repertorium edierter Texte des Mittelalters* (Berlin: Akademie Verlag, 1994); and Steven Nadler and T. M. Rudavsky, *The Cambridge History of Jewish Philosophy* (Cambridge: Cambridge University Press, 2009). At present, general reference works freely available on the web, most notably Wikipedia, are extremely unreliable for medieval philosophy.

Emden	*A Biographical Register of the University of Oxford to A.D. 1500*
FA	*Franciscan Authors, 13th–18th Century* (Van Der Heijden and Roest)
Glorieux	*Répertoire des maîtres en théologie de Paris au XIIIᵉ siècle*
HIP	*History of Islamic Philosophy* (Nasr and Leaman)
HJP	*History of Jewish Philosophy* (Frank and Leaman)
Kaeppeli	*Scriptores Ordinis Praedicatorum Medii Aevi*
Lohr	"Medieval Latin Aristotle Commentaries," supplemented by *Latin Aristotle Commentaries*
ODB	*Oxford Dictionary of Byzantium* (Kazhdan *et al.*)
ODNB	*Oxford Dictionary of National Biography*, rev. edn (Matthew and Harrison)
Pennington	*Medieval Canonists: A Bio-Bibliographical Listing*
PG	*Patrologiae cursus completus: series graeca* (Migne)
PL	*Patrologiae cursus completus: series latina* (Migne)
REP	*Routledge Encyclopedia of Philosophy* (Craig)
Roensch	*Early Thomistic School*
SEP	*Stanford Encyclopedia of Philosophy* (Zalta)
Sirat	*A History of Jewish Philosophy in the Middle Ages*
Weijers	*Le travail intellectuel à la Faculté des arts de Paris*

ABBO OF FLEURY b. Orléanais, 945/50; d. Gascony, 1004. Influential teacher and monastic leader, notable for his scientific and mathematical interests. Early eduation at the Benedictine monastery at Fleury. Studied at Paris, Rheims, and Orléans, returning to Fleury to teach. Traveled to England, teaching at Ramsey Abbey from 985 to 987, before becoming abbot at Fleury from 988 until his death. Killed in a quarrel between feuding monks. Among his works pertaining to philosophy are *Questiones grammaticales* [*ca.* 988] (ed. and [Fr] tr. Guerreau-Jalabert 1982); a *De ratione spere* [978] (ed. Thomson, in "Two Astronomical Tractates" 1985); a commentary on the *Calculus* of Victorius of Aquitaine (ed. Peden, in *Abbo of Fleury* 2003); a *Computus* for calculating Easter; an early logical treatise, the *Syllogismorum categoricorum et hypotheticorum enodatio* (ed. van de Vyver and Raes 1966); and a treatise *De syllogismis hypotheticis* (ed. Schupp 1997). The bulk of his works are collected in PL 139. A contemporary *vita* by Aimoin of Fleury is also extant (ed. and [Fr] tr. Bautier *et al.* 2004).

Secondary sources. Cousin, *Abbon de Fleury* (1954); Germann, *De temporum ratione* (2006); Mostert, *Political Theology* (1987); Obrist (ed.) *Abbon de Fleury* (2004); Riché, *Abbon de Fleury* (2004); CALMA; DMA (Morelle and Lemoine); ODNB (Pfaff).

ʿABD AL-JABBĀR b. Asadabad (western Iran) *ca.* 935; d. 1025. Muʿtazilite theologian. Studied in Basra and elsewhere; subsequently lived in Baghdad, then in Rayy, where he was appointed chief judge. Principal work is a vast theological summa, *Al-Mughnī fī abwāb al-tawḥīd wa-al-ʿadl* (*Summa on Matters of Unity and Justice*) [970–80] (ed. 1960–).

Secondary sources. Reynolds, "Rise and Fall" (2005); Frank, "Autonomy of the Human Agent" (1982); Heemskerk, *Suffering* (2000); Hourani, *Islamic Rationalism* (1971); Peters, *God's Created Speech* (1976); Vasalou, "Equal Before the Law" (2003); EI (Stern).

AL-ABHARĪ (Athīr al-Dīn) b. Mosul, *ca.* 1200; d. 1264 (?). Author of several brief, influential philosophical textbooks. Student of Fakhr al-Dīn al-Rāzī. Best known for the *Hidāyat al-ḥikma* (*Guide to Philosophy*) (ed. Mumtāz al-Dīn 1960/5), which ranges over logic, physics, and theology. Also influential is *Al-Isāghūjī fī al-manṭiq* (*Introduction to Logic*), an adaptation of Porphyry (tr. Calverly 1933). Both were the subject of many later commentaries.

Secondary sources. BEIP (Thomas); EI (Brockelmann).

ABNER OF BURGOS (Alfonso of Valladolid) b. *ca.* 1270; d. *ca.* 1348. Jewish convert to Christianity, best known for his rejection of free will. Studied medicine, philosophy, and astronomy. Converted to Christianity *ca.* 1320. Subsequently wrote a series of polemical treatises against Judaism, including the dialogue *Mostrador de justicia*, surviving only in Castillian (ed. Mettmann 1994–6); the *Minḥat Kena'ot* (*Offering of Jealousy*) (ed. [Castillian] Mettmann 1990), a response to criticisms from Isaac Pulgar; and the *Tesuvot la-Meharef* (*Response to the Blasphemer*) (ed. [Castillian] Mettmann 1998).

Secondary sources. Baer, "Abner of Burgos" (1940); Sirat.

ABRAHAM ABULAFIA b. Saragossa (Spain), *ca.* 1240; d. Comino [Malta], *ca.* 1291. Mystical theologian. Founding figure of prophetic Kabbalah, an attempt to access the ancient, hidden truths of the Torah. Excerpts from various works are available in translation (tr. Meltzer *et al.* 1976).

Secondary sources. Idel, *Mystical Experience* (1988); Tirosh-Samuelson, "Philosophy and Kaballah" (2003); Wolfson, *Abraham Abulafia* (2000).

ABRAHAM BAR ḤIYYA (bar Hayya) b. *ca.* 1065; d. Barcelona, *ca.* 1140. Scientist, philosopher. Born into a prominent Jewish family; held a position at the court of Alfonso I of Aragon. A pioneer in writing philosophical and scientific texts in Hebrew. Philosophical works include the *Hegyon ha-Nefesh ha-Aẓuvah* (*Meditation of the Sad Soul*) (ed. Wigoder 1971; tr. Wigoder 1969) and the *Megillat ha-Megalleh* (*Scroll of the Revealer*) (ed. Poznanski 1924), a treatise on the arrival of the Messiah. Important scientific works include the first Hebrew scientific encyclopedia, the *Yesode ha-Tevuna u-Migdal ha-'Emuna* (*Foundations of Understanding and Tower of Faith*) (ed. and [Sp] tr. Millás Vallicrosa 1952); the *Heshbon Mahalkhot ha-Kokhavim* (*Book of Calculation and the Movement of the Stars*) (ed. and [Sp] tr. Millás Vallicrosa 1959); *Sefer ha-'Ibur* (*Book of Intercalation*) (ed. Filipowski 1851), on the Jewish calendar; and the *Sefer Ṣurat ha-'Ares* (*Sphaera mundi*) (ed. Hebrew and Latin 1546). Perhaps the Abraham who collaborated with Plato of Tivoli on various Latin scientific translations.

Secondary sources. Sela, *Rise of Medieval Hebrew Science* (2003); DSB (Levey); REP (Wigoder); Sirat.

ABRAHAM IBN DAUD (ben David; Rabad) b. southern Spain, *ca.* 1110; d. Toledo, *ca.* 1180. Philosopher and historian, author of the first systematic attempt to integrate Aristotelianism into Jewish thought. Studied with his uncle in Cordoba, moving to Toledo *ca.* 1147. Principal philosophical work is the *Ha-Emunah ha-Ramah* (*The Exalted Faith*) [*ca.* 1160] (ed. and tr. Samuelson and Weiss 1986), originally in Arabic but extant only in Hebrew translation. Also well known is the Hebrew *Sefer ha-Qabbalah* (*The Book of Tradition*) [*ca.* 1160] (ed. and tr. Cohen 1967), a survey of the history of Judaism. Perhaps to be identified with the Arabic–Latin translator known as Avendauth, who collaborated with Dominicus Gundisalvi in Toledo.

Secondary sources. Eran, "Substance and Accident" (1997); Fontaine, *In Defense of Judaism* (1990), "Polemics" (2005); Samuelson, "Causation and Choice" (1979); REP (Samuelson); SEP (Fontaine).

ABRAHAM IBN EZRA (ben Meïr; Abraham Avenezra) b. Tudela (southern Spain), *ca.* 1093; d. 1167. Poet, astrologer, scientist, mystic, and Neoplatonic philosopher. Lived in Tudela until *ca.* 1140, when the Almohad conquests prompted him to wander through Europe, spending time in Italy, southern France, and England. Nearly all of the large body of his extant works dates from this later period (1140–60). His writings are mainly brief treatises in Hebrew (with a few written directly into Latin with the assistance of a Christian scholar) on a wide variety of topics ranging over the arts, sciences, and theology (ed. 1970 in 4 vols.; ed. Levin 1985). Among the more philosophical of his works are the visionary allegory *Hayy ben Meqitz* (*Texture of the Divine*) [prob. before 1140] (tr. Hughes, in *Texture of the Divine* 2004) and the *Yesod Mora* (*The Foundation of Reverence*) [1158] (ed. Cohen and Simon 2002), on the commandments of the Jewish religion. Important astrological treatises include the *Reshit Hokhmah* (*The Beginning of Wisdom*) [1148] (ed. and tr. Levy and Cantera 1939), the *Sefer ha-Yesodot* (*Book of Foundations*) (tr. [Fr] Halbronn 1977), and the *Sefer ha-Teʾamim* (*Book of Reasons*) [1148; rev. 1154] (ed. and tr. Sela 2007). Also extant are important commentaries on the Hebrew Bible: available translations include Isaiah [1145] (ed. and tr. Friedländer 1873/1960), Hosea (ed. and tr. Lipshitz 1988), and the Pentateuch (tr. Strickman *et al.* 1988–2004). His poetry is also available in various anthologies (ed. 1975; tr. Weinberger 1997).

Secondary sources. Sela and Freudenthal, "Scholarly Writings" (2006) (bibliography); Díaz Esteban (ed.), *Abraham Ibn Ezra* (1990); Friedländer, *Essays* (1877/1963); Goldstein, "Astronomy and Astrology" (1996); Greive, *Studien* (1973); Levy, *Astrological Works* (1927); Sela, *Rise of Medieval Hebrew Science* (2003); Tomson (ed.), *Abraham Ibn Ezra* (2000); Twersky and Harris (eds.), *Rabbi Abraham ibn Ezra* (1993); REP (Jospe); SEP (Langermann); Sirat.

ABRAHAM MAIMONIDES (ben Moses, Maimuni, he-Hasid [the Pious]) b. Fustat (Egypt), 1186; d. 1237. Theologian, physician, rabbinical authority. The only son of Moses Maimonides, he continued his father's work as a scholar and community leader. Principal work is the *Kifāyat al-ʿābidīn* (*Complete Guide for Devotees*) [*ca.* 1230] (part. ed. Dana 1989; [Hebrew and English] tr. Wincelberg 2008), a monumental compendium of jurisprudence and religious philosophy that departs from his father's views in stressing ethical perfection as the ultimate human goal. Among various other extant works is the *Milhamot ha-Shem* (*Wars of the Lord*) [after 1235] (ed. Margaliot 1953); the *Maʾaseh nisim* (*Act of Miracles*) (ed. and [Hebrew] tr. Goldberg 1867), both defenses of his father's work; and a brief treatise in defense of his ethical pietism (tr. Goitein 1965).

Secondary sources. Eppenstein, *Abraham Maimuni* (1914) [life and works]; Cohen, "Soteriology" (1967–8); Goitein, "Pietist Circle" (1967); REP (Fenton).

ABŪ BISHR MATTĀ (ibn Yūnus al-Qunnā'ī) d. Baghdad, 940. Logician, translator, founding figure of the Baghdad Peripatetics. A Nestorian Christian, of Syriac origins. Worked in Baghdad, where he was the teacher of al-Fārābī and Yaḥyā ibn ʿAdī. Famously argued for the universal validity of logic in a debate with the grammarian Abū Saʿīd al-Sīrāfī [932] (ed. and tr. Margoliouth, in "Discussion" 1905). Responsible for a great many translations from the Syriac of both Aristotle and his commentators, as well as commentaries on the logical works and on the *Physics* (part. tr. McGinnis and Reisman, in *Classical Arabic Philosophy* 2007).

Secondary sources. Endress, "Grammatik und Logik" (1986); Mahdi, "Language and Logic" (1970); Rescher, *Development* (1964); EI (Endress).

ABŪ ḤANĪFA (al-Nuʿmān ibn Thābit; Imām al-Aʿẓam) b. *ca.* 699; d. Baghdad 767. Theologian and legal scholar, founder of prominent schools of thought in both law and theology. Lived in Kufa, where he studied religious law and became an authority and teacher, though without becoming a judge (*qāḍī*). Died in prison. Although he did not compose any writings on religious law, his efforts at a theoretically systematic account have survived in the work of his disciples, to whom he dictated his ideas. His theological thought is represented by various prominent works, most prominently *Al-ʿĀlim wa-al-mutaʿallim* (*The Scholar and the Student*) and the *Fiqh al-Absat* (*The Comprehensive Book of Jurisprudence*) (both ed. al-Kawthari 1949), although these are now thought to be the work of his disciples. Of the *Fiqh al-akbar* (*The Great Book of Jurisprudence*), only the first part represents his views (ed. 1907; tr. Ibn Yusuf 2007).

Secondary sources. Hallaq, *Origins and Evolution of Islamic Law* (2005); Shibli Numani, *Abu Hanifah* (1988); BEIP (Kiliç); EI (Schacht).

ABŪ HĀSHIM (ʿAbd al-Salām al-Jubbāʾī) b. Basra; d. Baghdad, 933. Muʿtazilī theologian. Son of al-Jubbāʾī. No writings are extant, but his views are discussed extensively in later polemical works. Best known for his account of the divine attribute in terms of modes.

Secondary sources. Frank, "Attribute" (1982); Gimaret, "Théorie des *aḥwāl*" (1970), "Matériaux" (1976); EI (Gardet).

ABŪ AL-HUDHAYL AL-ʿALLĀF b. Basra *ca.* 750; d. Samarra, 840/50. Foundational Muʿtazilī theologian. Spent most of his life in Basra; later joined the court circle at Baghdad. Although a prolific author, no works are extant. His influence on later thought was nevertheless considerable, both through his writings and through the disciples he attracted.

Secondary sources. Frank, *Metaphysics of Created Being* (1966); BEIP (İskenderoğlu); EI (Nyberg).

ABŪ MAʿSHAR (Jaʿfar ibn Muḥammad ibn ʿUmar al-Balkhī; Albumasar) b. 787; d. 886. Leading Arabic advocate of astrology, active in Baghdad, where he was at first a rival and then an associate of al-Kindī. Grounded his astrological theory in a well-developed astronomical system, drawing above all on the work of Aristotle, but also Neoplatonism and a wide range of other sources. Influential on Latin authors in the twelfth and thirteenth centuries; regarded as a principal authority in astrology. Major works include the *Madkhal al-kabīr* (*Greater Introduction to Astronomy*) (ed. [Arabic/Latin] Lemay 1995); an abridgement of that work (ed. [Arabic/Latin] and tr. Burnett *et al.* 1994); and the *Kitāb al-milal wa-al-duwal* (*Book of Great Conjunctions*) (ed. [Arabic/Latin] and tr. Yamamoto and Burnett 2000).

Secondary sources. Adamson, "Defense of Astrology" (2002); Lemay, *Abu Maʿshar and Latin Aristotelianism* (1962); BCPMA (Hackett); DSB (Pingree); EI (Burnett).

ABŪ SAʿĪD AL-SĪRĀFĪ d. 979. Judge and grammarian. Famous for his Baghdad debate with Abū Bishr Mattā [932] (ed. and tr. Margoliouth, in "Discussion" 1905), in which he argued that Greek logic is valid only for the Greek language and that Arabic grammar requires its own logic. His magnum opus is a massive commentary on Sībawayhi's *Kitāb* (ed. ʿAbd al-Tawwāb *et al.* 1986–).

Secondary sources. Endress, "Grammatik und Logik" (1986); Gunaydin, "Theory of 'Lingua-Logical' Grammar" (2006); Mahdi, "Language and Logic" (1970); EI (Humbert).

ABŪ TAMMĀM *fl.* Khurasan, tenth century. Ismāʿīlī missionary and philosopher. Disciple of Muḥammad al-Nasafī. Probably the author of the *Kitāb al-shajara* (pt. 2 ed. Tāmir 1965, as *Kitāb al-īḍāḥ*; pt. 1 part. ed. and tr. Madlung and Walker 1998).

Secondary sources. Walker, "Abū Tammām" (1994), "The Ismāʿīlīs" (2005).

ABŪ ZAYD AL-BALKHĪ b. near Balkh (Afghanistan), *ca.* 850; d. 934. Wide-ranging scholar. Traveled to Iraq as a young man, where he was a student of al-Kindī. His only known philosophical work is the recently discovered *Maṣāliḥ al-abdān wa-al-anfus* (*Sustenance for Body and Soul*) (ed. Miṣrī 2005).

Secondary sources. Rosenthal, "Politics" (1989); EI (Dunlop).

ACCURSIUS b. near Florence, *ca.* 1184; d. Bologna, *ca.* 1260. Italian jurist. A student of Azo, becoming professor at Bologna. Composed the *Glossa ordinaria* or *Magna glossa* [1220/50] (ed. 1488/1968, etc.) on Roman law as codified by Justinian.

Secondary sources. Landsberg, *Glosse* (1883); Tierney, "Origins of the Modern State" (1968); Weigand, *Naturrechtslehre* (1967); DBI (Fiorelli); CALMA.

ACHARD OF ST. VICTOR b. England; d. *ca.* 1170/1. Theologian and spiritual author. Studied at St. Victor in Paris, becoming abbot in 1155. Elected bishop of Avranches in 1161. Extant works include treatises *De discretione animae et spiritus et mentis* (ed. Häring 1960) and *De trinitate* (*De unitate divinae essentiae et pluralitate creaturarum*) (ed. Martineau 1987), as well as a set of fifteen sermons (ed. Châtillon 1970), all available in translation (tr. Feiss 2001).

Secondary sources. Châtillon, "Le *De discretione*" (1964), *Theologie, spiritualité et métaphysique* (1969); Ilkhani, *Philosophie de la création* (1999); CALMA.

ADAM OF BALSHAM (Parvipontanus) b. near Cambridge, 1100/2; d. 1157/69. Logician. Studied in Paris from *ca.* 1120. Master of a school on the Petit Pont in Paris by 1132, which gave rise to one of the main schools of twelfth-century logic, the *Adamiti* or *Parvipontani*. Canon of the Paris Cathedral from 1146. Took part in several Church councils investigating Gilbert of Poitiers. His chief work, the *Ars disserendi* [1132] (ed. Minio-Paluello 1956), is an important and influential early text in medieval logic. Also extant is a treatise on rare words, the *De utensilibus ad domum regendam* (or *Phalae tolum*) (ed. Hunt, in *Teaching and Learning* 1991).

Secondary sources. De Rijk, *Logica modernorum* (1962–7); Minio-Paluello, "Ars disserendi" (1954); CALMA; DMA (de Libera); Dronke; ODNB (Klibansky).

ADAM OF BUCKFIELD (Bockenfield, Bocfeld) b. Northumberland, *ca.* 1220; d. 1279/92. Oxford arts master and author of influential commentaries on Aristotle. Studying at Oxford by 1238; master by 1243. Canon of Lincoln Cathedral by 1263. Commentaries on a large number of Aristotelian works are extant in many manuscripts, often in multiple redactions (mostly unedited), including the *Metaphysics* (part. ed. Maurer 1955), *Physics*, *De caelo*, *De generatione*, *Meteorologica*, *De anima* [*ca.* 1145] (part. ed. Callus, in "Two Early Oxford Masters" 1939), and the *Parva naturalia*, as well as the *De causis*. Commentaries on the *De somno et vigilia*, the *De somnis*, and the *De divinatione per somnum* have been edited as works of Aquinas (ed. 1852–73, etc.).

Secondary sources. Grabmann, "Aristoteleskommentatoren" (1936); Noone, "Evidence" (1992); Thomson, "Works" (1944), "Further Note" (1958); CALMA; DMA (Beyer de Ryke); Lohr; ODNB (Long); Weijers.

ADAM MARSH (de Marisco) b. Bath, *ca.* 1200; d. 1259. Theologian, founding figure of the Franciscan chapter at Oxford. Master of arts at Oxford by 1226. Joined the Franciscan order in 1232. Studied theology under Robert Grosseteste, becoming the first Franciscan theology master at Oxford from 1242 to 1250. Despite his scholarly reputation, particularly as a biblical scholar, the only extant writings ascribed with certainty are a collection of letters [1241–59] (ed. Brewer 1858).

Secondary sources. Lawrence, "Letters" (1991); Little, "Franciscan School" (1926); CALMA; ODNB (Lawrence).

ADAM PULCHRAE MULIERIS (Bellefemme) *fl. ca.* 1230. Paris master of theology. Almost nothing is known about Adam's life (even the name is suspected of being corrupt). Extant works are fragments of a *Sentences* commentary (unedited), and the *Memoriale rerum difficilium naturalium* (or *Liber de intelligentiis*) [*ca.* 1230] (ed. Baeumker, in *Witelo* 1908), a work seemingly inspired by Robert Grosseteste's metaphysics of light, which would later be cited by Aquinas and others.

Secondary sources. Baeumker, "Zur Frage" (1924); CALMA; DMA (Beyer de Ryke); Weijers.

ADAM WODEHAM (Wodham, Wodam, Godam) b. *ca.* 1298; d. 1358. Franciscan friar and theologian. Lectured on the *Sentences* in London and again in Norwich in the late 1320s, before moving to Oxford in the early 1330s, where he became regent master around 1338. A younger contemporary of Ockham's, and perhaps his assistant, but an independent thinker in many respects, and often cited by later scholastics. His principal surviving philosophical work is his *Sentences* commentary, in multiple redactions. The interrelationship of these redactions is controversial. The so-called *Lectura secunda* [Bk. I up to d. 26] (ed. Wood and Gál 1990; d. 1 q. 1 tr. CTMPT III), a *reportatio* found in a single manuscript, has been identified by its editors with his lectures in Norwich, but has also been claimed to be a version of his Oxford lectures. The Oxford lectures (*ca.* 1332–4) have survived in three redactions, and are also printed in an abbreviated form (ed. Major 1512). No full edition from the manuscripts has been made, even though this is clearly Wodeham's most important work. Also surviving are two works on the continuum, the brief *Quaestio de divisione et compositione continui* (ed. Murdoch and Synan, in "Two Questions" 1966) and the book-length *Tractatus de indivisibilibus* (ed. and tr. Wood 1988), both written between 1322 and 1331.

Secondary sources: Courtenay, *Adam Wodeham* (1978); Brower-Toland, "Facts vs. Things" (2006); Grassi, *Intuizione e significato* (1986); Kretzmann, "Adam Wodeham's Anti-Atomism" (1984); Perler, "Seeing and Judging" (2008); Wood, "Adam Wodeham on Sensory Illusions" (1982); BCPMA (Wood); CALMA; ODNB (Courtenay).

ADELARD OF BATH b. Bath, *ca.* 1080; d. *ca.* 1152. English natural philosopher. Also published in metaphysics and translated mathematical works into Latin from Arabic. Studied at Tours, taught at Laon. Spent seven years in Salerno, Sicily, and the near East, where he learned Arabic. An influence on thirteenth-century English thinkers, such as Grosseteste and Roger Bacon, although his work in natural philosophy would largely be overshadowed by Aristotle. His most important work in natural philosophy is the *Quaestiones naturales* [before 1137, probably much earlier] (ed. and tr. Burnett *et al.* 1998), written in dialogue form. The metaphysical *De eodem et diverso* [before 1116] (ibid.) attempts a reconciliation of Plato and Aristotle, and offers a theory of universals. Among his many other scientific and mathematical treatises are a work on hawking, *De avibus* (ibid.), and an early work *Regulae abaci* (ed. Boncompagni 1881). Particularly influential were three versions of Euclid's *Elements*, in differing formats, all of which circulated widely, although only the first is ascribed to Adelard with confidence (ed. Busard 1983; ed. Busard and Folkerts 1992; ed. Busard 2001).

Secondary sources: Burnett, *Adelard of Bath* (1987); Burnett, "Algorismi" (1996); Clagett, "The Medieval Latin Translations of Euclid" (1953); Cochrane, *Adelard of Bath* (1994); Dickey, *Adelard of Bath* (1982); Jolivet, *Philosophie médiévale arabe et latine* (1995); BCPMA (Hackett); CALMA; DMA (Ricklin); Dronke; DSB (Clagett); ODNB (Burnett).

ADHEMAR OF ST. RUF d. *ca.* 1184. Theologian from the "little school" of Porretanians. Augustinian canon regular at St. Ruf (Avignon). Author of a *De Trinitate* (ed. Häring 1964) in defense of Gilbert of Poitiers. Assembled a large collection of patristic texts (unedited).

Secondary sources. Dondaine, *Écrits* (1962); Häring, "Vatersammlung" (1963), "Patristic Collection" (1966); Pelster, "Verteidigungsschrift" (1948); CALMA.

AEGIDIUS, *see* Giles.

AELRED OF RIEVAULX (Ailred) b. Hexham (Northumberland), *ca.* 1110; d. 1167. Cistercian monastic leader and spiritual author. Educated at Hexham and probably Durham; joined the court of the Scottish king after 1124. Entered the Cistercian monastery at Rievaulx (Yorkshire) in *ca.* 1134. Abbot from 1147 until his death, during which time he exercised considerable political and ecclesiastical influence. His writings include a *De anima* [*ca.* 1165] (ed. Talbot 1952; tr. Talbot 1981) and various spiritual works, including the *Speculum caritatis* [1142] (tr. Webb and Walker 1962) and a dialogue *De spiritali amicitia* [*ca.* 1160] (tr. Williams 1994). Also extant are a large number of sermons and various historical and hagiographical works (PL 195). An edition of the *Opera omnia* is in progress (ed. Hoste and Talbot 1971–). There is also a contemporary *Vita Ailredi* by Walter Daniel (ed. and tr. Powicke 1950/1978/1994).

Secondary sources. Hoste, *Bibliotheca Aelrediana* (1962); Burton, *Bibliotheca Aelrediana Secunda* (1997); Nouzille and Boulnois, *Expérience de Dieu* (1999); Squire, *Aelred of Rievaulx* (1981); CALMA; DMA (Nouzille); ODNB (Bell).

ALAN OF LILLE (Alanus ab Insulis, Alain de l'Isle, von Ryssel) b. Lille, *ca.* 1120; d. Cîteaux, 1202/3. Theologian, philosopher, and poet. Studied with Gilbert of Poitiers in Chartres or Paris, and probably with Bernard Silvestris in Tours. Taught in Paris and Montpellier, after *ca.* 1150. Later retired to the monastery of Cîteaux, where he remained until his death. His best-known works are two allegorical treatises: *De planctu Naturae* [late 1160s] (ed. Häring 1978; tr. Sheridan 1980), in which Nature plays a role like that of Philosophy in Boethius's *Consolation of Philosophy*, and the verse epic *Anticlaudianus* [*ca.* 1182–83] (ed. Bossuat 1955; tr. Sheridan 1973), which takes as its subject "the good and perfect man." Also extant are a treatise *De virtutibus et vitiis* (ed. Lottin, in *Psychologie et morale* VI [1960]), a *Liber penitentialis* (ed. Longère 1965) and three major works of theology: *Regulae caelestis iuris* (*Theologicae regulae*) [1170–80] (ed. Häring 1981); *Summa 'Quoniam homines'* [1170–80] (ed. Glorieux 1953); and *De fide catholica* (*Summa contra haereticos*) [1185–1200] (ed. PL 210; excerpts tr. Wakefield and Evans, in *Heresies* 1969), the last a guide to preaching against heretics and unbelievers. For various shorter works and further bio-bibliographical information, see *Textes inédits* (ed. d'Alverny 1965).

Secondary sources. Evans, *Alan of Lille* (1983); Raynaud de Lage, *Alain de Lille* (1951); Sweeney, *Logic, Theology, and Poetry* (2006); BCPMA (Marenbon); CALMA; DMA (Erismann); Dronke.

ALBERIC OF PARIS *fl.* 1130s–40s. Influential logician, opponent of nominalism. Replaced Peter Abaelard at the school of Mount St. Geneviève near Paris in 1137. Traveled to Bologna, perhaps studying parts of Aristotle's new logic there; subsequently returned to teach at Mount St. Geneviève. No works are extant, but Alberic's influence is evident in the writings of his followers, the Albricani and the Montani.

Secondary sources. De Rijk, "New Evidence" (1966); Iwakuma, "Influence" (2004); Marenbon, *Aristotelian Logic* (2000).

ALBERT THE GREAT (Albertus Magnus, Albert of Cologne) b. *ca.* 1200; d. 1280. Dominican philosopher and theologian, and one of the great masters of the scholastic era; the first medieval Latin author to attempt a comprehensive study of the entire Aristotelian corpus. An important figure in subsequent centuries, as shown by the enduring legacy of Albertists among later scholastics. Joined the Dominican order in 1223 while study-ing law at Padua, continued his studies under the Dominicans, probably in Cologne, and subsequently taught at various Dominican schools in Germany throughout the 1230s. Sent to Paris to study theology *ca.* 1241 and subsequently became regent master of theology from 1245 to 1248, the period when Aquinas commenced his studies at Paris (although Aquinas was perhaps at first studying in the arts faculty). Returned to Cologne in 1248 to found a Dominican *studium generale*, taking Aquinas with him. The remainder of his career was divided between various ecclesiastical and teaching positions throughout Germany.

Early major works include the *De natura boni* [1230s], *Summa de creaturis* [by 1246], and a *Sentences* commentary [completed 1249], works that already display his extensive familiarity with Aristotle and the Greco-Arabic commentary tradition. Beginning in Cologne, and for the next twenty years, he undertook a series of commentaries on nearly all of Aristotle's corpus, mostly in the form of paraphrases. This is the most extensive such set of commentaries from the Middle Ages. Among the most notable are the *Physics* [circa 1250], *Ethics* [1250–52, and again in 1262–63] (Bk. X of the earlier, tr. CTMPT II), the Organon [1252–6], and *Metaphysics* [1263–7]. Albert also produced commentaries on many other works, including those of pseudo-Dionysius [late 1240s] (*Mystical Theology* tr. Tugwell 1988), Euclid's *Elements* [1262–3], and an extensive set of biblical commentaries. Two comparable older versions of Albert's *Opera omnia* are available (ed. Jammy 1651, 21 vols.; ed. Borgnet 1890–9, 38 vols.). A critical edition is in progress, but less than half complete (ed. Geyer *et al.* [Cologne] 1951–, 40 vols. projected).

Secondary sources. Resnick and Kitchell, *Albert the Great: Bibliography (1900–2000)* (2004); Craemer-Ruegenberg, *Albert the Great* (2005); de Libera, *Métaphysique et noétique* (2005); Hoenen and de Libera (eds.), *Albertus Magnus und der Albertismus* (1995); Kovach and Shahan (eds.), *Albert the Great* (1980); Meyer and Zimmermann (eds.), *Albertus Magnus* (1980); Senner and Anzulewicz (eds.), *Albertus Magnus* (2001); Weisheipl (ed.), *Albertus Magnus and the Sciences* (1980); Zimmermann (ed.), *Albert der Große* (1981); BCPMA (Dreyer); CALMA; Kaeppeli; REP (de Libera); SEP (Führer); Weijers.

ALBERT OF ORLAMÜNDE *fl.* late thirteenth century. Dominican friar, teacher in Thüringen. Author of a short textbook on natural philosophy, the *Philosophia paupe-rum* or *Summa naturalium* (ed. Venice 1496, etc.; part. ed. Geyer, in *Summa naturalium* 1938), based on the writings of Albert the Great.

Secondary sources. Grabmann, "Philosophia pauperum" (1918); CALMA; Kaeppeli.

ALBERT OF SAXONY (Albert of Rickmersdorf, Albertus Parvus, Albertutius) b. *ca.* 1316; d. 1390. Arts master at Paris from 1351 to 1361, author of influential works in logic and natural philosophy. Founder and first rector of the University of Vienna in 1365. Bishop of Halberstadt from 1366 until his death. Later regarded as one of the principal adherents of nominalism, along with his near contemporaries at Paris, John Buridan and Marsilius of Inghen, whose works are often so similar as to be confused with each other. The subsequent wide circulation of Albert's work made him a better-known figure in some areas than more talented contemporaries like Buridan and Nicole Oresme.

Albert's principal logical work is the *Perutilis logica* [*ca.* 1360] (tr. [Sp] Muñoz García 1988, with text of 1522/1974 ed.; tract. II ed. Kann, *Eigenschaften* 1993; tract. VI. c. 1, *De insolubilibus*, tr. CTMPT I); he also authored a *Sophismata* [*ca.* 1359] (ed. 1502/1975, etc.]) and a set of twenty-five *Quaestiones logicales* [*ca.* 1356] (ed. Fitzgerald 2002), as well as commentaries on the *ars vetus* [*ca.* 1356] (ed. Muñoz García 1988) and the *Posterior Analytics* (ed. 1497/1986, etc.). His surviving Aristotle commentaries are mostly in natural philosophy, most prominently the *Physics* [*ca.* 1351] (ed. Patar 1999); *De caelo* [*ca.* 1354] (ed. 1492/1986 etc.); and *De generatione et corruptione* (ed. 1505/1970, etc.). Commentaries on the *Nicomachean Ethics* and the *Economics* also survive (both unedited), as well as several short mathematical texts, most notably the *Tractatus proportionum* [*ca.* 1353] (ed. Busard 1971). Although Albert studied theology in Paris, no theological writings survive.

Secondary sources. Sarnowsky, *Theorie der Bewegung* (1989) [life and works]; Muñoz García, "Albert of Saxony, Bibliography" (1990) [texts, manuscripts, editions]; Berger, "Bibliographie der Sekundärlitteratur" (1994); Biard (ed.), *Itinéraires d'Albert de Saxe* (1991); Heidingsfelder, *Kommentar zur Nikomachischen Ethik* (1927); Kann, *Die Eigenschaften der Termini* (1993); BCPMA (Grant); CALMA; DMA (de Libera); DSB (Moody); Lohr; REP (Biard); SEP (Biard); Weijers.

ALCHER OF CLAIRVAUX d. *ca.* 1165. Cistercian monk. Once thought the author of the influential pseudo-Augustinian *De spiritu et anima* (PL 40; tr. McGinn 1977) [mid-twelfth century], but this is now generally doubted. Various other works have also questionably been ascribed to Alcher, including *De diligendo Deo*, *Soliloquium animae ad Deum*, *Liber meditationum* (all PL 40), and *De anima* (PL 177 and 184).

Secondary sources. Raciti, "Autore" (1961); CALMA; DS (Canivez).

ALCUIN (Albinus) b. Northumbria, *ca.* 740; d. Tours, 804. Poet, historian, theologian, philosopher, and political force; central figure in the Carolingian renaissance. Educated at the cathedral school at York, where he remained until 786, when he journeyed to the court of Charlemagne. Returned to York in 790, and then back to the French court in 793. Appointed abbot of St. Martin's at Tours in 796. Alcuin's philosophical importance lies in his role in reviving the study of the arts and theology in both England and France. His extant works reflect his core pedagogical interests in the *trivium*, and include treatises *De orthographica* (ed. Bruni 1997), *De grammatica*, *De dialectica*, *De rhetorica et virtutibus* (ed. and tr. Howell 1941), as well as a *De vera philosophia* and a *De vitiis et virtutibus*. Among his theological writings, the *De fide sanctae trinitatis* and the *Contra haeresim Felicis* (ed. Blumenshine 1980) are particularly notable. His works are collected in PL 100-1. A great many letters are also extant (ed. Dümmler 1895; tr. Allot 1974).

Secondary sources. Germann, *De temporum ratione* (2006); Houwen and MacDonald (eds.), *Alcuin of York* (1998); Jullien and Perelman, *Clavis des auteurs Latins* (1999); Marenbon, *Circle of Alcuin* (1981); Wallach, *Alcuin and Charlemagne* (1959); CALMA; DMA (Veyrard-Cosme); ODNB (Bullough).

ALEXANDER OF ALEXANDRIA (Bonini) b. Alessandria (Piedmont), *ca.* 1268; d. Rome, 1314. Franciscan theologian. Became a friar as a youth. Sent to Paris to study theology;

after an interruption in his studies caused by ecclesiastical controversy, he became regent master in Paris in 1307–8, succeeding Scotus. Named Franciscan provincial minister of Genoa in 1308 and minister general in 1313. Extant works include commentaries on the *Metaphysics* [1304/6] (ed. 1572) and *De anima* [*ca.* 1306] (ed. 1481, etc.); an early *Sentences* commentary heavily dependent on Bonaventure [1301–3]; a rewritten and original commentary [1307–8]; and a *Quodlibet* [1307–8] (all unedited). In addition, various biblical commentaries survive (unedited), as well as several treatises concerning the Franciscan spiritualist controversy, which he took a strong role in combatting: a *Responsio ad Ubertinum de Casale* (ed. Chiappini 1914) and a *Tractatus de usu paupere* (ed. Heysse 1917). Also extant is a *Tractatus de usuris* (ed. Hamelin 1962).

Secondary sources. Amerini, "Nature of Essence" (2004), "Natura degli accidenti" (2005); Krause, "Abriss der Erkenntnistheorie" (1980); Rossini, "Quod coexsistit exsistit" (1995); Schabel and Rossini, "Time and Eternity" (2005); Veuthey, "Alexandre d'Alexandrie" (1931–2); DBI (Manselli); DMA (Boulnois); FA; Lohr; Weijers.

ALEXANDER OF HALES b. Gloucestershire, *ca.* 1185; d. Paris, 1245. Founding father of scholastic theology, insisted on the independence of philosophy and gave considerable impetus to the later medieval project of systematic theology. Son of a wealthy English family, he studied at Paris, became master of arts before 1210 and master of theology *ca.* 1220. Entered the Franciscan order in 1236, and became the first Franciscan at Paris to hold a chair in theology. Remained regent master in Paris for most of his life, and his chair would subsequently be reserved for a Franciscan. Alexander instituted the practice of commenting on Lombard's *Sentences*, and his *Glossa* on the Sentences [1223–7] (ed. 1951–7) is his earliest known work. Traditionally he is best known for the *Summa theologica* (*Summa Halesiana, Summa Fratris Alexandri*) (ed. 1924–48), but it is now clear that although he began this influential work, it was in large part written by others, albeit under his direction, and often using material from his earlier work. His other principal surviving works are a series of theological disputations; those dating from before 1236 have been edited (ed. 1960); an equally large number of later questions awaits an edition.

Secondary sources. Osborne, "Alexander of Hales" (1994) [biography]; Herscher, "Bibliography" (1945); Boehner, "System of Metaphysics" (1945); Gössmann, *Metaphysik und Heilsgeschichte* (1964); BCPMA (Cullen); CALMA; REP (Gál).

ALEXANDER LANGELEY *fl.* 1330s. Franciscan theologian. Lectured on the *Sentences* at Oxford between 1335 and 1340, from which a commentary on Bks. I–III is extant (Bk. I ed. Edwards 1999). An earlier set of lectures has not been found.

Secondary sources. Edwards, "Themes and Personalities" (2002); CALMA.

ALEXANDER NECKAM (Nequam) b. St. Albans (Hertfordshire), 1157; d. Kempsey (Worcestershire), 1217. Encyclopedic scholar. Studied first at the grammar school at St. Albans, and then in Paris from 1175 to 1182. Subsequently returned to England, teaching at St. Albans and later teaching theology at Oxford in the 1190s. Became an Augustinian canon at Cirencester in 1197/1202; elected abbot in 1213. Best known for two encyclopedic works, the *De naturis rerum* [before 1205] (Bks. I–II ed. Wright 1863) and the verse *De laudibus divinae sapientiae* [*ca.* 1213] (ed. Wright 1863), supplemented by the *Suppletio defectuum* [*ca.* 1213] (Bk. I ed. and tr. McDonough 1999). His many theological works include a scholastic *summa*, the *Speculum speculationum* (ed. Thomson 1988). Also extant is a commentary on Martianus Capella [*ca.* 1177] (ed. McDonough 2006), collections of fables (ed. Garbugino 1987), and a number of biblical commentaries and sermons (unedited).

Secondary sources. Hunt, *Schools and the Cloister* (1984); CALMA; DMA (Grondeux); Dronke; ODNB (Goering).

ALEXANDER OF VILLA DEI b. near Avranches, *ca.* 1160/70; d. Avranches, *ca.* 1240. Mathematician and grammarian. Educated at Paris, becoming canon of the cathedral of Avranches. Extant works include the verse grammar *Doctrinale* (ed. Reichling 1893/1974); the *Ecclesiale* (ed. and tr. Lind 1958); a *Massa compoti* (or *Computus ecclesiasticus*) ranging widely over canon law, theology, and science (ed. and [Fr] tr. Van Wijk 1936); and the *Carmen de musica* (ed. Seay 1977).

Secondary sources. Gutiérrez Galindo, *El Doctrinal* (1993) [Sp. tr. with introduction and notes]; CALMA; Weijers.

ALFARABI, *see* Fārābī.

ALFRED OF SHARESHILL (Shareshel, Alfredus Anglicus) b. Shareshill (near Lichfield); *fl. ca.* 1197 – *ca.* 1222. Scientist, translator. Little is known of his life, but he likely spent time in Toledo, since his translations of Aristotle seem part of the larger project advanced there by Gerard of Cremona and Michael Scot. Translated the pseudo-Aristotelian *De plantis* of Nicholas of Damascus (ed. Drossaart Lulofs and Poortman 1989) and *De mineralibus* [from Avicenna's *Shifā'*] (ed. Holmyard and Mandeville 1927/1982). Wrote commentaries on these works (*In De plantis* ed. Long 1985) and on the *Meteorology* (ed. Otte 1988). Best known for an independent treatise, the *De motu cordis* (ed. Baeumker 1923), an early example of the influence of the new Aristotle on Latin philosophy. A large number of other Aristotelian commentaries, no longer extant, testify to his importance in that movement.

Secondary sources. Baeumker, *Stellung* (1913); Otte, "Life and Writings" (1972), "Reception of Aristotle (1990); Struve, "Anthropologie" (1973); CALMA; DMA (Beyer de Ryke); Dronke; ODNB (Burnett); Weijers.

ALGAZALI, *see* Ghazālī.

ALGER OF LIÈGE b. Lìège, *ca.* 1060; d. Cluny, 1132/5. Theologian, historian. Studied at Liège, where he became deacon of St. Bartholomew. Canon of the St. Lambert Cathedral *ca.* 1100–21, subsequently retiring to the monastery at Cluny. Author of the *Liber de misericordia et iusticia* (ed. Kretzschmar 1985), an early source for canon law; a treatise on the Eucharist, *De sacramento corporis et sanguinis Domini* (ed. 1873); and a *Libellus de gratia et libero arbitrio* (PL 180).

Secondary sources. Brigué, *Alger de Liège* (1936); BBK (Bautz); CALMA.

ALHAZEN, *see* Ibn al-Haytham.

ʿALĪ IBN AL-ʿABBĀS AL-MAJŪSĪ (Haly Abbas) b. al-Ahwāz; d. 982/95. Leading medical authority. Lived in Shiraz. Author of the *Kitāb kāmil al-ṣināʿa al-ṭībbīyya* (*The Complete Book of the Medical Art*) (ed. Sezgin 1985), which became an important medical textbook in both Arabic and Latin. The first Latin translation was by Constantine the African [*ca.* 1080], who called it the *Pantegni* (ed. 1515). It was translated again by Stephan of Antioch in 1127, as the *Liber regalis dispositionis* (ed. 1492).

Secondary sources. Burnett and Jacquart (eds.), *Constantine the African* (1994); EI (Elgood).

ALKINDI, *see* Kindī.

ʿALLĀMA AL-ḤILLĪ b. Hilla (Iraq), 1250; d. 1325. Influential Shīʿite theologian. Born into a family of distinguished scholars; studied philosophy with al-Ṭūsī. Moved to Persia in 1305, where he was influential in the adoption of Shīʿism as the state religion. Hundreds of works are attested, mostly lost. His *Bāb al-ḥādī ʿashar* (ed. Muḥaqqiq 1986; tr. Miller 1928) and *Sharḥ tajrīd al-iʿtiqād* (*Commentary on* [*al-Ṭūsī's*] *Abstract of Theology*) (ed. 1988) are fundamental texts of Imāmī Shīʿism.

Secondary sources. Schmidtke, *Theology* (1991); BEIP (Leaman); EI (Jafri).

ALPHONSUS VARGAS OF TOLEDO d. 1366. Augustinian friar and theologian. Lectured on the *Sentences* at Paris [1344–45] (Bk. I only, ed. 1490/1952). Succeeded Gregory of Rimini to the Augustinian chair of theology at Paris in 1346/7. Elected archbishop of Seville in 1361. A set of questions on the *De anima* is also extant (ed. 1477, etc.).

Secondary sources. Kürzinger, *Alfonsus Vargas* (1930); Schabel, *Theology at Paris* (2000); Trapp, "Augustinian Theology" (1956); CALMA; Weijers.

ALRAZI, *see* Rāzī.

AMALRIC OF BENE (Amaury) b. Bène (near Chartres); d. *ca.* 1206. Studied the arts in Paris, becoming master there. Censured by the university shortly before his death. Condemned posthumously in 1210, along with his disciples, for his alleged pantheistic statement that *quicquid est est Deus*. No works survive; his views are known only through the criticisms of others (ed. Capelle, in *Amaury* 1932).

Secondary sources. D'Alverny, "Fragment du procès" (1950–1); Lucentini, "L'eresia" (1987); Thijssen, "Master Amalric" (1996); DMA (Casadei); Dronke; Weijers.

AL-ʿĀMIRĪ (Abū al-Ḥasan Muḥammad ibn Yūsuf) b. Khorasan; d. Nishapur, 992. Philosopher and theologian. Studied with Abū-Zayd al-Balkhī; subsequently lived in Rayy, Baghdad, Bukhara, and Nishapur. His work (ed. Khalifat 1996), while philosophical, tends to defend Islam against philosophical encroachment. Among his extant works are a treatise on the afterlife, *Kitāb al-amad ʿalā al-abad* (*On the Afterlife*) [986] (ed. and tr. Rowson 1988) and a paraphrase of Proclus's *Elements of Theology* (ed. and [German] tr. Wakelnig 2006).

Secondary sources. Wakelnig, "Hierarchy of Being" (2007); REP (Gaskill); HIP (Rowson); EI (Rowson).

ANDREW OF CORNWALL b. Cornwall; *fl.* late thirteenth century. Master of arts in Paris. Extant works are questions on the *Isagoge* and on the *Liber de sex principiis* (both unedited).

Secondary sources. Andrews, "Reception of Modism" (1999); CALMA; Lohr; Weijers.

ANDREW OF NEUFCHÂTEAU (Andreas de Novo Castro) b. Lorraine; d. *ca.* 1400. Franciscan theologian at Paris. Commented on the first book of Lombard's *Sentences* in 1358–9 (ed. 1514; part. ed. Friedman, in "Divine Omnipotence" 1994; part. ed. and tr. Idziak 1997). His work has attracted particular attention for its treatment of the semantics of propositions. Also composed a treatise on the immaculate conception (ed. Piana *et al.* 1954).

Secondary sources. Elie, *Le complexe significabile* (1936); Tachau, "Questiones" (1992); CALMA; FA.

ANDREW OF ST. VICTOR b. England, *ca.* 1110; d. Wigmore (Herefordshire), 1175. Biblical scholar. Studied in Paris, becoming an Augustinian canon at St. Victor. Returned to England *ca.* 1147 to become the first abbot of Wigmore. His exegetical treatises are distinctive for their use of the Hebrew text, but are not highly theological in character. Extant works include commentaries on Samuel, Kings, Wisdom, Ezechiel, and Daniel (ed. Lohr *et al.* 1986–).

Secondary sources. Smalley, *Study of the Bible* (1983); CALMA; ODNB (Gibson).

ANGELO OF FOSSOMBRONE *fl.* 1395–1402. Arts master and logician. Taught at Bologna from 1395 to 1400 and Padua from 1400 to 1402. Author of an *Insolubilia* (unedited) and a commentary on part of William Heytesbury's *Regulae* (unedited).

Secondary sources. Federici Vescovini, "Commento" (1982); Spade, *Mediaeval Liar* (1975); DBI (Leonardi); CALMA.

ANSELM OF CANTERBURY (of Aosta, of Bec) b. Aosta (northwest Italy), 1033; d. Canterbury, 1109. Philosopher and theologian whose ontological argument is only the most famous of his many important ideas. Left his native land as a young man; arrived in 1059 at the Benedictine monastery at Le Bec (Normandy), where he studied with Lanfranc. Quickly became prior and eventually abbot. Consecrated archbishop of Canterbury in 1093, a position he held until his death, although twice in exile. A contemporary biography by Eadmer (ed. and tr. Southern 1962) presents a clear picture of his life.

Best-known works in philosophical theology are the *Monologion* [1075–6] and *Proslogion* [1077–8], as well as the later *Cur Deus Homo* [1095–8], on the incarnation. Of special philosophical interest are the early *De grammatico* [1059–60] and three closely related dialogues: *De veritate*, *De libertate arbitrii*, and *De casu diaboli* [1080–86], which focus on issues of freedom and responsibility to which he later returned in the *De concordia* [1107–8]. The standard edition is Schmitt (1946/1968); many translations are available.

Secondary sources. Davies and Leftow, *Cambridge Companion* (2004); Southern, *Portrait* (1990); Evans, *Concordance* (1984), *Anselm* (1989); Henry, *Logic of Saint Anselm* (1967); Williams and Visser, *Anselm* (2008); CALMA; BCPMA (Hopkins); DBI (Schmitt); ODNB (Southern); REP (Hopkins); SEP (Williams).

ANSELM OF COMO *fl.* 1335–44. Master of arts at Bologna. Regarded as an Averroist. Extant works include a short *Quodlibet* and various other brief works (ed. Kuksewicz, in *Averroïsme bolonais* 1965).

Secondary sources. CALMA.

ANSELM OF LAON (Anselmus Laudinensis) b. Laon, before 1050; d. 1117. Renowned exegete and teacher. Probably studied at Bec with Anselm of Canterbury. Taught at Paris from 1076 to 1080, then returned to Laon to take over the direction of the cathedral school with his brother Ralph of Laon. His most important literary legacy is his commentaries on the Bible, including the Psalms (PL 116) and the Song of Songs (ed. and tr. Dove 1997). He seems, with his brother, to have begun what would become the *Glossa ordinaria* on the entirety of the Bible, which would circulate anonymously for centuries (ed. *Biblia latina*, 1480–1/1998; part. ed. PL 113–14). Various theological *Sententiae* are also attributed to Anselm (ed. Bliemetzrieder 1919; ed. Lottin, in *Psychologie* 1959, vol. V), though it is difficult to distinguish his from his students' contribution.

Secondary sources. Bliemetzrieder, "Autour de l'œuvre théologique" (1929); Flint, "School of Laon" (1976); Lefévre, *De Anselmo Laudunensi* (1895); Smalley, *Study of the Bible* (1983); CALMA; DMA (Brouwer).

ANTONINUS OF FLORENCE b. Florence, 1389; d. Florence, 1459. Theologian and famed preacher, particularly influential for his ethical and social thought. Entered the Dominican order as a youth, quickly assuming an important administrative role. Archbishop of Florence from 1446. Principal writings are his *Summa theologica* (*Summa moralis*) [1440–54] (ed. 1740/1959, etc.) and *Confessionale "Defecerunt"* (ed. 1490, etc.)

Secondary sources. Gaughan, *Social Theories* (1951); Howard, *Beyond the Written Word* (1995); Orlandi, *Antonino* (1959); CALMA; DBI; Kaeppeli.

ANTONIUS ANDREAE b. Aragon, *ca.* 1280; d. Catalonia, *ca.* 1320/5. Influential disciple of Scotus. Franciscan friar, studied at Lérida (Catalonia) and then at Paris under Scotus in 1304/7. His published works, which would circulate widely, include a *Sentences* commentary (ed. 1572, etc.), questions on the *ars vetus* (ed. 1508, etc.) and the *Metaphysics* (ed. 1491, etc.), a further *Expositio* of the *Metaphysics* (printed in older Scotus editions), and two shorter works: a *Tractatus formalitatum* and *Quaestiones de tribus principiis rerum naturalium* (both ed. 1475, etc.).

Secondary sources. Bérubé, "Antoine André" (1979); Gensler, "Catalogue of Works" (1992), "Concept of the Individual" (1996); Pini, "Una lettura scotista" (1991), "Scotistic Aristotelianism" (1995); CALMA; FA; Weijers.

ANTONIUS DE CARLENIS DE NEAPOLI b. Monte Aquilo (Cassino), 1386; d. 1460. Philosopher and Dominican theologian. Master of arts in Bologna from 1406 to 1408; subsequently joined the Dominican order. Studied theology in Bologna in 1439; master by 1447. Archbishop of Amalfi from 1449. Extant works include a *Sentences* commentary [1439–40] (part. ed. and tr. Livesey 1994), and questions on both the *Posterior Analytics* [1340s] and *Metaphysics* (both unedited).

Secondary sources. Meersseman, "Antonius de Carlenis" (1933); CALMA; Kaeppeli.

ARETHAS OF CAESAREA b. Patras, *ca.* 850; d. *ca.* 944. Byzantine scholar and politician. Elected archbishop of Caesarea in 902. Extant works include a commentary on the Apocalypse (PG 106) as well as various scholia on Plato, Aristotle, and other classical texts, including comments on the *Isagoge* and *Categories* (ed. Share 1994). In addition to the scholia and letters in PG 106, various works are edited by Westerink (1968–72).

Secondary sources. Lemerle, *Le premier humanisme byzantin* (1971); ODB (Kazhdan).

ARLOTTO OF PRATO b. Tuscany; d. 1286. Franciscan theologian. Studied theology in Paris in the 1270s, becoming regent master in 1284–5. His only extant philosophical work is a disputed question from that period on the eternity of the world (ed. Dales and Argerami, in *Medieval Latin Texts* 1991). Elected minister general of the Franciscan order in 1285.

Secondary sources. CALMA; DBI (Pratesi); FA.

ARMAND OF BELLEVUE (de Belvézer) b. Provence; d. after 1348. Dominican theologian. Appointed master of theology by papal order in 1326. Taught at the Montpellier *studium*, and then in Avignon until 1333. Extant works include a treatise on "difficult terms" in philosophy and theology [*ca.* 1326?] (ed. 1500, etc.); a commentary on Aquinas's *De ente et essentia* [*ca.* 1319] (ed. in Thomas Aquinas 1496, etc.); a response to Durand of St. Pourçain and Thomas Waleys [1333] (ed. van Liere 1992); and various biblical commentaries.

Secondary sources. Barbour, *Byzantine Thomism* (1993); Laurent, "Armandus de Bevézer" (1930); CALMA; DMA (Trottmann); Kaeppeli; Roensch.

ARNALD OF VILLANOVA b. prob. Valencia, 1238/40; d. at sea near Genoa, 1311. Physician, theologian, translator, and natural scientist. Studied in his youth with the Dominicans, subsequently pursuing theology and medicine at Montpellier. Traveled widely through Europe, becoming professor of medicine in Montpellier in 1291. Active as translator of Arabic natural philosophy. Often a controversial figure and repeatedly subject to banishment, in part because of his apocalyptic speculations and agitations for ecclesiastical reform that had affinities with the spiritual Franciscans. His medical renown led to his becoming the physician of rulers and popes. In alchemy too, his subsequent reputation was considerable, although most of the works ascribed to him in this area are spurious. His authentic medical works (ed. García Ballester *et al.* 1975–88) include the *Speculum medicinae* and the *Regimen sanitatis* (tr. Paynell 1597). His writings in Catalan have also been edited (ed. Batllori 1947), as have his spiritual writings (ed. Carreras y Artau 1971). There are multiple Renaissance editions of his complete works (Lyon 1504, etc.).

Secondary sources. Haven, *La vie et les œuvres* (1896/1972); Mensa i Valls, *Arnau de Vilanova* (1994) [bibliography]; Gerwing, *Vom Ende der Zeit* (1996); Perarnau (ed.), *Actes* (1995); Santi, *Arnau de Vilanova* (1986); Ziegler, *Medicine and Religion* (1998); BCPMA (Bertelloni); CALMA; DMA (Suarez-Nani); DSB (McVaugh).

ARNOLD OF SAXONY (Arnoldus Luca) b. Saxony; *fl.* 1225–50. Encyclopedist. Probably a physician. Author of a five-part encyclopedia, the *Liber de floribus rerum naturalium* [*ca.*

1225–50] (ed. Stange 1905–7). Also extant are a treatise on practical medicine and a dialogue on virtue and vice (both unedited).

Secondary sources. Draelants, "Une mise au point" (1992–3), "Encyclopédiste méconnu" (2000); CALMA; DMA (Beyer de Ryke); Lohr; Weijers.

ARNOLD OF STRELLEY b. near Nottingham; d. 1349. Dominican theologian. Lectured on the *Sentences*, probably at Oxford, between 1323 and 1330. Prior of the English province from *ca.* 1340 until his death; king's confessor in 1348. The *Sentences* commentary seems to have survived in an anonymous Erfurt manuscript (unedited). Apparently authored the *Centiloquium theologicum*, formerly ascribed to Ockham (ed. *Opera phil.* VII). Also authored a paraphrase of Ockham's *Tractatus de praedestinatione* (ed. Gelber, in "Ockham's Early Influence" 1988).

Secondary sources. Gelber, *It Could Have Been Otherwise* (2004); Kaeppeli.

AL-ASHʿARĪ (Abū al-Ḥasan) b. Basra, 873/4; d. Baghdad, 935/6. Founder of the Ashʿarite school of Islamic theology. Initially a student of Muʿtazilite theology, he turned against it in 912/13 and subsequently inspired the movement that bears his name. Of the many works ascribed to him, only a few have survived, most prominently his *Maqālāt al-islāmiyyīn* (*Discourses of the Proponents of Islam*) (ed. Ritter 1963); the *Kitāb al-Lumaʿ* (*Book of Lights*) (ed. and tr. McCarthy 1953); and the *Al-Ibānaʿan uṣūl al-dīyāna* (*Elucidation of Islam's Foundation*) (tr. Klein 1940).

Secondary sources. Allard, *Le problème des attributs divins* (1965); Frank, "Ashʿarite Ontology" (1999); Gimaret, *La doctrine d'al-Ashʿarī* (1990); BEIP (İskenderoğlu); EI (Watt).

ASTESANUS OF ASTI d. *ca.* 1330. Franciscan legal scholar and theologian. Author of an important confessional treatise, the *Summa de casibus conscientiae* (*Summa Astesana*) [*ca.* 1317] (ed. 1478, etc.).

Secondary sources. Dietterle, "Die *Summae confessorum*" (1905); Michaud-Quantin, *Sommes de casuistique* (1962); DBI (Abbondanza); CALMA.

AUBRY OF RHEIMS (Albericus) *fl.* 1260s–70s. Arts master at Paris. Rector in 1272. Author of a *Philosophia* [*ca.* 1265] (ed. Gauthier, in "Notes sur Siger " 1984) describing the study of philosophy as the ultimate end of human life.

Secondary sources. Gauthier, "Notes sur Siger" (1984); CALMA; Weijers.

AUGUSTINE OF ANCONA (Augustinus Triumphus) b. Ancona (Italy), 1270/3; d. 1328. Augustinian friar, theologian, and political theorist. Lectured at the Augustinian convent in Padua, then studied theology at Paris, lecturing on the *Sentences ca.* 1303. Returned to lecture at the Augustinian convent at Padua, then returned to Paris, where he became regent master of theology from 1313 to 1315. Subsequently lived in Naples, where he was the chaplain to Charles d'Anjou, son of King Robert of Naples in 1322. Best known as an advocate of papal authority, in his *Summa de potestate ecclesiastica* [1326] (ed. 1473, etc.; part. tr. CTMPT II) and *Tractatus brevis de duplici potestate prelatorum et laicorum* [*ca.* 1314/16] (ed. Scholz 1903/1962). A great many other works are extant but unedited, including his *Sentences* commentary (Bk. I only), commentaries on the *Prior Analytics* and *Metaphysics*, and a large number of biblical commentaries.

Secondary sources. Kölmel, "Einheit und Zweiheit der Gewalt" (1963); McCready, "The Papal Sovereign" (1977); McGrade, "Righteousness of Dissent" (1994–7); Ministeri, *De vita et operibus* (1953); Schmaus, "Die Gotteslehre" (1935); Wilks, *Problem of Sovereignty* (1963); CALMA; CHLMP; DBI (Ministeri); DMA (Solère); Lohr; Weijers.

AVEMPACE, *see* Ibn Bājja.

AVENDAUTH, *see* Abraham ibn Daud.

AVERROES (Abū al-Walīd Muḥammad ibn Aḥmad ibn Muḥammad ibn Rushd; The Commentator) b. Cordoba, *ca.* 1126; d. Marrakech, 1198. Famed commentator on Aristotle, his work helped define Latin Aristotelianism. Averroes is the Latin form of his name; in Arabic, he is known as Ibn Rushd. Born into an influential Andalusian family, he became influential himself among the Almohad rulers. Controversy over his views led to exile late in life, although he was restored to influence before his death. Best known for his commentaries on Aristotle: a series of epitomes or *Short Commentaries* (*jāmiʿ*); the paraphrases known as the *Middle Commentaries* (*talkhīṣ*); and finally his definitive works, the five *Long Commentaries* (*shurūḥ* or *tafsīr*): *Posterior Analytics* [1180] (ed. [Arabic] Badawī 1984); *Physics* [1186] (Arabic not extant); *De caelo* [1188] (ed. [Arabic] Endress 1994; ed. [Latin] Carmody and Arnzen 2003); *De anima* [*ca.* 1186] (ed. [Latin] Crawford 1953; tr. Taylor 2009; Arabic not extant); and *Metaphysics* [1190] (ed. Bouyges 1938–52). Prominent among his many other important works are his refutation of al-Ghazālī, the *Tahāfut al-tahāfut* (*Incoherence of the Incoherence*) [1180] (ed. Bouyges 1930; tr. Van den Bergh 1954/1978); the *Faṣl al-maqāl* (*Decisive Treatise*) [1179] (tr. Butterworth 2001, with facing Arabic); the *Kashf al-manāhij* (*Explanation of the Sorts of Proofs in the Doctrines of Religion*) [1180] (ed. Jābirī 1998; tr. Najjar 2001); and the *De substantia orbis* (ed. [Hebrew] and tr. Hyman 1986), with its influential discussion of matter. Many works do not survive, or survive only in Hebrew or Latin translation; much of what has survived has not been translated, and remains most accessible in Latin Renaissance editions (ed. Juntas 1552 and 1562/1962) (see Appendix B4). The Thomas-Institut maintains a useful on-line database of editions and manuscripts.

Secondary sources. Anawati, *Bibliographie* (1978); Endress, "Averrois Opera" (1999); Rosemann, "Catalogue of Editions," (1988); Aertsen and Endress (eds.), *Averroes and the Aristotelian Tradition* (1999); Arnaldez, *Rationalist in Islam* (2000); Hayoun and de Libera (eds.), *Averroès et l'averroisme* (1991); Leaman, *Averroes* (1988); Urvoy, *Ibn Rushd* (1991); Wolfson, "Plan for the Publication" (1931), "Revised Plan" (1963); BCPMA (Taylor); EI (Arnaldez); HIP (Urvoy); REP (Leaman).

AVICEBRON, *see* Solomon ibn Gabirol.

AVICENNA (Abū ʿAlī al-Ḥusayn ibn ʿAbd Allāh ibn Sīnā) b. Afshana (Uzbekistan), 980; d. Isfahan, 1037. The leading figure of medieval Islamic philosophy and one of the greatest philosophers of any era. Avicenna is the Latinized form of Ibn Sīnā. A youthful prodigy, according to the testimony of his autobiography (ed. and tr. Gohlman 1974), whose work eventually covered all aspects of learning, from philosophical treatises in the Aristotelian tradition (with a Neoplatonic influence) to medicine, natural science, and poetry. Principal philosophical work is the *Kitāb al-Shifāʾ* (*Book of the Healing*) [1020–7] (ed. Madkur and Zāyid 1983, etc.), which contains four parts (*jumal*): I. Logic (part. tr. Shehaby 1973); II. Natural Science; III. Mathematics; IV. Metaphysics (tr. Marmura 2005, with facing Arabic). The vast second *jumla*, known in Latin as the *Naturalia*, is further divided into eight sections (*funūn*), including the highly influential sections on physics (*fann* 1; known in Latin as the *Sufficientia*) and on the soul (*fann* 6) (ed. Rahman 1959). Among the many other surviving works are his classic medical treatise, the *Qānūn fī al-ṭibb* (*Canon of Medicine*) (ed. 1877/1970; Latin ed. 1507; part. tr. Gruner 1930/1999); the *Kitāb al-najāt* (*Book of Salvation* [*from Error*]) (ed. Dānishpāzhūh 1985; II.6 [on soul] tr. Rahman 1952); and the *Ishārāt wa-al-tanbīhāt* (*Remarks and Admonitions*) (ed. Forget 1892, Dunyā 1960; part. tr. Inati 1984, 1996; [Fr] tr. Goichon 1951), a philosophical summa in two parts: first logic, and second natural philosophy and metaphysics. Extensive excerpts from various works are translated in McGinnis and Reisman, *Classical Arabic Philosophy* (2007). The series *Avicenna latinus* has published much of the medieval Latin translation of the *Shifāʾ*, including the metaphysics (ed. Van Riet 1977–80) and the bulk of the *Naturalia*, including the *Sufficientia* (ed. Van Riet 1992) and the *Liber de anima* (ed. Van Riet 1968–72) (see Appendix B4).

Secondary sources. Janssens, *Annotated Bibliography* (1991), *First Supplement* (1999); Belo, *Chance and Determinism* (2007); Goodman, *Avicenna* (1992); Gutas, *Avicenna and the Aristotelian Tradition* (1988); Janssens, *Ibn Sina* (2006) [collected papers]; Janssens and De Smet (eds.), *Avicenna and his Heritage* (2002); Reisman and al-Rahīm (ed.), *Before and After Avicenna* (2003); Wisnovsky (ed.), *Aspects of Avicenna* (2001); Wisnovsky, *Avicenna's Metaphysics* (2003), "Avicenna and the Avicennian Tradition" (2005); BCPMA (Burrell); EI (Goichon); HIP (Inati, Nasr); REP (Kemal).

AZO (Azzo Portius, Soldanus) b. Bologna, *ca.* 1150; d. ca. 1230. Important legal scholar. Professor of civil law in Bologna from 1190. Author of the enormously influential *Summa Codicis*, a systematic summary of Justinian's code (ed. 1578/1966; excerpts tr. Maitland 1895/1978), supplemented by the *Apparatus ad Codicem* or *Lectura* (ed. 1577/1966). Secondary sources. DBI (Fiorelli); CALMA.

AL-BAGHDĀDI ('Abd al-Laṭīf ibn al-Labbād) b. Baghdad, 1162/3; d. Baghdad, 1231/2. Wide-ranging scholar in medicine, mathematics, and philosophy. Studied in Baghdad; subsequently traveled widely throughout the Middle East, returning to his native city only shortly before his death. Principal extant philosophical work is the *Fī ʿilm mā baʿd al-ṭabīʿa* (*On the Science of Metaphysics*) (part. ed. and [German] tr. Neuwirth 1976). Secondary sources. EI (Stern) [= BEIP (Leaman)].

AL-BAGHDĀDĪ (Abū al-Barakāt) b. Balad (near Mosul), *ca.* 1077; d. Baghdad, *ca.* 1166. Philosopher and physician. Born into a Jewish family; converted to Islam late in life. Famed in his life chiefly for his medical accomplishment, although his medical works, if any survive, have not been studied. Author of the voluminous *Kitāb al-muʿtabar* (*Book of Personal Reflection*) (ed. 1938–9), a work modeled on Avicenna's *Shifāʾ*, ranging over logic, natural science, and metaphysics.

Secondary sources. Davidson, *On Intellect* (1992); Pines, *Studies* (1979); Strousma, "Maimonidean Controversy" (1993); DSB (Pines); EI (Pines); REP (Langermann).

BAHMANYĀR (Abū al-Ḥasan ibn al-Marzubān) b. Azerbaijan; d. 1067. Leading disciple of Avicenna. A Zoroastrian. Most important work is a lengthy exposition of Avicenna, his *Kitāb al-taḥṣīl* (*The Summation*) (ed. Mutahhari 1970; brief excerpt tr. Rowson, in Nasr and Aminrazavi, *Anthology* 1999). Also extant are his *Mā baʿd al-ṭabīʿa* (*Metaphysics*) and *Kitāb fī-marātib al-wujūd* (*On the Grades of Existence*) (both ed. and [German] tr. Poper 1851). Avicenna's *Kitāb al-mubāḥathāt* (*Discussions*) consists mainly in answers to questions raised by Bahmanyār.

Secondary sources. Janssens, "Faithful Disciple?" (2003), "Revision of Ibn Sīnā" (2007); Reisman, *Making of the Avicennan Tradition* (2002); BEIP (Kalin and Aminrazavi); EI (Rahman).

BAHYA IBN PAQŪDĀ (ben Joseph ibn Pakuda) *fl.* Saragossa, mid-eleventh century. Founding figure of Jewish pietism. Rabbinic judge, probably the author of a collection of Hebrew hymns. Principal work is the *Al-Hidāya ʾilā farāʾiḍ al-qulūb* (*Guidance to the Duties of the Heart*) [1040] (ed. Yahuda 1912), translated initially into Hebrew (*Hovot ha-Levavot*) and then into all the major European languages (tr. Mansoor 1973).

Secondary sources. Eisenberg, "Reason and Emotion" (1981); Goodman, "Free Will" (1983); Vajda, "Dialogue" (1937), *Théologie ascétique* (1947); REP (Goodman); Sirat.

BALDUS DE UBALDIS b. Perugia, *ca.* 1327; d. Pavia, 1400. Roman lawyer and canonist. Studied law in Pisa. Lectured at Perugia from *ca.* 1351, with subsequent stints at Pisa, Florence, Padua, and Pavia. A practical legal theorist, whose theoretical views emerge from the large collection of *consilia* he produced regarding specific cases. Grounded the sovereignty of the commonwealth in the political authority of the people. Articulated an influential theory of just war. Principal works are the five volumes of *Consilia* (ed. 1575, etc.) and a large collection of commentaries on various legal texts (ed. 1599/2004, etc.).

Secondary sources. Canning, *Political Thought* (1987); Pennington, "Consilia" (1988); Wahl, "Foundations of the Nation-State" (1977); CALMA; CHLMP.

AL-BĀQILLĀNĪ (Muḥammad ibn al-Ṭayyib) b. Basra; d. 1013. Influential Ashʿarite theologian. Lived as an adult in Baghdad, serving for a time as judge. Among his extant works are the *Iʿjāz al-Qurʾān* (*The Uniqueness of the Quran*) (part. tr. von Grunebaum 1950) and the *Kitāb al-tamhīd* (*Book of Introduction*) (ed. McCarthy 1957).

Secondary source. EI (McCarthy).

BARLAAM THE CALABRIAN b. Seminara (Calabria), *ca.* 1290; d. Avignon (?), 1348. Byzantine theologian, philosopher, and mathematician. A monk in his youth, he moved to Constantinople in 1330, becoming *hegoumenos* of the Akataleptos monastery until 1341. Served as an ambassador in discussions with the Western Church. His involvement in various theological controversies led to the condemnation of some of his writings, and he subsequently converted to Catholicism in 1342, becoming bishop of Gerace (Calabria) until his death. Extant work in Greek includes eight letters (ed. and [Ital] tr. Phyrigos, in *Dalla controversia* 2005), often with substantial philosophical content, especially the exchange with Gregory Palamas (ed. and [Ital] tr. Phyrigos 1975); a series of philosophically interesting anti-Latin works (ed. and [Ital] tr. Phyrigos 1998); the *Logistike*, concerning mathematics (ed. and [German] tr. Carelos 1996); and two treatises on solar eclipses (ed. and [Fr] tr. Mogenet *et al.* 1977). His only purely philosophical work known to be genuine is the *Solutions to the Questions Addressed by Georgios Lapithes* [*ca.* 1334] (ed. Sinkewicz 1981).

Secondary sources. Demetrakopoulos, "Further Evidence" (2003); Hogg, *Ethica secundum stoicos* (1997); Ierodiakonou, "Anti-Logical Movement" (2002); Sinkewicz, "Knowledge of God" (1982); ODB (Talbot).

BARTHOLOMAEUS ANGLICUS b. England before 1203; d. 1272. Encyclopedist. A Franciscan friar. Perhaps studied at Oxford. Arts master at Paris in 1224. Served as lector at Magdeburg in Saxonia from 1331. Provincial minister of Austria in 1247, then Bohemia before 1255 and Saxonia from 1262 to 1272. Famous for his encyclopedic *De proprietatibus rerum* [*ca.* 1245] (ed. 1601/1964; Bks. III–IV [soul and body] ed. Long 1979), in nineteen books, which circulated widely and was translated into many languages including English [1398] (tr. John Trevisa 1975–88).

Secondary sources. Seymour, *Bartholomaeus Anglicus* (1992); CALMA; DMA (Beyer de Ryke); ODNB (Seymour); Weijers.

BARTHOLOMEW OF BOLOGNA b. Bologna; d. after 1294. Franciscan theologian. Studied theology in Paris in the 1260s, apparently serving as regent master in the 1270s. Returned to Bologna in the 1280s, becoming provincial minister there in 1285. Extant works include a *Sentences* commentary (unedited), a *Tractatus de luce* (ed. Squadrani 1932), various disputed questions, including *De fide* (ed. Mückshoff 1940), and various sermons (unedited).

Secondary sources. Longpré, "Bartolommeo di Bologna" (1923); DBI; CALMA; FA; Glorieux.

BARTHOLOMEW OF BRUGES b. *ca.* 1286; d. 1356. Arts master and physician. Master of arts in Paris from 1307 to 1309. Studied medicine at Montpellier, becoming regent master in 1329. Extant works include questions on the *Physics*, *De anima*, *De generatione et corruptione*, and *Economics* (all unedited), a short commentary on Averroes's paraphrase of the *Poetics* (ed. Dahan 1980), and various sophismata/disputed questions (part. ed. in secondary sources).

Secondary sources. Ebbesen and Pinborg, "Sophisma on the Nature of Logic" (1981); Pattin, *Sens agens* (1988); Roos, "Die Kontroverse" (1974); CALMA; Weijers.

BARTHOLOMEW OF SALERNO *fl.* mid-twelfth century. Leading figure in the Salerno medical school. Author of the *Practica Bartholomaei* (ed. de Renzi, in *Collectio Salernitana*

IV [1856/1967]) and of commentaries on various Greek and Arabic medical texts (unedited).

Secondary sources. Jacquart, "Aristotelian Thought in Salerno" (1988); CALMA; Dronke.

BARTOLUS OF SASSOFERRATO (Saxoferrato) b. near Sassoferrato, 1313/14; d. Perugia, 1357. Famous civil lawyer, both in Italy and subsequently throughout Europe. Studied at Perugia and then Bologna. Professor at Pisa from 1339, and then Perugia from 1342, where Baldus was his student and then his colleague. His many works were prized for their practical character and clarity. Principal works are his various academic disputations or *Quaestiones* [1333–57], assorted commentaries or *Lecturae* [1339–52], and his advisory opinions or *Consilia*. These are printed separately in various Renaissance editions, and collected, more or less extensively, together with many falsely ascribed works, in various *Opera omnia* (ed. 1481–2 etc.). A modern edition is available of the *Tractatus testimoniorum* (ed. Lepsius 2003). Excerpts have been translated on conflicting laws (tr. Beale, in *Conflict of Laws* 1914/1979; tr. Clarence Smith, in "Bartolo" 1970) and just war (tr. Reichberg *et al.*, in *Ethics of War* 2006).

Secondary sources. Ryan, "Bartolus and Free Cities" (2000); Segoloni (ed.), *Bartolo da Sassoferrato* (1962); Sheedy, *Bartolus on Social Conditions* (1942); Woolf, *Bartolus of Sassoferrato* (1913); Ullmann, "Bartolus on Customary Law" (1940); CALMA; REP (Gordon).

BEDE b. Northumbria, 672/3; d. Jarrow, 735. Historian, theologian, poet, scientist. Placed in the Benedictine monastery at Wearmouth at age seven; spent his life there and at the sister monastery of Jarrow. Most famous for his history of England [731], but also important for his biblical commentaries (excerpts tr. Holder and Foley 1999), his treatises *De natura rerum* and *De temporum ratione* (tr. Wallis 1999), and various grammar handbooks. His works are published in the *Corpus Christianorum*.

Secondary sources. Brown, *Bede, the Venerable* (1987), *Bede the Educator* (1996); DeGregorio (ed.), *Innovation and Tradition* (2006); Germann, *De temporum ratione* (2006); Ward, *The Venerable Bede* (1990); CALMA; ODNB (Campbell).

BERENGAR OF TOURS b. Tours, *ca.* 1000; d. Tours, *ca.* 1088. Theologian, famous for his controversial teachings on the Eucharist. Studied at Chartres under Fulbert, eventually becoming master of the school of St. Martin in Tours. Controversy over his Eucharistic views – particularly his claim that no material change is necessary for Christ to be present in the host – began in 1049–54 and flared up twice more in 1059 and 1079. His principal extant work is a response to his critic Lanfranc of Bec, the *Rescriptum contra Lanfrancum* [1059] (ed. Huygens 1988); much of his position is inferred from works written against him.

Secondary sources. Chadwick, "Ego Berengarius" (1989); de Montclos, *Lanfranc et Bérenger* (1971); Holopainen, *Dialectic and Theology* (1996); Liebeschütz, "Debate on Philosophical Learning" (1970); CALMA; DMA (Brouwer).

BERNARD OF AREZZO (Bernardus Aretinus) b. Tuscany; d. 1342. Franciscan theologian. Lectured on the *Sentences* in Paris, *ca.* 1335. None of his writings is extant; his views are known only through two notorious letters (and fragments of seven more) written to him by Nicholas of Autrecourt [1335/7] (ed. and tr. de Rijk 1994). Although overshadowed by Nicholas, Bernard's views are themselves interesting for their skeptical tendencies.

Secondary sources. Kaluza, *Nicolas d'Autrécourt* (1995); Tachau, *Vision and Certitude* (1988).

BERNARD OF AUVERGNE b. Gannat (Auvergne); d. after 1307. Dominican theologian. Bachelor of theology at Paris, *ca.* 1294–7, perhaps becoming master. His principal works are his defenses of Aquinas against Henry of Ghent, James of Viterbo (both unedited), and Godfrey of Fontaines (part. ed. Stella, in "Teologi e teologia" 1957) [all dating 1298/1315]. Also extant is a brief commentary on Bk. I of the *Sentences* commentary (unedited), of uncertain attribution.

Secondary sources. Friedman, "Dominican Quodlibetal Literature" (2007); Pattin, "La structure de l'être" (1962); Zuckerman, "Some Texts on Papal Power" (1982); CALMA; Kaeppeli; Roensch.

BERNARD OF CHARTRES (Bernardus Carnotensis) b. Brittany; d. *ca.* 1130. Influential teacher. Master at the cathedral school of Chartres before 1117; subsequently chancellor. Perhaps the elder brother of Thierry of Chartres. Only extant work is a commentary on the *Timaeus* (ed. Dutton 1991).

Secondary sources. CALMA; Dronke; DSB (Jeauneau).

BERNARD OF CLAIRVAUX b. Fontaines-les-Dijon, 1090; d. Clairvaux, 1153. Mystic and leading spiritual authority of the twelfth century, deeply influential on the character of monastic life and on wider developments in philosophy and theology. Studied at Châtillon. Joined the Cistercian order at Cîteaux in 1113, and two years later was named abbot of the new monastery at Clairvaux, a position he held until his death, despite many opportunities for ecclesiastical advancement. Traveled widely, preaching throughout Western Europe. Involved in disputes with Peter Abaelard (1140) and Gilbert of Poitiers (1147–8). His own theology was conservative, firmly rooted in authority, eschewing philosophical subtleties. Most of his writings – sermons and treatises – focus on a moral and contemplative reading of Scripture, as in his long, unfinished *Sermones super Cantica canticorum* [1135–53]. His most influential philosophical work is the *De gratia et libero arbitrio* [*ca.* 1127]; his *De consideratione* [his last work, *ca.* 1148] influenced later medieval political thought. A modern edition of his complete works is available (ed. Leclerq *et al.* 1957–77, 8 vols.), as are translations of many of his writings.

Secondary sources. Association Bourguignonne, *Saint Bernard théologien* (1956); Brague (ed.), *Saint Bernard* (1993); Casey, *Thirst for God* (1988); Doyle, *Bernard of Clairvaux and the Schools* (2005); Elm (ed.), *Bernhard von Clairvaux* (1994); Evans, *Mind of St. Bernard* (1983), *Bernard of Clairvaux* (2000); Gilson, *The Mystical Theology* (1940); Leclercq, *Monks and Love* (1979); McGuire, *The Difficult Saint* (1991); BCPMA (McGuire); CALMA; REP (Murphy).

BERNARD LOMBARDI *fl.* 1323–32. Dominican theologian. Lectured on the *Sentences* in Paris in 1327–8, defending a broadly Thomistic line. His commentary on all four books is extant in six mss., in several redactions (unedited). Probably regent master in 1331–2, from when survives a *Quodlibet* (unedited).

Secondary sources. Koch, *Durandus de S. Porciano* (1927); Porebski, "La question" (1973); CALMA; Kaeppeli.

BERNARD SILVESTRIS b. *ca.* 1100; d. *ca.* 1160. Teacher, poet, Platonist. Taught at the cathedral school at Tours. Principal work is a prose-poem on creation and providence, the *Cosmographia* [1147] (ed. Dronke 1978; tr. Wetherbee 1973). Also extant is a long poem concerned with fate, the *Mathematicus* [*ca.* 1150] (ed. and tr. Stone 1996). Perhaps also by Bernard are two earlier commentaries, on the *Aeneid* [*ca.* 1125/30] (ed. Jones and Jones 1977; tr. Schreiber and Maresca 1979) and on Martianus Capella's *De nuptiis* [*ca.* 1130/5] (ed. Westra 1986).

Secondary sources. Stock, *Myth and Science* (1972); CALMA; DMA (Ricklin); Dronke.

BERNARD OF TRILIA b. Nimes, *ca.* 1240; d. Avignon, 1292. Thomistic theologian. Entered the Dominican order as a young man and studied in Paris *ca.* 1260/5. Lectured at various Dominican houses of study in southern France before returning to Paris in 1279 to lecture on the *Sentences* in 1281–3 (commentary not extant), becoming master from 1283 to 1286. Extant works include several disputed questions, including sets on the soul's cognition when separated from body [*ca.* 1285] (ed. Künzle 1969) and when joined to body (part. ed. Goris, in *Kritik* 1998), three *Quodlibeta* (part. ed. André, in "Les *Quodlibeta*" 1921), and various biblical commentaries.

Secondary sources. Friedman, "Dominican Quodlibetal Literature" (2007); CALMA; DMA; Kaeppeli; Roensch; Weijers.

BERNARDINO OF SIENA b. Massa (Tuscany), 1380; d. Aquila, 1444. Popular preacher and moralist. Joined the Franciscan order in 1402. Famous for his preaching tours throughout north and central Italy. Accused of heresy in 1423, but subsequently acquitted. Canonized as saint in 1450. His sermons and treatises have been edited in a modern nine-volume edition (ed. 1950–65).

Secondary sources. Origo, *World of San Bernardino* (1962); McAodha, "The Nature and Efficacy of Preaching" (1967); Mormando, *The Preacher's Demons* (1999); Thureau-Dangin, *Un prédicateur populaire* (1926); CALMA; DBI (Manselli).

BERTHOLD OF MOOSBURG b. *ca.* 1300; d. after 1361. German Dominican. Taught between 1335 and 1361 at the Dominican *studium* in Cologne, succeeding Eckhart as its head. Advocated a Platonism drawn from Proclus, in preference to Aristotelianism. Sole surviving work is a vast commentary on Proclus's *Elements of Theology* (ed. Pagnoni-Sturlese and Sturlese 1984–, 9 vols.), the only such commentary known from the Middle Ages.

Secondary sources. De Libera, *Introduction à la mystique rhénane* (1984); Iremadze, *Konzeptionen des Denkens im Neuplatonismus* (2004); BCPMA (Milem); CALMA; Kaeppeli; Lohr.

BESSARION b. Trebizond; d. Ravenna, 1472. Cardinal, theologian, translator. Educated in Constantinople and Mistra, becoming a monk in 1423 and subsequently *hegoumenos* of the monastery of St. Basil in Constantinople. Appointed metropolitan of Nicaea in 1437. Converted to Catholicism in 1439; elected cardinal that same year. After a trip to Greece in 1439–40, he spent the rest of his career in Italy. Led a circle in Rome devoted to Greek–Latin and Latin–Greek translations (see Appendix B5). His monumental *In calumniatorem Platonis* [1469] (ed. Mohler, in *Kardinal Bessarion* 1923–42/1967) defended Plato against the attacks of George Trapezountios. Other writings are edited in PG 161.

Secondary sources. Mohler, *Kardinal Bessarion* (1923–42/1967); Monfasani, *Byzantine Scholars* (1995); Moraux, *D'Aristote à Bessarion* (1970); ODB (Talbot).

AL-BIṬRŪJĪ, Nūr al-Dīn Abū Ishāq (Alpetragius) b. Morocco; d. Seville, *ca.* 1204. Influential astronomer, author of the *Kitāb al-hay'a* (*De motibus coelorum*), which would be translated into Latin and Hebrew (ed. [Latin] Carmody 1952).

Secondary source. EI (Vernet).

BLASIUS OF PARMA (Pelacanus, de Pelacanis, Biagio Pelacanbii) b. Parma, *ca.* 1345; d. Parma, 1416. Heterodox philosopher whose views often pushed the limits of medieval tolerance. Received his doctorate from Pavia *ca.* 1374, spent time in Paris, taught all across the arts curriculum in Bologna, Padua, Pavia, and Florence. Reprimanded by the bishop of Pavia in 1396, without evident impact on his career, although his subsequent works are more cautious. Popularized the logic of Ockham and William Heytesbury, as well as the natural philosophy of John Buridan and Albert of Saxony. Most notoriously, he argued for the materiality and mortality of the human soul. His focus in natural philosophy is quantitative, after the Oxford Calculators. Many works survive, including two works on the soul [1382; 1385] (both ed. Federici Vescovini 1974), two redactions of the *Physics* [1382/8; 1397] (unedited), various works on logic, including a set of questions on Paul of Spain (ed. Biard and Federici Vescovini 2001), and works on quantitative natural philosophy, including questions on Bradwardine's *Tractatus proportionum* (ed. Biard and Rommevaux 2006) and a *quaestio* on the intension and remission of forms (ed. Federici Vescovini 1994).

Secondary sources. Barocelli, "Per Biagio Pelacani" (1992) [bibliography]; Federici Vescovini, *Astrologia e scienza* (1979); Federici Vescovini (ed.), *Filosofia, scienza e astrologia* (1992); CALMA; DMA (Biard); REP (Federici Vescovini); Weijers.

BOETHIUS OF DACIA (Dacus) b. Denmark, *ca.* 1240; d. after 1277. A leading arts master at Paris in the late thirteenth century and a key figure among the "Radical Aristotelians," so-called because of their aggressive defense of various philosophical theses, seemingly at the expense of Church doctrine. He was in Paris from 1262, teaching in the arts faculty there from as early as 1265 until *ca.* 1277, when he was one of the main targets of Stephen Tempier's condemnation. All his works are prior to this date. Subsequently seems to have left the arts faculty, perhaps joining the Dominican order. Treatises on the eternity of the world and on human happiness (both tr. Wippel 1987) were especially controversial. A leading figure among the speculative grammarians for his works on logic and language, including sets of questions on the *Topics* and on Priscian (tr. Senape

McDermott 1980), and a collection of sophismata (part. tr. CTMPT I). The complete works are available in a modern edition (ed. J. Pinborg *et al.* 1969–).

Secondary sources. Ebbesen, "Science is a Serious Game" (2000); Pinborg, *Medieval Semantics* (1984); BCPMA (Bazán); CALMA; DMA (de Libera); Kaeppeli; REP (Ebbesen); Weijers.

BONAVENTURE (John of Fidanza) b. near Orvieto, *ca.* 1217; d. Lyon, 1274. Franciscan theologian and the most eminent counterweight to the prevailing Aristotelian tendencies of the scholastic era. Studied in Paris from 1235, where he was master of arts *ca.* 1243. Joined the Franciscan order in 1243/4, and after four years of study began to lecture and hold disputations [1248–54]. Served as master of theology from 1254 to 1257, at which time he was elected minister general of the Franciscan order. His remaining years were largely occupied with administrative duties, culminating in his appointment as cardinal in 1273. His writings from after 1257, which are strikingly unscholastic in style, are focused on moral and spiritual questions, and are often hostile to the Aristotelianism of the universities.

Principal academic works are his lengthy *Sentences* commentary [1250–2] ("Conscience and synderesis" [II.39] tr. CTMPT II; part. tr. *The Franciscan Archive*: www.franciscan-archive.org/bonaventura/sent.html) and three sets of disputed questions: *De scientia Christi* [*ca.* 1254] (tr. Hayes 1992); *De mysterio Trinitatis* [*ca.* 1257] (tr. Hayes 1979), and *De perfectione evangelica*, a defense of the mendicant orders. His most-read works are various shorter, less technical opuscula, above all the *Itinerarium mentis in Deum* [1259] (tr. Boehner 1993), and also the *De reductione artium ad theologiam* (tr. Hayes 1996), the *Breviloquium* (tr. de Vinck 1960–70), and his sermon *Unus est magister vester Christus* (tr. CTMPT III) (the last three from his years as master of theology). The major work from the end of his life is the *Collationes in Hexaemeron* [1273]. The complete works are available in a modern edition (ed. 1882–1902).

Secondary sources. Bougerol, *Introduction* (1st edn tr. 1964; 2nd edn 1988); Emery, "Bonaventure's Doctrine of the Cardinal Virtues" (1983); Gilson, *Philosophy of Bonaventure* (tr. 1965); Quinn, *Historical Constitution* (1973); Speer, "Bonaventure and the Question of a Medieval Philosophy" (1997); BCPMA (Speer); CALMA; DBI (Gregory); REP (Kent); SEP (Noone and Houser).

BRUNETTO LATINI b. Florence, *ca.* 1220; d. Florence, 1294. Encyclopedist and rhetorician. A prominent political figure in Florence and an important influence on Dante. Exiled in France from 1260 to 1266, he wrote during this period an Italian treatise on rhetoric based on Cicero (ed. Maggini 1915); an incomplete didactic poem *Il Tesoretto* (ed. and tr. Holloway 1981); and in French his encyclopedic three-book *Li livres dou Tresor* (ed. Carmody 1948/1975 etc.).

Secondary sources. Holloway, *Brunetto Latini* (1986), *Twice-Told Tales* (1993); DMA (Connochie).

BULGARUS b. Bologna; d. after 1159. Leading scholar of Roman law. Active teaching in Bologna by 1141. Principal work is *De regulis iuris* (ed. Beckhaus 1856/1967).

Secondary sources. Kantorowicz and Buckland, *Studies in the Glossators* (1938); CALMA; DBI (Paradisi).

BURCHARD OF WORMS b. *ca.* 950; d. 1025. Legal authority. Educated in Koblenz (Rhineland), eventually becoming bishop of Worms. Compiled an important collection of canon law, the *Decretum* or *Brocardus* [1008–11], which would remain authoritative until Gratian. His works are edited in PL 140.
Secondary sources. BBK (Bautz); CALMA.

BURGUNDIO OF PISA b. Pisa, *ca.* 1110; d. 1193. Jurist, physician, translator. Served as ambassador from Pisa to Constantinople. Known for his translations from Greek (see Appendices B1-2), including John of Damascus's *De fide orthodoxa* [1154/5] (ed. Buytaert 1955) and Nemesius of Emesa's *De natura hominis* [1165] (ed. Verbeke and Moncho 1975), as well as various patristic texts, medical treatises by Galen and others, and most likely translations of Aristotle's *De generatione et corruptione* and parts of the *Ethics*.
Secondary sources. Bossier, "L'élaboration du vocabulaire philosophique" (1997); Classen, *Burgundio von Pisa* (1974); Vuillemin-Diem and Rashed, "Burgundio de Pise" (1997); CALMA; DBI (Liotta); DMA (Bonmariage); Dronke.

CAJETAN OF THIENE (Gaetano, Caietanus) b. Gaeta, 1387; d. Padua, 1465. Italian natural philosopher. Student of Paul of Venice, and his successor as professor of philosophy – first logic, then natural philosophy – at Padua from 1422 until 1462. Not to be confused with the later saint by the same name, or with the Renaissance Thomistic theologian Cardinal Cajetan (Thomas de Vio). His influence can be gauged from the many Renaissance editions of his work. These include Aristotelian commentaries – on the *Physics* [1439] (ed. 1476, etc.), the *De caelo* (ed. 1476, etc.), the *Meteora* (ed. 1476, etc.) and the *De anima* (ed. 1475, etc.) – as well as treatises on William Heytesbury's *Regulae* and *Sophismata* (ed. 1494) and on the intention and remission of forms (ed. 1491).
Secondary sources. Silvestro da Valsanzibio, *Vita e dottrina* (1949); Bottin, "Gaetano da Thiene e i 'calculatores'" (1983); BCPMA (Lahey); CALMA; CHLMP; Lohr.

CAMBIOLUS OF BOLOGNA *fl.* 1330s. Arts master at the University of Bologna. Regarded as an Averroist. His extant works consist in five relatively long disputed questions on natural philosophy (ed. Kuksewicz, in *Averroïsme bolonais* 1965).
Secondary source. CALMA.

CANDIDUS WIZO (Hwita) b. England, prob. before 770; *fl.* 793–803. Early medieval theologian. A student of Alcuin, he journeyed to the continent in 793, eventually becoming part of Charlemagne's court circle. Extant works include *De passione domini* (PL 106) and perhaps several other theological works from the Carolingian circle (ed. Marenbon, in *Circle of Alcuin* 1981).
Secondary sources. CALMA; ODNB (Marenbon).

CATHERINE OF SIENA (Benincasa) b. Siena, 1347; d. Rome, 1380. Mystic and Church reformer, canonized in 1461. Joined the Dominican tertiaries at age seventeen, living a life of extreme asceticism and serving the poor and sick. Entered the political sphere in her last decade, actively campaigning for Church reform and an end to the papal schism. Extensive correspondence from this period survives (ed. Misciattelli and Tommaseo 1913–22; tr. Noffke 2000–). Her most important work, based on her mystical experiences, is the *Libro della divina dottrina* or *Dialog* (ed. Fiorilli and Caramella 1928; tr. Noffke 1980). Raymond of Capua, a devoted disciple and later Dominican minister general, recounts her life in the *Legenda maior* (ed. Jungmayr 2004; tr. Kearns 1980).

Secondary sources. Luongo, *Saintly Politics* (2006); Undset, *Catherine of Siena* (1954); CALMA; DBI (Dupré Theseider); DMA (Mornet).

CHRISTINE DE PIZAN b. Venice, 1364; d. Poissy (Paris), *ca.* 1430. Poet, moralist, political essayist. Lived in France from a young age, in the circle of the French court. A widow with three children at twenty-five, she came to support herself by writing. Among her most philosophically significant works are the *Livre de la cité des dames* [1404] (ed. Hicks and Moreau 1986; tr. Richards 1982); *Le livre des trois vertus* [1405] (ed. Willard and Hicks 1989; tr. Lawson 1985); and the *Livre du corps de policie* [1407] (ed. Kennedy 1998; tr. Forhan 1994). Various anthologies of her work are also available (tr. Willard 1994, Blumenfeld-Kosinski 1997).

Secondary sources. Kennedy, *Bibliographical Guide* (1984); Birk, *Biblical Wisdom* (2005); Forhan, *Political Theory* (2002); Richards (ed.), *Reinterpreting Christine de Pizan* (1992); Willard, *Christine de Pizan* (1984); CALMA; DBI (Tilliette); DMA (Dulac).

CLAREMBALD OF ARRAS b. *ca.* 1110; d. *ca.* 1187. Teacher and philosophical commentator. Studied under Hugh of St. Victor and Thierry of Chartres, probably at Paris. Served as provost and archdeacon in Arras, and later as chaplain in Laon. Author of commentaries on Boethius's *De trinitate* and *De hebdomadibus*, both *ca.* 1157–8 (tr. George and Fortin 2002; ed. Häring 1965), and a *Tractatulus super librum Genesis* [1160/70] (ed. Häring 1965) that serves as a sequel to Thierry's *De sex dierum operibus*.

Secondary sources. Fortin, *Boethian Commentator* (1995); Häring, "Creation and Creator" (1955); CALMA; DMA (Brouwer); Dronke; REP (Brown).

CONSTANTINE THE AFRICAN b. Tunis; d. Monte Cassino, 1087. Important translator of Arabic medical texts. Studied medicine in Tunis, then settled in Italy and converted to Christianity. Later entered the Benedictine monastery of Monte Cassino. Most influential of the many texts he translated was 'Alī ibn al-'Abbās al-Majūsī's *Kitāb kāmil al-ṣinā'a al-ṭibbīyya* (*The Complete Book of the Medical Art*), which Constantine entitled the *Pantegni* (ed. 1515).

Secondary sources. Burnett and Jacquart (eds.), *Constantine the African* (1994).

COSTA BEN LUCA, *see* Quṣta ibn Lūqā.

DANIEL OF MORLEY b. Norfolk, *ca.* 1140; d. *ca.* 1210. Champion of Islamic thought. Studied in Oxford and Paris. Traveled to Toledo, where he studied Arabic philosophy and science with Gerard of Cremona. Returned to England *ca.* 1187, bringing this new learning with him. Sole extant work is the *Philosophia*, or *De naturis inferiorum et superiorum* [before 1187] (ed. Maurach 1979).

Secondary sources. Burnett, *Introduction of Arabic Learning* (1997); Silverstein, "Daniel of Morley" (1948); DMA (Beyer de Ryke); Dronke; ODNB (Burnett).

DANTE ALIGHIERI b. Florence, 1265; d. Ravenna, 1321. Italian poet who found consolation in philosophy after the death of his beloved Beatrice. A prominent member of the ruling class in Florence, forced into exile by political events in 1302. Although outside both academia and religious orders, Dante was keenly interested in philosophy and was particularly influenced by the work of Aquinas. His major poems, most famously the epic *Divine Comedy*, are infused with philosophical ideas. Also produced a series of explicitly philosophical (although non-technical) works, most importantly the *Convivio* [1304–7] (tr. Lansing 1990, etc.), an extended reflection on the value of philosophy, and the *De monarchia* [*ca.* 1318] (ed. and tr. Shaw 1995, etc.), a defense of absolute monarchy that gives voice to his disenchantment with the republicanism of Florence. These and other philosophical works are edited, with commentary, in the *Opere minori* (ed. Vasoli et al. 1979–84).

Secondary sources. Boyde, *Dante Philomythes and Philosopher* (1981), *Perception and Passion in Dante's Comedy* (1993), *Human Vices and Human Worth in Dante's Comedy* (2000); Cassell, *The* Monarchia *Controversy* (2004); Gilson, *Dante and Philosophy* (tr. 1949); Imbach, *Dante* (1996); Minio-Paluello, "Dante's Reading of Aristotle" (1980); Moevs, *The Metaphysics of Dante's Comedy* (2005); Nardi, *Saggi di filosofia Dantesca* (1967), *Dante e la cultura medievale* (1985); BCPMA (Noone); DBI (D'Addario); REP (Perler); SEP (Wetherbee).

DAVID OF DINANT b. Dinant (Belgium); d. *ca.* 1214. Physician and philosopher, censured for his interpretation of Aristotle. Probably master of arts at Paris. Translated many Aristotelian texts from the Greek, manuscripts of which he discovered while traveling in Greece. Served as chaplain to Innocent III *ca.* 1206. Condemned for heresy by a Parisian synod in 1210 for his pantheistic view that matter, intellect, and God are really identical. All that remains of his writings are fragments from his lectures in Paris, known as the *Quaternuli* (ed. Kurdziałek 1963, Casadei 2008).

Secondary sources. Maccagnolo, "Beginning of Aristotelianism" (1988); Vuillemin-Diem, "Aristoteles Latinus" (2003); DMA (Casadei); Dronke; Weijers.

DĀWŪD IBN KHALAF b. Kufa (Iraq), 815/18; d. Baghdad, 884. Founder of the Zāhiriyya school of religious law, which insists on a literal reading of the Quran, against the imposition of any rational analysis. Although numerous works are attested, none are extant.

Secondary source. EI (Schacht).

DĀWŪD IBN MARWĀN (al-Muqammis) b. Raqqa (Syria); *fl.* ninth century. Early Judaeo-Arabic philosopher and theologian. A prolific author, most of whose work has been lost. Converted to Christianity and subsequently back to Judaism. Authored several anti-Christian polemics, surviving only in fragments. His extant philosophical work is the ʿ*Ishrūn maqāla* (*Twenty Chapters*) (ed. and tr. Stroumsa 1989).

Secondary source. REP (Stroumsa).

DEMETRIOS KYDONES b. Thessaloniki, 1320/5; d. Crete, 1397/8. Scholar and translator. Deprived of his family's wealth by a political uprising in 1345, he entered into political service in Constantinople. Translated many Latin works into Greek (see Appendix B5), particularly Thomas Aquinas, which propelled the rise of Thomism in Byzantium. Defended Latin Aristotelianism, using it to attack the theology of Gregory Palamas. An advocate for unity with Rome (see tr. Likoudis 1983); converted to Catholicism in 1357. A large body of correspondence is extant (ed. Loenertz 1956–60; tr. [German] Tinnefeld 1981–2003), as is an essay on *The Disdain for Death* (ed. Deckelmann 1901). Various pro-Latin apologetics and anti-Palamite treatises are also extant (PG 154 [some works here are spurious]). His younger brother Prochoros Kydones was also an active translator and advocate of Latin thought.

Secondary sources. Kianka, *Demetrius Cydones* (1981); Demetracopoulos, "Translation of the *Summa theologiae*" (1982); BBK (Todt); ODB (Kianka).

DENYS THE CARTHUSIAN (Dionysius, de Leeuwis) b. Rijkel (Belgium), 1402/3; d. 1472. Encyclopedic scholar and leading Albertist. Studied at the University of Cologne from 1421, becoming master of arts in 1424. Subsequently entered the Carthusian monastery at Roermond, where he spent most of the remainder of his life. His voluminous writings (ed. 1896–1935, in 43 vols.) include commentaries on the whole Bible, on Boethius, pseudo-Dionysius, Aquinas, Lombard's *Sentences*, as well as various compendia of his own philosophical and theological views, and over 900 sermons. Among his most important philosophical works are his *De lumine christianae theoriae* [*ca.* 1451] and *Elementatio philosophica* [*ca.* 1465]. An edition of *Opera selecta* is underway (ed. Emery 1991–).

Secondary sources. Palazzo, "Ulrich of Strasbourg and Denys the Carthusian" (2004–6); Wassermann, *Dionysius der Kartäuser* (1996); BCPMA (Emery); REP (Emery).

DIETRICH OF FREIBERG (Theodoric, Thierry, Theodoricus Teutonicus, of Saxony) b. Freiberg, *ca.* 1250; d. after 1310. Dominican scholar, active in natural philosophy, metaphysics, and theology. Friar from an early age; taught at the Dominican convent in Freiberg *ca.* 1271. Studied in Paris, probably 1272–4, and after time in Germany returned to Paris to lecture on the *Sentences*, beginning in 1281. Returned to Germany, probably in 1293, as prior in Würzburg, and then as provincial superior of the German province. Returned again to Paris as master of theology from 1296/7 to 1300. His surviving works (ed. Flasch 1977–85 in 4 vols.) take the form of treatises rather than disputed questions or commentaries. Although inspired by Albert the Great and Aquinas, Dietrich's work is highly original. His treatises in natural philosophy – *De luce*, *De coloribus*, and *De iride* (part. tr. Wallace and Grant 1974) – have been extensively studied by historians of science, with the last of these containing the first known correct optical account of the rainbow. In metaphysics, his most important works are *De ente et essentia*, *De quiditatibus entium* (tr. Maurer, in "The *De quidditatibus*" 1956), *De intellectu et intelligibili* (tr. Führer 1992), and *De accidentibus*.

Secondary sources. Kandler *et al.* (eds.), *Dietrich von Freiberg* (1999); Flasch (ed.), *Von Meister Dietrich zu Meister Eckhart* (1987); Sturlese, *Dokumente und Forschungen zu Leben und Werke* (1984); Wallace, *Scientific Methodology* (1959); BCPMA (Teske); DMA (Suarez-Nani); DSB (Wallace); Kaeppeli; REP (Somerset); SEP (Führer).

ḌIRĀR IBN ʿAMR b. *ca.* 728; d. 815. Muʿtazilī theologian. Of Arab extraction. A student of Wāṣil ibn ʿAṭā. Taught in Basra, then Baghdad. A prolific and influential author, but none of his works is extant.

Secondary sources. van Ess, "Ḍirār b. ʿAmr" (1967–8); EI (van Ess).

DOMINICUS GUNDISALVI (Gundissalinus, Domingo González) *fl.* 1162–90. Translator and philosopher active in Toledo. Archdeacon of Cuéllar, and canon of the cathedral at Segovia and later Toledo. An important bridge between Islamic and Christian thought, both through translations of important Arabic treatises and through new works grounded in Islamic philosophy. Credited with translations of Solomon ibn Gabirol's *Fons vitae*, al-Ghazālī's *Intentions of the Philosophers* (*Summa theoricae philosophiae*), and Avicenna's *Metaphysics*, as well as various works by al-Fārābī and others (see Appendix B4). His philosophical treatises, largely syntheses of the works of others, include *De unitate* (ed. Correns 1891), *De scientiis* (ed. Alonso Alonso 1954), *De processione mundi* (ed. Bülow 1925; tr. Laumakis 2002), *De anima* (ed. Muckle 1940), and *De divisione philosophiae* (ed. Baur 1903). A recent suggestion that translator and philosopher are different men has not been generally accepted (see Rucquoi, "Gundisalvus ou Dominicus Gundisalvi" 1999, and the response by Fidora and Soto Bruna, "Algunas observaciones" 2001).

Secondary sources. Burnett, "Arabic into Latin" (2005); Fidora, *Wissenschaftstheorie* (2003); Jolivet, "Arabic Inheritance" (1988); BCPMA (Houser); DMA (Caiazzo); DSB (Kren).

DŪNASH IBN TĀMĪM (Abū Sahl) b. North Africa, *ca.* 900; d. *ca.* 960. Scientist, philologist, theologian. Student of Isaac Israeli. Author of a commentary on the Kabbalistic *Sefer Yesira* (*Book of Creation*) [955–6] (ed. and [Fr] tr. Vajda and Fenton 2002). Also known to have studied Hebrew and Arabic philology.

Secondary source. Sirat.

DURAND OF ST. POURÇAIN b. 1270/5; d. Meaux, 1334. Controversial Dominican theologian. Entered the Dominican order at Clermont. Studied at Paris, lecturing on the *Sentences* there, probably in 1307–8. Master of theology in 1312–13. Taught at the papal curia in Avignon between 1313 and 1317; subsequently appointed to a series of bishoprics. His principal and most controversial work is his *Sentences* commentary, in three versions. The first, stemming from lectures at a provincial Dominican *studium*, dates from 1304–7 (unedited). In response to criticism for departing from the teachings of Aquinas, Durand composed a second version in 1310–11 (unedited). Despite adhering more closely to Aquinas, this met with further criticisms and led to two formal investigations [1313–14, 1316/17]. These processes eventually gave rise to the third and best-known version [1317/27] (ed. 1571/1964, etc.; digital repr. on web at Thomas-Institut), in which Durand returned to many of his original views. Other extant works include five

Quodlibeta [1312–16] (ed. Stella 1965, Takada 1968) and questions *De habitibus* [prob. 1312–13] (ed. Koch 1930).

Secondary sources. Fumagalli Beonio Brocchieri, *Durando di S. Porziano* (1969); Emery, "Dieu, la foi et la théologie" (1999); Iribarren, *Durandus of St. Pourçain* (2005); Koch, *Durandus de S. Porciano* (1927); Lowe, *Contested Theological Authority* (2003); BCPMA (Friedman); DMA (Emery); Kaeppeli; REP (Fumagalli Beonio Brocchieri); Weijers.

DURANDELLUS (Nicholas Medensis) *fl.* 1320s. Author of a Thomistic critique of Durand of St. Pourçain, the *Evidentiae contra Durandum* [*ca.* 1325–6] (ed. Stella 2003).

Secondary source. Emery, "La théologie trinitaire" (1997).

ECKHART OF HOCHHEIM (Meister Eckhart) b. Hochheim (Thuringia) *ca.* 1260; d. prob. Avignon, 1328. Controversial scholastic philosopher, theologian, and mystic. Entered the Dominican order at a young age. Educated first at Cologne and then Paris from 1286. Prior of the Dominican convent at Erfurt from 1294 to 1298; subsequently master of theology at Paris in 1302–3. Provincial minister of the new Saxony province from 1303–11. Served as regent master for an exceptional second term in Paris in 1311–13; spent the following decade in Strasbourg, where he was active as a preacher. Returned to Cologne in 1324, where his views gave rise to an inquisition on suspicions of quietism and pantheism that culminated, after his death, in a papal bull [1329] condemning seventeen theses as heretical and another eleven as suspect of heresy. Long known for his German sermons and treatises, which are heavily influenced by Neoplatonic views of the intellect and reflect his more mystical side. His Latin works, discovered only in 1886, depict him as a more conventional academic philosopher. Most important of these is the incomplete *Opus tripartitum* [begun in 1305]. His most influential German work is *Das Buch der göttlichen Tröstung* [*ca.* 1315]. A critical edition of both the German and Latin works (ed. 1936–) is nearly complete.

Secondary sources. Largier, *Bibliographie* (1989); Albert, *These vom Sein* (1976); Davies, *Meister Eckhart* (1991); de Libera, *Introduction à la Mystique rhénane* (1984); Goris, *Einheit als Prinzip und Ziel* (1997); McGinn, *Mystical Thought* (2001); Mojsisch, *Meister Eckhart* (2001); BCPMA (Aertsen); DMA (de Libera); Kaeppeli; REP (Aertsen); SEP (Mojsisch and Summerell).

EDWARD UPTON b. Winchester; d. 1418/19. Logician. Studied the arts and theology at Oxford. Principal of St. Edmund Hall, 1384–90; subsequently associated with Exeter and University colleges. Ordained subdeacon in 1400, he was enlisted in the cause of combatting Wycliffism in the last decades of his life. Extant works are a *De probationibus propositionum* (ed. de Rijk, in *Some 14th Century Tracts* 1982), a *De actione interiori elementorum simplicium*, and two brief logical treatises (all unedited).

Secondary sources. Ashworth and Spade, "Logic in Late Medieval Oxford" (1992); Emden; ODNB (Lahey).

EUSTACHIUS OF ARRAS (Atrebatensis, Eustace) b. Arras (northern France) *ca.* 1225; d. 1291. Franciscan theologian. Student at Paris of Bonaventure and Gilbert of Tournai, whom he succeeded as regent master of theology (1263–6). Elected bishop of Coutances in 1282. Extant works (mostly unedited) include fragments of a *Sentences* commentary, three *Quodlibeta*, and a great many disputed questions, including a set on the eternity of the world (ed. Dales and Argerami 1986–7).

Secondary sources. Glorieux, "Maîtres franciscains" (1930); Putallaz, *Figures franciscaines* (1997); FA.

EUSTRATIOS OF NICAEA b. *ca.* 1050; d. *ca.* 1120. Philospher and theologian. A student of John Italos, he escaped Italos's condemnation to become metropolitan of Nicaea. A later condemnation in 1117 was lifted only after his death. His writings insist on the importance of philosophy for theology, and take a nominalistic position on the problem of universals. Extant works include commentaries on the *Nicomachean Ethics* (ed. Heylbut 1892; Bks. I and VI tr. [Latin] Robert Grosseteste [ed. Mercken 1973, Trizio forthcoming]) and on Bk. II of the *Posterior Analytics* (ed. Hayduck 1907; tr. [Latin] Andreas Gratiolus 1542/2001). A number of theological writings have also been edited (in Demetrakopulos, *Bibliotheca ecclesiastica* 1866/1965).

Secondary sources. Giocarinis, "Doctrine of Ideas" (1964); Joannou, "Définition des Seins" (1954); Lloyd, "Aristotelianism" (1987); ODB (Kazhdan).

EVERARD OF YPRES (Eberhard) b. Ypres (Flanders), *ca.* 1115; d. after 1191. Theologian and disciple of Gilbert of Poitiers. Studied under Gilbert at Chartres (1130s), Paris (*ca.* 1137) and Poitiers (1142). Joined the Cistercians at Clairvaux sometime after 1185. His *Dialogus Ratii et Everardi* [1191/8] (ed. Häring 1953) defends Gilbert's teachings. Also extant are two letters on the Trinity (ed. Häring, in "Everard of Ypres" 1955) and a *Summula decretalium* [*ca.* 1180] (unedited), whose attribution to Everard is uncertain.

Secondary source. Dronke.

EVRARD OF BÉTHUNE *fl.* 1200. Grammarian, possibly Flemish. Author of the *Grecismus* [*ca.* 1212] (ed. Wrobel 1887), a popular commentary in verse on Donatus's *Barbarismus*. Secondary source. Grondeux, *Le Graecismus* (2000).

AL-FĀRĀBĪ, Abū Naṣr Muḥammad (Alfarabi, Alpharabius) b. prob. Farab (Turkestan), *ca.* 870; d. Damascus, *ca.* 950. Leading Islamic philosopher, influential in logic and language as well as metaphysics and political philosophy. Little is known of his life. Studied in Baghdad, then lived in Damascus, where he died. Combined Aristotelian and Neoplatonic influences; an important source for Avicenna and Maimonides, among many others. Of the more than 100 works attributed to him, only a fraction are extant. Important treatises include the classic metaphysical and political treatise *Al-Madīna al-fāḍila* (*On the Perfect State*) (ed. and tr. Walzer 1985); *Fuṣūl al-madanī* (*Aphorisms of the Statesman*) (ed. and tr. Dunlop 1961); *Risāla fī al-ʿaql* (*The Treatise on Intellect*) (ed. Bouyges 1938; part. tr. Hyman and Walsh, in *Philosophy in the Middle Ages* 1973); *Kitāb al-ḥurūf* (*The Book of Letters*) (ed. Mahdi 1969; part. tr. Khalidi, in *Medieval Islamic Writings* 2005); *Kitāb iḥṣāʾ al-ʿulūm* (*Survey of the Sciences*) (ed. Amīn 1968); *Qāmūs al-Fārābī al-falsafī* (*The Philosophical Lexicon*) (ed. and tr. Alon 2002); and various writings in metaphysics (ed. Dieterici 1890). See also *Political Writings* (tr. Butterworth 2001), and *Philosophy of*

Plato and Aristotle (tr. Mahdī 1969), which contain assorted translations, as do McGinnis and Reisman, *Classical Arabic Philosophy* (2007). Various Aristotelian commentaries have survived, including the *Prior Analytics* (tr. Rescher 1963) and the *De interpretatione* (ed. Kutsch and Marrow 1960; tr. Zimmermann 1981).

Secondary sources. Fakhry, *Al-Fārābī* (2002) [life; works]; Abed, *Aristotelian Logic* (1991); Davidson, *Alfarabi, Avicenna, and Averroes on Intellect* (1992); Galston, *Politics and Excellence* (1990); Lameer, *Al-Fārābī and Aristotelian Syllogistics* (1994); Mahdi, *Alfarabi and the Foundation of Islamic Political Philosophy* (2001); Menn, "Senses of Being" (2008); Netton, *Al-Farabi* (1992); Reisman, "Philosophical Curriculum" (2005); BCPMA (Black); BEIP (Yavuz); EI (Walzer); HIP (Black); REP (Netton).

FERRANDUS OF SPAIN (de Hispania) *fl.* 1290s. Master of arts at Paris. Later bishop of Calahorra. An early example of the sort of Latin Averroism that would become more prominent in John of Jandun. Author of commentaries on the *Metaphysics* and perhaps also on the *Economics* and on Averroes's *De substantia orbis* (all unedited). Also extant is a *Quaestio de specie intelligibili* (ed. Kuksewicz 1977).

Secondary sources. Zimmermann, "Ein Averroist" (1968), "Kritik an Thomas von Aquin" (1976); Weijers.

FERRARIUS THE CATALAN (Ferrer, Catalanus) *fl.* 1265–75. Dominican theologian. Studied in Paris in 1274–5; regent master of theology in 1275–6. Extant works are two *Quodlibeta* [1275/7] and various sermons (only excerpts edited).

Secondary sources. Grabmann, "Quaestiones tres" (1930); Kaeppeli.

FRANCIS OF MARCHIA (de Appignano, de Esculo, de Ascoli, Franciscus Rubeus) b. Appignano del Tronto, *ca.* 1285–90; d. after 1344. Strikingly original Franciscan theologian and natural philosopher. Entered the Franciscan order at an early age; studied at Paris, *ca.* 1310, and subsequently taught at *studia* in Paris and elsewhere. His most important work is his lectures on the *Sentences*, delivered at Paris during the academic year 1319–20 and later revised. Taught at the Franciscan convent in Avignon in 1328, when conflict with John XXII over the mendicant concept of poverty led to his fleeing Avignon with Ockham and others. After many years as a fugitive, speaking out against the pope, Francis was captured and put on trial, perhaps in 1341. He subsequently confessed and recanted. His lectures on the *Sentences* survive in multiple manuscript versions, but were never printed. Editorial efforts are now underway, with several volumes already published (ed. Mariani) and a coordinated effort at a critical edition in progress. Other principal works [dates uncertain] include a *Quodlibet* (ed. Mariani 1997), and commentaries on the *Physics* (ed. Mariani 1998) and *Metaphysics*. Dating to Francis's years in exile, the *Improbatio* offers an extended statement of his political stance against John XXII (ed. Mariani 1993).

Secondary sources. Friedman and Schabel, "Commentaries on the Sentences" (2001) [bibliography]; Duba, "Authenticity" (2007), "Continental Franciscan *Quodlibeta*" (2007); Friedman and Schabel (eds.), *Francis of Marchia* (2006); Priori and Balena (eds.), *Atti del Convegno Internazionale su Francesco d'Appignano* (2004, etc.); Schneider, *Die Kosmologie* (1991); BCPMA (Friedman); DBI (Vian); FA; SEP (Schabel); Weijers.

FRANCIS OF MEYRONNES (de Mayronis) b. Provence, *ca.* 1288; d. Piacenza, 1328. Franciscan theologian. Studied at Paris. An independent-minded disciple of Scotus, and possibly his student at the University of Paris, *ca.* 1304–7. Lectured on the *Sentences* in Paris 1320–1; appointed master of theology in 1323. Served as Franciscan provincial minister of Provence from 1323 to 1328, during which time he continued to lecture in Avignon. His major work is his *Sentences* commentary, which has survived in multiple redactions; the revised version is known as the *Conflatus* (ed. 1520/1966, etc.). Other works include his dispute over the Trinity with Pierre Roger [1320–1] (ed. Barbet 1961); lectures on the *ars vetus* (*Passus*, ed. 1479, etc.) and the *Physics* (ed. 1490, etc.); a treatise on the transcendentals (ed. Möhle 2004); his *Quodlibeta* (ed. 1520/1966, etc.); a large number of sermons (*Quadragesimale*, ed. 1491, etc.); a treatise on intuitive cognition (ed. Etzkorn, in "Franciscus de Mayronis" 1994–7); and various political treatises.

Secondary sources. Roth, *Franz von Mayronis* (1936); Duba, "Continental Franciscan *Quodlibeta*" (2007); Lapparent, "L'œuvre politique" (1940–2); Luscombe, "François de Meyronnes and Hierarchy" (1991); Maurer, "Epistemological Realism" (1971); Maurer, "Role of Infinity" (1971); Möhle, *Formalitas* (2007); Rossmann, *Hierarchie der Welt* (1972); Vignaux, "L'être comme perfection" (1962); BCPMA (Lambertini); FA; Lohr; REP (Hause); Weijers.

FRANCIS OF PRATO b. Prato (Tuscany), *fl.* 1340s. Dominican philosopher, advocate of metaphysical realism. Became a friar as a youth. Studied and lectured at convents throughout central Italy. Principal extant works are his *Logica* [1344–5] (ed. Amerini 2005) and *De universalibus* [1341/3] (ed. Amerini 2003), as well as various treatises, including the *Tractatus de voce univoca* (ed. Amerini 2005), *Tractatus de prima et secunda intentione* (ed. Mojsisch 2000), *Tractatus de sex transcendentibus* (ed. Mojsisch and Maasen 2000), and *Tractatus de suppositionibus terminorum* (ed. Amerini 1999/2000). Also extant are a large number of disputed questions (mostly unedited).

Secondary sources. Amerini, "La dottrina della *significatio*" (2000), "What is Real" (2005); Rode, *Franciscus de Prato* (2004); Kaeppeli.

FREDEGISUS OF TOURS *fl.* 800–30. Carolingian philosopher and theologian. A student of Alcuin. Principal philosophical work is *De nihilo et tenebris* [800/14] (PL 104; tr. Jun 2003), a letter arguing for the reality of nothingness and shadows. His views on the soul are described in a contemporary letter by Agobard of Lyon [*ca.* 830] (PL 104).

Secondary sources. Ahner, *Fredegis von Tours* (1878); Marenbon, *Circle of Alcuin* (1981).

FULBERT OF CHARTRES b. *ca.* 960; d. 1028. Scholar, preacher, poet, and influential teacher. Studied at Rheims and then Chartres, becoming bishop there in 1006. The cathedral school became famous under his leadership; students included Berengar of Tours. His extant works include many letters and hymns (ed. and tr. Behrends 1976) as well as various sermons and treatises (PL 141).

Secondary sources. Association des amis du Centre médiéval européen de Chartres (ed.), *Enseigner le Moyen Age* (1996); Jeauneau, *L'âge d'or* (1995); DMA (Giordanengo).

GABRIEL BIEL b. Speyer (Rhineland), before 1425; d. Einsiedel (Thuringia), 1495. Eclectic theologian, influential on reformation thought. Studied at Heidelberg, Erfurt, and Cologne. Professor of theology at Tübingen from 1484; served several times as rector. Drew on both realist and nominalist traditions and was especially influenced by Ockham. Biel's spiritual interests are pronounced, and he played an important role in the Brethren of the Common Life (*devotio moderna*) movement. His *Sentences* commentary [mid-1480s on] is his most important philosophical work (ed. Rückert *et al.* 1973–92). Also philosophically rich is his commentary on the Canon of the Mass [1488] (ed. Oberman and Courtenay 1963–76). His *Defensiorum obedientiae apostolicae* [1462] (ed. and tr. Oberman *et al.* 1968) makes a case for papal authority. His thought has received particular attention for its voluntarism and alleged Pelagianism; on the latter, see his *Quaestiones de justificatione* (ed. Feckes 1929).

Secondary sources. Oberman, *Harvest* (1963) [bibliography]; Burkard, *Philosophische Lehrgehalte* (1974); Faix, *Gabriel Biel und die Brüder vom Gemeinsamen Leben* (1999); Farthing, *Thomas Aquinas and Gabriel Biel* (1988); BCPMA (Friedman); REP (Farthing).

GAETANO, *see* Cajetan.

GARLAND OF BESANÇON (Gerlandus) *fl.* 1075/1130 (?). Nominalist logician from the circle of Roscelin. Author of an important early logical treatise, the *Dialectica* [1100/20] (ed. de Rijk 1959; part. tr. Bosley and Tweedale, *Basic Issues* 2006). A summary of the *ars vetus*, the *Dialectica* is nominalist in the sense that it treats logic, including the categories and universals, as concerned entirely with words. The treatise devotes particular attention to the hypothetical syllogism. Both the date of this treatise and even the correct name of the author are uncertain.

Secondary sources. Henry, "Singular Syllogism" (1975); Iwakuma, "Vocales" (1992); Stump, "Dialectic" (1980); Tweedale, "Logic" (1988).

GARLAND THE COMPUTIST (Garlandus Compotista) b. Lorraine, *ca.* 1015; d. Besançon, 1084/1102. Scholar and scientist. Studied at Liège. Lived in England from 1036/40 to 1066. Master at Besançon in 1084. A prolific author on subjects such as chronology (*Compotus*), astronomy (*Tabulae astronomicae*), arithmetic (*De abaco*), music (*De fistulis, De nolis*), theology (*Candela*), and of commentaries on the Psalms and Gospels (all unedited). It has recently been shown that the important logical treatise, the *Dialectica*, is by a different Garlandus.

Secondary sources. CHLMP; Dronke.

GENTILIS DA CINGULO b. Cingoli [Marche]; d. before 1334. Arts master; prominent modist grammarian. Studied at Paris, *ca.* 1290. Professor of arts at Bologna before 1295. Extant works include questions on Priscian minor (ed. Martorelli Vico 1985), a commentary on Martin of Dacia (ed. Alessio 1992), and various treatises on the *Ars vetus* (unedited).

Secondary sources. Grabmann, *Gentile da Cingoli* (1941); Lohr; Weijers.

GEOFFREY OF ASPALL (Galfridus de Hasphall) b. Suffolk; d. Gascony, 1287. Arts master at Oxford; subsequently enjoyed a long career in royal service. Studied at Paris in the 1240s, probably as a student of Adam of Buckfield. Subsequently served as arts master in the 1250s, until at least 1262. By 1265 his scholarly career seems to have concluded. Almost all the surviving works are Aristotelian commentaries, which are notably composed as a series of questions. Twelve have been identified: the *Metaphysics*, *Physics* (twice), *De caelo* (twice), *De generatione et corruptione* (twice), *De anima*, and various *parva naturalia*. None have been printed, except for books III–IV of the question commentary on the *Physics* (ed. Trifogli, in *Liber Quartus Physicorum* 2007).

Secondary sources. Callus, "The Introduction of Aristotelian Learning" (1943); Macrae, "Commentaries on Aristotle" (1968); Plevano, "Instant of Change" (1993); Zwiercan, "Note sur deux manuscrits" (1961); CHLMP; Lohr; ODNB (Long); Weijers.

GEORGE GEMISTOS PLETHON b. Constantinople, *ca.* 1360; d. Mistra, 1452/4. Leading Byzantine scholar and proponent of Platonism. Little is known about the first half of his life: he seems to have studied at the Islamic court at Adrianople, and later to have taught in Constantinople. Probably expelled to Mistra *ca.* 1410, on suspicions of heresy and paganism. He remained there the rest of his life, aside from a visit to Florence in 1438–9, which gave rise to his pro-Platonic *On the Points on which Aristotle Contentiously Disagrees with Plato* [1439] (ed. Lagarde 1973; tr. Woodhouse, in *George Gemistos Plethon* 1986), which (at least according to legend) subsequently inspired Cosimo de' Medici's Platonic Academy. Other extant works include a treatise on virtues (ed. and [Fr] tr. Tambrun-Krasker 1987); an essay attacking George Scholarios's Aristotelianism (ed. Maltese 1988); and his partially extant *Laws* (ed. and [Fr] tr. Alexandre and Pellissier 1858/1966), which became controversial for its embrace of paganism. Further works are available in PG 160, and in German translation (tr. Blum 1988).

Secondary sources. Demetrakopoulos, "Dependence on Thomas Aquinas" (2006); Karamanolis, "Plethon and Scholarios on Aristotle" (2002); Masai, *Pléthon et le platonisme* (1956); Tambrun, *Pléthon* (2006); Tatakis, *Byzantine Philosophy* (2003); Woodhouse, *George Gemistos Plethon* (1986); ODB (Talbot).

GEORGE PACHYMERES b. Nicaea, 1242; d. Constantinople, after 1307. Historian and teacher of philosophy. Studied in Nicaea and then in Constantinople from 1261. Various ecclesiastical positions followed. Best known for his history of the Byzantine empire from 1260 to 1308 (PG 143–4). More philosophical writings include an encyclopedia of the *quadrivium* (ed. Tannery and Stéphanou 1940); a sequel to Proclus's commentary on the *Parmenides* (ed. Gadra *et al.* 1989); an *explicatio* of the entire corpus of pseudo-Dionysius (PG 3–4); and a monumental *Philosophia* (in twelve books) in which he paraphrases Aristotle's principal works (known in Latin as the "epitome" [ed. 1560]), which is only now being edited in full (Organon ed. Bechius 1548; *Metaphysics* ed. Pappa 2002; *Ethics* ed. Ikonomakos 2005).

Secondary sources. Tatakis, *Byzantine Philosophy* (2003); ODB (Talbot).

GEORGE SCHOLARIOS – GENNADIOS II b. Constantinople, 1400/5; d. Mt. Menoikeion, *ca.* 1472. Theologian, Aristotelian philosopher, patriarch of Constantinople. Taught philosophy in Constantinople, subsequently becoming a leading ecclesiastical figure. Captured by the Turks in 1453, he was released and appointed patriarch. An adamant opponent of unification with the Roman church. His many extant works (all ed. Petit *et al.* 1928–36) show the influence of Latin authors, especially Aquinas, whose work he translated and commented on, along with that of some other Latin scholastics (see Appendix B5).

Secondary sources. Barbour, *Byzantine Thomism* (1993); Ebbesen and Pinborg, "Gennadios and Western Scholasticism" (1981–2); Karamanolis, "Plethon and Scholarios on Aristotle" (2002); Livanos, *Greek Tradition* (2006); Turner, "Career" (1969); ODB (Talbot).

GEORGE TRAPEZOUNTIOS (of Trebizond) b. Crete, 1395; d. Rome, 1472/3. Rhetorician, translator, Aristotelian philosopher. Studied as a youth in Crete, moving to Italy at age twenty and converting to Catholicism in 1426. Taught Greek and rhetoric in Vicenza, Venice, and Rome. Entered into papal service in the 1440s. Translated into Latin almost all of Aristotle's *libri naturales*, Plato's *Laws*, and other works. A dispute with Bessarion beginning in the 1450s led to his most important work, the *Comparatio Philosophorum Aristotelis et Platonis* [1458] (ed. 1523/1965). Also wrote an earlier, very popular logic textbook, the *Isagoge Dialectica* [ca. 1438] (ed. 1539/1966), and a treatise, the *Protectio Aristotelis Problematum* [1456] (ed. Mohler, in *Kardinal Bessarion* 1923–42/1967), attacking the opponents of Aristotelianism. Various theological works are edited in PG 161.

Secondary sources. Monfasani, *George of Trebizond* (1976), *Collectanea Trapezuntiana* (1984); ODB (Kahzdan, Talbot); REP (Monfasani).

GERALD OF ODO (Gerardus Odonis, Guiral Ot, Odon, Eudes) b. Camboulit (southern France), *ca.* 1285/90; d. Sicily, 1349. Franciscan theologian, best known for his long commentary on Aristotle's *Ethics*. Bachelor of theology at Toulouse by 1316, where he lectured on the *Sentences* (only fragments extant). Assigned to Paris in 1327–8, he lectured on the *Sentences* a second time (extant but unedited). Served as Franciscan minister general from 1329 to 1342. Subsequently named patriarch of Antioch and bishop of Catania (Sicily). The most-discussed aspect of his *Sentences* commentary is his argument that a continuum is composed of indivisible, extensionless points. The influential *Ethics* commentary [1320s] (ed. 1482, etc.) gives heavy emphasis to human freedom and the role of the will. A quodlibetal dispute from Paris [1333] concerns the vision of God (ed. and tr. [Fr] Trottmann 2001). Also extant are various logical treatises (ed. de Rijk 1997–), a treatise *De intentionibus* (ed. de Rijk 1997–), various works on physics and metaphysics (ed. in progress), an economic treatise *De contractibus* [ca. 1316] (ed. in progress), and numerous biblical commentaries (unedited).

Secondary sources. de Rijk, "Works by Gerald Ot" (1993); Bakker, "Guiral Ot et le mouvement" (2003); Duba and Schabel (eds.), *Vivarium* (2009); Kent, *Aristotle and the Franciscans* (1984), "Aristotle's Ethics" (2008); Langholm, *Price and Value* (1979); Murdoch, "Infinity and Continuity" (1982); Saarinen, *Weakness of Will* (1994); Schabel, "Questions on Divine Foreknowledge" (2002), "*Sentences* Commentary" (2004); Spruyt, "Gerardus Odonis on the Universal" (1996); Walsh, "Commentaries on Aristotle's 'Ethics'" (1975); Zoubov, "Catton, Odon et Bonet" (1959); CHLMP; DMA (Trottmann); Lohr; REP (Kent); Weijers.

GERARD OF ABBEVILLE b. Abbeville (Picardy), *ca.* 1225; d. 1272. Paris theologian and leading critic of the mendicant orders at Paris. Studied at Paris, becoming master of theology before 1257. His principal work is the *Contra adversarium perfectionis christianae* [*ca.* 1269] (ed. Clasen 1938–9). Also extant are a full twenty *Quodlibeta* from his regency as theology professor [*ca.* 1260s] (four qq. on the mendicant controversy ed. Teetaert 1951), as well as various further disputed questions (*De cogitationibus* ed. Pattin, in *L'anthropologie* 1993, along with many quodlibetal questions).

Secondary sources. Congar, "Aspects ecclésiologiques" (1961); BBK (Marschler); Glorieux.

GERARD OF BOLOGNA b. Bologna, 1240s; d. Avignon, 1317. Carmelite theologian. Studied theology in Paris, becoming the first master of theology from among his order, *ca.* 1295. Prior general of his order from 1297, and subsequently much involved in ecclesiastical affairs, although also active at Paris for many years, debating four *Quodlibeta* [1305–11] there and a fifth at Avignon, where he probably composed his unfinished *Summa theologiae* [1313/17] (only excerpts of these edited).

Secondary sources. Brown, "Nature of the Good" (2003); Schabel, "Early Carmelites" (2003), "Carmelite *Quodlibeta*" (2007); Xiberta, *De scriptoribus scholasticis* (1931); DBI (Vecchio); Glorieux.

GERARD OF CREMONA (Gerardus Cremonensis) b. Cremona, 1114; d. Toledo, 1187. Leading translator of Arabic philosophical and scientific work, active in Toledo. According to the *Vita* written by his students (ed. Burnett, in "Coherence" 2001), Gerard learned Arabic so as to be able to translate the massive collection of Arabic texts available in Toledo. Of around seventy translations he is reputed to have made, the most significant include Aristotle's *Posterior Analytics*, *Physics*, *De caelo*, *De generatione et corruptione*, and *Meteorologica* [Bks. I–III], as well as Ptolemy's *Almagest*, various treatises by al-Kindī and al-Fārābī, and the *Liber de causis* (ed. Pattin 1966); he also translated a large number of medical, astronomical, mathematical, and alchemical treatises. (See Appendices B1 and B4.)

Secondary sources. Brams, *Riscoperta di Aristotele* (2003); d'Alverny, "Translations and Translators" (1982); Burnett, "Arabic into Latin" (2005); Dod, "Aristoteles Latinus" (1982); DBI; DMA (Draelants); Dronke.

GERARD OF SIENA b. Tuscany; d. 1336. Augustinian theologian. Lectured on the *Sentences* in Paris, *ca.* 1325 (Bk. I ed. 1598; Bk. II–III extant but unedited); master of theology by 1330. Also extant are some quodlibetal questions [1330] (unedited), from which is drawn a *Tractatus de usuris et restitutionibus* (ed. 1556).

Secondary sources. Schabel and Courtenay, "Augustinian Quodlibeta" (2007); Trapp, "Augustinian Theology" (1956); DBI (Vecchio).

GERHOH OF REICHERSBERG b. Polling (Bavaria), *ca.* 1093; d. Reichersberg (upper Austria), 1169. Scholar and Church reformer. Studied at Hildesheim; taught at Augsburg. After becoming a regular canon, he became provost at the Augustinian house of Reichersberg in 1132, where he spent most of his remaining life. His principal work is a very long commentary on the Psalms. Also extant are sixteen treatises and various letters. Most of his work is printed in PL 193–94; the rest has been edited in Van den Eynde *et al.* (1955–6).

Secondary sources. Classen, *Gerhoch von Reichersberg* (1960); Van den Eynde, *L'œuvre littéraire* (1957).

GERSHOM BEN SOLOMON *fl.* Arles, second half of thirteenth century. Encyclopedic author, perhaps the father of Levi ben Gershom. Only known work is the encyclopedic *Sha'ar ha-Shamayim* (*Gate of Heaven*) [1242/75] (ed. 1876/1967; tr. Bodenheimer 1953).

Secondary source. Sirat.

GERSONIDES, *see* Levi ben Gershom.

GERTRUDE THE GREAT (of Helfta) b. 1256; d. 1302. Mystic. An orphan, raised from age five at the monastery of Helfta (Saxony). Educated by Mechthild of Hackeborn, she in turn became a spiritual counselor and educator. Her numerous spiritual visions are described in two works: the *Exercitia spiritualia* (tr. Lewis and Lewis 1989) and the *Legatus divinae pietatis* (*Herald of Divine Love*) (tr. Windworth 1993), much of which was compiled after her death (both ed. and [Fr] tr. Hourlier *et al.* 1967–86).

Secondary sources. Finnegan, *Women of Helfta* (1991); Bynum, *Jesus as Mother* (1982).

AL-GHAZĀLĪ, Abū Ḥāmid Muḥammad ibn Muḥammad (Algazel) b. Tus (Khurasan), *ca.* 1058; d. Tus, 1111. Brilliant Persian philosopher and theologian who gave up a distinguished teaching career to embrace the mystical practices of Sufism. Studied in Tus, Jurjan, and Nishapur; eventually came to Baghdad, where he was appointed head of Niẓāmīya College in 1091. The leading intellectual figure in the capital of the Moslem world, al-Ghazālī nevertheless resigned his position in 1095, in the wake of a spiritual crisis (as well as perhaps a political one). Withdrawing from public life, he taught at small private schools in Damascus and Jerusalem, and ultimately returned to Tus, where he taught and wrote, founding a small private school and a Sufi convent. In 1106, citing the widespread theological confusion of the time, he returned to a high-profile, state-sponsored position at Nishapur, but ultimately returned to his school in Tus.

Al-Ghazālī's autobiography, *Al-Munqidh min al-ḍalāl* (*The Deliverer from Error*) [*ca.* 1108] (ed. Ṣalībā and 'Ayyād 1934; tr. McCarthy 1980), describes his renunciation of academic philosophy in favor of Sufism, which he came to regard as the only path to certainty. His best-known philosophical work, ironically, is a work that he wrote to summarize the philosophical thinking that he came to reject, the *Maqāṣid al-falāsifa* (*Intentions of the Philosophers*) [1094] (ed. Dunyā 1961). The only work of al-Ghazālī's to be translated during the Middle Ages (into both Latin [ed. Lohr 1965 (logic); ed. Muckle 1933 (metaphysics and physics)] and Hebrew), it gave Christians and Jews the impression that he was a vigorous defender of an Avicennian philosophical program. Al-Ghazālī's true philosophical masterpiece is the *Tahāfut al-falāsifa* (*The Incoherence of the Philosophers*) [1095] (ed. and tr. Marmura 1997), in which he challenges twenty theses alleged to have been demonstrated by the *falāsifa* – embracing, most famously, an occasionalist theory of causality. Averroes would later reply to this work, point by point, in his *Tahāfut al-tahāfut*

(*The Incoherence of the Incoherence*). Other important works include various theological works: *Al-Iqtiṣād fī al-iʿtiqād* (*The Middle Path in Theology*) [*ca.* 1095] (ed. Çubukçu and Atay 1962; part. tr. Abū Zayd 1970); *Al-Risāla al-Qudsiyya* (*The Jerusalem Epistle*) [*ca.* 1096] (ed. and tr. Tibawi 1965); *Fayṣal al-tafriqa bayna al-Islām wa-al-zandaqa* (*The Decisive Criterion for Distinguishing Islam from Clandestine Unbelief*) (ed. Dunyā 1961; tr. Jackson 2002); three works on Aristotelian logic: *Miʿyār al-ʿilm* (*The Standard Measure of Knowledge*) [1095] (ed. Shams al-Dīn 1990); *Miḥakk al-naẓar fī al-manṭiq* (*The Touchstone of Proof in Logic*) [1095] (ed. al-Naʿsani 1966); and *Al-Quṣṭās al-mustaqīm* (*The Just Balance*) [1095–6] (ed. Shalḥat 1959; tr. Brewster 1978); an ethical treatise, *Mizān al-ʿamal* (*The Balance of Action*) [1095] (ed. Dunyā 1964; [Fr] tr. Hachem 1945); and various later Sufi-influenced treatises, including the multi-volume *Iḥyāʾ ʿulūm al-dīn* (*The Revivification of the Religious Sciences*) [1096–7] (ed. 2002, etc.; many partial trs.) and *Mishkāt al-anwār* (*The Niche of the Lights*) [1106–7] (ed. and tr. Buchman 1998).

Secondary sources. D'Alverny, "Algazel dans l'occident latin" (1986); Dutton, "Al-Ghazālī on Possibility" (2001); Frank, *Creation* (1992); Frank, *Al-Ghazali and the Ashʿarite School* (1994); Griffel, *Apostasie und Toleranz* (2000), *Philosophical Theology* (forthcoming); Jabre, *La notion de certitude* (1958); Kukkonen, "Possible Worlds" (2000); Laoust, *La politique de Gazali* (1970); Marmura, "Ghazalian Causes" (1995), "Al-Ghazālī" (2005); Moose, *Ghazali and the Poetics of Imagination* (2006); Ormsby, *Theodicy* (1984); Ormsby, *Ghazali* (2007); Perler and Rudolph, *Occasionalismus* (2000); Shehadi, *Ghazali's Unique Unknowable God* (1964); Sherif, *Ghazali's Theory of Virtue* (1975); Whittingham, *Al-Ghazali and the Quran* (2007); BCPMA (Druart); EI (Watt); HIP (Campanini); REP (Nakamura); SEP (Griffel).

GILBERT OF POITIERS (Gilbertus Porreta, Porretanus, de la Porrée) b. Poitiers, 1085/90; d. 1154. Theologian and logician who shaped much of subsequent twelfth-century thought. Studied in Chartres under Bernard and then at Laon under Anselm and Ralph of Laon. Left Laon by 1116; after time in Poitiers became canon in 1124 and then chancellor at Chartres from 1126 until *ca.* 1137. Taught at both Chartres and Paris during these years. Founded a school of philosophy in Paris which survived well into the second half of the twelfth century and whose members, the Porretani, produced a large body of work building on Gilbert's ideas. Bishop of Poitiers from 1142. His views on the Trinity led to charges of heresy, pushed by Bernard of Clairvaux, but Gilbert successfully defended himself (1147–8) and died with his reputation intact. His only surviving work is theological: commentaries on Boethius's theological works [1146–7] (ed. Häring 1966), and still unedited commentaries on the Psalms [before 1116] and Pauline letters [*ca.* 1135]. His distinctive ideas in logic emerge from the works of others, including the *Compendium* of an anonymous student (ed. Ebbesen *et al.* 1983). Gilbert was traditionally but is no longer credited as the author of the *Liber sex principiorum* (see Lewry, "Liber sex principiorum" 1987).

Secondary sources. Nielsen, *Theology and Philosophy* (1982) [biography etc.]; de Rijk, "Semantics and Metaphysics" (1988–9); Gross-Diaz, *Psalms Commentary* (1996); Gammersbach, *Gilbert von Poitiers und seine Prozesse* (1959); Jacobi, "Einzelnes" (1995); Jolivet and de Libera, *Aux origines de la logica modernorum* (1987); Maioli, *Gilberto Porretano* (1979);

Marenbon, "Gilbert of Poitiers" (1988), "Note on the Porretani" (1988); BCPMA (Marenbon); DMA (de Libera); Dronke; REP (Jacobi).

GILBERT OF STRATTON d. *ca.* 1294. Oxford theologian. Secular master, incepted *ca.* 1288. Various disputed questions are extant (unedited except for a question on the eternity of the world in Dales and Argerami, *Medieval Latin Texts* 1991).

Secondary sources. Dales, "Gilbert of Stratton" (1994); Little and Pelster, *Oxford Theology* (1934); Emden.

GILBERT OF TOURNAI (Guibert, van Doornik, de Tornaco) b. Tournai, 1200/10; d. Tournai, 1284/8. Franciscan theologian, notable for the spiritual, non-technical character of his work. Studied the arts in Paris, becoming master of arts before 1240. Began the study of theology and joined the Franciscan order, taking the Franciscan chair of theology *ca.* 1260. His *Sentences* commentary has not been found. What remains are a great many sermons and non-scholastic treatises, most notably the *Rudimentum doctrinae* [1259–68] (ed. in progress; part. ed. Gieben, in "Four Chapters" 1963), which includes the *De modo addiscendi* (ed. Bonifacio 1953). Also extant is a *Tractatus de pace* [*ca.* 1275] and a treatise written for Louis IX, the *Eruditio regum et principum* [1259] (ed. de Poorter 1914).

Secondary source. FA.

GILES OF LESSINES b. Lessines (southwest Belgium), *ca.* 1230; d. *ca.* 1304. Dominican theologian and early Thomist. A student of Albert the Great, perhaps in Cologne, and later of Aquinas in Paris around 1270. His only extant philosophical work is the *De unitate formae* [1278] (ed. de Wulf 1901).

Secondary sources. Iribarren, "Responsio" (2001); CALMA; Kaeppeli; Roensch; Weijers.

GILES OF ORLEANS (Aegidius Aurelianensis) *fl.* second half of thirteenth century; d. after 1277. Paris arts master, known only for various Aristotelian commentaries, of which only the *De generatione et corruptione* (ed. Kuksewicz 1993) has been edited.

Secondary sources. Korolec, "Conceptions de philosophie morale" (1990); Kuksewicz, "Theorie der Materie" (1991); CALMA; Lohr; Weijers.

GILES OF ROME (Aegidius Romanus, Egidius Colonna) b. prob. Rome, *ca.* 1243/7; d. Avignon, 1316. Innovative theologian and philosopher with Thomistic leanings; his work was deeply influential on later scholastic thought. Joined the order of the Augustinian Hermits as a youth, studied the arts at Paris, and then theology from 1269 to 1272, probably under Aquinas. Lectured on the *Sentences* before 1271; books I–II were later revised (Bk. I ed. 1521/1968). Subsequently commented on a wide range of Aristotelian and associated texts. Attacked in 1277 for heterodox views, to which he responded, unrepentant, in his *Apologia* (ed. Wielockx 1985). Abandoned Paris, presumably for Italy, where he stayed until 1285, when – after papal intervention – he returned to Paris, becoming master of theology by 1287. Elected prior general of the Augustinian order in 1292 and archbishop of Bruges in 1295. Heavily involved in ecclesiastical affairs during these later years, as evidenced by the treatises *De renuntiatione papae* [1297] (ed.

Eastman 1992) and *De ecclesiastica potestate* [1301–2] (ed. and tr. Dyson 2004). Giles's work is available in various Renaissance editions, many of which have been reprinted by Minerva (1966–70). A critical *Opera omnia* is in the early stages. In addition to the works already mentioned, other important treatises include the *Theoremata de esse et essentia* [1278/85] (ed. Hocedez 1930; tr. Murray 1952), the *Theoremata de corpore Christi* [*ca.* 1274] (ed. 1481, 1554–5/1968), the *Contra gradus et pluralitatem formarum* [1278] (ed. 1500/1982), the *De regimine principum* (ed. 1556/1968; part. tr. CTMPT II), and also Aristotelian and biblical commentaries, as on the Song of Songs (ed. 1554–5/1968; tr. Rotelle 1998). There is also a *Quodlibet* from Italy [1281] (ed. Bruni, in "Quaestiones" 1939–40), some *Quodlibeta* from his second stay in Paris (ed. 1646/1966), and various disputed questions (ed. 1503/1968). The traditional attribution to Giles of the *Errores philosophorum* [*ca.* 1270] (ed. and tr. Koch and Riedl 1944) is doubtful (see Donati, "Studi per una cronologia" 1990).

Secondary sources. Conti, "Conscenza e verità" (1992); Donati, "La dottrina delle dimensioni indeterminate" (1988); Eardley, "Foundations of Freedom" (2006); Pini, "Giles of Rome" (2006); Trifogli, "Natural Motion in the Void" (1992); Trifogli, "Instant of Change" (1993); BCPMA (Donati); CALMA; DBI (Del Punta, Donati and Luna); REP (Del Punta and Trifogli); SEP (Lambertini); Weijers.

GODFREY OF FONTAINES (Godefridus de Fontibus) b. Liège, *ca.* 1250; d. 1306/9. Paris theologian and philosopher. Studied arts at Paris in the early 1270s and theology from at least 1274, studying with Henry of Ghent among others. Master of theology from 1285 to *ca.* 1303–4. Also served as canon of Liège and Tournai and as provost of San Severin at Cologne from 1287 to 1295; elected bishop of Tournai in 1300 but declined the position, apparently because the election was contested. Godfrey's views are quite independent but often set off in directions suggested by Aquinas. His work also reflects an interest in the radical Aristotelianism of the arts faculty, as is demonstrated by the presence of such works in the library of manuscripts he left the Sorbonne. This includes a "Student Notebook," which contains his own transcriptions of Siger of Brabant, Boethius of Dacia, Aquinas, Giles of Rome, and others. Principal work is fifteen wide-ranging quodlibetal questions (ed. 1904–37; X.6, XI.17, XIII.1 tr. CTMPT II), numbered in chronological order and running from Christmas 1285 until 1303/4. Generally, there is one from each year, with a gap of around five years between the last two. Also surviving are various briefer, ordinary disputed questions, some of which have been edited in scattered books and articles.

Secondary sources. Wippel, *Metaphysical Thought of Godfrey of Fontaines* (1981) [biobib-liography, etc.]; de Lagarde, "La philosophie sociale" (1943–5); De Wulf, *Un théologien-philosophe* (1904); Duin, "La bibliothèque" (1959); Lambertini, "Political *Quodlibeta*" (2006); Tihon, *Foi et théologie* (1966); Wippel, "Godfrey of Fontaines at the University of Paris" (2001), "Godfrey of Fontaines' Quodlibet XIV" (2006); BCPMA (Wippel); DMA (de Libera); REP (Wippel); SEP (Wippel).

GONSALVO OF SPAIN (Gonsalvus Hispanus, Gonsalvus of Balboa) b. Galicia, *ca.* 1255; d. *ca.* 1313. Franciscan philosopher and theologian. Sometimes referred to as Gonsalvus de Vallebona, although this is actually the name of a different Spanish Franciscan. Completed his early studies in Spain and his bachelor of theology at Paris by 1288. Elected provincial minister for the province of Santiago of Compostela in 1290. Returned to Paris *ca.* 1297 as master of theology; served as Franciscan regent master in 1302–3, supervising Scotus at this time. Forced, with Scotus, to leave Paris in 1303 for refusing to support King Philip IV over Pope Boniface VIII. Returning to Spain, he was appointed Franciscan minister general in 1304, a position he held until his death. Gonsalvo's philosophical views are characteristically Franciscan, defending the plurality of substantial forms, spiritual matter, and the primacy of will over intellect. His principal surviving works are a collection of disputed questions [1302–3] (ed. Amorós 1935) and his *Conclusiones metaphysicae*, formerly ascribed to Scotus (ed. Wadding, 1639, vol. IV; Vivès 1892, vol. VI). His *Sentences* commentary has not been found.

Secondary sources. Gracia, "Agent and Possible Intellects" (1969); Longpré, "Gonsalve de Balboa" (1924–5); Martel, *La psychologie* (1968); BCPMA (Traver); FA; Weijers.

GOSVIN OF MARBAIS b. Marbais (Belgium); *fl.* 1270s. Arts master at Paris. Only known work is the grammar textbook *Tractatus de constructione* [*ca.* 1270] (ed. Rosier-Catach 1998). Perhaps the same man as Gosvin de la Chapelle, a Paris arts master who fell under suspicion of heresy along with Siger of Brabant in 1276.

Secondary sources. Rosier-Catach, *La parole comme acte* (1994); Weijers.

GOTTSCHALK OF ORBAIS b. *ca.* 805; d. Hautvillers, 868. Theologian, controversial for his theory of predestination. Educated first at the monastery of Fulda, then at Reichenau. Controversy ensued in 829 when Gottschalk resisted becoming a monk. Released from his vows, which he had claimed were forced upon him, he subsequently traveled widely, spending some time at the monasteries of Corbie and Orbais. In 848 and again in 849 his doctrine of "dual predestination" was condemned; when Gottschalk refused to disavow it, he was sentenced to life imprisonment in the abbey of Hautvillers. His various surviving works – many discovered only in 1931 – are available in a modern edition (ed. Lambot 1945).

Secondary sources. Ganz, "Debate on Predestination" (1990); Jolivet, *Godescalc d'Orbais et la trinité* (1958); Tavard, *Trina Deitas* (1996); Weber, *Die Gedichte* (1992).

GRATIADEUS AESCULANUS (Giovanni Graziadei of Ascoli) *fl.* first half of fourteenth century. Dominican philosopher. Professor of philosophy at Bologna and Padua. Extant works include a series of Aristotelian commentaries, including the *Ars vetus* (ed. 1491, etc.), the *Physics* [both literal and questions] (ed. 1517, etc.), and the *De anima* (unpublished). Some editions of Aquinas use his commentary on the *De interpretatione* to complete Aquinas's unfinished commentary.

Secondary sources. DBI (Gentili); Kaeppeli; Lohr.

GRATIAN *fl.* Bologna, 1140s. Foundational figure in canon law. All that is known of his life with certainty is that he composed the *Concordia discordantium canonum*, the fundamental work of canon law that became known as the *Decretum* (ed. 1558, etc.; part. tr. Thompson 1993). The work is an attempt to harmonize thousands of passages from various Church authorities, which Gratian organized and commented on. This quickly became the basic textbook of canon law. Included as part of the *Corpus iuris canonici* (ed. Richter and Friedberg 1879/1959), it remained authoritative within the Church until 1917. A searchable edition is available on the web through the Bayerische Staatsbibliothek.

Secondary sources. Chodorow, *Christian Political Theory* (1972); Kuttner, *Gratian* (1983); Noonan, "Gratian Slept Here" (1979); Reuter, *Wortkonkordanz zum Decretum Gratiani* (1990); Tierney, *Foundations* (1998); Winroth, *Making of Gratian's Decretum* (2000); Vetulani, *Sur Gratien et les Décrétales* (1990); Pennington.

GREGORY PALAMAS b. Constantinople, *ca.* 1296; d. 1357. Leading Orthodox theologian, controversial for his real distinction between God's unknowable essence and "energies," a doctrine that became known as Palamism. Joined the monastery of Mt. Athos as a young man, becoming a priest in 1322. Imprisoned in 1342 for five years, but on his release made metropolitan of Thessalonica. Prominent works include the *Triads in Defense of the Holy Hesychasts* [1334–40] (ed. Meyendorff 1973; tr. Gendle 1983), written against Barlaam of Calabria; a *Dialogue* also against Barlaam (ed. and tr. Ferwerda 1999); the *One Hundred and Fifty Chapters* [1347/8] (ed. and tr. Sinkewicz 1988); an extensive correspondence with Barlaam and others (ed. Bobrinsky *et al.* 1962–70); as well as many homilies (tr. Veniamin 2002). For other works, see PG 150–1.

Secondary sources. Ierodiakonou, "Anti-Logical Movement" (2002); Meyendorff, *Study of Gregory Palamas* (1974); ODB (Papadakis).

GREGORY OF RIMINI (Gregorius Ariminensis, de Arimino) b. Rimini, *ca.* 1300; d. Vienna, 1358. Prominent Paris theology master; the last great scholastic theologian of the Middle Ages. Joined the Augustinian Hermits as a youth. Studied in Paris from 1322/3 until 1328/9. Subsequently taught at various Augustinian *studia* in Italy, and then returned to Paris *ca.* 1342 to lecture on the *Sentences* [1343–4]. Appointed master of theology in 1345, then returned to Italy, teaching at Padua from 1347 to 1351 and then Rimini from 1351 to 1356. Elected prior general of the Augustinian order in 1357. Rimini's views are not easily characterized: he championed the new ideas coming out of England, and would subsequently be listed among the nominalists, but at the same time he was deeply influenced by Augustine. His work was subsequently much cited and even copied by later scholastics, and was printed many times during the Renaissance. By far the most important work is the *Sentences* commentary (ed. Trapp 1979–84), of which only Books I–II circulated. Also surviving are a treatise *De usura* (ed. 1508, etc.) and various unpublished works, including a treatise on the cardinal virtues.

Secondary sources. Biblioteca civica Gambalunga, *Gregorio da Rimini filosofo* (2003); Bermon, *L'assentiment* (2007); Courtenay, "Whether God Can Undo the Past" (1972–3); Cross, "Infinity, Continuity" (1998); Eckermann, *Wort und Wirklichkeit* (1978); García Lescún, *La teología trinitaria* (1970); Leff, *Gregory of Rimini* (1961); Oberman (ed.), *Gregor von Rimini* (1981); Santos-Noya, *Die Sünden und Gnadenlehre* (1990); Schabel, *Theology at Paris* (2000); BCPMA (Zupko); DBI (Lambertini, Tabarroni, and Conti); REP (Brown); SEP (Schabel).

GUALTERUS, *see* Walter.

GUARINO VERONESE (da Verona) b. Verona, 1374; d. Ferrara, 1460. Early Italian humanist. Studied in Padua and in Constantinople [1403–8]. Taught in Florence 1410–14, Verona 1419–29, and Ferrara 1429–60. Composed the earliest humanist Latin grammar, the *Regulae grammaticales* [before 1418] (ed. 1508, etc.), a brief but influential work that is most notable for omitting any trace of scholastic metaphysics and logics. A pioneer in editing and translating classical texts. His letters have been edited in three volumes (ed. Sabbadini 1915–19).

Secondary sources. Sabbadini, *Guariniana* (1891–6); Canfora, *La controversia* (2001); Percival, "Changes in the Approach to Language" (1982); Schweyen, *Guarino Veronese* (1973); CHLMP; DBI (Pistilli).

GUERRIC OF ST. QUENTIN b. Picardy; d. 1245. Arts master and Dominican theologian. Doctor of medicine and master of arts at Paris. Joined the Dominican order *ca.* 1225. After studying theology at Bologna and Paris, he became regent master from 1233 to 1242. Held some of the first quodlibetal disputations (ed. Principe 2002). Also extant are various sermons and biblical commentaries, and questions on the *Sentences* (only excerpts edited).

Secondary sources. Côté, "Problème de l'infinité divine" (1995); DMA (Côté); Glorieux.

GUY TERRENA (Guido Terreni) b. Perpignan, *ca.* 1260–70; d. Avignon, 1342. Carmelite theologian. Student of Godfrey of Fontaines in Paris. Master of theology at Paris from 1312 to 1317. Prior general of the Carmelite order 1318–21. Bishop of Majorca 1321–32; bishop of Elna 1332–42. Prominent critic of the voluntarism associated with Franciscan thought. An outspoken advocate of papal authority. Many works survive, mostly unedited, including six *Quodlibeta*, disputed questions *De verbo* and another set of disputed questions (both unedited), six more theological questions (ed. Etzwiler 1988), fragments of his *Sentences* commentary, commentaries on Aristotle's *Physics*, *Ethics* (both unedited), and *De anima* (fragments, ed. Etzwiler 1974), a philosophically interesting commentary on the *Decretum* (unedited), a treatise on papal infallibility (ed. Xiberta 1926), and a *Summa de haeresibus* (ed. 1631).

Secondary sources. Xiberta, *Guiu Terrena* (1932); Brown, "Unity of the Concept of Being" (1992); Schabel, "Early Carmelites" (2003), "Carmelite Quodlibeta" (2007); Tierney, *Origins of Papal Infallibility* (1972); BCPMA (Bertelloni); DMA (Trottmann); Lohr; Weijers.

GUY VERNANI OF RIMINI b. Vergnano (near Rimini); d. *ca.* 1345. Dominican friar, best known for his writings on church and state. Lector at the Bologna convent in 1312. At the Rimini convent 1324–44. Commentaries have survived on the *De anima*, *Ethics*, *Politics*, and *Rhetoric* (all unedited). Wrote a treatise *De potestate summi pontificis* [1327] (ed. Cheneval 1995), and a fierce *Refutation* of Dante's *Monarchia* [1329] (ed. Matteini 1958; tr. Cassell, in *Historical Study* 2004), both in defense of papal authority. Composed a *Liber de virtutibus* (ed. Cova forthcoming), organized along the lines of the second part of Aquinas's *Summa theologiae*.

Secondary sources. Dunbabin, "Commentary on Aristotle's *Politics*" (1988); CHLMP; Kaeppeli; Weijers.

GUILLELMUS, *see* William.

ḤASDAI CRESCAS b. Barcelona, *ca.* 1340; d. 1410/11. Strikingly original Jewish philosopher, often standing in opposition to Aristotelianism. Studied in Barcelona, and attained a considerable reputation by 1370. Moved to Saragossa in 1389, where he wielded considerable authority as rabbi and liaison to the king, and helped Jewish communities rebuild after the devastating riots of 1391. His major work, the *Sefer Or Adonai* (*Light of the Lord*) [1405–10] (ed. Fischer 1990; part. tr. Wolfson, in *Crescas' Critique* 1929; part. tr. Manekin, in *Writings* 2007), attacks the Aristotelianism of Maimonides and Levi ben Gershom, advancing in the process many provocative theses, such as a substantival theory of space and a defense of determinism that expressly precludes free will. Also composed a polemic against Christianity, the *Sefer Biṭṭul 'Iqqarei ha-Nosrim* (*Refutation of the Principles of the Christians*) [1397–8] (tr. Lasker 1992; ed. and [Sp] tr. Valle Rodriguez), and a sermon on the Passover, *Derashat ha-Pesaḥ* (ed. Ravitzky 1988).

Secondary sources. Feldman, "Theory of Eternal Creation" (1980); Harvey, *Physics and Metaphysics* (1988); Pines, *Scholasticism* (1967); Robinson, "Hasdai Crescas" (2003); Rudavsky, "Theory of Time" (1990); Tobiass and Ifergan, *Crescas* (1995); Touati, "La providence" (1983); Wolfson, *Crescas' Critique* (1929); BCPMA (Rudavsky); HJP (Lasker); REP (Feldman).

HEIRIC OF AUXERRE b. 841; d. 876/7. Scholar, poet, teacher. Entered the monastery of St. Germanus of Auxerre at age seven. Became master of the school there, and had among his students Remigius, who succeeded him as master at Heiric's death. A collection of homilies (ed. Quadri 1992–) survives, and a plausible case can be made for Heiric's authorship of various glosses on the *Categoriae decem* (ed. Marenbon, in *Circle of Alcuin* 1981) and Boethius's *Opuscula sacra* (ed. Rand, in *Johannes Scottus* 1906).

Secondary sources. Marenbon, *Circle of Alcuin* (1981); BBK (Bautz).

HENRY ARISTIPPUS b. Calabria (?), *ca.* 1100; d. *ca.* 1162. Sicilian translator of Greek texts. Archdeacon of Catania in 1156. Ambassador to Constantinople 1158–60, where he obtained many Greek manuscripts. Chief minister of Sicily in 1160, but subsequently put in prison by the king, where he died. Translated Plato's *Phaedo* [1156] (ed. Minio-Paluello 1950) and *Meno* [1154/60] (ed. Kordeuter and Labowsky 1940), works that would have little influence on subsequent thought. Also translated Aristotle's *Meteorologica* Bk. IV (unedited).

Secondary sources. Dod, "Aristoteles Latinus" (1982); DMA (Lambert); Dronke.

HENRY BATE OF MALINES (Henricus Batenus) b. Mechelen (Belgium), 1246; d. Tongerloo (?), after 1310. Encyclopedist and astronomer. Studied at the Paris arts faculty *ca.* 1266–70, becoming master of arts before 1274. Perhaps became master of theology there, but mainly studied and wrote outside of the university context. His major work is the *Speculum divinorum et quorundam naturalium* [1285–1305] (part. ed. van de Vyver *et al.*

1960–), a twenty-three part synthesis of Aristotelian, Platonic, Jewish, and Islamic scientific and philosophical thought. Many minor works survive, including his *Nativitas* [1280] (unedited), which amounts to an astrological autobiography, and a treatise on the construction of the astrolabe, the *Magistralis compositio astrolabii* (ed. 1485). Henry also translated and wrote commentaries on various Jewish and Arabic treatises of astronomy.

Secondary sources. Gregory, "Platone e Aristotele" (1961); Guldentops, "Encyclopaedism" (1997), "Metamorphosis of Averroës" (1996); Wallerand, "Henri Bate et saint Thomas d'Aquin" (1934); DMA (Beyer de Ryke); DSB (Poulle); Weijers.

HENRY OF BRATTON (Bracton) b. near Barnstaple (Devon); d. Exeter, 1268. English jurist. Traditionally identified as the author of the most ambitious English legal work of the Middle Ages, the *De legibus et consuetudinibus Angliae* [*ca.* 1230–50s] (ed. and tr. Woodbine and Thorne 1968–77), which attempts to summarize all of English common law. Although the unfinished treatise is often known simply as *Bracton*, Bratton himself seems only to have been responsible for revisions and updates to a work begun much earlier. Also associated with Bratton is a notebook that transcribes some two thousand cases taken from plea rolls dating from 1217 to 1240 (ed. Maitland 1887/1983/1999).

Secondary sources. Barton, "Mystery of Bracton" (1993); Brand, "Age of Bracton" (1996); Nederman, "Kingship Revisited" (1984); "Royal Will" (1988); CHLMP; ODNB (Brand).

HENRY OF FRIEMAR b. Friemar (Thuringia), *ca.* 1245; d. Erfurt, 1340. Augustinian friar and theologian. Joined the order of Augustinian Hermits at a young age; studied theology in Bologna before 1264. Provincial minister in Germany 1290–9; subsequently studied theology in Paris, becoming regent master 1305–12. Later served as master in Erfurt. Extant works include *De quatuor instinctibus* (ed. Warnock and Zumkeller 1977); *De decem preceptis* (ed. Guyot 2005); various ascetic-mystical treatises (ed. Zumkeller 1975); a *Quodlibet*; and a commentary on the *Ethics* (both unedited).

Secondary sources. Stroick, *Heinrich von Friemar* (1954); BBK (Bautz); Lohr.

HENRY OF GHENT (Henricus Gandavensis, de Gandavo) b. Ghent, *ca.* 1217; d. 1293. Leading Paris theologian whose views would be extensively debated by subsequent generations. Master of theology at Paris in 1275/6 until shortly before his death. Canon of Tournai, archdeacon of Bruges in 1277 and then of Tournai from 1278/9 until his death. Member of the commission of theologians who advised Stephen Tempier prior to his issuing the Condemnation of 1277. A secular master (unaffiliated with any religious order), his ideas are quite distinct from those of the great Dominican and Franciscan theologians of the previous generation, such as Aquinas and Bonaventure. His principal works are a vast number of disputed questions defended over the length of his career, divided into a series of fifteen *Quodlibeta*, and a massive collection of *Quaestiones ordinariae*, which are organized in the form of a theological *Summa*. A critical edition of both these works is well underway (*Opera omnia* 1979–); parts not yet edited are accessible in reliable Renaissance editions (ed. 1518/1961 and 1520/1953). A growing number of translations are available: on political philosophy (tr. CTMPT II); divine illumination (CTMPT III); free will (tr. Teske 1993); God's existence and essence (tr. Decorte and Teske 2005); God's unity and simplicity (tr. Teske 2006). Other works, of uncertain authenticity, are a set of questions on the *Liber de causis* (ed. Zwaenepoel 1974); various lectures on the Bible (*Opera* vol. XXXVI); and commentaries on the *Physics* and *Metaphysics* (unedited).

Secondary sources. Flores, *Metaphysics and the Trinity* (2006); Guldentops and Steel (eds.), *Henry of Ghent* (2003); Gómez Caffarena, *Ser participado* (1958); Laarmann, *Deus, primum cognitum* (1999); Marrone, *Truth and Scientific Knowledge* (1985); Paulus, *Henri de Gand* (1938); Pasnau, "Twilight of Divine Illumination" (1995); Pickavé, *Metaphysik als erste Wissenschaft* (2007); Vanhamel (ed.), *Henry of Ghent* (1996); BCPMA (Wielockx); DMA (Porro); Lohr; REP (Marrone).

HENRY OF HARCLAY b. *ca.* 1270; d. Avignon, 1317. English theologian. Studied arts at Oxford, becoming master by 1296. Moved to Paris to study theology, where he was deeply influenced by Scotus's lectures. Lectured on the *Sentences* himself *ca.* 1300. Returned to Oxford, becoming master of theology before 1312, in which year he was appointed chancellor, a position he retained until his death. Though traditionally described as a Scotist, Harclay developed many original and controversial views. His principal work is a wide-ranging, philosophically rich series of twenty-nine *Quaestiones ordinariae* (ed. and tr. Henninger 2008), all dating from his years as master of theology in Paris. Of his earlier *Sentences* commentary, only Book I is extant (unedited).

Secondary sources. Dales, "Henry of Harclay on the Infinite" (1984); Henninger, *Relations* (1989); Maurer, "Univocity of Being" (1954); Murdoch, "Henry of Harclay and the Infinite" (1981); Pelster, "Heinrich von Harclay" (1924); Thijssen, "Response to Thomas Aquinas" (1990); BCPMA (Henninger); ODNB (Henninger); REP (Molland).

HENRY HOPTON *fl.* 1350s–60s. Oxford arts master. Fellow of University College in 1357. Author of an *Insolubilia* (unedited) and a treatise *De veritate et falsitate propositionis* (ed. in William Heytesbury 1494).

Secondary sources. Ashworth and Spade, "Logic in Late Medieval Oxford" (1992); Biard, "La signification" (1983); Maierù, "The Sophism" (1993); Spade, *Mediaeval Liar* (1975); Emden.

HENRY OF LANGENSTEIN (Henry Heimbuch, of Hesse) b. near Marburg, 1325; d. Vienna, 1397. Secular theologian. Studied in Paris, becoming master of arts in 1363 and master of theology in 1375. Professor of theology at Vienna in 1384. Lectured on the *Sentences*, most likely at Paris in the 1370s, and subsequently revised (Bks. II–IV ed. and [German] tr. Damerau 1980). Also extant and largely unedited are various ecclesiastical treatises, many defending Urban IV and suggesting ways of achieving ecclesiastical peace during the papal schism, as well as some brief philosophical–scientific treatises.

Secondary sources. Pirzio, "Le prospettive filosofiche" (1969); Shank, *Unless You Believe* (1988); Steneck, *Science and Creation* (1976); BBK (Bautz).

HENRY OF LÜBECK *fl.* 1312–36. Dominican theologian. German provincial minister 1325–36. Only extant works are three very wide-ranging and philosophically interesting

Quodlibeta [1312/25] (ed. in progress), probably delivered at the *studium generale* in Cologne.

Secondary sources. Bucichowski, "Le principe d'individuation" (1975); Friedman, "Dominican Quodlibetal Literature" (2007); Sturlese, "Gottebenbildichkeit" (1977); Kaeppeli.

HENRY RUYN OF ROSTOCK (of Runen) *fl.* 1430s–40s. Erfurt master, 1430s–40s. Extant works include a *Disputata Metaphysicae* [before 1438] (ed. Tabarroni 1991).

HENRY OF SUSA, *see* Hostiensis.

HENRY SUSO (Seuse) b. Swabia, *ca.* 1295; d. Ulm, 1366. Dominican mystic. A Dominican novice at thirteen; experienced a radical conversion at eighteen, followed by a decade of intense contemplation and self-deprivation. Studied at Cologne 1324–8, where he met John Tauler and perhaps studied under Eckhart. Lector and then prior at Constance until moving to Ulm [1348]. His works (German works ed. Hofmann 1966) include a theological dialogue, *Das Büchlein der Wahrheit* [1328]; the immensely popular devotional treatise *Das Büchlein der ewigen Weisheit* [1327–34] (both tr. Clark 1953), translated into Latin as the *Horologium sapientiae* (ed. Künzle 1977); and *Das Briefbüchlein* [1362]. His autobiography, compiled with his cooperation by the Dominican nun Elsbeth Stagel, a close friend and disciple, is *Das Buch von dem Diener* [1362] (tr. Clark 1952).

Secondary sources. Filthaut (ed.), *Seuse-Studien* (1966); Haas, *Nim din selbes war* (1971); Kieckhefer, *Unquiet Souls* (1984); Tobin, "Henry Suso and Elsbeth Stagel" (1999); Kaeppeli; REP (Bussanich).

HENRY TOTTING OF OYTA b. Oyta (Lower Saxony); d. 1397. Arts master and theologian. Studied in Erfurt and Prague. Master of arts at Prague in 1365. Bachelor of theology in 1371, when he was accused of heresy in Avignon, but subsequently acquitted. Subsequently studied theology in Paris, returning to Prague *ca.* 1381, becoming professor of theology there and subsequently in Vienna, from 1384. Extant works include a wide range of Aristotelian commentaries (unedited), a set of questions on the *Isagoge* (ed. Schneider 1979), and both a literal commentary and the more usual question-commentary on the *Sentences* (all unedited). Also the editor of a popular abbreviation of Adam Wodeham's *Sentences* commentary (ed. Major 1512).

Secondary sources. Lang, *Heinrich Totting von Oyta* (1937); Maierù, "Logica aristotel-ica" (1981); Lohr; Weijers.

HERMANN OF CARINTHIA (of Dalmatia, Hermannus Dalmata, Sclavus, Secundus) b. St. Peter im Holz (southern Austria), *ca.* 1110; d. after 1143. Scientist, philosopher, Arabic translator. Student of Thierry of Chartres in the 1130s; probably learned Arabic in Spain; subsequently moved to the south of France in the early 1140s. Principal translations include Ptolemy's *Planisphere* [1143] (ed. Heiberg 1907), Abū Maʿshar's *Greater Introduction to Astrology* (ed. Lemay 1995), and probably Euclid's *Elements* (ed. Busard 1967–77) (see Appendix B4). Main philosophical work is his *De essentiis* [1143] (ed. and tr. Burnett 1982), a treatise on the origins of the world and human nature.

Secondary sources. Burnett, "Hermann of Carinthia" (1988); DMA (Caiazzo); Dronke.

HERMANN THE GERMAN (Hermannus Alemannus) *fl.* 1240s–60s. Translator from Arabic into Latin. Worked in Toledo. Likely the same Hermannus who became bishop of Astorga (Léon) in 1266 and died in 1272. Translations include the *Rhetoric*, with fragments of Averroes's middle commentary; the *Summa Alexandrinorum*, an Arabic epitome of the *Ethics* [1243/4]; Averroes's middle commentary on the *Poetics* [1256]; and probably his middle commentary on the *Ethics* [1240] (see Appendices B1 and B4).
   Secondary sources. Dod, "Aristoteles Latinus" (1982).

HERMANN OF REICHENAU (Hermannus Contractus, Hermann the Lame) b. Altshausen (Swabia), 1013; d. Reichenau, 1054. Scholar, composer, mathematician, astronomer. Born into nobility. Severely disabled from birth. Entered into the abbey of Reichenau at age seven, eventually becoming abbot in 1043. A composer, he also wrote treatises on music (ed. and tr. Ellinwood 1936), mathematics, astronomy, and history. An extensive web site, including texts, is at http://flaez.ch/hermannus/.
   Secondary sources. Germann, *De temporum ratione* (2006) (edits several treatises).

HERVAEUS BRITO d. 1276 (?). Master of arts at Paris. Author of several commentaries on the *Ars vetus* (unedited), and a brief *Philosophia* (ed. Lafleur and Carrier, in "La 'Philosophia'" 1994–5). Perhaps to be identified with Hervaeus Sophista.
   Secondary sources. Lohr; Weijers.

HERVAEUS NATALIS (Hervé, Harvey Nedellec) b. Brittany, *ca.* 1250/60; d. Narbonne, 1323. French theologian and champion of Aquinas. Entered the Dominican order in 1276. Lectured on the *Sentences* at Paris, probably in 1302–3, becoming regent master in 1307–9 and again in 1316–18. He headed the Dominican's French province in 1309–18, and served as master general in 1318–23. Regarded as an early Thomist, Hervaeus is at the same time an original, independent thinker. A vast and wide-ranging body of work has survived, most prominently his *Sentences* commentary [1303–4; rev. 1309] (ed. 1647/1966), many *Quodlibeta* [1307–9] (ed. 1513/1966), a *Defensio doctrinae fr. Thomae* [1303–12] (ed. Piccari 1995), and a large number of treatises on philosophical and theological topics (including *De intellectu et specie* [ed. Stella, "La prima critica" 1959]; *De secundis intentionibus* [ed. and tr. Doyle 2008]; and eight others edited with the *Quodlibeta*). His long engagement with ecclesiastical issues yielded further treatises, including *De iurisdictione* [1311] (ed. Hödl 1959), *De potestate papae* [*ca.* 1319] (ed. with *Sentences*), and *De paupertate Christi et apostolorum* [1322] (ed. Sikes 1937–8; tr. Jones 1999).
   Secondary sources. Allen, "Notion of Being" (1960); Conforti, "*De cognitione primi principii*" (1997), "Natural and Theological Knowledge" (1999); Friedman, "Dominican Quodlibetal Literature" (2007); Henninger "Hervaeus Natalis" [Individuation] (1994); Kelley, "Some Observations on the Fictum Theory" (1978); Lowe, *Contested Theological Authority* (2003); Mannath, "Proofs for the Existence of God" (1969); Perler, "Peter Aureol vs. Hervaeus Natalis on Intentionality" (1994); Plotnik, *Controversies over the Real Presence* (1970); Schöllgen, *Das Problem der Willensfreiheit* (1927/1975); Senko, "L'essence

et l'existence" (1961); Trottmann "Verbe mentale" (1997); Wengert "Three Senses of Intuitive Cognition" (1983); BCPMA (Teske); DMA (Bonino); Kaeppeli; REP (Perler); Roensch; Weijers.

HERVAEUS SOPHISTA *fl.* 1220s. Paris arts master. Author of a collection of sophisms known as the *Abstractiones* (unedited). Perhaps to be identified with Hervaeus Brito.
  Secondary sources. De Libera, "Les *Abstractiones*" (1986); Weijers.

HEYMERIC DE CAMPO (van de Velde) b. near Eindhoven (Low Countries), *ca.* 1395; d. Leuven, 1460. Theologian and leading reviver of Albertism. Studied arts and theology at Paris, beginning *ca.* 1410. Moved to Cologne in 1422, becoming master of theology there in 1428. Rector at Cologne in 1432. Professor at the University of Louvain from 1435 to 1460, and was rector five times. Author of around fifty works ranging over philosophy, theology, and ecclesiastic politics. Friend of Nicholas of Cusa. His *Problemata inter Albertum Magnum et Sanctum Thomam* (*Tractatus problematicus*) [*ca.* 1425] (ed. 1496, etc.) takes the Albertist side in the controversy with Thomism, and became the fundamental work for later Albertism. Other works include the *Reparationes totius naturalis philosophiae* (ed. 1494), as well as a large metaphysics handbook, the *Compendium divinorum* [1420–2] (ed. Korolec 1967–8); a treatise on the trinity, *De signis notionalibus* (ed. Hoenen 1998); and a catalogue of one hundred fifteenth-century theologies, the *Centheologicon* [after 1453] (unedited). Also authored a defense of Birgitta of Sweden's *Revelationes* [1434/5] (ed. Fredriksson Adman 2003). A first volume of selected works has recently been published (ed. Imbach and Ladner 2001–).
  Secondary sources. Burie, "Proeve tot inventarisatie" (1977); Cavigioli, "Les écrits" (1981); Cavigioli and Imbach, "Quelques compléments" (1981); Hamann, *Das Siegel* (2006); Hoenen, *Heymeric van de Velde* (1990), "Academics and Intellectual Life" (1994), "Academic Theology" (2002); Ladner, *Revolutionäre Kirchenkritik?* (1985); BCPMA (Casarella); DMA (Hoenen); Weijers.

HILDEGARD OF BINGEN b. Bermersheim (Germany), 1098; d. near Bingen, 1179. Benedictine nun and influential abbess, renowned for her mystical visions and for her theological, scientific, political, and musical contributions. Entered a hermitage at the age of eight, and a Benedictine convent at fourteen. Beginning in the 1140s, she became an influential public figure, completing four preaching tours throughout Germany and engaging in extensive correspondence with religious and political leaders across Europe – unprecedented roles at the time for a woman. Founded her own convent at Rupertsberg, near Bingen *ca.* 1150. Her three major works describe in detail and present allegorical commentaries on her mystical visions, which had begun at the age of five. These works are *Scivias* [1141–51] (tr. Hart and Bishop 1990); *Liber vitae meritorum* [1158–63] (tr. Hozeski 1994); *Liber divinorum operum* [1163–73] (part. tr. Cunningham and Fox 1987). All three are edited in the *Corpus Christianorum*, as is a contemporary biography by Godefridus and others (ed. Klaes 1993; tr. McGrath and Palmquist 1995) and her extensive letters (tr. Baird and Ehrman 1994–), which are often of philosophical interest. Also authored two scientific/medical treatises, *Physica* (ed. PL 197; tr. Throop 1998) and *Causae et curae* (ed. Moulinier and Berndt 2003; part. tr. Berger 1999) [both 1150–60], as well as numerous poems and hymns, some of which Hildegard set to music. Many popular treatments of her life and work are available.

Secondary sources. Dronke, *Women Writers* (1984); Gössmann, "Hildegard of Bingen" (1989); McInerney (ed.), *Hildegard of Bingen* (1998); Maddocks, *Hildegard of Bingen* (2001); Newman, *Sister of Wisdom* (1987); Newman (ed.), *Voice of the Living Light* (1998); BCPMA (Milem); REP (Murphy).

HILLEL BEN SAMUEL OF VERONA b. *ca.* 1220; d. 1295. Physician, translator, philosopher, Talmudic scholar. Studied medicine at Montpellier; subsequently lived in Barcelona and in various Italian cities. His major work is the *Tagmule ha-Nefesh* (*The Rewards of the Soul*) [1291] (ed. Sermoneta 1981), a study of the soul's nature and its fate after death. Also translated many texts from Latin into Hebrew.

Secondary sources. Sermoneta, "Hillel ben Shemuel" (1962); REP (Rigo).

HINCMAR OF RHEIMS b. 806; d. Epernay, 882. Archbishop of Rheims and influential theologian. Educated at the abbey of St. Denis, he subsequently attained influence at the imperial court, becoming an advisor to Charles the Bald in 840 and archbishop in 845. Hincmar was at the center of various ecclesiastical controversies, notably the condemnation of Gottschalk of Orbais in 848–9 for his views on predestination. Hincmar's own first treatise on predestination [857–8] is not extant, but we have a later treatise, *De praedestinatione Dei et libero arbitrio* (PL 125). Other extant works include *De cavendis vitiis et virtutibus exercendis* (ed. Nachtmann 1998) and a large collections of letters (ed. Perels 1975–).

Secondary sources. Devisse, *Hincmar, archevêque de Reims* (1975–6); Ganz, "Debate on Predestination" (1990); Schrörs, *Hinkmar, Erzbischof von Reims* (1884); Tavard, *Trina Deitas* (1996).

HONORIUS AUGUSTODUNENSIS (of Autun) b. *ca.* 1080; d. Regensburg, *ca.* 1157. English, or perhaps German, scholar with wide-ranging interests in philosophy and theology. Studied at Anselm's school in Canterbury; subsequently lived in a convent in Regensburg. Two encyclopedic works were widely circulated and translated into vernacular languages: the *Imago mundi* (ed. Flint 1982), a treatise on cosmography, meteorology, and astronomy; and the *Elucidarium* (ed. Lefèvre 1954), a summary in dialogue form of Christian theology. Most philosophically significant work is the *Clavis physicae* (ed. Lucentini 1974), a compendium of Eriugena's *Periphyseon*. His vast corpus is collected in PL 172.

Secondary sources. Endres, *Honorius Augustodunensis* (1906); Flint, *Honorius Augustodunensis* (1995); Sanford, "Honorius" (1948); DMA (Beyer de Ryke); Dronke.

HOSTIENSIS (Henry of Susa, de Segusio) b. *ca.* 1200; d. Lyon, 1271. Eminent canon lawyer. Studied law in Bologna in the 1220s. Archdeacon of Paris by 1239; seems to have spent time in England in the royal household. Chaplain to Innocent IV, with whom he had studied in Bologna. Elected bishop of Sisteron in 1243/4, served as archbishop of Embrun in 1250–61, and finally as cardinal-bishop of Ostia in 1262–71 (the origin of his customary name). His two most important works are the *Summa aurea* [*ca.* 1253], on the Decretals of Gregory IX (ed. 1537/1962, etc.), and the *Lectura* or *Commentaria* on the Decretals [rev. 1271] (ed. 1581/1965, etc.).

Secondary sources. Gallagher, *Canon Law* (1978); Pennington.

HRABANUS MAURUS b. Mainz, *ca.* 783; d. Mainz, 856. Teacher and ecclesiastical authority. Educated in the monastery of Fulda from an early age. Took part in the circle of Charlemagne; studied with Alcuin at Tours *ca.* 800. Returned to Fulda at Alcuin's death in 804, eventually becoming abbot in 822. Elected archbishop of Mainz from 847 to 856. Among his many works (PL 107–12) are the encyclopedic *De rerum naturis* or *De universo* [842–6], a *De praedestinatione* [842] aimed at refuting the views of Gottschalk, and a large number of biblical commentaries.

Secondary sources. Bohne (ed.), *Hrabanus Maurus* (1980); Felten (ed.), *Hrabanus Maurus* (2006); Luscombe, "Predestination Controversy" (2006); Ribémont, *Les origines des encyclopédies médiévales* (2001); DMA (Morelle and Bouhot).

HUGH ETHERIAN b. Pisa; d. Constantinople, 1182. Theologian influential on controversies over the Trinity. Studied in Paris in the 1150s; moved to Constantinople *ca.* 1160. Authored a work on the Trinity, the *Liber de differentia naturae et personae* [1170s] (ed. Häring 1962), which was used in support of Gilbert of Poitiers's controversial views. Also wrote an influential work on the Trinitarian controversy dividing the Orthodox and Catholic churches, *De haeresibus quas Graeci in Latinos devolvunt* [*ca.* 1177] (ed. PL 202), and a treatise *Contra Patarenos* (ed. and tr. Hamilton *et al.* 2004).

Secondary sources. Dondaine, "Hugues Éthérien" (1952), *Écrits de la "petite école"* (1962); Marenbon, "Note on the Porretani" (1988).

HUGH OF HONAU (Hugo Honaugiensis) b. near Strasbourg *ca.* 1125; d. after 1180. Student of Gilbert of Poitiers, member of the so-called "little school" of Porretani. Visited Constantinople twice on diplomatic missions (1171, 1179), returning to Germany the second time with Hugh Etherian's *Liber de differentia naturae et personae.* Subsequently authored his own work with a similar title [*ca.* 1180] (ed. Häring 1962), relying heavily on patristic sources that he collected in his *Liber de homoysion et homoeysion* [before 1179] (ed. Häring 1967–8). More philosophical is his brief *Liber de ignorantia* [*ca.* 1180] (ed. Häring 1963). Also surviving are two letters from the 1170s to Hugh Etherian (ed. in Hugh Etherian 1962).

Secondary sources. Marenbon, "Note on the Porretani" (1988).

HUGH OF LAWTON (Lanton) *fl.* 1320s. Dominican theologian. Lectured on the *Sentences* at Oxford, 1326/30. Portions of those lectures are extant but unedited (save for excerpts in secondary sources).

Secondary sources. Gelber, "I Cannot Tell a Lie" (1984), "Eternal Questions" (1990), *It Could Have Been Otherwise* (2004); Schabel and Friedman, "Trinitarian Theology V" (2005); Kaeppeli.

HUGH OF NOVUM CASTRUM b. *ca.* 1280; d. after 1322. Franciscan theologian, a disciple of Scotus. Almost nothing is known about his life. Regent master of theology at Paris *ca.* 1321–2. His lectures on the *Sentences* in Paris [1307/17] (unedited) survive in many manuscripts and in two redactions.

Secondary sources. Heynck, "Der Skotist" (1961); Schabel and Rossini, "Time and Eternity" (2005); FA.

HUGH RIPELIN OF STRASBOURG b. Alsace, *ca.* 1200/10; d. 1268. Dominican theologian. Prior of the Zurich convent for many years beginning in 1232; prior of the Strasbourg convent in 1261. Author of the widely circulated *Compendium theologicae veritatis* [1265/70] (ed. in Albert the Great, ed. Borgnet vol. XXXIV, etc.), a straightforward summary of early Dominican theology.

Secondary sources. Steer, *Hugo Ripelin von Strassburg* (1981); BBK; Kaeppeli.

HUGH OF ST. CHER b. near Vienne, *ca.* 1190; d. Orvieto, 1263. Early Dominican theologian. Studied in Paris; became doctor of law there before 1226. Entered the Dominican order in 1225, and served as French provincial in 1227–30 and again in 1236–44. Read the *Sentences* in 1229–30 (unedited), and served as master of theology from 1230 to 1235. Named cardinal in 1244. In addition to his *Sentences* commentary and a set of disputed questions [*ca.* 1230] (unedited), surviving works include a great many biblical commentaries (ed. 1669 in 8 vols., etc.), an influential concordance on the Bible (ed. Lucas and Phalèse 1837, etc.), a *Speculum ecclesiae* on the mass (ed. Sölch 1940), a treatise *De prophetia* (ed. Torrell 1977), and various sermons (unedited).

Secondary sources. Bataillon *et al.* (eds.), *Hugues de Saint-Cher* (2004); Fisher, "Development" (1956); Principe, *Hypostatic Union* (1970); Quinto, "Use of Stephen Langton" (1999); DMA (Dahan); DTC (Mangenot); Kaeppeli; Glorieux.

HUGH OF ST. VICTOR b. Saxony, *ca.* 1096; d. Paris, 1141. Wide-ranging theologian, influential teacher, and mystic. Entered the abbey of St. Victor in Paris between 1115 and 1118, where he studied with William of Champeaux. Served as prior there from 1133. The founding intellectual figure in the "Victorine" school, concerned more with the fundamentals of education than with philosophical or theological controversies. Two most important philosophical works are his *summa* of theology, *De sacramentis christianae fidei* [1130–3] (ed. PL 176; tr. Deferrari 1951), and the *Didascalicon de studio legendi* [1120–5] (ed. Buttimer 1939; tr. Taylor 1961), which defines the parts of philosophy and its relationship to Christian teachings. Briefer works include an epitome of philosophy and treatises on geometry (tr. Homann 1991) and grammar (all three edited by Baron 1966); a *De contemplatione et eius speciebus* (ed. Baron 1958); various spiritual works, including *Noah's Ark* (ed. Sicard 2001; tr. 1962); and *De tribus diebus* (ed. Poirel 2001), a meditation on creation. The full corpus is edited in PL 175–7.

Secondary sources. Baron, *Science et sagesse* (1957), *Études sur Hugues de Saint-Victor* (1963); Ehlers, *Studien zum Geschichtsdenken* (1973); Girolimon, "*De sacramentis*" (1994); Goy, *Überlieferung* (1976); Hofmeier, *Die Trinitätslehre* (1964); Illich, *In the Vineyard* (1993); Moore, *Jews and Christians* (1998); Rudolph, *First, I Find the Center Point* (2004); Schütz, *Deus absconditus* (1967); Sicard, *Hugues de Saint-Victor* (1991); BCPMA (Gorman); Dronke; REP (Jordan).

HUGOLIN OF ORVIETO (de Urbe Veteri) b. Orvieto, *ca.* 1300; d. Acquapendente (Viterbo), 1373. Theologian and philosopher. An Augustinian Hermit, sent to study at Paris *ca.* 1334–6. Lectured on the *Sentences* at Paris in 1348–9, becoming master of theology in 1352. In 1357 he directed the Augustinian *studium* in Perugia, and in 1364 he co-founded the theology faculty in Bologna, subsequently teaching there. Appointed general of the Augustianian Hermits in 1368 and patriarch of Constantinople in 1371. Principal work is his *Sentences* commentary (ed. Eckermann 1980–8). A commentary on the *Physics* is also extant [1352] (part. ed. Eckermann, in *Physikkommentar* 1972), as is a treatise *De Deo trino* [1372] (ed. Stegmüller, in "Tractatus" 1954) and various sermons (unedited).

Secondary sources. Eckermann, *Schwerpunkte* (1990); Eckermann and Hucker (eds.), *Hugolin von Orvieto* (1992); Zumkeller, *Theologische Erkenntnislehre* (1941); Lohr.

HUGUCCIO d. 1210. Influential canon lawyer. Taught in Bologna in the 1180s, becoming bishop of Ferrara in 1190. Principal work is his *Summa* on Gratian's *Decretum* [*ca.* 1188–90] (ed. Přerovský 2006–), which he left incomplete upon becoming bishop. Sometimes identified with Huguccio of Pisa, the author of various grammatical treatises [*ca.* 1160] (unedited), but this is doubtful.

Secondary sources. Müller, "Huguccio of Pisa" (1991); Pennington.

HUMBERT OF ROMANS b. Romans (Vienne), *ca.* 1200; d. Valence, 1277. Dominican ecclesiastical leader. A student in Paris by 1215. Entered the Dominican order in 1224. Elected provincial minister first of the Roman province in 1240, then of the French province in 1244, and ultimately minister general in 1254–63, a position he voluntarily resigned, retiring to the monastery of Valence. Notable among his many works are his sermons (part. ed. Casagrande, in *Prediche* 1978) and the *Liber de eruditione praedicatorum* [1263] (ed. Berthier 1888/1956), a theoretical treatise on preaching.

Secondary sources. Heintke, *Humber von Romans* (1933); Betts, *Humbert of Romans* (1984); Kaeppeli.

ḤUNAYN IBN ISḤĀQ AL-ʿIBĀDĪ (Johannitius) b. al-Ḥīra (Iraq), 808; d. 877. Prolific translator and leading medical authority. A Nestorian Christian; studied medicine in Baghdad, until he was forced to leave, allegedly for asking too many questions. Journeyed to Alexandria, where he became fluent in Greek. Returning to Baghdad, he completed his studies, eventually becoming chief court physician. Ḥunayn translated hundreds of works from Greek into Arabic and Syriac, especially in medicine but also in philosophy, astronomy, and mathematics. (His own account of these activities is extant [ed. and (German) tr. Bergsträsser 1925].) Also produced treatises of his own, the most influential of which is *Al-Masāʾil fī al-ṭibb* (*Questions on Medicine*) (ed. Abū Rayyān *et al.* 1978; tr. Ghalioungui 1980). Fragments of this became an important Latin medical text under the title *Isagoge ad artem Galeni* (ed. Maurach 1978). His son, Isḥāq ibn Ḥunayn, would also become an eminent translator and physician.

Secondary sources. Bergsträsser, *Hunain ibn Ishak und seine Schule* (1913); Gutas, *Greek Thought* (1998); Saʿdi, "Bio-Bibliographical Study" (1934); DSB (Anawati and Iskandar); EI (Strohmaier).

IBN AL-ʿARABĪ (Muḥyi al-Dīn) b. Murcia (southeast Spain), 1165; d. Damascus, 1240. Prominent Sufi mystic and wide-ranging author. An early mystical experience shaped the course of his subsequent life. After periods in Seville and North Africa, he made the pilgrimage to Mecca in 1202 and subsequently lived in Baghdad and Anatolia before ultimately moving to Damascus. Principal works are *Al-Fuṣūṣ al-ḥikam* (*The Ringstones of Wisdom*) [1229] (ed. Affifi 1946; tr. Austin 1980, etc.) and the massive *Al-Futūḥāt al-makkiyya* (*The Meccan Revelations*) [1231; rev. 1238] (ed. Yahia 1972–91; part. tr. Chodkirwicz *et al.* 2002–4).

Secondary sources. Addas, *Quest for Red Sulphur* (1993); Affifi, *Mystical Philosophy* (1938); Bashier, *Ibn al-ʿArabī's Barzakh* (2004); Chittick, *Sufi Path of Knowledge* (1989), *Imaginal Worlds* (1994); Chodkiewicz, *Ocean without Shore* (1993); Corbin, *Creative imagination* (1969); Rizvi, "Mysticism and Philosophy" (2005); Yousef, *Time and Cosmology* (2007); BEIP (Hirtenstein); EI (Ateş); HIP (Chittick); REP (Robinson); SEP (Chittick).

IBN BĀJJA, Abū Bakr Muḥammad ibn al-Ṣāʾigh (Avempace) b. Saragossa, 1085/90; d. Fez, 1139. Founding philosopher in the Western Islamic tradition. Lived in Seville and Granada; imprisoned several times for political views. Spent his last years in Fez, where he is said to have died from poisoning by a rival. His surviving work includes medical treatises, commentaries on Aristotle and al-Fārābī, and original philosophical treatises. Prominent among these are three works apparently written toward the end of his life: the unfinished ethico-political treatise, *Tadbīr al-mutawaḥḥid* (*Governance of the Solitary*) (part. tr. Berman 1963), the *Risālat al-wadāʾ* (*Essay on Bidding Farewell*), and the *Risālat al-ittiṣāl al-ʿaql al biʾl-insān* (*Essay on the Conjunction of the Intellect with Human Beings*) (all three ed. Fakhry 1968). His commentaries on Aristotle include the *Physics* (part. ed. Lettinck, in *Aristotle's Physics* 1994), the *Meteorology* (ed. and tr. Lettinck, in *Aristotle's Meteorology* 1999), the *De generatione et corruptione* (ed. and [Sp] tr. Montada 1995), and the *De anima* (*Kitāb fī al-nafs*) (ed. al-Maʿṣūmī 1960/1999; tr. al-Maʿṣūmī 1961/1999). Among the many shorter treatises are *Man's Ultimate Felicity* (tr. Altmann, in "Ibn Bajja" 1965). Many more works are available in Spanish translation, while many others remain unedited.

Secondary sources. al-ʿAlawi, *Muʾallafat* (1983) [works]; Harvey, "Place of the Philosopher" (1992); Leaman, "Society and Philosophy" (1980); Montada, "Philosophy in Andalusia" (2005); Moody, "Galileo and Avempace" (1951); Sezgin (ed.), *Ibn Bajja* (1999); Zainaty, *La morale d'Avempace* (1979); BCPMA (Hamid); BEIP (Akbaş); EI (Dunlop); HIP (Goodman); REP (Inati); SEP (Montada).

IBN FŪRAK (Abū Bakr Muḥammad) b. Isfahan, *ca.* 941; d. 1015. Ashʿarite theologian who sought to systematize al-Ashʿarī's views. Studied in Basra and Baghdad, before taking charge of a *madrasa* built for him in Nishapur. Allegedly poisoned after a debate in Ghazni against the Karrāmiyya sect, he died while returning to Nishapur. Principal works are the *Kitāb mushkil al-ḥadīth* (*Ambiguity of the Hadith*) (ed. Gimaret 2003); the *Mujarrad maqālāt al-Ashʿarī* (*Summary of Ashʿarī's Treatises*) (ed. Gimaret 1986); and the *Kitāb al-ḥudūd fī al-uṣūl* (*Book of Definitions on the Foundations of Law*) (ed. al-Sulaymānī 1999).

Secondary sources. Gimaret, *La doctrine d'al-Ash'arī* (1990); BEIP (İskenderoğlu); EI (Watt).

IBN GABIROL, *see* Solomon ibn Gabirol.

IBN ḤANBAL (Aḥmad) b. Baghdad, 780; d. Baghdad, 855. Theologian and jurist, founder of the Hanbali school of religious law. An Arab, he was educated in Baghdad, and traveled widely from an early age studying the prophetic tradition (*ḥadīth*). His opposition to the Mu'tazilite theory of the divine attributes resulted in his persecution for many years, and he became renowned for his defense of traditional Sunnī beliefs. Most famous of his works is his vast collection of traditional sayings, the *Musnad* (ed. 1949–56, etc.). His principal theological work is the *Kitāb al-sunna* (*Book of Theological Traditions*) (ed. Qahtani 1986).

   Secondary sources. Hallaq, *Origins and Evolution of Islamic Law* (2005); Melchert, *Ahmad ibn Hanbal* (2006); BEIP (Kiliç); EI (Laoust).

IBN AL-HAYTHAM, Abū 'Alī al-Ḥasan ibn al-Ḥasan (Alhacen, Alhazen) b. Basra, 965; d. Cairo, *ca.* 1040. Natural philosopher and mathematician, famous for his work in optics. Very little about his life is known, although it is generally thought that he left modern-day Iraq for Egypt *ca.* 1021, and subsequently lived a withdrawn, scholarly life at the Azhar mosque in Cairo, from which period most of his vast corpus dates. Lists have survived of over 180 treatises, largely scientific and mathematical, a good number of which are extant. His scientific–philosophical masterpiece is the *Kitāb al-manāẓir* (*Book of Optics*) [1028/38] (Bks. I–V ed. Sabra 1983–2002; Bks. I–III tr. Sabra 1989) – translated into Latin before 1200 as the *De aspectibus* (Bks. I–VI ed. and tr. Smith 2001–8) – which, over the course of seven books, presents a highly sophisticated treatment of mathematical optics and the psychology of visual perception. This would serve as the fundamental treatise on these topics until the seventeenth century. Many other works are extant, mostly in Arabic, including a study of conics (ed. and tr. Hogendijk 1985) and a cluster of short treatises on burning mirrors and lenses. The astronomical treatise *Maqāla fī hay'at al-'ālam* (*On the Configuration of the World*) (ed. and tr. Langermann 1990) seems to have been written by someone else.

   Secondary sources. Lindberg, *Theories of Vision* (1976); Omar, *Optics* (1977); Rashed, *Géométrie et dioptrique au Xᵉ siècle* (1993), *Les mathématiques infinitésimales* (1993–2006, in 6 vols.); Sabra, *Optics* (1994) [collected papers]; Schramm, *Weg zur Physik* (1963); BCPMA (Lindberg); DSB (Sabra); EI (Vernet).

IBN ḤAZM (Abū Muḥammad 'Alī ibn Aḥmad ibn Sa'īd) b. Cordoba, 994; d. 1063. Influential jurist and philosopher. After a stormy political career in Cordoba, during which he was imprisoned and exiled on multiple occasions, he left politics and devoted himself to scholarly pursuits. Most influential as the leading exponent of the Zahirite school of jurisprudence, which insists on a literal reading of religious texts. In philosophy, one of his best-known works is a treatise on love, *Ṭawq al-hamāma* (*The Dove's Neck Ring*) (ed. Bercher 1949; tr. Arberry 1953/1997). Also composed an ethical treatise, *Kitāb al-akhlāq wa-al-siyar* (*Book of Morals and Behavior*) (ed. Tomiche 1961; tr. Abū Laylah 1990);

a study of the different branches of science, *Marātib al-ʿulūm* (*The Categories of the Sciences*) (ed. and tr. Chejne 1982); a study of differences among religions, the *Kitāb al-fiṣal fī al-milal wa-al-aḥwāʾ wa-al-niḥal* (*Book of Distinctions between Religions and Sects*) (ed. and part [Sp] tr. Asín Palacios 1927–32); and lengthy polemics against Judaism and Christianity.

Secondary sources. Aasi, *Muslim Understanding* (1999); Adang, *Muslim Writers* (1996); Arnaldez, *Grammaire et théologie* (1984); Behloul, *Evangelienkritik* (2002); Chejne, *Ibn Hazm* (1982), "Ibn Hazm on Logic" (1984); Hourani, "Reason and Revelation" (1985); Pulcini, *Exegesis as Polemical Discourse* (1998); EI (Arnaldez); REP (Leaman and Albdour).

IBN JAMĀʿA (Badr al-Dīn Muḥammad) b. Hamat (northern Syria), 1241; d. 1333. Leading member of a family of jurists from the Mamluk period. Studied in Damascus. Appointed chief judge in Egypt and Damascus. Author of numerous works on Islamic law, most prominently the *Taḥrīr al-aḥkām fī tadbīr ahl al-Islām* (*Summary of the Rules for the Governance of the People of Islam*) (ed. and [German] tr. Kofler 1934–8).

Secondary sources. Lambton, *State and Government* (1981); EI (Salibi).

IBN KAMMŪNA (Saʿd ibn Manṣūr) d. 1284. Physician and scholar. A Jew who spent most of his life in Baghdad. The *Tanqīḥ al-abḥāth li al-milal al-thalāth* (*Examination of the Inquiries into the Three Faiths*) [1280] (ed. Perlmann 1967; tr. Perlmann 1971) is a comparative study of Islam, Judaism, and Christianity. Despite its dispassionate tone, its criticisms of Islam provoked riots in Baghdad. Also extant is a treatise on the immortality of the soul (ed. Nemoy 1944; tr. Nemoy 1958) and lengthy commentaries on al-Suhrawardī (ed. Ziai and Alwishah 2003) and Avicenna (unedited).

Secondary sources. EI (Perlmann); REP (Langermann).

IBN KHALDŪN (Walī al-Dīn ʿAbd al-Raḥmān) b. Tunis, 1332; d. Cairo, 1406. Sociologist, historian, and philosopher. Studied in Tunis, then served in the Merinid court in Fez in 1354–62. Served the sultan of Granada for two years before returning to North Africa. After more than a decade of political turmoil and intrigue, departed for Egypt, where he continued to live an active political life and to serve as teacher and judge. Deeply versed in Islamic culture, his work attempts to understand the social and cultural legacy of Islam. His chief work is a history of the Arabs and Berbers, the *Kitāb al-ʿibar* (*Book of Advice*) (ed. 1961), whose very long methodological introduction (the *Muqaddima*) [1374–8] (tr. Rosenthal 1967) is his philosophical masterpiece. His philosophical ideas were deeply influenced by both Averroes and al-Ghazālī but tended to follow the latter, as in his most prominent discussion of mysticism, the *Shifāʾ al-sāʾil* (*The Healing of the Seeker*) [ca. 1373] (ed. al-Ṭanjī 1958; tr. [Fr] Pérez 1991).

Secondary sources. al-Azmeh, *Ibn Khaldūn in Modern Scholarship* (1981) [bibliography, etc.], *Ibn Khaldūn: Essay* (1990); Issawi, *Arab Philosophy of History* (1986); Lacoste, *Birth of History* (1984); Lawrence, *Islamic Ideology* (1984); Mahdi, *Philosophy of History* (1957); Nassar, *La pensée réaliste* (1967); Rosenthal, "Theory of the Power-State" (1956); BEIP (Ahmad); EI (Talbi); HIP (Lakhsassi); REP (Issawi and Leaman).

IBN MASARRA (Muḥammad ibn ʿAbd Allāh) b. Cordoba, 883; d. near Cordoba, 931. Formative Andalusian philosopher and mystic. An influential teacher, he founded a hermitage near Cordoba for friends and students. Although his works were viewed with suspicion, it was only after his death that his followers were subject to persecution. Two works are extant: *Risālat al-iʿtibār* (*On Reflection*) and *Khawāṣṣ al-ḥurūf* (*Characteristics of Letters*) (both ed. Jaʿfar 1982).

Secondary sources. Asín Palacios, *Mystical Philosophy* (1978); BEIP (Leaman); EI (Arnaldez); HIP (Goodman); REP (Atiyeh).

IBN MISKAWAYH, *see* Miskawayh.

IBN AL-MUQAFFAʿ b. Firuzabad (Persia), *ca.* 720; d. Basra, *ca.* 756. Prolific translator and scholar. A career in government made him rich, but also involved him in political conflict that led him to be executed at a young age. Author of many translations from Middle Persian into Arabic, although the traditional ascription of a synopsis of the Organon is probably incorrect. Several of his own treatises are also extant, including a mirror for princes, *Al-Adab al-kabīr* (*The Greater Work on Courtly Manners*) (ed. Fawwāl 1994).

Secondary sources. Gabrieli, "L'opera" (1931–2); Kraus, "Zu Ibn al-Muqaffaʿ" (1934); BEIP (Cooperson); EI (Gabrieli).

IBN AL-RĀWANDĪ b. Rawand (near Isfahan); d. *ca.* 910. Notorious atheist and critic of Islam. Little is known of his life other than that he lived in Baghdad. Initially an adherent of Muʿtazilism, he later became its opponent and an opponent of religion in general. Of the more than 100 books he is said to have written, only parts of a few remain. Most important of these is the *Faḍīḥat al-muʿtazila* (*The Scandal of the Muʿtazilites*) (ed. Nyberg 1925; tr. [Fr] Nadir 1957), which has survived largely intact. Subsequent authors attack Ibn al-Rāwandī ruthlessly for his opposition to Islam and lack of faith.

Secondary sources. al-Aʿsam, *History of Ibn ar-Riwandi* (1975); Stroumsa, *Freethinkers* (1999); BEIP (Leaman); EI (Kraus); REP (Inati).

IBN RUSHD, *see* Averroes.

IBN SABʿĪN (ʿAbd al-Ḥaqq ibn Ibrāhīm) b. Murcia (Spain), 1217/18; d. Mecca, 1269/71. Leading Sufi philosopher. Studied in Spain, where he acquired a reputation for learning, but was forced into exile *ca.* 1248 in Ceuta (northwest Africa). Forced to leave again, he traveled east to Tunis, Egypt, and finally Mecca. Although he acquired many students, controversy followed him the entire way. Most important philosophical work is the *Budd al-ʿārif* (*Escape of the Gnostic*) (ed. Kattūra 1978). Also extant is a philosophical correspondence with Frederick II of Sicily (ed. and [German] tr. Akasoy, in *Philosophie und Mystik* 2006).

Secondary sources. BEIP (İskenderoğlu); EI (Faure); HIP (Taftazani and Leaman); REP (Omran).

IBN SINA, *see* Avicenna.

IBN SUWĀR IBN AL-KHAMMĀR (al-Ḥasan) b. Baghdad, 942; d. *ca.* 1030. Translator, physician, and scholar. Disciple of Yaḥyā ibn ʿAdī. Translated, from the Syriac, various works of Aristotle, especially the logic. Various philosophical treatises are extant (part. tr. [Fr] in Lewin, "Ideal antique" 1955).

Secondary sources. Kraemer, *Humanism in the Renaissance* (1992); Lewin, "La notion de *muḥdath*" (1954), "L'idéal antique" (1955); Walzer, *Greek into Arabic* (1962).

IBN TAYMIYYA (Taqī al-Dīn Aḥmad) b. Harran (southeast Turkey), 1263; d. Damascus, 1328. Leading jurist and theologian. Educated in Damascus, where as a boy he had taken refuge from the Mongol invasion. Became an influential teacher there and in Cairo, but his extensive polemics led to his being imprisoned on several occasions. A wide-ranging and prolific author, many of whose works are still extant, he criticized various contemporary movements for departing from pure Sunnī beliefs. Important works include a treatise on judicial policy, the *Kitāb al-siyāsa al-sharʿiyya* (*The Governance according to Religious Law*) [1311–15] (ed. Mubārak 1966; tr. Farrukh 1966); the *Kitāb al-imān* (*Book of Faith*) (ed. Albānī 1980; tr. al-Ani and Tel 1999); *Jahd al-qrīḥah fī tajrīd al-naṣīḥah* (*Against the Greek Logicians*) (ed. and tr. Hallaq 1993); *Darʾ taʿāruḍ al-ʿaql wa-al-naql* (*Rejecting the "Contradiction" between Intellect and Transmission*) (ed. al-Raḥmān 1997); and *Al-Jawāb al-ṣaḥīḥ li-man baddala dīn al-masīḥ* (*The Right Answer to Those Who Changed the Message of Jesus Christ*) (ed. Ibn Nāṣir et al. 1993–9; part. tr. Michel 1984). Selected writings are translated in Ansari (2000).

Secondary sources. Khan, *Political Thought* (1973); Lambton, *State and Government* (1981); BEIP (Kiliç); EI (Laoust); REP (Pavlin).

IBN AL-ṬAYYIB (Abū al-Faraj ʿAbdallāh) d. 1043. Nestorian Christian philosopher and physician, active in Baghdad. Extant works include various theological treatises, such as a commentary on Genesis (ed. and [Fr] tr. Sanders 1967), and philosophical commentaries, including the *Isagoge* (ed. Gyekye 1975; tr. Gyekye 1979) and the *Categories* (ed. Ferrari 2006).

Secondary sources. Ferrari, "Duft des Apfels" (2004); EI (Vernet).

IBN TIBBON, *see* Samuel Ibn Tibbon.

IBN ṬUFAYL al-Qaysī, Abū Bakr Muḥammad (Abubacer) b. Guadix (northeast of Granada), *ca.* 1110; d. Marrakech, 1185. Prominent Andalusian philosopher. Studied medicine, became friend and physician to the Almohad rulers, to which position he was succeeded by Averroes. Aside from some poetry fragments, the only extant work is *Ḥayy ibn Yaqẓān* (ed. Gauthier 1936; tr. Goodman 1972), a philosophical fable that recapitulates all of science, philosophy, and theology through the story of a child's solitary intellectual development on a deserted island.

Secondary sources. Gauthier, *Sa vie, ses œuvres* (1909/1983); Conrad (ed.), *World of Ibn Ṭufayl* (1996); Hawi, *Islamic Naturalism and Mysticism* (1974); Hawi, "Appraisal" (1976); Hourani, "Principal Subject" (1956); Kukkonen, "No Man Is an Island" (2008); Montada, "Philosophy in Andalusia" (2005); BEIP (Leaman); EI (Carra de Vaux); HIP (Goodman); REP (Inati).

AL-ĪJĪ (ʿAḍud al-Dīn) b. Īj (southern Iran), prob. after 1281; d. Īj, 1355. Ashʿarite theologian. Served as chief judge in Shiraz *ca.* 1336. Political intrigue led to his being put in prison, where he died. Best known for his theological *summa*, the *Kitāb al-mawāqif fī 'ilm al-kalām* (*Book of Stations Concerning the Science of Theology*) (ed. 'Umayrah 1997; Bk. I tr. [German] van Ess, *Erkenntnislehre* 1966).

Secondary sources. Van Ess, "Biobibliographische Notizen" (1978); BEIP (Leaman); EI (van Ess).

IKHWĀN AL-ṢAFĀ' (Brethren of Purity) *fl.* ninth to tenth century (?). Anonymous authors of an influential Arabic encyclopedia that ranges widely over science, philosophy, and theology. There is controversy over the members of this secret society, and over their doctrinal affiliations. Even the date of composition is unclear, and the work may have been revised over the course of a century or more. The *Rasā'il Ikhwān al-Ṣafā' wa Khullān al-Wafā'* (*Epistles of the Pure Brethren and Sincere Friends*) (ed. Ghālib 1957, etc.) consists of fifty-two epistles divided into four parts (introduction; natural science [part. tr. (Fr) Gauthier-Dalché 1988]; psychology [tr. (German) Diwald 1975]; metaphysics–theology [part. tr. Van Reijn 1995]). It draws heavily on Greek and other non-Arabic material. The most famous section depicts a debate between animals and man (tr. Goodman 1978). A critical edition of the whole work, with translation, is in progress.

Secondary sources. De Callataÿ, *Ikhwān al-Ṣafā'* (2005); El-Bizri (ed.), *Epistles of the Brethren* (2008); Nasr, *Introduction* (1993); Netton, *Muslim Neoplatonists* (1982); BEIP (El-Bizri); EI (Marquet); HIP (Netton); SEP (Baffioni).

IMMANUEL BEN SOLOMON b. Rome, *ca.* 1261; d. before 1336. Poet, biblical commentator. Studied in Rome; forced to leave after the loss of his property, after which he lived in various Italian cities. Both his many biblical commentaries (largely unedited) and his poetical work contain considerable philosophical content. Notable among the former are his commentary on Genesis (ch. 1 ed. and [Ital] tr. Michelini Tocci 1963). His principal literary work is the *Maḥbarot* (*Compositions*) (ed. Jarden 1957; part. tr. Gollancz 1921).

Secondary source. REP (Rigo).

INNOCENT IV (Sinibaldo dei Fieschi, Fliscus) b. Genoa, before 1200; d. Naples, 1254. Influential canon lawyer and pope. Studied law in Parma and perhaps Bologna. Left academia for the papal curia in 1226. Elected cardinal in 1227 and pope in 1243, a tenure that was marked by his clash with the Holy Roman Emperor Frederick II. His most influential work is the long *Apparatus* or *Commentaria* on the Decretals of Gregory IX (ed. 1570/1968), on which he worked for much of his life. The *Novelle* collects his own Decretals, on which he also commented (unedited).

Secondary sources. Melloni, *Innocenzo IV* (1990); Watt, *Theory of Papal Monarchy* (1966); Pennington.

IRNERIUS OF BOLOGNA (Guarneris) b. Bologna, *ca.* 1055; d. Bologna, *ca.* 1130. Legal scholar who revived the study of Roman law. Taught in Rome, then returned to Bologna to found a new school of jurisprudence in 1088. The first of the glossators, whose marginal commentaries on the code of Justinian (the *Corpus iuris civilis*) stand at the beginning of systematic European law. Chief work is the *Summa codices* (ed. Fitting

1894/1971). Also associated with the *Quaestiones de iuris subtilitatibus* (ed. Zanetti 1958), although the true author may be Placentinus.

Secondary sources. Besta, *L'opera* (1896); Kantorowicz and Buckland, *Studies* (1938/1969); Radding, *Origins of Medieval Jurisprudence* (1988); von Savigny, *Geschichte* (1834–51/1961); Weigand, *Die Naturrechtslehre* (1967); DBI (Cortese).

ʿĪSĀ IBN ZURʿA b. Baghdad, 943; d. 1008. Translator, philosopher, Christian apologist. A Jacobite Christian; studied with Yaḥyā ibn ʿAdī. Translated various works of Aristotle, probably from the Syriac. His surviving treatises include discussions on the intellect and on the existence of God (both ed. Sbath, in *Vingt traités* 1929).

Secondary sources. Pines, "La loi naturelle" (1961); EI.

ISAAC ALBALAG *fl.* Catalonia, 1280s–90s. Philosopher, heavily influenced by Averroes's brand of Aristotelianism. Origins in the Pyrenees. Insisted on the philosophical truth of Aristotelianism, even when this appeared to conflict with biblical accounts. Translated into Hebrew, with commentary, parts of al-Ghazālī's *Intentions of the Philosophers* [1292] (part. tr. Manekin, *Writings* 2007). Also extant is the *Sefer Tikkun ha-Deʿot* (*Book of Setting Doctrines Right*) (ed. Vajda 1973).

Secondary sources. Vajda, *Isaac Albalag* (1960); HIP (Leaman); REP (Leaman); Sirat.

ISAAC BEN JOSEPH PULGAR (Pollegar) *fl.* Spain, first half of fourteenth century. Philosopher and controversialist. Little is known of his life, other than that he was close to Isaac Albalag, whose translation of al-Ghazālī he finished, and also to Abner of Burgos, of whom he became a bitter adversary after Abner's conversion to Christianity. Principal work is his *Ezer ha-Dat* (*Support of the Faith*) (ed. Levinger 1984).

Secondary source. Sirat.

ISAAC ISRAELI b. *ca.* 855; d. *ca.* 955. Early Jewish Neoplatonist and physician. Spent the first half of his life in Egypt; moved to Tunisia *ca.* 905. Served as doctor to a series of Fatimid rulers. Little more is known of his life, and his dates are likewise uncertain. His numerous writings include various philosophical and medical works, all written in Arabic, but surviving mainly in Hebrew and Latin. His best-known philosophical treatise is the *Book of Definitions*, a collection of fifty-seven definitions largely taken from al-Kindī, which has survived in Latin (ed. Muckle 1937–8) and Hebrew (*Sefer ha-Gvulim*) (ed. Hirschfeld 1896), and in fragments of the original (ed. Hirschfeld 1902). His most extended philosophical work is his *Book on the Elements*, also surviving in Latin (ed. 1515) and in Hebrew (*Sefer ha-Yesodot*) (ed. Fried 1900). A distinct *Chapter on the Elements* has also survived in Hebrew (*Shaʿar ha-Yesodot*, ed. Altmann 1956), and fragments are extant from the original *Kitāb al-jawāhir* (*Book of Substances*) (ed. Stern 1956). All of these except the *Book on the Elements* have been translated by Altmann and Stern (1958/1979). His medical works were most influential among medieval readers, both Islamic and Christian. Among these are the *Book of Fevers* and the *Book of Urine* (both ed. [Latin] 1515).

Secondary sources. Pessin, "Jewish Neoplatonism" (2003); Veit, *Das Buch der Fieber* (2003); BCPMA (Pessin); EI (Altmann); HJP (Rudavsky); REP (Lasker); SEP (Levin and Walker).

ISAAC OF STELLA b. England, early twelfth century; d. *ca.* 1177. Cistercian theologian and spiritual leader. Studied in France, joined the Cistercian order and in 1147 became abbot at the monastery of l'Étoile (*Stella*) near Poitiers. Moved to the island of Ré, near La Rochelle, *ca.* 1167, where he founded a new Cistercian monastery. His *Epistola de anima* (ed. PL 194; tr. McGinn, *Three Treatises* 1977) depicts the soul standing between God and the world, an image of both. This brief work would indirectly achieve wide circulation through its absorption into the pseudo-Augustinian treatise *De spiritu et anima* (also tr. McGinn 1977). Also surviving is a large collection of sermons, often with substantial philosophical and theological content (ed. and [Fr] tr. Hoste *et al.* 1967–87, in 3 vols.; part. tr. McCaffrey 1979; Deme 2007).

Secondary sources. McGinn, *Golden Chain* (1969); Raciti, "Isaac de l'Étoile" (1971); REP (Wetherbee).

ISIDORE OF SEVILLE b. Carthagena or Seville, *ca.* 560; d. 636. Influential encyclopedist. Born into a prominent religious family, becoming a monk *ca.* 589. Bishop of Seville from *ca.* 600. Primarily a compiler rather than an original thinker, his aim was to preserve the disappearing knowledge of antiquity. Best known for his *Etymologies* [*ca.* 620–35] (ed. Lindsay 1911; tr. Barney 2006), a twenty-volume attempt at a compendium of all knowledge, which would be enormously influential on later medieval thought. Composed another encyclopedia, the *De natura rerum* (ed. and tr. [Fr] Fontaine 1960/2002), as well as two further works on the meanings of terms, the *Differentiae* and the *Synonyms*. His explicitly theological works include *De fide catholica*, *De ecclesiasticis officiis*, *De ordine creaturarum*, and *Sententiarum libri tres* (ed. Cazier 1998). Letters have also survived (tr. Ford 1970). The complete works are available in PL 81–4, and are being reedited in *Corpus Christianorum* (1989–).

Secondary sources. Brehaut, *Encyclopedist* (1964); Fontaine, *Isidore de Séville* (1984), *Tradition et actualité* (1988) [papers]; Henderson, *Medieval World* (2007); Ribémont, *Les origines* (2001); BCPMA (d'Onofrio); DMA (Reydellet).

IVO OF CHARTRES (Carnotensis) b. prob. near Beauvais, *ca.* 1040; d. 1115. Important scholar of canon law. Studied with Lanfranc and Anselm at Bec. Bishop of Chartres from 1090 until his death. Author of three efforts to systematize canon law: the *Collectio tripartita* (unedited), the *Decretum* (ed. PL 161), and the *Panormia* (ed. PL 161). The "Prologue" to these is particularly interesting (ed. Brasington 2004). A large corpus of letters has also survived, almost all concerned with ecclesiastical business (part. ed. Leclercq 1949; letter 222 tr. Fairweather, in *Scholastic Miscellany* 1956).

Secondary sources. Kéry, *Canonical Collections* (1999); Sprandel, *Ivo von Chartres* (1962).

JĀBIR IBN ḤAYYĀN (Geber) b. 721; d. 815. Foundational authority on alchemy. Prolific, wide-ranging scholar, whose works are said to have numbered over 1,000, although Jābir's very existence has been debated by some modern scholars, and his authorship of many traditionally attributed works is seriously in doubt. Among these, the influential *Summa perfectionis* is now known not to be an Arabic treatise at all, and is instead ascribed to Paul of Taranto. It, along with other Latin works associated with Jābir, were translated into English in the seventeenth century (tr. Russel 1678/1928). Selections from the *Kitāb al-Ahjar* (*Book of Stones*) are available in a modern edition (ed. and tr. Haq 1990).

Secondary sources. Hill, "Literature of Arabic Alchemy" (1990); Kraus, *Jābir ibn Ḥayyān* (1942–3); EI (Kraus).

JACOB, JACQUES, *see also* James.

JACOB ANATOLI b. southern France, *ca.* 1194; d. 1258. Prominent Arabic-to-Hebrew translator. Son-in-law of Samuel ibn Tibbon. Physician at the court of Frederick II in Naples *ca.* 1231, where he came to know and perhaps work alongside the great Latin translator Michael Scot. Translated Averroes's middle commentary on the Organon [*ca.* 1232], as well as various astronomical treatises (see Appendix B6). His only original work is the *Malmad ha-Talmidim* (*Incentive to the Pupils*) [*ca.* 1249] (ed. 1866/1968), a collection of moralizing sermons.

Secondary source. Sirat.

JAHM IBN ṢAFWĀN (Abū Muḥriz) b. Khurasan; d. 746. Early Islamic theologian. Spent most of his life in Tirmidh (Uzbekistan). Executed after taking part in a political revolt. His theological views were influential enough to have inspired a later sect of Jahmiyya, but none of his works are extant.

Secondary sources. Van Ess, *Theologie und Gesellschaft* (1991–7); EI (Watt); BEIP (el-Kaisy).

JAMES OF ASCOLI (Jacobus de Aesculo) *fl.* 1310s. Franciscan theologian and follower of Scotus. Master of theology at Paris by 1309; regent master in 1310–11. Active in inquisitions against Marguerite of Porete and Peter of John Olivi. Extant works include various quodlibetal and disputed questions (part. ed. Yokoyama 1967) and an incomplete *Sentences* commentary (unedited).

Secondary sources. Hödl, "Die Seinsdifferenz" (1988); BBK (Madey); FA; Glorieux.

JAMES OF DOUAI (Jacobus de Duaco) *fl.* 1275. Master of arts in Paris. Extant commentaries (mainly unedited) on both *Analytics*, the *De anima* (ed. Raedemaeker 1962), the fourth book of the *Meteorology*, the *Parva Naturalia*, and perhaps the *Ethics*. Also extant is a treatise on the soul's knowledge of itself (ed. Bazán 1969).

Secondary sources. Grabmann, "Jakob von Douai" (1947); Guldentops, "Theory of Knowledge" (2006), "Philosophy of Mind" (2007); CHLMP; Lohr; Weijers.

JAMES OF LAUSANNE d. 1322. Dominican theologian. Student of Peter of Palude. Read the *Sentences* at Paris in 1314–15, becoming master of theology in 1317. Both a literal and a question commentary survive (unedited).

Secondary sources. Schabel *et al.*, "Peter of Palude" (2001) [edits three questions on divine foreknowledge]; Kaeppeli.

JAMES OF METZ (Jacobus Mettensis) *fl. ca.* 1300. Dominican theologian. Lectured on the *Sentences*, perhaps at Paris, *ca.* 1300–1, and again *ca.* 1302–3 (unedited). This is his only known work. James was by no means a Thomist, although the degree of his anti-Thomism remains subject to dispute. Influential on subsequent heterodox Dominicans, such as Durand of St. Pourçain. James's views would later be the subject of a short polemical treatise by Hervaeus Natalis (unedited).

Secondary sources. Decker, *Die Gotteslehre* (1967); Koch, "Jakob von Metz" (1929); Köhler, *Der Begriff der Einheit* (1971), "Wissenschaft und Evidenz" (1974); Solère, "Thomistes et antithomistes" (1997); Ullrich, *Fragen der Schöpfungslehre* (1966); BCPMA (Friedman); DMA (Solère); Kaeppeli.

JAMES OF PIACENZA (Jacobus de Placentia, Jacques de Plaisance) *fl.* 1340s. Arts master at Bologna. Regarded as a proponent of radical Averroism. Extant works include disputed questions, various commentaries on the logical curriculum (all unedited), and questions on *De anima* III (ed. Kuksewicz 1967).

Secondary sources. Kuksewicz, *De Siger de Brabant à Jacques de Plaisance* (1968); Lohr; Weijers.

JAMES OF THÉRINES b. Thérines (Picardy); d. 1321. Cistercian theologian. Studied in Paris as early as 1290, becoming regent master of theology in 1306. Left Paris in 1309 to serve as abbot of the monastery at Chaalis, where he had originally joined the order. Abbot of Pontigny from 1317/18 until his death. His extant works consist of two *Quodlibeta* from 1306–7 (ed. Glorieux 1958).

Secondary sources. Jordan, *Unceasing Strife* (2005); Sullivan, "*Quodlibeta*" (2007).

JAMES OF VENICE b. Venice; d. after 1147. The most important twelfth-century Greek-to-Latin translator. Studied in Constantinople. Translated large parts of Aristotle's corpus, including the *Posterior Analytics*, *Physics*, *De anima*, some of the *Parva Naturalia*, and *Metaphysics* I–IV.4 (ed. *Aristoteles Latinus* 1953–). These were the standard Latin translations until William of Moerbeke's [1260s], and in some cases beyond (see Appendix B1).

Secondary sources. Brams, *Riscoperta di Aristotele* (2003); Dod, "Aristotles Latinus" (1982); Minio-Paluello, *Opuscula* (1972); DMA (Bonmariage); Dronke.

JAMES OF VITERBO (Jacobus Capocci) b. Viterbo, *ca.* 1255; d. 1307/8. Parisian master of theology. Joined the order of Augustinian Hermits *ca.* 1270. Studied philosophy and theology at Paris *ca.* 1275–82. After another period in Italy, he returned to Paris as bachelor of theology in 1288, studying under Giles of Rome, whom he succeeded as master of theology from 1293 to 1300. Lecturer at the Augustinian *studium generale* in Naples until 1302; archbishop of Naples from 1303 until his death. Principal works are his four *Quodlibeta* [1293–7] (ed. Ypma 1968–75; II.20 and IV.30 tr. CTMPT II) and his thirty-two *Quaestiones de divinis praedicamentis* [before 1296] (part. ed. Ypma 1983–6, with further questions appearing in *Augustiniana* 1988–). His *De regimine christiano* [1301–2] (ed. and tr. Dyson 1995) argues in favor of papal authority. Various other works survive, mainly unedited, including a series of disputed questions *De verbo* (quest. 1 ed. Scanzillo 1972).

Secondary sources. Ypma, "Recherches sur la carrière" (1974), "Recherches sur la productivité" (1975); Gossiaux, "Essence and Existence" (1999), "Reality of the Possibles" (2007); Gutierrez, "De vita et scriptis" (1937–8); Mahoney, "Themistius and the Agent Intellect" (1973); Phelps, "Theory of Seminal Reasons" (1980); Ruello, "Fondements de la liberté humaine" (1974–5); Wippel, "Relationship between Essence and Existence" (1982); BCPMA (Gossiaux); CHLMP; DMA (Bonino); REP (Mahoney); Glorieux.

JAN VAN RUUSBROEC (van Ruysbroeck) b. *ca.* 1293; d. 1381. Dutch mystic. Educated at the cathedral school in Brussels; ordained priest in 1317. Founded a monastic community outside Brussels, of which he became prior from 1350 until his death. His eleven extant works are in Middle Dutch. Most important is the *Die gheestelike brulocht* (*The Spiritual Espousals*) (tr. Wiseman 1985), whose three books address the active, the inner, and the contemplative life. His complete works are available in a modern edition (ed. de Baere 1988–).

Secondary source. DMA (Hoenen).

JEAN, *see* John.

JEROME OF PRAGUE b. Prague, 1370/1; d. Constance, 1416. Disciple of John Hus, burned at the stake for supporting the doctrines of Hus and John Wyclif. Studied at the University of Prague; journeyed to Oxford in 1399, then returned to Prague with copies of Wyclif's theological writings. An edict at Prague against Wyclif's doctrines led Jerome to relocate as master of arts at Paris, from where he was forced to flee in 1406, moving first to Heidelberg and then to Cologne, and finally back to Prague. After more years of controversy, including charges of heresy – motivated largely by his outspoken demands for ecclesiastical reform – Jerome was arrested and brought to Constance. After initially making the recantation that would have saved his life, he retracted it and was burned at the stake. The principal philosophical tenet at issue in these controversies is thought to be a strong form of realism regarding universals, but Jerome wrote little, and all that has survived are a few speeches (ed. Höfler, *Geschichtsschreiber* 1856–66, vol. II) and various brief philosophical treatises (mostly unedited).

Secondary sources. Bernard, "Jerome of Prague" (1958); Betts, "Jerome of Prague" (1969); Kaluza, "Jérôme de Prague" (1994); Pilný, *Jérôme de Prague* (1974); Vilém, "Der Streit" (1995); BCPMA (Sanford); Weijers.

JOACHIM DE FIORE b. Calabria, *ca.* 1135; d. 1202. Monastic reformer and reputed prophet of the coming Antichrist. Son of a notary, he gave up his father's profession after a religious experience while traveling in the Middle East. Eventually returned to Calabria and joined a Cistercian monastery in 1159, but left the Cistercians in 1189 to found a new monastic order in Fiore. Most famous for his Apocalypse commentary (ed. 1527/1964); other significant works are the *Liber de concordia novi ac veteris testamenti* (ed. Daniel 1983), the *Tractatus super quatuor evangelia* (ed. Buonaiuti 1930), and the *Psalterium decem chordarum* (ed. 1527/1965). His most philosophical work is the brief *De prescientia Dei et predestinatione electorum* (ed. de Leo 1988).

Secondary sources. McGinn, *Calabrian Abbot* (1985); Reeves, *Influence of Prophecy* (1969); West and Zimdars-Swartz, *Joachim of Fiore* (1983); DMA (De Fraja); DS (Baraut); REP (Eisen Murphy).

JOHANNES, *see also* John.

JOHANNES TEUTONICUS b. *ca.* 1170; d. 1245. Influential canon lawyer. Studied and taught at Bologna before retiring to Halberstadt *ca.* 1219. His efforts at synthesizing earlier material were so successful that his gloss on Gratian's *Decretum* (as revised by Bartholomew of Brescia) became known as the *Glossa ordinaria* [*ca.* 1215] (ed. 1601, etc.; part. tr. Thompson and Gordley 1993). Other principal works are the *Compilatio quarta*, together with an apparatus of glosses (ed. Augustín 1576), and an *Apparatus glossarum* on the *Compilatio tertia* (Bks. I–II ed. Pennington 1981).

Secondary sources. Weigand, *Die Naturrechtslehre* (1967); Pennington.

JOHANNITIUS, *see* Ḥunayn ibn Isḥāq.

JOHN AURIFABER *ca.* 1295–1333. Arts master and critic of modist grammar. Studied at Paris. Arts master at Erfurt. Known for his *Determinatio de modis significandi* [1332] (ed. Pinborg, in *Entwicklung* 1967), which formulates an influential attack on the doctrine of modism. Also extant are a *Tractatus de demonstratione*, a sophism on dimensions, and a question on mixtures (all unedited). A distinct John Aurifaber served as master of arts at Paris in 1397; his only extant work is a few questions on the *Physics* (unedited).

Secondary sources. Biard, *Logique et théorie* (1989); Kuksewicz, "Some Remarks" (1997); Lorenz, *Studium generale erfordense* (1989); Pinborg, "A Note" (1975), "Speculative Grammar" (1982); CHLMP; Lohr; Weijers.

JOHN BACONTHORPE (Baco, Bacconis) b. Norfolk, *ca.* 1290; d. 1345/52. Carmelite theologian. Entered the Carmelite convent at Blakeney at a young age. Studied at Oxford. Read the *Sentences* at Paris, most likely in 1320–1, becoming regent master there by 1323. Provincial prior in England in 1327–33. Probably taught at Cambridge, and later Oxford. Although commonly categorized as an Averroist, it remains unclear to what extent this is accurate. His *Sentences* commentary survives in several redactions, the earlier version surviving in manuscript form (part. ed. Borchert 1974) and a later version [after 1325] surviving only in a printed edition (ed. 1618/1969, etc.). Also surviving are three *Quodlibeta* [the first two probably in 1323–5, the third, also in Paris, in 1330] (ed. 1618/1969, etc.), questions on canon law [*ca.* 1340] (ed. Borchert 1974), as well as commentaries on the Gospel of Matthew [1336/7] and on Augustine and Anselm (all unedited).

Secondary sources. Di S. Brocardo, "Profilo storico" (1948); Etzwiler, "Doctrine of the Unique Intellect" (1971), "Prince of the Averroists" (1976); Lynch, "De distinctione intentionali" (1931); Schabel, "Carmelite Quodlibeta" (2007); Smalley, "Postill on St

Matthew" (1958); Turley, "Papal Infallibility" (1982); Xiberta, *De scriptoribus* (1931); BCPMA (Cross); DMA (Schmutz); ODNB (Marenbon).

JOHN OF BASSOLIS d. 1333. Franciscan theologian, a disciple of Scotus. Lectured on the *Sentences* in Rheims in 1313 [rev. *ca.* 1317] (ed. 1516–17).

Secondary sources. Pasiecznik, "John de Bassolis" (1953–4); Volz, *Die Lehre des Johannes de Bassolis* (1969); FA.

JOHN BLUND b. *ca.* 1175; d. 1248. Early lecturer on the new Aristotle. Studied arts at Paris; apparently lectured at both Oxford and Paris around the turn of the century. Returned to Paris to study theology; eventually incepted as master *ca.* 1220. Unrest in Paris brought him back to England in 1229. Elected archbishop of Canterbury in 1232, he was denied consecration by Gregory IX, and instead appointed chancellor of York Minster from 1234–48. The only extant work is a treatise on the soul [*ca.* 1200/10] (ed. Callus and Hunt 1970), probably composed at Oxford, and remarkable as a very early instance of Aristotle's and Avicenna's appearance in the curriculum of the new universities.

Secondary sources. Callus, "Introduction of Aristotelian Learning to Oxford" (1943), "Treatise of John Blund" (1955); Dronke; ODNB (Lawrence); Weijers.

JOHN BODE (Bodi) *fl.* 1357. Benedictine monk and doctor of theology at Oxford. Only known work is a collection of twenty-two sophisms known by its incipit, *A est unum calidum* (unedited), written in the tradition of the Oxford Calculators. The John Bode listed as a fellow of Merton College in 1338 is probably a different man.

Secondary sources. CHLMP; Emden; ODNB (North).

JOHN BURIDAN b. Picardy, 1295/1300; d. 1358/61. Parisian arts master; the most influential philosopher of the later fourteenth century. Educated in Paris; earned master of arts degree by the mid-1320s. Taught in the arts faculty at Paris for his entire career, serving twice as rector [1328, 1340]. Never became theology master, but remained a secular cleric (unaffiliated with any religious order). Although later classified as a nominalist, his views are highly original and not easily labeled, in some areas showing the influence of Ockham but in other places diverging quite dramatically. Although heavily influential on later scholastic thought, scholars no longer speak of a true "Buridan School," but simply regard his influence as pervasive both in Paris and elsewhere. His main philosophical achievement is found in his question-commentaries, which are extant for most of Aristotle's major works, often in multiple redactions. Of particular philosophical interest are the commentaries on the *Physics* (ed. 1509/1964), *Metaphysics* (ed. 1518/1964), and *De anima* (ed. and tr. Zupko 1989 [Bk. III only, from the third redaction]; ed. Patar 1991 [an earlier redaction]; ed. Lokert 1516, etc. [seemingly a mix of various redactions]), critical editions of which are all underway. Also edited are questions on Porphyry (ed. Tatarsynski 1986); the *Categories* (ed. Schneider 1983); the *De interpretatione* (ed. Van der Lecq 1983); *De generatione et corruptione* (ed. Streijger forthcoming); and *De caelo* (ed. Moody 1942). In logic, Buridan authored the massive *Summulae de dialectica* (various part. eds.; the whole tr. Klima 2001), one of the key texts of the *via moderna*, which consists in nine large parts, the ninth being the *Sophismata* (ed. Pironet 2004; tr. Klima

2001 and Scott 1966), which also circulated as a separate treatise. Another important logical work is the *Tractatus de consequentiis* (ed. Hubien 1976; tr. King 1985). The main ethical work is the commentary on the *Ethics* (ed. 1513/1968; part. tr. CTMPT II); the *Politics* commentary published under Buridan's name is not authentic. Many other commentaries and briefer treatises are extant.

Secondary sources. Michael, *Johannes Buridan* (1985) [biobibliography]; de Rijk, "On Universals" (1992); Hughes, *Self-Reference* (1982); Klima, *John Buridan* (2009); Krieger, *Begriff der praktischen Vernunft* (1986), *Subjekt und Metaphysik* (2003); Normore, "Buridan's Ontology" (1985); Schönberger, *Relation als Vergleich* (1994); Thijssen, "Buridan School" (2004); Thijssen and Zupko (eds.), *Metaphysics and Natural Philosophy* (2001); Walsh, "Connection of the Virtues" (1986); Zupko, *Portrait* (2003); BCPMA (Klima); DMA (de Libera); SEP (Zupko); REP (Zupko); Weijers.

JOHN THE CANON (Mambres, Marbres) b. Catalonia; *fl.* 1320s/30s. Master of arts at Toulouse. Canon of Tortosa, and possibly also Barcelona. Influenced by Francis of Marchia, although not a Franciscan. Only known work is a *Physics* commentary (ed. 1475, etc.). His identity with John Mambres is supposed, but not certain.

Secondary sources. Bakker and Dekker, "Antoine Andrée ou Jean le Chanoine?" (2000); Lohr; Weijers.

JOHN CAPREOLUS (Jean Cabrol) b. near Rodez (southern France), 1380; d. Rodez, 1444. Key figure in the Thomist movement. Known in the Renaissance as the *Princeps Thomistarum* – not quite the "Prince of Thomists" (as he is often called), but more literally the Founding Father of the Thomists. Joined the Dominican order in southern France. Assigned to lecture on the *Sentences* at Paris in 1407; licensed as master of theology in 1411. Subsequently taught at Dominican convents in Toulouse and Rodez. Worked for the remainder of his life on his commentary on the *Sentences*, also known as the *Defensiones theologiae divi Thomae Aquinatis* (ed. Paban and Pègues 1900–8/1967). This work takes the form of a massive defense of Aquinas's doctrines against a host of critics, particularly Henry of Ghent, Scotus, Peter Auriol, Ockham, Adam Wodeham, and Gregory of Rimini. The material on virtues from Bk. III is available in translation (tr. White and Cessario 2001).

Secondary sources. Bedouelle *et al.* (eds.), *Jean Capreolus* (1997); Forster, *Verteidigung der Lehre* (1955); Grabmann, "Johannes Capreolus" (1956); Hegyi, *Die Bedeutung des Seins* (1959); Müller, "Ethics" (2004), "Sprache" (2004); BCPMA (White); Kaeppeli; REP (Tavuzzi).

JOHN CHILMARK d. *ca.* 1396. Mathematician and philosopher. Master of arts and fellow of Merton College in 1384. Subsequently lectured at Exeter College. At least eight extant works of logic and natural philosophy, in the Mertonian tradition, are ascribed to Chilmark (all unedited).

Secondary sources. Keele, "Logical and Scientific Treatises" (2007).

JOHN OF DACIA (Johannes Dacus) *fl.* 1280s. Master of arts at Paris. Most important extant work is a modist grammar, the *Summa gramatica* [*ca.* 1280], a very long but incomplete record of lectures on Priscian. Also extant is a *Divisio scientiae* [*ca.* 1280] and *De gradibus formarum* (all ed. Otto 1955).

Secondary sources. Rosier-Catach, *Grammaire spéculative* (1983); Sirridge, "Science of Language" (1995); Weijers.

JOHN DORP b. near Leyden; *fl.* 1393–1418. Logician, traditionally numbered among the nominalists. Received his bachelor of arts at Paris in 1393; named master in that same year. Became master of medicine in 1404 and left Paris in 1405 to serve as a physician in Holland. Listed as master of arts at Cologne in 1413. Authored a commentary on Buridan's *Summulae* [*ca.* 1393] (ed. 1499/1965, etc.), of which tract 4 (on the properties of terms) is in fact a commentary on Marsilius of Inghen.

Secondary sources. Ashworth, "Infinite Sets" (1977), "Medieval Theories of Singular Terms" (2006); Bos, "Die Rezeption" (2000); Read, "Material Supposition" (1999); Weijers.

JOHN DUMBLETON b. Gloucestershire, *ca.* 1310; d. *ca.* 1349. Natural philosopher; one of the Oxford Calculators. Fellow of Merton College by 1338. Studied theology in Paris, perhaps in 1345–6. Author of a large *Summa logicae et philosophiae naturalis* [1340s] (unedited), mostly focused on natural philosophy and extant in over twenty manuscripts, and a brief *Compendium sex conclusionum* [1348] (ed. Weisheipl, in "Early Fourteenth-Century Physics" 1956; tr. Moody, in *Rise of Mechanism* 1950), a discussion of circular motion.

Secondary sources. Molland, "Geometrical Optics" (1995); Sylla, *Oxford Calculators* (1991) [outline of *Summa* pts. II–VI], "Latitude of Forms" (1973), "John Dumbleton's *Summa*" (1991); Weisheipl, "Early Fourteenth-Century Physics" (1956), "Place of Dumbleton" (1959), "Ockham and some Mertonians" (1968), "Repertorium Mertonense" (1969); BCPMA (Sylla); ODNB (Molland); Weijers.

JOHN DUNS SCOTUS b. Duns (Scotland), 1265/6; d. Cologne, 1308. Vastly influential Franciscan theologian and philosopher. Studied with the Franciscans at Oxford from an early age; began his theological studies there *ca.* 1288. Lectured on the *Sentences ca.* 1298. Sent to Paris in 1302, where he lectured on the *Sentences* again (interrupted by a year in England in 1303–4). Regent master of theology at Paris in 1305–7, after which he was assigned to the Franciscan *studium* in Cologne. Principal work is the *Sentences* commentary, extant in a bewildering number of versions. The earliest version is the *Lectura*, dating from Oxford, for which we have Bks. I–III. These were revised [1300–4], and this *Ordinatio* includes Bk. IV (but has gaps elsewhere). The Paris lectures have survived in the form of various more or less polished lecture notes, the *Reportatio Parisiensis*. There are multiple versions for each of the four books, and also the so-called *Additiones magnae* compiled by William of Alnwick [1312/25]. At present, the Vatican critical edition (ed. Balić *et al.* 1950–) has completed the *Lectura* and is partway through the *Ordinatio*. For the Paris lectures, one must still consult the old *Opera omnia* (ed. Wadding 1639; ed. Vivès 1891–5), although a version of Bk. I is newly available (ed. and tr. Wolter and Bychkov 2004).

Other important works are the *Quodlibeta* [1306/7] (ed. Alluntis 1968; tr. Alluntis and Wolter 1975); the *De primo principio* [*ca.* 1308] (ed. and tr. Wolter 1966), on God's existence and nature; the *Collationes* [1302–8], a set of disputations from Oxford and Paris; and the doubtfully authentic *Theoremata*. In addition, there are many question-commentaries on Aristotle, mostly from early in Scotus's career, with the exception of the *Metaphysics* (tr. Etzkorn and Wolter 1997–8), which mixes early and late material. These works have been edited as the *Opera philosophica* (ed. Noone *et al.* 1997–2006). Most of Scotus's work has never been translated, although useful collections are available on will and morality (ed. and tr. Wolter 1986); universals (tr. Spade, in *Five Texts* 1994); contingency and freedom (ed. and tr. Vos 1994), individuation (ed. and tr. Wolter 2005), as well as a general *Philosophical Writings* (ed. and tr. Wolter 1962/1987).

Secondary sources. Cross, *Physics* (1998), *Duns Scotus* (1999), *Duns Scotus on God* (2005); Frank and Wolter, *Duns Scotus, Metaphysician* (1995); Honnefelder, *Ens inquantum ens* (1979); Kent, *Virtues of the Will* (1995); Pini, *Categories* (2002); Ryan and Bonansea (eds.), *John Duns Scotus* (1965); Vos, *Philosophy* (2006); Williams (ed.), *Cambridge Companion* (2003); Wolter, *Philosophical Theology* (1990) [collected papers]; Wolter (ed.), *Duns Scotus* (1993); Wood *et al.* (eds.), *John Duns Scotus* (1996); BCPMA (Dumont); REP (Dumont); SEP (Williams); Weijers. Tobias Hoffmann maintains an internet bibliography.

JOHN OF ERFURT (Erfurdensis, Alemannus, of Saxony) b. Saxony, *ca.* 1255; d. *ca.* 1320/40. Franciscan canon lawyer and perhaps theologian. Lectured at Erfurt, beginning *ca.* 1275, and Magdeburg *ca.* 1285–95. Studied law in Bologna in 1295. Particularly influential for his *Summa confessorum* [1295; rev. 1302] (ed. Brieskorn 1981). The popular *Sentences* commentary [1294/1304] (unedited) may have been authored by a younger man by the same name.

Secondary sources. Heynck, "Studien" (1958–60); FA; Pennington.

JOHN OF FREIBURG b. *ca.* 1250; d. *ca.* 1304. Dominican moral theologian. Author of a *Summa confessorum* [1298] (ed. 1476, etc.), which draws on the moral theory of Aquinas to update Raymond of Pennafort's *Summa de paenitentia*.

Secondary sources. Boyle, "*Summa confessorum*" (1974); Kaeppeli.

JOHN OF GARLAND b. Berkshire, *ca.* 1195; d. *ca.* 1272. Grammarian and poet. Studied at Oxford in 1210–13; subsequently taught at Paris. Master of grammar at Toulouse in 1229–32, afterwards returning to Paris, where he seems to have remained. Principal work is the *Compendium gramatice* [*ca.* 1232] (ed. Haye 1995), with an accompanying guide, the *Clavis compendii* [*ca.* 1234] (ed. Marguin-Hamon 2008). Also extant is the *Ars lectoria Ecclesie* or *Accentarius* [1234] (ed. Marguin-Hamon 2003) and commentaries on the verse grammars of Evrard of Béthune and Alexander of Villa Dei (unedited). His youthful *Dictionarius* [*ca.* 1218] (ed. and tr. Rubin 1981) marks the first known use of that term. Many poems are also extant. The musical theorist John of Garland is a different man.

Secondary sources. Grondeux and Marguin. "L'œuvre grammaticale" (1999); Hunt, *Teaching and Learning* (1991); ODNB (Traugott); Weijers.

JOHN GERSON (Jean Le Charlier) b. Gerson-les-Barbey (Ardennes), 1363; d. Lyon, 1429. Ecclesiastical and spiritual leader. Early education in Rheims. Studied philosophy and theology at the College of Navarre in Paris from 1377. Student of Peter of Ailly. Master of arts in 1382. Sent to Avignon in 1387 as part of a delegation intent on defending the rights of the university against the papacy. Master of theology in 1392. Appointed university chancellor in 1395, a position he retained until his death, even after he left Paris for the last time in 1415. Heavily involved in efforts at curricular reform at Paris, and at ending the papal schism. An influential voice at the Council of Constance [1414–17]. Spent the last decade of his life in Lyon, where he was active as an author and advisor on spiritual matters. An extremely prolific author, his complete works are edited in ten volumes (ed. Glorieux 1960–73). In philosophy, he was sympathetic toward nominalism, in the *De modis significandi* [1426] and *De concordia metaphysicae cum logica* [1426]. He is much better known, however, as a proponent of educational reform, in works such as *Contra curiositatem studentium* [1402] (part. tr. Ozment 1969), and for his spiritual and mystical writings, including *De mystica theologia* [1402–3] (part. tr. McGuire 1998), *De consolatione theologiae* [1418] (ed. and tr. Miller 1998), and *De elucidatione scholastica mysticae theologiae* [1424]. Many letters have also survived.

Secondary sources. McGuire, *Jean Gerson* (2005); McGuire (ed.), *Companion* (2006); Brown, *Pastor and Laity* (1987); Burger, *Aedificatio* (1986); Burrows, *Consolation* (1991); Connolly, *Jean Gerson* (1928); Mourin, *Jean Gerson* (1952); Pascoe, *Jean Gerson* (1973); Vial, *Jean Gerson* (2006); BCPMA (South); DMA (Solère); REP (Burrows).

JOHN HILTALINGEN OF BASEL b. Basel, *ca.* 1315; d. Freiburg, 1392. Augustinian friar and theologian. Studied in Avignon; taught at the Augustinian *studium generale* in Strasbourg. Lectured on the *Sentences* in Paris in 1365–6, receiving his doctorate in 1371. Subsequently active in ecclesiastical affairs, becoming prior general of his order in 1379 and bishop of Lombez in 1389. An edition of his substantial *Sentences* commentary is in progress.

Secondary sources. Marcolino, "Leben und Schrifftum" (2003); Trapp, "Augustinian Quotations" (1954); Zumkeller, "Der Augustinertheologe" (1980); BBK (Zumkeller).

JOHN OF HOLLAND b. near Amsterdam; d. after 1371. Arts master. Studied at Oxford. Arts master at Prague beginning in 1366, becoming dean of the faculty in 1369. Author of at least six logical treatises: *Suppositiones, Fallacie, Obligationes, Insolubilia* (all ed. Bos 1985), plus *Sophismata* and *Consequentie* (both unedited). Also extant are several treatises of natural philosophy: a *De motu* (part. ed. Clagett, in *Science of Mechanics* 1959) and a *De primo et ultimo instanti* [1369] (unedited).

Secondary sources. D'Ors, "Sobre les 'Obligationes'" (1988); Weijers.

JOHN HUNTMAN (Hunter, Johannes Venator) *fl.* second half of fourteenth century. English logician. Fellow of Oriel College [1373–87]; accused of excessive sympathy for the views of John Wyclif. Author of a *Logica* (ed. de Rijk 1999) and an *Insolubilia* (unedited).

Secondary sources. De Rijk, "Semantics" (1982); Spade, *Mediaeval Liar* (1975); Emden.

JOHN HUS (Jan Huss) b. Husinec (Czech Republic), *ca.* 1369; d. Constance, 1415. Ecclesiastical critic; proponent of John Wyclif. Studied at the University of Prague, becoming bachelor of arts in 1393 and master of arts in 1396. University dean in 1401–2 and then rector in 1409–10. Involved in controversies at Prague between German students and Czech students who were advocating Wyclif's condemned views. A strident critic of clerical abuses, Hus broke with the archbishop of Prague and then the pope, and was consequently excommunicated in 1410. Forced to leave Prague in 1412, he took refuge in southern Bohemia, until he was summoned to appear before the general council at Constance in 1414. Although guaranteed safe conduct, he was imprisoned. His offer to abandon any view that could be proved heretical on the basis of Scripture made matters worse, since it implied the rejection of Church authority. Unwilling to recant, he was burned at the stake. His *Opera omnia* runs to eight volumes (ed. Flajshans 1903–7), and includes a *Sentences* commentary. Associated documents have been edited separately (ed. Palacky 1869). His most important treatise is the *Tractatus de ecclesia* (ed. Thomson 1956; tr. Schaff 1915/1974). Many letters are extant (ed. Novotný 1920; tr. Spinka 1972), as is a contemporary account of his trial (tr. Spinka, in *John Hus at the Council* 1966).

Secondary sources. De Vooght, *L'hérésie* (1960); Hilsch, *Johannes Hus* (1999); Kaminsky, *Hussite Revolution* (1967); Novotný and Kybal, *Zivot a Ucení* [Life and Teachings] (1919–31, in 5 vols.); Spinka, *Concept of the Church* (1966), *John Hus* (1968/1979); DMA (Marin); REP (Bostick).

JOHN ITALOS b. southern Italy, *ca.* 1025; d. after 1082. Byzantine philosopher, notable for his forceful defense of philosophy's preeminence even with regards to theology. Moved to Constantinople *ca.* 1049, becoming the student of Michael Psellos and eventually succeeding him as professor of philosophy. Condemned for heresy and paganism in 1082. His extant works (ed. Ketschakmadze 1966) include a set of ninety-three "quodlibetal" questions; commentaries on the *Topics* and *De interpretatione*; and various other logical treatises.

Secondary sources. Clucas, *Trial of John Italos* (1981); Ierodiakonou, "John Italos on Universals" (2007); Stephanou, *Jean Italos* (1949); Tatakis, *Byzantine Philosophy* (2003); ODB (Kazhdan).

JOHN OF JANDUN b. near Rheims, 1280s; d. Todi (Umbria), 1328. Influential Averroist philosopher. Master of arts in Paris in 1310. Joined the faculty at the newly formed College of Navarre in Paris in 1315. Fled to the court of Ludwig of Bavaria in 1326; condemned as a heretic in 1327. An enthusiastic Aristotelian, as read through an Averroistic lens, Jandun was controversial for pursuing philosophical conclusions even when they conflicted with Church teachings, leaving those teachings to be embraced purely on faith. His work was particularly influential in Italy, where it was copied and later printed many times over. His principal works take the form of question-commentaries on Aristotle: on the *Physics* [*ca.* 1315] (ed. 1587/1969), *De anima* (ed. 1587/1966), *De caelo* (ed. 1552), *Metaphysics* (ed. 1553/1966), and *Parva naturalia* (ed. 1505). Various separate disputations have also survived, including *De habitu intellectus* (ed. Kuksewicz 1961); *De infinitate vigoris Dei* (ed. Kuksewicz 1965); *De notioritate universalium* (ed. Kuksewicz

1970); *De principio individuationis* (ed. Kuksewicz 1963), as well as treatises on the agent sense (ed. Pattin 1988) and on the city of Paris (ed. Le Roux de Lincy and Tisserand 1867).

Sometimes erroneously known as John of Ghent (de Gandavo). Jandun is to be distinguished both from the earlier Paris theology master (*ca.* 1303) by that name, whose works are unknown, as well as from the later Johannes Dullardus of Ghent (1470–1513), whose works were printed.

Secondary sources. Brenet, "Perfection" (2001), *Transferts du sujet* (2003); Ermatinger, "Relations" (1969); Grignaschi, "Pensiero politico" (1958); Kuksewicz, *Théorie de l'intellect* (1968); Lambertini, "Felicitas politica" (1998); MacClintock, *Perversity and Error* (1956); Mahoney, "Themes and Problems in the Psychology" (1987); Maurer, "Divine Causality" (1955/1990); Pattin, *Sens agent* (1988); Schmugge, *Johannes von Jandun* (1966); Vitali and Kuksewicz, "Les deux rédactions" (1984); BCPMA (South); DMA (Brenet); REP (Mahoney); Weijers.

JOHN OF LA ROCHELLE (de Rupella) b. La Rochelle, 1190/1200; d. 1245. Early Franciscan philosopher and theologian. Entered Franciscan order *ca.* 1230. Studied theology at Paris, becoming master in 1236. Assumed the Franciscan chair of theology after Alexander of Hales (1238/41), and held that position until his death. A close associate of Alexander's; played a leading role in assembling his *Summa theologica*. Most studied philosophical works are two treatises on the soul, the *Tractatus de divisione multiplici potentiarum animae* [*ca.* 1233] (ed. Michaud-Quantin 1964), and the *Summa de anima* [*ca.* 1235] (ed. Bougerol 1995; tr. [Fr] Vernier 2001). Also extant are *summae* on the virtues, vices, the articles of the faith, and the ten commandments (all unedited); many biblical commentaries; sermons (part. ed. Lynch 1961); and disputed questions on grace (ed. Hödl 1964) and other theological topics.

Secondary sources. Bougerol, "Œuvres et manuscrits" (1994); Michaud-Quantin, "Les puissances de l'âme" (1949); Salman, "L'averroïsme latin" (1947–8); BCPMA (Sondag); FA; REP (Jordan); Glorieux; Weijers.

JOHN LE PAGE (Pagus, Pago) *fl.* 1230s–40s. Early University of Paris master of arts and theology. Master of arts at Paris in 1225–30; bachelor of theology *ca.* 1240/2 to 1245. One of the first lecturers on Aristotle at the University of Paris. Influential for his logical work [*ca.* 1225–35], including commentaries on the *logica vetus*, all unedited except the *Categories* (ed. Franceschini 1934), and treatises on *appellationes* (ed. de Libera, in "Appellationes" 1984) and *syncategoremata* (ed. Braakhuis, in *Syncategorematische Termen* 1979). A *Sentences* commentary is extant in a *reportatio* and a corrected version (unedited).

Secondary sources. Chenu, "Description du manuscrit" (1932); Gründel, "Sentenzenglose" (1958); Pelster, "Literaturgeschichtliches" (1930); BBK (Schneider); DMA (de Libera); Weijers.

JOHN OF LEGNANO b. Milan, *ca.* 1320; d. Bologna, 1383. Renowned jurist. Educated at the University of Bologna. Taught both civil and canon law there by 1350; professor of both by the mid-1360s. An important advocate of Urban VI during the schism, as argued in his *De fletu ecclesiae* [1378–80] (unedited). His many writings, largely unedited, extend to legal commentaries, theological and moral treatises, and astronomy. Notable works include *De bello* [1360] (ed. Holland 1917/1964/1995); *De pace* [1364]; *De pluritalite beneficiorum* [1365]; *De iuribus ecclesiæ in civitatem Bononiae* [1376]; and an astrological treatise, *De adventu Christi* [1375]. His fame was judged comparable to Petrarch's in the *Canterbury Tales.*

Secondary sources. Bosdari, *Giovanni da Legnano* (1901); Ermini, *Trattati della guerra e della pace* (1923); Gianazza and D'Ilario, *Vita e opere* (1983); McCall, "Chaucer" (1965), "Writings" (1967); Schork and McCall, "Lament" (1972); Smoller, "Astrology" (2007).

JOHN LESAGE (Johannes Sapiens) b. Belgium; *fl.* 1300–11. Secular theologian. Regent master at Paris *ca.* 1300–2. Dean of the cathedral at Liège in 1304–11. Extant works are a question on whether free will requires the will to move itself (unedited) and a brief *Quodlibet* [1302] (ed. Glorieux 1958).

Secondary source. Glorieux.

JOHN OF MECHLINIA (Hulshot, de Malines) b. Malines (Belgium), 1405; d. 1475. Albertist theologian and philosopher. Matriculated at the University of Cologne in 1424; master of arts in 1426. At Louvain in 1428. Returned to Cologne first as professor of arts in 1430–9 and then of theology in 1440–75. Author of a *Tractatus de homine* (ed. Pattin 1977) and commentaries on the old and new logic (unedited), the *De anima* (ed. 1491, etc.), the *Parva naturalia* (ed. 1491, etc.), *De motu animalium*, and the *De divinis nominibus* (unedited). Also extant is a treatise on demonology, his *Determinatio utrum perfecta Dei opera possint impediri daemonis malitia* (ed. 1493).

Secondary sources. Pattin, "Jan van Hulshout" (1976), "Een vijftiende-eeuws commentaar" (1995); Lohr.

JOHN OF MIRECOURT (de Mercuria, Monachus Albus) *fl.* 1344–7. Cistercian theologian, condemned for his unorthodox philosophical views. Taught at the Cistercian college in Paris. Lectured on the *Sentences* in 1344–5. In 1347, the chancellor of the university condemned forty-one propositions, including the denial of all qualities and motions, even acts of the soul (ed. Denifle and Châtelain, in *Chartularium* II: 1147). The *Sentences* commentary, on Bk. I only, has been published only in part (qq. 2–6 ed. Franzinelli 1958; qq. 13–16 ed. Parodi 1978), but the whole text (ed. Parodi *et al.*) is available on the internet. The only other extant works are two sets of replies made to the censure against him (ed. Stegmüller 1933).

Secondary sources. Caroti, "Les *modi rerum*" (2004); Courtenay, "Whether God Can Undo the Past" (1972–3); Murdoch, "*Subtilitates Anglicanae*" (1978); Parodi, "Linguaggio delle proportiones" (1984); Tessier, "Jean de Mirecourt" (1974); Van Neste, "Epistemology" (1976); BCPMA (Beuchot); REP (Somerset).

JOHN OF MURRO (Johannes Minus de Murrovalle) b. Marche; d. Avignon, 1312. Franciscan theologian. Provincial minister of the Marche province in the 1270s. Studied theology in Paris by 1283; licensed as master in 1289. Subsequently taught at the Roman curia. Elected Franciscan minister general from 1296 to 1304, and cardinal-bishop of

Porto from 1302. Various disputed questions and fragments of a *Sentences* commentary survive (unedited except excerpts on free will in Longpré, "Œuvre scolastique" 1947).
Secondary sources. FA; Glorieux.

JOHN OF NAPLES d. *ca.* 1350. Dominican theologian. Studied in Bologna in 1298–1300; subsequently taught in Naples. Studied theology in Paris, becoming regent master in 1315. Returned to Naples in 1317. His principal works are various *Quodlibeta* [*ca.* 1315] (unedited) and disputed questions (ed. 1618; excerpt tr. CTMPT II). A defense of Aquinas, arguing that the Condemnation of 1277 does not affect his teachings, has been edited in his name (ed. Jellouschek 1925).
Secondary sources. Friedman, "Dominican Quodlibeta Literature" (2007); Schneider, *Trinitätslehre* (1972); Kaeppeli.

JOHN OF NOVA DOMUS (Maisonneuve) d. 1418. Flemish arts master. Taught in the Paris arts faculty his entire career, beginning *ca.* 1395. A transitional figure between the innovations of the fourteenth century and the schools and doctrinal conflicts of the fifteenth. Defends a traditional Albertist realism against the innovations of Ockham, Buridan, and others. Extant works include a *Tractatus de esse et essentia* (ed. Meersseman 1933); *Tractatus universalium* (ed. Meersseman 1936); *De universali reali* [attribution in doubt] (ed. Weiler 1968); a commentary on the *Metaphysics* [1413/18]; and a *Commentum aureum super secundum partem Doctrinalis Alexandri* [*ca.* 1405] (both unedited).
Secondary sources. Hoenen and de Libera (eds.), *Albertus Magnus and Albertismus* (1995); Kaluza, *Querelles* (1988); Meersseman, "Les origines" (1932); Wels, *Wissen und Glauben* (2004); DMA (Hoenen); Weijers.

JOHN OF PARIS (John Quidort) b. Paris; d. Bordeaux, 1306. Dominican theologian and early Thomist. Studied at Paris as a Dominican by 1279. Lectured on the *Sentences* there *ca.* 1292/5. Master of theology in 1304. His earliest work is a defense of Aquinas, the *Correctorium "Circa"* [1283/4] (ed. Müller 1941). A vast *reportatio* of his *Sentences* commentary is also extant [1292/6] (Bks. I–II ed. Müller 1961–4). Sixteen theses from this work were investigated as suspect. John's successful *Apologia* [1296/9] survives (ed. Müller 1952), as does a disputed question on the central issue of whether being and essence are distinct [1296/9] (ed. Glorieux, in "La distinction réelle," 1951). A later treatise on the Eucharist [1304/5] again brought John under suspicion, and he was censured and suspended as master in Paris; he died while appealing the matter to Pope Clement V. His most studied work is a political treatise, *De potestate regia et papali* [1302/3] (ed. and [German] tr. Bleienstein 1969; tr. Watt 1971). Also extant, among other things, is at least one set of quodlibetal questions (ed. Heiman 1955), a *Quaestio de principio individuationis* (Müller 1974), and a treatise *De modo existendi corpus Christi in sacramento altaris* (ed. Pattin 1977).
Secondary sources. Coleman, "Property" (1983); Dunbabin, "Commentary" (2002); Leclercq, *Jean de Paris* (1942); Grabmann, "Studien" (1922/1979); Müller, "La date" (1959); BCPMA (Friedman); DMA (Solère); Kaeppeli; REP (Jordan); Roensch; Weijers.

JOHN PECHAM (Peckham) b. Patcham (Sussex), *ca.* 1230; d. 1292. Conservative Franciscan champion of Augustinianism. Educated as a youth at the Benedictine monastery at Lewes. Perhaps studied the arts in Paris in the 1240s. Joined the Franciscans at Oxford in the early 1250s; sent to Paris in the 1260s, where he completed his theological studies. Appointed regent master of theology at Paris in spring 1270; served as regent master of theology at Oxford in 1272–5. Elected Franciscan provincial minister of England in 1275. Lecturer to the Papal curia in 1277. Archbishop of Canterbury from 1279 until his death. A follower of Bonaventure's Augustinianism, and an early critic of Aquinas. Many works are extant, including eleven sets of disputed questions (ed. Etzkorn *et al.* 2002); four *Quodlibeta* [1270–7] (ed. Etzkorn and Delorme 1989); treatises on the soul (ed. Melanus 1948) and on optics (ed. Lindberg 1972); an introduction to optics called the *Perspectiva communis* (ed. and tr. Lindberg 1970); questions on the eternity of the world (ed. and tr. Brady and Potter 1993); treatises on poverty (ed. Kingsford *et al.* 1910/1969; ed. Wyngaert 1925); and a treatise on mystical numbers (ed. Hughes 1985). Only the first book of the *Sentences* commentary survives [mid/late 1260s] (unedited). Many letters are extant (ed. Martin 1882–5 in 3 vols.), as well as various sermons, hymns, and poems.

Secondary sources. Doucet, "Notulae bibliographicae" (1933); Boureau, *Théologie et censure* (1999); Brady, "Background" (1974); Douie, *Archbishop Pecham* (1952); Etzkorn, "Career" (1989); Lindberg, "Perspectiva" (1965); Spettmann, "Psychologie" (1919); Wilson, "Critique" (1998); BCPMA (Etzkorn); FA; ODNB (Thompson); REP (Etzkorn); Weijers.

JOHN PETRIZI *fl.* twelfth century. Georgian philosopher, strongly influenced by Neo-platonism. Almost nothing is known of his life. Most important work is his commentary on Proclus's *Elements of Theology* (ed. Nuzubidse and Kauchtschischvili 1937), together with a translation, both in Old Georgian. Also translated Nemesius's *On the Nature of Man*.

Secondary source. SEP (Iremadze).

JOHN PICARDI OF LICHTENBERG d. after 1313. Dominican theologian. Lecturer at the Cologne *studium* in 1303. Bachelor of theology at Paris, *ca.* 1305–8; regent master in 1310–11. Principal extant work is a collection of disputed questions from Cologne (ed. in progress).

Secondary sources. Sturlese, "Johannes Picardi von Lichtenberg" (1982); Glorieux; Kaeppeli; Weijers.

JOHN OF POUILLY (de Polliaco) b. prob. near Laon; d. *ca.* 1328. Paris theologian. Studied the arts and theology in Paris under Godfrey of Fontaines and Henry of Ghent, becoming master of arts in 1295 and then regent master of theology in 1307–12, holding one of the secular chairs. Censured in 1321 by John XXII for views that limited papal authority. Extant works include five *Quodlibeta* and various disputed questions (unedited except for fragments in secondary literature).

Secondary sources. Hödl, "Aulien" (1960), "Non est malitia" (1999), "Die Opposition" (2004), "Quodlibeta" (2007); Koch, "Der Prozess" (1933); Valois, "Jean de Pouilli" (1914); DMA (Bonino); Weijers.

JOHN QUIDORT, *see* John of Paris.

JOHN OF READING b. *ca.* 1270; d. Avignon, 1346. Franciscan theologian. Early years unknown. Ordained subdeacon in 1292, at which point he was already a friar. Studied with the Franciscans at Oxford. Regent master of theology *ca.* 1319, after lecturing on the *Sentences* as a bachelor. Master of theology at the Franciscan *studium* in Avignon beginning in 1322, where he seems to have remained. A devoted follower of Scotus, and (in the Avignon revisions to his *Sentences* commentary) a frequent critic of Ockham. The *Sentences* commentary – his only extant work – survives in only one manuscript, which runs only to distinction 6 of book I. Various partial editions have been made (prol. q. 2 in Brown, "Sources" 1966; prol. qq. 6–7, 10 in Livesey, *Theology and Science* 1989; I.2.2–3 in Etzkorn, "The Existence and Unicity of God" 1981; I.4.3.3 in Gál, "De necessitate specierum intelligibilium" 1969).

Secondary sources. Alliney, "Fra Scoto e Ockham" (1996); Longpré, "Jean de Reading" (1924); Percan, *Teologia* (1986); BCPMA (Georgedes); FA; ODNB (Brown).

JOHN RIGAUD (Rigaldus) b. Limoges; d. Avignon, 1323. Franciscan moral theologian. Author of the moral handbook *Compendium pauperis* [1311/17] (ed. 1501), and the *Formula confessionis* [1309/12] (unedited).

Secondary sources. Valois, "Jean Rigaud" (1914); Teetaert, "La 'Formula confessionis'" (1946); FA.

JOHN OF RIPA (de la Marche) b. *ca.* 1325. Innovative Franciscan theologian. Bachelor of theology at Paris *ca.* 1354/5; master of theology *ca.* 1360/8. Known as the *doctor difficilis* and *doctor supersubtilis*, his views tend toward Scotism and were influential enough that Paul of Venice would compose an abbreviation [before 1402] of his *Sentences* commentary (ed. Ruello 1980–2000). Of the commentary itself [*ca.* 1357], only Bk. I has survived complete (prologue ed. Combes and Ruello 1961–70; d. 37 ed. Combes *et al.* 1967). Also extant is a summary, known as the *Conclusiones* (ed. Combes 1957); a response to criticisms, the *Determinationes* [1358] (ed. Combes 1957); and a *Quaestio de gradu supremo* [1354/5] (ed. Combes and Vignaux 1964).

Secondary sources. Borchert, *Trinitätslehre* (1974); Coleman, "Oxford Calculators" (1975); Combes, "Présentation" (1956), "La métaphysique" (1963), "L'intensité" (1970); Kaluza, "Nature des écrits" (1987); Ruello, *La pensée* (1990), "Projet théologique" (1994); Vignaux, "Forme intensive" (1964), "Preuve ontologique" (1975), "L'averroisme" (1988), "Concept de Dieu" (1981); DMA (Boulnois); FA.

JOHN RODINGTON b. *ca.* 1290; d. Bedford, 1348. Franciscan theologian. Studied theology at Oxford, lecturing on the *Sentences* there in the 1320s. Regent master in 1332–3. Provincial minister of England in 1336–40. His extant works (all unedited) are some *Quodlibeta* and the *Sentences* commentary [prob. 1328–9], which is extant in two redactions and circulated very widely.

Secondary sources. Barbet, "Le commentaire" (1954); Lechner, "Die Quästionen" (1935); Schabel and Friedman, "Trinitarian Theology" (2003); Tweedale, "Knowledge, Science, and Theology" (1965); FA; ODNB (Courtenay).

JOHN OF ST. GERMANS b. St. Germans (Cornwall); *fl.* 1298–1320. Benedictine theologian. A monk of the Worcester Cathedral Priory. Studied theology at Oxford *ca.* 1298–1302, subsequently becoming lector at the abbey of St. Augustine in Canterbury, in 1308–10. Resumed his theological studies at Paris, serving as regent master in 1312–15, when he returned to England. He returned to teach at Canterbury in 1320. His commentary on the *Posterior Analytics* has been edited under Scotus's name (ed. Vivès vol. II, etc.). Perhaps also by John are a *Sentences* commentary and a collection of disputed questions, each found in Worcester mss (unedited).

Secondary sources. Sullivan, *Benedictine Monks* (1995); Weijers.

JOHN OF SALISBURY (Sarisberiensis) b. Old Sarum (Wiltshire), *ca.* 1115/20; d. Chartres, 1180. Scholar and diplomat. Studied at Paris from 1136, under Peter Abaelard, William of Conches, and other leading scholars. Began to teach while still studying in Paris, from 1141 to 1147. Served as clerk to the archbishop of Canterbury in 1147–63, crossing Europe many times in transit to and from the papal court. Conflict between Archbishop Thomas Becket and King Henry II forced him into exile in Rheims in 1164–70. Returned to England with Becket in 1170, and after the latter's murder stayed on until 1176, when he was elected bishop of Chartres. John's writings are important as an early expression of humanism, and for the light they shed on educational and ecclesiastical practices. His *Entheticus de dogmate philosophorum* [*ca.* 1155] (ed. and tr. Laarhoven 1987) is a satirical poem offering advice to a young student. The *Metalogicon* [1159] (ed. Hall and Keats-Rohan 1991; tr. McGarry 1962) is a defense of the liberal arts against careerism. Most influential was his political–moral treatise, the *Policraticus* [1156–9] (ed. Webb 1909; Bks. I–IV ed. Keats-Rohan 1993; part. tr. Dickinson 1927; Pike 1938; Nederman 1990). Also extant are his brief, unfinished memoirs of the papal court, the *Historia pontificalis* [1164–70] (ed. and tr. Chibnall 1956/1986), as well as 325 letters (ed. and tr. Millor *et al.* 1955–79), and brief lives of St. Anselm [1163] and Thomas Becket [1173] (both ed. Biffi 1990).

Secondary sources. Luscombe, "Bibliography" (1984); Nederman, *John of Salisbury* (2005); Guth, *Johannes von Salisbury* (1978); Kerner, *Logische Struktur* (1977); Liebeschütz, *Medieval Humanism* (1950); Olsen, "Humanism" (1988); Ullmann, *"Policraticus"* (1980); Webb, *John of Salisbury* (1932/1971); Wilks (ed.), *World of John of Salisbury* (1984); BCPMA (Kneepkens); Dronke; ODNB (Luscombe); REP (Jordan); SEP (Guilfoy).

JOHN SCOTTUS ERIUGENA (Scotus, Erigena) b. Ireland, *ca.* 800; d. *ca.* 877. Leading philosopher of the Carolingian era. Presumably received his early education in an Irish monastic school. First mentioned in 850/1 as residing in the itinerant court of Charles the Bald, where he had probably served as arts master, and perhaps physician, for some years. Retained the king's patronage for the remainder of his life, perhaps spending some years in Soissons. Most important work is the *Periphyseon* (or *De divisione naturae*) [862–6] (tr. Sheldon-Williams and O'Meara 1987, etc.), a dialogue in five books on the nature of the universe as understood by Christians. The complex manuscript tradition of this work – revisions in Eriugena's own hand apparently survive – has inspired two separate attempts at a critical edition (ed. Sheldon-Williams 1968–; ed. Jeauneau 1996–). Eriugena's earliest extant works are a commentary on Martianus Capella's *De nuptiis Philologiae et Mercurii*

[840s] (ed. Lutz 1939), and a collection of biblical glosses, *Glossae Divinae Historiae* (ed. Contreni and Ó Néill 1997). His controversial *De divina praedestinatione* [850/1] (ed. Madec 1978, Mainoldi 2003; tr. Brennan 1998) rebuts Gottschalk's dual theory of predestination. It was condemned as Pelagian shortly after being written, and subject to various written attacks. Apparently during this period, Eriugena learned Greek, and went on to make a series of important translations (see Appendix B2): of Maximus the Confessor's *Ambigua* [861/2] (ed. Jeauneau 1988) and *Quaestiones ad Thalassium* (*Scoliae*) [862–6] (ed. Laga and Steel 1980–90), of Gregory of Nyssa's *De hominis opificio* (*De imagine*) [*ca.* 862] (ed. Cappuyns 1965), and most importantly of the corpus of pseudo-Dionysius [860–2] (ed. PL 122), which would be the standard translation until the thirteenth century. Eriugena also wrote a long commentary on pseudo-Dionysius's *Celestial Hierarchy* [*ca.* 865–70] (ed. Barbet 1975), as well as a partial commentary on the Gospel of John [*ca.* 865–70] (ed. and tr. [Fr] Jeauneau 1972), and a sermon on the prologue to John [*ca.* 865–70] (ed. and tr. [Fr] Jeauneau 1969).

Secondary sources. Brennan, *Guide* (1989) [bibliography]; Allard (ed.), *Jean Scot écrivain* (1986); Beierwaltes, *Eriugena* (1994); Carabine, *John Scottus Eriugena* (2000); Jeauneau, *Études érigéniennes* (1987); Madec, *Jean Scot et ses auteurs* (1988); McGinn and Otten, *Eriugena: East and West* (1994); Marenbon, *Circle of Alcuin* (1981); Moran, *Philosophy of Eriugena* (1989); O'Meara, *Eriugena* (1988); Otten, *Anthropology* (1991); Rudnick, *Das System* (1990); Schrimpf, *Das Werk* (1982); Wohlman, *L'Homme, le monde sensible et le péché* (1987); BCPMA (Steel and Hadley); DMA (Erismann); ODNB (Marenbon); REP (Moran); SEP (Moran). Among the many edited volumes, see in particular the proceedings of the Society for the Promotion of Eriugenian Studies.

JOHN SHARPE (Scharpe) b. near Münster, *ca.* 1360; d. after 1414. Oxford theologian and philosopher; leading Oxford realist. Bachelor of arts at the University of Prague in 1379; subsequently studied and taught at Oxford, eventually becoming doctor of theology. Fellow at Queen's College from 1391 to 1403. By 1415 he had returned to Germany as a lecturer at Lüneburg (Saxony). His only edited work is the *Quaestio super universalia* (ed. Conti 1990). Remaining extant writings are commentaries on the *De anima* and *Physics*, an abbreviation of Scotus's *Quodlibeta*, and several short philosophical and theological treatises.

Secondary sources. Conti, "Ontology and Semantics" (2005); de Libera, "Questions de réalisme" (1992); Kennedy, "*De anima*" (1969); Lohr; SEP (Conti); Weijers.

JOHN OF STERNGASSEN d. before 1327. Dominican theologian. In residence at the Strasbourg convent in 1310 and again in 1316. Only major extant work is his lectures on the *Sentences*, delivered perhaps at Paris in 1290/5, or perhaps later (ed. Senner 1995).

Secondary sources. Senner, "Jean de Sterngassen" (1997); Kaeppeli.

JOHN TARTEYS *fl. ca.* 1400. Oxford arts master; realist follower of John Wyclif. Fellow of Balliol College. Extant works include a *Problema correspondens libello Porphyrii* (part. ed. Conti 1990) and various logical treatises, unedited except for his *Obligationes* (ed. Ashworth 1992). The *Summa insolubilium* edited under the name of John Wyclif is sometimes attributed to Tarteys.

Secondary source. Emden.

JOHN TAULER b. Strasbourg, *ca.* 1300; d. 1361. Influential Dominican preacher and mystic. A Dominican friar from his youth, he studied at the Dominican *studium* in Cologne in 1324, when Eckhart was a master and Henry Suso a fellow student. Lived in Strasbourg and Basel; devoted himself to preaching and spiritual direction. A popular figure among later Reformers, Tauler published nothing during his life; his literary output consists of seventy-nine sermons in Middle High German collected by Dominican nuns.

Secondary sources. Gnädinger, *Johannes Tauler* (1993); Ozment, *Homo spiritualis* (1969); Kaeppeli; REP (Bussanich).

JOHN VENATOR, *see* John Huntman.

JOHN VERSOR d. after 1482. Arts master and theologian. Master of arts at Paris in 1435, and subsequently master of theology there for many years. His work has both Thomistic and Albertist elements. Author of commentaries on almost all of Aristotle's principal works, as well as on Peter of Spain and Donatus minor. All are available in early printed editions.

Secondary sources. Lohr; Weijers.

JOHN OF WALES (Wallensis, Gallensis) b. north Wales, *ca.* 1220; d. Paris, 1285. Franciscan theologian and moralist. Studied theology in Oxford; joined the Franciscans in 1258. Served as Franciscan master at Oxford in 1259–62. Relocated to Paris by 1270, eventually serving as regent master there in 1281–3. Many works survive, of which the most popular were pastoral handbooks, especially the *Communiloquium* or *Summa collationum* [1265/69] (ed. 1489/1964).

Secondary sources. Swanson, *John of Wales* (1989); Glorieux; ODNB (Swanson).

JOHN WENCK b. Herrenberg (southwest Germany), *ca.* 1396; d. Heidelberg, 1459. Albertist philosopher and opponent of Nicholas of Cusa. Student at the University of Paris, becoming master of arts in 1415. At the University of Heidelberg from 1426, studying theology and receiving his doctorate in 1432. Taught on the theology faculty there until his death, serving as rector repeatedly. Wenck is best known for his *De docta ignorantia* [1442/3] (ed. and tr. Hopkins 1988), an attack on Nicholas of Cusa, to which Cusa made a fierce reply in his *Apologia doctae ignorantiae* [1449] (tr. Hopkins 1988). Various brief treatises are extant but unedited, except for a Middle High German *Büchlein von der Seele* (ed. Steer 1967).

Secondary sources. Haubst, "Johannes Wenck" (1951); BBK (Olszewsky); Weijers.

JOHN WENT d. 1348. Franciscan theologian. Lectured on the *Sentences* at Oxford in 1336–7 (unedited). Lector at the Franciscan house in Oxford [1339–40]; subsequently served as provincial minister in England until his death.

Secondary sources. Edwards, "Themes and Personalities" (2002); Kennedy and Romano, "Divine Omnipotence" (1987).

JOHN OF WESEL (Vessalia) *fl.* mid-fourteenth century. Parisian arts master. At Paris from 1344 to 1353. Four works have been tentatively ascribed to him: questions on the *Ars vetus* and on the *Prior Analytics* (both unedited), and sets of questions on *obligationes* and *insolubilia* (part. ed. Spade, in "Three Questions" 1996).

Secondary sources. Lohr; Weijers.

JOHN WYCLIF (Wycliffe) b. Wycliffe (Yorkshire), *ca.* 1325; d. Lutterworth, 1384. Heterodox and influential philosopher and theologian; a leading advocate of metaphysical realism. Studied at Oxford from *ca.* 1350. Ordained priest in 1351. Master of Balliol in 1360. Began studying theology by 1362, receiving his doctorate in 1372/3. Condemned for his ecclesiastical views by Pope Gregory XI in 1377, and by the university in 1381 for his denial of the doctrine of transubstantiation. That same year he withdrew to the parish church in Lutterworth where he was rector. There he continued to write, even as further charges of heresy were brought against him. His philosophical views and criticisms of the Church spread widely in England and abroad even before his death: the so-called Lollards were influential in England all through the following century, and the Hussite rebellion in Bohemia took many ideas directly from Wyclif's work. Only in 1415 was he formally condemned as a heretic, at the Council of Constance.

Wyclif's very extensive writings, in both Latin and English, have not yet been completely edited, and still await systematic philosophical study. Many of the Latin writings have been edited by the Wyclif Society (1883–1922, in 36 vols.). Of these the early works are largely logical and philosophical: a *De logica* [*ca.* 1360], a *Continuatio logicae* [prob. 1360/3] (both ed. Dziewicki 1893), and a *Summa insolubilium* [1368–9] (ed. Spade and Wilson 1986); *De ente in communi* [*ca.* 1365] and *De ente primo in communi* [*ca.* 1365] (both ed. Thomson 1930); *De actibus animae* [*ca.* 1365] (ed. Dziewicki 1902); *Purgans errores circa universalia in communi* [1366/8] (ed. Dziewicki 1909); *De ente praedicamentali* [*ca.* 1369] (ed. Beer 1891); *De intelleccione Dei* and *De volucione Dei* [both *ca.* 1370] (both ed. Dziewicki 1909); *Tractatus de universalibus* [*ca.* 1368–9, or 1373–4] (ed. Müller 1985; tr. Kenny 1985); *De materia et forma* [*ca.* 1370–5] (ed. Dziewicki 1902), and *De Trinitate* [1371–4] (ed. du Pont Breck 1962). Wyclif organized many of these shorter treatises – and other works yet to be edited – into a *Summa de ente*, whose structure scholars have had to piece together. Beginning *ca.* 1373, Wyclif turned his attention increasingly to theological and ecclesiastical issues: these include works on law and dominion such as *De civili dominio* [1375/6] (ed. Poole and Loserth 1885–1904; part. tr. CTMPT II), *De ecclesia* [1378] (ed. Loserth and Matthew 1886), and *De potestate papae* [*ca.* 1379] (ed. Loserth 1907); works asserting the authority and inerrancy of Scripture, such as *De veritate sacrae scripturae* [1377/8] (ed. Buddensieg 1905–7; tr. Levy 2001) and the *Trialogus* [1382/3] (ed. Lechler 1869); and, most notoriously of all, Wyclif's rejection of transubstantiation, the *De eucharistia* (ed. Loserth 1892). In addition to these academic Latin treatises, there are Latin polemical works (ed. Buddensieg 1883/1966) and English works (part. ed. Matthew 1880/1978; Lindberg 1991). For later English Wycliffite texts, see Hudson, *Selections* (1997).

Secondary sources. Thomson, *Latin Writings* (1983) [works]; Catto, "Wyclif and Wycliffism" (1992); Conti, "Analogy and Formal Distinction" (1997); Daly, *Political Theory* (1962); Evans, *Myth and Reality* (2005); Farr, *Legal Reformer* (1974); Fumagalli

Beonio Brocchieri and Simonetta (eds.), *Wyclif* (2003); Ghosh, *Wycliffite Heresy* (2001); Hudson, *Premature Reformation* (1988); Hudson and Wilks (eds.), *From Ockham to Wyclif* (1987); Kenny, *Wyclif* (1985); Kenny (ed.), *Wyclif in his Times* (1986); Lahey, *Philosophy and Politics* (2003); Levy, *Scriptural Logic* (2003); Levy (ed.), *Companion* (2006); McFarlane, *English Non-Conformity* (1952); Michael, "Body and Mind" (2003); Mallard, "Biblical Authority" (1961); Robson, *Oxford Schools* (1961); Thomson, "Philosophical Basis" (1931); Wilks, *Political Ideas* (2000); Workman, *John Wyclif* (1926); BCPMA (Kronen); ODNB (Hudson and Kenny); REP (Catto); SEP (Conti, Lahey); Weijers.

JORDANUS *fl. ca.* 1240. Grammarian. Master of arts at Paris. Author of the *Notulae super Priscianum Minorem* [*ca.* 1240] (part. ed. Sirridge 1980).
   Secondary sources. Gauthier, "Notes sur les débuts" (1982); Sirridge, "Socrates' Hood" (1983); Weijers.

JOSEPH ALBO b. Aragon, *ca.* 1380; d. Castile, 1444. Systematic theologian and philosopher. Studied with Ḥasdai Crescas in Saragossa. Spiritual leader of the community of Daroca (Aragon) during a time of violent persecution, and, after Daroca's destruction, of the community of Soria (Castile). Played a leading role in the debate between Christians and Jews at Tortosa in 1413–14. Although the debate was an exercise in Christian propaganda, it gave rise to Albo's masterpiece, the four-part *Sefer ha-ʿIqqarim* (*Book of Principles*) [finished *ca.* 1425] (ed. and tr. Husik 1929, in 5 vols.; part. tr. Manekin, in *Writings* 2007). Organized around three core principles of belief – in God's existence, in revelation, and in divine justice – the treatise would become widely read both in its original Hebrew and in Latin translation.
   Secondary sources. Back, *Joseph Albo's Bedeutung* (1869); Bleich, "Providence" (1997); Harvey, "Albo's Discussion of Time" (1979–80); Husik, "Last of the Mediaeval Jewish Philosophers" (1928–30); Lasker, *Jewish Philosophical Polemics* (1977); Lerner "Natural Law" (1964); Rauschenbach, *Jüdische Philosophie* (2002); REP (Frank); SEP (Ehrlich).

JOSEPH IBN CASPI b. Languedoc, 1279; d. after 1332. Prolific commentator and scholar. Traveled widely. Strongly Aristotelian in outlook, he was influenced by both Jewish and Islamic authors. Author of a commentary on Maimonides (ed. Werbluner 1848), as well as various biblical commentaries, such as the *Gevia' Kesef* (ed. and tr. Herring 1982).
   Secondary sources. Mesch, "Principles of Judaism" (1982); HIP (Leaman); REP (Leaman); Sirat.

JOSEPH IBN ṢADDIQ d. 1149. Poet and Neoplatonic philosopher. Little is known of his life, beyond that he was a rabbinical judge at Cordoba from 1138. His major work, *Al-ʿĀlam al-ṣaghīr*, is extant only in Hebrew translation, as *Ha-Olam ha-Katan* (*The Microcosm*) (ed. and tr. Haberman 2003). It treats human beings as a microcosm of the world.
   Secondary sources. Vajda, "Philosophie et théologie" (1949); Wolfson, "Divine Attributes" (1965); REP (Rudavsky).

AL-JUBBĀʾĪ (Abū ʿAlī Muḥammad) b. Jubba (Khuzistan); d. 915/16. Leading Muʿtazilī theologian. Studied in Basra, becoming master there and training two prominent students: his son, Abū Hāshim, and al-Ashʿarī, who would found a rival tradition. No complete works are extant.

Secondary sources. Frank, "Attribute" (1982); Gimaret, "Matériaux" (1976); EI (Gardet).

JUDAH BEN SOLOMON HA-COHEN (Ibn Matqa) b. Toledo, *ca.* 1215. Encyclopedist. Born into a family of celebrated astrologists. Composed a three-part philosophical-scientific encyclopedia, the *Midrash ha-Ḥokhmah*, first in Arabic [1230s] (not extant) and then in Hebrew [1247] (only excerpts edited), while at the court of Frederick II in Lombardy.

Secondary sources. Harvey (ed.), *Medieval Hebrew Encyclopedias* (2000); Sirat.

JUDAH HALEVI b. Tudela (northeast Spain), *ca.* 1075; d. 1141. Physician, philosopher, poet. Moved to Andalusia as a youth, where he became well known for his poetry and settled in Granada. After marrying and establishing a thriving medical practice in Toledo, he moved with his wife and daughter to Cordoba. Attempted to emigrate to the Holy Land in 1140, but died either in Egypt or soon after arriving in Israel. His principal philosophical work is a dialogue between a philosopher and a Jewish king, the *Khazari* [1130–40] (ed. Baneth 1977; tr. Hirschfeld 1964).

Secondary sources. Kogan, "Use of Philosophy in the *Kuzari*" (2003); Silman, *Philosopher and Prophet* (1995); HIP (Kogan); HJP (Goodman); REP (Goodman); SEP (Kogan).

JUDAH ROMANO (ben Moses ben Daniel) b. *ca.* 1292; d. after 1330. Translator and philosopher. Active in the Naples court of Robert II of Anjou. Hebrew translator of Latin scholastic texts; his own views were influenced by Maimonides and Aristotle, as interpreted by Latin scholastics. (See Appendix B6.)

Secondary source. REP (Rigo).

JULIAN OF NORWICH b. England, 1342; d. *ca.* 1416. Anchoress and mystic. Perhaps a Benedictine nun. By 1394 she had chosen the solitary existence of an anchorite at St. Julian's Church in Norwich. A series of sixteen visions during a grave illness at the age of thirty inspired her only work, the celebrated *Revelations of Divine Love* or *Book of Showings* (ed. [Middle English] Colledge and Walsh 1978; tr. [modern English] Colledge and Walsh 1978, etc.). The short version of this work [1373/93] confines itself to describing these mystical experiences; the long version [1393] interprets the original visions and describes the mystical experiences that had been continuous for the following twenty years.

Secondary sources. Jantzen, *Julian of Norwich* (1987); Upjohn, *In Search* (1989); ODNB (Bhattacharji).

AL-JURJĀNĪ, ʿAlī ibn Muḥammad (al-Sayyid al-Sharīf) b. Astarabad (Persia), 1339; d. Shiraz, 1434. Wide-ranging philosopher and theologian. Studied in Harat and subsequently traveled to Egypt, Constantinople, and Shiraz, where he was appointed teacher in 1377. His theological works are heavily philosophical, including most prominently his commentary on al-Ījī's *Mawāqif* (*Stations*) (ed. Mahdi 1977). Other prominent philosophical writings include a philosophical lexicon, *Al-Taʿrīfāt* (ed. ʿUmayrah 1987; tr. [Fr] Gloton 2006) and a *Risālat al-wujud* (*Treatise on Being*) (ed. Taqawi 1942).

Secondary sources. Anawati, "La doctrine des accidents" (1974); BEIP (Aminrazavi); EI (Tritton).

AL-JUWAYNI (Abū al-Maʿālī Abd al-Malik) b. near Nishapur, 1028; d. near Nishapur, 1085. Ashʿarite theologian. From a family of famous teachers, he took over his father's teaching position at an early age. Political events forced him to leave for Baghdad. Eventually he taught in Mecca and Medina in 1058–61. With a change in the political situation back home, Juwaynī returned to Nishapur, where he taught until his death, numbering al-Ghazālī among his students. Principal interests are jurisprudence and *kalām*. His *Burhān fī uṣūl al-fiqh* (*The Proofs of Jurisprudence*) (ed. al-Dīb 1980) aims to set out an Ashʿarite juridical method. In *kalām*, two prominent works are *Al-Shāmil fī uṣūl al-dīn* (*Totality of the Foundations of Law*) (ed. Klopfer 1959) and *Al-Irshād ila qawāṭiʿ al-adillah fī uṣūl al-iʿtiqād* (*The Guide to the Cogent Proofs of the Principles of Faith*) (ed. Mūsa and ʿAbd al-Ḥamīd 1950).

Secondary sources. BEIP (İskenderoğlu); EI (Brockelmann); REP (Leaman and Albdour).

AL-KINDĪ, ʿAbd al-Masīḥ *fl.* early tenth century (?). Author of a letter written in defense of Christianity. The author's identity is otherwise unknown, and even the dating is uncertain, with the early ninth century sometimes suggested. He is generally thought to be a Nestorian Christian. The letter (ed. Tien 1880; tr. Muir 1882), written in response to a Muslim friend, attacks Islam in some detail. It was translated into Latin in 1141 (ed. González Muñoz 2005).

Secondary source. EI (Troupeau).

AL-KINDĪ (Abū Yūsuf Yaʿqūb ibn Isḥāq) b. Basra, *ca.* 800; d. *ca.* 870. Foundational figure in Arabic philosophy. An ethnic Arab from the fabled Kinda tribe. Educated in Baghdad; served as a scholar and tutor in the court of successive ʿAbbāsid caliphs. Although he himself probably did not know Greek, he oversaw a group of scholars who were systematically translating Greek philosophical and scientific texts into Arabic. A tenth-century list of titles indicates that al-Kindī wrote hundreds of treatises, mainly scientific and mathematical, most of which are no longer extant. His scientific work was highly influential, particularly the *De radiis stellarum* (ed. D'Alverny and Hudry 1974), which accounts for all physical interaction in geometric terms, and a treatise on optics, the *De aspectibus* (ed. Björnbo and Vogel 1912), both of which survive only in Latin. Of the surviving philosophical works (ed. Abū Rīda 1950–3), the most influential is the *Fī al-falsafa al-ūlā* (*On First Philosophy*) (tr. Ivry 1974), which combines Neoplatonic and Aristotelian influences into a treatise that understands metaphysics as the study of God. Another influential treatise is a collection of philosophical definitions, the *Fi ḥudūd al-ashyāʾ wa-rusūmihā* (*On the Definitions of Things and their Descriptions*) (tr. Klein-Franke 1982). Al-Kindī surveys the work of Aristotle in his *Fī kammiya kutub Arisṭūṭālīs* (*On the Quantity of Aristotle's Books*) (tr. [Ital] Guidi and Walzer 1940); his *Risālat al-ʿaql* (*On the*

Intellect) (tr. McCarthy 1964) is the first Arabic attempt to grapple with the notorious Aristotelian divisions of intellect, and was translated into Latin. Some brief translations are contained in McGinnis and Reisman (*Classical Arabic Philosophy* 2007), and more are forthcoming (tr. Adamson and Pormann forthcoming). Still more is in French, for both the philosophical and the scientific work (tr. Gimaret 1976; tr. Rashed and Jolivet 1997–8 [with Arabic], tr. Mestiri and Dye 2004).

Secondary sources. Adamson, "Before Essence" (2002), "Reception" (2005), *Al-Kindi* (2007); Butterworth, "Beginnings of Islamic Political Philosophy" (1992); Druart, "Ethics" (1993); Endress, "Circle" (1997); Gutas, *Greek Thought, Arabic Culture* (1998); Ivry, *Metaphysics* (1974); Jolivet, *L'intellect* (1971); Lindberg, "Theory of Vision" (1971); Staley, "Creation" (1989); Tornero Poveda, *La transformacion* (1992); Travaglia, *Doctrine of Rays* (1999); BCPMA (Jolivet); EI (Jolivet and Rashed); HIP (Klein-Franke); REP (Kennedy-Day); SEP (Adamson).

AL-KIRMĀNĪ (Ḥamīd al-Dīn) b. Kerman (Iran); d. after 1020. Ismāʿīlī missionary and philosopher. Active in the Ismāʿīlī cause mainly in Iraq, though he journeyed to Cairo in the early eleventh century to intervene in a dispute over the nature of the imamate. His work attempts to point Ismāʿīlī thought in an Aristotelian direction. Principal texts are the *Kitāb al-riyāḍ* (*Book of Gardens*) (ed. Tāmir 1960) and the *Kitāb rāḥa al-ʿaql* (*The Peace of Intellect*) [1020/1] (ed. Ḥusayn and Ḥilmī 1953). His main work regarding the imamate has recently been translated (ed. and tr. Walker 2007).

Secondary sources. De Smet, *Quiétude de l'intellect* (1995); Walker, *Ḥamīd al-Dīn al-Kirmānī* (1999), "The Ismāʿīlīs" (2005); EI (de Bruijn).

LAMBERT *fl.* 1250s. Author of the *Logica* or *Summa Lamberti* [1253/7] (ed. Alessio 1971), a work in the terminist tradition of Peter of Spain. The identity of this Lambert is uncertain: he is perhaps Lambert of Auxerre, a friar at the Dominican house in Auxerre, or the contemporary Lambert of Lagny. The *Logica* contains chapters *De propositionibus*, *De praedicabilibus*, *De praedicamentis*, *De postpraedicamentis*, *De syllogismo*, *De locis*, *De fallaciis*, *De suppositionibus et significationibus* [the last tr. CTMPT I].

Secondary sources. Ashworth, "Signification and Modes" (1991); Read, "Properties of Terms" (2006); CHLMP; Kaeppeli; Weijers.

LANDULPH CARACCIOLO (de Mazoriis) b. Naples; d. 1351. Franciscan theologian. Lectured on the *Sentences* at Paris, probably 1318–19. Master of theology by 1325, at which point he was the Franciscan provincial minister of Terra Laboris (southern Italy). Bishop of Castellammare in 1327; archbishop of Amalfi from 1331 until his death. His *Sentences* commentary, on all four books, circulated very widely (Bk. II ed. Venice 1487). Also extant are various biblical commentaries (unedited) and sermons (part. ed. 1637).

Secondary sources. Schabel, "Divine Foreknowledge" (1999), "Predestination" (2002), "Parisian Commentaries" (2002); BCPMA (Schabel); FA.

LANFRANC OF BEC b. Pavia, *ca.* 1010; d. 1089. Theologian and ecclesiastical leader. Early education in Italy; left for France *ca.* 1031, teaching in various locations and possibly studying at Chartres. Taught at Avranches (Normandy) beginning *ca.* 1039, before joining the newly founded monastery at Bec in 1042. He quickly became prior and opened a school that achieved a wide reputation, attracting many of the foremost minds of the era, including Anselm of Canterbury (as of 1059). In 1066 he was appointed abbot of St. Stephen's Abbey in Caen (Normandy) by William, duke of Normandy, and was subsequently consecrated archbishop of Canterbury in 1070. From that post, which he held until his death, Lanfranc exerted considerable influence on the shaping of Norman England. The surviving works are less impressive than his reputation would suggest. Chief among these is the treatise *De corpore et sanguine Domini* [*ca.* 1066] (ed. and tr. [Ital] Martello 2001), an attack on the eucharistic theology of Berengar of Tours. From his time at Bec we have annotations on various patristic texts, focused largely on grammatical and textual matters. His commentaries on the Pauline epistles circulated widely (PL 150). While archbishop, Lanfranc composed his influential monastic constitutions (ed. and tr. Knowles and Brooke 2002). Many letters have also survived (ed. and tr. Clover and Gibson 1979).

Secondary sources. Collins, *Teacher in Faith* (2007); Cowdrey, "Enigma" (1994), *Lanfranc* (2003); de Montclos, *Lanfranc et Bérenger* (1971); d'Onofrio (ed.), *Lanfranco di Pavia* (1993); Gibson, *Lanfranc* (1978); Holopainen, *Dialectic and Theology* (1996); Huygens, "Bérenger, Lanfranc" (1965); Mantienne, *Lanfranc* (2006); DBI (Cowdrey); DMA (Brouwer); ODNB (Cowdrey).

AL-LAWKARĪ (Abū al-ʿAbbās) b. Lawkar (Persia); d. *ca.* 1123. Second-generation disciple of Avicenna; studied with Avicenna's prominent student Bahmanyar. Principal work is his multi-volume *Bayān al-ḥaqq bi-ḍamān al-ṣidq* (*The Explanation of Truth from the Point of View of Trust*), an account of Avicenna's logic (part ed. Dībājī 1985), natural philosophy (unedited), and metaphysics (ed. Dībājī 1995), as filtered through Bahmanyar.

Secondary sources. Marcotte, "Preliminary Notes" (2006); Reisman, *Making of the Avicennan Tradition* (2002); BEIP (Kalin).

LEVI BEN GERSHOM (Gersonides, ben Gerson, Leon of Bagnols, Ralbag) b. Provence, 1288; d. Provence, 1344. Influential philosopher and biblical scholar. Spent his entire life in southern France. His major philosophical work, *Sefer Milḥamot ha-Shem* (*The Wars of the Lord*) [1329] (ed. 1866/1923; tr. Feldman 1984–99), argues that religion could be defended on rational, philosophical grounds. Distinguished by its precise, analytic style, its six books range over questions about creation, the soul's immortality, prophecy, divine providence, and astronomy. Gershom's controversial views in all these areas were sharply criticized by later Jewish authors. His Aristotelianism is heavily influenced by Averroes, on whose commentaries he composed a series of supercommentaries [1321–4] (only excerpts published). A distinguished scholar of Jewish law, whose commentaries on the Torah have been printed many times. Various critical editions are in progress; available translations include the Song of Songs [1326] (ed. and tr. Kellner 1998), and the Book of Job [1325] (tr. Lassen 1946). Also authored a logical treatise, *Sefer ha-Heqesh ha-Yashar* (*Book of the Correct Syllogism*) [1319] (tr. Manekin 1992), which was translated anonymously into Latin. His strong interests in mathematics led to his *Sefer Maʿaseh Hoshev* (*The Work of a Counter*) [1321] (ed. and tr. [German] Lange 1909).

Secondary sources. Freudenthal, *Studies* (1992) [bibliography by Keller]; Dahan, *Gersonide* (1991); Eisen, *Gersonides on Providence* (1995); Feldman, "Debate Concerning Determinism" (1984); Glasner, "Levi ben Gershom and the Study of Ibn Rushd" (1995); Manekin, "Conservative Tendencies" (2003); Rudavsky, *Time Matters* (2000); Sirat *et al.* (eds.), *Méthodes de travail* (2003); Touati, *La pensée philosophique et théologique* (1973); BCPMA (Pessin); HIP (Freudenthal); REP (Feldman); SEP (Rudavsky).

LUDOLPH MEISTERMANN OF LÜBECK *fl.* 1390s. Logician, active at the universities of Prague and Vienna. Known works are a lengthy set of questions *De significatione propositionum* [1392], and sets of questions on supposition, appellation, and *insolubilia* [1393] (all unedited).

Secondary sources. Bos, "Logic of Fiction" (1998); Spade, *Mediaeval Liar* (1975).

MANEGOLD OF LAUTENBACH b. Lautenbach (Alsace), *ca.* 1045; d. prob. Marbach, after 1103. Scholar and ecclesiastical polemicist. Studied in both France and Germany. A married itinerant teacher in the 1060s, he later became an Augustinian monk in Rottenbuch. In 1094 he was prior at Marbach. The two intact works known to be his are a defense of the papacy against philosophical encroachments, the *Liber contra Wolfelmum* [*ca.* 1085] (ed. Hartmann 1972/1991; tr. Ziomkowski 2002), and the *Liber ad Gebehardum* [*ca.* 1085] (ed. Francke 1891), which takes the pope's side in the investiture controversy and develops an interesting account of sovereignty. There are also various surviving references to, and fragments of, commentaries and scholia on classical texts and the Bible (largely unedited).

Secondary sources. Endres, "Manegold von Lautenbach" (1904); Gross, "Erbsündenlehre" (1960); Hartmann, "Anfänge" (1970); Herren, "Scholia" (2004); Koch, *Manegold von Lautenbach* (1902/1965); Laakmann, *Königsgewalt* (1969); Stead, "Manegold of Lautenbach" (1914); BBK (Schmidt); CHLMP; Dronke.

MARGUERITE OF OINGT b. Lyonnais, *ca.* 1240; d. 1310. Carthusian nun and mystic. Entered a women's Carthusian community at Poleteins (near Lyon), becoming prioress by 1288. Extant works (ed. Duraffour *et al.* 1965; tr. Blumenfeld-Kosinski 1990) include the influential *Pagina meditationum* [Latin] and the *Speculum* [Franco-Provencal].

Secondary sources. McGinn, *Flowering of Mysticism* (1998); Muller, *Autre côté du miroir* (1999); Petroff, *Body and Soul* (1994).

MARGUERITE OF PORETE b. *ca.* 1250; d. Paris, 1310. French mystic. Described as a beguine, she was living around Valencienne (Belgium) in the early 1300s, when her book, *Le mirouer des simples ames aneanties* [*ca.* 1300] (ed. Guarnieri 1986; tr. Colledge *et al.* 1999), was condemned and publicly burnt. Written in Old French, and extant in Latin translation as well, the book characterizes the final goal of human life as a single, simple unitive act of will with God. It was subsequently enlarged, clarified, and eventually approved by a commission of theologians, but her repeated refusal to submit to ecclesiastical authority led her to be condemned as an unrepentant heretic, and she was burned at the stake.

Secondary sources. Hollywood, *Soul as Virgin Wife* (1995); Leicht, *Marguerite Porete* (1999); McGinn, *Flowering of Mysticism* (1998), *Meister Eckart* (1994); Muller, *Autre côté du miroir* (1999); Petroff, *Body and Soul* (1994); Richir, *Marguerite Porete* (2002); DMA (Boulnois).

MARSILIUS OF INGHEN b. Nijmegen, *ca.* 1340; d. Heidelberg, 1396. Influential natural philosopher and famed master of arts at the University of Paris from 1362 to 1379, where he twice served as rector. Served as the University of Heidelberg's first rector in 1386, where he taught until his death, becoming doctor of theology in 1396. Traditionally described as a nominalist and heavily influenced by the views of John Buridan, but an independent thinker in many respects. His most influential works are his question-commentaries on Aristotle: *De generatione et corruptione* (ed. 1505/1970, etc.), *De anima*, *Metaphysics*, *Parva naturalia*, and the *Ethics* (all unedited), and an *Abbreviationes* on the *Physics* (ed. 1521, etc.). (A question-commentary on the *Physics* printed under the name "Johannes Marcilius Inguen" [ed. 1518/1964] is not by Marsilius.) Also important are various logical treatises, surviving in many manuscripts but unedited except for a treatise on the properties of terms (ed. and tr. Bos 1983). His last work was his *Sentences* commentary [1392–6] (ed. Wieland *et al.* 2000).

Secondary sources. Hoenen, "Bibliographie" (1989–90); Bakker, "Aristotelian Metaphysics" (2001); Braakhuis and Hoenen (eds.), *Marsilius of Inghen* (1992); Hoenen, *Divine Knowledge* (1993), "Commentary on the *Sentences*" (2002); Hoenen and Bakker (eds.), *Philosophie und Theologie* (2000); Marshall, "Parisian Psychology" (1983); Reina, "Comprehensio veritatis" (1994), *Hoc Hic et Nunc* (2002); Ritter, *Studien* (1921); Wielgus (ed.), *Werk und Wirkung* (1993); BCPMA (Hoenen); DMA (Hoenen); Lohr; REP (Bos); SEP (Hoenen); Weijers.

MARSILIUS OF PADUA (Marsiglio dei Mainardini) b. Padua, 1275/80; d. 1342/3. Famous political theorist. Practiced medicine and lectured on natural philosophy at the University of Paris, becoming rector in 1312–13. His major work is the *Defensor pacis* [before June 1324] (ed. Previté-Orton 1928, etc.; tr. Gewirth 1956/2001, Brett 2005), which argues for the supremacy of the temporal powers of the state over the spiritual powers of the papacy. Left Paris in 1325, entering into the service of Emperor Ludwig of Bavaria. Other works in this same vein include *De translatione imperii* [prob. 1326–7] and *Defensor minor* [1341] (both ed. Jeudy and Quillet 1979; tr. Nederman 1993), a summary of the *Defensor pacis* which responds to criticisms made by William of Ockham.

Secondary sources. Miethke, "Literaturbericht" (1993); Garnett, *The Truth of History* (2006); Gewirth, *Marsilius of Padua* (1951), "Republicanism" (1979); Lewis, "Positivism" (1963); Moreno-Riano, *World of Marsilius* (2006); Nederman, *Community and Consent* (1995); Quillet, *Philosophie politique* (1970); Tierney, "Marsilius on Rights" (1991); BCPMA (Bertelloni); REP (McGrade); Weijers; vols. 5–6 of *Medioevo* (1979–80) are devoted to Marsilius.

MARTIN (Magister Martinus) *fl. ca.* 1200. Paris theologian known only as the author of the *Compilatio quaestionum theologiae* (unedited). Influenced by Gilbert of Poitiers.

Secondary sources. Heinzmann, *Die Compilatio* (1964); Landgraf, *Introduction* (1973); Munsch, "Treatise on the Incarnation" (2002) (edits the material on the incarnation).

MARTIN OF ALNWICK (Martinus Anglicus) b. Northumberland; d. Newcastle, 1336. Franciscan theologian. Studied at Oxford, where he incepted as regent master in 1304. Took part in disputes over mendicant poverty at Avignon in 1311. Various questions from his *Sentences* commentary are extant (unedited). The logical treatises of "Martinus Anglicus" are now viewed as the work of a different, later author.
Secondary source. ODNB (Brown).

MARTIN OF DACIA (Dacus) b. Denmark; d. Paris, 1304. Philosopher and grammarian. Professor on the arts faculty at Paris in the 1270s and master of theology at Paris *ca.* 1285. Appointed chancellor to the Danish King Erik VI in 1287/8, a position he retained until close to his death. Most influential was his grammatical treatise *De modis significandi* [*ca.* 1270], an important early attempt at a systematic theory of grammar. Also authored question-commentaries on the *ars vetus*. His complete work is available in a critical edition (ed. Roos 1961).
Secondary sources. Bursill-Hall, *Speculative Grammars* (1971); Pinborg, "Speculative Grammar" (1982); Roos, *Die Modi significandi* (1952); BCPMA (Rivera); CHLMP; Weijers.

MARTINUS ANGLICUS *fl.* 1335/70. English logician. Author of treatises *De veritate et falsitate propositionis* (ed. de Rijk, in *Some 14th Century Tracts* 1982), *De obligationibus* (ed. Schupp 1993), and *Consequentiae* (unedited). His identification with Martin of Alnwick is now generally rejected.
Secondary source. Ashworth, "English *Obligationes*" (1983).

MATTHEW OF AQUASPARTA b. near Todi (Umbria), *ca.* 1238; d. 1302. Franciscan theologian in the Augustinian tradition. Joined the Franciscan order *ca.* 1260; sent to Paris *ca.* 1268. Lectured on the *Sentences* [prob. 1271–2], and was then apparently assigned to teach at the Bologna *studium* in 1273–7 before incepting as regent master at Paris *ca.* 1278–9. Subsequently appointed to the Roman *studium* in 1279–87. His academic career came to an end when he was elected minister general of the Franciscan order in 1287–9 and then also cardinal in 1288–1302. Matthew's main influences are his older contemporaries Bonaventure and John Pecham, whom he follows in attempting to craft an Augustinian Aristotelianism that is more conservative than that of the Dominicans Aquinas and Albert the Great. His principal works are his *Sentences* commentary (Bks. I, II, and IV are extant in a single autograph copy, unedited) and a series of *Quodlibeta* [1278–5] (unedited), as well as a great many disputed questions, among the more philosophical of which are questions on illumination (ed. Quaracchi 1883), the soul (ed. Gondras 1957–61), the separated soul (ed. Quaracchi 1959), faith and cognition (ed. Quaracchi 1957; part tr. McKeon, *Selections* 1930; part. tr. Fairweather, *Scholastic Miscellany* 1956), the production of things and providence (ed. Gál 1956), and grace (ed. Doucet 1935 [with detailed biobibliographical information]).

Secondary sources. Beha, "Theory of Cognition" (1961); Bérubé, "Henri de Gand et Mathieu d'Aquasparta" (1974); Dowd, "*De productione rerum*" (1974); Grabmann, *Erkenntnislehre* (1906); Hayes, *General Doctrine of Creation* (1964); Marrone, "Augustinian Epistemology" (1983); *Matteo d'Acquasparta* (1993); Mazzarella, *La dottrina* (1969); Payne, "Cognitive Intuition of Singulars" (1981); Prezioso, "L'attività del soggetto pensente" (1950); Putallaz, *La connaissance de soi* (1991); BCPMA (Houser); DMA (de Libera); FA; Glorieux; REP (Brown); Weijers.

MATTHEW OF BOLOGNA *fl.* 1270s. Grammarian. Master of arts, perhaps at Bologna. Author of *Quaestiones super modos significandi* (ed. Rosier-Catach 1992), a modistic grammar.

MATTHEW OF GUBBIO *fl. ca.* 1333–47. Arts master at Bologna. Central figure among the Italian Averroists. Extant works include various commentaries on the logical curriculum (unedited), various disputed questions on physics and the soul (ed. Kuksewicz, in *Averroisme bolonais* 1965), and perhaps a *De anima* commentary (ed. Ghisalberti 1981). Secondary source. Lohr.

MATTHEW OF ORLEANS *fl.* 1220s. Logician. Known only as the author of the *Sophistaria* or *Summa communium distinctionum circa sophismata accidentium* (ed. Spruyt 2001). Secondary source. Weijers.

AL-MĀTURĪDĪ (Abū Manṣūr) b. Maturid (Samarkand), before 873; d. Maturid, *ca.* 944. Theologian and jurist, founder of the Maturidiyya school of Sunnī *kalām* that is the main rival to the Ashʿariyya. Seems to have remained in Maturid his entire life, leading an ascetic, scholarly life. Principal work is the *Kitāb al-tawḥīd* (*Book of Unity*) (ed. Kholeif 1970). A long Quran commentary (ed. al-Khaymī 2004) is probably the work of his students.
Secondary sources. Ceric, *Roots of Synthetic Theology* (1995); Rudolph, *Al-Māturīdī* (1996); BEIP (İskenderoğlu); EI (Madelung).

AL-MĀWARDĪ (Abū al-Ḥasan ʿAlī ibn Muḥammad) b. Basra, 974; d. Baghdad, 1058. Renowned jurist. Studied in Basra and then in Baghdad. Eventually became chief judge in Baghdad and was active in diplomatic affairs. Principal political work is *Al-Aḥkām al-sulṭāniyya* (*The Laws of Islamic Governance*) (ed. al-Sirjānī 1978; tr. Yate 1996). Also extant, among many other works, is an important moral treatise, the *Kitāb adab al-dunyā wa-al-dīn* (*Right Conduct in Matters Worldly and Religious*) (ed. Abū Bakr 1988).
Secondary sources. Khan, *Theory of the State* (1983); Mikhail, *Politics and Revelation* (1995); BEIP (İskenderoğlu); EI (Brockelmann).

MECHTILD OF HACKEBORN b. Helfta (Saxony), 1241; d. Helfta, 1299. Cistercian (or possibly Benedictine) nun and mystic. Born into an aristocratic family, she entered the monastery of Helfta at age seven, where her sister Gertrude would become famous as abbess. Eventually put in charge of the monastery school, she counted Gertrude the Great among her students. In her last years she began to speak about the visions she had had from an early age. The *Liber specialis gratiae* [1292–] (ed. 1877) is the record of these accounts, written down by two nuns, one of whom was likely Gertrude the Great. Many vernacular translations, including Middle English (ed. Halligan 1979) are extant.

Secondary sources: Finnegan, *Women of Helfta* (1991); Bynum, *Jesus as Mother* (1982).

MECHTILD OF MAGDEBURG b. Saxony, 1209; d. Helfta, 1282/4. Mystic, ecclesiastical critic, poet. Took up the life of a beguine in Magdeburg (Saxony) at around the age of twenty-three, under Dominican direction. Her life of prayer and asceticism was combined with an outspoken criticism of Church abuses, which led to her ongoing persecution. Eventually she sought refuge in the Cistercian (or possibly Benedictine) convent at Helfta in 1270, where she joined other renowned figures such as Gertrude the Great and Mechtild of Hackeborn. The work for which she is famous is *The Flowing Light of the Godhead*, which stresses the soul's role as the bride of Christ; although originally written in Middle Low German, it survives only in Middle High German (ed. Vollmann-Profe 2003; tr. Tobin 1998) and Latin translation (minus the seventh book).

Secondary sources. Finnegan, *Women of Helfta* (1991); Hollywood, *Soul as Virgin Wife* (1995); McGinn, *Meister Eckart* (1994); Newman, "La Mystique Courtoise" (1995); Bynum, *Jesus as Mother* (1982).

MEISTER ECKHART *see* Eckhart.

MICHAEL OF EPHESUS b. *ca.* 1050; d. 1129. Philosopher and Aristotelian commentator, an important figure in the Byzantine revival of Neoplatonic Aristotelianism. Little is known of his life, and even his dates are uncertain. Extant works are commentaries (many published in *Commentaria in Aristotelem Graeca* (CAG); many extant in Latin translations) on the biological works (CAG XIV.3, XXII.2; *De motu* and *De incessu* tr. Preuss 1981), the *Ethics* (CAG XX, XXII.3; Bks. V, IX–X tr. [Latin] Robert Grosseteste [ed. Mercken 1991, Trizio forthcoming]; Bk. IX tr. Konstan 2001), *Politics* (ed. Susemihl and Immisch, in Aristotle, *Politica* 1929), *Parva naturalia* (CAG XXII.1), *Sophistical Refutations* (CAG II.3), and *Metaphysics*.

Secondary sources. Browning, "Funeral Oration" (1962/1990); Ebbesen, *Commentators and Commentaries* (1981); ODB (Kazhdan and Tkacz).

MICHAEL OF MARBAIS b. Brabant; *fl. ca.* 1300. Master of arts at Paris. Proponent of modistic grammar. Author of a *Summa de modis significandi* (ed. Kelly 1995) and *Quaestiones super Priscianum minorem* (unedited).

Secondary sources. Bursill-Hall, *Speculative Grammars* (1971); Covington, *Syntactic Theory* (1984); Kelly, *Mirror of Grammar* (2002); Weijers.

MICHAEL OF MASSA b. Siena; d. prob. Paris, 1337. Theologian. Little is known about his life or work. An Augustinian Hermit, he probably composed his *Sentences* commentary in the late 1320s (Bks. I–II only, unedited). Seemingly an important influence on his confrère Gregory of Rimini.

Secondary sources. Schabel, "Questions on Future Contingents" (1998) (edits Bk. I dd. 35–8); Courtenay, "Redating" (1995), "Categories" (2003); Hödl, "Schöpfungsbegriff" (1975); Trapp, "Augustinian Theology" (1956), "Notes on Some Manuscripts" (1965); BCPMA (Schabel); Weijers.

MICHAEL PSELLOS b. Constantinople, 1018; d. after 1081 (?). Byzantine scholar whose work ranged over history, rhetoric, law, and theology. His philosophy advocated the revival of ancient Hellenism, especially Platonism. A career administrator, he served as well as a kind of court philosopher, the *hypatos ton philosophon* in Constantinople. His best-known work is his *Chronographia* (ed. Renauld 1926–8; tr. Sewter 1966). His more philosophical works include a collection of "quodlibetal" questions, the *De omnifaria doctrina* (ed. Westerink 1948); various *Scripta minora* (ed. Kurtz and Drexl 1936–41), and collections of various brief theological (ed. Gautier 1989) and philosophical texts (ed. Duffy and O'Meara 1989–92). Also extant are various commentaries on Aristotle, including the *De interpretatione* (ed. Manutius 1503; tr. [Latin] 1541).

Secondary sources. Barber and Jenkins (ed.), *Reading Michael Psellos* (2006); Benakis, "Studien zu den Aristoteles-Kommentaren" (1961–2), "Kritik an Aristoteles" (1963); Duffy, "Hellenistic Philosophy" (2002); Ierodiakonou, "Psellos' Paraphrasis" (2002); Kaldellis, *Argument* (1999); Tatakis, *Byzantine Philosophy* (2003); ODB (Kazhdan).

MICHAEL SCOT b. perhaps in Fife; d. *ca.* 1236. Important Arabic–Latin translator. In Toledo from 1210, at which point he was already translating Arabic scientific texts. Moved to Bologna in 1220, entering into the employment of Frederick II and enjoying close relationships with successive popes. Among his most important translations are al-Biṭrūjī's *De motibus coelorum* [1217] (ed. Carmody 1952), Aristotle's *De animalibus* [before 1220], Averroes's long commentary on the *De caelo*, and perhaps also the long commentaries on the *Physics*, *De anima*, and *Metaphysics*. (See Appendices B1 and B4.) Various original treatises are also extant, most notably the *Liber introductorius* (part. ed. 1508, etc.), an introduction to astrology with wider reflections on the nature of the universe.

Secondary sources. Brams, *Riscoperta di Aristotele* (2003); Dod, "Aristoteles Latinus" (1982); Thorndike, *Michael Scot* (1965); ODNB (Morpurgo); Weijers.

MISKAWAYH b. Rayy (Persia), *ca.* 932; d. 1030. Historian and humanistic philosopher. Combined his scholarly work with an active political career in Baghdad, Isfahan, and Rayy. Most studied philosophical work is an ethical treatise, the *Tahdhīb al-akhlāq* (*The Refinement of Character*) (ed. Zurayk 1966; tr. Zurayk 1968). Among his other works is an epistle on the intellect and the intelligible (ed. Arkoun 1964; tr. Marcotte 1996). His principal historical work is the *Tajārib al-umam* (*Experiences of Nations*) (ed. and tr. Amedroz and Margoliouth 1920–1).

Secondary sources. Adamson, "Miskawayh's Psychology" (2007); Arkoun, *Humanisme arabe* (1982); Kraemer, *Humanism* (1986); EI (Arkoun); HIP (Leaman); REP (Leaman).

MONACHUS NIGER *fl.* 1330s–40s. Benedictine theologian whose proper name is uncertain. Although very little is known about this figure, his lectures on the *Sentences* [at

Oxford or perhaps Cambridge, 1335–41] (unedited) are often cited by contemporaries. Perhaps to be identified with the Benedictine Johannes Normanus.

Secondary sources. Courtenay, *Adam Wodeham* (1978); Edwards, "Themes and Personalities" (2002).

MOSES IBN EZRA b. Granada, *ca.* 1055; d. after 1135. Hebrew poet and scholar. Studied in Lucena; forced by the Almoravid invasion to flee Andalusia in 1090. The remainder of his life was spent in exile, in Christian Spain, longing for his home. Although most famous for his poetry, two interesting Arabic works of philosophy and literary criticism are extant: the *Kitāb al-muḥāḍara wa-al-mudākara* (*Book of Conversation and Discussion*) (ed. and [Sp] tr. Abumalhan Mas 1985–6), and the *Maqālat al-ḥadīqa fī maʿnā al-majāz wa-al-ḥaqīqa* (*The Treatise of Garden on Metaphorical and Literal Meaning*) (ed. and [Hebrew] tr. Fenton 1989).

Secondary sources. Fenton, *Philosophie et exégèse* (1997); REP (Fenton).

MOSES IBN TIBBON b. Marseille; *fl.* 1244–83. Physician, scholar, and prolific translator. Lived in Montpellier. Son of Samuel ibn Tibbon and father of Judah ben Moses ibn Tibbon, who would play a prominent role in the Maimonidean controversy at Montpellier in 1304. Greatest influence is his many translations into Hebrew of Arabic philosophical and scientific works, particularly those of Averroes but also including works by Euclid, al-Biṭrūjī, and Maimonides. His own work includes a commentary on the Song of Songs (ed. 1874).

Secondary sources. Fraisse, *Kommentar zum Hohenlied* (2004); Robinson, "Ibn Tibbon Family" (2005); SEP (Robinson); Sirat.

MOSES MAIMONIDES (ben Maimon, Rambam) b. Cordoba, 1138; d. Cairo, 1204. Pre-eminent Jewish philospher and religious authority. Born into a prominent rabbinic family. Forced to leave Cordoba after the Almohad conquest of 1148, eventually settling in Fez in 1160 and then Cairo, *ca.* 1165, where he remained for the rest of his life, becoming a leading figure in the local Jewish community and serving as court physician from 1185. His work, which joins Neoplatonic and Aristotelian ideas, grew out of Judeo-Islamic thought, and deeply influenced philosophers in the Latin West, from Aquinas to Spinoza and beyond. Although well known during his life for his many medical writings, his enduring philosophical fame rests on the *Dalālat al-ḥāʾirīn* (*Moreh Nevukhim; Guide of the Perplexed*) [1185–90], written in Arabic with Hebrew characters (ed. and [Fr] tr. Munk 1856/1964; tr. Pines 1963). Also of enduring significance are his rabbinic treatises, principally the *Kitāb al-siraj* (*Sefer ha-Maor; Commentary on the Mishnah Avot*) [1168] (ed. [Hebrew] Rabinowitz 1948); the *Kitāb al-faraʿid* (*Sefer ha-Mitzvot; Book of the Commandments*) [1170] (ed. Bloch 1888; tr. Chavel 1967); and, above all, the *Mishneh Torah* [*ca.* 1180] (ed. Frankel 2000, in 12 vols.; part. tr. *Code of Maimonides* 1949–72), his monumental and still authoritative study of rabbinic law. Of special philosophical interest are the ethical treatise from the introduction to the *Kitāb al-siraj* known as the *Eight Chapters* (ed. Wolff and Niewöhner 1903/2003; tr. Gorfinkle 1912/1966), and the first book of the *Mishneh Torah*, known as *The Book of Knowledge* (tr. Hyamson 1974). Maimonides's many other works include a youthful treatise on logic (ed. and tr. Efros 1938/1978). Various treatises and letters are translated in anthologies (Halkin and Hartman 1985; Lerner, *Empire of Light* 2000; Twersky 1972; Weis and Butterworth 1975).

Secondary sources. Seeskin, *Cambridge Companion to Maimonides* (2005); Buijs (ed.), *Maimonides* (1988); Davidson, *Moses Maimonides* (2005); Frank, "Anger as a Vice" (1990), "Maimonides and Aristotelianism" (2003); Harris, *After 800 Years* (2008); Kraemer (ed.), *Perspectives* (1991); Langermann, "Maimonides and the Sciences" (2003); Leaman, *Moses Maimonides* (1997); Pessin, "Influence of Islamic Thought" (2005); Pines and Yovel (eds.), *Maimonides and Philosophy* (1985); Rubio, *Aquinas and Maimonides* (2007); Seeskin, *Searching for a Distant God* (2000), *The Origin of the World* (2005); BCPMA (Ivry); HIP (Broadie); HJP (Kreisel); REP (Goodman); SEP (Seeskin).

MOSES NAHMANIDES (Ramban, Bonastrug de Porta) b. Gerona (Catalonia), *ca.* 1194; d. Acre (Palestine) 1270. Philosopher, Talmudist, founding figure of Kabbalah. A cautious critic of philosophy, who played a leading role in the anti-rationalist attack on Maimonides's work, seeking to keep it from a general audience [1232–3]. A debate in Barcelona with the apostate Pablo Christiani in 1263 led to charges of abusing Christianity, and he was forced to flee to Palestine. His own ideas are presented largely in scriptural commentaries, most notably his commentary on the Torah (ed. Chavel 1959–63; tr. Chavel 1976). An anthology of other speculative works is also available (ed. Chavel 1963; tr. Chavel 1978).

Secondary sources. Caputo, *Nahmanides in Medieval Catalonia* (2008); Chazen, *Barcelona and Beyond* (1992); Novak, *Theology* (1992); Twersky (ed.), *Rabbi Moses Nahmanides* (1983); REP (Stern).

MOSES OF NARBONNE (Narboni) b. Perpignan, *ca.* 1300; d. *ca.* 1362. Jewish Aristotelian. Spent most of his life in Spain, working as a physician. Author of many commentaries on religious and philosophical texts, including a commentary on Averroes's theory of the active intellect (ed. and tr. Bland 1981). Best known for his commentary on Maimonides's *Guide of the Perplexed* [1355–62] (part. ed. and [Fr] tr. Hayoun 1986). Also extant is a response to Abner of Burgos's deterministic views, *Ma'amar ha-Behira* (*Treatise on Choice*) [1361] (ed. Hayoun 1982; tr. Manekin, *Writings* 2007).

Secondary sources. HIP (Leaman), REP (Leaman); Sirat.

AL-NASAFĪ (Abū al-Muʿīn) b. Nasaf (Bukhara), *ca.* 1046; d. Nasaf, 1114/15. Leading Maturidite theologian. Principal works are the *Bahr al-kalām* (*Ocean of Theology*) (ed. Farfūr 1997) and the *Tabsirat al-adilla* (*Instructing the Evidences*) (ed. Salāma 1990).

Secondary sources. Madelung, "Abu'l Muʿīn al-Nasafī" (2000); BEIP (İskenderoğlu); EI (Wensinck).

AL-NASAFĪ (Muhammad) b. Nasaf (Bukhara); d. 943. Ismāʿīlī missionary and Neoplatonic philosopher. Head of the Ismāʿīlī *da'wa* in Nishapur; enjoyed some success in converting local rulers before he and many of his followers were massacred after a political reversal. Principal work, extant only in fragments, is *Al-Mahsūl* (*The Result*), a founding work in Ismāʿīlī philosophy that would be much criticized by subsequent generations.

Secondary sources. Daftary, *Ismāʿīlīs* (1990); Stern, *Studies* (1983); Walker, *Early Philosophical Shiism* (1993), "The Ismāʿīlīs" (2005); EI (Poonawala).

AL-NAẒẒĀM (Abū Isḥāq) d. 835/45. Muʿtazilī theologian and poet. Studied in Basra, in the circle of his uncle Abū al-Hudhayl; came to the court at Baghdad sometime after 819. Only fragments of his work are extant, but he is known to have rejected the atomism characteristic of the *mutakallimūn*.

Secondary sources. van Ess, *Theology and Science* (1978); EI (van Ess).

NICHOLAS OF AMIENS *fl.* later twelfth century. French theologian. Author of the *Ars fidei catholicae* (ed. Dreyer 1993), which sets out Christian doctrine in an axiomatic form inspired by Euclid. Perhaps also the author of the brief *Potentia est vis* (ed. Dreyer 1993).

Secondary source. BBK (Wesseling).

NICHOLAS OF AMSTERDAM (Nicholaus Theoderici) b. *ca.* 1388; d. Greifswald, *ca.* 1437. German arts master. Studied the arts at Cologne from 1407 and at Erfurt from 1412, becoming master at Erfurt in 1414. Taught for most of his career at Rostock [1422–37]. Commentaries are extant on the *Ethics, Metaphysics, Physics, De anima, De caelo, De generatione, Meteorology,* and *Parva naturalia* (all unedited).

Secondary sources. Pinborg, "Aristoteles-Quaestionen" (1964); Pluta, "Materialism" (2007); Pluta (ed.), *Nicholas of Amsterdam* (2008); Włodek, "Commentaire sur le *De anima*" (1963); Lohr.

NICHOLAS OF AUTRECOURT (Ultricuria) b. Autrécourt (Lorraine), *ca.* 1298; d. Metz, 1369. Radical critic of Aristotelianism, condemned in Avignon and Paris. Studied the arts in Paris, obtaining his master's degree *ca.* 1318/20. Studied civil law outside of Paris, then returned *ca.* 1330 to teach on the arts faculty and study theology at the Sorbonne. He completed the degree requirements in theology, including lecturing on the *Sentences* [*ca.* 1335–6], but apparently did not incept as master. Summoned to Avignon in 1340 to respond to charges of false teaching. A trial focusing on a list of sixty-six erroneous propositions lasted until 1346, when he was convicted of teaching various erroneous and heretical statements. His sentence was to recant publicly and to burn his works, an exercise he performed first in Avignon and then in Paris, in November 1347. Deprived of his license to teach, he spent the remainder of his life in Metz, where he had been appointed canon in 1339 and later dean of the cathedral chapter. Just a few of Nicholas's works have survived. Most important is an extended treatise on atomistic natural philosophy commonly known by its opening words, *Exigit ordo* (but more properly called the *Tractatus utilis ad videndum an sermones peripateticorum fuerint demonstrativi*) [1330, later revised] (ed. O'Donnell 1939; tr. Kennedy *et al.* 1971). The most notorious of his works, in which he expresses doubts over whether we have any certainty in philosophy, are the letters to Bernard of Arezzo (two of nine have survived) [1335–6] and to a Master Giles (one brief and fragmentary letter) [*ca.* 1337] (ed. and tr. de Rijk 1994). The only other surviving work is a brief theological dispute on the intention and remission of forms [1336–9] (ed. with the *Exigit ordo*).

The text of the *Exigit ordo* presents substantial problems, since it is the product of revisions and additions over several years and survives in only a single manuscript. (The only currently available edition and translation misreads the title of the work, wrongly calling it the "Universal Treatise," and so badly scrambles the order in which the text itself is to be read as to make the all-important prologue and first chapter virtually unintelligible. For the essential corrections, see Kaluza, *Ami de la vérité* 1995.)

Secondary sources. Kaluza, *Ami de la vérité* (1995) [biography]; Caroti and Grellard (eds.), *Nicolas d'Autrécourt* (2006); Dutton, "Atomism, Nominalism" (1996); Grellard, *Croire et savoir* (2005); Perler, *Zweifel und Gewissheit* (2006); Scott, "Autrecourt, Buridan, and Ockhamism" (1971); Thijssen, *Censure and Heresy* (1998), "Quest for Certain Knowledge" (2000); Weinberg, *Nicolaus of Autrecourt* (1948/1969); Zupko, "On Certitude" (2001); DMA (Grellard); REP (Perler); SEP (Thijssen); Weijers.

NICHOLAS BONET (Bonetus) b. Touraine, *ca.* 1280; d. 1343. Franciscan philosopher and theologian. Student of theology in Paris, apparently studying with Scotus, and later master of theology at Paris. Appointed bishop of Malta in 1342. Various studies of Aristotle have survived: a *Categories*, *Metaphysics*, and *Physics* (*Philosophia naturalis*), as well as a *Theologia naturalis* (all ed. 1505). Also credited with a Scotistic treatise, *Formalitates* (ed. 1475), although his authorship is uncertain. Best known today for his indivisibilism regarding the continuum.

Secondary sources. Martin de Barcelona, "Nicolás Bonet" (1925); Alliney, "Tempus naturae" (2002); Murdoch, "Mathesis" (1969); Zoubov, "Catton, Odon, Bonet" (1959); CHLMP; FA; Lohr; Weijers.

NICHOLAS BYARD d. 1261. Famous preacher and moral theologian, variously described as a Franciscan or a Dominican. Did not pursue advanced study in theology, and his sermons (extant in many mss., but unpublished) have a popular, non-technical character. Other extant works are his *Distinctiones* (unedited) and his *Summa de abstinentia* or *Dictionarius pauperum* (ed. 1498), which are handbooks for preachers.

Secondary sources. BBK (Hödl); DS (Schmitt); DTC (Teetaert); FA; Kaeppeli; ODNB (Summerson).

NICHOLAS OF CUSA (Cusanus, Cues, Krebs) b. Kues (Rhineland), 1401; d. Todi (Umbria), 1464. Innovative philosopher and theologian, often regarded as a key precursor to modern thought. Studied at Heidelberg in 1416–17, then at Padua, receiving his doctorate in canon law in 1423. Lectured and took up theological studies at the University of Cologne. Entered into the service of the archbishop of Trier by 1427, whom he represented at the Council of Basel beginning in 1432, playing an important role there. Ordained priest in the late 1430s, and elected cardinal in 1448. Bishop of Brixen (Tirolia) from 1450. Although largely occupied with diplomatic and ecclesiastical duties, Cusa authored treatises on a wide range of topics, from canon law to philosophy, mysticism, mathematics, and Islam. His earliest works are associated with the Council of Basel, most notably the *De concordantia catholica* [1433] (tr. Sigmund 1991), a powerful argument for the authority of Church councils, and *De auctoritate praesidendi in concilio generali* [1434] (tr. Bond *et al.* 1990). His most famous work is *De docta ignorantia* [1440] (tr. Hopkins 1985), a meditation on our inability to grasp infinite being, which was later followed by an *Apologia doctae ignorantiae* [1449] (tr. Hopkins, *Debate* 1988). Other important works include the *Idiota de sapientia* and *Idiota de mente* [both 1450] (both tr. Hopkins 1996), and the *De visione Dei* [1453] (tr. Hopkins 1988). Other philosophically interesting treatises are also extant (see the translations of Hopkins 1994, 1997–2000), as are many sermons and mathematical writings. The modern edition of Cusa's *Opera omnia* is now virtually complete (Hoffmann *et al.* 1932–, in 22 vols.).

Secondary sources. Haubst *et al.* (eds.), *Mitteilungen* (1961–) [bibliography]; Meuthen, *Nikolaus von Kues* (1979) [biography]; Casarella, *Cusanus* (2006); Haubst, *Striefzüge* (1991); Hopkins, *Concise Introduction* (1986); Hudson, *Becoming God* (2007); Flasch, *Nikolaus von Kues* (1998); Jacobi, *Die Methode* (1969); Leinkauf, *Einführung* (2006); Meuthen and Hallauer (eds.), *Acta Cusana* (1976–); Sigmund, *Medieval Political Thought* (1963); Vansteenberghe, *Le Cardinal* (1920/1963); BCPMA (Dupré and Hudson); DMA (Counet); REP (Hopkins); Weijers.

NICHOLAS DRUKKEN OF DACIA d. *ca.* 1357. Paris logician. Studied at Paris, becoming arts master in 1341 and rector in 1344. Exant works are a *Tractatus de suppositionibus* and questions on the *Prior Analytics* (both ed. in *Opera* 1997).

Secondary sources. Lagerlund, *Modal Syllogistics* (2000); Weijers.

NICHOLAS KABASILAS (Chamaetos) b. Thessaloniki, 1319/23; d. Constantinople, after 1397. Byzantine theologian and philosopher. Born into a noble family; studied in Thessaloniki and then Constantinople. His work draws not only on Patristic authors but also on Aristotle as well as Aquinas and other Latin sources. Among his theological works (PG 150), most notable are his study of the sacraments, *The Life in Christ* (tr. deCatanzaro 1974; ed. and [Fr] tr. Congourdeau 1989–90); and his *Commentary on the Divine Liturgy* (tr. Hussey and McNulty 1960/2002; ed. Périchon and [Fr] tr. Salaville 1967). More philosophical is the unfinished anti-skeptical *Contra Pyrrhonem* [1355/9] (ed. Demetracopoulos 1999) and the *De rationis valore* [1355/9] (ed. Demetracopoulos 1998), in which he argues that beatitude requires cultivating reason. Far from being a follower of Gregory Palamas, as often reported, he in fact criticizes Palamism in both of these works. His correspondence has also been edited (ed. Enepekides 1953). Selections of his work have been translated into Italian (tr. Spiteris 1996).

Secondary sources. Angelopoulos, *Nikolaos Kabasilas* (1970); Conticello and Conticello, *La théologie byzantine* (2002); Lot-Borodine, *Maître de la spiritualité* (1958); Tsirpanlis, "Career and Writing" (1979), *Liturgical and Mystical Theology* (1979); Völker, *Sakramentmystik* (1977); BBK (Tinnefeld); ODB (Talbot).

NICHOLAS OF LYRA b. Lyre (Normandy), *ca.* 1270; d. Paris, 1349. Prominent biblical commentator. Joined the Franciscan order *ca.* 1300 and was sent to Paris to study theology, becoming regent master in 1308. Subsequently much involved in Franciscan administrative affairs, serving as provincial minister of Francia in 1319–24 and later Burgundy from 1324/5, before retiring to Paris. The principal project of his later years, and the work for which he is famous, is his massive *Postilla litteralis super totam Bibliam* [1322–31] and the briefer *Postilla moralis seu mystica* [1339] (both ed. Lyon 1545, etc.), intended as a handbook for preachers. The first – which makes use of Nicholas's impressive knowledge of Hebrew – became a standard biblical commentary and was widely printed. Translations have been published of the commentaries on the Apocalypse (tr. Krey 1997) and the Song of Songs (tr. Kiecker 1998). Also extant are four *Quodlibeta* [*ca.* 1309] (only excerpts ed.), along with various other disputed questions (unedited) and a treatise *De visione divinae essentiae* [1334] (ed. Woodward 2005), on the controversy over the beatific vision of the saints in heaven.

Secondary sources. Brown, "Critique of Scotus' Univocity" (1991); Duba, "Continental Franciscan *Quodlibeta*" (2007); Krey and Smith (ed.), *Nicholas of Lyra* (2000); FA.

NICHOLAS OF NORMANDY *fl. ca.* 1270. Paris arts master whose only known work is a grammatical sophism *Albus musicus est* (ed. Ebbesen 1988).

Secondary source. Weijers.

NICHOLAS OF OCKHAM b. *ca.* 1245; d. 1320. Franciscan theologian. Studied at Paris *ca.* 1270–4; subsequently studied theology at Oxford, becoming regent master there in 1286–7. His *Sentences* commentary, dating from his years at Oxford [prob. 1280–2], is extant in all four books (unedited). Also extant are various disputed questions (ed. Saco Alarçón 1981, 1993).

Secondary source. Saco Alarçón, "Vida y obras" (1978).

NICHOLAS OF PARIS *fl. ca.* 1240. Arts master at Paris, known for his logical writings. Probably the author of the *Summe de dialectica* (*Summe Metenses*) (part. ed. de Rijk, *Logica modernorum* II.1 1967), as well as important early examples of treatises on *obligationes* (ed. Braakhuis 1998) and *syncategoremata* (ed. Braakhuis 1979; part. tr. CTMPT I), and also various commentaries on the *ars vetus* and on Priscian minor (unedited)

Secondary sources. Grabmann, "Logischen Schriften" (1926); CHLMP; Lohr; Weijers.

NICHOLAS OF STRASBOURG *fl. ca.* 1323–9. Dominican theologian and mystic. Educated in Paris; lector at the Dominican convent in Cologne. Best known for defending his confrère Eckhart from censure in 1326, for which he himself was briefly excommunicated before the sentence was voided by the pope. Author of a Thomistic *Summa philosophiae* (ed. Suarez-Nani *et al.* 1990–), as well as various theological writings, including a set of treatises and sermons in German (ed. Pfeiffer, in *Deutsche Mystiker* 1845–57/1962).

Secondary sources. Hillenbrand, *Nikolaus von Strassburg* (1968); Imbach and Lindblad, "Compilatio" (1985); Trusen, *Der Prozess* (1988); Wagner, *Materie im Mittelalter* (1986) [ed. and study of *Summa* II.1]; Kaeppeli.

NICHOLAS TRIVET (Trevet) b. Somerset, 1257/65; d. *ca.* 1335. Dominican theologian, historian, and classical scholar. Joined the London convent as a young man; subsequently sent to Oxford to study, serving as master of theology, prob. in 1303–7. Lived in Paris *ca.* 1307–14, but traveled widely throughout France and Italy. Recalled to Oxford in 1314, where he served as master for another year. The most philosophical of his extant works are various disputed questions and six *Quodlibeta* [five from the first regency; the last from the second] (part. ed. Hauke, in *Die Lehre* 1967, and in Dales and Argerami, *Medieval Latin Texts* 1991), but he is more famous for his historical chronicles and his commentaries on Boethius, Seneca, Livy, Virgil, and Augustine (available in a variety of editions).

Secondary sources. Ehrle, *Nikolaus Trivet* (1923); Friedman, "Dominican Quodlibetal Literature" (2007); Kaeppeli; ODNB (Clark); Weijers.

NICOLE ORESME b. near Caen (Normandy), *ca.* 1320; d. 1382. Leading natural philosopher of the later Middle Ages. Studied the arts at the University of Paris in the 1330s, becoming master of arts by 1341. In residence at the College of Navarre in Paris by 1348, studying theology; became doctor of theology in 1356, and also grand master of the college. Closely connected to the royal family and tutor to Charles V, upon whose ascension in 1364 Oresme became dean of the cathedral at Rouen. Appointed bishop of Lisieux in 1377.

His work, which ranges widely over philosophy and theology, is celebrated for its quantitative orientation. The mathematical–scientific treatises are most studied, in particular the *Tractatus de configurationibus qualitatum et motuum* [*ca.* 1350] (ed. and tr. Clagett 1968), with its proof of the mean-speed theorem and its attempt at a quantitative theory of qualities; the *De proportionibus proportionum* [*ca.* 1356] (ed. and tr. Grant 1966); and *De causis mirabilium* [*ca.* 1370] (ed. and tr. Hansen 1985), which displays Oresme's orientation toward naturalism. Of equal if not greater philosophical interest are the Aristotle commentaries: the *De anima* (ed. Patar 1995), the *De generatione et corruptione* (ed. Caroti 1996), the *De caelo* (ed. and tr. Kren 1965), the *Meteorology* (part. ed. and tr. McCluskey 1974), and especially the recently discovered *Physics* (ed. Caroti *et al.* in progress), all written in the late 1340s. Standing in between these commentaries and the later treatises are the questions on Euclid's *Elements* [*ca.* 1350] (ed. Busard 1961). In the 1370s, at the request of the king, he produced French translations with accompanying commentaries of Aristotle's *Politics* (ed. Menut 1970), *Ethics* (ed. Menut 1940), *Economics* (ed. and tr. Menut 1957), and *De caelo* (ed. and tr. Menut and Denomy 1968). Also noteworthy are the *De visione stellarum,* which is a treatise on optics and atmospheric refraction (ed. Burton 2007), and a treatise on money (ed. Wolowski 1864/1976).

Secondary sources. Menut, "Provisional Bibliography" (1966); Babbitt, *Oresme's Livre de Politiques* (1985); Caroti, "La position" (1994), "Les modi rerum" (2000); Celeyrette and Mazet, "La hiérarchie" (1998); Courtenay, "Early Career" (2000); Grant, *Studies* (1981), "Natural Knowledge" (1993); Kaye, *Economy and Nature* (1998); Kirschner, *Kommentar zur Physik* (1997) [prelim. part. ed.]; Molland, "Scientific Progress" (1974); Piron, *Violence, langage* (1997); Quillet (ed.), *Autour de Nicole Oresme* (1990); Souffrin and Segonds (eds.), *Nicolas Oresme* (1988); Taschow, *Frühling der Moderne* (2003); BCPMA (Grant); DMA (Celeyrette); REP (Molland); Weijers.

NIKEPHOROS BLEMMYDES b. 1197; d. Ephesus, 1272. Byzantine scholar and influential teacher. Studied in Bithynia (northern Turkey), focusing on medicine – his father's profession – before taking up a career in the church in 1224. Joined a monastery *ca.* 1235, quickly becoming its head. Founded his own monastery near Ephesus in 1241. Extant works include extensive epitomes of logic and physics (PG 142), as well as an autobiography [1264–5] (ed. Munitiz 1984; tr. Munitiz 1988); a mirror for princes, the *Imperial Statue* (ed. and tr. Hunger and Ševčenko 1986); a pair of discourses on the soul and body (ed. 1784); and a treatise on predestination (ed. and [German] tr. Lackner 1985). A collection of theological writings has also recently been published (ed. and [Fr] tr. Stavrou 2007).

Secondary sources. Bydén, *Theodore Metochites* (2003); Codellas, "Philosophical Works" (1949); Tatakis, *Byzantine Philosophy* (2003); ODB (Macrides).

NIKEPHOROS CHOUMNOS b. 1250/5; d. Constantinople, 1327. Byzantine scholar and statesman. Studied rhetoric and philosophy in Constantinople, becoming an important political figure. His philosophical works (ed. Boissonade, in *Anecdota graeca* 1833/1962; *Anecdota nova* 1844/1962; PG 140) advocate the classical tradition, against the modernism of his rival Theodore Metochites. A nominalist, he rejected both Plato's Ideas and Aristotle's forms.

Secondary sources. Bydén, *Theodore Metochites* (2003); Ševčenko, *Études sur la polémique* (1962); Tatakis, *Byzantine Philosophy* (2003); Verpeaux, *Nicéphore Choumnos* (1959); ODB (Talbot).

NIKEPHOROS GREGORAS b. Herakleia Pontike, 1293; d. Constantinople, 1361. Scholar and teacher whose work ranges over history, philosophy, theology, and astronomy. Orphaned as a child. Studied philosophy in Constantinople with Theodore Metochites. Founded a school at the monastery of Chora in Constantinople, where he was an influential teacher. Involvement in the dispute over hesychasm led to his being condemned and anathematized in 1351; placed under house arrest, he lived the remainder of his life in disgrace. In his dialogue *Phlorentios* or *On Wisdom* [*ca.* 1333] (ed. and [Ital] tr. Leone 1975), Aristotle's views are rejected in favor of Platonism. His best-known work is a history, in thirty-seven books, of thirteenth- and fourteenth-century Byzantium (ed. Schopen and Bekker 1829–55). Many letters are also extant (ed. Leone 1982–3).

Secondary sources. Bydén, *Theodore Metochites* (2003); Ierodiakonou, "Anti-Logical Movement" (2002); Tatakis, *Byzantine Philosophy* (2003); ODB (Talbot).

ODO OF OURSCAMP, *see* Odo of Soissons.

ODO RIGALDUS (Eudes of Rouen, Odon Rigaud, Rigaldi, Rigauld) b. Brie-Comte-Robert (Île-de-France), *ca.* 1205; d. Gaillon (Normandy), 1275. Early Franciscan theologian. Entered the Franciscan order *ca.* 1236 and studied in Paris under Alexander of Hales. Lectured on the *Sentences*, probably in 1243–5, then served as regent master in 1245–7 at Paris. Elected archbishop of Rouen in 1248 and was subsequently much involved in ecclesiastical and diplomatic matters, even accompanying Louis IX to Tunis on his second crusade in 1270. Extant work includes his *Sentences* commentary (part. ed. Sileo 1984); various sermons (part. ed. Duval-Arnould 1976–7; Bougerol 1995); and sixteen disputed questions, including *De scientia theologiae* (ed. Sileo 1984), *De libero arbitrio* (ed. Lottin 1931), *De gratia* (ed. Pergamo 1935), and *De aeternitate mundi* (ed. Dales and Argerami, in *Medieval Latin Texts* 1991). A remarkable look at Odo's daily activities from 1248 to 1269 is preserved in his journal (ed. Bonnin 1852; tr. Brown and O'Sullivan 1964).

Secondary sources. Andrieu-Guitrancourt, *L'archevêque* (1938); Bouvy, "Les questions sur la grâce" (1960), "Les necessité de la grâce" (1961); Davis, *The Holy Bureaucrat* (2006); Henquinet, "Les manuscrits" (1939); Lottin, "Un commentaire" (1935); Pobst, "Visition" (2002); Sileo, "Dalla lectio alla disputatio" (1997); Wood, "Distinct Ideas" (1993); Glorieux.

ODO OF SOISSONS (of Ourscamp) b. Soissons; d. *ca.* 1172. Paris theologian. A student of Peter Lombard at the cathedral school in Paris and subsequently a teacher, becoming chancellor there *ca.* 1164–8. Joined the Cistercian cloister in Ourscamp (northeast of Paris) in 1168; elected abbot soon after. Bishop of Tusculum from 1170. Extant works include various letters and sermons and a large number of theological questions (part. ed. Pitra 1888), although some of the questions edited under his name stem from his followers, and others seem entirely unconnected to Odo.

Secondary sources. Hödl, "Sentenzen" (2002); Leclercq, "Lettres" (1955); Lottin, "Le premier" (1938); DS (Longère).

ODO OF TOURNAI (of Cambrai) b. Orleans, *ca.* 1060; d. Anchin, 1113. Educator and theologian. An influential teacher in Tournai (Belgium), he became a Benedictine monk at St. Martin's Abbey there in 1095, and eventually abbot. Elected bishop of Cambrai in 1105, but was forced to withdraw from the position five years later for political reasons. His most important extant works (PL 160) are *De peccato originali* and *Dispositio contra Judaeum Leonem* (both tr. Resnick 1994), as well as an *Expositio in canonem missae.*

Secondary source. Resnick, "Problem of Universals" (1997).

OLIVER BRITO *fl. ca.* 1250–60. Paris arts master. Author of an introductory textbook, the *Philosophia* (ed. Lafleur and Carrier, in *L'enseignement* 1997).

Secondary sources. Lafleur, *Quatre introductions* (1988); Weijers.

PAUL OF GELRIA (Paul Fabri) b. Saxony, *ca.* 1352; d. Cologne, 1404. German arts master and theologian. Studied the arts at Paris under Thomas of Cleves, incepting as master in 1376. Taught at Paris until 1382, at that point leaving for the University of Prague. Went on to study theology in Vienna, becoming doctor in 1396. Subsequently taught at Cologne until his death. Only known work is *De conceptibus* [1380s] (ed. Bos and Read 2001).

Secondary sources. Read, "Material Supposition" (1999); Weijers.

PAUL OF PERGULA b. *ca.* 1400; d. Venice, 1455. Logician. Student of Paul of Venice in Padua, becoming master of arts *ca.* 1420, and doctor of theology by 1430. Taught in Venice from 1420 until his death. Extant works include an introductory *Logica*; a *Tractatus de sensu composito et diviso* (both ed. Brown 1961); *Dubia super Consequentiis Strodi* (ed.

1477, etc.); *Sophismata asinina* (ed. Pironet 1998), as well as commentaries on the *ars vetus* and William Heytesbury (unedited).

Secondary sources. Boh, "Suppositions and Consequences" (1965); Braakhuis, "Commentary on the Sophismata" (1982); Brown, "*Tractatus de obligationibus*" (1966); Karger, "La supposition matérielle" (1982); Spade, *Mediaeval Liar* (1975); BCPMA (Lahey); CHLMP; Lohr; Weijers.

PAUL OF PERUGIA d. Paris, *ca.* 1346. Carmelite theologian. Lectured on the *Sentences* at Paris in 1344–5 (unedited except for excerpts in the secondary literature), dying before he could become master.

Secondary sources. Etzwiler, "Nature of Theological Knowledge" (1987); Schabel, "*Sentences* Commentary" (2005); Xiberta, *De scriptoribus scholasticis* (1931).

PAUL OF TARANTO (Tarento) b. Taranto (southern Italy); *fl. ca.* 1260/1300. Franciscan alchemist. Lectured at the *studium* in Assisi. Author of the influential alchemist treatise *Summa perfectionis* (ed. and tr. Newman 1991), traditionally ascribed to Jābir ibn Ḥayyān, as well as the briefer *Liber tam theoricae quam practicae veritatis in arte alkimica* (ed. and tr. Newman, in "Summa perfectionis" 1986).

Secondary sources. Haage, "Die Korpuskulartheorie" (1994); Newman, "New Light" (1985).

PAUL OF VENICE (Paolo Nicoletti Veneto) b. Udine, *ca.* 1369; d. Padua, 1429. Eminent logician and natural philosopher. Joined the Augustinian order in his youth; studied in Padua before being assigned to study theology at Oxford in 1390–3. Taught mainly at Padua, with stints in Siena in 1420–4 and Perugia in 1424–8. Also served both as an active administrator in his order and as a Venetian diplomat. His works, concentrated on logic and natural philosophy, are among the most influential of later scholasticism, surviving in hundreds of manuscripts and many editions. Particularly influential are his *Summa philosophiae naturalis* [1408] (ed. 1503/1974) and *Logica parva* [*ca.* 1393–5] (ed. Perreiah 2002; tr. Perreiah 1984). Other major logical works are the *Sophismata aurea* [*ca.* 1399] (ed. 1493) and the vast *Logica magna* [*ca.* 1396–9] (ed. 1499; various modern part. eds. and trs.), which largely reports on the work of others. Many commentaries on Aristotle circulated widely, including the *Posterior Analytics* [1406] (ed. 1477/1976), *Physics* [1409] (ed. 1499), *Metaphysics* [*ca.* 1420–4] (unedited), *De generatione et corruptione* (ed. 1498), *De anima* [*ca.* 1415–20] (ed. 1504), and *ars vetus* [1428] (ed. 1494). Various influences shaped Paul's work, including Parisian Averroism, English logic, and Wycliffite realism.

Secondary sources. Perreiah, *Bibliographical Guide* (1986); Amerini, "Nature of Essence" (2004); Bottin, "Logica e filosofia naturale" (1983); Conti, *Esistenza e verità* (1996), "Individuation" (1998), "Divine Ideas" (2003); Kuksewicz, "Teoria dell'anima" (1983); Maierù (ed.), *English Logic in Italy* (1982); Nardi, "Aristotelismo padovano" (1958); Perreiah, "Insolubilia" (1978); Ruello, "Théologien 'averroiste'?" (1978); BCPMA (Perreiah); REP (Ashworth); SEP (Conti); Weijers.

PETER ABAELARD (Abailard, Abelard) b. Le Pallet (Brittany), 1079; d. Chalon-sur-Saône (Burgundy), 1142. Famous and controversial philosopher and theologian; one of the greatest logicians of the Middle Ages. Traveled in his youth to study with the leading scholars of the Latin world, including Roscelin and William of Champeaux. Soon attracted his own students; by 1113, he was master of the school of Notre Dame in Paris. His affair with Héloïse and subsequent castration led to his entering the Benedictine monastery of St. Denis *ca.* 1119, where he continued to teach, increasingly on theology. His first work in that area was condemned and burned by a synod at Soissons in 1121 for controversy surrounding its claims about the Trinity. Subsequently established his own monastery, the Paraclete (where Héloïse later became abbess), then left to become abbot of St. Gildas in Brittany, *ca.* 1126. After much conflict there, he returned to Paris, still writing and teaching at Mount St. Geneviève *ca.* 1132–8. Again his views came under suspicion, with Bernard of Clairvaux leading the attack, and in 1140 the Council of Sens condemned nineteen propositions. Abaelard sought to appeal directly to Rome, but Bernard prevailed, and Abaelard's sentence (to silence) was lifted only due to the intervention of Peter the Venerable, under whose protection he spent his remaining days.

Abaelard's principal works are logical, ethical, and theological; their dating is problematic because they were revised over time. The logical works, often rich with metaphysical ideas, are concerned almost entirely with the *ars vetus*, Aristotle's new logic having become available only later in Abaelard's life. The main works are the *Dialectica* [*ca.* 1110] (ed. de Rijk 1970) and the *Logica "Ingredientibus"* [*ca.* 1120] (ed. Geyer 1919–27; part. tr. Spade, *Five Texts* 1994), the latter a formal commentary on the *ars vetus*. Also extant are a later commentary on the *Isagoge* known as the *Glossulae* (or *Logica "Nostrorum petitioni sociorum"*) [*ca.* 1125] (ed. Geyer 1933); an early *Introductiones parvulorum* (ed. Dal Pra 1969); a *Tractatus de intellectibus* (ed. Morin 1994; tr. King, *Problem of Universals* 1982); and a *Sententiae* (ed. Minio-Paluello 1958) concerned with puzzles over wholes and parts. The ethical works consist of his most widely read philosophical treatise, the *Scito teipsum* (*Know Thyself*, also known as the *Ethics*) [1130s] (ed. Ilgner 2001; tr. Spade 1995; ed. and tr. Luscombe 1971) and the *Collationes* [*ca.* 1128] (ed. and tr. Orlandi and Marenbon 2001), a dialogue between a Christian, a Jew, and a philosopher. In theology, his first condemned treatise, the *Theologia summi boni* [1120] was expanded into the *Theologia Christiana* [*ca.* 1125–6], and further revised into the *Theologia scholarium* [*ca.* 1134], which seems to have been the focus of attack at Sens (all three ed. in *Opera theologica*). His *Sic et non* (ed. Boyer and McKeon 1977) is not an original work, but rather collects patristic texts on a series of 158 questions. We know a great deal about Abaelard's life because of his *Historia calamitatum* (ed. Monfrin 1974) and the famous correspondence with Héloïse (ed. Muckle 1953–5), both translated many times. Other letters, sermons, and various lesser works survive as well (see PL 178).

Secondary sources. Brower and Guilfoy (eds.), *Cambridge Companion* (2004); Jacobi, "Speech Sign 'Est'" (1986); King, *Problem of Universals* (1982); Kretzmann, "Culmination" (1982); Luscombe, *School of Peter Abelard* (1969); Marenbon, *Philosophy of Peter Abelard* (1997); Mews, *Abelard and Heloise* (2005); Pinziani, *Logical Grammar* (2003); de Rijk, "Semantics" (1986); Thomas (ed.), *Petrus Abaelardus* (1980); Tweedale, *Abailard on Universals* (1976); Wilks, "Essential Predication" (1998); BCPMA (Marenbon); CALMA; Dronke; REP (Tweedale); SEP (King).

PETER OF ABANO (de Apono, Aponensis) b. Abano (Veneto), *ca.* 1250; d. 1315. Physician, philosopher, translator. Studied in Padua; subsequently journeyed to Constantinople, *ca.* 1270–85. Studied and taught in Paris in the 1290s, then perhaps taught medicine in Montpellier. Returned to Padua in 1306, where he ultimately died in prison after coming under theological suspicions. His two major works are the *Conciliator differentiarum philosophorum et praecipue medicorum* [1303; rev. 1310] (ed. 1565/1985), which is a comparative study of Greek and Arabic medicine and philosophy, and a commentary on the pseudo-Aristotelian *Problemata* [1310] (ed. 1501, etc.). His best-known medical work is a treatise on poison, the *De venenis atque eorundem commodis remediis* [1303] (ed. 1537, etc.). His scientific interests are reflected in the *Lucidator dubitabilium astronomiae* [1303; rev. 1310] (ed. Federici Vescovini 1988).

Secondary sources. Ferrari, *Tempi* (1900); Hasse, "Theory of the Soul" (2001); Lagerlund, "Anatomy of Perception" (2008); Nardi, *Saggi* (1958); Olivieri, *Pietro d'Abano* (1988); Paschetto, *Pietro d'Abano* (1984); Siraisi, "*Expositio Problematum*" (1970); Thorndike, *History* (1923–58), "Manuscripts" (1944); DSB (Premuda); Weijers.

PETER OF AILLY (Petrus de Alliaco) b. Compiègne (Picardy), 1350; d. Avignon, 1420. Progressive philosopher and theologian, associated with nominalism. Studied in Paris at the College of Navarre beginning in 1364; master of arts in 1368. Studied theology from 1368, obtaining his doctorate in 1381. Grand master of Navarre in 1384–9; chancellor of the university in 1389–95. Bishop of Le Puy in 1395 and Cambrai in 1397, and finally cardinal of Cambrai in 1411. Participated in the Council of Constance in 1414–18, where he played a leading role in the condemnation of John Hus. Authored over 170 works, mainly devoted to ecclesiastical questions, especially the Great Schism. His philosophical and theological work dates from his early years at Paris and includes a *Sentences* commentary [1376–7] (ed. 1490/1968), a *Tractatus de anima* [1377/81] (ed. Pluta 1987), a treatise on Boethius's *Consolation* (part. ed. Chappuis 1993), and various logical works, including studies of concepts (ed. Kaczmarek 1980; tr. Spade 1980) and insolubles [early 1370s] (ed. 1499, etc.; tr. Spade 1980). A polemic against the *modi significandi* (ed. Kaczmarek 1980, 1994) has been wrongly ascribed to him. Although the treatise on the soul is his only surviving work in natural philosophy, Peter became well known for his scientific interests, particularly his cosmographical treatise, the *Imago mundi* [*ca.* 1410] (ed. and [Fr] tr. Buron 1930). Various treatises and sermons were collected in a Renaissance edition (1490/1971).

Secondary sources. Chappuis *et al.*, "Die philosophischen Schriften" (1986); Biard, "Présence et représentation" (1992); Calma, "Commentaire sur les *Sentences*" (2007); Kennedy, *Harvest* (1986); Meller, *Erkenntnislehre* (1954); Oakley, *Political Thought* (1964); Pluta, "Unsterblichkeit" (1990); Smoller, *History, Prophecy, and the Stars* (1994); BCPMA (Lee); CHLMP; DMA (Beyer de Ryke); DSB (Kren); REP (Pluta); Weijers.

PETER ALFONSI b. Huesca (Aragon), *ca.* 1060; d. *ca.* 1140. A former rabbi who converted to Christianity in 1106. Court physician to Alfonso I of Aragon and Henry I of England. Most famous for a collection of Oriental tales, the *Disciplina clericalis* (tr. Hermes and Quarrie 1977). His *Dialogus* (PL 157; [Sp] tr. Tolan *et al.* 1996) argues for converting

Jews. Also the author of works of astronomy and probably a study of the elements (ed. and tr. Dales 1976).

Secondary sources. Burnett, "Works" (1997); d'Alverny, "De elementis" (1986); Lasker, "Jewish–Christian Polemics" (1996); Dronke.

PETER OF AQUILA b. *ca.* 1275; d. Agnone (Molise), 1361. Franciscan theologian. Studied at Paris, lecturing on the *Sentences* probably in 1337–8 (ed. Paolini 1907–9, etc.). Also extant are a compendium of the *Sentences* and a commentary on the *Ethics* (both unedited). A follower of Scotus, for which he became known as the *Scotellus* or "Little Scotus."

Secondary sources. Bernards, "Zum Schrifttum" (1953); Schmitt, "Compendium" (1950); Vittorini, "La teoria delle idee" (2008); BBK (Meier-Oeser); FA; Weijers.

PETER AURIOL (Aureol, Aureoli, Oriel) b. near Cahors (southern France), *ca.* 1280; d. 1322. Innovative Franciscan theologian. Probably joined the Franciscan order before 1300 and subsequently studied in Paris. Lectured at Franciscan *studia* in Bologna in 1312 and Toulouse in 1314–16 before returning to Paris to study theology in 1316. Regent master from 1318 to 1320. Elected provincial minister of Aquitaine in 1320 and archbishop of Aix-en-Provence in 1321. Auriol's philosophical thought is extremely original but dense and difficult. His views were often discussed by subsequent authors, but almost always critically. His principal work is his *Sentences* commentary. The first version, the *Scriptum*, covers only Book I (ed. Rome, 1596; prol. and dd. 1-8 ed. Buytaert 1952–6; part. tr. CTMPT III). It was begun in Toulouse and finished soon after his arrival in Paris. He began a new series of lectures in Paris, and *reportationes* on all four books survive, in various more or less revised redactions (Bks. II–IV ed. 1605). (The 1596–1605 edition is extremely unreliable, and work on a critical edition is in the early stages. Various preliminary partial editions have been published in journals. See Friedman's web page www.peterauriol.net for further texts and bibliography.) Other extant works include a *Quodlibet* [1320] (ed. 1605); an extremely popular treatise on scriptural interpretation, the *Compendium sensus litteralis totius divinae Scripturae* (ed. Seeboeck 1896); and two early treatises, a *Tractatus de paupertate et usu paupere* [1311] (ed. 1512), and an unfinished philosophical work, his *Tractatus de principiis naturae* [1312] (unedited).

Secondary sources. Boehner, "*Notitia Intuitiva*" (1948); Denery, *Seeing and Being Seen* (2005); Dreiling, *Konzeptualismus* (1913); Duba, "Aristotle's *Metaphysics*" (2001); Friedman, "Intentions and Essential Predication" (1999); Friedman and Nielsen (eds.), *Vivarium* (2000); Halverson, *Predestination* (1998); Goris, "Implicit Knowledge" (2002); Nielsen, "Dictates of Faith" (1996), "Intelligibility of Faith" (1999), "Way with Words" (2002), "*Quodlibet*" (2007); Perler, "Intentionality" (1994), "What Am I Thinking About?" (1994); Schabel, *Theology at Paris* (2000); Vignaux, *Justification* (1934); BCPMA (Nielsen); DMA (Cesalli); DTC (Teetaert); REP (Pasnau); SEP (Friedman); Weijers.

PETER OF AUVERGNE (de Alvernia) b. Crocq (Auvergne); d. Clermont-Ferrand, 1304. Parisian arts master and theologian. Studied at Paris, perhaps under Aquinas, although he remained unaffiliated to any religious order. Rector of the University of Paris in 1275 and regent master of theology from 1296 to 1302, at which point he was named bishop of Clermont. Although sometimes regarded as a Thomist, Peter's work is quite independent. His literal and question commentaries on Aristotle are among the most important of the thirteenth century: he commented on virtually the whole Aristotelian corpus, including extant works on the *ars vetus* (*Categories* ed. Andrews 1987; *Isagoge* ed. Tiné 1997), the *Metaphysics* (part. ed. Hocedez, in "*Quaestiones*" 1932; Monahan 1955), the *Ethics* (ed. Celano 1986), the *Posterior Analytics* (part. ed. Pinborg, in "A New MS," 1973), the *parva naturalia* (ed. White 1986); *De memoria* (ed. Bloch 2007); *De brev. vitae* (ed. Dunne 2002), *De plantis* (ed. Poortman 2003), and perhaps the *Physics*, if a commentary traditionally ascribed to Siger of Brabant is in fact Peter's (ed. Delhaye 1941). He also completed Aquinas's commentaries on the *Politics* (part. ed. Grech 1967; part. tr. CTMPT II), *De caelo*, and *Meteora* (all edited with Aquinas's work). The separate questions on the *De caelo* have also been edited (Galle 2003). Peter's logical works, which include a collection of *sophismata* (part. ed. Ebbesen, in "*Animal est omnis homo*" 1993), show him to have been associated with the speculative grammarians. From his later years as master of theology we have six *Quodlibeta* (unedited) and fragments from his *Sentences* commentary.

Secondary sources. Galle, "Bibliography" (2000/5); Andrews, "Denomination" (1988); Dunphy, "Similarities" (1953), "Twofold Efficient Cause" (1966); Ebbesen, "*Termini accidentales concreti*" (1986); Galle, "Whether or Not the Heaven" (2001), "Unicity of the World" (2001); Gauthier, "Questiones super librum Ethicorum" (1964); Hocedez, "La théologie" (1930), "La vie et les œuvres" (1933), "L'individuation" (1934), "La philosophie des Quodlibets" (1935); de Leemans, "*De motu animalium*" (2004); Monahan, "Subject of Metaphysics" (1954); Rosier-Catach and Ebbesen, "Syllogizantem" (2004); Schabel, "Quodlibeta" (2007); White, "Aquinas and the Prologue" (1990); BCPMA (Andrews); CHLMP; DMA (Bonino); Lohr; REP (Andrews); Roensch; Weijers; www.paleography.unifr.ch/petrus_de_alvernia/.

PETER OF CANDIA (Petros Philargis; Pope Alexander V) b. Crete, *ca.* 1340; d. Bologna, 1410. Franciscan theologian. Orphaned as a child and educated by the local Franciscans, joining the order in 1357. Studied the arts in Padua, and then theology at Franciscan *studia* in Norwich, Oxford, and Paris. Lectured on the *Sentences* at Paris in 1378–80, becoming master in 1381. A series of ecclesiastical appointments culminated in his election as pope in 1409. His philosophical importance rests on his *Sentences* commentary, which circulated widely in the fifteenth century, although it was never printed. Containing few original ideas, it was nevertheless an important conduit by which a wide range of earlier, progressive fourteenth-century ideas were transmitted to later scholasticism. An electronic edition is well underway: www.ucy.ac.cy/isa/Candia/texts.htm.

Secondary sources. Brown, "Believing and Knowing" (1994–7) [edits *Sent.* prologue], "Hundred-Year 'History'" (1991), "Sermons" (1976); Ehrle, *Sentenzenkommentar* (1925); Schabel, "Prelude to the Quarrel" (1998); BCPMA (Schabel); FA.

PETER CEFFONS *fl.* 1350. Cistercian theologian. Lectured on the *Sentences* at Paris in 1348–9; later became abbot of Clairvaux. His lengthy commentary is extant in just a single manuscript and remains almost entirely unstudied and unedited. Its introductory letter (ed. Trapp, in "Peter Ceffons" 1957) is notable for its criticisms of the condemnations of 1347.

Secondary sources. Elderidge, "Changing Concepts" (1978); Genest, "Dieu trompeur" (1984); Murdoch, "*Subtilitates Anglicanae*" (1978); BCPMA (Schabel).

PETER THE CHANTER (Cantor) b. near Beauvais, *ca.* 1130; d. Longpont Abbey, (northern France) 1197. Paris theologian. Educated at the cathedral school at Rheims, where he subsequently taught and became both canon and cantor. Master of the Notre Dame cathedral school in Paris by 1173, again serving as cantor. Died en route to Rheims, where he had been elected dean of the cathedral chapter. Best known for his *Verbum abbreviatum* [before 1187] (short vers. ed. PL 205; long vers. ed. Boutry 2004), an instruction manual for preachers and teachers. Also extant is a *Summa de sacramentis et animae consiliis* [*ca.* 1191] (ed. Dugauquier 1954–7), as well as the *De tropis loquendi* (unedited) and various biblical commentaries (unedited).

Secondary sources. Baldwin, *Masters, Princes, and Merchants* (1970); Evans, "Work of 'Terminist Theology'" (1982); BBK (Reinhardt).

PETER COMESTOR b. Troyes; d. Paris, *ca.* 1180. Theologian and historian. Educated at the cathedral school at Troyes, where he subsequently taught. Chancellor of Notre Dame Cathedral by 1168, a position that gave him authority over the cathedral school and that he retained even after retiring from teaching to the abbey of St. Victor in 1169. Most popular work was his biblical history, the *Historia scholastica* [1169/73] (PL 198; *Liber Genesis*, ed. Sylwan 2005), which soon became a required text in the theology curriculum. Philosophically most important is his theological *summa*, the *Sententiae de sacramentis* (ed. Martin 1937). Also extant are a large number of sermons (PL 171, 198).

Secondary sources. Daly, "Peter Comestor" (1957); BBK (Rappenecker).

PETER DAMIAN b. Ravenna, *ca.* 1007; d. Faenza, 1072. Monastic leader and Church reformer, suspicious of philosophical learning. Studied the arts and law in various Italian universities; subsequently became well known as a teacher of rhetoric. After a religious conversion *ca.* 1035, he entered the Benedictine monastery at Fonte Avellana (near Gubbio), becoming prior in 1043. His work displays a persistent animosity to philosophy, which he regards as at best the servant of theology. These writings, usually in the form of letters (which number over 180) (ed. Reindel 1983–93; tr. Blum 1989–2005), are typically concerned with spiritual matters, or with ecclesiastical and monastic reform. The best known of the latter kind is his *Liber gomorrhianus* [*ca.* 1051] (Letter 31). His main contribution to philosophy comes in his *De divina omnipotentia* [1065] (Letter 119), in which he has famously been read to suggest that God could make it the case that a past event did not occur. A collection of his spiritual writings is available in English (tr. McNulty 1959), and his sermons are available in a modern edition (ed. Lucchesi 1983). The complete works are edited in PL 144–5.

Secondary sources. Dressler, *Leben und Werk* (1954); Endres, *Petrus Damiani* (1910); Gaskin, "Divine Power" (1997); Gonsette, *La culture profane* (1956); Holopainen, *Dialectic and Theology* (1996), "Necessity" (1999); Leclercq, *Saint Pierre Damien* (1960); Moonan,

"Impossibility" (1980); Ranft, *Theology of Work* (2006); Remnant, "Could God Change the Past?" (1978); Resnick, *Divine Power* (1992); BCPMA (Sanford); REP (Mann); SEP (Holopainen).

PETER OF FALCO *fl.* 1280s. Paris theology master. His traditional identification as a Franciscan has been confirmed by a recently discovered document placing him at the Barcelona convent in 1281. Only fragments of his *Sentences* commentary are extant, but both a *Quodlibet* (ed. Gondras 1966) and a large collection of disputed questions (ed. Gondras 1968) have survived.

Secondary sources. Piron, "Franciscan *Quodlibeta*" (2006); FA.

PETER HELIAS (Petrus Heliae) b. Poitiers, *ca.* 1100; d. Poitiers, after 1166. Grammarian. Student of Thierry of Chartres at Paris in the 1130s; became a renowned teacher of grammar and rhetoric in Paris. Returned to Poitiers *ca.* 1155, where he was a cathedral official. Author of a commentary on Cicero's *De inventione* [1130–9] (unedited) and a widely used grammar textbook, the *Summa super Priscianum* [*ca.* 1150] (ed. Reilly 1993). His followers became known as the Heliste.

Secondary sources. Fredborg, "Dependence" (1973), "On Rhetoric" (1974), "Speculative Grammar" (1988); Hunt, "Studies I" (1941–3); Kneepkens, "Grammar and Semantics" (2000); Rosier-Catach, "Les acceptions" (1987); BCPMA (Kneepkens); Dronke.

PETER OF IRELAND *fl.* 1250s. Arts master who taught at Naples in the 1250s. Traditionally identified as Aquinas's teacher at Naples in the 1240s – a thesis that is now in doubt. Extant works include commentaries on the *De interpretatione* (ed. Dunne 1996) and the *De longitudine et brevitate vitae* (ed. Dunne 1993). Questions on the *Posterior Analytics* (part. ed. Ebbesen and Pinborg, in "Studies" 1970) have also been ascribed to him.

Secondary sources. Robiglio, "Neapolitan Gold" (2002); Lohr; Weijers.

PETER OF JOHN OLIVI (Olieu) b. Sérignan (Languedoc), 1247/8; d. Narbonne, 1298. Controversial, iconoclastic theologian. Joined the Franciscan order at the age of twelve. Studied in Paris from 1267 to 1272, but did not incept as master of theology. Subsequently lectured at various Franciscan convents, mainly in Montpellier and Narbonne, but also in Florence in 1287–9. These years were punctuated by various controversies, with his views condemned by the Franciscan authorities in 1283. Although he was subsequently allowed to teach again, his views remained under a cloud of suspicion even after his death, with various doctrines condemned at the Council of Vienne in 1311–12 and again by John XXII in 1326. Because of this controversy, Olivi's work was not widely circulated and has only recently been recognized as brilliantly anticipating many of the leading theological and philosophical movements of the next century.

Olivi was most controversial and influential as an early proponent of Franciscan spiritualism, with its strict understanding of mendicant poverty (see his *Tractatus de usu paupere* [1281/2] (ed. Burr 1992) and its inflammatory reading of the *Apocalypse*. (Olivi's commentary on that work [1296–7] (unedited) was condemned by John XXII in 1326.) Olivi's philosophical views were equally unorthodox, as highlighted by his uncompromising rejection of Aristotle's authority. His philosophical masterpiece is his

Summa [*ca.* 1274–95] – not a *Sentences* commentary but a revised collection of various disputed questions (Bk. II ed. Jansen 1922–6; Bk. III ed. Emmen and Stadter 1981; some parts still unedited). A *reportatio* of his lectures on the *Sentences* (from his years in Florence) remains unedited. His many other works include *Quodlibeta* [1289–95] (ed. Defraia 2002), questions on logic [*ca.* 1285] (ed. Brown 1986), and many biblical commentaries, including Genesis (ed. Flood 2007), Proverbs and Ecclesiastes (ed. Schlageter 2003), Acts (ed. Flood 2001), and the Gospel of John (part. ed. Pasnau 1993; part. tr. CTMPT III). For documents pertaining to his 1283 condemnation, see his *Epistola ad fratrem R.* (ed. Piron *et al.* 1998) and also Laberge, "Tria scripta" (1935) and Fussenegger, "Littera septem sigillorum" (1954).

Secondary sources. Piron, "Parcours d'un intellectuel franciscain" (1999) [biobib-liography], "Les œuvres perdues" (1998), "Franciscan *Quodlibeta*" (2006); Bettoni, *Le dottrina filosofiche* (1959); Boureau and Piron (eds.), *Pierre de Jean Olivi* (1999); Burr, "Olivi and the Philosophers" (1971), "Persecution" (1976), *Franciscan Poverty* (1989), *Peaceable Kingdom* (1993); Cross, "Absolute Time" (2002); Dumont, "Origin" (1995); Gieben, "Bibliographia" (1968); Jansen, *Erkenntnislehre* (1921); Kaye, "Liberty of Indifference" (2004); Madigan, *Interpretation of Matthew* (2003); Maranesi, "IV libro della *Summa*" (2002); Martin, "Self-Knowledge and Cognitive Ascent" (2007); Pasnau, *Theories of Cognition* (1997), "Metaphysics of Soul" (1997), "Human Freedom" (1999); Perler, *Theorien der Intentionalität* (2002); Putallaz, *Insolente liberté* (1995), "Les idées divines" (2003); BCPMA (Putallaz); DMA (Putallaz); REP (Pasnau); SEP (Pasnau); Weijers.

PETER LOMBARD b. Novara (Piedmont), 1095/1100; d. 1160. Theologian and author of the *Sentences*, which became the standard medieval theology textbook. Studied at Bologna, then Rheims and Paris in 1136, probably under Hugh of St. Victor. A master in his own right by 1142. Named canon of Notre Dame in 1145 and bishop of Paris in 1159. The *Sententiae in quattuor libris distinctae* [1148–52; rev. 1155–7] (ed. Brady 1971–81; tr. Silano 2007–) is a systematic compilation of biblical texts and Church authorities organized into four books, beginning with God (I), then creatures (II), then Christ (III), and finally the sacraments (IV). Also composed commentaries on the Psalms [before 1138] (PL 191) and Paul's epistles [1139–41] (PL 191–2). His sermons [1140–60] have been printed as the work of Hildebert of Lavardin (in PL 171).

Secondary sources. Colish, *Peter Lombard* (1994); Delhaye, *Pierre Lombard* (1961); Monagle, *Christological Nihilism* (2007), *Pietro Lombardo* (2007); Rosemann, *Peter Lombard* (2004), *Story of a Great Medieval Book* (2007); BCPMA (Rosemann); DMA (Boulnois); DTC (de Ghellinck); REP (Colish).

PETER OF MANTUA (de Alboinis) d. 1400. Logician. Student at Padua in 1389; professor of natural and moral philosophy in Bologna from 1392 until his death. Author of an extensive *Logica* (ed. 1477, etc.), an important source for the transmission of English logic to Italy. Also composed a *De primo et ultimo instanti* (ed. with *Logica*).

Secondary sources. Boh, *Epistemic Logic* (1993); Bos, "Tract on *appellatio*" (1982), "Rejection of *Ampliatio*" (1983), "Treatise *De veritate et falsitate*" (1985); de Libera, "Apol-linaire Offredi" (1982); James, "Philosopher-Humanist" (1974); Maierù, "Problema del significato" (1974); Pasnau, "William Heytesbury on Knowledge" (1995); Spade, *Mediaeval Liar* (1975); Weijers.

PETER OF NAVARRE (de Atarrabia) b. Spain; d. 1347. Franciscan theologian. Lectured on the *Sentences* in the early 1320s, probably in Barcelona; only Bk. I is extant (ed. Azcona 1974).

Secondary sources. Azanza Elío, *El conocimiento de Dios* (1997); FA.

PETER OF PALUDE b. Bresse (eastern France), *ca.* 1275; d. Paris, 1342. Dominican theologian. Entered the Dominican order as a youth in Lyon. Studied theology in Paris, lecturing on the *Sentences* in 1309–10. Regent master in 1314–17. Patriarch of Jerusalem in 1329. Much involved in ecclesiastical affairs, including processes against Durand of St. Pourçain in 1313–17, Peter of John Olivi in 1320, and controversies over the beatific vision in 1333. In philosophy and theology he aspired to faithful Thomism. Principal works are his *Sentences* commentary [1310–15] (ed. 1495, etc.) and various sermons (ed. 1491, etc.). Also extant are a *Tractatus de potestate papae* [*ca.* 1317] (ed. Stella 1966), a concordance to Aquinas's *Summa theologiae* (ed. 1552), several *Quodlibeta* (unedited), and an extensive set of biblical commentaries (unedited).

Secondary sources. Dunbabin, *Hound of God* (1991); Schabel *et al.*, "The Parisian Reaction" (2001); DS (Duval); DTC (Hedde and Amman); Kaeppeli; Roensch.

PETER OF PISA b. 744; d. Italy, before 799. Grammarian. Taught at Pavia, where he held a public disputation with a Jew named Lullus. Came to the court of Charlemagne after the conquest of Lombardy in 773–4, where he is famously said to have taught grammar to the emperor. Extant writings are an elementary grammar based on Donatus (in three versions); a collection of extracts from Priscian, Diomedes, and Pompeius; and a commentary on Daniel. An edition of the grammatical works is in progress (ed. Luhtala).

Secondary sources. Holtz, "La grammaire carolingienne" (1992); Law, *Grammar and Grammarians* (1997).

PETER OF POITIERS (Pictaviensis) b. Poitiers, *ca.* 1130; d. Paris, 1205. Studied in Paris, perhaps under Peter Lombard and Peter Comestor, becoming master of the cathedral school of Notre Dame in 1169. Appointed chancellor of the new university at Paris from 1193 until his death. Author of a theological *Sententiae* in five books [*ca.* 1170] (PL 211; Bks. I–II ed. Moore and Dulong 1943–50), a work notable for departing from Lombard by introducing a fifth book devoted to ethics. Also extant are many sermons and a *Summa de confessione* (ed. Longère 1980).

Liable to be confused with other Peters from Poitiers, including one who authored his own book of *Sentences*, the *Zwettler Summe* [*ca.* 1150] (ed. Häring 1977) [see Peter of Vienna], and the canon of St. Victor who died circa 1216.

Secondary source. Moore, *Works* (1936).

PETER OF SPAIN (Petrus Hispanus non papa) *fl.* late twelfth century. Author of the *Summa "Absoluta cuiuslibet"* (ed. Kneepkens, in *Het Iudicium Constructionis* 1987), a grammatical treatise based on the *Priscianus minor*. Not to be confused with other figures of the same name (see below).

Secondary sources. Hunt, *"Absoluta"* (1975); Kneepkens, "The *Absoluta cuiuslibet*" (2000).

PETER OF SPAIN (Petrus Hispanus) *fl.* 1230s–40s. Renowned logician. Author of the highly influential *Summulae logicales* or *Tractatus* [1230/45] (ed. de Rijk 1972; tr. Dinneen 1990; part. tr. CTMPT I) and also the *Syncategoreumata* [1235/45] (ed. and tr. de Rijk and Spruyt 1992). Traditionally identified as the future Pope John XXI (see below), but now generally thought to be a Dominican friar. His precise identity remains in dispute.

Secondary sources. D'Ors, "Petrus Hispanus" (1997–2003); Dinneen, "Suppositio" (1990); de Rijk, "Origins of the Theory" (1982); Tugwell, "Petrus Hispanus" (1999), "Auctor Summularum" (2006); Yrjönsuuri, "Words and Things" (2000); BCPMA (Klima); REP (Longeway); SEP (Spruyt).

PETER OF SPAIN (Petrus Juliani; Pope John XXI; Petrus Hispanus Portugalensis) b. Lisbon, *ca.* 1205; d. Viterbo, 1277. Scholar and pope. Studied the arts at Paris in the 1220s, then medicine, probably in southern France. Professor of medicine in Siena from 1245. Physician of Pope Gregory X in 1272. Elected archbishop and cardinal in 1273 and then Pope John XXI in 1276; died when the roof of his study collapsed. Apparently provided the impetus for the Condemnation of 1277. His authorship of various works is contested: perhaps the author of two famous logical treatises (see above); of the *Thesaurus pauperum* (on medical prescriptions) and other medical works (ed. Pereira 1973; ed. Salmón 1998); of one or more of three different works on the soul (ed. Alonso 1941–52); and/or of commentaries on pseudo-Dionysius (ed. Alonso 1957) and Aristotle's *De animalibus* (unedited).

Secondary sources. De Asúa, "Medicine and Philosophy" (1999); Bazán, "13th-Century Commentaries on *De anima*" (2002); Lohr; REP (Longeway); Weijers.

PETER SUTTON b. England; *fl.* 1310. Franciscan theologian. Regent master of theology at Oxford *ca.* 1308/11. Extant are various disputed questions (ed. Etzkorn 1964) and *Quodlibeta* (ed. Etzkorn 1963), as well as a separate question on the univocity of being (ed. Schmaus 1933), all dating from his regency.

Secondary source. Glorieux, "Peut-on identifier" (1960).

PETER OF TARENTAISE (Pope Innocentius V) b. Isère (French Alps), *ca.* 1224; d. Rome, 1276. Dominican theologian, later pope. Studied theology in Paris, becoming regent master in 1258–60 and again in 1267–9. Dominican provincial minister of France in 1264–7 and 1269–72; archbishop of Lyon in 1272; cardinal in 1273. Elected pope in 1276. Most influential for his *Sentences* commentary [1256–8] (ed. 1649–52/1964). Also extant are a *Quodlibet* [1264] (ed. Glorieux 1937) and various disputed questions (unedited, except for a question on the eternity of the world in Dales and Argerami, *Medieval Latin Texts* 1991), as well as commentaries on Paul's letters (ed. 1478, etc., under the name 'Nicolas de Gorran').

Secondary sources. Friedman, "Dominican Quodlibetal Literature" (2007); Gillet, *Studia et documenta* (1953); Laurent, *Le bienheureux Innocent V* (1947); DMA (Bonino); Glorieux; Kaeppeli.

PETER THOMAE b. Catalonia, *ca.* 1280; d. *ca.* 1340. Franciscan philosopher. Studied theology in Paris. Lector at the Barcelona *studium ca.* 1316–32. Subsequently investigated for sorcery and witchcraft. Imprisoned in 1340, where he died. A follower, albeit critically, of Scotus. Edited works include a *Quodlibet* from Barcelona (ed. Hooper and Buytaert 1957), as well as treatises *De distinctione predicamentorum* [*ca.* 1320] (ed. Bos 2000), *De ente* (part. ed. Dumont, in "Univocity" 1988), and *De unitate minori* (ed. Bos 2002). Also extant are Bk. I of his *Sentences* commentary [1323/6] and several other philosophical treatises (all unedited).

Secondary sources. Bridges, *Identity and Distinction* (1959); Dumont, "Univocity" (1988); Gál, "Proof for the Existence of God" (1998); Hoeres, "Zur Ontologie" (1961); Maierù, "Logica e teologia trinitaria" (1991); Schabel, "Divine Foreknowledge" (2003); FA; Weijers.

PETER OF TRABES *fl.* 1290s. Franciscan theologian, probably Italian. Taught at the Florence *studium generale*, where he was influenced by Peter of John Olivi. Apparently never became master at Paris. His extant works (all unedited) include a *Sentences* commentary, which survives both as a *reportatio* of Bks. II–III [1294–6] and as an *ordinatio* of Bks. I, II, and IV [1297/1300]. Some disputed questions and two *Quodlibeta* [1295–6] also survive.

Secondary sources. Huning, "Stellung" (1964); Piron, "Franciscan *Quodlibeta*" (2006).

PETER THE VENERABLE (of Montboissier) b. Auvergne, *ca.* 1092; d. Cluny, 1156. Theologian and monastic leader. Raised in the Cluniac monastery of Sauxillanges. Abbot of Cluny from 1122 until his death, making it a center of learning and influence in the Christian world. Commissioned the first Latin translation of the Quran and subsequently authored a polemic against Islam (ed. Kritzeck, *Peter the Venerable and Islam* 1964). Also wrote treatises against Judaism (ed. Friedman 1985) and the heretic Peter de Bruis (ed. Fearns 1968); despite their polemical character, these treatises are notable for being charitable and fair-minded. His theological works include a treatise *De miraculis* (ed. Bouthillier 1988). The *Opera omnia* is printed in PL 189. His correspondence is available in a modern edition (ed. Constable 1967).

Secondary sources. Torrell and Bouthillier, *Pierre le Vénérable* (1986) [biography]; Constable and Kritzeck (eds.), *Petrus Venerabilis* (1956); Kritzeck, *Peter the Venerable and Islam* (1964); BCPMA (Sanford).

PETER OF VIENNA (Peter of Poitiers?) b. *ca.* 1120; d. 1183. Theologian, disciple of Gilbert of Poitiers. Lived in Paris; moved to Vienna before 1153, when he exchanged heated letters with Gerhoh of Reichersberg over the Trinity. In addition to these and other letters (ed. Häring, in "Liber de differentia" 1962), Peter is perhaps the author of the so-called *Zwettler Summe* [*ca.* 1150] (ed. Häring 1977).

Secondary source. Fichtenau, "Magister Petrus von Wien" (1975).

PHILIP THE CHANCELLOR b. Paris, *ca.* 1160s; d. 1236. Influential early theologian at the University of Paris. Studied and taught in Paris. Appointed archdeacon of Noyon before 1211 and chancellor of Notre Dame Cathedral from 1217 until his death, which gave him jurisdiction over the university and involved him in long-running disputes over university politics. His principal work is his massive *Summa de bono* [1225/36] (ed. Wicki 1985; part. tr. Houser, in *Cardinal Virtues* 2004), a comprehensive theological treatise organized around the concept of the good, and one of the earliest Latin works to take account of the newly recovered Islamic–Aristotelian material. Also extant are a large collection of sermons (part. ed. Davy, in *Sermons* 1931) and poetry, most of which survives in musical settings.

Secondary sources. Dronke, "Lyrical Compositions" (1987); McCluskey, "Roots of Ethical Voluntarism" (2001); MacDonald, "Goodness as Transcendental" (1992); Principe, *Hypostatic Union* (1963–75); BCPMA (Houser); DMA (Imbach); Dronke; REP (MacDonald); SEP (McCluskey).

PHOTIOS (Photius) b. *ca.* 810; d. after 893. Scholar and patriarch of Constantinople, a major force in the revival of classical education in Byzantium. Served as patriarch for two terms, and at the same time played a vital pedagogical role in Constantinople. A nominalist, he rejected both Plato's ideas and Aristotle's forms. His main philosophical work is a large set of questions known as the *Amphilochia* (ed. Laourdas and Westerink 1983–8). Also extant are many letters (ed. Laourdas and Westerink 1983–8; part. tr. in White, *Patriarch Photios* 1981) and homilies (ed. Laourdas 1959; tr. Mango 1958), and the mammoth *Bibliotheca* (ed. Schamp and Kindt 2003), a descriptive catalogue of ancient works.

Secondary sources. Schamp, *Photios* (1987); Tatakis, *Byzantine Philosophy* (2003); ODB (Kazhdan).

PIERRE, *see also* Peter.

PIERRE ROGER (Pope Clement VI) b. Maumont (Corrèze), 1291; d. 1352. Benedictine theologian, later pope. Studied in Paris, reading the *Sentences* in 1320–1 and becoming master in 1323. Various ecclesiastical positions culminated in his election to the papacy in 1342. Best known as a scholar for his dispute with Francis of Meyronnes concerning the Trinity [1320–1] (ed. Barbet 1961). His *Sentences* commentary has not been found.

Secondary sources. Wood, *Clement VI* (1989); BBK (Bautz); Weijers.

PLACENTINUS b. Piacenza; d. Montpellier, 1192. Jurist and glossator. Studied in Bologna; taught both there and in Mantua before leaving for Montpellier, where he founded the school of law in 1160. Subsequently returned to Bologna and Piacenza as a teacher, returning to Montpellier just a few years before his death. His legal work was extremely influential on later generations, and would often be cited and reprinted. The principal work is the *Summa Codicis* [1170s] (ed. 1536/1962). He also authored a *Summa Institutionum* [1170s] (ed. 1536) and a *Summa de actionum varietatibus* [*ca.* 1160] (ed. Wahrmund 1925/1962). He may also be the author of the *Quaestiones de iuris subtilitatibus* (ed. Zanetti 1958), traditionally ascribed to Irnerius.

Secondary sources. Kantorowicz, "Poetical Sermon" (1938); de Tourtoulon, *Placentin* (1896/1972).

PLETHON, *see* George Gemistos Plethon.

PROCHOROS KYDONES b. Thessalonike, *ca.* 1335; d. *ca.* 1371. Byzantine scholar and translator; younger brother of Demetrios Kydones. Took monastic vows as a youth at the Great Lavra monastery in Athos, becoming a priest *ca.* 1364. Expelled from the monastery in 1367 because of his opposition to Palamism. Condemned and excommunicated in Constantinople in 1368. Translated Augustine, Boethius, and Aquinas (see Appendix B5). His own principal work is the Thomistic *On Essence and Energy* [1367], formerly ascribed to Gregory Akindynos (ed. Filovski and Petrusevski 1973–6). Also extant is a brief note on the value of syllogisms in theology (ed. Tinnefeld, in "Ein Text" 1994).

Secondary sources. Russell, "Prochoros Cydones" (2006); BBK (Todt); ODB (Talbot).

PROFIAT DURAN (Efodi, Isaac ben Moses Levi) d. *ca.* 1414. Theologian, historian, and anti-Christian polemicist. Studied the Talmud in Germany, settled in Catalonia, employed as a tutor. Forced to convert to Christianity, he nevertheless continued his literary work, dedicating scientific treatises to important Christian figures but writing anti-Christian polemics on the side. By 1403 he was able to return openly to Judaism. His most important philosophical works are a commentary on Maimonides's *Guide* (ed. in early editions of the *Guide*) and the introduction to his grammatical treatise, *Maʿaseh Efod* [1403] (ed. 1865). Most famous of his polemical works is a satirical letter, "Do not be as your fathers" [1391/7] (tr. Kobler, in *Letters of Jews* 1953), written to a friend who backed out of a plan to emigrate to Palestine.

Secondary sources. Lasker, *Jewish Philosophical Polemics* (1977); REP (Kellner and Leaman); Sirat.

PROSPER OF REGGIO EMILIA b. 1270s; d. 1332/3. Augustinian Hermit and Paris theologian. Studied in Paris, then served as lector at Milan. Returned to Paris to lecture on the *Sentences*, incepting as master of theology in 1316. Returned to Italy in 1318, becoming regent at the Augustinian convent at Bologna by 1321, where he taught until his death. Extant works include a *Sentences* commentary (prologue and Bk. I only) [prob. 1314–15] and various disputed questions [*ca.* 1313] (all unedited).

Secondary sources. Courtenay, "Reflections" (2007); Pelzer, "Prosper de Reggio Emilia" (1928).

PRUDENTIUS OF TROYES (Galindo) b. Spain; d. Troyes (northeast France) 861. Historian engaged in predestination dispute. Left Spain in his youth; studied at the court of Charles the Bald and became bishop of Troyes by 847. Attacked Hincmar's views on predestination *ca.* 849, seemingly taking the side of Gottschalk. Subsequently attacked John Scottus Eriugena's views in this same area in 851. His *Annales Bertiniani* are an important source for ninth-century French history. His work is edited in PL 115.

PTOLEMY OF LUCCA (Bartholomew, Tolomeo dei Fiadoni) b. Lucca (Tuscany); d. Torcello, 1327. Political theorist and historian; Dominican friar and student of Aquinas. Served as prior of convents in Lucca and Florence from 1287 to 1307; lived in the papal court of Avignon in 1309–19; bishop of Torcello from 1318. Best known for completing Aquinas's *De regimine principum* (from II.4) [*ca.* 1300] (ed. Spiazzi 1954, etc; tr. Blythe 1997). Other works include the *Determinatio compendiosa* [*ca.* 1280] (ed. Krammer 1909); an *Exaemeron* (*De operibus sex dierum*) [1285–95] (ed. Masetti 1880); and various historical works, most notably the *Annales* [1303–6] (ed. Schmeidler 1955) and the *Historia ecclesiastica nova* [1313–16] (ed. Muratori 1727).

Secondary sources. Blythe, "Aristotle's *Politics*" (2002); Davis, "Roman Patriotism" (1975); König, *Tolomeo von Lucca* (1878); Krüger, *Leben und Werke* (1874); La Salle and Blythe, "Civic Humanist" (2005); Nederman and Sullivan, "Reading Aristotle through Rome" (2008); Kaeppeli.

AL-QUSHAYRĪ (Abū al-Qāsim) b. Ustuwa (northeast Iran), 986; d. Nishapur, 1072. Sufi scholar and theologian. Born into a wealthy family; fell under the influence of the Sufi master Abū ʿAlī al-Daqqāq while in Nishapur and subsequently devoted himself to religious study. Becoming the head of the Sufi madrasa in Nishapur, he eventually came into conflict with the local authorities, and after a brief imprisonment left for Baghdad in 1056. With a change in the political situation, he returned to Nishapur *ca.* 1063. His many extant works range widely over theology, law, and mysticism. Most prominent is his *Risāla* [1045–6] (ed. Mahmūd and Ibn al-Sharīf 1966; tr. Knysh 2007), which argues for the conformity of Sufi beliefs with Islamic law and theology. His *Al-taḥbīr fī al-tadhkīr* (*The Reminder Tractate*) (ed. Busyūnī 1968) is a mystical commentary on God's ninety-nine names.

Secondary sources. Ahmad, "Theologian and Commentator" (1969); BEIP (Kuşpinar); EI (Halm).

QUSṬĀ IBN LŪQĀ (Costa ben Luca) b. Baalbek (Lebanon); d. Armenia, 912/13. Scientist, philosopher, and translator. Of Christian origin, he lived for many years in Baghdad, where he was an eminent scholar and physician. Relocated to Armenia to serve as the royal physician there. Best known for his *De differentia animae et spiritus*, which was especially influential in its Latin translation by John of Seville [1125/52] (ed. Barach 1878/1968; Wilcox 1985).

Secondary sources. Daiber, "Einteiling der Wissenschaften" (1990); EI (Hill).

RADULPHUS ARDENS (Raoul Ardent) b. Beaulieu (Poitou); d. *ca.* 1200. Theologian and popular preacher. Probably studied at the cathedral school in Poitiers; a student of Gilbert of Poitiers after 1141. Became chaplain of Richard I. His principal extant theological work is the *Speculum universale* [1193–1200] (table of chapters ed. Gründel 1961), also known as the *Summa de vitiis et virtutibus*. His preaching seems to have given rise to the surname 'Ardent'; his extant homilies are collected in PL 155.

Secondary sources. D'Alverny, "L'obit" (1940); Gründel, "L'œuvre encyclopédique" (1966), *Lehre des Radulfus Ardens* (1976); Landgraf, "Der Porretanismus" (1940);

Michaud-Quantin, "Die Psychologie" (1958); Wolf, "La préface" (1979); DMA (Beyer de Ryke).

RADULPHUS BRITO (Ralph the Breton, Raoul de Hotot) b. *ca.* 1270; d. *ca.* 1320. Prominent philosopher and logician. Master of arts at the University of Paris by 1296, incepted as master of theology, probably in 1314; provisor of the Sorbonne in 1315–20. A leading figure among the *modistae*. Although Brito's philosophical writings were both original and widely influential, his many extant works have been only partly edited. These include questions on *De anima* III (ed. Fauser 1974); on Boethius's *Topics* (ed. Green-Pedersen and Pinborg 1978); on Priscian minor (ed. Enders and Pinborg 1980); on the *ars vetus* (ed. 1499); and excerpts from his *Sophismata* (various eds.) and his questions on the *Isagoge* (part. ed. Pinborg, in "Radulphus Brito" 1980). Unedited works (except for excerpts in the secondary literature) include questions on the *Prior* and *Posterior Analytics*, *Sophistical Refutations*, *Physics*, *Meteorology*, and perhaps the *Metaphysics*. From his theological studies there is a *Sentences* commentary [1308–9], a *Quodlibet*, and *Quaestiones in vesperis*.

Secondary sources. Courtenay, "Master of Arts and Theology" (2005); Ebbesen, "Rationale est animal" (1978), "Dead Man is Alive" (1979), "Brito on the Metaphysics" (2000), "The Last of the Great Arts Masters" (2000); Jolivet, "L'intellect et le langage" (1985); McMahon, "Sufficiency of the Categories" (1981); Marmo, *Semiotica e linguaggio* (1994); Pinborg, *Entwicklung der Sprachtheorie* (1967), *Logic und Semantik* (1972), *Medieval Semantics* (1984) [papers]; Roos, "Zwei Quaestionum" (1978); Sirridge, "Universal Living Thing" (2007); BCPMA (Wilson); REP (Ebbesen).

RADULPHUS DE LONGO CAMPO b. 1153/60; d. Provence, after 1213. Physician and arts master. Cistercian monk. Spent time in the abbey of Cîteaux, but lived mainly in Provence, teaching in Montpellier. His edited works are an encyclopedic *Distinctiones* [*ca.* 1190] (ed. Sulowski 1976) and a commentary on Alan of Lille's *Anticlaudianus* (to Bk. IV) [1212/13] (ed. Sulowski 1972) which offers a straightforward exposition of Alan's allegorical treatment of the seven liberal arts. Unedited works include a youthful *Cornicula, seu Summula de philosophia*, and a *Computus*.

Secondary source. Dronke.

RALPH OF BEAUVAIS b. England, *ca.* 1100; d. after 1180. Grammar master. Studied in France under Peter Abaelard. Became an influential teacher at Beauvais. Extant works are his *Glosae super Donatum* (ed. Kneepkens 1982) and the *Liber Tytan* (ed. Kneepkens 1991), a set of grammatical notes on Ovid and Lucan.

Secondary source. Hunt, "Studies on Priscian II" (1950).

RALPH OF LAON (RAOUL) b. Laon; d. 1131. Arts master. Brother of Anselm of Laon, with whom he achieved fame at the school they founded in Laon in 1076. Seems, with his brother, to have begun what would become the *Glossa ordinaria* on the entirety of the Christian Bible (PL 113–14; *Biblia latina* 1480–1/1992), which circulated anonymously for centuries. Authored the mathematical treatise, *Liber de abaco* (ed. Nagl, in

Abhandlungen 1890). Various theological *Sententiae* have also been attributed to him (ed. Lottin, in *Psychologie* 1959, vol. V).

Secondary sources. Flint, "School of Laon" (1976); Smalley, *Study of the Bible* (1983).

RALPH STRODE d. 1387. Logician. Fellow of Merton College in 1359–60. Author of a series of treatises [*ca.* 1359] known collectively as the *Logica*, consisting of *De arte logica*, *De principiis logicalibus*, *De suppositionibus*, *Consequentiae* (ed. and tr. Seaton 1973), *Obligationes* (ed. 1493–4, etc.), and *De insolubilibus*. The *Consequentiae* and *Obligationes* became immensely popular in Italy in subsequent centuries, and were copied and printed many times. Engaged in theological controversy with Wyclif, although only the latter's side of the debate survives.

Secondary sources. Ashworth, "Ralph Strode on Inconsistency" (1993); Novaes, "*Obligationes*" (2006); Ashworth and Spade, "Logic in Late Medieval Oxford" (1992); BCPMA (Georgedes); CHLMP; ODNB (North).

RAMBERT DE' PRIMADIZZI OF BOLOGNA b. Bologna; d. Venice, 1308. Dominican theologian. A friar by 1268, he eventually obtained his theology doctorate at Paris, becoming regent master in 1295–9. Prior of the Bologna convent in 1301; bishop of Castellum in 1303. His principal work is the *Apologeticum veritatis* [1286/8] (ed. Müller 1944), the last of the Thomistic *correctoria* written in response to William de la Mare.

Secondary sources. Glorieux; Kaeppeli.

RAOUL, *see* Radulphus *or* Ralph.

RATRAMNUS OF CORBIE b. *ca.* 800; d. after 868. Prominent early medieval theologian. Benedictine monk at the abbey of Corbie (Picardy); little else is known of his life. Best known for his Eucharistic treatise *De corpore et sanguine Domini* (ed. Bakhuizen van den Brink 1974; tr. McCracken, in *Early Medieval Theology* 1957). Also of philosophical interest are two treatises *De anima* (ed. Wilmart 1931; ed. Lambot 1952) and *De praedestinatione* (PL 121).

Secondary sources. Bouhot, *Ratramne de Corbie* (1976); Marenbon, *Circle of Alcuin* (1981); BBK (Wesseling).

RAYMOND LULL (Llull) b. Majorca, 1232/3; d. Tunis, 1316. Idiosyncratic philosopher, theologian, mystic. Spent his youth as a royal courtier until a religious experience at age thirty led him to pursue a life of religious study. Devoted himself to refuting the Muslim faith; to that end, he learned Arabic and attempted to establish a new method of demonstrating the doctrines of the Christian faith. Traveled extensively, promoting his ideas among Christians, attacking Latin Averroism, and evangelizing among Muslims. Suspected of unorthodoxy at various points, Lull's work became more influential during the Renaissance than it was in the Middle Ages. Some 240 works are extant in Catalan and Latin (still more writings, in Arabic, have not survived). The most prominent philosophical works are those describing his novel method of inquiry, including the *Ars demonstrativa* [*ca.* 1283] and the *Ars brevis* [1308]. This method is applied to Christian apologetics in the *Libre del gentili i dels tres savis* [*ca.* 1275] and to medicine in the *Liber principiorum medicinae* [*ca.* 1276] (all four tr. Bonner 1985). A critical edition of the Latin works is ongoing (*Opera latina* 1975–), although the older *Opera omnia* remains useful (ed. Salzinger 1721–40/1965). Many of the Catalan works are collected in *Obres* (ed. Obrador y Benassar *et al.* 1906–50), with a *Nova edició de les obres* in progress (ed. 1990–). Most of our biographical information comes from a contemporary anonymous *Vida* [*ca.* 1311] (ed. Batllori and Hillgarth 1982).

Secondary sources. Brummer, *Bibliographia* (1976); Salleras i Carolà, "Bibliografia" (1986); Garcías, *Llull y el Islam* (1981); Hames, *Art of Conversion* (2000); Hillgarth, *Lull and Lullism* (1971); Johnston, *Spiritual Logic* (1987), *Evangelical Rhetoric* (1995); Moreno Rodríguez, *La lucha contra el averroismo* (1982); Platzeck, *Raimund Lull* (1962–4); Urvoy, *Penser l'Islam* (1980); Yates, "Art of Ramon Lull" (1954); BCPMA (Lohr); DMA (Tenge-Wolf); REP (Johnston). The journal *Studia Lulliana* (1957–) is published in Majorca (formerly *Estudios Lulianos*).

RAYMOND OF PENNAFORT b. near Barcelona, *ca.* 1175; d. Barcelona, 1275. Dominican canon lawyer. Studied first in Barcelona, then in Bologna *ca.* 1210–20. Returned to Barcelona, where he entered the Dominican order in 1222. Served as chaplain to Pope Gregory IX in 1230–6, producing the standard compilation of post-Gratian canon law known as the *Liber extra* [1234]. Appointed master general of the Dominican order in 1238–40, during which time he revised the constitutions of the order. Subsequently returned to Barcelona, where he was active in organizing missionary work among Muslims and Jews. Raymond's most influential work is the *Summa de paenitentia* (*Summa de casibus conscientiae*, or *Raymundina*) [*ca.* 1221] (ed. Ochoa and Diez 1976), to which a fourth part on matrimony was added *ca.* 1335 (ed. Ochoa and Diez 1978; tr. Payer 2005). Also authored a *Summa de iure canonico* [*ca.* 1216] (ed. Ochoa Sanz and Diez Garcia 1975).

Secondary sources. Longo (ed.), *Magister Raimundus* (2002); Mas i Solench, *Ramon de Penyafort* (2000); Rius y Serra (ed.), *Diplomatario* (1954); Schwertner, *Saint Raymond of Pennafort* (1935); Valls i Taberner, *San Ramón de Penyafort* (1936/1979); Kaeppeli.

AL-RĀZĪ, Abū Bakr Muḥammad ibn Zakariyāʾ (Rhazes) b. Rayy (Persia), *ca.* 865; d. Rayy, 925/35. Physician, philosopher, and director of hospitals in Rayy and Baghdad. Principal area of influence was medicine, where he was a leading authority throughout the Middle Ages. His main surviving works are in this area, including a diary of clinical observations and various medical treatises. Foremost among these is his nine-volume *Al-Ḥāwī* (*Compendium*) (ed. 1955–68), a collection of case notes compiled by his students, which was translated into Latin in 1279 as the *Continens Liber* (ed. 1486, etc.). His opposition to revealed religion made him a controversial figure – all the more so because he took Socrates and Plato, rather than Aristotle, as his inspiration. Among his few surviving works in philosophy (ed. Kraus 1939), the most significant are concerned with ethical issues, *Al-Sīra al-falsafiyya* (*The Philosophical Life* – a philosophical autobiography) (tr., with other works, in McGinnis and Reisman, *Classical Arabic Philosophy* 2007) and *Al-Ṭibb al-rūḥānī* (*The Spiritual Medicine*) (tr. Arberry 1950).

Secondary sources. Druart, "Al-Razi's Conception of the Soul" (1996), "Al-Razi's Ethics" (1997); Goodman, "Razi's Psychology" (1972), "Fall of the Soul" (1975);

Stroumsa, *Freethinkers* (1999); Walker, "Political Implications" (1992); BCPMA (Druart); BEIP (Leaman); EI (Goodman); HIP (Goodman); REP (Walker).

AL-RĀZĪ (Abū Ḥātim) b. near Rayy; d. Azerbaijan, *ca.* 934. Leading figure in the Ismāʿīlī movement in Persia; reputedly succeeded in converting various local rulers, but ultimately forced into exile. Best-known work is a theological dictionary, the *Kitāb al-zīna* (*Book of Ornament*) (ed. al-Hamadānī 1994). Also extant are a *Kitāb al-iṣlāḥ* (*Book of Correction*) (ed. Muḥaqqiq *et al.* 1998), aimed at al-Nasafī, and the *Aʿlām al-nubūwwah* (*Signs of Prophethood*) (ed. 2003), which records his controversies with Abū Bakr al-Rāzī.

Secondary sources. Poonawala, *Biobibliography* (1977); Daftary, *Ismāʿīlīs* (1990); Stern, *Studies* (1983); Walker, "The Ismāʿīlīs" (2005); BEIP (Aminrazavi); EI (Stern).

AL-RĀZĪ (Fakhr al-Dīn) b. Rayy (Persia), 1149/50; d. Herat, 1209/10. Influential theologian and philosopher. Studied in Rayy and subsequently traveled widely, settling in Herat *ca.* 1203 to found an academy. Although suspicious of philosophy, his theological works depend extensively on it. The vast number and range of his extant works defies brief summary. In philosophy, his most important works are *Al-Mabāḥith al-mashriqiyya* (*Eastern Studies*) [before 1185] (ed. 1990), and his commentary on the physics and metaphysics of Avicenna's *Ishārāt wa-al-tanbīhāt* (part. ed. with Avicenna's text, in Dunyā, 1957–60). Also important is his theological treatise, *Muḥaṣṣal afkār* (*The Harvest of Thought*) (ed. 1905). Most prominent of all is his massive commentary on the Quran, the *Mafātīḥ al-ghayb* (*The Keys to the Unknown*), also known as *Al-Tafsīr al-kabīr* (*The Great Commentary*) (ed. 1934–62, etc.).

Secondary sources. Kholeif, *Study* (1966); Shihadeh, *Teleological Ethics* (2006); BEIP (Leaman); EI (Anawati); REP (Cooper).

REMIGIO DE' GIROLAMI (Remi of Florence) d. Florence, 1319. Dominican theologian, political theorist, and influential preacher. Studied the arts in Paris and entered the Dominican order there *ca.* 1269. Lector in the Florence convent from *ca.* 1274, and then elsewhere in Italy. Subsequently served as provincial minister of the Roman Province in 1309–11, and prior of his convent in Florence. Notable works are his *Contra falsos ecclesiae professores* [before 1298] (ed. Tamburini 1981), celebrating the authority and wisdom of the Church; the *De subiecto theologiae* [1297–9] (ed. Panella 1982); the political treatises *De bono communi* [1302] and *De bono pacis* (both ed. Panella, in "Dal bene commune" 1985); the metaphysical *De modis rerum* (ed. Gavric 2007); and a *Quodlibet* (ed. Panella 1983).

Secondary sources. Davis, "Early Florentine Political Theorist" (1960); de Matteis, *La "teologia politica communale"* (1977); Panella, "Remigiana" (1982); Rupp, "Damnation" (2000); Kaeppeli.

REMIGIUS OF AUXERRE (Autissiodorensis) b. West Franconia, *ca.* 841; d. 908. Benedictine monk and noted commentator. Taught in Auxerre and served as director of the monastery school there from 876, in Rheims from 893, and in Paris from 900. Author of many marginal glosses and commentaries on Scripture, Priscian, Donatus, Bede, and Phocas, inter alia. Particularly notable are his commentary on the *De nuptiis* of Martianus

Capella (ed. Lutz 1962–5); his *Expositio super Genesim* (ed. Edwards 1999); his commentary on Boethius's *Consolatio* (part. ed. Silk, in *Saeculi noni* 1935; Troncarelli, in *Tradizioni perdute* 1981; tr. Stewart 1916); and his *Ennarationes in Psalmos* (PL 131).

Secondary sources. Iogna-Prat and Jeudi (eds.), *L'école caroligienne d'Auxerre* (1991); Marenbon, *Circle of Alcuin* (1981).

RICHARD BILLINGHAM *fl.* 1340s–50s. English logician and theologian. Fellow of Merton College *ca.* 1344 – *ca.* 1361 and author of several influential logic textbooks, most notably the *Speculum puerorum* (also known by its incipit: *Terminus est in quem*) (ed. Maierù 1970; ed. de Rijk, in *Some 14th-Century Tracts* 1982), which would later circulate widely in Italy. Also extant are treatises *De consequentiis* (ed. Weber 2003), *De significato propositionis*, and *De sensu composito et diviso* (both unedited). Parts of a later *Sentences* commentary also seem to have survived (unedited).

Secondary sources. Bos, "Richard Billingham's *Speculum*" (2007); de Rijk, "The Place" (1975), "Works on Logic" (1976), "Semantics in Billingham and Venator" (1982); DMA (de Libera); ODNB (Fletcher).

RICHARD BRINKLEY *fl.* 1350–73. English logician and theologian. Joined the Franciscan order in Oxford, where he was active. Only complete surviving work is the *Summa nova de logica* [1355/73], a basic textbook of logic, parts of which have been edited: *De propositionibus* (part. ed. and tr. Fitzgerald 1987); *De insolubilibus* (ed. Spade 1969); *De obligationibus* (ed. Wilson and Spade 1995). Also extant are portions of his *Sentences* commentary (part. ed. Kaluza, in "Œuvre théologique" 1989). His theological *Determinationes* are now lost.

Secondary sources. Gál and Wood, "Richard Brinkley" (1980); Spade, "Logic of *sit verum*" (1994–7); BCPMA (Georgedes); CHLMP; ODNB (Fitzgerald); REP (Andrews).

RICHARD OF BROMWICH *fl.* 1300s. Benedictine theologian. Studying at Oxford by 1304 and master by 1312. Sole surviving work is a *Sentences* commentary [1305/9] extant in a single autograph manuscript (unedited).

Secondary source. Schabel and Friedman, "Trinitarian Theology IV" (2004).

RICHARD OF CAMPSALL b. Campsall (Yorkshire), 1280/5; d. *ca.* 1330. Theologian. Bachelor of arts at Balliol College and regent master of arts by 1306 at Merton College, with which he remained affiliated through the remainder of his life. Master of theology by 1322. Remained unaffiliated with any religious order. His extant writings are a series of twenty disputed questions on the *Prior Analytics* [*ca.* 1306] and treatises on prime matter, divine foreknowledge, and universals [*ca.* 1318] (all ed. Synan 1968–82). His *Sentences* commentary [1316–17] is no longer extant, though it is widely cited by later English theologians. The anti-Ockhamist *Logica* is now credited to an unknown pseudo-Campsall (ed. Synan 1982). It cannot be authentic, because Campsall's own views are similar to Ockham's and indeed may have influenced Ockham.

Secondary sources. Gelber, "Logic and Trinity" (1974); McDermott, "Materials" (1990); Tachau, "Influence" (1987), "New Evidence" (1991); BCPMA (Georgedes); ODNB (Synan).

RICHARD OF CLIVE *fl.* 1276–1306. Oxford theologian. Master of arts and fellow of Merton College by 1276; doctor of theology by 1288. Continued studies of theology at Paris in 1291–2. Chancellor of Oxford in 1297–8. Extant works include commentaries on the *Physics* and *Metaphysics* (unedited).

Secondary sources. Little and Pelster, *Oxford Theology* (1934); Andrews and Noone, "Newly Identified Redaction" (1994); Ebbesen, "Talking About What Is No More" (1987); Emden; Lohr.

RICHARD OF CONINGTON d. Cambridge, 1330. Franciscan theologian. Perhaps studied theology in Paris in the 1290s but was studying at Oxford by 1300. Lectured on the *Sentences* at Oxford *ca.* 1302–3, becoming regent master *ca.* 1306. Subsequently lectured on the Bible at Cambridge. Provincial minister of the English Franciscans in 1310–16. Although a contemporary and confrère of Scotus, Richard's views owe more to Henry of Ghent. No record of his *Sentences* commentary has been found, although several disputed questions are extant (unedited). Several treatises on apostolic poverty have survived: one from 1312 (ed. Heysse 1930) and another from 1322 (ed. Douie, in "Three Treatises" 1931).

Secondary sources. Brown, "Analogy of the Concept of Being" (1966); Doucet, "L'œuvre scolastique" (1937); Dumont, "William of Ware" (1996); FA; ODNB (Courtenay).

RICHARD OF FERRYBRIDGE (Feribrigge) *fl.* 1350s–60s. Logician and natural philosopher. Master of arts at Oxford; subsequently served as rector at several churches in Nottinghamshire in the 1360s. Two works on logic are extant: a *Logica seu de veritate propositionum* (part. ed. Del Punta, in "La *Logica*" 1982), and a *Consequentiae* (ed. 1493; part. ed. Pozzi, in *Consequentiae* 1978). Also surviving, in a single manuscript, is a treatise *De motu* (part. ed. Clagett, in *Science of Mechanics* 1959).

Secondary sources. Ashworth and Spade, "Logic in Late Medieval Oxford" (1992); Bertagna, "Richard Ferrybridge's *Logica*" (1993); Green-Pedersen, "Early British Treatises on Consequences" (1985); DMA (de Libera); ODNB (Ashworth).

RICHARD FISHACRE b. Exeter, *ca.* 1205; d. Oxford, 1248. Early Dominican theologian. Joined the Dominican order as a young man; studied theology at Oxford. Master of theology from *ca.* 1240, during which time he composed the first Oxford commentary on Lombard's *Sentences* [*ca.* 1245] (ed. Rödler *et al.* 2003–). Subsequently authored a treatise on heresies, *Adnotationes in S. Augustini librum de haeresibus* (ed. Long 1993) and various philosophical *quaestiones*, including ones on the eternity of the world (ed. Long, in "First Oxford Debate" 1998) and on the nature of light (ed. Long and Noone, in "Metaphysics of Light" 1998).

Secondary sources. Brown, "Need for Philosophy" (1988); Callus, "Introduction" (1943); Long, "Science of Theology" (1972), "Way to God" (1988), "Moral and Spiritual Theology" (1990), "*De libero arbitrio*" (1995), "Angels and Pinheads" (1998); BCPMA (Long); Kaeppeli; ODNB (Long).

RICHARD FITZRALPH (Armachanus) b. Dundalk (Ireland), 1295/1300; d. Avignon, 1360. Theologian, best known for his vehement opposition to the mendicant orders. Studied arts at Oxford by 1315, becoming master of arts in 1325. Lectured on the *Sentences* in 1327–8 or the following year (unedited), becoming master of theology in 1331. Chancellor of Oxford in 1332–34, during a tense period at the university. Subsequently traveled repeatedly to Avignon, becoming immersed in ecclesiastical issues. Appointed dean of Lichfield Cathedral in 1335; elected archbishop of Armagh in 1346, a position he held until his death. Disputes in Avignon with the Armenian Church led to his *Summa de quaestionibus Armenorum* [1340s] (ed. 1512), which would be read into the sixteenth century. During his last years he became heavily involved in criticizing the mendicant friars, a case he made in his *De pauperie Salvatoris* [1357] (part. ed. Poole 1890) and in various sermons, most notably the *Defensio curatorum* [1350], which also circulated in Middle English (tr. John Trevisa [*ca.* 1380] 1925/1987).

Secondary sources. Walsh, *Richard FitzRalph* (1981); Coleman "Antimendicant" (1984); Dawson, "Poverty Controversies" (1983); Genest, "Contingence et révélation" (1991), "Aux origines" (2002); Gwynn, "Sermon-Diary" (1937–8); Leff, *Commentator of the Sentences* (1963); BCPMA (Georgedes); ODNB (Walsh).

RICHARD KILVINGTON b. Yorkshire, 1302/5; d. London, 1361. Philosopher and theologian, one of the Oxford Calculators. Began his studies at Oxford by 1319, becoming master of arts in 1324/5 and doctor of theology *ca.* 1335. Probably a fellow of Oriel College. Lived in the London household of Richard Bury, and became active in the service of Edward III. Archdeacon of London by 1350, from which office he supported Richard Fitzralph's campaign against the mendicant friars. His only edited scholarly works are a philosophically rich collection of *Sophismata* [early 1320s] (ed. Kretzmann and Kretzmann 1990; tr. Kretzmann and Kretzmann 1990). Also extant are questions on the *Generation and Corruption* [before 1325], *Physics* [1325/6], and *Ethics* [1326/32], as well as a short *Sentences* commentary [*ca.* 1333–4].

Secondary sources. Jung-Palczewska, "Works" (2000), "Motion in a Vacuum" (1997), "Concept of Time" (2000); Katz, "On a *Sophisma*" (1996); BCPMA (Sylla); REP (Kretzmann); SEP (Jung).

RICHARD KNAPWELL d. Bologna, 1289. Early English Thomist. Dominican friar; bachelor of the *Sentences* at Oxford during the 1270s, becoming master of theology in 1284. Author of the *Correctorium "Quare"* [*ca.* 1283] (ed. Glorieux 1927), responding to William de la Mare's anti-Thomistic treatise. His *Quaestio de unitate formae* [1285/6] (ed. Kelley 1982) resulted in his excommunication by the Franciscan John Pecham; his appeal to Pope Nicholas IV, also a Franciscan, led to a sentence of perpetual silence in 1288. Also extant are various *Quodlibeta* and disputed questions [1284–6] (unedited).

Secondary sources. Callus, "Unity of Form" (1959); Jordan, "Controversy" (1982); Iribarren, "Responsio" (2001); DMA (Bonino); Kaeppeli; ODNB (Tugwell); Roensch.

RICHARD LAVENHAM b. Lavenham (Suffolk); *fl.* 1399 – *ca.* 1403. Logician, natural philosopher, and theologian. Entered the Carmelite order at Ipswich. Educated at Oxford, advancing to the study of theology. Prior of Carmelite convents at London and perhaps Bristol in 1399. Credited with over sixty works, many of which are still extant but mostly unedited. In theology, he is best known for a list of heresies he drew from the works of the Wycliffite John Purvey [1400/3] (ed. Netter and Shirley, *Fasciculi zizaniorum* 1858 [pp. 383–9]; tr. Foxe, *Actes* 1570 [pp. 649–53]). In philosophy, his logical writings have received the most attention, including a brief *De syncategorematibus* (ed. 1510, etc.) and various other brief works edited by Paul Spade (in "Treatises" 1973; "Five Logical Tracts" 1974; "Notes" 1975; *"Obligationes"* 1978; "Notes" 1980; "Treatise *Scire"* 1984 [with G.A. Wilson]). There are also various extant works in natural philosophy (all unedited), including a *Speculum naturalis philosophiae* and a *Parvus tractatus de anima*. In Middle English, there survives *A Litil Tretys* (ed. van Zutphen 1956) on the seven deadly sins.

   Secondary sources. Ashworth and Spade, "Logic in Late Medieval Oxford" (1992); d'Ors, "Sobre las *Obligationes*" (1991); Spade, "Richard Lavenham and the Cambridge Logic" (1980); CHLMP; Lohr; ODNB (Spade).

RICHARD OF MIDDLETON (de Mediavilla, Menneville) b. *ca.* 1249; d. Rheims, 1302/3. Franciscan theologian in the Augustinian tradition. Native of either England or France. Studied in Paris in 1276–84, becoming regent master of theology in 1284–7. Provincial minister of France in 1295. His *Sentences* commentary [*ca.* 1280; rev. *ca.* 1290?] (ed. 1591/1963) offers an early Franciscan reaction to the work of Aquinas – a reaction that becomes more critical in his three *Quodlibeta* [1284–7] (ed. 1590/1963). A large number of disputed questions [early 1280s] remain unedited (q. 13 ed. Fidelis a Fanna 1874; q. 38, ed. Vanni Rovighi, *L'immortalita* 1936). The treatise *De gradu formarum* (ed. Zavalloni, *La controverse* 1951) is an important work in the dispute over the plurality of substantial forms.

   Secondary sources. Hocedez, "Sa vie, ses œuvres" (1925); Sharp, "Richard of Middleton" (1930); Cunningham, *"Esse* and Existence" (1970); Henninger, "Natalis and Mediavilla" (1994); van Veldhuijsen, "The Created World" (1990); Zavalloni, *La controverse* (1951); BCPMA (Cross); DMA (Lambert); ODNB (Brown); REP (Brown).

RICHARD ROLLE (de Hampole) b. Thornton Dale (Yorkshire), 1305/10; d. Hampole, 1349. English mystic and contemplative author. Studied at Oxford, but left without a degree after a religious conversion. Subsequently lived as a recluse, writing and serving as a spiritual advisor. His devotional writings, written both in Latin (such as *De emendatione vitae* and *De incendio amoris*) and in Middle English (such as *The Pricke of Conscience* and *The Form of Perfect Living*), were extremely influential and have been edited and translated extensively (ed. Ogilvie-Thomson 1988, etc.; tr. Allen 1988, etc.).

   Secondary sources. Watson, *Invention of Authority* (1991); ODNB (Hughes).

RICHARD RUFUS OF CORNWALL (Cornubiensis) b. Cornwall; d. after 1259. Franciscan theologian and philosopher. Studied the arts at Paris before becoming a friar in 1238. Studied theology at Oxford, lecturing on the *Sentences* there in 1250–3. Returned to Paris, giving further lectures on the *Sentences* in 1253–5. Appointed regent master of theology at Oxford in 1256. Two sets of lectures on the *Sentences* survive (both unedited): the Oxford lectures (Bks. I–III only) and a later lecture that builds on Bonaventure's commentary and might date either from Paris or from Richard's later regency in Oxford. In addition to several brief disputed questions, he is the author of a *Contra Averroem* [1236–7] and a *Speculum animae* [1245]. There is controversy over whether Rufus is also the author of various Aristotelian commentaries: on the *Physics*, *Posterior Analytics*, *De anima*, *De generatione et corruptione*, and two on the *Metaphysics* [all dated to 1235–8, assuming Rufus is the author]. A critical edition of the whole corpus is in progress: to date only the uncertainly attributed *Physics* has been published (ed. Wood 2003).

Secondary sources. Donati, "Anonymous" (2005); Gál, "Viae" (1956), "Opiniones" (1975); Karger, "Substantial Transmutation" (2002); Noone, *Edition and Study* (1987), "Authorship" (1989), "Creation" (1993); Plevano, "Instant of Change" (1993); Raedts, *Richard Rufus* (1987); Wood, "Physics" (1992), "*Speculum animae*" (1995), *De anima* (2001); BCPMA (Wood); DMA (Wood); ODNB (Raedts); REP (Wood).

RICHARD OF ST. VICTOR d. 1173. Augustinian theologian, mystic, and contemplative author. Born in Britain (by tradition Scotland, but possibly either England or Ireland). Entered the Augustinian abbey at St. Victor (near Paris) in the 1140s or early 1150s, becoming sub-prior by 1159 and prior in 1162. A follower of Hugh of St. Victor, though perhaps not his student, Richard followed Hugh as master of the famous monastery school. His writings can be divided into the exegetical, contemplative, and analytical. The major exegetical work is the *Liber exceptionum* [prob. 1153–9] (ed. Châtillon 1958), an introduction to the Bible. Among the contemplative writings, the most influential were the so-called *Benjamin maior* [1153/62] (also known as the *The Mystical Ark* or the *De gratia contemplationis*) (ed. PL 196; tr. Zinn 1979) and *Benjamin minor* [1153/62] (also known as *The Twelve Patriarchs* or the *De praeparatione animi ad contemplationem*) (ed. Châtillon *et al.* 1997; tr. Zinn 1979). His most influential work of analytical theology is the *De trinitate* (ed. Ribaillier 1958; part. tr. Zinn 1979), often cited by scholastic authors. Also significant is the *De statu interioris hominis* (ed. Ribaillier 1967). A further assortment of contemplative writings is available in English (tr. Kirchberger 1957). The *Opera omnia* is printed in PL 196; various later collections are also available (ed. and tr. [Fr] Châtillon *et al.* 1951; ed. Ribaillier 1967; ed. Châtillon *et al.* 1986).

Secondary sources. Chase, *Angelic Wisdom* (1995); Dumeige, *L'idée chrétienne de l'amour* (1952); Spijker, *Fictions of the Inner Life* (2004); BCPMA (Emery); ODNB (Haren); REP (Emery).

RICHARD THE SOPHISTER (Ricardus Sophista, Magister Abstractionum) *fl.* 1230s/40s. Logician. Author of a large collection of sophisms called the *Abstractiones* (unedited), which is perhaps the earliest clear example of the genre and which circulated widely over the next century as a textbook used to identify logical fallacies. Various attempts to identify the author – most prominently, as Richard Rufus of Cornwall – have been met with skepticism.

Secondary sources. De Libera, "La littérature" (1983); Pinborg, "Magister Abstractionum" (1976); CHLMP; SEP (Streveler).

RICHARD SWINESHEAD (Calculator, Suisseth) b. Swineshead (Lincolnshire); *fl. ca.* 1340–54. Leading Mertonian natural philosopher. Educated at Oxford; a fellow at Merton

College by 1344. Famous for the *Liber calculationum* [*ca.* 1350] (ed. 1477, etc.), for which he became known as "the Calculator." This large and difficult work, composed of sixteen treatises, applies quantitative reasoning to natural philosophy. Also extant are three brief treatises: *De motu*, *De motu locali*, and *De caelo* (unedited). Richard was sometimes confused with his older contemporary and perhaps brother, Roger Swineshead, whose work is similar in character.

Secondary sources. Clagett, "Richard Swineshead" (1950); Hoskin and Molland, "Falling Bodies" (1966–7); Murdoch, "*Mathesis*" (1969); Sylla, "Oxford Calculators" (1982); BCPMA (Sylla); DSB (Murdoch and Sylla); ODNB (Molland).

ROBERT ALYNGTON d. Leicestershire, 1398. Oxford philosopher and theologian, a proponent of metaphysical realism. Fellow of Queen's College in 1379–86 and master of arts; doctor of theology by 1393. Chancellor in 1393 and 1395. Extant works include commentaries on the *Categories* (part. ed. Conti 1993) and the *Liber sex principiorum*, as well as treatises on supposition and on the genera of being (all unedited).

Secondary sources. Ashworth and Spade, "Logic in Late Medieval Oxford" (1992); Conti, "Linguaggio e realtà" (1993), "Realist Interpretation" (2008); SEP (Conti).

ROBERT BACON b. 1170s/80s; d. Oxford, 1248. Early Dominican theologian at Oxford. Probably studied in Paris and Oxford; master by 1219. Entered the Dominican order *ca.* 1229, continuing to teach in Oxford for the remainder of his life. Thought to be the author of a *Syncategoremata* from early in his career (unedited). A commentary on the Psalms (unedited) dates from after he became a friar. Bacon's once famous sermons have been almost entirely lost.

Secondary sources. Smalley, "Robert Bacon" (1948); Braakhuis, *De 13de eeuwse tractaten* (1979), "English Tracts on Syncategorematic Terms" (1981); Kaeppeli; ODNB (Dunbabin).

ROBERT BLUND *fl.* 1170s. English grammarian. Author of the *Summa in arte grammatica* (ed. Kneepkens, in *Het Iudicium Constructionis* 1987).

Secondary source. Emden.

ROBERT OF COURSON d. 1219. English moral theologian. Studied in Paris under Peter the Chanter *ca.* 1190–5, teaching there from 1200. Subsequently much involved in ecclesiastical affairs. Elected cardinal in 1212 and was responsible for the statutes of 1215 that structured the University of Paris. Only extant work is his *Summa theologica* [1208/12] (unedited), which is heavily focused on moral questions.

Secondary sources. Dickson and Dickson, "Cardinal Robert de Courson" (1934); ODNB (Sayers).

ROBERT COWTON b. Cowton (Yorkshire); *fl.* 1300–15. Franciscan theologian. Entered the Franciscan order in his youth, studying at Oxford by 1300. His only extant work, a *Sentences* commentary [*ca.* 1309–11] (ed. in progress), survives in many manuscripts (and later abbreviations). Did not become regent master in England, but perhaps in Paris.

Although a contemporary confrère of Scotus, Robert's views owe more to Henry of Ghent.

Secondary sources. Brown, "Analogy of Being" (1971); Friedman, "Trinitarian Theology" (2001); Lottin "Robert Cowton et Jean Duns Scot" (1954); Theissing, *Glaube und Theologie* (1970); FA; ODNB (Courtenay).

ROBERT OF FLAMBOROUGH d. 1224. Moral theologian. Master and canon of the abbey of St. Victor (Paris). Author of the *Liber poenitentialis* [1208/13] (ed. Firth 1971), a guide to confessors in administering penance.

ROBERT FLAND *fl.* mid-fourteenth century. Logician. Perhaps of Flemish origins. Probably associated with Oxford. Our information comes entirely from a single manuscript containing three short treatises (ed. Spade 1976–80) – *Consequentiae, Insolubilia*, and *Obligationes* – written between 1335 and 1370.

Secondary sources. CHLMP; ODNB (Brown).

ROBERT GRAYSTANES (Greystones) b. Durham, before 1290; d. Durham, 1334. Oxford theologian and Benedictine monk at the Durham monastery from an early age. Studied philosophy and theology at the Durham house of studies in Oxford, lecturing on the *Sentences ca.* 1321–2 (unedited). Elected bishop of Durham in 1333; forced to renounce the position a month later. In addition to the unedited *Sentences* commentary, Robert is perhaps the author of a chronicle of Durham for the years 1215–34 (ed. Raine, in *Historiae* 1839).

Secondary sources. Kennedy, "Commentary" (1986), "Essence and Existence" (1989); Livesey, "Subalternation" (1994); Schabel and Friedman, "Trinitarian Theology" (2003); Tachau, *Vision and Certitude* (1988); ODNB (Foster).

ROBERT GROSSETESTE (Lincolniensis) b. Suffolk, *ca.* 1170; d. Buckden (Cambridgeshire), 1253. Natural philosopher, translator, theologian, and influential bishop. Seems to have studied at Lincoln and then Cambridge. Between 1196 and 1220 he appears to have been mainly engaged in administrative work in Hereford, with some time spent in Paris. Began teaching at Oxford *ca.* 1225 (although possibly much earlier); elected chancellor, probably *ca.* 1228/30. Gave up his various university and ecclesiastical positions in 1231, becoming lector to the newly established Franciscan community at Oxford (but without himself becoming a friar). Elected bishop of Lincoln in 1235, he devoted most of the remainder of his life to ecclesiastical matters.

Grosseteste's earliest works from his years in Hereford focus on natural philosophy, including *De artibus liberalibus, De generatione sonorum, De sphaera*, and *De impressionibus aeris* (all ed. Baur 1912). These were followed by commentaries on the *Posterior Analytics* [*ca.* 1228] (ed. Rossi 1981) and the *Physics* [*ca.* 1222–32] (ed. Dales 1963) – the earliest known Latin commentaries on these works. His teaching at Oxford yielded a series of philosophical treatises, including *De veritate, De veritate propositionis, De scientia Dei* (all three tr. McKeon, in *Selections* 1930), *De statu causarum, De intelligentiis*, and *De unica forma* (all ed. Baur 1912), as well as a *De libero arbitrio* (in two recensions) (1st vers. edn Lewis, in "First Recension" 1991; 2nd vers. part. edn Lewis, in "Time and

Modality" 1988; 1st vers. tr. Lewis, in "Time and Modality" 1988). He continued this work while lecturing to the Franciscans, writing a *Hexaëmeron* (ed. Dales and Gieben 1982; tr. Martin 1996) and various short treatises in natural philosophy, including *De impressionibus elementorum*, *De lineis*, *De natura locorum*, *De iride*, *De colore*, and, most importantly, *De luce* (all ed. Baur 1912; the last tr. Riedl 1942), which lays out his famous metaphysics of light. His study of the Greek language, which perhaps began in the 1220s, yielded an impressive set of translations produced during his years as bishop (see Appendices B1–2), including the works of John of Damascus [*ca.* 1237], pseudo-Dionysius (with commentaries) [*ca.* 1240] (*Mystical Theology* ed. and tr. McEvoy 2003), and the first complete Latin translation of Aristotle's *Nicomachean Ethics* [1246–7], together with translations of various ancient commentators on the *Ethics*, supplemented by Grosseteste's own glosses (part. ed. Mercken 1973–91). Several biblical commentaries have been edited as the first volume of a projected *Opera* (ed. McEvoy *et al.* 1995).

Secondary sources. Southern, *Robert Grosseteste* (1986/1992) [biography]; Thomson, *Writings* (1940); Gieben, "Bibliographia" (1969), "Bibliographia" (1995); Callus (ed.), *Robert Grosseteste* (1955); Crombie, *Origins of Experimental Science* (1953); Dales, "Scientific Works" (1961); McEvoy, *Philosophy* (1982), *Robert Grosseteste* (1994) [papers], *Robert Grosseteste* (2000); McEvoy (ed.), *New Perspectives* (1995); Mackie and Goering, *Editing* (2003); Marrone, *New Ideas of Truth* (1983), *Light of Thy Countenance* (2001); BCPMA (Lewis); DMA (Beyer de Ryke); ODNB (Southern); REP (MacDonald); SEP (Lewis). There is also an extensive website, *The Electronic Grosseteste*: www.grosseteste.com.

ROBERT OF HALIFAX b. Yorkshire, *ca.* 1300; d. after 1350. Franciscan theologian. Joined the Franciscan order *ca.* 1318 and studied at Oxford from *ca.* 1324, eventually lecturing on the *Sentences*. Master of theology at Cambridge *ca.* 1336. The *Sentences* commentary [1333/40, Bks. I–II only] (unedited) is his only known work; it was popular enough to have survived in sixteen manuscripts, all on the continent.

Secondary sources. Courtenay, "Some Notes" (1973); BCPMA (Georgedes).

ROBERT HOLCOT (Holkot) b. Holcot (Northamptonshire), *ca.* 1290; d. Northampton, 1349. Influential Dominican theologian and popular author. Joined the Dominicans as a youth and studied at Oxford *ca.* 1326–34. Master of theology at Oxford, probably 1333–4, and then (perhaps) at Cambridge in 1334–6. Subsequently worked as an assistant for Richard Bury, bishop of Durham; eventually returned to Northampton, where he continued to write until his death. Holcot enjoyed a tremendous reputation for centuries, not only for his academic theology but also for more popular works on the Bible. His most important philosophical work is his *Sentences* commentary [1331–3] (ed. 1518/1967, etc.), but also significant are the *Sex articuli*, or *Quaedam conferentiae* [1332] (ed. Hoffmann 1993), a set of *Determinationes* (ed. with *Sent.* commentary), and his quodlibetal questions [1332–4] (part. ed. Gelber 1983; Streveler *et al.* 1995; Courtenay, in "Revised Text" 1971 [tr. CTMPT III]; Jensen, in "Killing Infidels" 1993; Kennedy, in *Skeptic* 1993; Molteni, in *Dottrina della grazia* 1967; Muckle, in "Utrum theologia" 1958). Two shorter surviving treatises are *De imputabilitate peccati* (ed. with *Sent.* commentary) and *De stellis* (ed. Thorndike, in "New Work" 1957). Among his popular works, foremost is his vast and very popular commentary on Wisdom (*Postilla super librum Sapientiae*)

[1334–6] (ed. 1494/1974). Also well known are a work for preachers, the *Moralitates* [late 1330s] (ed. 1514, etc.) and his *Commentary on Ecclesiasticus* [late 1340s] (ed. 1509, etc.). His *Sermo finalis* from the end of his regency in Oxford is extant (ed. Wey, in "*Sermo finalis*" 1949), and his collected sermons survive in a single manuscript (unedited).

Secondary sources. Gelber, "Logic and Trinity" (1974), *It Could Have Been Otherwise* (2004); Gillespie, "Quodlibeta" (1971); Grassi, "Conoscenza teologica" (1979); Hoffmann, *Theologische Methode* (1972); Incandela, "Prophecy" (1994); Oberman, "Facientibus" (1962); Schepers, "Holkot contra dicta Crathorn" (1970–2); Moody, "Objects of Knowledge" (1964); Tachau, "Contingency" (1994), "Logic's God" (1996); BCPMA (Georgedes); DMA (Robert); Kaeppeli; ODNB (Swanson); REP (Pasnau); SEP (Gelber).

ROBERT KILWARDBY b. 1215; d. Viterbo, 1279. Dominican philosopher and theologian, archbishop of Canterbury. Studied the arts at Paris *ca.* 1231–7. Served as arts master until *ca.* 1245, then joined the Dominican order, probably in England, and began studying theology at Oxford. Achieved his doctorate *ca.* 1256 and subsequently served as regent master in 1256–61. Elected Dominican provincial minister of England in 1261; consecrated archbishop of Canterbury in 1273. Entered into philosophical controversy as archbishop in 1277 by condemning thirty propositions, some quite clearly contrary to Aquinas's teaching. Appointed cardinal-bishop of Porto in 1278.

Extensive commentaries survive from his years in Paris, including commentaries on Donatus (ed. Schmücker 1984); pseudo-Priscian's *De accentibus* (ed. Lewry 1988); Priscian minor (unedited) [but not Priscian major, as formerly thought]; perhaps sets of *sophismata* (unedited); and commentaries on the old and new logic (unedited except for *Prior an.* [ed. 1516/1968, etc.], as by 'Giles of Rome') and on *Ethics* I–III (unedited). In Oxford, he wrote an introductory treatise classifying the different sciences, *De ortu scientiarum* [*ca.* 1250] (ed. Judy 1976; part. tr. CTMPT I), and brief treatises [*ca.* 1256–61] *De natura relationis* (ed. Schmücker 1980), *De tempore*, and *De spiritu fantastico* (both ed. and tr. Lewry and Broadie 1987). His major theological work is his *Sentences* commentary [*ca.* 1255] (ed. Leibold *et al.* 1982–93). Two letters with substantial philosophical content survive from his last decade, to John of Vercelli (ed. Dondaine 1977) and to Peter Conflans (ed. Birkenmajer 1922).

Secondary sources. Braakhuis, "Kilwardby vs Bacon?" (1985), "Convertibility of Being and One" (1999); Lewry, "Writings on the Logica Vetus" (1978); Sirridge, "Scientific Grammarian" (1990), "Utrum idem" (2007); Thom, *Logic and Ontology* (2007); DMA (de Libera); Kaeppeli; ODNB (Tugwell); REP (Conti).

ROBERT OF MELUN b. England, *ca.* 1100; d. Hereford, 1167. Theologian, influential teacher, and bishop. Studied in Paris under Hugh of St. Victor and probably Peter Abaelard. Taught in France for over forty years, including at Paris and Melun, founding a school of logic known as the Meludinenses. Joined the attack on Gilbert of Poitiers in 1147, but defended Abaelard. Consecrated as bishop of Hereford in 1163; his remaining years were dominated by the conflict over Thomas Becket. His three extant theoretical works are *Questiones de epistolis Pauli* and *Questiones de divina pagina* [both 1145/57], and a twice revised but never finished *Sententie* [1150s/60s] (all ed. Martin 1932–52). Perhaps also the author of a brief treatise on universals (ed. Dijs, in "Two Anonymous" 1990).

Secondary sources. Horst, *Die Trinitätslehre* (1964); Luscombe, *School of Peter Abelard* (1969); ODNB (Rampolla).

ROBERT ORFORD (Erfort, Oxford) b. *ca.* 1250; d. after 1293. Early English Thomist and Dominican friar. Bachelor of the *Sentences* at Oxford in 1284; became master of theology at Oxford *ca.* 1289 and was still regent in 1293. His extant works all defend Thomism as he understands it and include his *Correctorium corruptorii "Sciendum"* [*ca.* 1283] (ed. Glorieux 1956), in response to William de la Mare's anti-Thomistic treatise; *Contra dicta Fr. Aegidii Romani* [1288/92] (ed. Vella 1968); and *Contra dicta Magistri Henrici de Gandavo* [1289/93] (unedited). Also the likely author of the pseudo-Aquinian *De natura materiae* (ed. Spiazzi 1954, etc.).

Secondary sources. Friedman, "Dominican Quodlibetal Literature" (2007); Iribarren, "Responsio" (2001); Jordan, "Controversy of the Correctoria" (1982); Kelley, "Two Early English Thomists" (1981), "Attack on Giles of Rome" (1987); Kaeppeli; ODNB (Gaine); Roensch.

ROBERT OF PARIS *fl.* 1160s. Parisian arts master. Author of the grammar treatise *Summa "Breve sit"* [1160s] (ed. Kneepkens, in *Het Iudicium Constructionis* 1987).

ROBERT WALSINGHAM b. prob. Norfolk; d. after 1312. Carmelite theologian. Studied at Oxford by at least 1280; became master of theology in 1312. Main influence is Henry of Ghent. His work survives in two *Quodlibeta* [1312–13], and in excerpts from his earlier *Quaestiones ordinariae* and *Sentences* commentary (all unedited).

Secondary sources. Goris, "La critique" (2000); Schabel, "Carmelite Quodlibeta" (2007); Schabel and Friedman, "Trinitarian Theology III" (2003); ODNB (Brown).

ROBERTUS ANGLICUS. Many thirteenth-century texts are attributed to a "Robert the Englishman," and it is often difficult to distinguish the different authors. One such Robert is the author of the *Sophistria* [1260/70] (ed. Grondeux and Rosier-Catach 2006), a collection of grammatical sophisms, who is perhaps also the author of a *Lectura super Priscianum minorem* (unedited). An unedited mid-thirteenth-century commentary on the *Ars vetus* is associated with a different Robertus Anglicus (see Piché, *Le problème des universaux* 2005), and two commentaries on Peter of Spain [1250/70] (ed. Ebbesen and Rosier-Catach, in "Two Roberts" 1997) are associated with still two more men by this name, although it is not clear that either of the two is in fact English (see Ebbesen and Rosier-Catach, "Robertus Anglicus" 2000). There is also an astronomer by this name [*fl. ca.* 1271] (see ODNB [Pedersen]), and moreover Robert Kilwardy is often so-called (see Lewry, "Robertus Anglicus" 1982).

ROGER BACON b. Somerset, *ca.* 1214/20; d. England, *ca.* 1292. Natural philosopher. Educated at Oxford; master of arts at Paris by 1245 (and perhaps from 1237). Subsequently taught on the arts faculty for various periods at both universities, although even the rough chronology is unclear. Joined the Franciscan order *ca.* 1257. His last years, from

1270 or at least from 1280, were spent in England. His works were condemned by the Franciscans in 1278 for reasons that are unclear, although his notoriously difficult and arrogant personality was presumably a factor. On some accounts, he was subsequently imprisoned, but the evidence is thin.

His works are many and wide-ranging. The earliest relate to his teaching in the arts, including two sets of questions on both the *Physics* and *Metaphysics*; questions on the *Liber de causis* (all ed. Steele *et al.* 1909–40); and various treatises on logic and grammar, including the *Summulae dialectices* [*ca.* 1250] (ed. de Libera 1986–7), *Summa grammatica* and *Summa de sophismatibus et distinctionibus* [1240s] (both ed. Steele *et al.* 1909–40). His work from the 1260s takes a more original turn, focusing more on an empirically grounded natural philosophy, and stressing the importance of mathematics and the study of languages. His *Perspectiva* (ed. and tr. Lindberg 1996) and *De multiplicatione specierum* (ed. and tr. Lindberg 1983) [both *ca.* 1266] initiate the quantitative study of optics in the Latin tradition. In 1267 he sent Pope Clement IV his best-known work, the *Opus Maius* (ed. Bridges 1897–1900/1964 [pt. III ed. Fredborg *et al.* 1978]; tr. Burke 1928), soon followed by a summary, the *Opus minus*, and a further retreatment, the *Opus tertium* (both ed. Brewer 1859/1965). These were regarded as preliminary studies, however, for an even larger work, never completed, of which only two sections survive: the *Communia naturalium* and the *Communia mathematica* [*ca.* 1270] (both ed. Steele *et al.* 1909–40). Also from this period is an introduction to Bacon's views, his *Compendium studii philosophiae* (ed. Brewer 1859/1965), as well as Greek and Hebrew grammars (ed. Nolan and Hirsch 1902). Other notable works include writings on moral philosophy (ed. Massa 1953) and an incomplete *Compendium studii theologiae* [1292] (ed. and tr. Mahoney 1988). His writings on universals have also been translated (tr. Maloney 1989).

Secondary sources. Hackett and Mahoney, "Bibliography" (1987); Hackett (ed.), *Bacon and the Sciences* (1997), *Bacon and Aristotelianism* (1997); Clegg, *First Scientist* (2003); Crowley, *Problem of the Soul* (1950); Little, *Essays* (1914); BCPMA (Hackett); DMA (de Libera); DSB (Crombie and North); FA; ODNB (Molland); REP (Sinkler); SEP (Hackett).

ROGER MARSTON b. England, *ca.* 1235; d. Norwich, 1303. Franciscan theologian in the Augustinian tradition. Studied theology in Paris under John Pecham *ca.* 1269–71. Subsequently incepted as master at Cambridge *ca.* 1276, where he lectured on the *Sentences* (now lost), and at Oxford *ca.* 1281. Provincial minister of the English Franciscans in 1292–8. Only extant works are three sets of disputed questions (ed. van de Woestyne *et al.* 1932) and four *Quodlibeta* (ed. Etzkorn and Brady 1994) [both 1282–4].

Secondary sources. Belmond, "Théorie de la connaissance" (1934); Etzkorn, "Grades of the Form" (1962); Hissette, "Hylemorphisme universel?" (1972); Gilson, "Augustinisme avicennisant" (1933); BCPMA (Wilson); DMA (Lambert); FA; ODNB (Brown); REP (Etzkorn).

ROGER NOTTINGHAM d. after 1358. Franciscan theologian. Bachelor of theology by 1343 at the Oxford convent. Author of a brief collection of *Insolubilia* [1343] (ed. Synan 1964) and an *Introitus ad Sententias* (ed. Synan 1963).

Secondary sources. Spade, *Mediaeval Liar* (1975); Emden; FA.

ROGER ROSETH (Rosetus) *fl.* 1330s. English Franciscan theologian. Only surviving work is his lectures on the *Sentences* at Oxford [mid-1330s] (qq. 3–5 ed. Hallamaa 2005), a witness to the influence of the Oxford Calculators on English theology.

Secondary sources. Hallamaa, "On the Borderline" (2000), "Defending Common Rationality" (2003); Murdoch, "From Social to Intellectual Factors" (1975); Spade, *Mediaeval Liar* (1975); Tachau, "*Species in medio*" (1982).

ROGER SWINESHEAD (Swyneshed, Suisseth) b. Swineshead (Lincolnshire); d. *ca.* 1365. Natural philosopher in the Mertonian tradition. Educated at Oxford. Went on to study theology and became a Benedictine monk at Glastonbury. Extant are two logical treatises from the early 1330s – his *Insolubilia* (ed. Spade 1979) and *Obligationes* (ed. Spade 1977) – and a mathematical treatment of motion, *De motibus naturalibus* (unedited). To be distinguished from his younger contemporary and perhaps brother, Richard Swineshead.

Secondary sources. Weisheipl, "Roger Swyneshed" (1964); Sylla, "Mathematical Physics" (1987); ODNB (Molland).

ROGER WHELPDALE d. London, 1423. Oxford philosopher, a proponent of metaphysical realism. Fellow of Balliol College before 1400, and subsequently fellow and provost from 1404 to 1420 of Queen's College. Elected bishop of Carlisle in 1419. Extant works include commentaries on Porphyry and *Posterior Analytics* I (both unedited), and a treatise *De universalibus* (part. ed. Conti 1990).

Secondary sources. Emden; Lohr; ODNB (Summerson).

ROLAND OF BOLOGNA *fl.* 1140s–50s. Legal scholar, theologian. A student of Gratian at Bologna, and subsequently a distinguished professor there. Author of one of the earliest commentaries on Gratian's *Decretum*, known as the *Stroma* (ed. Thaner 1874/1962), although it is perhaps a composite of two different works by Roland (see Kuttner, "Did Rolandus Write?" 1994). Also the author of a theological *summa* or *Sententiae* (ed. Gietl 1891/1969). The Roland who authored these works is not, as formerly thought, Roland Bandinelli (Pope Alexander III).

Secondary sources. Noonan, "Who was Rolandus?" (1977); Liotta and Tofanni (eds.), *Miscellanea* (1986).

ROLAND OF CREMONA b. 1178; d. Bologna, 1259. Early Dominican theologian. Master of arts in Bologna. Joined the Dominicans there in 1219, subsequently studying theology. Became the first Dominican theology master in Paris in 1229–30. Lecturer in theology at Toulouse in 1230–33, then returned to Bologna, where he continued to preach and teach until his death. Principal work is his *Summa* of theology [1228] (prologue ed. Cremascoli, in "La 'Summa'" 1975; Bk. III ed. Cortesi 1962).

Secondary sources. Brungs, "Definition der Tugend" (1998); Filthaut, *Roland von Cremona* (1936); Glorieux; Kaeppeli.

ROSCELIN OF COMPIÈGNE b. Brittany, *ca.* 1050; d. after 1120. Controversial logician and theologian. Taught in France, where he was a leading proponent of nominalism. None of his works survive; our information comes entirely from his critics, particularly

Anselm of Canterbury and Peter Abaelard (his former student). In 1092 he was charged with heresy for his theory of the Trinity, which he was forced to renounce.

Secondary sources. Kluge, "Problem of Universals" (1976); Meier, *Macht und Wahnwitz* (1974); Mews, "Nominalism and Theology" (1992); Picavet, *Roscelin* (1911); Tweedale, "Logic" (1988); REP (Tweedale).

RUFINUS *fl.* 1150–91. Canon lawyer and theologian. Studied at Bologna, perhaps under Gratian, becoming master *ca.* 1150. Perhaps elected bishop of Assisi *ca.* 1164, and archbishop of Sorrento 1180/6. His most influential work was his *Summa decretorum* [*ca.* 1164] (ed. Singer 1902/1963), the first full-length commentary on Gratian's *Decretum*. Also extant is his treatise on peace, *De bono pacis* [*ca.* 1180–6] (ed. Brunacci and Catanzaro 1986).

Secondary sources. Gouron, "Sur les sources" (1986); CHLMP.

RUPERT OF DEUTZ (Robert) b. Liège, *ca.* 1075; d. Deutz, 1129. Theologian and Benedictine monk. Entered the Abbey of St. Lawrence (Liège) as a boy. Ecclesiastical conflict led him into a period of exile in 1092–6, and further theological conflict, eventually including charges of heresy, forced him to leave permanently. Eventually he settled in the Cologne area, becoming abbot of the Deutz monastery from 1120. A prolific and widely known author during the first half of the twelfth century, Rupert's principal theoretical works are *De Sancta Trinitate et operibus eius* [1117] (ed. Haacke 1971–2); *De voluntate Dei* [1113/14]; *De omnipotentia Dei* [1117] (both PL 170); a commentary on the Gospel of John [1115–16] (ed. Haacke 1969); *De victoria Verbi Dei* [1123/4] (ed. Haacke 1970); and a commentary on the Song of Songs [1126] (ed. Deutz and Deutz 2005).

Secondary sources. Van Engen, *Rupert of Deutz* (1983); Beitz, *Rupert von Deutz* (1930); DMA (Bouhot).

SAADIAH GAON (Saadya ben Joseph; Saʾid ibn Yusuf al-Fayyūmi) b. Fayyoum (upper Egypt), 882; d. Baghdad, 942. Rabbi, poet, exegete; the first systematic Jewish philosopher. Left Egypt for Palestine at a young age, and quickly became an influential scholar, becoming involved in a controversial reform of the Jewish calendar in 922. Appointed head (*gaon*) of the Jewish academy of Sura (Babylon) in 928, a prestigious position that he held on and off, amidst much conflict, for the remainder of his life. Earliest major work is a Hebrew–Arabic lexicon [913, later enlarged] (ed. Allony 1969). His most important philosophical work is the *Amānāt wa-al-iʿtiqādāt* (*The Book of Beliefs and Convictions*), written in Arabic but commonly known by its Hebrew title, *Sefer Emunot ve-Deʿot* [933] (ed. Landauer 1880, Kafih 1970; tr. Rosenblatt 1948; part. tr. Altmann in Lewy *et al.*, *Three Jewish Philosophers* 1985; part. tr. Manekin, in *Writings* 2007). Also important is his commentary on the Hebrew esoteric work *Sefer Yeẓira* (*Book of Creation*), the *Tafsīr kitāb al-mabādī* (ed. and [Fr] tr. Lambert 1891). Saadiah translated the Bible into Arabic, and wrote many biblical commentaries, which are often of considerable philosophical interest (part. ed. Derenbourh *et al.* 1893–9), most notably that on Job (tr. Goodman 1988).

Secondary sources. Efros, *Studies* (1974); Finkelstein (ed.), *Rab Saadia Gaon* (1944); Goodman, "Interpretive Technique" (1990); Katz (ed.), *Saadiah Gaon* (1980); Malter, *Life and Works* (1921/1969); Rosenthal (ed.), *Saadya Studies* (1943/1980); Stroumsa, "Saadya and Jewish Kalam" (2003); Vajda, "Théorie de la connassance" (1967); BCPMA (Pessin); HIP (Goodman); REP (Goodman); SEP (Pessin).

AL-SAMARQANDĪ (Shams al-Dīn) b. Samarkand (Uzbekistan), *ca.* 1250; d. *ca.* 1303. Astronomer, mathematician, logician, and theologian. Almost nothing is known of his life. Best known for his *Risāla fī ādāb al-baḥth* [*ca.* 1276] (ed. al-Manṣūrī 1934), which offers a general theory of dialectical disputation applicable in any scholarly domain.

   Secondary sources. Miller, "Islamic Disputation Theory" (1984); EI (Miller).

SAMUEL IBN TIBBON b. Lunel (Provence), *ca.* 1165; d. 1232. Translator, philosopher, exegete. Educated by his scholarly father, Judah ibn Tibbon. Traveled widely as an adult, both for business and for scholarly purposes, eventually settling in Marseilles. Along with those of his father, his son Moses, and his son-in-law Jacob Anatoli, his translations into Hebrew created both a philosophical library and a technical terminology in Hebrew. Samuel's main influence was Maimonides; among other works, he translated the commentary on Avot from the Mishnah (*Sefer ha-Maor*) [1202] (ed. Rabinowitz 1948; tr. David 1968); and the *Guide of the Perplexed* (*Moreh ha-Nevukhim*) [1204] (ed. Even-Shemuel 1987). He also translated Aristotle's *Meteorology* [1210] (ed. Fontaine 1995), and works by Averroes, Avicenna, and others. As a complement to his translation activity, he produced the first Hebrew philosophical lexicon, the *Perush ha-Millot ha-Zarot* (ed. with *Guide*). His two main original treatises are a commentary on Ecclesiastes [1213/21] (ed. and tr. Robinson 2007) and the treatise *Ma'amar Yiqqavu ha-Mayim* (ed. Bisliches 1837), a discussion of Genesis 1: 9, "Let the waters be gathered."

   Secondary sources. Freudenthal, "Sciences" (1993); Ravitzky, "Esoteric Character" (1981); Robinson, "Commentary on Ecclesiastes" (2000), "Ibn Tibbon Family" (2005); SEP (Robinson).

AL-SARAKHSĪ (Aḥmad ibn al-Ṭayyib) b. *ca.* 835; d. 899. Leading disciple of al-Kindī. An educator of the future caliph, he came to be a member of the inner circle of the court, but eventually was thrown in prison in 896, where he died. Although a productive scholar, and an important advocate of Greek learning, only fragments of his work survive.

   Secondary sources. Rosenthal, *As-Sarakhsī* (1943); EI (Rosenthal).

SEDULIUS SCOTTUS b. prob. Leinster (Ireland); *fl.* 840s–860s. Poet, grammarian, biblical commentator. Little is known about his life, other than that he describes himself as a priest, and that he lived in France, mainly in Liège. His extant grammatical works are commentaries on Eutyches, Priscian, and Donatus (ed. Löfstedt 1977). His *De rectoribus Christianis* (ed. Hellmann 1906) is a mirror for princes, in alternating prose and verse. Also extant are a large set of poems (ed. Meyers 1991), and commentaries on Paul's epistles (ed. Frede and Stanjek 1996), on Matthew (ed. Löfstedt 1989), and an *Explanationes in canones et argumenta evangeliorum* (PL 103). A florilegium of excerpts from classical authors, the *Collectaneum miscellaneum* (ed. Simpson 1988) also survives.

   Secondary sources. Düchting, *Sedulius Scottus* (1968); Marenbon, *Circle of Alcuin* (1981); ODNB (Davies).

SERVAIS OF MOUNT ST. ELOI (Gervais) d. 1313/14. Theologian. A canon regular at the monastery of Mount St. Eloi, he came to Paris to study theology and became regent master by 1282. Returning to his monastery, he was elected abbot in 1291, a position he held until his death. Aside from various sermons, his extant works are a series of quodlibetal questions [1280s] (unedited), focused largely on moral and canon law issues.

Secondary sources. Glorieux, *La littérature quodlibétique* (1925–35); Hissette, "Une question quodlibétique" (1982); Schabel, *Theological Quodlibeta* (2006–7); Sullivan, "*Quodlibeta*" (2007).

SERVASANTO OF FAENZA b. near Faenza, 1220/30; d. Florence, *ca.* 1300. Preacher and moral theologian. Joined the Franciscan order at Bologna, where he probably studied. Seems not to have done advanced work in theology at the university. As a member of the Florence convent, he was very active as a preacher, and many sermons have been preserved. His extant treatises, all collections of material intended as a guide for preachers, are the *Liber de exemplis naturalibus* and *Liber de virtutibus et vitiis* (both unedited), and the *Summa de poenitentia* or *Antidotarium animae* (ed. 1485).

Secondary sources. Casagrande, "Predicare la penitenza" (1996); Grabmann, "*Liber de exemplis naturalibus*" (1920); Oliger, "Liber de virtutibus et vitiis" (1924); FA.

AL-SHĀFIʿĪ (Muḥammad ibn Idrīs) b. prob. Gaza, 767; d. Cairo, 819. Leading religious scholar, founder of the Shāfiʿite legal school. Raised in Mecca. Studied in Medina and Baghdad before moving to Egypt where he developed a dramatically new legal system. His principal work is *Al-Risāla fī al-uṣūl* (*A Treatise on Legal Theory*) (ed. Shākir 1979, etc.; tr. Khadduri 1987), a foundational treatise on the science of jurisprudence.

Secondary sources. Burton, *Sources of Islamic Law* (1990); Hallaq, *Origins and Evolution of Islamic Law* (2005); Schacht, *Origins of Jurisprudence* (1967); BEIP (Kiliç); EI (Chaumont).

AL-SHAHRASTĀNĪ (Abū al-Fatḥ Muḥammad ibn ʿAbd al-Karīm) b. Shahristan (Khurasan), *ca.* 1086; d. Shahristan, 1153. Theologian and historian, probably Ismāʿīlī. Studied in Nishapur. Journeyed to Mecca in 1117, and subsequently taught at al-Niẓāmiyya in Baghdad. His last years were spent as a confidant of the Seljuk ruler of Khurasan. Among his many works, the best known is a monumental study of comparative religion, the *Kitab al-milal wa-al-niḥal* (*Book of Religions and Sects*) [1127/8] (ed. Badrān 1951; [Fr] tr. Gimaret and Monnot 1986–93; part. tr. Lawrence 1976, Kazi and Flynn 1983). Also extant is a theological *summa*, the *Nihāyat al-aqdām fī ʿilm al-kalām* (*Furthest Steps in the Science of Theology*) [after 1128] (ed. and tr. Guillaume 1934); a critique of Avicenna's metaphysics, the *Muṣāraʿat al-falāsifa* (*Struggling with the Philosopher*) (ed. and tr. Madelung and Mayer 2001); a brief treatise on atoms (ed. with the *Nihāyat*); and a Persian speech on creation (ed. and [Fr] tr. Steigerwald 1998).

Secondary sources. Monnot, "Controverses théologiques" (1995); Daftary, *Ismāʿīlīs* (1990); BEIP (İskenderoğlu); EI (Monnot).

SHEM TOV IBN FALAQUERA b. northern Spain, 1223/8; d. after 1290. Hebrew translator, scholar, and poet. Urged the harmony of faith and reason, and defended the importance of philosophy. His many extant works include a commentary on Maimonides's *Guide* [1280] (ed. Shiffman 1990); a book defending the study of Maimonides, *Iggeret ha-Vikuah* (*Epistle of the Debate*) (ed. Jellinek 1875/1970; tr. Harvey 1987); a long philosophical encyclopedia, *De'ot ha-Philosofim* (*The Opinions of the Philosophers*) (unedited); the *Sefer ha-Mevaqqesh* (*Book of the Seeker*) [1263] (ed. Tamah 1778/1970; tr. Levine 1976); and various treatises on ethics and psychology (part. ed. and tr. Jospe, in *Torah and Sophia* 1988).

Secondary sources. REP (Jospe); Sirat.

SĪBAWAYHI b. Shiraz, *ca.* 760; d. *ca.* 796. Pioneering figure of Arabic grammar. Little is known of his life beyond his one book, the *Kitāb Sībawayhi* (ed. Hārūn 1966–77, etc.; tr. [German] Jahn 1895–1900/1969), which is the foundational text for Islamic grammar and the subject of many later commentaries.

Secondary sources. Carter, *Sibawayhi* (2004); EI (Carter).

SIGER OF BRABANT b. Low Countries, *ca.* 1240; d. Orvieto, 1282/4. Controversial arts master, a leading figure among the so-called Latin Averroists. Initially studied at Liège, then Paris in 1255/7. Master of arts by 1266, his views were condemned in 1270 and again in 1277, though he himself was never convicted of heresy, and he modified his views over time. Left Paris for Liège by the end of 1276; spent his final years in Italy, where he was allegedly killed by his demented secretary. His extant writings range widely over the arts curriculum. In logic, we have several *sophismata*, a set of *Quaestiones logicales*, and a treatise on *Impossibilia* (all ed. Bazán 1974). There are commentaries on *De anima* III [*ca.* 1265] (ed. Bazán 1972); the *De generatione* (ed. Bazán 1974); *Physics* (ed. Zimmermann, in Bazán 1974); and *Metaphysics* [*ca.* 1273/5] (in four mss., representing four distinct *reportationes*, ed. Dunphy 1981, Maurer 1983). Also extant is a commentary on the *Liber de causis* [1274/6] (ed. Marlasca 1972) and treatises *De necessitate et contingentia causarum* (ed. Duin, *La doctrine de la providence* 1954); *De aeternitate mundi* [*ca.* 1272] (ed. Bazán 1972; tr. Vollert *et al.* 1964); and *De anima intellectiva* [*ca.* 1271] (ed. Bazán 1972).

Secondary sources. Van Steenberghen, *Maître Siger de Brabant* (1977), *La philosophie au XIIIe siècle* (1991); Bianchi, *Il vescovo e i filosofi* (1990); Dod, *Life and Thought* (1998); Gauthier, "Notes" (1983–4); Putallaz, *Insolente liberté* (1995); Putallaz and Imbach, *Profession, philosophe* (1997); Ryan, "Man's Free Will" (1983); BCPMA (Bazán); REP (Wippel).

SIGER OF COURTRAI b. *ca.* 1280; d. 1341. Logician and grammarian. Studied in Paris *ca.* 1300. Dean of the Church of Our Lady at Courtrai (Flanders) from *ca.* 1305 until *ca.* 1330. A leading proponent of modism. Extant works are a *Summa modorum significandi*; *Sophismata* (both ed. Wallerand and Pinborg 1977); a treatise *Ars priorum* and fragments on fallacies (both ed. Wallerand 1913); and a commentary on the *De interpretatione* (ed. Verhaak 1964).

Secondary sources. Bursill-Hall, *Speculative Grammars* (1971); Marmo, *Semiotica e linguaggio* (1994); Rosier-Catach, *La grammaire spéculative* (1983); CHLMP.

AL-SIJISTĀNĪ, Abū Sulaymān (al-Manṭiqī) b. Sistan (southeast Iran), *ca.* 912; d. *ca.* 985. Leading advocate of philosophy in tenth-century Baghdad. After spending his youth in

Sistan, he moved to Baghdad as a young man, joining the circle of Yaḥyā ibn ʿAdī and Abū Bishr Mattā. He came to assemble an important circle of friends and followers, and his influence as a teacher is more important than his written works, only parts of which have survived. Most significant of these is *Ṣiwān al-ḥikma* (*Vessel of Wisdom*) (ed. Badawi 1974), a collection of sayings from Greek and Islamic philosophers that survives only in part, and perhaps is only partly the work of al-Sijistānī. A few brief treatises (ed. Badawi 1974) are also extant, including *On the Proper Perfection of the Human Species* (tr. McGinnis and Reiman, in *Classical Arabic Philosophy* 2007).

Secondary sources. Kraemer, *Philosophy in the Renaissance* (1986); BEIP (Kalin); EI (Stern); REP (Atiyeh).

AL-SIJISTĀNĪ, Abū Yaʿqūb (al-Sijzī) *fl.* tenth century. Leading Ismāʿīlī theologian. Said to have been executed toward the end of the tenth century. His two principal works are the *Kitāb al-yanābīʾ* (*Book of Wellsprings*) (ed. and part. [Fr] tr. Corbin 1961; tr. Walker 1994), and the *Kashf al-maḥjūb* (*Unveiling of the Hidden*), which is extant only in a Persian translation (ed. Corbin 1949; tr. [Fr] Corbin 1988).

Secondary sources. Daftary, *Ismāʿīlīs* (1990); Walker, *Early Philosophical Shiism* (1993); BEIP (Aminrazavi); EI (Stern).

SIMEON DURAN (ben Zemaḥ) b. Majorca, 1361; d. 1444. Theologian and expert on Jewish law (*halakha*). Forced by anti-Jewish violence in 1391 to flee Spain for North Africa. Most important works pertaining to philosophy are a commentary on Job, *Ohev Mishpat* (*Lover of Justice*) (ed. 1590), with an extensive discussion of providence, and a commentary on Avot, *Magen Avot* (ed. 1785/1969).

Secondary sources. Pfeffer, *Providence in the Book of Job* (2005); REP (Kellner); Sirat.

SIMON OF DACIA *fl.* 1260s. Modist grammarian, seemingly a member of the arts faculty at Paris. Author of the *Domus gramatice* [1255/70] and a set of questions on Priscian minor [1260/70] (both ed. Otto 1963). A set of *Quaestiones super modos significandi* is attested but seems to have been lost.

SIMON OF FAVERSHAM (Simon Anglicus) b. Kent, prob. 1240s; d. Avignon, 1306. Philosopher and theologian, author of important Aristotelian commentaries. Probably studied at Oxford. Subsequently seems to have lectured on the arts at Paris in the late 1270s and early 1280s before returning to teach theology at Oxford, where he is known to have been present in 1301. Chancellor of Oxford in 1304–6. His extant writings cover much of the Aristotelian corpus, sometimes in multiple versions, including questions on the *Isagoge*, the *Categories*, the *De interpretatione* (all ed. Mazzarella 1957), the *Sophistical Refutations* [*ca.* 1280] (ed. Ebbesen *et al.* 1984), *De anima* III (part. ed. Sharp 1934), the *Physics*, and the *Metaphysics* (both unedited). There are commentaries on Priscian and Peter of Spain's *Summulae logicales* (both unedited). A sophism is also extant (ed. Yokoyama, in "Universale est intentio" 1969).

Secondary sources. De Rijk, "Genuine Text II" (1968); Grabmann, *Aristoteleskommentare* (1933); Longeway, "Questions on the 'Posterior Analytics'" (1977); BCPMA (Longeway); Lohr; ODNB (Brown).

SIMON OF HINTON *fl.* 1248–62. Oxford Dominican theologian. Studied theology at Oxford in the 1240s, probably becoming regent master after Richard Fishacre, in 1248. Subsequently served as provincial minister of the English province in 1254–61, when he was removed from the position and sent to teach in Germany for a year before returning to England. Extant works include various questions from his theological study at Oxford, various biblical commentaries, and, most prominently, his *Summa iuniorum* [prob. after 1261] (ed. 1706), a compendium of essential Christian doctrines and morals.

Secondary sources. BBK (Senner); Kaeppeli; ODNB (Tugwell).

SIMON OF TOURNAI b. Tournai (Belgium), *ca.* 1130; d. 1201. Theologian, grammarian, influential teacher. Received his early education in Tournai. Subsequently studied in the cathedral school in Paris from before 1155, taking over as head in 1165. Appointed canon at Tournai, but nevertheless remained in Paris, going on to serve as master of the school at Mount St. Geneviève and continuing to teach into the new century. Although probably not a student of Gilbert of Poitiers, his work bears Gilbert's strong influence, and also that of the newly available Aristotle. His strong, provocatively worded views made him both popular and controversial. His two principal works are his theological *Sentences* or *Summa*, or *Institutiones in sacra pagina* [1160–5?] (part. ed. Schmaus 1932, Heinzmann 1967), and a large collection of theological *Disputationes* [after 1160] (ed. Warichez 1932). Only one sermon survives, containing a commentary on the Athanasian creed (ed. Häring 1976).

Secondary sources. Häring, "Simon of Tournai" (1965); ODNB (Luscombe).

SINIBALDO FIESCHI, *see* Innocent IV.

SOLOMON IBN GABIROL (Avicebron, Avencebrol) b. Malaga, 1021/2; d. Valencia, prob. 1057/8. Jewish Neoplatonic philosopher and poet. Orphaned at a young age, grew up in Saragossa, then lived in Granada and Valencia. Of the many philosophical works he claims to have written, only two survive. The *Mekor Ḥayyim* (*Fountain of Life*), composed in Arabic, is extant only in a twelfth-century Latin translation, the *Fons vitae* (ed. Bauemker 1892–5; part. tr. Manekin, *Writings* 2007), and in Hebrew fragments (ed. Munk 1857–9/1927). It was extremely influential on medieval Christian thought, particularly for its support of universal hylomorphism. The *Tikkun Middot ha-Nefesh* (*On the Improvement of Moral Qualities*) [1045] (ed. and tr. Wise 1909/1966), also composed in Arabic, is a treatise on practical ethics. There is also a large body of Hebrew poetry, much of which is striking for its wholly secular character, as elegies, love poems, etc. (part. tr. Cole 2001). Other poetry is more philosophical (part. tr. Davidson 1923/1973), most significantly the *Keter Malkhut* (*The Kingly Crown*) (ed. and tr. Slavitt 1998, etc.), a series of forty songs devoted to metaphysical and cosmological themes, which forms the text of the Yom Kippur service. The *Mibhar Peninim* (*Choice of Pearls*) [*ca.* 1045] (tr. Cohen 1925), a collection of proverbs and maxims, is perhaps also the work of Ibn Gabirol.

Secondary sources. Brunner, *Platonisme et Aristotelisme* (1965), *Métaphysique* (1997); Goodman (ed.), *Neoplatonism* 1992; Pessin, *Universal Hylomorphism* (2000), "Jewish

Neoplatonism" (2003); Loewe, *Ibn Gabirol* (1989); Rudavsky, "Matter and Evil" (1978); BCPMA (Rudavsky); HIP (Lancaster); HJP (Rudavsky); REP (Frank).

STEPHEN LANGTON b. Langton (Lincolnshire), *ca.* 1150; d. 1228. Theologian, archbishop of Canterbury. Studied in Paris, perhaps under Peter the Chanter, becoming an influential master of theology there from the 1180s to 1206. Elected cardinal and archbishop of Canterbury in 1206, from which point he was immersed in a long and stormy set of political conflicts. Many works are extant and largely unedited, especially sermons (part. ed. Roberts 1980) and commentaries on nearly the whole of the Bible (on Chronicles, ed. Saltman 1978). A commentary on Lombard's *Sentences* is extant (ed. Landgraf 1952), as is a treatise *De persona* (ed. Bieniak 2006). His writings are assumed to date from his years in Paris, although he may have made later revisions.

Secondary sources. Bejczy, "Cardinal Virtues" (2006); Powicke, *Stephen Langton* (1928/1965); Roberts, *Stephanus de Lingua Tonante* (1968); ODNB (Holdsworth).

STEPHEN OF RIETI (de Reate) *fl.* 1340s. Dominican philosopher, advocate of metaphysical realism. Studied the arts at Rome and Florence in 1331–3. Lectured at various Dominican *studia* in central Italy, where he also studied theology alongside Francis of Prato. Extant works include a *Tractatus de universalibus* (ed. Amerini 2003), a commentary on the *Ars vetus* [*ca.* 1343] (part. ed. with the *De univ.*), and treatises *De secundis intentionibus* and *De ente reali et rationis* (both ed. de Rijk, in Gerald of Odo, *Opera philosophica* 1997–).

Secondary sources. Amerini, "What is Real" (2005); Kaeppeli; Lohr.

STEPHEN OF TOURNAI (Tornacensis) b. Orléans, 1128; d. 1203. Canon lawyer. Studied first in his native city, then took up law in Bologna beginning *ca.* 1160. Appointed abbot of St. Euverte in Orléans in 1167, and then abbot of Mount St. Geneviève in Paris in 1177. Bishop of Tournai from 1192. His influential *Summa decretorum* [1165/6] (part. ed. Schulte 1891) became a basic text for canon lawyers north of the Alps. Also extant are collections of letters (ed. Desilve 1893; PL 211) and sermons (PL 211).

Secondary sources. Kalb, *Studien* (1983); Weigand, "Studien" (1986); Pennington.

AL-SUHRAWARDĪ (Abū Ḥafṣ ʿUmar) b. Suhraward (northwest Iran), 1145; d. Baghdad, 1234. Important Sufi theologian. Came to Baghdad as a youth, where he studied with his uncle Abū al-Najīb al-Suhrawardī (d. 1168), himself a prominent Sufi. (In all, the *nisba* 'al-Suhrawardī' refers to three prominent, contemporary theologians.) A famed preacher, his disciples would found the Sufi order of Suhrawardiyya. Principal work is the *ʿAwārif al-maʿārif* (*Advantages of Knowledge*) [by 1215/16] (ed. 1983; tr. [German] Gramlich 1978), a handbook on Sufi practices that remains influential today. A fourteenth-century Persian translation/elaboration of this work is available in English (tr. Clarke 1891/1980).

Secondary sources. BEIP (Leaman); EI (Hartmann).

AL-SUHRAWARDĪ (Shihāb al-Dīn Yaḥyā) b. Suhraward (northwest Iran) 1154; d. Aleppo (northwest Syria), 1191. Founder of the Illuminationist school of Islamic thought. Studied in Maraghah and then Isfahan. After journeying through Anatolia, he settled in

Aleppo in 1183, where he became a prominent scholar and developed close ties with the rulers. For reasons that are unclear, but that seemingly involve both religious and political factors, he was executed at the age of thirty-seven. His four major philosophical works, in Arabic, are *Al-Talwīḥāt* (*Intimations*) (ed. with Ibn Kammūna's commentary, Ziai and Alwishah 2003); *Al-Muqāwamāt* (*Oppositions*); *Al-Mashāriʿ wa-al-muṭāraḥāt* (*Pathways and Conversations*); and, above all, *Ḥikmat al-ishrāq* (*Philosophy of Illumination*) [1186] (ed. and tr. Walbridge and Ziai 1999). These, and other works are edited in a three-volume edition (ed. Corbin and Nasr 1976–7). Many of his writings in Persian have been translated (tr. Thackston 1982; tr. [Fr] Corbin 1976, with very useful annotations).

Secondary sources. Aminrazavi, *Suhrawardi* (1997); Walbridge, "Suhrawardī and Illuminationism" (2005); Ziai, *Knowledge and Illumination* (1990); BEIP (Leaman); EI (Ziai); HIP (Ziai); REP (Cooper); SEP (Marcotte).

AL-TAFTĀZĀNĪ, Saʿd al-Dīn (al-ʿAllāma) b. Taftazan (Khurasan), 1322; d. Samarkand, 1390. Leading Ashʿarite theologian and wide-ranging scholar. His education is uncertain, but it left him a gifted scholar from an early age. In his subsequent career he traveled widely through central Asia. Of his extant work, his theology is best known, especially his commentaries on central texts, as on the creed of Najm al-Dīn al-Nasafī [1367] (ed. Salāma 1974; tr. Elder 1950/1980), and his *Sharh al-maqāṣid* (*Explanation of Purposes*) (ed. Umayra 1984–9).

Secondary sources. BEIP (İskenderoğlu); EI.

AL-TAWḤĪDĪ (Abū Ḥayyān) b. *ca.* 930; d. Shiraz, 1023. Persian scholar whose accounts of Baghdad intellectual circles provide important information on the views of his contemporaries. Most of his life was spent in Baghdad, where he arrived before 959, and Rayy, from 968, at the court of the Buyid princes. His *Al-Imtāʿ wa-al-muʾānasa* (*Enjoyment and Conviviality*) [980–5] (ed. Amīn and Zayn 1953) records a series of thirty-seven conversations held at the Baghdad court. His main philosophical work is the Neoplatonic *Al-Muqābasāt* (*Borrowed Lights*) (ed. Husayn 1970).

Secondary sources. Bergé, *Pour un humanisme* (1979); BEIP (Akbaş); EI (Stern); REP (Genequand).

THĀBIT IBN QURRA b. Harran (southeast Turkey), *ca.* 830; d. Baghdad, 901. Mathematician, astronomer, philosopher, and translator. Discovered while working as a money changer in Harran, Thābit was brought to Baghdad to study in the Banū Mūsā circle of mathematicians. Many astronomical treatises are extant, in Arabic and in Latin translation (ed. and [Fr] tr. Morelon 1987; ed. Carmody 1960). His translations from Greek into Arabic include Ptolemy's *Almagest* and works by Apollonius and Archimedes.

Secondary sources. Rashed, *Mathématiques infinitésimales* (1996); Sabra, "Infinite" (1997); Sezgin *et al.* (eds.), *Texts and Studies* (1997); BEIP (El-Bizri); DSB (Rosenfeld and Grigorian); EI (Rashed and Morelon).

THADDEUS OF PARMA d. 1341. Philosopher. Perhaps studied at Paris. Master of arts at Bologna from at least 1318 and also at Siena in 1321–5. Important source for the transmission of Latin Averroism from Paris to Italy. Extant works include questions on the *De anima* [*ca.* 1320] (Bk. III ed. Vanni Rovighi 1951), which are simply a summary of John of Jandun's questions; a few questions on the *Metaphysics* (unedited), a question on necessity (ed. Cheneval, in "*Utrum omnia*" 1988); and an *Expositio super theoricam planetarum* [*ca.* 1318] (unedited).

Secondary sources. Ermatinger, "Averroism in Bologna" (1954); Federici Vescovini, "La classification des mathématiques" (1994), "L'exorde de l'*Arithmetica*" (2003); Grabmann, "Studien" (1936); Kuksewicz, *Averroïsme bolonais* (1965); Sorge, *Profili dell'averroismo bolognese* (2001), "L'ente e l'uno" (2002); Vanni Rovighi, "La psicologia" (1931); Lohr.

THEMON JUDAEUS b. Münster; *fl.* 1349–60. Paris arts master, whose work is in the circle of John Buridan. Likely a Jew who converted to Christianity, he became an arts master at Paris by 1349, and was subsequently prominent in university affairs. His extant works are a set of questions on Aristotle's *Meteorology* (ed. 1516, etc.), a commentary on Sacrobosco's *Sphere*, and a set of questions on the motion of the moon [1350] (both ed. Hugonnard-Roche 1973).

Secondary sources. Crombie, *Robert Grosseteste* (1953); Lohr.

THEODORE II DUKAS LASKARIS b. 1221/2; d. 1258. Emperor of Nicaea who left philosophical, scientific, and theological works. Trained in philosophy from a young age by leading scholars, such as Nikephoros Blemmydes, he succeeded his father as emperor in 1254. Extant philosophical works include *De naturali communione libri VI* (*Physike koinonia*) (PG 140); *Kosmikē dēlōsis* (*A Description of the Natural World*) (ed. Festa 1897–9); *A Treatise on Virtue* and *A Praise of Wisdom* (both ed. Palaiologou 2007); and a *Concise Ethics* (unedited). Also extant are various works of rhetoric (ed. Tartaglia 2000) and theology (ed. Krikones 1988).

Secondary sources. Georgiopoulou, "Theodore II Dukas Laskaris" (1990); Papadopoulos, *Théodore II Lascaris* (1908); Richter, *Theodoros Dukas Laskaris* (1989); ODB (Angold).

THEODORE ABŪ QURRAH b. Edessa (Syria), *ca.* 750; d. prob. after 816. Theologian and Christian apologist, an early participant in Christian–Islamic dialogue. Very little is known about his life. Traditionally said to have joined the monastery of Mar Sabas (Palestine), where John of Damascus (d. 749) had been a lively intellectual force, but the evidence for this claim is thin. Chalcedonian bishop of Harran from an unknown date. The story of his being deposed as bishop *ca.* 813 on grounds of heresy is now judged unlikely. Works are extant in both Arabic (part. ed. Bacha 1904) and Greek (PG 97). More recently edited Arabic works are a treatise on icons (ed. Dick 1986) and a treatise on the existence of God and the true religion (ed. Dick 1982). Most of his writings have recently been published in English (tr. Lamoreaux 2005).

Secondary sources. Griffith, *Theodore Abu Qurrah* (1992); Lamoreaux, "Biography" (2002); Samir and Nielsen, *Christian Arabic Apologetics* (1994).

THEODORE GAZES (Gaza) b. Thessaloniki, *ca.* 1415; d. Calabria, 1475/6. Translator, grammarian. Moved to Italy by 1440, studying Latin in Mantua and then teaching

Greek at Ferrara. In 1451 joined the circle of Bessarion in Rome, where he was active as a translator from Greek into Latin and vice versa (see Appendix B5). His *Eisagogē* to Greek grammar (ed. Donnet 1979) became a standard textbook. His *De fato* (ed. and tr. Taylor 1925) responds to Plethon's necessitarian reading of Plato.

Secondary sources. Geanakoplos, "Theodore Gaza" (1989); ODB (Kahzdan, Talbot).

THEODORE METOCHITES b. 1270; d. Constantinople, 1332. Prominent statesman and prolific scholar. Despite being forced into exile with his father at the age of thirteen, Theodore came to occupy a series of prominent administrative positions at an early age, culminating in his appointment as prime minister in 1305. With the overthrow of Emperor Andronicus II, he was imprisoned and then exiled in 1328, returning two years later to live out his life at the monastery of Chora. His many writings – almost all extant, but many unedited – range over philosophy, astronomy, history, and poetry. Most prominent is his *Miscellanea* (ed. Müller and Kiessling 1821/1966; part ed. and tr. Hult 2002), an encyclopedic collection of philosophical, scientific, and historical essays. Also extant is a paraphrase of Aristotle's *Physics* and *Parva naturalia* (ed. 1559/1992), an introduction to astronomy (ed. Bydén, in *Theodore Methochites* 2003), and an ethical treatise (ed. Polemes 1995).

Secondary sources. Beck, *Theodoros Metochites* (1952); de Vries-Van der Velden, *Théodore Métochite* (1987); Ševčenko, *Études sur la polémique* (1962); Tatakis, *Byzantine Philosophy* (2003); ODB (Talbot).

THIERRY OF CHARTRES (Theodoricus Carnotensis) b. Brittany; d. after 1156. Philosopher and influential teacher. Perhaps the younger brother of Bernard of Chartres. Taught at the cathedral school at Chartres and perhaps in Paris as well, *ca.* 1130. Chancellor of Chartres in the 1140s. Resigned his position in the 1150s and lived the remainder of his life in a monastery, perhaps the Cistercian abbey of Vaux-de-Cernay. His chief works are a series of commentaries on Boethius's theological works [1140s], the cosmological *De sex dierum operibus* [1130s] (both ed. Häring 1971), and a prologue and notes to his massive, unfinished encyclopedic collection of texts on the liberal arts, the *Heptateuchon* (prol. ed. Jeauneau, in *Lectio philosophorum* 1973). Also extant are two earlier works on rhetoric [1130s] (ed. Fredborg 1988).

Secondary sources. Dronke, "Thierry of Chartres" (1988); Maccagnolo, *Rerum universitas* (1976); Speer, *Entdeckte Natur* (1995); Dronke.

THOMAS AQUINAS (d'Aquino) b. Roccasecca (Italy), 1224/5; d. Fossanova, 1274. Philosopher and theologian; the foundational figure of scholastic thought. Studied first at the nearby abbey of Monte Cassino, then in Naples in 1239, where, against his family's wishes, he joined the Dominican order *ca.* 1242/4. Sent first to Paris in 1246 and then to Cologne in 1248, studying under Albert the Great. Returned to Paris in 1252 as a student of theology, becoming regent master in 1256. After three years, Aquinas was sent back to Italy in 1259, where he taught in houses of study in Orvieto in 1261–5 and Rome in 1265–8. From there he was sent back to Paris for an unusual second term as regent master, in the midst of considerable turmoil over the status of the mendicant orders and the proper interpretation of Aristotle. After four academic years, he returned to Italy for the last time in 1272, teaching in Naples.

Aquinas's works, except where noted, are available in the critical Leonine edition (ed. 1882–), and are available in searchable form at www.corpusthomisticum.org. Except where noted, they have been translated into English (see Thérèse Bonin's translation bibliography on the internet). His massive literary output can be divided into five main categories. Foremost are his major theological syntheses: his early *Sentences* commentary [1252–6] (ed. Mandonnet and Moos through IV.22; no translation); his *Summa contra gentiles* [1259–65]; and his *Summa theologiae* [1266–73], the third and last part of which was never completed, and which was "supplemented" (from q. 90) soon after his death by parts of the *Sentences* commentary. Second in philosophical significance are his disputed questions: *De veritate* [1256–9]; *De potentia* [1265–6]; *De anima* [1265-6]; *De spiritualibus creaturis* [1267–8]; *De malo* [1269–71]; *De virtutibus* [1271–2]; and his *Quodlibeta* [VII–XI from 1256–9; I–VI and XII from 1268–72]. Third are his Aristotelian commentaries, a project he began in 1267 and which extends to nearly all of Aristotle's major philosophical works. (There are also commentaries on Boethius's *De trinitate* [*ca.* 1258] and *De hebdomadibus*, on pseudo-Dionysius's *De divinis nominibus* [1260s], and on the *Liber de causis* [1272].) Fourth is his quite extensive set of biblical commentaries, including Job [1261–5], the Gospels [1264, 1269–72], and Paul's letters [1265–73]. Finally, there are many shorter treatises, including the early *De principiis naturae* [*ca.* 1252] and *De ente et essentia* [*ca.* 1254]; the *De regimine principum* (*De regno*) [*ca.* 1267]; and the polemical *De unitate intellectus* [1270] and *De aeternitate mundi* [1271].

Secondary sources. Torrell, *Saint Thomas Aquinas* (1996) (biobibliography), *Spiritual Master* (2003); Davies, *Thought of Thomas Aquinas* (1992); Finnis, *Moral, Political, and Legal Theory* (1998); Kretzmann, *Metaphysics of Theism* (1997), *Metaphysics of Creation* (1999); Kretzmann and Stump (eds.), *Cambridge Companion* (1993); Pasnau, *Thomas Aquinas on Human Nature* (2002); Pasnau and Shields, *Philosophy of Aquinas* (2004); Stump, *Aquinas* (2003); Wippel, *Metaphysical Thought* (2000); BCPMA (Davies); DMA (Imbach); Kaeppeli; REP (Kretzmann and Stump); SEP (McInerny and O'Callaghan).

THOMAS OF BAILLY b. Bailly (near Versailles); d. 1328. Secular master of theology at Paris. Studied at Paris, serving as regent master in 1301–7, from which time are extant six *Quodlibeta* (ed. Glorieux 1960).

Secondary source. Glorieux.

THOMAS BRADWARDINE b. England, *ca.* 1300; d. Canterbury, 1349. Influential philosopher, theologian, and mathematician. Fellow of Balliol College in 1321, becoming master of arts by 1323, by which time he had become a fellow of Merton College. After several years teaching on the arts faculty, he began studying theology. Left Merton in 1335, subsequently joining the household of bishop Richard Bury. After serving as master of theology *ca.* 1336–7, he was appointed chancellor of St. Paul's Cathedral in London in 1337–49. During these years his career was outside academia, including an appointment as royal chaplain in 1339, and as archbishop of Canterbury in 1349, just a month before his death from the plague. In philosophy, he is a foundational figure among the Oxford Calculators. Most significant is the *Tractatus de proportionibus*

velocitatum in motibus [1328] (ed. and tr. Crosby 1955). Also extant [1322/5] are *De insolubilibus* (ed. Roure 1970; ed. and tr. Read forthcoming); *De incipit et desinit* (ed. Nielsen
1982); *Geometria speculativa* (ed. and tr. Molland 1989); *Arithmetica speculativa* (ed. 1495);
Opus artis logicae (ed. Pinborg 1982); and *De continuo* [1328/35] (ed. Murdoch 1957).
A treatise on consequences seems unlikely to be his (ed. Green-Pedersen, in "Bradwardine (?)" 1982). His extant theological works include fragments from his *Sentences*
commentary [*ca.* 1333] (unedited), a treatise *De futuris contingentibus* [perhaps from that
commentary] (ed. Genest 1979), a sermon celebrating God's providence [1346] (ed.
Oberman and Weisheipl in "The *Sermo epinicius*" 1958); and, most importantly, his mas-
terwork on grace, foreknowledge, and human freedom, the *De causa Dei contra Pelagium
et de virtute causarum ad suos Mertonenses* [1344] (ed. 1618/1964).

     Secondary sources. Dolnikowski, *View of Time* (1995); Genest, *Prédétermination et liberté*
(1992); Genest and Tachau, "Sur les *Sentences*" (1990); Leff, *Bradwardine* (1957); Murdoch, "Mathematics and Continuity" (1984); Molland, "Geometry" (1978); Oberman,
Archbishop Thomas Bradwardine (1957); Spade, "*Insolubilia*" (1981); DMA (Celeyrette);
DSB (Murdoch); ODNB (Leff); REP (Sylla).

THOMAS BUCKINGHAM b. prob. Buckinghamshire; d. 1349. English theologian. Fellow
of Merton College from 1324, becoming master of arts *ca.* 1330 and then turning
to theology. Lectured on the *Sentences* by 1338, becoming doctor by 1346, when he
became chancellor of Exeter Cathedral. Extant works include his *Sentences* commentary
(ed. 1505) and *Quaestiones theologicae* (*Ostensio meriti liberae actionis*) [*ca.* 1347] (q. 1 ed.
Genest, in *Prédétermination* 1992), a response to Thomas Bradwardine's *De causa Dei*.
     Secondary sources. De la Torre, *Contingency of Futures* (1987); ODNB (Benbow).

THOMAS OF CANTIMPRÉ (Brabantinus, van Bellegham, Cantimpratensis) b. near Brussels, *ca.* 1201; d. 1270/2. Encyclopedist, hagiographer. Studied as a boy at Liège, becoming an Augustinian canon in 1217 at the abbey of Cantimpré (near Cambrai). Joined
the Dominican order at Louvain in 1232 and began studying theology under Albert the
Great, first in Cologne and then in Paris. In 1246 he returned to Louvain, where he
taught and preached throughout the region. His principal work is the vast *Liber de natura
rerum* [1230-44] (ed. Boese 1973), an encyclopedia in twenty books ranging widely over
the natural sciences. His *Bonum universale de apibus* (ed. and [Fr] tr. Platelle 1997) takes
the life of bees as an allegory for the human good. Also extant are various hagiographical
writings (available in translation).
     Secondary sources. Engels, "Thomas Cantimpratensis redivivus" (1974); DMA (Beyer
de Ryke); Kaeppeli.

THOMAS OF CHOBHAM b. Chobham (Surrey); d. 1233/6. Moral theologian. Studied
arts and theology in Paris in the 1180s under Peter the Chanter. Back in England by
1192, serving in the household of several wealthy patrons. Canon of Salisbury Cathedral
by 1214. Returned to Paris after 1217, teaching theology there between 1222 and
1228, after which time he returned to Salisbury and might have become bishop but
for his illegitimate birth. His most influential work is his *Summa confessorum* [1216] (ed.
Broomfield 1968), an immensely popular handbook on the pastoral care of souls. Other

extant works are his *Summa de arte praedicandi* [1222/28] (ed. Morenzoni 1988), *Summa de commendatione virtutum et extirpatione vitiorum* [1222/8] (unedited), as well as many sermons (ed. Morenzoni 1993).

Secondary sources. Baldwin, *Masters, Princes and Merchants* (1970); ODNB (Goering).

THOMAS OF CLEVES (Thomas Zeghenans, de Berca, de Clivis) b. Kleve (Saxony), *ca.* 1340; d. Kleve, 1412. Philosopher in the tradition of John Buridan and Albert of Saxony. Studied the arts at Paris under William Buser, becoming master in 1365. Continued to teach at Paris until 1375; then at the Vienna cathedral school in 1376–83; and subsequently at the universities of Vienna and Cologne. Extant works are a *De conceptibus* [1370s] (ed. Bos and Read 2001) and a partial *Logica* (ed. Bos, in *Logica modernorum* 2004).

Secondary source. Read, "Collective Supposition" (1991).

THOMAS OF ERFURT (de Erfordia) *fl.* early 1300s. Logician and grammarian. Presumably a student at Paris. Later taught in Erfurt. His famous *Tractatus de modis significandi seu Grammatica speculativa* [before 1310] (ed. Bursill-Hall 1972) became the standard text of modistic grammar; until 1922 it was thought to be the work of Scotus. It shows the strong influence of Radulphus Brito and Siger of Courtrai. Other extant works are commentaries on the *ars vetus* (unedited) and a very brief collection of mnemonic verses for teaching grammar to schoolboys (ed. Gansiniec 1960).

Secondary sources. Lorenz, *Studium Generale Erfordense* (1989) [biography]; Ashworth, *Tradition* (1978); Gabler, *Die semantischen und syntaktischen Funktionen* (1987); Grabmann, *Thomas von Erfurt* (1943); Pinborg, *Entwicklung* (1967); Rosier-Catach, *La grammaire spéculative* (1983); BCPMA (Beuchot); SEP (Zupko).

THOMAS GALLUS (Vercellensis) b. France; d. 1246. Commentator on pseudo-Dionysius. An Augustinian canon, he spent his early years teaching theology at the Abbey of St. Victor in Paris. Joined the newly founded abbey in Vercelli (northern Italy) in 1219, becoming abbot in 1225. Forced out by political conflicts in 1243. His studies of the pseudo-Dionysian corpus come in three stages. First is the *Expositio*, a set of glosses [compl. 1233] (ed. in Denys the Carthusian, *Opera* vols. XV–XVI; *Mystical Theology* ed. and tr. McEvoy 2003; letters ed. Walsh, in "Expositions" 1963); then a widely circulated *Extractio* [1238] summarizing the four works (unedited); then a literal commentary on the whole corpus, the *Explanacio* [1241–3] (*Mystical Theology* ed. Théry 1934). Also extant is a commentary on the Song of Songs (ed. Barbet 1967).

Secondary sources. McEvoy, "Commentators" (2002); DS (Barber).

THOMAS MANLEVELT (Manlefelt, Maulfelt) *fl.* 1320s–30s. English logician, associated with nominalism. Parisian master of arts; subsequently taught in Leuven. Extant works include treatises *De suppositionibus*, *De consequentiis*, and *De confusionibus* (ed. in progress). Various other logical works are also attested to Manlevelt, including *Quaestiones super veteri arte* (part. ed. Andrews, "Thomas Maulevelt").

Secondary sources. Lorenz, *Studium Generale Erfurdense* (1989), "Thomas Manlefelt" (1996); Brands, "Referenztheorie" (1995); Grass, *Schlußfolgerungslehre in Erfurter Schulen* (2003); Lohr.

THOMAS OF STRASBOURG (Strassburg, de Argentina) b. Haguenau (Alsace); d. Vienna, 1357. Theologian. Augustinian hermit. Studied in Strasbourg and later in Paris. Prior general of his order in 1345–57. His *Sentences* commentary [1330s] (ed. 1490/1989, etc.), which is fairly conservative in character, was popular enough to have been reprinted many times during the Renaissance.

Secondary sources. Lindner, *Erkenntnislehre* (1930); Shannon, *Good Works and Predestination* (1940).

THOMAS OF SUTTON (Thomas Anglicus) b. Yorkshire, *ca.* 1250; d. after 1315. Early Thomist. Ordained deacon at Blyth (northeast England) in 1274. Fellow of Merton College, then a Dominican friar at Oxford, perhaps by 1282. Taught in the arts faculty; incepted as master of theology [1290/5]; still active in 1311. His most substantial edited works are his *Quaestiones ordinariae* (ed. Schneider 1977) and four *Quodlibeta* [1290s] (ed. Schmaus and Gonzalez-Haba 1969). Also extant are a *Contra quodlibet* (ed. Schneider 1978) aimed against Scotus and a critique of Robert Cowton's *Sentences* commentary [after 1312] (unedited). Various *opuscula* survive, sometimes confused with Aquinas's own, including *De instantibus* (ed. Aquinas, *Opera* 1852–73, vol. XVI); *Contra pluralitatem formarum* [1284] (ibid., vol. XVII); *De esse et essentia* (ed. Senko 1970); and *De productione formarum substantialium* (ed. Wlodek 1979). There is a commentary on the *Categories* [1270s] (part. ed. Conti, in "Commentary" 1985) and perhaps on *Metaphysics* VII (unedited), as well as continuations of Aquinas's unfinished commentaries on the *De generatione et corruptione* (ed. Kelley 1976) and the *De interpretatione* (unedited). Probably not by Sutton is the *Liber propugnatorius super primum Sententiarum contra Johannem Scotum* [1311/23] (ed. 1523/1966; part. ed. Schmaus 1930).

Secondary sources. Conti, "Le composizione metafisica" (1991); Friedman, "Trinitarian Theology" (2001); Kelley, "Two Early English Thomists" (1981); Klima, "Nature of the Intellective Soul" (2001); Lewry, "Two Continuators" (1981); BCPMA (Klima); DMA (Cesalli); Kaeppeli; ODNB (Luscombe); Roensch.

THOMAS WALEYS *fl.* 1318–40. English Dominican theologian. A friar from his youth, becoming bachelor of theology at Oxford by 1318, and incepting as master *ca.* 1323. Sent in 1326 to serve as lector at the Dominican convent in Bologna. Chaplain in Avignon in 1331, where he ran into trouble for attacking John XXII's controversial views regarding the beatific vision. Jailed in 1333, the charges against him were dropped after nineteen months, though he was not permitted to return to England until *ca.* 1342. Thomas's work shows a special affinity for classical texts: in addition to biblical commentaries, he wrote commentaries on Augustine's *City of God* and Boethius's *Consolation of Philosophy* (both available in various Renaissance editions). Also extant is a treatise *De modo componendi sermones* [*ca.* 1340] (ed. Charland, in *Artes praedicandi* 1936).

Secondary sources. Kaeppeli, *Le procès* (1936); Smalley, *English Friars* (1960); Trottmann, *La vision béatifique* (1995); Kaeppeli; ODNB (Tugwell).

THOMAS WYLTON (Wilton) *fl. ca.* 1288–1322. Philosopher, theologian. Fellow of Merton College *ca.* 1288–1301. Master of arts at Oxford in 1301–4. Subsequently pursued theological studies in Paris, serving as master of theology there in 1312–22. An influential realist, he was Walter Burley's teacher. His extant works include questions on the *Physics* and *De anima* [both before 1304] (unedited); one *Quodlibet* [1315/16] (almost entirely edited in various papers; see below); and various disputed questions (unedited).

Secondary sources. Dumont, "New Questions" (1998); Etzkorn and Andrews, "Multiple Accidents" (1994); Henninger, "Relations" (1990); Jung-Palczewska, "God's Infinite Power" (1996), "La question" (1997); Nielsen, "Theology and Virtue" (2000); Nielsen, Noone, and Trifogli, "Formal Distinction" (2003); Nielsen and Trifogli, "Beatific Vision" (2006); Senko, "De anima intellectiva" (1964); Trifogli, "Statuto ontologico del tempo" (1990), "Wylton on Motion" (1995), "Immobility of Place" (1998), "Final Causality" (2007), "*Quodlibet*" (2007); Trifogli and Nielsen, "Number, the Instant, and Time" (2005); BCPMA (Trifogli); ODNB (Lohr).

THOMAS OF YORK (de Eboraco) b. *ca.* 1220; d. before 1269. Theologian. Joined the Franciscan order by 1245. Sent to Oxford to study theology by 1249. Appointed master of theology in 1253, without having served as master of arts. Lector at Cambridge *ca.* 1256. His major work is the *Sapientale* [1250s] (unedited), an unsystematic compendium of philosophical and theological questions, drawing on a vast range of Christian and non-Christian sources. Also extant is a defense of the mendicant orders, *Manus quae contra omnipotentem* [1253/6] (ed. Bierbaum 1920).

Secondary sources. Grabmann, "Metaphysik" (1913); Longpré, "Thomas d'York" (1926); Reilly, "Efficacy of Secondary Causes" (1953); Sharp, *Franciscan Philosophy* (1930); Scully, "Power of Physical Bodies" (1962); ODNB (Catto); REP (Somerset).

THUO OF VIBORG (Thuo Nicholai de Vibergia) b. Dacia; d. Lund, 1472. Studied philosophy in Erfurt from 1426, becoming master of arts in 1428 and doctor of theology in 1439. Author of a *Disputata metaphysicae* [1438–9] (ed. Tabarroni 1998) and *De pluralitate formarum* (ed. Ebbesen 1998).

Secondary sources. Bos, "Thuo of Viborg" (1999); Lohr.

AL-ṬŪSĪ (Khwājah Naṣīr al-Dīn) b. Tus (Iran), 1201; d. Baghdad, 1274. Scientist, philosopher, and theologian. Born into a Twelver Shīʿī family; studied in Tus and then Nishapur. Took refuge from Genghis Khan in the mountain fortresses of Khorasan in 1227 and later Alamut, embracing the Ismāʿīlī faith of his hosts. With the fall of Alamut in 1256, he became scientific advisor to the Mongols and returned to Twelver Shīʿism. A large observatory and library were built for him at Maraghah, which became a center for philosophical and scientific inquiry. Al-Ṭūsī authored over 100 works, mostly in Arabic but also in Persian. In ethics, his best-known work is the *Akhlāq-i nāṣirī* (*Nasirean Ethics*) [1235; rev. 1265] (ed. M. Mīnuwi and A. R. Ḥaydarī 1977; tr. Wickens 1964). In theology, his major works are the *Tajrīd al-ʿaqāʾid* (*Abstract of Theology*) (ed. Sulayman 1996) and, from his Ismāʿīlī period, the *Tasawwurat* or *Rawdat-al-taslim* (*Paradise of Submission*) (ed. and tr. Badakhchani 2005). In logic, his main work is the *Asās al-iqtibās* (*The Ground for the Acquisition of Knowledge*) [1244] (ed. Radawi 1947). Other central works include his commentary on Avicenna's *Ishārāt* [before 1258] (with Avicenna's text, in Dunyā 1957–60) and his memoir on astronomy, the *Tadhkira fī ʿilm al-hayʾa* (ed. and tr. Ragep 1993). An autobiography is also extant from his Ismāʿīlī period [prob. after 1246] (ed. and tr. Badakhchani 1998). Selected translations of al-Ṭūsī's metaphysics are available in Morewedge (1992).

Secondary sources. Mudarris Raḍawī, *Aḥwal wa ātār-i* (1975) [*Life and Works*]; Madelung, "Ethics" (1985); Morewedge, "Analysis of 'Substance'" (1975); Street, "Logical Connectives" (1995); DSB (Nasr); HIP (Dabashi); REP (Cooper).

UBERTINO DA CASALE b. Casale Monferrato (Piedmont), 1259; d. after 1328. Preacher and leader of the Spiritual Franciscans. Joined the Franciscan order in 1273. Studied in Paris, probably 1274–83, and subsequently lived in Florence, preaching there and in the surrounding communities, and serving as chaplain to Cardinal Orsini from 1306. Active in Avignon from 1309, attempting to resolve the conflicts over Franciscan spiritualism. Charges of heresy in 1319 and 1325 eventually forced him to flee Avignon, perhaps seeking protection at the court of Louis the Bavarian. His principal work is his lengthy eschatological treatise, the *Arbor vitae crucifixae Iesu* [1305] (ed. 1485/1961; part. tr. Armstrong *et al.*, *Francis of Assisi* 1999). Various shorter works defend the spiritualist movement and their conception of poverty, including the *Rotulus Iste*, the *Sanctitati apostolicae*, and the *Declaratio* [all 1311] (all ed. Ehrle 1887).

Secondary sources. Burr, *Spiritual Franciscans* (2001); Callaey, *L'idéalisme franciscain* (1911); Potestà, *Storia ed escatologia* (1980); DS (Potestà).

ULRICH OF STRASBOURG (de Argentina) b. Strasbourg, *ca.* 1220; d. Paris, 1277. Dominican theologian and philosopher, heavily influenced by Neoplatonism. Joined Dominican order *ca.* 1245, studying with Albert the Great in Paris and then in Cologne in 1248–54. Appointed lector in theology at the Strasbourg convent, then provincial minister of the Teutonic Province in 1272–7. Subsequently resumed his theology studies in Paris, but died before becoming master. His only extant work is the massive *Liber de summo bono* (*Summa de bono*) [1265–72] (ed. Mojsisch *et al.* 1989), a work heavily influenced by pseudo-Dionysius.

Secondary sources. Backes, *Christologie* (1975); Breuning, *Erhebung und Fall* (1959); de Libera, *Introduction* (1984), "Ulrich de Strasbourg" (1985); Grabmann, "Studien" (1926); Lescoe, *God as First Principle* (1979); Palazzo, "Ulrich of Strasbourg" (2004–6); Putnam, "Aristotelian Causes" (1961); BCPMA (Emery); Kaeppeli; REP (Bussanich).

URSO OF SALERNO b. Calabria; d. *ca.* 1225. Physician and last of the great masters of the school of Salerno. His work extends beyond the narrowly medical into fundamental questions of philosophy and natural science. Extant treatises include *Aphorismi cum glossulis* (ed. Creutz, in "Aphorismen" 1936), *De commixtionibus elementorum* (ed. Stürner 1976), *De effectibus qualitatum* (ed. Matthaes, *Salernitaner Arzt* 1918), *De effectibus medicinarum* (ed. ibid.), *De effectibus qualitatum accidentalibus* (ed. Sudhoff, in "Salernitaner Handschrift" 1920), *De gradibus* (ed. ibid.), *De saporibus et odoribus* (ed. Hartmann, *Literatur* 1919), *De coloribus* (ed. Thorndike 1959).

Secondary sources. Creutz, "Letzte des Hochsalerno" (1934); Jacquart, "Aristotelian Thought in Salerno" (1988); Kristeller, "School of Salerno" (1956); Dronke.

VINCENT OF BEAUVAIS (Bellovacensis) b. Beauvais (Picardy), *ca.* 1190; d. near Beauvais, *ca.* 1264. Encyclopedist. Among the first generation of Dominican friars, charged by the order with the task of producing a compilation of all knowledge for his fellow friars. The result was the encyclopedic *Speculum maius* [finished *ca.* 1260] (ed. Douai 1624/1964–5), in three parts: *Speculum naturale*, *Speculum doctrinale*, and *Speculum historiale*, with a prefatory *Libellus apologeticus* (ed. von den Brincken, in "Geschichtsbetrachtung" 1978). Lector at the Cistercian monastery of Royaumont (near Paris) from 1246, where he developed close ties with the royal family. His lesser works include the *De eruditione filiorum nobilium* [1247/50] (ed. Steiner 1938/1970), the *De morali principis institutione* [1260/2] (ed. Schneider 1995), the *Liber consolatorius pro morte amici* and the *Liber gratiae* (both ed. Amerbach 1481).

Secondary sources. Aerts *et al.* (eds.), *Studies on the* Speculum maius (1986); Gabriel, *Educational Ideas* (1956), *Mittelalterlicher Erzieher* (1967); Paulmier-Foucart *et al.* (eds.), *Vincent de Beauvais* (1990); Paulmier-Foucart and Duchenne, *Le grand miroir du monde* (2004); Tobin, *Education of Women* (1984); Weigand, *Scholastische Universalchronistik* (1991); DMA (Paulmier-Foucart); Kaeppeli. See also the Vincent of Beauvais Newsletter (1976–) and Johannes Voorbij's internet bibliography.

VINCENT FERRER b. Valencia, 1350; d. Vannes (Brittany), 1419. Dominican philosopher and preacher. Joined the order as a youth, studying at convents in Valencia and Barcelona. After further study in Lérida and Toulouse, he returned to Valencia to teach theology at the cathedral school, *ca.* 1385. A close relationship with Cardinal Pedro de Luna led him to Avignon once Pedro was elected to the papacy as Benedict XIII. In 1399 he left the papal court, dedicating himself largely to missionary work and preaching, for which he became famous. Many of those sermons are extant in Catalan (ed. Sanchis y Sivera and Schib 1971–). His philosophical writings are a *Tractatus de suppositionibus* (ed. Trentman 1977) and a *Quaestio de unitate universalis* (ed. Trentman 1982). His best-known work is his *Tractatus de vita spirituali* (ed. Rousset 1899; tr. 1957). Other sermons and treatises have also been edited (ed. Fages 1909).

Secondary sources. Fages, *Histoire* (1901); BBK (Frenken); DMA (Pujol Gómez); Kaeppeli.

VITAL DU FOUR (Vitalis de Furno) b. Bazas (Aquitaine), *ca.* 1260; d. Avignon, 1327. Franciscan philosopher and theologian. Became a friar at an early age. Studied theology at Paris in 1285–91, apparently without then receiving the doctorate or serving as regent master. Lectured at the Montpellier *studium* in 1292–6, then the University of Toulouse in 1296–1307. Elected provincial minister of the Aquitaine province in 1307, perhaps receiving the doctorate at this time by papal fiat. Elected cardinal in 1312 and then cardinal-bishop of Albano in 1321. During his later years he played a leading role in shaping the mainstream Franciscan response to the spiritualist movement. Vital's philosophical ideas are in line with the conservative Franciscans of the thirteenth century. His principal philosophical works are a *Sentences* commentary [1295–6] (unedited); three

Quodlibeta [1296–1300] (ed. Delorme 1947); and disputed questions *De rerum principio* [1292–5] (ed. 1891) and *De cognitione* (ed. Delorme 1927). There is also a popular *Speculum morale totius sacrae Scripturae* [1305] (ed. 1513, etc.) and a commentary on the Apocalypse (ed. Bonelli 1773).

Secondary sources. Lynch, *Theory of Knowledge* (1972); Mann, "Best of All Possible Worlds" (1991); Mauro, "Disputata de anima" (1997); Piron, "Franciscan Quodlibeta" (2006); Putallaz, "La connaissance de soi" (1990); BCPMA (Traver); DMA (Brumberg-Chaumont); Glorieux; REP (Mann).

WALAHFRID STRABO b. Swabia, 808/9; d. Reichenau, 849. Poet, scholar, Benedictine monk. A student of Rabanus Maurus at the abbey school of Fulda. Tutor of Charles the Bald in 829–38; abbot of the monastery of Reichenau in 839–49. Most famous as a poet (ed. Dümmler, *Poetae Latini* 1884), particularly for his *Visio Wettini* [824/5] (ed. and tr. Traill 1974), describing the vision of a journey to the next life. Also the author of the *Life of St. Gall* (tr. Joynt 1927) and other saints' lives; of biblical commentaries; and of a history of church liturgical practices, the *Libellus de exordiis et incrementis quarundam in observationibus ecclesiasticis rerum* (ed. and tr. Harting-Correa 1996). Not the originator of the *Glossa ordinaria*, as traditionally thought.

Secondary source. BBK (Wesseling).

WALTER OF AILLY (Gualterus de Alliaco) *fl.* thirteenth century. Parisian arts master, known only from the colophon of several manuscripts containing sophisms, two logical (unedited) and one grammatical (ed. Rosier-Catach 1989).

Secondary source. Weijers.

WALTER OF BRUGES b. Zande (western Flanders), *ca.* 1225; d. Poitiers, 1307. Franciscan theologian. Joined the order at a young age, and was sent to study at Paris, where he was a student of Bonaventure. Lectured on the *Sentences ca.* 1261–5, serving as regent master in 1267–8. Subsequently served as provincial minister for France until 1279, when he was elected bishop of Poitiers, a position he held until the year before his death. All but Bk. III of his *Sentences* commentary is extant (unedited except for excerpts below), with Bk. I seemingly a later redaction [shortly after 1270]. Also extant are various disputed questions from his tenure in Paris (ed. Longpré 1928).

Secondary sources. Decorte, "Einfluss der Willenspsychologie" (1983); Eardley, "Foundations of Freedom" (2006); Kent, *Virtues of the Will* (1995); FA; Glorieux.

WALTER BURLEY (Burleigh) b. England, 1274/5; d. 1344/5. Philosopher and logician, an influential advocate of metaphysical realism. Began studying the arts at Oxford *ca.* 1296; master of arts by 1301; fellow of Merton College in 1305. Left for Paris in 1307/9 to study theology, receiving his doctorate by 1323. (His *Sentences* commentary is not extant.) Returned to England in 1327, where he entered into royal service, leaving his academic career behind. Joined Richard Bury's household in Durham in 1334–40. Spent his last few years abroad, in Italy and southern France.

His surviving works are exclusively philosophical. From his years on the arts faculty at Oxford, or shortly thereafter, are questions on *De anima* III [1301] (ed. Synan 1997); the

De interpretatione [in 1301 and again before 1310] (ed. Brown 1974, 1973); the *Posterior Analytics* [before 1310] (ed. Sommers 2000); the *De generatione* [*ca.* 1307] (ed. Gensler 2007); and the *Categories* [before 1310] (unedited). Also extant from this period [*ca.* 1302] are a series of logical treatises: *De suppositionibus* (ed. Brown 1972); *De exclusivis* (ed. de Rijk 1985); *De exceptivis* (ed de Rijk 1986); *De consequentiis* (ed. Green-Pedersen 1980); *De insolubilibus* (ed. Roure 1970); and *De obligationibus* (ed. Green 1963; part. tr. CTMPT I). Early commentaries on the *Topics*, *De anima*, and *Physics* are extant (all unedited), as is a later *Physics* commentary [after 1324] (ed. 1501/1972). From the 1320s there are treatises *De potentiis animae* (ed. Kitchel 1971), *De primo et ultimo instanti* (ed. Shapiro and Shapiro 1965), *De formis* (ed. Scott 1970), *De relativis* (ed. Shapiro and Kiteley 1962), and *De intensione et remissione formarum* (ed. 1496). Also from this period is his principal work of logic, the *De puritate artis logicae* [a short version and a long version are extant] (ed. Boehner 1955; tr. Spade 2000). From Burley's last years come commentaries on the *Ethics* [1334] and *Politics* [1343] (both unedited), a treatise *De universalibus* [after 1337] (ed. Wöhler 1999), and a last set of commentaries on the *ars vetus* [1337] (ed. 1509), offering a major reconsideration of his metaphysics and logic.

Secondary sources. Krieger, "Studies" (1999); Ottman and Wood, "Life and Works" (1999); Cesalli, "Le réalisme propositionnel" (2001); Conti, "Ontology" (1990), "Significato e verità" (2000); Gambra, "Compromiso de existencia" (1996); Karger, "Realism" (1999); Nederman, "Kings, Peers and Parliament" (1992); Normore, "Continuity" (1982); Pinborg, "Meaning of Proposition" (1969); Spade, "How to Start and Stop" (1994), "Kinds of Simple Supposition" (1999); Uña, *Contexto cultural* (1978); Wood, "*Physics* Commentaries" (1984), "Motion in a Vacuum" (1989/90), "Willing Wickedly" (1999); BCPMA (Sommers); DMA (Sylla); ODNB (Sommers); REP (Sylla); SEP (Conti); Weijers.

WALTER CHATTON (Catton) b. Chatton (Northumbria), 1285/90; d. Avignon, 1343/4. Theologian and philosopher, an important influence on Ockham. Entered the Franciscan order as a boy, probably at Carlisle, where he would have received his early education. Studied theology at Oxford *ca.* 1317–19. Lectured on the *Sentences*, either in London or Oxford, in 1321–3 and again in 1323–4, engaging in extensive disputations with Ockham. Regent master of theology in 1329–30. In Avignon from 1333. His principal works are two versions of his *Sentences* commentary – a *Reportatio* [*ca.* 1323] (ed. Wey and Etzkorn 2002–5) and a revised version up to Bk. I d. 17, of the *Lectura* [1324/30] (ed. Etzkorn and Wey 2007–). (The *Collatio* and *Prologus* are edited separately [ed. Wey 1989].) Also extant is a *Quodlibet* [1329–30] (ed. forthcoming) and a treatise *De paupertate evangelica* (ed. Douie 1931–2).

Secondary sources. Fitzpatrick, "Univocity of Being" (1971); Karger, "Objects of Knowledge" (1995); Keele, "*Res* Theory" (2003), "Divine Power" (2007); Kelley, "Universal Concept" (1981); Maurer, "Ockham's Razor" (1984); Schabel, "Oxford Franciscans" (2000); Tachau, *Vision and Certitude* (1988); BCPMA (Etzkorn); DMA (Etzkorn); ODNB (Biller); REP (Brown); SEP (Keele).

WALTER HILTON b. *ca.* 1343; d. 1396. Influential English contemplative, mystic, and ascetic. Studied canon law at Cambridge, apparently without becoming master.

Subsequently spent some time as a solitary, and then from *ca.* 1386 as an Augustinian canon at Thurgarton (Nottinghamshire), where he remained until his death. His principal works, in Middle English, are *The Scale of Perfection* [1386/96] (ed. Underhill 1923/1948; tr. Clark and Dorward 1991), exhorting the contemplative life, and his epistle on *The Mixed Life* (ed. Ogilvie-Thomson 1986), written for those attempting to combine contemplation with an active life.

Secondary source. ODNB (Clark).

WALTER OF MORTAGNE (de Mauritania) b. Mortagne (Flanders), *ca.* 1100; d. Laon, 1174. Influential logician and theologian. Educated at Tournai and then Rheims, he subsequently taught at Laon from *ca.* 1120. Elected bishop of Laon in 1155 and subsequently much involved in ecclesiastical affairs. His "indifference" theory of universals is described by John of Salisbury, and in a *Tractatus "Quoniam de generali"* [1120s] (ed. Dijs, in "Two Anonymous" 1990; tr. King in *Peter Abailard* 1982), which seems likely to be Walter's. Other extant works include a *Liber de trinitate* (PL 209) and a philosophically interesting letter to Peter Abaelard [1140] (ed. Ostlender, in *Sententiae* 1929).

Secondary source. Ott, *Theologischen Briefliteratur der Frühscholastik* (1937).

WĀṢIL IBN ʿAṬĀʾ d. 748/9. Theologian and preacher. Lived mainly in Basra. An important teacher who played a formative role in subsequent Islamic theology, especially Muʿtazilism. Although many theological writings are attested, none have survived (there is an extant sermon, ed. and [German] tr. Daiber 1988).

Secondary sources. Van Ess, *Theologie und Gesellschaft* (1991–7); Watt, *Formative Period* (1973); BEIP (El-Kaisy); EI (van Ess).

WILLIAM OF ALNWICK b. Northumberland, *ca.* 1275; d. Avignon, 1333. Franciscan philosopher and theologian, a disciple of Scotus. A friar from an early age. Probably studied at the Franciscan *studium* at Newcastle, and subsequently in Paris, under Scotus. Regent master at Oxford in 1315–16 and perhaps in Paris in 1317–18; subsequently lectured in Montpellier and Bologna. His opposition to John XXII on the issue of apostolic poverty led to a process of censure in 1323 and his flight to Naples. Seven years later, Alnwick (pronounced ANick) was appointed bishop of Giovinazzo. During his years studying in Paris, he served as secretary for Scotus's *Ordinatio* and reported one of his *Collationes*. After Scotus's death, he produced the lengthy *Additiones magnae* [1312/25], completing Scotus's unfinished lectures. Alnwick's own thought, often original despite the strong Scotistic influence, survives in his own *Sentences* commentary from Paris [prob. 1313–15] (unedited); disputed questions *De esse intelligibile* [1315–16] (ed. Ledoux 1937; part. tr. CTMPT III); a *Quodlibet* [1315–16] (ed. Ledoux 1937), and a lengthy set of *Disputationes* [1322–3] (only selections edited; see secondary sources). Three questions on time are also extant (ed. Alliney, *Time and Soul* 2002).

Secondary sources. Dumont, "Univocity" (1987); D'Souza, "Problem of Faith and Reason" (1973); Kuksewicz, "Trois questions anti-averroistes" (1966); Maier, "Gegen den Averroismus" (1949); Noone, "Formal Distinction" (1993); Prezioso, *Evoluzione del volontarismo* (1964); Schmaus, "Futura contingentia" (1932); Veliath, "Scotism" (1970); BCPMA (Dumont); Emden; ODNB (Brown); Weijers.

WILLIAM OF ARNAUD (Arnaldi) *fl. ca.* 1270s. Logician. Author of a *Lectura tractatuum* [1270s] (ed. de Rijk, in "Genuine Text" 1969), a commentary on Peter of Spain's *Tractatus*. Not an arts master at Toulouse from the 1230s/40s, as de Rijk argued.

Secondary sources. Gondras, "Liber de sex principiis" (1975); d'Ors, "Petrus Hispanus II" (2001); Tabarroni, "Lo Pseudo-Egidio" (1988); BCPMA (Lahey); Lohr.

WILLIAM OF AUVERGNE (William of Paris, Guillelmus Alvernus) b. Aurillac (Auvergne), 1180/90; d. 1249. Theologian and bishop. Master of theology at Paris by 1223; canon of the cathedral of Notre Dame. Appointed bishop of Paris in 1228–49, which gave him authority over the university. William's thought attempts to grapple with the influence of Islamic philosophy and the new Aristotle. Most of his philosophical works are part of a massive *summa*, the *Magisterium divinale ac sapientiae* [1228/40], consisting of *De trinitate* [*De primo principio*] (ed. Switalski 1976; tr. Teske and Wade 1989); *De universo creaturum* (tr. Teske 1998–2007); *De anima* [*ca.* 1240] (tr. Teske 2000); *Cur Deus homo*; *De fide et legibus*; *De sacramentis*; and *De virtutibus et moribus*. Other important philosophical works include his *De immortalitate animae* (ed. Bülow 1897; tr. Teske 1991), *De bono et malo* (ed. O'Donnell 1946–54), *De gratia et libero arbitrio* (ed. Corti 1966); *De arte predicandi* (ed. de Poorter 1923); and *De errore Pelagii* (ed. Landgraf 1930). Works not available in a modern edition can be found in his *Opera omnia* (ed. Le Feron 1674/1963, etc.).

Secondary sources. Morenzoni and Tilliette (eds.), *Autour de Guillaume d'Auvergne* (2005) [bio-bibliography]; Baumgartner, *Erkenntnislehre* (1893); Jüssen, "Transformation der scholastischen Philosophie" (1987); Lewis, "Enuntiable" (1995); Marrone, *New Ideas of Truth* (1983); Moody, "*De anima*" (1975); Quentin, *Naturkenntness* (1976); Rohls, *Wilhelm von Auvergne* (1980); Teske, *Studies* (2006); Valois, *Sa vie et ses ouvrages* (1880); BCPMA (Teske); DMA (Brenet); DS (Viard); REP (Marrone); Weijers.

WILLIAM OF AUXERRE (Guillelmus Altissiodorensis) b. Auxerre, *ca.* 1150; d. Rome, 1231. Influential early university theologian. Master of theology at Paris during its earliest years. Archdeacon of Beauvais. Died before carrying out Pope Gregory IX's commission in 1231 to reform the university study of Aristotle. His philosophical thought survives in his influential *Summa aurea* [1215/29] (ed. Ribaillier 1980–7), a comprehensive theological work modeled on Peter Lombard's *Sentences*, but developed more systematically, and influenced by the broader philosophical corpus of the thirteenth century. The only other extant work ascribed to him with confidence is the *Summa de officiis ecclesiasticis* [*ca.* 1200] (unedited), an account of Church offices and liturgical practices.

Secondary sources. Saint Pierre, "Bibliography" (1966); Coolman, *Knowing God* (2004); Lottin, *Psychologie et morale* (1942–60); MacDonald, "Goodness as Transcendental" (1992); Ottaviano, *La vita, le opere* (1929); Principe, *Hypostatic Union* (1963–75); Solère, "Question du possible" (2000); BCPMA (Zupko); DMA (Lambert and Solère); DS (Ribaillier); REP (MacDonald); Weijers.

WILLIAM OF BONKES *fl.* 1290s. Oxford philosopher. Fellow of Balliol College in 1291 and regent master of arts in 1293. Sets of questions are extant on Priscian, and on the *De interpretatione*, *Metaphysics*, *Physics*, *De caelo*, *De generatione*, and *Meteora* (all unedited). *Sophismata* are also extant (ed. Ebbesen, in "*Animal est*" 1993).

Secondary source. Lohr.

WILLIAM BUSER b. Heusden (Brabant), before 1339; d. after 1413. Logician. Student of Albert of Saxony. Master of arts at Paris from 1357; rector in 1364. Teacher of Thomas of Cleves and Marsilius of Inghen. Only known work is an *Obligationes* [1360] (ed. Pozzi, *La coerenza logica* 1990).

Secondary sources. Kneepkens, "Mysterious Buser" (1982), "Obligationes" (1993); Weijers.

WILLIAM OF CHAMPEAUX b. Champeaux (Île-de-France), *ca.* 1060/70; d. Clairvaux, 1122. Realist logician and theologian, the leading philosopher of his day. Studied under Anselm of Laon. Information about much of his life is uncertain, but taught in Paris, first at the school of Notre Dame beginning in 1094, then at the abbey of St. Victor *ca.* 1108–13, which he helped to found. Elected bishop of Châlons-sur-Marne in 1113. Died shortly after joining the Cistercian order. In addition to his influential teaching, William was extremely active as an ecclesiastical reformer. His logical ideas – distinguished foremost by their realism – are known largely through the uncharitable criticisms of his most famous student, Peter Abaelard. A number of surviving logical treatises have recently been identified, however, including two *Introductiones dialecticae* [*ca.* 1094] (ed. Iwakuma, in "Introductiones" 1993), as well as commentaries on the *ars vetus* (unedited), on Boethius's *Topics* (part. ed. Green-Pedersen, in "William of Champeaux" 1974), and on Cicero's rhetoric (part. ed. Fredborg, in "Commentaries" 1976). His theological views survive as a collection of theological *sententiae* (ed. Lottin, in *Psychologie et morale* vol. V 1959).

Secondary sources. Iwakuma, "Étude préliminaire" (1999), "Categories" (2003), "*Introductiones*" (2003); Marenbon, *Aristotelian Logic* (2000) [papers]; Tweedale, *Abailard on Universals* (1976), "Logic" (1988); DMA (de Libera); Dronke; REP (Tweedale); SEP (Guilfoy).

WILLIAM OF CLIFFORD d. 1306. Arts master at Oxford by 1265. Bishop of Emly (Ireland) in 1286. Only work attributed with certainty is a commentary extant in one manuscript on the *Physics* (Bks. III–IV ed. Trifogli, in *Liber Quartus* 2007), although William seems likely to be the author of commentaries from the same manuscript on the *De anima*, *De generatione et corruptione*, *Meteora*, *De somno et vigilia*, and *De vegetabilibus*.

Secondary sources. Donati, "Alcuni commenti anonimi" (2008); Trifogli, *Oxford Physics* (2000); Zimmermann, "Bemerkungen" (1996); Lohr.

WILLIAM OF CONCHES b. Conches (Normandy), *ca.* 1085; d. after 1154. Natural scientist, Platonist, and influential teacher. Student of Bernard of Chartres, probably teaching at Chartres himself thereafter, and perhaps also at Paris. Tutor from *ca.* 1122 to Geoffrey Plantagenet, duke of Normandy. Best known for two comprehensive philosophical surveys: the *Philosophia mundi* [*ca.* 1125] (ed. and [German] tr. Maurach and Telle 1980; ed. Dutton in progress) and, in dialogue form, the *Dragmaticon philosophiae* [1144–9] (ed. Ronca *et al.* 1997; tr. Ronca and Curr 1997). (The second retracts certain positions of the first that had been criticized by William of St. Thierry.) Also extant are commentaries on Boethius's *Consolation of Philosophy* [*ca.* 1125] (ed. Nauta 1999), on Macrobius's commentary on Cicero's *Somnium Scipionis* (part. ed. Dronke, in *Fabula* 1974; ed. Lemay in progress), on Priscian's *Institutiones grammaticae* (part. ed. Jeauneau, in *Lectio* 1973; ed. Jeauneau in progress), on Juvenal's *Satires* (ed. Wilson 1980), and on the *Timaeus* [*ca.* 1130] (ed. Jeauneau 2006). Perhaps also the author of the influential ethical compilation, *Moralium dogma philosophorum* (ed. Holmberg 1929).

Secondary sources. Dutton, *Mystery* (2006); Elford, "William of Conches" (1988); Ellard, *Sacred Cosmos* (2007); Gregory, *Anima mundi* (1955); DMA (Ricklin); Dronke; REP (Marenbon).

WILLIAM CRATHORN b. northern England; *fl.* 1330s. Eccentric Dominican theologian and philosopher. Lectured on *Sentences* Bk. I at Oxford [1330–1] (ed. Hoffmann 1988; q. 1 tr. CTMPT III). His psychology and metaphysics were the subject of extensive attacks by Robert Holcot. A *Quodlibet* may also be extant (unedited).

Secondary sources. Kirjavainen, "Transcendental Elements" (2000); Pasnau, *Theories of Cognition* (1997); Perler, "Mental Language" (1997); Richter, "Handschriftliches" (1972); Schepers, "Holkot contra dicta Crathorn" (1970–2); Sprengard, *Systematische-Historische Untersuchungen* (1968); Tachau, "*Complexe significabile*" (1987), *Vision and Certitude* (1988), "Introduction" (1995); BCPMA (Pasnau); Kaeppeli; REP (Pasnau); SEP (Robert).

WILLIAM OF DURHAM d. Rouen, 1249. Paris theologian. Master of theology at Paris from 1220/3 until 1229. Subsequently held various ecclesiastical appointments in France and England, amassing enough wealth to make the bequest that would eventually help found University College at Oxford. The only extant work known to be his is a large set of questions [late 1220s] surviving in a single manuscript (unedited except for a question on the eternity of the world in Dales and Argerami, *Medieval Latin Texts* 1991).

Secondary sources. Glorieux; ODNB (Summerson).

WILLIAM OF FALEGAR (Falgar, Falagar) d. 1297/8. Franciscan theologian. Became a friar in Toulouse. Studied in Paris under John Pecham from *ca.* 1270, becoming regent master *ca.* 1280–2. Elected provincial minister of Aquitania in 1285. Lector at the papal curia in 1287–91; bishop of Viviers in 1296. Author of a *Sentences* commentary (unedited) and various disputed questions (part. ed. Gondras, in "Guillaume de Falegar" 1972), including a *De gradibus formarum* [1271–2] (ed. Glorieux, in "Le *De gradibus*" 1957). Also extant are various sermons (unedited). Not to be identified with Peter of Falco, as has been suggested.

Secondary sources. Burr, *Eucharistic Presence* (1984); Cenci, "Guglielmo de Falgar" (1985); Heysse, "Pierre de Falco" (1940); BBK (Kohl); FA; Glorieux; Weijers.

WILLIAM HEYTESBURY b. prob. Wiltshire, before 1313; d. 1372/3. Logician and natural philosopher; leading Oxford Calculator. Educated at Oxford; fellow of Merton College from 1330; regent arts master 1331–9. Doctor of theology in 1348. University chancellor in 1370–2, and perhaps earlier (1352–4). Rector at Ickham Church (Kent) from 1354. Surviving works, all dating from 1331 to 1339, are mainly in logic, where he was extremely influential, particularly in Italy. The *Regulae solvendi sophismata* [1335] (ed. 1494, etc.) consists in six chapters: on insolubles (tr. Spade 1979); on knowing and doubting (tr. CTMPT I); on relative pronouns; on beginning and ceasing; on maxima and minima (tr. Longeway 1984); and on place, quantity, and quality. His two other principal works are the *De sensu composito et diviso* (ed. 1494, etc.; tr. CTMPT I) and the *Sophismata* (ed. 1494, etc.; a provisional ed. by Pironet is available on the internet). Other works include a treatise on consequences, *Juxta hunc textum* (internet ed. Pironet); a *Sophismata asinina* (ed. Pironet 1994); and a beginner's guide to definitions in natural philosophy, the *Termini naturales* (unedited). No theological works are extant.

Secondary sources. Boh, "Epistemic and Alethic Iteration" (1984); Buzzetti, "Linguaggio e ontologia" (1992); Lecq, "Necessity" (1983); Pasnau, "Knowledge" (1995); Spade, "Manuscripts" (1989); Sylla, "Medieval Quantifications" (1971); Weisheipl, "Repertorium" (1969); Wilson, *William Heytesbury* (1956/1960); BCPMA (Longeway); DMA (de Libera); ODNB (Ashworth); REP (Longeway); SEP (Longeway); Weijers.

WILLIAM HOTHUM b. Yorkshire, *ca.* 1245; d. Dijon, 1298. Early English Thomist. Dominican friar. Studied theology in Oxford by 1269. Lectured on the *Sentences* in Paris in the late 1270s, becoming regent master there in 1280–2. Dominican provincial minister in England in 1282–7, during which time he was perhaps active teaching at Oxford, and was directly involved in conflicts with John Pecham over Thomism. Subsequently appointed to a second term as master in Paris, which he never began, perhaps because he was busy with diplomatic missions for the English king, with which his later years were much occupied. Elected to a second term as English provincial in 1290–6, and subsequently archbishop of Dublin in 1296–8. Of his academic writings very little survives: aside from a few sermons, there is only a set of seventeen quodlibetal questions [1280] (unedited), and perhaps a *De anima* commentary ascribed to a Guillelmus Hedonensis (unedited).

Secondary sources. Hinnebusch, *Early English Friars Preachers* (1951); Kaeppeli; ODNB (Haines); Roensch.

WILLIAM DE LA MARE (de Mara) b. England; *fl.* 1270s. Franciscan theologian, known for his early opposition to Thomism. Little is known about his life. Studied theology in Paris, probably under John Pecham, and probably succeeding him as regent master in 1271–2. Thereafter returned to England. Most famous for his *Correctorium fratris Thomae* [1277/9; later revised] (ed. Glorieux 1927, with Richard Knapwell's response; revised text part. ed. Oliva 2005), which comprised a lengthy attack on Aquinas's views. In 1282 the Franciscans made this work mandatory for any friar reading the *Summa theologiae*. By 1284, there were four point-by-point Dominican responses, each known as a *Correctorium corruptorii*. William's other principal extant works are his *Sentences* commentary [1268–70] (ed. Kraml 1989–2001), a set of disputed questions [1274] (unedited), and several studies of the Hebrew and Greek texts of the Bible (unedited).

Secondary sources. Creytens, "Littérature des correctoires" (1942); Heynck, "Datierung" (1967); FA; ODNB (Marenbon).

WILLIAM OF LUCCA b. Lucca (Tuscany); d. 1178. Italian scholar. Studied in northern France, under the influence of the Porretani. Returned to teach in Lucca and Bologna, where he is buried. The only extant work ascribed with certainty is the first part of a commentary on pseudo-Dionysius's *De divinis nominibus* [1169–77] (ed. Gastaldelli

1983), which bears the influence of both Gilbert of Poitiers and John Scottus Eriugena. Perhaps also by this William is a *Summa dialectice artis* (ed. Pozzi 1975), much influenced by Peter Abaelard. Ascribed to that same author is a *De arithmetica compendiose tractata* (ed. Arrighi 1964).

Secondary sources. Jeauneau, "Commentaire sur les Noms Divins" (2000); Dronke.

WILLIAM OF MACCLESFIELD b. Macclesfield; d. Canterbury, 1303. Early English Thomist. Dominican friar. Studied theology at Paris in the early 1290s, then at Oxford, incepting there as master *ca.* 1298. Generally credited with the authorship of the *Correctorium* "*Quaestione*" [*ca.* 1284] (ed. Müller 1954), a response to William de la Mare, which suggests he was studying at Oxford well before his theological studies in Paris. Also extant and probably William's are questions on the prologue and Bk. I of the *Sentences* (unedited), and some disputed questions (unedited).

Secondary sources. Jordan, "Controversy" (1982); Schabel and Friedman, "Trinitarian Theology V" (2005); DMA (Bonino); Kaeppeli; ODNB (Marenbon); Roensch.

WILLIAM OF MIDDLETON (Milton, de Militonia, de Meliton) d. *ca.* 1257/60. Franciscan theologian. Studied theology under Alexander of Hales at Paris, becoming regent master there in 1248–53, and then at Cambridge in 1253–6. His extant works include various sets of disputed questions, including a set on the sacraments (ed. Piana and Gál 1961), a treatise on the Mass (ed. Lampen 1931), and a great many biblical commentaries (unedited). Involved in completing Alexander's *Summa* from 1255, but died before it was finished.

Secondary sources. DS (Van Dijk); FA; Glorieux; ODNB (d'Avray).

WILLIAM MILVERLEY *fl. ca.* 1400. English logician. Oxford arts master, a proponent of metaphysical realism, whose logical treatises circulated widely in England and on the continent. The only one of these to be edited is the *Compendium de quinque universalibus* (part. ed. Conti 1990).

Secondary sources. Ashworth and Spade, "Logic in Late Medieval Oxford" (1992); Emden; ODNB (Fletcher).

WILLIAM OF MOERBEKE b. Belgium, *ca.* 1215; d. Corinth, 1286. Prolific Aristotelian translator. Joined the Dominican order as a youth, probably entering the convent at Louvain. Living in Greece by 1260, and probably from much earlier. Confessor to the pope in Viterbo *ca.* 1267–78. Archbishop of Corinth in 1278–86. Responsible for new or revised translations from the Greek of practically the whole Aristotelian corpus [mainly 1260s; see Appendix B1] (ed. *Aristoteles Latinus* 1953–), along with various Greek commentators (ed. Verbeke *et al.*, in *Corpus latinum* 1957–), Proclus's *Elementatio theologica* [1268] (ed. Boese 1987), and the works of Archimedes. It is no longer supposed that William had a close relationship with Aquinas.

Secondary sources. Brams, *Riscoperta di Aristotele* (2003); Brams and Vanhamel (eds.), *Guillaume de Moerbeke* (1989); Dod, "Aristoteles Latinus" (1982); Grabmann, *Guglielmo di Moerbeke* (1946); Minio-Paluello, *Opuscula* (1972); DSB (Minio-Paluello); DMA (Flüeler); Kaeppeli.

WILLIAM OF NOTTINGHAM b. *ca.* 1282; d. 1336. Franciscan theologian. Master at Oxford *ca.* 1312–14, provincial minister of the English Franciscans in 1316–30. Philosophical writings include a *Sentences* commentary [1306–8] (unedited except for fragments, including IV.8–13 [on the Eucharist] ed. Barbarić 1976). Various biblical studies are also extant. To be distinguished from an earlier William of Nottingham, also a Franciscan, and also English minister provincial [1240–54].

Secondary sources. Friedman, "Trinitarian Theology" (2001); Longpré, "Le commentaire sur les *Sentences*" (1929); Meier, "*Distinctio formalis*" (1930); Schmaus, "De aeternitate mundi" (1932), "Neue Mitteilungen" (1932); Smalley, "Which William?" (1954); BBK (Wöhrer); FA.

WILLIAM OF OCKHAM (Occam) b. Ockham (Surrey), *ca.* 1287; d. Munich, 1347. Brilliantly innovative theologian and philosopher, the inceptor of late medieval nominalism. Joined the Franciscan order as a youth, probably studying at the London convent. Began his theological studies *ca.* 1310, either in London or Oxford. Eventually sent to Oxford, lecturing on the *Sentences* in 1317–19 and subsequently the Bible. Lectured at a Franciscan *studium*, probably in London, in 1321–4, without incepting as regent master. Summoned to Avignon in 1324 to respond to charges of heretical teaching. Various lists of propositions were drawn up, but no formal condemnation was ever made. While in Avignon, Ockham and several other Franciscans, including Michael of Cesena, minister general of the order, concluded that John XXII's position on apostolic poverty was heretical, and they fled Avignon in 1328 for Italy and then Germany, taking refuge with Emperor Ludwig of Bavaria. Ockham, excommunicated, spent the remainder of his life at the Franciscan convent in Munich.

Ockham's work divides in half. The first half consists in the scholastic theology and philosophy he wrote in England and Avignon (all ed. *Opera philosophica et theologica* 1967–89), the most important of which are his initial *Sentences* lectures, known as the *Reportatio* (covering Bks. II–IV); his revised version of Bk. I, known as the *Ordinatio* [1321/4] (part. tr. Boehner 1990; Spade, *Five Texts* 1994; CTMPT II–III); seven *Quodlibeta* [1321/4; rev. in Avignon] (tr. Freddoso and Kelley 1991); the enormously influential *Summa logicae* [*ca.* 1323] (pt. I tr. Loux 1974; pt. II tr. Freddoso and Schuurman 1980; pt. III–2 tr. Longeway 2007; pt. III–3 part. tr. CTMPT I); commentaries on the *ars vetus* (*Isagoge*, tr. Kluge 1973–4); the *Sophistical Refutations* [all 1321/4]; and a series of studies on Aristotle's physics [1321/4] (*Brevis summa* tr. Davies 1989). Other philosophically important works from this period are treatises on the Eucharist and on quantity [both 1323/4] (both tr. Birch 1930); a study of the connection of the virtues [1319] (tr. Wood 1997); a question on the eternity of the world (tr. Bosley and Tweedale, in *Basic Issues* 2006); and a treatise on divine foreknowledge (tr. Adams and Kretzmann 1983).

The second half of Ockham's literary career, from the time he left Avignon until his death, is concerned exclusively with political and ecclesiastical issues. The principal works from this period are the *Opus nonaginta dierum* [1332/4] (tr. Kilcullen and Scott 2001); *Epistola ad fratres minores* [1334] (tr. McGrade and Kilcullen 1995); *Octo quaestiones de potestate papae* [1340–1] (part. tr. McGrade and Kilcullen 1995); *Breviloquium* [1341/2] (tr. McGrade and Kilcullen 1992); *De imperatorum et pontificum potestate* [1346–7] (tr. Brett 1998); and the *Dialogus* [1334/46] (part. tr. CTMPT II). The last is available on the internet in a critical edition with translation (ed. and tr. Kilcullen *et al.*). The rest is printed in the *Opera politica* (ed. Offler *et al.* 1940–97).

Secondary sources. Spade (ed.), *Cambridge Companion* (1999); Beckmann, *Bibliographie* (1992); Adams, *William Ockham* (1987); Freppert, *Basis of Morality* (1988); Hirvonen, *Passions* (2004); Goddu, *Physics* (1984); Knysh, *Political Ockhamism* (1996), *Ockham Hermeneutics* (1997); McGrade, *Political Thought* (1974/2002); Maurer, *Philosophy of William of Ockham* (1999); Michon, *Nominalisme* (1994); Miethke, *Weg zur Sozialphilosophie* (1969); Moody, *Logic* (1935); Müller, *Handeln in einer kontingenten Welt* (2000); Panaccio, *Les mots* (1991), *Ockham on Concepts* (2004); Pasnau, *Theories of Cognition* (1997); Shogimen, *Political Discourse* (2007); Tachau, *Vision and Certitude* (1988); BCPMA (Noone); FA; ODNB (Courtenay); REP (Panaccio); SEP (Spade); Weijers.

WILLIAM OF PAGULA b. prob. Paull (Yorkshire), *ca.* 1290; d. 1332 (?). Canon lawyer and theologian. Studied canon law at Oxford, receiving his doctorate *ca.* 1320. Vicar of the church of Winkfield (Salisbury) from 1314 until his death. Authored three treatises on practical theology (all unedited): a popular manual of pastoral theology, the *Oculus sacerdotis* [1320s] (tr. Mirk 1868/1975); the *Summa summarum* [1320/3], a hefty treatise on the responsibilities of the clergy; and the even heftier *Summa praelatorum* [1320/3], which was intended as a comprehensive sourcebook for parish priests, but did not achieve the popularity of the first two works. Also composed two recensions of a *Speculum regis* for Edward III [1331–2] (ed. Moisant 1891; tr. Nederman, in *Political Thought* 2002).

Secondary sources. Boyle, "*Summa summarum*" (1965); Nederman and Neville, "Origins of the *Speculum regis*" (1997); ODNB (Nederman).

WILLIAM PENBYGULL (Penbegyll) b. Exeter; d. Oxford, 1420. Oxford follower of John Wyclif's controversial realism. Studied at Oxford, becoming master of arts. Fellow at Exeter College in 1399; rector in 1406–7. Studied theology by 1417. Extant works are treatises *De universalibus* (ed. Conti 1982) and *Divisio entis in praedicamenta* (unedited).

Secondary sources. Conti, "Categories and Universals" 2008; Lohr; SEP (Conti).

WILLIAM PERALDUS b. Perault, *ca.* 1200; d. Lyon, 1261. Dominican moral theologian. Studied at Paris, becoming a friar there and subsequently living at the convent in Lyon. Author of the enormously influential *Summa de vitiis* [*ca.* 1236] and *Summa de virtutibus* [*ca.* 1248], compendia for preachers and confessors that often circulated together as a single work (ed. 1497, etc.) and would be loosely adapted into Middle English as the anonymous *Book for a Simple and Devout Woman* (ed. Diekstra 1998). Other extant works are the *De eruditione religiosorum* [*ca.* 1260/5] (ed. 1512, etc.) and *De eruditione principum* [*ca.* 1265] (ed. in Thomas Aquinas, *Opera omnia* 1852–73).

Secondary sources. Dondaine, "Vie et œuvres" (1948); Verweij, "*Summa de virtutibus*" (2006); Wenzel, "Continuing Life" (1992); Kaeppeli.

WILLIAM OF PETER GODIN b. Bayonne (Gascony), *ca.* 1260; d. Avignon, 1336. Early French Thomist. Joined the Dominican order at an early age. Studied at Béziers in 1279 and Montpellier in 1284–7. Subsequently lectured at various Dominican houses of study in France. Sent to Paris to acquire a doctorate in theology in 1292, eventually incepting as master in 1304–6. Subsequently served as lector at the papal curia in 1306–12. His later years were occupied with ecclesiastical affairs for the Dominican order and for the papacy. Appointed cardinal in 1312 and cardinal-bishop of Sabina in 1317. Much involved in various inquiries into heresy. Principal philosophical work is his *Sentences* commentary, known as the *Lectura Thomasina* [1299–1301] (unedited). Also extant are a *Quaestio de individuationis principio* [*ca.* 1305] (unedited) and a *Tractatus de causa immediata ecclesiastice potestatis* [1318] (ed. McCready 1982), which should likely be ascribed to William rather than to Peter of Palude.

Secondary sources. Decker, *Gotteslehre* (1967); Fournier, "Cardinal Guillaume" (1925); Goris and Pickavé, "Lectura Thomasina" (1998); Grabmann, "Kardinal Guilelmus" (1926); Kaeppeli; Roensch.

WILLIAM OF RUBIO b. Spain, *ca.* 1290. Franciscan theologian. Student of Francis of Marchia. Lectured on the *Sentences* either in Paris or perhaps Barcelona [1324/32] (ed. 1518). Served from 1334 as provincial minister of Aragon. Quodlibetal questions are attested but not extant.

Secondary sources. Duba, "Continental Franciscan *Quodlibeta*" (2007); Rubert Candáu, *La filosofia del siglo XIV* (1952); Schabel, "Parisian Commentaries" (2002); FA.

WILLIAM OF ST. AMOUR b. Burgundy, *ca.* 1200; d. Burgundy, 1272. Paris theologian and leading controversialist against the mendicant orders. Studied at Paris in the 1220s, becoming master of arts in 1228. Doctor of canon law by 1238; master of theology by 1250. William was a leader in the anti-mendicant movement of the 1250s, but with Alexander IV's election as pope in 1254, the friars were again ascendant, and Willliam was suspended from teaching in 1255. This gave rise to his most famous work, the virulently anti-mendicant *De periculis novissimorum temporum* [1256] (ed. and tr. Geltner 2007), which precipitated an inquiry that led to the book's being burned and William's excommunication and exile from Paris. Various briefer anti-mendicant works are extant (ed. Traver 2003; ed. Traver, in "Disputed Questions" 1995), as well as a lengthy *Collectiones catholicae et canonicae scripturae* [1266] (ed. 1632/1997). William seems not to be the author of extant commentaries on the *Prior* and *Posterior Analytics* (unedited) once ascribed to him. The anti-mendicant *Liber de Antichristo* (ed. Martène and Durand 1733/1968) should be ascribed to his student, Nicholas of Lisieux.

Secondary sources. Dawson, "Apostolic Tradition" (1978); Dufeil, *Guillaume de Saint-Amour* (1972); Faral, "Responsiones" (1950–1); Fleming, "Collations" (1965); BBK (Menzel); DS (Delhaye); Lohr; Glorieux.

WILLIAM OF ST. THIERRY (a Sancto Theodorico) b. Liège, *ca.* 1080; d. Signy (Ardennes), *ca.* 1148. Benedictine theologian and mystic. Studied at cathedral schools in Liège and Rheims. Joined the Benedictine monastery of St. Nicaise near Rheims *ca.* 1100. Elected abbot of the St. Thierry monastery near Rheims in 1121–35; subsequently retired to the Cistercian abbey at Signy. His numerous works have been edited in PL 180; a critical edition is in progress (ed. Verdeyen and van Burink 1989–). His spiritual writings include the *Epistola ad fratres de Monte Dei* (also known as *De vita solitaria* or *The Golden*

Epistle) [1144] (tr. Berkeley and Déchanet 1971), and the treatises *De Deo contemplando* (tr. Penelope 1971); *De natura et dignitate amoris* (tr. Davis 1981); *Speculum fidei* (tr. Davis 1979); and *Aenigma fidei* (tr. Anderson 1974). William wrote several more theoretical treatises, including a *De natura corporis et animae* (ed. and [Fr] tr. Lemoine 1988; tr. McGinn, *Three Treatises* 1977) and a *De sacramento altaris*, and also polemical treatises against Peter Abaelard and William of Conches. Also extant are commentaries on the Song of Songs and on Romans (tr. Hasbrouck and Anderson 1980).

Secondary sources. Sergent, "Bibliography" (2004); Bell, *Image and Likeness* (1984); Baudelet, *Expérience spirituelle* (1985); Carfantan (ed.), *William, Abbot of St. Thierry* (1987); Déchanet, *William of St. Thierry* (1972); Verdeyen, *La théologie mystique* (1990), *Guillaume de Saint-Thierry* (2003); Vuillaume, "La connaissance de Dieu" (1995); BBK (Lautenschläger).

WILLIAM OF SHERWOOD b. Nottinghamshire, 1200/5; d. 1266/72. Influential logician. Probably studied at Oxford, where he became master of arts by 1249. Treasurer of Lincoln from *ca.* 1255. The two works ascribed to Willliam with certainty are his *Introductiones in logicam* (ed. Brands and Kann 1995; tr. Kretzmann 1966/1975) and *Syncategoremata* (ed. O'Donnell 1941; tr. Kretzmann 1968). Possibly also by William are treatises on *Insolubilia* (ed. Roure 1970) and on *Obligationes* (ed. Green 1963).

Secondary sources. Braakhuis, "Views" (1977); Jacobi, *Modalbegriffe* (1980); Kirchhoff, *Syntcategoremata* (2008); Pinborg and Ebbesen, "Thirteenth-Century Notes" (1984); Spade and Stump, "*Obligationes*" (1983); Stump, "Treatise on Obligations" (1980); BCPMA (Longeway); DMA (de Libera); ODNB (Ashworth); REP (Longeway); Weijers.

WILLIAM OF SOISSONS *fl.* 1140s. Logician. Student of John of Salisbury and Adam of Balsham. Described by his student William of Tyre as a man of halting speech but sharp mind. No works are extant.

WILLIAM OF WARE b. Hertfordshire; *fl.* 1290–1305. Franciscan theologian; apparently the teacher of Scotus. Entered the Franciscan order at a young age. Studied at Oxford and lectured on the *Sentences* there, but without incepting as master. Perhaps lectured on the *Sentences* at Paris as well. Only work ascribed with certainty is the *Sentences* commentary [1290/1305], extant in three or perhaps four different redactions (unedited except fragments).

Secondary sources. Bissen, "L'incarnation" (1934); Daniels, "Menschliche Erkenntnis" (1913); Hödl, "Sentenzenkommentar" (1990); Gál, "Doctrina philosophica" (1954); Ledoux, "De gratia" (1930); Longpré, "Maîtres franciscains" (1922); Muscat, "De unitate Dei" (1927); Schabel and Friedman, "Trinitarian Theology IV" (2004); BCPMA (Cross); FA; ODNB (Marenbon).

WITELO b. Silesia, *ca.* 1230; d. *ca.* 1290. Theologian and philosopher, best known for his work in optics. Studied the arts in Paris in the 1250s and canon law at Padua from 1262/3 to 1268. Spent time at the papal court in Viterbo from 1268. Best known for his *Perspectiva* [1270/8] (Bks. I–III ed. and tr. Unguru 1977–91; Bk. V ed. and tr. Smith

1983), a study in ten books of the optics and psychology of vision that is heavily indebted to Ibn al-Haytham. Other extant works are the *De natura daemonum* and the *De causa primaria poenitentiae* (both ed. Burchardt 1979).

Secondary sources. Baeumker, *Witelo* (1908/1991); Birkenmajer, "Études sur Witelo" (1920–5); Lindberg, "Alhazen's Theory of Vision" (1967), "Lines of Influence" (1971), *Theories of Vision* (1976).

YAḤYĀ IBN ʿADĪ (Abū Zakariyāʾ) b. Takrit (Iraq), 893; d. 974. Translator and logician. Jacobite Christian, moved to Baghdad as a youth where he studied with al-Fārābī and Abū Bishr Mattā. An important translator of Greek philosophical texts from Syriac into Arabic, and the author of numerous original treatises, including the ethical treatise *Tahdhīb al-akhlāq* (*Reformation of Morals*) (ed. and tr. Griffith 2002); a treatise on God's unity, the *Maqāla fī al-tawḥīd* (ed. Khalīl 1980); a treatise on free action (ed. and tr. Pines and Schwarz 1979); and a treatise *On the Possible* (ed. Ehrig-Eggert 1989; part. tr. McGinnis and Reisman, in *Classical Arabic Philosophy* 2007). Collections are available of other works both philosophical (ed. Khulayfāt 1988) and apologetical (ed. Périer 1920). An anti-Nestorian treatise has also been edited (ed. and [Fr] tr. Platti 1981).

Secondary sources. Endress, *Works* (1977); Ehrig-Eggert, *Die Abhandlung* (1990); Fakhry, *History* (2004); Platti, *Yahya Ibn ʿAdi* (1983); REP (Inati).

BIBLIOGRAPHY OF PRIMARY SOURCES

Included among the primary texts are all cited works written before 1800, including manuscripts, with the exception of modern multi-author anthologies, which are listed among the secondary sources under the editor's name. Authors prior to 1600 are organized by first name, unless that name is not standardly used. The bibliography does not generally list individual works published as part of collected editions. For information on editions and translations of specific works, consult Appendix C. For more information on medieval translations, consult Appendix B.

Abbo of Fleury. *De syllogismis hypotheticis*, ed. F. Schupp (Leiden: Brill, 1997).

    Opera inedita, ed. A. van de Vyver and R. Raes (Bruges: De Tempel, 1966).

    Questiones grammaticales, ed. A. Guerreau-Jalabert (Paris: Les Belles Lettres, 1982).

ʿAbd al-Jabbār. *Al-Mughnī fī abwāb al-tawḥīd wa-al-ʿadl* (Cairo: Wizārat al-Thaqāfah wa-al-Irshād al-Qawmī, 1960–).

al-Abharī. *Hidāyat al-ḥikma*, ed. U. Mumtāz al-Dīn (Dhaka: Imdādīya Lāʾibrayrī, 1960–5).

    Al-Isāghūjī fī al-manṭiq, tr. E. Calverley, in *The Macdonald Presentation Volume* (Princeton, NJ: Princeton University Press, 1933) 75–85.

Abner of Burgos. *Mostrador de justicia*, ed. W. Mettmann (Opladen: Westdeutscher Verlag, 1994–6).

    Ofrenda de Zelos (Minhat Kenaʾot) und Libro de la Ley, ed. W. Mettman (Opladen: Westdeutscher Verlag, 1990).

    Tesuvot la-Meharef: Spanische Fassung, ed. W. Mettmann (Opladen: Westdeutscher Verlag, 1998).

Abraham Abulafia. *The Path of the Names: Writings*, tr. D. Meltzer *et al.* (Berkeley, CA: Tree Books, 1976).

Abraham bar Ḥiyya. *Hegyon ha-Nefesh ha-Azuvah*, ed. G. Wigoder (Jersualem: Mosad Bialik, 1971).

    The Meditation of the Sad Soul, tr. G. Wigoder (London: Routledge and Kegan Paul, 1969).

    Megillat ha-Megalleh, ed. A. Poznanski (Berlin: Mekitzei Nirdamim, 1924).

    La obra enciclopédica, ed. J. M. Millás Vallicrosa (Madrid: Consejo Superior de Investigaciones Científicas, Instituto Arias Montano, 1952).

    La obra Séfer Hesbón mahlekot ha-kokabim, ed. and tr. J. M. Millás Vallicrosa (Barcelona: Consejo Superior de Investigaciones Científicas, 1959).

    Sefer ha-ʿIbur, ed. H. Filipowski (London: Longmans, 1851).

    Sphaera mundi (Basel: Petrus, 1546).

Abraham ibn Daud. *The Book of Tradition (Sefer ha-qabbalah)*, ed. G. D. Cohen (Philadelphia, PA: Jewish Publication Society of America, 1967).

    The Exalted Faith, ed. and tr. N. M. Samuelson and G. Weiss (Rutherford, NJ: Fairleigh Dickinson University Press, 1986).

Abraham ibn Ezra. *Abraham Ibn Ezra Reader: Annotated Texts with Introductions and Commentaries*, ed. I. Levin (New York: Israel Matz, 1985).

The Book of Reasons: A Parallel Hebrew–English Critical Edition of the Two Versions of the Text, ed. and tr. S. Sela (Leiden: Brill, 2007).

The Commentary of Ibn Ezra on Isaiah, ed. and tr. M. Friedländer (London: Society of Hebrew Literature, 1873; repr. New York: Feldheim, 1960).

The Commentary of Rabbi Abraham Ibn Ezra on Hosea, ed. and tr. A. Lipshitz (New York: Sepher-Hermon Press, 1988).

Ibn Ezra's Commentary on the Pentateuch, tr. H. N. Strickman et al. (New York: Menorah, 1988–2004).

Kitvei R. Avraham ibn Ezra (Jerusalem: Makor, 1970), 4 vols.

Le livre des fondements astrologiques, tr. J. Halbronn (Paris: Retz, 1977).

The Religious Poems of Abraham Ibn Ezra (Jerusalem: Israel Academy of Sciences and Humanities, 1975).

Reshit Hokhmah (The Beginning of Wisdom), ed. and trans. R. Levy and F. Cantera (Baltimore, MD: Johns Hopkins University Press, 1939).

Twilight of a Golden Age: Selected Poems of Abraham Ibn Ezra, tr. L. J. Weinberger (Tuscaloosa: University of Alabama Press, 1997).

Yesod Mora ve-Sod Torah, ed. J. Cohen and U. Simon (Ramat-Gan: Bar-Ilan University Press, 2002).

Abraham Maimonides. *The Guide to Serving God*, ed. and tr. Y. Wincelberg (Jerusalem: Feldheim, 2008).

Kitāb Kifāyat al-ʿābidīn (Part Two, Volume Two), The Arabic Original with an Introduction and an Annotated Hebrew Translation, ed. and tr. N. Dana (Ramat-Gan: Bar-Ilan University, 1989).

Maʿaseh nisim, ed. B. Goldberg. (Paris: Y. Bril, 1867).

Milhamot ha-Shem, ed. R. Margaliot (Jerusalem: Mosad Harav Kook, 1953).

A Treatise in Defence of the Pietists, tr. S. D. Goitein, Journal of Jewish Studies 16 (1965) 105–14.

Abū Ḥanīfa. *Al-ʿĀlim wa-al-mutaʿallim*, ed. M. Z. al-Kawthari (Cairo: Maṭbaʿat al-Anwar, 1949).

Al-Fiqh al-akbar fī al-tawḥīd (Cairo: al-Maṭbaʿah al-ʿĀmirah, 1907).

Iman Abu Hanifa's al-Fiqh al-akbar Explained, tr. A.-R. Ibn Yusuf (Santa Barbara, CA: White Thread Press, 2007).

Abū Maʿshar. *The Introduction To Astrology: Together With The Medieval Latin Translation of Adelard of Bath*, ed. C. Burnett et al. (Leiden: Brill, 1994).

Introductorium ad astronomiam Albumasaris abalachi, tr. Hermann of Carinthia (Augsburg, 1489).

Kitāb al-madkhal al-kabīr ilā ʿilm aḥkām al-nujūm = Liber introductorii maioris ad scientiam judiciorum astrorum, ed. R. Lemay (Naples: Istituto universitario Orientale, 1995–).

On Historical Astrology: The Book of Religions and Dynasties (On the Great Conjunctions), ed. K. Yamamoto and C. Burnett (Leiden: Brill, 2000).

Abū Muḥammad ʿAbdallāh Ibn Rushd. *On Whether the Active Intellect Unites with the Material Intellect whilst it is Clothed with the Body*, ed. [Arabic, Hebrew, Latin] and tr. C. Burnett and M. Zonta, Archives d'histoire doctrinale et littéraire du moyen âge 67 (2000) 295–335.

Abū Saʿīd al-Sīrāfī. *Sharḥ Kitab Sibawayh*, ed. R. ʿAbd al-Tawwāb et al. (Cairo: al-Hayʾah al-Miṣrīya al-ʿĀmmah lil-Kitāb, 1986–).

Abū Tammām. *An Ismaili Heresiography: The "Bāb al-shaytān" from Abū Tammām's Kitāb al-shajara*, ed. and tr. W. Madlung and P. E. Walker (Leiden: Brill, 1998).

Kitāb al-īḍāḥ, ed. A. Tāmir (Beirut: al-Maṭbaʿah al-Kāthūlikīyah, 1965) (formerly ascribed to Shihāb al-Dīn Abū Firās).

Abū Wafāʾ al-Mubashshir ibn Fātik. *Liber philosophorum moralium antiquorum*, tr. John of Procida (?), ed. E. Franceschini, *Atti del Reale Istituto Veneto di Scienze, Lettere ed Arti* 91 (1931–2) 393–597.

Abū Zayd al-Balkhī. *Maṣaliḥ al-abdān wa-al-anfus*, ed. M. al-Misrī (Cairo: Maʿhad al-Makhṭūṭāt al-ʿArabīyah, 2005).

Accursius. *Glossa in Codicem [Glossa ordinaria]* (Venice, 1488; repr. Turin: Ex officina Erasmiana, 1968).

Achard of St. Victor. *De discretione animae et spiritus et mentis*, ed. N. M. Häring, *Mediaeval Studies* 22 (1960) 174–91.

    Sermons inédits, ed. J. Châtillon (Paris: Vrin, 1970).

    L'unité de Dieu et la pluralité des créatures, ed. E. Martineau *et al.* (Saint-Lambert des Bois: Authentica, 1987).

    Works, tr. H. Feiss (Kalamazoo, MI: Cistercian Publications, 2001).

Adam of Balsham. *Ars disserendi (Dialectica Alexandri)*, ed. L. Minio-Paluello (Rome: Edizioni di Storia e Letteratura, 1956).

    De utensilibus ad domum regendam, in B. Hauréau (ed.) *Notices et extraits de quelques manuscrits latins de la Bibliothèque Nationale* (Paris, 1890–3) vol. III.

Adam of Buckfield. *Sententia super secundum Metaphysicae*, ed. A. Maurer, in J. R. O'Donnell (ed.) *Nine Mediaeval Thinkers: A Collection of Hitherto Unedited Texts* (Toronto: Pontifical Institute of Mediaeval Studies, 1955) 99–144.

Adam Marsh. "Adae de Marisco epistolae," ed. J. S. Brewer, *Monumenta Franciscana* 1 (1858) 77–489.

Adam Wodeham. *Lectura secunda in librum primum Sententiarum*, ed. R. Wood and G. Gál (St. Bonaventure, NY: St. Bonaventure University, 1990).

    Super quattuor libros sententiarum, ed J. Major (Paris, 1512).

    Tractatus de indivisibilibus, ed. R. Wood (Dordrecht: Kluwer, 1988).

Adelard of Bath. *Conversations with his Nephew: On the Same and the Different, Questions on Natural Science, and On Birds*, ed. and tr. C. Burnett *et al.* (Cambridge: Cambridge University Press, 1998).

    Regulae abaci, ed. B. Boncompagni, *Bollettino di bibliografia e di storia delle scienze matematiche e fisiche* 14 (1881) 1–134.

Adhemar of St. Ruf. "The Tractatus de Trinitate of Adhemar of Saint-Ruf (Valence)," ed. N. M. Haring, *Archives d'histoire doctrinale et littéraire du moyen âge* 31 (1964) 111–206.

Aelred of Rievaulx. *De anima*, ed. C. H. Talbot (London: Warburg Institute, 1952).

    Dialogue on the Soul, tr. C. H. Talbot (Kalamazoo, MI: Cistercian Publications, 1981).

    The Mirror of Charity, tr. G. Webb and A. Walker (London: Mowbray, 1962).

    Opera omnia, ed. A. Hoste and C. H. Talbot (Turnhout: Brepols, 1971–).

    Sermones, ed. G. Raciti (Turnhout: Brepols, 1989).

    Spiritual Friendship: A New Translation, tr. M. F. Williams (Scranton, PA: University of Scranton Press, 1994).

Aimoin de Fleury. *Vita et passio sancti Abbonis*, ed. R.-H. Bautier *et al.* (Paris: CNRS, 2004).

Alan of Lille. *Anticlaudianus*, ed. R. Bossuat (Paris: Vrin, 1955).

    Anticlaudianus: Or the Good and Perfect Man, tr. J. Sheridan (Toronto: Pontifical Institute of Mediaeval Studies, 1973).

    Ars praedicandi, in J.-P. Migne (ed.) *Patrologiae cursus completus: series latina* (Paris, 1844–91) vol. CCX.

    De planctu naturae, ed. N. M. Häring, *Studi Medievali* 19 (1978) 797–879.

    Liber poenitentialis, ed. J. Longère (Leuven: Nauwelaerts, 1965).

    The Plaint of Nature, tr. J. Sheridan (Toronto: Pontifical Institute of Mediaeval Studies, 1980).

Regulae caelestis iuris, ed. N. M. Häring, *Archives d'histoire doctrinale et littéraire du moyen âge* 48 (1981) 97–226.

Summa "Quoniam homines", ed. P. Glorieux, *Archives d'histoire doctrinale et littéraire du moyen âge* 20 (1953) 113–364.

Textes inédits, ed. M.-T. d'Alverny (Paris: Vrin, 1965).

Albert the Great. *Commentary on Dionysius' Mystical Theology*, in S. Tugwell (tr.) *Albert and Thomas: Selected Writings* (New York: Paulist Press, 1988).

Opera omnia, ed. B. Geyer *et al.* [Cologne] (Münster: Aschendorff, 1951–).

Opera omnia, ed. E. Borgnet (Paris: Vivès, 1890–9).

Opera omnia, ed. P. Jammy (Lyon, 1651).

Albert of Orlamünde. *Philosophia pauperum* (Venice, 1496).

Albert of Saxony. *Expositio et Questiones in Aristotelis libros Physicorum ad Albertum de Saxonia attributae*, ed. B. Patar (Louvain-la-Neuve: Peeters, 1999).

Perutilis logica (Venice, 1522; repr. Hildesheim: Olms, 1974).

Perutilis logica, tr. A. Muñoz García (Maracaibo: La Universidad del Zulia, 1988).

Quaestiones in artem veterem, ed. A. Muñoz García (Maracaibo: La Universidad del Zulia, 1988).

Questiones circa logicam, ed. M. J. Fitzgerald (Leiden: Brill, 2002).

Questiones subtilissime in libros Aristotelis De celo et mundo (Venice, 1492; repr. Hildesheim: Olms, 1986).

Questiones subtilissime in libros de generatione (Venice, 1505; repr. Frankfurt: Minerva, 1970).

Questiones subtilissime super libros posteriorum (Venice, 1497; repr. Hildesheim: Olms, 1986).

Sophismata (Paris, 1502; repr. Hildesheim: Olms, 1975).

Tractatus proportionum, ed. H. L. L. Busard (Vienna: Springer in Komm, 1971).

Alcuin. *Alcuin of York, c. A.D. 732 to 804: His Life and Letters*, ed. S. Allott (York: W. Sessions, 1974).

Contra haeresim Felicis, ed. G. Blumenshine (Vatican: Biblioteca Apostolica Vaticana, 1980).

De orthographia, ed. S. Bruni (Florence: SISMEL, Edizioni del Galluzzo, 1997).

Epistolae Karolini aevi, ed. E. Dümmler (Berlin: Weidmann, 1895).

The Rhetoric of Alcuin and Charlemagne, ed. and tr. W. S. Howell (Princeton, NJ: Princeton University Press, 1941).

Alexander of Alexandria. *Commentarium De anima* (Oxford, 1481).

Commentarium in Metaphysicam (Venice, 1572) (published as Alexander of Hales).

Responsio ad Ubertinum de Casale, in A. Chiappini (ed.) "Communitatis Responsio 'Religiosi Viri' ad Rotulum fr. Ubertini de Casali," *Archivum Franciscanum Historicum* 7 (1914) 654–75; 8 (1915) 56–80.

Tractatus de usu paupere, in A. Heysse (ed.) "Ubertini de Casali Opusculum 'Super tribus Sceleribus'," *Archivum Franciscanum Historicum* 10 (1917) 103–74.

Tractatus de usuris, in A. M. Hamelin (ed.) *Un traité de morale économique au XIVe siècle* (Leuven: Nauwelaerts, 1962).

Alexander of Aphrodisias. *On Aristotle's On Coming-to-be and Perishing 2.2–5*, ed. E. Gannagé (London: Duckworth, 2005).

Praeter commentaria scripta minora, ed. I. Bruns (Berlin: Reimer, 1887–92).

Traité de la providence (Peri pronoias), version arabe de Abū Bisr Matta ibn Yūnus, ed. and tr. P. Thillet (Lagrasse: Verdier, 2003).

Alexander of Hales. *Glossa in quattuor libros Sententiarum Petri Lombardi* (Quaracchi: Editiones Collegii S. Bonaventurae, 1951–7).

Quaestiones disputatae "Antequam esset frater" (Quaracchi: Editiones Collegii S. Bonaventurae, 1960).

Alexander of Hales *et al. Summa theologica* (Quaracchi: Editiones Collegii S. Bonaventurae, 1924–48).

Alexander Langeley. "Reportatio super librum primum Sententiarum," ed. R. Edwards (D.Phil. thesis: University of Oxford, 1999).

Alexander Neckam. *Commentum super Martianum,* ed. C. McDonough (Tavarnuzze: SISMEL, Edizioni del Galluzzo, 2006).

    De naturis rerum libri duo, with the Poem of the Same Author, De laudibus divinae sapientiae, ed. T. Wright (London: Longman, 1863).

    Novus Aesopus, ed. G. Garbugino (Genoa: Dipartimento di Archeologia, Filologia classica e loro Tradizioni, 1987).

    Speculum speculationum, ed. R. M. Thomson (London: British Academy, 1988).

    Suppletio defectuum. Alexander Neckam on Plants, Birds and Animals: A Supplement to the Laus Sapientie divine, Book I, ed. and tr. C. McDonough (Tavarnuzze: SISMEL, Edizioni del Galluzzo, 1999).

Alexander of Villa Dei. *Carmen de musica cum glossis,* ed. A. Seay (Colorado Springs, CO: Colorado College Music Press, 1977).

    Doctrinale, ed. D. Reichling (Berlin: A. Hofmann, 1893; repr. New York: Franklin, 1974).

    Ecclesiale, ed. L. R. Lind (Lawrence: University of Kansas Press, 1958).

    Le nombre d'or: étude de chronologie technique suivie du texte de la "Massa compoti" d'Alexandre de Villedieu, ed. and tr. W. E. van Wijk (The Hague: Nijhoff, 1936).

Alfred of Shareshill. *Commentary on the "Metheora" of Aristotle,* ed. J. K. Otte (Leiden: Brill, 1988)

    "Commentary on the pseudo-Aristotelian *De plantis*: A Critical Edition," ed. R. J. Long, *Mediaeval Studies* 47 (1985) 125–67.

    De motu cordis, ed. C. Baeumker (Münster: Aschendorff, 1923).

Alger of Liège. *De misericordia et iustitia,* ed. R. Kretzschmar (Sigmaringen: Thorbecke, 1985).

    De sacramentis corporis et sanguinis dominici (London: Nutt, 1873).

ʿAlī ibn al-ʿAbbās al-Majūsī. *The Complete Medical Art – Kāmil al-ṣināʿa al-ṭibbīyya,* ed. F. Sezgin (Frankfurt: Institute for the History of Arabic-Islamic Sciences, 1985).

    Liber medicinae, sive Regalis dispositio, tr. Stephan of Antioch (Venice, 1492).

    Pantegni, in Constantine the African (tr.) *Opera Omnia Ysaac* (Lyon, 1515).

ʿAllāma al-Ḥillī. *Al-Bāb al-ḥādī ʿashar,* ed. M. Muhaqqiq (Tehran: Muʾassasah-i Muṭālaʿāt-i, 1986).

    Al-Bāb al-ḥādī ʿashar, A Treatise on the Principles of Shīʿite Theology, tr. W. M. Miller (London: Royal Asiatic Society, 1928).

    Kashf al-murād fī Sharḥ tajrīd al-iʿtiqād (Beirut: Muʾassasat al-Aʿlamī, 1988).

Alphonsus Vargas. *Lectura in primum librum Sententiarum,* ed. Thomas de Spilimbergo (Venice, 1490; repr. Meriden Gravure, 1952).

    Quaestiones super libris Aristotelis de anima (Florence, 1477).

Ambrose. *De officiis,* ed. I. J. Davidson (Oxford: Oxford University Press, 2001).

    Opera, ed. K. Schenkl *et al.* (Prague: Tempsky, 1897–).

al-ʿĀmirī. *Feder, Tafel, Mensch: al-ʿĀmirīs Kitāb al-Fuṣūl fī l-maʿālim al-ilāhīya und die arabische Proklos-Rezeption im 10. Jh,* ed. and tr. E. Wakelnig (Leiden: Brill, 2006).

    A Muslim Philosopher on the Soul and its Fate: Al-ʿAmiri's Kitāb al-Amad ʿalā al-abad, ed. and tr. E. K. Rowson (New Haven, CT: American Oriental Society, 1988).

    Rasāʾil-i Abū al-Ḥasan ʿĀmirī, ed. S. Khalīfāt (Tehran: Markaz-i Nashr-i Dānishgāhī, 1996).

Ammonius. *In Porphyrii Isagogen sive V Voces,* ed. A. Busse (*Commentaria in Aristotelem Graeca* IV.3) (Berlin: Reimer, 1891).

Andrew of Neufchateau. *Primum scriptum Sententiarum* (Paris: J. Grantion, 1514).

Questions on an Ethics of Divine Commands, ed. J. Idziak (Notre Dame, IN: University of Notre Dame Press, 1997).

Tractatus de immaculata conceptione B. M. Virginis, ed. C. Piana *et al.* (Quaracchi: Editiones Collegii S. Bonaventurae, 1954).

Andrew of St. Victor. *Opera*, ed. C. H. Lohr *et al.* (Turnhout: Brepols, 1986–).

Anonymous. *Book for a Simple and Devout Woman*, ed. F. N. M. Diekstra (Groningen: Forsten, 1998).

Categoriae Decem, ed. L. Minio-Paluello (*Aristoteles Latinus* 1.1–5) (Bruges: Desclée de Brouwer, 1961).

Centiloquium, in William of Ockham, *Opera Philosophica* (St. Bonaventure, NY: St. Bonaventure University, 1988) VII: 384–95.

"The Cloud of Unknowing" and Related Treatises on Contemplative Prayer, ed. P. Hodgson (Salzburg: Institut für Anglistik und Amerikanistik, Universität Salzburg, 1982).

Compendium logicae porretanum, ed. S. Ebbesen *et al.*, *Cahiers de l'Institut du Moyen Age Grec et Latin* 46 (1983) 1–113.

De anima et potentiis eius, ed. R. A. Gauthier, *Revue des sciences philosophiques et théologiques* 66 (1982) 3–55.

De potentiis animae et obiectis, ed. D. A. Callus, *Recherches de théologie ancienne et médiévale* 19 (1952) 131–70.

Dialogus Eberardi et Ratii, ed. N. M. Häring, *Mediaeval Studies* 15 (1953) 243–89.

Glosa "Promisimus", ed. K. M. Fredborg, *Cahiers de l'Institut du Moyen Age Grec et Latin* 70 (1999) 81–228.

Grammatica Porretana, ed. K. M. Fredborg and C. H. Kneepkens, *Cahiers de l'Institut du Moyen Age Grec et Latin* 57 (1988) 11–67.

A Latin Dialogue on the Doctrine of Gilbert of Poitiers, ed. N. M. Häring, *Mediaeval Studies* 15 (1953) 243–89.

Lectura in librum de anima, ed. R. Gauthier (Grottaferrata: Collegii S. Bonaventurae, 1985).

Liber de pomo: versio latina Manfredi, ed. M. Plezia (Warsaw: Academia Scientiarum Polona, 1960).

Liber de spiritu et anima, tr. E. Leiva in B. McGinn (ed.) *Three Treatises on Man: A Cistercian Anthropology* (Kalamazoo, MI: Cistercian Publications, 1977).

Liber sex principiorum, ed. L. Minio-Paluello, *Aristoteles Latinus* I.7 (Bruges: Desclée de Brouwer, 1966).

Libri feudorum, in D. Godefroy *et al.* (eds.) *Corpus juris civilis romani* (Basel, 1756).

Logica "Cum sit nostra," in L. M. de Rijk (ed.) *Logica modernorum* (Assen: Van Gorcum, 1962–7) II.2: 413–51.

The Prose Salernitan Questions. An Anonymous Collection Dealing with Science and Medicine Written by an Englishman c. 1200 with an Appendix of Ten Related Collections, ed. B. Lawn (London: British Academy, 1979).

Quaestiones super Posteriora Analytica (ms. in Paris, Bibliothèque Nationale lat. 16096).

The Sea of Precious Virtue (Bahr Aava'id'): A Medieval Islamic Mirror for Princes, tr. J. Meisami (Salt Lake City: Utah University Press, 1991).

The Tractatus de successivis Attributed to William Ockham, ed. P. Boehner (St. Bonaventure, NY: Franciscan Institute, 1944).

Turba philosophorum, ed. J. Ruska, *Quellen und Studien zur Geschichte der Naturwissenschaften und der Medizin* 1 (1931).

Vida de Ramon Llull: les fonts escrites i la iconografia coetànies, ed. M. Batllori and J. N. Hillgarth (Barcelona: Associació de Bibliòfils de Barcelona, 1982).

Anselm of Canterbury. *Monologion and Proslogion with the Replies of Gaunilo and Anselm*, tr. T. Williams (Indianapolis: Hackett, 1996).

Proslogion, tr. M. J. Charlesworth (Notre Dame, IN: University of Notre Dame Press, 1965).

Opera omnia, ed. F. S. Schmitt (Edinburgh: Nelson, 1946; repr. Stuttgart: Frommann, 1968).

Anselm of Laon. *Anselms von Laon systematische Sentenzen*, ed. F. Bliemetzrieder (Münster: Aschendorff, 1919).

Glossa ordinaria: Pars 22, In Canticum canticorum, ed. M. Dove (Turnhout: Brepols, 1997).

Antoninus of Florence. *Confessionale "Defecerunt"* (Florence, 1490).

Summa theologica (Verona, 1740; repr. Graz: Akademische Druck, 1959).

Antonius Andreae. *Commentarium in libros Sententiarum* (Venice, 1572).

Quaestiones de tribus principiis rerum naturalium, ed. T. Penketh (Padua, 1475).

Quaestiones super duodecim libros Metaphysicae (Venice, 1491).

Scriptum in arte veteri et in divisionibus Boetii cum questionibus (Venice, 1508).

Antonius de Carlenis. *Four Questions on the Subalternation of the Sciences*, ed. S. Livesey (Philadelphia: American Philosophical Society, 1994).

Apuleius. *De philosophia libri*, ed. C. Moreschini (Stuttgart: Teubner, 1991).

Arethas of Caesarea. *Scholia on Porhyry's Isagoge and Aristotle's Categories (Codex Vaticanus Graecus 35)*, ed. M. Share (Athens: Academy of Athens, 1994).

Scripta minora, ed. L. G. Westerink (Leipzig: Teubner, 1968–72).

Aristotle. *Aristoteles Latinus*, ed. L. Minio-Paluello *et al.* (Bruges: Desclée de Brouwer, 1953–).

The Complete Works of Aristotle: The Revised Oxford Translation, ed. J. Barnes (Princeton, NJ: Princeton University Press, 1984).

De anima Books II and III, tr. D. W. Hamlyn, 2nd edn (Oxford: Clarendon Press, 1993).

De anima, tr. [Hebrew] Zerahyah ben Isaac ben Shealtiel Hen, ed. G. Bos (Leiden: Brill, 1994).

Al-Naṣṣ al-kāmil li-manṭiq Arisṭū, ed. F. Jabr (Beirut: Dār al-Fikr al-Lunānī, 1999).

The Nicomachean Ethics, tr. T. Irwin (Indianapolis, IN: Hackett, 1985).

Omnia quae extant opera . . . additis . . . Averrois Cordubensis in ea opera omnes qui ad nos pervenere commentarii (Venice, 1550–2).

Otot ha-shamayim: Samuel ibn Tibbon's Hebrew Version of Aristotle's Meteorology, ed. and tr. R. Fontaine (Leiden: Brill, 1995).

Politica, ed. F. Susemihl and O. Immisch (Leipzig: Teubner, 1929).

Posterior Analytics, tr. J. Barnes, 2nd edn (Oxford: Clarendon Press, 1993).

Sefer ha-middot le-Aristutalis, ed. I. Satanow (Berlin: Orientalische Buchdruckerey, 1790).

"La traduzione arabo-ebraica del *De generatione et corruptione* di Aristotele," ed. A. Tessier, in *Atti dell'Accademia Nazionale dei Lincei: memorie della Classe di Scienze Moralis* VIII 28 (1984) 5–122.

Armand of Bellevue. "Armand of Belvézer on Eschatology: An Edition of his *Responsiones ad 19 Articulos* (1333)," ed. F. A. van Liere, *Archivium Historicum Ordinis Praedicatorum* 62 (1992) 7–134.

De declaratione difficilium terminorum theologie philosophie atque logice (Lyon, 1500).

Arnald of Villanova. *Espiritual*, ed. J. Mensa (Barcelona: Institut d'Estudis Catalans, 1994).

Obres catalanes, ed. M. Batllori (Barcelona: Editorial Barcino, 1947).

Opera medicina omnia, ed. L. García Ballester *et al.* (Barcelona: Institut d'Estudis Catalans, 1975–88).

Opera omnia (Lyon, 1504).

Regimen sanitatis Salerni, this booke teaching all people to gouerne them in health, tr. T. Paynall (London: T. Creede, 1597).

Scripta spiritualia, ed. J. Carreras y Artau (Barcelona: Institut d'Estudis Catalans, 1971).

Arnold of Saxony. *Die Encyklopädiedes Arnoldus Saxo, zum ersten Mal nach einem Erfurter Codex*, ed. E. Stange (Erfurt: F. Bartholomäus, 1905–7).

al-Ashʿarī. *Al-Ibāna ʿan uṣūl ad-dīyāna (The Elucidation of Islam's Foundation)*, tr. W. Klein (New Haven, CT: American Oriental Society, 1940).

Maqālāt al-islāmiyyīn, ed. H. Ritter, 2nd edn (Wiesbaden: Steiner, 1963).

The Theology of al-Ashʿari: The Arabic Texts of al-Ashʿari's Kitāb al-Lumaʿ and Risālat istiḥsān al-khawḍ fī ʿilm al-kalām, ed. and tr. R. McCarthy (Beirut: Catholic Press, 1953).

Astesanus of Asti. *Summa de casibus conscientiae* (Venice, 1478).

Augustine. *Augoustinou Peri Triados biblia pentekaideka, haper ek tēs tōn Latinōn dialektou eis tēn Hellada metēnegke Maximos ho Planoudēs*, ed. M. Papathomopoulos *et al.* (Athens: Academy of Athens, 1995).

Commentary on the Lord's Sermon on the Mount, tr. D. J. Kavanagh (Washington, DC: Catholic University of America Press, 1951).

Confessions, tr. E. B. Pusey (London: Dent, 1907).

Opera (Corpus Christianorum, series latina) (Turnhout: Brepols, 1954–81).

Opera (Corpus scriptorum ecclesiasticorum latinorum) (Vienna: Tempsky, 1887).

Prochoros Kydones' Übersetzungen von Augustinus, De libero arbitrio I 1–90 und Ps.-Augustinus, De decem plagis Aegyptiorum (lateinisch-griechisch) ed. H. Hunger (Vienna: Österreichischen Akademie der Wissenschaften, 1990).

Augustine of Ancona. *Summa de potestate ecclesiastica ad Ioannem XXII* (Augsburg, 1473).

Tractatus brevis de duplici potestate prelatorum et laicorum, ed. R. Scholz, *Die Publizistik zur Zeit Philippe des Schönen und Bonifaz VIII* (Stuttgart: Enke, 1903; repr. Amsterdam, 1962).

Aulus Gellius. *A. Gellii Noctae Atticae*, ed. P. K. Marshall (Oxford: Clarendon Press, 1968).

Averroes. *Aristotelis opera cum Averrois commentariis* (Venice, 1562; repr. Frankfurt: Minerva, 1962).

La béatitude de l'âme, ed. M. Geoffroy and C. Steel (Paris: Vrin, 2001).

Beʾur Even Rushd le-Sefer ha-halasah le-Aristu, ed. J. Goldenthal (Leipzig: H. Franke, 1842).

The Book of the Decisive Treatise Determining the Connection Between the Law and Wisdom; and Epistle Dedicatory, ed. and tr. C. E. Butterworth (Provo, UT: Brigham Young University Press, 2001).

Commentarium magnum in Aristotelis De anima libros, ed. F. S. Crawford (Cambridge, MA: Mediaeval Academy of America, 1953).

Commentarium magnum in Aristotelis Physicorum librum septimum (Vindobonensis, lat. 2334) (Paderborn: Schöningh, 2007).

Commentarium medium et Epitome in Aristotelis De generatione et corruptione libros, ed. S. Kurland (Cambridge, MA: Medieval Academy of America, 1958).

Commentarium medium in Porphyrii Isagogen et Aristotelis Categorias, ed. H. Davidson (Cambridge, MA: Medieval Academy of America, 1969).

The Commentary of Averroes on Aristotle's De anima in the Hebrew Translation of Moses b. Samuel Ibn Tibbon, ed. A. L. Ivry (Jerusalem: Israel Academy of Arts and Sciences, 2003).

"Commentary on Alexander of Aphrodisias' *Treatise On the Intellect* (in Hebrew)," ed. H. Davidson, *Jerusalem Studies in Jewish Thought* 7 (1988) 205–17.

Commentary on Aristotle's Book on the Heaven and the Universe: Sharḥ Kitāb fī al-samāʾ wa-al-ʿālam, ed. G. Endress (Frankfurt: Publications of the Institute for the History of Arabic-Islamic Science, 1994).

Commentary on Plato's Republic, ed. E. I. J. Rosenthal, 2nd edn (Cambridge: Cambridge University Press, 1966).

Il commento medio di Averroè alla Poetica di Aristotele, ed. F. Lasinio (Pisa: Annali delle Università Toscane, 1872).

Il commento medio di Averroè alla Retorica, ed. F. Lasinio (Florence: Le Monnier, 1877).

Commentum magnum super libro De celo et mundo Aristotelis, ed. F. J. Carmody and R. Arnzen (Leuven: Peeters, 2003).

Commentum medium in Categorias Aristotelis, tr. William of Luna, ed. R. Hissette (Leuven: Peeters, forthcoming).

Commentum medium super libro Peri hermeneias Aristotelis, tr. William of Luna (?), ed. R. Hissette (Leuven: Peeters, 1996).

Compendia librorum Aristotelis qui Parva naturalia vocantur, ed. [Arabic] H. Blumberg (Cambridge, MA: Mediaeval Academy of America, 1972).

Compendia librorum Aristotelis qui Parva naturalia vocantur, ed. [Hebrew] H. Blumberg (Cambridge, MA: Mediaeval Academy of America, 1954).

Compendia librorum Aristotelis qui Parva naturalia vocantur, ed. [Latin] A. L. Shields (Cambridge, MA: Mediaeval Academy of America, 1949).

De separatione primi principii, ed. C. Steel and G. Guldentops, *Recherches de théologie et philosophie médiévales* 64 (1997) 86–135.

De substantia orbis: Critical Edition of the Hebrew Text with English Translation and Commentary, ed. A. Hyman (Cambridge, MA: Medieval Academy of America, 1986).

Epitome of Parva naturalia, tr. H. Blumberg (Cambridge, MA: Mediaeval Academy of America, 1961).

Faith and Reason in Islam: Averroes' Exposition of Religious Arguments, tr. I. Najjar (Oxford: Oneworld, 2001).

Al-Kashf ʿan manāhij al-adillah fī ʿaqāʾid al-millah, ed. M. ʿĀbid al-Jābirī (Beirut: Markaz Dirāsāt al-Waḥdah al-ʿArabīyah, 1998).

Kol melʾeket higgayon le-Aristotelo, ed. J. Marcaria (Riva di Trento: A. Braun, 1559).

Long Commentary on the De anima of Aristotle, tr. R. C. Taylor (New Haven, CT: Yale University Press, 2009).

Middle Commentary on Aristotle's De anima, ed. A. Ivry (Provo, UT: Brigham Young University Press, 2002).

Middle Commentary on Aristotle's Nicomachean Ethics in the Hebrew Version of Samuel ben Judah, ed. L. V. Berman (Jerusalem: Israel Academy of Arts and Sciences, 1999).

Qizzurey Even Roshd ʿal Shemaʿ tivʿi le-Aristoteles, ed. J. Marcaria (Riva di Trento: A. Braun, 1559).

Sharḥ al-Burhān li-Arisṭū wa-Talkhīṣ al-Burhān, ed. ʿA. Badawī (Kuwait: Qism al-Turāth al-ʿArabi, 1984).

Tafsīr mā baʿd al-ṭabīʿa, ed. M. Bouyges (Beirut: Imprimerie Catholique, 1938–52).

Tahāfut al-tahāfut, ed. M. Bouyges (Beirut: Imprimerie Catholique, 1930).

Tahāfut al-tahāfut (The Incoherence of the Incoherence), tr. S. van den Bergh (London: Luzac, 1954; repr. 1978).

Talkhīṣ Kitāb al-nafs, ed. A. F. al-Ahwānī (Cairo: Maktabat al-Nahḍah al-Miṣrīyah, 1950).

Avicenna. *Avicenna's De anima (Arabic Text): Being the Psychological Part of* Kitab al-Shifāʾ, ed. F. Rahman (London: Oxford University Press, 1959).

Avicenna's Psychology: An English Translation of Kitāb al-najāt, *Book II, Chapter VI*, tr. F. Rahman (London: Oxford University Press, 1952).

Canon of Medicine [Bk. I] in O. C. Gruner (tr.) *A Treatise on the Canon of Medicine of Avicenna* (London: Luzac, 1930; rev. edn Chicago: KAZI, 1999).

De celo et mundo, ed. M. Renaud, *Bulletin de philosophie médiévale* 15 (1973) 92–130.

De congelatione et conglutinatione lapidum, ed. E. J. Holmyard and D. C. Mandeville (Paris: Guenther, 1927; repr. New York: AMS Press, 1982).

De medicinis cordialibus, in S. Van Riet (ed.) *Liber de anima seu Sextus de naturalibus IV–V* (Leiden: Brill, 1972) 187–210.

"Essay on the Secret of Destiny," in G. F. Hourani (tr.) *Reason and Tradition in Islamic Ethics* (Cambridge: Cambridge University Press, 1985) 229–31.

Al-ishārāt wa-al-tanbīhāt, ed. J. Forget (Leiden: Brill, 1892).

Al-ishārāt wa-al-tanbīhāt, ed. S. Dunyā (Cairo: Dār al-Maʿārif, 1957–60).

Liber Canonis (Venice, 1507; repr. Hildesheim: Olms, 1964).

Liber de anima seu Sextus de naturalibus, ed. S. Van Riet (*Avicenna Latinus*) (Leiden: Brill, 1968–72).

Liber de philosophia prima sive scientia divina, ed. S. Van Riet (*Avicenna Latinus*) (Leuven: Peeters, 1977–80).

Liber primus naturalium, ed. S. Van Riet et al. (*Avicenna Latinus*) (Louvain-la-Neuve: Peeters, 1992–2006).

Liber quartus naturalium de actionibus et passionibus qualitatum primarum, ed. S. Van Riet (*Avicenna Latinus*) (Louvain-la-Neuve: Peeters, 1989).

Liber tertius naturalium de generatione et corruptione, ed. S. Van Riet (*Avicenna Latinus*) (Louvain-la-Neuve: Peeters, 1987).

The Life of Ibn Sina, ed. and tr. W. E. Gohlman (Albany: State University of New York Press, 1974).

Le livre des directives et remarques (Kitāb al-Iŝarat wa l-tanbihat), tr. A. M. Goichon (Paris: Vrin, 1951).

Maqāla fī al-nafs ʿalā sunnat al-ikhtiṣār [Compendium on the Soul], ed. S. Landauer, "Die Psychologie des Ibn Sīnā," *Zeitschrift der deutschen morgenländischen Gesellschaft* 29 (1875) 335–418.

The Metaphysics of "The Healing", tr. M. Marmura (Provo, UT: Brigham Young University Press, 2005).

Al-Najāt, ed. M. Dānishpāzhūh (Tehran: Dānishgāh-yi Tihrān, 1985).

The Propositional Logic of Ibn Sina, ed. N. Shehaby (Dordrecht: Reidel, 1973).

Al-Qānūn fī al-ṭibb (Cairo, 1877; repr. Baghdad, 1970).

Remarks and Admonitions, Part 1: Logic, tr. S. C. Inati (Toronto: Pontifical Institute for Mediaeval Studies, 1984).

Remarks and Admonitions: Part 4, tr. S. C. Inati (London: Kegan Paul, 1996).

Al-Shifāʾ, ed. I. Madkur and S. Zāyid (Cairo: Hayʾa al-miṣriyya al-ʿāmma li-al-kitāb, 1983).

Al-Shifāʾ: al-Ilāhiyyāt, ed. M. Y. Mūsā, S. Dunyā and S. Zāʾid (Cairo: al-Hayʾah al-ʿĀmmah li-Shuʾūn al-Maṭābi al-Amirīyah, 1960).

Sufficientia, in *Opera philosophica* (Venice, [etc.]; repr. Leuven: Édition de la bibliothèque S.J., 1961).

Al-taʿlīqāt [Annotations], ed. ʿA. Badawī (Cairo: Hayʾa al-miṣriya al-ʿāmma li-al-kitāb, 1973).

Azo. *Lectura super Codicem* (Paris, 1577; repr. Turin: Ex officina Erasmiana, 1966).

Select Passages from the Works of Bracton and Azo, ed. F. W. Maitland (London: Quaritch, 1895; repr. Abingdon: Professional Books, 1978).

Summa super Codicem (Turin, 1578; repr. Turin: Ex officina Erasmiana, 1966).

Babin, François. *Journal ou relation fidelle de tout ce qui s'est passé dans l'université d'Angers au sujet de la philosophie de Des Carthes en l'execution des ordres du Roy pendant les années 1675, 1676, 1677, et 1678* (Angers, 1679).

Bacon, Francis. *De principiis atque originibus*, in G. Rees (ed.) *Philosophical Studies c.1611–c.1619 (The Oxford Francis Bacon VI)* (Oxford: Clarendon Press, 1996) 195–267.

al-Baghdādī, ʿAbd al-Laṭīf. *Bearbeitung von Buch Lambda der aristotelischen Metaphysik*, ed. and tr. A. Neuwirth (Wiesbaden: Steiner, 1976).

al-Baghdādī, Abū al-Barakāt. *Kitāb al-muʿtabar* (Hyderabad: Osmania Publication Bureau, 1938–9).

Bahmanyār. *Behmenjār ben el-Marzubān, der persische Aristoteliker aus Avicenna's Schule*, ed. S. Poper (Leipzig: L. Voss, 1851).

    Kitāb al-taḥṣīl, ed. M. Mutahhari (Tehran: Tehran University Press, 1970).

Baḥya ibn Paqūdā. *The Book of Direction to the Duties of the Heart*, tr. M. Mansoor (London: Routledge, 1973).

    Al-Hidāya ʾilā farāʾid al-qulūb, ed. A. S. Yahuda (Leiden: Brill, 1912).

Baldus de Ubaldis. *Commentaria omnia* (Venice: Juntas, 1599; repr. Goldbach: Keip Verlag, 2004).

    Consiliorum, sive responsorum, volumen primum [-qvintum] (Venice, 1575).

al-Bāqillānī. *Kitāb al-tamhīd*, ed. R. J. McCarthy (Beirut: Librairie Orientale, 1957).

    A Tenth-Century Document of Arabic Literary Theory and Criticism, tr. G. von Grunebaum (Chicago: University of Chicago Press, 1950).

Barlaam the Calabrian. *Epistole a Palamas*, ed. and tr. A. Phyrigos (Rome: Catholic Book Agency, 1975).

    Logistikē, ed. and tr. P. Carelos (Athens: Akademia Athenon, 1996).

    Opere contro i Latini, ed. and tr. A. Phyrigos (Vatican: Biblioteca Apostolica Vaticana, 1998).

    Solutions Addressed to George Lapithes, ed. R. E. Sinkewicz, *Mediaeval Studies* 43 (1981) 151–217.

    Traités sur les éclipses de soleil de 1331 et 1337, ed. J. Mogenet *et al.* (Leuven: Peeters, 1977).

Bartholomaeus Anglicus. *De rerum proprietatibus* (Frankfurt, 1601; repr. Frankfurt: Minerva, 1964).

    On the Properties of Soul and Body = De proprietatibus rerum, libri III et IV, ed. R. J. Long (Toronto: Pontifical Institute of Mediaeval Studies, 1979).

    On the Properties of Things, tr. John Trevisa (Oxford: Clarendon Press, 1975–88).

Bartholomew of Bologna. *Quaestiones disputatae de fide*, ed. M. Mückshoff (Münster: Aschendorff, 1940) 3–104.

    Tractatus de luce, ed. I. Squadrani, *Antonianum* 7 (1932) 139–238; 337–76; 465–94.

Bartholomew of Bruges. *Commentarius in Aristotelis Poeticam*, in G. Daham (ed.) "Notes et textes sur la poétique au moyen âge," *Archives d'histoire doctrinale et littéraire du moyen âge* 47 (1980) 228–39.

Bartolus of Sassoferrato. *Opera omnia* (Lyon, 1481–2).

Basil of Caesarea. *Eusthatius ancienne version latine des neuf homélies sur l'Hexaëmeron de Basile de Césarée*, ed. E. Amand de Mendieta and S. Y. Rudberg (Berlin: Akademie Verlag, 1958).

Bayle, Pierre. *Historical and Critical Dictionary: Selections*, tr. R. Popkin (Indianapolis, IN: Hackett, 1991).

Bede. *A Biblical Miscellany*, tr. A. Holder and W. Foley (Liverpool: Liverpool University Press, 1999).

    Opera, ed. C. W. Jones and D. Hurst (Turnhout: Brepols, 1955–).

    The Reckoning of Time, tr. F. Wallis (Liverpool: Liverpool University Press, 1999).

Benedict of Nursia. *Regula (Corpus scriptorum ecclesiasticorum latinorum 75)* (Vienna: Tempsky, 1977).

Berengar of Tours. *Rescriptum contra Lanfrannum*, ed. R. B. C. Huygens (Turnhout: Brepols, 1988).

Bernard of Chartres. *The "Glosae super Platonem" of Bernard of Chartres*, ed. P. E. Dutton (Toronto: Pontifical Institute of Mediaeval Studies, 1991).

Bernard of Clairvaux. *Opera*, ed. J. Leclerq *et al.* (Rome: Editiones Cistercienses, 1957–77).

    Works (Kalamazoo, MI: Cistercian Publications, 1973–80).

Bernard Silvestris. *The Commentary on Martianus Capella's De nuptiis Philologiae et Mercurii Attributed to Bernardus Silvestris*, ed. H. H. Westra (Toronto: Pontifical Institute of Mediaeval Studies, 1986).
  The Commentary on the First Six Books of the Aeneid of Vergil, ed. J. W. Jones and E. F. Jones (Lincoln: University of Nebraska Press, 1977).
  The Commentary on the First Six Books of the Aeneid of Vergil, tr. E. G. Schreiber and T. E. Maresca (Lincoln: University of Nebraska Press, 1979).
  Cosmographia, ed. P. Dronke (Leiden: Brill, 1978).
  The Cosmographia of Bernardus Silvestris, tr. W. Wetherbee (New York: Columbia University Press, 1973).
  Mathematicus, ed. and tr. D. M. Stone, *Archives d'histoire doctrinale et littéraire du moyen âge* 63 (1996) 209–83.
Bernard of Trilia. *Quaestiones disputatae de cognitione animae separatae*, ed. P. Künzle (Bern: Francke, 1969).
Bernardino of Siena. *Opera omnia* (Quaracchi: Editiones Collegii S. Bonaventurae, 1950–65).
Berthold of Moosburg. *Expositio super Elementationem theologicam Procli*, ed. M. R. Pagnoni-Sturlese and L. Sturlese (Hamburg: Meiner, 1984–).
Biblia latina cum glossa ordinaria (Strasbourg, 1480–1; repr. Turnhout: Brepols, 1992).
Biblia sacra juxta vulgatam Clementinam (Rome: Societatis S. Joannis Evangelis, 1927; repr. 1956).
al-Biṭrūjī. *De motibus coelorum*, ed. F. J. Carmody (Berkeley: University of California Press, 1952).
Blasius of Parma. "La 'quaestio de intensione et remissione formarum' di Biagio Pelacani da Parma," ed. G. Federici-Vescovini, *Physis: Rivista internazionale di storia della scienza* 31 (1994) 433–535.
  Quaestiones circa Tractatum proportionum magistri Thome Braduardini, ed. J. Biard and S. Rommevaux (Paris: Vrin, 2006).
  Les quaestiones de anima, ed. G. Federici Vescovini (Florence: Olschki, 1974).
  Questiones super Tractatus logice Magistri Petri Hispani, ed. J. Biard and G. Federici Vescovini (Paris: Vrin, 2001).
Boethius. *Eine byzantinische Übersetzung von Boethius' De hypotheticis syllogismis*, ed. D. Z. Nikitas (Göttingen: Vandenhoeck und Ruprecht, 1982).
  Contra Eutychen, in H. F. Stewart and E. K. Rand (eds.) *The Theological Tractates* (Cambridge, MA: Harvard University Press, 1918).
  De consolatione philosophiae; Opuscula theologica, ed. C. Moreschini (Munich: K. G. Saur, 2000).
  De consolatione philosophiae: traduction grecque de Maxime Planude, ed. M. Papathomopoulos (Athens: Academy of Athens, 1999).
  De consolatione philosophiae: traduzione ebraica di 'Azaria ben r. Joseph Ibn Abba Mari detto Bonafous Bonfil Astruc, ed. S. J. Sierra (Turin and Jerusalem: Istituto di Studi Ebraici and Scuola Rabbinica Margulies-Disegni, 1967).
  De divisione, ed. J. Magee (Leiden: Brill, 1998).
  De hebdomadibus [*Quomodo substantiae*], in H. F. Stewart and E. K. Rand (eds.) *The Theological Tractates* (Cambridge, MA: Harvard University Press, 1918).
  De hypotheticis syllogismis, ed. L. Obertello (Brescia: Paideia, 1969).
  De institutione arithmetica, De institutione musica, ed. G. Friedlein (Leipzig: Teubner, 1867; repr. Frankfurt: Minerva, 1966).
  De topiciis differentiis kai hoi metaphraseis tōn Manouēl Holobōlou kai Prochorou Kydōnē, ed. D. Z. Nikitas (Athens: Academy of Athens, 1990).
  De Trinitate, in H. F. Stewart and E. K. Rand (eds.) *The Theological Tractates* (Cambridge, MA: Harvard University Press, 1918).

In librum Aristotelis Peri hermeneias commentarii editio duplex, ed. K. Meiser (Leipzig: Teubner, 1877–80).

In Porphyrii Isagogen commentorum editio duplex, ed. S. Brandt (*Corpus Scriptorum Ecclesiasticorum Latinorum*, vol. XLVIII) (Vienna: F. Tempsky, 1906).

"Manuel Calecas' Translation of Boethius' *De Trinitate:* Introduction, New Critical Edition, Index Latinograecitatis," ed. J. A. Demetracopoulos, *Synthesis Philosophica* 39 (2005) 83–118.

Opera omnia, in J.-P. Migne (ed.) *Patrologiae cursus completus: series latina* (Paris, 1844–91) vols. LXIII–LXIV.

Opuscula sacra, ed. A. Galonnier (Leuven: Peeters, 2007).

Philosophiae consolatio, ed. L. Bieler (*Corpus Christianorum, Series latina* XCIV) (Turnhout: Brepols, 1957).

Boethius of Dacia. *Godfrey of Fontaines's Abridgement of Boethius of Dacia's Modi significandi sive Quaestiones super Priscianum majorem*, tr. A. C. Senape McDermott (Amsterdam: Benjamins, 1980).

On the Supreme Good, On the Eternity of the World, On Dreams, ed. J. F. Wippel (Toronto: Pontifical Institute of Mediaeval Studies, 1987).

Opera, ed. J. Pinborg *et al.* (Copenhagen: DSL/Gad, 1969–).

Bonaventure. *Breviloquium*, tr. J. de Vinck (Paterson, NJ: St. Anthony Guild, 1960–70).

Disputed Questions on the Knowledge of Christ, ed. Z. Hayes (New York: St. Bonaventure Press, 1992).

Disputed Questions on the Mystery of the Trinity, ed. Z. Hayes (New York: St. Bonaventure Press, 1979).

The Journey of the Mind to God, tr. P. Boehner, ed. S. Brown (Indianapolis, IN: Hackett, 1993).

On the Eternity of the World, tr. C. Vollert *et al.* (Milwaukee, WI: Marquette University Press, 1964).

On the Reduction of the Arts to Theology, tr. Z. Hayes (St. Bonaventure, NY: Franciscan Institute, 1996).

Opera omnia (Quaracchi: Editiones Collegii S. Bonaventurae, 1882–1902).

Bouju, Théophraste. *Corps de toute la philosophie* (Paris: Vesue Marc Orry, 1614).

Boyle, Robert. *The Works of Robert Boyle*, ed. M. Hunter and E. B. Davis (London: Pickering and Chatto, 1999–2000).

Brunetto Latini. *Li livres dou tresor*, ed. and tr. F. J. Carmody (Berkeley: University of California Press, 1948; repr. Geneva: Slatkine, 1975).

La rettorica, ed. F. Maggini (Florence: Galletti e Cocci, 1915).

Il tesoretto = The Little Treasure, ed. and tr. J. B. Holloway (New York: Garland, 1981).

Bryson. *Der OIKONOMIKOΣ der Neupythagoräers Bryson und sein Einfluss auf die islamiche Wissenschaft*, ed. M. Plessner (Heidelberg: Winter, 1928).

Bulgarus. *Ad digestorum titulum de diversis regulis iuris antiqui commentarius*, ed. F. W. K. Beckhaus (Bonn: Henry und Cohen, 1856; repr. Frankfurt: Minerva, 1967).

Cajetan (Thomas de Vio). *Scripta philosophica: commentaria in Praedicamenta Aristotelis*, ed. M. H. Laurent (Rome: Angelicum, 1939).

Cajetan of Thiene. "Declaratio super tractatu Hentisberi Regularum," in *Tractatus Gulielmi Hentisberi de sensu composito et diviso* (Venice, 1494).

Expositio in libros Aristotelis De anima (Padua, 1475).

Expositio in libros De caelo et mundo (Padua, 1476).

Expositio in libros meterologicorum Aristotelis (Padua: Petrus Maufer, 1476).

Recollecte super octo libros Physicorum Aristotelis (Treviso: Johannes de Hassia, 1476).

Recollectae super Sophismatibus Hentisberi, in *Tractatus Gulielmi Hentisberi de sensu composito et diviso* (Venice, 1494).

Tractatus de reactione per Gaetanum de Thienis (Venice: Joannis de Foriivio et Gregorii Fratrum, 1491).

Cassiodorus. *Institutiones,* ed. R. A. B. Mynors (Oxford: Clarendon Press, 1937; repr. 1961).

Opera, ed. Å. J. Fridh and J. W. Halporn (*Corpus Christianorum, Series Latina 96–98*) (Turnhout: Brepols, 1958–73).

Catherine of Siena. *The Dialogue,* tr. S. Noffke (New York: Paulist Press, 1980).

Le lettere di S. Caterina da Siena, ed. P. Misciattelli and N. Tommaseo (Siena: G. Bentivoglio, 1913–22).

The Letters of Catherine of Siena, tr. S. Noffke (Tempe, AZ: Arizona Center for Medieval and Renaissance Studies, 2000–).

Libro della divina dottrina, ed. M. Fiorilli and S. Caramella, 2nd edn (Bari: G. Laterza, 1928).

Christine de Pizan. *The Book of the Body Politic,* tr. K. L. Forhan (Cambridge: Cambridge University Press, 1994).

The Book of the City of Ladies, tr. E. J. Richards (New York: Persea Books, 1982).

Le livre de la cité des dames, ed. E. Hicks and T. Moreau (Paris: Stock, 1986).

Le livre des trois vertus, ed. C. C. Willard and E. Hicks (Paris: Champion, 1989).

Le livre du corps de policie, ed. A. J. Kennedy (Paris: Champion, 1998).

The Selected Writings of Christine de Pizan, tr. R. Blumenfeld-Kosinski (New York: Norton, 1997).

The Treasure of the City of Ladies, or, The Book of the Three Virtues, tr. S. Lawson (Harmondsworth: Penguin, 1985).

The Writings of Christine de Pizan, tr. C. C. Willard (New York: Persea Books, 1994).

Cicero. *De divinatione; De fato; Timaeus,* ed. O. Plasberg and W. Ax (Leipzig: Teubner, 1938).

Liber De senectute in Graecum translatus, tr. Theodorus Gazes, ed. G. Salanitro (Leipzig: Teubner, 1987).

Scripta quae manserunt omnia, ed. W. Trillitzsch (Leipzig: Teubner, 1964–).

Somnium Scipionis in graecum translatum, tr. Maximos Planudes, ed. A. Pavano (Rome: Gruppo editoriale internazionale, 1992).

Tusculanae Disputationes, ed. M. Pohlenz (Leipzig: Teubner, 1918).

Clarembald of Arras. *The Boethian Commentaries,* tr. D. B. George and J. R. Fortin (Notre Dame, IN: University of Notre Dame Press, 2002).

Life and Works of Clarembald of Arras, a Twelfth-Century Master of the School of Chartres, ed. N. M. Häring (Toronto: Pontifical Institute of Mediaeval Studies, 1965).

Columban. *Opera,* ed. G. S. M. Walker (Dublin: Dublin Institute for Advanced Studies, 1957).

Daniel of Morley. *Philosophia,* ed. G. Maurach, *Mittellateinisches Jahrbuch* 14 (1979) 204–55.

Dante Alighieri. *Convivio,* tr. R. Lansing (New York: Garland, 1990).

The Divine Comedy, tr. J. Ciardi (New York: Norton, 1977).

Monarchia, ed. and tr. P. Shaw (Cambridge: Cambridge University Press, 1995).

Opere minori, ed. C. Vasoli *et al.* (Milan: R. Ricciardi, 1979–84).

d'Argentré, Charles Duplessis. *Collectio judiciorum de novis erroribus* (Paris: apud A. Cailleau, 1728–36; repr. Brussels: Culture et Civilisation, 1963).

David. *Prolegomena et in Porphyrii Isagogen commentarium,* ed. A. Busse (*Commentaria in Aristotelem Graeca* XVIII.2) (Berlin: Reimber, 1904).

David of Dinant. *Davidis de Dinanto Quaternulorum fragmenta,* ed. M. Kurdziałek (Warsaw: Panstwowe Wydawnictwo Naukowe, 1963).

I testi di David di Dinant: filosofia della natura e metafisica a confronto col pensiero antico, ed. E. Casadei (Spoleto: Centro italiano di studi sull'alto medioevo, 2008).

Dāwūd ibn Marwān. *Twenty Chapters ('Ishrūn maqāla)*, ed. and tr. S. Stroumsa (New York: Brill, 1989).

de Launoy, Jean. *De varia Aristotelis fortuna in Academia Parisiensi*, 2nd edn (Hages-Comitum: Apud Adrianum Vlacq, 1656).

Demetrios Kydones. *Briefe*, tr. F. H. Tinnefeld (Stuttgart: Hiersemann, 1981–2003).

    Correspondance, ed. R. J. Loenertz (Rome: Biblioteca Apostolica Vaticana, 1956–60).

    De contemnenda morte oratio, ed. H. Deckelmann (Lepizig: Teubner, 1901).

    Ending the Byzantine Greek Schism: The 14th c. Apologia of Demetrios Kydones for Unity with Rome, tr. J. Likoudis (New Rochelle, NY: Catholics United for the Faith, 1983).

Denys the Carthusian. *Opera omnia* (Montreuil: Typis Cartusiae S. M. de Pratis, 1896–1935).

    Opera selecta, ed. K. Emery (Turnhout: Brepols, 1991–).

Descartes, René. *Œuvres de Descartes*, ed. C. Adam and P. Tannery (Paris: Cerf, 1897; repr. Paris: Vrin, 1996).

Dietrich of Freiberg. "On the Rainbow and Radiant Impressions," in W. A. Wallace and E. Grant (eds.) *A Source Book in Medieval Science* (Cambridge, MA: Harvard University Press, 1974).

    Opera omnia, ed. K. Flasch (Hamburg: Meiner, 1977–85).

    Treatise on the Intellect and the Intelligible, tr. M. Führer (Milwaukee, WI: Marquette University Press, 1992).

Diogenes Laertius. *Vitae philosophorum*, ed. M. Marcovich (Leipzig: Teubner, 1999).

Domingo de Soto. *Commentaria in octo libros Physicorum Aristotelis* (Burgos, 1665).

Dominicus Gundisalvi. *De anima*, in T. J. Muckle, *Mediaeval Studies* 2 (1940) 23–103.

    De divisione philosophiae, ed. L. Baur (Münster: Aschendorff, 1903).

    De processione mundi, ed. G. Bülow (Münster: Aschendorff, 1925).

    De scientiis, ed. M. Alonso Alonso (Madrid: Escuelas de Estudios Arabes, 1954).

    De unitate, ed. P. Correns (Münster: Aschendorff, 1891).

    The Procession of the World, ed. J. Laumakis (Milwaukee, WI: Marquette University Press, 2002).

Duhamel, Jean-Baptiste. *Philosophia universalis, sive commentarius in universam Aristotelis philosophiam, ad usum scholarum comparatam* (Paris: C. Thiboust, 1705).

Dūnash ibn Tāmīm. *Le commentaire sur le "Livre de la création" de Dūnaš ben Tāmīm de Kairouan (Xᵉ siècle)*, ed. and tr. G. Vajda and P. Fenton, rev. edn (Leuven: Peeters, 2002).

Durand of St. Pourçain. *In Petri Lombardi Sententias theologicas commentarium libri quatuor* (Venice: ex typographia Guerraea, 1571; repr. Ridgewood, NJ: Gregg, 1964).

    Quaestio de natura cognitionis et disputatio cum anonymo quodam, ed. J. Koch (Münster: Aschendorff, 1935).

    Quaestiones de habitibus, ed J. Koch (Münster: Aschendorff, 1930).

    Quodlibeta avenionensia tria, additis correctionibus Hervei Natalis supra dicta Durandi in primo quolibet, ed. P. T. Stella (Zurich: Pas-Verlag, 1965).

    Quodlibeta Paris I (Q.I-Q.IV), ed. T. Takada (Kyoto: Takada, 1968).

Durandellus. *Evidentiae contra Durandum*, ed. P. T. Stella (Tübingen: Francke, 2003).

Eadmer. *The Life of St Anselm, Archbishop of Canterbury*, ed. R. W. Southern (London: Nelson, 1962).

Eckhart of Hochheim. *Die deutschen und lateinischen Werke* (Stuttgart: Kohlhammer, 1936–).

    Eine lateinische Rechtfertigungsschrift des Meister Eckhart, ed. A. Daniels (Münster: Aschendorff, 1923).

    Utrum in deo sit idem esse et intelligere, ed. B. Mojsisch, in *Bochumer Philosophisches Jahrbuch für Antike und Mittelalter* 4/1999 (2000) 179–97.

Elias. *In Porphyrii Isagogen et Aristotelis Categorias commentaria*, ed. A. Busse (*Commentaria in Aristotelem Graeca* XVIII.1) (Berlin: Reimer, 1900).

Epictetus. *Enchiridion*, tr. G. Long (Amherst, NY: Prometheus Books, 1991).

Euclid. *Elements*, tr. Hermann of Carinthia, ed. H. Busard, *Janus* 54 (1967) 1–140 [Books I–VI]; *Mathematical Centre Tracts* (Amsterdam) 84 (1977) [Books VII–XII].

   The First Latin Translation of Euclid's "Elements" Commonly Ascribed to Adelard of Bath, ed. H. L. L. Busard (Toronto: Pontifical Institute of Mediaeval Studies, 1983).

   Johannes de Tinemue's Redaction of Euclid's Elements, the So-Called Adelard III Version, ed. H. L. L. Busard (Stuttgart: Steiner, 2001).

   The Latin Translation of the Arabic Version of Euclid's Elements Commonly Ascribed to Gerard of Cremona, ed. H. L. L. Busard (Leiden: Brill, 1984).

   The Mediaeval Latin Translation of Euclid's Elements: Made Directly from the Greek, ed. H. L. L. Busard (Stuttgart: Steiner, 1987).

   Robert of Chester's (?) Redaction of Euclid's Elements, the So-Called Adelard II Version, ed. H. Busard and M. Folkerts (Basel: Birkhäuser, 1992).

Eustachius of Arras. *Quaestiones septem de aeternitate mundi*, ed. R. C. Dales and O. Argerami, *Archives d'histoire doctrinale et littéraire du moyen âge* 53 (1986) 116–37; 54 (1987) 59–102.

Eustratios of Nicea. *Commentaria in II librum Posteriorum analyticorum Aristotelis*, tr. Andreas Gratiolus (Venice, 1542; repr. Stuttgart-Bad Cannstatt: Frommann-Holzboog, 2001).

   In Analyticorum posteriorum librum secundum commentarium, ed. M. Hayduck (*Commentaria in Aristotelem Graeca* XXI) (Berlin: Reimer, 1907).

   In Ethica Nicomachea commentaria, ed. G. Heylbut (*Commentaria in Aristotelem Graeca* XX) (Berlin: Reimer, 1892).

   In Ethicam Nicomacheam, tr. Robert Grosseteste, in H. P. F. Mercken (ed.) *The Greek Commentaries on the Nicomachean Ethics of Aristotle in the Latin Translation of Robert Grosseteste* (Leiden: Brill, 1973).

Everard of Ypres. *Dialogus Ratii et Everardi*, ed. N. M. Häring, *Mediaeval Studies* 15 (1953) 243–89.

Evrard de Béthune. *Graecismus*, ed. J. Wrobel (Breslau: G. Koebner, 1887).

al-Fārābī. *Alfarabi's philosophische Abhandlungen aus Londoner, Leidener und Berliner Handschriften*, ed. F. Dieterici (Leiden: Brill, 1890).

   Commentary and Short Treatise on Aristotle's De Interpretatione, tr. F. W. Zimmermann (Oxford: Oxford University Press, 1981).

   Commentary on Aristotle's Per Hermeneias (De interpretatione), ed. W. Kutsch and S. Marrow (Beirut: Imprimerie Catholique, 1960).

   De scientiis: secundum versionem Dominici Gundisalvi, ed. and [German] tr. J. H. J. Schneider (Freiburg: Herder, 2006).

   De scientiis = Über die Wissenschaften nach der lateinischen Übersetzung Gerhards von Cremona, ed. and [German] tr. F. Schupp (Hamburg: Meiner, 2005).

   Fuṣūl al-madanī: Aphorisms of The Statesman, ed. D. M. Dunlop (Cambridge: Cambridge University Press, 1961).

   L'harmonie entre les opinions de Platon et d'Aristote: Texte arabe et traduction, ed. F. M. Najjar and D. Mallet (Damascus: Institut français de Damas, 1999).

   Introduction to the Book of Rhetoric, tr. [Latin] Hermann the Germann, in M. Grignaschi and J. Langhade (eds.) *Deux ouvrages inédits sur la réthorique* [*sic*] (Beirut: Dār el-Mashriq, 1971).

   Kitāb al-ḥurūf, ed. M. Mahdi (Beirut: Dār al-Mashriq, 1969).

   Kitāb iḥṣāʾ al-ʿulūm [*Survey of the Sciences*], ed. ʿU. Amīn (Cairo: Dār al-Fikr al-ʿArabī, 1931–48).

   Liber exercitationis ad viam felicitatis, ed. D. Salman, *Recherches de théologie ancienne et médievale* 12 (1940) 33–48.

"*Long Commentary* on Aristotle's *Categoriae* in Hebrew and Arabic: A Critical Edition and English Translation of the Newly-Found Extant Fragments," ed. M. Zonta, in B. Abrahamov (ed.) *Studies in Arabic and Islamic Culture* (Ramat-Gan: Bar-Ilan University Press, 2006) II: 185–254.

On the Perfect State: Abū Naṣr al-Fārābī's Mabādiʾ ārāʾ ahl al-madīna al-fāḍila, ed. and tr. R. Walzer (Oxford: Clarendon Press, 1985).

Philosophical Lexicon = *Qāmūs al-Fārābī al-falsafī*, ed. and tr. I. Alon (Cambridge: E. J. W. Gibb Memorial Trust, 2002).

Philosophy of Plato and Aristotle, tr. M. Mahdi (Ithaca, NY: Cornell University Press, 1962).

The Political Writings, tr. C. Butterworth (Ithaca, NY: Cornell University Press, 2001).

Risāla fī al-ʿaql, ed. M. Bouyges (Beirut: Imprimerie Catholique, 1938).

Short Commentary on Aristotle's Prior Analytics, ed. N. Rescher (Pittsburgh: University of Pittsburgh Press, 1963).

"Le sommaire du livre des 'Lois' de Platon (Djawāmiʾ Kitāb al-Nawāmīs li-Aflātūn) par Abū Nasr al-Fārābī," ed. T.-A. Druart, *Bulletin d'études orientales* 50 (1998) 109–55.

Ferrandus of Spain. *De specie intelligibili*, ed. Z. Kuksewicz, *Medioevo* 3 (1977) 187–235.

Ferrarius the Catalan. *Quodlibet* (ms. in Paris, Bibliothèque de l'Arsenal 379).

Foxe, John. *The First Volume of the Ecclesiasticall History Contayning the Actes and Monumentes of Thynges Passed* (London: J. Daye, 1570).

Francis of Assisi. *Die Opuscula des hl. Franziskus von Assisi. Neue textkritische Edition*, ed. K. Esser (Grottaferrata: Editiones Collegii S. Bonaventurae, 1976).

Francis of Marchia. *Commentarius in IV libros Sententiarum Petri Lombardi. Distinctiones primi libri prima ad decimam*, ed. N. Mariani (Grottaferrata: Editiones Collegii S. Bonaventurae, 2006).

Commentarius in IV libros Sententiarum Petri Lombardi. Quaestiones praeambulae et Prologus, ed. N. Mariani (Grottaferrata: Editiones Collegii S. Bonaventurae, 2003).

Improbatio contra libellum Domini Johannis qui incipit Quia vir reprobus, ed. N. Mariani (Grottaferrata: Editiones Collegii S. Bonaventurae, 1993).

Quodlibet cum quaestionibus selectis ex commentario in librum Sententiarum, ed. N. Mariani (Grottaferrata: Editiones Collegii S. Bonaventurae, 1997).

Sententia et compilatio super libros Physicorum Aristotelis, ed. N. Mariani (Grottaferrata: Editiones Collegii S. Bonaventurae, 1998).

Francis of Meyronnes. *Expositio in VIII libros Physicorum* (Ferrara, 1490).

In libros sententiarum (Venice, 1520; repr. Frankfurt: Minerva, 1966).

Passus super Universalia, Praedicamenta et Perihermenias Aristotelis (Bologna, 1479).

Quadragesimale doctoris illuminati Francisci de Mayronis (Venice: Bernardinum de Nouaria, 1491).

Quodlibeta (Venice, 1520; repr. Frankfurt: Minerva, 1966).

Der Tractatus de transcendentibus des Franciscus de Mayronis, ed. H. Möhle (Dudley, MA: Peeters, 2004).

Francis of Meyronnes and Pierre Roger. *Disputatio* (1320–1), ed. J. Barbet (Paris: Vrin, 1961).

Francis of Prato. *De universalibus*, in F. Amerini (ed.) *I trattati De universalibus di Francesco da Prato e Stefano da Rieti (secolo XIV)* (Spoleto: Centro italiano di studi sull'alto medioevo, 2003) 57–132.

La logica di Francesco da Prato: con l'edizione critica della Loyca e del Tractatus de voce univoca, ed. F. Amerini (Florence: SISMEL, Edizioni del Galluzzo, 2005).

Tractatus de prima et secunda intentione, ed. B. Mojsisch, *Bochumer Philosophisches Jahrbuch für Antike und Mittelalter* 5 (2000) 147–74.

Tractatus de sex transcendentibus, ed. B. Mojsisch and J. Maasen, *Bochumer Philosophisches Jahrbuch für Antike und Mittelalter* 5 (2000) 175–217.

Tractatus de suppositionibus terminorum, ed. F. Amerini, *Medioevo* 25 (1999/2000) 486–547.

Francisco Suárez. *De anima: Commentaria una cum quaestionibus in libros Aristotelis De anima*, ed. S. Castellote (Madrid: Sociedad de Estudios y Publicaciones, 1978).

Disputationes metaphysicae (Paris, 1866; repr. Hildesheim: Olms, 1965).

Frassen, Claude. *Philosophia Academica, quam ex selectissimis Aristotelis et Doctoris Subtilis Scoti rationibus* (Paris, 1668).

Fredegisus of Tours. "The Letter of Fredegisus of Tours on Nothingness and Shadow: A New Translation and Commentary," tr. N. Jun, *Comitatus* 34 (2003) 150–69.

Frey, Jean-Cécile. *Opuscula varia nusquam edita, philosophis, medicis, et curiosis omnibus utilissima*, ed. A. Morand (Paris, 1646; repr. Lecce: Conte Editore, 2003).

Fulbert of Chartres. *The Letters and Poems of Fulbert of Chartres*, ed. and tr. F. Behrends (Oxford: Oxford University Press, 1976).

Gabriel Biel. *Canonis misse expositio*, ed. H. A. Oberman and W. J. Courtenay (Wiesbaden: Steiner, 1963–76).

Collectorium circa quattuor libros Sententiarum, ed. H. Rückert *et al.* (Tübingen: Mohr, 1973–92).

Defensorium obedientiae apostolicae et alia documenta, ed. H. A. Oberman *et al.* (Cambridge, MA: Harvard University Press, 1968).

Quaestiones de justificatione, ed. C. Feckes (Münster: Aschendorff, 1929).

Galen. *Burgundio of Pisa's Translation of Galen's Peri kraseōn* (*De complexionibus*), ed. R. J. Durling (Berlin: De Gruyter, 1976).

Burgundio of Pisa's Translation of Galen's Peri ton peponthoton topon *(De interioribus)*, ed. R. J. Durling (Weisbaden: Steiner, 1992).

Compendium Timaei Platonis, ed. and tr. P. Kraus and R. Walzer (London: Warburg Institute, 1951).

"De alimentorum facultatibus: tekstkritisch onderzoek en uitgave van de Latijnse vertaling van Willem Van Moerbeke," ed. M. Camps (Ph.D. dissertation: University of Leuven, 1987).

De causis procatarcticis libellus a Nicolao Regino in sermonem Latinum translatus, ed. K. Bardong (Leipzig: Teubner, 1937).

In Platonis Timaeum commentarii fragmenta, ed. H. O. Schröder, P. Kahle, *et al.* (Leipzig: Teubner, 1934).

Kitāb Jālīnūs fī Firaq al-ṭibb li-al-mutaʿallimīn, ed. M. S. Sālim (Cairo: Matbaʿat Dār al-Kutub, 1977).

Kitāb al-Usṭuquṣṣāt ʿalā raʾ y Buqrāṭ, ed. M. S. Sālim (Cairo: al-Hayʾah al-Miṣrīyah al-ʿĀmmah lil-Kitāb, 1987).

On the Parts of Medicine; On Cohesive Causes; On Regimen in Acute Diseases in Accordance with the Theories of Hippocrates, ed. M. C. Lyons *et al.* (Berlin: Akademie-Verlag, 1969).

Über die Medizinischen Namen, ed. and tr. M. Meyerhof and J. Schacht, *Abhandlungen der Preussischen Akademie der Wissenschaften* 3 (1931).

Garland of Besançon. *Dialectica*, ed. L. M. de Rijk (Assen: Van Gorcum, 1959).

Garland the Computist. *De computo* (ms. in Paris, Bibliothèque Nationale lat. 15118).

Gassendi, Pierre. *Dissertations en forme de paradoxes contre les Aristotéliciens (Exercitationes paradoxicae adversus Aristoteleos)* Livres I et II, ed. B. Rochot (Paris: Vrin, 1959).

Syntagmatis philosophici, in *Opera omnia* (Lyon, 1658; repr. Stuttgart-Bad Cannstatt: Frommann-Holzboog, 1964).

Gentilis da Cingulo. "Il commento di Gentile da Cingoli a Martino di Dacia," ed. G. C. Alessio, in D. Buzzetti *et al.* (eds.) *L'insegnamento della logica a Bologna nel XIV secolo* (Bologna: Presso l'Istituto per la storia dell'Università, 1992) 3–71.

Quaestiones supra Prisciano Minori, ed. R. Martorelli Vico (Pisa: Scuola Normale Superiore, 1985).

George Gemistos Plethon. *Contra Scholarii pro Aristotele obiectiones*, ed. E. V. Maltese (Leipzig: Teubner, 1988).

De differentiis, ed. B. Lagarde, *Byzantion* 43 (1973) 312–43.

Nomōn syngraphēs ta sōzomena = Traité des lois, ed. C. Alexandre, tr. A. Pellissier (Paris, 1858; repr. Amsterdam: Hakkart, 1966).

Peri aretōn = Traité des vertus, ed. and tr. B. Tambrun-Krasker (Athens: Akademia Athenon, 1987).

Politik, Philosophie und Rhetorik im spätbyzantinischen Reich, tr. W. Blum (Stuttgart: Hiersemann, 1988).

George Pachymeres. *Epitomē tēs Aristotelikēs logikēs*, ed. P. Bechius (Paris, 1548).

Hypomnema eis ton Parmeniden Platonos: anonymou synecheia tou hypomnematos Proklou, ed. T. A. Gadra *et al.* (Paris: Vrin, 1989).

In universam fere Aristotelis philosophiam epistome, tr. P. Bechio (Basel, 1560).

Philosophia, Buch 10: Kommentar zur Metaphysik des Aristoteles, editio princeps, ed. E. Pappa (Paris: Vrin, 2002).

Philosophia, editio princeps: Vivlia hendekaton, Ta ethika, etoi, Ta Nikomacheia, ed. K. Ikonomakos (Athens: Akademia Athenon, 2005).

Quadrivium, ed. P. Tannery and E. Stéphanou (Vatican: Biblioteca Apostolica Vaticana, 1940).

George Scholarios – Gennadios II. *Florilegium Thomisticum I*, ed. J. A. Demetracopoulos, *Recherches de théologie et philosophie médiévales* 69 (2002) 117–71.

Florilegium Thomisticum II (De fato), ed. J. A. Demetracopoulos, *Recherches de théologie et philosophie médiévales* 74 (2007) 301–76.

Œuvres complètes, ed. L. Petit *et al.* (Paris: Maison de la Bonne Presse, 1928–36).

George Trapezountios. *Comparationes Philosophorum Aristotelis et Platonis* (Venice: Iacobus Pentius, 1523; repr. Frankfurt: Minerva, 1965).

Isagoge Dialectica (Cologne: Eucharius, 1539; repr. Frankfurt: Minerva, 1966).

Gerald of Odo. *De suppositionibus*, ed. S. Brown, *Franciscan Studies* 35 (1975) 5–44.

Expositio in Aristotelis Ethicam (Brescia, 1482).

Opera philosophica, ed. L. M. de Rijk (Leiden: Brill, 1997–).

Sententia et expositio cum quaestionibus in Aristotelis Ethicam (Venice, 1500).

La vision de Dieu aux multiples forms, ed. C. Trottmann (Paris: Vrin, 2001).

Gerard of Abbeville. *Contra adversarium perfectionis christianae*, ed. S. Clasen, *Archivum Franciscanum Historicum* 31 (1938) 276–329; 32 (1939) 89–200.

"Quatre questions inédites de Gérard d'Abbeville pour la défense de la superiorité du clergé séculier," ed. A. Teetaert, *Archivio italiano per la storia della pietà* 1 (1951) 83–178.

Gerard of Siena. *In primum librum Sententiarum doctissimae quaestiones* (Padua, 1598).

Tractatus de usuris et restitutionibus (Rome, 1556).

Gerhoh of Reichersberg. *Opera inedita*, ed. D. van den Eynde *et al.* (Rome: Pontificium Athenaeum Antonianum, 1955–6).

Gershom ben Solomon. *The Gate of Heaven: Sha'ar ha-Shamayim*, tr. F. S. Bodenheimer (Jerusalem: Kiryath Sepher, 1953).

Sefer Shaar ha-Shamayim (Warsaw, 1875; repr. Jerusalem, 1967).

Gertrude the Great. *The Herald of Divine Love*, tr. M. Winkworth (New York: Paulist Press, 1993).

Œuvres spirituelles, ed. and tr. J. Hourlier *et al.* (Paris: Cerf, 1967–86).

Spiritual Exercises, tr. G. J. Lewis and J. Lewis (Kalamazoo, MI: Cistercian Publications, 1989).

al-Ghazālī. *Algazels's Metaphysics: A Medieval Translation*, ed. J. T. Muckle (Toronto: St. Michael's College, 1933).

The Book of Knowledge, Being a Translation with Notes of the Kitab al-ʿIlm of al-Ghazzali's Ihya
    ʿUlum al-Din, tr. N. A. Faris (Lahore: Shaykh Muhammad Ashraf, 1962).
Book XX of al-Ghazali's Ihya' ʿUlum al-Din, ed. L. Zolondek (Leiden: Brill, 1963).
Critère de l'action (Mizān al-ʿamal): traité d'éthique psychologique et mystique, tr. H. Hachem (Paris:
    Maisonneuve, 1945).
Faith in Divine Unity and Trust in Divine Providence (Book 35 of The Revival of Religious Sciences),
    ed. D. Burrell (Louisville, KY: Fons Vitae, 2001).
Faysal al-tafriqa bayna al-Islām wa-al-zandaqa, ed. S. Dunyā (Cairo: ʿĪsā al-Bābī al-Ḥalabī,
    1961).
*The Foundation of the Articles of Faith: Being a Translation with Notes of the Kitab Qawaʿid al-
    ʿAqaʾid of al-Ghazzali's Ihya' ʿUlum al-Din*, ed. N. A. Faris (Lahore: Shaykh Muḥammad
    Ashraf, 1963).
*Freedom and Fulfillment: An Annotated Translation of al-Ghazali's al-Munqidh min al-Dalal and
    Other Relevant Works of al-Ghazali*, ed. R. J. McCarthy (Boston: Twayne, 1980).
*Al-Ghazali on Divine Predicates and their Properties: A Critical and Annotated Translation of these
    Chapters in al-Iqtiṣād fī al-iʿtiqād*, tr. A. Abū Zayd (Lahore: Shaykh Muḥammad Ashraf,
    1970).
Al-Ghazali on Patience and Thankfulness: Book XXXII of the Revival of the Religious Sciences, tr.
    H. T. Littlejohn (Cambridge: Islamic Texts Society, 2001).
Ihya' ʿulūm al-dīn (Beirut: Dār al-kutub al-ʿilmīyya, 2002).
The Incoherence of the Philosophers / Tahāfut al-falāsifa: A Parallel English–Arabic Text, ed. M. E.
    Marmura (Provo, UT: Brigham Young University Press, 1997).
Invocations and Supplications: Book IX of the Revival of the Religious Sciences, ed. K. Nakamura
    (Cambridge: Islamic Text Society, 1990).
Al-Iqtiṣād fī al-iʿtiqād, ed. I. A. Çubukçu and H. Atay (Ankara: Nur Matbaasi, 1962).
The Just Balance: al-Quṣṭās al-mustaqīm, tr. D. P. Brewster (Lahore: Shaykh Muḥammad Ashraf,
    1978).
Logica, ed. C. H. Lohr, *Traditio* 21 (1965) 223–90.
Al-Maqṣad al-asnā fī sharḥ maʿānī asmāʾ Allāh al-ḥusnā, ed. F. Shehadi, 2nd edn (Beirut: Dār
    al-Mashriq, 1982).
Maqāṣid al-falāsifa, ed. S. Dunyā (Cairo: Dār al-Maʿārif, 1961).
Miḥakk al-naẓar fī al-manṭiq, ed. M. al-Naʿsani (Beirut: Dār al-Nahḍa al-Ḥadītha, 1966).
Miʿyār al-ʿilm, ed. A. Shams al-Dīn (Beirut: Dār al-Kutub al-ʿIlmīya, 1990).
Mizān al-ʿamal, ed. S. Dunyā (Cairo: Dār al-Maʿārif, 1964).
Al-Munqidh min al-ḍalāl, ed. J. Ṣalībā and K. ʿAyyād (Damascus: Maktab al-Nashr al-ʿArabī,
    1934).
The Niche of Lights = Mishkāt al-anwār: A Parallel English–Arabic Text, ed. D. Buchman (Provo,
    UT: Brigham Young University Press, 1998).
*On the Boundaries of Theological Tolerance in Islam: Abū Hāmid al-Ghazālī's Faysal al-tafriqa
    bayna al-Islām wa-al-zandaqa*, ed. S. A. Jackson (Karachi: Oxford University Press, 2002).
Al-Quṣṭās al-mustaqīm, ed. V. Shalhat (Beirut: Imprimerie Catholique, 1959).
The Remembrance of Death and the Afterlife: Book XL of the Revival of Religious Sciences, ed. T. J.
    Winter (Cambridge: Islamic Text Society, 1989).
Al-Risāla al-Qudsiyya, ed. A. L. Tibawi, *Islamic Quarterly* 9 (1965) 62–122.
Worship in Islam: Al-Ghazali's Book of the Ihya' on the Worship, ed. E. E. Calverley (London:
    Luzac, 1957).
Gianfrancesco Pico della Mirandola. *Examen vanitatis doctrinae gentium, et veritatis Christianae
    doctrinae*, in Giovanni Pico della Mirandola, *Opera omnia* (Basel, 1557; repr. Hildesheim:
    Olms, 1969) II: 710–1264.

Gilbert of Poitiers. *The Commentaries on Boethius by Gilbert of Poitiers*, ed. N. M. Häring (Toronto: Pontifical Institute of Mediaeval Studies, 1966).

Gilbert of Tournai. *De modo addiscendi*, ed. E. Bonifacio (Turin: Società editrice internazionale, 1953).

    Eruditio regum et principum, ed. A. de Poorter (*Les Philosophes Belges* IX) (Leuven: Institut Supérieur de Philosophie de l'Université, 1914).

    Tractatus de pace, ed. E. Longpré (Quaracchi: Editiones Collegii S. Bonaventurae, 1925).

Giles of Lessines. *De unitate formae* ed. M. De Wulf (*Les Philosophes Belges* I) (Leuven: Institut Supérieur de Philosophie de l'Université, 1901).

Giles of Orleans. *Quaestiones super De generatione et corruptione*, ed. Z. Kuksewicz (Amsterdam: Grüner, 1993).

Giles of Rome. *Apologia (Opera omnia* III.1), ed. R Wielockx (Florence: Olschki, 1985).

    Commentaria in octo libros Physicorum Aristotelis (Venice 1502; repr. Frankfurt: Minerva, 1968).

    Commentary on the Song of Songs and Other Writings, tr. J. Rotelle (Villanova, PA: Augustinian Press, 1998).

    Contra gradus et pluralitatem formarum (Venice, 1500; repr. Frankfurt: Minerva, 1982).

    De regimine principum libri III (Rome, 1556; repr. Frankfurt: Minerva, 1968).

    De renunciatione pape, ed. J. Eastman (Lewiston, NY: E. Mellen Press, 1992).

    Errores philosophorum, ed. J. Koch, tr. J. Riedl (Milwaukee, WI: Marquette University Press, 1944).

    In librum Solomonis qui Cantica canticorum inscribitur commentaria, in *Opera exegetica: Opuscula I* (Rome: Antonio Blado, 1554–5; repr. Frankfurt: Minerva, 1968).

    In primum librum Sententiarum (Venice, 1521; repr. Frankfurt: Minerva, 1968).

    On Ecclesiastical Power: A Medieval Theory of World Government, ed. and tr. R. W. Dyson (New York: Columbia University Press, 2004).

    Quaestiones disputatae de esse et essentia, De mensura angelorum, et De cognitione angelorum (Venice, 1503; repr. Frankfurt: Minerva, 1968).

    Quodlibeta (Leuven, 1646; repr. Frankfurt: Minerva, 1966).

    Theoremata de corpore Christi (Bologna, 1481).

    Theoremata de corpore Christi in *Opera exegetica: Opuscula I* (Rome: Antonio Blado, 1554–5; repr. Frankfurt: Minerva, 1968).

    Theoremata de esse et essentia, ed. E. Hocedez (Leuven: Museum Lessianum, 1930).

    Theorems on Essence and Existence, tr. M. Murray (Milwaukee, WI: Marquette University Press, 1952).

Godefridus et al. *The Life of the Holy Hildegard*, tr. J. McGrath and M. Palmquist (Collegeville, MN: Liturgical Press, 1995).

    Vita Sanctae Hildegardis, ed. M. Klaes (Turnhout: Brepols, 1993).

Godfrey of Fontaines. *Le huitième Quodlibet, Le Neuvième Quodlibet, Le dixième Quodlibet (Les Philosophes Belges* IV), ed. J. Hoffmans (Leuven: Institut Supérieur de Philosophie de l'Université, 1924–31).

    Notulae (ms. in Paris, Bibliothèque Nationale lat. 16297).

    Les quatre premiers Quodlibets (Les Philosophes Belges II), ed. M. De Wulf and A. Pelzer (Leuven: Institut Supérieur de Philosophie de l'Université, 1904).

    Les Quodlibets cinq, six et sept (Les Philosophes Belges III), ed. M. De Wulf and J. Hoffmans (Leuven: Institut Supérieur de Philosophie de l'Université, 1914).

    Le Quodlibet XV et trois Questions ordinaires de Godefroid de Fontaines (Les Philosophes Belges XIV), ed. O. Lottin (Leuven: Institut Supérieur de Philosophie de l'Université, 1937).

    Les Quodlibets onze et douze, Les Quodlibets treize et quatorze (Les Philosophes Belges V), ed. J. Hoffmans (Leuven: Institut Supérieur de Philosophie de l'Université, 1932–5).

Gonsalvo of Spain. *Quaestiones disputatae et de quodlibet*, ed. L. Amóros (Quaracchi: Editiones Collegii S. Bonaventurae, 1935).

Gosvin of Marbais. *Tractatus de constructione*, ed. I. Rosier (Nijmegen: Artistarium, 1998).

Gottschalk of Orbais. "Lettre inédite de Godescalc d'Orbais," ed. C. Lambot, *Revue Bénédictine* 68 (1958) 41–51.

    Œuvres théologiques et grammaticales, ed. C. Lambot (Leuven: Spicilegium sacrum Lovaniense, 1945).

Goudin, Antoine. *Philosophia juxta inconcussa tutissimaque Divi Thomae dogmata* (Paris, 1668).

Gratiadeus Aesculanus. *Acutissime questiones de physico auditu Fratris Gratiadei Esculani ordinis predicatorum: item questiones disputate eiusdem* (Venice, 1517).

    Commentaria in artem veterem Aristotelis (Venice, 1491).

Gratian. *Corpus iuris canonici*, ed. A. Richter and E. Friedberg (Leipzig: Tauchnitz, 1879; repr. Graz: Akademische Druck, 1959).

    Decretum d. Gratiani, universi iuris cononici pontificias constitutiones (Lyon, 1558).

    The Treatise on Laws: (Decretum DD. 1–20), with the Ordinary Gloss, tr. A. Thompson and J. Gordley (Washington, DC: Catholic University of America Press, 1993).

Gregor Reisch. *Margarita philosophica* (Strasbourg, 1504).

Gregory VII. *Das Register Gregors VII*, ed. E. Caspar (Berlin: Weidmann, 1955).

Gregory the Great. *Moralia in Iob*, ed. M. Adriaen (Turnhout: Brepols, 1979).

    Morals on the Book of Job, tr. J. Bliss (Oxford: J. H. Parker, 1844–50).

Gregory of Nazianzus. *Tyrannii Rufini Orationum novem interpretatio*, ed. J. Wrobel and A. Engelbrecht (Vienna: Tempsky, 1910).

Gregory of Nyssa. *De imagine*, tr. John Scottus Eriugena, ed. M. Cappuyns, *Recherches de théologie ancienne et médiévale* 32 (1965) 205–62.

Gregory Palamas. *Défense des saints hésychastes*, ed. and tr. J. Meyendorff (Leuven: Spicilegium sacrum Lovaniense, 1973).

    Dialogue between an Orthodox and a Barlaamite, ed. and tr. R. Ferwerda (Binghamton, NY: Global Publications/CEMERS, 1999).

    Homilies, tr. C. Veniamin (South Canaan, PA: St. Tikhon's Seminary Press, 2002).

    The One Hundred and Fifty Chapters, ed. and tr. R. E. Sinkewicz (Toronto: Pontifical Institute of Mediaeval Studies, 1988).

    Syngrammata, ed. B. Bobrinsky *et al.* (Thessaloniki: Chrestu, 1962–70).

    The Triads, tr. N. Gendle (New York: Paulist Press, 1983).

Gregory of Rimini. *Lectura super primum et secundum Sententiarum*, ed. D. Trapp *et al.* (Berlin: De Gruyter, 1979–84).

    Tractatus de imprestantiis venetorum et de usura (Reggio Emilia, 1508).

Guarino Veronese. *Epistolario*, ed. R. Sabbadini (Venice: A spese della Società 1915–19; repr. Torino: Bottega d'Erasmo, 1967).

    Grammaticales regulae (Venice: Per Petrum de Quarengis Bergomensem, 1508).

Guerric of St. Quentin. *Quaestiones de quolibet*, ed. W. H. Principe (Toronto: Pontifical Institute of Mediaeval Studies, 2002).

Guy Terrena. *Quaestio de magisterio infallibili romani pontificis*, ed. B. M. Xiberta (Münster: Aschendorff, 1926).

    "Six Questions of Guideo Terreni, O.Carm. (†1342) Vat. lat. 901, ff. 140r–145v," ed. J. P. Etzwiler, *Carmelus* 35 (1988) 138–77.

    "Some Fragments from the Commentary on the *De anima* of Guido Terreni," ed. J. P. Etzwiler, *Carmelus* 21 (1974) 198–232.

    Summa de haeresibus ab intitio mundi usque ad a. 1300 et ultra (Cologne, 1631).

Guy Vernani. *Liber de virtutibus*, ed. L. Cova (Turnhout: Brepols, forthcoming).

Il più antico oppositore politico di Dante: *Guido Vernani da Rimini*; *testo critico del "De reprobatione monarchiae*," ed. N. Matteini (Padua: CEDAM, 1958).

Tractatus de potestate summi pontificis, in F. Cheneval (ed.) *Die Rezeption der Monarchia Dantes bis zur Editio Princeps im Jahre 1559: Metamorphosen eines philosophischen Werkes* (Munich: Fink, 1995).

Ḥasdai Crescas. *Bittul ʿiqqare ha-Nosrim* [*Refutation of Christian Principles*], ed. C. del Valle Rodríguez (Madrid: Aben Ezra Ediciones, 2000).

Derashat ha-Pesah le-R. Hasdai Kreskas u-mehkarim be-mishnato ha-filosofit, ed. A. Ravitzky (Jerusalem: Israel Academy of Sciences and Humanities, 1988).

Or Adonai, ed. S. Fischer (Jerusalem: Sifrei Ramot, 1990).

The Refutation of Christian Principles, tr. D. J. Lasker (Albany: State University of New York Press, 1992).

Heiric of Auxerre. *Homiliae per circulum anni*, ed. R. Quadri (Turnhout: Brepols, 1992–).

Helperic of Auxerre. "Liber de computo," in J.-P. Migne (ed.) *Patrologiae cursus completus: series latina* (Paris, 1844–91) vol. CXXXVII.

Henry Bate of Malines. *Magistralis compositio astrolabii* (Venice, 1485).

Speculum divinorum et quorundam naturalium, ed. C. Steel and E. van de Vyver (Leuven: Publications universitaires, 1960–7; Leuven: Leuven University Press, 1990–).

Henry of Bratton. *Bracton's Note Book*, ed. F. W. Maitland (London; C. J. Clay, 1887; repr. Littleton, CO: F. B. Rothman, 1983; Buffalo: W. S. Hein, 1999).

On the Laws and Customs of England, ed. G. E. Woodbine, tr. S. E. Thorne (Cambridge, MA: Harvard University Press, 1968–77).

Henry of Friemar. *De decem preceptis*, ed. B. G. Guyot (Pisa: Scuola Normale Superiore, 2005).

De quatuor instinctibus, in R. G. Warnock and A. Zumkeller (ed. and tr.) *Der Traktat Heinrichs von Friemar über die Unterscheidung der Geister* (Würzburg: Augustinus-Verlag, 1977).

Tractatus ascetico-mystici, ed. A. Zumkeller (Würzburg: Augustinus-Verlag, 1975).

Henry of Ghent. *Henry of Ghent's Summa: The Questions on God's Existence and Essence (Articles 21–24)*, tr. J. Decorte and R. J. Teske (Paris: Peeters, 2005).

Henry of Ghent's Summa: The Questions on God's Unity and Simplicity (Articles 25–30), tr. R. J. Teske (Paris: Peeters, 2006).

Opera omnia, ed. R. Macken *et al.* (Leiden: Brill, 1979–).

Les Quaestiones in Librum de causis attribuées à Henri de Gand, ed. J. P. Zwaenepoel (Leuven: Publications universitaires, 1974).

Quodlibeta (Paris, 1518; repr. Leuven: Bibliothèque S.J., 1961).

Quodlibetal Questions on Free Will, tr. R. J. Teske (Milwaukee, WI: Marquette University Press, 1993).

Summa quaestionum ordinariarum (Paris, 1520; repr. St. Bonaventure, NY: Franciscan Institute, 1953).

Henry of Harclay. *Ordinary Questions*, ed. M. G. Henninger (Oxford: Oxford University Press, 2008).

Henry of Langenstein. *Der Sentenzenkommentar*, ed. and tr. R. Damerau (Marburg: Damerau, 1980).

Henry Ruyn. *Disputata Metaphysicae*, ed. A. Tabarroni, *Cahiers de l'Institut du Moyen Age Grec et Latin* 61 (1991) 185–428.

Henry Suso. *Deutsche mystische Schriften*, ed. G. Hofmann (Dusseldorf: Patmos-Verlag, 1966).

Horologium sapientiae, ed. P. Künzle (Freiburg: Universitätsverlag, 1977).

The Life of the Servant, ed. J. M. Clark (London: Clarke, 1952).

Little Book of Eternal Wisdom and Little Book of Truth, ed. J. M. Clark (London: Faber and Faber, 1953).

Henry Totting of Oyta. *Quaestiones in Isagogen Porphyrii*, ed. J. Schneider (Munich: Bayerische Akademie der Wissenschaften, 1979).

Hermann of Carinthia. *De essentiis: A Critical Edition with Translation and Commentary*, ed. C. Burnett (Leiden: Brill, 1982).

Hermann of Reichenau. *Musica*, ed. and tr. L. W. Ellinwood (Rochester: Eastman School of Music, 1936).

Hermes Trismegistus. *Corpus Hermeticum*, ed. A. D. Nock; tr. [French] A. J. Festugière (Paris: Les Belles Lettres, 1945–54).

Hervaeus Natalis. *De iurisdictione*, ed. L. Hödl (Munich: Hueber, 1959).

De paupertate Christi et apostolorum, ed. J. Sikes, *Archives d'histoire doctrinale et littéraire du moyen âge* 12–13 (1937–8) 209–97.

De potestate papae (Paris, 1647; repr. Farnborough: Gregg, 1966).

Defensa doctrinae D. Thomae, in E. Krebs (ed.) *Theologie und Wissenschaft nach der Lehre der Hochscholastik an der Hand der bisher ungedruckten Defensa Doctrinae D. Thomae des Hervaeus Natalis mit Beifügung gedruckter und ungedruckter Paralleltexte* (Münster: Aschendorff, 1912).

In quattor libros Sententiarum commentaria (Paris, 1647; repr. Farnborough: Gregg, 1966).

Opinio de difficultatibus contra doctrinam fratris Thome [Defensio doctrinae fr. Thomae], ed. P. Piccari, *Memorie Domenicane* n.s. 26 (1995) 5–193.

The Poverty of Christ and the Apostles, tr. J. D. Jones (Toronto: Pontifical Institute of Mediaeval Studies, 1999).

Quodlibeta cum octo ipsius profundissimis tractatibus (Venice, 1513; repr. Ridgewood, NJ: Gregg, 1966).

A Treatise of Master Hervaeus Natalis (d. 1323), The Doctor Perspicacissimus, On Second Intentions, ed. J. P. Doyle (Milwaukee, WI: Marquette University Press, 2008).

Heymeric de Campo. *Compendium divinorum*, ed. J. Korolec, *Studia Mediewistyczne* 8 (1967) 19–75; 9 (1968) 3–90.

De signis notionalibus trinitatis et unitatis supernae, ed. M. Hoenen, *Freiburger Zeitschrift für Philosophie und Theologie* 45 (1998) 207–63.

Dyalogus Super Reuelacionibus Beate Birgitte: A Critical Edition with an Introduction, ed. A. Fredriksson Adman (Uppsala: Uppsala University Press, 2003).

Opera selecta, ed. R. Imbach and P. Ladner (Freiburg: Universitätsverlag, 2001–).

Problemata inter Albertum Magnum et Sanctum Thomam ad intelligentiam utriusque opinionis multum conferentia (Cologne, 1496).

Reparationes totius naturalis philosophiae (Cologne, 1494).

Hildegard of Bingen. *Analecta Sanctae Hildegardis opera spicilegio solesmensi parata*, ed. J.-B. Pitra (Monte Cassino: Typis Sacri Montis Casinensis, 1882).

Book of Divine Works with Letters and Songs, tr. R. Cunningham and M. Fox (Santa Fe, NM: Bear and Company, 1987).

The Book of the Rewards of Life, tr. B. Hozeski (New York: Garland, 1994).

Cause et cure, ed. L. Moulinier and R. Berndt. (Berlin: Akademie Verlag, 2003).

Epistolarium, ed. L. van Acker (Turnhout: Brepols, 1991–3).

The Letters, tr. J. Baird and R. Ehrman (New York: Oxford University Press, 1994–).

Liber divinorum operum, ed. A. Derolez and P. Dronke (Turnhout: Brepols, 1996).

Liber vitae meritorum, ed. A. Carlevaris (Turnhout: Brepols, 1995).

On Natural Philosophy and Medicine: Selections from Cause et Cure, tr. M. Berger (Cambridge: Brewer, 1999).

Opera omnia, in J.-P. Migne (ed.) *Patrologiae cursus completus: series latina* (Paris, 1844–91) vol. CXCVII.

Physica (Argentorati, 1533).

Physica: The Complete English Translation of her Classic Work on Health and Healing, tr. P. Throop (Rochester, VT: Healing Arts Press, 1998).

Scivias, ed. A. Führkötter and A. Carlevaris (Turnhout: Brepols, 1978).

Scivias, tr. C. Hart and J. Bishop (New York: Paulist Press, 1990).

Hillel ben Samuel of Verona. *Sefer tagmule ha-nefesh le-ha-hakam ha-filosof we-ha-rofeʾ r. Hillel ben . . . r. Shemuʾel ben . . . r. Eliʿezer mi-Verona*, ed. S. Z. H. Halberstam (Lyck: Meqitsey Nirdamim, 1874).

Sefer tagmulei ha-nefesh, ed. G. Sermoneta (Jerusalem: Israel Academy of Sciences and Humanities, 1981).

Hincmar of Rheims. *De cavendis vitiis et virtutibus exercendis*, ed. D. Nachtmann (Munich: Monumenta Germaniae Historica, 1998).

Epistolae, ed. E. Perels (Munich: Monumenta Germaniae Historica, 1975–).

Honorius Augustodunensis. *Clavis physicae*, ed. P. Lucentini (Rome: Edizioni di Storia e Letteratura, 1974).

L'elucidarium et les lucidaires, ed. Y. Lefèvre (Paris: De Boccard, 1954).

Imago mundi, ed. V. I. J. Flint, *Archives d'histoire doctrinale et littéraire du moyen âge* 49 (1982) 7–153.

Hostiensis. *In I–VI Decretalium libros commentaria* (Venice, 1581; repr. Turin: Bottega d'Erasmo, 1965).

Summa aurea (Lyon, 1537; repr. Aalen: Scientia Verlag, 1962).

Hugh Etherian. *Contra Patarenos*, ed. and tr. J. Hamilton *et al.* (Leiden: Brill, 2004).

Liber de differentia naturae et personae, ed. N. M. Häring, *Mediaeval Studies* 24 (1962) 1–34.

Hugh of Honau. *Liber de diversitate naturae et personae proprietatumque personalium non tam Latinorum quam ex Graecorum auctoritatibus extractus*, ed. N. M. Häring, *Archives d'histoire doctrinale et littéraire du moyen âge* 29 (1962) 103–216.

Liber de homoysion et homoeision, ed. N. M. Häring, *Archives d'histoire doctrinale et littéraire du moyen âge* 34 (1967) 129–253; 35 (1968) 211–95.

Liber de ignorantia, ed. N. M. Häring, *Mediaeval Studies* 25 (1963) 209–30.

Hugh of St. Cher. *De prophetia*, in J.-P. Torrell (ed.) *Théorie de la prophétie et philosophie de la connaissance aux environs de 1230: la contribution d'Hugues de Saint-Cher (Ms. Douai 434, Question 481)* (Leuven: Spicilegium sacrum Lovaniense, 1977).

Opera omnia in universum Vetus et Novum Testamentum (Lyon: J. A. Huguetan et G. Barbier, 1669).

Sacrorum Bibliorum vulgatae editionis concordantiae, ed. F. Lucas and H. Phalèse (Insulis: L. Lefort, 1837).

Tractatus super Missam, seu, Speculum Ecclesiae, ed. G. M. Sölch (Münster: Aschendorff, 1940).

Hugh of St. Victor. *De archa Noe; Libellus de formatione arche* (Turnhout: Brepols, 2001).

De contemplatione et eius speciebus, ed. R. Baron (Tournai: Desclée, 1958).

De sacramentis christianae fidei, in J.-P. Migne (ed.) *Patrologiae cursus completus: series latina* (Paris, 1844–91) vol. CLXXVI.

De tribus diebus, ed. D. Poirel (Turnhout: Brepols, 2001).

Didascalicon: A Medieval Guide to the Arts, tr. J. Taylor (New York: Columbia University Press, 1961).

Didascalicon de studio legendi, ed. C. H. Buttimer (Washington, DC: Catholic University of America Press, 1939).

On the Sacraments of the Christian Faith, tr. R. J. Deferrari (Cambridge, MA: Mediaeval Academy of America, 1951).

Opera propaedeutica, ed. R. Baron (Notre Dame, IN: University of Notre Dame Press, 1966).

Practical Geometry, tr. F. A. Homann (Milwaukee, WI: Marquette University Press, 1991).

Selected Spiritual Writings (New York: Harper and Row, 1962).

Hugolin of Orvieto. *Commentarius in quattuor libros Sententiarum*, ed. W. Eckermann (Würzburg: Augustinus-Verlag, 1980–8).

Huguccio. *Summa decretorum, 1: Distinctiones I–XX*, ed. O. Přerovský (Vatican: Biblioteca Apostolica Vaticana, 2006–).

Humbert of Romans. *Opera de vita regulari*, ed. J. J. Berthier (Rome: A. Befani, 1888; repr. Turin: Marietti, 1956).

Hume, David. *Dialogues Concerning Natural Religion*, ed. R. Popkin (Indianapolis, IN: Hackett, 1980).

Enquiry Concerning the Human Understanding and Concerning the Principles of Morals, ed. L. A. Selby-Bigge, 2nd edn (Oxford: Clarendon Press, 1902).

Ḥunayn ibn Isḥāq al-ʿIbādī. *Hunain ibn Isḥāq über die syrischen und arabischen Galen-Übersetzungen*, ed. and tr. G. Bergsträsser (Leipzig: Brockhaus, 1925).

Isagoge ad artem Galeni, ed. G. Maurach, *Sudhoffs Archiv* 62 (1978) 148–74.

Al-Masāʾil fī al-ṭibb lil-mutaʿallimīn, ed. M. Abū Rayyān et al. (Cairo: Dār al-Jāmiʿāt al-Misrīyah, 1978).

Questions on Medicine for Scholars, ed. P. Ghalioungui (Cairo: al-Ahram Center for Scientific Translations, 1980).

Ibn al-ʿArabī, Muḥyi al-Dīn. *The Bezels of Wisdom*, tr. R. W. J. Austin (New York: Paulist Press, 1980).

Al-Fuṣūṣ al-ḥikam, ed. A. E. Affifi (Cairo: Dār Iḥyāʾ al-Kutub al-ʿArabīyah, 1946).

Al-Futūḥāt al-makkiyya, ed. O. Yahia (Cairo: al-Hayʾah al-Miṣrīyah al-ʿĀmmah lil-Kitāb, 1972–91).

The Meccan Revelations, tr. M. Chodkiewicz et al. (New York: Pir Press, 2002–4).

Ibn Bājja. "The Governance of the Solitary," tr. L. Berman, in R. Lerner and M. Mahdi (eds.) *Medieval Political Philosophy: A Source Book* (Toronto: Free Press of Glencoe, 1963) 122–33.

ʿIlm al-nafs, tr. M. S. H. al-Maʿṣūmī (Karachi: Pakistan Historical Society, 1961; repr. Frankfurt: Publications of the Institute for the History of Arabic and Islamic Science, 1999).

Kitāb an-nafs, ed. M. S. H. al-Maʿṣūmī (Damascus: Majmaʿ al-ʿLughah al-ʿArabīyah bi-Dimashq, 1960; repr. Frankfurt: Publications of the Institute for the History of Arabic and Islamic Science, 1999).

Libro de la generación y la corrupción, ed. and tr. J. Puig Montada (Madrid: CSIC, 1995).

Rasāʾil Ibn Bājjah al-ilāhīyah, ed. M. Fakhry (Beirut: Dār al-Nahār, 1968).

Ibn Fūrak, Abū Bakr Muḥammad. *Kitāb al-ḥudūd fī al-uṣūl*, ed. M. al-Sulaymānī (Beirut: Dār al-Gharb al-Islāmī, 1999).

Kitāb mushkil al-ḥadīth, ed. D. Gimaret (Damascus: al-Maʿhad al-Faransī lil-Dirāsāt al-ʿArabīyah bi-Dimashq, 2003).

Mujarrad maqālāt al-Ashʿarī, ed. D. Gimaret (Beirut: Dār al-Mashriq, 1987).

Ibn Ḥanbal. *Kitāb al-sunna*, ed. M. al-Qahtani (Dammam: Dār Ibn al-Qayyīm, 1986).

Al-Musnad (Miṣr: Dār al-Maʿārif, 1949–56).

Ibn al-Haytham (Alhacen). *Completion of the Conics*, ed. and tr. J. P. Hogendijk (New York: Springer, 1985).

De aspectibus I–III, ed. and tr. A. M. Smith (Philadelphia, PA: American Philosophical Society, 2001).

De aspectibus IV–V, ed. and tr. A. M. Smith (Philadelphia, PA: American Philosophical Society, 2006).

De aspectibus VI, ed. and tr. A. M. Smith (Philadelphia, PA: American Philosophical Society, 2008).

De configuratione mundi, ed. J. L. Mancha, in M. Comes *et al.* (eds.) *"Ochava Espera" y "Astrofísica": Textos y estudios sobre las fuentes árabes de la astronomía de Alfonso X* (Barcelona: Universidad de Barcelona, 1990) 133–207.

On the Configuration of the World, ed. Y. T. Langermann (New York: Garland, 1990).

The Optics of Ibn al-Haytham, Books I–III: On Direct Vision, tr. A. I. Sabra (London: Warburg Institute, 1989).

The Optics of Ibn al-Haytham, Books I-II-III: On Direct Vision. The Arabic Text, ed. A. I. Sabra (Kuwait: National Council for Culture, Arts and Letters, 1983).

The Optics of Ibn al-Haytham, Edition of the Arabic Text of Books IV–V: On Reflection and Images Seen by Reflection, ed. A. I. Sabra (Kuwait: National Council for Culture, Arts and Letters, 2002).

Ibn Ḥazm. *Le collier du pigeon, ou, De l'amour et des amants = Ṭawq al-hamāma fī al-ulfa wa-al-ullāf*, ed. L. Bercher (Algiers: Carbonel, 1949).

  Épitre morale: Kitāb al-ahlāq wa-l-siyar, ed. N. Tomiche (Beirut: Commission Internationale pour la Traduction des Chefs-d'Œuvre, 1961).

  In Pursuit of Virtue: The Moral Theology and Psychology of Ibn Hazm al-Andalusi with a Translation of his Book al-Akhlāq wa'l-siyar, ed. M. Abū Laylah (London: Ta-Ha, 1990).

  Kitāb al-fiṣal fī al-milal wa-al-ahwā' wa-al-nihal, in M. Asín Palacios (ed. and tr.) *Abenházam de Córdoba y su historia crítica de las ideas religiosas* (Madrid: Real Academia de la Historia, 1927–32; repr. Madrid: Turner, 1984).

  Marātib al-ʿulūm = The Categories of the Sciences, in A. G. Chejne (ed. and tr.) *Ibn Hazm* (Chicago: Kazi Publications, 1982).

  The Ring of the Dove: A Treatise on the Art and Practice of Arab Love, tr. A. Arberry (London: Luzac, 1953; repr. 1997).

Ibn Jamāʿa. Badr al-Dīn Muḥammad. *Taḥrīr al-ahkām fī tadbīr ahl al-Islām*, ed. and tr. H. Kofler, *Islamica* 6 (1934) 349–414; 7 (1935) 1–64; Schlussheft (1938) 18–129.

Ibn Kammūna. *The Arabic Treatise on the Immortality of the Soul by Saʿd ibn Mansur ibn Kammuna*, ed. L. Nemoy (New Haven, CT: Yale University Library, 1944).

  Examination of the Inquiries into the Three Faiths: A Thirteenth-Century Essay in Comparative Religion, ed. M. Perlmann (Berkeley: University of California Press, 1967).

  Examination of the Inquiries into the Three Faiths: A Thirteenth-Century Essay in the Comparative Study of Religion, tr. M. Perlmann (Berkeley: University of California Press, 1971).

  "Ibn Kammuna's Treatise on the Immortality of the Soul," tr. L. Nemoy in S. Löwinger *et al.* (eds.) *Ignace Goldziher Memorial Volume* (Jerusalem: Rubin Mass, 1958) II: 83–99.

  Al-Tanqīḥāt fī sharḥ al-talwīḥāt: Refinement and Commentary on Suhrawardi's Intimations, a Thirteenth-Century Text on Natural Philosophy and Psychology, ed. H. Ziai and A. Alwishah (Costa Mesa, CA: Mazda, 2003).

Ibn Khaldun. *Muqaddima*, ed. and trans. F. Rosenthal (Princeton, NJ: Princeton University Press, 1967).

  Shifāʾ al-sāʾil li-tahdīb al-masāʾil, ed. M. al-Ṭanjī (Istanbul: Osman Yalcin Matbaasi, 1958).

  Taʾrīkh al-ʿAllāmat Ibn Khaldūn: Kitāb al-ʿibar wa-dīwān al-mubtadaʾ wa-al-khabar fī ayyām al-ʿArab wa-al-ʿAjam wa-al-Barbar wa-man ʿaṣarahum min dhawī al-Sulṭān al-Akbar (Beirut: Maktabat al-Madrasah wa-Dār al-Kitab al-Lubnani, 1961).

  La voie et la loi ou le maître et le juriste, tr. R. Pérez (Paris: Sindbad, 1991).

Ibn Masarra. *Min al-turāth al-falsafī*, ed. M. Jaʿfar (Cairo: al-Majlis al-Aʿla lil-Thaqāfa, 1982).

Ibn al-Muqaffaʿ. *Al-Adab al-ṣaghīr wa-al-adab al-kabīr*, ed. I. Fawwāl (Beirut: Dār al-Kitāb al-ʿArabī, 1994).

  Al-Manṭiq li-Ibn al-Muqaffaʿ, Ḥudūd al-manṭiq li-Ibn Bahrīz, ed. M. T. Dānishpāzhūh (Tehran: Anjuman-i Shāhanshāhī-i Falsafah-i Īrān, 1978) 1–93.

Ibn al-Nadīm. *Kitāb al-Fihrist*, ed. G. Flügel (Leipzig: Vogel, 1871–2).

Ibn al-Rāwandī. *Faḍīḥat al-muʿtazila*, ed. H. S. Nyberg, in Ibn al-Khayyāṭ, *Kitāb al-intiṣār wa-al-radd ʿala Ibn ar-Rawandī al-Mulhid* (Cairo: Maṭbaʿat al-Kutub al-Misrīyya, 1925).

    Le livre du triomphe et de la réfutation d'Ibn al Rawandi l'hérétique, tr. A. N. Nadir (Beirut: Catholic Press, 1957).

Ibn Sabʿīn. *Budd al-ʿārif*, ed. J. Kattūra (Beirut: Dār al-Andalus, 1978).

Ibn Taymiyya. *Darʾ taʿāruḍ al-ʿaql wa-al-naql*, ed. ʿAbd al-Laṭīf ʿAbd al-Raḥmān (Beirut: Dār al-Kutub al-ʿIlmiyyah, 1997).

    Ibn Taymiyya against the Greek Logicians, ed. and tr. W. B. Hallaq (Oxford: Clarendon Press, 1993).

    Ibn Taymiyyah Expounds on Islam: Selected Writings of Shaykh al-Islam Taqi ad-Din Ibn Taymiyyah on Islamic Faith, Life, and Society, tr. M. A. Ansari (Riyadh: General Administration of Culture and Publication, 2000).

    Ibn Taimiyya on Public and Private Law in Islam: Or Public Policy in Islamic Jurisprudence, tr. O. A. Farrukh (Beirut: Khayats, 1966).

    Jawāb al-ṣaḥīḥ li-man baddala dīn al-masīḥ, ed. A. ibn Nāṣir et al. (Riyadh: al-Mamlakah al-ʿArabīya al-Saʿūdiya, 1993–9).

    Kitāb al-imān, ed. M. al-Albānī (Egypt: Maktabat Anis Ibn Mālik, 1980).

    Kitāb al-imān: Book of Faith, tr. S. H. al-Ani and S. A. Tel (Bloomington, IN: Iman, 1999).

    Kitāb al-Siyāsa al-sharʿiyya, ed. M. al-Mubārak (Beirut: Dār al-Kutub al-Arabīya, 1966).

    A Muslim Theologian's Response to Christianity, tr. T. F. Michel (Delmar, NY: Caravan Books, 1984).

Ibn al-Ṭayyib. *Arabic Logic: Ibn al-Ṭayyib's Commentary on Porphyry's Eisagoge*, tr. K. Gyekye (Albany: State University of New York Press, 1979).

    Commentaire sur la Genèse, ed. and tr. J. C. J. Sanders (Leuven: Secrétariat du Corpus scriptorum Christianorum orientalium, 1967).

    Der Kategorienkommentar von Abū l-Farag ʿAbdallāh ibn aṭ-Ṭayyib: Text und Untersuchungen, ed. C. Ferrari (Leiden: Brill, 2006).

    Tafsīr kitāb Isāghūji li-Furfūriyūs, ed. K. Gyekye (Beirut: Dār al-Mashriq, 1975).

Ibn Ṭufayl. *Ḥayy ibn Yaqẓān*, ed. L. Gauthier, 2nd edn (Beirut: Imprimerie Catholique, 1936).

    Ḥayy ibn Yaqzan, a Philosophical Tale, tr. L. Goodman (New York: Twain Publishers, 1972).

al-Ījī, ʿAḍud al-Dīn. *Kitāb al-mawāqif*, ed. A. R. ʿUmayrah (Beirut: Dār al-Jīl, 1997).

Ikhwān al-Ṣafāʾ. *Arabische Philosophie und Wissenschaft in der Enzyklopädie: Kitāb Ihwān as-ṣafāʾ (III): Die Lehre von Seele und Intellekt*, ed. S. Diwald (Wiesbaden: Harrassowitz, 1975).

    The Case of Animals versus Man before the King of the Jinn: A Tenth-Century Ecological Fable of the Pure Brethren of Basra, tr. L.E. Goodman (Boston: Twayne, 1978).

    The Epistles of the Sincere Brethren (Rasāʾil Ikhwān al-Ṣafāʾ): An Annotated Translation of Epistles 43 to 47, tr. E. van Reijn (Montreux: Minerva Press, 1995).

    Epistola fratrum sincerorum in cosmographia, ed. P. Gauthier-Dalché, *Revue d'histoire des texts* 18 (1988) 137–67.

    Liber de quatuor confectionibus, ed. A. Sannino, *Studi Medievali* 41 (2000) 151–89.

    Rasāʾil Ikhwān al-Ṣafāʾ wa Khullān al-Wafāʾ, ed. M. Ghālib (Beirut: Dār al-Sādir, 1957).

Immanuel ben Solomon. *Il commento di Emanuele Romano al Capitolo I della Genesi*, ed. and tr. F. Michelini Tocci (Rome: Centro di studi semitici, Istituto di studi del vicino Oriente, 1963).

    Machberot Immanuel ha-Romi, ed. D. Jarden (Jerusalem: Mossad Bialik, 1957).

    Tophet and Eden (Hell and Paradise), tr. H. Gollancz (London: University of London Press, 1921).

Innocent IV. *Commentaria super libros quinque decretalium [Apparatus]* (Frankfurt, 1570; repr. Frankfurt: Minerva, 1968).

Irnerius (?). *Questiones de iuris subtilitatibus*, ed. G. Zanetti (Florence: La Nuova Italia, 1958).

Summa codicis, ed. H. Fitting (Berlin: Guttentag, 1894; repr. Frankfurt: Minerva, 1971).

Isaac Abarbanel. *Principles of Faith = Rosh amanah*, tr. M. M. Kellner (Rutherford, NJ: Fairleigh Dickenson University Press, 1982).

Sefer rosh amanah (Tel Aviv: Sifriyati, 1958).

Isaac Albalag. *Sefer Tikkun ha-De'ot*, ed. G. Vajda (Jerusalem: ha-Akademyah ha-leumit ha-Yisreelit le-mada'im, 1973).

Isaac ben Joseph Pulgar. *Ezer ha-dat*, ed. J. S. Levinger (Tel Aviv: University of Tel Aviv, 1984).

Isaac Israeli. *Isaac Israeli, a Neoplatonic Philosopher of the Early Tenth Century: His Works Translated with Comments and an Outline of his Philosophy*, tr. A. Altmann and S. M. Stern (London: Oxford University Press, 1958; repr. Westport, CT: Greenwood, 1979).

Kitāb al-ḥudud wa-al-rusūm, ed. H. Hirschfeld, *Jewish Quarterly Review* 15 (1902) 689–93.

Kitāb al-jawāhir, ed. S. M. Stern, *Journal of Jewish Studies* 7 (1956) 13–29.

Liber de definicionibus, ed. J. T. Muckle, *Archives d'histoire doctrinale et littéraire du moyen âge* 11 (1937–8) 299–340.

Omnia opera Ysaac in hoc volumine contenta cum quibusdam aliis opusculis (Lyon, 1515).

Sefer ha-Gvulim, ed. H. Hirschfeld, in *Festschrift zum 80. Geburtstag Moritz Steinschneiders* (Leipzig: Harrassowitz, 1896) 131–42.

Sefer ha-Yesodot, ed. S. Fried (Drohobycz: Bi-defus A. H. Zupnik, 1900).

Sha'ar ha-Yesodot, ed. A. Altmann, *Journal of Jewish Studies* 7 (1956) 31–57.

Isaac of Stella. *Epistola de anima*, in B. McGinn (tr.) *Three Treatises on Man: A Cistercian Anthropology* (Kalamazoo, MI: Cistercian Publications, 1977).

The Selected Works of Isaac of Stella: A Cistercian Voice from the Twelfth Century, tr. D. Deme (Aldershot: Ashgate, 2007).

Sermones, ed. A. Hoste, G. Raciti, and G. Salet (Paris: Cerf, 1967–87).

Sermons for the Christian Year, tr. H. McCaffrey (Kalamazoo, MI: Cistercian Publications, 1979).

Isidore of Seville. *Etymologiae*, ed. W. M. Lindsay (Oxford: Clarendon Press, 1911).

The Etymologies of Isidore of Seville, tr. S. A. Barney (Cambridge: Cambridge University Press, 2006).

The Letters of St. Isidore of Seville, tr. G. B. Ford, 2nd edn (Amsterdam: Hakkert, 1970).

Sententiae, ed. P. Cazier (Turnhout: Brepols, 1998).

Traité de la nature, ed. and tr. J. Fontaine (Paris: Institut d'Études Augustiniennes, 1960; repr. 2002).

Ivo of Chartres. *Correspondance* (1090–8), ed. J. Leclercq (Paris: Les Belles Lettres, 1949).

Opera omnia, in J.-P. Migne (ed.) *Patrologiae cursus completus: series latina* (Paris, 1844–91) vols. CLXI–CLXII.

Ways of Mercy: The Prologue of Ivo of Chartres, ed. B. C. Brasington (Münster: LIT, 2004).

Jābir ibn Ḥayyān. *Names, Natures and Things: The Alchemists Jabir ibn Hayyan and his Kitāb al-Ahjar (Book of Stones)*, ed. S. N. Haq (Dordrecht: Kluwer, 1994).

(?). *The Works of Geber, the Most Famous Arabian Prince and Philosopher*, tr. R. Russel (London, 1678; repr. London: Dent, 1928).

Jacob Anatoli. *Malmad ha-talmidim* (Lyck: Mekitze Nirdamim, 1866; repr. Jerusalem: Miketze Nirdamim, 1968).

James of Ascoli. "Zwei Quästionen des Iacobus de Aesculo über das 'Esse Objectivum'," ed. T. Yokoyama, in L. Scheffczyk *et al.* (eds.) *Wahrheit und Verkündigung: Michael Schmaus zum 70. Geburtstag* (Munich: Paderborn, 1967) I: 31–74.

James of Douai. *Een commentaar op de Anima*, ed. J. de Raedemaeker (Leuven: Licentiaatsverhandeling Wijsbegeerte en Letteren, 1962).

De scientia animae et de cognitione suiipsius, ed. B. C. Bazán, *Philosophia* 35 (1969) 111–53.

James of Piacenza. *Lectura cum quaestionibus super tertium De anima*, ed. Z. Kuksewicz (Wroclaw: Ossolineum, 1967).

James of Thérines. *Quodlibets I and II*, ed. P. Glorieux (Paris: Vrin, 1958).

James of Viterbo. *Disputationes de quolibet*, ed. E. Ypma (Würzburg: Augustinus, 1968–75).

   On Christian Government: De regimine Christiano, ed. and tr. R. W. Dyson (Woodbridge: Boydell Press, 1995).

   Prima quaestio disputata de verbo, ed. C. Scanzillo, *Asprenas* n.s. 19 (1972) 25–61.

   Quaestiones de divinis praedicamentis, ed. E. Ypma (Rome: Augustinianum, 1983–6).

Jan van Ruusbroec. *Opera omnia*, ed. G. de Baere (Turnhout: Brepols, 1988–).

   The Spiritual Espousals and Other Works, tr. J. A. Wiseman (New York: Paulist Press, 1985).

Jerome. *Lettres*, ed. and tr. J. Labourt (Paris: Les Belles Lettres, 1949–63).

   Opera (Corpus Christianorum, Series latina 72–) (Turnhout: Brepols, 1958–).

Joachim de Fiore. *Aspetti inediti della Vita e delle Opere*, ed. P. De Leo (Soveria Manelli: Rubbettino Editore, 1988).

   Expositio in apocalypsim (Venice, 1527; repr. Frankfurt: Minerva, 1964).

   Liber de concordia novi ac veteris testamenti, ed. E. R. Daniel, *Transactions of the American Philosophical Society* 73 (1983).

   Psalterium decem chordarum (Venice, 1527; repr. Frankfurt: Minerva, 1965).

   Tractatus super quatuor evangelia, ed. E. Buonaiuti (Rome: Tipografia del Senato, 1930).

Johannes Teutonicus. *Apparatus glossarum in Compilationem tertiam*, ed. K. Pennington (Vatican: Biblioteca Apostolica Vaticana, 1981).

   Apparatus glossarum in Compilationem quartam, in A. Augustín (ed.) *Antiquae collectiones decretalium* (Lerida, 1576).

   Glossa ordinaria, in Gratian, *Decretum Gratiani emendatum et annotationibus illustratum una cum glossis* (Paris, 1601).

John Baconthorpe. *Quaestiones in quatuor libros Sententiarum, et quodlibetales* (Cremona, 1618; repr. Westmead, UK: Gregg, 1969).

   Die "Quaestiones speculativae et canonicae" des Johannes Baconthorp über der sakramentalen Charakter, ed. E. Borchert (Munich: Schöningh, 1974).

John of Bassol. *Opera* (Paris, 1516–17).

John Blund. *Tractatus de anima*, ed. D. A. Callus and R. W. Hunt (London: Oxford University Press, 1970).

John Buridan. *In Metaphysicam Aristotelis questiones acutissimae* (Paris, 1518; repr. Frankfurt: Minerva, 1964).

   Jean Buridan's Logic: The Treatise on Supposition, the Treatise on Consequences, tr. P. King (Dordrecht: Reidel, 1985).

   "John Buridan's Philosophy of Mind: An Edition and Translation of Book III of his 'Questions on Aristotle's De anima' (Third Redaction), with Commentary and Critical and Interpretative Essay," ed. J. Zupko (Ph.D. dissertation: Cornell University, 1989).

   Questiones in Aristotelis tres libros de anima, ed. G. Lokert (Paris, 1516; repr. in B. Patar, *Le traité de l'âme* [Leuven: Éditions de l'Institut Supérieur de Philosophie, 1991]).

   Quaestiones in Praedicamenta, ed. J. Schneider (Munich: Beck, 1983).

   Quaestiones libri Porphyrii, ed. R. Tatarsynski, *Przeglad Tomistyczny* 2 (1986) 111–95.

   Quaestiones super De generatione et corruptione, ed. M. Streijger (Leiden: Brill, forthcoming).

   Quaestiones super decem libros Ethicorum Aristotelis ad Nicomachum (Paris, 1513; repr. Frankfurt: Minerva, 1968).

   Quaestiones super octo Physicorum (Venice, 1509: repr. Frankfurt: Minerva, 1964).

   Questiones longe super Librum Perihermeneias, ed. R. van der Lecq (Nijmegen: Ingenium, 1983).

Quaestiones super libris quattuor de caelo et mundo, ed. E. A. Moody (Cambridge, MA: Mediaeval Academy of America, 1942).

Sophismata, ed. T. K. Scott (Stuttgart-Bad Cannstatt: Frommann-Holzboog, 1977).

Sophisms on Meaning and Truth, tr. T. K. Scott (New York: Appleton-Century-Crofts, 1966).

Summulae de demonstrationibus, ed. L. M. de Rijk (Groningen: Ingenium, 2001).

Summulae de dialectica, tr. G. Klima (New Haven, CT: Yale University Press, 2001).

Summulae de practica sophismatum, ed. F. Pironet (Turnhout: Brepols 2004).

Summulae de praedicabilibus, ed. L. M. de Rijk (Nijmegen: Ingenium, 1995).

Summulae: de propositionibus, ed. R. van der Lecq (Turnhout: Brepols, 2005).

Summulae de suppositionibus, ed. R. van der Lecq (Nijmegen: Ingenium, 1998).

Summulae in praedicamenta, ed. E. P. Bos (Nijmegen: Ingenium, 1994).

Tractatus de consequentiis, ed. H. Hubien (Leuven: Publications universitaires, 1976).

Tractatus de differentia universalis ad individuum, ed. S. Szyller, *Przeglad Tomistyczny* 3 (1987) 135–78.

Le traité de l'âme de Jean Buridan (De prima lectura), ed. B. Patar (Leuven: Éditions de l'Institut Supérieur de Philosophie, 1991).

John the Canon. *Quaestiones super Physica Aristotelis* (Padua, 1475).

John Capreolus. *Defensiones theologiae divi Thomae Aquinatis*, ed. C. Paban and T. Pègues (Turin: A. Cattier, 1900–8; repr. Frankfurt: Minerva, 1967).

On the Virtues, tr. K. White and R. Cessario (Washington, DC: Catholic University of America Press, 2001).

John Cassian. *Conlationes XXIIII*, ed. M. Petschenig (Vienna: apud C. Geroldi filium, 1886; repr. Vienna: Verlag der Österreichischen Akademie der Wissenschaften, 2004).

De institutis coenobiorum et de octo principalium vitiorum remediis, ed. M. Petschenig (Vienna: Tempsky, 1888; repr. Vienna: Verlag der Österreichischen Akademie der Wissenschaften, 2004).

John of Celaya. *Expositio in librum Praedicabilium Porphyri cum questionibus eiusdem secundum triplicem viam beate Thome, realium et nominalium* (Paris, 1516).

John Climacus. *Scala paradisi*, in J.-P. Migne (ed.) *Patrologiae cursus completus: series graeca* (Paris, 1857–66) LXXXVIII: 631–1164.

John of Dacia. *Opera*, ed. A. Otto (Copenhagen: Gad, 1955).

John of Damascus. *De fide orthodoxa: The Versions of Burgundio and Cerbanus*, ed. E. M. Buytaert (St. Bonaventure, NY: Franciscan Institute, 1955).

Dialectica, in B. Kotter (ed.) *Die Schriften des Johannes von Damaskos* (Berlin: De Gruyter, 1969).

Dialectica: Version of Robert Grosseteste, ed. O. A. Colligan (St. Bonaventure, NY: Franciscan Institute 1953).

"An Edition of Three Unpublished Translations by Robert Grosseteste of Three Short Works of John of Damascus," ed. M. Holland (Ph.D. dissertation: Harvard University, 1980).

John Dorp. *Perutile compendium totius logicae Joannis Buridani cum praeclarissima . . . Joannis Dorp expositione* (Venice, 1499; repr. Frankfurt: Minerva, 1965).

John Duns Scotus. *Contingency and freedom = Lectura I 39*, ed. and tr. A. Vos (Dordrecht: Kluwer, 1994).

Cuestiones Cuodlibetales, ed. and tr. F. Alluntis (Madrid: Biblioteca De Autores Cristianos, 1968).

Duns Scotus on the Will and Morality, tr. A. B. Wolter (Washington, DC: Catholic University of America Press, 1986).

Early Oxford Lecture on Individuation, ed. and tr. A. B. Wolter (St. Bonaventure, NY: Franciscan Institute, 2005).

God and Creatures: The Quodlibetal Questions, tr. F. Alluntis and A. B. Wolter (Princeton, NJ: Princeton University Press, 1975; repr. Washington, DC: Catholic University of America Press, 1987).

Opera omnia, ed. C. Balić *et al.* (Vatican City: Typis Polyglottis Vaticanis, 1950–).

Opera omnia, ed. L. Wadding (Lyon, 1639; repr. Hildesheim: Olms, 1968).

Opera omnia (Paris: Vivès, 1891–5).

Opera philosophica, ed. T. Noone *et al.* (St. Bonaventure, NY: Franciscan Institute, 1997–2006).

Philosophical Writings, tr. A. B. Wolter (Edinburgh: Nelson, 1962; repr. Indianapolis, IN: Hackett, 1987).

Questions on the Metaphysics of Aristotle, tr. G. J. Etzkorn and A. B. Wolter (St. Bonaventure, NY: Franciscan Institute, 1997–98).

Reportatio I-A, ed. A. B. Wolter and O. V. Bychkov (St. Bonaventure, NY: St. Bonaventure University Press, 2004).

Reportatio IIA (manuscript in Turin K, ii, 26).

A Treatise on God as First Principle [De primo principio], ed. and tr. A. B. Wolter (Chicago: Franciscan Herald Press, 1966; rev. edn, 1983).

John of Erfurt. *Summa confessorum*, ed. N. Brieskorn (Frankfurt: Lang, 1980–1).

John of Freiburg. *Summa confessorum* (Augsburg, 1476).

John of Garland. *Ars lectoria Ecclesie*, ed. E. Marguin-Hamon (Turnhout: Brepols, 2003).

La Clavis compendii de Jean de Garlande: édition critique, traduite et commentée, ed. and tr. E. Marguin-Hamond (Turnhout: Brepols, 2008).

Compendium gramatice, ed. T. Haye (Weimar: Böhlau, 1995).

The Dictionarius, ed. and tr. B. B. Rubin (Lawrence, KS: Coronado Press, 1981).

John Gerson. *The Consolation of Theology = De consolatione theologiae*, ed. and tr. C. L. Miller (New York: Abaris Books, 1998).

Early Works, tr. B. McGuire (New York: Paulist Press, 1998).

Œuvres complètes, ed. P. Glorieux (Paris: Desclée de Brouwer, 1960–73).

Opus tripartitum, in G. Ouy (ed.) *Gerson bilingue: Les deux rédactions latine et française de quelques œuvres du chancelier parisien* (Paris: Champion, 1998).

Selections from A Deo exivit, Contra curiositatem studentium and De mystica theologia speculative, tr. S. Ozment (Leiden: Brill, 1969).

John of Holland. *Four Tracts on Logic (Suppositiones, Fallacie, Obligationes, Insolubilia)*, ed. E. P. Bos (Nijmegen: Artistarium, 1985).

John Huntman. *Logica*, ed. L. M. de Rijk (Stuttgart-Bad Cannstatt: Frommann-Holzboog, 1999).

John Hus. *De ecclesia: The Church*, tr. D. S. Schaff (New York: C. Scribner's Sons, 1915; repr. Westport, CN: Greenwood Press, 1974).

Documenta magistri Johannis Hus, ed. F. Palacky (Prague: Tempsky, 1869).

Korespondence a dokumenty, ed. V. Novotný (V Praze, Nákl: Komise pro vydávání pramenů náboženského hnutí českého, 1920).

The Letters of John Hus, tr. M. Spinka (Manchester: Manchester University Press, 1972).

Opera omnia, ed. V. Flajshans (Prague: J. Bursík and J. R. Vilímek, 1903–7).

Tractatus de ecclesia, ed. S. H. Thomson (Boulder: University of Colorado Press, 1956).

John Italos. *Opera*, ed. N. Ketschakmadze (Tbilisi: Mezniereba, 1966).

Quaestiones Quodlibetales (ΑΠΟΡΙΑΙ ΚΑΙ ΛΥΣΕΙΣ), ed. P. Joannou (Ettal: Buch-Kunstverlag, 1956).

John of Jandun. *In libros Aristotelis De coelo et mundo quae extant quaestiones subtilissimae* (Venice: Iuntas, 1552).

Quaestio de habitu intellectus, ed. Z. Kuksewicz, *Mediaevalia philosophica Polonorum* 9 (1961) 3–30.

Quaestio de infinitate vigoris Dei, ed. Z. Kuksewicz, *Manuscripta* 9 (1965) 167–70.

Quaestio de notioritate universalium, ed. Z. Kuksewicz, *Mediaevalia philosophica Polonorum* 14 (1970) 87–97.

Quaestio de principio individuationis, ed. Z. Kuksewicz, *Mediaevalia philosophica Polonorum* 11 (1963) 93–106.

Quaestiones in duodecim libros Metaphysicae iuxta Aristotelis et magni Commentatoris intentionem disputatae (Venice: Hieronymus Scotus, 1553; repr. Frankfurt: Minerva, 1966).

Super libros Aristotelis De anima subtilissimae quaestiones (Venice, 1587; repr. Frankfurt: Minerva, 1966).

Super octo libros Aristotelis de physico auditu subtilissimae quaestiones (Venice, 1587; repr. Frankfurt: Minerva, 1969).

Super parvis naturalibus Aristotelis quaestiones perutiles ac eleganter discussae, ed. M. Zimara (Venice, 1505).

Tractatus de laudibus Parisius, in Le Roux de Lincy and L. M. Tisserand (ed.) *Paris et ses historiens aux XIVe et XVe siècles* (Paris: Imprimerie Impériale, 1867) 32–79.

Tractatus de sensu agente, in A. Pattin (ed.) *Pour l'histoire du sens agent: La controverse entre Barthélemy de Bruges et Jean de Jandun, ses antécédents et son évolution* (Leuven: Leuven University Press, 1988) 166–222.

John of La Rochelle. *Eleven Marian Sermons*, ed. K. F. Lynch (St. Bonaventure, NY: Franciscan Institute, 1961).

Die neuen Quästionen der Gnadentheologie, ed. L. Hödl (Munich: Huber, 1964).

Somme de l'âme, tr. J.-M. Vernier (Paris: Vrin, 2001).

Summa de anima, ed. J. G. Bougerol (Paris: Vrin, 1995).

Summa de vitiis (ms. in Paris, Bibliothèque Nationale lat. 16417).

Tractatus de divisione multiplici potentiarum animae, ed. P. Michaud-Quantin (Paris: Vrin, 1964).

John le Page. *Rationes super predicamenta Aristotelis*, ed. E. Franceschini, *Sophia* 2 (1934) 172–82, 329–50, 476–86.

John of Legnano. *Tractatus de bello, de represaliis et de duello*, ed. T. E. Holland (Oxford: Oxford University Press, 1917; repr. New York: Oceania, 1964; Buffalo: Hein, 1995).

John Lesage. *Quodlibet I*, ed. P. Glorieux (Paris: Vrin, 1958)

John of Mechlinia. *Determinatio utrum perfecta Dei opera possint impediri daemonis malitia* (Heidelberg, 1493).

Textum parvorum naturalium Aristotelis: cum commentario clarissimo secundum doctrinam magni Episcopi Ratisponensis (Cologne, 1491).

Textus trium librorum De anima Aristotelis cum commentario secundum doctrinam venerabilis domini Alberti Magni (Cologne, 1491).

Le Tractatus de homine de Jean de Malines: Contribution à l'histoire de l'albertisme à l'Université de Cologne, ed. A. Pattin (Leuven: Uitgave Tijdschrift voor filosofie, 1977).

John of Mirecourt. "Questioni inedite di Giovanni di Mirecourt sulla conoscenza," ed. A. Franzinelli, *Rivista critica di storia della filosofia* 13 (1958) 319–40, 415–49.

"Questioni inedite tratte dal I libro del commento alle Sentenze di Giovanni di Mirecourt (qq. 13–16)," ed. M. Parodi, *Medioevo* 3 (1978) 237–84; 4 (1978) 59–92.

"Die zwei Apologien des Jean de Mirecourt," ed. F. Stegmüller, *Recherches de théologie ancienne et médiévale* 5 (1933) 40–78, 192–204.

John of Naples. *Quaestiones disputatae* (Naples: D. Gravina, 1618).

Utrum licite possit doceri Parisius doctrina fratris Thome quantum ad omnes conclusiones eius, in C. Jellouschek (ed.) *Xenia Thomistica* (Rome: Typis polyglottis Vaticanis, 1925) 73–104.

John of Nova Domus. *Tractatus universalium*, in G. Meersseman (ed.) *Jahrbuch des Kölnischen Geschichtsvereins* 18 (1936) 144–68.

Tractatus de esse et essentia, in G. Meersseman (ed.) *Geschichte des Albertismus* (Paris: Haloua, 1933) I: 91–200.

De universali reali, ed. A. G. Weiler, *Vivarium* 6 (1968) 108–54.

John of Paris. *Apologia*, in J.-P. Müller (ed.) "À propos du Mémoire justificatif de Jean Quidort," *Recherches de théologie ancienne et médiévale* 19 (1952) 344–51.

Commentaire sur les Sentences, ed. J.-P. Müller (Rome: Herder, 1961–4).

Correctorium corruptorii "Circa", ed. J.-P. Müller (Rome: Herder, 1941).

De modo existendi corpus Christi in sacramento altaris, ed. A. Pattin, *Angelicum* 54 (1977) 184–206.

De potestate regia et papali, ed. F. Bleienstein (Stuttgart: Klett, 1969).

Determinatio de modo existendi corporis Christi in sacramento altaris, ed. and tr. J. H. Martin, *Viator* 6 (1975) 214–40.

On Royal and Papal Power, tr. J. A. Watt (Toronto: Pontifical Institute of Mediaeval Studies, 1971).

Quaestio de principio individuationis, ed. J.-P. Müller, in J. Möller and H. Kohlenberger (eds.) *"Virtus Politica": Festgabe zum 75. Geburstag von Alfons Hufnagel* (Stuttgart-Bad Cannstatt: F. Frommann, 1974) 335–56.

Quodlibeta, ed. A. J. Heiman, in J. R. O'Donnell (ed.) *Nine Mediaeval Thinkers: A Collection of Hitherto Unedited Texts* (Toronto: Pontifical Institute of Mediaeval Studies, 1955).

John Pecham. *De numeris misticis*, ed. B. Hughes, *Archivum Franciscanum Historicum* 78 (1985) 3–28, 333–83.

Perspectiva communis, in D. C. Lindberg (ed. and tr.) *John Pecham and the Science of Optics* (Madison: University of Wisconsin Press, 1970).

Quaestiones disputatae, ed. G. J. Etzkorn *et al.* (Grottaferrata: Editiones Collegii S. Bonaventurae, 2002).

Quaestiones tractantes de anima, ed. H. Spettmann (Münster: Aschendorff, 1918).

Questions Concerning the Eternity of the World, ed. and tr. I. Brady and V. Potter (New York: Fordham University Press, 1993).

Quodlibeta quatuor, ed. G. J. Etzkorn and F. M. Delorme (Grottaferrata: Editiones Collegii S. Bonaventurae, 1989).

Registrum epistolarum fratris Johannis Peckham, archiepiscopi Cantuariensis, ed. C. T. Martin (London: Longman, 1882–5).

Summa de esse et essentia, ed. F. Delorme (Rome: Studi Franciscani, 1928).

Tractatus de anima, ed. G. Melanus (Florence: Studi Franciscani, 1948).

Tractatus tres de paupertate, ed. C. Kingsford *et al.* (Aberdoniae: Typis Academicis, 1910; repr. Farnborough: Gregg, 1969).

Tractatus de perspectiva, ed. D. C. Lindberg (St. Bonaventure, NY: Franciscan Institute, 1972).

Tractatus pauperis, ed. A. ven den Wyngaert (Paris: Éditions de la France Franciscaine, 1925).

John Petrizi. *Commentaria in Procli Diadochi Stoicheiosein Theologiken*, ed. S. Nutsubidse and S. Kauchtschischvili (Tbilisi: Sumptibus Universitatis Tblisiensis, 1937).

John of Pouilly. *Quodlibeta* (ms. in Paris, Bibliothèque Nationale lat. 15372).

John Rigaud. *Compendium pauperis*, ed. F. Willer (Basel: Jakob de Pforsten, 1501).

John of Ripa. *Conclusiones*, ed. A. Combes (Paris: Vrin, 1957).

Determinationes, ed. A. Combes (Paris: Vrin, 1957).

"Jean de Ripa I Sent. Dist. XXXVII: 'De modo inexistendi divinae essentiae in omnibus creaturis'," ed. A. Combes *et al.*, *Traditio* 23 (1967) 191–268.

Lectura super Primum sententiarum, ed. A. Combes and F. Ruello (Paris: Vrin, 1961–70).

Quaestio de gradu supreme, ed. A. Combes and P. Vignaux (Paris: Vrin, 1964).

Super primum Sententiarum Johannis de Ripa lecturae abbreviatio: Prologus, abbrev. Paul of Venice, ed. F. Ruello (Florence: Olschki, 1980).

Super primum Sententiarum Johannis de Ripa lecturae abbrevatio: Liber 1, abbrev. Paul of Venice; ed. F. Ruello (Florence: SISMEL, Edizioni del Galluzzo, 2000).

John of Salisbury. *Entheticus maior et minor*, ed. and tr. J. van Laarhoven (Leiden: Brill, 1987).

    Frivolities of Courtiers and Footprints of Philosophers: Being a Translation of the Policraticus of John of Salisbury, ed. and tr. J. B. Pike (Minneapolis: University of Minnesota Press 1938).

    The Letters of John of Salisbury, ed. and tr. W. J. Millor *et al.*, rev. edn (London: Nelson, 1955–79; rev. edn Oxford: Clarendon Press, 1986–).

    Memoirs of the Papal Court [Historia pontificalis], ed. and tr. M. Chibnall (London: Nelson, 1956; repr. Oxford: Oxford University Press, 1986).

    Metalogicon, ed. J. B. Hall and K. S. B. Keats-Rohan (Turnhout: Brepols, 1991).

    The Metalogicon, tr. D. McGarry (Berkeley: University of California Press, 1962).

    Policratici, sive, de nugis curialium et vestigiis philosophorum libri VIII, ed. C. C. J. Webb (Oxford: Clarendon Press, 1909; reprinted New York: Arno Press, 1979).

    Policraticus, tr. C. J. Nederman (Cambridge: Cambridge University Press, 1990).

    Policraticus I–IV, ed. K. S. B. Keats-Rohan (Turnhout: Brepols, 1993).

    The Statesman's Book of John of Salisbury, tr. J. Dickinson (New York: Knopf, 1927).

    Vita Sancti Anselmi and Vita Sancti Thomae, in I. Biffi (ed.) *Anselmo e Becket, due vite* (Milan: Jaca, 1990).

John Scottus Eriugena. *Annotationes in Marcianum*, ed. C. Lutz (Cambridge, MA: Medieval Academy of America, 1939).

    Commentaire sur l'Evangile de Jean, ed. E. Jeauneau (Paris: Cerf, 1972).

    De divina praedestinatione liber, ed. G. Madec (Turnhout: Brepols, 1978).

    De praedestinatione liber: Dialettica e teologia all'apogeo della rinascenza carolingia, ed. E. Mainoldi (Florence: SISMEL, Edizioni del Galluzzo, 2003).

    Expositiones in Ierarchiam coelestem, ed. J. Barbet (Turnhout: Brepols, 1975).

    Glossae Divinae Historiae: The Biblical Glosses of John Scottus Eriugena, ed. J. Contreni and. P. Ó Néill (Florence: SISMEL, Edizioni del Galluzzo, 1997).

    L'homélie sur le Prologue de Jean, ed. E. Jeauneau (Paris: Cerf, 1969).

    Periphyseon, ed. E. Jeauneau (Turnhout: Brepols, 1996–).

    Periphyseon, ed. I.-P. Sheldon-Williams (Dublin: Institute for Advanced Studies, 1968–).

    Periphyseon (The Division of Nature), tr. I.-P. Sheldon-Williams and J. J. O'Meara (Montréal: Bellarmin, 1987).

    Treatise on Divine Predestination, tr. M. Brennan (Notre Dame, IN: University of Notre Dame Press, 1998).

John Sharpe. *Quaestio super universalia*, ed. A. D. Conti (Florence: Olschki, 1990).

John of Sterngassen. *Johannes von Sterngassen und sein Sentenzenkommentar*, ed. W. Senner (Berlin: Akademie, 1995).

John Tarteys. *Obligationes*, ed. E. J. Ashworth, *Documenti e studi sulla tradizione filosofica medievale* 3 (1992) 653–703.

    Problema correspondens libello Porphyrii (ms. in Lambeth Palace, ms. 393).

    Problema correspondens libello Porphyrii [excerpts], ed. A. D. Conti, in John Sharpe, *Quaestio super universalia* (Florence: Olschki, 1990) 165–87.

John Tauler. *Sermons*, ed. A. L. Corin (Liège: H. Vaillant-Carmanne, 1924–9).

    Sermons, tr. M. Shrady (New York: Paulist Press, 1985).

John of Wales. *Communiloquium sive Summa collationum* (Strasbourg, 1489; repr. Wakefield: S. R. Publishers, 1964).

John Wenck. *Das Büchlein von der Seele*, ed. G. Steer (Munich: Fink, 1967).

    Nicholas of Cusa's Debate with John Wenck, ed. and tr. J. Hopkins (Minneapolis, MN: Banning, 1988).

John Wyclif. *De civili dominio*, ed. R. L. Poole and J. Loserth (London: Trübner, 1885–1904).
   De dominio divino libri tres, ed. R. L. Poole (London: Trübner, 1890).
   De ecclesia, ed. J. Loserth and F. D. Matthew (London: Trübner, 1886).
   De ente librorum duorum excerpta, ed. M. Dziewicki (London: C. K. Paul, 1909).
   De ente praedicamentali, ed. R. Beer (London: Trübner, 1891).
   De eucharistia, ed. J. Loserth (London: Trübner, 1892).
   De logica, ed. M. H. Dziewicki (London: Trübner, 1893–9).
   De potestate papae, ed. J. Loserth (London: Trübner, 1907).
   De Trinitate, ed. A. du Pont Breck (Boulder: University of Colorado Press, 1962).
   De veritate sacrae scripturae, ed. R. Buddensieg (London: Trübner, 1905–7).
   The English Works of Wyclif, Hitherto Unprinted, ed. F. D. Matthew (London: Trübner, 1880; repr. New York: Kraus, 1978).
   English Wyclif Tracts 1–3, ed. C. Lindberg (Oslo: Novus Forlag, 1991).
   Miscellanea philosophica, ed. M. H. Dziewicki (London: Trübner, 1902).
   On the Truth of the Holy Scripture, tr. I. C. Levy (Kalamazoo, MI: Medieval Institute Publications, 2001).
   On Universals, tr. A. Kenny (Oxford: Clarendon Press, 1985).
   Polemical Works in Latin, ed. R. Buddensieg (London: Trübner, 1883; repr. New York: Johnson, 1966).
   Summa de ente libri primi tractatus primus et secundus, ed. S. H. Thomson (Oxford: Clarendon Press, 1930).
   Summa insolubilium, ed. P. V. Spade and G. A. Wilson (Binghamton, NY: Medieval and Renaissance Texts and Studies, 1986).
   Tractatus de universalibus, ed. I. J. Müller (Oxford: Clarendon Press, 1985).
   Trialogus, ed. G. Lechler (Oxford: Clarendon Press, 1869).
Jordanus. *Notulae super Priscianum Minorem: Partial Edition and Introduction*, ed. M. Sirridge, *Cahiers de l'Institut du Moyen Age Grec et Latin* 36 (1980) 1–104.
Joseph Albo. *Sefer ha-'Ikkarim: Book of Principles*, ed. and tr. I. Husik (Philadelphia, PA: Jewish Publication Society of America, 1929).
Joseph ibn Caspi. *'Amude kesef u-maskiyot kesef: shene perushim 'al sefer ha-Moreh leha-Rambam*, ed. S. Werbluner (Frankfurt: Y. F. Bakh, 1848).
   Gevia' Kesef, ed. and tr. B. Herring (New York: Ktav, 1982).
Joseph ibn Ṣaddiq. *The Microcosm*, ed. and tr. J. Haberman (Madison, NJ: Fairleigh Dickinson University Press, 2003).
Juan Luis Vives. *De anima et vita* (Basel, 1538; repr. Turin: Bottega d'Erasmo, 1963).
Judah Halevi. *Kitāb al-radd wa al-dalīl fī al-dīn al-dhalīl [Khazari]*, ed. D. Z. Baneth (Jerusalem: Magnes Press, 1977).
   The Kuzari = Kitab al Khazari: An Argument for the Faith of Israel, tr. H. Hirschfeld (New York: Schocken, 1964).
Julian of Norwich. *A Book of Showings*, ed. E. Colledge and J. Walsh (Toronto: Pontifical Institute of Mediaeval Studies, 1978).
   Showings, tr. E. Colledge and J. Walsh (New York: Paulist Press, 1978).
al-Jurjānī, 'Alī ibn Muḥammad. *Le livre des définitions*, tr. M. Gloton (Beirut: Dār Albouraq, 2006).
   Risālat al-wujud, ed. N.-A. Taqawi (Tehran: Rangi Press, 1942).
   Sharh al-mawāqif fī 'ilm al-kalām, ed. A. al-Mahdi (Cairo: Maktabat al-Azhar).
   Al-Ta'rīfāt, ed. A. R. 'Umayrah (Beirut: 'Ālam al-Kutub, 1987).
Justinian. *Corpus juris civilis*, ed. P. Krueger *et al.* (Berlin: Weidmann, 1954).
al-Juwaynī. *Al-Burhān fī uṣūl al-fiqh*, ed. A. al-Dīb (Cairo: Dār al-Anṣār, 1980).

Al-Irshād ila qawāṭiʿ al-adillah fī uṣūl al-iʿtiqād (The Guide to the Cogent Proofs of the Principles of Faith), ed. M. Mūsa and A. ʿAbd al-Ḥamīd (Cairo: Maktabat al-Khānjī, 1950).

Al-Shāmil fī uṣūl al-dīn, ed. H. Klopfer (Cairo: Dār al-ʿarab, 1959).

al-Kindī, ʿAbd al-Masīḥ. *The Apology of al Kindy*, tr. W. Muir (London: Smith Elder, 1882).

Exposición y refutación del Islam: la versión latinade las epistolas de al-Hasimi y al-Kindi, ed. F. González Muñoz (Coruña: Universidade da Coruña, 2005).

Risālat, ed. A. Tien (London, 1880).

al-Kindī, Abū Yūsuf. "Al-Kindi's 'On Definitions and Descriptions of Things'," tr. F. Klein-Franke *Le Muséon: Revue des études orientales* 95 (1982) 191–216.

Cinq épîtres, ed. D. Gimaret (Paris: Centre National de la Recherche Scientifique, 1976).

De aspectibus, in A. Björnbo and S. Vogel (eds.) *Alkindī, Tideus und Pseudo-Euklid: Drei optische Werke* (Leipzig: Teubner, 1912).

De radiis stellarum, ed. M.-T. D'Alverny and F. Hudry, *Archives d'histoire doctrinale et littéraire du moyen âge* 41 (1974) 139–260.

Essay on How to Banish Sorrow, in H. Ritter and R. Walzer (eds.) *Uno scritto morale inedito di al-Kindi* (Rome: Tipografo della Reale Accademia Nazionale dei Lincei, 1938).

Fī al-ṣināʿa al-ʿuẓmā, ed. A. T. al-Sayyid Aḥmad (Cyprus: Dār al-Shabbāb, 1987).

Metaphysics: A Translation of Yaʿqub ibn Ishaq al-Kindi's Treatise "On First Philosophy", tr. A. Ivry (Albany: State University of New York Press, 1974).

Le moyen de chasser les tristesses et autres textes éthiques, ed. S. Mestiri and G. Dye (Paris: Fayard, 2004).

Œuvres philosophiques et scientifiques d'al-Kindi: vol. I: *L'optique et la catoptrique*, ed. R. Rashed (Leiden: Brill, 1997).

Œuvres philosophiques et scientifiques d'al-Kindi: vol. II: *Métaphysique et cosmologie*, ed. R. Rashed and J. Jolivet (Leiden: Brill, 1998).

The Philosophical Works of al-Kindi tr. P. Adamson and P. E. Pormann (Karachi: Oxford University Press, forthcoming).

Rasāʾil al-falsafiyya, ed. M. Abū Rīda (Cairo: Dār al-Fikr al-ʿArabī, 1950–3).

Uno scritto introduttivo allo studio di Aristotele, tr. M. Guidi and R. Walzer (Rome: Reale Accademia Nazionale dei Lincei, 1940).

Treatise on the Intellect, ed. R. J. McCarthy, *Islamic Studies* 3 (1964) 119–49.

al-Kirmānī. *Kitāb al-riyāḍ*, ed. A. Tāmir (Beirut: Dār al-Thaqāfa, 1960).

Kitāb rāḥa al-ʿaql, ed. M. K. Ḥusayn and M. Ḥilmī (Cairo: Dār al-Fikr al-ʿArabī, 1953).

Master of the Age: An Islamic Treatise on the Necessity of the Imamate, ed. and tr. P. E. Walker (London: I. B. Tauris, 2007).

La Grange, Jean-Baptiste de. *Les principes de la philosophie contre les nouveaux philosophes, Descartes, Rohault, Regius, Gassendi, le P. Maignan, etc.* (Paris: Georges Josse, 1682).

Lambert. *Logica (Summa Lamberti)*, ed. F. Alessio (Florence: La Nuova Italia, 1971).

Landulph Caracciolo. *Commentarium in secundum librum Sententiarum* (Naples, 1487).

Sermones in quatuor Evangelia (Naples, 1637).

Lanfranc. *The Letters of Lanfranc, Archbishop of Canterbury*, ed. and tr. H. Clover and M. Gibson (Oxford: Clarendon Press, 1979).

Liber de corpore et sanguine Domini, ed. C. Martello (Catania: CUECM, 2001).

The Monastic Constitutions, ed. D. Knowles and C. Brooke (New York: Oxford University Press, 2002).

al-Lawkarī. *Bayān al-ḥaqq bi-ḍamān al-ṣidq: al-ʿIlm al-ilāhī*, ed. I. Dībājī (Tehran: International Institute of Islamic Thought and Civilization, 1995).

Bayān al-ḥaqq bi-ḍamān al-ṣidq: al-Manṭiq 1. al-Madkhal, ed. I. Dībājī (Tehran: Amīr Kabīr, 1985).

Le Bossu, René. *Parallele des principes de la Physique d'Aristote et de celle de René Des Cartes* (Paris, 1674; repr. Paris: Vrin, 1981).

Leibniz, Gottfried Wilhelm. *Philosophical Essays*, tr. R. Ariew and D. Garber (Indianapolis, IN: Hackett, 1989).

 Die philosophischen Schriften, ed. C. I. Gerhardt (Berlin, 1875–90; repr. Hildesheim: Olms, 1965).

Levi ben Gershom. *The Commentary of Levi ben Gerson on the Book of Job*, ed. A. L. Lassen (New York: Bloch, 1946).

 Commentary on Song of Songs, ed. M. Kellner (New Haven, CT: Yale University Press, 1998).

 The Logic of Gersonides: An Analysis of Selected Doctrines, ed. C. H. Manekin (Dordrecht: Kluwer, 1992).

 Sefer Maʿaseh Hoshev, ed. G. Lange (Frankfurt: Golde, 1909).

 Sefer Milhamot Ha-Shem (Leipzig, 1866; repr. Berlin: L. Lames, 1923).

 The Wars of the Lord, tr. S. Feldman (Philadelphia, PA: Jewish Publication Society, 1984–99).

Locke, John. *Second Treatise of Government*, ed. C. B. Macpherson (Indianapolis, IN: Hackett, 1980).

Lorenzo Valla. *Encomium Sancti Thomae de Aquino*, in E. Garin (ed.) *Opera omnia* (Turin: Bottega d'Erasmo, 1962), vol. II.

Macrobius. *Maximou Planoudē tou Hypomnēmatos eis ton Oneiron tou Skipiōnos tou Makrobiou metaphrasis*, ed. A. C. Megas (Thessaloniki: Art of Text, 1995).

 Saturnalia apparatu critico instruxit, In Somnium Scipionis commentarios selecta varietate lectionis ornavit, ed. J. Willis (Leipzig: Teubner, 1970).

Manegold of Lautenbach. *Ad Gebehardum liber*, in K. Francke (ed.) *Libelli de lite* (Hannover: Impensis Bibliopolii Hahniani, 1891) I: 308–430.

 Liber contra Wolfelmum, tr. R. Ziomkowski (Paris: Peeters, 2002).

 Liber Magistri Manegaldi contra Wolfelmum Coloniensem, ed. W. Hartmann (Weimar: Böhlau, 1972; repr. Munich: Monumenta Germaniae Historica, 1991).

Marguerite of Oingt. *Les œuvres de Marguertie d'Oingt*, ed. and tr. A. Duraffour *et al.* (Paris: Les Belles Lettres, 1965).

 The Writings of Margaret of Oingt, Medieval Prioress and Mystic (d. 1310), tr. R. Blumenfeld-Kosinski (Newburyport, MA: Focus Information Group, 1990).

Marguerite Porete. *Le mirouer des simple âmes*, ed. R. Guarnieri (Turnhout: Brepols, 1986).

 The Mirror of Simple Souls, tr. E. Colledge *et al.* (Notre Dame, IN: University of Notre Dame Press, 1999).

Marsilius of Inghen. *Abbreviationes libri Physicorum* (Venice, 1521).

 Quaestiones de generatione et corruptione (Venice, 1505; repr. Frankfurt: Minerva, 1970).

 Quaestiones super quattuor libros Sententiarum, ed. G. Wieland *et al.* (Leiden: Brill, 2000–).

 Treatises on the Properties of Terms: A First Critical Edition of the Suppositiones, Ampliationes, Appellationes, Restrictiones and Alienationes, ed. and tr. E. P. Bos (Dordrecht: Kluwer, 1983).

Marsilius of Padua, *The Defender of the Peace*, tr. A. Brett (Cambridge: Cambridge University Press, 2005).

 Defensor pacis, ed. C. W. Previté-Orton (Cambridge: Cambridge University Press, 1928).

 Defensor pacis, tr. A. Gewirth (New York: Columbia University Press, 1956; repr. 2001).

 Œuvres mineures, ed. C. Jeudy and J. Quillet (Paris: Éditions de Centre National de la Recherche Scientifique, 1979).

 Writings on the Empire: Defensor minor and De translatione Imperii, tr. C. J. Nederman (Cambridge: Cambridge University Press, 1993).

Martianus Capella. *De nuptiis Philologiae et Mercurii*, ed. J. Willis (Leipzig: Teubner, 1983).

Martin of Dacia. *Opera*, ed. H. Roos (Copenhagen: Gad, 1961).

Martinus Anglicus. *De obligationibus = Uber die Verpflichtungen*, ed. F. Schupp (Hamburg: Meiner, 1993).

Māshā'allāh. *On the Elements and Orbs*, tr. [Latin] Gerard of Cremona, ed. J. Heller (Nuremberg, 1549).

Matthew of Aquasparta. *Quaestiones disputatae de anima VI*, ed. A.-J. Gondras, *Archives d'histoire doctrinale et littéraire du moyen âge* 32 (1957) 203–352.

Quaestiones disputatae de anima XIII, ed. A.-J. Gondras (Paris: Vrin, 1961).

Quaestiones disputatae de anima separata, de anima beata, de ieiunio et de legibus (Quaracchi: Editiones Collegii S. Bonaventurae, 1959).

Quaestiones disputatae de fide et de cognitione, 2nd edn (Quaracchi: Editiones Collegii S. Bonaventurae, 1957).

Quaestiones disputatae de gratia, ed. V. Doucet (Quaracchi: Editiones Collegii S. Bonaventurae, 1935).

Quaestiones disputatae de illuminatione, in Bonaventure, *De humanae cognitionis ratione* (Quaracchi: Editiones Collegii S. Bonaventurae, 1883) 87–177.

Quaestiones disputatae de productione rerum et de providentia, ed. G. Gál (Quaracchi: Editiones Collegii S. Bonaventurae, 1956).

Matthew of Bologna. *Quaestiones super modos significandi*, in I. Rosier (ed.) "Mathieu de Bologne et les divers aspects du pré-modisme," in D. Buzzetti *et al.* (eds.) *L'insegnamento della logica a Bologna nel XIV secolo* (Bologna: Istituto per la Storia dell'Università, 1992) 73–164.

Matthew of Gubbio. *Le "Quaestiones de anima" attribuite a Matteo da Gubbio: edizione del testo (cod. Fesulano 161, ff. 84v–103v, Florence, Biblioteca Medicea Laurenziana)*, ed. A. Ghisalberti (Milan: Vita e Pensiero, 1981).

Matthew of Orleans. *Sophistaria sive Summa communium distinctionum circa sophismata accidentium*, ed. J. Spruyt (Leiden: Brill, 2001).

al-Māturīdi, Abū Mansūr. *Kitāb al-tawḥīd*, ed. F. Kholeif (Beirut: Dār el-Machreq, 1970).

Tafsīr al-Qur'ān al-'azim, al-musamma Ta'wīlāt ahl al-sunnah, ed. F. Y. al-Khaymī (Beirut: Mu'assasat al-Risālah Nāshirūn, 2004).

al-Māwardī. *Al-Aḥkām al-sulṭāniyya wa-al-wilāyāt al-dīnīyya*, ed. M. F. al-Sirjānī (Cairo: al-Maktabah al-Tawfīqīyya, 1978).

Al-Ahkam as-Sultaniyyah = The Laws of Islamic Governance, tr. A. Yate (London: Ta-Ha, 1996).

Kitāb adab al-dunyā wa-al-dīn, ed. M. F. Abū Bakr (Cairo: Dār al-Miṣrīyah al-Lubnānīyah, 1988).

Maximus the Confessor. *Ambigua*, tr. [Latin] John Scottus Eriugena, ed. E. Jeauneau (Turnout: Brepols, 1988).

Censurae de caritate, tr. [Latin] Cerbanus, ed. I. Boronkai, *Acta Antiqua Academiae Scientiarum Hungaricae* 23 (1975) 305–18.

Mystagogia, tr. [Latin] Anastasius Bibliothecarius, *Revue de l'Orient Chrétien* 10 (1905) 289–313.

Quaestiones ad Thalassium II. Q. LVI-LXV, tr. [Latin] John Scottus Eriugena, ed. C. Laga and C. Steel (Turnhout: Brepols, 1990).

Scripta saeculi VII vitam Maximi Confessoris illustrantia: una cum latina interpretatione Anastasii Bibliothecarii iuxta posita, ed. P. Allen and B. Neil (Turnhout: Brepols, 1999).

Mechtild of Hackeborn. *The Booke of Gostlye Grace*, ed. T. A. Halligan (Toronto: Pontifical Institute of Mediaeval Studies, 1979).

Liber specialis gratiae (Revelationes Gertrudianae et Mechtildianae, vol. II) (Poitiers: H. Oudin, 1877).

Mechtild of Magdeburg. *Das fließende Licht der Gottheit*, ed. and tr. G. Vollmann-Profe (Frankfurt: Deutscher Klassiker Verlag, 2003).

The Flowing Light of the Godhead, tr. F. Tobin (New York: Paulist Press, 1998).

Mersenne, Marin. *La correspondance du P. Marin Mersenne, religieux minime*, ed. C. de Waad *et al.* (Paris: Presses universitaires de France, 1933–88).

Methodius of Olympus. *De resurrectione*, in G. N. Bonwetsch (ed.) *Methodius* (Leipzig: J. C. Hinrichs, 1917).

Michael of Ephesus. *On the Movement and Progression of Animals*, tr. A. Preuss (Hildesheim: Olms, 1981).

Michael of Ephesus and Aspasius. *On Aristotle's Nicomachean Ethics 8 and 9*, tr. D. Konstan (Ithaca, NY: Cornell University Press, 2001).

Michael of Marbais. *Summa de modis significandi*, ed. L. G. Kelly (Stuttgart-Bad Cannstatt: Frommann-Holzboog, 1995).

Michael Psellos. *Aristotelis per Hermenias liber* (Venice: H. Scotus, 1541).

   Chronographie, ed. E. Renauld (Paris: Les Belles Lettres, 1926–8).

   De omnifaria doctrina, ed. L. G. Westerink (Utrecht: Beigers, 1948).

   Fourteen Byzantine Rulers: The Chronographia, tr. E. R. A. Sewter, rev. edn (Baltimore, MD: Penguin, 1966).

   In Aristotelis De interpretatione paraphrasis, ed. A. Manutius (Venice, 1503).

   Philosophica minora, ed. J. M. Duffy and D. J. O'Meara (Leipzig: Teubner, 1989–92).

   Scripta minora, ed. E. Kurtz and F. Drexl (Milan: Vita e Pensiero, 1936–41).

   Theologica, ed. P. Gautier (Leipzig: Teubner, 1989).

Michael Scott. *Liber phisionomie* (Cologne: C. de Syrickzee, 1508).

The Mishnah, tr. H. Danby (Oxford: Clarendon Press, 1933).

Miskawayh. "De l'intellect et de l'intelligible (Fī l-ʿaql wa-l-maʿqūl)," ed. M. Arkoun *Arabica* 11 (1964) 80–7.

   An Epistle on the Intellect and the Intelligible, tr. R. Marcotte, *Islamic Culture* 70 (1996) 1–17.

   The Refinement of Character, tr. C. K. Zurayk (Beirut: American University of Beirut, 1968).

   Tahdhīb al-akhlāq, ed. C. Zurayk (Beirut: American University of Beirut Centennial Publications, 1966).

   Tajārib al-umam, in H. F. Amedroz and D. S. Margoliouth (ed. and tr.) *The Eclipse of the Abbasid Caliphate* (Oxford: Blackwell, 1920–1).

Moses ibn Ezra. *Kitāb al-muḥāḍara wal-mudākara*, ed. M. Abumalhan Mas (Madrid: Consejo Superior de Investigaciones Scientiíficas, Instituto de Filologia, 1985–6).

   Maqālat al-ḥadīqa fī maʿnā al-majāz wa-al-ḥaqīqa, ed. P. Fenton (Jerusalem: Mekize Nirdamim, 1989).

Moses ibn Tibbon. *Perush ʿal Shir ha-shirim* (Lyck: Mekitse nirdamim, 1874).

Moses Maimonides. *Acht Kapitel: Eine Abhandlung zur jüdischen Ethik und Gotteserkenntnis*, ed. M. Wolff and F. Niewöhner, 2nd edn (Leiden: Brill, 1903; repr. Frankfurt: Institute for the History of Arabic-Islamic Science, 2003).

   The Book of Knowledge, tr. M. Hyamson (Jerusalem: Feldheim, 1974).

   The Code of Maimonides (New Haven, CT: Yale University Press, 1949–72).

   The Commandments (Sefer ha-Mitzvot), tr. C. B. Chavel (London: Soncino, 1967).

   The Commentary to Mishnah Aboth, tr. A. David (New York: Bloch, 1968).

   Crisis and Leadership: Epistles of Maimonides, ed. A. Halkin and D. Hartman (Philadelphia, PA: Jewish Publication Society, 1985).

   Dalālat al-ḥāʾirīn, ed. S. Munk (Paris: Franck, 1856; repr. Osnabrück: Zeller, 1964).

   The Eight Chapters of Maimonides on Ethics: A Psychological and Ethical Treatise, tr. J. Gorfinkle (New York: Columbia University Press, 1912; repr. New York: AMS, 1966).

   The Ethical Writings of Maimonides, ed. R. Weis and C. Butterworth (New York: New York University Press, 1975).

The Guide of the Perplexed, tr. S. Pines (Chicago: University of Chicago Press, 1963; repr. 1974).

Le livre des préceptes [*Kitāb al-Faraʿid*], ed. M. Bloch (Paris: E. Bouillon et E. Vieweg, 1888).

A Maimonides Reader, ed. I. Twersky (West Orange, NJ: Behrman House, 1972).

Mishnah im Perush, ed. and [Hebrew] tr. J. Kafih (Jerusalem: Mossad ha-Rav Kook, 1963).

Mishneh Torah, ed. S. Frankel (Jerusalem: Hotzaat Shabse Frankel, 2000).

Moreh ha-Nevukhim, ed. Y. Even-Shemuel (Jerusalem: Mosad ha-Rav Kook, 1987).

Sefer ha-Maor, hu Perush ha-Mishnah, ed. M. D. Rabinowitz (Tel Aviv: Rishonim, 1948).

Treatise on Logic, ed. and tr. I. Efros (New York: American Academy for Jewish Research, 1938; repr. 1978).

Moses Nahmanides. *Commentary on the Torah*, tr. C. B. Chavel (New York: Shilo, 1976).

Kitvei Ha-Ramban, ed. C. B. Chavel (Jerusalem: Mosad Ha-Rav Kook, 1963).

Perush ha-Torah, ed. C. B. Chavel (Jerusalem: Mosad ha-Rav Kook, 1959–63).

Writings and Discourses, tr. C. B. Chavel (New York: Shilo, 1978).

Moses of Narbonne. *The Epistle on the Possibility of Conjunction with the Active Intellect by Ibn Rushd with the Commentary of Moses Narboni*, ed. and tr. K. Bland (New York: Jewish Theological Seminary of America, 1981).

"L'épître du libre-arbitre de Moise de Narbonne," ed. M.-R. Hayoun, *Revue des Études Juives* 141 (1982) 139–67.

Moshe Narboni, ed. and tr. M.-R. Hayoun (Tübingen: Mohr, 1986).

Mullā Ṣadrā (Ṣadr al-Dīn Shīrāzī). *Al-ḥikma al-mutaʿāliya fī al-Asfār al-aqliyya al-arbaʿa* [*Transcendent Wisdom in Four Intellectual Journeys*], ed. R. Lutfī *et al.* (al-Najaf: Dār al-maʿārif al-islamiyya, 1958).

Kitāb al-mashāʿir [*The Book of Stations*], in P. Morewedge (tr.) *The Metaphysics of Mulla Sadra* (New York: Society for the Study of Islamic Philosophy and Science, 1992).

al-Nasafī, Abū al-Muʿīn. *Baḥr al-kalām*, ed. M. S. Farfūr (Damascus: Maktabat Dār al-Farfūr, 1997).

Tabṣirat al-adilla fī uṣūl al-dīn, ed. K. Salāma (Damascus: Institut français de Damas, 1990).

Nemesius of Emesa. *De natura hominis*, ed. M. Morani (Leipzig: Teubner, 1987).

De natura hominis: traduction de Burgundio de Pise, ed. G. Verbeke and J. R. Moncho (Leiden: Brill, 1975).

Premnon physicon, sive Peri physeōs anthrōpou liber, tr. [Latin] Alphanus, ed. K. Burkhard (Leipzig: Teubner, 1917).

Nicholas of Amiens. *Ars fidei catholicae: ein Beispielwerk axiomatischer Methode*, ed. M. Dreyer (Münster: Aschendorff, 1993).

Nicholas of Autrecourt. *Exigit ordo*, ed. J. R. O'Donnell, *Mediaeval Studies* 1 (1939) 179–280.

Nicholas of Autrecourt, his Correspondence with Master Giles and Bernard of Arezzo: A Critical Edition and English Translation, ed. L. M. de Rijk (Leiden: Brill, 1994).

The Universal Treatise [*Exigit ordo*], tr. L. A. Kennedy *et al.* (Milwaukee, WI: Marquette University Press, 1971).

Nicholas Bonet. *Formalitates* (Padua, 1475).

Quattuor volumina: Metaphysica, Naturalis philosophia, Praedicamenta, Theologia naturalis (Venice, 1505).

Nicholas Byard. *Dictionarius pauperum* (Paris, 1498).

Nicholas of Cusa. *De auctoritate praesidendi in concilio generali*, tr. H. L. Bond *et al.*, *Church History* 59 (1990) 19–34.

De concordantia catholica (The Catholic Concordance), tr. P. Sigmund (Cambridge: Cambridge University Press, 1991).

Dialectical Mysticism, tr. J. Hopkins (Minneapolis, MN: Banning, 1988).

Metaphysical Speculations, tr. J. Hopkins (Minneapolis, MN: Banning, 1997–2000).

A Miscellany on Nicholas of Cusa, tr. J. Hopkins (Minneapolis, MN: Banning, 1994).

On Learned Ignorance, tr. J. Hopkins (Minneapolis, MN: Banning, 1985).

On Wisdom and Knowledge, tr. J. Hopkins (Minneapolis, MN: Banning, 1996).

Opera omnia, ed. E. Hoffmann *et al.* (Leipzig: Meiner, 1932–).

Nicholas of Damascus. *De plantis: Five Translations*, ed. H. J. Drossaart Lulofs and E. L. Poortman (Amsterdam: North-Holland, 1989).

Nicholas Drukken of Dacia. *Opera*, ed. N. J. Green-Pedersen and S. Ebbesen (Copenhagen: Reitzel, 1997).

Nicholas Kabasilas. "Der Briefwechsel des Mystikers Nikolaos Kabasilas," ed. P. Enepekides, *Byzantinische Zeitschrift* 46 (1953) 18–46.

Cabasilas, teologo e mistico bizantino: Nicola Cabasilas Chamaetos, e la sua sintesi teologica, tr. Y. Spiteris (Rome: Lipa, 1996).

A Commentary on the Divine Liturgy, tr. J. M. Hussey and P. McNulty (London: SPCK, 1960; repr. Crestwood, NY: St. Vladimir's Press, 2002).

Explication de la divine liturgie, ed. P. Périchon, tr. S. Salaville, 2nd edn (Paris: Cerf, 1967).

Kata Pyrrhonos: Platonikos philo-skeptikismos kai aristotelikos anti-skeptikismos ste byzantine dianoese tou 14ºᵘ aiona, ed. J. A. Demetracopoulos (Athens: Parousia, 1999).

The Life in Christ, tr. C. J. de Catanzaro (Crestwood, NY: St. Vladimir's Press, 1974).

Quaestio de rationis valore, ed. J. A. Demetracopoulos, *Byzantina* 19 (1998) 53–93.

La vie en Christ, ed. and tr. M.-H. Congourdeau (Paris: Cerf, 1989–90).

Nicholas of Lisieux. *Liber de Antichristo*, in E. Martène and U. Durand (eds.) *Veterum scriptorum amplissima collectio* (Paris, 1733; repr. New York: Franklin, 1968) IX: 1273–1446.

Nicholas of Lyra. *Apocalypse Commentary*, tr. P. Krey (Kalamazoo, MI: Medieval Institute Publications, 1997).

Biblia sacra cum glossis, interlineari et ordinaria, Nicolai Lyrani Postilla et moralitatibus (Lyon, 1545).

De visione divinae essentiae, ed. M. Woodward, *Franciscan Studies* 63 (2005) 325–407.

The Postilla of Nicholas of Lyra on the Song of Songs, tr. J. G. Kiecker (Milwaukee, WI: Marquette University Press, 1998).

Nicholas of Normandy. "A Grammatical Sophisma by Nicholas of Normandy: *Albus musicus est*," ed. S. Ebbesen, *Cahiers de l'Institut du Moyen Age Grec et Latin* 56 (1988) 103–16.

Nicholas of Ockham. *Quaestiones disputatae de dilectione Dei*, ed. C. Saco Alarçón (Grottaferrata: Editiones Collegii S. Bonaventurae, 1981).

Quaestiones disputatae de traductione humanae naturae a primo parente, ed. C. Saco Alarçón (Grottaferrata: Editiones Collegii S. Bonaventurae, 1993).

Nicholas of Paris. *Obligationes*, in H. A. G. Braakhuis (ed.) "Obligations in Early Thirteenth Century Paris: The *Obligationes* of Nicholas of Paris(?)," *Vivarium* 36 (1998) 152–233.

Summe Metenses [extracts], in L. M. de Rijk (ed.) *Logica modernorum* (Assen: Van Gorcum, 1962–7) II.1: 449–90.

Syncategoremata, in H. A. G. Braakhuis (ed.) *De 13de eeuwse tractaten over syncategorematische termen: inleidende studie en uitgave van Nicolaas van Parijs' Sincategoreumata* (Nijmegen: Krips Repro, 1979).

Nicholas of Strasbourg. *Summa*, ed. T. Suarez-Nani *et al.* (Hamburg: Meiner, 1990–).

Nicole Oresme. *De proportionibus proportionum and Ad pauca respicientes*, ed. E. Grant (Madison: University of Wisconsin Press, 1966).

De visione stellarum (On Seeing the Stars): A Critical Edition of Oresme's Treatise on Optics and Atmospheric Refraction, ed. D. Burton (Leiden: Brill, 2007).

Expositio et quaestiones in Aristotelis De anima, ed. B. Patar (Leuven: Peeters, 1995).

Kommentar zur Physik des Aristoteles: Kommentar mit Edition der Quaestionen zu Buch 3 und 4 der aristotelischen Physik sowie von vier Quaestionen zu Buch 5, ed. S. Kirschner (Stuttgart: Steiner, 1997).

Le livre de éthiques d'Aristote, ed. A. D. Menut (New York: G. E. Stechert, 1940).

Le Livre de Politiques d'Aristote, ed. A. D. Menut (Philadelphia, PA: American Philosophical Society, 1970).

Le livre de yconomique d'Aristote; Critical Edition of the French Text from the Avranches Manuscript with the Original Latin Version, Introduction and English Translation, ed. A. D. Menut (Philadelphia, PA: American Philosophical Society, 1957).

Le livre du ciel et du monde, ed. A. D. Menut and A. J. Denomy (Madison: University of Wisconsin Press, 1968).

Nicole Oresme and the Marvels of Nature: A Study of his De causis mirabilium *with Critical Edition, Translation and Commentary*, ed. B. Hanson (Toronto: Pontifical Institute of Mediaeval Studies, 1985).

Nicole Oresme and the Medieval Geometry of Qualities and Motions: A Treatise on the Uniformity and Difformity of Intensities known as Tractatus de configurationibus qualitatum et motuum, ed. M. Clagett (Madison: University of Wisconsin Press, 1968).

Quaestiones super De generatione et corruptione, ed. S. Caroti (Munich: Bayerische Akademie der Wissenschaften, 1996).

Quaestiones super Geometriam Euclidis, ed. H. L. L. Busard (Leiden: Brill, 1961).

Questiones super De celo, ed. and tr. C. Kren (Ph.D. dissertation: University of Wisconsin, 1965).

Questiones super quatuor libros meteororum, in S. C. McCluskey (ed.) "Nicole Oresme on Light, Color, and the Rainbow: An Edition and Translation, with Introduction and Critical Notes, of Part of Book Three of His *Questiones super quatuor libros meteororum*" (Ph.D. dissertation: University of Wisconsin, 1974).

Traictie de la première invention des monnoies: textes français et latin d'après les manuscrits de la Bibliothèque impériale, ed. L Wolowski (Paris: Guillaumin, 1864; repr. Geneva: Slatkine Reprints, 1976).

Nikephoros Blemmydes. *Autographia sive curriculum vitae*, ed. J. A. Munitiz (Turnhout: Brepols, 1984).

Des Nikephoros Blemmydes βασιλικὸς ἀνδριάς und dessen Metaphrase von Georgios Galesiotes und Georgios Oinaiotes: ein weiterer Beitrag zum Verständnis der byzantinischen Schrift-Koine, ed. H. Hunger and I. Ševčenko (Vienna: Österreichischen Akademie der Wissenschaften, 1986).

Epitomē logikēs [etc.] (Leipzig, 1784).

Gegen die Vorherbestimmung der Todesstunde, ed. and tr. W. Lackner (Leiden: Brill, 1985).

Œuvres théologiques, ed. and tr. M. Stavrou (Paris: Cerf, 2007).

A Partial Account, tr. J. A. Munitiz (Leuven: Spicilegium sacrum Lovaniense, 1988).

Nikephoros Gregoras. *Byzantina historia*, ed. L. Schopen and I. Bekker (Bonn: Weber, 1829–55).

Epistulae, ed. P. L. Leone (Matino: Tipografia di Matino, 1982–3).

Fiorenzo: o, intorno alla sapienza, ed. and tr. P. L. Leone (Naples: Università di Napoli, Cattedra di filologia bizantina, 1975).

Odo Rigaldus. *Quaestio de gratia*, in B. Pergamo (ed.) "Il desiderio innato del sopranaturale," *Studi francescani* 7 (1935) 414–17; 8 (1936) 308–49.

Quaestio de libero arbitrio, ed. O. Lottin, *Revue Thomiste* 36 (1931) 886–95.

The Register of Eudes of Rouen, Archbishop of Rouen, ed. S. M. Brown and J. F. O'Sullivan (New York: Columbia University Press, 1964).

Registrum visitationum archiepiscopi rothomagensis: journal des visites pastorales, ed. T. Bonnin (Rouen: A. Le Brument, 1852).

"Un sermon inédit d'Eudes Rigaud," ed. J. G. Bougerol, *Archives d'histoire doctrinale et littéraire du moyen âge* 62 (1995) 343–58.

Sermones in Synodi Rothomagensi, ed. L. Duval-Arnould, *Archivum Franciscanum Historicum* 69 (1976) 336–400; 70 (1977) 35–71.

Teoria della scienza teologica: Quaestio de scientia theologicae di Odo Rigaldi e altri testi inediti (1230–1250), ed. L. Sileo (Rome: Pontificium Athenaeum Antonianum, 1984).

Odo of Soissons. *Quaestiones*, ed. J. B. Pitra (Paris: Typis Tusculanis, 1888).

Odo of Tournai. *On Original Sin and a Disputation with the Jew, Leo, Concerning the Advent of Christ, the Son of God: Two Theological Treatises*, tr. I. M. Resnick (Philadelphia: University of Pennsylvania Press, 1994).

Olympiodorus. *Prolegomena et in Categorias commentarium*, ed. A. Busse (*Commentaria in Aristotelem Graeca* XII.1) (Berlin: Reimer, 1902).

Origen. *Commentaire sur le Cantique des cantiques,* tr. [Latin] Rufinus, ed. L. Brésard and H. Crouzel (Paris: Cerf, 1991–2).

De principiis libri IV, ed. H. Görgemanns and H. Karpp (Darmstadt: Wissenschafliche Buchgesellschaft, 1976).

Der Römerbriefkommentar des Origenes: Kritische Ausgabe der Uebersetzung Rufins, ed. C. P. Hammond Bammel (Freiburg: Herder, 1990–).

Traité des principes, tr. [Latin] Rufinus, ed. H. Crouzel and M. Simonetti (Paris: Cerf, 1978–84).

Werke, ed. P. Koetschau *et al.* (Leipzig: Hinrichs, 1899–1955).

Pascal, Blaise. *Œuvres complètes*, ed. L. Lafuma (Paris: Éditions du Seuil, 1963).

Paul of Gelria. *Concepts: The Treatises of Thomas of Cleves and Paul of Gelria, an Edition of the Texts with a Systematic Introduction*, ed. E. P. Bos and S. Read (Louvain-la-Neuve: Éditions de l'Institut Supérieur de Philosophie, 2001).

Paul of Pergula. *Dubia super Consequentiis Strodi* (Padua, 1477).

Logica and Tractatus de sensu composito et diviso. ed. M. A. Brown (St. Bonaventure, NY: Franciscan Institute, 1961).

Sophismata asinina, ed. F. Pironet, *Documenti e studi sulla tradizione filosofica medievale* 9 (1998) 441–64.

Paul of Taranto. *Summa perfectionis*, ed. and tr. W. Newman (Leiden: Brill, 1991).

Paul of Venice. *Expositio in libros Posteriorum Aristotelis* (Venice, 1477; repr. Hildesheim: Olms, 1976).

Expositio super libros De generatione et corruptione (Venice, 1498).

Expositio super octo libros Physicorum nec non super commento Averrois (Venice, 1499).

Expositio super Universalia Porphyrii et artem veterem Aristotelis (Venice, 1494).

Lectura super libros Metaphysicorum (ms. in Pavia, Biblioteca Universitaria, fondo Aldini, ms. 324).

Logica magna (Venice, 1499).

Logica parva: First Critical Edition from the Manuscripts with Introduction and Commentary, ed. A. R. Perreiah (Leiden: Brill, 2002).

Logica parva, tr. A. R. Perreiah (Washington, DC: Catholic University of America Press, 1984).

Quaestio de universalibus [excerpts], ed. A. D. Conti in John Sharpe, *Quaestio super universalia* (Florence: Olschki, 1990) 199–207.

Scriptum super libros De anima (Venice, 1504).

Sophismata aurea (Venice, 1493).

Summa philosophiae naturalis (Venice, 1503; repr. Hildesheim: Olms, 1974).

Peter Abaelard. *Collationes*, ed. G. Orlandi, tr. J. Marenbon (Oxford: Clarendon Press, 2001).

Des intellections [Tractatus de intellectibus], ed. P. Morin (Paris: Vrin, 1994).

Dialectica, ed. L. M. de Rijk, 2nd edn (Assen: Van Gorcum, 1970).

Ethica seu Scito teipsum, ed. R. M. Ilgner in *Petri Abaelardi opera theologica* (Turnhout: Brepols, 2001).

Ethical Writings, tr. P. Spade (Indianapolis, IN: Hackett, 1995).

Ethics, ed. and tr. D. E. Luscombe (Oxford: Oxford University Press, 1971).

Historia calamitatum, ed. J. Monfrin, 4th edn (Paris: Vrin, 1974).

Introductiones parvulorum, in M. Dal Pra (ed.) *Pietro Abelardo: Scritti di logica*, 2nd edn (Florence: La Nuova Italia, 1969).

Letters IX–XIV: An Edition with an Introduction, ed. E. R. Smits (Groningen: Rijksuniversiteit, 1983).

Logica "Ingredientibus", ed. B. Geyer (Münster: Aschendorff, 1919–27).

Logica "Nostrorum petitioni sociorum", ed. B. Geyer (Münster: Aschendorff, 1933).

Sententiae secundum Magistrum Petrum, in L. Minio-Paluello (ed.) *Twelfth-Century Logic: Texts and Studies* (Rome: Edizioni di Storia et Letteratura, 1958) vol. II.

Sic et non, ed. B. Boyer and R. McKeon (Chicago: University of Chicago Press, 1977).

Opera theologica, ed. E. Buytaert and C. Mews (Turnhout: Brepols, 1969–87).

Peter Abaelard and Héloïse. "The Letter of Heloise on Religious Life and Abelard's First Reply," ed. J. T. Muckle., *Mediaeval Studies* 17 (1955) 241–81.

"The Personal Letters between Abelard and Heloise," ed. J. T. Muckle, *Mediaeval Studies* 15 (1953) 68–94.

Peter of Abano. *Conciliator differentiarum philosophorum et praecipue medicorum* (Venice, 1565; repr. Padua: Antenore, 1985).

De venenis atque eorundem commodis remediis (Marpurgi, 1537).

Il "Lucidator dubitabilium astronomiae" di Pietro d'Abano: opere scientifiche inedite, ed. G. Federici Vescovini (Padua: Programma e 1+1, 1988).

Problemata Aristotelis cum expositione Petri Aponi (Venice, 1501).

Peter of Ailly. *Concepts and Insolubles*, tr. P. V. Spade (Dordrecht: Reidel, 1980).

Conceptus, in L. Kaczmarek (ed.) *Modi significandi und ihre Destruktionen: zwei Texte zur scholastischen Sprachtheorie im 14. Jahrhundert* (Münster: Münsteraner Arbeitskreis f. Semiotik, 1980).

Conceptus et insolubilia (Paris: G. Marchant, 1499).

Consistorio per eundem contra M. Joannem de Montesano, in C. D. d'Argentré (ed.) *Collectio judiciorum de novis erroribus* (Paris: apud A. Cailleau, 1728–36; repr. Brussels: Culture et Civilisation, 1963) I: 69–74.

Quaestiones super libros Sententiarum cum quibusdam in fine adjunctis (Strasbourg, 1490; repr. Frankfurt: Minerva, 1968).

Tractatus de anima, in O. Pluta (ed.) *Die philosophische Psychologie des Peter von Ailly* (Amsterdam: Grüner, 1987).

Tractatus et sermones (Strasbourg, 1490; repr. Frankfurt: Minerva, 1971).

Tractatus super De consolatione philosophiae Boethii, ed. M. Chappuis (Amsterdam: Grüner, 1993).

Ymago mundi de Pierre d'Ailly, cardinal de Cambrai et chancelier de l'université de Paris (1350–1420): Texte latin et traduction française des quatre traités cosmographiques de d'Ailly et des notes marginales de Christophe Colomb, ed. and tr. E. Buron (Paris: Maisonneuve Frères, 1930).

Peter Alfonsi. *Diálogo contra los judíos*, tr. J. Tolan *et al.* (Huesca: Instituto de Estudios Altoaragoneses, 1996).

The Disciplina clericalis, tr. E. Hermes and P. Quarrie (Berkeley: University of California Press, 1977).

On the Elements, ed. and tr. R. C. Dales (Berkeley: University of California Press, 1976).

Peter of Aquila. *Commentaria in quatuor libros Sententiarum*, ed. C. Paolini (Levanto: Conv. SSmae Annuntiationis, 1907–9).

Peter Auriol. *Commentariorum in primum librum Sententiarum, pars prima et secunda* (Rome, 1596).
Commentariorum in secundum, tertium et quartum Sententiarum et Quodlibeti (Rome, 1605).
Compendium sensus litteralis totius divinae Scripturae, ed. P. Seeboeck (Quaracchi: Editiones Collegii S. Bonaventurae, 1896).
De paupertate et usu paupere, in B. de Ceva (ed.) *Firmamenta trium ordinum beatissimi patris nostri Francisci* (Paris, 1512) IV: 116–30.
Scriptum super primum sententiarum, ed. E. M. Buytaert (St. Bonaventure, NY: Franciscan Institute, 1952–6).
Peter of Auvergne. *The Commentary of Peter of Auvergne on Aristotle's Politics*, ed. G. M. Grech (Rome: Desclée de Brouwer, 1967).
Commentary on Aristotle's On Length and Shortness of Life, ed. M. Dunne, *Archives d'histoire doctrinale et littéraire du moyen âge* 69 (2002) 153–200.
Quaestiones in Metaphysicam, ed. A. Monahan, in J. R. O'Donnell (ed.) *Nine Mediaeval Thinkers: A Collection of Hitherto Unedited Texts* (Toronto: Pontifical Institute of Mediaeval Studies, 1955) 145–81.
Quaestiones super De memoria et reminiscentia, ed. D. Bloch, *Cahiers de l'Institut du Moyen Age Grec et Latin* 78 (2007).
Quaestiones super parva naturalia, in K. White (ed.) "Two Studies Related to St. Thomas Aquinas' Commentary on Aristotle's *De sensu et sensato*, together with an Edition of Peter of Auvergne's *Quaestiones super parva naturalia*" (Ph.D. dissertation: University of Ottawa, 1986).
Quaestiones super Praedicamentis, ed. R. Andrews, *Cahiers de l'Institut du Moyen Age Grec et Latin* 55 (1987) 3–84.
Le questioni su Porfirio, ed. A. Tiné, *Archives d'histoire doctrinale et littéraire du moyen âge* 64 (1997) 235–333.
Questions on Aristotle's De caelo, ed. G. Galle (Leuven: Leuven University Press, 2003).
Questions on Books I and II of Aristotle's Nicomachean Ethics, ed. A. Celano, *Mediaeval Studies* 48 (1986) 1–110.
Sententia super librum De vegetabilibus et plantis, ed. E. Poortman (Leiden: Brill, 2003).
Peter the Chanter. *Summa de sacramentis et animae consiliis*, ed. J. A. Dugauquier (Leuven: Éditions Nauwelaerts, 1954–7).
Verbum abbreviatum: textus conflatus, ed. M. Boutry (Turnhout: Brepols, 2004).
Peter Comestor. *Scolastica historia: Liber Genesis*, ed. A. Sylwan (Turnhout: Brepols, 2005).
Sententiae de sacramentis, ed. R. M. Martin, in *Maitre Simon et son groupe De sacramentis* (Leuven: Spicilegium sacrum Lovaniense, 1937).
Peter Damian. *Die Briefe des Petrus Damiani*, ed. K. Reindel (Munich: Monumenta Germaniae Historica, 1983–93).
De divina omnipotentia, ed. A. Cantin (Paris: Cerf, 1972).
Letters, tr. O. Blum (Washington, DC: Catholic University of America Press, 1989–2005).
Selected Writings on the Spiritual Life, tr. P. McNulty (London: Faber and Faber, 1959).
Sermones, ed. G. Lucchesi (Turnhout: Brepols, 1983).
Peter of Falco. *Quaestiones disputatae de quolibet*, ed. A.-J. Gondras, *Archives d'histoire doctrinale et littéraire du moyen âge* 33 (1966) 105–236.
Quaestiones disputatae ordinariae, ed. A.-J. Gondras (Leuven: Éditions Nauwelaerts, 1968).
Peter Helias. *Summa super Priscianum*, ed. L. A. Reilly (Toronto: Pontifical Institute of Mediaeval Studies, 1993).
Peter of Ireland. *Expositio et quaestiones in Aristotelis librum De longitudine et brevitate vitae*, ed. M. Dunne (Louvain-la-Neuve: Peeters, 1993).
Expositio et quaestiones in Peryermenias Aristotelis, ed. M. Dunne (Louvain-la-Neuve: Peeters, 1996).

Peter of John Olivi. *Epistola ad fratrem R.*, ed. S. Piron *et al. Archivum Franciscanum Historicum* 91 (1998) 33–64.

Lectura super Proverbia et Lectura super Ecclesiasten, ed. J. Schlageter (Grottaferrata: Editiones Collegii S. Bonaventurae, 2003).

On Genesis, ed. D. Flood (St. Bonaventure, NY: Franciscan Institute, 2007).

On the Acts of the Apostles, ed. D. Flood (St. Bonaventure, NY: Franciscan Institute, 2001).

Quaestio de usu paupere and Tractatus de usu paupere, ed. D. Burr (Florence: Olschki, 1992).

Quaestiones de incarnatione et redemptione. Quaestiones de virtutibus [*Summa* III], ed. A Emmen and E. Stadter (Grottaferrata: Editiones Collegii S. Bonaventurae, 1981).

Quaestiones in secundum librum Sententiarum [*Summa II*], ed. B. Jansen (Quaracchi: Editiones Collegii S. Bonaventurae, 1922–26).

Quaestiones logicales, ed. S. Brown, *Traditio* 42 (1986) 335–88.

Quodlibeta quinque, ed. S. Defraia (Grottaferrata: Editiones Collegii S. Bonaventurae, 2002).

Summa quaestionum super Sententias (ms. in Biblioteca Apostolica Vaticana, ms. Borgh. 322 and Borgh. 328).

Tractatus de verbo, ed. R. Pasnau, *Franciscan Studies* 53 (1993) 121–53.

Peter Lombard. *Collectanea in omnes d. Pauli Epistolas*, in J.-P. Migne (ed.) *Patrologiae cursus completus: series latina* (Paris, 1844–91) vols. CXCI–CXCII.

The Sentences, tr. G. Silano (Toronto: Pontifical Institute of Mediaeval Studies, 2007–).

Sententiae in quatuor libros distinctae, ed. I. C. Brady, 3rd edn (Grottaferrata: Editiones Collegii S. Bonaventurae, 1971–81).

Peter of Mantua. *Logica* (Padua, 1477).

Peter of Navarre. *In primum Sententiarum scriptum*, ed. P. S. Azcona (Madrid: Consejo Superior de Investigaciones Científicas, Instituto Francisco Suarez, 1974).

Peter of Palude. *Commentarium in IV libros Sententiarum* (Venice, 1495).

Concordantiae ad Summam S. Thomae (Salamanca, 1552).

Quartus sententiarum liber, ed. V. Haerlem (Paris, 1514).

Sermones thesauri novi dominicales (Strasbourg: Martin Flach, 1491).

Tractatus de potestate papae, ed. P. T. Stella (Zurich: Pas Verlag, 1966).

Peter of Poitiers. *Sententie I–II*, ed. P. S. Moore and M. Dulong (Notre Dame, IN: University of Notre Dame Press, 1943–50).

[*Summa de confessione*] *Compilatio praesens*, ed. J. Longère (Turnhout: Brepols, 1980).

Peter of Spain. *Exposição sobre os livros do Beato Dionisio Areopagita*, ed. M. A. Alonso (Lisbon: Instituto de Alta Cultura, 1957).

Language in Dispute: An English Translation of Peter of Spain's Tractatus, *Called Afterwards* Summulae logicales, tr. F. P. Dinneen (Amsterdam: Benjamins, 1990).

Medical Classroom Practice: Petrus Hispanus' Questions on Isagoge, Tegni, Regimen Acutorum and Prognostica (c. 1245–50), ed. F. Salmón (Cambridge: Cambridge Wellcome Unit for the History of Medicine, 1998).

Obras filosóficas, ed. M. A. Alonso (Madrid: Bolaños y Aguilar, 1941–52).

Obras médicas, ed. M. Pereira (Coimbra: Por ordem da Universidade de Coimbra, 1973).

Questiones super tractatus logice magistri Petri Hispani, ed. G. Federici-Vescovini *et al.* (Paris: Vrin, 2001).

Syncategoreumata, ed. L. M. de Rijk, tr. J. Spruyt (Leiden: Brill, 1992).

Tractatus Called Afterwards Summule Logicales, ed. L. M. de Rijk (Assen: Van Gorcum, 1972).

Peter Sutton. "Petrus Sutton (?), O.F.M.: Quaestiones disputatae," ed. G. J. Etzkorn, *Franciscan Studies* 24 (1964) 101–43.

"Petrus Sutton(?), O.F.M.: Quodlibeta," ed. G. J. Etzkorn, *Franciscan Studies* 23 (1963) 68–139.

"Die Quaestio des Petrus Sutton OFM, über die Univokation des Seins," ed. M. Schmaus, *Collectanea Franciscana* 3 (1933) 5–25.

Peter of Tarentaise. *In IV librum sententiarum commentaria* (Toulouse, 1649–52; repr. Ridgewood, NJ: Gregg Press, 1964).

Postilla super epistolas Pauli (Cologne: J. Koelhoff, 1478) (edited under the name "Nicolas de Gorran").

"Le quodlibet de Pierre de Tarantasia," ed. P. Glorieux, *Recherches de théologie ancienne et médiévale* 9 (1937) 237–80.

Peter Thomae. *De distinctione predicamentorum*, ed. E. P. Bos, in M. Kardaun and J. Spruyt (eds.) *The Winged Chariot: Collected Essays on Plato and Platonism in Honour of L.M. de Rijk* (Leiden: Brill, 2000) 277–312.

Quodlibet, ed. M. R. Hooper and E. M. Buytaert (St. Bonaventure, NY: Franciscan Institute, 1957).

The Tract De unitate minori *of Petrus Thomae*, ed. E. P. Bos (Leuven: Peeters, 2002).

Peter the Venerable. *Adversus Iudeorum inveteratam duritiem*, ed. Y. Friedman (Turnhout: Brepols, 1985).

Contra Petrobrusianos hereticos, ed. J. Fearns (Turnhout: Brepols, 1968).

De miraculis libri duo, ed. D. Bouthillier (Turnhout: Brepols, 1988).

The Letters of Peter the Venerable, ed. G. Constable (Cambridge, MA: Harvard University Press, 1967).

Peter of Vienna (?). *Die Zwettler Summe*, ed. N. M. Häring (Münster: Aschendorff, 1977).

Philip the Chancellor. *Summa de bono*, ed. N. Wicki (Berne: Francke, 1985).

Philo of Alexandria. *About the Contemplative Life*, ed. F. C. Conybeare (Oxford: Clarendon Press, 1895).

L'ancienne version latine des Questions sur la genèse de Philon d'Alexandrie, ed. F. Petit (Berlin: Akademie Verlag, 1973).

Philoponus. *In Aristotelis Categorias commentarium*, ed. A. Busse (*Commentaria in Aristotelem Graeca* XIII.1) (Berlin: Reimer, 1898).

Philoponus against Aristotle on the Eternity of the World, tr. C. Wildberg (Ithaca, NY: Cornell University Press, 1987).

Photios. *Bibliotheca*, ed. J. Schamp and B. Kindt (Turnhout: Brepols, 2003).

Epistulae et amphilochia, ed. V. Laourdas L. G. Westerink (Leipzig: Teubner, 1983–8).

Homiliai, ed. B. Laourdas (Thessaloniki, 1959).

Homilies, tr. C. A. Mango (Cambridge, MA: Harvard University Press, 1958).

Placentinus. *In summam Institutionum* (Lyon, 1536).

Summa codicis (Mainz, 1536; repr. Turin: Bottega d'Erasmo, 1962).

Die summa De actionum varietatibus, ed. L. Wahrmund (Innsbruck: Wagner, 1925; repr. Aalen: Scientia Verlag, 1962).

Plato. *Meno*, tr. Henry Aristippus, ed. V. Kordeuter and C. Labowsky (*Plato Latinus* I) (London: Warburg Institute, 1940).

Parmenides usque ad finem primae hypothesis, nec non Procli Commentarium in Parmenidem, tr. W. Moerbeke, ed. R. Klibansky and C. Labowsky (*Plato Latinus* III) (London: Warburg Institute 1953).

Phaedo, tr. Henry Aristippus, ed. L. Minio-Paluello (*Plato Latinus* II) (London: Warburg Institute, 1950).

Opera, ed. J. Burnet (Oxford: Clarendon Press, 1905–13).

Timaeus a Calcidio translatus commentarioque instructus, ed. J. H. Waszink (*Plato Latinus* IV) 2nd edn (London: Warburg Institute, 1975).

Pliny the Elder. *Natural History*, tr. H. Rackham (Cambridge, MA: Harvard University Press, 1938–63).

Plotinus. *Enneads*, ed. A. H. Armstrong (Cambridge, MA: Harvard University Press, 1984).

Porphyry. *Introduction [Isagoge]*, tr. J. Barnes (Oxford: Clarendon Press, 2003).

    Isagoge, ed. A. Busse (*Commentaria in Aristotelem Graeca* IV.1) (Berlin: G. Reimer, 1887).

    Isagoge, translatio Boethii, ed. L. Minio-Paluello (*Aristoteles Latinus* I.6–7) (Brugues: Desclée de Brouwer, 1966).

    On the Life of Plotinus, in P. Henry and H.-R. Schwyzer (eds.) *Plotini Opera* (Oxford: Oxford University Press, 1964) vol. I.

Priscian. *Institutiones grammaticae*, ed. M. Hertz (Leipzig: Teubner, 1855–59; repr. Hildesheim: Olms, 1961).

    Opera (Venice: G. Arrivabenus, 1488).

Prochoros Kydones. *Pragmateia eis to peri ousias kai energeias zetema*, ed. J. Filovski and M. D. Petrusevski, *Ziva Antika* 23 (1973) 317–67; 26 (1976) 161–92.

Proclus. *Commentaire sur le Parménide de Platon, traduction de Guillaume de Moerbeke*, ed. C. Steel (Leuven: Presses universitaires, 1982–5).

    Elementatio theologica, translata a Guillelmo de Morbecca, ed. H. Boese (Leuven: University Press, 1987).

    The Elements of Theology, ed. E. R. Dodds, 2nd edn (Oxford: Oxford University Press, 1963).

    In Platonis Timaeum commentaria, ed. E. Diehl (Leipzig: Teubner, 1903–6).

    Liber de causis, tr. Gerard of Cremona, ed. A. Pattin, *Tijdschrift voor Filosofie* 28 (1966) 90–203.

    Tria opuscula (De providentia, libertate, malo), latine Guilelmo de Moerbeka vertente et graece ex Isaacii Sebastocratoris aliorumque scriptis collecta, ed. H. Boese (Berlin: De Gruyter, 1960).

Profiat Duran. *Maʿaseh Efod* (Vienna, 1865).

Pseudo-Albert the Great. *Quaestiones Alberti de modis significandi*, ed. and tr. L. G. Kelly (Amsterdam: Benjamins, 1977).

Pseudo-Andronicus of Rhodes. *Peri pathōn*, ed. A. Gilbert-Thirry (Leiden: Brill, 1977).

Pseudo-Apollonius. *On the Secrets of Nature*, tr. [Latin] Hugo of Santalla, ed. F. Hudry, in *Chrysopoeia* 6 (1997–9) 1–154.

Pseudo-Aristotle. "The Hebrew Version of the *Secretum Secretorum*," ed. M. Gaster, *Journal of the Royal Asiatic Society* (1907) 879–912; (1908) 111–62, 1065–84.

    Iggeret ha-musar le-Aristotelos, ed. J. Marcaria (Riva di Trento: A. Braun, 1559).

    Liber de causis, ed. I. Schreiber (Budapest: Athenaeum, 1916).

    "*Nutaf min al-ḥiyal:* A Partial Arabic Version of Pseudo-Aristotle's *Problemata Mechanica*," ed. M. Abattouy, *Early Science and Medicine* 6 (2001) 96–122.

    On the Causes of the Properties of the Four Elements, tr. Gerard of Cremona, ed. S. L. Vodraska (Ph.D dissertation: University of London, 1969).

    The Problemata Physica Attributed to Aristotle: The Arabic Version of Hunain ibn Ishaq and the Hebrew Version of Moses Ibn Tibbon, ed. L. S. Filius (Leiden: Brill, 1999).

    Secret of Secrets, tr. [Latin] John of Seville, in H. Suchier (ed.) *Denkmäler Provenzalischer Literatur und Sprache* (Halle: M. Niemeyer, 1883) 473–80.

    Sefer ha-tappuah le-Aristotelos, ed. J. Marcaria (Riva di Trento: A. Braun, 1562).

Pseudo-Campsall. *Logica Campsale Anglicj, valde utilis et realis contra Ocham*, in E. A. Synan (ed.) *The Works of Richard Campsall* (Toronto: Pontifical Institute of Mediaeval Studies, 1982) II: 51–420.

Pseudo-Cicero. "La traduzione greca di Rhetorica ad Herennium III,16–24," ed. S. Bernardinello, *Aevum* 47 (1973) 387–416.

Pseudo-Dionysius. *The Complete Works*, tr. C. Luibheid (New York: Paulist Press, 1987).

Corpus Dionysiacum, ed. B. R. Suchla, G. Heil, and A. M. Ritter (Berlin: De Gruyter, 1990–1).

Dionysiaca: recueil donnant l'ensemble des traductions latines des ouvrages attribués au Denys de l'aréopage, ed. P. Chevallier (Paris: Desclée de Brouwer, 1937–50).

Pseudo-Galen. *Dialog über die Seele: aus dem Arabischen übersetzt von Jehuda ben Salomo Alcharisi*, ed. A. Jellinek (Leipzig, 1852).

Pseudo-Grosseteste. *Tractatus de grammatica: eine fälschlich Robert Grosseteste zugeschriebene spekulative Grammatik*, ed. K. Reichl (Munich: Schöningh, 1976).

Pseudo-Kilwardby. "The Commentary on 'Priscianus Maior' ascribed to Robert Kilwardby," ed. K. M. Fredborg *et al.*, *Cahiers de l'Institut du Moyen Age Grec et Latin* 15 (1975) 1–143.

Pseudo-Peter of Ailly. *Destructiones modorum significandi*, ed. L. Kaczmarek (Amsterdam: Grüner, 1994).

Pseudo-Polemon. *Physiognomica*, [Arabic] ed. and tr. R. Hoyland, in S. Swain *et al.* (eds.) *Seeing the Face, Seeing the Soul: Polemon's Physiognomy from Classical Antiquity to Medieval Islam* (Oxford: Oxford University Press, 2007).

Ptolemy. *Almagest*, tr. G. J. Toomer (New York: Springer, 1984; repr. Princeton, NJ: Princeton University Press, 1998).

Opera quae exstant omnia, ed. J. L. Heiberg (Leipzig: Teubner, 1898–1907).

Ptolemy of Lucca. *Die Annalen des Tholomeus von Lucca*, ed. B. Schmeidler (Berlin: Weidmannsche Buchhandlung, 1955).

De regimine principum ad regem Cypri, in Thomas Aquinas, *Opuscula philosophica*, ed. R. M. Spiazzi (Rome: Marietti, 1954) 253–358.

Determinatio compendiosa de iurisdictione imperii, ed. M. Krammer (Hannover: Impensis Bibliopolii Hahniani, 1909).

Exaemeron seu De opera sex dierum tractatus, ed. T. Masetti (Siena: Ex typographia S. Bernardini, 1880).

Historia ecclesiastica nova, in L. Muratori (ed.) *Rerum italicarum scriptores* (Milan, 1727) XI: 751–1242.

On the Government of Rulers, tr. J. Blythe (Philadelphia: University of Pennsylvania Press, 1997).

al-Qushayrī. *Epistle on Sufism*, tr. A. D. Knysh (Reading: Garnet, 2007).

Al-Risāla al-Qushayrīya, ed. A. Mahmūd and M. Ibn al-Sharīf (Cairo: Dār al-Kutub al-Ḥadīthah, 1966).

Al-Tahbīr fī al-tadhkīr, ed. I. Busyūnī (Cairo: Dār al-kātib al-ʿarabī, 1968).

Qusṭā ibn Lūqā. *De differentia animae et spiritus liber*, ed. C. Barach (Innsbruck, 1878; repr. Frankfurt: Minerva, 1968).

De differentia animae et spiritus liber, in J. Wilcox (ed.) "The Transmission and Influence of Qusṭā ibn Lūqā's *On the Difference between Spirit and the Soul*" (Ph.D. dissertation: City University of New York, 1985).

On Physical Ligatures, tr. [Latin] Constantine the African, ed. J. Wilcox and J. M. Riddle, *Medieval Encounters* 1 (1995) 1–50.

Radulphus Ardens. *Speculum universale*, ed. J. Gründel (Munich: Hueber, 1961).

Radulphus Brito. *Quaestiones super arte veteri* (Venice, 1499).

Quaestiones super libros Topicarum Boethii, ed. N. J. Green-Pedersen and J. Pinborg, *Cahiers de l'Institut du Moyen Age Grec et Latin* 26 (1978).

Quaestiones super librum De anima, ed. W. Fauser (Münster: Aschendorff, 1974).

Quaestiones super Priscianum minorem, ed. H. W. Enders and J. Pinborg (Stuttgart-Bad Cannstatt: Frommann-Holzboog, 1980).

Radulphus de Longo Campo. *Distinctiones: vocabularium semanticum saeculi XII (circa 1190) dictionibus illustratum*, ed. J. Sulowski (Warsaw: Ossolineum, 1976).
  In Anticlaudianum Alani commentum, ed. J. Sulowski (Warsaw: Zaklad Narodowy im Ossolinskich, 1972).
Ralph of Beauvais. *Glose super Donatum*, ed. C. H. Kneepkens (Nijmegen: Ingenium, 1982).
  Liber Tytan, ed. C. H. Kneepkens (Nijmegen: Ingenium, 1991).
Ralph Strode. *Consequentiae et Obligationes, cum commentis* (Venice, 1493–4).
  Tractatus de consequentiis, ed. W. Seaton (Ph.D. dissertation: University of California at Berkeley, 1973).
Rambert de' Primadizzi of Bologna. *Apologeticum veritatis contra corruptorium*, ed. J.-P. Müller (Vatican: Biblioteca Apostolica Vaticana, 1944).
Ratramnus of Corbie. *De anima*, ed. A. Wilmart, *Revue Bénédictine* 43 (1931) 207–23.
  De anima ad Odonem, ed. C. Lambot (Namur: Éditions Godenne, 1952).
  De corpore et sanguine Domini, ed. J. N. Bakhuizen van den Brink, 2nd edn (Amsterdam: North-Holland, 1974).
Raymond of Capua. *The Life of Catherine of Siena*, tr. C. Kearns (Wilmington, DE: Glazier, 1980).
  Die Legenda maior (Vita Catharinae Senensis), ed. J. Jungmayr (Berlin: Weidler, 2004).
Raymond Lull. *Compendium logicae Algazelis*, ed. C. H. Lohr (Ph.D. dissertation: Universität zu Freiburg, 1967).
  Nova edició de les obres de Ramon Llull (Palma de Mallorca: Patronat Ramon Llull, 1990–).
  Obres de Ramon Lull, ed. M. Obrador y Benassar *et al.* (Palma de Mallorca: Comissió Editora Lulliana, 1906–17; Diputació Provincial de Balears and Institut d'Estudis Catalans, 1923–50).
  Opera latina (Palma de Mallorca: Maioricensis Schola Lullistica del CSIC, 1959–67; Turnhout: Brepols, 1975–).
  Opera omnia, ed. I. Salzinger (Mainz, 1721–40; repr. Frankfurt: Minerva, 1965).
  Selected Works of Ramon Llull, tr. A. Bonner (Princeton, NJ: Princeton University Press, 1985).
Raymond of Pennafort. *Summa de iure canonico*, ed. J. Ochoa Sanz and L. Diez Garcia (Rome: Commentarium pro religiosis, 1975).
  Summa de matrimonio, ed. X. Ochoa and A. Diez (Rome: Commentarium pro religiosis, 1978).
  Summa de paenitentia, ed. X. Ochoa and A. Diez (Rome: Commentarium pro religiosis, 1976).
  Summa on marriage, tr. P. Payer (Toronto: Pontifical Institute of Mediaeval Studies, 2005).
al-Rāzī, Abū Bakr. *Kitāb al-ḥāwī fī al-ṭibb* (Haydarabad al-Dakkan: Maṭbaʿat Majlis Dairat al-Maʿārif al-ʿUthmaniyah, 1955–68).
  Liber Elhavi id est Continens artem medicinae (Brescia: Jacobus Britannicus, 1486).
  Rasāʾil falsafiyya, ed. P. Kraus (Cairo: Fouad I University Faculty of Letters, 1939; repr. Beirut: Dār al-Afaq al-Jadida, 1973).
  The Spiritual Physick of Rhazes, tr. A. Arberry (London: John Murray, 1950).
al-Rāzī, Abū Ḥātim. *Aʿlām al-nubūwwah* (Beirut: Dār al-Saqi, 2003).
  Kitāb al-Iṣlāḥ, ed. M. Muhaqqiq *et al.* (Tehran: Muʾassasah-ʾi Muṭālaʿāt-i Islāmī, 1998).
  Kitāb al-Zīna, ed. H. al-Hamadānī (Sanaa: Markaz al-Dirāsāt, 1994).
al-Rāzī, Fakhr al-Dīn. *Al-Mabāḥith al-mashriqiyya* (Beirut: Dār al-Kitāb al-ʿArabī, 1990).
  Muḥaṣṣal afkār (Cairo: al-Maṭbaʿah al Ḥusaynīyyah al-Miṣrīyyah, 1905).
  Al-Tafsīr al-kabīr (Cairo: al-Maṭbaʿah al Bahīyya al-Miṣrīyya, 1934–62).
Regula non bullata, ed. C. Paolozzi, *Archivum Franciscanum Historicum* 100 (2007) 5–148.
Remigio de' Girolami. *Contra falsos ecclesie professores*, ed. F. Tamburini (Rome: Pontificia Università Lateranense, 1981).

De subiecto theologiae, ed. E. Panella (Milan: Massimo, 1982).

Une métaphysique à l'école de Thomas d'Aquin: le De modis rerum *de Rémi de Florence*, ed. A. Gavric (Fribourg: Academic Press, 2007).

"I Quodlibeti di Remigio dei Girolami," ed. E. Panella, *Memorie Domenicane* 14 (1983) 1–149.

Remigius of Auxerre. "A Commentary by Remigius Autissiodorensis on the 'De consolatione philosophiae' of Boethius," tr. H. F. Stewart, *Journal of Theological Studies* 17 (1916) 22–42.

Commentum in Martianum Capellam, ed. C. Lutz (Leiden: Brill, 1962–5).

Expositio super Genesim, ed. B. Edwards (Turnhout: Brepols, 1999).

Richard Billingham. *De consequentiis*, ed. S. Weber (Amsterdam: Grüner, 2003).

Speculum puerorum sive Terminus est in quem, ed. A. Maierù, *Studi Medievali*, 3rd ser., 10 supp. (1970) 297–398.

Richard Brinkley. "An Anonymous Fourteenth-Century Treatise on 'Insolubles': Text and Study," ed. P. V. Spade (Ph.D. dissertation: Pontifical Institute of Mediaeval Studies, Toronto, 1969).

Obligationes, ed. G. A. Wilson and P. V. Spade (Münster: Aschendorff, 1995).

Theory of Sentential Reference, ed. and tr. M. J. Fitzgerald (Leiden: Brill, 1987).

Richard of Campsall. *The Works of Richard of Campsall*, ed. E. A. Synan (Toronto: Pontifical Institute of Mediaeval Studies, 1968–82).

Richard of Conington. *Tractatus de paupertate*, ed. A. Heysse, *Archivum Franciscanum Historicum* 23 (1930) 57–105, 340–60.

Richard of Ferrybridge. *Consequentiae* (Venice, 1493).

Richard Fishacre. *In tertium librum Sententiarum*, ed. K. Rödler *et al.* (Munich: Bayerische Akademie der Wissenschaften, 2003–).

"Richard Fishacre's *Super S. Augustini librum de haeresibus adnotationes*: an Edition and Commentary," ed. R. J. Long, *Archives d'histoire doctrinale et littéraire du moyen âge* 60 (1993) 207–79.

Richard Fitzralph. *De pauperie Salvatoris*, in R. L. Poole (ed.) *Iohannis Wycliffe De dominio divino libri tres; to Which are Added the First Four Books of the Treatise De pauperie Salvatoris* (London: Trübner, 1890).

Defensio curatorum, tr. J. Trevisa (London: Oxford University Press, 1925; repr. Millwood, NY: Kraus Reprint, 1987).

Summa Domini Armacani in questionibus Armenorum, ed. J. Le Sueur (Paris, 1512).

Richard Kilvington. *The Sophismata of Richard Kilvington*, ed. N. Kretzmann and B. Ensign Kretzmann (Oxford: Oxford University Press, 1990).

The Sophismata of Richard Kilvington, tr. N. Kretzmann and B. Ensign Kretzmann (Cambridge: Cambridge University Press, 1990).

Richard Knapwell. *Le Correctorium corruptorii "Quare"*, ed. P. Glorieux (Kain: Saulchoir, 1927).

Quaestio disputata de unitate formae, ed. F. E. Kelley (Paris: Vrin, 1982).

Richard Lavenham. *De syncategorematibus, in Libellus sophistarum ad usum Cantabrigiensis* (London, 1510).

A Litil Tretys on the Seven Deadly Sins, ed. J. P. W. M. van Zutphen (Rome: Institutum Carmelitanum, 1956).

Richard of Middleton. *De ratione cognoscendi seu utrum quidquid certitudinaliter cognoscitur a nobis cognoscatur in rationibus aeternis quaestio anecdota*, ed. Fidelis a Fanna (Turin: Marietti, 1874).

Quodlibeta quaestiones octuaginta (Brescia, 1590; repr. Frankfurt: Minerva, 1963).

Super IV libros Sententiarum Petri Lombardi quaestiones subtilissimae (Brescia, 1591; repr. Frankfurt: Minerva, 1963).

Richard Rolle. *The English Writings*, tr. R. Allen (New York: Paulist Press, 1988).

    Prose and Verse, ed. S. J. Ogilvie-Thomson (Oxford: Early English Text Society, 1988).

Richard Rufus of Cornwall. *De ideis* (ms. in Erfurt, Universitätsbibliothek, cod. Amplonianus Q. 312).

    De ideis (ms. in Archiv Prazskeho Hradu [Prague, Library of the Metropolitan Chapter], ms. 1437).

    Disssertatio in Metaphysicam Aristotelis (ms. in Salamanca, Bibl. Gen. Hist. cod. 2322).

    In Physicam Aristotelis, ed. R. Wood (Oxford: Oxford University Press, 2003).

Richard of St. Victor. *De statu interioris hominis*, ed. J. Ribaillier, *Archives d'histoire doctrinale et littéraire du moyen âge* 34 (1967) 7–128.

    De Trinitate: texte critique, ed. J. Ribaillier (Paris: Cerf, 1958).

    Les douze patriarches, ou, Beniamin minor, ed. J. Châtillon *et al.* (Paris: Cerf, 1997).

    Liber exceptionum, ed. J. Châtillon (Paris: Vrin, 1958).

    Opuscules théologiques, ed. J. Ribaillier (Paris: Vrin, 1967).

    Selected Writings on Contemplation, ed. C. Kirchberger (London: Faber and Faber, 1957).

    Sermons et opuscules spirituels inédits: l'édit d'Alexandre ou les trois processions, ed. and tr. J. Châtillon *et al.* (Paris: Desclée de Brouwer, 1951).

    Trois opuscules spirituels de Richard de Saint-Victor: textes inédits accompagnés d'études critiques et de notes, ed. J. Châtillon *et al.* (Paris: Études Augustiniennes, 1986).

    The Twelve Patriarchs; The Mystical Ark; Book Three of the Trinity, tr. G. A. Zinn (New York: Paulist Press, 1979).

Richard Swineshead. *Liber calculationum* (Padua, 1477).

Robert Alyngton. *Litteralis sententia super Praedicamenta Aristotelis* [excerpts], in A. D. Conti (ed.) "Linguaggio e realtà nel commento alle Categorie di Robert Alyngton," *Documenti e studi sulla tradizione filosofica medievale* 4 (1993) 179–306.

Robert of Basevorn. *Forma praedicandi*, in T.-M. Charland (ed.) *Artes praedicandi: contribution à l'histoire de la rhétorique au moyen âge* (Ottawa: Institut d'Études Médiévales, 1936).

Robert of Flamborough. *Liber poenitentialis*, ed. J. J. F. Firth (Toronto: Pontifical Institute of Mediaeval Studies, 1971).

Robert Fland. *Consequentiae*, ed. P. V. Spade, *Mediaeval Studies* 38 (1976) 54–84.

    Insolubilia, ed. P. V. Spade, *Mediaeval Studies* 40 (1978) 56–80.

    Obligationes, ed. P. V. Spade, *Mediaeval Studies* 42 (1980) 41–60.

Robert Grosseteste. *Commentarius in Posteriorum analyticorum libros*, ed. P. Rossi (Florence: Olschki, 1981).

    Commentarius in VIII libros physicorum Aristotelis, ed. R. C. Dales (Boulder: University of Colorado Press, 1963).

    (tr.). *The Greek Commentaries of the Nicomachean Ethics of Aristotle in the Latin Translation of Robert Grosseteste*, ed. H. Mercken (*Corpus Latinum Commentariorum in Aristotelem Graecorum* VI) (Leiden: Brill, 1973–91).

    (tr.). *The Greek Commentaries of the Nicomachean Ethics of Aristotle in the Latin Translation of Robert Grosseteste*, ed. M. Trizio (*Corpus Latinum Commentariorum in Aristotelem Graecorum* VI.2) (Leuven: Leuven University Press, forthcoming).

    Hexaëmeron, ed. R. C. Dales and S. Gieben (London: British Academy, 1982).

    Mystical Theology: The Glosses by Thomas Gallus and the Commentary of Robert Grosseteste on De mystica theologia, ed. J. McEvoy (Paris: Peeters, 2003).

    On Light, ed. C. Riedl (Milwaukee, WI: Marquette University Press, 1942).

    On the Six Days of Creation, tr. C. F. J. Martin (Oxford: British Academy, 1996).

    Opera, ed. J. McEvoy *et al.* (Turnhout: Brepols, 1995).

Die philosophischen Werke des Robert Grosseteste, ed. L. Baur (Münster: Aschendorff, 1912).

Robert Holcot. *Exploring the Boundaries of Reason: Three Questions on the Nature of God by Robert Holcot, OP*, ed. H. G. Gelber (Toronto: Pontifical Institute of Mediaeval Studies, 1983).

In quattuor libros Sententiarum quaestiones (Lyon, 1518; repr. Frankfurt: Minerva, 1967).

Moralitates Roberti Olchot verbum Dei evangelizantibus per utiles (Venice, 1514).

Seeing the Future Clearly: Questions on Future Contingents, ed. P. Streveler *et al.* (Toronto: Pontifical Institute of Mediaeval Studies, 1995).

Sex articuli, in F. Hoffmann (ed.) *Die "Conferentiae" des Robert Holcot O.P. und die akademischen Auseinandersetzungen an der Universität Oxford 1330–1332* (Münster: Aschendorff, 1993).

Super libros Sapientiae (Hagenau, 1494; repr. Frankfurt: Minerva, 1974).

Super librum Ecclesiastici (Venice, 1509).

Robert Kilwardby. *De natura relationis*, ed. L. Schmücker (Lenggries: Schmücker, 1980).

De ortu scientiarum, ed. A. G. Judy (London: British Academy, 1976).

Epistula ad Petrum de Confleto, in A. Birkenmajer (ed.) *Vermischte Untersuchungen zur Geschichte der mittelalterlichen Philosophie* (Münster: Aschendorff, 1922) 36–69.

In Donati Artem maiorem III, ed. L. Schmücker (Brixen/Bressanone: Typographia A. Weger Fund. 1550, 1984).

[pseudo-Giles of Rome]. *In Libros priorum analyticorum expositio* (Venice, 1516; repr. Frankfurt: Minerva, 1968).

Notulae super librum Porphyrii (ms. in Cambridge, Peterhouse, ms. 206) 33ra–42ra.

Notulae super librum Praedicamentorum (ms. in Cambridge, Peterhouse, ms. 206) 42rb–65va.

Notule libri Prisciani de accentibus, ed. P. O. Lewry, *Mediaeval Studies* 50 (1988) 96–185.

On Time and Imagination: De tempore, De spiritu fantastico, ed. and tr. P. O. Lewry and A. Broadie (Oxford: Oxford University Press for the British Academy, 1987).

Quaestiones in librum primum Sententiarum, ed. J. Schneider (Munich: Bayerische Akademie der Wissenschaften, 1986).

Quaestiones in librum quartum Sententiarum, ed. R. Schenk (Munich: Bayerische Akademie der Wissenschaften, 1993).

Quaestiones in librum secundum Sententiarum, ed. G. Leibold (Munich: Bayerische Akademie der Wissenschaften, 1992).

Quaestiones in librum tertium Sententiarum, Part I: Christologie, ed. E. Gössmann (Munich: Bayerische Akademie der Wissenschaften, 1982).

Quaestiones in librum tertium Sententiarum, Part II: Tugendlehre, ed. G. Leibold (Munich: Bayerische Akademie der Wissenschaften, 1985).

Responsio de 43 quaestionibus Iohannis Vercellensis, ed. H.-F. Dondaine, *Archivum Fratrum Praedicatorum* 47 (1977) 5–50.

Robert of Melun. *Œuvres*, ed. R. M. Martin (Leuven: Spicilegium sacrum Lovaniense, 1932–52).

Robert Orford. *Le Correctorium corruptorii "Sciendum"*, ed. P. Glorieux (Paris: Vrin, 1956).

De natura materiae, in Thomas Aquinas, Opuscula philosophica, ed. R. M. Spiazzi (Rome: Marietti, 1954) 131–45.

Reprobationes dictorum a fratre Egidio in primum Sententiarum, ed. A. Vella (Paris: Vrin 1968).

Robertus Anglicus. *Sophistria*, ed. A. Grondeux and I. Rosier-Catach (Paris: Vrin, 2006).

Roger Bacon. *Compendium of the Study of Theology*, ed. and tr. T. S. Mahoney (Leiden: Brill, 1988).

De multiplicatione specierum and De speculis comburentibus, ed. D. C. Lindberg (Oxford: Clarendon Press, 1983).

De signis, ed. K. M. Fredborg *et al.*, *Traditio* 34 (1978) 75–136.

The Greek Grammar of Roger Bacon and a Fragment of his Hebrew Grammar, ed. E. Nolan and S. A. Hirsch (Cambridge: Cambridge University Press, 1902).

Moralis philosophia, ed. E. Massa (Zurich: Thesaurus Mundi, 1953).

Opera hactenus inedita Rogeri Bacon, ed. R. Steele *et al.* (Oxford: Clarendon Press, 1909–40).

Opera quaedam hactenus inedita, ed. J. S. Brewer (London: Longman, 1859; repr. 1965).

Opus maius, ed. J. H. Bridges (Oxford: Clarendon Press, 1897–1900; repr. Frankfurt: Minerva, 1964).

The Opus Majus, tr. R. B. Burke (Philadelphia: University of Pennsylvania Press, 1928; repr. New York: Russell, 1962).

Perspectiva, in D. C. Lindberg (ed. and tr.) *Roger Bacon and the Origins of Perspectiva in the Middle Ages* (Oxford: Clarendon Press, 1996).

Summulae dialectices, ed. A. de Libera, *Archives d'histoire doctrinale et littéraire du moyen âge* 53 (1986) 139–289; 54 (1987) 171–278.

Three Treatments of Universals, ed. T. S. Maloney (Binghamton, NY: MARTS, 1989).

Roger Marston. *Quaestiones disputatae de emanatione aeterna, de statu naturae lapsae et de anima*, ed. Z. van. de Woestyne *et al.* (Quaracchi: Editiones Collegii S. Bonaventurae, 1932).

Quodlibeta quatuor, ed. G. J. Etzkorn and I. Brady, 2nd edn (Grottaferrata: Editiones Collegii S. Bonaventurae, 1994).

Roger Nottingham. *Insolubilia*, ed. E. Synan, *Mediaeval Studies* 26 (1964) 257–70.

Introitus ad Sententias, ed. E. Synan, *Mediaeval Studies* 25 (1963) 259–79.

Roger Roseth. *Lectura super Sententias: Quaestiones 3, 4 & 5*, ed. O. Hallamaa (Helsinki: Luther-Agricola Society, 2005).

Roger Swineshead. *Insolubilia*, ed. P. V. Spade, *Archives d'histoire doctrinale et littéraire du moyen âge* 46 (1979) 177–220.

Obligationes, ed. P. V. Spade, *Archives d'histoire doctrinale et littéraire du moyen âge* 44 (1977) 243–85.

Roger Whelpdale, *Tractatus de universalibus* [excerpts], ed. A. D. Conti, in John Sharpe, *Quaestio super universalia* (Florence: Olschki, 1990) 189–97.

Roland of Bologna. *Die Sentenzen Rolands*, ed. A. Gietl (Freiburg: Herder, 1891; repr. Amsterdam: Rodopi, 1969).

Summa Magistri Rolandi, ed. F. Thaner (Innsbruck: Wagner, 1874; repr. Aalen: Scientia Verlag, 1962).

Roland of Cremona. *Summae Magistri Rolandi Cremonensis O.P. Liber tercius*, ed. A. Cortesi (Bergamo: Edizioni Monumenta Bergomensia, 1962).

Rufinus. *De bono pacis*, ed. A. Brunacci and G. Catanzaro (Assisi: Fonteviva Editrice, 1986).

Summa decretorum, ed. H. Singer (Paderborn: Schöningh, 1902; repr. Aalen: Scientia Verlag, 1963).

Rupert of Deutz. *Commentaria in Canticum Canticorum*, ed. H. Deutz and I. Deutz (Turnhout: Brepols, 2005).

De Sancta Trinitate et operibus eius, ed. R. Haacke (Turnhout: Brepols, 1971–2).

De victoria Verbi Dei, ed. R. Haacke (Weimar: Böhlau, 1970).

In evangelium sancti Iohannis, ed. R. Haacke (Turnhout: Brepols, 1969).

Saadiah Gaon. *The Book of Beliefs and Opinions*, tr. S. Rosenblatt (New Haven, CT: Yale University Press, 1948).

Commentaire sur le Sefer Yesira, ed. M. Lambert (Paris: Bouillon, 1891).

Ha-Egron: Kitāb ʿusul al-shiʾr al-ʾibrani, ed. N. Allony (Jerusalem: Academy of the Hebrew Language, 1969).

Kitāb al-Amānāt wa-al-iʿtiqādāt, ed. S. Landauer (Leiden: Brill, 1880).

Kitāb al-Amānāt wa-al-iʿtiqādāt, ed. J. Kafiḥ (Jerusalem: Sura, 1970).

Les œuvres complètes, ed. J. Derenbourh *et al.* (Paris: E. Leroux, 1893–9).

The Book of Theodicy: Translation and Commentary on the Book of Job, tr. L. Goodman (New Haven, CT: Yale University Press, 1988).

al-Samarqandī. *Risāla fī ādāb al-baḥth*, in M. al-Manṣūrī (ed.) *Majmuʿah mushtamilah ʿala al-ātī bayānuhū* (Mahabad: Kitābfurūshī-yi Sayyidyān, 1934).

Samuel ibn Tibbon. *Commentary on Ecclesiastes: The Book of the Soul of Man*, ed. and tr. J. T. Robinson (Tübingen: Mohr Siebeck, 2007).

Maʾamar Yiqqawu ha-Mayim, ed. M. Bisliches (Pressburg: Anton Edler von Schmid, 1837).

Sedulius Scottus. *Carmina*, ed. J. Meyers (Turnhout: Brepols, 1991).

Collectaneum in apostolum, ed. H. Frede and H. Stanjek (Freiburg: Herder, 1996).

Collectaneum miscellaneum, ed. D. Simpson (Turnhout: Brepols, 1988).

De rectoribus Christianis, in S. Hellmann (ed.) *Sedulius Scottus* (Munich: Beck, 1906).

In Donati artem maiorem, ed. B. Löfstedt (Turnhout: Brepols, 1977).

In Donati artem minorem; In Priscianum; In Eutychem, ed. B. Löfstedt (Turnhout: Brepols, 1977).

Kommentar zum Evangelium nach Matthäus, ed. B. Löfstedt (Freiburg: Herder, 1989).

Seneca. *L. Annaei Senecae ad Lucilium epistulae morales*, ed. L. D. Reynolds (Oxford: Clarendon Press, 1965).

Sennert, Daniel. *Thirteen Books of Natural Philosophy* (London, 1659).

Servasanto of Faenza. *Summa de poenitentia* (Louvain, 1485).

al-Shāfiʿī, Muḥammad ibn Idrīs. *Al-Risāla fī al-uṣūl*, ed. A. M. Shākir (Cairo: Dār al-Turāth, 1979).

Al-Risāla fī uṣūl al-fiqh: Treatise on the Foundations of Islamic Jurisprudence, tr. M. Kahadduri, 2nd edn (Cambridge: Islamic Texts Society, 1987).

al-Shahrastānī, Abū al-Fatḥ. *Kitāb al-milal wa-al-niḥal*, ed. M. Badrān (Cairo: Maṭbaʿat al-Azhar, 1951).

Livre des religions et des sectes, tr. D. Gimaret and G. Monnot (Paris: Peeters, 1986–93).

Majlis: discours sur l'ordre et la création, ed. and tr. D. Steigerwald (Sainte-Foy, Quebec: Presses de l'Université Laval, 1998).

Muslim Sects and Divisions: The Section on Muslim Sects in Kitāb al-milal wa'l nihal, tr. A. K. Kazi and J. G. Flynn (London: Kegan Paul, 1983).

Shahrastani on the Indian Religions, tr. B. B. Lawrence (The Hague: Mouton, 1976).

Struggling with the Philosopher: A Refutation of Avicenna's Metaphysics, ed. and tr. W. Madelung and T. Mayer (London: I. B. Taurus, 2001).

Summa philosophiae: Kitāb nihāyat al-iqdām fī ʿilm al-kalām, ed. A. Guillaume (London: Oxford University Press, 1934).

Shem Tov ibn Falaquera. *Book of the Seeker*, tr. M. H. Levine (New York: Yeshiva University Press, 1976).

Epistle of the Debate: An Introduction to Jewish Philosophy, tr. S. Harvey (Cambridge, MA: Harvard University Press, 1987).

Iggeret ha-Vikuah, ed. A. Jellinek (Vienna, 1875; repr. in *Kitvei Rabbi Shem Tov Falaquera* [Jerusalem: Maqor, 1970]).

Moreh ha-Moreh, ed. Y. Shiffman, in "Rabbi Shem Tov ben Joseph Falaquera's *More ha-More*: A Philosophical and Philological Analysis" (Ph.D. dissertation: Hebrew University of Jerusalem, 1990).

Sefer ha-Mevaqqesh, ed. M. Tamah (The Hague, 1778; repr. in *Kitvei Rabbi Shem Tov Falaquera* [Jerusalem: Maqor, 1970]).

Sībawayhi. *Kitāb Sībawayhi*, ed. A. S. M. Hārūn (Cairo: Dār al-Qalam, 1966–77).

Sîbawaihi's Buch über die Grammatik, übersetzt und erklärt, tr. G. Jahn (Berlin: Reuther und Reichard, 1895–1900; repr. Hildesheim: Olms, 1969).

Siger of Brabant. *Écrits de logique, de morale, et de physique: édition critique*, ed. B. C. Bazán (Leuven: Publications universitaires, 1974).

    On the Eternity of the World, tr. C. Vollert *et al.* (Milwaukee, WI: Marquette University Press, 1964).

    Quaestiones in Metaphysicam: Édition revue de la reportation de Munich; Texte inédit de la reportation de Vienne, ed. W. Dunphy (Louvain-la-Neuve: Éditions de l'Institut Supérieur de Philosophie, 1981).

    Quaestiones in Metaphysicam: Texte inédit de la reportation de Cambridge; Édition revue de la reportation de Paris, ed. A. Maurer (Louvain-la-Neuve: Éditions de l'Institut Supérieur de Philosophie, 1983).

    Quaestiones in tertium De anima; De anima intellectiva; De aeternitate mundi, ed. B. C. Bazán (Leuven: Publications universitaires, 1972).

    Les Quaestiones super librum de causis, ed. A. Marlasca (Leuven: Publications universitaires, 1972).

Siger of Courtrai. *Commentator van Perihermenaias*, ed. C. Verhaak (Brussels: Paleis der Academiën, 1964).

    Les œuvres de Siger de Courtrai (étude critique et textes inédits), ed. G. Wallerand (Leuven: Institut Supérieur de Philosophie de l'Université, 1913).

    Summa modorum significandi; Sophismata, ed. G. Wallerand and J. Pinborg (Amsterdam: Benjamins, 1977).

al-Sijistānī, Abū Sulaymān. *Ṣiwān al-ḥikma wa-thalāth rasāʾil*, ed. A. Badawī (Teheran: Bunyād Farhang, 1974)

al-Sijistānī, Abū Yaʿqūb. *Kashf al-maḥjūb*, ed. H. Corbin (Tehran: Institute français de recherche en Iran, 1949).

    Kashf al-maḥjub: Le devoilement des choses cachées, tr. H. Corbin (Lagrasse: Verdier, 1988).

    Kitāb al-yanābīʿ, in H. Corbin (ed.) *Trilogie ismaélienne* (Tehran: Département d'Iranologie de l'Institut francoiranien, 1961).

    The Wellsprings of Wisdom: A Study of Abū Yaʿqūb al-Sijistānī's Kitāb al-Yanābīʿ, tr. P. E. Walker (Salt Lake City: University of Utah Press, 1994).

Silhon, Jean de. *De l'immortalité de l'âme* (Paris, 1634).

Simeon Duran. *Magen Avot* (Livorno, 1785; repr. Jerusalem: Mekor, 1969).

    Ohev Mishpat (Venice, 1590).

Simon of Dacia. *Opera*, ed. A. Otto (Copenhagen: Gad, 1963).

Simon of Faversham. *Opera omnia*, vol. I: *Opera logica*, ed. P. Mazzarella (Padua: CEDAM, 1957).

    Quaestiones super libro elenchorum, ed. S. Ebbesen *et al.* (Toronto: Pontifical Institute of Mediaeval Studies, 1984).

    Quaestiones super tertium De anima, ed. D. Sharp, *Archives d'histoire doctrinale et littéraire du moyen âge* 9 (1934) 307–68.

Simon of Hinton. *Summa iuniorum*, in John Gerson, *Opera omnia* (Antwerp, 1706) I: 233–422.

Simon of Tournai. *Disputationes*, ed. J. Warichez (Leuven: Spicilegium sacrum Lovaniense, 1932).

    Institutiones in sacram paginam: Einleitung und Quästionenverzeichnis, ed. R. Heinzmann (Munich: Paderborn, 1967).

    "Simon of Tournai's Commentary on the So-Called Athanasian Creed," ed. N. M. Häring, *Archives d'histoire doctrinale et littéraire du moyen âge* 43 (1976) 135–99.

"Die Texte der Trinitätslehre in den *Sententiae* des Simon von Tournai," ed. M. Schmaus, *Recherches de théologie ancienne et médiévale* 4 (1932) 59–72, 187–98, 294–307.

Simplicius. *Commentarius In Epicteti Enchiridion*, in F. Dübner (ed.) *Theophrasti Characteres* (Paris: A. Firmin-Didot, 1840).

In Aristotelis physicorum libros octo commentaria, ed. H. Diels (*Commentaria in Aristotelem Graeca* IX–X) (Berlin: Reimer, 1882, 1895).

In libros De anima commentaria, ed. M. Hayduck (*Commentaria in Aristotelem Graeca* XI) (Berlin: Reimer, 1882).

Sirmond, Antoine. *De immortalitate animae demonstratio physica et Aristotelica, adversus Pomponatium et asseclas* (Paris, 1635).

Démonstration de l'immortalité de l'ame. Tirée des principes de la nature. Fortifiée de ceux d'Aristote. Où plusieurs beaux secrets de la philosophie sont mis en leur jour (Paris, 1637).

Solomon ibn Gabirol. *Choice of Pearls*, tr. A. Cohen (New York: Bloch, 1925).

A Crown for the King, ed. and tr. D. R. Slavitt (New York: Oxford University Press, 1998).

Fons vitae, ed. C. Baeumker (Münster: Aschendorff, 1892–5).

The Improvement of the Moral Qualities, ed. and tr. S. Wise (New York: Columbia University Press, 1909; repr. New York: AMS Press, 1966).

"Liqqutim min ha-Sefer Makor Hayyim," ed. S. Munk, in *Mélanges de philosophie juive et arabe* (Paris: Franck, 1857–9; repr. Paris: Gamber, 1927).

Selected Poems, tr. P. Cole (Princeton, NJ: Princeton University Press, 2001).

Selected Religious Poems of Solomon ibn Gabirol, ed. I. Davidson (Philadelphia, PA: Jewish Publication Society of America, 1923; repr. New York: Arno Press, 1973).

Stephen Langton. *Commentary on the Book of Chronicles*, ed. A. Saltman (Ramat-Gan: Bar-Ilan University Press, 1978).

De persona, ed. M. Bieniak, *Cahiers de l'Institut du Moyen Age Grec et Latin* 77 (2006) 85–109.

Selected Sermons, ed. P. B. Roberts (Toronto: Pontifical Institute of Mediaeval Studies, 1980).

Der Sentenzenkommentar, ed. A. M. Landgraf (Münster: Aschendorff, 1952).

Stephen of Rieti. *De universalibus*, in F. Amerini, *I trattati De universalibus di Francesco da Prato e Stefano da Rieti (secolo XIV)* (Spoleto: Centro italiano di studi sull'alto medioevo, 2003) 133–45.

Stephen of Tournai. *Die Summa des Stephan von Doornick über das Decretum Gratiani*, ed. J. F. Schulte (Giessen: Roth, 1891; repr. Aalen: Scientia Verlag, 1965).

Lettres, ed. J. Desilve (Valenciennes: Lemaître, 1893).

al-Suhrawardī, Abū Ḥafṣ ʿUmar. *ʿAwārif al-maʿārif* (Beirut: Dār al-kitāb al-ʿarabī, 1983).

A Dervish Textbook from the ʿAwarifu-l-maʿarif, tr. H. W. Clarke (London: Octagon Press, 1980; orig. publ. 1891).

Die Gaben der Erkenntnisse, tr. R. Gramlich (Wiesbaden: Steiner, 1978).

al-Suhrawardī, Shihāb al-Dīn Yaḥyā. *L'Archange empourpré: quinze traités et récits mystiques*, ed. H. Corbin (Paris: Fayard, 1976).

The Mystical and Visionary Treatises of Shihabuddin Yahya Suhrawardi, tr. W. M. Thackston, Jr (London: Octagon Press, 1982).

Œuvres philosophiques et mystiques, ed. H. Corbin and S. H. Nasr (Tehran: Académie Impériale Iranienne de Philosophie, 1976–7).

The Philosophy of Illumination: A New Critical Edition of the Text of Ḥikmat al-Ishrāq, with English Translation, ed. J. Walbridge and H. Ziai (Provo, UT: Brigham Young University Press, 1999).

Syrianus. *In Metaphysica commentaria* ed. W. Kroll (*Commentaria in Aristotelem Graeca* VI.1) (Berlin: Reimer, 1902).

al-Taftāzānī. *A Commentary on the Creed of Islam: Saʿd al-Din al-Taftazani on the Creed of Najm al-Din al-Nasafi*, tr. E. E. Elder (New York, Columbia University Press, 1950; repr. New York: Books for Libraries, 1980).

Sharḥ al-ʿaqāʾid al-Nasafiyya (Cairo: 1916).

Sharḥ al-ʿaqāʾid al-Nasafiyya, ed. K. Salāma (Damascus: Wizārat al-Thaqāfah wa-al-Irshād al-Qawmī, 1974).

Sharḥ al-Maqāṣid, ed. A. Umayra (Cairo: ʿĀlam al-Kutub, 1984–9).

al-Tawḥīdī. *Al-Imtāʿ wa al-muʾānasa*, ed. A. Amīn and A. al-Zayn (Cairo: Maṭbaʿat Lajnat al-Taʾlīf wa-al-Tarjamah wa-al-Nashr, 1953).

Al-Muqābasāt, ed. M. T. Husayn (Baghdad: Maṭbaʿat al-Irshad, 1970).

Thābit ibn Qurra. *Astronomical Works*, ed. F. J. Carmody (Berkeley: University of California Press, 1960).

Œuvres d'astronomie, ed. R. Morelon (Paris: Les Belles Lettres, 1987).

Thaddeus of Parma. *Quaestiones de anima*, ed. S. Vanni Rovighi (Milan: Vita e Pensiero, 1951).

Themistius. *In Aristotelis Metaphysicorum librum Λ, paraphrasis hebraice et latine*, ed. S. Landauer (Berlin: Reimer, 1903).

In libros Aristotelis De caelo paraphrasis hebraice et latine, ed. S. Landauer (Berlin: Reimer, 1902).

Paraphrasis of the Posterior Analytics, tr. [Latin] Gerard of Cremona, ed. J. R. O'Donnell, *Mediaeval Studies* 20 (1958) 239–315.

Themon Judaeus. *In quatuor libros Meteorum*, ed. G. Lokert (Paris, 1516).

L'œuvre astronomique de Themon Juif, maître parisien du XIVᵉ siècle, ed. H. Hugonnard-Roche (Geneva: Droz, 1973).

Theodore II Dukas Laskaris. "Deux traités inédits de Theodore II Doucas Lascaris," ed. P.-M. Palaiologou, *Byzantina* 27 (2007) 51–90.

Kosmikē dēlōsis, ed. N. Festa, *Giornale della Società Asiatica Italiana* 11 (1897/8) 101–14; 12 (1899) 39–52.

Opuscula rhetorica, ed. A. Tartaglia (Leipzig: Teubner, 2000).

Per christianikes theologias logoi, ed. C. T. Krikones, 2nd edn (Thessaloniki: Patriarchikon Hidryma Paterikon Meleton, 1988).

Theodore Abū Qurrah. *Mayāmir Thāwdūrus Abī Qurra usquf Ḥarrān*, ed. C. Bacha (Beirut: Maṭbaʿat al-Fawāʾid, 1904).

Maymar fī ikrām al-ayqūnāt = Traité du culte des icônes, ed. I. Dick (Jounieh: Librairie Saint Paul, 1986).

Maymar fī wujūd al-khāliq wa-al-dīn al-qawīm = Traité de l'existence du Créateur et de la vraie religion, ed. I. Dick (Jounieh: Librairie Saint Paul, 1982).

Theodore Abu Qurrah, tr. J. C. Lamoreaux (Provo, UT: Brigham Young University Press, 2005).

Theodore Gazes. *De fato*, ed. and tr. J. W. Taylor (Toronto: University of Toronto Library, 1925).

"Introduction à la grammaire, libri IV," ed. D. Donnet, *Byzantion* 49 (1979) 133–55.

Theodore Metochites. *Ethikos e Peri paideias*, ed. I. D. Polemes (Athens: Ekdoseis Kanake, 1995).

Miscellanea philosophica et historica, ed. C. G. Müller and T. Kiessling (Leipzig: Vogelii, 1821; repr. Amsterdam: Hakkert, 1966).

Paraphrasis in Aristotelis universam naturalem philosophiam (Basel, 1559; repr. Stuttgart-Bad Cannstaat: Frommann-Holzboog, 1992).

Theodore Metochites on Ancient Authors and Philosophy: Semeioseis gnomikai 1–26 & 71, ed. and tr. K. Hult (Gothenburg: Acta Universitatis Gothoburgensis, 2002).

Theodulf of Orleans. *Opus Caroli Regis contra Synodum (Libri Carolini)*, ed. A. Freeman (Hannover: Hahnsche Buchhandlung, 1998).

Thierry of Chartres. *Commentaries on Boethius*, ed. N. M. Häring (Toronto: Pontifical Institute of Mediaeval Studies, 1971).

The Latin Rhetorical Commentaries, ed. K. M. Fredborg (Toronto: Pontifical Institute of Mediaeval Studies, 1988).

Thomas Aquinas. *The Basic Writings*, ed. A. C. Pegis (New York: Random House, 1945).

De ente et essentia (Venice, 1496).

Dēmētriou Kydōnē, Thōma Akuinatou Summa theologikē exellēnistheisa, eds. G. Leontsinis *et al.* (Athens: Publication de la Fondation de Recherche et d'Éditions de Philosophie Néohellénique, 1976–2002).

An Exposition of the "On the Hebdomads" of Boethius, tr. J. L. Schultz and E. A. Synan (Washington, DC: Catholic University of America Press, 2001).

In Aristotelis libros De caelo et mundo, De generatione et corruptione, Meteorologicorum expositio, ed. R. M. Spiazzi (Rome: Marietti, 1952).

In De divinis nominibus expositio, ed. C. Pera *et al.* (Turin: Marietti, 1950).

In duodecim libros Metaphysicorum Aristotelis expositio, ed. M. R. Cathala and R. M. Spiazzi (Rome: Marietti, 1971).

In octo libros Physicorum Aristotelis expositio, ed. P. M. Maggiòlo (Turin: Marietti, 1965).

On Being and Essence, tr. A. Maurer (Toronto: Pontifical Institute of Mediaeval Studies, 1968).

On the Eternity of the World, tr. C. Vollert *et al.* (Milwaukee, WI: Marquette University Press, 1964).

On the Unity of the Intellect Against the Averroists, tr. B. Zedler (Milwaukee, WI: Marquette University Press, 1968).

Opera omnia (Parma: Fiaccadori, 1852–73).

Opera omnia, ed. Leonine Commission (Rome: Commissio Leonina, 1882–).

Opuscula theologica, ed. R. A. Verardo *et al.* (Rome: Marietti, 1954).

Super epistolas S. Pauli lectura, ed. R. Cai (Turin: Marietti, 1953).

Super librum de causis expositio, ed. H. D. Saffrey (Fribourg: Société Philosophique, 1954).

Thomas of Bailly. *Quodlibeta*, ed. P. Glorieux (Paris: Vrin, 1960).

Thomas Bradwardine. *Arithmetica speculativa* (Paris, 1495).

De causa Dei contra Pelagium et de virtute causarum ad suos Mertonenses, libri tres, ed. H. Savile (London: apud I. Billium, 1618; repr. Frankfurt: Minerva, 1964).

De continuo, in J. Murdoch (ed.) "Geometry and the Continuum in the Fourteenth Century: A Philosophical Analysis of Thomas Bradwardine's *Tractatus de continuo*" (Ph.D. dissertation, University of Wisconsin, 1957).

De futuris contingentibus, ed. J.-F. Genest, *Recherches Augustiniennes* 14 (1979) 249–336.

De incipit et desinit, ed. L. O. Nielsen, *Cahiers de l'Institut du Moyen Age Grec et Latin* 42 (1982) 1–83.

De insolubilibus, ed. M. L. Roure, *Archives d'histoire doctrinale et littéraire du moyen âge* 37 (1970) 205–326.

De proportionibus velocitatum in motibus, ed. and tr. H. L. Crosby (Madison: University of Wisconsin Press, 1955).

Geometria speculativa, ed. and trans. A. G. Molland (Wiesbaden: Steiner, 1989).

Insolubilia, ed. and tr. S. Read (Leuven: Peeters, forthcoming).

Opus artis logicae, ed. J. Pinborg, *Cahiers de l'Institut du Moyen Age Grec et Latin* 42 (1982) 151–64.

Quaestiones circa tractatum proportionum magistri Thome Braduardini, ed. S. Rommevaux *et al.* (Paris: Vrin, 2006).

Thomas Buckingham. *In quatuor libros Sententiarum* (Paris, 1505).

Thomas of Cantimpré. *Les exemples du "Livre des abeilles": une vision médiévale*, ed. H. Platelle (Turnhout: Brepols, 1997).

Liber de natura rerum, ed. H. Boese (Berlin: De Gruyter, 1973).

Thomas of Celano. *Vita secunda S. Francisci Assisiensis* (Quaracchi: Editiones Collegii S. Bonaventurae, 1927).

Thomas of Chobham. *Sermones*, ed. F. Morenzoni (Turnhout: Brepols, 1993).

Summa confessorum, ed. F. Broomfield (Leuven: Éditions Nauwelaerts, 1968).

Summa de arte praedicandi, ed. F. Morenzoni (Turnhout: Brepols, 1988).

Thomas of Cleves. *Concepts: The Treatises of Thomas of Cleves and Paul of Gelria, an Edition of the Texts with a Systematic Introduction*, ed. E. P. Bos and S. Read (Louvain-la-Neuve: Éditions de l'Institut Supérieur de Philosophie, 2001).

Thomas of Erfurt. *Fundamentum puerorum*, in R. Gansiniec (ed.) *Metrificale marka z opatowca i traktaty gramatyczne XIV i XV wieku* (Warsaw: Zaklad Narodowy im. Ossolinskich, 1960).

Grammatica speculativa, ed. and tr. G. L. Bursill-Hall (London: Longmans, 1972).

Thomas Gallus. *Commentaires du Cantique des Cantique*, ed. J. Barbet (Paris: Béatrice-Nauwelaerts, 1972).

Grand commentaire sur la Théologie Mystique, ed. G. Théry (Paris: Haloua, 1934).

Mystical Theology: The Glosses by Thomas Gallus and the Commentary of Robert Grosseteste on "De Mystica Theologia", ed. and tr. J. McEvoy (Paris: Peeters, 2003).

Thomas of Strasbourg. *Super quatuor libros Sententiarum* (Strasbourg, 1490; repr. Frankfurt, 1989).

Thomas of Sutton. *Contra quodlibet Iohannis Duns Scoti*, ed. J. Schneider (Munich: Bayerische Akademie der Wissenschaften, 1978).

Der liber propugnatorius des Thomas Anglicus und die Lehrunterschiede zwischen Thomas von Aquin und Duns Scotus, ed. M. Schmaus (Münster: Aschendorff, 1930).

Expositionis D. Thomae Aquinatis in libros Aristotelis de generatione et corruptione continuatio, ed. F. Kelley (Munich: Bayerische Akademie der Wissenschaften, 1976).

Liber propugnatorius super primum Sententiarum contra Johannem Scotum (Venice, 1523; repr. Frankfurt: Minerva, 1966).

Quaestiones ordinariae, ed. J. Schneider (Munich: Bayerische Akademie der Wissenschaften, 1977).

Quodlibeta, ed. M. Schmaus and M. Gonzalez-Haba (Munich: Bayerische Akademie der Wissenschaften, 1969).

Tractatus de esse et essentiae, ed. W. Senko, *Studia Mediewistycne* 11 (1970) 233–59.

Tractatus de productione formarum substantialium, ed. Z. Wlodek, *Archives d'histoire doctrinale et littéraire du moyen âge* 54 (1979) 142–68.

Thomas of York. *Manus quae contra omnipotentem*, ed. M. Bierbaum, *Franziskanische Studien* 2 (1920) 37–168

Thuo of Viborg. *Opera*, ed. A. Tabarroni and S. Ebbesen (Copenhagen: Reitzel, 1998).

al-Ṭūsī. *Akhlāq-i nāṣirī*, ed. M. Mīnuwi and A. R. Ḥaydarī (Tehran: Khvārazmī, 1977).

Asās al-iqtibās, ed. M. Radawi (Tehran: Tehran University Press, 1947).

Contemplation and Action: The Spiritual Autobiography of a Muslim Scholar, ed. and tr. S. J. Badakhchani (London: I. B. Taurus, 2005).

Memoir on Astronomy: al-tadhkira fī 'ilm al-hay'a, ed. and tr. F. J. Ragep (New York: Springer, 1993).

The Metaphysics of Tusi: Treatise on the Proof of a Necessary Being, Treatise on Determinism and Destiny, Treatise on Division of Existents, tr. P. Morewedge (New York: SSIPS, 1992).

The Nasirean Ethics, tr. G. M. Wickens (London: George Allen and Unwin, 1964).

Paradise of Submission: A Medieval Treatise on Ismaili Thought, ed. and tr. S. J. Badakhchani (London: I. B. Taurus, 1998).

Tajrīd al-ʿaqāʾid, ed. A. Sulayman (Alexandria: Dār al-Maʿrifah al-Jāmiʿīyah, 1996).

Ubertino da Casale. *Arbor vitae crucifixae Jesu*, ed. Andrea de Bonetis (Venice, 1485; repr. Turin: Bottega d'Erasmo, 1961).

Declaratio, ed. F. Ehrle, *Archiv für Literatur- und Kirchengeschichte des Mittelalters* 3 (1887) 162–96.

Rotulus Iste, ed. F. Ehrle, *Archiv für Literatur- und Kirchengeschichte des Mittelalters* 3 (1887) 93–137.

Sanctitati apostolicae, ed. F. Ehrle, *Archiv für Literatur- und Kirchengeschichte des Mittelalters* 3 (1887) 377–416.

Ulrich of Strasbourg. *De summo bono*, ed. B. Mojsisch *et al.* (Hamburg: Meiner, 1989).

Urso of Salerno. *De coloribus*, ed. L. Thorndike, *Ambix* 7 (1959) 7–16.

De commixtionibus elementorum libellus, ed. W. Stürner (Stuttgart: Klett, 1976).

Vincent of Beauvais. *De eruditione filiorum nobilium*, ed. A. Steiner (Cambridge, MA: Mediaeval Academy of America, 1938; repr. New York: Kraus, 1970).

De morali principis institutione, ed. R. Schneider (Turnhout: Brepols, 1995).

Opuscula, scilicet: libri de gratia: libri laudum Virginis gloriose: liber de sancto Johanne evangelista: liber de eruditione puerorum regalium: liber consolatorius de morte amici, ed. J. Amerbach (Basel, 1481).

Speculum quadruplex, naturale, doctrinale, morale, historiale (Douai, 1624; repr. Graz: Akademische Druck, 1964–5).

Vincent Ferrer. *Œuvres*, ed. P.-H. Fages (Paris: Picard, 1909).

Opuscula ascetica, ed. M.-J. Rousset (Paris: Lethielleux, 1899).

Quaestio de unitate universalis, ed. J. A. Trentman, *Mediaeval Studies* 44 (1982) 122–37.

Sermons, ed. J. Sanchis y Sivera and G. Schib (Barcelona: Edit. Barcino, 1971–).

Tractatus de suppositionibus, ed. J. A. Trentman (Stuttgart-Bad Cannstatt: Fromman Holzboog, 1977).

A Treatise on the Spiritual Life (Westminster, MD: Newman Press, 1957).

Vital du Four. *De rerum principio*, in John Duns Scotus, *Opera omnia* (Paris: Vivès, 1891) IV: 257–471.

Expositio in Apocalypsim, in B. Bonelli (ed.) *Supplementum operum omnium S. Bonaventurae* (Trente, 1773) II: 5–1035.

Quaestiones disputatae de cognitione, ed. F. Delorme, *Archives d'histoire doctrinal et littéraire du moyen âge* 2 (1927) 151–337.

Quodlibeta tria, ed. F. Delorme (Rome: Pontificium Athenaeum Antonianum, 1947).

Speculum morale totius sacrae Scripturae (Lyon: J. Moylin, 1513).

Walahfrid Strabo. *Libellus de exordiis et incrementis quarundam in observationibus ecclesiasticis rerum*, ed. A. Harting-Correa (Leiden: Brill, 1996).

The Life of St. Gall, tr. M. Joynt (Toronto: Macmillan, 1927).

Visio Wettini, ed. and tr. D. Traill (Bern: Lang, 1974).

Walter of Ailly. "Un sophisme grammatical modiste de maître Gauthier d'Ailly," ed. I. Rosier, *Cahiers de l'Institut du Moyen Age Grec et Latin* 59 (1989) 181–232.

Walter of Bruges. *Quaestiones disputatae*, ed. E. Longpré (*Les Philosophes Belges* X) (Leuven: Institut Supérieur de Philosophie, 1928).

Walter Burley. *Commentarius in librum Perihermeneias*, ed. S. F. Brown, *Franciscan Studies* 33 (1973) 42–134.

De consequentiis, ed. N. J. Green-Pedersen, *Franciscan Studies* 40 (1980) 102–66.

De exceptivis, ed. L. M. de Rijk, *Vivarium* 24 (1986) 22–49.

De exclusivis, ed. L. M. de Rijk, *Vivarium* 23 (1985) 23–54.

De insolubilibus, ed. M. L. Roure, *Archives d'histoire doctrinale et littéraire du moyen âge* 45 (1970) 205–326.

De intensione et remissione formarum (Venice, 1496).

De obligationibus, in R. Green (ed.) "An Introduction to the Logical Treatise De obligationibus, with Critical Texts of William of Sherwood [?] and Walter Burley" (Ph.D. dissertation: Katholieke Universiteit Leuven, 1963).

De potentiis animae, ed. M. J. Kitchel, *Mediaeval Studies* 33 (1971) 85–113.

De primo et ultimo instanti, ed. H. Shapiro and C. Shapiro, *Archiv für Geschichte der Philosophie* 47 (1965) 159–73.

De puritate artis logicae. Tractus longior, with a Revised Edition of the Tractatus brevior, ed. P. Boehner (St. Bonaventure, NY: Franciscan Institute, 1955).

De relativis, ed. H. Shapiro and M. Kiteley, *Franciscan Studies* 22 (1962) 155–71.

De suppositionibus, ed. S. Brown, *Franciscan Studies* 32 (1972) 15–64.

Expositio in libros octo Physicorum Aristotelis (Venice, 1501; repr. Hildesheim: Olms, 1972).

Expositio super artem veterem Porphyrii et Aristotelis (Venice, 1509).

Klopotliwa zmiana czyli Waltera Burleya zmagania ze zmiennoscia rzeczy [*Commentarius in libros De generatione et corruptione*], ed. M. Gensler (Lódz: Wydawnictwo Uniwersytetu Lódziego, 2007).

On the Purity of the Art of Logic: The Shorter and the Longer Treatises, tr. P. V. Spade (New Haven, CT: Yale University Press, 2000).

Quaestiones circa tertium De anima, ed. E. A. Synan (Leiden: Brill, 1997).

Quaestiones in librum Perihermeneias, ed. S. F. Brown, *Franciscan Studies* 34 (1974) 200–95.

Quaestiones super librum Posteriorum, ed. M. C. Sommers (Toronto: Pontifical Institute of Mediaeval Studies, 2000).

Tractatus de formis, ed. by J. D. Scott (Munich: Bayerische Akademie der Wissenschaften, 1970).

Tractatus de universalibus, ed. H.-U. Wöhler (Leipzig: Verlag der Sächsischen Akademie der Wissenschaften, 1999).

Tractatus super librum Praedicamentorum (ms. in Cambridge, Peterhouse, ms. 184) 171ra–89va.

Walter Chatton. *Collatio ad Librum Primum et Prologus*, ed. J. C. Wey (Toronto: Pontifical Institute of Mediaeval Studies, 1989).

De paupertate evangelica, ed. D. Douie, *Archivum Franciscanum Historicum* 24 (1931) 341–69; 25 (1932) 36–58; 26 (1932) 210–40.

Lectura super Sententias, ed. G. J. Etzkorn and J. C. Wey (Toronto: Pontifical Institute of Mediaeval Studies, 2007–).

Reportatio et lectura super Sententias: Collatio ad librum primum et prologus, ed. J. C. Wey (Toronto: Pontifical Institute of Mediaeval Studies, 1989).

Reportatio super Sententias, ed. J. C. Wey and G. J. Etzkorn (Toronto: Pontifical Institute of Mediaeval Studies, 2002–5).

Walter Daniel. *The Life of Ailred of Rievaulx*, ed. and tr. F. M. Powicke (London: Nelson, 1950; repr. Oxford: Oxford University Press, 1978; repr. Kalamazoo, MI: Cistercian Publications, 1994).

Walter Hilton. *Mixed Life*, ed. S. J. Ogilvie-Thomson (Salzburg: Institut für Anglistik und Amerikanistik, Universität Salzburg, 1986).

The Scale of Perfection, ed. E. Underhill (London: J. M. Watkins, 1923; repr. 1948).

The Scale of Perfection, tr. J. P. H. Clark and R. Dorward (New York: Paulist Press, 1991).

Wāṣil ibn ʿAṭāʾ. *Wāṣil ibn ʿAṭāʾ als Prediger und Theologe: ein neuer Text aus dem 8. Jahrhundert n. Chr.*, ed. H. Daiber (Leiden: Brill, 1988).

William of Alnwick. *Quaestiones disputatae de esse intelligibili et de quodlibet*, ed. A. Ledoux (Quaracchi: Editiones Collegii S. Bonaventurae, 1937).

William of Auvergne. *De arte predicandi*, ed. A. de Poorter, *Revue néoscolastique de philosophie* 25 (1923) 192–209.

De bono et malo, ed. J. R. O'Donnell, *Mediaeval Studies* 8 (1946) 245–99; 16 (1954) 219–71.

De errore Pelagii, ed. A. Landgraf, *Speculum* 5 (1930) 168–80.

De immortalitate animae, in G. Bülow (ed.) *Des Dominicus Gundissalinus Schrift von der Unsterblichkeit der Seele* (Münster: Aschendorff, 1897).

De Trinitate, ed. B. Switalski (Toronto: Pontifical Institute of Mediaeval Studies, 1976).

The Immortality of the Soul, tr. R. J. Teske (Milwaukee, WI: Marquette University Press, 1991).

Opera omnia, ed. B. Le Feron (Paris, 1674; repr. Frankfurt: Minerva, 1963).

The Providence of God Regarding the Universe: Part Three of the First Principal Part of The Universe of Creatures, tr. R. J. Teske (Milwaukee, WI: Marquette University Press, 2007).

The Soul, tr. R. J. Teske (Milwaukee, WI: Marquette University Press, 2000).

Tractatus de gratia, ed. G. Corti (Rome: Lateran University, 1966).

The Trinity, or, The First Principle, tr. R. J. Teske and F. C. Wade (Milwaukee, WI: Marquette University Press, 1989).

The Universe of Creatures, tr. R. J. Teske (Milwaukee, WI: Marquette University Press, 1998).

William of Auxerre. *Summa aurea*, ed. J. Ribaillier (Paris: Centre National de la Recherche Scientifique, 1980–7).

William of Conches. *A Dialogue on Natural Philosophy (Dragmaticon philosophiae)*, tr. I. Ronca and M. Curr (Notre Dame, IN: University of Notre Dame Press, 1997).

Dragmaticon, ed. I. Ronca et al. (Turnhout: Brepols, 1997).

Glosae in Iuvenalem, ed. B. Wilson (Paris: Vrin, 1980).

Glosae super Boetium, ed. L. Nauta (Turnhout: Brepols, 1999).

Glosae super Platonem, ed. E. Jeauneau (Turnhout: Brepols, 2006).

Moralium dogma philosophorum, ed. J. Holmberg (Uppsala: Almquist, 1929).

Philosophia, ed. G. Maurach and H. Telle (Pretoria: University of South Africa Press, 1980).

William Crathorn. *Quästionen zum ersten Sentenzenbuch*, ed. F. Hoffmann (Münster: Aschendorff, 1988).

William Heytesbury. *On 'Insoluble' Sentences: Chapter One of his Rules for Solving Sophisms*, tr. P. V. Spade (Toronto: Pontifical Institute of Medieval Studies, 1979).

On Maxima and Minima: Chapter 5 of Rules for Solving Sophismata, with an Anonymous Fourteenth-Century Discussion, ed. and tr. J. Longeway (Dordrecht: Kluwer, 1984).

Sophismata asinina, ed. F. Pironet (Paris: Vrin, 1994).

Tractatus Gulielmi Hentisberi de sensu composito et diviso, Regulae ejusdem cum Sophismatibus, ed. J. M. Mapellus (Venice, 1494).

William de la Mare. *Commentarium in libros Sententiarum*, ed. H. Kraml (Munich: Beck, 1989–2001).

Correctorium Fratris Thomae, in P. Glorieux (ed.) *Les premières polémiques thomistes: I. Le correctorium corruptorii "Quare"* (Kain: Le Saulchoir, 1927).

Correctorium Fratris Thomae, 2nd redaction, in A. Oliva (ed.) "La deuxième rédaction du Correctorium de Guillaume de la Mare: les questions concernant la I pars," *Archivium Franciscanum Historicum* 98 (2005) 421–64.

William of Lucca. *Commentum in tertiam ierarchiam Dionisii que est de divinis nominibus*, ed. F. Gastaldelli (Florence: Olschki, 1983).

De arithmetica compendiose tractata: dal codice 614 (sec. XII) della Biblioteca capitolare Feliniana di Lucca, ed. G. Arrighi (Pisa: Domus Galilaeana, 1964).

Summa dialetice artis, ed. L. Pozzi (Padua: Liviana, 1975).

William of Macclesfield. *Le Correctorium Corruptorii "Quaestione"*, ed. J. P. Müller (Rome: Herder, 1954).

William of Middleton. *Opusculum super missam*, ed. W. Lampen (Quaracchi: Editiones Collegii S. Bonaventurae, 1931).

Quaestiones de sacramentis, ed. C. Piana and G. Gál (Quaracchi: Editiones Collegii S. Bonaventurae, 1961).

William Milverley. *Compendium de quinque universalibus* [excerpts], ed. A. D. Conti, in Johannes Sharpe, *Quaestio super universalia* (Florence: Olschki, 1990) 159–64.

William of Nottingham. *Quaestiones sex de Eucharistiae sacramento* [*Sent.* IV.8–13], ed. J. Barbarić (Vicenza: LIEF, 1976).

William of Ockham. *Commentary on Porphyry*, tr. E.-H. Kluge, *Franciscan Studies* 33 (1973) 171–254; 34 (1974) 306–82.

The De sacramento altaris, tr. T. B. Birch (Burlington, IA: Lutheran Literary Board, 1930).

Demonstration and Scientific Knowledge in William of Ockham: A Translation of Summa Logicae *III-II: De Syllogismo Demonstrativo, and Selections from the Prologue to the* Ordinatio, tr. J. Longeway (Notre Dame, IN: University of Notre Dame Press, 2007).

Dialogus, ed. and tr. J. Kilcullen *et al.*: www.britae.ac.uk/pubS/dialogus/ockdial.html.

A Letter to the Friars Minor, and Other Writings, tr. A. S. McGrade and J. Kilcullen (Cambridge: Cambridge University Press, 1995).

Ockham on Aristotle's Physics: A Translation of Ockham's Brevis Summa Libri Physicorum, tr. J. Davies (St. Bonaventure, NY: Franciscan Institute, 1989).

Ockham on the Virtues, tr. R. Wood (West Lafayette, IN: Purdue University Press, 1997).

Ockham's Theory of Propositions, tr. A. Freddoso and H. Schuurman (Notre Dame, IN: Notre Dame University Press, 1980).

Ockham's Theory of Terms, tr. M. Loux (Notre Dame, IN: Notre Dame University Press, 1974).

On the Power of Emperors and Popes, tr. A. S. Brett (Durham, NC: University of Durham Press, 1998).

Opera philosophica et theologica (St. Bonaventure, NY: Franciscan Institute, 1967–89).

Opera politica, ed. H. S. Offler *et al.* (Manchester: Manchester University Press, 1940–97).

Philosophical Writings, tr. P. Boehner, rev. S. Brown (Indianapolis, IN: Hackett, 1990).

Predestination, God's Foreknowledge, and Future Contingents, tr. M. Adams and N. Kretzmann, 2nd edn (Indianapolis, IN: Hackett, 1983).

Quodlibetal Questions, tr. A. Freddoso and F. Kelley (New Haven, CT: Yale University Press, 1991).

A Short Discourse on the Tyrannical Government, tr. A. S. McGrade and J. Kilcullen (Cambridge: Cambridge University Press, 1992).

Work of Ninety Days, tr. J. Kilcullen and J. Scott (Lewiston, NY: E. Mellen Press, 2001).

William of Pagula. *De speculo regis Edwardi III*, ed. J. Moisant (Paris: Picard, 1891).

Instructions for Parish Priests, tr. J. Mirk, ed. E. Peacock (London: Trübner, 1868; repr. Milwood, NY: Kraus, 1975).

William Penbygull. *De universalibus*, ed. A. D. Conti, *Medioevo* 8 (1982) 137–203.

William Peraldus. *De eruditione seu de institutione religiosorum* (Paris, 1512).

Summa de virtutibus et vitiis (Cologne, 1497).

William of Peter Godin. *Tractatus de causa immediata ecclesiastice potestatis*, ed. W. D. McCready (Toronto: Pontifical Institute of Mediaeval Studies, 1982).

William of Rennes. *Glossa, in Raymond of Pennafort, Summa de poenitentia* (Rome, 1603).

William of Rubio. *Disputatorum in quatuor libros magistri Sententiarum tomus prior [et secundus]* (Paris, 1518).

William of St. Amour. *De periculis novissimorum temporum*, ed. and tr. G. Geltner (Paris: Peeters, 2007).

Opera omnia (Constance, 1632; repr. Hildesheim: Olms, 1997).

The Opuscula of William of Saint-Amour: The Minor Works of 1255–1256, ed. A. Traver (Münster: Aschendorff, 2003).

William of St. Thierry. *De natura corporis et animae*, ed. M. Lemoine (Paris: Les Belles Lettres, 1988).

The Enigma of Faith, tr. J. Anderson (Washington, DC: Cistercian Publications, 1974).

Exposition on the Epistle to the Romans, tr. J. Hasbrouck and J. Anderson (Kalamazoo, MI: Cistercian Publications, 1980).

The Golden Epistle: A Letter to the Brethren at Mont Dieu, tr. T. Berkeley and J. Déchanet (Spencer, MA: Cistercian Publications, 1971).

The Mirror of Faith, tr. T. Davis (Kalamazoo, MI: Cistercian Publications, 1979).

The Nature and Dignity of Love, tr. T. Davis (Kalamazoo, MI: Cistercian Publications, 1981).

On Contemplating God, tr. Sister Penelope (Spencer, MA: Cistercian Publications, 1971).

Opera omnia, ed. P. Verdeyen and. A van Burink (Turnhout: Brepols, 1989–).

William of Sherwood. *De obligationibus*, in R. Green (ed.) "An Introduction to the Logical Treatise *De obligationibus*, with Critical Texts of William of Sherwood [?] and Walter Burley" (Ph.D. dissertation: Katholieke Universiteit Leuven, 1963).

Insolubilia, ed. M. L. Roure, *Archives d'histoire doctrinale et littéraire du moyen âge* 37 (1970) 205–326.

Introduction to Logic, tr. N. Kretzmann (Minneapolis: University of Minnesota Press, 1966; repr. Westport, CT: Greenwood Press, 1975).

Introductiones in Logicam: Einführung in die Logik, ed. H. Brands and C. Kann (Hamburg: Meiner, 1995).

Syncategoremata, ed. J. R. O'Donnell, *Mediaeval Studies* 3 (1941) 46–93.

Treatise on Syncategorematic Words, tr. N. Kretzmann (Minneapolis: University of Minnesota Press, 1968).

Witelo. *Book V of Witelo's* Perspectiva: *An English Translation, with Introduction and Commentary and Latin Edition of the First Catoptrical Book of Witelo's* Perspectiva, ed. and tr. A. M. Smith (Warsaw: Polish Academy of Sciences Press, 1983).

De causa primaria poenitentiae in hominibus et de natura daemonum, ed. G. Burchardt, *Studia Copernicana* 19 (1979) 155–208.

Perspectiva, ed. F. Risner (Basel, 1572; repr. New York: Johnson, 1972).

Perspectivae liber primus, ed. and tr. S. Unguru (Warsaw: Polish Academy of Sciences Press, 1977).

Perspectivae liber secundus et liber tertius, ed. and tr. S. Unguru (Warsaw: Polish Academy of Sciences Press, 1991).

Yaḥyā ibn ʿAdī. *La grande polémique antinestorienne*, ed. and tr. E. Platti (Leuven: Peeters, 1981).

Maqāla fī al-tawḥīd, ed. S. Khalīl (Rome: al-Maʿhad al-Bābawī al-Sharqī, 1980).

Maqālāt Yaḥyā ibn ʿAdī al-falsafiyya, ed. S. Khulayfāt (Amman: al-Jāmiʿa al-Urdunīyya, 1988).

Petits traités apologétiques de Yahia ben ʿAdī, ed. A. Périer (Gabalda: Geuthner, 1920).

The Reformation of Morals: A Parallel English–Arabic Text, ed. and tr. S. H. Griffith (Provo, UT: Brigham Young University Press, 2002).

Refutation of the Doctrine of Acquisition, ed. and tr. S. Pines and M. Schwarz, in S. Blau et al. (eds.) *Studia Orientalia Memoriae D.H. Baneth Dedicata* (Jerusalem: Magnes Press, 1979) 49–94.

Über den Nachweis der Natur des Möglichen [On the Possible], ed. C. Ehrig-Eggert, *Zeitschrift für Geschichte der arabisch-islamischen Wissenschaften* 5 (1989) 283–97.

BIBLIOGRAPHY OF SECONDARY SOURCES

Aasi, Ghulam Haider. *Muslim Understanding of Other Religions: A Study of Ibn Hazm's Kitāb al faṣl fī al-milal wa-al-ahwā' wa-al-niḥal* (Islamabad: International Institute of Islamic Thought and Islamic Research Institute, 1999).

Abed, Shukri. *Aristotelian Logic and the Arabic Language in Alfarabi* (Albany: State University of New York Press, 1991).

Acar, Rahim. *Talking about God and Talking about Creation: Avicenna's and Thomas Aquinas' Positions* (Leiden: Brill, 2005).

Adams, Marilyn McCord. "Ockham on Final Causality: Muddying the Waters," *Franciscan Studies* 56 (1998) 1–46.

"Ockham on Identity and Distinction," *Franciscan Studies* 36 (1976) 5–74.

"Scotus and Ockham on the Connection of the Virtues," in L. Honnefelder *et al.* (eds.) *John Duns Scotus: Metaphysics and Ethics* (Leiden: Brill, 1996) 499–522.

William Ockham (Notre Dame, IN: University of Notre Dame Press, 1987).

Adamson, Peter. "Abū Ma'shar, al-Kindī and the Philosophical Defense of Astrology," *Recherches de théologie et philosophie médiévales* 69 (2002) 245–70.

The Arabic Plotinus (London: Duckworth, 2002).

"The Arabic Sea Battle: al-Fārābī on the Problem of Future Contingents," *Archiv für Geschichte der Philosophie* 88 (2006) 163–88.

"Before Essence and Existence: Al-Kindi's Conception of Being," *Journal of the History of Philosophy* 40 (2002) 297–312.

Al-Kindī (Oxford: Oxford University Press, 2007).

"Al-Kindi and the Reception of Greek Philosophy," in P. Adamson and R. Taylor (eds.) *The Cambridge Companion to Arabic Philosophy* (Cambridge: Cambridge University Press, 2005) 32–51.

"Miskawayh's Psychology," in P. Adamson (ed.) *Classical Arabic Philosophy: Sources and Reception* (London: Warburg Institute, 2007) 39–54.

Adang, Camilla. *Muslim Writers on Judaism and the Hebrew Bible: From Ibn Rabban to Ibn Hazm* (Leiden: Brill, 1996).

Addas, Claude. *Quest for Red Sulphur: The Life of Ibn 'Arabī*, tr. P. Kingsley (Cambridge: Islamic Texts Society, 1993).

Adnés, Pierre. "Pénitence," in M. Viller *et al.* (eds.) *Dictionnaire de spiritualité* (Paris: Beauchesne, 1984) XII.1: 943–1004.

Aerts, W. J. *et al.* (eds.). *Vincent of Beauvais and Alexander the Great: Studies on the* Speculum maius *and its Translations into Medieval Vernaculars* (Groningen: Forsten, 1986).

Aertsen, Jan A. *Medieval Philosophy and the Transcendentals: The Case of Thomas Aquinas* (Leiden: Brill, 1996).

"Ontology and Henology in Medieval Philosophy (Thomas Aquinas, Master Eckhart and Berthold of Moosburg)," in E. Bos and P. Meyer (eds.) *On Proclus and his Influence in Medieval Philosophy* (Leiden: Brill, 1992) 120–40.

Aertsen, Jan A. and Gerhard Endress (eds.). *Averroes and the Aristotelian Tradition: Sources, Constitution, and Reception of the Philosophy of Ibn Rushd (1126–1198)* (Leiden: Brill, 1999).

Aertsen, Jan A. and Andreas Speer (eds.). *Was ist Philosophie im Mittelalter? Qu'est-ce que la philosophie au moyen âge? What is Philosophy in the Middle Ages?* (Berlin: De Gruyter, 1998).

Aertsen, Jan A., Kent Emery, and Andreas Speer (eds.). *Nach der Verurteilung von 1277: Philosophie und Theologie an der Universität von Paris im letzten Viertel des 13. Jahrhunderts: Studien und Texte* (Berlin: De Gruyter, 2001).

Affifi, Abul Ela. *The Mystical Philosophy of Muhyid Din-Ibnul Arabi* (Cambridge: Cambridge University Press, 1938).

Ahmad, Rashid. "Abu al-Qasim al-Qushairi as a Theologian and Commentator," *Islamic Quarterly* 13 (1969) 16–69.

Ahner, Moritz Max. *Fredegis von Tours: ein Beitrag zur Geschichte der Philosophie im Mittelalter* (Leipzig: Brückner und Niemann, 1878).

Aiello, Andrea and Robert Wielockx. *Goffredo di Fontaines, aspirante baccelliere Sentenziario: le autografe "Notule de scientia theologie" e la cronologia del ms. Paris BNF Lat. 16297* (Turnhout: Brepols, 2008).

Akasoy, Anna. *Philosophie und Mystik in der späten Almohadenzeit die Sizilianischen Fragen des Ibn Sab'in* (Leiden: Brill, 2006).

al-'Alawi, J. D. *Mu'allafat Ibn Bajja* (Beirut: Dar ath-Thaqafa, 1983).

Albert, Karl. *Meister Eckarts These vom Sein: Untersuchungen zur Metaphysik des Opus tripartitum* (Saarbrücken: Universitäts- und Schulbuchverlag, 1976).

Alessio, Gian Carlo. "Il commento di Gentile da Cingoli a Martino di Dacia," in D. Buzzetti *et al.* (eds.) *L'insegnamento della logica a Bologna nel XIV secolo* (Bologna: Istituto per la Storia dell'Università, 1992) 4–71.

Allard, Guy (ed.). *Jean Scot écrivain* (Montréal: Bellarmin, 1986).

Allard, Michel. *Le problème des attributs divins dans la doctrine d'al-As'ari et de ses premiers grands disciples* (Beirut: Imprimerie Catholique, 1965).

Allen, Elliot B. "Hervaeus Natalis: An Early 'Thomist' on the Notion of Being," *Mediaeval Studies* 22 (1960) 1–14.

Alliney, Guido. "Fra Scoto e Ockham: Giovanni di Reading e il dibattito sulla libertà a Oxford (1310–1320)," *Documenti e studi sulla tradizione filosofica medievale* 7 (1996) 243–68.

"'Tempus naturae' e 'tempus mathematicum' in Nicola Bonet," in A. Cacciotti and P. Sella (eds.) *Revirescunt chartae codices documenta textus: miscellanea in honorem P. Caesaris Cenci OFM*, vol. II (Rome: Edizioni Antonianum, 2002) 1089–113.

Time and Soul in Fourteenth-Century Theology: Three Questions of William of Alnwick on the Existence, the Ontological Status and the Unity of Time (Florence: Olschki, 2002).

Alonso, Manuel. *Teología de Averroes: estudios y documentos* (Madrid: Consejo Superior de Investigaciones Científicas, 1947).

al-Alousi, Husām Muhī al-Dīn. *The Problem of Creation in Islamic Thought* (Baghdad: National Printing and Publishing Co., 1968).

Altmann, Alexander. "Creation and Emanation in Isaac Israeli: A Reappraisal," in I. Twersky (ed.) *Studies in Medieval Jewish History and Literature* (Cambridge, MA: Harvard University Press, 1979) 1–15.

"Ibn Bajja on Man's Ultimate Felicity," in S. Lieberman (ed.) *Harry Austryn Wolfson Jubilee Volume on the Occasion of his Seventy-Fifth Birthday*, vol. I (Jerusalem: American Academy for Jewish Research, 1965) 47–87.

Studies in Religious Philosophy and Mysticism (Ithaca, NY: Cornell University Press, 1969).

Amerini, Fabrizio. "Alessandro di Alessandria sulla natura degli accidenti," *Documenti e studi sulla tradizione filosofica medievale* 16 (2005) 179–235.

"La dottrina della significatio di Francesco da Prato O. P. (XIV secolo). Una critica tomista a Guglielmo di Ockham," *Documenti e studi sulla tradizione filosofica medievale* 11 (2000) 375–408.

"Thomas Aquinas, Alexander of Alexandria and Paul of Venice on the Nature of Essence," *Documenti e studi sulla tradizione filosofica medievale* 15 (2004) 541–91.

"What is Real? A Reply to Ockham's Ontological Program," *Vivarium* 43 (2005) 187–212.

Aminrazavi, Mehdi. *Suhrawardi and the School of Illumination* (Richmond, UK: Curzon, 1997).

Anawati, Georges. "La doctrine des accidents chez les penseurs musulmans d'après le commentaire du K. al-Mawaqif de Iji par Jurjani," in *Dirāsāt falsafiyya muhdāt ilā al-duktūr Ibrāhīm Madkūr* (Cairo: al-Hayah al-Misrīyah al-ʿĀmmah lil-Kitāb, 1974) 91–120.

Anawati, Georges *et al.* (eds.). *Muʾallafāt Ibn Rushd (Bibliographie d'Averroes)* (al-Jazāʾir: Jāmiʿat al-Duwal al-ʿArabīya, 1978).

Anciaux, Paul. *La théologie du sacrament de pénitence au XIIᵉ siècle* (Leuven: Nauwelaerts, 1949).

André, G. S. "Les *Quodlibeta* de Bernard de Trilia," *Gregorianum* 2 (1921) 226–65.

Andrews, Robert. "Andrew of Cornwall and the Reception of Modism in England," in S. Ebbesen and R. L. Friedman (eds.) *Medieval Analyses in Language and Cognition* (Copenhagen: Reitzels, 1999) 105–15.

"Denomination in Peter of Auvergne," in N. Kretzmann (ed.) *Meaning and Inference in Medieval Philosophy: Studies in Memory of Jan Pinborg* (Dordrecht: Kluwer, 1988) 91–106.

"Thomas Maulevelt's Denial of Substance," in L. Newton (ed.) *Medieval Commentaries on Aristotle's Categories* (Leiden: Brill, 2008) 347–68.

Andrews, Robert and Timothy B. Noone. "A Newly Identified Redaction of Richard Clive's 'Quaestiones metaphysicae': With Edition of Three Questions on Relation," *Manuscripta* 38 (1994) 23–41.

Andrieu-Guitrancourt, Pierre. *L'archevêque Eudes Rigaud et la vie de l'église au 13ᵉ siècle* (Paris: Sirey, 1938).

Angelopoulos, Athanasios. *Nikolaos Kabasilas Hamaetos, he zoe kai to ergon autou* (Thessaloniki: Patriarchikon Hidryma Paterikon Meleton, 1970).

Arberry, A. J. *The Koran Interpreted* (London: Macmillan, 1955).

Arbesmann, Rudolph. "The Concept of '*Christus medicus*' in St. Augustine," *Traditio* 10 (1954) 1–28.

Ariew, Roger. "Cartesian Empiricism," *Revue roumaine de philosophie* 50 (2006) 71–85.

Descartes and the Last Scholastics (Ithaca, NY: Cornell University Press, 1999).

"Oratorians and the Teaching of Cartesian Philosophy in Seventeenth-Century France," *History of Universities* 17 (2001–2) 47–80.

Ariew, Roger, John Cottingham, and Tom Sorell (trs.). *Cambridge Texts in Context: Descartes' Meditations* (Cambridge: Cambridge University Press, 1998).

Arikha, Noga. *Passions and Tempers: A History of the Humours* (New York: Ecco, 2007).

Arjomand, Said Amir. *The Shadow of God and the Hidden Imam: Religion, Political Order, and Societal Change in Shiʿite Iran from the Beginning to 1890* (Chicago: University of Chicago Press, 1984).

Arkoun, Mohammed. *Contribution à l'étude de l'humanisme arabe au IVᵉ/Xᵉ siècle: Miskawayh, philosophe et historien*, 2nd edn (Paris: Vrin, 1982).

Armstrong, Regis *et al.* (eds.). *Francis of Assisi. Early Documents* (Hyde Park, NY: New City Press, 1999).

Arnaldez, Roger. *Averroes: A Rationalist in Islam*, tr. D. Streight (Notre Dame, IN: University of Notre Dame Press, 2000).

Grammaire et théologie chez Ibn Hazm de Cordoue: essai sur la structure et les conditions de la pensée musulmane (Paris: Vrin, 1984).

Arquillière, Henri Xavier. *L'augustinisme politique: essai sur la formation des théories politiques du Moyen-Age*, 2nd edn (Paris: Vrin, 1955).

al-Aʿsam, ʿAbd al-Amīr. *History of Ibn ar-Riwandi the Heretic* (Beirut: Manshūrāt Dār al-Afāq al-Jadīdah, 1975).

Ashworth, E. Jennifer. "Analogy and Equivocation in Thirteenth-Century Logic: Aquinas in Context," *Mediaeval Studies* 54 (1992) 94–135.

"'Can I Speak More Clearly Than I Understand?' A Problem of Religious Language in Henry of Ghent, Duns Scotus, and Ockham," *Historiographia Linguistica* 7 (1980) 29–38.

"An Early Fifteenth Century Discussion of Infinite Sets," *Notre Dame Journal of Formal Logic* 18 (1977) 232–4.

"English *Obligationes* Texts after Roger Swyneshed: The Tracts Beginning *Obligatio est quaedam ars*," in O. P. Lewry (ed.) *The Rise of British Logic* (Toronto: Pontifical Institute of Mediaeval Studies, 1983) 309–33.

Language and Logic in the Post-Medieval Period (Dordrecht: Reidel, 1974).

"Medieval Theories of Singular Terms," in E. Zalta (ed.) *The Stanford Encyclopedia of Philosophy* (Fall 2006 edition): http://plato.stanford.edu/archives/fall2006/entries/singular-terms-medieval/.

"Mental Language and the Unity of Propositions: A Semantic Problem Discussed by Early Sixteenth-Century Logicians," *Franciscan Studies* 41 (1981) 61–96.

"Ralph Strode on Inconsistency in Obligational Disputations," in K. Jacobi (ed.) *Argumentationstheorie. Scholastische Forschungen zu den logischen und semantischen Regeln korrekten Folgerns* (Leiden: Brill, 1993) 363–86.

"Signification and Modes of Signifying in Thirteenth-Century Logic: A Preface to Aquinas on Analogy," *Medieval Philosophy and Theology* 1 (1991) 39–67.

Studies in Post-Medieval Semantics (London: Variorum Reprints, 1985).

"Theories of Propositions: Some Early Sixteenth-Century Discussions," *Franciscan Studies* 38 (1978) 81–121.

The Tradition of Medieval Logic and Speculative Grammar from Anselm to the End of the Seventeenth Century. A Bibliography from 1836 Onwards (Toronto: Pontifical Institute of Mediaeval Studies, 1978).

Ashworth, E. Jennifer and Paul Vincent Spade. "Logic in Late Medieval Oxford," in J. I. Catto and R. Evans (eds.) *The History of the University of Oxford*, vol. II: *Late Medieval Oxford* (Oxford: Clarendon Press, 1992) 35–64.

Asín Palacios, Miguel. *The Mystical Philosophy of Ibn Masarra and his Followers*, tr. E. H. Douglas and H. W. Yoder (Leiden: Brill, 1978).

Association des amis du Centre médiéval européen de Chartres (ed.). *Enseigner le Moyen Age à partir d'un monument, la cathédrale de Chartres: le temps de Fulbert* (Chartres: Société archéologique d'Eure-et-Loir, 1996).

Association Bourguignonne des Sociétés Savantes. *Saint Bernard théologien: actes du Congres de Dijon*, 2nd edn (Rome: Editiones Cistercienses, 1956).

Azanza Elío, Ana. *El conocimiento de Dios según Pedro de Atarrabia* (Pamplona: Ediciones Eunate, 1997).

al-Azmeh, Aziz. *Ibn Khaldūn: An Essay in Reinterpretation* (London: Routledge, 1990).

Ibn Khaldūn in Modern Scholarship: A Study in Orientalism (London: Third World Centre, 1981).

Babbitt, Susan M. *Oresme's Livre de Politiques and the France of Charles V* (Philadelphia, PA: American Philosophical Society, 1985).

Bachrach, David. *Religion and the Conduct of War c. 300–1215* (Woodbridge: Boydell Press, 2003).

Bäck, Allan. *On Reduplication: Logical Theories of Qualification* (Leiden: Brill, 1996).

Back, Samuel. *Joseph Albo's Bedeutung in der Geschichte der jüdischen Religionsphilosophie: ein Beitrag zur genauern Kenntniss der Tendenz des Buches "IKKARIM"* (Breslau: Heidenfeld, 1869).

Backes, Ignaz. *Die Christologie, Soteriologie und Mariologie des Ulrich von Strassburg: ein Beitrag zur Geistegeschichte des 13. Jahrhunderts* (Trier: Paulinus-Verlag, 1975).

Backus, Irene (ed.). *The Reception of the Church Fathers in the West: From the Carolingians to the Maurists* (Leiden: Brill, 1997).

Baer, Yitzhak. "Abner of Burgos' *Minhat Qena'ot* and its Influence on Hasdai Crescas," *Tarbiz* 11 (1940) 188–206.

Baeumker, Clemens. *Die Stellung des Alfred von Sareshel (Alfredus Anglicus) und seiner Schrift De motu cordis in der Wissenschaft des beginnenden XIII. Jahrhunderts* (Munich: Königlich Bayerischen Akademie der Wissenschaften, 1913).

  Witelo: ein Philosoph und Naturforscher des dreizehnten Jahrhunderts (Münster: Aschendorff, 1908; repr. 1991).

  "Zur Frage nach Abfassungszeit und Verfasser des irrtümlich Witelo zugeschriebenen *Liber de intelligentiis*," in *Miscellanea Francesco Ehrle* (Rome: Biblioteca Apostolica Vaticana, 1924) I: 87–202.

Bainton, Roland. *Christian Attitudes toward War and Peace* (Nashville, TN: Abingdon Press, 1960).

Bakker, Paul J. J. M. "Aristotelian Metaphysics and Eucharistic Theology: John Buridan and Marsilius of Inghen on the Ontological Status of Accidental Being," in J. M. M. H. Thijssen and J. Zupko (eds.) *The Metaphysics and Natural Philosophy of John Buridan* (Leiden: Brill, 2001) 247–64.

  "Guiral Ot et le mouvement autour de la question *De motu* conservée dans le manuscrit Madrid, Biblioteca nacional, 4229," *Early Science and Medicine* 8 (2003) 298–319.

  La raison et le miracle: les doctrines eucharistiques (c. 1250–c.1400). Contribution à l'étude des rapports entre philosophie et théologie (Nijmegen: Katholieke Universiteit Nijmegen, 1999).

  "Réalisme et rémanence: La doctrine eucharistique de Jean Wyclif," in M.-T. Fumagalli, Beonio Brocchieri and S. Simonetta (eds.) *John Wyclif: logica, teologia, politica* (Florence: SISMEL, Edizioni del Galluzzo, 2003) 87–112.

Bakker, Paul J. J. M. and D.-J. Dekker. "Antoine Andrée ou Jean le Chanoine? À propos de l'authenticité du commentaire de la *Physique* conservé dans le ms. Cambridge, Gonville & Caius College, 368 (590)," *Bulletin de philosophie médiévale* 42 (2000) 101–31.

Baldwin, John. *Masters, Princes and Merchants: The Social Views of Peter the Chanter and his Circle* (Princeton, NJ: Princeton University Press, 1970).

Baltes, Matthias. *Die Weltentstehung des platonischen Timaios nach den Antiken interpreten* (Leiden. Brill, 1976–8).

Barad, Judith. "Aquinas on the Role of Emotion in Moral Judgement and Activity," in B. C. Bazán et al. (eds.) *Les philosophies morales et politiques au Moyen Âge*, vol. II (New York: Legas, 1995) 642–53.

Barber, Charles. "Living Painting, or the Limits of Pointing? Glancing at Icons with Michael Psellos," in C. Barber and D. Jenkins (eds.) *Reading Michael Psellos* (Leiden: Brill, 2006) 117–30.

Barber, Charles and David Jenkins (eds.). *Reading Michael Psellos* (Leiden: Brill, 2006).

Barbet, Jeanne. "Le commentaire des Sentences de Jean de Rodington, O.F.M. (†1348) d'après les manuscrits Reims 503 et Toulouse 192," *Bulletin d'information de l'Institut de recherche et d'histoire des textes* 3 (1954) 55–63.

Barbour, Hugh Christopher. *The Byzantine Thomism of George Gennadios Scholarios and his Translation of Armandus de Bellovise on the* De Ente et Essentia *of Thomas Aquinas* (Vatican: Libreria Editrice Vaticana, 1993).

Barker, Ernest. *Social and Political Thought in Byzantium: From Justinian I to the Last Palaeologus* (Oxford: Clarendon Press, 1957).

Barnes, Jonathan. "The Just War," in N. Kretzmann *et al.* (eds.) *Cambridge History of Later Medieval Philosophy* (Cambridge: Cambridge University Press, 1982) 771–84.

Barocelli, Francesco. "Per Biagio Pelacani, un Convegno e un 'Centro Studi'," in G. Federici Vescovini (ed.) *Filosofia, scienza e astrologia nel Trecento europeo* (Padua: Il Poligrafo, 1992) 21–38.

Baron, Roger. *Études sur Hugues de Saint-Victor* (Paris: De Brouwer, 1963).
   Science et sagesse chez Hugues de Saint-Victor (Paris: Lethielleux, 1957).

Barton, J. L. "The Mystery of Bracton," *Journal of Legal History* 14 (1993) 1–42.

Bashier, Salman. *Ibn al'Arabī's Barzakh: The Concept of the Limit and the Relationship between God and the World* (Albany: State University of New York Press, 2004).

Bataillon, Louis J., Gilbert Dahan, and Pierre-Marie Gy (eds.). *Hugues de Saint-Cher (†1263): Bibliste et théologien* (Turnhout: Brepols, 2004).

Baudelet, Yves-Anselme. *L'expérience spirituelle selon Guillaume de Saint-Thierry* (Paris: Cerf, 1985).

Baumgartner, Matthias. *Die Erkenntnislehre des Wilhelm von Auvergne* (Münster: Aschendorff, 1893).

Bautz, Friedrich (ed.). *Biographisch-Bibliographisches Kirchenlexikon* (Herzberg: Bautz, 1970–2007).

Bazán, Bernardo C. "13th-Century Commentaries on *De anima*: From Peter of Spain to Thomas Aquinas," in G. Fioravanti *et al.* (eds.) *Il commento filosofico nell'Occidente latino, secoli XIII–XV* (Turnhout: Brepols, 2002) 119–84.
   "The Human Soul: Form *and* Substance? Thomas Aquinas's Critique of Eclectic Aristotelianism," *Archives d'histoire doctrinale et littéraire du moyen âge* 64 (1997) 95–126.

Beale, Joseph. *Bartolus on the Conflict of Laws* (Cambridge, MA: Harvard University Press, 1914; repr. Westport, CT: Hyperion Press, 1979).

Beck, Hans Georg. *Theodoros Metochites, die Krise des byzantinischen Weltbildes im 14. Jahrhundert* (Munich: Beck, 1952).

Becker, Adam. *Fear of God and the Beginning of Wisdom. The School of Nisibis and Christian Scholastic Culture in Late Antique Mesopotamia* (Philadelphia, PA: University of Pennsylvania Press, 2006).

Beckmann, Jan. *Ockham-Bibliographie: 1900–1990* (Hamburg: Meiner, 1992).

Beckwith, Sarah. *Christ's Body: Identity, Culture, and Society in Late Medieval Writings* (London: Routledge, 1993).

Bedouelle, Guy, Romanus Cessario, and Kevin White (eds.). *Jean Capreolus et son temps 1380–1444* (Paris: Cerf, 1997).

Beer, Samuel. "The Rule of the Wise and the Holy: Hierarchy in the Thomistic System," *Political Theory* 14 (1984) 391–422.

Beggiani, Seely J. "Theology at the Service of Mysticism: Method in Pseudo-Dionysius," *Theological Studies* 57 (1996) 201–23.

Beha, H. M. "Matthew of Aquasparta's Theory of Cognition," *Franciscan Studies* 20 (1960) 161–204; 21 (1961) 383–465.

Behloul, Samuel-Martin. *Ibn Hazms Evangelienkritik: eine methodische Untersuchung* (Leiden: Brill, 2002).

Beierwaltes, Werner (ed.). *Begriff und Metapher: Sprachform des Denkens bei Eriugena* (Heidelberg: Carl Winter Universitätsverlag, 1990).

Eriugena: Grundzüge seines Denkens (Frankfurt am Main: Klostermann, 1994).

Beitz, Egid. *Rupert von Deutz: seine Werke und die bildende Kunst* (Cologne: Verlag des kölnischen Geschichtsvereins, 1930).

Bejczy, István Pieter. "Two Questions of Stephen Langton on the Cardinal Virtues," *Medioevo* 31 (2006) 299–336.

Bejczy, István Pieter and Richard Newhauser (eds.). *Virtue and Ethics in the Twelfth Century* (Leiden: Brill, 2005).

Bell, David. *The Image and Likeness: The Augustinian Spirituality of William of St Thierry* (Kalamazoo, MI: Cistercian Publications, 1984).

Bell, Joseph N. *Love Theory in Later Hanbalite Islam* (Albany: State University of New York Press, 1979).

Belmond, Séraphin. "La théorie de la connaissance d'après Roger Marston," *La France Franciscaine* 17 (1934) 153–87.

Belo, Catarina. *Chance and Determinism in Avicenna and Averroes* (Leiden: Brill, 2007).

Benakis, Linos. "Bibliographie internationale sur la philosophie Byzantine (1949–1990)," in *Bibliographie Byzantine publié à l'occasion du XVIIIe Congrès Internationale d'Études Byzantines* (Athens: Comité hellénique des études byzantines, 1991) 319–77.

"Michael Psellos' Kritik an Aristoteles und seine eigene Lehre zur Physis- und Materie-Form-Problematik," *Byzantinische Zeitschrift* 56 (1963) 213–27.

"The Problem of General Concepts in Neoplatonism and Byzantine Thought," in D. J. O'Meara (ed.) *Neoplatonism and Christian Thought* (Albany: State University of New York Press, 1982) 75–86 and 248–9.

"Studien zu den Aristoteles-Kommentaren des Michael Psellos," *Archiv für Geschichte der Philosophie* 43 (1961) 215–38; 44 (1962) 33–61.

"Die theoretische und praktische Autonomie der Philosophie als Fachdisziplin in Byzanz," in M. Asztalos *et al.* (eds.) *Knowledge and the Sciences in Medieval Philosophy: Proceedings of the Eighth International Congress of Medieval Philosophy* (Helsinki: Yliopistopaino, 1990) I: 223–7.

Bergé, Marc. *Pour un humanisme vécu: Abu Hayyan al-Tawhidi* (Damascus: Institut français de Damas, 1979).

Berger, Harald. "Albert von Sachsen (1316?–1390). Bibliographie der Sekundärlitteratur," *Bulletin de philosophie médiévale* 36 (1994) 148–85; 37 (1995) 175–86; 38 (1996) 143–52; 40 (1998) 103–16.

Bergsträsser, Gotthelf. *Hunain ibn Ishak und seine Schule: Sprach- und literargeschichtliche untersuchungen zu den arabischen Hippokrates- und Galen-übersetzungen* (Leiden: Brill, 1913).

Berkowitz, Luci and Karl A. Squitier (eds.). *Thesaurus Linguae Graecae: Canon of Greek Authors and Works*, 3rd edn (Oxford: Oxford University Press, 1990).

Berlioz, Jacques and Marie Anne Polo de Beaulieu. *Les exempla médiévaux: nouvelles perspectives* (Paris: Champion, 1998).

Bermon, Pascale. *L'assentiment et son objet chez Grégoire de Rimini* (Paris: Vrin, 2007).

Bernard, Paul. "Jerome of Prague, Austria and the Hussites," *Church History* 35 (1958) 3–22.

Bernards, Mathäus. "Zum Schrifttum des Petrus von Aquila OFM († 1361)," *Franziskanische Studien* 35 (1953) 113–15.

Bertagna, Mario. "Richard Ferrybridge's *Logica*: A Handbook for Solving Sophismata," in S. Read (ed.) *Sophisms in Medieval Logic and Grammar: Acts of the Ninth European Symposium for Medieval Logic and Semantics* (Dordrecht: Kluwer, 1993) 31–44.

Bertola, Ermenegildo. "La dottrina dell'immortalità dell'anima in Johannes Blundus," *Aquinas* 9 (1966) 28–48.

Bertolacci, Amos. "A Community of Translators: The Latin Medieval Versions of Avicenna's *kitāb al-Shifā' (Book of the Cure)*," in C. Mews and J. Crossley (eds.) *Communities of Learning, Religious Diversity, and the Written Record 1085–1453* (forthcoming).

Bérubé, Camille. "Antoine André, témoin et interprète de Duns Scot." *Antonianum* 54 (1979) 385–466.

   "Henri de Gand et Mathieu d'Aquasparta interprètes de saint Bonaventure," *Naturaleza y gracia* 21 (1974) 131–72.

Bérubé, Camille and Servus Gieben. "Guibert de Tournai et Robert Grosseteste: sources inconnues de la doctrine de l'illumination suivi de l'édition critique de trois chapitres du *Rudimentum doctrinae* de Guibert de Tournai," in *Sanctus Bonaventura: 1274–1974* (Grottaferrata: Collegium Sancti Bonaventurae, 1973) 627–54.

Besnier, Bernard, Pierre-François Moreau, and Laurence Renault (eds.). *Les passions antiques et médiévales* (Paris: Presses universitaires de France, 2003).

Besta, Enrico. *L'opera d'Irnerio: contributo alla storia del diritto italiano* (Turin: Loescher, 1896).

Bettoni, Efrem. *Le dottrina filosofiche di Pier di Giovanni Olivi* (Milan: Vita e Pensiero, 1959).

Betts, Edward Tracy. *Humbert of Romans: His Life and Views of Thirteenth-Century Society* (Toronto: Pontifical Institute of Medieval Studies, 1984).

Betts, R. R. "Jerome of Prague," in *Essays in Czech History* (London: Athlone, 1969) 195–235.

Bianchi, Luca. *Censure et liberté intellectuelle à l'Université de Paris (XIII*^e*–XIV*^e *siècles)* (Paris: Les Belles Lettres, 1999).

   Il vescovo e i filosofi. La condanna Parigina del 1277 e l'evoluzione dell'aristotelismo scolastico (Bergamo: Pierluigi Lubrina Editore, 1990).

Biard, Joël. "Les controverses sur l'objet du savoir et les 'complexe significabilia' à Paris au XIVe siècle," in S. Caroti (ed.) *Quia inter doctores est magna dissensio: les débats de philosophie naturelle à Paris au XIV*^e *siècle* (Florence: Olschki, 2004) 1–31.

   Guillaume d'Ockham: Logique et philosophie (Paris: Presses universitaires des France, 1997).

   Guillaume d'Ockham et la théologie (Paris: Cerf, 1999).

   Logique et théorie du signe au XIVe *siècle* (Paris: Vrin, 1989).

   "The Natural Order in John Buridan," in J. M. M. H. Thijssen and J. Zupko (eds.) *The Metaphysics and Natural Philosophy of John Buridan* (Leiden: Brill, 2001) 77–95.

   (ed.). *Paris–Vienne au XIV*^e *siècle. Itinéraires d'Albert de Saxe* (Actes de la Table ronde internationale, Paris, 19–22 juin 1990) (Paris: Vrin, 1991).

   "Présence et représentation chez Pierre d'Ailly: quelques problèmes de théorie de la connaissance au XIVe siècle," *Dialogue* 31 (1992) 459–74.

   "La signification d'objets imaginaires dans quelques texts anglais du XIVe siècle (Guillaume Heytesbury, Henry Hopton)," in O. Lewry (ed.) *The Rise of British Logic* (Toronto: Pontifical Institute of Mediaeval Studies, 1983) 265–83.

Biblioteca civica Gambalunga. *Gregorio da Rimini filosofo: atti del convegno* (Rimini: Raffaelli, 2003).

Bignami-Odier, Jeanne. "Le manuscrit Vatican latin 2186," *Archives d'histoire doctrinale et littéraire du moyen âge* 11 (1938) 133–66.

Biller, Peter. *The Measure of Multitude: Population in Medieval Thought* (Oxford: Oxford University Press, 2000).

Biller, Peter and A. J. Minnis. *Handling Sin: Confession in the Middle Ages* (Woodbridge, UK: York Medieval Press, 1998).

Birk, Bonnie A. *Christine de Pizan and Biblical Wisdom: A Feminist-Theological Point of View* (Milwaukee, WI: Marquette University Press, 2005).

Birkenmajer, Aleksander. "Avicennas Vorrede zum 'Liber Sufficientiae' und Roger Bacon," in A. Birkenmajer (ed.) *Études d'histoire des sciences et de la philosophie du moyen âge* (Wroclaw: Zakład Narodowy im. Ossolińskich, 1970) 89–101.

"Études sur Witelo, I–IV," *Bulletin international de l'Académie polonaise des sciences et des lettres, Classe d'histoire et de philosophie* année 1918 (1920) 4–6; année 1919–20 (1922–4) 354–60; année 1922 (1925) 6–9.

Bissen, Jean-Marie. "Question inédite de Guillaume de Ware, OFM, sur le motif de l'incarnation," *Études Franciscaines* 46 (1934) 218–22.

Black, Antony. *The History of Islamic Political Thought: From the Prophet to the Present* (London: Routledge, 2001).

Political Thought in Europe, 1250–1450 (Cambridge: Cambridge University Press, 1992).

"Society and the Individual from the Middle Ages to Rousseau: Philosophy, Jurisprudence and Constitutional Theory," *History of Political Thought* 1 (1980) 145–66.

The West and Islam: Religion and Political Thought in World History (Oxford: Oxford University Press, 2008).

Black, Deborah L. "Avicenna on Self-Awareness and Knowing that One Knows," in S. Rahman *et al.* (eds.) *The Unity of Science in the Arabic Tradition: Science, Logic, Epistemology and their Interactions* (Dordrecht: Springer, 2008) 63–87.

"Estimation (*Wahm*) in Avicenna: The Logical and Psychological Dimensions," *Dialogue* 32 (1993) 219–58.

"Imagination and Estimation: Arabic Paradigms and Western Transformations," *Topoi* 19 (2000) 59–75.

"Knowledge (*'ilm*) and Certitude (*yaqīn*) in al-Fārābī's Epistemology," *Arabic Sciences and Philosophy* 16 (2006) 11–45.

Blanchet, Léon. *Les antécédents historiques du "Je pense, donc je suis"* (Paris: Alcan, 1920).

Bleich, J. David. "Providence in the Philosophy of Hasdai Crescas and Joseph Albo," in Y. Elman and J. S. Gurock (eds.) *Hazon Nahum: Studies in Jewish Law, Thought, and History Presented to Dr. Norman Lamm* (New York: Yeshiva University Press, 1997) 311–58.

Bliemetzrieder, Franz. "Autour de l'œuvre théologique d'Anselme de Laon," *Recherches de théologie ancienne et médiévale* 1 (1929) 434–83.

Blomme, Robert. *La doctrine du péché dans les écoles théologiques de la première moitié du XIIᵉ siècle* (Leuven: Publications universitaires, 1958).

Bloomfield, Morton. *The Seven Deadly Sins: An Introduction to the History of a Religious Concept* (East Lansing, MI: Michigan State College Press, 1952).

Blumenthal, David. "On the Intellect and the Rational Soul," *Journal of the History of Philosophy* 15 (1977) 207–11.

Blythe, James. "Aristotle's *Politics* and Ptolemy of Lucca," *Vivarium* 40 (2002) 103–36.

Bobik, Joseph. *Aquinas on Matter and Form and the Elements* (Notre Dame, IN: University of Notre Dame Press, 1998).

Boehner, Philotheus. *Medieval Logic: An Outline of its Development from 1250–c. 1400* (Manchester: Manchester University Press, 1952).

"*Notitia Intuitiva* of Non Existents According to Peter Aureoli, O.F.M. (1322)," *Franciscan Studies* 8 (1948) 388–416.

"The System of Metaphysics of Alexander of Hales," *Franciscan Studies* 5 (1945) 366–414.

Boh, Ivan. "Consequences," in N. Kretzmann *et al.* (eds.) *The Cambridge History of Later Medieval Philosophy* (Cambridge: Cambridge University Press, 1982) 300–14.

"Epistemic and Alethic Iteration in Later Medieval Logic," *Philosophia naturalis* 21 (1984) 492–506.

Epistemic Logic in the Middle Ages (London: Routledge, 1993).

"Paul of Pergula on Suppositions and Consequences," *Franciscan Studies* 25 (1965) 30–89.

Bohn, Eva. "Candidus and the Continuity of Carolingian Intellectual Life after Alcuin" (Ph.D. dissertation: University of Cambridge, 2004).

Bohne, Winfried (ed.). *Hrabanus Maurus und seine Schule* (Fulda: Rabanus-Maurus-Schule, 1980).

Boissonade, Jean François. *Anecdota graeca* (Paris, 1833; repr. Hildesheim: Olms, 1962). *Anecdota nova* (Paris, 1844; repr. Hildesheim: Olms, 1962).

Boland, Vivian. *Ideas in God According to Saint Thomas Aquinas: Sources and Synthesis* (Leiden: Brill, 1996).

Bolland, Johannes, Jean Baptiste Carnandet, Godefridus Henschenius, and Daniel von Papenbroeck (eds.) *Acta sanctorum quotquot toto orbe coluntur vel a catholicis scriptoribus celebrantur* (Paris: Palme, 1863–1940).

Bolton, Brenda. *Innocent III: Studies on Papal Authority and Pastoral Care* (Aldershot: Variorum, 1995).

Bonin, Therese. *Creation as Emanation. The Origin of Diversity in Albert the Great's On the Causes and the Procession of the Universe* (Notre Dame, IN: University of Notre Dame Press, 2001).

Borchert, Ernst. *Die Trinitätslehre des Johannes de Ripa* (Munich: Schöningh, 1974).

Borst, Arno. "Ein Forschungsbericht Hermanns des Lahmen," *Deutsches Archiv* 40 (1984) 379–477.

Bos, E. P. "An Anonymous Commentary on the Second Part of Alexander de Villa Dei's *Doctrinale* (circa 1400)," in M. C. Pacheco and J. F. Meirinhos (eds.) *Intellect et imagination dans la philosophie médiévale: actes du XIe Congrès international de philosophie médiévale de la Société internationale pour l'étude de la philosophie médiévale* (Turnhout: Brepols, 2006) 1743–56.

Logica modernorum in Prague about 1400: The Sophistria Disputation "Quoniam quatuor" with a Partial Reconstruction of Thomas of Cleves' Logica (Leiden: Brill, 2004).

"Peter of Mantua and his Rejection of *Ampliatio* and *Restrictio*," in O. Lewry (ed.) *The Rise of British Logic* (Toronto: Pontifical Institute of Mediaeval Studies, 1983) 384–99.

"Peter of Mantua's Tract on *appellatio* and his Interpretation of Immanent Forms," in A. Maierù (ed.) *English Logic in Italy in the 14th and 15th Centuries* (Naples: Bibliopolis, 1982) 231–52.

"Peter of Mantua's Treatise *De veritate et falsitate, sive De taliter et qualiter*," in E. P. Bos (ed.) *Medieval Semantics and Metaphysics. Studies Dedicated to L. M. de Rijk* (Nijmegen: Artistarium, 1985) 291–307.

"Die Rezeption der *Suppositiones* des Marsilius von Inghen in Paris (Johannes Dorp) und Prag (ein anonymer *Sophistria* Traktat) um 1400," in M. J. F. M. Hoenen and P. J. J. M. Bakker (eds.) *Philosophie und Theologie des ausgehenden Mittelalters: Marsilius von Inghen und das Denken seiner Zeit* (Leiden: Brill, 2000) 213–38.

"Richard Billingham's Logic in his Mirror of the Youngsters," in F. Beets and M.-A. Gavray (eds.) *Logique et ontologie: perspectives diachroniques et synchroniques* (Liège: Éditions Université de Liège, 2005) 73–94.

"Richard Billingham's *Speculum puerorum*, Some Medieval Commentaries and Aristotle," *Vivarium* 45 (2007) 360–73.

"Thuo of Viborg and Marsilius of Inghen," in S. Ebbesen and R. L. Friedman (eds.) *Medieval Analyses in Language and Cognition* (Copenhagen: Reitzels, 1999) 523–39.

"Towards a Logic of Fiction: Ludolph Meistermann of Lübeck," in J. A. Aertsen and A. Speer (eds.) *Was ist Philosophie im Mittelalter?* (*Miscellanea Mediaevalia* 26) (Berlin: De Gruyter, 1998) 809–17.

Bos, Gerrit and Charles Burnett. *Scientific Weather Forecasting in the Middle Ages: The Writings of al-Kindi* (London: Kegan Paul, 2000).

Bosdari, Filippo. *Giovanni da Legnano, canonista e uomo politico del 1300* (Bologna, 1901).

Bosl, Karl. *"Potens und Pauper,"* in A. Bergengruen and L. Deike (eds.) *Alteuropa und die Moderne Gesellschaft: Festschrift für Otto Brunner* (Göttingen: Vandenhoeck und Ruprecht, 1963) 60–87.

Bosley, Richard and Martin Tweedale (eds.). *Basic Issues in Medieval Philosophy: Selected Readings Presenting the Interactive Discourses among Major Figures*, 2nd edn (Peterborough, Ont.: Broadview Press, 2006).

Bossier, Fernand. "L'élaboration du vocabulaire philosophique chez Burgundio de Pise," in J. Hamesse (ed.) *Aux origines du lexique philosophique européen* (Louvain-la-Neuve: Fédération internationale des instituts d'études médiévales, 1997) 81–116.

Bossy, John. "Moral Arithmetic: Seven Sins into Ten Commandments," in E. Leites (ed.) *Conscience and Casuistry in Early Modern Europe* (Cambridge: Cambridge University Press, 1988) 214–34.

Bottin, Francesco. "Gaetano da Thiene e i 'calculatores'," in A. Poppi (ed.) *Scienza e filosofia all'Università di Padova nel Quattrocento* (Padua: Edizioni LINT, 1983) 125–34.

"Logica e filosofia naturale nelle opere di Paolo Veneto," in A. Poppi (ed.) *Scienza e filosofia all'Università di Padova nel Quattrocento* (Padua: Edizioni LINT, 1983) 85–124.

Bougerol, Jacques Guy. "The Church Fathers and the *Sentences* of Peter Lombard," in I. Backus (ed.) *The Reception of the Church Fathers in the West: From the Carolingians to the Maurists* (Leiden: Brill, 1997) I: 113–64.

Introduction à l'étude de saint Bonaventure (Paris: Vrin, 1988).

Introduction to the Works of Bonaventure, tr. J. de Vinck (Patterson, NJ: St. Anthony Guild Press, 1964).

"Jean de la Rochelle – les œuvres et les manuscrits," *Archivum Franciscanum Historicum* 87 (1994) 205–15.

Bouhot, Jean Paul. *Ratramne de Corbie: histoire littéraire et controverses doctrinales* (Paris: Études Augustiniennes, 1976).

Boulnois, Olivier. "Le besoin de métaphysique. Théologie et structure des métaphysiques médiévales," in J.-L. Solère and Z. Kaluza (eds.) *La servante et la consolatrice: la philosophie dans ses rapports avec la théologie au Moyen Âge* (Paris: Vrin, 2002) 45–94.

"Duns Scot: existe-t-il des passions de la volonté?," in B. Besnier *et al.* (eds.) *Les passions antiques et médiévales: theories et critiques des passions*, vol. I (Paris: Presses universitaires de France, 2003) 281–95.

Être et representation: une généalogie de la métaphysique moderne à l'époque de Duns Scotus (XIIIe–XIVe siècle) (Paris: Presses universitaires de France, 1999).

Boureau, Alain. *Théologie, science et censure au XIIIe siècle: le cas de Jean Peckham* (Paris: Les Belles Lettres, 1999).

Boureau, Alain and Sylvain Piron. *Pierre de Jean Olivi (1248–1298): pensée scolastique, dissidence spirituelle et société* (Paris: Vrin, 1999).

Bouvy, Jean. "La nécessité de la grâce dans le Commentaire des Sentences d'Odon Rigaud," *Recherches de théologie ancienne et médiévale* 28 (1961) 59–96.

"Les questions sur la grâce dans le Commentaire des Sentences d'Odon Rigaud," *Recherches de théologie ancienne et médiévale* 27 (1960) 290–343.

Bowman, Leonard. "The Development of the Doctrine of the Agent Intellect in the Franciscan School of the Thirteenth Century," *Modern Schoolman* 50 (1973) 251–79.

Boyde, Patrick. *Dante Philomythes and Philosopher: Man in the Cosmos* (Cambridge: Cambridge University Press, 1981).

Perception and Passion in Dante's Comedy (Cambridge: Cambridge University Press, 1993).

Human Vices and Human Worth in Dante's Comedy (Cambridge: Cambridge University Press, 2000).

Boyle, Leonard E. "The Fourth Lateran Council and Manuals of Popular Theology," in T. J. Hefferman (ed.) *The Popular Literature of Medieval England* (Knoxville: University of Tennessee Press, 1985) 30–43.

"The Inter-Conciliar Period 1179–1215 and the Beginnings of Pastoral Manuals," in F. Liotta (ed.) *Miscellanea, Rolando Bandinelli, Papa Alessandro III* (Siena: Accademia senese degli intronati, 1986) 45–56.

Pastoral Care, Clerical Education and Canon Law, 1200–1400 (London: Variorum, 1981).

"The *Quodlibets* of St. Thomas and Pastoral Care," *The Thomist* 38 (1974) 232–56.

"The *Summa confessorum* of John of Freiburg and the Popularization of the Moral Teaching of St. Thomas and some of his Contemporaries," in A. Maurer (ed.) *St. Thomas Aquinas, 1274–1974: Commemorative Studies* (Toronto: Pontifical Institute of Mediaeval Studies, 1974) II: 245–68.

"Summae confessorum," in R. Bultot (ed.) *Les genres littéraires dans les sources théologiques et philosophiques médiévales: définition, critique et exploration* (Louvain-la-Neuve: Université catholique de Louvain, 1982) 227–37.

"The *Summa summarum* and some Other English Works of Canon Law," in S. Kuttner and J. J. Ryan (eds.) *Proceedings of the Second International Congress of Medieval Canon Law* (Vatican: S. Congregatio de seminariis et studiorum universitatibus, 1965) 415–56.

Braakhuis, H. A. G. *Die 13de Eeuwse Tractaten over Syncategorematische Termen* (Meppel: Krips Repro, 1979).

"Convertibility of Being and One in a Sophism Attributed to Robert Kilwardby," in S. Ebbesen and R. L. Friedman (eds.) *Medieval Analyses in Language and Cognition* (Copenhagen: Reitzels, 1999) 117–38.

"English Tracts on Syncategorematic Terms from Robert Bacon to Walter Burley," in H. A. G. Braakhuis et al. (eds.) *English Logic and Semantics from the End of the Twelfth Century to the Time of Ockham and Burleigh* (Nijmegen: Ingenium, 1981) 131–65.

"Kilwardby vs Bacon? The Contribution to the Discussion on Univocal Signification of Beings and Non-Beings Found in a Sophism Attributed to Robert Kilwardby," in E. P. Bos (ed.) *Medieval Semantics and Metaphysics* (Nijmegen: Ingenium, 1985) 111–42.

"Paul of Pergula's Commentary on the Sophismata of William Heytesbury," in A. Maierù (ed.) *English Logic in Italy in the 14th and 15th Centuries* (Naples: Bibliopolis, 1982) 343–57.

"School Philosophy and Philosophical Schools. The Semantic-Ontological Views in the Cologne Commentaries on Peter of Spain, and the 'Wegestreit'," *Miscellanea Mediaevalia* 20 (1989) 1–18.

"The Views of William of Sherwood on some Semantical Topics and their Relation to those of Roger Bacon," *Vivarium* 15 (1977) 111–42.

Braakhuis, H. A. G. and M. J. F. M. Hoenen (eds.). *Marsilius of Inghen: Acts of the International Marsilius of Inghen Symposium* (Nijmegen: Ingenium, 1992).

Brachtendorf, Johannes. "Cicero and Augustine on the Passions," *Revue des Études Augustiniennes* 43 (1997) 289–308.

Brady, Ignatius. "John Pecham and the Background of Aquinas's *De aeternitate mundi*," in A. Maurer (ed.) *St. Thomas Aquinas (1274–1974): Commemorative Studies* (Toronto: Pontifical Institute of Mediaeval Studies, 1974) II: 11–71.

Brague, Remi (ed.). *Saint Bernard et la philosophie* (Paris: Cerf, 1993).

Brams, Jozef. *La riscoperta di Aristotele in Occidente*, tr. A. Tombolini (Milan: Jaca, 2003).

Brams, Jozef and Willy Vanhamel (eds.). *Guillaume de Moerbeke: recueil d'études à l'occasion du 700e anniversaire de sa mort (1286)* (Leuven: Leuven University Press, 1989).

Brand, Paul. "The Age of Bracton," *Proceedings of the British Academy* 89 (1996) 65–89.

Brands, Hartmut. "Referenztheorie und freie Logik im Spätmittelalter," *Philosophisches Jahrbuch* 102 (1995) 33–60.

Brennan, Mary. *A Guide to Eriugenian Studies: A Survey of Publications 1930–87* (Paris: Cerf, 1989).

Brehaut, Ernest. *An Encyclopedist of the Dark Ages, Isidore of Seville* (New York: Franklin, 1964).

Brenet, Jean-Baptiste. "Perfection de la philosophie ou philosophe parfait? Jean de Jandun lecteur d'Averroès," *Recherches de théologie et philosophie médiévales* 68 (2001) 310–48.

Transferts du sujet: la noétique d'Averroès selon Jean de Jandun (Paris: Vrin, 2003).

Breuning, Wilhelm. *Erhebung und Fall des Menschen nach Ulrich von Strassburg* (Trier: Paulinus-Verlag, 1959).

Bridges, Geoffrey. *Identity and Distinction in Petrus Thomae, O.F.M.* (St. Bonaventure, NY: Franciscan Institute, 1959).

Brigué, Louis. *Alger de Liège: un théologien de l'eucharistie au début du XIIe siècle* (Paris: Gabalda, 1936).

Brock, Sebastian. "From Antagonism to Assimilation. Syriac Attitudes to Greek Learning," in N. Garsoian *et al.* (eds.) *East of Byzantium: Syria and Armenia in the Formative Period* (Washington, DC: Dumbarton Oaks, Center for Byzantine Studies, Trustees for Harvard University, 1980) 17–34.

"The Syriac Background to Ḥunayn's Translation Techniques," *Aram* 3 (1991) 139–62.

"The Syriac Commentary Tradition," in C. Burnett (ed.) *Glosses and Commentaries on Aristotelian Logical Texts* (London: Warburg Institute, University of London, 1993) 3–18.

"A Syriac Intermediary for the Arabic Theology of Aristotle? In Search of a Chimera," in C. D'Ancona (ed.) *The Libraries of the Neoplatonists* (Leiden: Brill, 2007) 293–306.

Syriac Perspectives on Late Antiquity (London: Variorum Reprints, 1984).

"Towards a History of Syriac Translation Technique," in R. Lavenant (ed.) *Symposium Syriacum III: les contacts du monde syriaque avec les autres cultures* (Rome: Pontificium Institutum Studiorium Orientalium, 1983) 1–14.

Brock, Stephen. *Action and Conduct: Thomas Aquinas and the Theory of Action* (Edinburgh: T&T Clark, 1998).

Brooke, Christopher. *The Medieval Idea of Marriage* (Oxford: Oxford University Press, 1989).

Brooke, Rosalind B. (ed. and tr.). *Scripta Leonis, Rufini et Angeli sociorum S. Francisci: The Writings of Leo, Rufinus and Angelo, Companions of St Francis* (Oxford: Clarendon Press, 1970; corrected edn 1990).

Brosch, Hermann Josef. *Der Seinsbegriff bei Boethius mit besonderer Berücksichtigungder Beziehung von Sosein und Dasein* (Innsbruck: Felizian Rauch, 1931).

Brousseau-Beuermann, Christine. "Les Questiones de Johannes de Wolve et les Sophismata artis grammaticae du ms. Paris BNF lat. 15037," in A. de Libera and J. Jolivet (eds.) *Gilbert de Poitiers et ses contemporains, aux origines de la Logica modernorum* (Naples: Bibliopolis, 1987) 91–105.

"Le sophisme anonyme 'Amatus sum vel fui' du codex Parisinus BN lat. 16135," *Cahiers de l'Institut du Moyen Age Grec et Latin* 61 (1991) 147–83.

Brower, Jeffrey and Kevin Guilfoy. *The Cambridge Companion to Abelard* (Cambridge: Cambridge University Press, 2004).

Brower-Toland, Susan. "Facts vs. Things: Adam Wodeham and the Later Medieval Debate about Objects of Judgment," *Review of Metaphysics* 60 (2006) 597–642.

Brown, Barry. *Accidental Being: A Study in the Metaphysics of Thomas Aquinas* (Washington, DC: Catholic University Press of America, 1985).

Brown, D. Catherine. *Pastor and Laity in the Theology of Jean Gerson* (Cambridge: Cambridge University Press, 1987).

Brown, George H. *Bede the Educator* (Jarrow: St. Paul's Church, 1996).

Bede, the Venerable (Boston: Twayne, 1987).

Brown, Mary Anthony. "The Role of the *Tractatus de obligationibus* in Mediaeval Logic," *Franciscan Studies* 26 (1966) 26–35.

Brown, Peter. *Augustine of Hippo* (London: Faber and Faber, 1967).

Brown, Stephen F. "Gerard of Bologna on the Nature of the Good (Text and Commentary)," in M. Pickavé (ed.) *Der Logik des Transzendentalen: Festschrift für Jan A. Aertsen zum 65. Geburtstag* (Berlin: De Gruyter, 2003) 285–303.

"Guido Terrena and the Unity of the Concept of Being," *Documenti e studi sulla tradizione filosofica medievale* 3 (1992) 599–631.

"Nicholas of Lyra's Critique of Scotus' Univocity," in B. Mojsisch and O. Pluta (eds.) *Historia philosophiae medii aevi: Studien zur Geschichte der Philosophie des Mittelalters: Festschrift für Kurt Flasch* (Amsterdam: Benjamins, 1991) 115–27.

"Peter of Candia on Believing and Knowing," *Franciscan Studies* 54 (1994–7) 251–76.

"Peter of Candia's Hundred-Year 'History' of the Theologian's Role," *Medieval Philosophy and Theology* 1 (1991) 156–90.

"Peter of Candia's Sermons in Praise of Peter Lombard," in R. Almagno and C. Harkins (eds.) *Studies Honoring Ignatius Charles Brady, Friar Minor* (St. Bonaventure, NY: Franciscan Institute, 1976).

"Richard Fishacre on the Need for Philosophy," in R. Salinger-Link (ed.) *A Straight Path: Studies in Medieval Philosophy and Culture – Essays in Honor of Arthur Hyman* (Washington, DC: Catholic University of America Press, 1988) 23–35.

"Richard of Conington and the Analogy of the Concept of Being," *Franziskanische Studien* 48 (1966) 297–307.

"Robert Cowton O.F.M. and the Analogy of the Concept of Being," *Franciscan Studies* 31 (1971) 5–40.

"Sources for Ockham's Prologue to the *Sentences* (pt 1)," *Franciscan Studies* 26 (1966) 36–65.

Browning, Robert. "An Unpublished Funeral Oration of Anna Comnena," *Proceedings of the Cambridge Philological Society* 188 (n.s. 8) (1962) 1–12; repr. in R. Sorabji (ed.) *Aristotle Transformed* (London: Duckworth, 1990) 393–406.

Brummer, Rudolf. *Bibliographia Lulliana: Ramon-Llull-Schrifttum 1870–1973* (Hildesheim: Gerstenberg, 1976).

Brundage, James. *Law, Sex, and Christian Society in Medieval Europe* (Chicago: University of Chicago Press, 1987).

Medieval Canon Law (London: Longman, 1995).

Brungs, Alexander. "Roland von Cremona O.P., die Geschichte des geistigen Lebens im frühen 13. Jahrhundert und die Definition der Tugend," in J. Hamesse (ed.) *Roma, magistra mundi: itineraria culturae medievalis: mélanges offerts au Père L. E. Boyle à l'occasion de son 75ᵉ anniversaire* (Louvain-la-Neuve: Fédération des instituts d'études médiévales, 1998) 27–51.

Bruni, Gerardo. "Quaestiones I–XX a fratre Aegidio Romano Paduae disputatae in Capitulo Generali O.E.S.A. 1281," *Analecta Augustiniana* 17 (1939–40) 125–50.

Brunner, Fernand. *Métaphysique d'Ibn Gabirol et de la tradition platonicienne*, ed. D. Schulthess (Aldershot: Ashgate, 1997).

Platonisme et Aristotelisme: la critique d'Ibn Gabirol par St. Thomas d'Aquin (Leuven: Publications universitaires, 1965).

Bucichowski, Wacław. "Le principe d'individuation dans la question de Henri de Lubeck 'Utrum materia sit principium individuationis'," *Mediaevalia Philosophica Polonorum* 21 (1975) 89–113.

Buijs, Joseph A. (ed.). *Maimonides: A Collection of Critical Essays* (Notre Dame, IN: Notre Dame University Press, 1988).

Burge, Tyler. "Buridan and Epistemic Paradox," *Philosophical Studies* 34 (1978) 21–35.

Burger, Christoph. *Aedificatio, fructus, utilitas. Johannes Gerson als Professor der Theologie und Kanzler der Universität Paris* (Tübingen: Mohr, 1986).

Burie, Luc. "Proeve tot inventarisatie van de in handschrift of in druk bewaarde werken van de Leuvense theologieprofessoren uit de XVe eeuw," in E. van Eijl and A. Black (eds.) *Facultas S. Theologiae Lovaniensis, 1432–1797* (Leuven: Leuven University Press, 1977) 221–37.

Burkard, Franz. *Philosophische Lehrgehalte in Gabriel Biels Sentenzenkommentar unter besonderer Berücksichtigung seiner Erkenntnislehre* (Meisenheim am Glan: Hain, 1974).

Burnett, Charles. *Adelard of Bath: An English Scientist and Arabist of the Early Twelfth Century* (London: Warburg Institute, University of London, 1987).

   "*Algorismi vel helcep decentior est diligentia*: The Arithmetic of Adelard of Bath and his Circle," in M. Folkerts (ed.) *Mathematische Probleme im Mittelalter: der lateinische und arabische Sprachbereich* (Wiesbaden: Harrassowitz, 1996) 221–331.

   "Arabic into Latin: The Reception of Arabic Philosophy into Western Europe," in P. Adamson and R. Taylor (eds.) *The Cambridge Companion to Arabic Philosophy* (Cambridge: Cambridge University Press, 2005) 370–404.

   "The Coherence of the Arabic–Latin Translation Program in Toledo in the Twelfth Century," *Science in Context* 14 (2001) 249–88.

   "Euclid and al-Fārābī in MS Vatican Reg. Lat. 1268," in R. Arnzen and J. Thielmann (eds.) *Words, Texts and Concepts Cruising the Mediterranean Sea: Studies on the Sources, Contents and Influences of Islamic Civilization and Arabic Philosophy and Science* (Leuven: Peeters, 2004) 411–36.

   "Hermann of Carinthia," in P. Dronke (ed.) *A History of Twelfth-Century Western Philosophy* (Cambridge: Cambridge University Press, 1988) 386–404.

   The Introduction of Arabic Learning into England (London: British Library, 1997).

   "Physics before the *Physics*. Early Translations from Arabic of Texts Concerning Nature in MSS British Library, Additional 22719 and Cotton Galba E IV," *Medioevo* 27 (2002) 53–109.

   "'Ptolemaeus in Almagesto dixit': The Transformation of Ptolemy's Almagest in its Transmission via Arabic into Latin," in H. Böhme and G. Toepfer (eds.) *Was ist Wissenschaft? Wissensformen der Antike und ihre Transformationen* (Berlin: De Gruyter, 2009).

   "The Works of Petrus Alfonsi: Questions of Authenticity," *Medium Aevum* 66 (1997) 42–79.

Burnett, Charles and Danielle Jacquart (eds.). *Constantine the African and ʿAli ibn al-ʿAbbas al-Magusi: The Pantegni and Related Texts* (Leiden: Brill, 1994).

Burnyeat, Myles. "Aquinas on 'Spiritual Change' in Perception," in D. Perler (ed.) *Ancient and Medieval Theories of Intentionality* (Leiden: Brill, 2001) 129–53.

Burr, David. *Eucharistic Presence and Conversion in Late Thirteenth-Century Franciscan Thought* (Philadelphia, PA: American Philosophical Society, 1984).

   Olivi and Franciscan Poverty: The Origins of the Usus Pauper Controversy (Philadelphia: University of Pennsylvania Press, 1989).

   Olivi's Peaceable Kingdom: A Reading of the Apocalypse Commentary (Philadelphia: University of Pennsylvania Press, 1993).

   The Persecution of Peter Olivi (Philadelphia, PA: American Philosophical Society, 1976).

   "Peter John Olivi and the Philosophers," *Franciscan Studies* 31 (1971) 41–71.

   The Spiritual Franciscans: From Protest to Persecution in the Century after Saint Francis (University Park: Pennsylvania State University Press, 2001).

Burrell, David. *Faith and Freedom: An Interfaith Perspective* (Oxford: Blackwell, 2004).

Burrows, Mark. *Jean Gerson and "De Consolatione Theologiae" (1418): The Consolation of a Biblical and Reforming Theology for a Disordered Age* (Tübingen: Mohr, 1991).

Bursill-Hall, Geoffrey. *A Census of Medieval Latin Grammatical Manuscripts* (Stuttgart: Frommann-Holzboog, 1981).

  Speculative Grammars of the Middle Ages: The Doctrine of Partes orationis of the Modistae (The Hague: Mouton, 1971).

Burton, John. *The Sources of Islamic Law: Islamic Theories of Abrogation* (Edinburgh: Edinburgh University Press, 1990).

Burton, Pierre-André. *Bibliotheca Aelrediana Secunda: Une bibliographie cumulative (1962–1996)* (Louvain-la-Neuve: Fédération internationale des instituts d'études médiévales, 1997).

Busard, H. L. L. "Unendliche Reihen in *A est unum calidum*," *Archive for History of Exact Sciences* 2 (1965) 387–97.

Butterworth, Charles E. "Al-Kindi and the Beginnings of Islamic Political Philosophy," in C. Butterworth (ed.) *The Political Aspects of Islamic Philosophy* (Cambridge, MA: Harvard University Press, 1992) 14–32.

Buzzetti, Dino. "Linguaggio e ontologia nei commenti di autore bolognese al *De tribus praedicamentis* di William de Heytesbury," in D. Buzzetti (ed.) *L'insengamento della logica a Bologna nel XIV secolo* (Bologna: Presso l'Istituto per la Storia dell'Università, 1992) 579–604.

Bydén, Börje. "'Strangle Them with These Meshes of Syllogisms!': Latin Philosophy in Greek Translations of the Thirteenth Century," in J. O. Rosenqvist (ed.) *Interaction and Isolation in Late Byzantine Culture* (Stockholm: Swedish Research Institute in Istanbul, 2004) 133–57.

  Theodore Metochites' Stoicheiosis astronomike and the Study of Natural Philosophy and Mathematics in Early Palaiologan Byzantium (Gothenburg: Acta Universitatis Gothoburgensis, 2003).

Bynum, Caroline Walker. *Fragmentation and Redemption: Essays on Gender and the Human Body in Medieval Religion* (New York: Zone Books, 1992).

  Holy Feast, Holy Fast: The Religious Significance of Food to Medieval Women (Berkeley: University of California Press, 1987).

  Jesus as Mother: Studies in the Spirituality of the High Middle Ages (Berkeley: University of California Press, 1982).

  The Resurrection of the Body in Western Christianity 200–1336 (New York: Columbia University Press, 1995).

  Wonderful Blood: Theology and Practice in Late Medieval Northern Germany and Beyond (Philadelphia: University of Pennsylvania Press, 2007).

Cacouros, Michel. "De la pensée grecque à la pensée byzantine," in J.-F. Mattéi (ed.) *Encyclopédie philosophique universelle* (Paris: Presses universitaires de France, 1998) IV: 1362–84.

  "Georges Scholarios et le *Paris. Gr. 1932:* Jean Chortasménos, l'enseignement de la logique, le thomisme à Byzance," in *The Greek Script in the 15th and 16th Century* (Athens: National Hellenic Research Foundation, 2000) 397–442.

  "Recherches sur le commentaire inédit de Théodore Prodrome aux *Analytiques postérieurs*, livre II d'Aristote," *Atti della Accademia Pontaniana* n.s. 38 (1990) 313–38.

Cacouros, Michel and Marie-Hélène Congourdeau. *Philosophie et sciences à Byzance de 1204 à 1453* (Leuven: Peeters, 2006).

Callaey, Frédégand. *L'idéalisme franciscain spirituel au xive siècle: étude sur Ubertino de Casale* (Leuven: Bureau du Recueil, 1911).

Callus, D. A. *The Condemnation of St Thomas at Oxford*. The Aquinas Society of London, Aquinas Paper 5 (London: Blackfriars Publications, 1955).

  "The Introduction of Aristotelian Learning to Oxford," *Proceedings of the British Academy* 29 (1943) 229–81.

"The Problem of the Unity of Form and Richard Knapwell, O.P.," *Mélanges offerts à Étienne Gilson* (Toronto: Pontifical Institute of Mediaeval Studies, 1959) 123–60.

(ed.). *Robert Grosseteste: Scholar and Bishop* (Oxford: Clarendon Press, 1955).

"The Treatise of John Blund on the Soul," *Autour d'Aristote: recueil d'études de philosophie ancienne et médiévale offert à Mgr. A. Mansion* (Leuven: Publications universitaires, 1955) 471–95.

"Two Early Oxford Masters on the Plurality of Forms: Adam of Buckfield – Richard Rufus of Cornwall," *Revue neo-scholastique de philosophie* 42 (1939) 411–45.

Calma, Monica. "Pierre d'Ailly: le commentaire sur les *Sentences* de Pierre Lombard," *Bulletin de philosophie médiévale* 49 (2007) 139–94.

Cameron, Averil. *Christianity and the Rhetoric of Empire: The Development of Christian Discourse* (Berkeley: University of California Press, 1991).

Cameron, Margaret. "Boethius on Utterances, Understanding, and Reality," in J. Marenbon (ed.) *The Cambridge Companion to Boethius* (Cambridge: Cambridge University Press, 2009) 85–104.

Canfora, Davide. *La controversia di Poggio Bracciolini e Guarino Veronese su Cesare e Scipione* (Florence: Olschki, 2001).

Canning, Joseph. *A History of Medieval Political Thought 300–1450* (Cambridge: Cambridge University Press, 1994).

The Political Thought of Baldus de Ubaldis (New York: Cambridge University Press, 1987).

Capelle, G. C. *Amaury de Bène: étude sur son panthéisme formel* (Paris: Vrin, 1932).

Cappuyns, Maieul. *Jean Scot Érigène: sa vie, son œuvre, sa pensée* (Paris: De Brouwer, 1933).

Caputo, Nina. *Nahmanides in Medieval Catalonia: History, Community and Messianism* (Notre Dame, IN: University of Notre Dame Press, 2008).

Carabine, Deirdre. *John Scottus Eriugena* (Oxford: Oxford University Press, 2000).

Carfantan, Jerry (ed.). *William, Abbot of St. Thierry: A Colloquium at the Abbey of St. Thierry* (Kalamazoo, MI: Cistercian Publications, 1987).

Caron, Pier Giovanni. "Aequitas et interpretatio dans la doctrine canonique aux XIIIe et XIVe siècles," in S. Kuttner (ed.) *Proceedings of the Third International Congress of Medieval Canon Law* (Vatican: Biblioteca Apostolica Vaticana, 1971) 131–41.

"Aequitas romana, 'Misericordia' patristica e 'Epicheia' aristotelica nella dottrina decretalistica del Duecento e Trencento," *Studia Gratiana* 14 (1967) 309–47.

Caroti, Stefano. "La critica contro l'astrologia di Nicole Oresme e la sua influenza nel Medioevo e nel Rinascimento," *Atti della Accademi nazionale, Classe di scienze morali* 238 (1979) 543–685.

"*Mirabilia*, scetticismo, e filosofia della natura nei *Quodlibeta* di Nicole Oresme," *Annali dell'Istituto e museo di storia della scienza di Firenze* 9 (1984) 3–20.

"Les *modi rerum* . . . Encore une fois. Une source possible de Nicole Oresme: le commentaire sur le livre 1er des *Sentences* de Jean de Mirecourt," in S. Caroti and J. Celeyrette (eds.) *Quia inter doctores est magna dissensio: Les débats de philosophie naturelle à Paris au XIVe siècle* (Florence: Olschki, 2004) 195–222.

"Nicole Oresme et les *modi rerum*," *Oriens–Occidens: Sciences, mathématiques et philosophie de l'Antiquité à l'Âge classique* 3 (2000) 115–44.

"Oresme on Motion (Questiones super Physicam, III, 2–7)," *Vivarium* 31 (1993) 8–36.

"La position de Nicole Oresme sur la nature du mouvement (Quaestiones super Physicam III, 1–8): problèmes gnoséologiques, ontologiques et sémantiques," *Archives d'histoire littéraire et doctrinale du moyen âge* 61 (1994) 303–85.

Caroti, Stefano and Christophe Grellard (eds.). *Nicolas d'Autrécourt et la faculté des arts de Paris (1317–1340)* (Cesena: Stilgraf Editrice, 2006).

Carter, M. G. *Sibawayhi* (London: I. B. Tauris, 2004).

Casagrande, Carla. "Predicare la penitenza: La *Summa de poenitentia* di Servasanto da Faenza," in *Dalla penitenza all'ascolto delle confessioni: il ruolo dei frati mendicanti* (Spoleto: Centro italiano di studi sull'alto medioevo, 1996) 59–101.

Casagrande, Carla and Silvana Vecchio. "La classificazione dei peccati tra settenario e decalogo (secoli XIII–XV)," *Documenti e studi sulla tradizione filosofica medievale* 5 (1994) 331–95.

I peccati della lingua: disciplina ed etica della parola nella cultura medievale (Rome: Istituto della Enciclopedia Italiana, 1987).

I sette vizi capitali: storia dei peccati nel medioevo (Turin: Einaudi, 2000).

Casarella, Peter. *Cusanus: The Legacy of Learned Ignorance* (Washington, DC: Catholic University of America Press, 2006).

Casey, Michael. *A Thirst for God: Spiritual Desire in Bernard of Clairvaux's Sermons on the Song of Songs* (Kalamazoo, MI: Cistercian Publications, 1988).

Casini, Lorenzo. "Cognitive and Moral Psychology in Renaissance Philosophy: A Study of Juan Luis Vives' *De anima et vita*" (Ph.D. dissertation: University of Uppsala, 2006).

Cassell, Anthony. *An Historical Study with Accompanying Translations of Dante Alighieri's Monarchia, Guido Vernani's Refutation of the Monarchia composed by Dante, and Pope John XXII's Bull Si fratrum* (Washington, DC: Catholic University of America Press, 2004).

Caster, Kevin. "William of Auvergne and St. Thomas Aquinas on the Real Distinction between Being and Essence," in J. Hackett *et al.* (eds.) *Being and Thought in Aquinas* (Binghamton, NY: Global Academic Publications, 2004) 75–108.

Catto, J. I. (ed.). *The History of the University of Oxford*, vol. I: *The Early Oxford Schools* (Oxford: Oxford University Press, 1984).

"Theology and Theologians 1220–1320," in J. I. Catto (ed.) *The History of the University of Oxford* (Oxford: Oxford University Press, 1984) I: 471–517.

"Wyclif and Wycliffism in Oxford, 1356–1430," in J. I. Catto and R. Evans (eds.) *The History of the University of Oxford* (Oxford: Clarendon Press, 1992) II: 175–261.

Catto, J. I. and Ralph Evans (eds.). *The History of the University of Oxford*, vol. II: *The Late Middle Ages* (Oxford: Oxford University Press, 1993).

Cavigioli, Jean-Daniel. "Les écrits d'Heymericus de Campo (1395–1460) sur les œuvres d'Aristote," *Freiburger Zeitschrift für Philosophie und Theologie* 28 (1981) 293–371.

Cavigioli, Jean-Daniel and Ruedi Imbach. "Quelques compléments aux catalogues des œuvres d'Heymericus de Campo," *Codices Manuscripti* 7 (1981) 1–3.

Celeyrette, Jean and Edmond Mazet. "La hiérarchie des degrés d'être chez Nicole Oresme," *Arabic Sciences and Philosophy* 8 (1998) 45–65.

Cenci, Cesare. "Fr. Guglielmo de Falgar o Fr. Guglielmo Farinier?" *Archivum Franciscanum Historicum* 78 (1985) 481–9.

Ceric, Mustafa. *Roots of Synthetic Theology in Islam: A Study of the Theology of Abū Mansūr al-Māturīdī* (Kuala Lumpur: International Institute of Islamic Thought and Civilization, 1995).

Cesalli, Laurent. "Le 'pan-propositionnalisme' de Jean Wyclif," *Vivarium* 43 (2005) 124–55.

"Le réalisme propositionnel de Walter Burley," *Archives d'histoire doctrinale et littéraire du moyen âge* 68 (2001) 155–221.

Chadwick, Henry. "Ego Berengarius," *Journal of Theological Studies* 40 (1989) 414–45.

"Origen, Celsus, and the Resurrection of the Body," *Harvard Theological Review* 41 (1948) 83–102.

Chandler, Hugh. "Plantinga and the Contingently Possible," *Analysis* 36 (1976) 106–9.

Chappuis, Marguerite, Ludger Kaczmarek, and Olaf Pluta. "Die philosophischen Schriften des Peter von Ailly: Authentizität und Chronologie," *Freiburger Zeitschrift für Philosophie und Theologie* 33 (1986) 593–615.

Charland, Thomas-Marie. *Artes praedicandi: contribution à l'histoire de la rhétorique au Moyen Age* (Paris: Vrin, 1936).

Chase, Steven. *Angelic Wisdom: The Cherubim and the Grace of Contemplation in Richard of St. Victor* (Notre Dame, IN: University of Notre Dame Press, 1995).

Châtillon, Jean. "Achard de St Victor et le De discretione anime, spiritus et mentis," *Archives d'histoire doctrinale et littéraire du moyen âge* 31 (1964) 7–35.

 Théologie, spiritualité et métaphysique dans l'œuvre oratoire d'Achard de Saint-Victor (Paris: Vrin, 1969).

Chazen, Robert. *Barcelona and Beyond: The Disputation of 1263 and its Aftermath* (Berkeley: University of California Press, 1992).

Chejne, Anwar. *Ibn Hazm* (Chicago: Kazi Publications, 1982).

 "Ibn Hazm of Cordova on Logic," *Journal of the American Oriental Society* 104 (1984) 57–72.

Cheneval, Francis. "'Utrum omnia eveniant de necessitate': Textedition und Studie der gleich-namigen Quaestio von Thaddeus von Parma (Cod. Vat. Lat. 6768)," *Freiburger Zeitschrift für Philosophie und Theologie* 35 (1988) 175–99.

Chenu, Marie-Dominique. "Maîtres et bacheliers de l'Université de Paris v. 1240. Description du manuscrit Paris, Bibl. Nat. lat. 15652," *Études d'histoire littéraire et doctrinale du XIIIe siècle* 1 (1932) 11–39.

 La théologie au douzième siècle (Paris: Vrin, 1966).

 La théologie comme science au XIIIe siècle (Paris: Vrin, 1957).

Chittick, William. *Imaginal Worlds: Ibn al-'Arabī and the Problem of Religious Diversity* (Albany: State University of New York Press, 1994).

 The Sufi Path of Knowledge: Ibn al-'Arabī's Metaphysics of Imagination (Albany: State University of New York Press, 1989).

Chodkiewicz, Michel. *An Ocean without Shore: Ibn 'Arabī, the Book, and the Law* (Albany: State University of New York Press, 1993).

Chodorow, Stanley. *Christian Political Theory and Church Politics in the Mid-Twelfth Century: The Ecclesiology of Gratian's Decretum* (Berkeley: University of California Press, 1972).

Cipolla, Carlo. *Before the Industrial Revolution: European Society and Economy, 1000–1700*, 2nd edn (New York: Norton, 1980).

Clagett, Marshall. "The Medieval Latin Translations from the Arabic of the Elements of Euclid, with Special Emphasis on the Versions of Adelard of Bath," *Isis* 44 (1953) 16–42.

 "Richard Swineshead and Late Medieval Physics," *Osiris* 9 (1950) 131–61.

 The Science of Mechanics in the Middle Ages (Madison: University of Wisconsin Press, 1959; repr. 1961).

Clanchy, M. T. *From Memory to Written Record*, 2nd edn (Oxford: Blackwell, 1993).

Clarence Smith, J. A. "Bartolo on the Conflict of Laws," *American Journal of Legal History* 14 (1970) 157–74, 247–75.

Classen, Peter. *Burgundio von Pisa: Richter, Gesandter, Übersetzer* (Heidelberg: Carl Winter Universitätsverlag, 1974).

 Gerhoch von Reichersberg: eine Biographie (Wiesbaden: Steiner, 1960).

Clegg, Brian. *The First Scientist: A life of Roger Bacon* (New York: Carroll and Graf, 2003).

Clucas, Lowell. *The Trial of John Italos and the Crisis of Intellectual Values in Byzantium in the Eleventh Century* (Munich: Institut für Byzantinistik, Neugriechische Philologie und Byzantinische Kunstgeschichte der Universität, 1981).

Cochrane, Louise. *Adelard of Bath: The First English Scientist* (London: British Museum Press, 1994).

Code, Alan. "Aristotle's Metaphysics as a Science of Principles," *Revue internationale de philosophie* 51 (1997) 357–78.

Codellas, P. S. "Nikephoros Blemmydes' Philosophical Works and Teachings," *Proceedings of the Xth International Congress of Philosophy* (Amsterdam: North-Holland, 1949) 1117–18.

Cohen, Gerson D. "The Soteriology of Abraham Maimuni," *Proceedings of the American Academy for Jewish Research* 35 (1967) 75–98; 36 (1968) 33–56.

Coleman, Janet. "*Dominium* in Thirteenth- and Fourteenth-Century Political Thought and its Seventeenth-Century Heirs: John of Paris and Locke," *Political Studies* 33 (1985) 73–100.

"FitzRalph's Antimendicant 'proposicio' (1350) and the Politics of the Papal Court at Avignon," *Journal of Ecclesiastical History* 35 (1984) 376–90.

"Jean de Ripa and the Oxford Calculators," *Mediaeval Studies* 37 (1975) 130–89.

A History of Political Thought from the Middle Ages to the Renaissance (Oxford: Blackwell, 2000).

"Medieval Discussions of Property: *Ratio* and *Dominium* according to John of Paris and Marsilius of Padua," *History of Political Thought* 4 (1983) 209–28.

"Poverty, Property and Political Thought in Fourteenth-Century Scholastic Philosophy," in C. Wenin (ed.) *L'homme et son univers au moyen age* (Louvain-la-Neuve: Éditions de l'Institut Supérieur de Philosophie, 1986) 845–55.

"Property and Poverty," in J. Burns (ed.) *The Cambridge History of Medieval Political Thought* (Cambridge: Cambridge University Press, 1988) 607–48.

Colish, Marcia. "*Habitus* Revisited: A Reply to Cary Nederman," *Traditio* 48 (1993) 77–92.

Peter Lombard (Leiden: Brill, 1994).

Collins, Ann Ryan. *Teacher in Faith and Virtue: Lanfranc of Bec's Commentary on Saint Paul* (Leiden: Brill, 2007).

Colomer, Eusebio. "Heimeric van de Velde entre Ramón Llull y Nicolas de Cusa," in J. Vincke (ed.) *Spanische Forschungen der Görres-Gesellschaft* (Münster: Aschendorff, 1963) XXI: 216–32.

Combes, André. "L'intensité des formes après Jean de Ripa," *Archives d'histoire doctrinale et littéraire du moyen âge* 37 (1970) 17–147.

"La métaphysique de Jean de Ripa," in *Die Metaphysik im Mittelalter* (*Miscellanea Mediaevalia* 2) (Berlin: De Gruyter, 1963) 543–73.

"Présentation de Jean de Ripa," *Archives d'histoire doctrinale et littéraire du moyen âge* 23 (1956) 145–242.

Conforti, Patrizia. "Hervé de Nédellec et les questiones ordinaires *De cognitione primi principii*," *Revue Thomiste* 97 (1997) 63–82.

"'Naturali cognitione probare': Natural and Theological Knowledge in Hervaeus Natalis," in J. A. Aertesen and A. Speer (eds.) *Was ist Philosophie im Mittelalter?* (*Miscellanea Mediaevalia* 26) (Berlin: De Gruyter, 1999) 614–21.

Congar, Yves. "Aspects ecclésiologiques de la querelle entre mendicants et séculiers dans la seconde moitié du XIIIe siècle et le début du XIVe siècle," *Archives d'histoire doctrinale et littéraire du moyen âge* 28 (1961) 35–151.

Connolly, James. *Jean Gerson: Reformer and Mystic* (London: Herder, 1928).

Conrad, Lawrence I. (ed.). *The World of Ibn Tufayl: Interdisciplinary Perspectives on Hayy Ibn Yaczan* (Leiden: Brill, 1996).

Constable, Giles. *The Reformation of the Twelfth Century* (Cambridge: Cambridge University Press, 1996).

Constable, Giles and James Kritzeck (eds.). *Petrus Venerabilis, 1156–1956: Studies and Texts Commemorating the Eighth Centenary of his Death* (Rome: Herder, 1956).

Conti, Alessandro D. "Analogy and Formal Distinction: On the Logical Basis of Wyclif's Metaphysics," *Medieval Philosophy and Theology* 6 (1997) 133–65.

"Categories and Universals in the Later Middle Ages," in L. Newton (ed.) *Medieval Commentaries on Aristotle's* Categories (Leiden: Brill, 2008) 369–409.

"Le composizione metafisica dell'ente finito corporeo nell'ontologia di Thomas Sutton," *Documenti e studi sulla tradizione filosofica medievale* 2 (1991) 317–60.

"Conoscenza e verità in Egidio Romano," *Documenti e studi sulla tradizione filosofica medievale* 3 (1992) 305–61.

Esistenza e verità: forme e strutture del reale in Paolo Veneto e nel pensiero filosofico del tardo medioevo (Rome: Edizioni dell'Istituto Storico Italiano per il Medioevo, 1996).

"Johannes Sharpe's Ontology and Semantics: Oxford Realism Revisited," *Vivarium* 43 (2005) 156–86.

"Linguaggio e realtà nel commento alle *Categorie* di Robert Alyngton," *Documenti e studi sulla tradizione filosofica medievale* 4 (1993) 179–306.

"Ontology in Walter Burley's Last Commentary on the *Ars Vetus*," *Franciscan Studies* 50 (1990) 121–76.

"Paul of Venice on Individuation," *Recherches de théologie et philosophie médiévales* 65 (1998) 107–32.

"Paul of Venice's Theory of Divine Ideas and its Sources," *Documenti e studi sulla tradizione filosofica medievale* 14 (2003) 409–48.

"A Realist Interpretation of the *Categories* in the Fourteenth Century: The *Litteralis sententia super Praedicamenta Aristotelis* of Robert Alyngton," in L. Newton (ed.) *Medieval Commentaries on Aristotle's* Categories (Leiden: Brill, 2008) 317–46.

"Significato e verità in Walter Burley," *Documenti e studi sulla tradizione filosofica medievale* 11 (2000) 317–50.

"Teoria degli universali e teoria della predicazione nel trattato *De universalibus* di William Penbygull: discussione e difesa della posizione di Wyclif," *Medioevo* 8 (1982) 137–203.

"Thomas Sutton's Commentary on the 'Categories' according to Ms Oxford, Merton College 289," in P. O. Lewry (ed.) *The Rise of British Logic* (Toronto: Pontifical Institute of Mediaeval Studies, 1985) 173–213.

"Wyclif's Logic and Metaphysics," in I. C. Levy (ed.) *A Companion to John Wyclif* (Leiden: Brill, 2006) 67–125.

Conticello, G. C. and Vassa Conticello. *La théologie byzantine et sa tradition* (Turnhout: Brepols, 2002).

Contreni, John. "The Carolingian Renaissance: Education and Literary Culture," in R. McKitterick (ed.) *The New Cambridge Medieval History*, vol. II: *c.700–c.900* (Cambridge: Cambridge University Press, 1991) 709–57.

Conybeare, F. C., J. Rendel Harris, and Agnes Smith Lewis (ed.). *The Story of Ahikar from the Aramaic, Syriac, Arabic, Armenian, Ethiopic, Old Turkish, Greek and Slavonic Versions* (London: C. J. Clay and Sons, 1898).

Cook, Michael. *Commanding Right and Forbidding Wrong in Islamic Thought* (Cambridge: Cambridge University Press, 2000).

Coolman, Boyd. *Knowing God by Experience: The Spiritual Senses in the Theology of William of Auxerre* (Washington, DC: Catholic University of America Press, 2004).

Cooper, John. *Reason and Emotion: Essays on Ancient Moral Psychology and Ethical Theory* (Princeton, NJ: Princeton University Press, 1999).

Cooperson, Michael. "Ibn al-Muqaffa'," in O. Leaman (ed.) *The Biographical Encyclopaedia of Islamic Philosophy* (London: Thoemmes, 2006) I: 280–6.

Copleston, Frederick. *A History of Philosophy* (Westminster, MD: Newman Press, 1946–75).

Corbin, Henry. *Creative Imagination in the Sufism of Ibn ʿArabī* (Princeton, NJ: Princeton University Press, 1969).

Côté, Antoine. "Guerric de Saint-Quentin et le problème de l'infinité divine," in B. C. Bazán et al. (eds.) *Les philosophies morales et politiques au Moyen Âge* (Ottawa: Legas, 1995) 1132–48.

Courtenay, William J. "The Academic and Intellectual Worlds of Ockham," in P. V. Spade (ed.) *The Cambridge Companion to Ockham* (Cambridge: Cambridge University Press, 1999) 17–30.

Adam Wodeham: An Introduction to his Life and Writings (Leiden: Brill, 1978).

"The Categories, Michael of Massa and Natural Philosophy at Paris, 1335–1340," in J. Biard and I. Rosier-Catach (eds.) *La tradition médiévale des Catégories (XIIe–XVe siècles): XIIIe Symposium européen de logique et de sémantique médiévales* (Leuven: Peeters, 2003) 243–60.

"Covenant and Causality in Pierre d'Ailly," *Speculum* 46 (1971) 94–119.

"The Dialectic of Omnipotence in the High and Late Middle Ages," in T. Rudavsky (ed.) *Divine Omniscience and Omnipotence in Medieval Philosophy* (Dordrecht: Reidel, 1985) 243–69.

"The Early Career of Nicole Oresme," *Isis* 91 (2000) 542–8.

"John of Mirecourt and Gregory of Rimini on Whether God Can Undo the Past," *Recherches de théologie ancienne et médiévale* 39 (1972) 224–53; 40 (1973) 147–74.

"Necessity and Freedom in Anselm's Conception of God," *Analecta Anselmiana* 4 (1975) 39–64.

"The *Quaestiones in Sententias* of Michael de Massa, OESA. A Redating," *Augustiniana* 45 (1995) 191–207.

"Radulphus Brito, Master of Arts and Theology," *Cahiers de l'Institut du Moyen Age Grec et Latin* 76 (2005) 131–58.

"Reflections on Vat. Lat. 1086 and Prosper of Reggio Emilia O.E.S.A.," in C. Schabel (ed.) *Theological Quodlibeta in the Middle Ages: The Fourteenth Century* (Leiden: Brill, 2007) 345–57.

"The Registers of the University of Paris and the Statutes Against the 'Scientia Occamica'," *Vivarium* 29 (1991) 13–49.

"A Revised Text of Robert Holcot's Quodlibetal Dispute on Whether God is Able to Know More Than He Knows," *Archiv für Geschichte der Philosophie* 53 (1971) 1–21.

Schools and Scholars in Fourteenth-Century England (Princeton, NJ: Princeton University Press, 1987).

"Some Notes on Robert of Halifax, O.F.M.," *Franciscan Studies* 33 (1973) 135–42.

Cousin, P. *Abbon de Fleury-sur-Loire: un savant, un pasteur, un martyr à la fin du Xᵉ siècle* (Paris: Lethielleux, 1954).

Cousin, Victor. *Ouvrages inédits d'Abélard pouvant servir à l'histoire de la philosophie scolastique en France* (Paris: Imprimerie Royale, 1836).

Coutre, R. A. "The Use of Epikeia in Natural Law: Its Early Developments," *Église et théologie* 4 (1973) 71–93.

Couvreur, Gilles. *Les pauvres ont-ils des droits? Recherches sur le vol en cas d'extrême nécessité depuis la Concordia de Gratien (1140) jusqu'à Guillaume d'Auxerre († 1231)* (Rome: Libreria Editrice dell'Università Gregoriana, 1961).

"Pauvreté et droits des pauvres à la fin du XIIe siècle," in G. Couvreur (ed.) *La pauvreté: des sociétés de pénurie à la société d'abondance* (Paris: Fayard, 1964) 13–37.

Covington, Michael. *Syntactic Theory in the High Middle Ages: Modistic Models of Sentence Structure* (Cambridge: Cambridge University Press, 1984).

Cowdrey, H. E. J. "The Enigma of Archbishop Lanfranc," *Haskins Society Journal* 6 (1994) 129–52.

Lanfranc: Scholar, Monk, and Archbishop (Oxford: Oxford University Press, 2003).

Cox, Virginia and John O. Ward (eds.). *The Rhetoric of Cicero in its Medieval and Early Renaissance Commentary Tradition* (Leiden: Brill, 2006).

Craemer-Ruegenberg, Ingrid. *Albert the Great* (Leipzig: Benno, 2005).

Craig, Edward (ed.). *Routledge Encyclopedia of Philosophy* (London: Routledge, 1998).

Craig, William Lane. *The Problem of Divine Foreknowledge and Future Contingents from Aristotle to Suarez* (Leiden: Brill, 1988).

Cremascoli, Giuseppe. "La 'Summa' di Rolando da Cremona, Il testo del prologo," *Studi Medievali* 16 (1975) 825–76.

Creutz, Rudolf. "Die Medizinisch–naturaphilosophische Aphorismen und Kommentar des Magister Urso Salernitanus," *Quellen und Studien zur Geschichte der Naturwissenschaften und der Medizin* 5 (1936) 1–192.

Urso, der Letzte des Hochsalerno, Arzt, Philosoph, Theologe (Berlin: Ebering, 1934).

Creytens, Raymond. "Autour de la littérature des correctoires," *Archivum Fratrum Praedicatorum* 12 (1942) 313–30.

Crombie, Alistair. *Robert Grosseteste and the Origins of Experimental Science 1100–1700* (Oxford: Clarendon Press, 1953; 2nd edn, 1962).

Crone, Patricia. *Medieval Islamic Political Thought* (Edinburgh: Edinburgh University Press, 2004).

Crone, Patricia and Martin Hinds. *God's Caliph: Religious Authority in the First Centuries of Islam* (Cambridge: Cambridge University Press, 1986).

Cross, Richard. "Absolute Time: Peter John Olivi and the Bonaventurean Tradition," *Medioevo* 27 (2002) 261–300.

Duns Scotus (Oxford: Oxford University Press, 1999).

Duns Scotus on God (Aldershot: Ashgate, 2005).

"Infinity, Continuity, and Composition: The Contribution of Gregory of Rimini," *Medieval Philosophy and Theology* 7 (1998) 89–110.

"Philosophy of Mind," in T. Williams (ed.) *The Cambridge Companion to Duns Scotus* (Cambridge: Cambridge University Press, 2003) 263–84.

The Physics of Duns Scotus: The Scientific Context of a Theological Vision (Oxford: Clarendon Press, 1998).

Crowley, Theodore. *Roger Bacon: The Problem of the Soul in his Philosophical Commentaries* (Leuven: Institut Supérieur de Philosophie, 1950).

Cullen, Christopher. *Bonaventure* (New York: Oxford University Press, 2006).

Cunningham, F. A. "Richard of Middleton, O.F.M. on esse and essence," *Franciscan Studies* 30 (1970) 49–76.

Cusato, Michael F. "The Renunciation of Power as a Foundational Theme in Early Franciscan History," in M. Gosman *et al.* (eds.) *The Propagation of Power in the Medieval West* (Groningen: Forsten, 1997) 265–86.

"To Do Penance / Facere penitentiam," *The Cord* 57 (2007) 3–24.

Daftary, Farhad. *The Ismāʿīlīs: Their History and Doctrines* (Cambridge: Cambridge University Press, 1990).

Dahan, Gilbert (ed.). *Gersonide en son temps* (Leuven: Peeters, 1991).

Daiber, Hans. "Die Aristotelesrezeption in der syrischen Literatur," in D. Kuhn and H. Stahl (eds.) *Die Gegenwart des Altertums* (Heidelberg: Edition Forum, 2001) 327–45.

Bibliography of Islamic Philosophy (Leiden: Brill, 1999).

Bibliography of Islamic Philosophy: Supplement (Leiden: Brill, 2007).

"Qosṭā ibn Lūqā (9. Jh.) über die Einteilung der Wissenschaften," *Zeitschrift für Geschichte der arabisch-islamischen Wissenschaften* 6 (1990) 93–129.

Dales, Richard C. "Gilbert of Stratton. An Early Oxford Defense of Aquinas's Teaching on the Possibility of a Beginningless World," *Documenti e studi sulla tradizione filosofica medievale* 5 (1994) 259–96.

"Henry of Harclay on the Infinite," *Journal of the History of Ideas* 45 (1984) 295–302.

Medieval Discussions of the Eternity of the World (Leiden: Brill, 1990).

The Problem of the Rational Soul in the Thirteenth Century (Leiden: Brill, 1995).

"Robert Grosseteste's Scientific Works," *Isis* 52 (1961) 381–402.

Dales, Richard C. and Omar Argerami (eds.). *Medieval Latin Texts on the Eternity of the World* (Leiden: Brill, 1991).

Dalfert, Ingolf. *Malum: Theologische Hermeneutik des Bösen* (Tübingen: Mohr Siebeck, 2008).

d'Alverny, Marie-Thérèse. *Alan of Lille's Textes inédits* (Paris: Vrin, 1965).

"Algazel dans l'occident latin," in *Un trait d'union entre l'orient et l'occident: al-Ghazzali et Ibn Maimoun* (Agadir: Académie royale du Maroc, 1986) 125–46.

"Un fragment du procès des Amauriciens," *Archives d'histoire doctrinale et littéraire du moyen âge* 18 (1950–1) 325–36.

"Notes sur les traductions médiévales des œuvres philosophiques d'Avicenne," *Archives d'histoire doctrinale et littéraire du moyen âge* 19 (1952) 337–58.

"L'obit de Raoul Ardent," *Archives d'histoire doctrinale et littéraire du moyen âge* 15/17 (1940) 403–5.

"Pseudo-Aristotle, 'De elementis'," in J. Kraye et al. (eds.) *Pseudo-Aristotle in the Middle Ages: The Theology and Other Texts* (London: Warburg Institute, 1986) 63–83.

"Translations and Translators," in R. L. Benson and G. Constable (eds.) *Renaissance and Renewal in the Twelfth Century* (Cambridge, MA: Harvard University Press, 1982) 421–62.

Daly, Lowrie J. *The Political Theory of John Wyclif* (Chicago: Loyola University Press, 1962).

Daly, Saralyn R. "Peter Comestor: Master of Histories," *Speculum* 32 (1957) 62–73.

Damerow, Peter, Gideon Freudenthal, Jürgen Renn, and Peter McLaughlin (eds.). *Exploring the Limits of Preclassical Mechanics* (Dordrecht: Springer, 1992).

D'Ancona, Cristina. "From Latin Antiquity to the Arab Middle Ages: The Commentaries and the Harmony between the Philosophies of Plato and Aristotle," in L. Honnefelder et al. (eds.) *Albertus Magnus und die Anfänge der Aristoteles-Rezeption in lateinischen Mittelalter* (Münster: Aschendorf, 2005) 45–69.

"Historiographie du platonisme médiéval: le cas de saint Thomas," in S.-T. Bonino (ed.) *Saint Thomas au XXᵉ siècle (Colloque du centenaire de la "Revue thomiste")* (Paris: Éditions Saint-Paul, 1994) 198–217.

(ed.). *The Libraries of the Neoplatonists* (Leiden: Brill, 2007).

(ed.). *Storia della filosofia nell'Islam medievale* (Turin: Einaudi, 2005).

Daniels, Augustinus. *Quellenbeiträge und Untersuchungen zur Geschichte der Gottesbeweise im XIII. Jahrhundert* (Münster: Aschendorff, 1909).

"Wilhelm von Ware über das menschliche Erkenntnis," *Studien zur Geschichte der Philosophie: Festgabe zum 60. Geburtstag Clemens Baeumker* (Münster: Aschendorff, 1913) 309–18.

D'Anna, Gabriella. "Abelardo e Cicerone," *Studi Medievali* 10 (1969) 333–419.

Davidson, Herbert. *Alfarabi, Avicenna, and Averroes on Intellect: Their Cosmologies, Theories of the Active Intellect, and Theories of Human Intellect* (Oxford: Oxford University Press, 1992).

Moses Maimonides (Oxford: Oxford University Press, 2005).

Proofs for Eternity, Creation, and the Existence of God in Medieval Islamic and Jewish Philosophy (Oxford: Oxford University Press, 1987).

"The Relation between Averroes' Middle and Long Commentaries on the De Anima," *Arabic Sciences and Philosophy* 7 (1997) 139–51.

Davies, Brian. *The Thought of Thomas Aquinas* (Oxford: Clarendon Press, 1992).

Davies, Brian and Brian Leftow (eds.). *The Cambridge Companion to Anselm* (Cambridge: Cambridge University Press, 2004).

Davies, Oliver. *Meister Eckhart: Mystical Theologian* (London: SPCK, 1991).

Davis, Adam. *The Holy Bureaucrat: Eudes Rigaud and Religious Reform in Thirteenth-Century Normandy* (Ithaca, NY: Cornell University Press, 2006).

Davis, Charles. "An Early Florentine Political Theorist: Fra Remigio de' Girolami," *Proceedings of the American Philosophical Society* 104 (1960) 662–76.

"Roman Patriotism and Republican Propaganda: Ptolemy of Lucca and Pope Nicholas III," *Speculum* 50 (1975) 411–33.

d'Avray, David. *Medieval Marriage: Symbolism and Society* (Oxford: Oxford University Press, 2005).

The Preaching of the Friars: Sermons Diffused from Paris before 1300 (Oxford: Clarendon Press, 1985).

Davy, M.-M. *Les sermons universitaires parisiens de 1230–1231: contribution à l'histoire de la prédication médiévale* (Paris: Vrin, 1931).

Dawson, James Doyne. "William of Saint-Amour and the Apostolic Tradition," *Mediaeval Studies* 40 (1978) 223–38.

"Richard FitzRalph and the Fourteenth-Century Poverty Controversies," *Journal of Ecclesiastical History* 34 (1983) 315–44.

de Asúa, M. "Medicine and Philosophy in Peter of Spain's Commentary on 'De animalibus'," in C. Steel *et al.* (eds.) *Aristotle's Animals in the Middle Ages and the Renaissance* (Leuven: Leuven University Press, 1999).

de Barcelona, Martin. "Nicolás Bonet (†1343), Tourangeau, doctor proficuus, O.M.," *Études Franciscaines* 37 (1925) 638–57.

de Callataÿ, Godefroid. *Ikhwān al-Ṣafāʾ: A Brotherhood of Idealists on the Fringe of Orthodox Islam* (Oxford: Oneworld, 2005).

de Certeau, Michel. *La fable mystique: XVI–XVII siècle* (Paris: Gallimard, 1982).

Heterologies (Manchester: Manchester University Press, 1986).

de la Torre, Bartholomew. *Thomas Buckingham and the Contingency of Futures: The Possibility of Human Freedom* (Notre Dame, IN: University of Notre Dame Press, 1987).

de Lagarde, Georges. *La naissance de l'espirit laïque au declin du moyen age* (Leuven: Nauwelaerts, 1956–70).

"La philosophie sociale d'Henri de Gand et de Godefroid de Fontaines," *Archives d'histoire doctrinale et littéraire du moyen âge* 18–20 (1943–5) 73–142.

de Leemans, Pieter. "Peter of Auvergne on Aristotle's *De motu animalium* and the MS Oxford, Merton College 275," *Archives d'histoire doctrinale et littéraire du moyen âge* 71 (2004) 129–202.

de Libera, Alain. "Les *Abstractiones* d'Hervé le Sophiste (Hervaeus Sophista)," *Archives d'histoire doctrinale et littéraire du moyen âge* 52 (1986) 163–230.

"Apollinaire Offredi critique de Pierre de Mantoue: Le *Tractatus de instanti* et la logique du changement," in A. Maierù (ed.) *English Logic in Italy in the 14th and 15th Centuries* (Naples: Bibliopolis, 1982) 253–91.

"Les *Appellationes* de Jean le Page," *Archives d'histoire doctrinale et littéraire du moyen âge* 51 (1984) 193–255.

Introduction à la mystique rhénane d'Albert le Grand à Maître Eckhart (Paris: OEIL, 1984).

"La littérature des *Abstractiones* et la tradition logique d'Oxford," in P. O. Lewry (ed.) *The Rise of British Logic* (Toronto: Pontifical Institute of Mediaeval Studies, 1983) 63–114.

"La littérature des *Sophismata* dans la tradition terministe parisienne de la seconde moitié du XIIIe siècle," in M. Asztalos (ed.) *The Editing of Theological and Philosophical Texts from the Middle Ages* (Stockholm: Almqvist and Wiksell International, 1986) 213–44.

Métaphysique et noétique: Albert le Grand (Paris: Vrin, 2005).

"The Oxford and Cambridge Traditions in Logic," in N. Kretzmann *et al.* (eds.) *The Cambridge History of Later Medieval Philosophy* (Cambridge: Cambridge University Press, 1982) 174–87.

Penser au Moyen Âge (Paris: Seuil, 1991).

La philosophie médiévale (Paris: Presses universitaires de France, 1993).

La querelle des universaux de Platon à la fin du Moyen Age (Paris: Seuil, 1996).

"Questions de réalisme: sur deux arguments antiockhamistes de John Sharpe," *Revue de metaphysique et de morale* 97 (1992) 83–110.

La référence vide: théories de la proposition (Paris: Seuil, 2002).

"Supposition naturelle et appellation: aspects de la sémantique parisienne au XIIIe siècle," *Histoire Epistémologie Langage* 3 (1981) 63–77.

"Ulrich de Strasbourg, lecteur d'Albert le Grand," *Freiburger Zeitschrift für Philosophie und Theologie* 32 (1985) 105–36.

de Libera, Alain and Irène Rosier. "La pensée linguistique médiévale," in S. Auroux (ed.) *Histoire des idées linguistiques* (Liège: Mardaga, 1992) II: 115–86.

de Matteis, Maria Consiglia. *La "teologia politica comunale" di Remigio de' Girolami* (Bologna: Pàtron, 1977).

de Montclos, Jean. *Lanfranc et Bérenger: la controverse eucharistique du XIe siècle* (Leuven: Spicilegium sacrum Lovaniense, 1971).

de Renzi, Salvatore. *Collectio Salernitana* (Naples: Dalla tipografia del Filiatre-Sebezio, 1852–9; repr. Bologna: Forni Editore, 1967).

de Rijk, L. M. "Each Man's Ass is not Everybody's Ass: On an Important Item in Thirteenth-Century Semantics," *Historiographia Linguistica* 7 (1980) 221–30.

"John Buridan on Universals," *Revue de métaphysique et de morale* 97 (1992) 35–59.

Logica modernorum: A Contribution to the History of Early Terminist Logic (Assen: Van Gorcum, 1962–7).

"On the Genuine Text of Peter of Spain's 'Summule Logicales', Part II: Simon Faversham (d. 1306) as a Commentator of the Tract I–V of the *Summule*," *Vivarium* 6 (1968) 69–101.

"On the Genuine Text of Peter of Spain's 'Summule Logicales', Part IV: The *Lectura Tractatum* by Guillelmus Arnaldi, Master of Arts at Toulouse (1235–1244). With a Note on the Date of Lambert of Auxerre's *Summule*," *Vivarium* 7 (1969) 120–62.

"The Origins of the Theory of the Properties of Terms," in N. Kretzmann *et al.* (eds.) *The Cambridge History of Later Medieval Philosophy* (Cambridge: Cambridge University Press, 1982) 161–73.

"Peter Abailard's Semantics and his Doctrine of Being," *Vivarium* 24 (1986) 85–127.

"The Place of Billingham's *Speculum puerorum* in the 14th and 15th Century Logical Tradition," *Studia Mediewistyczne* 16 (1975) 99–153.

"Richard Billingham's Works on Logic," *Vivarium* 14 (1976) 121–38.

"Semantics and Metaphysics in Gilbert of Poitiers: A Chapter of Twelfth-Century Platonism," *Vivarium* 26 (1988) 73–112; 27 (1989) 11–35.

"Semantics in Richard Billingham and Johannes Venator," in A. Maierù (ed.) *English Logic in Italy in the 14th and 15th Centuries* (Naples: Bibliopolis, 1982) 167–84.

Some Earlier Parisian Tracts on Distinctiones Sophismatum (Nijmegen: Ingenium, 1988).

Some 14th Century Tracts on the Probationes terminorum: *Martin of Alnwick, O.F.M., Richard Billingham, Edward Upton and Others* (Nijmegen: Ingenium, 1982).

"Some New Evidence on Twelfth-Century Logic: Alberic and the School of Mont Ste. Geneviève (Montani)," *Vivarium* 4 (1966) 1–57.

"Some Thirteenth-Century Tracts on the Game of Obligation I," *Vivarium* 12 (1974) 94–123.

"Some Thirteenth-Century Tracts on the Game of Obligation II," *Vivarium* 13 (1975) 22–54.

"Works by Gerald Ot (Gerardus Odonis) on Logic, Metaphysics and Natural Philosophy Rediscovered in Madrid, Bibl. nac. 4229," *Archives d'histoire doctrinale et littéraire du moyen âge* 60 (1993) 173–93.

De Smet, Daniel. *La quiétude de l'intellect: néoplatonisme et gnose ismaélienne dans l'œuvre de Hamīd ad-Dīn al-Kirmānī, Xe/XIe s.* (Leuven: Peeters, 1995).

de Töth, Pietro Tommaso. *Storia di S. Chiara da Montefalco secondo un antico documento dell'anno 1308* (Siena, 1908).

de Tourtoulon, Pierre. *Placentin, sa vie, ses œuvres: étude sur l'enseignement du droit romain au moyen âge dans le midi de la France* (Paris: Librairie Maresq, 1896; repr. Glashütten im Taunus: Detlev Auvermann, 1972).

de Vaux, Roland. *Notes et textes sur l'avicennisme latin aux confins des XIIᵉ et XIIIᵉ siècles* (Paris: Vrin, 1934).

de Vooght, Paul. *L'hérésie de Jean Huss* (Leuven: Publications universitaires, 1960).

de Vries-Van der Velden, Eva. *Théodore Métochite: une réévaluation* (Amsterdam: Gieben, 1987).

De Wulf, Maurice. *Un théologien-philosophe du XIIIᵉ siècle: étude sur la vie, les œuvres et l'influence de Godefroid de Fontaines* (Brussels: Hayez, 1904).

de Zedelghem, Amédée. "L'attritionisme d'Abélard," *Estudis Franciscans* 35 (1925).

Deane, Herbert A. *The Political and Social Ideas of St. Augustine* (New York: Columbia University Press, 1963).

Déchanet, Jean. *William of St Thierry: The Man and his Work* (Spencer, MA: Cistercian Publications, 1972).

Decker, Bruno. *Die Gotteslehre des Jakob von Metz: Untersuchungen zur Dominikanertheologie zu Beginn des 14. Jahrhunderts* (Münster: Aschendorff, 1967).

Decorte, Jos. "Der Einfluss der Willenspsychologie des Walter von Brügge OFM auf die Willenspsychologie und Freiheitlehre das Heinrich von Gent," *Franziskanische Studien* 65 (1983) 215–40.

Degen, Rainer. "Galen im Syrischen: eine Übersicht über die syrische Überlieferung," in V. Nutton (ed.) *Galen: Problems and Prospects* (London: Wellcome Institute for the History of Medicine, 1981) 131–66.

DeGregorio, Scott (ed.). *Innovation and Tradition in the Writings of the Venerable Bede* (Morgantown: West Virginia University Press, 2006).

del Punta, Francesco. 'La *Logica* di R. Feribrigge nella tradizione manoscritta italiana," in A. Maierù (ed.) *English Logic in Italy in the 14th and 15th Centuries* (Naples: Bibliopolis, 1982) 53–85.

del Punta, Francesco, Silvia Donati, and Concetta Luna. "Egidio Romano," in *Dizionario biografico degli Italiani* (Rome: Istituto della Enciclopedia Italiana, 1993) XLII: 319–41.

Delaney, David. *Law and Nature* (Cambridge: Cambridge University Press, 2003).

Delhaye, Philippe. "Le dossier anti-matrimonial de l'*Adversus Jovinianum* et son influence sur quelques écrits latins du XIIe siècle," *Mediaeval Studies* 13 (1951) 65–86.

Pierre Lombard: sa vie, ses œuvres, sa morale (Montréal: Institut d'études médiévales, 1961).

Delio, Ilia. *Simply Bonaventure: An Introduction to his Life, Thought and Writings* (Hyde Park, NY: New City Press, 2001).

Delorme, Ferdinand. "Le Cardinal Vital Du Four: huit questions disputées sur le problème de la connaissance," *Archives d'histoire doctrinale et littéraire du moyen âge* 2 (1927) 333–7.

Delumeau, Jean. *L'aveu et le pardon: les difficultés de la confession xiiie–xviiie siècle* (Paris: Fayard, 1990).

Demetracopoulos, John A. *Apo tēn historia tou byzantinou thōmismou: Plēthōn kai Thōmas Akuinatēs* (Athens: Parousia, 2004).

"Demetrius Cydones' Translation of Bernardus Guidonis' List of Thomas Aquinas' Writings and the Historical Roots of Byzantine Thomism," in A. Speer and D. Wirmer (eds.) *1308: 36. Kölner Mediaevistentagung* (Berlin: De Gruyter, 2010).

"Demetrios Kydones' Translation of the *Summa theologiae*," *Jahrbuch der Österreichischen Byzantinistik* 32 (1982) 311–20.

"Further Evidence on the Ancient, Patristic, and Byzantine Sources of Barlaam the Calabrian's *Contra Latinos*: À propos de A. Fyrigos (ed.), *Barlaam Calabro, Opere contro i Latini*," *Byzantinische Zeitschrift* 96 (2003) 83–122.

"Georgios Gemistos – Plethon's Dependence on Thomas Aquinas' *Summa contra Gentiles* and *Summa Theologiae*," *Archiv für mittelalterliche Philosophie und Kultur* 12 (2006) 276–341.

"Nicholas Cabasilas's *Quaestio de rationis valore*: an anti-Palamite Defense of Secular Wisdom," *Byzantina* 19 (1998) 53–93.

Demetrakopulos, Andronikos K. *Bibliotheca ecclesiastica* (Leipzig, 1866; repr. Hildesheim: Olms, 1965).

Denery, Dallas. *Seeing and Being Seen in the Later Medieval World: Optics, Theology and Religious Life* (Cambridge: Cambridge University Press, 2005).

Denifle, Henri and Émile Chatelain (eds.). *Chartularium Universitatis Parisiensis* (Paris: Delalain, 1889–97).

Denzinger, Heinrich (ed.). *Enchiridion symbolorum definitionum et declarationum de rebus fidei et morum* (Freiburg: Herder, 1963).

Des Chene, Dennis. *Life's Form: Late Aristotelian Conceptions of the Soul* (Ithaca, NY: Cornell University Press, 2000).

Physiologia: Philosophy of Nature in Descartes and the Aristotelians (Ithaca, NY: Cornell University Press, 1995).

Devisse, Jean. *Hincmar, archevêque de Reims, 845–882* (Geneva: Droz, 1975–6).

Dhanani, Alnoor. *The Physical Theory of Kalām* (Leiden: Brill, 1994).

di S. Brocardo, Nilo. "Il profilo storico di Giovanni Baconthorp," *Ephemerides Carmeliticae* 2 (1948) 431–543.

Díaz Esteban, Fernando (ed.). *Abraham Ibn Ezra y su tiempo: actas del simposio internacional* (Madrid: Asociación Espanola de Orientalistas, 1990).

Dickey, Bruce. "Adelard of Bath: An Examination Based on Heretofore Unexamined Manuscripts" (Ph.D. dissertation: University of Toronto, 1982).

Dickson, Marcel and Christiane Dickson. "Le Cardinal Robert de Courson, sa vie," *Archives d'histoire doctrinale et littéraire du moyen âge* 9 (1934) 53–142.

Dietterle, Johann. "Die *Summae confessorum (sive de casibus conscientiae)* von inhren Anfängen an bis zu Silvester Prierias (unter besonderer Berücksichtigung über den Ablass)," *Zeitschrift für Kirchengeschichte* 24 (1903) 353–74, 520–48; 25 (1904) 248–72; 26 (1905) 59–81, 350–62; 27 (1906) 70–83, 166–88, 296–310, 431–42; 28 (1907) 401–31.

Dijs, Judith. "Two Anonymous 12th-Century Tracts on Universals," *Vivarium* 28 (1990) 85–117.

Dinneen, Francis P. "'Suppositio' in Petrus Hispanus: Linguistic Theories and Models," in G. L. Bursill-Hall (ed.) *De ortu grammaticae: Studies in Memory of Jan Pinborg* (Amsterdam: Benjamins, 1990) 69–85.

Dixon, Thomas. *From Passions to Emotions: The Creation of a Secular Psychological Category* (Cambridge: Cambridge University Press, 2003).

Dod, Bernard G. "Aristoteles Latinus," in N. Kretzmann *et al.* (eds.) *The Cambridge History of Later Medieval Philosophy* (Cambridge: Cambridge University Press, 1982) 45–79.

Dodd, Tony. *The Life and Thought of Siger of Brabant, Thirteenth-Century Parisian Philosopher: An Examination of his Views on the Relationship of Philosophy and Theology* (Lewiston, NY: E. Mellen Press, 1998).

Dodds, E. R. *The Greeks and the Irrational* (Berkeley: University of California Press, 1964).

Pagan and Christian in an Age of Anxiety (Cambridge: Cambridge University Press, 1965).

Dolnikowski, Edith Wilks. *Thomas Bradwardine: A View of Time and a Vision of Eternity in Fourteenth-Century Thought* (Leiden: Brill, 1995).

Donati, Silvia. "The Anonymous Commentary on the Physics in Erfurt," *Recherches de théologie et philosophie médiévales* 72 (2005) 232–362.

"La dottrina delle dimensioni indeterminate in Egidio Romano," *Medioevo* 14 (1988) 149–233.

"Guglielmo di Clifford († 1306) e alcuni commenti anonimi ai Libri naturales del ms. Cambridge, Peterhouse, 157 (De anima, De generatione et corruptione, Meteora, De somno et vigilia, De vegetabilibus)," *Documenti e studi sulla tradizione filosofica medievale* 19 (2008) 501–618.

"Per lo studio dei commenti alla Fisica del XIII secolo. I: Commenti di probabile origine inglese degli anni 1250–1270 *ca.*," *Documenti e studi sulla tradizione filosofica medievale* 2 (1991) 361–441; 4 (1993) 25–133.

"Studi per una cronologia delle opera di Egidio Romano. I: Le opera prima del 1285 – I commenti aristotelici," *Documenti e studi sulla tradizione filosofica medievale* 1 (1990) 1–111.

Dondaine, Antoine. *Écrits de la "petite école porrétaine"* (Paris: Vrin, 1962).

"Guillaume Peyraut, vie et œuvres," *Archivum Fratrum Praedicatorum* 18 (1948) 162–236.

"Hugues Éthérien et Léon Toscan," *Archives d'histoire doctrinale et littéraire du moyen âge* 19 (1952) 67–134.

d'Onofrio, Giulio (ed.). *Lanfranco di Pavia e l'Europa del secolo XI, nel IX centenario della morte (1089–1989): atti del convegno internazionale di studi* (Rome: Herder, 1993).

d'Ors, Angel. "Petrus Hispanus O.P., Auctor Summularum," *Vivarium* 35 (1997) 21–71; 39 (2001) 209–54; 41 (2003) 249–303.

"Sobre las *obligationes* de Juan de Holanda," *Anuario filosófico* 31 (1988) 33–70.

"Sobre las *obligationes* de Richard Lavenham," *Archives d'histoire doctrinale et littéraire du moyen âge* 58 (1991) 253–78.

Dossat, Yves. *Les crises de l'inquisition toulousaine au XIIIᵉ siècle, 1233–1273* (Bordeaux: Bière, 1959).

Doucet, Victorin. "Notulae bibliographicae de quibusdam operibus Fr. Ioannis Pecham, O.F.M.," *Antonianum* 8 (1933) 307–28, 425–59.

"L'œuvre scolastique de Richard de Conington," *Archivum Franciscanum Historicum* 29 (1937) 396–442.

Douie, D. L. *Archbishop Pecham* (Oxford: Clarendon Press, 1952).

"Three Treatises on Evangelical Poverty by Fr. Richard Conyngton, Fr. Walter Chatton and an Anonymous from MS V. iii. 18 in Bishop Cosin's library, Durham," *Archivum Franciscanum Historicum* 24 (1931) 341–69.

Dowd, John D. "Matthew of Aquasparta's *De productione rerum* and its Relation to St. Thomas Aquinas and St. Bonaventure," *Franciscan Studies* 34 (1974) 34–73.

Doyle, Matthew. *Bernard of Clairvaux and the Schools: The Formation of An Intellectual Milieu in the First Half of the Twelfth Century* (Spoleto: Fondazione Centro italiano di studi sull'alto medioevo, 2005).

Draelants, Isabelle. "Un encyclopédiste méconnu du XIIIe siècle: Arnold de Saxe. Œuvres, sources, réception" (Ph.D. dissertation: Université catholique de Louvain, 2000).

"Une mise au point sur les œuvres d'Arnoldus Saxo," *Bulletin de philosophie médiévale* 34 (1992) 163–80; 35 (1993) 130–49.

Dreiling, Raymund. *Der Konzeptualismus in der Universalienlehre des Petrus Aureoli* (Münster: Aschendorff, 1913).

Dressler, Fridolin. *Petrus Damiani. Leben und Werk* (Rome: Herder, 1954).

Dronke, Peter. *Fabula: Explorations into the Uses of Myth in Medieval Platonism* (Leiden: Brill, 1974).

"The Lyrical Compositions of Philip the Chancellor," *Studi Medievali* 28 (1987) 563–92.

"Thierry of Chartres," in P. Dronke (ed.) *A History of Twelfth Century Western Philosophy* (Cambridge: Cambridge University Press, 1988) 358–85.

Women Writers of the Middle Ages (Cambridge: Cambridge University Press, 1984).

Druart, Thérèse-Anne. "Al-Farabi, Emanation, and Metaphysics," in P. Morewedge (ed.) *Neoplatonism and Islamic Thought* (Albany: State University of New York Press, 1992) 127–48.

"Al-Ghazali's Conception of the Agent in the *Tahafut* and the *Iqtisad*: Are People Really Agents?," in J. E. Montgomery (ed.) *Arabic Theology, Arabic Philosophy: From the Many to the One* (Leuven: Peeters, 2006) 425–40.

"Al-Kindi's Ethics," *Review of Metaphysics* 47 (1993) 329–57.

"Al-Razi's Conception of the Soul: Psychological Background to his Ethics," *Medieval Philosophy and Theology* 5 (1996) 245–63.

"Al-Razi's Ethics," *Medieval Philosophy and Theology* 6 (1997) 47–71.

"The Human Soul's Individuation and its Survival after the Body's Death: Avicenna on the Causal Relation between Body and Soul," *Arabic Sciences and Philosophy* 10 (2000) 259–74.

"'Shay' or 'Res' as Concomitant of 'Being' in Avicenna," *Documenti e studi sulla tradizione filosofica medievale* 12 (2001) 125–42.

D'Souza, Joachim. "William of Alnwick and the Problem of Faith and Reason," *Salesianum* 35 (1973) 425–88.

Duba, William. "Aristotle's *Metaphysics* in Peter Auriol's Commentary on the *Sentences*," *Documenti e studi sulla tradizione filosofica medievale* 12 (2001) 549–72.

"The Authenticity of Francis of Marchia's *Quodlibet*: The Testimony of Paris, BNF, Ms. lat. 16110," *Bulletin de philosophie médiévale* 49 (2007) 91–102.

"Continental Franciscan *Quodlibeta* after Scotus," in C. Schabel (ed.) *Theological Quodlibeta in the Middle Ages: The Fourteenth Century* (Leiden: Brill, 2007) 569–649.

Duba, William O. and Chris Schabel (eds.). Special issue on Gerald of Odo, *Vivarium* 47.1 (2009).

Düchting, Reinhard. *Sedulius Scottus: seine Dichtungen* (Munich: Fink, 1968).

Dufeil, Michel-Marie. *Guillaume de Saint-Amour et la polémique universitaire parisienne, 1250–1259* (Paris: Picard, 1972).

Duffy, John. "Hellenistic Philosophy in Byzantium and the Lonely Mission of Michael Psellos," in K. Ierodiakonou (ed.) *Byzantine Philosophy and its Ancient Sources* (Oxford: Clarendon Press, 2002) 139–56.

Duggan, Charles. *Twelfth-Century Decretal Collections* (London: Athlone Press, 1963).

Duhem, Pierre. *Le système du monde: histoire des doctrines cosmologiques de Platon à Copernic* (Paris: Hermann, 1913–59).

Duin, Joannes Josef. "La bibliothèque philosophique de Godefroid de Fontaines," *Estudios Lulianos* 3 (1959) 21–36, 137–60.

La doctrine de la providence dans les écrits de Siger de Brabant; textes et étude (Leuven: Institut Supérieur de Philosophie, 1954).

Dumeige, Gervais. *Richard de Saint-Victor et l'idée chrétienne de l'amour* (Paris: Presses universitaires de France, 1952).

Dümmler, Ernst (ed.). *Poetae Latini aevi Carolini* (Berlin: Weidmann, 1881–1923).

Dumont, Stephen D. "Did Duns Scotus Change his Mind on the Will?," in J. Aertsen *et al.* (eds.) *Nach der Verurteilung von 1277: Philosophie und Theologie an der Universität von Paris im letzten Viertel des 13. Jahrhunderts: Studien und Texte* (Berlin: De Gruyter, 2001) 719–94.

"Duns Scotus's Parisian Question on the Formal Distinction," *Vivarium* 43 (2005) 7–62.

"New Questions by Thomas Wylton," *Documenti e studi sulla tradizione filosofica medievale* 10 (1998) 341–81.

"The Origin of Scotus's Theory of Synchronic Contingency," *Modern Schoolman* 72 (1995) 149–67.

"Univocity of the Concept of Being in the Fourteenth Century: John Duns Scotus and William of Alnwick," *Mediaeval Studies* 49 (1987) 1–75.

"The Univocity of the Concept of Being in the Fourteenth Century: II. The *De Ente* of Peter Thomae," *Mediaeval Studies* 50 (1988) 186–256.

"William of Ware, Richard of Conington and the *Collationes Oxonienses* of John Duns Scotus," in L. Honnefelder *et al.* (eds.) *John Duns Scotus. Metaphysics and Ethics* (Leiden: Brill, 1996) 59–85.

Dunbabin, Jean. "The Commentary of John of Paris (Quidort) on the *Sentences*," in G. R. Evans (ed.) *Mediaeval Commentaries on the* Sentences *of Peter Lombard: Current Research* (Leiden: Brill, 2002) 131–47.

"Guido Vernani of Rimini's Commentary on Aristotle's Politics," *Traditio* 44 (1988) 373–88.

A Hound of God: Pierre de la Palud and the Fourteenth-Century Church (Oxford: Clarendon Press, 1991).

Duneau, Jean-François. "Quelques aspects de la pénétration de l'hellénisme dans l'empire perse sassanide (IVᵉ–VIIᵉ siècles)," in P. Gallais and Y.-J. Riou (eds.) *Mélanges offerts à René Crozet* (Poitiers: Société d'études médiévales, 1966) I: 13–22.

Dunphy, William. "Peter of Auvergne and the Twofold Efficient Cause," *Mediaeval Studies* 28 (1966) 1–21.

"The Similarities between Certain Questions of Peter of Auvergne's *Commentary on the Metaphysics* and the Anonymous *Commentary on the Physics* Attributed to Siger of Brabant," *Mediaeval Studies* 15 (1953) 159–68.

Dunyā, Sulaymān. *Al-Shaykh Muḥammad ʿAbduh bayna al-falāsifa wa-al-kalāmīyyīn* (Cairo: ʿĪsā al-Bābī al-Ḥalabī, 1958).

Durling, R. J. "Corrigenda and Addenda to Diels' Galenica, II, Codices miscellanei," *Traditio* 37 (1981) 373–81.

Dutton, Blake D. "Al-Ghazālī on Possibility and the Critique of Causality," *Medieval Philosophy and Theology* 10 (2001) 23–46.

"Nicholas of Autrecourt and William of Ockham on Atomism, Nominalism, and the Ontology of Motion," *Medieval Philosophy and Theology* 5 (1996) 63–85.

Dutton, Paul E. *The Mystery of the Missing Heresy Trial of William of Conches* (Toronto: Pontifical Institute of Mediaeval Studies, 2006).

Dutton, Paul E. and Anneli Luhtala. "Eriugena in Priscianum," *Mediaeval Studies* 56 (1994) 153–63.

Dvornik, Francis. *Early Christian and Byzantine Political Philosophy* (Washington, DC: Dumbarton Oaks, 1966).

Eardley, Peter S. "The Foundations of Freedom in Later Medieval Philosophy: Giles of Rome and his Contemporaries," *Journal of the History of Philosophy* 44 (2006) 353–76.

"The Problem of Moral Weakness, the *Propositio Magistralis*, and the Condemnation of 1277," *Mediaeval Studies* 68 (2006) 161–203.

Eastwood, Bruce S. "Invention and Reform in Latin Planetary Astronomy," in M. W. Herren *et al.* (eds.) *Latin Culture in the Eleventh Century. Proceedings of the Third International Conference on Medieval Latin Studies* (Turnhout: Brepols, 2002) I: 264–97.

The Revival of Planetary Astronomy in Carolingian and Post-Carolingian Europe (Aldershot: Ashgate, 2002).

Ebbesen, Sten. "*Animal est omnis homo*: Questions and Sophismata by Peter of Auvergne, Radulphus Brito, William Bonkes, and Others," *Cahiers de l'Institut du Moyen Age Grec et Latin* 63 (1993) 145–208.

"Boethius of Dacia: Science is a Serious Game," *Theoria* 66 (2000) 145–58.

"Can Equivocation Be Eliminated?," *Studia Mediewistyczne* 18 (1977) 103–24.

Commentators and Commentaries on Aristotle's Sophistici Elenchi: *A Study of Post-Aristotelian Ancient and Medieval Writings on Fallacies* (Leiden: Brill, 1981).

"The Dead Man is Alive," *Synthese* 40 (1979) 43–70.

"Early Supposition Theory (12th–13th century)," *Histoire Epistémologie Langage* 3 (1981) 35–48.

"George Pachymeres and the *Topics*," *Cahiers de l'Institut du Moyen Age Grec et Latin* 66 (1996) 169–85.

"The Present King of France Wears Hypothetical Shoes with Categorical Laces. Twelfth Century Writers on Well-Formedness," *Medioevo* 7 (1981) 91–113.

"Radulphus Brito on the Metaphysics," *Miscellanea Mediaevalia* 28 (2000) 450–92.

"Radulphus Brito: The Last of the Great Arts Masters or: Philosophy and Freedom," in J. A. Aertsen und A. Speer (eds.) *Geistesleben im 13. Jahrhundert* (Berlin: De Gruyter, 2000) 231–51.

"The Sophism 'Rationale est animal' by Radulphus Brito," *Cahiers de l'Institut du Moyen Age Grec et Latin* 24 (1978) 85–120.

(ed.). *Sprachtheorien in Spätantike und Mittelalter* (Tübingen: Narr, 1995).

"Talking About What Is No More: Texts by Peter of Cornwall (?), Richard of Clive, Simon of Faversham, and Radulphus Brito," *Cahiers de l'Institut du Moyen Age Grec et Latin* 55 (1987) 135–68.

"*Termini accidentales concreti*: Texts from the Late Thirteenth Century," *Cahiers de l'Institut du Moyen Age Grec et Latin* 53 (1986) 37–150.

"What Must One Have an Opinion About," *Vivarium* 30 (1992) 62–79.

Ebbesen, Sten and Jan Pinborg. "Bartholomew of Bruges and his Sophisma on the Nature of Logic," *Cahiers de l'Institut du Moyen Age Grec et Latin* 39 (1981) iii–xxvi, 1–80.

"Gennadios and Western Scholasticism: Radulphus Brito's *Ars Vetus* in Greek Translation," *Classica et Mediaevalia* 33 (1981–2) 263–319.

"Studies in the Logical Writings Attributed to Boethius de Dacia," *Cahiers de l'Institut du Moyen Age Grec et Latin* 3 (1970) 1–54.

Ebbesen, Sten and Irène Rosier-Catach. "Petrus de Alvernia + Boethius de Dacia: Syllogizantem ponendum est terminos," *Cahiers de l'Institut du Moyen Age Grec et Latin* 75 (2004) 161–218.

"Robertus Anglicus on Peter of Spain," in I. Angelelli and P. Pérez-Ilzarbe (eds.) *Medieval and Renaissance Logic in Spain* (Hildesheim: Olms, 2000) 60–95.

"Le *trivium* à la Faculté des Arts," in L. Holtz and O. Weijers (eds.) *L'enseignement des disciplines à la Faculté des Arts (Paris et Oxford, XIIIe–XVe siècles)* (Turnhout: Brepols, 1997) 98–128.

"Two Roberts and Peter of Spain," *Cahiers de l'Institut du Moyen Age Grec et Latin* 67 (1997) 200–88.

Eckermann, Willigis. *Der Physikkommentar Hugolins von Orvieto OESA: ein Beitrag zur Erkenntnislehre des spätmittelalterlichen Augustinismus* (Berlin: De Gruyter, 1972).

Schwerpunkte und Wirkungen des Sentenzenkommentars Hugolins von Orvieto O.E.S.A. (Würzburg: Augustinus, 1990).

Wort und Wirklichkeit: Das Sprachverständnis in der Theologie Gregors von Rimini und Sein Weiterwirken in der Augustinerschule (Würzburg: Augustinus, 1978).

Eckermann, Willigis and Bernd Ulrich Hucker (eds.). *Hugolin von Orvieto: Ein spätmittelalterlicher Augustinertheologe in seiner Zeit* (Cloppenburg: Runge, 1992).

Edwards, Raymond. "Themes and Personalities in *Sentence* Commentaries at Oxford in the 1330s," in G. R. Evans (ed.) *Mediaeval Commentaries on the* Sentences *of Peter Lombard: Current Research* (Leiden: Brill, 2002) 379–93.

Efros, Israel. *Studies in Medieval Jewish Philosophy* (New York: Columbia University Press, 1974).

Ehrig-Eggert, Carl. *Die Abhandlung über den Nachweis der Natur des Möglichen von Yaḥyā ibn ʿAdī (gest. 974 A.D.)* (Frankfurt: Institut für Geschichte der Arabisch-Islamischen Wissenschaften an der Johann Wolfgang Goethe-Universität, 1990).

Ehrle, Franz. "Nikolaus Trivet, sein Leben, seine *Quodlibet* und seine *Quaestiones Ordinariae*," *Beiträge zur Geschichte der Philosophie des Mittelalters*, suppl. 2 (1923) 1–63.

Der Sentenzenkommentar Peters von Candia, des Pisaner Papstes Alexanders V (Münster: Aschendorff, 1925).

"Die Spiritualen, ihr Verhältnis zum Franziskanerorden und den Fraticellen," *Archiv für Literatur- und Kirchengeschichte des Mittelalters* 1 (1885) 509–69; 2 (1886) 106–64; 3 (1887) 553–623; 4 (1888) 1–190.

Ehlers, Joachim. *Hugo von St Victor: Studien zum Geschichtsdenken und der Geschichtsschreibung des 12. Jahrhunderts* (Wiesbaden: Steiner, 1973).

Eisen, Robert. *Gersonides on Providence, Covenant, and the Jewish People* (Albany: State University of New York Press, 1995).

Eisenberg, Y. "Reason and Emotion in *Duties of the Heart*," *Daat* 7 (1981) 5–35.

El-Bizri, Nader (ed.). *Epistles of the Brethren of the Purity. The Ikhwān al Ṣafāʾ and their Rasāʾil: An Introduction* (Oxford: Oxford University Press, 2008).

Elderidge, Laurence. "Changing Concepts of Church Authority in the Later Fourteenth Century: Pierre Ceffons of Clairvaux and William of Woodford, OFM," *Revue de l'Université d'Ottawa* 48 (1978) 170–8.

Elford, Dorothy. "William of Conches," in P. Dronke (ed.) *A History of Twelfth-Century Western Philosophy* (Cambridge: Cambridge University Press, 1988) 308–27.

Elie, Hubert. *Le complexe significabile* (Paris: Vrin, 1936).

Ellard, Peter. *The Sacred Cosmos: Theological, Philosophical, and Scientific Conversations in the Twelfth-Century School of Chartres* (Scranton, PA: University of Scranton Press, 2007).

Elm, Kaspar (ed.). *Bernhard von Clairvaux: Rezeption und Wirkung im Mittelalter und in der Neuzeit* (Wiesbaden: Harrassowitz, 1994).

Elshtain, Jean Bethke (ed.). *Just War Theory* (New York: New York University Press, 1992).

Emden, A. B. *A Biographical Register of the University of Oxford to A.D. 1500* (Oxford: Clarendon Press, 1957–9).

Emery, Gilles. "Dieu, la foi et la théologie chez Durand de Saint-Pourçain," *Revue Thomiste* 99 (1999) 659–99.

"La théologie trinitaire des *Evidentiae contra Durandum* de Durandellus," *Revue Thomiste* 97 (1997) 173–218.

Emery, Kent. "Reading the World Rightly and Squarely: Bonaventure's Doctrine of the Cardinal Virtues," *Traditio* 39 (1983) 183–218.

Endres, Josef. *Honorius Augustodunensis: Beitrag zur Geschichte des geistigen Lebens im 12. Jahrhundert* (Munich: Kempten, 1906).

"Manegold von Lautenbach, 'modernorum magister magistrorum'," *Historisches Jahrbuch* 25 (1904) 168–76.

Petrus Damiani und die weltliche Wissenschaft (Münster: Aschendorff, 1910).

Endress, Gerhard. *Der arabische Aristoteles und sein Leser: Physik und Theologie im Weltbild Alberts des Grossen* (Münster: Aschendorff, 2004).

"Averrois Opera: A Bibliography of Editions and Contributions to the Text," in J. A. Aertsen and G. Endress (eds.) *Averroes and the Aristotelian Tradition: Sources, Constitution, and Reception of the Philosophy of Ibn Rushd (1126–1198)* (Leiden: Brill, 1999) 339–81.

"Building the Library of Arabic Philosophy: Platonism and Aristotelianism in the Sources of al-Kindī," in C. D'Ancona (ed.) *The Libraries of the Neoplatonists* (Leiden: Brill, 2007) 319–50.

"The Circle of al-Kindi," in G. Endress and R. Kruk (eds.) *The Ancient Tradition in Christian and Islamic Hellenism* (Leiden: Research School CNWS, 1997) 43–76.

"Grammatik und Logik: arabische Philologie und griechische Philosophie im Widerstreit," in B. Mojsisch (ed.) *Sprachphilosophie in Antike und Mittelalter* (Amsterdam: Grüner, 1986) 163–299.

"Mathematics and Philosophy in Medieval Islam," in J. P. Hogendijk and A.I. Sabra (eds.) *The Enterprise of Science in Islam* (Cambridge: Cambridge University Press, 2003) 121–76.

"Mattā b. Yūnus," in H. A. R. Gibb *et al.* (eds.) *Encyclopaedia of Islam*, 2nd edn (Leiden: Brill, 1960–2004) VI: 844–6.

Proclus Arabus: zwanzig Abschnitte aus der Institutio theologica in arabischer Übersetzung (Beirut: Orient-Institut der Deutschen Morgenländischen Gesellschaft, 1973).

"Die wissenschaftliche Literatur," in H. Gätje and W. Fischer (eds.) *Grundriss der Arabischen Philologie* (Wiesbaden: Reichert, 1987–92) II: 400–506, III: 3–152.

The Works of Yahya Ibn 'Adi: An Analytical Inventory (Wiesbaden: Reichert, 1977).

Endress, Gerhard and Dimitri Gutas. *A Greek and Arabic Lexicon: Materials for a Dictionary of the Medieval Translations from Greek into Arabic* (Leiden: Brill, 1992–).

Engels, Joseph. "Thomas Cantimpratensis redivivus," *Vivarium* 12 (1974) 124–32.

Eppenstein, Simon. *Abraham Maimuni: sein Leben und seine Schriften* (Berlin: Louis Lamm Verlag, 1914).

Eran, Amira. "Abraham Ibn Daud's Definition of Substance and Accident," *Arabic Sciences and Philosophy* 7 (1997) 228–65.

Ermatinger, Charles. "Averroism in Early Fourteenth Century Bologna," *Mediaeval Studies* 16 (1954) 35–56.

"John of Jandun in his Relations with Arts Masters and Theologians," in *Arts libéraux et philosophie au moyen âge* (Montréal: Institut d'études médiévales, 1969) 1173–84.

Ermini, Giuseppe. *I trattati della guerra e della pace di Giovanni da Legnano* (Imola, 1923).

Etzkorn, Girard. "Franciscus de Mayronis: A Newly Discovered Treatise on Intuitive and Abstractive Cognition," *Franciscan Studies* 54 (1994–97) 15–50.

"The Grades of the Form according to Roger Marston, O.F.M.," *Franziskanische Studien* 44 (1962) 418–54.

"John of Reading on the Existence and Unicity of God, Efficient and Final Causality," *Franciscan Studies* 41 (1981) 125–221.

"John Pecham, O.F.M.: A Career of Controversy," in E. B. King *et al.* (eds.) *Monks, Nuns, and Friars in Mediaeval Society* (Sewanee, TN: Press of the University of the South, 1989) 71–82.

Etzkorn, Girard and Robert Andrews. "Tortosa Cathedral 88: A 'Thomas Wylton' Manuscript and the Question on the Compatibility of Multiple Accidents in the Same Subject," *Mediaevalia Philosophica Polonorum* 32 (1994) 57–99.

Etzwiler, James P. "Baconthorpe and Latin Averroism: The Doctrine of the Unique Intellect," *Carmelus* 18 (1971) 235–92.

"John Baconthorpe, 'Prince of the Averroists'," *Franciscan Studies* 36 (1976) 148–76.

"The Nature of Theological Knowledge According to Paul of Perugia, O.Carm. (*fl.* 1344)," *Carmelus* 34 (1987) 135–75.

Evans, G. R. *Alan of Lille: The Frontiers of Theology in the Later Twelfth Century* (Cambridge: Cambridge University Press, 1983).

Anselm (London: Chapman, 1989).

Anselm and Talking about God (Oxford: Clarendon Press, 1978).

Augustine on Evil (Cambridge: Cambridge University Press, 1982).

Bernard of Clairvaux (New York: Oxford University Press, 2000).

A Concordance to the Works of Saint Anselm (Millwood, NY: Kraus, 1984).

Fifty Key Medieval Thinkers (New York: Routledge, 2002).

John Wyclif: Myth and Reality (Downers Grove, IL: InterVarsity Press, 2005).

The Language and Logic of the Bible: The Earlier Middle Ages (Cambridge: Cambridge University Press, 1984).

(ed.). *Mediaeval Commentaries on the* Sentences *of Peter Lombard* (Leiden: Brill, 2002).

The Mind of St. Bernard of Clairvaux (Oxford: Clarendon Press, 1983).

"Why the Fall of Satan?," *Recherches de théologie ancienne et médiévale* 45 (1978) 130–46.

"A Work of 'Terminist Theology'? Peter the Chanter's *De tropis loquendi* and Some Fallacies," *Vivarium* 20 (1982) 40–58.

Fabro, Cornelio. *La nozione metafisica di partecipazione secondo S. Tommaso d'Aquino*, 3rd edn (Turin: Società editrice internazionale, 1963; repr. Segni: Editrice del Verbo Incarnato, 2005).

Participation et causalité selon S. Thomas d'Aquin (Leuven: Publications universitaires, 1961).

Fages, Pierre-Henri. *Histoire de Saint Vincent Ferrier, apôtre de l'Europe*, 2nd edn (Paris: Picard, 1901).

Fairweather, E. R. (ed.). *A Scholastic Miscellany: Anselm to Occam* (Philadelphia, PA: Westminster Press, 1956).

Faix, Gerhard. *Gabriel Biel und die Brüder vom Gemeinsamen Leben: Quellen und Untersuchungen zu Verfassung und Selbstverständnis des Oberdeutschen Generalkapitels* (Tübingen: Mohr, 1999).

Fakhry, Majid. *Al-Farabi: Founder of Islamic Neoplatonism: His Life, Works and Influence* (Oxford: Oneworld, 2002).

"The Classical Islamic Arguments for the Existence of God," *Muslim World* 47 (1957) 133–45.

Ethical Theories in Islam (Leiden: Brill, 1994).

A History of Islamic Philosophy (New York: Columbia University Press, 2004).

Faral, Edmond. "Les 'Responsiones' de Guillaume de Saint-Amour," *Archives d'histoire doctrinale et littéraire du moyen âge* 25–6 (1950–1) 337–94.

Farr, William E. *John Wyclif as Legal Reformer* (Leiden: Brill, 1974).

Farthing, John. *Thomas Aquinas and Gabriel Biel: Interpretation of St. Thomas Aquinas in German Nominalism on the Eve of the Reformation* (Durham, NC: Duke University Press, 1988).

Fedele, Pio. "Aequitas Canonica," *Apollinaris* 51 (1978) 415–38.

Federici Vescovini, Graziella. *Astrologia e scienza: la crisi dell'aristotelismo sul cadere del Trecento e Biagio Pelacani da Parma* (Florence: Vallecchi, 1979).

"La classification des mathématiques d'après le prologue de l'*Expositio super Theorica Planetarum* de l'averroiste Thaddée de Parme (Bologne, 1318)," in J. Hamesse (ed.) *Manuels, programmes de cours et techniques d'enseignement dans les universités médiévales* (Louvain-la-Neuve: Institut d'études médiévales de l'Université catholique de Louvain, 1994) 137–82.

"Il commento di Angelo di Fossambrone al *De tribus praedicamentis* di Guglielmo Heytesbury," in A. Maierù (ed.) *English Logic in Italy in the 14th and 15th Centuries* (Naples: Bibliopolis, 1982) 359–74.

"L'exorde de l'*Arithmetica* de Boèce et le Commentaire de l'avérroîste Thaddée de Parme (1318)," in E. Bonnefous and A. Galonnier (eds.) *Boèce ou la chaîne des savoirs* (Leuven: Éditions de l'Institut Supérieur de Philosophie, 2003) 57–71.

(ed.). *Filosofia, scienza e astrologia nel Trecento Europeo: Biagio Pelacani Parmense* (Padua: Il Poligrafo, 1992).

Feldman, Seymour. "Abravanel on Maimonides' Critique of the Kalam," *Maimonidean Studies* 1 (1990) 5–25.

"A Debate Concerning Determinism in Late Medieval Jewish Philosophy," *Proceedings of the American Academy for Jewish Research* 51 (1984) 15–54.

"The Theory of Eternal Creation in Hasdai Crescas and Some of his Predecessors," *Viator* 11 (1980) 289–320.

Felten, Franz J. (ed.). *Hrabanus Maurus: Gelehrter, Abt von Fulda, und Erzbischof von Mainz* (Mainz: Publikationen Bistum Mainz, 2006).

Fenton, Paul. *Philosophie et exégèse dans* Le Jardin de la métaphore *de Moïse Ibn ʿEzra* (Leiden: Brill, 1997).

Ferrari, Cleophea. "Der Duft des Apfels: Abū l-Faraj ʿAbdallāh ibn aṭ-Ṭayyib und sein Kommentar zu den *Kategorien* des Aristoteles," in V. Celluprica and C. D'Ancona Costa (eds.) *Aristotele e i suoi esegeti neoplatonici* (Napoli: Bibliopolis, 2004) 85–106.

Ferrari, Sante. *I tempi, la vita, le dottrine di Pietro d'Abano: Saggio storico-filosofico* (Genoa: Tipografia R. Istituto Sordomuti, 1900).

Ferruolo, Stephen. *The Origins of the University: The Schools of Paris and their Critics 1100–1215* (Stanford, CA: Stanford University Press, 1985).

Fichtenau, Heinrich. "Magister Petrus von Wien," *Beiträge zur Mediävistik* 1 (1975) 218–38.

Fidora, Alexander. *Die Wissenschaftstheorie des Dominicus Gundissalinus: Voraussetzungen und Konsequenzen des zweiten Anfangs der aristotelischen Philosophie im 12. Jahrhundert* (Berlin: Akademie-Verlag, 2003).

Fidora, Alexander and Maria Jesus Soto Bruna. "'Gundisalvus' ou 'Dominicus Gundisalvi'? Algunas observaciones sobre un reciente articulo de Adeline Rucquoi," *Estudios eclesiasticos* 76 (2001) 467–73.

Filthaut, Ephrem. *Roland von Cremona und die Anfänge der Scholastik im Predigerorden: ein Beitrag zur Geistesgeschichte der älteren Dominikaner* (Vechta i.O.: Albertus Magnus Verlag der Dominikaner, 1936).

(ed.). *Seuse-Studien: Heinrich Seuse, Studien zum 600. Todestag, 1366–1966* (Cologne: Albertus Magnus Verlag, 1966).

Finkelstein, L. (ed.) *Rab Saadia Gaon* (New York: Arno Press, 1944; repr. 1988).

Finnegan, Mary. *The Women of Helfta: Scholars and Mystics* (Athens: University of Georgia Press, 1991).

Finnis, John. *Aquinas: Moral, Political, and Legal Theory* (Oxford: Oxford University Press, 1998).

(ed.). *Natural Law* (Aldershot: Ashgate, 1991).

Natural Law and Natural Rights (Oxford: Clarendon Press, 1979).

Fisher, John. "Hugh of St. Cher and the Development of Mediaeval Theology," *Speculum* 31 (1956) 57–69.

Fitzpatrick, Noel. "Walter Chatton on the Univocity of Being: A Reaction to Peter Aureoli and William Ockham," *Franciscan Studies* 31 (1971) 88–177.

Flasch, Kurt. *Aufklärung im Mittelalter? Die Verurteilung von 1277* (Mainz: Dieterich, 1989).

    Nikolaus von Kues: Geschichte einer Entwicklung: Vorlesungen zur Einführung in seine Philosophie (Frankfurt: Klostermann, 1998).

    (ed.). *Von Meister Dietrich zu Meister Eckhart* (Hamburg: Meiner, 1987).

Fleming, John. "The 'Collations' of William of Saint-Amour against S. Thomas," *Recherches de théologie ancienne et médiévale* 32 (1965) 132–8.

Fletcher, J. M. "The Faculty of Arts," in J. I. Catto *et al.* (eds.) *The History of the University of Oxford* (Oxford: Clarendon Press, 1984) 369–99.

Flint, V. I. J. *Honorius Augustodunensis of Regensburg* (Aldershot: Variorum, 1995).

    "The 'School of Laon': A Reconsideration," *Recherches de théologie ancienne et médiévale* 43 (1976) 89–110.

Flood, David. "Assisi's Rules and People's Needs," *Franzikanische Studien* 66 (1984) 91–104.

    Francis of Assisi and the Franciscan Movement (Quezon City, Philippines: FIA Contact Publications, 1989).

Flores, Juan Carlos. *Henry of Ghent: Metaphysics and the Trinity* (Leuven: Leuven University Press, 2006).

Fontaine, Jacques. "Education and Learning," in P. Fouracre (ed.) *The New Cambridge Medieval History*, vol. I: *c.500–c.700* (Cambridge: Cambridge University Press, 2005) 735–59.

    Isidore de Séville et la culture classique dans l'Espagne wisigothique, 2nd edn (Paris: Études Augustiniennes, 1984).

    Tradition et actualité chez Isidore de Séville (London: Variorum, 1988).

Fontaine, Resianne. "Abraham Ibn Daud's Polemics against Muslims and Christians," in B. Roggema *et al.* (eds.) *The Three Rings, Textual Studies in the Historical Trialogue of Judaism, Christianity, and Islam* (Leuven: Peeters, 2005).

    In Defence of Judaism: Abraham Ibn Daud. Sources and Structure of ha-Emunah ha-Ramah (Assen: Van Gorcum, 1990).

Forhan, Kate L. *The Political Theory of Christine de Pizan* (Aldershot: Ashgate, 2002).

Forster, Karl. *Die Verteidigung der Lehre des heiligen Thomas von der Gottesschau durch Johannes Capreolus* (Munich: Karl Zink, 1955).

Forster, Regula. *Das Geheimnis der Geheimnisse: die arabischen und deutschen Fassungen des pseudo-aristotelischen Sirr al-asrār / Secretum secretorum* (Wiesbaden: Reichert, 2006).

Fortenbaugh, William. *Aristotle on Emotion*, 2nd edn (London: Duckworth, 2003).

Fortin, John R. *Clarembald of Arras as a Boethian Commentator* (Kirksville, MO: Thomas Jefferson University Press, 1995).

Fournier, Paul. "Le cardinal Guillaume de Peyre de Godin," *Bibliothèque de l'école des chartes* 86 (1925) 100–21.

Fox, Marvin. *Interpreting Maimonides: Studies in Methodology, Metaphysics, and Moral Philosophy* (Chicago: University of Chicago Press, 1990).

Fraisse, Otfried. *Moses Ibn Tibbons Kommentar zum Hohenlied und sein poetologisch-philosophisches Programm* (Berlin: De Gruyter, 2004).

Francis, Raymond. *Natural Law and Positive Law* (Washington, DC: Catholic University of America Press, 1959).

Franco, Abel. "Avempace, Projectile Motion, and Impetus Theory," *Journal of the History of Ideas* 64 (2004) 521–46.

Frank, Daniel H. "Anger as a Vice: A Maimonidean Critique of Aristotle's Ethics," *History of Philosophy Quarterly* 7 (1990) 269–81.

"Maimonides and Medieval Jewish Aristotelianism," in D Frank and O. Leaman (eds.) *Cambridge Companion to Medieval Jewish Philosophy* (Cambridge: Cambridge University Press, 2003) 136–56.

Frank, Daniel H. and Oliver Leaman (eds.). *Cambridge Companion to Medieval Jewish Philosophy* (Cambridge: Cambridge University Press, 2003).

(eds). *History of Jewish Philosophy* (London: Routledge, 1996).

Frank, Daniel H., Oliver Leaman, and Charles Manekin (eds.). *A Reader in Jewish Philosophy* (London: Routledge, 2000).

Frank, Richard M. "The Ashʿarite Ontology I: Primary Entities," *Arabic Sciences and Philosophy* 9 (1999) 165–231.

"Attribute, Attribution, and Being: Three Islamic Views," in P. Morewedge (ed.) *Philosophies of Existence Ancient and Medieval* (New York: Fordham University Press, 1982) 258–78.

"The Autonomy of the Human Agent in the Teaching of ʿAbd al-Jabbār," *Le Muséon* 95 (1982) 323–55.

"Can God Do What Is Wrong?," in T. Rudavsky (ed.) *Divine Omniscience and Omnipotence in Medieval Philosophy: Islamic, Jewish, and Christian Perspectives* (Dordrecht: Reidel, 1985) 69–79.

Creation and the Cosmic System: al-Ghazâlî and Avicenna (Heidelberg: Carl Winter Universitätsverlag, 1992).

Al-Ghazali and the Ashʿarite School (Durham, NC: Duke University Press, 1994).

Islamic Mysticism, Theology, and Philosophy: Texts and Studies on the Development of Kalam, ed. D. Gutas (Aldershot: Ashgate, 2005).

The Metaphysics of Created Being According to Abū al-Hudhayl al-ʿAllāf: A Philosophical Study of the Earliest Kalām (Istanbul: Nederlands Historisch-Archaeologisch Instituut in het Nabije Oosten, 1966).

"The Neoplatonism of Ğahm ibn Ṣafwān," *Le Muséon* 78 (1965) 395–424.

"The Use of the Enneads by John of Scythopolis," *Le Muséon* 100 (1987) 101–8.

Frank, William. "Duns Scotus on Autonomous Freedom and Divine Co-Causality," *Medieval Philosophy and Theology* 2 (1992) 142–64.

Frank, William and Allan B. Wolter. *Duns Scotus, Metaphysician* (West Lafayette, IN: Purdue University Press, 1995).

Fransen, Gérard. *Décrétales et les collections de décrétales* (Turnhout: Brepols, 1972).

Fraser, Kyle A. "Demonstrative Science and the Science of Being qua Being," *Oxford Studies in Ancient Philosophy* 22 (2002) 43–82.

Fredborg, Karin M. "Abelard on Rhetoric," in C. J. Mews et al. (eds.) *Rhetoric and Renewal in the Latin West 1100–1540: Essays in Honour of John O. Ward* (Leiden; Brill, 2003) 55–80.

"The Commentaries on Cicero's *De Inventione* and *Rhetorica ad Herennium* by William of Champeaux," *Cahiers de l'Institut du Moyen Age Grec et Latin* 17 (1976) 1–39.

"The Dependence of Petrus Helias' *Summa super Priscianum* on William of Conches' *Glose super Priscianum*," *Cahiers de l'Institut du Moyen Age Grec et Latin* 11 (1973) 1–57.

"Petrus Helias on Rhetoric," *Cahiers de l'Institut du Moyen Age Grec et Latin* 13 (1974) 31–41.

"The Priscian Commentary from the second half of the Twelfth Century: Ms Leiden BPL 154," *Histoire Epistémologie Langage* 12 (1990) 53–68.

"The Promisimus," in S. Ebbesen and R. L. Friedman (eds.) *Medieval Analyses in Language and Cognition* (Copenhagen: Royal Academy, 1999) 191–205.

"Some Notes on the Grammar of William of Conches," *Cahiers de l'Institut du Moyen Age Grec et Latin* 37 (1980) 21–41.

"Speculative Grammar," in P. Dronke (ed.) *A History of Twelfth-Century Western Philosophy* (Cambridge: Cambridge University Press, 1988) 177–95.

"Tractatus Glosarum Prisciani in Ms. Vat. Lat. 1486," *Cahiers de l'Institut du Moyen Age Grec et Latin* 21 (1977) 27–44.

"Universal Grammar According to Some Twelfth c. Grammarians," *Historiographia Linguistica* 7 (1980) 69–83.

Fredborg Karin M. and C. H. Kneepkens. "Grammatica Porretana," *Cahiers de l'Institut du Moyen Age Grec et Latin* 57 (1988) 11–67.

Frede, Dorothea. "On Mixture and Mixables," in J. Mansfeld and F. de Haas (eds.) *Aristotle: On Generation and Corruption, Book I* (Oxford: Clarendon Press, 2004) 289–314.

Freeman, Ann. *Theodulf of Orléans: Charlemagne's Spokesman against the Second Council of Nicaea* (Aldershot: Ashgate, 2003).

Freppert, Lucan. *The Basis of Morality According to William Ockham* (Chicago: Franciscan Herald Press, 1988).

Freudenthal, Gad. "Les Sciences dans les communautés juives médiévales de Provence: leur appropriation, leur rôle," *Revue des Études Juives* 152 (1993) 29–136.

(ed.). *Studies on Gersonides: A Fourteenth-Century Jewish Philosopher-Scientist* (Leiden: Brill, 1992).

Friedländer, Michael. *Essays on the Writings of Abraham ibn Ezra* (London: Society of Hebrew Literature, 1877; repr. Jerusalem: Mitshuf, 1963).

Friedman, Russell L. "Andreas de Novocastro (*fl.* 1358) on Divine Omnipotence and the Nature of the Past: I *Sentences*, Distinction Forty Five, Question Six," *Cahiers de l'Institut du Moyen Age Grec et Latin* 64 (1994) 101–50.

"Dominican Quodlibetal Literature, *ca.* 1260–1330," in C. Schabel (ed.) *Theological Quodlibeta in the Middle Ages: The Fourteenth Century* (Leiden: Brill, 2007) 401–91.

Intellectual Traditions in the Medieval University: The Use of Philosophical Psychology in Trinitarian Theology among the Franciscans and Dominicans, 1250–1350 (Leiden: Brill, 2008).

"Peter Auriol on Intentions and Essential Predication," in S. Ebbesen and R. L. Friedman (eds.) *Medieval Analyses in Language and Cognition* (Copenhagen: Royal Danish Academy of Sciences and Letters, 1999) 415–30.

"Trinitarian Theology and Philosophical Issues: Trinitarian Texts from the Late Thirteenth and Early Fourteenth Centuries," *Cahiers de l'Institut du Moyen Age Grec et Latin* 72 (2001) 89–168.

Friedman, Russell L. and Lauge Nielsen (eds.). Special issue on Peter Auriol, *Vivarium* 38 (2000).

Friedman, Russell L. and Chris Schabel (eds.). *Francis of Marchia, Theologian and Philosopher: A Franciscan at the University of Paris in the Early Fourteenth Century* (Leiden: Brill, 2006).

"Francis of Marchia's Commentaries on the Sentences. Question List and State of Research," *Mediaeval Studies* 63 (2001) 31–106.

Frugoni, Chiara. "Female Mystics, Visions, and Iconography," in D. Bornstein and R. Rusconi (eds.) *Women and Religion in Medieval and Renaissance Italy* (Chicago: University of Chicago Press, 1996) 130–64.

Fumagalli Beonio Brocchieri, Maria Teresa. *Durando di S. Porziano. Elementi filosofici della terza redazione del 'Commento alle Sentenze'* (Florence: La Nuova Italia, 1969).

Fumagalli Beonio Brocchieri, Maria Teresa and Stefano Simonetta (eds.). *John Wyclif: logica, teologia, politica* (Florence: SISMEL, Edizioni del Galluzzo, 2003).

Furlani, Giuseppe. "Di una presunte versione araba di alcuni scritti di Porfirio e di Aristotele," *Rendiconti della R. Accademia Nazionale dei Lincei (Classe di sc. mor., stor., e filol.)* 6 (1926) 205–13.

Fussenegger, Geroldus. "'Littera septem sigillorum' contra doctrinam Petri Ioannis Olivi edita," *Archivum franciscanum historicum* 47 (1954) 45–53.

Gabbay, Dov M. and John Woods (eds.). *Handbook to the History of Logic*, vol. II (Amsterdam: Elsevier, 2008).

Gabler, Darius. *Die semantischen und syntaktischen Funktionen im Tractatus "De modis significandi sive grammatica speculativa" des Thomas von Erfurt: die Probleme der mittelalterlichen Semiotik* (Bern: Lang, 1987).

Gabriel, Astrik. *The Educational Ideas of Vincent of Beauvais* (Notre Dame, IN: Mediaeval Institute, University of Notre Dame, 1956).

Vinzenz von Beauvais, ein mittelalterlicher Erzieher (Frankfurt: Knecht, 1967).

Gabrieli, Francesco. "L'opera di Ibn al-Muqaffaʿ," *Rivista degli Studi Orientali* 13 (1931–2) 197–247.

Gál, Gedeon. "Gulielmi de Ware, O.F.M. doctrina philosophica per summa capita proposita," *Franciscan Studies* 14 (1954) 155–80, 265–92.

"Opiniones Richardi Rufi Cornubiensis a Censore Reprobatae," *Franciscan Studies* 35 (1975) 136–93.

"Petrus Thomae's Proof for the Existence of God," *Franciscan Studies* 56 (1998) 115–51.

"Quaestio Ioannis de Reading de necessitate specierum intelligibilium: defensio doctrinae Scoti," *Franciscan Studies* 29 (1969) 66–156.

"Viae ad exsistentiam Dei probandum in doctrina Richari Rufi," *Franziskanische Studien* 38 (1956) 177–202.

Gál, Gedeon and Rega Wood. "Richard Brinkley and his *Summa logicae*," *Franciscan Studies* 40 (1980) 59–101.

Gallagher, Clarence. *Canon Law and the Christian Community: The Role of Law in the* Summa aurea *of Cardinal Hostiensis* (Rome: Università Gregoriana, 1978).

Gallagher, David M. "Free Choice and Free Judgment in Thomas Aquinas," *Archiv für Geschichte der Philosophie* 76 (1994) 247–77.

Galle, Griet. "A Comprehensive Bibliography on Peter of Auvergne," *Bulletin de philosophie médiévale* 42 (2000) 53–79; 47 (2005) 87–96.

"Peter of Auvergne on the Unicity of the World," *Recherches de théologie ancienne et médiévale* 68 (2001) 111–41.

"Peter of Auvergne's Question as to Whether or Not the Heaven is Generated and Perishable," in J. Aertsen *et al.* (eds.) *Nach der Verurteilung von 1277: Philosophie und Theologie an der Universität von Paris im letzten Viertel des 13. Jahrhunderts: Studien und Texte* (Berlin: De Gruyter, 2001) 535–76.

Galonnier, Alain. *Boèce. Opuscula sacra* (Leuven: Peeters, 2007).

Galston, Miriam. *Politics and Excellence: The Political Philosophy of Alfarabi* (Princeton, NJ: Princeton University Press, 1990).

Gambra, José Miguel. "El compromiso de existencia y la teoría de la predicación en la obra de Gualterio Burley," *Archives d'histoire doctrinale et littéraire du moyen âge* 63 (1996) 139–70.

Gammersbach, Suitbert. *Gilbert von Poitiers und seine Prozesse im Urteil der Zeitgenossen* (Cologne: Böhlau, 1959).

Ganz, David. "The Debate on Predestination," in M. T. Gibson and J. L. Nelson (eds.) *Charles the Bald: Court and Kingdom*, 2nd edn (Aldershot: Variorum, 1990) 283–302.

"Theology and the Organisation of Thought," in R. McKitterick (ed.) *The New Cambridge Medieval History*, vol. II: *c. 700– c. 900* (Cambridge: Cambridge University Press, 1995) 758–85.

Garber, Daniel. "Defending Aristotle/Defending Society in Early 17th C Paris," in C. Zittel and W. Detel (eds.) *Wissensideale und Wissenskulturen in der frühen Neuzeit* (Berlin: Akademie-Verlag, 2002) 135–60.

Descartes Embodied (Cambridge: Cambridge University Press, 2001).

Descartes' Metaphysical Physics (Chicago: University of Chicago Press, 1992).

García Lescún, Eliseo. *La teología trinitaria de Gregorio de Rimini: Contribución a la historia de la escolástica tardía* (Burgos: Ediciones Aldecos, 1970).

Garcías Palou, Sebastián. *Ramon Llull y el Islam* (Palma de Mallorca: Gráficas Planisi, 1981).

Garnett, George. *Marsilius of Padua and 'The Truth of History'* (Oxford: Oxford University Press, 2006).

Gaskin, Richard. "Peter Damian on Divine Power and the Contingency of the Past," *British Journal for the History of Philosophy* 5 (1997) 229–47.

Gaudemet, Jean. *Le Mariage en Occident: les mœurs et le droit* (Paris: Cerf, 1987).

Gaughan, William. *The Social Theories of Saint Antoninus from the Summa Theologica* (Washington, DC: Catholic University of America Press, 1951).

Gauthier, Léon. *Ibn Thofäil, sa vie, ses œuvres* (Paris: Leroux, 1909; repr. Paris: Vrin, 1983).

Gauthier, René-Antoine. "Notes sur les débuts (1225–1240) du premier 'averroïsme'," *Revue des sciences philosophiques et théologiques* 66 (1982) 322–73.

"Notes sur Siger de Brabant," *Revue des sciences philosophiques et théologiques* 67 (1983) 201–32; 68 (1984) 3–49.

"Les 'Questiones supra librum Ethicorum' de Pierre d'Auvergne," *Revue du Moyen Age Latin* 20 (1964) 233–60.

Gauvard, Claude, Alain de Libera, and Michel Zink (eds.). *Dictionnaire du Moyen Age* (Paris: Presses universitaires de France, 2002).

Geach, Peter. "Assertion," *Philosophical Review* 69 (1960) 221–5.

Geanakoplos, Deno J. "Theodore Gaza, a Byzantine Scholar of the Palaeologan 'Renaissance' in the Italian Renaissance," in *Constantinople and the West* (Madison: University of Wisconsin Press, 1989) 68–90.

Geiger, Louis-Bertrand. *La participation dans la philosophie de S. Thomas d'Aquin* (Paris: Vrin, 1942; 2nd edn 1953).

Gelber, Hester Goodenough. "Eternal Questions: The Dominican Hugh of Lawton on the Eternity of the World," in M. Asztalos *et al.* (eds.) *Knowledge and the Sciences in Medieval Philosophy: Proceedings of the Eighth International Congress of Medieval Philosophy* (Helsinki: Yliopistopaino, 1990) III: 71–8.

"I Cannot Tell a Lie: Hugh of Lawton's Critique of William of Ockham on Mental Language," *Franciscan Studies* 44 (1984) 141–79.

It Could Have Been Otherwise: Contingency and Necessity in Dominican Theology at Oxford 1300–1350 (Leiden: Brill, 2004).

"Logic and the Trinity: A Clash of Values in Scholastic Thought, 1300–1335" (Ph.D. dissertation: University of Wisconsin, 1974).

"Ockham's Early Influence: A Question about Predestination and Foreknowledge by Arnold of Strelley, O.P.," *Archives d'histoire doctrinale et littéraire du moyen âge* 55 (1988) 271–89.

Gendreau, Bernard. "The Quest for Certainty in Bonaventure," *Franciscan Studies* 21 (1961) 104–227.

Genest, Jean-François. "Aux origines d'une casuistique. La révélation des futurs contingents d'après la lecture de Richard Fitzralph sur les *Sentences*," *Archives d'histoire doctrinale et littéraire du moyen âge* 69 (2002) 239–98.

"Contingence et révélation des futurs: la *quaestio biblica* de Richard FitzRalph," in J. Jolivet *et al.* (eds.) *Lectionum varietates: hommage à Paul Vignaux* (Paris: Vrin, 1991) 199–246.

"Pierre de Ceffons et l'hypothèse du Dieu trompeur," in Z. Kaluza and P. Vignaux (eds.) *Preuve et raisons à l'Université de Paris: logique, ontologie et théologie au XIVe siècle* (Paris: Vrin, 1984) 197–214.

Prédétermination et liberté créé à Oxford au XIVe siècle: Buckingham contra Bradwardine (Paris: Vrin, 1992).

Genest, Jean-François and Katherine Tachau. "La lecture de Thomas Bradwardine sur les Sentences," *Archives d'histoire doctrinale et littéraire du moyen âge* 57 (1990) 301–6.

Gensler, Marek. "Catalogue of Works by or Ascribed to Antonius Andreae," *Mediaevalia Philosophica Polonorum* 31 (1992) 149–50.

"The Concept of the Individual in the *Sentences* Commentary of Antonius Andreae," in J. Aertsen and A. Speer (eds.) *Individuum und Individualität im Mittelalter* (Berlin: De Gruyter, 1996) 305–12.

George, Robert (ed.). *Natural Law* (Aldershot: Ashgate, 2003).

Georgiopoulou, Sophia. "Theodore II Dukas Laskaris (1222–1258) as an Author and an Intellectual of the XIIIth Century" (Ph.D. dissertation: Harvard University, 1990).

Georr, Khalil. *Les Catégories d'Aristote dans leurs versions syro-arabes* (Beirut: Institut français de Damas, 1948).

Germann, Nadja. *De temporum ratione: Quadrivium und Gotteserkenntnis am Beispiel Abbos von Fleury und Hermanns von Reichenau* (Leiden: Brill, 2006).

"Zwischen *veritas naturae* und *fides historiae*. Zeit und Dauer bei Abbo von Fleury," in A. Speer (ed.) *Das Sein der Dauer* (*Miscellanea Mediaevalia* 34) (Berlin: De Gruyter, 2008) 171–95.

Gersh, Stephen. *Middle Platonism and Neoplatonism: The Latin Tradition* (Notre Dame, IN: University of Notre Dame Press, 1986).

Gerwing, Manfred. *Vom Ende der Zeit: der Traktat des Arnald von Villanova über die Ankunft des Antichrist in der akademischen Auseinandersetzung zu Beginn des 14. Jahrhunderts* (Münster: Aschendorff, 1996).

Gewirth, Alan. *Marsilius of Padua and Medieval Political Philosophy* (New York: Columbia University Press, 1951).

"Republicanism and Absolutism in the Thought of Marsilius of Padua," *Medioevo* 5 (1979) 23–48.

Geyer, Bernhard. *Die Albert dem Grossen zugeschriebene* Summa naturalium (Philosophia pauperum)*: Texte und Untersuchungen* (Münster: Aschendorff, 1938).

Ghersetti, Antonella. *Il Kitāb Arisṭāṭalīs al-faylasūf nella traduzione di Ḥunayn b. Isḥāq* (Freiburg: Herder, 1999).

Ghisalberti, Alberto M. (ed.). *Dizionario biografico degli Italiani* (Rome: Istituto della Enciclopedia Italiana, 1960–).

Ghosh, Kantik. *The Wycliffite Heresy* (Cambridge: Cambridge University Press, 2001).

Gianazza, Egidio and Giorgio D'Ilario. *La vita e le opere di Giovanni da Legnano (sec. XIV)* (Legnano: Landoni, 1983).

Gibb, H. A. R. *et al.* (eds.). *Encyclopaedia of Islam*, 2nd edn (Leiden: Brill, 1960–2004).

Gibson, Margaret. "The Collected Works on Priscian: The Printed Editions 1470–1859," *Studi Medievali* 18 (1979) 249–60.

"The Early Scholastic Glosule to Priscian, *Institutiones Grammaticae*: The Text and its Influence," *Studi Medievali* 1 (1979) 35–54.

Lanfranc of Bec (Oxford: Clarendon Press, 1978).

Gieben, Servus. "Bibliographia Oliviana (1885–1967)," *Collectanea Franciscana* 38 (1968) 167–95.

"Bibliographia Universa Roberti Grosseteste ab an. 1473 ad an. 1969," *Collectanea Franciscana* 39 (1969) 362–418.

"Four Chapters on Philosophical Errors from the *Rudimentum Doctrinae* of Gilbert of Tournai," *Vivarium* 1 (1963) 141–66.

"Robertus Grosseteste: Bibliographia 1970–91," in J. McEvoy (ed.) *Robert Grosseteste: New Perspectives on his Thought and Scholarship* (Turnhout: Brepols, 1995).

Giet, Stanislas. "La doctrine de l'appropriation des biens chez quelques-uns des pères," *Recherches de science religieuse* 35 (1948) 55–91.

Giffen, Lois. *Theory of Profane Love among the Arabs* (New York: New York University Press, 1971).

Gilbert, Neal. "Ockham, Wyclif, and the 'Via Moderna'," *Miscellanea Mediaevalia* 9 (1974) 85–125.

Gillespie, Richard. "Robert Holcot's Quodlibeta," *Traditio* 27 (1971) 480–90.

Gillespie, Vincent. "*Doctrina* and *Predicacio*: The Design and Function of Some Pastoral Manuals," *Leeds Studies in English* (1980) 36–50.

Gillet, Martin Stanislas. *Beatus Innocentius PP. V (Petrus de Tarantasia O.P.): Studia et documenta* (Rome: Ad S. Sabinae, 1953).

Gillispie, Charles C. (ed.). *Dictionary of Scientific Biography* (New York: Scribner, 1970–80).

Gilson, Étienne. "Avicenne en occident au moyen-âge," *Archives d'histoire doctrinale et littéraire du moyen âge* 36 (1969) 89–121.

Dante and Philosophy, ed. D. Moore (London: Vrin, 1949).

History of Christian Philosophy in the Middle Ages (New York: Random House, 1955).

The Mystical Theology of St. Bernard, ed. A. H. C. Downes (New York: Sheed and Ward, 1940; repr. Kalamazoo, MI: Cistercian Publications, 1990).

"La notion d'existence chez Guillaume d'Auvergne," *Archives d'histoire doctrinale et littéraire du moyen âge* 15 (1946) 55–91.

The Philosophy of St. Bonaventure, tr. I. Trethowan and F. Sheed (Paterson, NJ: St. Anthony Guild, 1965).

"Pourquoi saint Thomas a critiqué saint Augustin," *Archives d'histoire doctrinale et littéraire du moyen âge* 1 (1926–7) 5–127.

"Roger Marston, un cas d'augustinisme avicennisant," *Archives d'histoire doctrinale et littéraire du moyen âge* 8 (1933) 37–42.

"Les sources gréco-arabes de l'augustinisme avicennisant," *Archives d'histoire doctrinale et littéraire du moyen âge* 4 (1929–30) 5–149.

Le thomisme: introduction au système de Saint Thomas d'Aquin (Strasbourg: Vix, 1919; 6th edn Paris: Vrin, 1983).

Gil-Sotres, Pedro. "Modelo teórico y observación clínica: las pasiones del alma en la psicología medica medieval," in *Comprendre et maîtriser la nature au Moyen Age: Mélanges d'histoire des sciences offerts à Guy Beaujouan* (Geneva: Droz, 1994) 181–204.

Gimaret, Daniel. *La doctrine d'al-Ashʿarī* (Paris: Cerf, 1990).

"Matériaux pour une bibliographie des Ǧubbāʾī," *Journal asiatique* 264 (1976) 277–332.

"Muʿtazila," in P. Bearman *et al.* (eds.) *Encyclopaedia of Islam*, new edn (Leiden: Brill Online, 1993) VII: 783–93.

"La théorie des aḥwāl d'Abū Hāšim Al-Ǧubbāʾī," *Journal asiatique* 258 (1970) 47–86.

Giocarinis, Kimon. "Eustratios of Nicaea's Defence of the Doctrine of Ideas," *Franciscan Studies* 24 (1964) 159–204.

Girolimon, Michael T. "Hugh of St Victor's *De sacramentis Christianae fidei*," *Journal of Religious History* 18 (1994) 127–38.

Glasner, Ruth. "Levi ben Gershom and the Study of Ibn Rushd in the Fourteenth Century," *Jewish Quarterly Review* 86 (1995) 51–90.

Glauche, Günter. *Schullektüre im Mittelalter: Entstehung und Wandlungen des Lektürekanons bis 1200 nach den Quellen dargestellt* (Munich: Arbeo-Gesellschaft, 1970).

Glorieux, Palémon. "Le *De gradibus formarum* de Guillaume de Falgar, OFM," *Recherches de théologie ancienne et médiévale* 24 (1957) 296–319.

"Jean Quidort et la distinction réelle de l'essence et de l'existence," *Recherches de théologie ancienne et médiévale* 18 (1951) 151–7.

La littérature quodlibétique de 1260 à 1320 (Paris: Vrin, 1925–35).

"Maîtres franciscains de Paris: Fr. Eustache," *La France Franciscaine* 13 (1930) 125–71.

"Peut-on identifier P. de Ang.?," *Recherches de théologie ancienne et médiévale* 27 (1960) 148–53.

Répertoire des maîtres en théologie de Paris au XIIIᵉ siècle (Paris: Vrin, 1933).

Gnädinger, Louise. *Johannes Tauler, Lebenswelt und mystische Lehre* (Munich: Beck, 1993).

Godart, G. C. "'Philosophy' or 'Religion'? The Confrontation with Foreign Categories in Late Nineteenth-Century Japan," *Journal of the History of Ideas* 69 (2008) 71–91.

Goddu, André. *The Physics of William of Ockham* (Leiden: Brill, 1984).

Goering, Joseph. "The Internal Forum and the Literature of Penance and Confession," *Traditio* 59 (2004) 175–227.

"Robert Grosseteste at the Papal Curia," in J. Brown and W. Stoneman (eds.) *A Distinct Voice: Medieval Studies in Honor of Leonard E. Boyle O.P.* (Notre Dame, IN: University of Notre Dame Press, 1997) 253–76.

William de Montibus (c. 1140–1213): The Schools and the Literature of Pastoral Care (Toronto: Pontifical Institute of Medieval Studies, 1992).

Goitein, Shlomo Dov. "Abraham Maimonides and his Pietist Circle," in A. Altmann (ed.) *Jewish Medieval and Renaissance Studies* (Cambridge, MA: Harvard University Press, 1967) 145–64.

Goldstein, B. R. "Astronomy and Astrology in the Works of Abraham ibn Ezra," *Arabic Sciences and Philosophy* 6 (1996) 9–21.

Gómez Caffarena, José. *Ser participado y ser subsistente e la metafísica de Enrique de Gante* (Rome: Pontificia Università Gregoriana, 1958).

Gómez-Lobo, Alfonso. "Aristotle's First Philosophy and the Principles of Particular Disciplines," *Zeitschrift für philosophische Forschung* 32 (1978) 183–94.

Gondras, Alexandre Jean. "Un commentaire avignonnais sur le *Liber de sex principiis* attribué à 'Maître Vital'," *Archives d'histoire doctrinale et littéraire du moyen âge* 42 (1975) 196–317.

"Guillaume de Falegar. Œuvre inédites," *Archives d'histoire doctrinale et littéraire du moyen âge* 39 (1972) 185–288.

Gonsette, J. *Pierre Damien et la culture profane* (Leuven: Publications universitaires, 1956).

Goodman, Lenn E. *Avicenna* (London: Routledge, 1992; rev. edn Ithaca, NY: Cornell University Press, 2006).

"Bahya on the Antinomy of Free Will and Predestination," *Journal of the History of Ideas* 44 (1983) 115–30.

God of Abraham (New York: Oxford University Press, 1996).

Islamic Humanism (New York: Oxford University Press, 2003).

(ed.). *Neoplatonism and Jewish Thought* (Albany, NY: State University of New York Press, 1992).

Rambam: Readings in the Philosophy of Moses Maimonides (New York: Viking, 1976).

"Rāzī vs Rāzī: Philosophy in the Majlis," in H. Lazarus-Yafeh *et al.* (eds.) *The Majlis: Interreligious Encounters in Medieval Islam* (Wiesbaden: Harrassowitz, 1999) 84–107.

"Razi's Myth of the Fall of the Soul: Its Function in his Philosophy," in G. Hourani (ed.) *Essays in Islamic Philosophy and Science* (Albany, NY: State University of New York Press, 1975) 25–40.

"Razi's Psychology," *Philosophical Forum* 4 (1972) 26–48.

"Saadiah Gaon's Interpretive Technique in Translating the Book of Job," in *Translating Scripture* (*Jewish Quarterly Review* supplement) (Philadelphia, PA: Annenberg Research Institute, 1990) 47–76.

Goris, Harm. *Free Creatures of an Eternal God. Thomas Aquinas on God's Infallible Foreknowledge and Irresistible Will* (Leuven: Peeters, 1996).

Goris, Wouter. "La critique de Richard de Conington par Robert de Walsingham," *Archives d'histoire doctrinale et littéraire du moyen âge* 67 (2000) 269–93.

Einheit als Prinzip und Ziel: Versuch über die Einheitsmetaphysik des Opus tripartitum *Meister Eckharts* (Leiden: Brill, 1997).

"Implicit Knowledge – Being as First Known in Peter of Oriel," *Recherches de théologie et philosophie médiévales* 69 (2002) 33–65.

"Die Kritik des Bernhard von Trilia an der Lehre von Gott als Ersterkanntem: Einleitung und Textausgabe," *Recherches de théologie et philosophie médiévales* 65 (1998) 248–319.

Goris, Wouter and Martin Pickavé. "Die 'Lectura Thomasina' des Guilelmus Petri de Godino (*ca.* 1260–1336)," in J. Hamesse (ed.) *Roma, magistra mundi: itineraria culturae medievalis: mélanges offerts au Père L.E. Boyle à l'occasion de son 75ᵉ anniversaire* (Louvain-la-Neuve: Fédération des instituts d'études médiévales, 1998) 83–109.

Gossiaux, Mark D. "James of Viterbo and the Late Thirteenth-Century Debate Concerning the Reality of the Possibles," *Recherches de théologie et philosophie médiévales* 74 (2007) 483–522.

"James of Viterbo on the Relationship between Essence and Existence," *Augustiniana* 49 (1999) 73–107.

Gössmann, Elisabeth. "Hildegard of Bingen," in M. E. Waithe (ed.) *A History of Women Philosophers*, vol. II (Dordrecht: Kluwer, 1989) 27–65.

Metaphysik und Heilsgeschichte: eine theologische Untersuchung der Summa Halesiana (Munich: Hueber, 1964).

Goulet, Richard. *Dictionnaire des philosophes antiques* (Paris: Éditions du Centre national de la recherche scientifique, 1999–).

Gouron, André. "Sur les sources civilistes et la datation des Sommes de Rufin e d'Étienne de Tournai," *Bulletin of Medieval Canon Law*, n.s. 16 (1986) 55–70.

Goy, Rudolf. *Die Überlieferung der Werke Hugos von St Viktor* (Stuttgart: Hiersemann, 1976).

Grabmann, Martin. *Die Aristoteleskommentare des Simon von Faversham: handschriftliche Mitteilungen* (Munich: Bayerische Akademie der Wissenschaften, 1933).

"Die Aristoteleskommentatoren Adam von Bocfeld und Adam von Bouchermefort: die Anfänge der Erklärung des 'neuen Aristotel' in England," *Mittelalterliches Geistesleben* (1936) 138–82, 613–16.

Gentile da Cingoli, ein italienischer Aristoteleserklärer aus der Zeit Dantes (Munich: Verlag der Bayerischen Akademie der Wissenschaften, 1941).

Guglielmo di Moerbeke O.P. il traduttore delle opere di Aristotele (Rome: Pontificia Università Gregoriana, 1946).

"Des heiligen Augustinus *Quaestio De ideis* (*De diversis quaestionibus* LXXXIII, qu. 46) in ihrer inhaltlichen Bedeutung und mittelalterlichen Weiterwirkung," in M. Grabmann (ed.) *Mittelalterliches Geistesleben* (Munich: Hueber, 1936) II: 25–34.

"Jakob von Douai, ein Aristoteleskommentator zur Zeit des hl. Thomas von Aquin und des Siger von Brabant," in M. A. Pelzer (ed.) *Mélanges Auguste Pelzer: études d'histoire littéraire et doctrinale de la scolastique médiévale offerts à Mgr. Auguste Pelzer à l'occasion de son soixante-dixième anniversaire* (Leuven: Éditions de l'Institut Supérieur de Philosophie, 1947) 389–413.

"Johannes Capreolus O.P., der *Princeps Thomistarum* (†1444), und seine Stellung in der Geschichte der Thomistenschule," in *Mittelalterliches Geistesleben: Abhandlungen zur Geschichte der Scholastik und Mystik* (Munich: Hueber, 1956) III: 370–410.

"Kardinal Guilelmus Petri O.P. († 1336) und seine Lectura Thomasina," *Divus Thomas* 4 (1926) 385–402.

"Der *Liber de exemplis naturalibus* des Franziskanertheologen Servasanctus," *Franziskanische Studien* 7 (1920) 85–117.

"Die logischen Schriften des Nikolaus von Paris und ihre Stellung in den aristotelischen Bewegung des XIII. Jahrhunderts," in M. Grabmann (ed.) *Mittelalterliches Geistesleben* (Munich: Hueber, 1926) I: 222–48.

"Die Metaphysik des Thomas von York," *Studien zur Geschichte der Philosophie: Festgabe zum 60 Geburtstag Clemens Baeumker* (Münster: Aschendorff, 1913) 181–93.

"Die *Philosophia pauperum* und ihr Verfasser Albert von Orlamünde," *Beiträge zur Geschichte der Philosophie des Mittelalters* 20 (1918) 1–29.

Die philosophische und theologische Erkenntnislehre des Kardinals Matthaeus von Aquasparta (Vienna: Mayer, 1906).

"Quaestiones tres Fratris Ferrarii Catalani, O.Pr. doctrinam sancti Augustini illustrantes ex codice Parisiensi editae," *Estudis Franciscans* 42 (1930) 382–90.

Die Sophismataliteratur des 12. und 13. Jahrhunderts mit Textausgabe eines Sophisma des Boethius von Dacien (Münster: Aschendorff, 1940).

"Studien über den Averroisten Taddeo da Parma," *Mittelalterliches Geistesleben*, vol. II (1936) 239–260.

"Studien über Ulrich von Strassburg," in *Mittelalterliches Geistesleben: Abhandlungen zur Geschichte der Scholastik und Mystik* (Munich: Hueber, 1926) I: 147–221.

"Studien zu Johannes Quidort von Paris, O.Pr.," in *Sitzungsberichte der Bayerischen Akademie der Wissenschaften zu München* (Munich: Die Akademie, 1922) [repr. in M. Grabmann, *Gesammelte Akademieabhandlungen* (Paderborn: Schöningh, 1979) I: 69–128].

Thomas von Erfurt und die Sprachlogik des mittelalterlichen Aristotelismus (Munich: Hueber, 1943).

Gracia, Jorge J. E. "The Agent and Possible Intellects in Gonsalvus Hispanus' Question XIII," *Franciscan Studies* 20 (1969) 5–36.

Gracia, Jorge J. E. and Timothy B. Noone (eds.). *A Companion to Philosophy in the Middle Ages* (Oxford: Blackwell, 2003).

Graetz, Heinrich. "The Significance of Judaism for the Present and the Future," *Jewish Quarterly Review* 1 (1888) 4–13.

Graf, Georg. *Geschichte der christlichen arabischen Literatur* (Vatican: Biblioteca Apostolica Vaticana, 1944–).

Grant, Edward. *The Foundations of Modern Science in the Middle Ages: Their Religious, Institutional and Intellectual Contexts* (Cambridge: Cambridge University Press, 1996).

God and Reason in the Middle Ages (Cambridge: Cambridge University Press, 2001).

"Jean Buridan and Nicole Oresme on Natural Knowledge," *Vivarium* 31 (1993) 84–105.

"The Medieval Doctrine of Place: Some Fundamental Problems and Solutions," in A. Maierù and A. Paravicini-Bagliani (eds.) *Studi sul XIV secolo in memoria di Anneliese Maier* (Rome: Edizioni di Storia e Letteratura, 1981) 57–79.

Studies in Medieval Science and Natural Philosophy (London: Variorum Reprints, 1981).

Grass, Rainer. *Schlußfolgerungslehre in Erfurter Schulen des 14. Jahrhunderts: eine Untersuchung der Konsequentientraktate von Thomas Maulfelt und Albert von Sachsen in Gegenüberstellung mit einer modernen Position* (Amsterdam: Grüner, 2003).

Grassi, Onorato. *Intuizione e significato: Adam Wodeham e il problema della conoscenza nel XIV secolo* (Milan: Jaca, 1986).

"Le tesi di Robert Holcot sul valore non scientifico della conoscenza teologica," *Rivista di filosofia neo-scolastica* 71 (1979) 49–79.

Green-Pedersen, Niels. "Bradwardine (?) on Ockham's Doctrine of Consequences: An Edition," *Cahiers de l'Institut du Moyen Age Grec et Latin* 42 (1982) 85–150.

"Early British Treatises on Consequences," in P. O. Lewry (ed.) *The Rise of British Logic* (Toronto: Pontifical Institute of Mediaeval Studies, 1985) 285–307.

"William of Champeaux on Boethius' Topics according to Orléans Bibl. Mun. 266," *Cahiers de l'Institut du Moyen Age Grec et Latin* 13 (1974) 13–30.

Gregory, Tullio. *Anima mundi: la filosofia di Guglielmo di Conches e la Scuola di Chartres* (Florence: Sansoni, 1955).

"Platone e Aristotele nello Speculum di Enrico Bate di Malines," *Studi Medievali* 3 (1961) 302–19.

"The Platonic Inheritance," in P. Dronke (ed.) *A History of Twelfth-Century Western Philosophy* (Cambridge: Cambridge University Press, 1988) 54–80.

Greive, Hermann. *Studien zum jüdischen Neuplatonismus: die Religionsphilosophie des Abraham Ibn Ezra* (Berlin: De Gruyter, 1973).

Grellard, Christophe. *Croire et savoir: les principes de la connaissance selon Nicolas d'Autrécourt* (Paris: Vrin, 2005).

Griffel, Frank. "Al-Ghazālī's Concept of Prophecy: The Introduction of Avicennan Psychology into Ash'arite Theology," *Arabic Sciences and Philosophy* 14 (2004) 101–44.

Al-Ghazālī's Philosophical Theology (Oxford: Oxford University Press, 2009).

Apostasie und Toleranz im Islam: die Entwicklung zu al-Gazālīs Urteil gegen die Philosophen und die Reaktionen der Philosophen (Leiden: Brill, 2000).

"MS London, British Library Or. 3126: An Unknown Work by al-Ghazālī on Metaphysics and Philosophical Theology," *Journal of Islamic Studies* 17 (2006) 1–42.

Griffith, Sidney H. *The Church in the Shadow of the Mosque: Christians and Muslims in the World of Islam* (Princeton, NJ: Princeton University Press, 2008).

Theodore Abu Qurrah: The Intellectual Profile of an Arab-Christian Writer of the First Abbasid Century (Tel Aviv: Tel Aviv University, 1992).

Grignaschi, Marc. "Il pensiero politico e religioso di Giovanni di Jandun," *Bollettino del'Istituto Storico Italiano per il Medioevo e Archivio Muratoriano* 70 (1958) 425–96.

"Les traductions latines des ouvrages de la logique arabe et l'abrégé d'Alfarabi," *Archives d'histoire doctrinale et littéraire du moyen âge* 39 (1972) 41–107.

Grondeux, Anne. *Le Graecismus d'Evrard de Béthune à travers ses gloses: entre grammaire positive et grammaire spéculative du XIIIᵉ au XIVᵉ siècle* (Turnhout: Brepols, 2000).

"Prologue, *prohemium*, glose du *prohemium* dans les manuscrits du Graecismus d'Evrard de Béthune," in *Les prologues médiévaux (Actes du colloque organisé par l'Academia Belgica et l'Ecole française de Rome, Rome 26–28 mars 1998)* (Turnhout: Brepols, 2000) 323–44.

"Sophismata Anonymi Avenionensis," *Cahiers de l'Institut du Moyen Age Grec et Latin* 73 (2002) 41–59.

"*Turba ruunt* (Ov. 'Her.' 1, 88?): Histoire d'un exemple grammatical," *Archivum Latinitatis Medii Aevi* 61 (2003) 175–222.

Grondeux, Anne and Elsa Marguin. "L'œuvre grammaticale de Jean de Garlande (*ca.* 1195–1272?), auteur, réviseur et glosateur. Un bilan," *Histoire Epistémologie Langage* 21 (1999) 133–63.

Grondeux, Anne and Irène Rosier-Catach. "Synthèse grammaticale," in I. Rosier-Catach (ed.) *Les Glosulae super Priscianum, Guillaume de Champeaux, Abelard: arts du langage et théologie aux confins des XIe/XIIe siècles* (Turnhout: Brepols, forthcoming).

Groppo, Guiseppe. "La teologia e il suo 'subiectum' secundo il prologo del commento alle sentenze di Pietro de Palude, O.P. († 1342)," *Salesianum* 23 (1961) 219–316.

Gross, Julius. "Die Erbsündenlehre Manegolds von Lautenbach nach seinem Psalmen-Kommentar," *Zeitschrift für Kirchengeschichte* 71 (1960) 253–61.

Gross-Diaz, Theresa. *The Psalms Commentary of Gilbert of Poitiers: From lectio divina to the Lecture Room* (Leiden: Brill, 1996).

Gründel, Johannes. *Die Lehre des Radulfus Ardens von den Berstandestugenden auf dem Hintergund seinen Seelenlehre* (Munich: Schöningh, 1976).

"L'œuvre encyclopédique de Raoul Ardent, le *Speculum universale*," *Cahiers d'histoire mondiale* 9 (1966) 553–70.

"Die Sentenzenglose des Johannes Pagus (circa 1243–1245) in Padua, Bibl. Ant. 139," *Münchener Theologische Zeitschrift* 9 (1958) 171–85.

Grundmann, Herbert. "Die Frauen und die Literatur im Mittelalter: ein Beitrag zur Frage nach der Entstehung des Schrifttums in der Volkssprache," *Archiv für Kulturgeschichte* 26 (1936) 129–61.

Religious Movements in the Middle Ages: The Historical Links between Heresy, the Mendicant Orders, and the Women's Religious Movement in the Twelfth and Thirteenth Century, with the Historical Foundations of German Mysticism (Notre Dame, IN: University of Notre Dame Press, 1995).

Gueroult, Martial. *Descartes' Philosophy Interpreted According to the Order of Reasons*, tr. R. Ariew *et al.* (Minneapolis: University of Minnesota Press, 1984–5).

Guldentops, Guy. "Henry Bate's Encyclopaedism," in P. Binkley (ed.) *Pre-Modern Encyclopaedic Texts* (Leiden: Brill, 1997) 227–37.

"Henry Bate's Metamorphosis of Averroës," *Alif* 16 (1996) 56–76.

"James of Douai's Theory of Knowledge," in M. C. Pacheco and J. F. Meirinhos (eds.) *Intellect et imagination dans la philosophie médiévale* (Turnhout: Brepols, 2006) II: 1143–54.

"A Short Introduction to James of Douai's Philosophy of Mind," in P. J. J. M. Bakker and J. M. M. H. Thijssen (eds.) *Mind, Cognition and Representation: The Tradition of Commentaries on Aristotle's De anima* (Aldershot: Ashgate, 2007) 21–43.

Guldentops, Guy and Carlos Steel (eds.). *Henry of Ghent and the Transformation of Scholastic Thought: Studies in Memory of Jos Decorte* (Leuven: Leuven University Press, 2003).

Gunaydin, Muhammet. "Al-Sīrāfī's Theory of 'Lingua-Logical' Grammar" (Ph.D. dissertation: University of Pennsylvania, 2006).

Gutas, Dimitri. "The 'Alexandria to Baghdad' Complex of Narratives. A Contribution to the Study of Philosophical and Medical Historiography among the Arabs," *Documenti e studi sulla tradizione filosofica medievale* 10 (1999) 155–93.

Avicenna and the Aristotelian Tradition, Introduction to Reading Avicenna's Philosophical Works (Leiden: Brill, 1988).

"Geometry and the Rebirth of Philosophy in Arabic with al-Kindī," in R. Arnzen and J. Thielmann (eds.) *Words, Texts and Concepts Cruising the Mediterranean Sea*, Festschrift for Gerhard Endress (Leuven: Peeters, 2004) 195–209.

Greek Thought, Arabic Culture: The Graeco-Arabic Translation Movement in Baghdad and Early 'Abbāsid Society (2nd–4th / 8th–10th Centuries) (London: Routledge, 1998).

"Intuition and Thinking: The Evolving Structure of Avicenna's Epistemology," in R. Wisnovsky (ed.) *Aspects of Avicenna* (Princeton, NJ: Princeton University Press, 2001) 1–38.

"The Logic of Theology (kalām) in Avicenna," in D. Perler and U. Rudolph (eds.) *Logik und Theologie: das Organon im arabischen und im lateinischen Mittelalter* (Leiden: Brill, 2005) 59–72.

"On Graeco-Arabic Epistolary 'Novels'," *Middle Eastern Literatures* (forthcoming).

"Paul the Persian on the Classification of the Parts of Aristotle's Philosophy: A Milestone between Alexandria and Baġdād," *Der Islam* 60 (1983) 231–67.

"Plato's *Symposion* in the Arabic Tradition," *Oriens* 31 (1988) 36–60.

Guth, Klaus. *Johannes von Salisbury (1115/20–1180): Studien zur Kirchen-, Kultur- und Sozialgeschichte Westeuropas im 12. Jh.* (St. Ottilien: Eos-Verlag, 1978).

Gutierrez, David. "De vita et scriptis Beati Iacobi de Viterbio," *Analecta Augustiniana* 16 (1937–8) 216–24, 282–305, 358–81.

Gutiérrez Galindo, Marco. *El Doctrinal: una gramática latina del Renacimiento del siglo XII* (Madrid: Akal, 1993).

Gwynn, Aubrey. "The 'Sermon-Diary' of Richard FitzRalph, Archbishop of Armagh," *Proceedings of the Royal Irish Academy*, 44 (1937–8) 1–57.

Gyekye, Kwame. "Al-Ghazâlî on Action," in *Ghazâlî, la raison et le miracle* (Paris: Maisonneuve et Larose, 1987) 83–91.

Haage, Bernhard Dietrich. "Die Korpuskulartheorie bei Geber latinus," *Würzburger medizinhistorische Mitteilungen* 12 (1994) 19–28.

Haakonssen, Knud. "The Moral Conservatism of Natural Rights," in I. Hunter and D. Saunders (eds.) *Natural Law and Civil Sovereignty: Moral Right and State Authority in Early Modern Political Thought* (Houndmills, Basingstoke: Palgrave, 2002) 13–26.

Haas, Alois M. *Nim din selbes war: Studien zur Lehre von der Selbsterkenntnis bei Meister Eckhart, Johannes Tauler und Heinrich Seuse* (Freiburg: Universitätsverlag, 1971).

Hackett, Jeremiah (ed.). *Roger Bacon and Aristotelianism*, special issue of *Vivarium* 35:2 (1997).

(ed.). *Roger Bacon and the Sciences: Commemorative Essays* (Leiden: Brill, 1997).

Hackett, Jeremiah and Thomas S. Mahoney. "Roger Bacon Bibliography (1957–1985)," *New Scholasticism* 61 (1987) 184–207.

Hadot, Ilsetraut. *Arts libéraux et philosophie dans la pensée antique* (Paris: Études Augustiniennes, 1984).

"Dans quel lieu le néoplatonicien Simplicius a-t-il fondé son école de mathématiques, et où a pu avoir lieu son entretien avec un manichéen?," *International Journal of the Platonic Tradition* 1 (2007) 42–107.

Hadot, Pierre. "La distinction de l'être et de l'étant dans le 'De Hebdomadibus' de Boèce," in *Die Metaphysik im Mittelalter (Miscellanea mediaevalia* 2) (Berlin: De Gruyter, 1963) 147–53.

Exercises spirituels et philosophie antique, 2nd edn (Paris: Études Augustiniennes, 1987).

"Forma essendi: interprétation philologique et interprétation philosophique d'une formule de Boèce," *Études Classiques* 38 (1970) 143–56.

Philosophy as a Way of Life: Spiritual Exegesis from Socrates to Foucault, tr. M. Chase (Oxford: Blackwell, 1995).

Haines, Roy. *"Ecclesia Anglicana": Studies in the English Church of the Later Middle Ages* (Toronto: University of Toronto Press, 1989).

Haldane, John. "The Metaphysics of Intellect(ion)," *Proceedings of the American Catholic Philosophical Association* 80 (2007) 39–55.

Haldon, John. *Byzantium in the Seventh Century: The Transformation of a Culture* (Cambridge: Cambridge University Press, 1990).

Hallamaa, Olli. "Defending Common Rationality: Roger Roseth on Trinitarian Paralogisms," *Vivarium* 41 (2003) 84–119.

  "On the Borderline between Logic and Theology: Roger Roseth, Sophismata, and Augmentation of Charity," *Documenti e studi sulla tradizione filosofica medievale* 11 (2000) 351–74.

Hallaq, Wael B. *The Origins and Evolution of Islamic Law* (Cambridge: Cambridge University Press, 2005).

Halm, Heinz. *Shiism* (Edinburgh: Edinburgh University Press, 1991; 2nd edn (New York: Columbia University Press, 2004).

Halverson, James L. *Peter Aureol on Predestination. A Challenge to Late Medieval Thought* (Leiden: Brill, 1998).

Hamann, Florian. *Das Siegel der Ewigkeit: Universalwissenschaft und Konziliarismus bei Heymericus de Campo* (Münster: Aschendorff, 2006).

Hames, Harvey. *The Art of Conversion: Christianity and Kabbalah in the Thirteenth Century* (Leiden: Brill, 2000).

Hammond, Robert. *The Philosophy of Alfarabi and its Influence on Medieval Thought* (New York: Hobson Book Press, 1947).

Hankey, Wayne. "Aquinas and the Platonists," in S. Gersh and M. J. F. M. Hoenen (eds.) *The Platonic Tradition in the Middle Ages. A Doxographic Approach* (Berlin: De Gruyter, 2002) 279–324.

Hansberger, R. E. "The Transmission of Aristotle's *Parva Naturalia* in Arabic" (Ph.D. dissertation: Oxford University, 2006).

Häring, N. M. "Chartres and Paris Revisited," in J. R. O'Donnell (ed.) *Essays in Honour of Anton Charles Pegis* (Toronto: Pontifical Institute of Medieval Studies, 1974) 268–329.

  "The Creation and Creator of the World According to Thierry of Chartres and Clarenbaldus of Arras," *Archives d'histoire doctrinale et littéraire du moyen âge* 22 (1955) 137–216.

  "Everard of Ypres and his Appraisal of the Conflict between St. Bernard and Gilbert of Poitiers," *Mediaeval Studies* 17 (1955) 143–72.

  "In Search of Adhemar's Patristic Collection," *Mediaeval Studies* 28 (1966) 336–46.

  "The *Liber de differentia naturae et personae* by Hugh Etherian and the Letters Addressed to him by Peter of Vienna and Hugh of Honau," *Mediaeval Studies* 24 (1962) 1–34.

  "Simon of Tournai and Gilbert of Poitiers," *Mediaeval Studies* 27 (1965) 325–30.

  "Die Vatersammlung des Adhemar von Saint-Ruf in Valence," *Scholastik* 38 (1963) 402–20.

Harris, Jay (ed.). *Maimonides after 800 Years: Essays on Maimonides and his Influence* (Cambridge, MA: Harvard University Press, 2008).

Harrison, Simon. "Do We Have a Will? Augustine's Way in to the Will," in G.B. Matthews (ed.) *The Augustinian Tradition* (Berkeley: University of California Press, 1999) 195–205.

Hart, H. L. A. "Are There Any Natural Rights?," *Philosophical Review* 64 (1955) 175–91.

  The Concept of Law (Oxford: Clarendon Press, 1961).

Hartmann, Friedrich. *Die Literatur von Früh- und Hochsalerno und der Inhalt des Breslauer Codex Salernitanus* (Leipzig: Noske, 1919).

Hartmann, Wilfried. "Manegold von Lautenbach und die Anfänge der Frühscholastik," *Deutsches Archiv für Erforschung des Mittelalters* 26 (1970) 47–149.

Harvey, E. Ruth. *The Inward Wits: Psychological Theory in the Middle Ages and the Renaissance* (London: Warburg Institute, 1975).

Harvey, Steven (ed.) *The Medieval Hebrew Encyclopedias of Science and Philosophy* (Dordrecht: Kluwer, 2000).

  "The Place of the Philosopher in the City according to Ibn Bajja," in C. E. Butterworth (ed.) *The Political Aspects of Islamic Philosophy: Essays in Honor of M. S. Mahdi* (Cambridge, MA: Harvard University Press, 1992) 199–233.

Harvey, Warren. "Albo's Discussion of Time," *Jewish Quarterly Review* 70 (1979–80) 210–38.
  Physics and Metaphysics in Hasdai Crescas (Amsterdam: Gieben, 1998).
Hasse, Dag Nikolaus. "Avicenna on Abstraction," in R. Wisnovsky (ed.) *Aspects of Avicenna* (Princeton, NJ: Markus Wiener, 2001) 39–72.
  Avicenna's De anima *in the Latin West: The Formation of a Peripatetic Philosophy of the Soul 1160–1300* (London: Warburg Institute; Turin: Nino Aragno Editore, 2000).
  "Pietro d'Abano's 'Conciliator' and the Theory of the Soul in Paris," in Jan A. Aertsen et al. (eds.) *Nach der Verurteilung von 1277: Philosophie und Theologie an der Universität von Paris im letzten Viertel des 13. Jahrhunderts: Studien und Texte* (Berlin: De Gruyter, 2001) 635–53.
  "Plato Arabico-latinus: Philosophy – Wisdom Literature – Occult Sciences," in S. Gersh and M. J. F. M. Hoenen (eds.) *The Platonic Tradition in the Middle Ages: A Doxographic Approach* (Berlin: De Gruyter, 2002) 31–65.
Haubst, Rudolf. "Johannes Wenck aus Herrenberg als Albertist," *Recherches de théologie ancienne et médiévale* 18 (1951) 308–23.
  Streifzüge in die cusanische Theologie (Münster: Aschendorff, 1991).
Haubst, Rudolf et al. (eds). *Mitteilungen und Forschungsbeiträge der Cusanus-Gesellschaft* (Mainz: Mattias-Grünewald, 1961–).
Hauke, Hermann. "Die Lehre von der Beseligenden Schau nach Nikolaus Trivet" (Inaugural Dissertation: University of Munich, 1967).
Hause, Jeffrey. "Aquinas on the Function of Moral Virtue," *American Catholic Philosophical Quarterly* 81 (2007) 1–20.
  "Thomas Aquinas and the Voluntarists," *Medieval Philosophy and Theology* 6 (1997) 167–82.
Haven, Mark. *La vie et les œuvres de Maître Arnaud de Villeneuve* (1896; reprint, Geneva: Slatkine Reprints, 1972).
Hawi, Sami. "Ibn Tufayl's Appraisal of his Predecessors and their Influence on his Thought," *International Journal of Middle East Studies* 7 (1976) 89–121.
  Islamic Naturalism and Mysticism: A Philosophical Study of Ibn Tufayl's Hayy Yaqzan (Leiden: Brill, 1974).
Hayes, Zachary. *The General Doctrine of Creation in the Thirteenth Century, with Special Emphasis on Matthew of Aquasparta* (Munich: Schöningh, 1964).
Hayoun, Moise-Ruben. *Moshe Narboni* (Tubingen: Mohr, 1986).
Hayoun, Moise-Ruben and Alain de Libera (eds.). *Averroès et l'averroïsme* (Paris: Presses universitaires de France, 1991).
Heemskerk, Margaretha. *Suffering in the Muʿtazilite Theology: ʿAbd al-Jabbar's Teaching on Pain and Divine Justice* (Leiden: Brill, 2000).
Hegyi, Johannes. *Die Bedeutung des Seins bei den klassischen Kommentatoren des heiligen Thomas von Aquin: Capreolus, Silvester von Ferrara, Cajetan* (Pullach bei München: Berchmanskolleg, 1959).
Heidingsfelder, Georg. *Albert von Sachsen: sein Lebensgang und sein Kommentar zur Nikomachischen Ethik des Aristoteles* (Münster: Aschendorff, 1927).
Hein, Christel. *Definition und Einteilung der Philosophie von der spätantiken Einleitungsliteratur zur arabischen Enzyklopädie* (Frankfurt: Lang, 1985).
Heintke, Fritz. *Humbert von Romans, der fünfte Ordermeister der Dominikaner* (Berlin: Ebering, 1933; repr. Vaduz: Kraus, 1965).
Heinzmann, Richard. *Die* Compilatio questionum theologiae secundum Magistrum Martinum (Munich: Hueber, 1964).
Henderson, John. *The Medieval World of Isidore of Seville: Truth from Words* (Cambridge: Cambridge University Press, 2007).

Henle, Robert J. *Saint Thomas and Platonism: A Study of Plato and Platonici Texts in the Writings of Saint Thomas* (The Hague: Nijhoff, 1956).

Henninger, Mark. "Hervaeus Natalis, b.1250/60; d. 1323, and Richard of Mediavilla, b.1245/49; d.1302/07," in J. J. E. Gracia (ed.) *Individuation in Scholasticism: The Later Middle Ages and the Counter-Reformation, 1150–1650* (Albany: State University of New York Press, 1994) 299–318.

Relations: Medieval Theories 1250–1325 (Oxford: Clarendon Press, 1989).

"Thomas Wylton's Theory of Relations," *Documenti e studi sulla tradizione filosofica medievale* 1 (1990) 457–90.

Henquinet, F. "Les manuscrits et l'influence des écrits theologiques d'Eudes Rigaud," *Recherches de théologie ancienne et médiévale* 11 (1939) 323–50.

Henry, Desmond P. *The Logic of Saint Anselm* (Oxford: Clarendon Press, 1967).

"The Singular Syllogism of Garlandus Compotista," *Revue internationale de philosophie* 113 (1975) 243–70.

Herren, Michael. "Manegold of Lautenbach's Scholia on the *Metamorphoses* – Are There More?" *Notes and Queries* 51 (2004) 218–23.

Herscher, Irenaeus. "A Bibliography of Alexander of Hales," *Franciscan Studies* 5 (1945) 434–54.

Heynck, Valens. "Der Skotist Hugo de Novo Castro," *Franziskanische Studien* 43 (1961) 244–70.

"Studien zu Johannes von Erfurt," *Franziskanische Studien* 40 (1958) 327–60; 42 (1960) 153–96.

"Zur Datierung des 'Correctorium fratris Thomae' Wilhelmus de La Mare," *Franziskanische Studien* 49 (1967) 1–21.

Heysse, Aubain. "Fr. Pierre de Falco ne peut être identifié avec Guillaume de Falegar O.F.M.," *Archivum Franciscanum Historicum* 33 (1940) 241–67.

Hill, Donald R. "The Literature of Arabic Alchemy," in M. J. L. Young *et al.* (eds.) *Religion, Learning and Science in the Abbasid Period* (Cambridge: Cambridge University Press, 1990) 328–41.

Hillenbrand, Eugen. *Nikolaus von Strassburg: religiöse Bewegung und dominikanische Theologie im 14. Jahrhundert* (Freiburg im Breisgau: Albert, 1968).

Hillgarth, Jocelyn N. *Ramon Lull and Lullism in Fourteenth-Century France* (Oxford: Clarendon Press, 1971).

Hilsch, Peter. *Johannes Hus (um 1370–1415): Prediger Gottes und Ketzer* (Rogensbourg: Pustet, 1999).

Hinnebusch, William. *The Early English Friars Preachers* (Rome: Ad S. Sabinae, 1951).

The History of the Dominican Order (State Island, NY: Alba House, 1966–73).

Hirschfield, Hartwig. *Festschrift zum 80. Geburtstag Moritz Steinschneiders.* (Leipzig: Harrassowitz, 1896)

Hirvonen, Vesa. *Passions in William Ockham's Philosophical Psychology* (Dordrecht: Kluwer, 2004).

Hissette, Roland. *Enquête sur les 219 articles condamnés à Paris le 7 mars 1277* (Leuven: Publications universitaires, 1977).

"Une question quodlibétique de Servais du Mont-Saint-Eloi sur le pouvoir papal de l'évêque," *Recherches de théologie ancienne et médiévale* 49 (1982) 234–42.

"Roger Marston, a-t-il professé l'hylemorphisme universel?," *Recherches de théologie ancienne et médiévale* 29 (1972) 205–23.

Hocedez, Edgar. "La philosophie des Quodlibets de Pierre d'Auvergne," in A. Long *et al.* (eds.) *Aus der Geisteswelt des Mittelalters: Studien und Texte Martin Grabmann zur Vollendung des 60. Lebensjahres von Freunden und Schülern gewidmet* (Münster: Aschendorff, 1935).

"Les *Quaestiones in metaphysicam* de Pierre d'Auvergne," *Archives de philosophie* 9 (1932) 515–70.

"Un question inédite de Pierre d'Auvergne sur l'individuation," *Revue néoscolastique de philosophie* 36 (1934) 355–86.

Richard de Middleton: sa vie, ses œuvres, sa doctrine (Leuven: Spicilegium Sacrum lovaniense, 1925).

"La théologie de Pierre d'Auvergne," *Gregorianum* 11 (1930) 526–55.

"La vie et les œuvres de Pierre d'Auvergne," *Gregorianum* 14 (1933) 3–36.

Hödl, Ludwig. "Die Aulien des Magisters Johannes von Pouilly und der scholastische Streit über die Begründung der menschlichen Willensfreiheit," *Scholastik* 35 (1960) 57–75.

"Literar- und problemgeschichtliche Untersuchungen zum Sentenzenkommentar des Wilhelm von Ware O.F.M. (nach 1305)," *Recherches de théologie ancienne et médiévale* 57 (1990) 122–41.

" 'Non est malitia in voluntate . . .' Die magistrale Entscheidung der Pariser Theologen von 1285/86 in der Diskussion des Johannes de Polliaco, Quodl. I, q. 10," *Archives d'histoire doctrinale et littéraire du moyen âge* 66 (1999) 247–97.

"Die Opposition des Johannes de Polliaco gegen die Schule der Gandavistae," *Bochumer Philosophisches Jahrbuch* 9 (2004) 115–77.

"The *Quodlibeta* of John of Pouilly († *ca.* 1328) and the Philosophical and Theological Debates at Paris 1307–1312," in C. Schabel (ed.) *Theological Quodlibeta in the Middle Ages: The Fourteenth Century* (Leiden: Brill, 2007) 199–229.

"Die Seinsdifferenz des möglichen im Quodlibet des Jacobus von Ascoli Ordinis Minorum," in O. Pluta (ed.) *Die Philosophie im 14. und 15. Jahrhundert* (Amsterdam: Grüner, 1988) 465–94.

"Die Sentenzen des Petrus Lombardus in der Diskussion seiner Schule," in G.R. Evans (ed.) *Mediaeval Commentaries on the* Sentences *of Peter Lombard: Current Research* (Leiden: Brill, 2002) 25–40.

"Studien zum nominalistischen Schöpfungsbegriff in der spätscholastischen Theologie des Michael de Massa OESA (†1337)," *Cassiciacum* 30 (1975) 234–56.

Hoenen, Maarten J. F. M. "Academic Theology in the Fifteenth Century: The Sentences Commentary of Heymericus de Campo (+ 1460)," in P. J. J. M. Bakker (ed.) *Chemins de la pensée médiévale: Études offertes à Zénon Kaluza* (Turnhout: Brepols, 2002) 513–59.

"Academics and Intellectual Life in the Low Countries. The University Career of Heymeric de Campo (†1460)," *Recherches de théologie ancienne et médiévale* 61 (1994) 173–209.

"The Commentary on the *Sentences* of Marsilius of Inghen," in G. Evans (ed.) *Mediaeval Commentaries on the* Sentences *of Peter Lombard* (Leiden: Brill, 2002) 465–506.

Heymeric van de Velde: Eenheid in de tegendelen (Baarn: Ambo, 1990).

"Heymeric van de Velde († 1460) und die Geschichte des Albertismus: Auf der Suche nach den Quellen der albertistischen Intellektlehre des *Tractatus problematicus*," in M. J. F. M. Hoenen and A. de Libera (eds.) *Albertus Magnus und der Albertismus. Deutsche philosophische Kultur des Mittelalters* (Leiden: Brill, 1995) 303–31.

Marsilius of Inghen: Divine Knowledge in Late Medieval Thought (Leiden: Brill, 1993).

"Marsilius von Inghen: Bibliographie. Appendix zu der geplanten Edition der wichtigsten Werk des Marsilius von Inghen," *Bulletin de philosophie médiévale* 31 (1989) 150–67.

"Marsilius von Inghen: Bibliographie. Ergänzungen," *Bulletin de philosophie médiévale* 31 (1990) 191–5.

"Nominalismus als universitäre Spekulationskontrolle," *Recherches de théologie et philosophie médiévales* 73 (2006) 349–74.

Hoenen, Maarten J. F. M. and Paul J. J. M. Bakker (eds.). *Philosophie und Theologie des ausgehenden Mittelalters: Marsilius von Inghen und das Denken seiner Zeit* (Leiden: Brill, 2000).

Hoenen, Maarten J. F. M and Alain de Libera. *Albertus Magnus und der Albertismus: Deutsche philosophische Kultur des Mittelalters* (Leiden: Brill, 1995).

Hoeres, Walter. "Wesen und Dasein bei Heinrich von Gent und Duns Scot," *Franziskanische Studien* 47 (1965) 121–86.

"Zur Ontologie von Petrus Thomae OFM," *Franziskanische Studien* 43 (1961) 374–9.

Hoffmann, Fritz. *Die theologische Methode des Oxforder Dominikanerlehrers Robert Holcot* (Münster: Aschendorff, 1972).

"Der Wandel in der Scholastischen Argumentation vom 13 Zum 14 Jahrhundert aufgezeigt an zwei Beispielen: Robert Holcot und William Crathorn," in A. Speer (ed.) *Die Bibliotheca Amploniana: ihre Bedeutung im Spannungsfeld von Aristotelismus, Nominalismus und Humanismus* (Berlin: De Gruyter, 1995) 301–22.

Hoffmann, Tobias. "Aquinas and Intellectual Determinism: The Test Case of Angelic Sin," *Archiv für Geschichte der Philosophie* 89 (2007) 122–56.

Hoffmann, Tobias, Jörn Müller, and Matthias Perkams (eds.). *Das Problem der Willensschwäche in der mittelalterlichen Philosophie* (Leuven: Peeters, 2006).

Höfler, Karl Adolf Constantin. *Geschichtschreiber der husitischen bewegung in Böhmen* (Vienna: Hof- und Staatsdruckerei, 1856–66).

Hofmeier, Johann. *Die Trinitätslehre des Hugo von St. Viktor* (Munich: Hueber, 1964).

Hogg, Charles R. Jr. "*Ethica secundum stoicos*: An Edition, Translation, and Critical Essay" (Ph.D. dissertation: Indiana University, 1997).

Holloway, Julia Bolton. *Brunetto Latini: An Analytic Bibliography* (London: Grant and Cutler, 1986).

Twice-Told Tales: Brunetto Latino and Dante Alighieri (New York: Lang, 1993).

Hollywood, Amy. "Inside Out: Beatrice of Nazareth and her Hagiographer," in C. Mooney (ed.) *Gendered Voices: Medieval Saints and their Interpreters* (Philadelphia: University of Pennsylvania Press, 1999) 78–98.

The Soul as Virgin Wife: Mechtild of Magdeburg, Marguerite Porete, and Meister Eckhart (Notre Dame, IN: University of Notre Dame Press, 1995).

Holopainen, Toivo. *Dialectic and Theology in the Eleventh Century* (Leiden: Brill, 1996).

"Necessity in Early Medieval Thought: Peter Damian and Anselm of Canterbury," in P. Gilbert *et al.* (eds.) *Cur Deus Homo* (Rome: Herder, 1999) 221–34.

Holtz, Louis. "La grammaire carolingienne," in S. Auroux (ed.) *Histoire des idées linguistiques*, tome II: *Le développement de la grammaire occidentale* (Liège: Mardaga, 1992) 96–106.

Holtz, Louis and Olga Weijers. *L'enseignement des disciplines à la Faculté des Arts (Paris et Oxford, XIIIᵉ–XVᵉ siècles)* (Turnhout: Brepols, 1997).

Honnefelder, Ludger. *Ens inquantum ens: der Begriff des Seienden als solchen als Gegenstand der Metaphysik nach der Lehre des Johannes Duns Scotus* (Münster: Aschendorff, 1979).

Hoover, J. "Ibn Taymiyya as an Avicennan Theologian: A Muslim Approach to God's Self-Sufficiency," *Theological Review* 27 (2006) 34–46.

"Perpetual Creativity in the Perfection of God: Ibn Taymiyya's Hadith Commentary on God's Creation of the World," *Journal of Islamic Studies* 15 (2004) 287–329.

Hopkins, Jasper. *A Companion to the Study of St. Anselm* (Minneapolis, MN: University of Minnesota Press, 1972).

A Concise Introduction to the Philosophy of Nicholas of Cusa, 3rd edn (Minneapolis, MN: Banning, 1986).

Nicholas of Cusa's Debate with John Wenck (Minneapolis, MN: Banning, 1988).

Horst, Ulrich. *Die Trinitäts und Gotteslehre des Robert von Melun* (Mainz: Matthias-Grünewald-Verlag, 1964).

Hoskin, Michael A. and A.G. Molland. "Swineshead on Falling Bodies: An Example of Fourteenth-Century Physics," *British Journal for the History of Science* 3 (1966–7) 150–82.

Hoste, Anselm. *Bibliotheca Aelrediana: A Survey of the Manuscripts, Old Catalogues, Editions and Studies Concerning St. Aelred of Rievaulx* (Steenbrugis: In Abbatia Sancti Petri, 1962).

Hourani, George. "Ibn Sina on Necessary and Possible Existence," *Philosophical Forum* 4 (1972) 74–86.

    Islamic Rationalism: The Ethics of ʿAbd al-Jabbar (Oxford: Clarendon Press, 1971).

    "The Principal Subject of Ibn Tufayl's Hayy Ibn Yaqzan," *Journal of Near Eastern Studies* 15 (1956) 40–6.

    "Reason and Revelation in Ibn Hazm's Ethical Thought," in G. Hourani (ed.) *Reason and Tradition in Islamic Ethics* (Cambridge: Cambridge University Press, 1985) 167–89.

    Reason and Tradition in Islamic Ethics (Cambridge: Cambridge University Press, 1985).

Houser, R. E. *The Cardinal Virtues: Aquinas, Albert and Philip the Chancellor* (Toronto: Pontifical Institute of Mediaeval Studies, 2004).

    "Philosophical Development through Metaphor: Light among the Greeks," *Proceedings of the American Catholic Philosophical Association* 64 (1990) 75–85.

    "The Real Distinction and the Principles of Metaphysics: Avicenna and Aquinas," in R. E. Houser (ed.) *Laudemus viros gloriosos: Essays in Honor of Armand Maurer, CSB* (Notre Dame, IN: University of Notre Dame Press, 2007) 74–108.

Houwen, L. A. J. R and A. A. MacDonald (eds.). *Alcuin of York: Scholar at the Carolingian Court* (Groningen: Forsten, 1998).

Howard, Peter. *Beyond the Written Word: Preaching and Theology in the Florence of Archbishop Antoninus 1427–1459* (Florence: Olschki, 1995).

Hoyland, R. G. and B. Gilmour. *Medieval Islamic Swords and Swordmaking* (Cambridge: Gibb Memorial Trust).

Hudson, Anne. *The Premature Reformation: Wycliffite Texts and Lollard History* (Oxford: Clarendon Press, 1988).

    (ed.) *Selections from English Wycliffite Writings* (Toronto: University of Toronto Press, 1997).

Hudson, Anne and Michael Wilks (eds.). *From Ockham to Wyclif* (Oxford: Blackwell, 1987).

Hudson, Nancy. *Becoming God: The Doctrine of Theosis in Nicholas of Cusa* (Washington, DC: Catholic University of America Press, 2007).

Hughes, Aaron. *The Texture of the Divine: Imagination in Medieval Islamic and Jewish Thought* (Bloomington, IN: Indiana University Press, 2004).

Hughes, G. E. *John Buridan on Self-Reference: Chapter Eight of Buridan's "Sophismata", An Edition and Translation with an Introduction and Philosophical Commentary* (Cambridge: Cambridge University Press, 1982).

Hughes, Kevin. "The *Ratio Dei* and the Ambiguities of History," *Modern Theology* 21 (2005) 645–61.

Hugonnard-Roche, Henri. "Aux origines de l'exégèse orientale de la logique d'Aristote: Sergius de Rešʿaina († 536), médecin et philosophe," *Journal asiatique* 277 (1989) 1–17.

    "Le corpus philosophique syriaque aux VIᵉ –VIIᵉ siècles," in C. D'Ancona (ed.) *The Libraries of the Neoplatonists* (Leiden: Brill, 2007) 279–91.

    La logique d'Aristote du grec au syriaque (Paris: Vrin, 2004).

Humbrecht, Thierry-Dominique. *Théologie négative et noms divins chez saint Thomas d'Aquin* (Paris: Vrin, 2005).

Hunger, Herbert. "Philosophie," in *Die hochsprachliche profane Literatur den Byzantiner* (Munich: Beck, 1978) I: 3–62.

Huning, H. A. "Die Stellung der Petrus de Trabibus zur Philosophie: nach dem zweiten Prolog zum ersten Buch seines Sentenzenkommentars ms 154, Biblioteca Comunale, Assisi," *Franziskanische Studien* 46 (1964) 193–287; 47 (1965) 1–43.

Hunt, R. W. "*Absoluta*: The *Summa* of Petrus Hispanus on Priscianus Minor," *Historiographia Linguistica* 2 (1975) 1–23.

The Schools and the Cloister: The Life and Writings of Alexander Nequam, ed. and rev. M. Gibson (Oxford: Clarendon Press, 1984).

"Studies on Priscian in the Eleventh and Twelfth Centuries. I. Petrus Helias and his Predecessors," *Medieval and Renaissance Studies* 1 (1941–3) 194–231; reprinted in G. L. Bursill-Hall (ed.) *The History of Grammar in the Middle Ages. Collected Papers* (Amsterdam: Benjamins, 1980).

"Studies on Priscian in the Twelfth Century. II: The School of Ralph of Beauvais," *Mediaeval and Renaissance Studies* 2 (1950) 1–56; reprinted in G. L. Bursill-Hall. (ed.) *The History of Grammar in the Middle Ages. Collected Papers* (Amsterdam: Benjamins, 1980).

Hunt, Tony. *Teaching and Learning Latin in Thirteenth-Century England* (Cambridge: Brewer, 1991).

Hurka, Thomas. "Virtuous Act, Virtuous Dispositions," *Analysis* 66 (2006) 69–76.

Husik, Isaac. "Joseph Albo: The Last of the Mediaeval Jewish Philosophers," *Proceedings of the American Academy for Jewish Research* 1 (1928–30) 61–72.

Huygens, R. B. C. "Bérenger de Tours, Lanfranc et Bernold de Constance," *Sacris erudiri* 16 (1965) 358–77.

Hyman, Arthur. "Aristotle's 'First Matter' and Avicenna's and Averroes's 'Corporeal Form'," in S. Lieberman *et al.* (eds.) *Harry Austryn Wolfson Jubilee Volume* (Jerusalem: American Academy for Jewish Research, 1965) 385–406.

"Maimonides on Creation and Emanation," in J. F. Wippel. (ed.) *Studies in Medieval Philosophy* (Washington, DC: Catholic University of America Press, 1987) 45–61.

Hyman, Arthur and James J. Walsh (eds.). *Philosophy in the Middle Ages: The Christian, Islamic, and Jewish Traditions*, 2nd edn (Indianapolis, IN: Hackett, 1973).

Idel, Moshe. *The Mystical Experience in Abraham Abulafia* (Albany, NY: State University of New York Press, 1988).

Idel, Moshe and Bernard McGinn (eds.). *Mystical Union in Judaism, Christianity, and Islam: An Ecumenical Dialogue* (New York: Continuum, 1999).

Ierodiakonou, Katerina. "The Anti-Logical Movement in the Fourteenth Century," in K. Ierodiakonou (ed.) *Byzantine Philosophy and its Ancient Sources* (Oxford: Clarendon Press, 2002) 219–36.

"Byzantine Commentators on the Epistemic Status of Ethics," in P. Adamson *et al.* (eds.) *Philosophy, Science, and Exegesis in Greek, Arabic, and Latin Commentaries* (London: Institute of Classical Studies, 2004) 221–38.

(ed.). *Byzantine Philosophy and its Ancient Sources* (Oxford: Oxford University Press, 2002).

"The Byzantine Reception of Aristotle's *Categories*," *Synthesis Philosophica* 39 (2005) 7–31.

"John Italos on Universals," *Documenti e studi sulla tradizione filosofica medievale* 18 (2007) 231–47.

"Metaphysics in the Byzantine Tradition: Eustratios of Nicaea on Universals," *Quaestio* 5 (2005) 67–82.

"Psellos' Paraphrasis on Aristotle's *De interpretatione*," in K. Ierodiakonou (ed.) *Byzantine Philosophy and its Ancient Sources* (Oxford: Clarendon Press, 2002) 157–81.

Ilkhani, Mohammad. *La philosophie de la création chez Achard de Saint-Victor* (Brussels: Ousia, 1999).

Illich, Ivan. *In the Vineyard of the Text: A Commentary to Hugh's* Didascalicon (Chicago: University of Chicago Press, 1993).

Imbach, Ruedi. "Averroistische Stellungnahmen zur Diskussion über das Verhältnis von *Esse* und *Essentia*. Von Siger von Brabant zu Thaddeus von Parma," in A. Maierù and A. Paravicini Bagliani (eds.) *Studi sul xiv secolo in memoria di Anneliese Maier* (Rome: Edizioni di Storia e Letteratura, 1981) 299–339.

"Das *Centheologicon* des Heymericus de Campo und die darin enthaltenen Casnus- Reminiszenzen," *Traditio* 39 (1983) 466–77.

Dante, la philosophie et les laïcs (Fribourg: Éditions universitaires, 1996).

"Notule sur le commentaire du 'Liber de causis' de Siger de Brabant et ses rapports avec Thomas d'Aquin," *Freiburger Zeitschrift für Philosophie und Theologie* 43 (1996) 304–23.

Imbach Ruedi and Ulrika Lindblad. "*Compilatio rudis ac puerilis*. Hinweise und Materialien zu Nikolaus von Strassburg O. P. und seiner *Summa*," *Freiburger Zeitschrift für Philosophie und Theologie* 32 (1985) 155–233.

Incandela, Joseph. "Robert Holcot, O.P., on Prophecy, the Contingency of Revelation, and the Freedom of God," *Medieval Philosophy and Theology* 4 (1994) 165–88.

Ingham, Mary Beth and Mechthild Dreyer. *The Philosophical Vision of John Duns Scotus* (Washington, DC: Catholic University Press, 2004).

Inglis, John. "Aquinas's Replication of the Acquired Moral Virtues," *Journal of Religious Ethics* 27 (1999) 3–27.

Spheres of Philosophical Inquiry and the Historiography of Medieval Philosophy (Leiden: Brill, 1998).

Inwood, Brad (ed.). *The Cambridge Companion to Stoicism* (Cambridge: Cambridge University Press, 2003).

Iogna-Prat, Dominique and Colette Jeudy. *L'école carolingienne d'Auxerre: de Murethach à Rémi, 830–908* (Paris: Beauchesne, 1991).

Iremadze, Tengiz. *Konzeptionen des Denkens im Neuplatonismus: zur Rezeption der proklischen Philosophie im deutschen und georgischen Mittelalter: Dietrich von Freiberg, Berthold von Moosburg, Joane Petrizi* (Amsterdam: Grüner, 2004).

Iribarren, Isabel. *Durandus of St. Pourçain: A Dominican Theologian in the Shadow of Aquinas* (New York: Oxford University Press, 2005).

"'Responsio secundum Thomam' and the Search for an Early Thomistic School," *Vivarium* 39 (2001) 255–96.

Irwin, Terence. "Stoic Naturalism and its Critics," in B. Inwood (ed.) *The Cambridge Companion to Stoicism* (Cambridge: Cambridge University Press, 2003) 345–64.

Issawi, Charles. *An Arab Philosophy of History: Selections from the* Prolegomena *of Ibn Khaldun of Tunis (1332–1406)* (Princeton, NJ: Princeton University Press, 1986).

Ivry, Alfred L. *Al-Kindi's Metaphysics* (Albany: State University of New York Press, 1974).

Ivry, Alfred. "Averroes' Three Commentaries on *De Anima*," in J. A. Aertsen and G. Endress (eds.) *Averroes and the Aristotelian Tradition* (Leiden: Brill, 1999) 199–216.

Iwakuma, Yukio. "Influence," in J. Brower and K. Guilfoy (eds.) *The Cambridge Companion to Abelard* (Cambridge: Cambridge University Press, 2004) 305–35.

"Pierre Abélard et Guillaume de Champeaux dans les premières années du XIIᵉ siècle: une étude préliminaire," in J. Baird (ed.) *Langage, sciences, philosophie au XIIe siècle* (Paris: Vrin, 1999).

"The *Introductiones dialecticae secundum Wilgelmum* and *secundum magistrum G. Paganellum*," *Cahiers de l'Institut du Moyen Age Grec et Latin* 63 (1993) 45–114.

"Vocales, or Early Nominalists," *Traditio* 47 (1992) 37–111.

"William of Champeaux and the *Introductiones*," in H. Braakhuis and C. H. Kneepkens (eds.) *Aristotle's* Peri hermeneias *in the Latin Middle Ages: Essays on the Commentary Tradition* (Groningen: Ingenium, 2003) 1–30.

"William of Champeaux on Aristotle's Categories," in J. Biard and I. Rosier-Catach (eds.) *La tradition médiévale des Catégories XIIe–XIVe siècles. Actes du XIIIe symposium européen de logique et de sémantique médiévales* (Leuven: Peeters, 2003) 313–28.

Iwakuma, Yukio and Sten Ebbesen. "Logico-Theological Schools from the Second Half of the Twelfth Century: A List of Sources," *Vivarium* 30 (1992) 173–210.

Jabre, Farid. *La notion de certitude selon Ghazali dans ses origines psychologiques et historiques* (Paris: Vrin, 1958).

Jacobi, Klaus. "Einzelnes-Individuum-Person. Gilbert von Poitier's Philosophie des Individuellen," in J. Aertsen and A. Speer (eds.) *Individuum und Individualität im Mittelalter* (Berlin: De Gruyter, 1995).

Gespräche lesen: philosophische Dialoge im Mittelalter (Tübingen: Narr, 1999).

Die Methode der cusanischen Philosophie (Munich: Alber, 1969).

Die Modalbegriffe in den logischen Schriften des Wilhelm von Shyreswood und in anderen Kompendien des 12. et 13. Jahrhunderts (Leiden: Brill, 1980).

"Peter Abelard's Investigations into the Meaning and Function of the Speech Sign 'Est'," in S. Knuutila and J. Hintikka (eds.) *The Logic of Being* (Dordrecht: Reidel, 1986) 145–80.

Jacobs, Louis. *Principles of the Jewish Faith: An Analytical Study* (New York: Basic Books, 1964).

Jacquart, Danielle. "Aristotelian Thought in Salerno," in P. Dronke (ed.) *A History of Twelfth-Century Western Philosophy* (Cambridge: Cambridge University Press, 1988) 407–28.

"De l'Arabe au Latin: l'influence de quelque choix lexicaux (*impressio, ingenium, intuitio*)," in J. Hamesse (ed.) *Aux origines du lexique philosophique europeen* (Louvain-la-Neuve: Fédération internationale des instituts d'études médiévales, 1997) 167–80.

James, T. E. "Peter Alboini of Mantua: Philosopher-Humanist," *Journal of the History of Philosophy* 12 (1974) 161–70.

Jansen, Bernhard. *Die Erkenntnislehre Olivis* (Berlin: Duemmlers, 1921).

Janssens, Jules L. *An Annotated Bibliography on Ibn Sînâ (1970–1989) including Arabic and Persian Publications and Turkish and Russian References* (Leuven: Leuven University Press, 1991).

An Annoted Bibliography on Ibn Sina: First Supplement (1990–1994) (Louvain-la-Neuve: Fédération internationale des instituts d'études médiévales, 1999).

"Bahmanyār, and his Revision of Ibn Sīnā's Metaphysical Project," *Medioevo* 32 (2007) 99–117.

"Bahmanyār ibn al-Marzubān: A Faithful Disciple of Ibn Sīnā?" in D. C. Reisman and A. H. al-Rahīm (eds.) *Before and After Avicenna: Proceedings of the First Conference of the Avicenna Study Group* (Leiden: Brill, 2003) 177–98.

Ibn Sina and his Influence on the Arabic and Latin World (Burlington, VT: Ashgate, 2006).

Janssens, Jules L. and Daniel de Smet (eds.). *Avicenna and his Heritage* (Leuven: Leuven University Press, 2002).

Jantzen, Grace. *Julian of Norwich: Mystic and Theologian* (London: Paulist Press, 1987).

Jeauneau, Édouard. *L'âge d'or des écoles de Chartres* (Chartres: Éditions Houvet, 1995).

"Le commentaire de Guillaume de Lucques sur les Noms Divins," in T. Boiadjiev *et al.* (eds.) *Die Dionysius-Rezeption im Mittelalter* (Turnhout: Brepols, 2000) 177–95.

"Deux rédactions des gloses de Guillaume de Conches sur Priscien," *Recherches de théologie ancienne et médiévale* 27 (1960) 212–47.

Études érigéniennes (Paris: Études Augustiniennes, 1987).

"L'héritage de la philosophie antique durant le haut Moyen Âge," *Settimane di studio del Centro Italiano di studi sull'alto medioevo* 22 (1975) 17–54.

Lectio philosophorum: recherches sur l'École de Chartres (Amsterdam: Hakkert, 1973).

Jensen, Kurt Villads. "Robert Holkot's *Questio* on Killing Infidels: A Reevaluation and an Edition," *Archivum Fratrum Praedicatorum* 63 (1993) 207–28.

Joannou, Périclès-Pierre. *Christliche Metaphysik in Byzanz: die Illuminationslehre des Michael Psellos und Johannes Italos* (Ettal: Buch-Kunstverlag, 1956).

"Die Definition des Seins bei Eustratios von Nikaia," *Byzantinische Zeitschrift* 47 (1954) 358–68.

"Der Nominalismus und die menschliche Psychologie Christ," *Byzantinische Zeitschrift* 47 (1954) 369–78.

Johnson, James Turner. *Ideology, Reason, and the Limitation of War: Religious and Secular Concepts, 1200–1740* (Princeton, NJ: Princeton University Press, 1975).

Just War Tradition and the Restraint of War. A Moral and Historical Inquiry (Princeton, NJ: Princeton University Press, 1981).

Johnston, Mark D. *The Evangelical Rhetoric of Ramon Llull* (New York: Oxford University Press, 1995).

The Spiritual Logic of Ramon Llull (Oxford: Clarendon Press, 1987).

Jolivet, Jean. *Abélard, ou la philosophie dans le langage* (Paris: Seghers, 1969).

"The Arabic Inheritance," in P. Dronke (ed.) *A History of Twelfth-Century Western Philosophy* (Cambridge: Cambridge University Press, 1988) 113–48.

Godescalc d'Orbais et la trinité (Paris: Vrin, 1958).

"L'intellect et le langage selon Radulphus Brito," in Z. Kaluza and P. Vignaux (eds.) *Preuve et raisons à l'Université de Paris: logique, ontologie et théologie au XIVe siècle* (Paris: Vrin, 1985) 83–91.

L'intellect selon Kindi (Leiden: Brill, 1971).

Philosophie médiévale arabe et latine (Paris: Vrin, 1995).

Jolivet, Jean and Alain de Libera (eds.). *Gilbert de Poitiers et ses contemporains: aux origines de la logica modernorum* (Naples: Bibliopolis, 1987).

Jordan, Mark D. "Aquinas's Construction of a Moral Account for the Passions," *Freiburger Zeitschrift für Philosophie und Theologie* 33 (1986) 71–97.

"The Controversy of the *Correctoria* and the Limits of Metaphysics," *Speculum* 57 (1982) 292–314.

"The Disappearance of Galen in Thirteenth-Century Philosophy and Theology," in A. Zimmermann *et al.* (eds.) *Mensch und Natur im Mittelalter* (Berlin: De Gruyter, 1992) 703–17.

Jordan, William C. *Unceasing Strife, Unending Fear: Jacques de Thérines and the Freedom of the Church in the Age of the Last Capetians* (Princeton, NJ: Princeton University Press, 2005).

Jospe, Raphael. *Torah and Sophia: The Life and Thought of Shem Tov ibn Falaquera* (Cincinnati, OH: Hebrew Union College Press, 1988).

Joutsivuo, Timo. *Scholastic Tradition and Humanist Innovation: The Concept of Neutrum in Renaissance Medicine* (Helsinki: Academia Scientiarum Fennica, 1999).

Jullien, Marie-Hélène and Françoise Perelman. *Clavis des auteurs latins du moyen age: territoire français, 735–987. Tomus II: Alcuin* (Turnhout: Brepols, 1999).

Jung-Palczewska, Elzbieta. "The Concept of Time in Richard Kilvington," in L. Cova and G. Alliney (eds.) *Tempus aevum aeternitatis: la concettualizzazione del tempo nel pensiero tardomedievale* (Florence: Olschki, 2000) 141–67.

"Motion in a Vacuum and in a Plenum in Richard Kilvington's Question: *Utrum aliquod corpus simplex posset moveri aeque velociter in vacuo et in pleno* from the 'Commentary on the Physics'," *Miscellanea Medievalia* 25 (1997) 179–93.

"La question quodlibétique *De infinitate vigoris Dei* de Thomas de Wylton," *Archives d'histoire doctrinale et littéraire du moyen âge* 64 (1997) 347–403.

"Works by Richard Kilvington," *Archives d'histoire doctrinale et littéraire du moyen âge* 67 (2000) 181–223.

"Wylton's Solution of the Aristotelian Problem of God's Infinite Power," in J. Marenbon (ed.) *Aristotle in Britain during the Middle Ages* (Turnhout: Brepols, 1996) 311–23.

Jüssen, Gabriel. "Wilhelm von Auvergne und die Transformation der scholastischen Philosophie im 13. Jahrhundert," in J. P. Beckmann *et al.* (eds.) *Philosophie im Mittelalter* (Hamburg: Meiner, 1987) 141–64.

Juste, David. "Neither Observation nor Astronomical Tables. An Alternative Way of Computing the Planetary Longitudes in the Early Western Middle Ages," in C. Burnett *et al.* (eds.) *Studies in the History of the Exact Sciences in Honour of David Pingree* (Leiden: Brill, 2004) 181–222.

Kaczmarek, Ludger. "Erhard Knab von Zwiefalten († 1480): *Improbatio modorum significandi*. Edition nach den Handschriften," in K. D. Dutz (ed.) *Individuation, Sympnoia panta, Harmonia, Emanation: Festgabe H. Schepers* (Münster: Nodus, 2000) 109–55.

"'Magister Sotphi': Gerhard von Zutphens *Glosa notabilis* (1487–88) und die Geschichter der Grammatik im 15. Jahrhundert," in K. D. Dutz and K.-A. Forsgren (eds.) *History and Rationality* (Münster: Nodus, 1995) 75–92.

Kaeppeli, Thomas. *Le procès contre Thomas Waleys, O.P.: étude et documents* (Rome: Ad S. Sabinae, 1936).

Scriptores Ordinis Praedicatorum Medii Aevi (Rome: Sabina, 1970–3).

Kalb, Herbert. *Studien zur Summa Stephans von Tournai* (Innsbruck: Universitätsverlag Wagner, 1983).

Kaldellis, Anthony. *The Argument of Psellos' Chronographia* (Leiden: Brill, 1999).

Kaluza, Zénon. "Le 'De universali reali' de Jean de Maisonneuve et les 'epicuri litterales'," *Freiburger Zeitschrift für Philosophie und Theologie* 33 (1986) 469–516.

"Les débuts de l'albertisme tardif (Paris et Cologne)," in M. J. F. M. Hoenen and A. de Libera (eds.) *Albertus Magnus und der Albertismus: Deutsche philosophische Kultur des Mittelalters* (Leiden: Brill, 1995) 207–95.

"Jérôme de Prague et le Timée de Platon," *Archives d'histoire doctrinale et littéraire du moyen age* 61 (1994) 59–104.

"La nature des écrits de Jean de Ripa," *Traditio* 43 (1987) 257–98.

Nicolas d'Autrécourt: ami de la vérité (*Histoire littéraire de la France: suite du quatorzième siècle*) (Paris: Académie des inscriptions et belles-lettres, 1995).

"L'œuvre théologique de Richard Brinkley, OFM," *Archives d'histoire doctrinale et littéraire du moyen âge* 56 (1989) 169–273.

Les querelles doctrinales à Paris: nominalistes et réalistes aux confins du XIVᵉ et du XVᵉ siècles (Bergamo: Lubrina, 1988).

"Les sciences et leurs langages: Note sur le statut du 29 décembre 1340 et le prétendu statut perdu contre Ockham," in L. Bianchi (ed) *Filosfia e teologia nel trecento: studi in ricordo di Eugenio Randi* (Louvain-la-Neuve: Fédération internationale des instituts d'études médiévales, 1994) 197–258.

Kaminsky, Herbert. *A History of the Hussite Revolution* (Berkeley: University of California Press, 1967).

Kandler, Karl-Hermann, Burkhard Mojsisch, and Franz-Bernhard Stammkötter (eds.). *Dietrich von Freiberg: neue Perspektiven seiner Philosophie, Theologie und Naturwissenschaft* (Amsterdam: Grüner, 1999).

Kann, Christoph. *Die Eigenschaften der Termini: eine Untersuchung zur "Perutilis Logica" des Alberts von Sachsen* (Leiden: Brill, 1994).

Kantorowicz, Hermann. "The Poetical Sermon of a Mediæval Jurist: Placentinus and His 'Sermo de Legibus'," *Journal of the Warburg Institute* 2 (1938) 22–41.

Kantorowicz, Hermann and W. W. Buckland. *Studies in the Glossators of the Roman Law: Newly Discovered Writings of the 12th Century* (Cambridge: Cambridge University Press, 1938; repr. Aalen: Scientia-Verlag, 1969).

Kapriev, Georgi. *Ipsa vita et veritas: der ontologische Gottesbeweis und die Ideenwelt Anselms von Canterbury* (Leiden: Brill, 1998).

"The Modern Study of Byzantine Philosophy," *Bulletin de philosophie médiévale* 48 (2006) 3–13.

Karamanolis, George. "Plethon and Scholarios on Aristotle," in K. Ierodiakonou (ed.) *Byzantine Philosophy and its Ancient Sources* (Oxford: Oxford University Press, 2002) 253–82.

Karger, Elizabeth. "Richard Rufus's Account of Substantial Transmutation," *Medioevo* 27 (2002) 168–91.

"La supposition materielle comme suppositions significative: Paul de Venice, Paul de Pergula," in A. Maierù (ed.) *English Logic in Italy in the 14th and 15th Centuries* (Naples: Bibliopolis, 1982) 331–41.

"Walter Burley's Realism," *Vivarium* 37 (1999) 24–40.

"William of Ockham, Walter Chatton and Adam Wodeham on the Objects of Knowledge and Belief," *Vivarium* 33 (1995) 171–96.

Katz, Bernard. "On a *Sophisma* of Richard Kilvington and a Problem of Analysis," *Medieval Philosophy and Theology* 5 (1996) 31–8.

Katz, Steven T. (ed.). *Saadiah Gaon* (New York: Arno Press, 1980).

Kaukua, Jari. *Avicenna on Subjectivity: A Philosophical Study* (Jyväskylä: University of Jyväskylä Press, 2007).

Kaye, Joel. *Economy and Nature in the Fourteenth Century: Money, Market Exchange, and the Emergence of Scientific Thought* (New York: Cambridge University Press, 1998).

Kaye, Sharon. "Why the Liberty of Indifference Is Worth Wanting: Buridan's Ass, Friendship, and Peter John Olivi," *History of Philosophy Quarterly* 21 (2004) 21–42.

Kazhdan, Alexander P. *et al. The Oxford Dictionary of Byzantium* (New York: Oxford University Press, 1991).

Keele, Rondo. "Can God Make a Picasso? William Ockham and Walter Chatton on Divine Power and Real Relations," *Journal of the History of Philosophy* 45 (2007) 395–411.

"The Logical and Scientific Treatises of John Chilmark (†1396)," *Bulletin de philosophie médiévale* 49 (2007) 119–37.

"Oxford *Quodlibeta* from Ockham to Holcot," in C. Schabel (ed.) *Theological Quodlibeta in the Middle Ages: The Fourteenth Century* (Leiden: Brill, 2007) 651–92.

"The So-Called *Res* Theory of Walter Chatton," *Franciscan Studies* 61 (2003) 37–53.

"Walter Chatton," in E. Zalta (ed.) *The Stanford Encyclopedia of Philosophy* (Fall 2006 edition): http://plato.stanford.edu/archives/fall2006/entries/walter-chatton/.

Keen, Maurice. *The Laws of War in the Late Middle Ages* (London: Routledge, 1965).

Kelley, Francis E. "Robert Orford's Attack on Giles of Rome," *The Thomist* 51 (1987) 70–96.

"Some Observations on the Fictum Theory in Ockham and its Relation to Hervaeus Natalis," *Franciscan Studies* 38 (1978) 260–82.

"Two Early English Thomists: Thomas Sutton and Robert of Orford vs. Henry of Ghent," *The Thomist* 45 (1981) 371–80.

"Walter Chatton vs. Aureoli and Ockham Regarding the Universal Concept," *Franciscan Studies* 41 (1981) 222–49.

Kellner, Menachem. "Dogma in Medieval Jewish Thought: A Bibliographical Survey," *Studies in Bibliography and Booklore* 15 (1984) 5–21.

Dogma in Medieval Jewish Thought: From Maimonides to Abravanel (Oxford: Oxford University Press, 1986).

Kelly, Louis G. *The Mirror of Grammar: Theology, Philosophy and the Modistae* (Amsterdam: Benjamins, 2002).

"La *Physique* d'Aristote et la phrase simple dans les traités de grammaire spéculative," in A. Joly and J. Stefanini (eds.) *La grammaire spéculative: des Modistes aux Idéologues* (Lille: Presses universitaires, 1977) 105–24.

Kempshall, M. S. *The Common Good in Late Medieval Political Thought* (Oxford: Clarendon Press, 1999).

Kennedy, Angus J. *Christine de Pizan: A Bibliographical Guide* (London: Grant and Cutler, 1984).

Kennedy, Leonard A. "The *De anima* of John Sharpe," *Franciscan Studies* 29 (1969) 249–70.

"Mediaevalia. I. Robert Graystanes' Commentary on the *Sentences*," *Recherches de théologie ancienne et médiévale* 53 (1986) 185–9.

Peter of Ailly and the Harvest of Fourteenth-Century Philosophy (Lewiston, PA: E. Mellen Press, 1986.)

The Philosophy of Robert Holcot, Fourteenth-Century Skeptic (Lewiston, PA: E. Mellen Press, 1993).

"Robert Graystanes, O.S.B., on Essence and Existence," *Recherches de théologie ancienne et médiévale* 56 (1989) 102–16.

Kennedy, Leonard A. and Margaret E. Romano. "John Went, O.F.M., and Divine Omnipotence," *Franciscan Studies* 47 (1987) 138–70.

Kenny, Anthony. "Divine Foreknowledge and Human Freedom," in A. Kenny (ed.) *Aquinas: A Collection of Critical Essays* (Notre Dame, IN: University of Notre Dame Press, 1969) 255–70.

"The Realism of *De Universalibus*," in A. Kenny (ed.) *Wyclif in his Times* (Oxford: Clarendon Press, 1986) 17–29.

Wyclif (Oxford: Clarendon Press, 1985).

(ed.). *Wyclif in his Times* (Oxford: Clarendon Press, 1986).

Kenny, Anthony and Jan Pinborg. "Medieval Philosophical Literature," in N. Kretzmann *et al.* (eds.) *The Cambridge History of Later Medieval Philosophy* (Cambridge: Cambridge University Press, 1982) 11–42.

Kent, Bonnie. "Aquinas and Weakness of Will," *Philosophy and Phenomenological Research* 75 (2007) 70–91.

"Aristotle and the Franciscans: Gerald Odonis' Commentary on the 'Nicomachean Ethics' " (Ph.D. dissertation: Columbia University, 1984).

"Aristotle's Ethics, Situationist Psychology, and a Fourteenth-Century Debate," *History of Philosophy Quarterly* 25 (2008) 95–114.

"Augustine's Ethics," in N. Kretzmann and E. Stump (eds.) *The Cambridge Companion to Augustine* (Cambridge: Cambridge University Press, 2001) 205–33.

"Evil in Later Medieval Philosophy," *Journal of the History of Philosophy* 45 (2007) 177–205.

"Habits and Virtues," in S. J. Pope (ed.) *The Ethics of Aquinas* (Washington, DC: Georgetown University Press, 2002) 116–30.

"Rethinking Moral Dispositions: Scotus on the Virtues," in Thomas Williams (ed.) *The Cambridge Companion to Duns Scotus* (Cambridge: Cambridge University Press, 2003) 352–76.

Virtues of the Will: The Transformation of Ethics in the Late Thirteenth Century (Washington, DC: Catholic University of America Press, 1995).

Kerby-Fulton, Kathryn. "Prophet and Reformer: Smoke in the Vineyard," in B. Newman (ed.) *Voice of the Living Light: Hildegard of Bingen and her World* (Berkeley: University of California Press, 1998).

Kerferd, G. B. *The Sophistic Movement* (Cambridge: Cambridge University Press, 1981).

Kerner, Max. *Johannes von Salisbury und die logische Struktur seines "Policraticus"* (Wiesbaden: Steiner, 1977).

Kéry, Lotte. *Canonical Collections of the Early Middle Ages (ca. 400–1140)* (Washington, DC: Catholic University of America Press, 1999).

Keys, Mary. *Aquinas, Aristotle, and the Promise of the Common Good* (Cambridge: Cambridge University Press, 2006).

Khalidi, Muhammad Ali (tr.). *Medieval Islamic Philosophical Writings* (Cambridge: Cambridge University Press, 2005).

Khan, Qamar-ud-Din. *Al-Mawardi's Theory of the State* (Lahore: Islamic Book Foundation, 1983).
  The Political Thought of Ibn Taymiyah (Islamabad: Islamic Research Institute, 1973).

Kholeif, Fathalla. *A Study on Fakhr al-Din al-Razi and his Controversies in Transoxania* (Beirut: Dar al-Machreq Éditeurs, 1966).

Kianka, Frances. "Demetrius Cydones (c. 1324–c. 1397): Intellectual and Diplomatic Relations between Byzantium and the West in the Fourteenth Century" (Ph.D. dissertation: Fordham University, 1981).

Kieckhefer, Richard. "Mysticism and Social Consciousness in the Fourteenth Century," *Revue de l'Université d'Ottawa* 48 (1978) 179–86.
  Unquiet Souls: Fourteenth-Century Saints and their Religious Milieu (Chicago: University of Chicago Press, 1984).

King, Peter. "Abelard's Intentionalist Ethics," *Modern Schoolman* 72 (1995) 213–31.
  "Aquinas on the Passions," in S. MacDonald and E. Stump (eds.) *Aquinas's Moral Theory: Essays in Honor of Norman Kretzmann* (Ithaca, NY: Cornell University Press, 1999) 101–32.
  "Duns Scotus on the Common Nature and Individual Difference," *Philosophical Topics* 20 (1992) 51–76.
  "Jean Buridan's Philosophy of Science," *Studies in History and Philosophy of Science* 18 (1987) 109–32.
  "Late Scholastic Theories of the Passions: Controversies in the Thomist Tradition," in H. Lagerlund and M. Yrjönsuuri (eds.) *Emotions and Choice from Boethius to Descartes* (Dordrecht: Kluwer, 2002) 229–58.
  "Peter Abailard and the Problem of Universals in the Twelfth Century" (Ph.D. dissertation: Princeton University, 1982).
  "Peter Abelard," in E. Zalta (ed.) *The Stanford Encyclopedia of Philosophy* (Fall 2004 edition): http://plato.stanford.edu/archives/fall2004/entries/abelard/.
  "Rethinking Representation in the Middle Ages," in H. Lagerlund (ed.) *Representation and Objects of Thought in Medieval Philosophy* (Aldershot: Ashgate, 2007) 68–86.
  "Scholasticism and the Philosophy of Mind: The Failure of Aristotelian Psychology," in T. Horowitz and A. Janis (eds.) *Scientific Failure* (Lanham, MD: Rowman and Littlefield, 1994) 109–38.
  "Scotus on Metaphysics," in T. Williams (ed.) *The Cambridge Companion to Duns Scotus* (Cambridge: Cambridge University Press, 2003).

Kirchhoff, Raina. *Die Syncategoremata des Wilhelm von Sherwood: Kommentierung und Historische Einordnung* (Leiden: Brill, 2008).

Kirjavainen, Heikki. "Transcendental Elements in the Semantics of Crathorn," in G. Holmström-Hintikka (ed.) *Medieval Philosophy and Modern Times* (Dordrecht: Kluwer, 2000) 45–58.

Kirschner, Stefan. *Nicolaus Oresmes Kommentar zur Physik des Aristoteles* (Stuttgart: Steiner, 1997).

Kirwan, Christopher. *Augustine* (London: Routledge, 1989).

Kitanov, Severin. "Beatific Enjoyment in Scholastic Philosophy and Theology 1240–1335" (Ph.D. dissertation: University of Helsinki, 2006).

Kleineidam, Erich. *Das Problem der hylomorphen Zusammensetzung der geistigen Substanzen im 13. Jahrhundert, behandelt bis Thomas von Aquin* (Breslau: Tesch, 1930).

Klibansky, Raymond. *The Continuity of the Platonic Tradition during the Middle Ages: Outlines of a Corpus Platonicum Medii Aevi* (London: Warburg Institute, 1939; repr. Munich: Kraus, 1981).

Klima, Gyula. "Buridan's Logic and the Ontology of Modes," in S. Ebbesen and R. L. Friedman (eds.) *Medieval Analyses in Language and Cognition* (Copenhagen: Royal Danish Academy of Sciences and Letters, 1999) 473–95.

"The Changing Role of *Entia Rationis* in Medieval Philosophy: A Comparative Study with a Reconstruction," *Synthese* 96 (1993) 25–59.

"Consequences of a Closed, Token-Based Semantics: The Case of John Buridan," *History and Philosophy of Logic* 25 (2004) 95–110.

" 'Debeo tibi equum': A Reconstruction of the Theoretical Framework of Buridan's Treatment of the Sophisma," in S. Read (ed.) *Sophisms in Medieval Logic and Grammar: Acts of the Ninth European Symposium for Medieval Logic and Semantics* (Dordrecht: Kluwer, 1993) 333–47.

"Existence and Reference in Medieval Logic," in A. Hieke and E. Morscher (eds.) *New Essays in Free Logic* (Dordrecht: Kluwer, 2001) 197–226.

John Buridan (Oxford: Oxford University Press, 2009).

"The Medieval Problem of Universals," in E. Zalta (ed.) *The Stanford Encyclopedia of Philosophy* (Winter 2004 edition): http://plato.stanford.edu/archives/win2004/entries/universals-medieval.

"Nominalism," in E. K. Brown (ed.) *Encyclopedia of Language and Linguistics*, 2nd edn (Boston: Elsevier, 2006) 8: 648–52.

"Ockham's Semantics and Ontology of the Categories," in P. V. Spade (ed.) *The Cambridge Companion to Ockham* (Cambridge: Cambridge University Press, 1999) 118–42.

"Peter of Spain, the Author of the *Summulae*," in J. J. E. Gracia and T. Noone (eds.) *A Companion to Philosophy in the Middle Ages* (Oxford: Blackwell, 2003) 526–31.

" 'Socrates est species': Logic, Metaphysics, and Psychology in St. Thomas Aquinas' Treatment of a Paralogism," in K. Jacobi (ed.) *Argumentationstheorie: Scholastische Forschungen zu den logischen und semantischen Regeln korrekten Folgerns* (Leiden: Brill, 1993) 489–504.

"Syncategoremata," in E. K. Brown and A. Anderson (eds.) *Encyclopedia of Language and Linguistics*, 2nd edn (Boston: Elsevier, 2006) 12: 353–6.

"Thomas of Sutton on the Nature of the Intellective Soul and the Thomistic Theory of Being," in J. Aertsen *et al.* (eds.) *Nach der Verurteilung von 1277: Philosophie und Theologie an der Universität von Paris im letzten Viertel des 13. Jahrhunderts: Studien und Texte* (Berlin: De Gruyter, 2001) 436–55.

Kluge, E.-H. "Roscelin and the Medieval Problem of Universals," *Journal of the History of Philosophy* 14 (1976) 405–14.

Kluxen, Wolfgang. "Literargeschichtliches zum lateinischen Moses Maimonides," *Recherches de théologie ancienne et médiévale* 21 (1954), 23–50.

Kneepkens, C. H. "The *Absoluta cuiuslibet* attributed to P.H. Some Notes on its Transmission and the Use Made of it by Robert Kilwardby and Roger Bacon," in I. Angelelli and P. Pérez-Ilzarbe (eds.) *Medieval and Renaissance Logic in Spain: Acts of the 12th European Symposium on Medieval Logic and Semantics* (Hildesheim: Georg Olms Verlag, 2000) 373–403.

"Absolutio: A Note on the Development of a Grammatical Notion," in I. Rosier (ed.) *L'héritage des grammairiens latins, de l'antiquité aux lumières* (Leuven: Peeters, 1988) 155–69.

"Erfurt, Ampl. Q.70A: A Quaestiones-Commentary on the Second Part of Alexander de Villa Dei's *Doctrinale* by Marsilius of Inghen? An Explorative Note on a Specimen of Conceptualist Grammar," *Vivarium* 28 (1990) 26–54.

"Grammar and Semantics in the Twelfth Century: Petrus Helias and Gilbert de la Porrée on the Substantive Verb," in M. Kardaun and J. Spruyt (eds.) *The Winged Chariot: Collected Essays on Plato and Platonism in Honour of L.M. de Rijk* (Leiden: Brill, 2000) 237–75.

Het Iudicium Constructionis: Het Leerstuk van de Constructio in de 2de Helft van de 12de Eeuw (Nijmegen: Ingenium, 1987).

"Master Guido and his View on Government: On Twelfth-Century Linguistic Thought," *Vivarium* 16 (1978) 108–41.

"*Mulier quae Damnavit Salvavit*. A Note of the Early Development of the Relatio Simplex," *Vivarium* 14 (1976) 1–25.

"The Mysterious Buser Again: William Buser of Heusden and the 'Obligationes' Tract 'Ob rogatum'," in A. Maierù (ed.) *Early Logic in Italy* (Naples: Bibliopolis, 1982) 147–66.

"On the Notion of *Constructio* in Conceptualist Grammar: Quaestio XXXV of the *Doctrinale*-Commentary Preserved in Erfurt, Amplon. Q. 70A and attributed to a Master Marcilius," in H. A. G. Braakhuis and M. J. F. M. Hoenen (eds.) *Marsilius of Inghen* (Nijmegen: Ingenium, 1992) 143–72.

"The Priscianic Tradition," in S. Ebbesen (ed.) *Sprachtheorien in Spätantike und Mittelalter* (Tübingen: Narr, 1995) 239–64.

"The *Relatio simplex* in the Grammatical Tracts of the Late Twelfth and Early Thirteenth Century," *Vivarium* 15 (1977) 1–30.

"Roger Bacon on the Double *intellectus*: A Note on the Development of the Theory of *Congruitas* and *Perfectio* in the First Half of the Thirteenth Century," in P. O. Lewry (ed.) *The Rise of British Logic* (Toronto: Pontifical Institute of Mediaeval Studies, 1985) 115–43.

"*Significatio generalis* and *significatio specialis*: Notes on Nicholas of Paris' Contribution to Early Thirteenth-Century Linguistic Thought," in S. Ebbesen and R. L. Friedman (eds.) *Medieval Analyses in Language and Cognition* (Copenhagen: Reitzels, 1999) 17–43.

"Some Notes on the Revival of Modistic Linguistics in the Fifteenth Century: Ps.-Johannes Versor and William Zenders of Weert," in R. L. Friedman and S. Ebbesen (eds.) *John Buridan and Beyond 1300–1700* (Copenhagen: Royal Danish Academy of Sciences and Letters, 2004) 69–119.

" 'Suppositio' and 'supponere' in 12th-Century Grammar," in J. Jolivet and A. de Libera (eds.) *Gilbert de Poitiers et ses contemporains: aux origines de la logica modernorum* (Naples: Bibliopolis, 1987) 325–51.

"The Tradition of Universal and Speculative Grammar in the Late Middle Ages," in C. Codoñer Merino *et al.* (eds.) *El Brocense y la Humanidades en el siglo XVI* (Salamanca: Ediciones Universidad, 2003) 33–60.

"Transitivity, Intransitivity and Related Concepts in Twelfth-Century Grammar. An Explorative Study," in G. L. Bursill-Hall *et al.* (eds.) *De ortu Grammaticae. Studies in Medieval Grammar and Linguistic Theory in Memory of Jan Pinborg* (Amsterdam: Benjamins, 1990) 161–89.

"The *Via antiqua* and the *Via moderna* in Grammar: The Late Medieval Discussions on the Subject of the Sentence," in A. Maierù and L. Valente (eds.) *Medieval Theories on Assertive and Non-Assertive Language* (Florence: Olschki, 2004) 219–44.

"Willem Buser of Heusden's Obligationes-Treatise 'Ob rogatum': A Ressourcement in the Doctrine of Logical Obligation?" in K. Jacobi (ed.) *Argumentationstheorie: scholastische Forschungen zu den logischen und semantischen Regeln korrekten Folgerns* (Leiden: Brill, 1993) 343–62.

Knowles, David. *The Evolution of Medieval Thought* (New York: Vintage Books, 1962).

The Religious Orders in England (Cambridge: Cambridge University Press, 1948–9).

Knuuttila, Simo. "The Emergence of the Logic of the Will in Medieval Thought," in G. B. Matthews (ed.) *The Augustinian Tradition* (Berkeley: University of California Press, 1999) 207–21.

Emotions in Ancient and Medieval Philosophy (Oxford: Clarendon Press, 2004).

Modalities in Medieval Philosophy (London: Routledge, 1993).

"Time and Creation in Augustine," in N. Kretzmann and E. Stump (eds.) *The Cambridge Companion to Augustine* (Cambridge: Cambridge University Press, 2001) 103–15.

"Trinitarian Sophisms in Robert Holcot's Theology," in S. Read (ed.) *Sophisms in Medieval Logic and Grammar: Acts of the Ninth European Symposium for Medieval Logic and Semantics* (Dordrecht: Kluwer, 1993) 348–56.

Knysh, George. *Fragments of Ockham Hermeneutics* (Winnipeg: WCU Council of Learned Societies, 1997).

Political Ockhamism (Winnipeg: WCU Council of Learned Societies, 1996).

Kobler, Franz. *Letters of Jews through the Ages: From Biblical Times to the Middle of the Eighteenth Century* (London: Ararat Publishing Society, 1953).

Koch, Georg. *Manegold von Lautenbach und die Lehre von der Volkssouveränität unter Heinrich IV* (Berlin: Ebering, 1902; repr. Vaduz: Kraus, 1965).

Koch, Josef. "Augustinischer und Dionysischer Neuplatonismus und das Mittelalter," in W. Beierwaltes (ed.) *Platonismus in der Philosophie des Mittelalters* (Darmstadt: Wissenschaftliche Buchgesellschaft, 1969) 317–42.

Durandus de S. Porciano, O.P.: Forschungen zum Streit um Thomas von Aquin zu Beginn des 14. Jahrhunderts (Münster: Aschendorff, 1927).

"Jakob von Metz O.P., der Lehrer des Durandus de S. Porciano, O.P.," *Archives d'histoire doctrinale et littéraire du moyen âge* 4 (1929) 169–229.

"Neue Aktenstücke zu dem gegen Wilhelm Ockham in Avignon geführten Prozess," in *Kleine Schriften* (Rome: Edizioni di Storia e Letteratura, 1973) II: 275–365.

"Der Prozess gegen den Magister Johannes de Polliaco und seine Vorgeschichte," *Recherches de théologie ancienne et médiévale* 5 (1933) 391–422.

Kogan, Barry. *Averroes and the Metaphysics of Causation* (Albany: State University of New York Press, 1985).

"Judah Halevi and his Use of Philosophy in the *Kuzari*," in D. H. Frank and O. Leaman (eds.) *The Cambridge Companion to Medieval Jewish Philosophy* (Cambridge: Cambridge University Press, 2003) 111–35.

Köhler, T.W. *Der Begriff der Einheit und ihr ontologisches Prinzip nach dem Sentenzenkommentar des Jakob von Metz O.P.* (Rome: Herder, 1971).

"Wissenschaft und Evidenz: Beobachtungen zum wissenschaftstheoretischen Ansatz des Jakob von Metz," in T. W. Köhler (ed.) *Sapientiae procerum amore: mélanges médiévistes offerts à Dom Jean-Pierre Müller* (Rome: Herder, 1974) 369–414.

Kölmel, W. "Einheit und Zweiheit der Gewalt im Corpus Mysticum: zur Souveränitätslehre des Augustinus Triumphus," *Historische Jahrbuch* 82 (1963) 103–47.

König, Dietrich. *Tolomeo von Lucca: ein biographischer versuch* (Harburg: Lühmann, 1878).

König-Pralong, Catherine. *Avènement de l'aristotélisme en terre chrétienne* (Paris: Vrin, 2005).

Konstan, David. *The Emotions of the Ancient Greeks: Studies in Aristotle and Classical Literature* (Toronto: University of Toronto Press, 2006).

Köpf, Ulrich. *Religiöse Erfahrung in der Theologie Bernhards von Clairvaux* (Tübingen: Mohr, 1980).

Korolec, J. B. "Gilles d'Orléans et ses conceptions de philosophie morale," in M. Asztalos *et al.* (eds.) *Knowledge and the Sciences in Medieval Philosophy: Proceedings of the Eighth International Congress of Medieval Philosophy* (Helsinki: Yliopistopaino, 1990) III: 224–33.

Kosman, L. A. "Aristotle's Definition of Motion," *Phronesis* 14 (1969) 40–62.

Kotzia, P. Περί του Μήλου ή Περί της Αριστοτέλους Τελευτής *(Liber de Pomo sive De morte Aristotilis)* (Thessaloniki: Ekdoseis Thyrathen, 2007).

Kovach, Francis Joseph and Robert W. Shahan (eds.). *Albert the Great: Commemorative Essays* (Norman: University of Oklahoma Press, 1980).

Kraemer, Joel L. *Humanism in the Renaissance of Islam: The Cultural Revival during the Buyid Age* (Leiden: Brill, 1986).

(ed.) *Perspectives on Maimonides: Philosophical and Historical Studies* (Oxford: Oxford University Press, 1991).

Philosophy in the Renaissance of Islam: Abu Sulayman al-Sijistani and his Circle (Leiden: Brill, 1986).

Kraus, Paul. *Jābir ibn Ḥayyān: contribution à l'histoire des idées scientifiques dans l'Islam* (Cairo: Institut français d'archéologie orientale, 1942–3).

"Zu Ibn al-Muqaffaʿ," *Rivista degli Studi Orientali* 14 (1934) 1–20; repr. in R. Brague (ed.) *Alchemie, Ketzerei, Apokryphen im frühen Islam* (Hildesheim: Olms, 1994) 89–108.

Krause, Feliks. "Abriss der Erkenntnistheorie bei Alexander von Alessandria," *Studia Mediewistyczne* 20 (1980) 91–125.

Kraye, Jill. "Moral Philosophy," in C. B. Schmitt and Q. Skinner (eds.) *The Cambridge History of Renaissance Philosophy* (Cambridge: Cambridge University Press, 1988) 303–86.

Kremer, Klaus. *Die neuplatonische Seinsphilosophie und ihre Wirkung auf Thomas von Aquin* (Leiden: Brill 1966).

Kretzmann, Norman. "Adam Wodeham's anti-Aristotelian anti-Atomism," *History of Philosophy Quarterly* 4 (1984) 381–98.

"The Culmination of the Old Logic in Peter Abelard," in R. L. Benson and J. Constable (eds.) *Renaissance and Renewal in the Twelfth Century* (Cambridge, MA: Harvard University Press, 1982) 488–511.

"A General Problem of Creation: Why Would God Create Anything at All?," in S. MacDonald (ed.) *Being and Goodness: The Concept of the Good in Metaphysics and Philosophical Theology* (Ithaca, NY: Cornell University Press, 1991) 208–28.

"Lex iniusta non est lex: Laws on Trial in Aquinas' Court of Conscience," in J. Finnis (ed.) *Natural Law* (Aldershot: Ashgate, 1991) II: 99–121.

The Metaphysics of Creation: Aquinas's Natural Theology in Summa Contra Gentiles II (Oxford: Clarendon Press, 1999).

The Metaphysics of Theism: Aquinas's Natural Theology in Summa Contra Gentiles I (Oxford: Clarendon Press, 1997).

"Socrates is Whiter than Plato Begins to be White," *Noûs* 11 (1977) 3–15.

"Syncategoremata, Exponibilia, Sophismata," in N. Kretzmann *et al.* (eds.) *The Cambridge History of Later Medieval Philosophy* (Cambridge: Cambridge University Press, 1982) 211–45.

Kretzmann, Norman, Anthony Kenny, and Jan Pinborg (eds.). *The Cambridge History of Later Medieval Philosophy: From the Rediscovery of Aristotle to the Disintegration of Scholasticism. 1100–1600* (Cambridge: Cambridge University Press, 1982).

Kretzmann, Norman and Eleonore Stump (eds.). *The Cambridge Companion to Aquinas* (Cambridge: Cambridge University Press, 1993).

The Cambridge Companion to Augustine (Cambridge: Cambridge University Press, 2001).

The Cambridge Translations of Medieval Philosophical Texts, vol. 1: *Logic and the Philosophy of Language* (Cambridge: Cambridge University Press, 1988).

Krey, Philip D. W. and Lesley Smith (eds.). *Nicholas of Lyra: The Senses of Scripture* (Leiden: Brill, 2000).

Krieger, Gerhard. *Der Begriff der praktischen Vernunft nach Johannes Buridanus* (Münster: Aschendorff, 1986).

"Studies on Walter Burley, 1989–1997," *Vivarium* 37 (1999) 94–100.

Subjekt und Metaphysik: Die Metaphysik des Johannes Buridan (Münster: Aschendorff, 2003).

Kristeller, Paul Oskar. "The School of Salerno: Its Development and its Contribution to the History of Learning," in *Storia e Letteratura: Raccolta di studi e testi 54: Studies in Renaissance Thought and Letters* (Rome: Edizioni di Storia e Letteratura, 1956) 287–336.

Kristeller, Paul Oskar et al. (eds.). *Catalogus translationum et commentariorum: Mediaeval and Renaissance Latin Translations and Commentaries: Annotated Lists and Guides* (Washington, DC: Catholic University of America Press, 1960–).

Kritzeck, James. *Peter the Venerable and Islam* (Princeton, NJ: Princeton University Press, 1964).

Krüger, Karl. *Des Ptolomäus Lucensis Leben und Werke* (Göttingen: Huth, 1874).

Kukkonen, Taneli. "Averroes and the Teleological Argument," *Religious Studies* 38 (2002) 405–28.

"The Impossible, insofar as it Is Possible: Ibn Rushd and Buridan on Logic and Natural Theology," in D. Perler and U. Rudolph (eds.) *Logik und Theologie: das Organon im arabischen und im lateinischen Mittelalter* (Leiden: Brill, 2005) 447–67.

"No Man Is an Island: Nature and Neo-Platonic Ethics in Ḥayy Ibn Yaqẓān," *Journal of the History of Philosophy* 46 (2008) 187–204.

"Possible Worlds in the *Tahâfut al-falâsifa:* Al-Ghazâlî on Creation and Contingency," *Journal of the History of Philosophy* 38 (2000) 479–502.

Kuksewicz, Zdzisław. *Averroïsme bolonais au XIVe siècle* (Wroclaw: Ossolineum, 1965).

De Siger de Brabant à Jacques de Plaisance: la théorie de l'intellect chez les averroïstes latins des XIIIe et XIVe siècles (Wroclaw: Editions de l'Academie Polonaise des Sciences, 1968).

"Guillaume d'Alnwick: trois questions anti-averroistes sur l'âme intellect," *Studia Mediewistyczne* 7 (1966) 3–76.

"Paolo Veneto e la sua teoria dell'anima," in L. Olivieri (ed.) *Aristotelismo veneto e scienza moderna* (Padua: Antenore, 1983) 130–64.

"Some Remarks on Erfurt Averroists," *Studia Mediewistyczne* 32 (1997) 93–121.

"Der Theorie der Materie des Aegidius von Orléans," in B. Mojsisch and O. Pluta (eds.) *Historia philosophiae medii aevi: Studien zur Geschichte der Philosophie des Mittelalters: Festschrift für Kurt Flasch* (Amsterdam: Benjamins, 1991) 521–34.

Kunitzsch, Paul. "Über das Frühstadium der arabischen Aneignung antiken Gutes," *Saeculum* 26 (1975) 268–82.

Künzle, Pius. *Das Verhältnis der Seele zu ihren Potenzen: Problemgeschichtliche Untersuchungen von Augustin bis und mit Thomas von Aquin* (Freiburg: Universitätsverlag, 1956).

Kürzinger, Josef. *Alfonsus Vargas Toletanus und seine theologische einleitungslehre: ein Beitrag zur Geschichte der Scholastik im 14. Jahrhundert* (Münster: Aschendorff, 1930).

Kuttner, Stephan. "Did Rolandus of Bologna Write a 'Stroma ex Decretorum, corpore captum'?", *Bulletin of Medieval Canon Law*, n.s. 20 (1990) 69–70.

Gratian and the Schools of Law, 1140–1234 (London: Variorum Reprints, 1983).

"Graziano: L'uomo e l'opera," *Studia Gratiana* 1 (1953) 17–29.

Laakmann, Reinhold. *Die Königsgewalt bei Manegold von Lautenbach* (Hamburg: Lüdke bei der Uni, 1969).

Laarmann, Matthias. *Deus, primum cognitum: die Lehre von Gott als dem Ersterkannten des menschlichen Intellekts bei Heinrich von Gent (†1293)* (Münster: Aschendorff, 1999).

Laberge, Damascus. "Fr. Petri Ioannis Olivi, O.F.M., tria scripta sui ipsius apologetica annorum 1283 et 1285," *Archivum Franciscanum Historicum* 28 (1935) 115–55, 374–407.

"Responsio quam fecit Petrus [Ioannis] ad litteram magistrorum, praesentatam sibi in Avinione," *Archivum Franciscanum Historicum* 28 (1935) 115–55, 374–407.

Lacoste, Yves. *Ibn Khaldun: The Birth of History and the Past of the Third World* (London: Verso, 1984).

Ladner, Pascal. *Revolutionäre Kirchenkritik am Basler Konzil? Zum Konziliarismus des Heymericus de Campo* (Basel: Verlag Helbing und Lichtenhahn, 1985).

Lafleur, Claude. *Quatre introductions à la philosophie au XIIIe siècle* (Paris: Vrin, 1988).

Lafleur, Claude and Joanne Carrier (eds.). *L'enseignement de la philosophie au XIIIe siècle: autour du "Guide de l'étudiant" du ms. Ripoll 109* (Turnhout: Brepols, 1997).

"La 'Philosophia' d'Hervé le Breton (alias Henri le Breton) et le recueil d'introductions à la philosophie du ms. Oxford, Corpus Christi College 283," *Archives d'histoire doctrinale et littéraire du moyen âge* 61 (1994) 149–226; 62 (1995) 359–442.

Lagerlund, Henrik. *Modal Syllogistics in the Middle Ages* (Leiden: Brill, 2000).

"Pietro d'Abano and the Anatomy of Perception," in S. Knuuttila and P. Kärkkäinen (eds.) *Theories of Perception in Medieval and Early Modern Philosophy* (Dordrecht: Springer, 2008) 117–30.

(ed.). *Representation and Objects of Thought in Medieval Philosophy* (Aldershot: Ashgate, 2007).

Lagerlund, Henrik and Mikko Yrjönsuuri (eds.). *Emotions and Choice from Boethius to Descartes* (Dordrecht: Kluwer, 2002).

Lahey, Stephen. *Philosophy and Politics in the Thought of John Wyclif* (Cambridge: Cambridge University Press, 2003).

Lambertini, Roberto. "Felicitas politica und speculatio: die Idee der Philosophie in ihrem Verhältnis zur Politik nach Johannes von Jandun," *Miscellanea Mediaevalia* 26 (1998) 984–90.

"Political Quodlibeta," in C. Schabel (ed.) *Theological Quodlibeta in the Middle Ages: The Thirteenth Century* (Leiden: Brill, 2006) 439–74.

"Sicut tabernarius vinum significat per circulum: Directions in Contemporary Interpretations of the Modistae," in U. Eco and C. Marmo (eds.) *On the Medieval Theories of Signs* (Amsterdam: Benjamins, 1989) 107–42.

Lambton, Ann. *State and Government in Medieval Islam: An Introduction to the Study of Islamic Political Thought: The Jurists* (Oxford: Oxford University Press, 1981).

Theory and Practice in Medieval Persian Government (London: Variorum Reprints, 1980).

Lameer, Joep. *Al-Farabi and Aristotelian Syllogistics: Greek Theory and Islamic Practice* (Leiden: Brill, 1994).

Lamoreaux, John C. "The Biography of Theodore Abū Qurrah Revisited," *Dumbarton Oaks Papers* 56 (2002) 25–40.

Landgraf, A. M. *Dogmengeschichte der Früh Scholastik* (Regensburg: Pustet, 1952–6).

Introduction à l'histoire de la littérature théologique de la scolastique naissante, tr. A.M. Landry and L.-B. Geiger (Montréal: Institut d'études médiévales, 1973).

"Der Porretanismus der Homilien des Radulphus Ardens," *Zeitschrift für katholische Theologie* 64 (1940) 132–48.

Landsberg, Ernst. *Die Glosse des Accursius und ihre Lehre vom Eigenthum: rechts-und dogmengeschichtliche Untersuchungen* (Leipzig: Brockhaus, 1883).

Lang, Albert. *Heinrich Totting von Oyta: ein Beitrag zur Entstehungsgeschichte der ersten deutschen Universitäten und zur Problemsgeschichte der Spätscholastik* (Münster: Aschendorff, 1937).

Lang, Helen. *The Order of Nature in Aristotle's Physics: Place and the Elements* (Cambridge: Cambridge University Press, 1998).

Langermann, Tzvi. "Maimonides and the Sciences," in D. H. Frank and O. Leaman (eds.) *The Cambridge Companion to Medieval Jewish Philosophy* (Cambridge: Cambridge University Press, 2003) 157–75.

Langholm, Odd. *The Aristotelian Analysis of Usury* (New York: Columbia University Press, 1984).

 Economics in the Medieval Schools: Wealth, Exchange, Value, Money and Usury According to the Paris Theological Tradition, 1200–1350 (Leiden: Brill, 1992).

 The Legacy of Scholasticism in Economic Thought: Antecedents of Choice and Power (Cambridge: Cambridge University Press, 1998).

 The Merchant in the Confessional: Trade and Price in Pre-Reformation Penitential Handbooks (Leiden: Brill, 2003).

 Price and Value in the Aristotelian Tradition (Bergen: Universitetsforlaget, 1979).

 Wealth and Money in the Aristotelian Tradition (New York: Columbia University Press, 1983).

Laoust, Henri. *La politique de Gazali* (Paris: Geuthner, 1970).

Lapidge, Michael, Claudio Leonardi, and Gian Carlo Garfagnini (eds.). *Compendium Auctorum Latinorum Medii Aevi: 500–1500* (Florence: SISMEL, Edizioni del Galluzzo, 2000–).

Lapparent, Pierre. "L'œuvre politique de François de Meyronnes, ses rapports avec celle de Dante," *Archives d'histoire doctrinale et littéraire du moyen âge* 15–7 (1940–2) 5–151.

Larchet, Jean-Claude. *Thérapeutique des maladies spirituelles: une introduction à la tradition ascétique de l'Eglise orthodoxe* (Paris: Cerf, 1997).

Largier, Niklaus. *Bibliographie zu Meister Eckhart* (Freiburg: Universitätsverlag Freiburg, 1989).

La Salle, John and James Blythe. "Was Ptolemy of Lucca a Civic Humanist? Reflections on a Newly-Discovered Manuscript of Hans Baron," *History of Political Thought* 26 (2005) 236–65.

Lasker, Daniel J. "Jewish-Christian Polemics at the Turning Point: Jewish Evidence from the Twelfth Century," *Harvard Theological Review* 89 (1996) 161–73.

 Jewish Philosophical Polemics against Christianity in the Middle Ages (New York: Ktav Publication House, 1977).

Laumakis, John. "Aquinas' Misinterpretation of Avicebron on the Activity of Corporeal Substances: *Fons Vitae* II, 9 and 10," *Modern Schoolman* 81 (2004) 135–49.

Laurent, M. H. "Armandus de Bevézer et son commentaire sur le *De ente et essentia*," *Revue Thomiste* 35 (1930) 426–36.

 Le bienheureux Innocent V (Pierre de Tarentaise) et son temps (Vatican: Biblioteca Apostolica Vaticana, 1947).

Law, Vivien. "La grammaire latine durant le haut moyen âge," in S. Auroux (ed.) *Histoire des idées linguistiques* (Liège: Mardaga, 1992) II: 83–95.

 Grammar and Grammarians in the Early Middle Ages (London: Longman, 1997).

 (ed.). *History of Linguistic Thought in the Early Middle Ages* (Amsterdam: Benjamins, 1993).

 The History of Linguistics in Europe, from Plato to 1600 (Cambridge: Cambridge University Press, 2003).

Lawn, Brian. *The Prose Salernitan Questions: An Anonymous Collection Dealing with Science and Medicine Written by an Englishman c. 1200 with an Appendix of Ten Related Collections* (London: Oxford University Press for the British Academy, 1979).

 The Salernitan Questions. An Introduction to the History of Medieval and Renaissance Problem Literature (Oxford: Clarendon Press, 1963).

Lawrence, Bruce. *Ibn Khaldun and Islamic Ideology* (Leiden: Brill, 1984).

Lawrence, C. H. "The Letters of Adam Marsh and the Franciscan School at Oxford," *Journal of Ecclesiastical History* 42 (1991) 218–38.

Lazzarini, Andrea. "Gratianus de Urbeveteri," *Studia Gratiana* 4 (1956) 1–15.

Lea, Henry. *A History of Auricular Confession and Indulgences in the Latin Church* (London: Swan Sonnenschein, 1896).

Leaman, Oliver. *Averroes and his Philosophy* (Oxford: Clarendon Press, 1988).

(ed.). *The Biographical Encyclopaedia of Islamic Philosophy* (London: Thoemmes, 2006).

"Ibn Bājja on Society and Philosophy," *Islam* 57 (1980) 109–19.

Moses Maimonides (London: Routledge, 1997).

Le Bras, Gabriel and Jean Gaudemet. *Histoire du droit et des institutions de l'Eglise en Occident* (Paris: Cujas, 1955–8).

Lechner, Joseph. "Die Quästionen des Sentenzkommentars des Joh. v. Rodington O.F.M.," *Franziskanische Studien* 22 (1935) 232–48.

Leclercq, Jean. "*Ad ipsam sophiam Christum*: das monastische Zeugnis Abaelards," in F. Hoffmann *et al.* (eds.) *Sapienter ordinare: Festgabe für Erich Kleineidam* (Leipzig: Benno, 1969) 179–98.

"'Ad ipsam sophiam Christum': le témoignage monastique d'Abélard," *Revue d'ascétique et de mystique* 46 (1970) 161–81.

L'amour des lettres et le désir de Dieu: initiation aux auteurs monastiques du moyen âge (Paris: Cerf, 1957).

Jean de Paris et l'écclésiologie du XIIIᵉ siècle (Paris: Vrin, 1942).

"Lettres d'Odon d'Ourscamp, cardinal cistercien," *Studia Anselmiana* 37 (1955) 145–57.

Monks and Love in Twelfth-Century France: Psycho-Historical Essays (Oxford: Clarendon Press, 1979).

"Pour l'histoire de l'expression 'philosophie chrétienne'," *Mélanges de sciences religieuses* 9 (1952) 221–6.

Saint Pierre Damien, ermite et homme d'eglise (Rome: Edizioni di Storia e Letteratura, 1960).

Ledoux, Athanasius. "De gratia creata et increata juxta Quaestionem ineditam Guillelmi de Ware," *Antonianum* 5 (1930) 148–56.

Lefebvre, Charles. "'Aequitas canonica' et 'periculum animae' dans la doctrine de l'Hostiensis," *Ephemerides Iuris Canonici* 8 (1952) 305–21.

"Épikie," in R. Naz (ed.) *Dictionnaire du droit canonique* (Paris: Letouzey et Ané, 1935–65) V: 364–75.

Les pouvoirs du juge en droit canonique (Paris: Sirey, 1938).

Lefévre, Georges. *De Anselmo Laudunensi Scholastico (1050–1117)* (Evreux: Hérissey, 1895).

Leff, Gordon. *Bradwardine and the Pelagians: A Study of His 'De Causa Dei' and its Opponents* (Cambridge: Cambridge University Press, 1957).

Gregory of Rimini: Tradition and Innovation in Fourteenth Century Thought (New York: Manchester, 1961).

Medieval Thought St Augustine to Ockham (Baltimore, MD: Penguin Books, 1958).

Richard Fitzralph, commentator of the Sentences: A Study in Theological Orthodoxy (Manchester: Manchester University Press, 1963).

Leicht, Irene. *Marguerite Porete: eine fromme Intellektuelle und die Inquisition* (Freiburg: Herder, 1999).

Leinkauf, Thomas. *Nicolaus Cusanus: eine Einführung* (Münster: Aschendorff, 2006).

Leinkauf, Thomas and Carlos Steel (eds.). *Platons Timaios als Grundtext der Kosmologie in Spätantike, Mittelalter und Renaissance* (Leuven: Leuven University Press, 2005).

Lemay, Richard J. *Abu Ma'shar and Latin Aristotelianism in the Twelfth Century: The Recovery of Aristotle's Natural Philosophy through Arabic Astrology* (Beirut: American University of Beirut, Publications of the Faculty of Arts and Sciences, 1962).

Lemerle, Paul. *Le premier humanisme byzantin* (Paris: Presses universitaires de France, 1971).

Leonardi, Claudio. "Intellectual Life," in T. Reuter (ed.) *The New Cambridge Medieval History*, vol. III: *c.900–c.1024* (Cambridge: Cambridge University Press, 1999) 186–211.

Lepsius, Susanne. *Der Richter und die Zeugen: eine Untersuchung anhand des Tractatus testimoniorum des Bartolus von Sassoferrato* (Frankfurt: Klostermann, 2003).

Lerner, Ralph (ed.). *Maimonides. Empire of Light: Popular Enlightenment in an Age of Belief* (Chicago: University of Chicago Press, 2000).

"Natural Law in Albo's *Book of Roots*," in J. Cropsey (ed.) *Ancients and Moderns: Essays on the Tradition of Political Philosophy in Honor of Leo Strauss* (New York: Basic Books, 1964) 132–47.

The Heresy of the Free Spirit in the Later Middle Ages (Berkeley: University of California Press, 1972).

Lescoe, Francis. *God as First Principle in Ulrich of Strasbourg* (New York: Alba House, 1979).

Lesne, Émile. *Histoire de la propriété ecclésiastique en France*, vol. V: *Les écoles de la fin du VIIIe siècle à la fin du XIIe* (Lille: Facultés catholiques, 1940).

Lettinck, Paul. *Aristotle's Meteorology and its Reception in the Arab World, with an Edition and Translation of Ibn Suwār's Treatise on Meteorological Phenomena and of Ibn Bajja's Commentary on the Meteorology* (Leiden: Brill, 1999).

Aristotle's Physics and its Reception in the Arabic World with an Edition of the Unpublished Parts of Ibn Bajja's Commentary on the Physics (Leiden: Brill, 1994).

Levenson, Jonathan. *Resurrection and the Restoration of Israel: The Ultimate Victory of the God of Life* (New Haven, CT: Yale University Press, 2006).

Levy, Ian C. *A Companion to John Wyclif: Late Medieval Theologian* (Leiden: Brill, 2006).

John Wyclif: Scriptural Logic, Real Presence, and the Parameters Of Orthodoxy (Milwaukee, WI: Marquette University Press, 2003).

Levy, Raphael. *The Astrological Works of Abraham Ibn Ezra* (Baltimore, MD: Johns Hopkins University Press, 1927).

Lewin, Bernhard. "L'ideal antique du philosophe dans la tradition arabe: un traité d'éthique du philosophe Baghdadien Ibn Suwar," *Lychnos 1954–55* (1955) 267–84.

"La notion de *muḥdath* dans le kalām et dans la philosophie: un petit traité du philosophe chrétien Ibn Suwar," *Orientalia Suecana* 3 (1954) 84–93.

Lewis, Bernard. *The Political Languages of Islam* (Chicago: University of Chicago Press, 1988).

Lewis, C. I. and C. H. Langford. *Symbolic Logic* (New York: The Century Co., 1932).

Lewis, Ewart. "The 'Positivism' of Marsilius of Padua," *Speculum* 38 (1963) 541–82.

Lewis, Neil. "The First Recension of Robert Grosseteste's *De libero arbitrio*," *Mediaeval Studies* 53 (1991) 1–88.

"Time and Modality in Robert Grosseteste" (Ph.D. dissertation: University of Pittsburgh, 1988).

"William of Auvergne's Account of the Enuntiable: Its Relations to Nominalism and the Doctrine of the Eternal Truths," *Vivarium* 33 (1995) 113–36.

Lewry, P. Osmund. "Grammar, Logic and Rhetoric 1220–1320," in J. Catto (ed.) *The History of the University of Oxford*, vol. I: *The Early Oxford Schools* (Oxford: Clarendon Press, 1984) 401–33.

"The *Liber sex principiorum*, a Supposedly Porretanean Work: A Study in Ascription," in J. Jolivet and A. de Libera (eds.) *Gilbert de Poitiers et ses contemporains* (Naples: Bibliopolis, 1987) 251–78.

"Robert Kilwardby's Writings on the *Logica Vetus* Studied with Regard to their Teaching and Method" (D. Phil. thesis: Oxford University, 1978).

"Robertus Angelicus and the Italian Kilwardby," in A. Maierù (ed.) *English Logic in Italy in the 14th and 15th Centuries* (Naples: Bibliopolis, 1983) 33–51.

"Two Continuators of Aquinas: Robertus de Vulgarbia and Thomas Sutton," *Mediaeval Studies* 43 (1981) 58–130.

Lewy, H., et al. (trs.). *Three Jewish Philosophers* (New York: Atheneum, 1985).

Liebeschütz, Hans. "The Debate on Philosophical Learning during the Transition Period (900–1080)," in A. H. Armstrong (ed.) *The Cambridge History of Later Greek and Early Medieval Philosophy* (Cambridge: Cambridge University Press, 1970) 587–610.

Medieval Humanism in the Writings of John of Salisbury (London: Warburg Institute of the University of London, 1950).

Lindberg, David C. "Alhazen's Theory of Vision and its Reception in the West," *Isis* 58 (1967) 321–41.

"Alkindi's Critique of Euclid's Theory of Vision," *Isis* 62 (1971) 469–89.

(ed. and tr.). *John Pecham and the Science of Optics* (Madison: University of Wisconsin, 1970).

"Lines of Influence in Thirteenth-Century Optics: Bacon, Witelo, and Pecham," *Speculum* 46 (1971) 66–83.

"The 'Perspectiva Communis' of John Pecham: Its Influence, Sources and Content," *Archives internationales d'histoire des sciences* 18 (1965) 37–53.

Roger Bacon and the Origins of Perspectiva *in the Middle Ages* (Oxford: Clarendon Press, 1996).

Theories of Vision from Al-Kindi to Kepler (Chicago: University of Chicago Press, 1976).

Lindner, Benedikt. *Die Erkenntnislehre des Thomas von Strassburg* (Münster: Aschendorff, 1930).

Liotta, Filippo and Roberto Tofanini (eds.). *Miscellanea, Rolando Bandinelli, Papa Alessandro III* (Siena: Accademia senese degli intronati, 1986).

Little, A. G. "The Franciscan School at Oxford in the Thirteenth Century," *Archivum Franciscanum Historicum* 19 (1926) 803–74.

Roger Bacon Essays (Oxford: Clarendon Press, 1914).

Little, A. G. and Franz Pelster. *Oxford Theology and Theologians, c.A.D. 1282–1302* (Oxford: Clarendon Press, 1934).

Little, Lester. *Religious Poverty and the Profit Economy in the High Middle Ages* (Ithaca, NY: Cornell University Press, 1978).

"Les techniques de la confession et la confession comme technique," in *Faire croire: modalités de la diffusion et de la réception des messages religieux du XIIe au XVe siècle* (Rome: École française de Rome, 1981) 87–99.

Livanos, Christopher. *Greek Tradition and Latin Influence in the Work of George Scholarios: Alone against All of Europe* (Piscataway, NJ: Gorgias Press, 2006).

Livesey, Steven. "Robert Graystanes O.S.B. on the Subalternation of Sciences," *Recherches de théologie ancienne et médiévale* 61 (1994) 236–72.

Theology and Science in the Fourteenth Century: Three Questions on the Unity and Subalternation of the Sciences from John of Reading's Commentary on the "Sentences" (Leiden: Brill, 1989).

Lloyd, A. C. *The Anatomy of Neoplatonism* (Oxford: Oxford University Press, 1990).

"The Aristotelianism of Eustratios of Nicaea," in J. Wiesner (ed.) *Aristoteles: Werk und Wirkung II* (Berlin: De Gruyter, 1987) 341–51.

"Neoplatonic Logic and Aristotelian Logic," *Phronesis* 1 (1955–6) 58–72, 146–60.

Lobel, Diana. " 'Silence is Praise to You': Maimonides on Negative Theology, Looseness of Expression, and Religious Experience," *American Catholic Philosophical Quarterly* 76 (2002) 25–49.

Lo Cascio, Renzo. "La predica del predicare di San Bernardino," in F. d'Episcopo (ed.) *San Bernardino da Siena Predicatore e Pellegrino* (Galatinna: Congedo, 1985) 63–73.

Lochrie, Karma. *Margery Kempe and Translations of the Flesh* (Philadelphia: University of Pennsylvania Press, 1991)

Loewe, Raphael. *Ibn Gabirol* (New York: Grove Weidenfeld, 1989).

Lohr, Charles H. *Latin Aristotle Commentaries, V: Bibliography of Secondary Literature* (Florence: SISMEL, Edizioni del Galluzzo, 2005).

"Medieval Latin Aristotle Commentaries," *Traditio* 23 (1967) 314–413; 24 (1968) 194–245; 26 (1970) 135–216; 27 (1971) 251–351; 28 (1972) 281–396; 29 (1973) 93–197; 30 (1974) 119–44

Long, A. A. and D. N. Sedley (tr.). *The Hellenistic Philosophers* (Cambridge: Cambridge University Press, 1987).

Long, R. James. "The First Oxford Debate on the Eternity of the World," *Recherches de théologie et philosophie médiévales* 65 (1998) 54–98.

"The Moral and Spiritual Theology of Richard Fishacre: Edition of Trinity Coll. (Cambridge) MS O.1.30," *Archivum Fratrum Praedicatorum* 60 (1990) 5–143.

"Of Angels and Pinheads: The Contributions of the Early Oxford Masters to the Doctrine of Spiritual Matter," *Franciscan Studies* 56 (1998) 237–52.

"Richard Fishacre's Treatise *De libero arbitrio*," in B. C. Bazán et al. (eds.) *Moral and Political Philosophies in the Middle Ages* (Ottawa: Legas, 1995) 879–91.

"Richard Fishacre's Way to God," in R. Link-Salinger et al. (eds.) *A Straight Path: Studies in Medieval Philosophy and Culture. Essays in Honor of Arthur Hyman* (Washington, DC: Catholic University of America Press, 1988) 174–82.

"The Science of Theology According to Richard Fishacre: Edition of the Prologue to his Commentary on the Sentences," *Mediaeval Studies* 34 (1972) 71–98.

Long, R. James and Timothy Noone. "Fishacre and Rufus on the Metaphysics of Light: Two Unedited Texts," in J. Hamesse (ed.) *Roma, magister mundi: itineraria culturae medievalis: mélanges offerts au Père L. E. Boyle à l'occasion de son 75e anniversaire* (Louvain-la-Neuve: Fédération des instituts d'études médiévales, 1998) 517–48.

Longère, Jean. "Pauvreté et richesse chez quelques prédicateurs durant la seconde moitié du XIIᵉ siècle," in M. Mollat (ed.) *Études sur l'histoire de la pauvreté* (Paris: Publications de la Sorbonne, 1974) I: 255–73.

Longeway, John. "Simon of Faversham's Questions on the 'Posterior Analytics': A Thirteenth-Century View of Science" (Ph.D. dissertation: Cornell University, 1977).

Longo, Carlo (ed.). *Magister Raimundus: atti del Convegno per il IV centenario della canonizzazione di San Raimondo de Penyafort, 1601–2001* (Rome: Istituto storico domenicano, 2002).

Longpré, Efrem. "Bartolommeo di Bologna, un maestro francescano del sec. XIII," *Studi Francescani* 9 (1923) 365–84.

"Le commentaire sur les *Sentences* de Guillaume de Nottingham O.F.M.," *Archivum Franciscanum Historicum* 22 (1929) 232–33.

"Fr Thomas d'York," *Archivum Franciscanum Historicum* 19 (1926) 875–930.

"Gonsalve de Balboa et le B. Duns Scot," *Études Franciscaines* 36 (1924) 640–5; 37 (1925) 170–82.

"Jean de Reading et le B. Jean Duns Scot," *La France Franciscaine* 7 (1924) 99–109.

"Maîtres franciscains de Paris: Guillaume de Ware OFM," *La France Franciscaine* 5 (1922) 71–82.

"L'œuvre scolastique du cardinal Jean de Murro, O.F.M. (†1312)," in *Mélanges Auguste Pelzer* (Leuven: Bibliothèque de l'Université, 1947) 467–92.

Lopez, Robert. *The Commercial Revolution of the Middle Ages, 950–1350* (Cambridge: Cambridge University Press, 1976).

Lorenz, Sönke. *Studium generale erfordense: zum Erfurter Schulleben im 13. und 14. Jahrhundert* (Stuttgart: Hiersemann, 1989).

"Thomas Manlefelt (Maulefelt): zu Leben und Werk," in M. Kintzinger *et al.* (eds.) *Schule und Schüler im Mittelalter: Beiträge zur europäischen Bildungsgeschichte des 9. bis 15. Jahrhunderts* (Cologne: Böhlau, 1996) 145–64.

Lot-Borodine, Myrrha. *Un maître de la spiritualité byzantine au XIVᵉ siècle: Nicolas Cabasilas* (Paris: Éditions de l'Orante, 1958).

Loth, Bernard and Albert Michel (eds.). *Dictionnaire de théologie catholique* (Paris: Letouzey et Ané, 1953–72).

Lottin, Odon. "Un commentaire sur les Sentences attribués d'Odon Rigaud," *Recherches de théologie ancienne et médiévale* 7 (1935) 402.

  Le droit naturel chez Thomas d'Aquin et ses prédécesseurs, 2nd edn (Bruges: Beyaert, 1931).

  "Le premier commentaire connu des Sentences de Pierre Lombard," *Recherches de théologie ancienne et médiévale* 8 (1938) 64–71.

  Psychologie et morale aux XIIᵉ et XIIIᵉ siècles (Gembloux: Duculot, 1948–60).

  "Robert Cowton et Jean Duns Scot," *Recherches de théologie ancienne et médiévale* 21 (1954) 281–94.

  "Les vertus morales acquises sont-elles vraies vertus? La réponse de théologiens de Pierre Abelard à St. Thomas d'Aquin," *Recherches de théologie ancienne et médiéval* 20 (1953) 13–39.

  "Les vertus morales acquises sont-elles vraies vertus? La réponse de théologiens de saint Thomas d'Aquin à Pierre Auriol," *Recherches de théologie ancienne et médiévale* 21 (1954), 100–29.

Lourdaux, Willem and Daniel Verhelst (eds.). *The Concept of Heresy in the Middle Ages (11th–13th c.)* (Leuven: Louvain University Press, 1976).

Lowe, Elizabeth. *The Contested Theological Authority of Thomas Aquinas: The Controversies between Hervaeus Natalis and Durandus of St. Pourcain* (New York: Routledge, 2003).

Lucentini, Paolo. "L'eresia di Amalrico," in W. Beierwaltes (ed.) *Eriugena Redivivus* (Heidelberg: Carl Winter Universitätsverlag, 1987) 174–91.

Luhtala, Anneli. "Early Medieval Commentary on Priscian's *Institutiones Grammaticae*," *Cahiers de l'Institut du Moyen Age Grec et Latin* 71 (2000) 115–88.

  "Glosses Based on Eriugena's Priscian Commentary," *Miscellanea Bibliothecae Apostolicae Vaticanae* 7 (2000) 199–213.

  "A Priscian Commentary Attributed to Eriugena," in S. Auroux (ed.) *History of Linguistics 1999: Selected Papers from the Eighth International Conference on the History of the Language Sciences* (Amsterdam: Benjamins, 2003) 19–30.

Luna, Concetta. "Review of Rainer Thiel, Simplikios und das Ende der neuplatonischen Schule in Athen," in *Mnemosyne* 54 (2001) 482–504.

Luongo, F. Thomas. *The Saintly Politics of Catherine of Siena* (Ithaca, NY: Cornell University Press, 2006).

Luscombe, David. "Francois de Meyronnes and Hierarchy," in M. Wilks and D. Wood (eds.) *The Church and Sovereignty c.590–1918: Essays in Honour of Michael Wilks* (Oxford: Blackwell, 1991) 225–31.

  "The Hierarchies in the Writings of Alan of Lille, William of Auvergne and St Bonaventure," in I. Iribarren and M. Lenz (eds.) *Angels in Medieval Philosophical Enquiry* (Aldershot: Ashgate, 2008) 15–28.

  "Hrabanus Maurus and the Predestination Controversy," in F. J. Felten and B. Nichtweiss (eds.) *Hrabanus Maurus. Gelehrter, Abt von Fulda und Erzbischof von Mainz* (Mainz: Publikationen Bistum Mainz, 2006) 141–58.

  "John of Salisbury: A Bibliography, 1953–82," in M. Wilks (ed.) *The World of John of Salisbury* (Oxford: Blackwell, 1984) 445–57.

"The *Lex divinitatis* in the Bull *Unam Sanctam* of Pope Boniface VIII," in C. Brooke *et al.* (eds.) *Church and Government in the Middle Ages* (Cambridge: Cambridge University Press, 1976) 205–21.

Medieval Thought (Oxford: Oxford University Press, 1997).

The School of Peter Abelard: The Influence of Abelard's Thought in the Early Scholastic Period (Cambridge: Cambridge University Press, 1969).

Lynch, John E. *The Theory of Knowledge of Vital du Four* (St. Bonaventure, NY: Franciscan Institute, 1972).

Lynch, Kilianus. "De distinctione intentionali apud mag. J. Baconthorpe," *Analecta Ordinis Carmelitarum* 7 (1931) 351–404.

McAodha, Loman. "The Nature and Efficacy of Preaching According to St. Bernandine of Siena," *Franciscan Studies* 27 (1967) 221–47.

Maccagnolo, Enzo. "David of Dinant and the Beginning of Aristotelianism in Paris," in P. Dronke (ed.) *A History of Twelfth-Century Western Philosophy* (Cambridge: Cambridge University Press, 1988) 429–42.

Rerum universitas: Saggio sulla filosofia di Teodorico di Chartres (Florence: Le Monnier, 1976).

McCall, John P. "Chaucer and John of Legnano," *Speculum* 40 (1965) 484–9.

"The Writings of John of Legnano," *Traditio* 23 (1967) 415–37.

MacClintock, Stuart. *Perversity and Error: Studies on the "Averroist" John of Jandun* (Bloomington: Indiana University Press, 1956).

McCluskey, Colleen. "The Roots of Ethical Voluntarism." *Vivarium* 39 (2001) 185–208.

McCracken, George. *Early Medieval Theology* (Philadelphia, PA: Westminster, 1957).

McCready, William. "The Papal Sovereign in the Ecclesiology of Augustinus Triumphus," *Medieval Studies* 39 (1977) 117–205.

McCullough, E. J. "St. Albert on Motion as Forma Fluens and Fluxus Formae," in J. A. Weisheipl (ed.) *Albertus Magnus and the Sciences: Commemorative Essays 1980* (Toronto: Pontifical Institute of Mediaeval Studies, 1980) 129–53.

McDermott, A. C. "Materials for an Archaeological Analysis of Richard Campsall's Logic," in G. L. Bursill-Hall *et al.* (eds.) *De Ortu Grammaticae: Studies in Memory of Jan Pinborg* (Amsterdam: Benjamins, 1990) 227–37.

MacDonald, Scott (ed.). *Being and Goodness: The Concept of the Good in Metaphysics and Philosophical Theology* (Ithaca, NY: Cornell University Press, 1991).

"Goodness as Transcendental: The Early Thirteenth-Century Recovery of an Aristotelian Idea," *Topoi* 11 (1992) 173–86.

McEvoy, James. "John Scottus Eriugena and Thomas Gallus, Commentators on the Mystical Theology," in J. McEvoy and M. Dunne (eds.) *History and Eschatology in Eriugena and his Time* (Leuven: Leuven University Press, 2002) 183–202.

The Philosophy of Robert Grosseteste (Oxford: Clarendon Press, 1982).

Robert Grosseteste (Oxford: Oxford University Press, 2000).

Robert Grosseteste, Exegete and Philosopher (Aldershot: Variorum, 1994).

(ed.). *Robert Grosseteste: New Perspectives on his Thought and Scholarship* (Turnhout: Brepols, 1995).

McFarlane, K. B. *John Wycliffe and the Beginnings of English Nonconformity* (London: English Universities Press, 1952).

McGinn, Bernard. *The Calabrian Abbot: Joachim of Fiore in the History of Western Thought* (New York: Macmillan, 1985).

The Flowering of Mysticism: Men and Women in the New Mysticism (1200–1350), vol. III of *The Presence of God: A History of Western Christian Mysticism* (New York: Crossroad Publishing, 1998).

The Golden Chain: A Study in the Theological Anthropology of Isaac of Stella (Washington, DC: Cistercian Publications, 1969).

Harvest of Mysticism in Medieval Germany, vol. IV of *The Presence of God: A History of Western Christian Mysticism* (New York: Crossroad Publishing, 2005).

Meister Eckhart and the Beguine Mystics: Hadwijch of Brabant, Mechtild of Magdeburg, and Marguerite of Porete (New York: Continuum, 1994).

The Mystical Thought of Meister Eckhart: The Man from Whom God Hid Nothing (New York: Crossroad Publishing, 2001).

(tr.). *Three Treatises on Man: A Cistercian Anthropology* (Kalamazoo, MI: Cistercian Publications, 1977).

McGinn, Bernard and Willemien Otten (eds.). *Eriugena: East and West* (Notre Dame, IN: University of Notre Dame Press, 1994).

McGinnis, Jon. "Positioning Heaven: The Infidelity of a Faithful Aristotelian," *Phronesis* 51 (2006) 140–61.

"Scientific Methodologies in Medieval Islam," *Journal of the History of Philosophy* 41 (2003) 307–27.

McGinnis, Jon and David C. Reisman (trs.). *Classical Arabic Philosophy: An Anthology of Sources* (Indianapolis, IN: Hackett, 2007).

McGrade, A. S. (ed.). *The Cambridge Companion to Medieval Philosophy* (Cambridge: Cambridge University Press, 2003).

"Enjoyment at Oxford after Ockham: Philosophy, Psychology and the Love of God," in A. Hudson and M. Wilks (eds.) *From Ockham to Wyclif* (Oxford: Blackwell, 1987) 63–88.

The Political Thought of William of Ockham: Personal and Institutional Principles (Cambridge: Cambridge University Press, 1974; repr. 2002).

"William of Ockham and Augustinus de Ancona on the Righteousness of Dissent," *Franciscan Studies* 54 (1994–7) 143–65.

McGrade, A. S., John Kilcullen, and Matthew Kempshall (trs.). *Cambridge Translations of Medieval Philosophical Texts*, vol. II: *Ethics and Political Philosophy* (Cambridge: Cambridge University Press, 2001).

McGrath, Alister. *Iustitia Dei: A History of the Christian Doctrine of Justification*, 3rd edn (Cambridge: Cambridge University Press, 1998).

McGuire, Brian Patrick (ed.). *A Companion to Jean Gerson* (Leiden: Brill, 2006).

The Difficult Saint: Bernard of Clairvaux and his Tradition (Kalamazoo, MI: Cistercian Publications, 1991).

Jean Gerson and the Last Medieval Reformation (University Park, PA: Pennsylvania State University Press, 2005).

McInerney, Maud Burnett (ed.). *Hildegard of Bingen: A Book of Essays* (New York: Garland, 1998).

McInerny, Ralph. *Aquinas against the Averroists: On There Being Only One Intellect* (West Lafayette, IN: Purdue University Press, 1993).

Aquinas and Analogy (Washington, DC: Catholic University of America Press, 1998).

Boethius and Aquinas (Washington, DC: Catholic University of America Press, 1990).

McKay, Angela. "The Infused and Acquired Virtues in Aquinas' Moral Philosophy" (Ph.D. dissertation: University of Notre Dame, 2004).

McKeon, Richard. *Selections from Medieval Philosophers* (New York: Scribners, 1930).

Mackie, Evelyn A. and Joseph Goering (eds.). *Editing Robert Grosseteste* (Toronto: University of Toronto Press, 2003).

Mackie, J. L. "Evil and Omnipotence," *Mind* 64 (1955) 200–12.

McMahon, William. "Radulphus Brito on the Sufficiency of the Categories," *Cahiers de l'Institut du Moyen Age Grec et Latin* 39 (1981) 81–96.

MacMullen, Ramsay. *Christianity and Paganism in the Fourth to Eighth Centuries* (New Haven, CT: Yale University Press, 1997).

Voting about God in Early Church Councils (New Haven, CT: Yale University Press, 2006).

McNeill, John. "Medicine for Sin as Prescribed in the Penitentials," *Church History* 1 (1932) 14–26.

Macrae, Enya. "Geoffrey of Aspall's Commentaries on Aristotle," *Mediaeval and Renaissance Studies* 6 (1968) 94–134.

Maddocks, Fiona. *Hildegard of Bingen: The Woman of her Age* (New York: Doubleday, 2001).

Madec, Goulven. *Jean Scot et ses auteurs: annotations érigéniennes* (Paris: Études Augustiniennes, 1988).

Madelung, Wilferd. "Abu'l Mu'in al-Nasafi and Ash'ari Theology," in C. Hillenbrand (ed.) *Studies in Honour of C.E. Bosworth* (Leiden: Brill, 2000) II: 318–30.

"Nasir al-Din Tusi's Ethics Between Philosophy, Shi'ism, and Sufism," in R. G. Hovannisian (ed.) *Ethics in Islam* (Malibu, CA: Undena, 1985) 85–101.

"The Origins of the Controversy Concerning the Creation of the Koran," in J. M. Barral (ed.) *Orientalia hispanica sive studia F.M. Pareja octogenario dicata* (Leiden: Brill, 1974) 504–25.

Madigan, Kevin. *Olivi and the Interpretation of Matthew in the High Middle Ages* (Notre Dame, IN: University of Notre Dame Press, 2003).

Mahdi, Muhsin. *Alfarabi and the Foundation of Islamic Political Philosophy* (Chicago: University of Chicago Press, 2001).

Ibn Khaldun's Philosophy of History (London: Allen and Unwin, 1957).

"Language and Logic in Classical Islam," in G. E. von Grunebaum (ed.) *Logic in Classical Islamic Culture* (Wiesbaden: Harrassowitz, 1970) 51–83.

Mahoney, E. P. "Themes and Problems in the Psychology of John of Jandun," in J. F. Wippel (ed.) *Studies in Medieval Philosophy* (Washington, DC: Catholic University of America, 1987) 273–88.

"Themistius and the Agent Intellect in James of Viterbo and Other Thirteenth-Century Philosophers," *Augustiniana* 23 (1973) 422–67.

Maier, Anneliese. *An der Grenze von Scholastik und Naturwissenschaft*, 2nd edn (Rome: Edizioni di Storia e Letteratura, 1952).

Metaphysische Hintergründe der Spätscholastischen Naturphilosophie (Rome: Edizioni di Storia e Letteratura, 1955).

"Das Problem der Evidenz in der Philosophie des 14. Jahrhunderts," in A. Maier (ed.) *Ausgehendes Mittelalter: Gesammelte Aufsätze zur Geistesgeschichte des 14. Jahrhunderts* (Rome: Edizioni di Storia e Letteratura, 1967) II: 367–418.

"Wilhelm von Alnwicks Bologneser Quaestiones gegen den Averroismus (1323)," *Gregorianum* 30 (1949) 265–308.

Zwei Grundprobleme der Scholastischen Naturphilosophie, 3rd edn (Rome: Edizioni di Storia e Letteratura, 1968).

Zwischen Philosophie und Mechanik (Rome: Edizioni di Storia e Letteratura, 1958).

Maierù, Alfonso (ed.) *English Logic in Italy in the 14th and 15th Centuries* (Naples: Bibliopolis, 1982).

"La linguistica medievale: filosofia del linguaggio," in G. Lepschy (ed.) *Storia della linguistica* (Bologna: Mulino, 1990) II: 101–37.

"Logica aristotelica e teologia trinitaria, Enrico Totting da Oyta," in A. Mairù and A. Paravicini Bagliani (eds.) *Studi sul XIV secolo in memoria di Anneliese Maier* (Rome: Edizioni di Storia e Letteratura, 1981) 496–512.

"Logica e teologia trinitaria nel commento alle sentenze attribuito a Petrus Thomae," in J. Jolivet *et al.* (eds.) *Lectionum varietates: hommage à Paul Vignaux, 1904–1987* (Paris: Vrin, 1991) 177–98.

"Il problema del significato nella logica di Pietro da Mantova," *Miscellanea Mediaevalia* 9 (1974) 155–70.

"The Sophism 'Omnis propositio est vera vel falsa' by Henry Hopton (Pseudo-Heytesbury's *De veritate et falsitate propositionis*," in S. Read (ed.) *Sophisms in Medieval Logic and Grammar: Acts of the Ninth European Symposium for Medieval Logic and Semantics* (Dordrecht: Kluwer, 1993) 103–15.

Maioli, Bruno. *Gilberto Porretano: dalla grammatica speculativa alla metafisica del concreto* (Rome: Bulzoni Editore, 1979).

Mäkinen, Virpi. "The Franciscan Background of Early Modern Rights Discussion: Rights of Property and Subsistence," in J. Kraye and R. Saarinen (eds.) *Moral Philosophy on the Threshold of Modernity* (Dordrecht: Kluwer, 2005) 165–80.

"Godfrey of Fontaine's Criticism Concerning Franciscan Poverty and the Birth of Individual Natural Rights," *Picenum seraphicum* 19 (2000): 69–85.

"The Rights of the Poor: An Argument against the Franciscans," in M. Korpiola (ed.) *Nordic Perspectives on Medieval Canon Law* (Helsinki: Matthias Calonius Society, 1999) 41–9.

Malcolm, John. "A Reconsideration of the Identity and Inherence Theories of the Copula," *Journal of the History of Philosophy* 17 (1979) 383–400.

Mallard, William. "John Wyclif and the Tradition of Biblical Authority," *Church History* 30 (1961) 50–60.

Malter, Henry. *Saadia Gaon, his Life and Works* (Philadelphia: Jewish Publication Society of America, 1921; repr. New York: Hermon Press, 1969).

Manekin, Charles. "Conservative Tendencies in Gersonides' Religious Philosophy," in D. H. Frank and O. Leaman (eds.) *The Cambridge Companion to Medieval Jewish Philosophy* (Cambridge: Cambridge University Press, 2003) 304–42.

(tr.). *Medieval Jewish Philosophical Writings* (Cambridge: Cambridge University Press, 2007).

Mann, William E. "The Best of All Possible Worlds," in S. MacDonald (ed.) *Being and Goodness: The Concept of the Good in Metaphysics and Philosophical Theology* (Ithaca, NY: Cornell University Press, 1991) 250–77.

"Divine Simplicity," *Religious Studies* 18 (1982) 451–71.

"Ethics," in J. Brower and K. Guilfoy (eds.) *The Cambridge Companion to Abelard* (Cambridge: Cambridge University Press, 2004) 279–304.

"Inner-Life Ethics," in G. B. Matthews (ed.) *The Augustinian Tradition* (Berkeley: University of California Press, 1998) 140–65.

Mannath, Joseph T. "Harvey of Nedellec's Proofs for the Existence of God: 'De cognicione primi principii, qq. III–IV'," *Salesianum* 31 (1969) 46–112.

Mantienne, Alain. *Lanfranc: le fidèle conseiller de Guillaume le Conquérant* (Condé-sur-Noireau: Corlet, 2006).

Maranesi, Pietro. "Il IV libro della *Summa Quaestionum* di Pietro di Giovanni Olivi. Un'ipotesi di soluzione," *Archivum Franciscanum Historicum* 95 (2002) 53–92.

Marcolino, Vénicio. "Leben und Schrifftum des Augustinereremiten Johannes von Basel (†1392)," *Augustiniana* 53 (2003) 319–81.

Marcotte, Roxanne D. "Preliminary Notes on the Life and Work of Abū al-ʿAbbās al-Lawkarī (d. *ca.* 517/1123)," *Anaquel de Estudios Árabes* 17 (2006) 133–57.

Marenbon, John. "Alcuin, the Council of Frankfurt and the Beginnings of Medieval Philosophy," in R. Berndt (ed.) *Das Frankfurter Konzil von 794: Kristallisationspunkt karolingischer Kultur* (Mainz: Selbstverlag der Gesellschaft für Mittelrheinische Kirchengeschichte, 1997) II: 603–15.

"Anselm Rewrites his Argument: *Proslogion* 2 and the *Response* to Gaunilo," in J. Hamesse and O. Weijers (eds.) *Écriture et réécriture des textes philosophiques médiévaux* (Turnhout: Brepols, 2006) 347–65.

Aristotelian Logic, Platonism and the Context of Early Medieval Philosophy in the West (Aldershot: Ashgate, 2000).

Boethius (Oxford: Oxford University Press, 2003).

(ed.). *The Cambridge Companion to Boethius* (Cambridge: Cambridge University Press, 2009).

"Carolingian Thought," in R. McKitterick (ed.) *Carolingian Culture: Emulation and Innovation* (Cambridge: Cambridge University Press, 1984) 171–92.

"Les Catégories au début du moyen âge," in O. Bruun and L. Corti (eds.) *Les Catégories et leur histoire* (Paris: Vrin, 2005) 223–43.

From the Circle of Alcuin to the School of Auxerre: Logic, Theology and Philosophy in the Early Middle Ages (Cambridge: Cambridge University Press, 1981).

"Gilbert of Poitiers," in P. Dronke (ed.) *A History of Twelfth-Century Western Philosophy* (Cambridge: Cambridge University Press, 1988) 328–52.

"Glosses and Commentaries on the *Categories* and *De interpretatione* before Abelard," in J. Fried (ed.) *Dialektik und Rhetorik im früheren und hohen Mittelalter*, Schriften des historischen Kollegs, Kolloquien 27 (Munich: Historisches Kolleg, 1997) 21–49.

"John Scottus and Carolingian Theology: from the *De praedestinatione*, its Background and its Critics, to the *Periphyseon*," in M. T. Gibson and J. L. Nelson (eds.) *Charles the Bald: Court and Kingdom*, 2nd edn (Aldershot: Variorum, 1990) 303–25.

Later Medieval Philosophy (1150–1350): An Introduction (London: Routledge, 1987).

"The Latin Tradition of Logic to 1100," in D. M. Gabbay and J. Woods (eds.) *Handbook to the History of Logic*, vol. II: *Medieval and Renaissance Logic* (Amsterdam: North-Holland, 2008) 1–63.

"Medieval Latin Commentaries and Glosses on Aristotelian Logical Texts, Before c. 1150 A.D.," in C. Burnett (ed.) *Glosses and Commentaries on Aristotelian Logical Texts: The Syriac, Arabic and Medieval Latin Traditions* (London: Warburg Institute, 1993) 77–127.

"A Note on the Porretani," in P. Dronke (ed.) *A History of Twelfth-Century Western Philosophy* (Cambridge: Cambridge University Press, 1988) 353–7.

The Philosophy of Peter Abelard (Cambridge: Cambridge University Press, 1997).

Le temps, la prescience et les futurs contingents de Boèce à Thomas d'Aquin (Paris: Vrin, 2005).

Margoliouth, D. S. "The Discussion Between Abu Bishr Matta and Abu Saʿid al-Sirafi on the Merits of Logic and Grammar," *Journal of the Royal Asiatic Society* (1905) 79–129.

Markowski, Mieczyslaw. "Komentarz Jana Aurifabera z Erfurtu do Fizyki Arystotelesa (Johannes Aurifabers von Erfurt Kommentar zur Physik des Aristoteles in der Handschrift 1423 der Universitätsbibliothek in Leipzig)," *Acta mediaevalia* 12 (1999) 335–43.

Markus, Robert A. "Saint Augustine's Views on the 'Just War'," in W. J. Sheils (ed.) *The Church and War* (Oxford: Blackwell, 1983) 1–13.

Marmo, Costantino. "Hoc autem etsi potest tollerari... Egidio Romano e Tommaso d'Aquino sulle passione dell' anima," *Documenti e studi sulla tradizione filosofica medievale* 2 (1991) 281–315.

"A Pragmatic Approach to Language in Modism," in S. Ebbesen (ed.) *Sprachtheorien in Spätantike und Mittelalter* (Tübingen: Narr, 1995) 169–83.

"Retorica e motti di spirito. Una 'quaestio' inedita di Giovanni di Jandun," in P. Magli, G. Manetti, and P. Violi (eds.) *Semiotica: storia, teoria, interpretazione* (Milan: Bompiani, 1992) 23–41.

"The Semantics of the Modistae," in S. Ebbesen and R. L. Friedman (eds.) *Medieval Analyses in Language and Cognition* (Copenhagen: Royal Danish Academy of Sciences and Letters, 1999) 83–104.

La semiotica e linguaggio nella Scolastica: Parigi, Bologna, Erfurt 1270–1330 (Rome: Istituto Storico Italiano per il Medioevo, 1994).

Marmura, Michael E. "Al-Ghazali," in P. Adamson and R. Taylor (eds.) *The Cambridge Companion to Arabic Philosophy* (Cambridge: Cambridge University Press, 2005) 137–54.

"Avicenna on Causal Priority," in P. Morewedge (ed.) *Islamic Philosophy and Mysticism* (Delmar: Caravan Books, 1981) 65–83.

"Avicenna's Chapter on Universals in the Isagoge of his Shifāʾ," in A. T. Welch and P. Cachia (eds.) *Islam: Past Influence and Present Challenge* (Edinburgh: Edinburgh University Press, 1979) 34–56.

"Avicenna's 'Flying Man' in Context," *The Monist* 69 (1986) 383–95.

"Ghazalian Causes and Intermediaries," *Journal of the American Oriental Society* 115 (1995) 89–100.

"The Metaphysics of Efficient Causality in Avicenna (Ibn Sina)," in M. Marmura (ed.) *Islamic Theology and Philosophy* (Albany: State University of New York Press, 1984) 172–87.

Marmura, Michael and John M. Rist. "Al-Kindi's Discussion of Divine Existence and Oneness," *Mediaeval Studies* 25 (1963) 338–52.

Marmursztejn, Elsa. *L'autorité des maîtres: scolastique, normes et société au xiiᵉ siècle* (Paris: Les Belles Lettres, 2007).

Maróth, Miklós. *The Correspondence between Aristotle and Alexander the Great: An Anonymous Greek Novel in Letters in Arabic Translation* (Piliscsaba: Avicenna Közel-Kelet Kutatások Intézete, 2006).

Marrone, Steven P. *The Light of Thy Countenance: Science and Knowledge of God in the Thirteenth Century* (Leiden: Brill, 2001).

"Matthew of Aquasparta, Henry of Ghent and Augustinian Epistemology after Bonaventure," *Franziskanische Studien* 65 (1983) 252–90.

Truth and Scientific Knowledge in the Thought of Henry of Ghent (Cambridge, MA: Medieval Academy, 1985).

William of Auvergne and Robert Grosseteste: New Ideas of Truth in the Early Thirteenth Century (Princeton, NJ: Princeton University Press, 1983).

Marrou, Henri I. *Saint Augustin et la fin de la culture antique* (Paris: Boccard, 1938–49).

Marshall, Peter. "Parisian Psychology in the Mid-Fourteenth Century," *Archives d'histoire doctrinale et littéraire du moyen âge* 50 (1983) 101–93.

Martel, Benoît. *La psychologie de Gonsalve d'Espagne* (Paris: Vrin, 1968).

Martin, Christopher J. "Abaelard on Modality: Some Possibilities and Some Puzzles," in T. Buchheim, C. H. Kneepkens, and K. Lorenz (eds.) *Potentialität und Possibilität Modalaussagen in der Geschichte der Metaphysik* (Stuttgart-Bad Cannstatt: Frommann-Holzboog 2001).

"Embarrassing Arguments and Surprising Conclusions in the Development of Theories of the Conditional in the Twelfth Century," in J. Jolivet and A. de Libera (eds.) *Gilbert de Poitiers et ses contemporains: aux origines de la logica modernorum* (Naples: Bibliopolis, 1987) 377–401.

"Formal Consequence in Scotus and Ockham: Towards an Account of Scotus' Logic," in O. Boulnois *et al.* (eds.) *Duns Scot à Paris 1302–2002* (Turnout: Brepols, 2005) 117–50.

"Logic," in J. Brower and K. Guilfoy (eds.) *The Cambridge Companion to Abelard* (Cambridge: Cambridge University Press, 2004) 158–99.

"The Logic of Negation in Boethius," *Phronesis* 36 (1991) 277–304.

"The Logic of the Nominales, or, The Rise and Fall of Impossible Positio," *Vivarium* 30 (1987) 110–26.

"Obligations and Liars," in M. Yrjönsuuri (ed.) *Medieval Formal Logic: Consequences, Obligations, Insolubles* (Dordrecht: Reidel, 2001) 63–94.

"Self-Knowledge and Cognitive Ascent: Thomas Aquinas and Peter Olivi on the *KK-Thesis*," in H. Lagerlund (ed.) *Forming the Mind: Essays on the Internal Senses and the Mind/Body Problem from Avicenna to the Medical Enlightenment* (Dordrecht: Springer, 2007) 93–108.

"Something Amazing About the Peripatetic of Pallet: Abelard's Development of Boethius' Account of Conditional Propositions," *Argumentation* 1 (1987) 420–36.

"William's Machine," *Journal of Philosophy* 83 (1986) 564–72.

Martin, C. F. J. "On a Mistake Commonly Made in Accounts of Sixteenth-Century Discussions of the Immortality of the Soul," *American Catholic Philosophical Quarterly* 69 (1995) 29–37.

Martin, John H. "The Eucharistic Treatise of John Quidort of Paris," *Viator* 6 (1975) 214–40.

"Inventing Sincerity, Refashioning Prudence: The Discovery of the Individual in Renaissance Europe," *American Historical Review* 102 (1997) 1309–42.

Mas i Solench, Josep Maria. *Ramon de Penyafort* (Barcelona: Rafael Dalmau, 2000).

Masai, François. *Pléthon et le platonisme de Mistra* (Paris: Les Belles Lettres, 1956).

Matteo d'Acquasparta: Francescano, filosofo, politico. Atti del xxix convegno storico internazionale (Spoleto: Centro italiano di studi sull'alto medioevo, 1993).

Matthaes, Curt. *Der Salernitaner Arzt Urso aus der 2. Hälfte des 12. Jahrhunderts und seine beiden Schriften "De effectibus qualitatum" und "De effectibus medicinarum"* (Leipzig: Noske, 1918).

Matthew, H. C. G. and Brian Harrison. *Oxford Dictionary of National Biography*, rev. edn (Oxford: Oxford University Press, 2004).

Matthews, Gareth B. *Augustine* (Oxford: Blackwell, 2005).

(ed.). *The Augustinian Tradition* (Berkeley: University of California Press, 1998).

Thought's Ego in Augustine and Descartes (Ithaca, NY: Cornell University Press, 1992).

Maurer, Armand. "The *De quidditatibus entium* of Dietrich of Freiberg and its Criticism of Thomistic Metaphysics," *Mediaeval Studies* 18 (1956) 173–203.

"Francis of Meyronnes' Defense of Epistemological Realism," in *Studia Mediaevalia et Mariologica in Honour of P. Carolo Balić* (Rome: Pontificium Athenaeum "Antonianum", 1971) 203–25; repr. in A. Maurer, *Being and Knowing* (Toronto: Pontifical Institute of Medieval Studies, 1990) 311–31.

"Henry of Harclay's Question on the Univocity of Being," *Mediaeval Studies* 16 (1954) 1–18.

"John of Jandun and the Divine Causality," *Mediaeval Studies* 17 (1955) 185–207; repr. in *Being and Knowing* (Toronto: Pontifical Institute of Mediaeval Studies, 1990) 275–308.

"Ockham's Razor and Chatton's Anti-Razor," *Mediaeval Studies* 46 (1984) 463–75.

The Philosophy of William of Ockham in the Light of its Principles (Toronto: Pontifical Institute of Mediaeval Studies, 1999).

"The Role of Infinity in the Thought of Francis of Meyronnes," *Mediaeval Studies* 33 (1971) 201–27; repr. in *Being and Knowing* (Toronto: Pontifical Institute of Medieval Studies, 1990) 333–59.

"St. Thomas and Eternal Truths," in *Being and Knowing: Studies in St. Thomas and Later Medieval Philosophers* (Toronto: Pontifical Institute of Medieval Studies, 1990) 43–58.

"St. Thomas and Historicity," in *Being and Knowing: Studies in St. Thomas and Later Medieval Philosophers* (Toronto: Pontifical Institute of Medieval Studies, 1990) 95–116.

Mauro, V. "La disputata *de anima* tra Vitale du Four e Pietro di Giovanni Olivi," *Studi Medievali* 38 (1997) 89–139.

May, Gerhard. *Schöpfung aus dem Nichts: Die Entstehung der Lehre von der Creatio ex nihilo* (Berlin: De Gruyter, 1978).

Mazzarella, Pasquale. *La dottrina dell'anima e della conoscenza in Matteo d'Acquasparta* (Padua: Gregoriana, 1969).

Meersseman, Gilles-Gérard. "Antonius de Carlenis O.P., Erzbischof von Amalfi," *Archivum Fratrum Praedicatorum* 3 (1933) 81–131.

Geschichte des Albertismus (Paris: Haloua, 1933–5).

"Les origines parisiennes de l'Albertisme Colonais," *Archives d'histoire doctrinale et littéraire du moyen âge* 7 (1932) 121–42.

Meier, H. C. *Macht und Wahnwitz der Begriffe: der Ketzer Roscellinus* (Aalen: Spieth, 1974).

Meier, L. "Wilhelm von Nottingham (†1336) ein Zeuge für die Entwicklung der *distinctio formalis* an der Universität Oxford," in F. J. von Rintelen (ed.) *Philosophia Perennis: Abhandlungen zu ihrer Vergangenheit und Gegenwart* (Regensburg: Habbel, 1930) 247–67.

Melamed, Abraham. *The Philosopher King in Medieval and Renaissance Jewish Philosophical Thought* (Albany: State University of New York Press, 2003).

Melchert, Christopher. *Ahmad ibn Hanbal* (Oxford: Oneworld, 2006).

Meller, Bernhard. *Studien zur Erkenntnislehre des Peter von Ailly* (Freiburg: Herder, 1954).

Melloni, Alberto and Nicolaus. *Innocenzo IV: La concezione e l'esperienza della cristianità come regimen unius personae* (Genoa: Marietti, 1990).

Menn, Stephen. *Descartes and Augustine* (Cambridge: Cambridge University Press, 1998).

"Al-Fārābī's *Kitāb al-ḥurūf* and his Analysis of the Senses of Being," *Arabic Sciences and Philosophy* 18 (2008) 59–97.

Mensa i Valls, Jaume. *Arnau de Vilanova, espiritual: guia bibliogràfica* (Barcelona: Institut d'Estudis Catalans, 1994).

Menut, Albert D. "A Provisional Bibliography of Oresme's Writings," *Mediaeval Studies* 28 (1966) 279–99.

Mercer, Christia. *Leibniz's Metaphysics: Its Origins and Development* (Cambridge: Cambridge University Press, 2001).

Mercken, H. P. F. "The Greek Commentators on Aristotle's *Ethics*," in R. Sorabji (ed.) *Aristotle Transformed: The Ancient Commentaries and their Influence* (London: Duckworth, 1990) 407–43.

Merlan, Philip. *Monopsychism, Mysticism, and Metaconsciousness* (The Hague: Nijhoff, 1963).

Mesch, Barry. "Principles of Judaism in Maimonides and Joseph ibn Caspi," in J. Reinharz and D. Schwetschinski (eds.) *Mystics, Philosophers and Politicians* (Durham, NC: Duke University Press, 1982) 85–98.

Meuthen, Erich. *Nikolaus von Kues, 1401–1464. Skizze einer Biographie*, 4th edn (Münster: Aschendorff, 1979).

Meuthen, Erich and Hermann Hallauer (eds). *Acta Cusana. Quellen zur Lebensgeschichte des Nikolaus von Kues* (Hamburg: Meiner, 1976–).

Mews, Constant. *Abelard and Heloise* (Oxford: Oxford University Press, 2005).

"Logica in the Service of Philosophy: William of Champeaux and his Influence," in R. Berndt (ed.) *Schrift, Schreiber, Schenker: Studien zur Abtei Sankt Viktor zu Paris und zu den Viktorinern* (Berlin: Akademie-Verlag, 2005) 61–101.

"Nominalism and Theology before Abaelard: New Light on Roscelin of Compiègne," *Vivarium* 30 (1992) 4–33.

Meyendorff, John. *A Study of Gregory Palamas*, tr. G. Lawrence, 2nd edn (London: Faith Press, 1974).

Meyer, Gerbert and Albert Zimmermann (eds.). *Albertus Magnus – Doctor Universalis* (Mainz: Matthias-Grüewald, 1980).

Meyer, Susan Suavé. *Aristotle on Moral Responsibility: Character and Cause* (Oxford: Blackwell, 1993).

Michael, Bernd. "Johannes Buridan: Studien zu seinem Leben, seinen Werken und zu Rezeption seiner Theorien im Europa des späten Mittelalters" (Ph.D. dissertation: University of Berlin, 1985).

Michael, Emily. "John Wyclif on Body and Mind," *Journal of the History of Ideas* 64 (2003) 343–60.

Michaud-Quantin, Pierre. "A propos des premières *summae confessorum*," *Recherches de théologie ancienne et médiévale* 26 (1959) 264–306.

"Die Psychologie bei Radulphus Ardens, einem Theologen des ausgehenden XII. Jahrunderts," *Münchener theologische Zeitschrift* 9 (1958) 81–96.

"Les puissances de l'âme chez Jean de la Rochelle," *Antonianum* 24 (1949) 489–505.

Sommes de casuistique et manuels de confession au moyen âge (Leuven: Nauwelaerts, 1962).

Michon, Cyrille. *Nominalisme: la théorie de la signification de Guillaume d'Ockham* (Paris: Vrin, 1994).

Michot, Jean. "La pandémie avicennienne," *Arabica* 40 (1993) 287–344.

Miethke, Jürgen. "Literaturbericht über Marsilius von Padua (1958–1992)," *Bulletin de philosophie médiévale* 35 (1993) 150–65.

"Papst, Ortsbischof und Universität in den Pariser Theologenprozessen des 13. Jahrunderts," in A. Zimmermann (ed.) *Die Auseinandersetzungen an der Pariser Universität im XIII. Jahrhundert* (Berlin: De Gruyter, 1976) 52–94.

Ockhams Weg zur Sozialphilosophie (Berlin: De Gruyter, 1969).

Migne, Jacques-Paul (ed.). *Patrologiae cursus completus: series graeca* (Paris, 1857–76).

(ed.). *Patrologiae cursus completus: series latina* (Paris, 1844–91).

Mikhail, Hanna. *Politics and Revelation: Mawardi and After* (Edinburgh: Edinburgh University Press, 1995).

Millás Vallicrosa, José Maria. *Las traducciones orientales en los manuscritos de la Biblioteca Catedral de Toledo* (Madrid: Consejo superior de investigaciones cientificas, 1942) 285–312.

Miller, Barry. "Necessarily Terminating Causal Series," *Mind* 91 (1982) 201–15.

Miller, L. B. "Islamic Disputation Theory: A Study of the Development of Dialectic in Islam from the Tenth through Fourteenth Centuries" (Ph.D. dissertation: Princeton University, 1984).

Minio-Paluello, Lorenzo. "The *'Ars disserendi'* of Adam of Balsham 'Parvipontanus'," *Mediaeval and Renaissance Studies* 3 (1954) 116–69.

"Dante's Reading of Aristotle," in C. Grayson (ed.) *The World of Dante* (Oxford: Clarendon Press, 1980) 61–80.

"Jacobus Veneticus Graecus, Canonist and Translator of Aristotle," *Traditio* 8 (1952) 265–304.

Opuscula: The Latin Aristotle (Amsterdam: Hakkert, 1972).

Ministeri, Blasio. *De vita et operibus Augustini de Ancona O.E.S.A. (1328)* (Rome: Analecta Augustiniana, 1953).

Miquel, André. *La géographie humaine du monde musulman jusqu'au milieu du 11e siecle* (Paris: La Haye, 1975).

Moevs, Christian. *The Metaphysics of Dante's Comedy* (Oxford: Clarendon Press, 2005).

Möhle, Hannes. *Formalitas und modus intrinsecus. Die Entwicklung der Scotischen Metaphysik bei Franciscus de Mayronis* (Münster: Aschendorff, 2007).

Mohler, Ludwig. *Kardinal Bessarion als Theologe, Humanist, und Staatsmann: Funde und Forschungen* (Paderborn: Schöningh, 1923–42; repr. Aalen: Scientia Verlag, 1967).

Mojsisch, Burkhard. *Meister Eckhart: Analogy, Univocity and Unity*, tr. O. F. Summerell (Amsterdam: Grüner, 2001).

Molland, A. George. "An Examination of Bradwardine's Geometry," *Archive for History of Exact Sciences* 19 (1978) 113–75.

"John Dumbleton and the Status of Geometrical Optics," in A. G. Molland (ed.) *Mathematics and the Medieval Ancestry of Physics* (Aldershot: Variorum, 1995).

"Nicole Oresme and Scientific Progress," *Miscellanea Mediaevalia* 9 (1974) 206–20.

Mollat, Michel. "Hospitalité et assistance au début du XIIIe siècle," in D. Flood (ed.) *Poverty in the Middle Ages* (Werl: Coelde, 1975).

Les pauvres au Moyen Age: étude sociale (Paris: Hachette, 1978).

Molteni, Paulo. *Roberto Holcot O.P.: dottrina della grazia e della giustificazione con due questioni quodlibetali inedite* (Pinerolo: Editrice Alzani, 1967).

Monagle, Clare. *Christological Nihilism in the Twelfth Century: The Contested Reception of Peter Lombard's* Sententiae (Turnhout: Brepols, 2007).

Monahan, Arthur. "The Subject of Metaphysics for Peter of Auvergne," *Mediaeval Studies* 16 (1954) 118–30.

Monfasani, John. *Byzantine Scholars in Renaissance Italy: Cardinal Bessarion and Other Émigrés: Selected Essays* (Aldershot: Variorum, 1995).

(ed.). *Collectanea Trapezuntiana: Texts, Documents, and Bibliographies of George of Trebizond* (Binghamton, NY: Medieval and Renaissance Texts and Studies, 1984).

George of Trebizond: A Biography and a Study of his Rhetoric and Logic (Leiden: Brill, 1976).

Monnot, Guy. "Les controverses théologiques dans l'œuvre de Shahrastani," in A. Le Boulluec (ed.) *La controverse religieuse et ses formes* (Paris: Cerf, 1995) 281–96.

Montada, Josef Puig. "Philosophy in Andalusia: Ibn Bājja and Ibn Ṭufayl," in P. Adamson and R. Taylor (eds.) *The Cambridge Companion to Arabic Philosophy* (Cambridge: Cambridge University Press, 2005) 155–79.

Moody, Ernest A. "Galileo and Avempace: The Dynamics of the Leaning Tower Experiment," *Journal for the History of Ideas* 12 (1951) 163–93, 375–422.

The Logic of William of Ockham (New York: Sheed and Ward, 1935).

"A Quodlibet Question of Robert Holcot, O.P. on the Problem of the Objects of Knowledge and of Belief," *Speculum* 39 (1964), 53–74.

The Rise of Mechanism in 14th Century Natural Philosophy: Translations of Texts on the Causal and Mathematical Analysis of Motion by John Buridan (ca. 1300–1358) and John Dumbleton (fl. 1328–1340) (New York: Columbia University Press, 1950).

"William of Auvergne and his Treatise *De anima*," in *Studies in Medieval Philosophy, Science, and Logic: Collected Papers, 1933–69* (Berkeley: University of California Press, 1975) 1–109.

Moonan, Lawrence. *Divine Power: The Medieval Power Distinction up to its Adoption by Albert, Bonaventure, and Aquinas* (Oxford: Clarendon Press, 1994).

"Impossibility and Peter Damian," *Archiv für Geschichte der Philosophie* 62 (1980) 146–63.

Mooney, Caroline. "The Authorial Role of Brother A. in the Composition of Angela of Foligno's Revelations," in A. Matter and J. Coakley (eds.) *Creative Women in Medieval and Early Modern Italy: A Religious and Artistic Renaissance* (Philadelphia: University of Pennsylvania Press, 1994).

Gendered Voices: Medieval Saints and their Interpreters (Philadelphia: University of Pennsylvania Press, 1999).

Moore, Philip. *The Works of Peter of Poitiers, Master in Theology and Chancellor of Paris (1193–1205)* (Notre Dame, IN: University of Notre Dame Press, 1936).

Moore, R. I. *The Formation of a Persecuting Society: Power and Deviance in Western Europe, 950–1250*, 2nd edn (Oxford: Blackwell, 2007).

Moore, Rebecca. *Jews and Christians in the Life and Thought of Hugh of St. Victor* (Atlanta, GA: Scholars Press, 1998).

Moore, W. L. "Via Moderna," in J. R. Strayer (ed.) *Dictionary of Middle Ages* (New York: Scribner, 1989) XII: 406–9.

Moose, Ebrahim. *Ghazali and the Poetics of Imagination* (Oxford: Oxford University Press, 2006).

Moran, Dermot. *The Philosophy of John Scottus Eriugena: A Study of Idealism in the Middle Ages* (Cambridge: Cambridge University Press, 1989).

Moraux, Paul. *D'Aristote à Bessarion: trois exposés sur l'histoire et la transmission de l'Aristotélisme grec* (Quebec: Les Presses de l'Université Laval, 1970).

Moreno-Riano, Gerson. *The World of Marsilius of Padua* (Turnhout: Brepols, 2006).

Moreno Rodríguez, Felipe. *La lucha de Ramón Llull contra el averroismo entre 1309 y 1311* (Madrid: Universidad Computense de Madrid, 1982).

Morenzoni, Franco and Jean-Yves Tilliette (eds.). *Autour de Guillaume d'Auvergne (+1249)* (Turnhout: Brepols, 2005).

Morewedge, Parviz. "The Analysis of 'Substance' in Tusi's *Logic* and in the Ibn Sinian Tradition," in G. Hourani (ed.) *Essays on Islamic Philosophy and Science* (Albany: State University of New York Press, 1975).

Mormando, Franco. *The Preacher's Demons: Bernardino of Siena and the Social Underworld of Early Renaissance Italy* (Chicago: University of Chicago Press, 1999).

Morris, Colin. *The Discovery of the Individual 1050–1200* (New York: Harper and Row, 1972).

Mostert, Marco. *The Political Theology of Abbo of Fleury: A Study of the Ideas about Society and Law of the Tenth-Century Monastic Reform Movement* (Hilversum: Verloren, 1987).

Mourin, Louis. *Jean Gerson prédicateur français* (Bruges: De Tempel, 1952).

Muckle, J. T. "Greek Works Translated into Latin before 1350," *Mediaeval Studies* 4 (1942) 33–42; 5 (1943) 102–14.

    "Isaac Israeli's Definition of Truth," *Archives d'histoire doctrinale et littéraire du moyen âge* 8 (1933) 5–8.

    "Utrum Theologia sit scientia. A Quodlibetal Question of Robert Holcot, O.P.," *Mediaeval Studies* 20 (1958) 127–53.

Mudarris Raḍawī, Muḥammad T. *Ahwal wa ātār-i Abū Ja'far Muḥammad al-Ṭūsī* (Tehran: Bunyād-i Farhang-i Irān, 1975).

Mulchahey, Marian Michèle. *"First the Bow is Bent in Study . . .": Dominican Education before 1350* (Toronto: Pontifical Institute of Mediaeval Studies, 1998).

Muldoon, James. *Popes, Lawyers, and Infidels: The Church and the Non-Christian World, 1250–1550* (Philadelphia: University of Pennsylvania Press, 1979).

Muller, Catherine M. *Marguerite Porete et Marguerite d'Oingt de l'autre côté du miroir* (New York: Lang, 1999).

Müller, Jean P. "La date de la lecture sur les Sentences de Jean Quidort," *Angelicum* 36 (1959) 129–62.

Müller, Sigrid. "The Ethics of John Capreolus and the *Nominales*," *Verbum: Analecta Neolatina* 6 (2004) 301–14.

    Handeln in einer kontingenten Welt: zu Begriff und Bedeutung der rechten Vernunft (recta ratio) bei Wilhelm von Ockham (Tübingen: Francke, 2000).

    "Sprache, Wirklichkeit und Allmacht Gottes: das Bild der *via moderna* bei Johannes Capreolus (1380–1444) und seine Bedeutung für die Schulbildung im 15. Jahrhundert," in J. Aertsen and M. Pickavé (eds.) *Herbst des Mittelalters? Fragen zur Bewertung des 14. und 15. Jahrhunderts* (Berlin: De Gruyter, 2004) 157–72.

Müller, Wolfgang. "Huguccio of Pisa: Canonist, Bishop, and Grammarian?," *Viator* 22 (1991) 121–52.

Muñoz García, Angel. "Albert of Saxony, Bibliography," *Bulletin de philosophie médiévale* 32 (1990) 161–90.

Munsch, Nathan. "The Treatise on the Incarnation of Master Martin: Christology in the Late Twelfth Century" (Ph.D. dissertation: Boston College, 2002).

Murdoch, John. "From Social to Intellectual Factors: An Aspect of the Unitary Character of Late Medieval Learning," in J. Murdoch and E. Sylla (eds.) *The Cultural Context of Medieval Learning* (Dordrecht: Reidel, 1975) 271–348.

  "Henry of Harclay and the Infinite," in A. Maierù and A. Paravicini Bagliani (eds.) *Studi sul XIV secolo in memoria di Anneliese Maier* (Rome: Edizioni di Storia e Letteratura, 1981) 219–61.

  "Infinity and Continuity," in N. Kretzmann *et al.* (eds.) *The Cambridge History of Later Medieval Philosophy* (Cambridge: Cambridge University Press, 1982) 564–91.

  "*Mathesis in philosophiam scholasticam introducta*: The Rise and Development of the Application of Mathematics in Fourteenth-Century Philosophy and Theology," *Arts libéraux et philosophie au moyen âge* (Montréal: Institut d'études médiévales, 1969) 215–54.

  "*Subtilitates Anglicanae* in Fourteenth-Century Paris: John of Mirecourt and Peter Ceffons," in M. P. Cosman and B. Chandler (eds.) *Machaut's World: Science and Art in the Fourteenth Century* (New York: New York Academy of Science, 1978) 51–86.

  "Thomas Bradwardine: Mathematics and Continuity in the Fourteenth Century," in E. Grant and J. Murdoch (eds.) *Mathematics and its Applications to Science and Natural Philosophy in the Middle Ages* (Cambridge: Cambridge University Press, 1984) 103–37.

Murdoch, John and Edith Sylla. "The Science of Motion," in D. Lindberg (ed.) *Science in the Middle Ages* (Chicago: University of Chicago Press, 1978) 206–65.

Murdoch, John and Edward Synan. "Two Questions on the Continuum: Walter Chatton (?), O.F.M. and Adam Wodeham, O.F.M.," *Franciscan Studies* 25 (1966) 212–88.

Murphy, Claudia Eisen. "Aquinas on our Responsibility for our Emotions," *Medieval Philosophy and Theology* 8 (1999) 163–205.

Murray, Alexander. "Confession before 1215," *Transactions of the Royal Historical Society* 3 (1993) 51–81.

  Reason and Society in the Middle Ages (Oxford: Clarendon Press, 1978).

  Suicide in the Middle Ages (Oxford: Oxford University Press, 1998–2002).

Murray, John Courtney. "Remarks on the Moral Problem of War," *Theological Studies* 20 (1959) 40–61.

Muscat, P. "Guillelmi de Ware quaestio inedita de unitate Dei," *Antonianum* 2 (1927) 335–50.

Nabulsi, Karma. "Conceptions of Justice in War: From Grotius to Modern Times," in R. Sorabji and D. Rodin (eds.) *The Ethics of War: Shared Problems in Different Traditions* (Aldershot: Ashgate, 2006) 44–60.

Nadler, Steven and T. M. Rudavsky (eds.). *The Cambridge History of Jewish Philosophy* (Cambridge: Cambridge University Press, 2009).

Nagl, Alfred. *Abhandlungen zur Geschichte der Mathematik* (Leipzig: Teubner, 1890).

Nagy, Albino. *Die philosophischen Abhandlungen des Jaʿqub ben Ishaq al-Kindi* (Münster: Aschendorff, 1897).

Nallino, Carlo A. "Tracce di opere greche giunte agli arabi per trafila pehlevica," in T. W. Arnold and R. A. Nicholson (eds.) *A Volume of Oriental Studies Presented to E.G. Browne* (Cambridge: Cambridge University Press, 1922) 345–63; repr. in M. Nallino and C. A. Nallino (eds.) *Raccolta di scritti editi e inediti* (Rome: Istituto per l'Oriente, 1948) VI: 285–303.

Nardi, Bruno. *Dante e la cultura medievale*, ed. P. Mazantini (Rome: Laterza, 1985).
    Saggi di filosofia dantesca (Florence: La Nuova Italia, 1967).
    Saggi sull'Aristotelismo padovano dal secolo XIV al XVI (Florence: Sansone, 1958).
Nash, Peter W. "The Accidentality of *Esse* According to Giles of Rome," *Gregorianum* 38 (1957) 103–15.
    "Giles of Rome on Boethius's 'Diversum est esse et id quod est'," *Mediaeval Studies* 20 (1950) 57–91.
Nasr, Seyyed Hossein. *An Introduction to Islamic Cosmological Doctrines: Conceptions of Nature and Methods Used for its Study by the Ikhwān al-Ṣafā', al-Bīrūnī, and Ibn Sīnā*, rev. edn (Albany: State University of New York Press, 1993).
Nasr, Seyyed Hossein and Oliver Leaman (eds.). *History of Islamic Philosophy* (London: Routledge, 1995).
Nasr, Seyyed Hossein and Aminrazavi Mehdi (eds.). *An Anthology of Philosophy in Persia* (Oxford: Oxford University Press, 1999).
Nassar, Nassif. *La pensée réaliste d'Ibn Khaldûn* (Paris: Presses universitaire de France, 1967).
National Conference of Catholic Bishops. *The Challenge of Peace: God's Promise and our Response* (Washington, DC: United States Catholic Conference, 1983).
Nederman, Cary J. "Bracton on Kingship Revisited," *History of Political Thought* 5 (1984) 61–77.
    Community and Consent: The Secular Political Theory of Marsiglio of Padua's Defensor Pacis (Lanham, MD: Rowman and Littlefield, 1995).
    John of Salisbury (Tempe: Arizona Center for Medieval and Renaissance Studies, 2005).
    "Kings, Peers and Parliament: Virtue and Corulership in Walter Burley's *Commentarius in VIII Libros Politicorum Aristotelis*," *Albion* 24 (1992) 391–407.
    Political Thought in Early Fourteenth-Century England: Treatises by Walter de Milemete, William of Pagula, and William of Ockham (Turnhout: Brepols, 2002).
    "The Royal Will and the Baronial Bridle: The Place of the *Addicio de cartis* in Bractonian Political Thought," *History of Political Thought* 9 (1988) 415–29.
Nederman, Cary J. and Cynthia J. Neville. "The Origins of the *Speculum regis Edwardi III* of William of Pagula," *Studi Medievali*, 3rd ser. 38 (1997) 317–29.
Nederman, Cary J. and Mary E. Sullivan. "Reading Aristotle through Rome: Republicanism and History in Ptolemy of Lucca's *De regimine principum*," *European Journal of Political Theory* 7 (2008) 223–40.
Needham, Paul. "Duhem's Theory of Mixture in the Light of the Stoic Challenge to the Aristotelian Conception," *Studies in History and Philosophy of Science* 33 (2002) 685–708.
Netter, Thomas and Walter W. Shirley (eds.). *Fasciculi zizaniorum magistri Johannis Wyclif cum tritico* (Rolls Series 5) (London: Longman, Brown, Green, Longmans, and Roberts, 1858).
Netton, Ian R. *Al-Farabi and his School* (New York: Routledge, 1992).
    Muslin Neoplatonists: An Introduction to the Thought of the Brethren of Purity, Ikhwān al-Ṣafā' (London: Allen and Unwin, 1982).
Newhauser, Richard. *The Early History of Greed: The Sin of Avarice in Early Medieval Thought and Literature* (Cambridge: Cambridge University Press, 2000).
    (ed.). *In the Garden of Evil: The Vices and their Culture in the Middle Ages* (Toronto: Pontifical Institute of Mediaeval Studies, 2005).
    (ed.). *The Seven Deadly Sins: From Communities to Individuals* (Leiden: Brill, 2007).
    The Treatise on Vices and Virtues in Latin and the Vernacular (Turnhout: Brepols, 1993).
Newhauser Richard and István Bejczy. *Towards a Revised Incipitarium: Corrections, Supplements, Deletions, and Additions to Update Morton Bloomfield et al., Incipits of Latin Works on the Virtues and Vices* (Turnhout: Brepols, 2007).

Newman, Barbara. *God and the Goddesses: Vision, Poetry, and Belief in the Middle Ages* (Philadelphia: University of Pennsylvania Press, 2003).

"Hildegard and her Hagiographers" in C. Mooney (ed.) *Gendered Voices: Medieval Saints and their Interpreters* (Philadelphia: University of Pennsylvania Press, 1999) 16–34.

"Hildegard of Bingen: Visions and Validation," *Church History* 54 (1985) 163–75.

"*La Mystique Courtoise*: Thirteenth-Century Beguines and the Art of Love," in *From Virile Woman to Woman Christ: Studies in Medieval Religion and Literature* (Philadelphia: University of Pennsylvania Press, 1995) 137–67.

Sister of Wisdom, St. Hildegard's Theology of the Feminine (Berkeley: University of California Press, 1987).

(ed.). *Voice of the Living Light: Hildegard of Bingen and her World* (Berkeley: University of California Press, 1998).

Newman, William R. *Atoms and Alchemy: Chymistry and the Experimental Origins of the Scientific Revolution* (Chicago: University of Chicago Press, 2006).

"New Light on the Identity of Geber," *Sudhoffs Archiv* 69 (1985) 76–90.

"The *Summa Perfectionis* and Late Medieval Alchemy: A Study of Chemical Traditions, Techniques, and Theories in Thirteenth-Century Italy" (Ph.D. dissertation: Harvard University, 1986).

Nicol, Donald. "Byzantine Political Thought," in J. H. Burns (ed.) *The Cambridge History of Medieval Political Thought c.350–c.1450* (Cambridge: Cambridge University Press, 1988) 51–82.

Nielsen, Lauge O. "The Debate between Peter Auriol and Thomas Wylton on Theology and Virtue," *Vivarium* 38 (2000) 35–98.

"Dictates of Faith versus Dictates of Reason: Peter Auriole on Divine Power, Creation, and Human Rationality," *Documenti e studi sulla tradizione filosofica medievale* 7 (1996) 213–41.

"The Intelligibility of Faith and the Nature of Theology: Peter Auriole's Theological Programme," *Studia Theologica* 53 (1999) 26–39.

"Peter Auriol's Way with Words: The Genesis of Peter Auriol's Commentaries on Peter Lombard's First and Fourth Books of the Sentences," in G. Evans (ed.) *Mediaeval Commentaries on the Sentences of Peter Lombard* (Leiden: Brill, 2002) 149–219.

"The *Quodlibet* of Peter Auriol," in C. Schabel (ed.) *Theological Quodlibeta in the Middle Ages: The Fourteenth Century* (Leiden: Brill, 2007) 267–331.

Theology and Philosophy in the Twelfth Century: A Study of Gilbert Porreta's Thinking and the Theological Expositions of the Doctrine of the Incarnation during the Period 1130–1180 (Leiden: Brill, 1982).

Nielsen, Lauge O., Timothy Noone, and Cecilia Trifogli. "Thomas Wylton's Question on the Formal Distinction as Applied to the Divine," *Documenti e studi sulla tradizione filosofica medievale* 14 (2003) 330–88.

Nielsen, Lauge O. and Cecilia Trifogli. "Questions on the Beatific Vision by Thomas Wylton and Sibert de Beka," *Documenti e studi sulla tradizione filosofica medievale* 17 (2006) 511–84.

Noonan, John. *Contraception: A History of its Treatment by the Catholic Theologians and Canonists* (Cambridge, MA: Harvard University Press, 1965).

"Gratian Slept Here: The Changing Identity of the Father of the Systematic Study of Canon Law," *Traditio* 35 (1979) 145–72.

The Scholastic Analysis of Usury (Cambridge, MA: Harvard University Press, 1957).

"Who was Rolandus?," in S. Kuttner *et al.* (eds.) *Law, Church and Society: Essays in Honor of Stephan Kuttner* (Philadelphia: University of Pennsylvania Press, 1977) 21–48.

Noone, Timothy. "Alnwick on the Origin, Nature, and Function of the Formal Distinction," *Franciscan Studies* 53 (1993) 231–61.

"An Edition and Study of the *Scriptum super Metaphysicam*, bk. 12, dist. 2: A Work Attributed to Richard Rufus of Cornwall" (Ph.D. dissertation: University of Toronto, 1987).

"Evidence for the Use of Adam of Buckfield's Writings at Paris," *Mediaeval Studies* 54 (1992) 308–16.

"The Franciscans and Epistemology: Reflections on the Roles of Bonaventure and Scotus," in R. E. Houser (ed.) *Medieval Masters: Essays in Memory of Msgr. E.A. Synan*, Thomistic Papers VII (Houston, TX: Center for Thomistic Studies, 1999) 63–90.

"Richard Rufus of Cornwall and the Authorship of the *Scriptum super metaphysicam*," *Franciscan Studies* 49 (1989) 55–91.

"Richard Rufus on Creation, Divine Immutability, and Future Contingency in the *Scriptum super Metaphysicam*," *Documenti e studi sulla tradizione filosofica medievale* 4 (1993) 1–23.

"Roger Bacon and Richard Rufus on Aristotle's *Metaphysics*: A Search for the Ground of Disagreement," *Vivarium* 25 (1997) 251–65.

Noone, Timothy and R. James Long. "Fishacre and Rufus on the Metaphysics of Light," in J. Hamesse (ed.), *Roma, magister mundi: itineraria culturae medievalis: mélanges offerts au Père L.E. Boyle à l'occasion de son 75e anniversaire* (Louvain-la-Neuve: Fédération internationale des instituts médiévales, 1998) I: 517–48.

Normore, Calvin G. "Buridan's Ontology," in J. Bogen and J. E. McGuire (eds.) *How Things Are: Studies in Predication and the History and Philosophy of Science* (Dordrecht: Reidel, 1985) 189–203.

"Duns Scotus's Modal Theory," in T. Williams (ed.) *The Cambridge Companion to Duns Scotus* (Cambridge: Cambridge University Press, 2003) 129–60.

"The Necessity in Deduction: Cartesian Inference and its Medieval Background," *Synthese* 96 (1993) 437–54.

"Picking and Choosing: Anselm and Ockham on Choice," *Vivarium* 36 (1998) 23–39.

"Walter Burley on Continuity," in N. Kretzmann (ed.) *Infinity and Continuity in Ancient and Medieval Thought* (Ithaca, NY: Cornell University Press, 1982) 258–69.

North, John. "Natural Philosophy in Late Medieval Oxford," in J. I. Catto and R. Evans (eds.) *The History of the University of Oxford*, vol. II: *Late Medieval Oxford* (Oxford: Oxford University Press, 1992) 76–95.

Nouzille, Phillippe and Olivier Boulnois. *Expérience de Dieu et théologie monastique au XIIe siècle* (Paris: Cerf, 1999).

Novaes, Catarina Dutilh. "Buridan's *consequentia*: Consequence and Inference within a Token-based Semantics," *History and Philosophy of Logic* 26 (2005) 277–97.

"Ralph Strode's *obligationes*: The Return of Consistency and the Epistemic Turn," *Vivarium* 44 (2006) 338–74.

Novak, David. *The Theology of Nahmanides Systematically Presented* (Atlanta, GA: Scholars Press, 1992).

Novotný, Václav, and Vlastimil Kybal. *M. Jan Hus, Zivot a Ucení* (Prague: Nákladem Jana Laichtera, 1919–31) 5 vols.

Nuchelmans, Gabriel. *Late-Scholastic and Humanist Theories of the Proposition* (Amsterdam: North-Holland, 1980).

Theories of the Proposition: Ancient and Medieval Conceptions of the Bearers of Truth and Falsity (Amsterdam: North-Holland, 1973).

Nussbaum, Martha. *The Therapy of Desire: Theory and Practice in Hellenistic Ethics* (Princeton, NJ: Princeton University Press, 1994).

Oakley, Francis. *Kingship: The Politics of Enchantment* (Oxford: Blackwell, 2006).

The Political Thought of Pierre d'Ailly: The Voluntarist Tradition (New Haven, CT: Yale University Press, 1964).

Oberman, Heiko A. *Archbishop Thomas Bradwardine* (Utrecht: Kemink and Zoon, 1957).

"Facientibus quod in se est Deus non denegat gratiam: Robert Holcot, OP and the Beginnings of Luther's Theology," *Harvard Theological Review* 55 (1962) 317–42.

(ed.). *Gregor von Rimini: Werk und Wirkung bis zur Reformation* (Berlin: De Gruyter, 1981).

The Harvest of Medieval Theology: Gabriel Biel and Late Medieval Nominalism (Cambridge, MA: Harvard University Press, 1963).

Werden und Wertung der Reformation: Vom Wegestreit zum Glaubenskampf (Tübingen: Mohr, 1977).

Oberman, Heiko A. and James A. Weisheipl. "The *Sermo epinicius* ascribed to Thomas Bradwardine," *Archives d'histoire doctrinale et littéraire du moyen âge* 25 (1958) 295–329.

O'Brien, Andrew. "Duns Scotus' Teaching on the Distinction between Essence and Existence," *New Scholasticism* 38 (1964) 61–77.

Obrist, Barbara (ed.). *Abbon de Fleury: philosophie, science et comput autour de l'an mil* (Paris: Centre d'histoire des sciences et des philosophies arabes et médiévales, 2004).

O'Carroll, Mary. *A Thirteenth-Century Preacher's Handbook: Studies in MS Laud misc. 511* (Toronto: Pontifical Institute of Medieval Studies, 1997).

O'Donnell, J. Reginald. "The Syncategoremata of William of Sherwood," *Mediaeval Studies* 3 (1941) 46–93.

O'Donovan, Oliver. *The Just War Revisited* (Cambridge: Cambridge University Press, 2003).

Oehler, Klaus. *Antike Philosophie und byzantinisches Mittelalter* (Munich: Beck, 1969).

Oliger, Livarius. "Servasanto da Faenza e il suo 'Liber de virtutibus et vitiis'," in *Miscellanea Francesco Ehrle* (Rome: Biblioteca Apostolica Vaticana, 1924) I: 148–89.

Olivieri, Luigi. *Pietro d'Abano e il pensiero neolatino* (Padua: Antenore, 1988).

Olsen, Glenn. "John of Salisbury's Humanism," in C. Leonardi (ed.) *Gli unamesimi medievali* (Florence: SISMEL, 1988).

O'Malley, John. "Medieval Preaching," in T. L. Amos *et al.* (eds.) *De ore Domini: Preacher and Word in the Middle Ages* (Kalamazoo, MI: Medieval Institute, 1989) 1–13.

Omar, Saleh Beshara. *Ibn al-Haytham's Optics: A Study of the Origins of Experimental Science* (Minneapolis, MN: Bibliotheca Islamica, 1977).

O'Meara, John J. *Eriugena* (Oxford: Clarendon Press, 1988).

Onuma, Yasuaki. *A Normative Approach to War: Peace, War and Justice in Hugo Grotius* (Oxford: Clarendon Press, 1993).

Origo, Iris. *The World of San Bernardino* (New York: Harcourt Brace, 1962).

Orlandi, Stefano. *Antonino, arcivescovo di Firenze, dottore della chiesa: studi* (Florence: Il Rosario, 1959).

Ormsby, Eric. *Ghazali* (Oxford: Oneworld, 2007).

Theodicy in Islamic Thought: The Dispute over al-Ghazâlî's "Best of All Possible Worlds" (Princeton, NJ: Princeton University Press, 1984).

Osborne, Kenan. "Alexander of Hales: Precursor and Promoter of Franciscan Theology," in *The History of Franciscan Theology, St Bonaventure* (New York: Franciscan Institute, 1994) 1–38.

Ostlender, Heinrich (ed.). *Sententiae florianenses* (Bonn: Hanstein, 1929).

Ott, Ludwig. *Untersuchungen zur theologischen Briefliteratur der Frühscholastik: unter besonderer Berücksichtigung des Viktorinerkreises* (Münster: Aschendorff, 1937).

Ottaviano, Carmelo. *Guglielmo d'Auxerre, d. 1231: la vita, le opere, il pensiero* (Rome: L'Universale tipografia poliglotta, 1929).

Otte, James. "Alfredus Anglicus and the Reception of Aristotle," *Proceedings of the Patristic, Mediaeval and Renaissance Conference* 15 (1990) 127–39.

"The Life and Writings of Alfredus Anglicus," *Viator* 3 (1972) 275–91.

Otten, Willemien. *The Anthropology of Johannes Scottus Eriugena* (Leiden: Brill, 1991).

Ottman, Jennifer and Rega Wood. "Walter Burley: His Life and Works," *Vivarium* 37 (1999) 1–24.

Ottosson, Per-Gunnar. *Scholastic Medicine and Philosophy: A Study of Commentaries on Galen's Tegni, ca. 1300–1450* (Naples: Bibliopolis, 1984).

Ouy, Gilbert. "Discovering Gerson the Humanist: Fifty Years of Serendipity," in B. P. McGuire (ed.) *A Companion to Jean Gerson* (Leiden: Brill, 2006) 79–132.

Owen, G. E. L. "Logic and Metaphysics in Some Early Works of Aristotle," in G. Owen and D. Ingemar (eds.) *Aristotle and Plato in the Mid-Fourth Century: Papers of the Symposium Aristotelicum* (Gothenburg: Elanders, 1960) 163–90.

"*Tithenai ta phainomena*," in J. Barnes *et al.* (eds) *Articles on Aristotle 1: Science* (London: Duckworth, 1975) 113–26.

Ozment, Steven. *Homo spiritualis: A Comparative Study of the Anthropology of Johannes Tauler, Jean Gerson and Martin Luther (1509–16)* (Leiden: Brill, 1969).

Palazzo, Alessandro. "Ulrich of Strasbourg and Denys the Carthusian," *Bulletin de philosophie médiévale* 46 (2004) 61–113; 48 (2006) 163–208.

Panaccio, Claude. "Aquinas on Intellectual Representation," in D. Perler (ed.) *Ancient and Medieval Theories of Intentionality* (Leiden: Brill, 2001) 185–201.

Le discours intérieur de Platon à Guilaume d'Ockham (Paris: Seuil, 1999).

"From Mental Word to Mental Language," *Philosophical Topics* 20 (1992) 125–47.

Les mots, les concepts et les choses. Le sémantique de Guillaume d'Occam et le nominalisme d'aujourd'hui (Montréal: Bellarmin, 1991).

Ockham on Concepts (Aldershot: Ashgate, 2004).

"Semantics and Mental Language," in P. V. Spade (ed.) *The Cambridge Companion to Ockham* (Cambridge: Cambridge University Press, 1999) 53–75.

Panaccio, Claude and Ernesto Perini-Santos. "Guillaume d'Ockham et la *suppositio materialis*," *Vivarium* 42 (2004) 202–24.

Panella, Emilio. "Dal bene comune al bene del comune: I trattati politici di Remigio dei Girolami nella Firenze dei bianchi-neri," in *Politica e vita religiosa a Firenze tra '300 e '500* (Pistoia: Centro riviste della provincia romana, 1985) 1–198.

"Remigiana: Note biografiche e fiologiche," *Memorie Domenicane* 13 (1982) 366–421.

Panizza, Letizia. "Stoic Psychotherapy in the Middle Ages and Renaissance: Petrarch's *De remedies*," in M. J. Osler (ed.) *Atoms, Pneuma, and Tranquility: Epicurean and Stoic Themes in European Thought* (Cambridge: Cambridge University Press, 1991) 39–65.

Papadopoulos, Jean B. *Théodore II Lascaris, empereur de Nicée* (Paris: Picard, 1908).

Park, Katharine. "The Organic Soul," in C. Schmitt *et al.* (eds.) *The Cambridge History of Renaissance Philosophy* (Cambridge: Cambridge University Press, 1988) 464–84.

Parodi, Massimo (ed.). "Il linguaggio delle proportiones nella distinctio prima di Giovanni di Mirecourt," *Rivista critica di storia della filosofia* 39 (1984) 657–86.

Parsons, Terence, "The Traditional Square of Opposition," in E. Zalta (ed.) *The Stanford Encyclopedia of Philosophy* (Winter 2006 edition): http://plato.stanford.edu/archives/o win2006/entries/ square/.

Paschetto, Eugenia. *Pietro d'Abano, medico e filosofo* (Florence: Nuovedizioni E. Vallecchi, 1984).

Pascoe, Louis B. *Jean Gerson: Principles of Church Reform* (Leiden: Brill, 1973).

Pasiecznik, Marcellus. "John de Bassolis, OFM," *Franciscan Studies* 13 (1953) 59–77; 14 (1954), 49–80.

Pasnau, Robert. "Aquinas and the Content Fallacy," *Modern Schoolman* 75 (1998) 293–314.
  (tr.). *Cambridge Translations of Medieval Philosophical Texts,* vol. III: *Mind and Knowledge* (Cambridge: Cambridge University Press, 2002).
  "Form, Substance, and Mechanism," *Philosophical Review* 113 (2004) 31–88.
  "Henry of Ghent and the Twilight of Divine Illumination," *Review of Metaphysics* 49 (1995) 49–75.
  "Olivi on Human Freedom," in A. Boureau and S. Piron (eds.) *Pierre de Jean Olivi (1248–1298): pensée scolastique, dissidence spirituelle et société* (Paris: Vrin, 1999) 15–25.
  "Olivi on the Metaphysics of Soul," *Medieval Philosophy and Theology* 6 (1997) 109–32.
  "Sensible Qualities: The Case of Sound," *Journal of the History of Philosophy* 38.1 (2000): 27–40.
  Theories of Cognition in the Later Middle Ages (Cambridge: Cambridge University Press, 1997).
  Thomas Aquinas on Human Nature: A Philosophical Study of Summa theologiae Ia 75–89 (Cambridge: Cambridge University Press, 2002).
  "William Heytesbury on Knowledge: Epistemology without Necessary and Sufficient Conditions," *History of Philosophy Quarterly* 12 (1995) 347–66.
Pasnau, Robert and Christopher Shields, *The Philosophy of Aquinas* (Boulder, CO: Westview, 2004).
Pattin, Adriaan. *L'anthropologie de Gérard d'Abbeville: étude préliminaire et édition critique de plusieurs Questions quodlibétiques concernant le sujet, avec l'édition complète du* De cogitationibus (Leuven: Leuven University Press, 1993)
  "Gilles de Rome, O.E.S.A. (ca 1243–1316) et la distinction réelle de l'essence et de l'existence," *Revue de l'Université d'Ottawa* 23 (1953) 80*–116*.
  "Jan van Hulshout (1405–1475) Vlaams wijsgeer en theoloog van de Universiteit te Keulen," *Tijdschrift voor Filosofie* 38 (1976) 104–38.
  Pour l'histoire du sens agent: la controverse entre Barthélemy de Bruges et Jean de Jandun, ses antécédents et son évolution (Leuven: Leuven University Press, 1988).
  "La structure de l'être fini selon Bernard d'Auvergne, O.P.," *Tijdschrift voor Filosofie* 24 (1962) 668–737.
  "Een vijftiende-eeuws commentaar op het *De divinis nominibus* van de Pseudo-Dionysius: een onbekend werk van Johannes Hulshout van Mechelen (1405–1475). Een studie over de bronnen van dit werk," in *Handelingen van de Koninklijke Kring voor Oudheidkunde, Letteren en Kunst van Mechelen,* 98e Boekdeel (Mechelen: The Kring, 1995) 53–64.
Paulmier-Foucart, Monique and Marie-Christine Duchenne. *Vincent de Beauvais et le Grand miroir du monde* (Turnhout: Brepols, 2004).
Paulmier-Foucart, Monique, Serge Lusignan, and Alain Nadeau (eds.). *Vincent de Beauvais: intentions et réceptions d'une œuvre encyclopédique au Moyen Âge* (Paris: Vrin, 1990).
Paulus, Jean. "Les disputes d'Henri de Gand et de Gilles de Rome sur la distinction de l'essence et l'existence," *Archives d'histoire doctrinale et littéraire du moyen âge* 13 (1940–2) 323–58.
  Henri de Gand. Essai sur les tendances de sa métaphysique (Paris: Vrin, 1938).
Payen, Jean Charles. "La penitence dans le contexte culturel des XIIᵉ et XIIIᵉ siècles: des doctrines contritionnistes aux pénitentiels vernaculaires," *Revue des sciences philosophiques et théologiques* 61 (1977) 399–428.
Payer, Pierre. *The Bridling of Desire: Views of Sex in the Later Middle Ages* (Toronto: University of Toronto Press, 1993).
Payne, Gordon. "Cognitive Intuition of Singulars Revisited (Matthew of Aquasparta versus B.J. Lonergan)," *Franciscan Studies* 41 (1981) 346–84.
Peden, A. M. *Abbo of Fleury and Ramsey: Commentary on the Calculus of Victorius of Aquitaine* (Oxford: Published for the British Academy by Oxford University Press, 2003).

Pedersen, Olaf. *The First Universities: Studium Generale and the Origins of University Education in Europe* (Cambridge: Cambridge University Press, 1997).

Pelster, Franz. "Die anonyme Verteidigungsschrift der Lehre Gilberts von Poitiers im Cod. Vat. 561 und ihr Verfasser Canonicus Adhemar von Saint-Ruf in Valence (um 1180)," *Studia mediaevalia in honorem Admodum Reverendi Patris Raymundi Josephi Martin* (Bruges: De Tempel, 1948) 113–46.

"Heinrich von Harclay, Kanzler von Oxford, und seine Quaestionen," in *Miscellanea Francesco Ehrle* (Rome: Biblioteca Apostolica Vaticana, 1924) I: 307–56.

"Literaturgeschichtliches zur Pariser theol. Schule aus den Jahren 1230–1256," *Scholastik* 5 (1930) 46–78.

Pelzer, A. "Les 51 articles de Guillaume Occam censurés, en Avignon, en 1326," *Revue d'histoire ecclésiastique* 18 (1922) 246–7.

"Prosper de Reggio Emilia des Ermites de Saint-Augustin et le manuscrit latin 1086 de la Bibliothèque Vaticane," *Revue néoscolastique de philosophie* 30 (1928) 316–51.

Pennington, Kenneth. "The Consilia of Baldus de Ubaldis," *Tijdschrift voor Rechtsgeschiedenis* 56 (1988) 85–92.

Medieval Canonists: A Bio-Bibliographical Listing: http://faculty.cua.edu/pennington/biobibl. htm.

Perarnau, Josep (ed.). *Actes de la I Trobada Internacional d'Estudis sobre Arnau de Vilanova* (Barcelona: Institut d'Estudis Catalans, 1995).

Percan, Josip. *Teologia come "scienza pratica" secondo Giovanni di Reading* (Grottaferrata: Editiones Collegii S. Bonaventurae, 1986).

Percival, W. Keith. "Changes in the Approach to Language," in N. Kretzmann *et al.* (eds.) *Cambridge History of Later Medieval Philosophy* (Cambridge: Cambridge University Press, 1982) 808–17.

Perler, Dominik (ed.). *Ancient and Medieval Theories of Intentionality* (Leiden: Brill, 2001).

"Crathorn on Mental Language," in C. Marmo (ed.) *Vestigia, Imagines, Verba. Semiotics and Logic in Medieval Theological Texts (XIIth–XIVth Century)* (Turnhout: Brepols, 1997) 337–54.

"Does God Deceive Us? Skeptical Hypotheses in Late Medieval Epistemology," in H. Lagerlund (ed.) *Skepticism in Medieval Philosophy* (Leiden: Brill, forthcoming).

"Essentialism and Direct Realism: Some Late Medieval Perspectives," *Topoi* 19 (2000) 111–22.

"Intentionality and Action: Medieval Discussions on the Cognitive Capacities of Animals," in M. C. Pacheco and J. F. Meirinhos (eds.) *Intellect et imagination dans la philosophie médiévale* (Turnhout: Brepols, 2006) I: 73–98.

"Peter Aureol vs. Hervaeus Natalis on Intentionality: A Text Edition with Introductory Remarks," *Archives d'histoire doctrinale et littéraire du moyen âge* 61 (1994) 227–62.

"Seeing and Judging: Ockham and Wodeham on Sensory Cognition," in S. Knuuttila and P. Kärkkäinen (eds.) *Theories of Perception in Medieval and Early Modern Philosophy* (Dordrecht: Springer, 2008) 151–69.

Theorien der Intentionalität im Mittelalter (Frankfurt: Klostermann, 2002).

"Things in the Mind: Fourteenth-Century Controversies over 'Intelligible *Species*'," *Vivarium* 34 (1996) 231–53.

"What Am I Thinking About? John Duns Scotus and Peter Aureol on Intentional Objects," *Vivarium* 32 (1994) 72–89.

Zweifel und Gewissheit: skeptische Debatten im Mittelalter (Frankfurt: Klostermann, 2006).

Perler, Dominik and Ulrich Rudolph. *Logik und Theologie: das Organon im arabischen und im lateinischen Mittelalter* (Leiden: Brill, 2005).

Occasionalismus: Theorien der Kausalität im arabisch-islamischen und im Europäischen Denken (Göttingen: Vandenhoeck und Ruprecht, 2000).

Perreiah, A. R. "Insolubilia in the Logica parva of Paul of Venice," *Medioevo* 4 (1978) 145–72.
  Paul of Venice: A Bibliographical Guide (Bowling Green, OH: Philosophy Documentation Center, 1986).
Pessin, Sarah. "The Influence of Islamic Thought on Maimonides," in E. Zalta (ed.) *The Stanford Encyclopedia of Philosophy* (Fall 2005 edition): http://plato.stanford.edu/archives/fall2005/entries/maimonides-islamic/.
  "Jewish Neoplatonism: Being above Being and Divine Emanation in Solomon Ibn Gabirol and Isaac Israeli," in D. H. Frank and O. Leaman (eds.) *The Cambridge Companion to Medieval Jewish Philosophy* (Cambridge: Cambridge University Press, 2003) 91–110.
  "Solomon Ibn Gabirol: Universal Hylomorphism and the Psychic Imagination" (Ph.D. dissertation: Ohio State University, 2000).
Peters, F. E. *Aristoteles Arabus: The Oriental Translations and Commentaries on the Aristotelian Corpus* (Leiden: Brill, 1968).
Peters, J. R. T. M. *God's Created Speech: A Study in the Speculative Theology of the Muʿtazilī Qāḍī l-quḍāt Abū l-Ḥasan ʿAbd al-Jabbār ibn Aḥmad al-Hamaḏānī* (Leiden: Brill, 1976).
Petroff, Elizabeth. *Body and Soul: Essays on Medieval Women and Mysticism* (New York: Oxford University Press, 1994).
Pfeffer, Jeremy. *Providence in the Book of Job: The Search for God's Mind* (Brighton: Sussex Academic Press, 2005).
Pfeiffer, Franz (ed.). *Deutsche Mystiker des vierzehnten Jahrhunderts* (Leipzig: Göschen, 1845–57; repr. Aalen: Scientia Verlag, 1962).
Phelps, Mary. "The Theory of Seminal Reasons in James of Viterbo," *Augustiniana* 30 (1980) 271–83.
Phyrigos, Antones. *Dalla controversia palamitica alla polemica esicastica, con un'edizione critica delle Epistole greche di Barlaam* (Rome: Antonianum, 2005).
Picavet, François. *Roscelin philosophe et theologien d'après la légende et d'après l'histoire; sa place dans l'histoire générale et comparée des philosophies medievales* (Paris: Alcan, 1911).
Piché, David (ed.). *La condamnation parisienne de 1277* (Paris: Vrin, 1999).
  Le problème des universaux à la Faculté des Arts de Paris entre 1230 et 1260 (Paris: Vrin, 2005).
Pickavé, Martin. *Heinrich von Gent über Metaphysik als erste Wissenschaft: Studien zu einem Metaphysikentwurf aus dem letzten Viertel des 13. Jahrhunderts* (Leiden: Brill, 2007).
Pietro Lombardo: Atti del XLIII Convegno storico internazionale (Spoleto: Fondazione Centro italiano di studi sull'alto medioevo, 2007).
Pilný, Josepha. *Jérôme de Prague: un orateur progressiste du Moyen Age* (Geneva: Perret-Gentil, 1974).
Pilsner, Joseph. *The Specification of Human Actions in St. Thomas Aquinas* (Oxford: Oxford University Press, 2006).
Pinborg, Jan. "Die Aristoteles-Quaestionen des Magister Nicolaus von Amsterdam," *Classica et Mediaevalia* 25 (1964) 244–62.
  Die Entwicklung der Sprachtheorie im Mittelalter (Münster: Aschendorff, 1967).
  Logik und Semantik im Mittelalter: ein Überblick (Stuttgart-Bad Cannstatt: Frommann-Holzboog, 1972).
  "Magister Abstractionum," *Cahiers de l'Institut du Moyen Age Grec et Latin* 18 (1976) 1–4.
  Medieval Semantics, Selected Studies on Medieval Logic and Grammar, ed. S. Ebbesen (London: Variorum, 1984).
  "A New MS of the Questions on the *Posteriora analytica* Attributed to Petrus de Alvernia," *Cahiers de l'Institut du Moyen Age Grec et Latin* 10 (1973) 48–62.
  "A Note on Some Theoretical Concepts of Logic and Grammar," *Revue internationale de philosophie* 21 (1975) 286–96.

"Radulphus Brito on Universals," *Cahiers de l'Institut du Moyen Age Grec et Latin* 35 (1980) 60–123.

"Speculative Grammar," in N. Kretzmann *et al.* (eds.) *The Cambridge History of Later Medieval Philosophy* (Cambridge: Cambridge University Press, 1982) 254–69.

"Walter Burleigh on the Meaning of Proposition," *Classica et Mediaevalia* 28 (1969) 394–404.

Pinborg, Jan and Sten Ebbesen. "Thirteenth-Century Notes on William of Sherwood's 'Treatise on Properties of Terms': An Edition of *Anonymi dubitationes et notabilia circa Guilelmi de Shyreswode introductionum logicalium Tractatum V* from MS Worcester Cath. Q.13," *Cahiers de l'Institut du Moyen Age Grec et Latin* 47 (1984) 103–41.

Pines, Shlomo. "La loi naturelle et la société: la doctrine politico-théologique d'Ibn Zurʿa," in U. Heyd (ed.) *Studies in Islamic History and Civilization* (Jerusalem: Magnes Press, 1961) 154–90.

"Les précurseurs musulmans de la theorie d l'impetus," *Archeion (Archivio di storia della scienza)* 21 (1938) 298–306.

Scholasticism after Thomas Aquinas and the Teachings of Hasdai Crescas and his Predecessors (Jerusalem: Israel Academy of Sciences and Humanities, 1967).

Studies in Abu'l-Barakat al-Baghdadi: Physics and Metaphysics, in The Collected Works of Shlomo Pines, vol. I (Leiden: Brill, 1979).

Pines, Shlomo and Yirmiyahu Yovel (eds.). *Maimonides and Philosophy* (Dordrecht: Nijhoff, 1985).

Pingree, David. *The Thousands of Abu Mashar* (London: Warburg Institute, 1968).

Pini, Giorgio. "Being and Creation in Giles of Rome," in J. Aertsen *et al.* (eds.) *Nach der Verurteilung von 1277: Philosophie und Theologie an der Universität von Paris im letzten Viertel des 13. Jahrhunderts: Studien und Texte* (Berlin: De Gruyter, 2001) 390–403.

Categories and Logic in Duns Scotus: An Interpretation of Aristotle's Categories in the Late Thirteenth Century (Leiden: Brill, 2002).

"Giles of Rome," in C. Schabel (ed.) *Theological Quodlibeta in the Middle Ages: The Thirteenth Century* (Leiden: Brill, 2006) 233–86.

"Una lettura scotista della *Metafisica* di Aristotele: l'*expositio in libros Metaphysicorum* di Antonio Andrea," *Documenti e studi sulla tradizione filosofica medievale* 2 (1991) 529–86.

"Scotistic Aristotelianism: Antonius Andreas' *Expositio* and *Quaestiones* on the *Metaphysics*," in L. Sileo (ed.) *Via Scoti: Methodologica ad mentem Joannis Duns Scoti* (Rome: Edizioni Antonianum, 1995) I: 375–89.

"Univocity in Scotus' *Quaestiones super Metaphysicam*: The Solution to a Riddle," *Medioevo* 30 (2005) 69–110.

Pinziani, Roberto. *The Logical Grammar of Abelard* (Dordrecht: Kluwer, 2003).

Piron, Sylvain. "Franciscan *Quodlibeta* in Southern *Studia* and at Paris, 1280–1300," in C. Schabel (ed.) *Theological Quodlibeta in the Middle Ages: The Thirteenth Century* (Leiden: Brill, 2006) 403–38.

Nicolas Oresme: Violence, langage et raison politique (Florence: European University Institute, 1997).

"Les œuvres perdues d'Olivi: essai de reconstitution," *Archivum Franciscanum Historicum* 91 (1998) 357–94.

"Parcours d'un intellectuel franciscain. D'une théologie vers une pensée sociale: l'œuvre de Pierre de Jean Olivi (ca. 1248–1298) et son traité 'De contractibus'" (Ph.D. dissertation: École des Hautes Études en Sciences Sociales, 1999).

Pironet, Fabienne. "Sophismata," in E. Zalta (ed.) *The Stanford Encyclopedia of Philosophy* (Spring 2006 edition): http://plato.stanford.edu/archives/win2002/entries/sophismata/.

"'The Sophismata asinina' of William Heytesbury," in S. Read (ed.) *Sophisms in Medieval Logic and Grammar: Acts of the Ninth European Symposium for Medieval Logic and Semantics* (Dordrecht: Kluwer, 1993) 128–43.

The Tradition of Medieval Logic and Speculative Grammar from Anselm to the End of the Seventeenth Century. A Bibliography (1977–1994) (Turnhout: Brepols, 1997).

Pirzio, Paola. "Le prospettive filosofiche del trattato di Enrico di Langenstein (1325–1397) 'De habitudine causarum'," *Rivista critica di storia della filosofia* 24 (1969) 363–73.

Plantinga, Alvin. *Does God Have a Nature?* (Milwaukee, WI: Marquette University Press, 1980).

The Nature of Necessity (Oxford: Oxford University Press, 1974).

Platti, Emilio. *Yaḥyā Ibn ʿAdī, théologien chrétien et philosophe arabe: sa théologie de l'Incarnation* (Leuven: Departement Orientalistiek, 1983).

Platzeck, Erhard-Wolfram. *Raimund Lull. Sein Leben – Seine Werke. Die Grundlagen seines Denkens (Prinzipienlehre)* (Rome: Editiones Franciscanae, 1962–64).

Plevano, Roberto. "Richard Rufus of Cornwall and Geoffrey of Aspall: Two Questions on the Instant of Change," *Medioevo* 19 (1993) 167–232.

Plotnik, Kenneth. *Hervaeus Natalis OP and the Controversies over the Real Presence and Transubstantiation* (Munich: Schöningh, 1970).

Pluta, Olaf. "Die Diskussion der Frage nach der Unsterblichkeit bei Nikolaus Oresme und Peter von Ailly," *Studia Mediewistyczne* 27 (1990) 115–30.

"Materialism in the Philosophy of Mind. Nicholas of Amsterdam's *Quaestiones* De anima," in P. J. J. M. Bakker and J. M. M. H. Thijssen (eds.) *Mind, Cognition and Representation: The Tradition of Commentaries on Aristotle's* De anima (Aldershot: Ashgate, 2007) 109–26.

(ed.). *Nicholas of Amsterdam: A Dutch Master of Arts in Fifteenth-Century Germany* (Amsterdam: Grüner 2008).

Pobst, Phyllis. "Visitation of Religious and Clergy by Archbishop Eudes Rigaud of Rouen," in T. Burman *et al.* (eds.) *Religion, Text, and Society in Medieval Spain and Northern Europe. Essays in Honor of J.N. Hillgarth* (Toronto: Pontifical Institute of Mediaeval Studies, 2002) 223–49.

Podskalsky, Gerhard. *Theologie und Philosophie in Byzanz* (Munich: Beck, 1977).

Poonawala, Ismail. *Biobibliography of Ismāʿīlī Literature* (Malibu, CA: Undena Publications, 1977).

Pope, Stephen J. (ed.). *The Ethics of Aquinas* (Washington, DC: Georgetown University Press, 2002).

"Overview of the Ethics of Thomas Aquinas," in S. J. Pope (ed.) *The Ethics of Aquinas* (Washington, DC: Georgetown University Press, 2002) 30–53.

Popkin, Richard. *The History of Scepticism: From Savonarola to Bayle*, rev. edn (Oxford: Oxford University Press, 2003).

Porebski, Stanisław. "La question de Bernard Lombardi concernant la différence réelle entre l'essence et l'existence," *Mediaevalia Philosophica Polonorum* 17 (1973) 157–85.

Porro, Pasquale. "An Historiographical Image of Henry of Ghent," in W. Vanhamel (ed.) *Henry of Ghent. Proceedings of the International Colloquium on the Occasion of the 700th Anniversary of his Death (1293)* (Leuven: Leuven University Press, 1996) 373–403.

"Possibilità e *Esse essentiae* in Enrico di Gand," in W. Vanhamel (ed.) *Henry of Ghent. Proceedings of the International Colloquium on the Occasion of the 700th Anniversary of his Death (1293)* (Leuven: Leuven University Press, 1996) 211–53.

Porter, Jean. *Nature as Reason: A Thomistic Theory of the Natural Law* (Grand Rapids, MI: Eerdmans, 2005).

"Responsibility, Passion, and Sin: A Reassessment of Abelard's *Ethics*," *Journal of Religious Ethics* 28 (2000) 367–94.

Post, Gaines. *Studies in Medieval Legal Thought: Public Law and the State 1100–1322* (Princeton, NJ: Princeton University Press, 1964).

Potestà, Gian Luca. *Storia ed escatologia in Ubertino da Casale* (Milan: Vita e Pensiero, 1980).

Pounds, Norman. *An Economic History of Medieval Europe*, 2nd edn (London: Longman, 1994).

Pourjavady, Reza and Sabine Schmidtke. *A Jewish Philosopher of Baghdad* (Leiden: Brill, 2006).

Powicke, F. M. *Stephen Langton, Being the Ford Lectures Delivered in the University of Oxford in Hilary term 1927* (Oxford: Clarendon Press, 1928; repr. New York: Barnes and Noble, 1965).

Pozzi, Lorenzo. *La coerenza logica nella teoria medioevale delle obbligazioni (con l'edizione del trattato "Obligationes" di Guglielmo Buser)* (Parma: Zara, 1990).

  Le consequentiae nella logica medievale (Padua: Liviana Editrice, 1978).

Prentice, Robert. "Univocity and Analogy According to Scotus's *Super libros Elenchorum Aristotelis*," *Archives d'histoire doctrinale et littéraire du moyen âge* 35 (1968) 39–64.

Prezioso, Faustino A. "L'attività del soggetto pensente nella gnoseologia di Matteo d'Acquasparta e di Ruggiero Marston," *Antonianum* 25 (1950) 259–326.

  L'evoluzione del volontarismo da Duns Scoto a Guglielmo Alnwick (Naples: Libreria scientifica editrice, 1964).

Principe, Walter. *The Theology of the Hypostatic Union in the Early Thirteenth Century* (Toronto: Pontifical Institute of Mediaeval Studies, 1963–75).

Prior, A. N. "The Possibly-True and the Possible," *Mind* 78 (1969) 481–92.

Priori, Domenico and Massimo Balena (eds.). *Atti del II Convegno Internazionale su Francesco d'Appignano* (Appignano del Tronto: Centro studi Francesco d'Appignano, 2004).

Pulcini, Theodore. *Exegesis as Polemical Discourse: Ibn Hazm on Jewish and Christian Scriptures* (New York: Oxford University Press, 1998).

Putallaz, François-Xavier. "La connaissance de soi au moyen âge: Vital du Four," *Collectanea Franciscana* 60 (1990) 507–37.

  La connaissance de soi au XIIIᵉ siècle. De Matthieu d'Aquasparta à Thierry de Freiberg (Paris: Vrin, 1991).

  Figures franciscaines, de Bonaventure à Duns Scot (Paris: Cerf, 1997).

  "Les idées divines dans la censure: le cas Olivi (1248–1298)," *Revue Thomiste* 103 (2003) 411–34.

  Insolente liberté: controverses et condamnations au XIIIᵉ siècle (Paris: Cerf, 1995).

Putallaz, François-Xavier and Ruedi Imbach. *Profession, philosophe: Siger de Brabant* (Paris: Cerf, 1997).

Putnam, C. "Ulrich of Strasbourg and the Aristotelian Causes," in J. K. Ryan (ed.) *Studies in Philosophy and the History of Philosophy* (Washington, DC: Catholic University of America Press, 1961) I: 139–59.

Putnam, Hilary. "On Negative Theology," *Faith and Philosophy* 14 (1997) 407–22.

Quentin, Albrecht. *Naturkenntness und Naturanschauungen bei Wilhelm von Auvergne* (Hildescheim: Gertenberg, 1976).

Quillet, Jeannine (ed.). *Autour de Nicole Oresme* (Paris: Vrin, 1990).

  La philosophie politique de Marsile de Padoue (Paris: Vrin, 1970).

Quinn, John. *The Historical Constitution of St. Bonventure's Philosophy* (Toronto: Pontifical Institute of Mediaeval Studies, 1973).

Quinto, Riccardo. "High of St.-Cher's Use of Stephen Langton," in S. Ebbesen and R. L. Friedman (eds.) *Medieval Analyses in Language and Cognition* (Copenhagen: Reitzels, 1999) 281–300.

Raciti, Gaetano. "L'autore del *De spiritu et anima*," *Rivista di filosofia neoscolastica* 53 (1961) 385–401.

"Isaac de l'Étoile," in M. Viller, G. Raciti, and A. Solignac (eds.) *Dictionnaire de spiritualité* (Paris: Beauchesne, 1971) VII: 2011–38.

Radding, Charles. *The Origins of Medieval Jurisprudence: Pavia and Bologna, 850–1150* (New Haven, CT: Yale University Press, 1988).

Raedts, Peter. *Richard Rufus of Cornwall and the Tradition of Oxford Theology* (Oxford: Oxford Historical Monographs, 1987).

Raine, James. *Historiae Dunelmensis scriptores tres: Gaufridus de Coldingham, Robertus de Graystanes, et Willielmus de Chambre* (London: J.B. Nichols and Son, 1839).

Ramsey, Paul. *The Just War: Force and Political Responsibility* (New York: Scribner, 1968).

Rand, E. K. *Johannes Scottus* (Munich: Beck, 1906).

Ranft, Patricia. *The Theology of Work: Peter Damian and the Medieval Religious Renewal Movement* (New York: Palgrave Macmillan, 2006).

Rashdall, Hastings. *The Universities of Europe in the Middle Ages*, rev. edn by F. M. Powicke and A. B. Emden (Oxford: Clarendon Press, 1936).

Rashed, Roshdi. *Géométrie et dioptrique au Xe siècle: Ibn Sahl, al-Qūhī et Ibn al-Haytham* (Paris: Les Belles Lettres, 1993).

"Al-Kindī's Commentary on Archimedes' 'The Measurement of the Circle'," *Arabic Sciences and Philosophy* 3 (1993) 7–53.

Les mathématiques infinitésimales du IXe au XIe siècle (London: Al-Furq-an Islamic Heritage Foundation, 1993–2006).

Rauschenbach, Sina. *Josef Albo: Jüdische Philosophie und christliche Kontroverstheologie in der Frühen Neuzeit* (Leiden: Brill, 2002).

Ravitzky, Aviezer. "Samuel Ibn Tibbon and the Esoteric Character of The Guide of the Perplexed," *Association of Jewish Studies Review* 6 (1981) 87–123.

Raynaud de Lage, Guy. *Alain de Lille, poète du XIIe siècle* (Montréal: Institut d'études médiévales, 1951).

Read, Stephen. "How Is Material Supposition Possible?," *Medieval Philosophy and Theology* 8 (1999) 1–20.

"The Liar Paradox from John Buridan back to Thomas Bradwardine," *Vivarium* 40 (2002) 189–218.

"Medieval Theories: Properties of Terms," in E. Zalta (ed.) *The Stanford Encyclopedia of Philosophy* (Spring 2006 edition): http://plato.stanford.edu/archives/spr2006/entries/medieval-terms/.

(ed.). *Sophisms in Medieval Logic and Grammar: Acts of the Ninth European Symposium for Medieval Logic and Semantics* (Dordrecht: Kluwer, 1993).

"Thomas of Cleves and Collective Supposition," *Vivarium* 29 (1991) 50–84.

Reeves, Marjorie. *The Influence of Prophecy in the Later Middle Ages: A Study in Joachimism* (Oxford: Clarendon, 1969; repr. Notre Dame, IN: University of Notre Dame Press, 1993).

Reichberg, Gregory M., Henrik Syse, and Endre Begby (eds.). *The Ethics of War: Classic and Contemporary Readings* (Indianapolis, IN: Wiley-Blackwell, 2006).

Reilly, James. "Thomas of York on the Efficacy of Secondary Causes," *Mediaeval Studies* 15 (1953) 225–33.

Reina, Maria. "Comprehensio veritatis: una questione di Marsilio di Inghen sulla metafisica," *Textes et Études du Moyen Age* 1 (1994) 283–335.

Hoc Hic et Nunc: Buridano, Marsilio di Inghen e la conoscenza del singolare (Florence: Olschki, 2002).

Reisman, David C. "Al-Fārābī and the Philosophical Curriculum," in P. Adamson and R. Taylor (eds.) *The Cambridge Companion to Arabic Philosophy* (Cambridge: Cambridge University Press, 2005) 52–71.

The Making of the Avicennan Tradition: The Transmission, Contents, and Structure of Ibn Sīnā's al-Mubāḥathāt (The Discussions) (Leiden: Brill, 2002).

Reisman, David C. and Ahmed H. al-Rahīm (eds.). *Before and after Avicenna: Proceedings of the First Conference of the Avicenna Study Group* (Leiden: Brill, 2003).

Remnant, Peter. "Peter Damian: Could God Change the Past?," *Canadian Journal of Philosophy* 8 (1978) 259–68.

Renan, Ernest. *Averroès et l'averroïsme (Œuvres complètes*, vol. III) (Paris: Calmann-Lévy, 1949).

Rescher, Nicholas. *The Development of Arabic Logic* (Pittsburgh, PA: University of Pittsburgh Press, 1964).

"A New Approach to Aristotle's Apodeictic Syllogisms," in N. Rescher (ed.) *Studies in Modality* (Oxford: Blackwell, 1974) 3–15.

Resnick, Irven M. *Divine Power and Possibility in St. Peter Damian's De divina omnipotentia* (Leiden: Brill, 1992).

"Odo of Tournai, the Phoenix, and the Problem of Universals," *Journal of the History of Philosophy* 35 (1997) 355–74.

Resnick, Irven M. and Kenneth Kitchell. *Albert the Great: A Selectively Annotated Bibliography (1900–2000)* (Tempe: Arizona Center for Medieval and Renaissance Studies, 2004).

Reuter, Timothy. *Wortkonkordanz zum Decretum Gratiani* (Munich: Monumenta Germaniae Historica, 1990).

Reynolds, Gabriel Said. "The Rise and Fall of Qadi ʿAbd al-Jabbar," *International Journal of Middle East Studies* 37 (2005) 3–18.

Reynolds, Philip. *Marriage in the Western Church: The Christianization of Marriage during the Patristic and Early Medieval Periods* (Leiden: Brill, 1994).

"Properties, Causality, and Epistemic Optimism in Thomas Aquinas," *Recherches de théologie et philosophie médiévales* 68 (2001) 270–309.

Ribémont, Bernard. *Les origines des encyclopédies médiévales d'Isidore de Séville aux Carolingiens* (Paris: Champion, 2001).

Richards, Earl Jeffrey (ed.). *Reinterpreting Christine de Pizan* (Athens: University of Georgia Press, 1992).

Riché, Pierre. *Abbon de Fleury: un moine savant et combatif (vers 950–1004)* (Turnhout: Brepols, 2004).

Écoles et enseignement dans le Haut Moyen Âge: fin du Vᵉ siècle – milieu du XIᵉ siècle (Paris: Picard, 1989).

Education and Culture in the Barbarian West, Sixth through Eighth Centuries, tr. J. J. Contreni (Columbia: University of South Carolina Press, 1976).

Richir, Luc. *Marguerite Porete: une âme au travail de l'Un* (Brussels: Ousia, 2002).

Richter, Gerhard. *Theodoros Dukas Laskaris, der natürliche Zusammenhang: ein Zeugnis vom Stand der byzantinischen Philosophie in der Mitte des 13. Jahrhundert* (Amsterdam: Hakkert, 1989).

Richter, Vladimir. "Handschriftliches zu Crathorn," *Zeitschrift für katholische Theologie* 94 (1972) 445–9.

Ritter, Gerhard. *Studien zur Spätscholastik I: Marsilius von Inghen und die okkamistische Schule in Deutschland* (Heidelberg: Carl Winter Universitätsverlag, 1921).

Rius y Serra, José (ed.). *San Raimundo de Penyafort: Diplomatario* (Barcelona: López Robert, 1954).

Rizvi, Sajjad H. "Mysticism and Philosophy: Ibn ʿArabī and Mullā Ṣadrā," in P. Adamson and R. Taylor (eds.) *The Cambridge Companion to Arabic Philosophy* (Cambridge: Cambridge University Press, 2005) 224–46.

Roberts, Phyllis B. *Stephanus de Lingua Tonante: Studies on the Sermons of Stephen Langton* (Toronto: Pontifical Institute of Mediaeval Studies, 1968).

Robertson, D. W. "A Note on the Classical Origins of 'Circumstances' in the Medieval Confessional," *Studies in Philology* 43 (1946) 6–14.

Robiglio, Andrea. *L'impossibile volere. Tommaso d'Aquino, i tomisti e la volontà* (Milan: Vita e Pensiero, 2002).

"'Neapolitan Gold': A Note on William of Tocco and Peter of Ireland," *Bulletin de philosophie médiévale* 44 (2002) 107–11.

Robinson, James T. "Hasdai Crescas and anti-Aristotelianism," in D. H. Frank and O. Leaman (eds.) *Cambridge Companion to Medieval Jewish Philosophy* (Cambridge: Cambridge University Press, 2003) 391–413.

"The Ibn Tibbon Family: A Dynasty of Translators in Medieval Provence," in J. Harris (ed.) *Be'erot Yitzhak: Studies in Memory of Isadore Twersky* (Cambridge, MA: Harvard University Press, 2005) 193–224.

"Samuel Ibn Tibbon's Commentary on Ecclesiastes and the Philosopher's Prooemium," in I. Twersky and J. Harris (eds.) *Studies in Medieval Jewish History and Literature* (Cambridge, MA: Harvard University Press, 2000) III: 83–146.

Robson, John. *Wyclif and the Oxford Schools* (Cambridge: Cambridge University Press, 1961).

Rocca, Gregory. "The Distinction between *res significata* and *modus significandi* in Aquinas' Theological Epistemology," *The Thomist* 55 (1990) 173–97.

Rochais, Henri. "Ipsa philosophia Christus," *Mediaeval Studies* 13 (1951) 244–7.

Rode, Christian. *Franciscus de Prato: Facetten seiner Philosophie im Blick auf Hervaeus Natalis und Wilhelm Ockham* (Stuttgart: Steiner, 2004).

Roensch, Frederick. *Early Thomistic School* (Dubuque, IA: Priory Press, 1964).

Roest, Bert. *A History of Franciscan Education (c. 1210–1517)* (Leiden: Brill, 2000).

Rohls, Jan. *Wilhelm von Auvergne und der mittelalterliche Aristotelismus* (Munich: Kaiser, 1980).

Rohmer, Jean. "La théorie de l'abstraction dans l'école franciscaine de Alexandre de Hales à Jean Peckham," *Archives d'histoire doctrinale et littéraire du moyen âge* 3 (1928) 105–84.

Roland-Gosselin, M.-D. *Le "De ente et essentia" de s. Thomas d'Aquin* (Paris: Vrin, 1926; repr. 1948).

Roos, Heinrich. "Die Kontroverse zwischen Bartholomaeus von Brügge und Radulphus Brito über die Frage 'Utrum genus possit salvari in unica specie'," in T. W. Köhler (ed.) *Sapientiae procerum amore: mélanges médiévistes offerts à Dom Jean-Pierre Müller* (Rome: Editrice Anselmiana, 1974) 323–42.

Die Modi significandi *des Martinus de Dacia* (Copenhagen: Frost-Hansen, 1952).

"Zwei Quaestionum des Radulphus Brito über das *Significatum generis*," *Cahiers de l'Institut du Moyen Age Grec et Latin* 24 (1978) 55–64.

Rosemann, Philipp W. "Ibn Rushd: A Catalogue of Editions and Scholarly Writings from 1821 onwards," *Bulletin de philosophie médiévale* 30 (1988) 153–215.

Peter Lombard (Oxford: Oxford University Press, 2004).

The Story of a Great Medieval Book: Peter Lombard's Sentences (Peterborough, ON: Broadview Press, 2007).

Rosenthal, Erwin I. J. (ed.). *Saadya Studies* (Manchester: Manchester University Press, 1943; repr. New York: Arno Press, 1980).

"The Theory of the Power-State: Ibn Khaldun's Study of Civilization," in E. Rosenthal (ed.) *Political Thought in Medieval Islam* (Cambridge: Cambridge University Press, 1956).

Rosenthal, Franz. "Abu Zayd al-Balkhi on Politics," in C. E. Bosworth *et al.* (eds.) *The Islamic World, from Classical to Modern Times: Essays in Honor of Bernard Lewis* (Princeton, NJ: Princeton University Press, 1989) 287–301.

Aḥmad b. aṭ-Ṭayyib as-Sarakhsī (New Haven, CT: American Oriental Society, 1943).

Das Fortleben der Antike im Islam (Zürich: Artemis Verlag, 1965).

Greek Philosophy in the Arab World (Aldershot: Ashgate, 1990).

"On the Knowledge of Plato's Philosophy in the Islamic World," *Islamic Culture* 14 (1940) 387–422; 15 (1941) 396–8.

"State and Religion according to Abū l-Ḥasan al-ʿĀmirī," *Islamic Quarterly* 3 (1956) 42–52.

Rosier-Catach, Irène. "Abélard et les grammairiens: sur la définition du verbe et la notion d'inhérence," in P. Lardet (ed.) *La tradition vive: Mélanges d'histoire des textes en l'honneur de Louis Holtz* (Turnhout: Brepols, 2003) 143–59.

"Abélard et les grammairiens: sur le verbe substantif et la prédication," *Vivarium* 41 (2003) 176–248.

"Les acceptions du terme 'substantia' chez Pierre Helie," in J. Jolivet and A. de Libera (eds.) *Gilbert de Poitiers et ses contemporains* (Naples: Bibliopolis, 1987) 299–324.

"The *Glosulae in Priscianum* and its Tradition," in N. McLelland and A. Linn (eds.) *Papers in Memory of Vivien Law* (Münster: Nodus Publikationen, 2004) 81–99.

(ed.). *Les Glosulae super Priscianum, Guillaume de Champeaux, Abelard: arts du langage et théologie aux confins des XIᵉ/XIIᵉ siècles* (Turnhout: Brepols, forthcoming).

"La grammaire dans le 'Guide de l'étudiant'," in C. Lafleur and J. Carrier (eds.) *L'enseignement de la philosophie au XIIIᵉ siècle. Autour du "Guide de l'étudiant" du ms. Ripoll 109* (Turnhout: Brepols, 1997) 255–79.

La grammaire spéculative des Modistes (Lille: Presses universitaires de Lille, 1983).

"Modisme, pré-modisme, proto-modisme, vers une définition modulaire," in S. Ebbesen and R. L. Friedman (eds.) *Medieval Analyses in Language and Cognition* (Copenhagen: Royal Academy, 1999) 45–81.

"O Magister . . . : Grammaticalité et intelligibilité selon un sophisme du XIIIᵉ siècle," *Cahiers de l'Institut du Moyen Age Grec et Latin* 56 (1988) 1–102.

La parole comme acte: sur la grammaire et la sémantique au XIIIᵉ siècle (Paris: Vrin, 1994).

La parole efficace: signe, rituel, sacré (Paris: Seuil, 2004).

"Priscien, Boèce, les *Glosulae in Priscianum*, Abélard: les enjeux des discussions autour de la notion de consignification," *Histoire Epistémologie Langage* 25 (2003) 55–84.

"*Res significata et modus significandi*: Les implications d'une distinction médiévale," in S. Ebbesen (ed.) *Sprachtheorien in Spätantike und Mittelalter* (Tübingen: Narr, 1995) 135–68.

"Roger Bacon: Grammar," in J. Hackett (ed.) *Roger Bacon and the Sciences: Commemorative Essays 1996* (Leiden: Brill, 1997) 67–102.

"Les sophismes grammaticaux au XIIIᵉ siècle," *Medioevo* 17 (1991) 175–230.

Rosier-Catach, Irène and Sten Ebbesen. "Petrus de Alvernia + Boethius de Dacia: Syllogizantem ponendum est terminos," *Cahiers de l'Institut du Moyen Age Grec et Latin* 75 (2004) 161–218.

Ross, James F. *Philosophical Theory* (Indianapolis, IN: Bobbs-Merrill, 1969).

Rossi, Pietro. "Robert Grosseteste and the Object of Scientific Knowledge," in J. McEvoy (ed.) *Robert Grosseteste: New Perspectives on his Thought and Scholarship* (Turnhout: Brepols, 1995) 53–76.

Rossini, M. "Quod coexsistit exsistit: Alessandro di Alessandria e i futuri contingenti," in L. Sileo (ed.) *Via Scoti: methodologica ad mentem Ioannis Duns Scoti* (Rome: Edizioni Antonianum, 1995) 1049–63.

Rossmann, Heribert. *Die Hierarchie der Welt: Gestalt und System des Franz von Meyronnes OFM mit besonderer Berücksichtigung seiner Schöpfungslehre* (Werl: Coelde, 1972).

Roth, Bartholomaeus. *Franz von Mayronis, O.F.M. Sein Leben, seine Werke, seine Lehre vom Formalunterschied in Gott* (Werl-in-Westfalen: Franziskus-Druckerei, 1936).

Roueché, Mossman. "Byzantine Philosophical Texts of the Seventh Century," *Jahrbuch der Österreichischen Byzantinistik* 23 (1974) 61–76.

"Did Medical Students Study Philosophy in Alexandria?," *Bulletin of the Institute of Classical Studies* 43 (1999) 153–69.

Rouse, Richard and Mary Rouse. *Preachers, Florilegia and Sermons: Studies on the "Manipulus florum" of Thomas of Ireland* (Toronto: Pontifical Institute of Mediaeval Studies, 1979).

Rubert Candáu, José Maria. *La filosofía del siglo XIV a través de G. Rubió* (Madrid: Ediciones Verdad y Vida, 1952).

Rubio, Mercedes. *Aquinas and Maimonides on the Possibility of the Knowledge of God: An Examination of the* Quaestio de attributis (Dordrecht: Springer, 2007).

Rucquoi, A. "Gundisalvus ou Dominicus Gundisalvi," *Bulletin de philosophie médiévale* 41 (1999) 85–106.

Rudavsky, T. M. "Conflicting Motifs in Ibn Gabirol's Discussion of Matter and Evil," *New Scholasticism* 52 (1978) 54–71.

"Gersonides," in E. Zalta (ed.) *The Stanford Encyclopaedia of Philosophy* (Spring 2007 edition): http://plato.stanford.edu/archives/spr2007/entries/gersonides.

"The Theory of Time in Maimonides and Crescas," *Maimonidean Studies* 1 (1990) 143–62.

Time Matters: Time, Creation and Cosmology in Medieval Jewish Philosophy (Albany: State University of New York Press, 2000).

Rudnick, Ulrich. *Das System des Johannes Scottus Eriugena: eine theologisch-philosophische Studie zu seinem Werk* (Frankfurt: Lang, 1990).

Rudolph, Conrad. *First, I Find the Center Point: Reading the Text of Hugh of Saint Victor's* The Mystic Ark (Philadelphia, PA: American Philosophical Society, 2004).

Rudolph, Ulrich. *Al-Māturīdī und die sunnitische Theologie in Samurkand* (Leiden: Brill, 1996).

Ruello, Francis. "Les fondements de la liberté humaine selon Jacques de Viterbe O.E.S.A. Disputatio 1ᵃ de Quolibet, q. VII (1293)," *Augustiniana* 24 (1974) 283–347; 25 (1975) 114–42.

"Paul de Venise théologien 'averroiste'?," in J. Jolivet (ed.) *Multiple Averroès* (Paris: Vrin, 1978) 257–72.

La pensée de Jean de Ripa OFM (XIVᵉ siècle), immensité divine et connaissance théologique (Fribourg: Éditions universitaires, 1990).

"Le projet théologique de Jean de Ripa O.F.M.," *Traditio* 49 (1994) 127–70.

Ruffing, Janet (ed.). *Mysticism and Social Transformation* (Syracuse, NY: Syracuse University Press, 2001).

Rupp, Teresa. "Damnation, Individual, and Community in Remigio dei Girolami's *De bono communi*," *History of Political Thought* 21 (2000) 217–36.

Rusconi, Roberto. "De la prédication à la confession: transmission et contrôle de modèles de comportement au XIIIᵉ siècle," in *Faire croire: modalités de la diffusion et de la réception des messages religieux du XIIᵉ au XVᵉ siècle* (Rome: École française de Rome, 1981) 67–85.

Russell, Bertrand. *A History of Western Philosophy* (London: Allen and Unwin, 1946).

Russell, Frederick H. "The Historical Perspective of the Bishops' Pastoral Letter: The View of One Medievalist," in C. Reid, Jr. (ed.) *Peace in a Nuclear Age: The Bishops' Pastoral Letter in Perspective* (Washington, DC: Catholic University of America Press, 1986) 86–97.

The Just War in the Middle Ages (Cambridge: Cambridge University Press, 1975).

"Love and Hate in Warfare: The Contribution of Saint Augustine," *Nottingham Medieval Studies* 31 (1987) 108–24.

"Persuading the Donatists: Augustine's Coercion by Words," in W. Klingshirn and M. Vessey (eds.) *The Limits of Ancient Christianity. Essays on Late Antique Thought and Culture in Honor of R. A. Markus* (Ann Arbor: University of Michigan Press, 1999) 115–30.

Russell, Norman. "Prochoros Cydones and the Fourteenth-Century Understanding of Orthodoxy," in A. Louth and A. Casiday (eds.) *Byzantine Orthodoxies* (Aldershot: Ashgate, 2006) 75–92.

Ryan, Christopher J. "Man's Free Will in the Works of Siger of Brabant," *Mediaeval Studies* 45 (1983) 155–99.

Ryan, John K. and Bernardino M. Bonansea. "John Duns Scotus, 1265–1965," in J. K. Ryan and B. M. Bonansea (eds.) *Studies in Philosophy and the History of Philosophy*, vol. III (Washington, DC: Catholic University of America Press, 1965).

Ryan, Magnus. "Bartolus of Sassoferrato and Free Cities," *Transactions of the Royal Historical Society* 10 (2000) 65–89.

Saak, Eric. *High Way to Heaven: The Augustinian Platform between Reform and Reformation, 1292–1524* (Leiden: Brill, 2002).

Saarinen, Risto. *Weakness of the Will in Medieval Thought from Augustine to Buridan* (Leiden: Brill, 1994).

Sabbadini, Remigio. *Guariniana*, ed. M. Sancipriano (Genoa: Tipografia del R. Istituto Sordo-Muti, 1891, 1896; repr. Turin: Bottega d'Erasmo, 1964).

Sabra, A. I. "Form in Ibn al-Haytham's Theory of Vision," *Zeitschrift für Geschichte der Arabisch-Isalmischen Wissenschaften* 5 (1980) 115–40.

   "*Kalām* Atomism as an Alternative Philosophy to Hellenizing *falsafa*," in J. Montgomery (ed.) *Arabic Theology, Arabic Philosophy: From the Many to the One: Essays in Celebration of Richard M. Frank* (Leuven: Peeters, 2006) 199–272.

   Optics, Astronomy and Logic: Studies in Arabic Science and Philosophy (Aldershot: Variorum, 1994).

   "Psychology versus Mathematics: Ptolemy and Alhazen on the Moon Illusion," in E. Grant and J. Murdoch (eds.) *Mathematics and its Applications in Science and Natural Philosophy in the Middle Ages* (Cambridge: Cambridge University Press, 1987) 217–47.

   "Thābit ibn Qurra on the Infinite and Other Puzzles: Edition and Translation of his Discussions with Ibn Usayyid," *Zeitschrift für Geschichte der arabisch-islamischen Wissenschaften* 11 (1997) 1–33.

Saco Alarcón, César. "Nicolás de Ockham OFM († c. 1320): Vida y obras," *Antonianum* 53 (1978) 493–573.

Saʿdi, Lutfi M. "A Bio-Bibliographical Study of Hunayn ibn Ishaq al-Ibadi," *Bulletin of the Institute of the History of Medicine* 2 (1934) 409–46.

Saffrey, H. D. "Nouveau liens objectifs entre le pseudo-Denys et Proclus," in *Recherches sur le Néoplatonisme après Plotin* (Paris: Vrin, 1990) 227–48.

Saint Pierre, J. A. "The Theological Thought of William of Auxerre: An Introductory Bibliography," *Recherches de théologie ancienne et médiévale* 33 (1966) 147–55.

Salleras i Carolà, Marcel. "Bibliografia lulliana (1974–1984)," *Randa* 19 (1986) 153–98.

Salman, Dominique. "Algazel et les latins," *Archives d'histoire doctrinale et littéraire du moyen âge* 10 (1936) 103–27.

Salman, H. D. "Jean de la Rochelle et l'averroïsme latin," *Archives d'histoire doctrinale et littéraire du moyen âge* 16 (1947–8) 133–42.

Salmon, Nathan. *Reference and Essence* (Princeton, NJ: Princeton University Press, 1981).

Samir, Khalil and Jørgen S. Nielsen. *Christian Arabic Apologetics during the Abbasid Period, 750–1258* (Leiden: Brill, 1994).

Samuelson, Norbert. "Causation and Choice in the Philosophy of ibn Daud," in *The Solomon Goldman Lectures*, vol. II (Chicago: Spertus College, 1979).

   "Gersonides' Account of God's Knowledge of Particulars," *Journal of the History of Philosophy* 10 (1972) 399–416.

San Cristóbal-Sebastián, Antonio. *Controversias acerca de la voluntad desde 1270 a 1300: estudio histórico-doctrinal* (Madrid: Editorial y librería co., 1958).

Sanford, Eva Matthews. "Honorius, Presbyter and Scholasticus," *Speculum* 23 (1948) 397–425.

Santi, Francesco. *Arnau de Vilanova: L'obra espiritual* (Valencia: Disputacio provincial de Valencia, 1986).

Santos-Noya, Manuel. *Die Sünden und Gnadenlehre des Gregors von Rimini* (Frankfurt: Lang, 1990).

Sarnowsky, Jürgen. *Die aristotelisch-scholastische Theorie der Bewegung: Studien zum Kommentar Alberts von Sachsen zur Physik des Aristoteles* (Münster: Aschendorff, 1989).

Sayers, Jane. *Innocent III: Leader of Europe, 1198–1216* (London: Longman, 1994).

Sbaraglia, Giovanni Giacinto (ed.). *Bullarium Franciscanum Romanorum Pontificum: Constitutiones, epistolas, ac diplomata* (Rome, 1759–68; repr. Santa Maria degli Angeli: Edizioni Porziuncola, 1983).

Sbath, Paul. *Vingt traités philosophiques et apologétiques d'auteurs arabes chrétiens du IXe au XIVe siècle* (Cairo: Friedrich, 1929).

Schabel, Chris. "Carmelite Quodlibeta," in C. Schabel (ed.) *Theological Quodlibeta in the Middle Ages: The Fourteenth Century* (Leiden: Brill, 2007) 493–544.

"Early Carmelites Between Giants: Questions on Future Contingents by Gerard of Bologna and Guy Terrena," *Recherches de théologie et philosophie médiévales* 70 (2003) 139–205.

"Francis of Marchia's *Virtus derelicta* and the Context of its Development," *Vivarium* 44 (2006) 60–80.

"Landulphus Caracciolo and a Sequax on Divine Foreknowledge," *Archives d'histoire doctrinale et littéraire du moyen âge* 66 (1999) 299–343.

"Landulph Caracciolo and Gerard Odonis on Predestination: Opposite Attitudes toward Scotus and Auriol," *Wissenschaft und Weisheit* 65 (2002) 62–81.

"*Non aliter novit facienda quam facta*: Gerard Odonis's Questions on Divine Foreknowledge," in P. J. J. M. Bakker (ed.) *Chemins de la pensée médiévale* (Turnhout: Brepols, 2002) 351–77.

"Oxford Franciscans after Ockham: Walter Chatton and Adam Wodeham," in G. R. Evans (ed.) *Mediaeval Commentaries on the* Sentences *of Peter Lombard: Current Research* (Leiden: Brill, 2002) 359–77.

"Parisian Commentaries from Peter Auriol to Gregory of Rimini, and the Problem of Predestination," in G. R. Evans (ed.) *Mediaeval Commentaries on the* Sentences *of Peter Lombard: Current Research* (Leiden: Brill, 2002) 221–65.

"Peter of Candia and the Prelude to the Quarrel at Louvain," *Epitirida of the Cyprus Research Centre* 24 (1998) 87–124.

"Peter Thomae's Question on Divine Foreknowledge from his Sentences Commentary," *Franciscan Studies* 61 (2003) 1–35

"Questions on Future Contingents by Michael of Massa, OESA," *Augustiniana* 48 (1998) 165–229.

"The *Quodlibeta* of Peter of Auvergne," in C. Schabel (ed.) *Theological Quodlibeta in the Middle Ages: The Fourteenth Century* (Leiden: Brill, 2007) 81–130.

"The *Sentences* Commentary of Gerard Odonis, OFM," *Bulletin de philosophie médiévale* 46 (2004).

"The *Sentences* Commentary of Paul of Perugia, O.Carm., with an Edition of his Question on Divine Foreknowledge," *Recherches de théologie et philosophie médiévales* 72 (2005) 54–112.

Theological Quodlibeta in the Middle Ages (Leiden: Brill, 2006–7).

Theology at Paris 1316–1345: Peter Auriol and the Problem of Divine Foreknowledge and Future Contingents (Aldershot: Ashgate, 2000).

Schabel, Chris and William J. Courtenay. "Augustinian *Quodlibeta* after Giles of Rome," in C. Schabel (ed.) *Theological Quodlibeta in the Middle Ages: The Fourteenth Century* (Leiden: Brill, 2007) 545–68.

Schabel, Chris and Russell L. Friedman. "Trinitarian Theology and Philosophical Issues III: Oxford 1312–1329: Walsingham, Graystanes, Fitzralph, and Rodington," *Cahiers de l'Institut du Moyen Age Grec et Latin* 74 (2003) 39–88.

"Trinitarian Theology and Philosophical Issues IV: English Theology *ca.* 1300: William of Ware and Richard of Bromwich," *Cahiers de l'Institut du Moyen Age Grec et Latin* 75 (2004) 121–60.

"Trinitarian Theology and Philosophical Issues V: Oxford Dominicans: William of Macclesfield and Hugh of Lawton," *Cahiers de l'Institut du Moyen Age Grec et Latin* 76 (2005) 31–44.

Schabel, Chris, Russell L. Friedman, and Irene Balcoyiannopoulou. "Peter of Palude and the Parisian Reaction to Durand of St. Pourcain on Future Contingents," *Archivum Fratrum Praedicatorum* 71 (2001) 183–300.

Schabel, Chris and Marco Rossini. "Time and Eternity among the Early Scotists. Texts on Future Contingents by Alexander of Alexandria, Radulphus Brito, and Hugh of Novocastro," *Documenti e studi sulla tradizione filosofica medievale* 16 (2005) 237–338.

Schacht, Joseph. *The Origins of Muhammadan Jurisprudence*, corrected edn (Oxford: Clarendon Press, 1967).

Schamp, Jacques. *Photios, historien des lettres: la bibliothèque et ses notices biographiques* (Paris: Les Belles Lettres, 1987).

Scheben, H. C. "Prediger und Generalprediger im Dominikanorden des 13. Jahrhunderts," *Archivum Fratrum Praedicatorum* 21 (1961) 112–41.

Schepers, Heinrich. "Holkot contra dicta Crathorn: I. Quellenkritik und biographische Auswertung der Bakkalareatsschriften zweier Oxforder Dominikaner des XIV. Jahrhunderts," *Philosophisches Jahrbuch* 77 (1970) 320–54.

"Holkot contra dicta Crathorn: II. Das 'significatum per propositionem'. Aufbau und Kritik einer nominalistischen Theorie über den Gegenstand des Wissens," *Philosophisches Jahrbuch* 79 (1972) 106–36.

Schmaltz, Tad. *Radical Cartesians* (Cambridge: Cambridge University Press, 2002).

Schmaus, Michael. "Die Gotteslehre des Augustinus Triumphus nach seinem Sentenzenkommentar," in *Aus des Geisteswelt des Mittelalters* (Münster: Aschendorff, 1935) 929–53.

"Guglielmi de Alnwick, O.F.M., doctrina de medio quo Deus cognoscit futura contingentia," *Bogoslovni vestnik* 12 (1932) 201–25.

"Guillelmi de Nottingham, O.F.M., doctrina de aeternitate mundi," *Antonianum* 7 (1932) 139–66.

"Neue Mitteilungen zum Sentenzenkommentar Wilhelms von Nottingham," *Franziskanische Studien* 19 (1932) 195–223.

Schmidtke, Sabine. "Creeds," in J. D. McAuliffe (ed.) *Encyclopaedia of the Qur'ān* (Leiden: Brill, 2001–6).

The Theology of al-ʿAllāma al-Ḥillī (d. 726/1325) (Berlin: Schwarz, 1991).

Schmitt, Charles. *Cicero Scepticus. A Study of the Influence of the Academica in the Renaissance* (The Hague: Nijhoff, 1972).

Schmitt, F. S. "Des Petrus von Aquila *Compendium supra librum sententiarum* aufgefunden," *Recherches de théologie ancienne et médiévale* 17 (1950) 267–82.

Schmitter, Amy. "17th and 18th Century Theories of Emotions," in E. Zalta (ed.) *The Stanford Encyclopaedia of Philosophy* (Summer 2006 edition): http://plato.stanford.edu/archives/sum2006/entries/emotions-17th18th.

Schmoll, Polykarp. *Die Busslehre der Frühscholastik: eine dogmengeschichte Untersuchung* (Munich: Lentner, 1909).

Schmugge, Ludwig. *Johannes von Jandun (1285/89–1328): Untersuchungen zur Biographie und Sozialtheorie eines lateinischen Averroisten* (Stuttgart: Hiersemann, 1966).

Schneider, Notker. *Die Kosmologie des Franciscus de Marchia: Texte, Quellen, und Untersuchungen zur Naturphilosophie des 14. Jahrhunderts* (Leiden: Brill, 1991).

Schneider, Richard. *Die Trinitätslehre in den* Quodlibeta *und* Quaestiones disputatae *des Johannes von Neapel OP (†1336)* (Munich: Schöningh, 1972).

Schneyer, Johannes Baptist. *Geschichte der katholischen Predigt* (Freiburg: Seelsorge, 1969).

Schöck, Cornelia. "Aussagenquantifizierung und -modalisierung in der frühen islamischen Theologie," in D. Perler und U. Rudolph (eds.) *Logik und Theologie* (Leiden: Brill, 2005) 19–43.

    Koranexegese, Grammatik und Logik: zum Verhältnis von arabischer und aristotelischer Urteils-, Konsequenz- und Schlusslehre (Leiden: Brill, 2006).

Schöllgen, Werner. *Das Problem der Willensfreiheit bei Heinrich von Gent und Herveus Natalis* (Dusseldorf: Pädagogischer Verlag Schwann, 1927; repr. 1975).

Schönberger, Rolf. *Relation als Vergleich: die Relationstheorie des Johannes Buridan im Kontext seines Denken und der Scholastik* (Leiden: Brill, 1994).

Schönberger, Rolf and Brigitte Kible. *Repertorium edierter Texte des Mittelalters* (Berlin: Akademie Verlag, 1994).

Schork, R. Joseph and John McCall. "A Lament on the Death of John of Legnano," *Studies in the Renaissance* 19 (1972) 180–95.

Schrörs, Heinrich. *Hinkmar, Erzbischof von Reims: sein Leben und seine Schriften* (Freiburg: Herder, 1884).

Schramm, Matthias. *Ibn al-Haythams Weg zur Physik* (Wiesbaden: Steiner, 1963).

Schrimpf, Gangolf. *Das Werk des Johannes Scottus Eriugena im Rahmen des Wissenscahftsverständnisses seiner Zeit: eine Hinführung zu Periphyseon* (Münster: Aschendorff, 1982).

Schütz, C. *Deus absconditus, Deus manifestus: die Lehre Hugos von St. Viktor über die Offenbarung Gottes* (Rome: Herder, 1967).

Schütz, Werner. *Geschichte der christliche Predigt* (Berlin: De Gruyter, 1972).

Schwertner, Thomas M. *Saint Raymond of Pennafort of the Order of Friars Preacher* (Milwaukee, WI: Bruce, 1935).

Schweyen, Renate. *Guarino Veronese: Philosophie und humanistische Pädagogik* (Munich: Fink, 1973).

Scott, Karen. "'This is why I have put you among your neighbors': St. Bernard's and St. Catherine's Understanding of the Love of God and Neighbor," in D. Maffei and P. Nardi (eds.) *Atti del Simposio Internazionale Cateriniano-Bernardiniano* (Siena: Accademia senese degli intronati, 1982) 279–94.

Scott, T. K. "Nicholas of Autrecourt, Buridan, and Ockhamism," *Journal of the History of Philosophy* 9 (1971) 15–41.

Scully, Edgar. "The Power of Physical Bodies According to Thomas of York," *Sciences ecclésiastiques* 14 (1962) 109–34.

Seaton, Wallace. "An Edition and Translation of the 'Tractatus de Consequentiis' by Ralph Strode, Fourteenth-Century Logician and Friend of Geoffrey Chaucer" (Ph.D. dissertation: University of California, Berkeley, 1973).

Seeskin, Kenneth (ed.). *The Cambridge Companion to Maimonides* (Cambridge: Cambridge University Press, 2005).

    Maimonides on the Origin of the World (Cambridge: Cambridge University Press, 2005).

"Sanctity and Silence: The Religious Significance of Maimonides' Negative Theology," *American Catholic Philosophical Quarterly* 76 (2002) 7–24.

Searching for a Distant God: The Legacy of Maimonides (New York: Oxford University Press, 2000).

Segoloni, Danilo (ed.). *Bartolo da Sassoferrato: studi e documenti per il VI centenario* (Milan: Giuffrè, 1962).

Sela, Shlomo. *Abraham Ibn Ezra and the Rise of Medieval Hebrew Science* (Leiden: Brill, 2003).

Sela, Shlomo and Gad Freudenthal. "Abraham Ibn Ezra's Scholarly Writings: A Chronological Listing," *Aleph* 6 (2006) 13–55.

Senko, Wladyslaw. "Les opinions d'Hervé Nédellec au sujet de l'essence et l'existence," *Mediaevalia Philosophica Polonorum* 10 (1961) 59–74.

"Tomasza Wiltona Quaestio disputata de anima intellectiva," *Studia Mediewistyczne* 5 (1964) 3–190.

Senner, Walter. "Jean de Sterngassen et son commentaire des *Sentences*," *Revue Thomiste* 97 (1997) 83–98.

Senner, Walter and Henryk Anzulewicz (eds.). *Albertus Magnus zum Gedenken nach 800 Jahren: neue Zugänge, Aspekte und Perspektiven* (Berlin: Akademie-Verlag, 2001).

Serene, Eileen. "Demonstrative Science," in N. Kretzmann *et al.* (eds.) *The Cambridge History of Later Medieval Philosophy* (Cambridge: Cambridge University Press, 1982) 496–517.

Sergent, F. Tyler. "A Bibliography of William of Saint-Thierry," in M. Dutton (ed.) *Truth as Gift: Studies in Medieval Cistercian History in Honor of John R. Sommerfeldt* (Kalamazoo, MI: Cistercian Publications, 2004) 457–82.

Sermoneta, Giuseppe. "Hillel ben Shemuel of Verona and his Philosophical Doctrine" (Ph.D. dissertation, Hebrew University of Jerusalem, 1962).

Ševčenko, Ihor. *Études sur la polémique entre Théodore Métochite et Nicéphore Choumnos* (Brussels: Éditions de Byzantion, 1962).

Seymour, M. C. *Bartholomaeus Anglicus and his Encyclopedia* (Aldershot: Variorum, 1992).

Sezgin, Fuat. *Geschichte des arabischen Schrifttums* (Leiden: Brill, 1967–).

(ed.). *Ibn Bajja Muhammad ibn Yahya ibn as-Saigh: Texts and Studies I* (Frankfurt: Institute for the History of Arabic-Islamic Science, 1999).

Sezgin, Fuat *et al.* (eds.). *Thābit ibn Qurra (d. 288/901): Texts and Studies* (Frankfurt: Institute for the History of Arabic-Islamic Science, 1997).

Shaked, Shaul. "Paymān: An Iranian Idea in Contact with Greek Thought and Islam," in *Transition Periods in Iranian History* (Paris: Association pour l'Avancement des Études Iraniennes, 1987) 217–40.

Shaki, Mansour. "The Dēnkard Account of the History of the Zoroastrian Scriptures," *Archív Orientální* 49 (1981) 114–25.

Shank, Michael H. *Unless You Believe, You Shall Not Understand: Logic, University, and Society in Late Medieval Vienna* (Princeton, NJ: Princeton University Press, 1988).

Shannon, Joseph. "Good Works and Predestination According to Thomas of Strassburg, O.S.A." (Ph.D. dissertation: Pontifical Gregorian University of Baltimore, 1940).

Shapiro, Marc. *Limits of Orthodox Theology: Maimonides' Thirteen Principles Reappraised* (Oxford: Littman Library of Jewish Civilization, 2004).

Sharp, Dorothea E. *Franciscan Philosophy at Oxford in the Thirteenth Century* (London: Milford, 1930).

"Richard of Middleton, Franciscan Philosophy at Oxford," *British Society of Franciscan Studies* 16 (1930) 211–76.

Sharples, R. W. *Alexander of Aphrodisias on Fate* (London: Duckworth, 1983).

Sheedy, Anna. *Bartolus on Social Conditions in the Fourteenth Century* (New York: Columbia University Press, 1942).

Sheehan, Michael W. "The Religious Orders 1220–1370," in J. I. Catto (ed.) *The History of the University of Oxford*, vol. I: *The Early Oxford Schools* (Oxford: Clarendon Press, 1984) 193–224.

Shehadi, Fadlou. *Ghazali's Unique Unknowable God: A Philosophical Critical Analysis of Some of the Problems Raised by Ghazali's View of God as Utterly Unique and Unknowable* (Leiden: Brill, 1964).

Sherif, Mohamed Ahmed. *Ghazali's Theory of Virtue* (Albany: State University of New York Press, 1975).

Shibli Numani, Muhammad. *Abu Hanifah: Life and Work*, tr. M. Hadi Hussain (New Delhi: Kitab Bhavan, 1988).

Shihadeh, Ayman. *The Teleological Ethics of Fakhr al-Din al-Razi* (Leiden: Brill, 2006).

Shogimen, Takashi. "From Disobedience to Toleration: William of Ockham and the Medieval Discourse of Fraternal Correction," *Journal of Ecclesiastical History* 52 (2001) 599–622.

  Ockham and Political Discourse in the Late Middle Ages (Cambridge: Cambridge University Press, 2007).

Sicard, Patrice. *Hugues de Saint-Victor et son école: introduction, choix de texte, traduction et commentaries* (Turnhout: Brepols, 1991).

Sigmund, Paul E. *Nicholas of Cusa and Medieval Political Thought* (Cambridge, MA: Harvard University Press, 1963).

Sihvola, Juha and Troels Engberg-Pedersen (eds.). *The Emotions in Hellenistic Philosophy* (Dordrecht: Kluwer, 1998).

Sikes, Jeffrey. *Peter Abailard* (Cambridge: Cambridge University Press, 1932).

Sileo, L. "Dalla *lectio* alla *disputatio*: le *Questioni de modo essendi Dei in creaturis*, *De existentia rerum in Deo* e *De voluntate Dei* di Odi Rigaldi," in A. Cacciotti and B. Faes de Mottoni (eds.) *Editori di Quaracchi, 100 anni dopo. Bilancio e prospettive* (Rome: Edizioni Antonianum, 1997) 109–31.

Silk, Edmund. *Saeculi noni auctoris in Boetii Consolationem philosophiae commentarius* (Rome: American Academy in Rome, 1935).

Silman, Yochanan. *Philosopher and Prophet: Judah Halevi, the Kuzari and the Evolution of his Thought*, tr. L. J. Schramm (Albany: State University of New York Press, 1995).

Silvas, Anna. *Jutta and Hildegard: The Biographical Sources* (Turnhout: Brepols, 1998).

Silverstein, Theodore. "Daniel of Morley, English Cosmologist and Student of Arabic Science," *Mediaeval Studies* 10 (1948) 179–96.

Silvestro da Valsanzibio. *Vita e dottrina di Gaetano di Thiene, filosofo dello studio di Padova, 1387–1465* (Padua: Studio filosofico dei FF.MM. cappuccini, 1949).

Sinkewicz, Robert E. "The Doctrine of the Knowledge of God in the Early Writings of Barlaam the Calabrian," *Mediaeval Studies* 44 (1982) 181–242.

Sinkler, Georgette. "Medieval Theories of Composition and Division" (Ph.D. dissertation: Cornell University, 1985).

Siraisi, Nancy. "The *Expositio Problematum Aristotelis* of Peter of Abano," *Isis* 61 (1970) 321–39.

Sirat, Colette. *A History of Jewish Philosophy in the Middle Ages* (Cambridge: Cambridge University Press, 1985).

Sirat, Colette, Sara Klein-Braslavy, and Olga Weijers (eds.). *Les méthodes de travail de Gersonide et le maniement du savoir chez les scolastiques* (Paris: Vrin, 2003).

Sirridge, Mary. "*Institutiones Grammaticae* XVII, 187: Three Reactions," in I. Rosier (ed.) *L'héritage des grammairiens latins de l'antiquité aux lumières* (Leuven: Peeters, 1988) 171–81.

  "Robert Kilwardby as 'Scientific Grammarian'," *Histoire Epistémologie Langage* 10 (1990) 7–28.

"Robert Kilwardby: Figurative Constructions and the Limits of Grammar," in G. L. Bursill-Hall (ed.) *De ortu grammaticae* (Amsterdam: Benjamins, 1990) 321–37.

"The Science of Language and Linguistic Knowledge: John of Denmark and Robert Kilwardby," in S. Ebbesen (ed.) *Sprachtheorien in Spätantike und Mittelalter* (Tübingen: Narr, 1995) 109–34.

"Socrates' Hood: Lexical Meaning and Syntax in Jordanus and Kilwardby," *Cahiers de l'Institut du Moyen Age Grec et Latin* 44 (1983) 102–21.

"'The Universal Living Thing is Either Nothing or Posterior.' Radulphus Brito's *Quaestiones super libros De anima*," in P. J. J. M. Bakker and J. M. M. H. Thijssen (eds.) *Mind, Cognition and Representation: The Tradition of Commentaries on Aristotle's De anima* (Aldershot: Ashgate, 2007) 45–68.

"'Utrum idem sint dicere et intelligere sive videre in mente': Robert Kilwardby, *Quaestiones in librum primum Sententiarum,*" *Vivarium* 45 (2007) 253–68.

Skinner, Quentin. *The Foundations of Modern Political Thought* (Cambridge: Cambridge University Press, 1978).

Smalley, Beryl. *The English Friars and Antiquity in the Early XIVth Century* (Oxford: Blackwell, 1960).

"John Baconthorp's Postill on St Matthew," *Mediaeval and Renaissance Studies* 4 (1958) 91–145.

"Robert Bacon and the Early Dominican School at Oxford," *Transactions of the Royal Historical Society* 30 (1948) 1–19.

The Study of the Bible in the Middle Ages, 3rd edn (Oxford: Blackwell, 1983).

"Which William of Nottingham?", *Medieval and Renaissance Studies* 3 (1954), 200–38.

Smith, A. Mark. "The Alhacenian Account of Spatial Perception and its Epistemological Implications," *Arabic Sciences and Philosophy* 15 (2005) 219–40.

Smith, Jane. "Islam and Christendom," in J. Esposito (ed.) *Oxford History of Islam* (Oxford: Oxford University Press, 1999).

Smoller, Laura Ackerman. "Astrology and the Sibyls: John of Legnano's *De adventu Christi* and the Natural Theology of the Later Middle Ages," *Science in Context* 20 (2007) 423–50.

History, Prophecy, and the Stars: The Christian Astrology of Pierre d'Ailly (Princeton, NJ: Princeton University Press, 1994).

Solère, Jean-Luc. "La logique d'un texte médiéval: Guillaume d'Auxerre et la question du possible," *Revue Philosophique de Louvain* 98 (2000) 250–93.

"Thomistes et antithomistes face à la question de l'infini créé: Durand de Saint-Pourçain, Hervé de Nédellec et Jacques de Metz," *Revue Thomiste* 97 (1997) 219–44.

Solignac, Aimé. "Péchés capitaux," in M. Viller, Gaetano Raciti, and Aimé Solignac (eds.) *Dictionnaire de spiritualité* (Paris: Beauchesne, 1937–95) XII.1: 853–62.

Solmsen, Friedrich. *Aristotle's System of the Physical World: A Comparison with his Predecessors* (Ithaca, NY: Cornell University Press, 1960).

Sorabji, Richard. *Emotion and Peace of Mind: From Stoic Agitation to Christian Temptation* (Oxford: Oxford University Press, 2000).

Matter, Space, and Motion (London: Duckworth, 1988).

The Philosophy of the Commentators, 200–600 AD: A Sourcebook (Ithaca, NY: Cornell University Press, 2005).

Self: Ancient and Modern Insights about Individuality, Life, and Death (Chicago: University of Chicago Press, 2006).

Time, Creation, and the Continuum (London: Duckworth, 1983).

Sorabji, Richard and David Rodin (eds.). *The Ethics of War: Shared Problems in Different Traditions* (Aldershot: Ashgate, 2006).

Sorge, Valeria. "L'ente e l'uno in una questione inedita di Taddeo da Parma," in G. Federici Vescovini (ed.) *Le problème des transcendentaux du XIV au XVII siècle* (Paris: Vrin, 2002) 23–34.

Profili dell'averroismo bolognese: metafisica e scienza in Taddeo da Parma (Naples: Luciano, 2001).

Souffrin, Pierre and Alain-Philippe Segonds (eds.). *Nicolas Oresme: tradition et innovation chez un intellectuel du XIV siècle* (Paris: Les Belles Lettres, 1988).

Southern, Richard W. *Robert Grosseteste: The Growth of an English Mind in Medieval Europe*, 2nd edn (Oxford: Clarendon Press, 1992).

Saint Anselm and his Biographer (Cambridge: Cambridge University Press, 1963).

Saint Anselm: Portrait in a Landscape (Cambridge: Cambridge University Press, 1990).

Scholastic Humanism and the Unification of Europe (Oxford: Blackwell, 1995–2001).

Spade, Paul Vincent (ed.). *The Cambridge Companion to Ockham* (Cambridge: Cambridge University Press, 1999).

"Five Logical Tracts by Richard Lavenham," in J. R. O'Donnell (ed.) *Essays in Honour of Anton Charles Pegis* (Toronto: Pontifical Institute of Mediaeval Studies, 1974) 70–124.

(tr.). *Five Texts on the Mediaeval Problem of Universals: Porphyry, Boethius, Abelard, Duns Scotus, Ockham* (Indianapolis, IN: Hackett, 1994).

"How to Start and Stop: Walter Burley on the Instant of Transition," *Journal of Philosophical Research* 19 (1994) 193–221.

"*Insolubilia* and Bradwardine's Theory of Signification," *Medioevo* 7 (1981) 115–34.

"Insolubles," in E. Zalta (ed.) *The Stanford Encyclopedia of Philosophy* (Fall 2005 edition): http://plato.stanford.edu/archives/fall2005/insolubles/.

"Introduction," in John Wyclif, *On Universals* (Oxford: Clarendon Press, 1985) vii–xlvii.

"The Logic of *sit verum* in Richard Brinkley and William of Ockham," *Franciscan Studies* 54 (1994–7) 227–50.

"The Logic of the Categorical: The Medieval Theory of Descent and Ascent," in N. Kretzmann (ed.) *Meaning and Inference in Medieval Philosophy* (Dordrecht: Kluwer, 1988) 187–224.

"The Manuscripts of William Heytesbury's *Regulae solvendi sophismata*: Conclusions, Notes and Descriptions," *Medioevo* 15 (1989) 271–313.

The Mediaeval Liar: A Catalogue of the Insolubilia-Literature (Toronto: Pontifical Institute of Mediaeval Studies, 1975).

"Medieval Theories of *Obligationes*," in E. Zalta (ed.) *Stanford Encyclopedia of Philosophy* (Fall 2003 edition): http://plato.stanford.edu/archives/fall2003/entries/obligationes/.

"Notes on Richard Lavenham's So Called *Summulae logicales*, with a Partial Edition of the Text," *Franciscan Studies* 40 (1980) 370–407.

"Notes on Some Manuscripts of Logical and Physical Works by Richard Lavenham," *Manuscripta* 19 (1975) 139–46.

"Ockham, Adams and Connotation: A Critical Notice of Marilyn Adams, *William Ockham*," *Philosophical Review* 99 (1990) 593–612.

"The Problem of Universals and Wyclif's Alleged 'Ultrarealism'," *Vivarium* 43 (2005) 111–23.

"Richard Lavenham and the Cambridge Logic," *Historiographia Linguistica* 7 (1980) 241–7.

"Richard Lavenham's *Obligationes*: Edition and Comments," *Rivista critica di storia della filosofia* 33 (1978) 225–42.

"The Semantics of Terms," in N. Kretzmann *et al.* (eds.) *The Cambridge History of Later Medieval Philosophy* (Cambridge: Cambridge University Press, 1982) 188–96.

"Three Questions by John of Wesel on *Obligationes* and *Insolubilia*" (1996): http://www.pvspade.com/Logic/docs/wesel.pdf.

"The Treatises *On Modal Propositions* and *On Hypothetical Propositions* by Richard Lavenham," *Mediaeval Studies* 35 (1973) 49–59.

"Walter Burley on the Kinds of Simple Supposition," *Vivarium* 37 (1999) 41–59.

Spade, Paul Vincent and Eleonore Stump. "Walter Burley and the *Obligationes* Attributed to William of Sherwood," *History and Philosophy of Logic* 4 (1983) 9–26.

Spade, Paul Vincent and Gordon Wilson. "Richard Lavenham's Treatise *Scire:* An Edition, with Remarks on the Identification of Martin (?) Bilond's *Obiectiones consequentiarum*," *Mediaeval Studies* 46 (1984) 1–30.

Speer, Andreas. "Bonaventure and the Question of a Medieval Philosophy," *Medieval Philosophy and Theology* 6 (1997) 25–46.

Die entdeckte Natur: Untersuchungen zu Begründungsversuchen einer scientia naturalis *im 12. Jahrhundert* (Leiden: Brill, 1995).

"*Lectio physica*: Anmerkungen zur *Timaios*-Rezeption im Mittelalter," in T. Leinkauf and C. Steel (eds.) *Platons* Timaios *als Grundtext der Kosmologie in Spätantike, Mittelalter und Renaissance* (Leuven: Leuven University Press, 2005) 213–34.

Spettmann, Hieronymus. "Die Psychologie des Johannes Pecham," *Beiträge zur Geschichte der Philosophie des Mittelalters* 20 (1919) 1–102.

Spinka, Matthew. *John Hus: A Biography* (Princeton, NJ: Princeton University Press, 1968; repr. Westport, CT: Greenwood, 1979).

John Hus at the Council of Constance (New York: Columbia University Press, 1966).

John Hus's Concept of the Church (Princeton, NJ: Princeton University Press, 1966).

Spitzig, Joseph. *Sacramental Penance in the Twelfth and Thirteenth Centuries* (Washington, DC: Catholic University of America Press, 1947).

Sprandel, Rolf. *Ivo von Chartres und seine Stellung in der Kirchengeschichte* (Stuttgart: Hiersemann, 1962).

Sprengard, Karl Anton. *Systematische-Historische Untersuchungen zur Philosophie des XIV Jahrhunderts* (Bonn: Mainzer Philosophische Forschungen, 1968).

Spruit, Leen. *Species Intelligibilis: From Perception to Knowledge* (Leiden: Brill, 1994–5).

Spruyt, Joke. "Gerardus Odonis on the Universal," *Archives d'histoire doctrinale et littéraire du moyen âge* 63 (1996) 171–208.

Spufford, Peter. *Money and its Use in Medieval Europe* (Cambridge: Cambridge University Press, 1988).

Squire, Aelred. *Aelred of Rievaulx: A Study* (Kalamazoo, MI: Cistercian Publications, 1981).

Stadter, Ernst. *Psychologie und Metaphysik der menschlichen Freiheit: die ideengeschichtliche Entwicklung zwischen Bonaventura und Duns Scotus* (Paderborn: Schöningh, 1971).

Stahl, William and Richard Johnson. *Martianus Capella and the Seven Liberal Arts* (New York: Columbia University Press, 1971).

Staley, Kevin. "Al-Kindi on Creation: Aristotle's Challenge to Islam," *Journal of the History of Ideas* 50 (1989) 355–70.

Staley, Lynn. "Julian of Norwich and the Late Fourteenth-Century Crisis of Authority," in D. Aers and L. Staley (eds.) *The Powers of the Holy: Religion, Politics, and Gender in Late Medieval English Culture* (University Park, PA: Pennsylvania State University Press, 1996) 107–78.

Stammerjohann, Harro and Sylvain Auroux (eds.). *Lexicon grammaticorum* (Tübingen: Niemeyer, 1996).

Stead, M. T. "Manegold of Lautenbach," *English Historical Review* 29 (1914) 1–15.

Steel, Carlos. *Der Adler und die Nachteule. Thomas und Albert über die Möglichkeit der Metaphysik* (Münster: Aschendorff, 2001).

"Das neue Interesse für den Platonismus am Ende des 13. Jahrhunderts," in T. Kobusch and B. Mojsisch (eds.) *Platon in der abendländischen Geistesgeschichte, Neue Forschungen zum Platonismus* (Darmstadt: Wissenschaftliche Buchgesellschaft, 1997) 120–33.

"Plato Latinus (1939–1989)," in J. Hamesse and M. Fattori (eds.) *Rencontres de cultures dans la philosophie médiévale: traductions et traducteurs de l'Antiquité tardive au XIVe siècle* (Louvain-la-Neuve: Publication de l'Institut d'études médiévales/Cassino: Università di Cassino, 1990) 301–16.

Steer, Georg. *Hugo Ripelin von Strassburg: zur Rezeptions- und Wirkungsgeschichte des "Compendium theologicae veritatis" im deutschen Spätmittelalter* (Tübingen: Niemeyer, 1981).

Stegmüller, Friedrich. "Der Tractatus de Deo Trino des Hugolins von Orvieto OESA," *Annali della biblioteca governativa e libreria civica di Cremona* 7 (1954) 19–57.

Steinschneider, Moritz. *Die hebräischen Übersetzungen des Mittelalters und die Juden als Dolmetscher* (Graz: Akademische Druck- und Verlagsanstalt, 1956).

Stella, Prospero T. "La prima critica di Hervaeus Natalis O. P. alla noetica di Enrico di Gand," *Salesianum* 21 (1959) 125–70.

"Teologi e teologia nelle *Reprobationes* de Bernardo d'Auvergne ai *Quodlibeti* di Goffredo di Fontaines," *Salesianum* 19 (1957) 171–214.

Steneck, Nicholas H. *Science and Creation in the Middle Ages: Henry of Langenstein (d. 1397) on Genesis* (Notre Dame, IN: University of Notre Dame Press, 1976).

Stephanou, Pelopidas Étienne. *Jean Italos, philosope et humaniste* (Rome: Pontificium Institutum Orientalium Studiorum, 1949).

Stern, Samuel M. *Studies in Early Isma'ilism* (Leiden: Brill, 1983).

Stevenson, William, Jr. *Christian Love and Just War: Moral Paradox and Political Life in St. Augustine and his Modern Interpreters.* (Macon, GA: Mercer University Press, 1987).

Stirnimann, Heinrich and Ruedi Imbach. *Eckardus Theutonicus, homo doctus et sanctus: Nachweise und Berichte zum Prozeß gegen Meister Eckhart* (Fribourg: Universitätsverlag, 1992).

Stock, Brian. *Myth and Science in the Twelfth Century: A Study of Bernard Silvester* (Princeton, NJ: Princeton University Press, 1972).

Stone, Abraham. "Simplicius and Avicenna on the Essential Corporeity of Material Substance," in R. Wisnovsky (ed.) *Aspects of Avicenna* (Princeton, NJ: Markus Wiener, 2001) 73–130.

Stone, M. W. F. "Equity and Moderation: The Reception and Uses of Aristotle's Doctrine of ΕΠΙΕΙΚΕΙΑ in Thirteenth-Century Ethics," *Documenti e studi sulla tradizione filosofica medievale* 17 (2006) 121–56.

"In the Shadow of Augustine: The Scholastic Debate on Lying from Robert Grosseteste to Gabriel Biel," in J. A. Aertsen and M. Pickavé (eds.) *Herbst des Mittelalters? Fragen zur Bewertung des 14. und 15. Jahrhunderts* (Berlin: De Gruyter, 2004) 277–317.

"'Initium omnis peccati est superbia': Jean Gerson's Account of Pride in his Mystical Theology, Pastoral Thought, and Hamartiology," in R. Newhauser (ed.) *In the Garden of Evil: The Vices and their Culture in the Middle Ages* (Toronto: Pontifical Institute of Mediaeval Studies, 2005) 293–323.

"The Soul's Relation to the Body: Thomas Aquinas, Siger of Brabant and the Parisian Debate on Monopsychism," in T. Crane and S. Patterson (eds.) *History of the Mind–Body Problem* (London: Routledge, 2000) 34–69.

Street, Tony. "Tusi on Avicenna's Logical Connectives," *History and Philosophy of Logic* 16 (1995) 257–68.

Streveler, Paul. "Richard the Sophister," in E. Zalta (ed.) *The Stanford Encyclopedia of Philosophy* (Spring 2005 edition): http://plato.stanford.edu/archives/spr2005/entries/richard-sophister/.

Stroick, Clemens. *Heinrich von Friemar: Leben, Werke, philosophisch-theologische Stellung in der Scholastik* (Freiburg: Herder, 1954).

Stroumsa, Sarah. *Freethinkers of Medieval Islam: Ibn al-Rāwandi, Abū Bakr al-Rāzī and their Impact on Islamic Thought* (Leiden: Brill, 1999).

"On the Maimonidean Controversy in the East: The Role of Abu'l-Barakat al-Baghdadi" [in Hebrew], in H. Ben-Shammai (ed.) *Hebrew and Arabic Studies in Honour of Joshua Blau* (Tel Aviv, 1993).

"Saadya and Jewish Kalam," in D. H. Frank and O. Leaman (eds.) *Cambridge Companion to Medieval Jewish Philosophy* (Cambridge: Cambridge University Press, 2003) 71–90.

Struve, Tilman. "Die Anthropologie des Alfredus in ihrer Stellung zwischen Platonismus und Aristotelismus," *Archiv für Kulturgeschichte* 55 (1973) 366–90.

Stump, Eleonore. *Aquinas* (London: Routledge, 2003).

"Aquinas' Account of Freedom: Intellect and Will," in B. Davies (ed.) *Thomas Aquinas: Contemporary Philosophical Perspectives* (Oxford: Oxford University Press, 2002) 275–94.

"Augustine on Free Will," in N. Kretzmann and E. Stump (eds.) *The Cambridge Companion to Augustine* (Cambridge: Cambridge University Press, 2001) 124–47.

"Dialectic in the Eleventh and Twelfth Centuries: Garlandus Compotista," *History and Philosophy of Logic* 1 (1980) 1–18.

"Saadya Gaon and the Problem of Evil," *Faith and Philosophy* 14 (1997) 523–49.

Wandering in Darkness: Narrative and the Problem of Suffering (Oxford: Oxford University Press, forthcoming).

"William of Sherwood's Treatise on Obligations," *Historiographia Linguistica* 7 (1980) 249–61.

Stump, Eleonore and Norman Kretzmann. "Absolute Simplicity," *Faith and Philosophy* 2 (1985) 353–91.

Sturlese, Loris. *Dokumente und Forschungen zu Leben und Werke Dietrichs von Freiberg* (Hamburg: Meiner, 1984).

"Gottebenbildichkeit und Beseelung des Himmels in den *Quodlibeta* Heinrichs von Lübeck OP," *Freiburger Zeitschrift für Philosophie und Theologie* 24 (1977) 191–233.

"Johannes Picardi von Lichtenberg," in W. Stammler *et al.* (eds.) *Die deutsche Literatur des Mittelalters: Verfasserlexikon* (Berlin: De Gruyter, 1977–) IV: 706–10.

Suárez, Gregorio. "El pensamiento de Egidio Romano en torno a la distinción de esencia y existencia," *La Ciencia Tomista* 75 (1948) 66–99, 230–72.

Sudhoff, Karl. "Die Salernitaner Handschrift in Breslau," *Archiv für Geschichte der Medizin* 12 (1920) 101–48.

Sullivan, Thomas. *Benedictine Monks at the University of Paris, A.D. 1229–1500: A Biographical Register* (Leiden: Brill, 1995).

"The *Quodlibeta* of the Canons Regular and the Monks," in C. Schabel (ed.) *Theological Quodlibeta in the Middle Ages: The Fourteenth Century* (Leiden: Brill, 2007) 359–400.

Swanson, Jenny. *John of Wales: A Study of the Works and Ideas of a Thirteenth-Century Friar* (Cambridge: Cambridge University Press, 1989).

Swanson, Scott G. "The Medieval Foundations of John Locke's Theory of Natural Rights: Rights of Subsistence and the Principle of Extreme Necessity," *History of Political Thought* 18 (1997) 403–12.

Sweeney, Eileen. *Logic, Theology, and Poetry in Boethius, Abelard, and Alan of Lille: Words in the Absence of Things* (New York: Palgrave Macmillan, 2006).

"Restructuring Desire: Aquinas, Hobbes, and Descartes on the Passions," in S. F. Brown (ed.) *Meeting of the Minds: The Relations between Medieval and Classical Modern European Philosophy* (Turnhout: Brepols, 1998) 215–33.

Swift, Louis J. "Augustine on War and Killing: Another View," *Harvard Theological Review* 66 (1973) 369–83.

Sylla, Edith. "Mathematical Physics and Imagination in the Work of the Oxford Calculators: Roger Swineshead's *On Natural Motions*," in M. Clagett, E. Grant and J. Murdoch (eds.) *Mathematics and its Applications to Science and Natural Philosophy in the Middle Ages: Essays in Honor of Marshall Clagett* (Cambridge: Cambridge University Press, 1987) 69–101.

"Medieval Concepts of the Latitude of Forms: The Oxford Calculators," *Archives d'histoire doctrinale et littéraire du moyen âge* 40 (1973) 251–71.

"Medieval Quantifications of Qualities: The 'Merton School'," *Archive for History of Exact Sciences* 8 (1971) 9–39.

"The Oxford Calculators," in N. Kretzmann *et al.* (eds.) *The Cambridge History of Later Medieval Philosophy* (Cambridge: Cambridge University Press, 1982) 540–64.

"The Oxford Calculators and Mathematical Physics: John Dumbleton's *Summa logicae et philosophiae naturalis*, Parts II and III," in S. Unguru (ed.) *Physics, Cosmology and Astronomy, 1300–1700: Tension and Accommodation* (Dordrecht: Kluwer, 1991) 129–61.

The Oxford Calculators and the Mathematics of Motion, 1320–1350: Physics and Measurement by Latitudes (New York: Garland, 1991).

"William Heytesbury on the Sophism '*Infinita sunt finita*'," in J. P. Beckmann and W. Kluxen (eds.) *Sprache und Erkenntnis im Mittelalter* (Berlin: De Gruyter, 1981) II: 628–36.

Synan, Edward. "The Insolubilia of Roger Nottingham, O.F.M.," *Mediaeval Studies* 26 (1964) 257–70.

"The 'Introitus ad sententias' of Roger Nottingham, O.F.M.," *Mediaeval Studies* 25 (1963) 259–79.

Tabarroni, Andrea. "Lo pseudo-Egidio (Guglielmo Arnaldi) e un'inedita continuazione del commento di Tommaso al 'Peryermenias'," *Medioevo* 14 (1988) 371–427.

Tachau, Katherine. "The Influence of Richard Campsall on Fourteenth-Century Oxford Thought," in A. Hudson and M. Wilks (eds.) *From Ockham to Wyclif* (Oxford: Blackwell, 1987) 109–23.

"Introduction," in P. Streveler *et al.* (eds.) *Seeing the Future Clearly: Questions on Future Contingents* (Toronto: Pontifical Institute of Mediaeval Studies, 1995) 1–98.

"Logic's God and the Natural Order in Late Medieval Oxford: The Teaching of Robert Holcot," *Annals of Science* 53 (1996) 235–67.

"The Problem of the *species in medio* at Oxford in the Generation after Ockham," *Mediaeval Studies* 44 (1982) 394–443.

"The 'Questiones in Primum Librum Sententiarum' of Andreas de Novocastro," *Archives d'histoire doctrinale et littéraire du moyen âge* 69 (1992) 289–318.

"Richard Campsall as a Theologian: New Evidence," in B. Mojsisch and O. Pluta (eds.) *Historia philosophiae medii aevi: Studien zur Geschichte der Philosophie des Mittelalters: Festschrift für Kurt Flasch* (Amsterdam: Benjamins, 1991) 979–1002.

"Robert Holcot on Contingency and Divine Deception," in L. Bianchi and R. Eugenio (eds.) *Filosofia e teologia nel trecento: studi in ricordo di Eugenio Randi* (Louvain-la-Neuve: Fédération internationale des instituts d'études médiévales, 1994) 157–96.

Vision and Certitude in the Age of Ockham: Optics, Epistemology and the Foundations of Semantics, 1250–1345 (Leiden: Brill, 1988).

"Wodeham, Crathorn, and Holcot: The Development of the *complexe significabile*," in L. M. de Rijk and H. Braakhuis (eds.) *Logos and Pragma* (Nijmegen: Ingenium, 1987) 161–87.

Talmon, Rafael. "Naẓra ǧadīda fī qaḍiyyat aqsām al-kalām: dirāsa ḥawl kitāb Ibn al-Muqaffaʿ fī al-manṭiq," *al-Karmil* 12 (1991) 43–67.

Tambrun, Brigitte. *Pléthon: le retour de Platon* (Paris: Vrin, 2006).

Tanner, Norman (ed.). *Decrees of the Ecumenical Councils* (London: Sheed and Ward, 1990).

Tardieu, Michel. "Chosroès," in *Dictionnaire des philosophes antiques* (Paris: CNRS Éditions, 1994) II: 309–18.

"La recension arabe des Magika logia," in B. Tambrun-Krasker (ed.) *Oracles Chaldaïques: recension de Georges Gémiste Pléthon* (Athens: Academy of Athens, 1995) 157–71.

Taschow, Ulrich. *Nicole Oresme und der Frühling der Moderne: die Ursprünge unserer modernen quantitativ-metrischen Weltaneignungsstrategien und neuzeitlichen Bewusstseins- und Wissenschaftskultur* (Halle: Avox Medien-Verlag, 2003).

Tatakis, Basil. *Byzantine Philosophy*, tr. N. J. Moutafakis (Indianapolis, IN: Hackett, 2003).

La philosophie Byzantine (Paris: Presses universitaires de France, 1949).

Tavard, George H. *Trina Deitas: The Controversy between Hincmar and Gottschalk* (Milwaukee, WI: Marquette University Press, 1996).

Teetaert, Amedeus. "La 'Formula confessionis' du frère mineur Jean Rigaud (d. 1323)," in *Miscellanea historica in honorem Alberti de Meyer* (Leuven: Bibliothèque de l'Université, 1946) 651–76.

"La littérature quodlibetique," *Ephemerides theologiae Lovanienses* 14 (1937) 77–105.

Teeuwen, Mariken. *The Vocabulary of Intellectual Life in the Middle Ages* (Turnhout: Brepols, 2003).

Teixidor, Javier. *Aristote en syriaque* (Paris: CNRS Éditions, 2003).

Tellenbach, Gerd. *The Church in Western Europe from the Tenth to the Early Twelfth Century* (Cambridge: Cambridge University Press, 1993).

Terian, Abraham. "The Hellenizing School: Its Time, Place, and Scope of Activities Reconsidered," in N. Garsoian *et al.* (eds.) *East of Byzantium: Syria and Armenia in the Formative Period* (Washington, DC: Dumbarton Oaks, 1980) 175–86.

Teske, Roland. *Studies in the Philosophy of William of Auvergne, Bishop of Paris (1228–1249)* (Milwaukee, WI: Marquette University Press, 2006).

"William of Auvergne's Debt to Avicenna," in J. Janssens and D. De Smet (eds.) *Avicenna and his Heritage* (Leuven: Leuven University Press, 2002) 153–70.

Tessier, Georges. "Jean de Mirecourt, philosophe et théologien," *Histoire litteraire de la France* 40 (1974) 1–52.

Teuffel, W. S. *Geschichte der Römische Literatur*, 6th edn (Teubner: Leipzig, 1910–16).

Theissing, Hermann. *Glaube und Theologie bei Robert Cowton OFM* (Münster: Aschendorff, 1970).

Théry, Gabriel. *Autour du décret de 1210: II. Alexandre d'Aphrodise* (Kain: Le Saulchoir, 1926).

Études dionysiennes (Paris: Vrin, 1937).

Thijssen, Johannes M. M. H. "The Buridan School Reassessed: Buridan and Albert of Saxony," *Vivarium* 42 (2004) 18–42.

Censure and Heresy at the University of Paris, 1200–1400 (Philadelphia: University of Pennsylvania Press, 1998).

"Master Amalric and the Amalricians: Inquisitorial Procedure and the Suppression of Heresy at the University of Paris," *Speculum* 71 (1996) 43–65.

"The Quest for Certain Knowledge in the Fourteenth Century: Nicholas of Autrecourt against the Academics," in J. Sihvola (ed.) *Ancient Scepticism and the Sceptical Tradition* (Helsinki: Societas Philosophica Fennica, 2000) 199–223.

"The Response to Thomas Aquinas in the Early Fourteenth Century: Eternity and Infinity in the Works of Henry of Harclay, Thomas of Wilton and William of Alnwick OFM," in J. B. M. Wissink (ed.) *The Eternity of the World in the Thought of Thomas Aquinas and his Contemporaries* (Leiden: Brill, 1990) 82–100.

Thijssen, Johannes M. M. H. and Jack Zupko (eds.). *The Metaphysics and Natural Philosophy of John Buridan* (Leiden: Brill, 2001).

Thom, Paul. *Logic and Ontology in the Syllogistic of Robert Kilwardby* (Leiden: Brill, 2007).

Thomas, Ivo. "Maxims in Kilwardby," *Dominican Studies* 7 (1954) 129–46.

Thomas, Rudolf (ed.). *Petrus Abaelardus: Person, Wirk, und Wirkung* (Trier: Paulinus-Verlag, 1980).

Thomson, R. B. "Two Astronomical Tractates of Abbo of Fleury," in J. D. North and J. J. Roche (eds.) *The Light of Nature: Essays in the History and Philosophy of Science Presented to A. C. Crombie* (Dordrecht: Nijhoff, 1985) 113–33.

Thomson, S. Harrison. "A Further Note on Master Adam of Bocfeld," *Medievalia et Humanistica* 12 (1958) 23–32.

   "The 'Notule' of Grosseteste on the Nicomachean Ethics," *Proceedings of the British Academy* 19 (1934) 3–26.

   "The Philosophical Basis of Wyclif's Theology," *Journal of Religion* 11 (1931) 86–116.

   "The Works of Magister Adam of Bocfield (Bouchermefort)," *Medievalia et Humanistica* 2 (1944) 55–87.

   The Writings of Robert Grosseteste, Bishop of Lincoln 1235–1253 (Cambridge: Cambridge University Press, 1940).

Thomson, W. R. *The Latin Writings of John Wyclyf: An Annotated Catalog* (Toronto: Pontifical Institute of Medieval Studies, 1983).

Thorndike, Lynn. *A History of Magic and Experimental Science* (New York: Columbia University Press, 1923–58).

   "Manuscripts of the Writings of Peter of Abano," *Bulletin of the History of Medicine* 15 (1944) 201–19.

   Michael Scot (London: Nelson, 1965).

   "A New Work by Robert Holcot (Corpus Christi College, Oxford, MS 138)," *Archives internationales d'histoire des sciences* 10 (1957) 227–35.

Thorndike, Lynn and Pearl Kibre. *A Catalogue of Incipits of Mediaeval Scientific Writings in Latin* (London: Mediaeval Academy of America, 1963).

Thureau-Dangin, Paul. *Un prédicateur populaire dans l'Italie de la Renaissance: Saint Bernardin de Sienne, 1380–1444* (Paris: Bloud et Gay, 1926).

Thurot, Charles. *Extraits de divers manuscrits latins, pour servir à l'histoire des doctrines grammaticales au Moyen Age* (Paris: Bibliothèque Impériale, 1869; repr. Frankfurt: Minerva, 1964).

Tierney, Brian. *Foundations of the Conciliar Theory: The Contribution of the Medieval Canonists from Gratian to the Great Schism*, new edn (Leiden: Brill, 1998).

   "Hierarchy, Consent and the 'Western Tradition'," *Political Theory* 15 (1987) 646–54.

   The Idea of Natural Rights: Studies on Natural Rights, Natural Law and Church Law, 1150–1625 (Atlanta, GA: Scholars Press, 1997).

   "Marsilius on Rights," *Journal of the History of Ideas* 52 (1991) 5–17.

   Medieval Poor Law (Berkeley: University of California Press, 1959).

   Origins of Papal Infallibility, 1150–1350: A Study on the Concepts of Infallibility, Sovereignty and Tradition in the Middle Ages (Leiden: Brill, 1972).

   "'The Prince is Not Bound by the Laws': Accursius and the Origins of the Modern State," in G. Rossi (ed.) *Atti del Convegno Internazionale di Studi Accursiani* (Milan: Giuffrè, 1968) III: 1245–74.

   "Tuck on Rights: Some Medieval Problems," *History of Political Thought* 4 (1983) 429–41.

Tihon, Paul. *Foi et théologie selon Godefroid de Fontaines* (Bruges: Desclée de Brouwer, 1966).

Tinnefeld, Franz. "Ein Text des Prochoros Kydones in *Vat. gr. 609* über die Bedeutung der Syllogismen für die theologische Erkenntnis," in A. Schoors and P. van Deun (eds.) *Philohistôr: miscellenea in honorem Caroli Laga septuagenarii* (Leuven: Peeters, 1994) 515–27.

Tirosh-Samuelson, Hava. *Happiness in Premodern Judaism: Virtue, Knowledge, and Well-Being* (Cincinnati, OH: Hebrew Union College Press, 2003).

"Philosophy and Kaballah: 1200–1600," in D. Frank and O. Leaman (eds.) *The Cambridge Companion to Medieval Jewish Philosophy* (Cambridge: Cambridge University Press, 2003) 218–57.

Tobiass, Marc and Maurice Ifergan. *Crescas: un philosophe juif dans l'Espagne médiévale* (Paris: Cerf, 1995).

Tobin, Frank. "Henry Suso and Elsbeth Stagel: Was the *Vita* a Cooperative Effort?," in C. Mooney (ed.) *Gendered Voices: Medieval Saints and their Interpreters* (Philadelphia: University of Pennsylvania Press, 1999) 118–35.

Tobin, Rosemary Barton. *Vincent of Beauvais' "De Eruditione Filiorum Nobilium": The Education of Women* (New York: Lang, 1984).

Tomson, Peter J. (ed.). *Abraham Ibn Ezra: savant universel* (Brussels: Institutum Judaicum, 2000).

Tornero Poveda, E. *Al-Kindi: la transformacion de un pensamiento religioso en un pensamiento racional* (Madrid: Consejo Superior de Investigaciones Científicas, 1992).

Torrell, Jean-Pierre. *Saint Thomas Aquinas*, vol. I: *The Person and his Work*, tr. R. Royal (Washington, DC: Catholic University of America Press, 1996).

Saint Thomas Aquinas, vol. II: *Spiritual Master* (Washington, DC: Catholic University of America Press, 2003).

Torrell, Jean-Pierre and Denise Bouthillier. *Pierre le Vénérable et sa vision du monde: sa vie, son œuvre, l'homme et le démon* (Leuven: Spicilegium sacrum Lovaniense, 1986).

Touati, Charles. *La pensée philosophique et théologique de Gersonide* (Paris: Éditions de Minuit, 1973).

"La providence divine chez Hasdai Crescas," *Da'at* 10 (1983) 15–31.

Trapp, Damasus. "Augustinian Theology of the 14th Century: Notes on Editions, Marginalia, and Booklore," *Augustiniana* 6 (1956) 146–274.

"Hiltalinger's Augustinian Quotations," *Augustiniana* 4 (1954) 412–49.

"Notes on Some Manuscripts of the Augustinian Michael de Massa (†1337)," *Augustinianum* 5 (1965) 58–133.

"Peter Ceffons of Clairvaux," *Recherches de théologie ancienne et médiévale* 24 (1957) 101–54.

Travaglia, Pinella. *Magic, Causality, and Intentionality: The Doctrine of Rays in al-Kindi* (Turnhout: Micrologus, 1999).

Traver, Andrew. "William of Saint-Amour's Two Disputed Questions 'De quantitate eleemosynae' and 'De valido mendicante'," *Archives d'histoire doctrinale et littéraire du moyen âge* 62 (1995) 295–342.

Trifogli, Cecilia. "Averroes's Doctrine of Time and its Reception in the Scholastic Debate," in P. Porro (ed.) *The Medieval Concept of Time* (Leiden: Brill, 2001) 57–82.

"La dottrina del luogo in Egidio Romano," *Medioevo* 14 (1988) 260–90.

"Giles of Rome on Natural Motion in the Void," *Mediaeval Studies* 54 (1992) 136–61.

"Giles of Rome on the Instant of Change," *Synthese* 96 (1993) 93–114.

Liber Quartus Physicorum Aristotelis: Repertorio delle Questioni, Commenti Inglesi ca. 1250–1270 (Florence: SISMEL, 2007).

"Il luogo dell'ultima sfera nei commenti tardo-antichi e medievali a Phyica IV.5," *Giornale critico della filosofia italiana* 68 (1989) 144–60.

Oxford Physics in the Thirteenth Century (ca. 1250–1270): Motion, Infinity, Place and Time (Leiden: Brill, 2000).

"Il problema dello statuto ontologico del tempo nelle 'Quaestiones super Physicam' di Thomas Wylton e di Giovanni di Jandun," *Documenti e studi sulla tradizione filosofica medievale* 1 (1990) 491–548.

"The *Quodlibet* of Thomas Wylton," in C. Schabel (ed.) *Theological Quodlibeta in the Middle Ages: The Fourteenth Century* (Leiden: Brill, 2007) 231–66.

"Thomas Wylton on Final Causality," in A. Fidora and M. Lutz-Bachmann (eds.) *Erfahrung und Beweis: die Wissenschaft von der Natur im 13. und 14. Jahrhundert* (Berlin: Akademie-Verlag, 2007) 249–64.

"Thomas Wylton on Motion," *Archiv für Geschichte der Philosophie* 77 (1995) 135–54.

"Thomas Wylton on the Immobility of Place," *Recherches de théologie et philosophie médiévales* 65 (1998) 1–39.

Trifogli, Cecilia and Lauge Nielsen. "Thomas Wylton's Questions on Number, the Instant, and Time," *Documenti e studi sulla tradizione filosofica medievale* 16 (2005) 57–117.

Trizio, Michele. "Byzantine Philosophy as a Contemporary Historiographical Project," *Recherches de théologie et philosophie médiévales* 74 (2007) 247–94.

Troeltsch, Ernst. *The Social Teaching of the Christian Churches*, tr. O. Wyon (New York: Macmillan, 1931; repr. New York: Harper, 1960).

Troncarelli, Fabio. *Tradizioni perdute. La 'Consolazione Philosophiae' nell'alto medioevo* (Padua: Antenore, 1981).

Trottmann, Christian. "Verbe mentale et noétique thomiste dans le *De verbo* d'Hervé de Nédellec," *Revue Thomiste* 97 (1997) 47–62.

La vision béatifique: des disputes scolastiques à sa définition par Benoît XII (Rome: École française de Rome, 1995).

Troupeau, Gérard. "ʿAbdīshūʿ ibn Bahrīz et son livre sur les définitions de la logique," in D. Jacquart (ed.) *Les voies de la science grecque* (Geneva: Droz, 1997).

"La logique d'Ibn al-Muqaffaʿ et les origins de la grammaire arabe," *Arabica* 28 (1981) 242–50.

Trusen, Winfried. *Der Prozess gegen Meister Eckhart: Vorgeschichte, Verlauf und Folgen* (Paderborn: Schöningh, 1988).

Tsirpanlis, Constantine. "The Career and Writings of Nicolas Cabasilas," *Byzantion* 49 (1979) 414–27.

The Liturgical and Mystical Theology of Nicolas Cabasilas (New York: Tsirpanlis, 1979).

Tuck, Richard. "Grotius's *Of the Law of War and Peace*," in J. H. Burns (ed.) *The Cambridge History of Political Thought, 1450–1700* (Cambridge: Cambridge University Press, 1991) 514–22.

Natural Rights Theories: Their Origin and Development (Cambridge: Cambridge University Press, 1979).

The Rights of War and Peace: Political Thought and the International Order from Grotius to Kant (Oxford: Oxford University Press, 1999).

Tugwell, Simon. "Auctor Summularum, Petrus Hispanus OP Stellensis?," *Archivum Fratrum Praedicatorum* 76 (2006) 103–15.

"Petrus Hispanus: Comments on Some Proposed Identifications," *Vivarium* 37 (1999) 103–13.

Turley, Thomas. "John Baconthorpe on Papal Infallibility," *Journal of Ecumenical Studies* 19 (1982) 744–58.

Turner, C. J. G. "The Career of George-Gennadius Scholarius," *Byzantion* 39 (1969) 420–55.

Turner, Denys. *The Darkness of God: Negativity in Christian Mysticism* (Cambridge: Cambridge University Press, 1995).

Tuve, Rosamond. "Notes on Virtues and Vices," *Journal of the Warburg and Courtauld Institutes* 26 (1963) 264–303.

Tweedale, Martin. *Abailard on Universals* (Amsterdam: North-Holland, 1976).

"John of Rodynton on Knowledge, Science, and Theology" (Ph.D. dissertation: UCLA, 1965).

"Logic (i): From the Late Eleventh Century to the Time of Abelard," in P. Dronke (ed.) *A History of Twelfth-Century Western Philosophy* (Cambridge: Cambridge University Press, 1988) 196–226.

Twersky, Isadore (ed.). *Rabbi Moses Nahmanides (Ramban): Explorations in his Religious and Literary Virtuosity* (Cambridge, MA: Harvard University Press, 1983).

Twersky, Isadore and Jay Harris (eds.). *Rabbi Abraham ibn Ezra: Studies in the Writings of a Twelfth-Century Jewish Polymath* (Cambridge, MA: Harvard University Press, 1993).

Työrinoja, Reijo. "God, Causality, and Nature. Some Problems of Causality in Medieval Theology," in E. Martikainen (ed.) *Infinity, Causality and Determinism: Cosmological Enterprises and their Preconditions* (Frankfurt: Lang, 2002) 45–60.

Ullmann, Manfred. "Ḥālid ibn Yazīd und die Alchemie: eine Legende," *Der Islam* 55 (1978) 181–218.

Die Medizin im Islam (Leiden: Brill, 1970).

Die Natur-und Geheimwissenschaften im Islam (Leiden: Brill, 1972).

Ullmann, Walter. "Bartolus on Customary Law," *Judicial Review* 52 (1940) 265–83.

The Growth of Papal Government in the Middle Ages: A Study in the Ideological Relation of Clerical to Lay Power (London: Methuen, 1955).

"John of Salisbury's *Policraticus* in the Later Middle Ages," in *Jurisprudence in the Middle Ages: Collected Studies* (London: Variorum Reprints, 1980) 519–45.

Medieval Papalism: The Political Theories of the Medieval Canonists (London: Methuen, 1949; repr. Westport, CT: Hyperion Press, 1979).

Ullrich, Lothar. *Fragen der Schöpfungslehre nach Jakob von Metz, O.P.* (Leipzig: Benno, 1966).

Uña Juarez, Agustín. *La filosoifa del siglo XIV. Contexto cultural de Walter Burley* (Madrid: Biblioteca 'Ciudad de Dios' Real monasterio de El Escorial, 1978).

Underhill, Evelyn. *The Essentials of Mysticism and Other Essays* (New York: Dutton, 1920).

Undset, Sigrid. *Catherine of Siena* (New York: Sheed and Ward, 1954).

Unguru, Sabetai. "Mathematics and Experiment in Witelo's Perspectiva," in E. Grant and J. Murdoch (eds.) *Mathematics and its Applications to Science and Natural Philosophy in the Middle Ages: Essays in Honor of Marshall Clagett* (Cambridge: Cambridge University Press, 1987) 269–301.

Upjohn, Sheila. *In Search of Julian of Norwich* (Darton, Longman and Todd, 1989).

Urvoy, Dominique. *Ibn Rushd* (London: Routledge, 1991).

Penser l'Islam: les présupposés islamiques de l'"Art" de Lull (Paris: Vrin, 1980).

Vajda, Georges. "Autour de la théorie de la connaissance chez Saadia," *Revue des Études Juives* 126 (1967) 375–97.

"Le dialogue de l'âme et de la raison dans les *Devoirs des Cœurs* de Bahya Ibn Paquda," *Revue des Études Juives* 102 (1937) 93–104.

Isaac Albalag: Averroiste juif, traducteur et commentateur d'Al-Ghazali (Paris: Vrin, 1960).

"La philosophie et la théologie de Joseph ibn Zaddiq," *Archives d'histoire doctrinale et littéraire du moyen âge* 24 (1949) 93–181.

La théologie ascetique de Bahya ibn Paquda (Paris: Cahiers de la Société Asiatique, 1947).

Valente, Luisa. *Logique et théologie: les écoles parisiennes entre 1150 et 1220* (Paris: Vrin, 2008).

"'*Talia sunt subiecta qualia praedicata permittunt,*' Le principe de l'approche contextuelle et sa genèse dans la théologie du XIIᵉ siècle," in J. Biard and I. Rosier-Catach (eds.) *La tradition médiévale des catégories (XIIᵉ–XVᵉ siècles)* (Leuven: Peeters, 2003) 289–311.

Valls i Taberner, Ferran. *San Ramón de Penyafort* (Barcelona: Editorial Labor, 1936; repr. 1979).

Valois, Noël. *Guillaume d'Auvergne, évèque de Paris (1228–1249); sa vie et ses ouvrages* (Paris: Picard, 1880)

"Jean de Pouilli, théologien," *Histoire littéraire de la France* 34 (1914) 220–81.

"Jean Rigaud, frère mineur," *Histoire littéraire de la France* 34 (1914) 286–91

Van Bladel, Kevin. "Hermes Arabicus" (Ph.D. dissertation: Yale University, 2004).

Van den Eynde, Damien. *L'œuvre littéraire de Géroch de Reichersberg* (Rome: Pontificio Ateneo Antoniano, 1957).

Van der Heijden, Maarten and Bert Roest. *Franciscan Authors, 13th–18th Century: A Catalogue in Progress*: http://users.bart.nl/~roestb/franciscan/.

Van der Lecq, Ria. "William Heytesbury on 'Necessity'," in O. Lewry (ed.) *The Rise of British Logic* (Toronto: Pontifical Institute of Mediaeval Studies, 1983) 249–63.

Van Dyke, Christina. "An Aristotelian Theory of Divine Illumination: Robert Grosseteste's Commentary on the Posterior Analytics," *British Journal for the History of Philosophy* (forthcoming).

"Metaphysical Amphibians: Aquinas on the Individuation and Identity of Human Beings" (Ph.D. dissertation: Cornell University, 2000).

Van Engen, John (tr.). *Devotio Moderna: Basic Writings* (New York: Paulist Press, 1988).

Rupert of Deutz (Berkeley: University of California Press, 1983).

Van Esbroeck, Michel. "La version géorgienne de deux commentaires d'Ammonius fils d'Hermias," in G. Fiaccadori (ed.) *Autori classici in lingue del vicino e medio oriente* (Rome: Istituto poligrafico e Zecca dello Stato, Libreria dello Stato, 1990) 55–64.

van Ess, Josef. "Biobibliographische Notizen zur islamischen Theologie," *Die Welt des Orients* 9 (1978) 255–83.

"Ḍirār b. ʿAmr und die 'Cahmīya'," *Islam* 43 (1967) 241–79; 44 (1968) 1–70, 318–20.

Die Erkenntnislehre des ʿAḍudaddīn al-Īcī: Ubersetzung und Kommentar des 1. Buches seiner Mawaqif (Wiesbaden: Steiner, 1966).

The Flowering of Muslim Theology, tr. J. M. Todd (Cambridge, MA: Harvard University Press, 2006).

Theologie und Gesellschaft im 2. und 3. Jahrhundert Hidschra: eine Geschichte des religiosen Denkens im fruhen Islam (Berlin: De Gruyter, 1991–7).

Theology and Science: The Case of Abū Isḥāq an-Naẓẓām (Ann Arbor: University of Michigan Press, 1978).

"Wrongdoing and Divine Omnipotence in the Theology of Abū Isḥāq an-Naẓẓām," in T. Rudavsky (ed.) *Divine Omniscience and Omnipotence in Medieval Philosophy: Islamic, Jewish, and Christian Perspectives* (Dordrecht: Reidel, 1985) 53–67.

Van Gelder, G. J. H. "Ancients and Moderns," in G. Krämer *et al.* (eds.) *Encyclopaedia of Islam*, 3rd edn (Leiden: Brill Online, 2008).

Vanhamel, Willy (ed.). *Henry of Ghent: Proceedings of the International Colloquium on the Occasion of the 700th Anniversary of His Death (1293)* (Leuven: Leuven University Press, 1996).

Van Hove, Alphonse. *Commentarium Lovaniense in codicem iuris canonici*, 2nd edn (Mechelen: Dessain, 1930).

Van Leeuwen, Henry. *The Problem of Certainty in English Thought: 1630–1690* (The Hague: Nijhoff, 1970).

Vanneste, Alfred. "La théologie de la pénitence chez quelques maîtres parisiens de la première moitié du xiiie siècle," *Ephemerides Theologicae Lovanienses* 28 (1952) 24–58.

Van Neste, Roy. "The Epistemology of John of Mirecourt: A Reinterpretation," *Citeaux* 27 (1976) 5–28.

Vanni Rovighi, Sofia. *L'immortalità dell'anima nei maestri francescani del secolo XIII* (Milan: Vita e Pensiero, 1936).

"La psicologia di Taddeo da Parma," *Rivista di Filosofia Neoscolastica* 23 (1931) 504–12.

Van Roo, William. *Grace and Original Justice according to St Thomas* (Rome: Gregorian University, 1955).

Vansteenberghe, Edmond. *Le Cardinal Nicolas de Cues* (Paris: Champion, 1920; repr. Frankfurt: Minerva, 1963).

Van Steenberghen, Fernand. *Maître Siger de Brabant* (Leuven: Publications universitaires, 1977).

    La philosophie au XIIIe siècle, 2nd edn (Louvain-la-Neuve: Institut Supérieur de Philosophie, 1991).

    Le problème de l'existence de Dieu dans les écrits de S. Thomas d'Aquin (Louvain-la-Neuve: Institut Supérieur de Philosophie, 1980)

    St. Thomas Aquinas and Radical Aristotelianism (Washington, DC: Catholic University of America Press, 1980).

Van't Spijker, Ienje. *Fictions of the Inner Life: Religious Literature and Formation of the Self in the Eleventh and Twelfth Centuries* (Turnhout: Brepols, 2004).

Van Veldhuijsen, Peter. "The Question on the Possibility of an Eternally Created World: Bonaventura and Thomas Aquinas," in J. B. M. Wissink (ed.) *The Eternity of the World in the Thought of Thomas Aquinas and his Contemporaries* (Leiden: Brill, 1990) 20–38.

Vasalou, Sophia. "Equal Before the Law: The Evilness of Human and Divine Lies: ʿAbd al-Ǧabbār's Rational Ethics," *Arabic Sciences and Philosophy* 13 (2003) 243–68.

Veit, Raphaela. *Das Buch der Fieber des Isaac Israeli und seine Bedeutung im lateinischen Westen: ein Beitrag zur Rezeption arabischer Wissenschaft im Abendland* (Stuttgart: Steiner, 2003).

Veliath, Dominic. "The Scotism of William of Alnwick in his *Determinationes de anima*," *Salesianum* 32 (1970) 93–134.

Verbeke, Gerard *et al.* (eds.). *Corpus latinum commentariorum in Aristotelem Graecorum* (Leuven: Publications universitaires, 1957–).

Verdeyen, Paul. *Guillaume de Saint-Thierry, premier auteur mystique des anciens Pays Bas* (Turnhout: Brepols, 2003).

    La théologie mystique de Guillaume de Saint-Thierry (Paris: FAC-éditions, 1990).

Verger, Jacques. *Les universités au moyen âge* (Paris: Presses universitaires de France, 1973).

Verpeaux, Jean. *Nicéphore Choumnos: homme d'état et humaniste byzantin (ca.1250/1255–1327)* (Paris: Picard, 1959).

Verweij, Michiel. "The Manuscript Transmission of the Summa de virtutibus by Guillelmus Peraldus. A Preliminary Survey of the Manuscripts," *Medioevo* 31 (2006) 103–298.

Vetulani, Adam. *Sur Gratien et les Décrétales*, ed. W. Uruszczak (Aldershot: Variorum, 1990).

Veuthey, Léon. "Alexandre d'Alexandrie, maître de Paris et ministre général des frères mineurs," *Études Franciscaines* 43 (1931) 145–76, 319–44; 44 (1932) 21–42, 193–207, 321–36, 429–67.

Vial, Marc. *Jean Gerson: théoricien de la théologie mystique* (Paris: Vrin, 2006).

Vignaux, Paul. "Un accès philosophique au spirituel: l'averroisme chez Jean de Ripa et Paul de Venise," *Archives de philosophie* 51 (1988) 385–400.

    "Le concept de Dieu chez Jean de Ripa," in A. Maierù (ed.) *Studi sul XIV sec. in memoria di Anneliese Maier* (Rome: Edizioni di Storia e Letteratura, 1981) 453–97.

    "L'être comme perfection selon François de Meyronnes," in *Études d'histoire littéraire et doctrinale* (Montréal: Institut d'études médiévales, 1962) 259–318.

    Justification et prédestination au XIVe siècle: Duns Scot, Pierre d'Auriole, Guillaume d'Occam, Grégoire de Rimini (Paris: Leroux, 1934; repr. Paris: Vrin, 1981).

    Nominalisme au xive siècle (Montréal: Institut d'études médiévales, 1948; repr. Paris: Vrin, 1981).

    "Note sur le concept de forme intensive dans l'œuvre de Jean de Ripa," *Mélanges Alexandre Koyré* (Paris: Hermann, 1964) I: 517–26.

'La preuve ontologique chez Jean de Ripa (I Sent. Dist. II Qu. I)', in H. Kohlenberger (ed.) *Die Wirkungsgeschichte Anselms von Canterbury* (Frankfurt: Minerva, 1975) 173–94.

Vilém, Herold. "Der Streit zwischen Hieronymus von Prag und Johann Gerson: eine spätmittelalterliche Diskussion mit tragischen Folgen," in Z. Włodek (ed.) *Société et église: textes et discussions dans les universités au moyen âge tardif* (Turnhout: Brepols, 1995) 77–89.

Viller, Marcel, Gaetano Raciti, and Aimé Solignac (eds.). *Dictionnaire de spiritualité ascétique et mystique, doctrine et histoire* (Paris: Beauchesne, 1937–95).

Villey, Michel. *Le droit et les droits de l'homme* (Paris: Presses universitaires de France, 1983).
  La formation de la pensée juridique modern, 4th edn (Paris: Montchrestien, 1975) 225–62.

Vineis, Edoardo. "La linguistica medievale: linguistica e grammatical," in G. Lepschy (ed.) *Storia della linguistica* (Bologna: Il Mulino, 1990) II: 11–101.

Visser, Sandra and Thomas Williams. "Anselm's Account of Freedom," in B. Davies and B. Leftow (eds.) *The Cambridge Companion to Anselm* (Cambridge: Cambridge University Press, 2004) 179–203.

Vitali, Mari and Zdzisław Kuksewicz. "Notes sur les deux rédactions des *Quaestiones de anima* de Jean de Jandun," *Mediaevalia Philosophica Polonorum* 27 (1984) 3–24.

Vittorini, Marta. "La teoria delle idee di Pietro d'Aquila ed i suoi fondamenti ontologici," in M. Carbajo Núñez (ed.) *Giovanni Duns Scoto: studi e ricerche nel VII centenario della sua morte in onore di P. César Saco Alarcón* (Rome: PAA – Edizioni Antonianum, 2008) II: 213–55.

Völker, Walther. *Die Sakramentmystik des Nikolaus Kabasilas* (Wiesbaden: Steiner, 1977).

Volz, Walter. *Die Lehre des Johannes de Bassolis von den Produktionen in Gott: ein Vergleich mit der Lehre des Johannes Duns Scotus* (Munich, 1969).

von den Brincken, Anna-Dorothee. "Geschichtsbetrachtung bei Vincenz von Beauvais: die *Apologia Actoris* zum *Speculum Maius*," *Deutsches Archiv für Erforschung des Mittelalters* 34 (1978) 410–99.

von Savigny, Friedrich Carl. *Geschichte des römischen Rechts im Mittelalter*, 2nd edn (Heidelberg: Mohr, 1834–51; repr. Bad Homburg: Gentner, 1961).

von Schulte, Johann Friedrich. *Geschichte der Quellen und Literatur des canonischen Rechts* (Stuttgart: Enke, 1875–80; repr. Graz: Akademische Druck, 1956).

Vorgrimler, Herbert. *Busse und Krankensalbung* (*Handbuch der Dogmengeschichte* IV.3) (Freiburg: Herder, 1978).

Vos, Antonie. *The Philosophy of John Duns Scotus* (Edinburgh: Edinburgh University Press, 2006).

Vuillaume, Christophe. "La connaissance de Dieu d'après Guillaume de Saint-Thierry," *Collectanea Cisterciensia* 57 (1995) 249–70.

Vuillemin-Diem, Gudrun. "Zum Aristoteles Latinus in den Fragmenten der Quaternuli des David von Dinant," *Archives d'histoire doctrinale et littéraire du moyen âge* 70 (2003) 27–136.

Vuillemin-Diem, Gudrun and Marwan Rashed. "Burgundio de Pise et ses manuscrits grecs d'Aristote: Laur. 87. 7. et Laur. 81. 18," *Recherches de théologie et philosophie médiévales* 64 (1997) 136–97.

Wada, Yoko (ed.). *A Companion to* Ancrene Wisse (Cambridge: Brewer, 2003).

Wagner, Claus. *Materie im Mittelalter: Edition und Untersuchungen zur Summa (II, 1) des Nikolaus von Strassburg OP* (Fribourg: Universitätsverlag, 1986).

Wahl, J.A. "Baldus de Ubaldis and the Foundations of the Nation-State," *Manuscripta* 21 (1977) 80–96.

Wakefield, Walter L. and Austin P. Evans. *Heresies of the High Middle Ages* (New York: Columbia University Press, 1969).

Wakelnig, Elvira. "Metaphysics in al-ʿĀmirī. The Hierarchy of Being and the Concept of Creation," *Medioevo* 32 (2007) 39–59.

Walbridge, John. "Suhrawardī and Illuminationism," in P. Adamson and R. Taylor (eds.) *The Cambridge Companion to Arabic Philosophy* (Cambridge: Cambridge University Press, 2005) 201–23.

Walker, Joel. *Legend of Mar Qardagh: Narrative and Christian Heroism in Late Antique Iraq* (Berkeley: University of California Press, 2006).

"The Limits of Late Antiquity: Philosophy between Rome and Iran," *The Ancient World* 33 (2002) 45–69.

Walker, Paul E. "Abū Tammām and his *Kitāb al-shajara*: A New Ismāʿīlī Treatise from Tenth-Century Khurasan," *Journal of the American Oriental Society* 114 (1994) 343–52.

Early Philosophical Shiism: The Ismāʿīlī Neoplatonism of Abū Yaʿqūb al-Sijistānī (Cambridge: Cambridge University Press, 1993).

Ḥamīd al-Dīn al-Kirmānī: Ismaili Thought in the Age of al-Ḥākim (London: I. B. Tauris, 1999).

"The Ismāʿīlīs," in P. Adamson and R. Taylor (eds.) *The Cambridge Companion to Arabic Philosophy* (Cambridge: Cambridge University Press, 2005) 72–91.

"The Political Implications of al-Razi's Philosophy," in C. Butterworth (ed.) *The Political Aspects of Islamic Philosophy* (Cambridge, MA: Harvard University Press, 1992) 61–94.

Wallace, William. *The Scientific Methodology of Theodoric of Freiberg: A Case Study of the Relationship Between Science and Philosophy.* (Fribourg: Fribourg University Press, 1959).

Wallach, Luitpold. *Alcuin and Charlemagne: Studies in Carolingian History and Literature* (Ithaca, NY: Cornell University Press, 1959).

Wallerand, Gaston. "Henri Bate de Malines et saint Thomas d'Aquin," *Revue néoscolastique de philosophie* 36 (1934) 387–411.

Wallis, Faith. "The Church, the World and the Time. Prolegomena to a History of the Medieval 'Computus'," in M.-C. Deprez-Masson (ed.) *Normes et pouvoirs à la fin du moyen âge* (Montréal: Ceres, 1990) 15–29.

Walsh, James. "Buridan on the Connection of the Virtues," *Journal of the History of Philosophy* 24 (1986) 453–82.

"The 'Expositions' of Thomas Gallus on the Pseudo-Dionysian Letters," *Archives d'histoire doctrinale et littéraire du moyen âge* 30 (1963) 199–220.

"Some Relationships Between Gerald Odo's and John Buridan's Commentaries on Aristotle's 'Ethics'," *Franciscan Studies* 35 (1975) 237–75.

Walsh, Katherine. *Richard FitzRalph in Oxford, Avignon, and Armagh: A Fourteenth-Century Scholar and Primate* (Oxford: Clarendon Press, 1981).

Walsham, Alexandra. *Providence in Early Modern England* (Oxford: Oxford University Press, 1999).

Walzer, Michael. *Just and Unjust Wars: A Moral Argument with Historical Illustrations*, 4th edn (New York: Basic Books, 2006).

Walzer, Richard. *Greek into Arabic: Essays on Islamic Philosophy* (Cambridge, MA: Harvard University Press, 1962).

Ward, Benedicta. *Miracles and the Medieval Mind*, rev. edn (Philadelphia: University of Pennsylvania Press, 1987).

The Venerable Bede (Harrisburg, PA: Morehouse, 1990).

Wassermann, D. *Dionysius der Kartäuser: Einführung in Werk und Gedankenwelt* (Salzburg: Institut für Anglistik and Amerikanistik, 1996).

Watson, Nicholas. "Middle English Mystics," in D. Wallace (ed.) *The Cambridge History of Medieval English Literature* (Cambridge: Cambridge University Press, 1999) 539–65.

Richard Rolle and the Invention of Authority (Cambridge: Cambridge University Press, 1991).

Watt, Alan. "Which Approach? Late 20th Century Interpretations of Augustine on War," *Journal of Church and State* 46 (2004) 99–113.

Watt, John A. "Spiritual and Temporal Powers," in J. H. Burns (ed.) *The Cambridge History of Medieval Political Thought c.350–c.1450* (Cambridge: Cambridge University Press, 1988) 367–423.

    The Theory of Papal Monarchy in the Thirteenth Century: The Contribution of the Canonists (London: Burns and Oates, 1966).

Watt, John W. "Syriac Translators and Greek Philosophy in Early Abbasid Iraq," *Journal of the Canadian Society for Syriac Studies* 4 (2004) 15–26.

Watt, W. Montgomery. "Aḳīda," in H. A. R. Gibb *et al.* (eds.) *Encyclopaedia of Islam*, 2nd edn (Leiden: Brill, 1960–2004).

    The Formative Period of Islamic Thought (Edinburgh: Edinburgh University Press, 1973).

    Islamic Creeds (Edinburgh: Edinburgh University Press, 1994).

Watts, Edward. "Justinian, Malalas, and the End of Athenian Philosophical Teaching in A.D. 529," *Journal of Roman Studies* 94 (2004) 168–82.

    "Where to Live the Philosophical Life in the Sixth Century? Damascius, Simplicius, and the Return from Persia," *Greek, Roman, and Byzantine Studies* 45 (2005) 285–315.

Wawrykow, Joseph. *God's Grace and Human Action: "Merit" in the Theology of Thomas Aquinas* (Notre Dame, IN: University of Notre Dame Press, 1995).

Webb, C. C. J. *John of Salisbury* (London: Methuen, 1932; repr. New York: Russell and Russell, 1971).

Weber, Marie-Luise. *Die Gedichte des Gottschalk von Orbais* (New York: Lang, 1992).

Weber, Max. *The Theory of Social and Economic Organization*, tr. A. M. Henderson and T. Parsons (New York: Oxford University Press, 1947).

Weigand, Rudolf. *Die Naturrechtslehre der Legisten und Dekretisten von Irnerius bis Accursius und von Gratian bis Johannes Teutonicus* (Munich: Hueber, 1967).

    "Studien zum kanonistischen Werk Stephans von Tournai," *Zeitschrift der Savigny-Stiftung für Rechtsgeschichte, kanonistische Abteilung* 72 (1986) 349–61.

    Vinzenz von Beauvais: Scholastische Universalchronistik als Quelle volkssprachiger Geschichtsschreibung (Hildesheim: Olms, 1991).

Weijers, Olga. *La "disputatio" à la Faculté des arts de Paris (1200–1350 environ). Esquisse d'une typologie* (Turnhout: Brepols, 1995).

    La "disputatio" dans les Facultés des arts au moyen âge (Turnhout: Brepols 2002).

    Le travail intellectuel à la Faculté des arts de Paris: textes et maîtres (ca. 1200–1500) (Turnhout: Brepols, 1994–).

Weijers, Olga and Louis Holtz (eds.). *L'enseignement des disciplines à la Faculté des arts, Paris et Oxford, XIIIe–XVe siècles: actes du colloque international* (Turnhout: Brepols, 1997).

Weiler, A. G. "Un traité de Jean de Nova Domo sur les universaux," *Vivarium* 6 (1968) 108–54.

Weinberg, J. R. *Nicolaus of Autrecourt. A Study in 14th Century Thought* (Princeton, NJ: Princeton University Press, 1948; repr. New York: Greenwood Press, 1969).

Weisheipl, James A. *Albertus Magnus and the Sciences: Commemorative Essays, 1980* (Toronto: Pontifical Institute of Mediaeval Studies, 1980).

    "Albertus Magnus and Universal Hylomorphism: Avicebron," in F. Kovach and R. Shahan (eds.) *Albert the Great Commemorative Essays* (Norman: University of Oklahoma Press, 1980) 239–60.

    "Curriculum of the Faculty of Arts at Oxford in the Early Fourteenth Century," *Mediaeval Studies* 26 (1964) 143–85.

    "Early Fourteenth-Century Physics of the Merton 'School' with Special Reference to Dumbleton and Heytesbury" (D.Phil. dissertation: University of Oxford, 1956).

    "Ockham and some Mertonians," *Mediaeval Studies* 30 (1968) 163–213.

"The Parisian Faculty of Arts in Mid-Thirteenth Century: 1240–1270," *American Benedictine Review* 25 (1974) 200–17.

"The Place of John Dumbleton in the Merton School," *Isis* 50 (1959) 439–54.

"Repertorium Mertonense," *Mediaeval Studies* 31 (1969) 174–224.

"Roger Swyneshed, OSB, logician, natural philosopher, and theologian," in *Oxford Studies Presented to Daniel Callus* (Oxford: Clarendon Press, 1964) 231–52.

Weisser, Ursula. *Das "Buch über das Geheimnis der Schöpfung" von Pseudo-Apollonios von Tyana* (Berlin: De Gruyter, 1980).

Wels, Henrik. *Aristotelisches Wissen und Glauben im 15. Jahrhundert: ein anonymer Kommentar zum Pariser Verurteilungsdekret von 1277 aus dem Umfeld des Johannes de Nova Domo: Studie und Text* (Amsterdam: Grüner, 2004).

Welter, Jean Thiébaut. *L'exemplum dans la littérature religieuse et didactique du Moyen Age* (Paris: Occitania, 1927).

Wengert, R. G. "Three Senses of Intuitive Cognition: A Quodlibetal Question of Harvey of Nedellec," *Franciscan Studies* 43 (1983) 408–31.

Wensinck, A. J. *The Muslim Creed: Its Genesis and Historical Development* (Cambridge: Cambridge University Press, 1932; repr. London: Cass, 1965).

Wenzel, Siegfried. "The Continuing Life of William Peraldus's *Summa vitiorum*," in M. D. Jordan and K. Emery (eds.) *Ad Litteram: Authoritative Texts and Medieval Readers* (Notre Dame, IN: University of Notre Dame Press, 1992) 135–64.

"The Seven Deadly Sins: Some Problems of Research," *Speculum* 43 (1968) 1–22.

West, Delno and Sandra Zimdars-Swartz. *Joachim of Fiore: A Study in Spiritual Perception and History* (Bloomington, IN: Indiana University Press, 1983).

Westerink, L. G. "Proclus commentateur des *Vers d'Or*," in G. Bos and G. Seel (eds.) *Proclus et son influence* (Zurich: Éditions du Grand Midi, 1987) 62–78.

Wey, Joseph. "The *Sermo finalis* of Robert Holcot," *Mediaeval Studies* 11 (1949) 219–24.

White, Despina S. *Patriarch Photios of Constantinople: His Life, Scholarly Contributions, and Correspondence Together with a Translation of Fifty-Two of his Letters* (Brookline, MA: Holy Cross Orthodox Press, 1981).

White, Kevin. "The Quodlibeta of Thomas Aquinas in the Context of his Work," in C. Schabel (ed.) *Theological Quodlibets in the Middle Ages: The Thirteenth Century* (Leiden: Brill, 2006) 49–134.

"St. Thomas Aquinas and the Prologue to Peter of Auvergne's *Quaestiones super De sensu et sensato*," *Documenti e studi* 1 (1990) 427–56.

Whittingham, Martin. *Al-Ghazali and the Quran: One Book, Many Meanings* (London: Routledge, 2007).

Wieland, George. "Plato or Aristotle – A Real Alternative in Medieval Philosophy?," in J. F. Wippel (ed.) *Studies in Medieval Philosophy* (Washington, DC: Catholic University of America Press, 1987) 63–83.

Wielgus, Stanislaw (ed.). *Marsilius von Inghen: Werk und Wirkung.* (Lublin: Akten des Zweiten Internationalen Marsilius-von-Inghen-Kongresses, 1993).

Wielockx, Robert, "Autour du procès de Thomas d'Aquin," in A. Zimmermann (ed.) *Thomas von Aquin: Werk und Wirkung im Licht neuerer Forschungen* (Berlin: De Gruyter, 1988) 413–38.

"Henry of Ghent," in J. J. E. Gracia and T. Noone (eds.) *A Companion to Philosophy in the Middle Ages* (Oxford: Blackwell, 2003) 296–304.

"Le ms. Paris Nat. lat. 16096 et la condemnation du 7 mars 1277," *Recherches de théologie ancienne et médiévale* 48 (1981) 227–37.

Wilks, Ian. "Peter Abelard and his Contemporaries," in D. M. Gabbay and J. Woods (eds.) *Handbook to the History of Logic*, vol. II: *Mediaeval and Renaissance Logic* (Amsterdam: North-Holland, 2008) 83–156.

"Peter Abelard and the Metaphysics of Essential Predication," *Journal of the History of Philosophy* 36 (1998) 356–85.

Wilks, Michael. *The Problem of Sovereignty in the Later Middle Ages; The Papal Monarchy with Augustinus Triumphus and the Publicists* (Cambridge: Cambridge University Press, 1963).

"Reformatio Regni: Wyclif and Hus as Leaders of Religious Protest Movements," *Studies in Church History* 9 (1972) 109–30.

(ed.). *The World of John of Salisbury* (Oxford: Blackwell, 1984).

Wyclif: Political Ideas and Practice, ed. A. Hudson (Oxford: Oxbow Books, 2000).

Willard, Charity Canon. *Christine de Pizan: Her Life and Works* (New York: Persea Books, 1984).

Williams, Thomas (ed.). *The Cambridge Companion to Duns Scotus* (Cambridge: Cambridge University Press, 2003).

"From Metaethics to Action Theory," in T. Williams (ed.) *The Cambridge Companion to Duns Scotus* (Cambridge: Cambridge University Press, 2003) 332–51.

Williams, Thomas and Sandra Visser. *Anselm* (Oxford: Oxford University Press, 2008).

Wilson, Curtis. *William Heytesbury: Medieval Logic and the Rise of Mathematical Physics* (Madison, WI: University of Wisconsin Press, 1956; repr. 1960).

Wilson, Gordon. "The Critique of Thomas Aquinas's Unicity Theory of Forms in John Peckam's Quodlibet IV (Romanum)," *Franciscan Studies* 56 (1998) 423–31.

Windeatt, Barry. *English Mystics of the Middle Ages* (Cambridge: Cambridge University Press, 1994).

Winroth, Anders. *The Makings of Gratian's Decretum* (Cambridge: Cambridge University Press, 2000).

Winship, Michael. *Seers of God: Puritan Providentialism in the Restoration and Early Enlightenment* (Baltimore, MD: Johns Hopkins University Press, 1996).

Wippel, John F. "The Dating of James of Viterbo's Quodlibet I and Godfrey of Fontaines' Quodlibet VIII," *Augustiniana* 24 (1974) 348–86.

"Godfrey of Fontaines and Henry of Ghent's Theory of Intentional Distinction Between Essence and Existence," in T. W. Köhler (ed.) *Sapientiae procerum amore: mélanges médiévistes offerts à Dom Jean-Pierre Müller* (Rome: Editrice Anselmiana, 1974) 289–321.

"Godfrey of Fontaines at the University of Paris in the Last Quarter of the Thirteenth Century," in J. Aertsen *et al.* (eds.) *Nach der Verurteilung von 1277: Philosophie und Theologie an der Universität von Paris im letzten Viertel des 13. Jahrhunderts: Studien und Texte* (Berlin: De Gruyter, 2001) 359–89.

"Godfrey of Fontaines' Quodlibet XIV on Justice as a General Virtue: Is It Really a Quodlibet?," in C. Schabel (ed.) *Theological Quodlibets in the Middle Ages: The Thirteenth Century* (Leiden: Brill, 2006) 287–344.

"James of Viterbo on the Essence–Existence Relationship (Quodlibet 1, q. 4), and Godfrey of Fontaines on the Relationship between Nature and Supposit (Quodlibet 7, q. 5)," in *Sprache und Erkenntnis im Mittelalter* (Berlin: De Gruyter, 1981) 777–87.

The Metaphysical Thought of Godfrey of Fontaines: A Study in Late Thirteenth-Century Philosophy (Washington, DC: Catholic University of America Press, 1981).

The Metaphysical Thought of Thomas Aquinas: From Finite Being to Uncreated Being (Washington, DC: Catholic University of America Press, 2000).

"Metaphysics and *Separatio* according to Thomas Aquinas," *Review of Metaphysics* 31 (1978) 431–70.

"The Parisian Condemnations of 1270 and 1277," in J. J. E. Gracia and T. Noone (eds.) *A Companion to Philosophy in the Middle Ages* (Oxford: Blackwell, 2003) 65–73.

"Possible Sources for Godfrey of Fontaines' Views on the Act-Potency Composition of Simple Creatures," *Mediaeval Studies* 44 (1984) 222–44.

"The Relationship Between Essence and Existence in Late Thirteenth-Century Thought: Giles of Rome, Henry of Ghent, Godfrey of Fontaines, and James of Viterbo," in P. Morewedge (ed.) *Philosophies of Existence Ancient and Medieval* (New York: Fordham University Press, 1982) 131–64.

"Thomas Aquinas and the Condemnation of 1277," *Modern Schoolman* 72 (1995) 233–72.

"Thomas Aquinas and Siger of Brabant on Being and the Science of Being as Being," *Modern Schoolman* 82 (2005) 143–68.

"Thomas Aquinas' Derivation of the Aristotelian Categories (Predicaments)," *Journal of the History of Philosophy* 25 (1987) 13–34.

Wippel, John F. and Allan B. Wolter (eds.). *Medieval Philosophy: From St. Augustine to Nicholas of Cusa* (New York: Free Press, 1969).

Wirszubski, Chaim. *Libertas as a Political Idea at Rome during the Late Republic and Early Principate* (Cambridge: Cambridge University Press, 1950).

Wisnovsky, Robert (ed.). *Aspects of Avicenna* (Princeton, NJ: Markus Wiener, 2001).

"Avicenna and the Avicennian Tradition," in P. Adamson and R. Taylor (eds.) *The Cambridge Companion to Arabic Philosophy* (Cambridge: Cambridge University Press, 2005) 92–136.

Avicenna's Metaphysics in Context (Ithaca, NY: Cornell University Press, 2003).

"The Nature and Scope of Arabic Philosophical Commentary in Post-Classical (*ca.* 1100–1900 AD) Islamic Intellectual History: Some Preliminary Observations," in P. Adamson *et al.* (eds.) *Philosophy, Science and Exegesis in Greek, Arabic and Latin Commentaries* (London: Institute of Classical Studies, 2004) II: 149–91.

"One Aspect of the Avicennian Turn in Sunnī Theology," *Arabic Sciences and Philosophy* 14 (2004) 65–100.

"Towards a History of Avicenna's Distinction between Immanent and Transcendent Causes," in D. C. Reisman and A. H al-Rahīm (eds.) *Before and after Avicenna* (Leiden: Brill, 2003) 49–68.

Wittwer, Roland. *Sextus Latinus: die erste lateinische Übersetzung von Sextus Empiricus' Pyrrhoneioi Hypotyposeis* (Leiden: Brill, forthcoming).

Włodek, Zofia. "Le commentaire de Nicolas d'Amsterdam sur le *De anima* d'Aristote. Introduction, textes inédits," *Mediaevalia Philosophica Polonorum* 11 (1963) 23–42.

Wohlhaupter, Eugen. *Aequitas Canonica: eine studie aus dem kanonischen Recht* (Paderborn: Schöningh, 1931).

Wohlman, Avital. *L'homme, le monde sensible et le péché dans la philosophie de Jean Scot Erigène* (Paris: Vrin, 1987).

Wolf, Georges. "La préface perdue des sermons de Raoul Ardent, chapelain de Richard Ier," *Archives d'histoire doctrinale et littéraire du moyen âge* 42 (1979) 35–9.

Wolfson, Elliot. *Abraham Abulafia – Kabbalist and Prophet: Hermeneutics, Theosophy and Theurgy* (Los Angeles: Cherub Press, 2000).

Wolfson, Harry A. *Crescas' Critique of Aristotle* (Cambridge, MA: Harvard University Press, 1929).

"The Internal Senses in Latin, Arabic, and Hebrew Philosophical Texts," *Harvard Theological Review* 28 (1935) 69–133.

"Joseph Ibn Saddik on Divine Attributes," *Jewish Quarterly Review* 55 (1965) 277–98.

"Meaning of Ex Nihilo in Isaac Israeli," *Jewish Quarterly Review* 50 (1959) 1–12.

"Notes on Isaac Israeli's Internal Senses," *Jewish Quarterly Review* 51 (1961) 275–87.

The Philosophy of the Kalam (Cambridge, MA: Harvard University Press, 1976).

"Plan for the Publication of a *Corpus commentariorum Averrois in Aristotele,*" *Speculum* 6 (1931) 412–27.

"Revised Plan for the Publication of a *Corpus commentariorum Averrois in Aristotele,*" *Speculum* 38 (1963) 88–104.

Wolter, Allan B. (ed.). *Duns Scotus*, special issue of *American Catholic Philosophical Quarterly*, 67 (1993).

"The Formal Distinction," in J. Ryan and B. Bonansea (eds.) *John Duns Scotus, 1265–1965* (Washington, DC: Catholic University of America, 1965) 45–60.

The Philosophical Theology of John Duns Scotus, ed. M. M. Adams (Ithaca, NY: Cornell University Press, 1990).

Wood, Diana. *Clement VI: The Pontificate and Ideas of an Avignon Pope* (Cambridge: Cambridge University Press, 1989).

Medieval Economic Thought (Cambridge: Cambridge University Press, 2002).

Wood, Rega. "Adam Wodeham on Sensory Illusions," *Traditio* 38 (1982) 214–52.

"Distinct Ideas and Perfect Solitude: Alexander of Hales, Richard Rufus and Odo Rigaldus," *Franciscan Studies* 53 (1993) 7–46.

Ockham on the Virtues (West Lafayette, IN: Purdue University Press, 1997).

"Richard Rufus of Cornwall and Aristotle's Physics," *Franciscan Studies* 53 (1992) 247–81.

"Richard Rufus of Cornwall on Creation: The Reception of Aristotelian Physics in the West," *Medieval Philosophy and Theology* 2 (1992) 1–30.

"Richard Rufus: Physics at Paris before 1240," *Documenti e studi sulla tradizione filosofica medievale* 5 (1994) 87–127.

"Richard Rufus's *De anima* Commentary: The Earliest Known, Surviving, Western *De anima* Commentary," *Medieval Philosophy and Theology* 10 (2001) 119–56.

"Richard Rufus's *Speculum animae*: Epistemology and the Introduction of Aristotle in the West," in A. Speer (ed.) *Die Bibliotheca Amploniana ihre Bedeutung im Spannungsfeld von Aristotelismus, Nominalismus und Humanismus* (Leiden: Brill, 1995) 86–109.

"Walter Burley on Motion in a Vacuum," *Traditio* 45 (1989–90) 191–217.

"Walter Burley's *Physics Commentaries,*" *Franciscan Studies* 44 (1984) 275–327.

"Willing Wickedly: Ockham and Burley Compared," *Vivarium* 37 (1999) 72–93.

"The Works of Richard Rufus: The State of the Question in 2008," *Recherches de théologie et philosophie médiévales* 76 (2009) 1–73.

Wood, Rega and Robert Andrews. "Causality and Demonstration: An Early Scholastic *Posterior Analytics* Commentary," *The Monist* 79 (1996) 325–56.

Wood, Rega, Ludger Honnefelder, and Mechthild Dreyer (eds.) *John Duns Scotus: Metaphysics and Ethics* (Leiden: Brill, 1996).

Wood, Rega and Michael Weisberg. "Interpreting Aristotle on Mixture: Problems about Elemental Composition from Philoponus to Cooper," *Studies in the History and Philosophy of Science* 35 (2004) 698–704.

Woodhouse, C. M. *George Gemistos Plethon: The Last of the Hellenes* (Oxford: Clarendon Press, 1986).

Woolf, Cecil. N. S. *Bartolus of Sassoferrato: His Position in the History of Medieval Political Thought* (Cambridge: Cambridge University Press, 1913).

Workman, H. B. *John Wyclif: A Study of the English Medieval Church* (Oxford: Clarendon Press, 1926).

Xiberta, Bartolomeu Maria. *De scriptoribus scholasticis saeculi XIV ex ordine Carmelitarum* (Leuven: Bureaux de La Revue, 1931).

Guiu Terrena: Carmelita de Perpinyà (Barcelona: Institució Patxot, 1932).

Yates, Frances. "The Art of Ramon Lull," *Journal of the Warburg and Courtauld Institutes* 17 (1954) 115–73.

Yokoyama, Tetsuo. "Simon of Faversham's *Sophisma: 'Universale est intentio'*," *Mediaeval Studies* 31 (1969) 1–14.

Yousef, Muḥammad ʿAlī Hajj. *Ibn ʿArabī – Time and Cosmology* (London: Routledge, 2007).

Ypma, Eelcko. "Recherches sur la carrière scolaire et la bibliothèque de Jacques de Viterbe +1308," *Augustiniana* 24 (1974) 247–82.

"Recherches sur la productivité littéraire de Jacques de Viterbe jusqu'à 1300," *Augustiniana* 25 (1975) 223–82.

Yrjönsuuri, Mikko. "Duties, Rules and Interpretations in Obligational Disputations," in M. Yrjönsuuri (ed.) *Medieval Formal Logic* (Dordrecht: Kluwer, 2001) 3–34.

"*Expositio* as A Method of Solving Sophisms," in S. Read (ed.) *Sophisms in Medieval Logic and Grammar: Acts of the Ninth European Symposium for Medieval Logic and Semantics* (Dordrecht: Kluwer, 1993) 202–16.

"Words and Things in Peter of Spain's *Syncategoreumata*," in I. Angelelli *et al.* (eds.) *Medieval and Renaissance Logic in Spain* (Hildesheim: Olms, 2000) 3–19.

Zagzebski, Linda. *The Dilemma of Freedom and Foreknowledge* (Oxford: Oxford University Press, 1991).

Zainaty, Georges. *La morale d'Avempace* (Paris: Vrin, 1979).

Zalta, Edward N. (ed.). *The Stanford Encyclopedia of Philosophy* (1997–): http://plato. stanford.edu/.

Zanin, Fabio. "Francis of Marchia, *Virtus derelicta*, and Modifications of the Basic Principles of Aristotelian Physics," *Vivarium* 44 (2006) 81–95.

Zavalloni, Roberto. *Richard de Mediavilla et la controverse sur la pluralité des formes* (Leuven: Éditions de l'Institut Supérieur de Philosophie, 1951).

Zawart, Anscar. *The History of Franciscan Preaching and of Franciscan Preachers (1290–1927): A Bio-bibliographical Study* (New York: Wagner, 1928).

Ziai, Hossein. *Knowledge and Illumination: A Study of Suhrawardī's Ḥikmat al-ishrāq* (Atlanta, GA: Scholars Press, 1990).

Ziegler, Josef. *Die Ehelehre der Pönitentialsummen von 1200–1350* (Regensburg: Pustet, 1956).

Medicine and Religion, c. 1300: The Case of Arnau de Vilanova (New York: Oxford University Press, 1998).

Zimmermann, Albert. *Albert der Große. Seine Zeit, sein Werk, seine Wirkung* (Berlin: De Gruyter, 1981).

"Ein Averroist des späten 13. Jahrhunderts: Ferrandus de Hispania," *Archiv für Geschichte der Philosophie* 50 (1968) 145–64.

"Bemerkungen zum Physikkommentar des William of Clifford," in J. Marenbon (ed.) *Aristotle in Britain during the Middle Ages* (Turnhout: Brepols, 1996) 299–310.

"Die Kritik an Thomas von Aquin in Metaphysikkommentar des Ferrandus de Hispania," in *Atti del Congresso Internazionale: Tommaso d'Aquino nel suo settimo centenario* (Naples: Edizioni domenicane italiane, 1976) II: 259–67.

Ontologie oder Metaphysik: Die Diskussion über den Gegenstand der Metaphysik im 13. und 14. Jahrhundert: Texte und Untersuchungen (Leuven: Peeters, 1998).

"Some Aspects of the Reception of Aristotle's Physics and Metaphysics in the Thirteenth Century," in M. Jordan and K. Emery (eds.) *Ad litteram: Authoritative Texts and their Medieval Readers* (Notre Dame, IN: University of Notre Dame Press, 1992) 217–27.

Zink, Michel. "La rhétorique honteuse et la convention du sermon *ad status* à travers la *summa de arte praedicatoria* d'Alan de Lille," in H. Roussel and F. Suard (eds.) *Alain de Lille, Gautier de Châtillon, Jakemart Giélée et leur temps* (Lille: Presses universitaires de Lille, 1978) 133–70.

Zoubov, Vasilii. "Walter Catton, Gérard d'Odon et Nicolas Bonet," *Physis* 1 (1959) 261–78.

Zuckerman, Charles. "Some Texts of Bernard of Auvergne on Papal Power," *Recherches de théologie ancienne et médiévale* 49 (1982) 174–204.

Zuckerman, Constantine. "A Repertory of Published Armenian Translations of Classical Texts," in G. Fiaccadori (ed.) *Autori classici in lingue del vicino e medio oriente* (Rome: Istituto poligrafico e Zecca dello Stato, Libreria dello Stato, 2001) 415–48.

Zumkeller, Adolar. "Der Augustinertheologe Johannes Hiltalingen von Basel (†1392) über Urstand, Erbsünde, Gnade und Verdienst," *Analecta Augustiniana* 43 (1980) 59–162.

Hugolin von Orvieto und seine theologische Erkenntnislehre (Würzburg: Rita, 1941).

Zupko, Jack. *John Buridan: Portrait of a Fourteenth-Century Arts Master* (Notre Dame, IN: University of Notre Dame Press, 2003).

"On Certitude," in J. M. M. H. Thijssen and J. Zupko (eds.) *The Metaphysics and Natural Philosophy of John Buridan* (Leiden: Brill, 2001) 165–82.

Zwiercan, Marian. "Note sur deux manuscrits du commentaire de Godefroid d'Aspale sur la Physique d'Aristote," *Mediaevalia Philosophica Polonorum* 10 (1961) 103–9.

INDEX NOMINUM

Authors prior to 1600 are listed by first name, unless that name is not standardly used.

INDEX RERUM

685 54214